EMANUEL

SUPPLEMENTS

TO

VETUS TESTAMENTUM

VOLUME XCIV

EMANUEL

STUDIES IN HEBREW BIBLE
SEPTUAGINT
AND DEAD SEA SCROLLS

IN HONOR OF
EMANUEL TOV

EDITED BY

SHALOM M. PAUL, ROBERT A. KRAFT,
LAWRENCE H. SCHIFFMAN AND WESTON W. FIELDS

WITH THE ASSISTANCE OF

EVA BEN-DAVID

BRILL
LEIDEN · BOSTON
2003

This book is printed on acid-free paper.

Bibliographic information published by Die Deutsche Bibliothek

Die Deutsche Bibliothek lists this publication in the Deutsche
Nationalbibliographie; detailed bibliographic data are
available on the Internet at http://dnb.dde.de.

Library of Congress Cataloging-in-Publication Data

Library of Congress Cataloging-in-Publication Data is also available.

ISSN 0083-5889
ISBN 90 04 12679 1

PRINTED IN THE NETHERLANDS

CONTENTS

PART ONE

QUMRAN

PART THREE

HEBREW BIBLE

ACKNOWLEDGMENTS

The editors wish to thank those who made this Festschrift possible: the Board of Directors of the Dead Sea Scrolls Foundation who conceived and supported the project; Mrs. Eva Meijering Ben-David, Executive Secretary of the Dead Sea Scrolls Foundation, who, as production manager, took over much of the responsibility for every stage of the book, and Hans van der Meij and Pim Rietbroek of Brill Academic Publishers, whose efforts and expertise brought it to completion.

EMANUEL TOV: A BIOGRAPHY

Born Menno Toff in Amsterdam on September 15, 1941, the son of Juda (Jo) Toff and Toos Neeter, Emanuel Tov was soon orphaned when his parents were deported to concentration camps during the German occupation of the Netherlands. As a vivid reminder of that period, his baby book contains a newspaper clipping in which his birth announcement is surrounded by Nazi prohibitions for Jews. Having survived the war in hiding with a Christian family, Emanuel was raised by his aunt and uncle as one of their children.

After the war, he began his primary studies at the Boerhave School, and continued at the Kohnstamm school in South Amsterdam. At the age of 12 he began a classical education in Latin and Greek at the Spinoza Lyceum, where Lika Aa, later to be his wife, was three classes below. By the time he finished the classical gymnasium at the age of 18, in addition to Latin and Greek and his native Dutch, Emanuel already knew, French, English, German as well as Hebrew, which he had studied from the age of bar mitzvah onwards at Talmud Torah.

Among the most important influences in his youth was his membership and leadership in Habonim ("the builders"), a zionistic youth movement that encouraged and trained young people to immigrate to Israel. In Habonim Emanuel met people of a similar background, and made friendships which have lasted his entire life.

During 1959–1960 he spent a year in Israel at the "Institute for Youth Leaders from Abroad" with about one hundred others, preparing himself for leadership in the movement, spending part of the year at Kfar Blum, a kibbutz in the north of Israel. During this year he sang in the choir and learned to play the flute. The following year he returned to the Netherlands (1960–61) to work full-time for the movement as the leader for the entire country, a position requiring extensive travel.

By October, 1961 Emanuel, now age twenty, decided he was ready to immigrate to Israel. Traveling all alone on his motor-scooter from Amsterdam across the Alps to southern Italy, by ship to the west coast of Greece, across Greece, and then from Piraeus by ship to

Haifa. After a one-month journey Emanuel arrived in Jerusalem just in time to enroll at the Hebrew University of Jerusalem.

His intention had been to study Hebrew Bible, but he discovered that a second major was required. For this he chose Greek literature, and ever since, these two topics have remained his favorites. He successfully completed the B.A. in 1964.

In the meantime, a chance meeting at the Customs Office in Jerusalem during the summer of 1963 reunited him with Lika Aa, whom he had known at school and in Habonim during his years in Amsterdam. What had been a childhood attraction now bloomed into full-blown love, and they were married on December 3, 1964.

During the next three years Emanuel pursued an M.A. in Hebrew Bible, and received his degree in 1967. At the Hebrew University he was influenced by a galaxy of prominent scholars. Among these were: Prof. Shemaryahu Talmon, for whom he served as a research assistant, who attracted him to textual studies, and introduced him to the Hebrew University Bible Project; Professor I. L. Seeligmann, himself originally Dutch, who supervised his Septuagint studies; Prof. Moshe Goshen-Gottstein who sparked an interest in the Peshitta and textual theory in general; and Prof. Meir Weiss, who taught him literary analysis and stylistics of the Hebrew Bible. Early in his career Emanuel realized that he preferred to work with solid data, such as manuscripts, rather than more theoretical, speculative matters.

Emanuel's mentor, Shemaryahu Talmon now made arrangements for the promising young scholar to continue his studies with Prof. Frank M. Cross, Jr. at the Department of Near Eastern Languages and Literatures at Harvard University for two years, 1967–1969, with Profs. Talmon and Cross co-directing his dissertation on behalf of the Hebrew University. During these two years he also served as a teaching fellow in Old Testament.

Emanuel recalls his two years at Harvard as one of the high points of his life. Not only did he study with Prof. Cross, but he also began what became a life-long professional and personal relationship with him. At Harvard he was exposed to new linguistic approaches by Prof. Thomas Lamdin, took New Testament courses with Prof. Krister Stendahl, supplementing his previous study of the New Testament in Jerusalem with Prof. David Flusser, and was introduced by Prof. John Strugnell to the study of the Apocrypha and Pseudepigrapha, as well as unpublished Cave 4 Qumran texts, at that time a privilege not enjoyed by all. He made many lasting friendships with his

classmates, too, among whom were Richard Saley, Paul Hanson, Zvi
Abusch, Dan Harrington, and Eric Meyers.

He returned to Jerusalem in the autumn of 1969. Shortly afterward Emanuel and Lika welcomed into their family a daughter,
Ophira; two years later their first son Ariel was born, and a second
son, Amitai joined them in 1974.

Meanwhile, with his family growing, Emanuel completed his requirements for the Ph.D. degree at the Hebrew University in 1973 with
a thesis on the Septuagint translation of Jeremiah (*summa cum laude*).
Additional readers were Profs. John Strugnell and Joseph Fitzmyer.

During his student years at the Hebrew University, Emanuel was
supported by scholarships and some odd jobs, including teaching outside the University. He particularly remembers his job in the Jewish
National and University Library mail room at the Givat Ram campus
of the university, where he "licked stamps" and entered each outgoing
letter in a ledger. In later years he shared with Prof. Jonas Greenfield
an interest in stamps, a hobby he had during his youth in the
Netherlands, and a visit to the Tov home on French Hill in Jerusalem
is likely to find his stamp books spread out on the dining room table,
awaiting his attention when he needs relaxation and escape. He is
also an avid table tennis player and an accomplished photographer.

Emanuel began teaching at the Hebrew University in 1973. Since
1986 he has been a professor in the Department of Bible, and in
1990 he was appointed to the J. L. Magnes Chair in Bible, held
until his retirement by Emanuel's mentor, Prof. Talmon. A natural
teacher, who enjoys his students and the classroom, he has taught
a wide variety of courses including textual criticism, Dead Sea Scrolls,
Septuagint, and exegesis of individual books of the Hebrew Bible.

Emanuel's career has been characterized by world-wide travel and
visiting professorships. He has served as a guest professor at the
University of Pennsylvania and Dropsie University in Philadelphia,
as well as at the University of Stellenbosch (South Africa), Macquarie
University (Sydney), Sydney University, and the Free University of
Amsterdam. Between 1982 and 1988 he gave the annual Grinfield
Lectures on the Septuagint at Oxford University. During the 1989–
1990 academic year he convened, together with Prof. M. Weinfeld,
a research group on the Dead Sea Scrolls at the Institute for Advanced
Studies of the Hebrew University in Jerusalem, and in 1990–1991
he was appointed a fellow at the Netherlands Institute for Advanced
Studies in Wassenaar. It was during this period that he accepted the

post of Editor-in-Chief of the International Team publishing the *Discoveries in the Judaean Desert* series, and it was in Wassenaar that he and I laid the plans for the Dead Sea Scrolls Foundation. In 2000 he was a fellow at the Center for Jewish Studies at Harvard University.

Over the years Emanuel has specialized in various aspects of the textual criticism of Hebrew and Greek Scripture, as well as the Dead Sea Scrolls. He has written eleven books, edited fourteen books and three electronic databases, and authored more than 170 studies on the Septuagint, the Qumran texts, and the text of the Hebrew and Greek Bible, as well as other aspects of biblical studies, in addition to the twenty-eight volumes of the *DJD* series whose production he has directed (see bibliography in this volume).

Emanuel continues to be involved in several research projects. Since 1964 he has served, first as an assistant, and later as one of the four editors of the Hebrew University Bible Project, which has so far produced new critical editions of Isaiah, Jeremiah, and Ezekiel, and twenty-five monographs. Together with Prof. Robert A. Kraft of the University of Pennsylvania, Emanuel has, since 1981, directed the CATSS project (Computer Assisted Tools for Septuagint Studies) in Jerusalem and Philadelphia. This project has produced several monographs as well as a module for comparing the Hebrew and Greek texts of the Bible incorporated in the Accordance computer program.

In 1982 he was invited by Father Pierre Benoit, then Editor-in-Chief of *The Discoveries in the Judaean Desert* series, to take over from Father Dominique Barthélemy, the editorship of the Greek Minor Prophets Scroll from Naḥal Ḥever, which was published as volume 8 of *Discoveries in the Judaean Desert*. In 1987 Prof. Eugene Ulrich asked him to edit the Cave 4 Jeremiah fragments, and he also published several additional texts in *DJD*.

Throughout his career Emanuel has received numerous awards and research grants. Among them are the Warburg Award of the Hebrew University 1969–1971, a Lady Davis Fellowship for study at Oxford University 1974–1975, a D.A.A.D. Summer Scholarship for work in Göttingen in 1977, a Wexler Fellowship from the Penn-Israel Foundation in 1980, and the Humboldt Research Prize from Germany in 1999.

Emanuel has also organized and co-organized three conferences: The Second International Congress on the Bible and the Computer (Jerusalem, 1988); the Summer Session of the Qumran Research Group, Institute for Advanced Studies, Hebrew University (1994); and the Dead

Sea Scrolls: Fifty Years After Their Discovery (Jerusalem, 1997).

For all of us who have been privileged to know and work with Prof. Emanuel Tov his oversight of the publication of the Dead Sea Scrolls stands as only one, but perhaps the most remarkable, of his many scholarly achievements.

For more than a decade he has focused most of his enormous energy and prodigious organizational ability on the direction of the Dead Sea Scrolls Publication Project, of which he was appointed Editor-in-Chief in late 1990. Since then he has directed a team of more than seventy scholars involved in the preparation of the Dead Sea Scrolls for publication in the *Discoveries in the Judaean Desert* series (Oxford University Press). Under Emanuel's editorship the international scrolls team was expanded, texts were reassigned to a wider variety of scholars, fragments were inventoried, and new photographs made.

Most important, perhaps, was the entire re-organization of the editorial and production teams. Under his guidance twenty-two volumes have been produced in Jerusalem, and an additional six in Notre Dame by Profs. Gene Ulrich and James VanderKam.

During his years as Editor-in-Chief of *DJD* Emanuel has worked closely with the Israel Antiquities Authority, which appointed him, with the Oxford Centre for Postgraduate Studies, and with the Qumran Forum (directed by Prof. Geza Vermes) at Yarnton Manor in Oxford.

It was Emanuel's appointment to his post as Editor-in-chief of *Discoveries in the Judaean Desert* that led to the formation of the Dead Sea Scrolls Foundation in 1991, of which he served as the Chairperson of the Board of Directors from its inception until 2000, when he was succeeded by Prof. Shalom Paul. Emanuel continues to serve on the Board as well as the Executive Committee.

With this volume Emanuel's colleagues honor him as a scholar and friend. He is generous and unassuming. To be his student is to be his friend as well. His classroom, his office, his home are equally open. He is always accessible, always gentle, always demanding and exact. His contribution to the scholarship of the Hebrew Bible, the Septuagint, and the Dead Sea Scrolls has already been immense, but we look forward with him to many more years of fruitful scholarship and happiness!

Weston W. Fields
Jerusalem

EMANUEL TOV

BIBLIOGRAPHY

Books

1. *The Book of Baruch Also Called I Baruch (Greek and Hebrew)* (Texts and Translations 8, Pseudepigrapha Series 6; Missoula, Mont.: Scholars Press, 1975). 51 pp.

2. *The Septuagint Translation of Jeremiah and Baruch: A Discussion of an Early Revision of Jeremiah 29–52 and Baruch 1:1–3:8* (HSM 8; Missoula, Mont.: Scholars Press, 1976). xi + 199 pp.

3. *The Text-Critical Use of the Septuagint in Biblical Research* (Jerusalem Biblical Studies 3; Jerusalem: Simor, 1981). 343 pp.

4. With J. R. Abercrombie, W. Adler, and R. A. Kraft: *Computer Assisted Tools for Septuagint Studies (CATSS), Volume 1, Ruth* (SCS 20; Atlanta, Georgia: Scholars Press, 1986). 325 pp.

5. *A Computerized Data Base for Septuagint Studies: The Parallel Aligned Text of the Greek and Hebrew Bible, CATSS Volume 2* (JNSLSup 1; 1986). xviii + 144 pp.

6. With D. Barthélemy, D. W. Gooding, and J. Lust: *The Story of David and Goliath, Textual and Literary Criticism, Papers of a Joint Venture* (OBO 73; Fribourg/Göttingen: Éditions universitaires/Vandenhoeck & Ruprecht, 1986). vii + 157 pp.

7. *The Textual Criticism of the Bible: An Introduction* (Heb.; Jerusalem: Bialik Institute, 1989). xxiv + 326 pp. and 30 plates.

8. With the collaboration of R. A. Kraft: *The Greek Minor Prophets Scroll from Naḥal Ḥever, (8ḤevXIIgr) (The Seiyal Collection I)* (DJD VIII; Oxford: Clarendon, 1990). xi + 169 pp. and xx plates.

7a. Expanded and updated version of 7: *Textual Criticism of the Hebrew Bible* (Minneapolis and Assen/Maastricht: Fortress Press and Van Gorcum, 1992). xl + 456 pp. (incl. 31 plates).

9. With the collaboration of S. J. Pfann: *The Dead Sea Scrolls on Microfiche: A Comprehensive Facsimile Edition of the Texts from the Judean Desert*, with a *Companion Volume* (Leiden: E. J. Brill/IDC, 1993). 134 microfiches and 187 pp.

8*. Revised edition of 8: *The Greek Minor Prophets Scroll from Naḥal Ḥever (8ḤevXIIgr) (The Seiyal Collection I)* (DJD VIII; Oxford: Clarendon, "Reprinted with corrections 1995"). xi + 169 pp. and xx plates.

9*. Revised edition of 9: *Companion Volume to The Dead Sea Scrolls Microfiche Edition* (2d rev. ed.; Leiden: E. J. Brill/IDC, 1995). 187 pp.

3*. *The Text-Critical Use of the Septuagint in Biblical Research* (Second Edition, Revised and Enlarged; Jerusalem Biblical Studies 8; Jerusalem: Simor, 1997). xxxv + 289 pp.

10. With C. Rabin and S. Talmon, *The Hebrew University Bible, The Book of Jeremiah* (Jerusalem: Magnes Press, 1997). xlv + 303 pp.

7*. Second corrected printing of: *The Textual Criticism of the Bible: An Introduction* (Heb.; Jerusalem: Bialik Institute, 1997). xxiv + 330 pp. and 30 plates.

7b. German version of 7a (revised and updated): *Der Text der Hebräischen Bibel: Handbuch der Textkritik* (trans. H.-J. Fabry; Stuttgart/Berlin/Cologne: Kohlhammer, 1997). xxxiv + 376 pp. (incl. 30 plates).

11. *The Greek and Hebrew Bible—Collected Essays on the Septuagint* (VTSup 72; Leiden/Boston/Cologne: E. J. Brill, 1999). xxxix + 570 pp.

7c. Russian version of 7b (revised and updated): *Tekstologiya Vetchoga Zaveta* (trans. K. Burmistrov and G. Jastrebov; Moscow: Biblisko-Bagaslovski Institut Sv. Apostola Andrjeya [St. Andrews Theological Seminary], 2001). xxxvii + 424 pp. and 30 plates.

7a*. *Textual Criticism of the Hebrew Bible* (2d rev. ed.; Minneapolis and Assen/Maastricht: Fortress Press/Royal Van Gorcum, 2001). xl + 456 pp. (incl. 31 plates).

ELECTRONIC PUBLICATIONS

1. *The Dead Sea Scrolls Database (Non-Biblical Texts)* (The Dead Sea Scrolls Electronic Reference Library, vol. 2; Prepared by the Foundation for Ancient Research and Mormon Studies [FARMS]) (Leiden: E. J. Brill, 1999).

2. In collaboration with A. Groves, the Hebrew text in חב״ד, *JPS Hebrew-English Tanakh: The Traditional Hebrew Text and the New JPS Translation* (2nd ed.; Philadelphia: The Jewish Publication Society, 1999).

3. *The Parallel Database of the MT and LXX*, Accordance computer program, version 5.5, Gramcord 2002 (division of the CATSS database, directed by R. A. Kraft and E. Tov).

BOOKS EDITED

1. *The Hebrew and Greek Texts of Samuel, 1980 Proceedings IOSCS, Vienna* (Jerusalem: Academon, 1980). 225 pp.

2. *A Classified Bibliography of Lexical and Grammatical Studies on the Language of the Septuagint and Its Revisions* (3rd ed.; Jerusalem: Academon, 1982). 46 pp.

3. With C. Rabin: *Textus, Studies of the Hebrew University Bible Project*, vol. 11 (Jerusalem: Magnes Press, 1984). 142 + 68* pp.

4. *Textus, Studies of the Hebrew University Bible Project*, vol. 12 (Jerusalem: Magnes Press, 1985). 199 + 66* pp.

5. *Textus, Studies of the Hebrew University Bible Project*, vol. 13 (Jerusalem: Magnes Press, 1986). 118 + 47* pp.

6. With M. Klopfenstein, U. Luz, and S. Talmon: *Mitte der Schrift? Ein jüdisch-christliches Gespräch. Texte der Berner Symposions 1985* (Judaica et Christiana 11; Bern: Peter Lang, 1987). 389 pp.

7. *Textus, Studies of the Hebrew University Bible Project*, vol. 14 (Jerusalem: Magnes Press, 1988). 183 pp.

8. *Textus, Studies of the Hebrew University Bible Project*, vol. 15 (Jerusalem: Magnes Press, 1990). 268 pp.

9. With M. Fishbane and with the assistance of W. Fields: *"Sha'arei Talmon": Studies in the Bible, Qumran, and the Ancient Near East Presented to Shemaryahu Talmon* (Winona Lake, IN: Eisenbrauns, 1992). xlix + 431 + 165* pp.

10. With A. Hurvitz and S. Japhet: I. L. Seeligmann, *Studies in Biblical Literature* (Heb.; Jerusalem: Magnes Press, 1992). 521 pp.

11. Max L. Margolis, *The Book of Joshua in Greek, Part V: Joshua 19:39–24:33* (Monograph Series, Annenberg Research Institute; Philadelphia 1992). xxvi + pp. 385–475.

12. J. Jarick with the collaboration of G. Marquis, *A Comprehensive Bilingual Concordance of the Hebrew and Greek Texts of the Book of Ecclesiastes* (CATSS: Basic Tools Volume 3; SCS 36; Atlanta, GA: Scholars Press, 1993). ix + 291 pp.

10*. With A. Hurvitz and S. Japhet: I. L. Seeligmann, *Studies in Biblical Literature* (Heb.; 2d rev. ed.; Jerusalem: Magnes Press, 1996). 521 pp.

13. Area editor (Dead Sea Scrolls) in *The Oxford Dictionary of the Jewish Religion* (ed. R. J. Z. Werblowsky and G. Wigoder; New York/Oxford: Oxford University Press, 1997).

14. Area editor in *Encyclopedia of the Dead Sea Scrolls*, vols. 1–2 (ed. L. H. Schiffman and J. C. VanderKam; Oxford/New York: Oxford University Press, 2000). xiv + 1132 pp.

15. With L. H. Schiffman and J. VanderKam, *The Dead Sea Scrolls: Fifty Years After Their Discovery—Proceedings of the Jerusalem Congress, July 20–25, 1997* (Jerusalem: Israel Exploration Society/The Shrine of the Book, Israel Museum, 2000).

In Press

16. F. H. Polak and G. Marquis, *A Classified Index of the Minuses of the Septuagint, Part I: Introduction; Part II: The Pentateuch* (CATSS Basic Tools, 4, 5; Stellenbosch: Print24.com, 2002).

17. With E. D. Herbert, *The Bible as Book—The Hebrew Bible and the Judaean Desert Discoveries* (London: British Library, 2002).

EDITOR-IN-CHIEF, *Discoveries in the Judaean Desert*

1. P. W. Skehan, E. Ulrich, and J. E. Sanderson, *Qumran Cave 4.IV: Palaeo Hebrew and Greek Biblical Manuscripts* (*DJD* IX; Oxford: Clarendon, 1992). xiii + 250 pp. + xlvii plates.

2. E. Qimron and J. Strugnell, *Qumran Cave 4.V: Miqsat Maʿaśe ha-Torah* (*DJD* X; Oxford: Clarendon, 1994). xiv + 235 pp. + viii plates.

3. E. Eshel et al., in consultation with J. VanderKam and M. Brady, *Qumran Cave 4.VI: Poetical and Liturgical Texts, Part 1* (*DJD* XI; Oxford: Clarendon, 1998). xi + 473 pp. + xxxii plates.

4. E. Ulrich and F. M. Cross, eds., *Qumran Cave 4.VII: Genesis to Numbers* (*DJD* XII; Oxford: Clarendon, 1994 [repr. 1999]). xv + 272 pp. + xlix plates.

5. H. Attridge et al., in consultation with J. VanderKam, *Qumran Cave 4.VIII: Parabiblical Texts, Part 1* (*DJD* XIII; Oxford: Clarendon, 1994). x + 470 pp. + xliii plates.

6. E. Ulrich and F. M. Cross, eds., *Qumran Cave 4.IX: Deuteronomy, Joshua, Judges, Kings* (*DJD* XIV; Oxford: Clarendon, 1995 [repr. 1999]). xv + 183 pp. + xxxvii plates.

7. E. Ulrich et al., *Qumran Cave 4.X: The Prophets* (*DJD* XV; Oxford: Clarendon, 1997). xv + 325 pp. + lxiv plates.

8. E. Ulrich et al., *Qumran Cave 4.XI: Psalms to Chronicles* (*DJD* XVI; Oxford: Clarendon, 2000). xv + 302 pp. + xxxviii plates.

9. J. M. Baumgarten, *Qumran Cave 4.XIII: The Damascus Document (4Q266–273)* (*DJD* XVIII; Oxford: Clarendon, 1996). xix + 236 pp. + xlii plates.

10. M. Broshi et al., in consultation with J. VanderKam, *Qumran Cave 4.XIV: Parabiblical Texts, Part 2* (*DJD* XIX; Oxford: Clarendon, 1995). xi + 267 pp. + xxix plates.

11. T. Elgvin et al., in consultation with J. A. Fitzmyer, S.J., *Qumran Cave 4.XV: Sapiential Texts, Part 1* (*DJD* XX; Oxford: Clarendon, 1997). xi + 246 pp. + xviii plates.

12. 1. S. Talmon, J. Ben-Dov, and U. Glessmer, *Qumran Cave 4.XVI: Calendrical Texts* (*DJD* XXI; Oxford: Clarendon, 2001). xii + 263 pp. + xiii plates.

13. G. Brooke et al., in consultation with J. VanderKam, *Qumran Cave 4.XVII: Parabiblical Texts, Part 3* (*DJD* XXII; Oxford: Clarendon, 1996). xi + 352 pp. + xxix plates.

14. F. García Martínez, E. J. C. Tigchelaar, and A. S. van der Woude, *Qumran Cave 11.II: 11Q2–18, 11Q20–31* (*DJD* XXIII; Oxford: Clarendon, 1998). xiii + 487 pp. + liv plates.

15. M. J. W. Leith, *Wadi Daliyeh I: The Wadi Daliyeh Seal Impressions* (*DJD* XXIV; Oxford: Clarendon, 1997). xxv + 249 pp. + xxiv plates.

16. É. Puech, *Qumran Cave 4.XVIII: Textes hébreux (4Q521–4Q528, 4Q576–4Q579)* (*DJD* XXV; Oxford: Clarendon, 1998). xii + 229 pp. + xv plates.

17. P. Alexander and G. Vermes. *Qumran Cave 4.XIX: 4QSerekh Ha-Yaḥad and Two Related Texts* (*DJD* XXVI; Oxford: Clarendon, 1998). xvii + 253 pp. + xxiv plates.

18. H. M. Cotton and A. Yardeni, *Aramaic, Hebrew, and Greek Documentary Texts from Naḥal Ḥever and Other Sites, with an Appendix Containing Alleged Qumran Texts (The Seiyâl Collection II)* (*DJD* XXVII; Oxford: Clarendon, 1997). xxvii + 381 pp. + 33 figures and lxi plates.

19. D. M. Gropp, *Wadi Daliyeh II: The Samaria Papyri from Wadi Daliyeh*; E. Schuller et al., in consultation with J. VanderKam and M. Brady, *Qumran Cave 4.XXVIII: Miscellanea, Part 2* (*DJD* XXVIII; Oxford: Clarendon, 2001). xv + 254 pp. + lxiii plates.

20. E. Chazon et al., in consultation with J. VanderKam and M. Brady, *Qumran Cave 4.XX: Poetical and Liturgical Texts, Part 2* (*DJD* XXIX; Oxford: Clarendon, 1999). xiii + 478 pp. + xxviii plates.

21. D. Dimant, *Qumran Cave 4.XXI: Parabiblical Texts, Part 4: Pseudo-Prophetic Texts* (*DJD* XXX; Oxford: Clarendon, 2001). xiv + 278 pp. + xii plates.

22. E. Puech, *Qumran Cave 4.XXII: Textes araméens, première partie: 4Q529–549* (*DJD* XXXI; Oxford: Clarendon, 2001). xviii + 439 pp. + xxii plates.

23. D. Pike and A. Skinner, in consultation with J. VanderKam and M. Brady, *Qumran Cave 4.XXIII: Unidentified Fragments* (*DJD* XXXIII; Oxford: Clarendon, 2001) xv + 376 pp. + xli plates.

24. J. Strugnell, D. J. Harrington, S. J., and T. Elgvin, in consultation with J. A. Fitzmyer, S.J., *Qumran Cave 4.XXIV: 4QInstruction (Mûsār lᵉMēvîn): 4Q415 ff.* (*DJD* XXXIV; Oxford: Clarendon, 1999). xvi + 584 pp. + xxxi plates.

25. J. Baumgarten et al., *Qumran Cave 4.XXV: Halakhic Texts* (*DJD* XXXV; Oxford: Clarendon, 1999). xi + 173 pp. + xii plates.

26. S. J. Pfann, *Cryptic Texts*; P. Alexander et al., in consultation with J. VanderKam and M. Brady, *Qumran Cave 4.XXVI: Miscellanea, Part 1* (*DJD* XXXVI; Oxford: Clarendon, 2000). xvi + 739 pp. + xlix plates.

27. H. Cotton et al., in consultation with J. VanderKam and M. Brady, *Miscellaneous Texts from the Judaean Desert* (*DJD* XXXVIII; Oxford: Clarendon, 2000). xvii + 250 pp. + xxxvi plates.

28. E. Tov (ed.), *The Texts from the Judaean Desert: Indices and an Introduction to the Discoveries in the Judaean Desert Series* (*DJD* XXXIX; Oxford: Clarendon, 2002). x + 452 pp.

In Press

1. F. M. Cross, D. W. Parry; E. Ulrich, *Qumran Cave 4.XII: 1–2 Samuel* (*DJD* XVII; Oxford: Clarendon, 2002). xxvii plates.

2. M. G. Abegg, Jr., *The Dead Sea Scrolls Concordance I. The Non-Biblical Texts from Qumran* (Leiden: E. J. Brill, 2002).

3. With D. Parry, *The Dead Sea Scrolls Arranged by Subject* (Leiden: E. J. Brill, 2002).

ARTICLES

1970

1. "Two Documentary Papyri," *ZPE* 5 (1970) 17–21 and plate II.

1971

2. "Pap. Giessen 13, 19, 22, 26: A Revision of the LXX?" *RB* 78 (1971) 355–83 and plates X–XI. Revised version: *The Greek and Hebrew Bible* (1999) 459–75.

1972

3. "Lucian and Proto-Lucian: Toward a New Solution of the Problem," *RB* 79 (1972) 101–13; repr. in *Qumran and the History of the Biblical Text* (ed. F. M. Cross

and S. Talmon; Cambridge, Mass.: Harvard University Press, 1975) 293–305. Revised version: *The Greek and Hebrew Bible* (1999) 477–88.

4. "L'incidence de la critique textuelle sur la critique littéraire dans le livre de Jérémie," *RB* 79 (1972) 189–99.

4a. Hebrew version of 4: *Beth Miqra* 50 (1972) 279–87.

5. "The Methodology of Textual Criticism in Jewish Greek Scriptures, with Special Attention to the Problems in Samuel-Kings: The State of the Question: Problems and Proposed Solutions," in *Septuagint and Cognate Studies* 2 (ed. R. A. Kraft; 1972) 3–15. Revised version: *The Greek and Hebrew Bible* (1999) 489–99.

1973

6. "Transliterations of Hebrew Words in the Greek Versions of the Old Testament: A Further Characteristic of the *kaige*-Th. Revision?" *Text* 8 (1973) 78–92. Revised version: *The Greek and Hebrew Bible* (1999) 501–12.

7. "Some Corrections to Reider-Turner's Index to Aquila," *Textus* 8 (1973) 164–74.

1974

8. "Une inscription grecque d'origine samaritaine trouvée à Thessalonique," *RB* 81 (1974) 43–8. Revised version: *The Greek and Hebrew Bible* (1999) 513–17.

1975

9. "On 'Pseudo-Variants' Reflected in the Septuagint," *JSS* 20 (1975) 165–77.

10. "The Contribution of Textual Criticism to the Literary Criticism and Exegesis of Jeremiah: The Hebrew *Vorlage* of the LXX of Chapter 27," *Shnaton* 1 (1975) 165–82 (Heb. with Eng. summ.).

1976

11. "The Relation between the Greek Versions of Baruch and Daniel," in *Armenian and Biblical Studies* (ed. M. E. Stone; Jerusalem: St. James, 1976) 27–34. Revised version: *The Greek and Hebrew Bible* (1999) 519–26.

12. "Some Thoughts on a Lexicon of the LXX," *BIOSCS* 9 (1976) 14–46. Revised version: *The Greek and Hebrew Bible* (1999) 95–108.

13. "Septuagint, Contribution to Old Testament Scholarship," *The Interpreter's Dictionary of the Bible, Supplementary Volume* (ed. K. Krim; New York/Nashville: Abingdon, 1976) 807–11.

14. "Three Dimensions of LXX Words," *RB* 83 (1976) 529–544. Revised version: *The Greek and Hebrew Bible* (1999) 453–64. Revised version: *The Greek and Hebrew Bible* (1999) 85–94.

1977

15. "Compound Words in the LXX Representing Two or More Hebrew Words," *Bib* 58 (1977) 189–212. Revised version: *The Greek and Hebrew Bible* (1999) 131–52.

16. "Recent Developments in Old Testament Textual Criticism," *Shnaton* 2 (1977) 279–86 (Heb. with Eng. summ.).

1978

17. "Old Testament Textual Criticism, Its Methods and Limitations," in *Studies in Bible and the Ancient Near East Presented to Samuel E. Loewenstamm on His Seventieth Birthday* (ed. Y. Avishur and J. Blau; Heb. with Eng. summ.; Jerusalem: Rubenstein, 1978) 207–21.

18. "The Textual History of the Song of Deborah in the A Text of the LXX," *VT* 28 (1978) 224–32. Revised version: *The Greek and Hebrew Bible* (1999) 501–8,

19. "The Use of Concordances in the Reconstruction of the Vorlage of the LXX," *CBQ* 40 (1978) 519–34.

20. "Midrash-Type Exegesis in the LXX of Joshua," *RB* 85 (1978) 50–61. Revised version: *The Greek and Hebrew Bible* (1999) 153–63.

21. "The Nature of the Hebrew Text Underlying the LXX: A Survey of the Problems," JSOT 7 (1978) 53–68.

22. "Studies in the Vocabulary of the Septuagint: The Relation between Vocabulary and Translation Technique," *Tarbiz* 47 (1978) 120–38 (Heb. with Eng. summ.; German summary in *Hebräische Beiträge zur Wissenschaft des Judentums deutsch angezeigt* 1 [Heidelberg: Lambert Schneider, 1985] 148).

23. "The Textual Character of the Leviticus Scroll from Qumran Cave 11," *Shnaton* 3 (1978) 238–44 (Heb. with Eng. summ.).

1979

24. "Loan-words, Homophony and Transliterations in the Septuagint," *Bib* 60 (1979) 216–36. Revised version: *The Greek and Hebrew Bible* (1999) 165–82.

25. "The Relationship between the Textual Witnesses of the Old Testament in the Light of the Scrolls from the Judean Desert," *Beth Miqra* 77 (1979) 161–70 (Heb.); repr. in *Studies in Biblical History* (ed. M. Cogan; Jerusalem: Zalman Shazar Center for Jewish History, 1997) 309–18.

26. "The Textual Affiliations of 4QSam[a]," JSOT 14 (1979) 37–53; repr. in *The Hebrew and Greek Texts of Samuel, 1980 Proceedings IOSCS, Vienna* (ed. E. Tov; Jerusalem: Academon, 1980) 189–205. Revised version: *The Greek and Hebrew Bible* (1999) 273–83.

10a. "Exegetical Notes on the Hebrew Vorlage of the LXX of Jeremiah 27 (34)," *ZAW* 91 (1979) 73–93. Revised version: *The Greek and Hebrew Bible* (1999) 363–84.

1980

27. "Determining the Relationship between the Qumran Scrolls and the LXX: Some Methodological Issues," in *The Hebrew and Greek Texts of Samuel, 1980 Proceedings IOSCS, Vienna* (ed. E. Tov; Jerusalem: Academon, 1980) 45–67.

28. "*Biblia Hebraica Stuttgartensia*," *Shnaton* 4 (1980) 172–80 (Heb. with Eng. summ.).

29. With S. Talmon: "A Commentary on the Text of Jeremiah, I. The LXX of Jer. 1:1–7," *Textus* 9 (1981) 1–15.

1981

30. "Tekstgetuigen en tekstgeschiedenis van het Oude en Nieuwe Testament, A. De tekst van het Oude Testament," in *Bijbels Handboek I, De Wereld van de Bijbel* (ed. A. S. van der Woude; Kampen: J. H. Kok, 1981) 217–62.

31. "The Impact of the LXX Translation of the Pentateuch on the Translation of the Other Books," in *Mélanges Dominique Barthélemy* (ed. P. Casetti, O. Keel and A. Schenker; OBO 38; Fribourg/Göttingen: Éditions universitaires/Vandenhoeck & Ruprecht, 1981) 577–92. Revised version: *The Greek and Hebrew Bible* (1999) 183–94.

32. "Some Aspects of the Textual and Literary History of the Book of Jeremiah," in *Le livre de Jérémie, le prophète et son milieu, les oracles et leur transmission* (ed. P.-M. Bogaert; BETL 54; Leuven: Leuven University Press/Peeters, 1981; rev. ed. 1997 [1998]) 145–67, 430. Revised version: *The Greek and Hebrew Bible* (1999) 363–84.

33. "The Discovery of the Missing Part of Margolis' Edition of Joshua," *BIOSCS* 14 (1981) 17–21. Revised version: *The Greek and Hebrew Bible* (1999) 21–30.

34. With R. A. Kraft: "Computer-Assisted Tools for Septuagint Studies," *BIOSCS* 14 (1981) 22–40.

1982

35. "The 'Lucianic' Text of the Canonical and the Apocryphal Sections of Esther: A Rewritten Biblical Book," *Textus* 10 (1982) 1–25. Revised version: *The Greek and Hebrew Bible* (1999) 535–48.

36. "Greek Translations," *Encyclopaedia Biblica*, vol. 8 (Heb.; Jerusalem: Bialik Institute, 1982), cols. 774–830.

37. "The Representation of the Causative Aspects of the *Hiph'il* in the LXX: A Study in Translation Technique," *Bib* 63 (1982) 417–24. Revised version: *The Greek and Hebrew Bible* (1999) 195–202.

38. "The Temple Scroll and Old Testament Textual Criticism," *ErIsr* 16 (Harry M. Orlinsky Volume) (ed. B. A. Levine and A. Malamat; Heb. with Eng. summ.; Jerusalem: Israel Exploration Society/Hebrew Union College-Jewish Institute of Religion, 1982) 100–11.

39. "A Modern Textual Outlook Based on the Qumran Scrolls," *HUCA* 53 (1982) 11–27.

40. "Criteria for Evaluating Textual Readings: The Limitations of Textual Rules," *HTR* 75 (1982) 429–48.

1983

41. "The Rabbinic Traditions concerning the 'Changes' Inserted in the Septuagint Translation of the Pentateuch and the Question of the Original Text of That Translation," in *I. L. Seeligmann Memorial Volume* (ed. A. Rofé and Y. Zakovitch; Heb. with Eng. summ.; Jerusalem: Magnes Press, 1983) 371–93.

1984

42. "Did the Septuagint Translators Always Understand Their Hebrew Text?" in *De Septuaginta, Studies in Honour of John William Wevers on His Sixty-Fifth Birthday* (ed. A. Pietersma and C. Cox; Mississauga, Ont.: Benben, 1984) 53–70. Revised version: *The Greek and Hebrew Bible* (1999) 203–18.

43. "The LXX Additions (Miscellanies) in 1 Kings 2," *Textus* 11 (1984) 89–118. Revised version: *The Greek and Hebrew Bible* (1999) 549–70.

44. "The Use of a Computerized Data Base for Septuagint Research: The Greek-Hebrew Parallel Alignment," *BIOSCS* 17 (1984) 36–47. Revised version: *The Greek and Hebrew Bible* (1999) 31–51.

45. With J. Cook: "A Computerized Database for the Qumran Biblical Scrolls with an Appendix on the Samaritan Pentateuch," *JNSL* 12 (1984) 133–7.

46. "The Fifth Fascicle of Margolis' The Book of Joshua in Greek," *JQR* 74 (1984) 397–407. Revised version: *The Greek and Hebrew Bible* (1999) 21–30.

47. "The LXX of Ezekiel," *The World of the Bible* (ed. G. Brin; Heb.; Jerusalem: Revivim, 1984) 17.

36a. Revised version of 36 in: *Bible Translations, An Introduction* (ed. C. Rabin; Heb.; The Biblical Encyclopaedia Library 2; Jerusalem: Bialik Institute, 1984) 49–120.

41a. "The Rabbinic Tradition concerning the 'Alterations' Inserted into the Greek Pentateuch and Their Relation to the Original Text of the LXX," *JSJ* 15 (1984) 65–89. Revised version: *The Greek and Hebrew Bible* (1999) 1–18.

1985

48. With B. G. Wright: "Computer-Assisted Study of the Criteria for Assessing the Literalness of Translation Units in the LXX," *Textus* 12 (1985) 149–87. Revised version: *The Greek and Hebrew Bible* (1999) 219–37.

49. "The Nature and Background of Harmonizations in Biblical MSS," *JSOT* 31 (1985) 3–29.

50. "Computer Assisted Alignment of the Greek-Hebrew Equivalents of the Masoretic Text and the Septuagint," in *La Septuaginta en la investigacion contemporanea (V Congreso de la IOSCS)* (ed. N. Fernández Marcos; Textos y Estudios "Cardenal Cisneros" 34; Madrid: Consejo Superior de Investigaciones Científicas, 1985) 221–42. Revised version: *The Greek and Hebrew Bible* (1999) 31–51.

51. "The Composition of 1 Samuel 17–18 in the Light of the Evidence of the Septuagint Version," in *Empirical Models for Biblical Criticism* (ed. J. H. Tigay; Philadelphia: University of Pennsylvania Press, 1985) 97–130. Revised version: *The Greek and Hebrew Bible* (1999) 333–60.

52. "The Literary History of the Book of Jeremiah in the Light of Its Textual History," in *Empirical Models for Biblical Criticism* (ed. J. H. Tigay; Philadelphia: University of Pennsylvania Press, 1985) 211–37. Revised version: *The Greek and Hebrew Bible* (1999) 345–64.

40a. Hebrew version of 40: *Beth Miqra* 100 (1985) 112–32.

1986

53. "The Growth of the Book of Joshua in the Light of the Evidence of the LXX Translation," ScrHier 31 (1986) 321–39. Revised version: *The Greek and Hebrew Bible* (1999) 385–396.

54. "Recensional Differences between the MT and LXX of Ezekiel," *ETL* 62 (1986) 89–101. Revised version: *The Greek and Hebrew Bible* (1999) 397–410.

55. "Jewish Greek Scriptures," in *Early Judaism and Its Modern Interpreters* (ed. R. A. Kraft and G. W. E. Nickelsburg; Atlanta, GA: Scholars Press, 1986) 223–37.

56. "The Orthography and Language of the Hebrew Scrolls Found at Qumran and the Origin of These Scrolls," *Textus* 13 (1986) 31–57.

57. "Bible Translations, Ancient," in *Illustrated Dictionary and Concordance of the Bible* (ed. G. Wigoder; New York/London: Macmillan, 1986) 181–84.

58. "A New Generation of Biblical Research," in *Proceedings of the First International Colloquium Bible and Computer, The Text, Louvain-la-Neuve (Belgique) 2–3–4 septembre 1985* (Paris/Genève: Champion-Sladkine, 1986) 413–43.

30a. Revised and updated English version of 30: "The Text of the Old Testament," in *The World of the Bible, Bible Handbook, Volume I* (ed. A. S. van der Woude; trans. S. Woudstra; Grand Rapids, Mich.: Eerdmans, 1986) 156–90.

51a. Abbreviated version: "The David and Goliath Saga," *BRev* 34 (1986) 35–41; reprinted in *Approaches to the Bible, The Best of Bible Review, I, Composition, Transmission and Language* (ed. H. Minkoff; Washington: Biblical Archaeology Society, 1994) 51–61.

1987

59. "Some Sequence Differences between the MT and LXX and Their Ramifications for the Literary Criticism of the Bible," *JNSL* 13 (1987) 151–60. Revised version: *The Greek and Hebrew Bible* (1999) 411–18.

60. "Die Septuaginta in ihrem theologischen und traditionsgeschichtlichen Verhältnis zur hebräischen Bibel," in *Mitte der Schrift? Ein jüdisch-christliches Gespräch. Texte der Berner Symposions 1985* (ed. M. Klopfenstein et al.; Judaica et Christiana 11; Bern: Peter Lang, 1987) 237–68.

61. "The Nature and Study of the Translation Technique of the LXX in the Past and Present," in *VI Congress of the International Organization for Septuagint and Cognate Studies* (ed. C. E. Cox; SCS 23; 1987) 337–59. Revised version: *The Greek and Hebrew Bible* (1999) 239–46.

36b. Revised and updated version of 36a: "Die griechischen Bibelübersetzungen," *Aufstieg und Niedergang der Römischen Welt* II, 20.1 (Berlin/New York: Walter de Gruyter, 1987) 121–89.

1988

62. "Computers and the Bible," *BRev* 4 (1988) 38–42.

63. "Hebrew Biblical Manuscripts from the Judaean Desert: Their Contribution to Textual Criticism," *JJS* 39 (1988) 1–37.

64. "The Bible and the Computer," *'Al Ha-perek* 4 (1988) 16–22 (Heb.).

65. "The Septuagint," in *Mikra, Compendia Rerum Iudaicarum ad Novum Testamentum*, Section Two, I (ed. M. J. Mulder; Assen-Maastricht and Philadelphia: Fortress Press/Van Gorcum, 1988) 161–88.

1989

66. "Achievements and Trends in Computer-Assisted Biblical Studies," *Proceedings of the Second International Colloquium Bible and Computer: Methods, Tools, Results, Jérusalem, 9–13 juin 1988* (Travaux de linguistique quantitative 43; ed. C. Muller; Paris/Genève: Champion-Sladkine, 1989) 33–60.

67. "Proto-Samaritan Texts and the Samaritan Pentateuch," in *The Samaritans* (ed. A. D. Crown; Tübingen: J. C. B. Mohr [Paul Siebeck], 1989) 397–407.

68. "An Urtext of the Hebrew Bible?" *Sefer H. M. Gevaryahu, Meḥqarim be-Miqra uwemaḥshevet yisrael muggash lo behagi'o leševah* (ed. B. Z. Lurie; Heb.; Jerusalem: Ḥevrah leḤeqer haMiqra beYisrael and Kiryat Sefer, 1989) 308–12.

69. "Computer Assisted Research of the Greek and Hebrew Bible," in *Computer Assisted Analysis of Biblical Texts, Papers Read at the Workshop on the Occasion of the Tenth Anniversary of the "Werkgroep Informatika", Faculty of Theology, Vrije Universiteit, Amsterdam, November, 5–6, 1987* (ed. E. Talstra; Amsterdam: Free University Press, 1989) 87–99.

70. "The Jeremiah Scrolls from Qumran," in *The Texts of Qumran and the History of the Community: Proceedings of the Groningen Congress on The Dead Sea Scrolls (20–23 August 1989)*, vol. I, Biblical Texts = *RevQ* 14 (ed. F. García Martínez; Paris: Gabalda, 1989) 189–206 and plates I–III.

1990

71. "Renderings of Combinations of the Infinitive Absolute Construction and Finite Verbs in the LXX: Their Nature and Distribution," in *Studien zur Septuaginta: Robert Hanhart zu Ehren* (ed. D. Fraenkel et al.; MSU XX; Göttingen: Vandenhoeck & Ruprecht, 1990) 64–73. Revised version: *The Greek and Hebrew Bible* (1999) 247–56.

72. "Greek Words and Hebrew Meanings," in *Melbourne Symposium on Septuagint Lexicography* (ed. T. Muraoka; SCS 28; Atlanta, Georgia: Scholars Press, 1990) 83–125. Revised version: *The Greek and Hebrew Bible* (1999) 109–28.

73. "Theologically Motivated Exegesis Embedded in the Septuagint," *Proceedings of a Conference at the Annenberg Research Institute May 15–16, 1989* (A Jewish Quarterly Review Supplement: 1990; Philadelphia: Annenberg Research Institute, 1990) 215–33. Revised version: *The Greek and Hebrew Bible* (1999) 257–69.

74. "Recensional Differences between the Masoretic Text and the Septuagint of Proverbs," in *Of Scribes and Scrolls, Studies on the Hebrew Bible, Intertestamental Judaism, and Christian Origins Presented to John Strugnell on the Occasion of His Sixtieth Birthday* (ed. H. W. Attridge et al.; College Theology Society Resources in Religion 5; Lanham, Maryland/New York/London: The College Theology Society University Press of America, 1990) 43–56. Revised version: *The Greek and Hebrew Bible* (1999) 419–31.

1991

75. "The Samaritan Pentateuch and the So-Called 'Proto-Samaritan Texts'," in *Studies on Hebrew and Other Semitic Languages Presented to Professor Chaim Rabin on the Occasion of His Seventy-Fifth Birthday* (ed. M. Goshen-Gottstein, S. Morag and S. Kogut; Heb.; Jerusalem: Academon, 1991) 133–46.

76. "A New Understanding of the Samaritan Pentateuch in the Wake of the Discovery of the Qumran Scrolls," *Proceedings of the First International Congress of the Société d'Études Samaritaines, Tel-Aviv, April 11–13, 1988* (ed. A. Tal and M. Florentin; Tel-Aviv: Chaim Rosenberg School for Jewish Studies, Tel Aviv University, 1991) 293–303.

77. "The Original Shape of the Biblical Text," *Congress Volume Leuven 1989* (ed. J. A. Emerton; VTSup 43; Leiden/New York/Copenhagen/Cologne: E. J. Brill, 1991) 345–59.

78. "*Deut.* 12 and *11QTemple* LII–LIII: A Contrastive Analysis," *RevQ* 15 (1991) 169–73.

79. "The CATSS Project: A Progress Report," in *VII Congress of the International Organization for Septuagint and Cognate Studies* (ed. C. E. Cox; SCS 31; Atlanta, GA: Scholars Press, 1991) 157–63.

80. "4QJer^c (4Q72)," in *Tradition of the Text: Studies Offered to Dominique Barthélemy in Celebration of His 70th Birthday* (ed. G. J. Norton and S. Pisano; OBO 109; Freiburg/Göttingen: Universitätsverlag/Vandenhoeck & Ruprecht, 1991) 249–76 and plates I–VII.

81. "The Unpublished Qumran Texts from Caves 4 and 11," *JJS* 43 (1992) 101–36.

63a. Revised and updated version of 63 in *Jewish Civilization in the Hellenistic-Roman Period* (ed. S. Talmon; JSPSup 10; Sheffield: Sheffield Academic Press, 1991) 107–37.

1992

82. "Interchanges of Consonants between the Masoretic Text and the *Vorlage* of the Septuagint," in *"Sha'arei Talmon": Studies in the Bible, Qumran, and the Ancient Near East Presented to Shemaryahu Talmon* (ed. M. Fishbane and E. Tov; Winona Lake, Ind.: Eisenbrauns, 1992) 255–66. Revised version: *The Greek and Hebrew Bible* (1999) 301–11.

83. "The Contribution of the Qumran Scrolls to the Understanding of the LXX," in *Septuagint, Scrolls and Cognate Writings: Papers Presented to the International Symposium on the Septuagint and Its Relations to the Dead Sea Scrolls and Other Writings (Manchester, 1990)* (ed. G. J. Brooke and B. Lindars; SCS 33; Atlanta, Georgia: Scholars Press, 1992) 11–47. Revised version: *The Greek and Hebrew Bible* (1999) 285–300.

84. "4QJosh^b," in *Intertestamental Essays in Honour of Józef Tadeusz Milik*, part I (ed. Z. J. Kapera; Qumranica Mogilanensia 6; Cracow: Enigma, 1992) 205–12 and plate II.

85. "Textual Criticism (OT)," in *ABD* (ed. D. N. Freedman; New York/London: Doubleday, 1992) 6.393–412.

86. "4QLev^d (4Q26)," in *The Scriptures and the Scrolls. Studies in Honour of A. S. van der Woude on the Occasion of His 65th Birthday* (ed. F. García Martínez, A. Hilhorst, and C. J. Labuschagne; VTSup 49; Leiden: E. J. Brill, 1992) 1–5 and plates 1–2.

87. "The Textual Base of the Corrections in the Biblical Texts Found at Qumran," in *The Dead Sea Scrolls: Forty Years of Research* (ed. D. Dimant and U. Rappaport; Leiden/New York/Cologne and Jerusalem: E. J. Brill, Magnes Press, and Yad Izhak Ben-Zvi, 1992) 299–314.

88. "The Textual Status of 4Q364–367 (4QPP)," in *The Madrid Qumran Congress: Proceedings of the International Congress on the Dead Sea Scrolls—Madrid, 18–21 March, 1991* (ed. J. Trebolle Barrera and L. Vegas Montaner; STDJ 11, 1–2; Leiden/Madrid: E. J. Brill/Complutense, 1992) 1.43–82.

89. "Some Notes on a Generation of Qumran Studies (by Frank M. Cross): Reply," in *The Madrid Qumran Congress: Proceedings of the International Congress on the Dead Sea Scrolls—Madrid, 18–21 March, 1991* (ed. J. Trebolle Barrera and L. Vegas Montaner; STDJ 11, 1–2; Leiden/Madrid: E. J. Brill/Complutense, 1992) 1.15–22.

63b. Hebrew version of 63 in *The Scrolls of the Judaean Desert: Forty Years of Research* (ed. M. Broshi et al.; Heb.; Jerusalem: Bialik Institute/Israel Exploration Society, 1992) 63–98.

90. "Three Fragments of Jeremiah from Qumran Cave 4," *RevQ* 15 (1992) 531–41.

65a. Translation of 65 into Japanese, in *Eusebian Studies*, vol. III (ed. G. Hata and H. W. Attridge; Tokyo: Lithon, 1992) 39–90, 438–44.

81a. Revised version of 82: "The Unpublished Qumran Texts from Caves 4 and 11," *BA* 55 (1992) 94–104.

1993

91. "The Qumran Scribal School," in *Studies in Bible and Exegesis, Vol. III, Moshe Goshen-Gottstein: in Memoriam* (ed. M. Bar-Asher et al.; Heb.; Ramat Gan: Bar-Ilan University Press, 1993) 135–53.

92. "Some Reflections on the Hebrew Texts from which the Septuagint Was Translated," *JNSL* 19 (1993) 107–22.

93. "Pentateuch, II, III, IV", "Qumran", in *A Companion to Samaritan Studies* (ed. A. D. Crown et al.; Tübingen: J. C. B. Mohr [Paul Siebeck], 1993) 180–83, 197–8.

1994

94. "Glosses, Interpolations, and Other Types of Scribal Additions in the Text of the Hebrew Bible," in *Language, Theology, and the Bible: Essays in Honour of James Barr* (ed. S. E. Balentine and J. Barton; Oxford: Clarendon, 1994) 40–66. Revised version: *The Greek and Hebrew Bible* (1999) 53–74.

94a. Hebrew version of 94 in *The Bible in the Light of Its Interpreters, Sarah Kamin Memorial Volume* (ed. S. Japhet; Heb.; Jerusalem: Magnes Press, 1994) 38–57.

95. Articles "Manuscripts, Hebrew Bible", "Dead Sea Scrolls," in *The Oxford Companion to the Bible* (ed. B. M. Metzger and M. D. Coogan; New York/Oxford: Oxford University Press, 1994) 159–60, 486–8.

96. "The Unpublished Qumran Texts from the Judean Desert," in *New Qumran Texts and Studies: Proceedings of the First Meeting of the International Organization for Qumran Studies, Paris 1992* (ed. G. J. Brooke with F. García Martínez; STDJ 15; Leiden/New York/Cologne: E. J. Brill, 1994) 81–8.

97. "The Exodus Section of 4Q422," *DSD* 1 (1994) 197–209.

98. "Biblical Texts as Reworked in Some Qumran Manuscripts with Special Attention to 4QRP and 4QParaGen–Exod," in *The Community of the Renewed Covenant, The Notre Dame Symposium on the Dead Sea Scrolls* (ed. E. Ulrich and J. VanderKam; Christianity and Judaism in Antiquity Series 10; Notre Dame, Ind.: University of Notre Dame Press, 1994) 111–34.

99. "The Qumran Scrolls in Light of Modern Research," in *Jewish Studies, Forum of the World Union of Jewish Studies* 34 (Jerusalem: Magnes Press, 1994) 37–67 (Heb.).

100. "4QJerᵃ: A Preliminary Edition," *Textus* 17 (1994) 1–41 and plates I–VII.

101. "4QLevᶜ," in *Qumran Cave 4.VII: Genesis to Numbers* (ed. E. Ulrich and F. M. Cross; DJD XII; Oxford: Clarendon, 1994) 189–92 and plate XXXV.

102. "4QLevᵈ," in *Qumran Cave 4.VII: Genesis to Numbers* (ed. E. Ulrich and F. M. Cross; DJD XII; Oxford: Clarendon, 1994) 193–95 and plate XXXVI.

103. "4QLevᵉ," in *Qumran Cave 4.VII: Genesis to Numbers* (ed. E. Ulrich and F. M. Cross; DJD XII; Oxford: Clarendon, 1994) 196–201 and plate XXXVII.

104. "4QLevᵍ," in *Qumran Cave 4.VII: Genesis to Numbers* (ed. E. Ulrich and F. M. Cross; DJD XII; Oxford: Clarendon, 1994) 203–4 and plate XXXVII.

105. With S. A. White: "4QReworked Pentateuchᵇ⁻ᵉ and 4QTemple?" in H. Attridge et al., in consultation with J. VanderKam, *Qumran Cave 4.VIII, Parabiblical Texts, Part 1* (*DJD* XIII; Oxford: Clarendon, 1994) 187–351, 459–63 and plates XIII–XXXXVI.

106. With T. Elgvin: "4QParaphrase of Genesis and Exodus," in: H. Attridge et al., in consultation with J. VanderKam, *Qumran Cave 4.VIII, Parabiblical Texts, Part 1* (*DJD* XIII; Oxford: Clarendon, 1994) 417–42, 468–70 and plates XLII–XLIII.

63c. Abbreviated French version of 63: "Les manuscrits bibliques," in *Les manuscrits de la Mer morte: Aux origines du christianisme, Les Dossiers d'Archéologie* 189 (1994) 42–8; also separately (Dijon: Faton, S. A., 1994) 42–8.

1995

107. "Groups of Hebrew Biblical Texts Found at Qumran," in *A Time to Prepare the Way in the Wilderness. Papers on the Qumran Scrolls by Fellows of the Institute for Advanced Studies of the Hebrew University, Jerusalem, 1989–1990* (ed. D. Dimant and L. H. Schiffman; STDJ 16; Leiden: E. J. Brill, 1995) 85–102.

108. "Letters of the Cryptic A Script and Paleo-Hebrew Letters Used as Scribal Marks in Some Qumran Scrolls," *DSD* 2 (1995) 330–39.

109. "Excerpted and Abbreviated Biblical Texts from Qumran," *RevQ* 16 (1995) 581–600.

110. With A. J. T. Jull, D. J. Donahue, and M. Broshi: "Radiocarbon Dating of Scrolls and Linen Fragments from the Judean Desert," *Radiocarbon* 37 (1995) 11–19.

111. "Three Manuscripts (Abbreviated Texts?) of Canticles from Qumran Cave 4," in *JJS* 46 (1995) 88–111.

112. "4QReworked Pentateuch: A Synopsis of Its Contents," *RevQ* 16 (1995) 647–53.

84a. "4QJosh^b," in *Qumran Cave 4.IX: Deuteronomy, Joshua, Judges, Kings* (ed. E. Ulrich and F. M. Cross; *DJD* XIV; Oxford: Clarendon, 1995) 151–8 and plate XXXV.

97a. "A Paraphrase of Exodus: 4Q422," in חיים ליונה, *Solving Riddles and Untying Knots: Biblical, Epigraphic, and Semitic Studies in Honor of Jonas C. Greenfield* (ed. Z. Zevit et al.; Winona Lake, Ind.: Eisenbrauns, 1995) 339–50.

102a. "4QLev^{c,e,g} (4Q25, 26a, 26b)," in *Pomegranates and Golden Bells: Studies in Biblical, Jewish, and Near Eastern Ritual, Law, and Literature in Honor of Jacob Milgrom* (ed. D. P. Wright et al.; Winona Lake, Ind.: Eisenbrauns, 1995) 257–66.

1996

113. "Scribal Practices Reflected in the Documents from the Judean Desert and in the Rabbinic Literature: A Comparative Study," in *Texts, Temples, and Traditions: A Tribute to Menahem Haran* (ed. M. V. Fox et al.; Winona Lake, Ind.: Eisenbrauns, 1996) 383–403.

114. "Special Layout of Poetical Units in the Texts from the Judean Desert," in *Give Ear to My Words: Psalms and Other Poetry in and around the Hebrew Bible, Essays in Honour of Professor N.A. van Uchelen* (ed. J. Dyk et al.; Amsterdam: Societas Hebraica Amstelodamensis, 1996) 115–28.

115. "Scribal Practices Reflected in the Paleo-Hebrew Texts from the Judean Desert," *Scripta Classica Israelica* 15 (1996) 268–73.

110a. Revised version of 110: *Atiqot* 28 (1996) 85–91.

116. "The History and Significance of a Standard Text of the Hebrew Bible," in *Hebrew Bible/Old Testament: The History of Its Interpretation*, Volume I, chapter 2.1 (ed. M. Saebø; Göttingen: Vandenhoeck & Ruprecht, 1996) 49–66.

117. "Scribal Markings in the Texts from the Judean Desert," in *Current Research and Technological Developments on the Dead Sea Scrolls: Conference on the Texts from the Judean Desert, Jerusalem, 30 April 1995* (ed. D. W. Parry and S. D. Ricks; STDJ 20; Leiden/New York/Cologne: E. J. Brill, 1996) 41–77.

118. "Discoveries in the Judaean Desert," in *Hommage à Józef Tadeusz Milik* = *RevQ* 17 (ed. F. García Martínez and E. Puech; 1996) 613–21.

119. "The Socio-Religious Background of the Paleo-Hebrew Biblical Texts Found at Qumran," in *Geschichte—Tradition—Reflexion, Festschrift für Martin Hengel zum 70. Geburtstag*, I–III (ed. H. Cancik et al.; Tübingen: J. C. B. Mohr [Paul Siebeck], 1996) I.353–74.

1997

30a. Revised edition of 30: "Tekstgetuigen en tekstgeschiedenis van het Oude en Nieuwe Testament, A. De tekst van het Oude Testament," in *Bijbels Handboek I, De Wereld van de Bijbel* (ed. A. S. van der Woude; Kampen: J. H. Kok, 1997) 223–69.

100a. "4QJer^a," in E. Ulrich et al., *Qumran Cave 4.X: The Prophets* (*DJD* XV; Oxford: Clarendon, 1997) 145–70 and plates XXIV–XXIX.

120. "4QJer^b," in E. Ulrich et al., *Qumran Cave 4.X: The Prophets* (*DJD* XV; Oxford: Clarendon, 1997) 171–6 and plate XXIX.

80a. "4QJer^c," in E. Ulrich et al., *Qumran Cave 4.X: The Prophets* (*DJD* XV; Oxford: Clarendon, 1997) 177–201 and plates XXX–XXXVI.

121. "4QJer^d," in E. Ulrich et al., *Qumran Cave 4.X: The Prophets* (*DJD* XV; Oxford: Clarendon, 1997) 203–5 and plate XXXVII.

122. "4QJer^e," in E. Ulrich et al., *Qumran Cave 4.X: The Prophets* (*DJD* XV; Oxford: Clarendon, 1997) 207 and plate XXXVII.

123. "The Book of Jeremiah in Qumran," *Shnaton* 11 (1997) 302–12 (Heb.).

124. Articles "Bible Text," "Bible Translations," "Masorah," "Septuagint," "Targum," and others. In: R. J. Z. Werblowsky and G. Wigoder, eds., *The Oxford Dictionary of the Jewish Religion* (New York/Oxford: Oxford University Press, 1997).

125. "The Biblical Texts from the Judean Desert," in *On a Scroll of a Book: Articles on The Dead Sea Scrolls: Lectures from Meetings on The Dead Sea Scrolls, The Hebrew University of Jerusalem, The Institute of Jewish Studies, November–December 1995* (ed. L. Mazor; Heb.; Jerusalem: Mount Scopus Publications, Magnes Press, 1997) 40–65.

125a. Revised form in *Qad* 30 (1997) 73–81 (Heb.).

126. "A Status Report on the Publication of the Judaean Desert Scrolls," *Qad* 30 (1997) 66–70 (Heb.).

127. "*Tefillin* of Different Origin from Qumran?" in *A Light for Jacob, Studies in the Bible and the Dead Sea Scrolls in Memory of Jacob Shalom Licht* (ed. Y. Hoffman and F. H. Polak; Jerusalem/Tel Aviv: Bialik Institute/Chaim Rosenberg School of Jewish Studies, 1997) 44*–54*.

128. "Different Editions of the Song of Hannah," in *Tehillah le-Moshe, Biblical and Judaic Studies in Honor of Moshe Greenberg* (ed. M. Cogan, B. L. Eichler, and J. H. Tigay; Winona Lake, Ind.: Eisenbrauns, 1997) 149–70. Revised version: *The Greek and Hebrew Bible* (1999) 433–55.

129. "The Scribes of the Texts Found in the Judean Desert," in *The Quest for Context and Meaning, Studies in Intertextuality in Honor of James A. Sanders* (ed. C. A. Evans and S. Talmon; Leiden/New York/Cologne: E. J. Brill, 1997) 131–52.

130. "The Text of Isaiah at Qumran," in *Writing & Reading the Scroll of Isaiah: Studies of an Interpretive Tradition*, I–II (ed. C. C. Broyles and C. A. Evans; VTSup 70, 1–2; Leiden: E. J. Brill, 1997) II.491–511.

131a. Revised French version of 131 (published in 1998): "L'Importance des textes du Désert de Juda pour l'histoire du texte de la Bible hébraïque: Une nouvelle synthèse," in *Qoumrân et les manuscrits de la Mer Morte: Un cinquantenaire* (ed. E.-M. Laperrousaz; Paris: Cerf, 1997) 215–52.

1998

131. "The Significance of the Texts from the Judean Desert for the History of the Text of the Hebrew Bible: A New Synthesis," in *Qumran between the Old and the New Testament* (ed. F. H. Cryer and Th. L. Thompson; Copenhagen International Seminar 6; JSOTSup 290; Sheffield: Sheffield Academic Press, 1998) 277–309.

132. "Scribal Practices and Physical Aspects of the Dead Sea Scrolls," in *The Bible as Book: The Manuscript Tradition* (ed. J. L. Sharpe III and J. Van Kampen; London/New Castle: The British Library/Oak Knoll Press, 1998) 9–33.

133. "The Rewritten Book of Joshua as Found at Qumran and Masada," in *Biblical Perspectives: Early Use and Interpretation of the Bible in Light of the Dead Sea Scrolls: Proceedings of the First International Symposium of the Orion Center for the Study of the Dead Sea Scrolls and Associated Literature, May 12–14 1996* (ed. M. E. Stone and E. G. Chazon; STDJ 28; Leiden/Boston/Cologne: E. J. Brill, 1998) 233–56.

134. Together with R. A. Kraft, "Introductory Essay," to: E. Hatch and H. A. Redpath, *A Concordance to the Septuagint and the Other Greek Versions of the Old Testament (Including the Apocryphal Books)* (2d ed.; Grand Rapids, Mich.: Baker Books, 1998) xi–xix.

135. "The Dimensions of the Qumran Scrolls," *DSD* 5 (1998) 69–91.

136. "Scribal Practices Reflected in the Texts from the Judean Desert," in *The Dead Sea Scrolls after Fifty Years: A Comprehensive Assessment* (ed. P. W. Flint and J. C. VanderKam; Leiden/Boston/Cologne: E. J. Brill, 1998) 1.403–29.

137. "Sense Divisions in the Qumran Texts, the Masoretic Text, and Ancient Translations of the Bible," in *Interpretation of the Bible, International Symposium on the Interpretation of the Bible on the Occasion of the Publication of the New Slovanian Translation of the Bible* (ed. J. Krasovec; Ljubljana/Sheffield: Slovenska Akademija Znanosti in Umetnosti/Sheffield Academic Press, 1998) 121–46.

138. "Rewritten Bible Compositions and Biblical Manuscripts, with Special Attention to the Samaritan Pentateuch," *DSD* 5 (1998) 334–54.

139. "Textual Criticism of the Hebrew Bible 1947–1997," in *Perspectives in the Study of the Old Testament and Early Judaism, Symposium in Honour of Adam S. van der Woude on the Occasion of His 70th Birthday* (ed. F. García Martínez and E. Noort; VTSup 73; Leiden/Boston/Cologne: E. J. Brill, 1998) 61–81.

155a. Revised form of 155 (published in 2000): "Fünf Jahrzehnte Erforschung der Rollen vom Toten Meer," *ThPQ* 149 (1998) 52–63.

1999

140. "The Characterization of the Additional Layer of the Masoretic Text of Jeremiah," *ErIsr* 26 (Frank Moore Cross Volume) (ed. B. A. Levine et al.; Heb. with Eng. summ.; Jerusalem: Israel Exploration Society and Hebrew Union College-Jewish Institute of Religion, 1999) 55–63.

141. "Correction Procedures in the Texts from the Judean Desert," in *The Provo International Conference on the Dead Sea Scrolls: Technological Innovations, New Texts and Reformulated Issues* (ed. D. W. Parry and E. Ulrich; STDJ 40; Leiden/Boston/Cologne: E. J. Brill, 1999) 232–63.

142. "Paratextual Elements in the Masoretic Manuscripts of the Bible Compared with the Qumran Evidence," in *Antikes Judentum und Frühes Christentum, Festschrift für Hartmut Stegemann zum 65. Geburtstag* (ed. B. Kolbmann et al.; BZNT 97; Berlin/New York: Walter de Gruyter, 1999) 73–83.

143. "The *Accordance* Search Program for the MT, LXX, and the CATSS Database," *BIOSCS* 30 (1997 [1999]) 36–44.

99a. Spanish version (revised) of 99: "Los manuscritos de Qumrán a la luz de la investigación reciente," in *Paganos, judíos y cristianos en los textos de Qumrán* (ed. J. Trebolle Barrera; Biblioteca de ciencias bíblicas y orientales 5; Madrid: Trotta, 1999) 19–53.

144. "A List of the Texts from the Judaean Desert," in *The Dead Sea Scrolls after Fifty Years: A Comprehensive Assessment* (ed. P. W. Flint and J. C. VanderKam; Leiden/Boston/Cologne: E. J. Brill, 1999) 2: 669–717.

145. Articles "Aquila," "Lucian," "Symmachus," "Theodotion" in *Dictionary of Biblical Interpretation* (ed. J. H. Hayes; Nashville: Abingdon Press, 1999).

146. "Die Schriftrollen vom Toten Meer," *Annex, Die Beilage zur Reformierten Presse* 28 (1999) 3–9.

147. "The Publication of the Texts from the Judaean Desert: Past, Present, and Future," in *The Dead Sea Scrolls at Fifty, Proceedings of the 1997 Society of Biblical Literature Qumran Section Meetings* (ed. R. A. Kugler and E. Schuller; SBLEJL 15; Atlanta, GA: Scholars Press, 1999) 21–7.

148. "Israeli Scholarship on the Texts from the Judean Desert," in *The Dead Sea Scrolls at Fifty, Proceedings of the 1997 Society of Biblical Literature Qumran Section Meetings* (ed. R. A. Kugler and E. Schuller; SBLEJL 15; Atlanta, GA: Scholars Press, 1999) 123–7.

149. "Opisthographs from the Judaean Desert," in *A Multiform Heritage: Studies on Early Judaism and Christianity in Honor of Robert A. Kraft* (ed. B. G. Wright; Scholars Press Homage Series; Atlanta, Georgia: Scholars Press, 1999) 11–8.

150. "The Papyrus Fragments Found in the Judean Desert," in *Lectures et relectures de la Bible, Festschrift P.-M. Bogaert* (ed. J.-M. Auwers and A. Wénin; Leuven: Leuven University Press/Peeters, 1999) 247–55.

144a. "Texts from the Judean Desert," in *The SBL Handbook of Style for Ancient Near Eastern, Biblical, and Early Christian Studies* (ed. P. H. Alexander et al.; Peabody, Mass.: Hendrickson, 1999) 176–233 (= Appendix F).

151. "The Greek Texts from the Judean Desert," *QC* 8 (1999) 161–8.

2000

111a. "4QCant$^{a–c}$," in E. Ulrich et al., *Qumran Cave 4.XI: Psalms to Chronicles* (*DJD* XVI; Oxford: Clarendon, 2000) 195–219 and plates XXIV–XXV.

152. Articles "Discoveries in the Judaean Desert," "Joshua," "Scribes," "Scribal Practices," "Scriptures: Texts" in *Encyclopedia of the Dead Sea Scrolls* (ed. L. H. Schiffman and J. C. VanderKam; Oxford/New York: Oxford University Press, 2000) 205–8, 431–4, 827–30, 830–1, 832–6.

153. "A Qumran Origin for the Masada Non-biblical Texts?" *DSD* 7 (2000) 57–73.

154. "The Book of Jeremiah: A Work in Progress," *BRev* 16 (2000) 32–8, 45.

155. "Five Decades of Discoveries, Editions, and Research," in *The Dead Sea Scrolls: Fifty Years After Their Discovery: Proceedings of the Jerusalem Congress, July 20–25, 1997* (ed. L. H. Schiffman et al.; Jerusalem: Israel Exploration Society and The Shrine of the Book, Israel Museum, 2000) 951–60.

156. "Further Evidence for the Existence of a Qumran Scribal School," in *The Dead Sea Scrolls: Fifty Years After Their Discovery: Proceedings of the Jerusalem Congress, July 20–25, 1997* (ed. L. H. Schiffman et al.; Jerusalem: Israel Exploration Society and The Shrine of the Book, Israel Museum, 2000) 199–216.

157. "Die biblischen Handschriften aus der Wüste Juda: Eine neue Synthese," in *Die Textfunde vom Toten Meer und der Text der Hebräischen Bibel* (ed. U. Dahmen et al.; Neukirchen-Vluyn: Neukirchener Verlag, 2000) 1–34.

158. "The Textual Basis of Modern Translations of the Hebrew Bible: The Argument against Eclecticism," *Textus* 20 (2000) 193–211.

2001

159. "The Background of the Sense Divisions in the Biblical Texts," in *Delimitation Criticism: A New Tool in Biblical Scholarship* (ed. M. C. A. Korpel and J. M. Oesch; Pericope 1; Assen: Van Gorcum, 2001) 312–50.

160. "The Nature of the Greek Texts from the Judean Desert," *NovT* 43 (2001) 1–11.

161. "Die Veröffentlichung der Schriftrollen vom Toten Meer," in *Qumran—Die Schriftrollen vom Toten Meer: Vorträge des St. Galler Qumran-Symposiums vom 2./3. Juli 1999* (ed. M. Flieger et al.; NTOA 47; Freiburg/Göttingen: Universitätsverlag/Vandenhoeck & Ruprecht, 2001) 1–21.

162. "A Categorized List of All the 'Biblical Texts' Found in the Judaean Desert," *DSD* 8 (2001) 67–84.

163. With B. Nitzan: "Recent Developments in the Publication and Research of the Dead Sea Scrolls," in: *Fifty Years of Dead Sea Scrolls Research, Studies in Memory of Jacob Licht* (ed. G. Brin and B. Nitzan; Heb.; Jerusalem 2001) 59–91.

164. "Scribal Features of Early Witnesses of Greek Scripture," in *The Old Greek Psalter, Studies in Honour of Albert Pietersma* (ed. R. J. V. Hiebert et al.; JSOTSup 332; Sheffield: Sheffield Academic Press, 2001) 125–48.

165. "The Publication of the Dead Sea Scrolls," in *On Scrolls, Artefacts and Intellectual Property* (ed. T. Lim et al.; JSPSup 38; Sheffield: Sheffield Academic Press, 2001) 199–213.

165a. Russian translation in *Stranitsy* 5 (Moscow: Biblisko-Bagaslovski Institut Sv. Apostola Andrjeya [St. Andrews Theological Seminary], 2000) 498–506.

165b. "The Decipherment and Publication of the Dead Sea Scrolls," in *Archaeology and Society in the 21st Century* (ed. N. A. Silberman and E. J. Frerichs; Jerusalem: Israel Exploration Society and the Dorot Foundation, 2001) 96–103.

2002

166. "The *Discoveries in the Judaean Desert* Series: History and System of Presentation," in *The Texts from the Judaean Desert: Indices and an Introduction to the* Discoveries in the Judaean Desert *Series* (ed. E. Tov; *DJD* XXXIX; Oxford: Clarendon, 2002) 1–25.
167. With the collaboration of S. Pfann: "List of the Texts from the Judaean Desert," *ibid.*, 27–113.
162a. "Categorized List of the 'Biblical Texts'," *ibid.*, 165–83.
168. "Lists of Specific Groups of Texts from the Judaean Desert," *ibid.*, 203–28.
169. "Scribal Notations in the Texts from the Judaean Desert," *ibid.*, 323–49.

In Press

170. "The Indication of Small Sense Units (Verses) in Biblical Manuscripts," in *Hamlet on a Hill. Semitic and Greek Studies Presented to Professor T. Muraoka on the Occasion of his Sixty-Fifth Birthday* (ed. M. F. J. Baasten and W. Th. van Peursen; Leuven: Peeters, 2003).
171. "The Corpus of the Qumran Papyri," in *Climate of Creativity: Semitic Papyrology in Context, Papers from a New York University Conference Marking the Retirement of Baruch A. Levine* (ed. L. H. Schiffman; Leiden: E. J. Brill, 2002/3).
172. "The Place of the Masoretic Text in Modern Text Editions of the Hebrew Bible: The Relevance of Canon," in *The Canon Debate* (ed. L. McDonald and J. A. Sanders; Peabody, Mass.: Hendrickson, 2002).
173. "The Text of the Hebrew/Aramaic and Greek Bible Used in the Ancient Synagogues," in *The Ancient Synagogue: From the Beginning to about 200 CE. Papers Presented at the International Conference Held at Lund University Oct. 14–17, 2001* (ed. B. Olsson and M. Zetterholm; ConBNT 39; Stockholm: Almqvist & Wiksell International 2002).
174. "Early Bible Translations into Greek and Renderings Derived from Them," in *An International Encyclopedia of Translation Studies*, chapter XXXVIII, article 348 (ed. K. H. Kittel).
175. "The Greek Biblical Texts from the Judean Desert," *The Bible as Book: The Transmission of the Greek Text* (London: British Library, 2002).
176. "The Nature of the Large-Scale Differences between the LXX and MT S T V, Compared with Similar Evidence from Qumran and the SP and with Reference to the Original Shape of the Bible," in *The Earliest Phase of the Text History of the Old Testament* (ed. A. Schenker; IOSCS 52; Atlanta, Georgia: Scholars Press, 2002).
177. "The Beginnings and Ends of Scrolls from the Judean Desert," *Festschrift F. Young.*
178. "Celebrating the Completion of the Publication of the Dead Sea Scrolls," *Proceedings, Denver Meeting of the SBL.*
179. "The Biblical Texts from the Judaean Desert—An Overview and Analysis of the Published Texts," in *The Bible as Book—The Hebrew Bible and the Judaean Desert Discoveries* (ed. E. D. Herbert and E. Tov; London: British Library, 2002) 139–66.
180. "The Copying of a Biblical Scroll," *Journal of Religious History* 26 (2002).
181. "The Biblical Scrolls from Masada: Their Nature and Origin," (Heb.).
182. "The *Ketiv-Qere* Variations in Light of the Manuscript Finds in the Judean Desert," *Festschrift J. de Waard.*
183. "The Writing of Biblical Texts with Special Attention to the Dead Sea Scrolls," *Festschrift M. Weinfeld* (Winona Lake, Ind.: Eisenbrauns, 2002).

REVIEWS

1. J. D. Schenkel, *Chronology and Recensional Development in the Greek Text of Kings*, in: *RB* 76 (1969) 427–31.

2. S. Jellicoe, *The Septuagint and Modern Study*, in: *RB* 77 (1970) 84–91.

3. K. G. O'Connell, *The Theodotionic Revision of the Book of Exodus*, in: *JBL* 93 (1974) 114–15.

4. E. Camilo dos Santos, *An Expanded Hebrew Index for the Hatch-Redpath Concordance to the Septuagint*, in: *JBL* 94 (1975) 477–80.

5. S. P. Brock et al., *A Classified Bibliography of the Septuagint*, in: *VT* 25 (1975) 803–10.

6. R. W. Klein, *Textual Criticism of the Old Testament*, in: *Shnaton* 2 (1977) 266–8 (Heb.).

7. C. A. Moore, *Daniel, Esther and Jeremiah, The Additions* (Anchor Bible vol. 44), in: *IEJ* 28 (1978) 132–4.

8. R. Weiss, *Mishut ba-Miqra'*, in: *Beth Miqra* 74 (1978) 399–401 (Heb.).

9. M. Delcor, *Religion d'Israel de proche orient ancien*, in: *BiOr* 35 (1978) 283–4.

10. *The Jewish People in the First Century*, vol. 2 (ed. S. Safrai and M. Stern), in: *Bibliotheca Orientalis* 35 (1978) 308–9.

11. L. Laberge, *La Septante d'Isaie 28–33, Etude de tradition textuelle*, in: *IEJ* 28 (1978) 295.

12. M. Caloz, *Étude sur la LXX origénienne du Psautier*, in: *BiOr* 36 (1979) 205–6.

13. D. Barthélemy, *Etudes d'histoire du texte de l'Ancien Testament*, in: *BiOr* 37 (1980) 74–5.

14. J. W. Olley, *'Righteousness' in the Septuagint of Isaiah: A Contextual Study*, in: *JBL* 100 (1981) 281–2.

15. R. Sollamo, *Renderings of Hebrew Semiprepositions in the Septuagint*, in: *Bib* 62 (1981) 437–41.

16. A. Diez Macho, *Biblia Polyglotta Matritensis*, IV, in: *JQR* 72 (1981–1982) 67.

17. *Biblia Babilonica, Edicion critica segun manuscritos hebreos de puntuacion babilonica*, in: *JQR* 72 (1981–1982) 656.

18. E. Verhoef, *Er staat geschreven. De Oud-Testamentische citaten in de Brief aan de Galaten*, in: *JQR* 72 (1981–1982) 149–50.

19. G. W. Anderson, ed., *Tradition and Interpretation*, in: *JQR* 72 (1981–1982) 227–8.

20. M. Teresa Ortega Monasterio, *Estudio masoretico interno de un manuscrito hebreo biblico español*, in: *JQR* 72 (1981–1982) 229–30.

21. I. Yeivin, *Introduction to the Tiberian Masorah*, translated by E. J. Revell, in: *JQR* 72 (1981–1982) 327–8.

22. A. van der Kooij, *Die alten Textzeugen des Jesajabuches*, in: *Shnaton* 5–6 (1982) 255–7 (Heb.).

23. G. Krautwurst, *Studien zu den Septuagintazusätzen in 1. (3.) Könige 2 und ihren Paralleltexten*, in: *BiOr* 39 (1982) 629–31.

24. Th. W. Franxman, *Genesis and the 'Jewish Antiquities' of Flavius Josephus*, in: *BiOr* 39 (1982) 644–7.

25. B. M. Zlotowitz, *The Septuagint Translation of the Hebrew Terms in Relation to God in the Book of Jeremiah*, in: *JBL* 102 (1983) 314–16.

26. C. McCarthy, *The Tiqqune Sopherim and Other Theological Corrections in the Masoretic Text of the Old Testament*, in: *JQR* 73 (1983) 284–7.

27. F. Perez Castro et al., *El codice de Profetas de El Cairo, Tomo VII, Profetas Meñores*, in: *JQR* 74 (1983) 98–9.

28. L. Vegas Montaner, *Biblia del Mar Muerto, Profetas Menores, Edicion critica segun manuscritos hebreos procedentes del Mar Muerto*, in: *JQR* 74 (1983) 400–403.

29. J. Koenig, *L'Herméneutique analogique du Judaisme antique d'après les témoins textuels d'Isaie*, in: *Bib* 65 (1984) 118–21.

30. L. J. Greenspoon, *Textual Studies in the Book of Joshua*, in: *JAOS* 105 (1985) 148–50.

31. W. R. Bodine, *The Greek Text of Judges, Recensional Developments*, in: *JQR* 75 (1985) 194–5.

32. C. Sirat, *Les papyrus en caractères hebraiques trouvés en Egypte*, in: *JQR* 76 (1986) 272–3.

33. J. Barr, *The Variable Spellings of the Hebrew Bible. The Schweich Lectures of the British Academy 1986*, in: *JSS* 35 (1990) 303–16.

34. *Sacred History and Sacred Texts in Early Judaism. A Symposium in Honour of A. S. van der Woude* (ed. J. N. Bremmer and F. García Martínez), in: *JSJ* 24 (1993) 83–7.

35. G. Veltri, *Eine Tora für den König Talmai: Untersuchungen zum Übersetzungsverständnis in der jüdisch-hellenistischen und rabbinischen Literatur*, in: *Scripta Classica Israelica* 14 (1995) 178–83. Revised version: *The Greek and Hebrew Bible* (1999) 75–83.

36. K. Bieberstein, *Lukian und Theodotion im Josuabuch, Mit einem Beitrag zu den Josuarollen von Hirbet Qumrân*, in: *JSJ* 26 (1995) 185–87.

37. *Mémorial Jean Carmignac* (ed. F. García Martínez and E. Puech) = *RevQ* 13 (1988), in: *Shnaton* 11 (1997) 323–6 (Heb.).

38. B. A. Taylor, *The Lucianic Manuscripts of 1 Reigns, Volume 1, Majority Text, Volume 2, Analysis*, in: *JAOS* 116 (1996) 551–3.

39. *Methods of Investigation of the Dead Sea Scrolls and the Khirbet Qumran Site: Present Realities and Future Prospects* (ed. M. O. Wise et al.) in: *DSD* 4 (1997) 241–3.

40. P. J. Gentry, *The Asterisked Materials in the Greek Job*, in: *JAOS* 118 (1998) 593–4.

41. J. G. Campbell, *The Use of Scripture in the Damascus Document 1–8, 19–20*, in: *JAOS* 119 (1999) 156–7.

42. E. D. Herbert, *Reconstructing Biblical Dead Sea Scrolls: A New Method Applied to the Reconstruction of 4QSam^a*, in: *DSD* 6 (1999) 215–20.

PART ONE

QUMRAN

1QSb AND THE ELUSIVE HIGH PRIEST

Martin G. Abegg, Jr.

> (Words of blessing) belonging to the Instructor, by which
> to bless the Prince of the Congregation whom [God chose . . .]
> 1QSb V, 20

Much of the limited study brought to bear upon 1QSb (Blessings)
since its discovery in 1947 has purposed, at least in part, to locate
the priestly consort to Messiah the Prince (נשיא)[1] among the fragmentary columns of the manuscript. J. T. Milik established the shape
of much of the subsequent discussion with his understanding that
the text exhibits the remains of four blessings, the blessing on the
faithful—those who keep his commandments (ושומרי מצוותיו, I, 1–21),
the blessing on the High Priest (I, 21–III, 19)—whose address formula is lost in the missing text of I, 21—, the blessing on the Zadokite
priesthood (בני צדוק הכוהנים, III, 22–V, 19), and the blessing on the
Prince of the Congregation (נשיא העדה, V, 20–VI, ?).[2] The order of
this outline has, with varying degrees of assurance, some modification
of the description of addresses, and the length of the blessings, been
followed by J. Carmignac,[3] G. Vermes,[4] and M. Wise.[5]

---

[1] For the equation between the Prince (נשיא) and the Messiah (משיח) compare,
"[. . . and a branch shall grow out of his roots' (Isa 10:34–11:1). This is the] Branch
of David. Then [all forces of Belial] shall be judged, [and the king of the Kittim
shall stand for judgment] and the Prince of the community—the Bra[nch of David]—
will have him put to death" (4Q285 7 3–4), and "the one who sits on the throne
of David [shall never] be cut off, because the 'ruler's staff' is the covenant of the
kingdom, [and the thous]ands of Israel are 'the feet,' until the Righteous Messiah,
the Branch of David, has come (4Q252 V, 2–4).

[2] O. P. Barthélemy and J. T. Milik, *Qumran Cave I* (*DJD* 1; Oxford: Clarendon
Press, 1955), 118–30.

[3] J. Carmignac, "Le recueil des bénédictions, in *Règle de la Congregation, Recueil des
Bénédictions, Interprétations de Prophètes et de Psaumes, Document de Damas, Apocryphe de
Génèse, Fragments des Grottes 1 et 4* (J. Carmignac, É. Cothenet and H. Lignée; vol. 2
of *Les Textes de Qumran*; Paris: Letouzey et Ané, 1963), 31.

[4] G. Vermes, *The Complete Dead Sea Scrolls in English* (London: Allen Lane/The
Penguin Press, 1997), 374–7.

[5] M. Wise, M. Abegg, and E. Cook, *The Dead Sea Scrolls: A New Translation* (San
Francisco: Harper SanFrancisco, 1996), 147–50.

In a recent study on 1QSa and 1QSb, Hartmut Stegemann places his blessing on Milik's physical reconstruction of the manuscript, but concludes that the High Priest of 1QSb is no priestly messiah.[6] This in part is due to his interpretation of 1QSa, which Stegemann understands to describe a regular practice rather than strictly eschatological event, and in part due to the order of the Blessings in 1QSb. He argues that the consensus model of the dual messiah, in which the priest is preeminent, would expect that the blessing on the High Priest should follow that of the Royal Messiah rather than preceding. According to Milik's model the blessing is instead tucked curiously between the common folk and the Zadokite priests. Therefore, Stegemann reasons that the priest of 1QSb I, 19–III, 21 is actually the High Priest who was serving at the time the blessings were to be spoken rather than he who was expected at the end of days.

Jacob Licht, in his important study,[7] noted that Milik's second blessing—that of the High Priest—is both too long (being two full columns) and, what is more significant, premature, coming as it does between the sect members and the Zadokite priests. He sought an alternate solution. He was unable to determine a definitive number or identification of the blessings beyond those that are clearly reflected in the manuscript (I, 1, III, 22, and V, 20), but countered Milik by finding evidence for the blessing of the High Priest from the bottom of column IV rather than from the bottom of column I.[8] In Licht's view the two key messianic personages were thus adjoined in the order of blessings, the High Priest followed directly by the Prince.[9]

---

[6] H. Stegemann, "Some Remarks to 1QSa, to 1QSb, and to Qumran Messianism," *RevQ* 17/65–68 (1996): 479–505.

[7] Jacob Licht, מגילת הסרכים ממגילות מדבר יהודה (Jerusalem: Bialik Institute, 1965), 273–89.

[8] The closest Licht comes to identifying any additional blessings is the following: "It is possible to establish, almost certainly, that the number of blessings which were recorded in the five columns was greater than the three preserved headings. For example, it is without doubt that some portion of the text witnessed to the High Priest, namely the Messiah of Aaron. Likewise, it can be assumed that the composition included specific blessings for those who held various positions and ranks in the congregation; e.g., 'men of renown' (קריאי השם), or 'the heads of the congregation's clans' (ראשי אבות העדה), however, the material that is in our possession is not sufficient for the identification of these expected blessings" (הסרכים, 274–75).

[9] For and alternate understanding of Licht's discussion see, L. H. Schiffman, *The Eschatological Community of the Dead Sea Scrolls* (SBLMS 38; Atlanta: Scholars Press, 1989), 73. Schiffman writes that Licht posited eight blessings, inserting an unknown group between the High Priest and the Prince of the Congregation. Licht, however, clearly states that "the beginning of the blessing for the High Priest is in the

The purpose of this present study is twofold, first it will examine the available evidence to determine the structure of 1QSb and the location of the blessing on the High Priest. This determination, as well as the evidence which supports it, will then allow conclusions concerning the *Sitz im Leben* of the composition as well as the character of the messianic (?) High Priest himself.

LITERARY STRUCTURE OF 1QSb

To set the stage, both Milik and Licht agreed on the nature of three blessings: that of the faithful (I, 1), the blessing on the Zadokite priests (III, 22), and the Blessing on the Prince of the congregation (V, 20). Each of these blessings exhibit the introductory formula למשכיל לברך את, "belonging to the Instructor, so as to bless . . .". In addition, the words, דברי ברכה, "words of blessing," precede this formula in the first two instances. It is noteworthy that both of these phrases are unique to 1QSb in all of Qumran Literature. In all three instances of blessing the introductory formula is followed immediately by the recipient of the benediction.

The blessing on the Zadokite priests (III, 22) exhibits the best preserved text and the greatest hope of discovering further structural clues. After recording the recipient of the blessing, the text continues from the end of line 22 with a relative clause describing the Sons of Zadok: "whom God chose" (אשר בחר בם אל), followed by three infinitives detailing the purpose of God's choice: 1) to uphold his covenant, 2) to prove and 3) to teach his precepts (III, 23). At the beginning of the manuscript, the compound nature of the recipient: "those who fear [God, who do] his will and keep his commandments, who hold fast to his holy co[ven]ant and walk blameless [in

---

missing middle section of column IV, and its end is preserved at the bottom of column V, adjoining the beginning of the blessing which is designated explicitly for the Prince. The two blessings designated for the two men of significance who would stand at the head of the community in the days to come were thus adjoining one another" (הסרכים, 275). Stegemann follows Schiffman in his interpretation of Licht contributing to his conclusion that the priest is not messianic after all ("Remarks," 500). J. H. Charlesworth and L. T. Stuckenbruck also follow Schiffman's reading of Licht, "Blessings (1QSb)," in *The Rule of the Community and Related Documents* (ed. J. H. Charlesworth et al.; vol. 1 of *The Dead Sea Scrolls: Hebrew, Aramaic, and Greek Texts with English Translations*, ed. J. H. Charlesworth; Tübingen/Louisville: J. C. B. Mohr (Paul Siebeck)/Westminster John Knox, 1994), 119.

all the paths of] his [truth]," compelled the author to recast his relative clause as a full sentence, but the verb remains the same: "and he (that is, God) chose them" (ויבחר בם), followed in this instance by a prepositional phrase giving the purpose of the choosing: "... for an eternal covenant that should endure forever" (I, 3). Unfortunately, an examination of V, 20 reveals that although the relative is present, the following clause has not survived. A search of the rest of the manuscript reveals another instance of the verb בחר ("to chose") followed by a pronominal object at IV, 22, בָחֹר בכה ("he chose you"). Again the purpose of the choosing follows: "to place you at the head of the holy ones" (קדושים, "angels"?). The context is missing, but it would seem likely from evidence elsewhere, that an introductory blessing formula could have been present in the lines just preceding. Based on these parallel structural patterns, it is reasonable to reconstruct בחר בו ("whom he chose") and a 5–6 word purpose statement in the lacuna at the end of V, 20 and the beginning of 21.

Returning to column III, after an additional sentence describing the nature of the Sons of Zadok, a second blessing formula, the beginning of the main body of the blessing, is found: "May the Lord bless you" (יברככה אדוני), followed by the place of origin: "from his holy habitation" (מ]מעון קו[דשו) and then the continuation of the prayer—"May he set you, perfected in honor, in the midst of the Holy Ones . . .," which continues to at least the end of the column. A check of column one reveals the same pattern as far as it is extant. The prayer for blessing begins at line three and continues through line seven where the column becomes too fragmentary to be of help. At column IV, no remains of the introductory formula exist, although the bottom of the column reveals the familiar prayer. Note line 27 as an example: "May he establish you as holy among his people. . . ." The bottom of column five preserves a variation of blessing formula: י[שׂ]א[כ]ה אדוני ("May the Lord lift you up . . ."). The following prayer, a reworking of Isa 11:4, begins with the Royal Messiah as the subject rather than God, as has been the case elsewhere. Note lines 24 and 25: "Thus may *you* be r[ighteous] by the might of your [mouth], laying waste the earth with your rod! With the breath of your lips may you kill the wicked!" before returning to the more familiar third person: "May he (God) give [you a spirit of coun]sel and may eternal might [rest upon you], the spirit of knowledge and the fear of God" (V, 25).

As to the second element of the blessing incipits, Licht notes that the name of God, אדוני ("Lord"), is itself an element that is found only at the beginning of each blessing (1QSb I, 3; III, 25; V, 23), "In general, the one who blesses avoids repeating the word Lord (אדוני) in the body of the blessings; he even reduces the references to God (אל)."[10] This would suggest that the occurrences of אדוני at II, 23 and III, 1 would signal the beginning of a new blessing.

One last pattern remains before we turn our attention to locating the High Priest. Returning to column III, it may prove significant that one of the elements of the prayer is the issue of covenant renewal. III, 26 reads וברית כהונת [עולם ית]ח[דש לכה ("may he re]new for you the [eternal] covenant of the priesthood"). Looking to column I we find no evident remains, although a similar statement may be lost in the lacuna at the end of line 4. A similar phrase is, however, extant at V, 5:]וחדש לכה ("and he shall renew for you"), and suggests "[the covenant of. . ." in the lacuna which follows. At line 21 of column V we again discover the renewal motif: ובריׄת הׄ[י]ׄׄחׄׄד יחדש לו ("And he shall renew for him (the Prince) the Covenant of the [Comm]unity").

These structural features: a blessing belonging to the Instructor, the named recipient, the qualification that God has chosen, the purpose of the choosing, a formula introducing a prayer invoking blessing, the name of the Lord, and finally, the indication of covenant renewal, appear to be the rather programmatic framework upon which our manuscript is built. One last offering in this regard: the only extant lines that reveal the end of a blessing are found at III, 21: לעולמי עד ("forever and ever"). This phrase is found 13 times elsewhere in Qumran literature, seven of these in the Hodayot where it is used only at the ends of sentences 1QH IV, 28; V, 7, 19; IX, 8, 31; XV, 31; XIX, 25.[11] Perhaps each of the Cave 1 "Blessings" ended with this phrase as well.

We are now prepared to recognize the individual benedictions within the text. The blessings beginning at I, 1, III, 22, and V, 20 are clear to all on the basis of the address to the instructor (למשכיל). Although no literary indicators exist at the bottom of column I, Milik notes that a horizontal stroke visible at the left side of the second

---

[10] Licht, הסרכים, 275.
[11] See also 4Q285 1 2 (11Q14 1–2 ii, 4), 4Q511 63 iv, 3, 4Q293 1 3, 4Q509 f18:1, and PAM 43.676 45 2.

column of 1QSa (thus the right margin of the 1QSb I) is echoed at III, 22 and V, 20.[12] As this stroke clearly indicates the end of a blessing in these latter cases it is safe to assume with Milik that a new blessing began at I, 21. The occurrence of אדוני ("Lord") at II, 22 and III, 1 and the verb of election (יבחר) at III, 2 are reflective of a new blessing which began in the vicinity of II, 21. The phrase בֿחר בכה [("he has chosen you") at IV, 22 is suggestive of a blessing beginning near IV, 20. Only ten lines of the last extant blessing, that of the Prince of the Congregation, remain, but it surely continued into column six. This last (?) column was unfortunately lost as the scroll was left in the cave with its beginning—1QS—on the inside, exposing the end of 1QSb to the elements.

Thus the literary and physical evidence suggest that the scroll contained six blessings, the first and general blessing of 20 lines followed by four blessings of approximately one column or 28 lines each. Only ten lines of the last blessing are preserved, but it is clear that it would have continued well into column VI. The following outline results:

  I. Blessing on the Faithful (I, 1–20)
 II. Blessing on an Unidentified Group or Individual (I, 21–II, 20?)
III. Blessing on an Unidentified Group or Individual (II, 21?–III, 21)
IV. Blessing on the Zadokite Priests (III, 22–IV, 19)
 V. Blessing on an Unidentified Group or Individual (IV, 20–V, 19)
VI. Blessing on the Prince of the Congregation (V, 20–VI, 20?)

Of these six blessings, one four, and six have preserved incipits, referring to the faithful (likely to be understood as the general membership), the Zadokite priests, and the Prince of the Congregation. It is noteworthy that each of the remaining three unidentified sections has been associated in the various studies on this text as referring to the High Priest, Milik in columns I–III and Licht in columns IV–V. Our study will now turn to an examination of these three blessings in search of the High Priest.

---

[12] Milik, *DJD* 1, 122.

QUEST FOR THE HIGH PRIEST: THE SECOND BLESSING

The second blessing, which ends somewhere near II, 20, contains the remains of thirteen words. None of these allows for any certain recognition of the group or person involved. The five occurrences of the pronominal suffix, "you," in the masculine singular, at first appear promising, until it is noticed that this inflection is also regular in the prayer of blessings one and four, both of which clearly address a group. It is important to note that the second person suffix is regular throughout (86×, counting the reconstructions), never appearing in the plural. The recipient of the second blessing must remain a mystery.

QUEST FOR THE HIGH PRIEST: THE THIRD BLESSING

From the bottom of column II to line 21 of column III a total of 102 words remain. The key word of this section is the verb חנן, "to be gracious." It appears six times in lines 22–26 of column II and, as has been pointed out by all discussions of this text, is a certain reflection of the priestly blessing of Num 6:24–27 which undergirds the entire manuscript: יאר יהוה פניו אליך ויחנך ("May the LORD make his face shine on you, and *be gracious* to you," Num 6:25). Although promising at first blush, the formulaic statement from Numbers 6 is found elsewhere in Qumran Literature addressing a wide range of recipients. At 1QS II, 3 the suffix refers to all the congregation and in the Hodayot it is twice directed to the teacher (VI, 25; VIII, 18). It also appears in the negative sense with Belial as its antecedent at 1QS II, 8 and 4Q280 1 3 (לוא יחונכה, "may he have no mercy").

The ברית עולם ("eternal covenant") indicated in line 25, which may be a reflection of covenant renewal from the missing incipit, is not the priestly covenant of Numbers 25, but rather a likely reference to the covenant of circumcision made with Abraham and interpreted in a metaphorical sense in 1QS V, 5–6. The eternal covenant is also mentioned in 1QSb I, 2–3 as the purpose of God's choice of the entire congregation.

At line 28, כול צאצ̇איכה, ("all [your] descend[ents]") is too generic to be of any help in identification. This terminology is used to refer to the offspring of the entire earth in 1QM X, 13 and 1QHᵃ V, 15.

Moving to the top of column III, וריח ניחֹֹ[חוה, 'sweet savor,' most often associated with offerings in the Hebrew Bible, appears indicative, but in its only occurrence in 1QS VIII, 9 the expression is used as a figure for the whole community. At 4Q266 18 v, 4 it is the sacrifice made by all Israel.

The phrase, לכהֹֹ[ונתכ]ֹה, 'your priesthood,' at the end of line 1 is rather a pointed reconstruction, but the preceding construct participle (יושבי, "those who dwell") makes it highly suspect. Although it is grammatically possible for the construct participle of ישב to be followed by a prepositional phrase in the genitive—יושבי בה ("those who dwell in it") is not uncommon[13]—there are no extant examples in Qumran literature with ל and only ישבי לבטח (Ezek 38:11 "those who live securely") in the Hebrew Bible. F. García-Martínez rejects Milik's reconstruction in his translation.[14]

The key to Milik's determination that columns I–III were to be understood as a blessing on the High Priest is in large part the occurrence of עדתכה ("your [singular] congregation") at III, 3.[15] As has been noted, however, the second singular suffix is regular in the document, even in those sections which are clearly focused on a plural recipient, and instances of "your (plural) congregation" are not lacking elsewhere (11Q14, 1 ii, 13, 15).[16]

These are the most suggestive readings of the section, falling far short of certainty in the quest for addressee. The identity of the recipient of the third blessing must remain indeterminate.

QUEST FOR THE HIGH PRIEST: THE FIFTH BLESSING

Finally we turn to the last unidentified blessing, IV, 20–V, 19. At first glance, the phrase בֹחר בכה ("he chose you") at the end of IV, 22 might appear to be a representative of the consistent pattern of second singular pronoun, even in instances, as in column I or the bottom of column III, where the antecedent is clearly plural. It is

---

[13] See 1QpHab IX, 8; XII, 1 and 4Q286 5 1.
[14] F. García Martínez, *The Dead Sea Scrolls Translated* (Brill: Leiden, 1994), 432; although he includes it in *The Dead Sea Scrolls Study Edition* (vol. 1; Brill: Leiden, 1997), 104–5.
[15] Milik, *DJD* 1, 121.
[16] See also "their congregation," 1QSa II, 9; 1QpHab V, 12; 4Q269 2 3; and "our congregation," 4Q509 3 5.

important to note, however, that elsewhere at this point in the structure, 1QSb I, 2 with the plural ויבחר בם ("he chose them, the general membership") and 1QSb III, 23 with אשר בחר בם ("whom [that
is the Zadokite priests] he chose"), the plural makeup of the recipients of blessing is made clear. It is thus evident from IV, 22 that
the recipient is an individual rather than a group.

The line following IV, 23 continues with an infinitive giving the
purpose of God's choice (as at III, 23): ולשאת ברוש קדושים ("to place
[you] at the head of the Holy Ones," namely the angels). This is
indicative in light of the fact that the Zadokite priests of blessing
4—1QSb III, 25—are "appointed, perfected in honor, in the *midst
of* the angels," (וישימכה מכלול הדר בתוך קדושים). The recipient of blessing five would thus be the head of the Zadokite Priests.

Another rather significant statement is made concerning this individual in IV, 24–25: ואתה כמלאך פנים במעון קודש ("And you are as an
angel of presence in the holy habitation"). This sentiment is echoed
in *Jub.* 31:14 concerning Levi, "God brought you and your seed to
himself from all humankind so that you might serve him in his sanctuary as the angels of presence and the holy ones." The community
are seen as in lot *together with* the angels of presence in 1QHᵃ XIV,
13, but the recipient of the fifth blessing is "*as* an angel of presence."

Further, the recipient of the fifth blessing is to serve in the "temple of his kingdom" (היכל מלכות) a phrase also preserved at 4Q301
5 2.[17] Another possible correspondence with 4Q301 occurs at 1QSb
IV, 27 where our character is described as the "great light" (מאור [גדול]).
This expression might also be reconstructed at 4Q301 5 4, a document which, like the Hodayot, is significantly couched in the first
person. Ed Cook suggests that: "although the name of the sage is
not preserved, one can hear the distinctive voice of a real, and
redoubtable, teacher."[18] Indeed, the statement at the end of 1QSb
IV, 27 appears to strengthen this connection, as we read that the
purpose of the establishment of the recipient of the fifth blessing is
ולהאיר פני רבים, "to illumine the face of many." This phrase is echoed
closely only at 1QHᵃ XII, 27: ובי האירותה פני רבים ("by me [the
teacher] you have illumined the face of many").

---

[17] See also 4Q287 2 11.
[18] Wise, Abegg, and Cook, *New Translation*, 174–5.

Although various combinations of columns I–III have been understood by many to speak of the High Priest, a review of this section
and that of IV–V has led to the conclusion that we should rather
affirm Jacob Licht's decision to place the blessing of the High Priest
at the end of column IV and the beginning of column V, immediately preceding the blessing of the Prince.

Sitz im Leben

Jacob Licht, having noted the three headings addressed to the *maskil*,
writes, "It follows that the composition is a collection of blessings
which were assigned to be recited on a ceremonial occasion, but the
nature of this occasion is not specified."[19] Yet clues do exist from
which to make a cogent suggestion.

Once a year, the Qumran sectarians celebrated the community
covenant, renewing the vows of the members-in-good standing and
admitting new converts who had completed the stipulated initiation
period.[20] The specific date for this covenant renewal is nowhere
explicit in the surviving texts but it is likely coincident with the celebration of the Festival of Weeks or Shavuot which according to the
calendars found in Cave 4 was celebrated on the fifteenth of the
third month.[21] Traditionally this festival has been associated with
important covenant making occasions. Rabbinic Judaism commem-
orates the giving of the law on Mount Sinai (*b. Šebu.* 88a, *b. Pesaḥ.*
68b) on the Festival of Weeks. The book of Jubilees echoes this
determination and locates the Sinai covenant (*Jub.* 6:10, 11, 17), the
covenants with Abraham (*Jub.* 14:10, 17) and Noah (*Jub.* 14:20),
and Abraham's circumcision (*Jub.* 15:1, 11) all on the very same
day. Three recently published scrolls from Cave 4 make it nearly
certain that the sectarian covenant renewal was also on this day:
"All [those who live] in camps shall convene in the third month"
(4Q266 11 16b–17, see also 4Q270 7 ii, 11 and 4Q275 1 3).

The covenant renewal ceremony—including excerpts of the liturgy—
is briefly outlined in 1QS I, 16–III, 6.[22] It is introduced by the priests

---

[19] Licht, הסרכים, 274.
[20] For an expanded discussion, see my forthcoming article, "The Covenant of
the Qumran Sectarians," in *Concepts of Covenant in the Second Temple Period* (ed. S. E.
Porter and J. C. R. de Roo; JSJSup; Leiden: Brill, 2002).
[21] 4Q319 12 2; 4Q320 4 iii, 5; 4 iv, 1; 4 v, 4; 4Q321 2 v, 1, 5; vi, 1, 8.
[22] Wise et al., *New Translation*, 127–9.

and Levites, clearly seen as the preservers of the covenant according to Deut 33:9 (4Q175 17) and Ezek 44:15 (CD III, 21–4:2; 1QS V, 2, 9). They rehearsed the righteous and merciful acts of God (1QS I, 21–22a) as well as the sins that Israel performed under the dominion of Belial (1QS I, 22b–24a). All of the initiates then made a strong confession of their sins (1QS I, 24b–26) ending in an acknowledgment of God's reward which is according to his merciful kindness rather than merit (1QS II, 1a).

The focus of the passage then shifts (1QS II, 1b) to a group described as the "men of God's lot," and "those who walk faultless in all his ways" (1QS II, 2). This is in reference to the full members of the community rather than initiates, the "faultless" conduct of those who have committed themselves to the sect (1QS III, 9; VIII, 18, 21; IX, 6, 8, 9; IX, 16). The similar expression "men of perfection" is also a description for the men of the community (CD XX, 2, 5, 7; 1QS VIII, 20).

The blessing spoken by the priests on this membership is a transparent expansion of the Priestly or Aaronic Blessing (Num 6:24–26). The words in italic in the following translation highlight the unmistakable origin of the blessing.

> May he *bless you* with every good thing and *keep you* from every evil. May he *enlighten your* mind with wisdom for living, *be gracious to you* with the knowledge of eternal things, and *lift up his* gracious *countenance upon you* for everlasting *peace* (1QS II, 2b–4a).

As noted, Licht recognized the same elements in the context of blessings and covenant renewal in 1QSb. Of the six blessing that make up this text, it is significant that the first and most general blessing is addressed to "those who hold fast to his holy co[ven]ant and *walk blameless* [in all the paths of] his [truth]" (1QSa I, 2), the very words of the excerpt quoted in 1QS II, 2. The following passages highlight the fact that key elements of the Priestly Blessing from Num 6:24–26 also form the framework of 1QSb.

> May the L[ord] *bless you* [from his holy habitation;] (1QSb I, 3)
> May he *be gracious to you* with the holy spirit and loving[kindness . . .] (1QSb II, 24)
> May the Lord *lift up his countenance upon you*. (1QSb III, 1)
> May he establish you as holy among his people, as the "greater [light" to illumine] the world with knowledge, and *to shine upon the face of many* [with wisdom leading to life.] 1QSb IV, 27–28
> [. . .] He has established *peace* for you forever and ever. (1QSb III, 21)

In addition, 1QSb is plainly a liturgical work the context of which
is covenant renewal. This renewal element was presumably a component of all six of the blessings but, given the fragmentary nature
of the text, the renewal vocabulary is only extant in the fourth blessing, on the Zadokite priests, the fifth blessing on the High Priest,
and the sixth blessing, for the Prince of the Congregation.

> May he set you, perfected in honor, in the midst of the Holy Ones;
> [may he *re*]*new* the [eternal] *covenant* of the priesthood for you. (1QSb
> III, 25–26)

> [. . .] and he shall *renew* [the *covenant* of peace . . .] for you [. . .] (1QSb
> V, 5)

> And he shall *renew* the *covenant* of the [con]gregation for him, so as to
> establish the kingdom of his people forev[er . . .] (1QSb V, 21)

The elements of liturgical blessing, a structure based on the Priestly
Blessing of Numbers 6, and covenant renewal are only present in
two passages in all of Qumran literature: 1QS II, 1b–4a and 1QSb.
Licht suggested that the two documents differed in their use of the
passage, the writer of 1QSb more consistently expanding and repeating elements of the text than the author of 1QS.[23] But from these
very characteristics, it would appear reasonable to suggest that 1QS
II, 1–4 is but a précis while 1QSb preserves the full text.

Character of the High Priest

The presence of the Prince in the last extant blessing suggested to
Licht that 1QSb is distinctly eschatological in nature.

> Since one blessing is designated for the Prince, who according to the
> view of the sect would arise in the end of days, it seems a reasonable
> assumption that the whole collection of blessings is intended for the
> days to come, for a ceremony that would be arranged by a congre-
> gation of the latter days, at a time described in Rule of the Congregation
> (1QSa).[24]

If, however, the relationship suggested in this study with 1QS is correct, 1QSb is not solely eschatological in nature. Rather it was recited
yearly at the time of covenant renewal. That there is an eschato-

---

[23] Licht, הסרכים, 276.
[24] Licht, הסרכים, 274.

logical aspect, however, is perhaps to be understood from the construction of the blessings. The first two instances of the verb לחדש,
"to renew" (1QSb III, 26; V, 5), are followed in the second person,
as if the recipient is present in the mind of the author. Of the
Zadokite priests it is said, "[may he re]new for *you* the [eternal]
covenant of the priesthood" (III, 26), and of the High Priest: "and
likewise for the High Priest: "may he renew for you [the covenant . . .]."
(V, 5). Whereas for the Prince of the Congregation our text reads:
"And he shall renew for *him* the Covenant of the [Comm]unity" (V,
21). The Prince, represented in the third person, is not present in
the mind of the writer; he is yet to come.

Stegemann, following Milik's determination that the blessing of
the High Priest is to be located at I, 19–III, 19, concludes that this
figure is "not a future Priestly Messiah but . . . the real high priest
of the time of the author of 1QSb."[25] Stegemann is at least partially
correct. Is it not possible that the presence of the priestly consort to
the Prince embodies the promise of 1 Sam 2:35, "I will raise up for
Myself a faithful priest who will do according to what is in My heart
and in My soul; and I will build him an enduring house, and he
will walk before My anointed always," and Jer 33:17–18, "David
shall never lack a man to sit on the throne of the house of Israel;
and the Levitical priests shall never lack a man before me to offer
burnt offerings, to burn grain offerings, and to prepare sacrifices continually."[26] Thus the *eschatological* High Priest is he who is faithfully
serving when—in the imagery of 1QSa—the Royal Messiah (the
Prince) arrives to take his seat at the banquet table before the faithful. Until then the blessings of 1QSb faithfully reflect the present
priest (you) and while looking forward to the coming Prince (him).

באחרית

The relative neglect that Qumran scholarship has displayed toward
1QSb is hardly justifiable. If the results of this study are valid, the

[25] Stegemann, "Remarks," 501.
[26] See William M. Schniedewind, "Structural Aspects of Qumran Messianism in
the Damascus Document," in *The Provo International Conference on the Dead Sea Scrolls:
New Texts, Reformulated Issues, and Technological Innovations* (ed. D. W. Parry and E. C.
Ulrich; Leiden: Brill, 1999), 523–36.

initial quest for the High Priest among the scraps of 1QSb has unexpectedly turned up an important liturgical connection: 1QSb is the full text (and thus no accidental appendix) of the blessings associated with the yearly renewal ceremony in 1QS I–III. In addition, it offers an important clue to the nature of the messianic High Priest: perhaps more important than his supposed preeminence was his potential omnipresence.

THE EVIL EMPIRE: THE QUMRAN ESCHATOLOGICAL WAR CYCLE AND THE ORIGINS OF JEWISH OPPOSITION TO ROME

Philip S. Alexander

I. The Evil Empire

The opposition of Jerusalem to Rome is one of the great political rivalries of history. Some Jews in late antiquity, admiring the Roman order—the peace it imposed, the roads, bridges, fora, baths and other public services it maintained—prayed for the well-being of the government, but many displayed an implacable hatred towards "wicked Rome" and daily called on God to overthrow the "arrogant kingdom". Jews fought two disastrous wars against Rome in Palestine (the First and Second Revolts of 66–74 and 132–135 c.e.), and in 115–117 during Trajan's reign rose in revolt in Egypt, Cyrenaica, Cyprus and Mesopotamia—the terrible "wars of Qitos (Quietus)" mentioned in Rabbinic literature. The Jews were the losers in all these conflicts, but many refused to regard the struggle as over. They looked forward to a final decisive show-down with Rome at the end of history when, under the leadership of a scion of the House of David (a sort of David Redivivus), they would defeat a coalition of gentile powers headed by Rome under its general Armillus (a sort of Romulus Redivivus).

When and why did these attitudes emerge? It is sometimes rather casually assumed that deep Jewish antagonism towards Rome stems from the period leading up to the First Revolt. I would suggest that it can be traced back much earlier—back almost to the moment in 63 B.C.E. when Pompey brought Jewish independence to an end and incorporated the Hasmonean State into the expanding Roman Empire. Though Israel was riven at that time by vicious political in-fighting, all the major parties, both pro- and anti-Hasmonean, were probably united in their opposition to Rome.[1] Some were prepared to use

---

[1] We should distinguish between nationalism and a pro-Hasmonean stance. The two should not necessarily be equated.

Rome for their own political ends, but this was a matter of expediency rather than conviction. The loss of independence seems to have come as a bitter blow to all and to have fuelled an outburst of apocalyptic speculation. This focused on a reinterpretation of the prophecies of Daniel. Daniel had traced a succession of four world empires, the fourth of which (the Greek) was to be succeeded by the universal rule of the "saints of God" (the Hasmonean State). The fourth empire was now identified with Rome and the events of Daniel were once more projected into the future. The Romans, the Kittim of Daniel, were transformed from being friends of Israel, who had curbed Greek power, into the "evil empire" which had succeeded the Greeks as Israel's eschatological foe. Some Jews, doubtless heartened by the political instability in Rome during the Roman civil wars, seriously contemplated the possibility of challenging Rome not merely to attain political independence but, more ambitiously, to succeed her as the dominant world power and so fulfil Daniel's prophecy of the ultimate triumph of the fifth monarchy of the saints. With the benefit of hindsight these aspirations seem wildly unrealistic. Though Rome was politically weakened by civil war, none of her enemies were able to exploit her weakness. She triumphed because the only other superpower in the region, Parthia, was reluctant to hold land permanently west of the Euphrates, and because Rome's legions finally proved a match for any army her foes could put into the field against them. The chaos was brought decisively to an end by Augustus. Instead of inaugurating the "fifth monarchy", the Jews in Palestine found themselves under the heel of the detested Roman "stooge", the "half-Jew" Herod. But the damage had been done. Hopes had been raised, heady ideas had been launched into the mainstream tradition—ideas which strengthened Jewish resolve over the next one hundred and fifty years in a series of forlorn rebellions against Rome, and which, insinuated into the Jewish political psyche, became central motifs of the messianic scenario of Judaism, keeping alive Jewish political ambitions down to the present day.

The evidence for seeing the thirty year period from around 60 to 30 B.C.E. as decisive in shaping subsequent Jewish attitudes towards Rome is found in a number of sources. Of these by far the most important is what I have called the eschatological war cycle at Qumran, and it is this cycle of texts which I want to analyse and contextualize in this paper.

II. The Eschatological War Cycle

Under the broad heading of the eschatological war cycle I include all those Qumran texts which speak of, and describe, the final great battle between the forces of good and evil. The central text of this cycle (because, by chance, it is the best preserved) is, of course, the great early Herodian-script scroll, 1QM (+ SHR 3332 and 1Q33, which indicate that the ending of the scroll is missing and that there was originally at least a twentieth column). There are also the 4QM fragments which overlap with, or are obviously related to, the great Cave 1 scroll:

1) 4Q491 (4QM^a) = 1QM V,16–17; VII,3–7, 10–11; IX,17; XII,1; XIII,8–9; XIV,4–18; XV,2–7; XVI,3–14; XVII,10–14. Palaeographically very close to 1QM, though possibly slightly later in date, this displays significant textual variants and differences in order, as well as additional material not closely paralleled in 1QM. It does not belong to the same recension of the war Scroll as 1QM.

2) 4Q492 (4QM^b) = 1QM XII,8–16; XIX,1–13. This is palaeographically and textually close to 1QM. The textual variants are only minor.

3) 4Q493 (4QM^c): cf. 1QM VII–VIII. This is the oldest copy of the War Scroll, dating palaeographically to the first half of the first century b.c.e. It is clearly part of a War Scroll but does not belong to the same recension as 1QM.

4) 4Q494 (4QM^d) = 1QM II,1–3. Written in a Herodian script later than 1QM, this contains only minor variants.

5) 4Q495 (4QM^e) = 1QM X,9–10; XIII,9–12. In early Herodian script, this shows minor variants from 1QM.

6) 4Q496 (4QM^f) = 1QM I,4–9, 11–17; II,5–6, 9–12, 13–14; II end–III,2; III,6–7, 9–11, 13–15; III end–IV,2; IV,6–7; IX,5–9. Palaeographically slightly younger than 4Q493, this contains some material not in 1QM, and in overlaps it shows minor variants. It is possibly not the same recension as 1QM.

Baillet suggested that 4Q497 is also a copy of the War Scroll, or of a related text, but the fragments are too small to yield certain identification.[2]

---

[2] M. Baillet, *Qumrân Grotte 4, III (4Q482–4Q520)* (DJD 7; Oxford: Clarendon, 1982), 69–72.

These texts can all be seen plausibly as recensions of a single work, 'The War Scroll'. In addition, however, there are several other texts dealing with the eschatological war which cannot for certain be identified as part of that work. The most important of these are as follows:

1) 4Q285: This clearly contains material about the eschatological war, but does not overlap textually with 1QM or 4QM. The script is early Herodian, very close to that of 1QM.
2) 11Q14: This can be linked to the eschatological war texts because of the overlap between 11Q14, 1–2 and 4Q285, 7–8. Indeed 11Q14 may be another copy of the same work. The script is Herodian.
3) 4Q471: The text is highly fragmentary, but there is a strong probability that it contained eschatological war material. The script is Herodian.

4Q529, entitled "Words of the book which Michael spoke to the angels of God" and preserved, according to Milik in another copy in 6Q23,[3] is also claimed to be part of the eschatological war cycle. Michael certainly plays a role in the final battle, and it is just possible that we may have here fragments of an address which he is supposed to give to his angelic troops, but the links with the war cycle are tenuous and speculative, and I am inclined, for the moment, to exclude this work.

These texts form a literary cycle in the sense that they are clearly all interrelated, but for the most part are not slavish copies of a single exemplar, or of one another, but rather represent a somewhat free reworking by different authors of a repertory of themes over a considerable period of time. The eschatological war tradition was, at least for a period, very active at Qumran and received a great deal of attention and elaboration.

III. ESCHATOLOGICAL SCENARIOS AND ESCHATOLOGICAL *SERAKHIM*

The material belonging to the eschatological war cycle may be classified according to its content and function into two broad, but

---

[3] J. T. Milik, *The Books of Enoch* (Oxford: Clarendon, 1976), 91.

quite distinct, types: (1) eschatological scenarios, i.e., descriptions of what is going to happen in the final eschatological war; and (2) eschatological *serakhim*, i.e., prescriptions as to the strategy and tactics which the eschatological community should adopt in the light of the eschatological scenario.

Of these two types of material the eschatological scenarios have logical priority. The tactics and strategy have to be shaped in response to events. But how did the Community know what was going to happen? They would not have been content with simply making it up. Within the theology of Qumran, and indeed more generally of Second Temple Judaism, knowledge of the future could only have come through prophetic revelation. The scenarios must be related, either directly or indirectly, to prophecy.

The motif of the eschatological war is common in early Jewish apocalyptic. Important non-Qumranic texts on this theme are found in the Psalms of Solomon, 1 Enoch, 4 Ezra, 2 Baruch, the Sibylline Oracles, the Assumption of Moses, and the Book of Revelation. There is also a great deal on the subject in the later Targumim, in Talmudic literature, and above all in the *Midrešê Geʾullāh* of the early Gaonic period, some of which may preserve Second Temple period traditions not otherwise attested. Close analysis of all these diverse accounts suggests that they go back, one way or another, ultimately to a small collection of Biblical prophecies. The key text was Dan 11:1–12:3. This is now generally recognized as a *vaticinium ex eventu*: it contains a thinly veiled account of the history of the Middle East from the time of Darius down to the time of the Diadochi, the writer's own time. Later apocalyptists, however, reinterpreted it, taking it as referring to events still in the future, at the end of history. Other passages were integrated into Daniel's picture, Ezek 38–39 (the wars of Gog and Magog) and Isa 10:24–11:10 (the defeat of Assyria) being particularly influential. These texts were regarded as divine revelation. They were studied closely, harmonized, and extended and clarified through exegesis and interpretation.

We can see this process in operation in the Scrolls. The Book of Daniel was clearly of great interest to the Community. Some eight manuscripts of Daniel or Pseudo-Daniel have turned up at Qumran, as well as references to Daniel as Scripture in 4Q174 (Florilegium) and reworkings of the Four Empires scenario in 4Q552–53. A similar story can be told about the use of Ezekiel and Isaiah. The relationship between these biblical prophecies and the Qumran eschatological scenarios is fundamentally exegetical. It can be modelled as a species of "Rewritten Bible". As much is stated in 1QM XI,7, "By the hand of your anointed ones, the seers of the appointed times [= the prophets, anointed, i.e., inspired by, the holy spirit], you have told us the times of the wars of your hands, to cover yourself with glory against your enemies, to bring down the troops of Belial, the seven nations of vanity, by the hand of the poor ones whom you have redeemed."

Belief in the imminent eschatological war elicited a twofold response from the Qumran Community. First, urgent clarification of what was going to happen. This could only be achieved, as we have noted, by searching the prophecies. Second, in the light of this understanding of prophecy, the formulation of strategy and tactics. In military terms the former corresponds to the gathering of political, military and economic intelligence, to the analysis of this data and to the construction of best-guess scenarios of the future course of events. The latter corresponds to the creation of a military doctrine in the form of a "war-book" which contains the broad strategies and tactics to be adopted in the light of the projected scenarios.

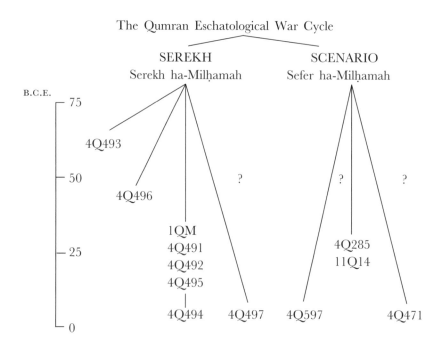

The Qumran Eschatological War Cycle

The Qumran Community classifies its tactics and strategy under the heading of *serakhim*. The term *serekh* seems to have been used by the Community to designate a rule or set of rules binding on them either now or at the eschaton. The rules are not seen as divinely revealed, nor should they be confused with divine commandments. The laws of the Pentateuch cannot be classified as *serakhim*, nor, for that matter, can those of the Temple Scroll. Though a *serekh* may contain some elements of Biblical law (as in the Sabbath Code in the Damascus Document),[4] it is basically a set of *man-made* rules, and was clearly recognized as such. These rules when promulgated and in force, are authoritative, and will be punished, sometimes severely, if breached, but they are not divinely revealed law. They can, therefore, be changed, if circumstances change. This is clearly illustrated from the *Serekh ha-Yaḥad*, a number of different recensions of which, spanning some one hundred and fifty years of community life, have been identified. The *serakhim* in 1QM, consequently, do not necessarily state what is actually going to happen, but what the Qumran tacticians and strategists though *should* happen in the light of their understanding of the circumstances. It is in complete harmony with this that the rules for the war seem, from time to time to have been changed. Two, possibly three, recensions of the War Scroll have been preserved.

IV. The Argument of 4Q285

I would like now to argue this fundamental distinction between eschatological scenarios and eschatological *serakhim* with respect both to 4Q285 and 1QM. First 4Q285.[5] In Frg. 1 the phrase "for the sake of your name" and the reference to "Michael, Gabriel, Sariel and Raphael" are more or less certain. They suggest that we have here a prayer to God on the field of battle, invoking angelic assistance, such as we find in 1QM I–IX. Such prayers belong to the *serekh*

---

[4] Note also that the war *serakhim*, like the eschatological scenarios, contain an element of biblical exegesis. They clarify Torah texts such as Deut 20:2–4 and Num 10:9 which relate to the conduct of war.

[5] See further Philip S. Alexander and Geza Vermes, "285. 4QSefer ha-Milḥamah," in *Qumran Cave 4. XXVI* (ed. Alexander et al.; *DJD* 36; Oxford: Clarendon, 2000), 228–46; P. S. Alexander, "A Reconstruction and Reading of 4Q285 (4QSefer ha-Milhamah)," *RevQ* 19 (2000): 333–48.

side of the war cycle. The Community believed that it would face spiritual as well as physical foes and that divine help would be needed if it was to emerge victorious. They therefore constructed prayers which would be appropriate for the invocation of divine help. There is nothing immutable or sacrosanct about the wording of these prayers. They are not revealed texts. They could be changed and other prayers substituted.

Frg. 3 seems to allude to the Levites blowing trumpets and rams horns to signal to the armies of the Sons of Light how to manoeuvre on the field of battle (cf. 1QM II,15–III,11). The use of trumpets in battle is sanctioned by Num 10:9 (quoted in 1QM X,6–8), so this element has an obvious exegetical basis. However, Scripture does not explain exactly how they are to be used, and working this out is part of the *serekh*. 1QM devotes a great deal of time to the problem. It is obviously necessary to signal clearly different manoeuvres on the field of battle (retreat and advance being the obvious ones). How 1QM envisages this being done is by using different types of instrument, which will have very different timbres (metal trumpets *v.* rams horns), and by blowing different notes or patterns of notes (staccato *v.* sostenuto). 1QM VIII,10 also recognizes the value of noise as psychological warfare: "the blowers of the rams horns shall sound a mighty alarm to terrify the heart of the enemy." It is unclear if any of this was originally included in 4Q285. I do not think there can have been much elaboration of this theme in the vicinity of frg. 3. 4Q285 may not, therefore, have gone beyond the biblical scenario at this point.

Frg. 4 seems to belong to the scenario side of the eschatological cycle. It appears to allude to the final victory of the Prince of the Congregation and all Israel over the King of the Kittim. The Kittim are routed in a land battle, flee westwards and embark on ships, pursued by the Israelites. They finally make a stand,[6] and a sea-battle ensues in which they are defeated. The Israelites return victoriously to dry land bearing with them the captured King of the Kittim who is brought for judgement before the Prince of the Congregation. The exegetical basis of the scenario here is reasonably clear. The quotation of Ezek 39:3–4 in lines 3–4 seems certain. It implies the identification of Gog in Ezekiel with the King of the Kittim. It is

---

[6] I am now strongly inclined to take line 8 as referring to the king of the Kittim and his forces making a stand against the pursuing Israelites.

possible that the eschatological war cycle identified the Kings of the North in Daniel 11–12 with the Parthians and the Kings of the South with the Ptolemies. They then identified the Kittim with the Romans, and in turn equated Rome with the land of Magog in Ezekiel 38–39, a land which Ezekiel could be read as implying lies far beyond the middle eastern theatre of war. The references to the sea battle are intriguing. The idea of the Israelites fighting a naval engagement in the eschatological war is not, to my knowledge, found elsewhere in Second Temple period eschatological texts. However, it might be influenced by Dan 11:30 which clearly envisages the Kittim arriving in the theatre of war in ships from the west. The reference here to the sea battle helps to illustrate the distinction I am trying to draw between scenario and *serekh*. The scenario indicates that Israel will have to fight a sea battle. But how is she going to fight it? What type of ships will she use? How will those ships be armed? In what formations will they be deployed? The Qumran strategists could have inserted here a *serekh* attempting to answer these questions, just as they produced *serakhim* for the land battles. They do not, however, seem to have chosen to do so.

Frg. 7 seems to allude to the Prince of the Congregation, the Branch of David, together with the High Priest, judging the King of the Kittim and putting him to death. This clearly belongs to the scenario, and is closely linked to Isa 10:24–11:10, which speaks of the final defeat of Assyria (= the Parthians) and the emergence of the victorious Branch of David (= the Prince of the Congregation). Isa 10:34 ("the thickets of the forest shall be hacked away, and Lebanon shall fall by a mighty one") is quoted in lines 3–4, but there is an exegetical puzzle here. In the context of 4Q285 one would expect the Mighty One to be identified with God or the Branch of David, his agent. Then "Lebanon" would naturally be equated with the King of the Kittim, and "the thickets of the forest" with his army. There may be a distant echo of such an interpretation in 1QM I,6, "And Assyria shall fall with none to help". But this runs right against the exegetical tradition, which identifies Lebanon with the Temple. Standard Rabbinic exegesis took "Lebanon" here as the Temple and the Mighty One as an allusion to Nebuchadnezzar.[7]

---

[7] See Geza Vermes, "'Car le Liban, c'est le Conseil de la Communauté'," in *Mélanges bibliques rédigés en l'honneur de André Robert* (Travaux de l'Institut Catholique de Paris 4; Paris: Bloud et Gay, 1957), 316–25; idem, "The Symbolical Interpretation of Lebanon in the Targums," *JTS* 9 (1958): 1–12.

I am not sure how we should explain this. It is possible that 4Q285 preserves an early reading of Isa 10:34, which, arguably, corresponds to the original meaning of the biblical text.

Though not directly quoted in the surviving text, Isa 11:4 probably played an important part in the construction of the eschatological scenario: The Branch of David "shall strike down a land [emendation: a ruthless one, *'ariṣ*] with the rod of his mouth, and slay a wicked one with the breath of his lips." The striking down by the "rod of the mouth" and "the breath of the lips" was taken as referring to the judicial sentence by which the Branch of David will condemn the King of the Kittim to death. It is interesting to note that this verse plays a prominent role in the messianism of the Psalms of Solomon (17, 27, 39).

I am now inclined to change the order of frgs. 8–10. I am more than ever convinced that 9–10 belong together, but feel there is a case to made for moving 9–10 to follow 7 and for putting 8 at the end of the series, following 9–10. This does not account for the damage patterns as well as the existing order, nor for the fact that physically (in texture, colour and line-spacing) 8 is very similar to 7, whereas 9–10 are quite different, so different in fact that I have toyed with the possibility that they belonged to a different sheet. However, in terms of *content* the sequence 7 + 9–10 + 8 has much to commend it. Frg. 7 seems to end with a reference to the High Priest giving a command to dispose of the polluting bodies of the slain Kittim. This theme is clearly continued on frgs. 9–10 (I would now definitely favour reading in line 4, "and [fire] shall devour them" rather than "and they shall eat"). Frg. 8 then forms a fitting climax in which the High Priest pronounces a blessing over all Israel, which sees the final defeat of the Kittim as inaugurating all the blessings promised in the Sinai covenant.

However we reconstruct the text there can be little doubt that the end of frg. 7 and frgs. 9–10 belong to the scenario. They are clearly based on Ezek 39:9–16, which refers to the disposal of the slain hosts of Gog, the burning of their weapons and the collection of the booty. There is, however, a possible element of *serekh* at 10:3, which may have stated that the collection of the booty should be entrusted only to those who can resist the temptation of material things, lest someone repeat the sin of Achan and bring disaster on Israel. Frg. 8, however, belongs primarily to the *serekh*. It is a benediction which someone composed as suitable for the High Priest to utter over Israel after the final victory. It is a pastiche of priestly benedictions drawn from the Bible, but there is no exegetical basis that I can find for such a priestly blessing in the biblical scenarios of the end. However, it would have seemed eminently proper to compose such a liturgy to solemnize the final deliverance.

V. THE ARGUMENT OF 1QM

1QM fails to convey any very clear structure or scenario, and appears to be anthological in character. In content it is predominantly a series of *serakhim*. Note the opening: "For the Maskil: The *Serekh* of War for the unleashing of the attack of the Sons of Light against the company of the Sons of Darkness", and the rubrics at II,15 [restored]; III,13; IV,9; V,3; IX,10; XVI,3. The *serakhim* cover a variety of topics: (1) the trumpets and their inscriptions; (2) the standards and their inscriptions; (3) manoeuvres on the field of battle; (4) the various elements of the army (cavalry, infantry, baggage-handlers etc.); (5) the role of the priests in the battle; (6) specifications for offensive and defensive weapons (swords, shields, spears, etc.); (7) hymns and prayers to be uttered on the field of battle. By way of contrast the scenario element is minimal and is found mainly at the beginning and end of the scroll. The key to understanding the scenario lies in the summary timetable of the eschatological war partly preserved in II,6–15. This implies that the war will last for forty years and that it will be divided into two major phases. The first is a war of independence fought by the whole people, which will result in the liberation of the Holy Land. This phase will last for six years and culminate in the seventh year, a sabbatical year, in the restoration of the Temple cult in Jerusalem. The second phase, covering the remaining thirty-three years, will be a war of world-conquest in which Israel will systematically defeat all the nations of the world as listed in Genesis 10. This war will not be fought by all the people, but only by part of them in turn. Nine years will be spent defeating the sons of Shem, ten defeating the sons of Ham, and ten defeating the sons of Japhet. During the four sabbatical years which will fall in this thirty-three year period military operations will be suspended.

This timetable seems to imply that the Kittim will be defeated at the end of the first phase of the war. They are the occupiers and oppressors of Israel, so their defeat has to come first. The war against them is covered in some detail in col. I. It is theoretically possible that a final engagement with them might be envisaged in the closing years of the forty-year war, when Israel defeats the Sons of Japhet, since the Kittim belong to the Japhetic branch of the sons of Noah. This might seem to be supported by the fact that the war against the Kittim crops up again at the end of the scroll in cols XVff., but the anthological nature of 1QM, and its somewhat haphazard arrangement, means that we should not assume that it is in chronological order. It is just as satisfactory to suppose that cols XV to the end are going over the same ground as col. I. In other words the Kittim are decisively and finally dealt with by year six of the eschatological war. There can be little doubt that the defeat of the Kittim and the recovery of national independence is what would have most interested the Qumran Community, or, for that matter, their fellow Jews: this is what would have tugged at the heart-strings. But the decision to prolong the war of liberation into a second phase, a war of world-conquest, is striking. The ambition is breathtaking. I shall return to this point presently.

The role of Dan 11:1–12:3 in the eschatological scenario of 1QM has long been recognized. There is still much force in J. van der Ploeg's proposal that 1QM grew from a primitive work based on Daniel 11–12, which has been more or less preserved at the beginning and end of the surviving War Scroll, and that into this work has been inserted a series of *serakhim* dealing with the practical conduct of the fighting.[8]

Though there are elements of armchair generalship in the eschatological war cycle, it is important to realise that 1QM is basically a real and practical warbook.[9] The battle-formations are real formations, the weapons are real weapons, the tactics are real tactics. It should be remembered that this material is unique in the early Jewish eschatological war texts. Certain eschatological war traditions seemed to have looked for dramatic divine intervention that would miraculously overwhelm the enemy. 1QM, however, holds that the Jews would actually have to take up arms and fight, and it held this

---

[8] J. van der Ploeg, *Le rouleau de la guerre* (Leiden: Brill, 1959), 11–22.
[9] For similarities between the War Scroll and ancient military manuals see J. Duhaime, "The *War Scroll* from Qumran and the Greco-Roman Tactical Treatises," *RevQ* 13 (1988): 133–51.

seriously enough to devise plausible tactics and weapons. As Yadin
above all has shown these reflect aspects of Roman military practice.[10] The Kittim in 1QM are the Romans. It is interesting, then,
that Israel is to adopt Roman tactics in order to defeat Rome.[11] The
detail and accuracy with which the tactics and weapons are described
suggests close acquaintance, either through direct observation, or possibly indirectly through study of Roman military manuals. I am not
suggesting that the Qumranites, when they were not studying Torah
or praying, were drilling and "square-bashing," or indulging in war-
games, though picturing them as early forerunners of the Knights
Templar is, perhaps, not quite as absurd as it sounds. However, they
believed that a real war was looming, and that they had a role to
play in it as leaders and as priests. They took that role seriously
enough to attempt to collect intelligence about the enemy, to formulate a war-doctrine, and to devise tactics, weapons and a sophisticated system of communication through trumpets and horns on the
field of battle.

VI. The Origins of the War Cycle

Two further observations and I have done. First, let me return to
the question of the relationship between 1QM and 4Q285. I am
now convinced that, although both clearly belong to the eschatological war cycle, 1QM and 4Q285 are two quite distinct documents.
I would now reject Milik's suggestion that 4Q285 represents the lost
ending of 1QM.[12] 4Q285 seems to describe, in 1QM's terms, the

---

[10] Y. Yadin, *The Scroll of the War of the Sons of Light against the Sons of Darkness*
(Oxford: Oxford University Press, 1962), 114–97. R. Gmirkin, "The War Scroll
and Roman Weaponry," *DSD* 3 (1996): 89–129, argues, not entirely persuasively,
that the weaponry and tactics point to the Roman army before the reforms of
Marius in 104–103 B.C.E. This does not necessarily disprove our post-63 date for
the composition of the War Scroll, which might have been relying on an older
Roman military manual. For a recent account of Roman battlefield tactics see Philip
Sabin, "The Face of Roman Battle," *JRS* 90 (2000): 1–17. Sabin and Gmirkin give
the more recent bibliography on Roman military practice.

[11] The adoption of Roman tactics is surely a Qumran innovation. It is highly
unlikely at the time the War Scroll was composed that the Judaean forces had reor-
ganized along Roman lines. They were presumably still basically following Hellenistic
military practice.

[12] J. T. Milik, "Milkî-ṣedeq et Milkî-reša' dans les anciens écrits juifs et chrétiens", *JJS* 23 (1972): 143.

eschatological war of liberation. In other words, it dovetails into the
first six years of the eschatological war in 1QM's timetable. None
of its surviving fragments alludes to the war of world conquest. The
two documents differ in their emphasis: 1QM, though it contains
some elements of scenario is fundamentally a *serekh* or series of *serakhim*.
4Q285, though it contains some elements of *serekh* was, I suspect,
fundamentally a scenario.

My second observation is of a more general kind, and concerns
the origins of Qumran war cycle. It is surely significant that the surviving copies of the war-cycle texts seem palaeographically to date
from around the mid to the late first century B.C.E.[13] They all seem
to reflect the equation of Rome with the Kittim, so they all probably date after 63 when Pompey arrived with his Roman legions and
put an end to the Jewish State. This was a period of political chaos
in the middle east in general and in Israel in particular. From the
standpoint of the Jews in Palestine there were two interlocking sources
of confusion: the first was the power-struggle among the survivors
of the Hasmoneans; the second was the civil war which raged in
Rome, and which, spilling over into the Middle East, saw Roman
armies from time to time rampaging across the region. It is hardly
surprising that this situation should have engendered apocalyptic fervour. This, as I noted earlier, took the form initially of revisiting
and reinterpreting the biblical prophecies, especially Daniel 11–12.
This is clear from 1QM I–II. The "kings of the north" in Daniel
(i.e., the Seleucids) become now the Parthians, referred to under the
names of "Asshur" and, somewhat oddly, the "Kittim of Asshur."
The "kings of the south" remain the Ptolemies. The "Kittim" are
still the Romans. The purpose of keeping the name Kittim was not
to avoid prying, hostile eyes but to preserve the link between contemporary events and biblical prophecy. The fourth empire of Daniel
is now Rome, not Greece. 1QM also picks up the references in
Daniel to Edom, Moab and Ammon. In 1QM these probably refer
primarily to the Nabataeans. 1QM also adds a reference to Phoenicia.
These allusions fit the political situation of 60–30 B.C.E., when, in
the political confusion engendered by the Roman civil war, the
statelets of Syria-Palestine, like the Jews, harboured hopes of win-

---

[13] Only 4Q493 causes problems for a post-63 date for the War Scroll, but they
are not acute. A date of around 60 for this text is not palaeographically out of the
question.

ning independence. The scenario in 1QM 1–2 is close to Daniel 11–12, but there are subtle differences. The picture it paints fits better the situation after 60. The writer is, of course, attempting to peer into the future, but he is broadly projecting forward a vision of the world based on the geo-political realities of his own time. In the dangerous and troubled time between 63 and *c.* 30 B.C.E. when Herod consolidated his hold on Palestine, there may well have been those in Judah who expected a final military conflict in which the Jews would be called upon to fight to regain their freedom. And in the broader global clashes they might have spied an opportunity for the Jews, by taking a leaf militarily out of Rome's book, to challenge her for world domination. This aspiration too could have had an exegetical basis and represent one way of reading Daniel's prediction of the triumph of the fifth monarchy. As I said before, the authors of the Qumran war cycle were certainly not lacking in ambition. They believed that Israel was the equal of Rome and was divinely destined one day to rule the world.

If this understanding of the Qumran war cycle is correct then its heyday was the period from 63 to 30 B.C.E. The impression is sometimes given that the Qumran Community became "zealot" only in the first century C.E. and that the real context for the war cycle is the years leading up to the first revolt against Rome. It is not improbable that interest in the war cycle would have revived at this period, but the texts definitely originated much earlier, and, judging by the existing evidence, the active phase of the tradition lay in the immediate aftermath of Pompey's incorporation of the Jewish State into the "evil empire."

THEOLOGICAL ELEMENTS IN THE
FORMULATION OF QUMRAN LAW[1]

Joseph M. Baumgarten

In the early stages of Qumran research scholarly interest in religious law ('halakha') was markedly limited. Even when it was recognized that the so-called *Damascus Document* (*CD*) from the Genizah stemmed originally from the Qumran community, doubts were expressed whether this held also for the law code, which constitutes a considerable part of the medieval text published and commented on by Schechter and elaborately re-evaluated by Ginzberg. After the discovery of the scrolls, the major focus of interest was on the theological tenets set forth in catechismal fashion in the *Rule of the Community* (*1QS*). This work does contain rules of discipline, but hardly any Torah-based 'halakha'. The admonition which precedes the law code in CD was of modern interest mainly for its allusions to biblical and sectarian history, not its critique of prevalent violations of religious law. In England some editions of the Damascus Document omitted the law code altogether.

The fact that religious law is now granted to have been a major concern of the Qumran community can be attributed to the noteworthy sequence of nomistic texts which belatedly became available in the latter phases of Scroll publication. We need only enumerate the para-pentateuchal *Temple Scroll*, the remarkable epistle about purity law known as מקצת מעשי התורה (*MMT*), and the Cave 4 'halakhic' texts, which include significant portions of the CD law code. The medieval Genizah manuscripts, it now turns out, preserve a substantially reliable text of some, but not all the laws advocated by the Qumran legists a millennium earlier.

The unexpected abundance of halakhic fragments has led some scholars to the hypothesis that halakhic rather than theological issues

---

[1] Dedicated with sincere הברת הטוב to Emanuel, whose balanced appreciation of both halakha and theology has brought the publication of the Scrolls to fruition.

An earlier form of this paper was presented on October 11, 2001 before the Qumran research group at the מכון ללימודים מתקדמים of the Hebrew University of Jerusalem.

were the decisive factors in the formation of Second Temple sectarian movements. I am inclined to a more moderate approach which
seeks to explore both ideological and legal differences among Jewish
movements of that period. This seems to me to be in accord with
the portrayal of Josephus and the recollections preserved in rabbinic
sources. I have maintained that the *Damascus Document* ought to be
viewed as a legal text, a פרוש המשפטים, as it is termed in its now
available conclusion, introduced by a paraenetic view of biblical and
sectarian history which supports the halakhic reforms advocated by
the Qumran teachers.

In this paper I propose to examine on the textual level five formulations of Qumran 'halakha' which contain theological allusions
of significance.

I. 4Q251 1–2

Frgs 1–2 (*olim* frg. 1)

ה]מֹשה [	] 1
]ות כול[	] 2
בהמה ולמשוך מים מבׄור [ ]○לש[	] 3
יוצא איש ממקומו כל השבת [ ]○○ אל]○ש המשיכה [	] 4
מן החוץ אל הבית]ומן הבית אל הה]ויץ]לו לדרוש ולקרׄא בספר ב]שב]ת	] 5
]מׄיא נדה בש]ר]וֹ ביוׄם] ה]שׄבת] החיל [	] 6
]בׄ[י]ם השׁשי בשר ער]וה[	] 7

This fragment concerns activities restricted on שבת, such as drawing
water from a well and carrying objects into and out of houses. Line
6 has the phrase מׄיא נדה which, differing from the editors,[2] I am
inclined to take as pertaining to sprinkling waters (מי נדה) which may
not be used for purification on Shabbat. This restriction appears
twice in other 4Q texts.

Line 7 insists that the cleansing of בשר ערוה should be accomplished on the sixth day, the eve of Shabbat. For our purposes, we
should like to determine what is meant by בשר ערוה. The editors
took it as a designation for the male sexual organ, but such specifically
localized cleansing would be rather anomalous. In the light of the

---

[2] The first editors' suggestion to restore the unknown Hiph'il הט]מׄיא is in my
opinion precluded by the context.

Qumran purification liturgies, which were intended to be recited after bathing on the eve of Shabbat and other holidays, it seems to me that the expression בשר ערוה designates the human body as a whole. Thus, a liturgical fragment refers in the plural to ערות בשרנו 'the shame of our flesh' (4Q512 36–38 ii,17). ערוה and בשר are the words used regularly for the dualistic portrayal of man's corporal nature. The author of the *Hodayot* describes himself as a "creature of clay, fashioned with water, and a foundation of shame (סוד הערוה)" [1QH[a] IX,22]. The counterpart in 1QS XI,9 is סוד בשר עול 'foundation of wicked flesh'.[3]

The scruples of the Essenes about exposure of the body and their use of a loincloth while bathing (*JW* 2.129, 161) may now be compared with the instruction וכסה את בנדיו (4Q512 11,4), which Baillet translated correctly, "il se couvrira de ses vetements" (*DJD* 7, p. 271). Not long ago I pointed out to the editor of 4Q472a (*DJD* 35, p. 156) that the phrase למכסי צו refers to the covering of excrements, צו being a short form of צואה (*DJD* 35, p. 156). Thus, two more specific Essene practices, the avoidance of nakedness and the scruples about leaving ordure exposed to the sun, may be added to the long list of parallels documented at Qumran.

II. 4Q269 8 ii,3–6 (= 4Q271 2)

4 [וזן כל הכלי אשר יעשה מ/לאכה ב/הם אשר יטמאו ל/נפש אדם כיא אם הוזו כמ/שפט]

5 [הטהרה במי הנדה ב/פֿקֿן הרשֿ/ע איש טהור מֿ]כֿ[ול טומֿאֿ]ה[אשר יעריב א]ת[ן

6 [שמשו וכול נער אשר לוא מלאו ימיו לעבור על הפקודים א]ל[יזה]

This passage sets forth two Qumran requirements concerning the person sprinkling the waters of purification on vessels contaminated with corpse impurity: a. he must himself be purified and wait until sundown b. he must be a mature adult, at least twenty years old; minors were not qualified to perform the sprinkling. Both of these rules, as we elucidated in *DJD* 18, were directed against the presumably Pharisaic practices of allowing a טבול יום and even young boys to do the sprinkling.

---

[3] This dualistic denigration of the body may be contrasted with the well-known story about Hillel who taught that the bathing of the body, in which the soul resides, was a prime מצוה (*Lev. Rab.* 34,3 ed. Margulies, p. 776).

For the present purpose we take note of the fact that these rules are said here to be valid "in the period of evil", בקץ הרשע. The periodization of history into קצים is a well known feature of Enochic and Qumranic theology; we now have an eschatological text (4Q416 1,13) which also refers to the future קץ האמת. However, here the terminology appears in the midst of a 'halakhic' text. One might suppose that purification from טומאה would only be needed in an epoch when evil exists, although the text here pertains to defilement from contact with the dead. Was corpse impurity, too, characteristic of the קץ הרשע?

A less radical hypothesis would be that the need to affirm these rules, which were controversial, only obtained as long as there was evil. This premise needs to be examined in the light of the use of קץ הרשע elsewhere in the *Damascus Document*.

CD XII,22–XIII,1 is an introductory heading for a group of organizational rules pertaining to those who dwell in camps: וזה סרך מושב המחנות המתהלכים באלה בקץ הרשעה עד עמוד משיח אהרן וישראל. This סרך deals primarily with inner communal matters, such as the roles of the priests and the מבקר, not controversial halakhic rulings. Yet these inner organizational concerns were also viewed as limited to the period of evil until the coming of the messiah/s.

The coming of the messiah/s is likewise mentioned in a similarly worded[4] and theologically pivotal passage in CD XIV,18–19. This passage is now available from 4Q266:

וזה פרוש [המשפטים אשר יש]פטו בם עד עמוד משיח אהרן וישראל
[ויכפר עוונם ממנ]חה וחטת

> And this is the explication of [the rules by which they shall be go]verned until the rise of the messiah of Aaron and Israel, [and he will atone their iniquity better than/through me]al and sin offerings.

I have elsewhere[5] argued for reading this passage in its literal, although theologically unexpected sense, attributing to the messiah/s the authority to forgive sins. Here, however, we may also inquire what the text implies about the status of the laws after the coming of the messiah/s. In my estimation the very need for the forgiveness of sins suggests that the laws of the Torah would not be abrogated in the

---

[4] E. Qimron would restore the gap in CD 14:18–19 to include the phrase [וישפטו בהם בקץ הרשעה], but 4Q266 10,12 clearly omit בקץ הרשעה.

[5] J. M. Baumgarten, "Messianic Forgiveness of Sin in CD 14:19 (4Q266 10 i 12–13)", *The Provo Conference on the Dead Sea Scrolls* (ed. D. W. Parry and E. Ulrich; Leiden: Brill, 1999), 537–44.

post-messianic age. This is further supported by the *Messianic Rule* (1QSᵃ) which specifies rules for the אחרית הימים and the order to be followed at the assembly headed by the messiahs of Aaron and Israel. Likewise, the author of MMT underlines his appeal for repentance and the proper observance of the laws by his judgment that the אחרית הימים has already arrived.

We would accordingly interpret the association of the laws with the קץ הרשע in line with the Qumran doctrine that the understanding of the laws was progressively revealed to the sect's teachers. This process continues during the period of evil, but is to culminate with the coming of the messiah/s who would finalize the true meaning of the Torah.

III. 4Q269 AND PARALLELS

4Q269 Frg. 9

4 [*vacat*   אל יבא איש אשה בברי]ת קוד[ש] אשר [ידעה]

5 [לעשות מעשה בדבר ואשר ידעה מעשה בבית אב]יה או אלמנה אשר

6 [נשכבה מאשר התארמלה וכול אשה אשר עליה ש]ם רע בבתולי[ה]

4Q415 Frg. 2 ii

1 [   ] כאב כבדי ∘[ ]∘ [ ]

  ∘ש

2 [אל תמישי בלבבך וע]

3 [כול היום ובחיקו בר]

4 [פן תפרעי ברית קוד]ש

5 [ואויבת לנפשך ול]ב

The characterization of marriage as a 'holy covenant' ברית קודש is now confirmed by 4Q415 2 ii, a wisdom instruction addressed in the feminine to a married woman. She is advised to honor her husband's parents and in other ways to enhance marital harmony. This is motivated by the caution "lest you disturb the holy covenant", פן תפרעי ברית קודש. Marriage is termed a ברית in biblical prophecy (Ezek 16:8, Mal 2:14). קודש and its cognates are employed in 4Q502 in the context of a man's relationship to his wife and companion, but the combination ברית קודש appears to emerge first in writings found at Qumran. The standard rabbinic term (לשנא דרבנן) for betrothal is קדושין, which is explained in the Talmud technically on the basis of the analogy to a sacred dedication (הקדש *b. Qidd.* 2b).

It is noteworthy that despite the misogynic reasons for Essene celibacy supplied by Philo and Josephus, Qumran texts portray the ideal wife as a person of understanding, apparently capable of admonishing her husband about the laws pertaining to their marital relationship.[6]

IV. 1QH[a] XII,5–12 and the Qumran concept of יום בפור

In a recent paper,[7] I proposed to use another source, beside פשר חבקוק, to throw light on the dramatic Yom Kippur confrontation between the Qumran sect and the Wicked Priest. It is one of the Hodayot hymns, attributable to the Teacher, which echoes Hab 2:15, the very lemma utilized in פשר חבקוק to describe the Yom Kippur incident. The lemma reads: הוי משקה רעיהו מספח חמתו אף שכר למען הבט אל מועדיהם "Woe to him who gives his neighbor drink, pouring out his wrath, making them drunk in order to gaze at their festivals". The author of the hymn applies this terminology to his opponents, the Pharisaic 'preachers of smooth things', who withhold the משקה of true knowledge from the thirsty; instead they give them vinegar to drink למען הבט אל תעותם להתהולל במועדיהם "in order to gaze at their error and to deport themselves foolishly on their holidays". The word תעות, I suggested, refers to the calendrical error of observing Yom Kippur and other holidays at the wrong time;[8] להתהולל alludes to the desecration of the somber spirit of Yom Kippur by inappropriate celebrations on this sacred day. Such celebrations are recorded in the Mishnah, which mentions that the high priest made a יום טוב for his friends after emerging unscathed from the Holy of Holies (m. Yoma 7:4), and that Yom Kippur was popularly celebrated by dancing and matchmaking (m. Ta'an. 4:8). Philo seems to be aware of the dual nature of the fastday which embodies both atonement and festive celebration. In Jubilees, by contrast, Yom Kippur was viewed as a day of mourning and weeping; its date was typologically anticipated by Jacob's grief when the brothers of Joseph brought his

---

[6] See the description of the wife as a בת אמת, possessing "intelligence and understanding" in 4Q502 Groupe I, 2 (DJD 7, p. 82) and my re-appraisal of 1QSa in DJD 18, p. 165.

[7] J. Baumgarten, "Yom Kippur in the Qumran Scrolls and Second Temple Sources", DSD 6 (1999): 184–91f.

[8] For this conotation of תעות see 4Q513 44.

bloodied garment to their father (*Jub.* 34:19). At Qumran, too, the תענית of Yom Kippur was associated with 'grief' ינון (4Q509 16 iv,4), and the fast was referred to not only as a צום, but as יום התענית 'the day of self-affliction' or מועד תענית (4Q508 2,2–4). In CD VI,19 the promise to keep the יום התענית כמצאת באי הברית החדשה "in accordance with what was revealed to the keepers of the new covenant" is listed as one of the duties incumbent upon the community. The central-ity of Yom Kippur is further underlined by its designation as יום גדול, a name which appears first at Qumran and is found later in talmudic and Samaritan sources.

In its description of the intrusion of the Wicked Priest פשר חבקוק depicts it as a grievous disturbance of the peaceful מנוחה appropri-ate to Yom Kippur as שבת שבתון. The aspect of tranquility is twice underlined by the identification of the day as קץ מועד מנוחת יום הכפורים and יום צום שבת מנוחתם. How did the Wicked Priest disturb the sabbath peace? The פשר indicates that he did so by intruding upon the congregation בכעס חמתו "with his wrathful anger". The peaceful מנוחה which they were striving for on this great Shabbat was shat-tered by his angry intrusion. This description calls for further explo-ration of the meta-halakhic dimension of spiritual rest as an element of Shabbat.

V. Shabbat מנוחה and tranquility

When one looks at the CD Shabbat code, extensive portions of which are extant, one notices immediately that it is not structured around archetypal categories of מלאכה. The forms of work explicitly pro-hibited in the Torah, such as plowing, harvesting, gathering wood, and kindling a fire are not mentioned, nor is there any trace of the thirty-nine categories of work enumerated in the Mishnah. After the initial rubric על השבת לשמרה כמשפטה there comes a precautionary rule forbidding מלאכה on the eve of Shabbat when the orb of the sun is still above the horizon by the distance of its diameter. This is followed by a series of restrictions, not of physical work, but of secular talk and planning and walking beyond the תחום. The wording and the substance of these rules were based on Isa 58:13: אם תשיב משבת רגלך עשות חפצך ביום קדשי וקראת לשבת ענג, "If you restrain your foot because of the Sabbath, from pursuing your business on my holy day; and call the Sabbath a delight"; the restriction on inappropriate talk derives from ודבר דבר. Interestingly, 4Q264a specifically sanctions talk about eating and drinking, which enhance the ענג of Shabbat, and approves of pronouncing blessings (*DJD* 35, p. 54).

Esther Chazon has observed that the Qumran liturgies which can be identified as intended for Shabbat are consistently doxological in character.[9] They do not embrace any petitional prayers, such as were recited on weekdays. One Shabbat prayer is entitled הודות ביום השבת, which recalls טוב להודות לה' in Psalm 92. Another liturgical fragment has the designation [מו]עד] מנוח ותענוג. The word ענג as we noted, already characterizes the Shabbat in Isa 58:13, and מנוח is twice juxtaposed with קודש. The avoidance of extraneous petitions was a salient aspect of the Shabbat prayers which also survived in rabbinic practice. The talmudic principle שבת היא מלזעוק (*b. Šabb. 12a*) derives from the concept that the spiritual tranquility of שבת must not be disturbed even by the urgency of human prayer.

The CD prohibitions of secular talk include litigating monetary claims. Tannaitic halakha took it for granted that courts cannot hold sessions on Shabbat, but the ostensible reason was that the proceedings could not be recorded. In CD the context suggests that the legal contentions would disturb the Sabbath peace. For the same reason one must not make financial claims against another, אל ישה ברעהו כל. The wording is taken from the ban on collecting debts which were cancelled by the sabbatical year (אשר ישה ברעהו, Deut 15:2).

The Shabbat code of CD does not deal with the question of waging war on Shabbat, but in *Jubilees* this is flatly prohibited, without any distinction between offensive and defensive actions. A fragmentary 4Q text dealing with Shabbat has the phrase להלחם עמו, but unfortunately the context is missing. We may, however, presume that the Qumranites accepted the prohibition of *Jubilees*. This is supported by the exclusion of warfare in the sabbatical years in the apocalyptic War Scroll. The stated reason is כיא שבת מנוח היאה לישראל (1QM II,8–9), which is an apparent extension of a Shabbat rule to the שמיטה year.

Two other rules found in the CD Shabbat code may be classified as disturbances of מנוחה. One forbids the owner of an animal to strike it with his fist in order to make it go in a particular direction (CD

---

[9] E. Chazon, "On The Special Character of Sabbath Prayer", *Journal of Jewish Music and Liturgy* 15 (1992–93): 1–21.

XI,6); this would violate the biblical injunction to grant it rest. Slaves, too, must be allowed their מנוחה, hence the prohibition אל ימר איש את עבדו ואת אמתו (CD XI,12).

In short, a significant portion of the Qumran Shabbat code reflects a conception of Shabbat as a day of peace and harmony free from the conflicts and confrontations which disturb the tranquility of life. This conception is compatible with later rabbinic thought, but it is substantially earlier.

In rabbinic theology the מנוחה of Shabbat derives not only from creation but foreshadows the tranquility of עולם הבא. Tannaitic exegesis characterized the world-to-come as יום שכולו שבת ומנוחה לחיי העולמים 'a day which is all Shabbat and tranquility for life evermore'. Yet, spiritual מנוחה may also be realized in the here and now with the arrival of Shabbat. R. Levi, a third generation Amora, commented on היום אם בקולו תשמעו (Ps 95:7): "If the children of Israel kept but one שבת as it ought to be kept, they would be redeemed forthwith". There is earlier evidence for the realization of ideal tranquility on Shabbat from the Second Temple period.

We may cite a Christian source preceding the destruction of the Temple; The anonymous author of the *Letter to the Hebrews*, wrote to a group of Christian believers who were apparently accustomed to practicing the biblical commandments and instructed them to maintain a form of sabbatical rest (Heb 4:1–11). Quoting Ps 95:7–8 ("Today, if you hear his voice, do not harden your hearts"), he infers that a Shabbat rest still remains for the people of God: 'Let us therefore make every effort to enter that rest (κατάπαυσις), so that no one may fall through such disobedience as theirs' (the Israelites of Ps 95:11). The quite similar exegesis of Psalm 95, especially the word היום, which both designates the sabbath and calls for its observance today, makes it probable that R. Levi's association of keeping שבת with redemptive rest derives from a tradition already known in the Second Temple period.

In sum, the foregoing sampling of religious laws, no doubt capable of more comprehensive extension, was intended to illustrate the affinity between the formulation of rules by the legists of the Qumran community and their theological tenets. These tenets are sometimes expressive of the particular catechism of the community, but they may also reflect beliefs held in common with other Jews in the Second Temple period.

4Q159 FRAGMENT 5 AND THE "DESERT THEOLOGY" OF THE QUMRAN SECT[1]

Moshe J. Bernstein

Introduction

One of the texts in *Discoveries in the Judaean Desert* 5 which I am in the process of re-editing together with Professor George Brooke is 4Q159, named by its initial editor, J. M. Allegro, "Ordinances."[2] The bulk of the substantial remains of this text, fragments 1 and 2–4, contains legal material which is related to laws found in the Pentateuch, hence its official designation. Virtually every scholar who has dealt with 4Q159, however, has questioned the relationship of fragment 5, which was also published by Allegro as part of this manuscript, to the other fragments, both on the grounds that it does not contain legal material as the other fragments do, and that it contains terminology, such as פשר and ואשר אמר, with which we are familiar from non-legal Qumran literature. As a result, frg. 5 has been ignored in almost all subsequent scholarly discussions of 4Q159.[3]

---

[1] I had the pleasure of presenting a paper on my preliminary work on 4Q159, including this fragment, at a monthly symposium of the Bible department of the Hebrew University held on December 12, 2001 in the home of Professor Emanuel Tov, in whose honor this essay is being published. Most of the work on this text was carried out during my tenure as a fellow at the Institute for Advanced Studies at the Hebrew University during the fall 2001 semester. In my work there on 4Q159, I profited from productive conversations with Professors Joseph Baumgarten and Elisha Qimron. At the penultimate stage of writing, I had the benefit of the criticism of Professor James C. VanderKam.

[2] J. M. Allegro, *Qumrân Cave 4, I (4Q158–186)* (*DJD* 5; Oxford: Clarendon, 1968), 6–9.

[3] Typical is the comment of J. A. Fitzmyer in his review of Allegro, *CBQ* 31 (1969): 237, "The fifth fragment of this text (4Q159) is so different in content from the rest that one wonders if it rightly belongs to this group of fragments." F. D. Weinert, "4Q159: Legislation for an Essene Community outside of Qumran?" *JSJ* 5 (1974): 179–207 (203–204) comments, "The total absence of any such [pesher] formulae in all the rest of 4Q159 makes the conclusion unavoidable that fragment 5 is not derived from the same text as 4Q159." L. H. Schiffman, "Ordinances and Rules," *The Dead Sea Scrolls: Hebrew, Aramaic and Greek Texts with English Translations. Volume 1. Rule of the Community and Related Documents* (ed. J. H. Charlesworth; Tübingen: J. C. B. Mohr, 1994), 145–57, writes (145) "Fragment 5 was misidentified and does

Joseph Baumgarten, I believe, has been the only scholar to continue
to work with the assumption that frg. 5 is part of 4Q159, working
from a starting point that there is an analogy between 4Q159 and
4Q265 ("Miscellaneous Rules") as texts which combine narrative and
halakhic material.[4] Although I cannot accept fully his typological
comparison between 4Q159 and 4Q265, some of his brief remarks
on 4Q159, in the introduction to his edition of 4Q265, anticipate
certain aspects of my treatment of 4Q159, although without the fuller
restoration of the fragment and its interpretation that I shall attempt.

The apparent reluctance of scholars to accept the initial identification
of fragment 5 as belonging to this text derives fundamentally from
two related concerns. The first, as noted above, is the insistence that
there is sufficient generic dissimilarity between frg. 5 and the other
fragments to preclude their belonging to the same MS.[5] I reject this
view which is predicated on what I believe to be an excessively rigid
sense of genres at Qumran, in this case the alleged phenomenon
that in a text which apparently is of a legal nature we cannot expect
to find non-legal material. The other argument consists of the absence
of any obvious connection in content between fragment 5 and the
remainder of the text that would lead us to consider them related,
even in the face of their apparent generic dissimilarity.

The former claim, which is an *a priori* assumption, is difficult to
refute. But in this essay, which I happily dedicate to the editor-in-
chief of the publication series in which my edition of this text will
appear, I shall attempt to demonstrate, by ordering the fragments
in a slightly different sequence, that there indeed exists a possible
connection between fragments 1 and 2–4, on the one hand, and
fragment 5, on the other. Following that demonstration, I shall venture a somewhat speculative suggestion regarding the possible signi-

---

not belong with this manuscript. It is in fact a *pesher*, probably to Leviticus 16:1."
J. Strugnell, "Notes en marge du volume V des 'Discoveries in the Judaean Desert
of Jordan'," *RevQ* 7 (1969–71): 175–79 must of course be consulted in any work
on this text.
    [4] "4Q265. Miscellaneous Rules," in *Qumran Cave 4.XXV: Halakhic Texts* (ed.
J. Baumgarten et al., *DJD* 35; Oxford: Clarendon, 1999), 58–60.
    [5] When I consulted Dr. Ada Yardeni for her paleographic evaluation of the frag-
ments, she asserted, after a brief examination of photographs of the fragments of
4Q159, that she felt that they were all written by a single hand. Paleographically,
then, fragment 5 qualifies to be part of 4Q159, and can only be excluded with the
admittedly not unreasonable claim that this scribe wrote more than one manuscript
which survived at Qumran.

ficance of the text of this fragment to the ideology of the community that lived at Qumran.

4Q159 FRAGMENT 5

Fragment 5, with minimal reconstruction, reads

[הדבר [פשר] אל וימחו אל ![מ⁶
[לו[ני בני vacat ![י
ר[אמ ואשר במשפט
[את[בקחת מושה]
ר[הדב[פשר שמה ![יצאו
[? ו בצוקה ⁷התורה[דל[רוש
[אש[ר דבר מושה]
[כול]

There can be little doubt that the central context of the fragment is that of Exod 33:7 ומשה יקח את האהל ונטה לו מחוץ למחנה הרחק מן המחנה וקרא לו אהל מועד והיה כל מבקש ה' יצא אל אהל מועד אשר מחוץ למחנה ("Moses would take the tent and pitch it outside the camp, far away from the camp and would call it the tent of meeting. Whoever was seeking the Lord would go out to the tent of meeting which was outside the camp."), based minimally on the occurrences of the words בקחת מושה and יצאו in the fragment.[8] At the first glance, then, the arguments against its belonging to the same document as the other fragments of 4Q159 seem plausible: on the one hand, fragment 5 does not contain legal material, but, on the other hand, it does contain the only occurrences in a Qumran narrative text of the idioms פשר הדבר and ואשר אמ]ר. Both of these formulas are characteristic of the pesharim and related texts, and we are not accustomed to finding them in legal (or narrative) documents.[9]

---

[6] Strugnell, 178–79, reads the *mem* as נ (noting both letters as doubtful), completing the word as פ]ני and connecting it with Lev 16:1 because before the word פשר we expect a biblical text. This reading has been accepted in several of the subsequent discussions of the text. I believe both that the *mem* is a more likely reading (VanderKam, in private communication, concurs, pointing to the נ in the next line), and that the context of Exodus 33 recommends a restoration along the lines which I shall suggest.

[7] The remains of the first *heh* of התורה are admittedly strangely shaped, but no other reading suggests itself, *pace* Weinert.

[8] We shall see further that לד]רוש התורה is probably related to כל מבקש ה' of the biblical text.

[9] The term פשר in CD is not to be drawn into the discussion, as it seems to be

It might be suggested that the so-called Reworked Pentateuch texts (4Q158, 364–367) can furnish an analogous genre to this document as a whole, since they, too, contain both legal and narrative material side by side. This loose descriptive analogy, however, is flawed since those texts are overtly modeled on the Pentateuch which itself is composed of a mixture of legal and non-legal material, while neither the legal nor the non-legal portions of 4Q159 can be said to follow a biblical paradigm. Fragment 5, in particular, which is the central text in our discussion, cannot be claimed to be similar stylistically to the non-legal sections of those texts in any way.[10] The peculiarity of a pesher on narrative text is not the only strange feature of this fragment; there is the added difficulty that the words before פשר] הדבר in line 1 do not coincide with any biblical text which we know.[11] Since this is the only example of a pesher in this type of text, we have no comparative data from which to derive any criteria for the nature of what we should expect to precede the pesher formula, be it text or paraphrase.[12] Since, however, the words פשר הדב]ר in line 5 also are not preceded by a biblical citation, we should not insist on restoring a citation before them in line 1.

---

employed there in the same sense as it is in the pesharim, indicating the interpretation or actualization of the prophetic message.

[10] Baumgarten, 60, draws an analogy between 4Q265 and 4Q159 "in the variety of [their] legal contents and in [their] mixed literary form," since both contain legal material which does not seem to be organized according to any overt pattern, as well as "biblical quotations and narrative allusions which are not strictly halakhic, but may have served as support for the rules propounded by Qumran exegetes." In the case of 4Q159, there may have been an ideological purpose in the inclusion of this non-narrative material, as we shall suggest.

[11] The suggestion of Strugnell to read something from Lev 16:1 would produce at best בקרבתם לפ]ני אל וימותו, which is also not a verbatim citation since the Tetragrammaton has been replaced by אל as occasionally occurs in the writings of Qumran (a point noted already by Schiffman, 157, n. 49). Furthermore, such a "quotation" does not connect with the following lines of the fragment in the way that the reading that we shall suggest later does. The same can be said for Weinert's restoration (203) [בקרבתם]ם אל וימותו], in which, he suggests, n. 72, that אל represents לפני ה' of the Pentateuchal text.

[12] I have touched upon this question with regard to "standard" pesharim in "Introductory Formulas for Citation and Re-Citation of Biblical Verses in the Qumran Pesharim: Observations on a Pesher Technique," *Dead Sea Discoveries* 1 (1994), 30–70. It seems clear that in 4QMMT citation formulas do not have to (and rarely do) introduce verbatim citations of Hebrew Bible; see my treatment in "The Employment and Interpretation of Scripture in 4QMMT: Preliminary Observations," *Reading 4QMMT: New Perspectives on Qumran Law and History*, John Kampen and Moshe J. Bernstein, eds. (Symposium 2; Atlanta: Scholars Press, 1996), 29–51 (39 and n. 23).

Context: Fragments 1–4

Before proceeding to the presentation of our arguments regarding fragment 5, we must first present the background against which, in my view, it appeared in 4Q159. The larger, "legal," fragments of 4Q159 cover the following themes (accepting, for the moment, the order of the fragments as published by Allegro):[13]

Fragment 1

Laws of leaving for poor in granary and field (Deut 23:25–26; 24:19–21) (lines 3–5)
Money of valuation/half-sheqel (Exod 30:12–13; 38:25–26) (lines 6–7)
"Digression" detailing the collection of the half-sheqel in the wilderness (lines 7–12)
Two lines concerning measurements *ephah* = *bath* and three *'esronim* (Cf. Ezek 45:11) (lines 13–14)
Two lines referring to Moses and burning (Exod 32:20?) (lines 16–17)

Fragments 2–4

Laws of Israelite sold to non-Jew (Lev 25:47, 53, 42) (lines 1–3)
Court of [ten] Israelites and two priests (no explicit biblical source, but relating to Deut 17) (lines 4–6)
Transvestism (Deut 22:5) (lines 6–7)
Bride accused of non-virginity (Deut 22:13–21) (lines 8–10)

I suggest that the final lines (16–17) of fragment 1 (which follow a *vacat*, and thus have no immediate surviving context) are to be reconstructed as follows:

הוה ע[ל הֹעם ועלב[נ]די[הם]¹⁴   16
ואת העגל אשר עשו בני י[שראל שרף מוש]ה[¹⁵   17

---

[13] There is no indication in Allegro's publication why he numbered the fragments 1 and 2–4 (as opposed to 1–3 and 4, for example), and the re-ordering which I shall propose does not run counter to any argument known to me.

[14] The proclitic spelling of ועל בנדיהם as one word is a phenomenon encountered occasionally in the Qumran corpus. Cf. E. Qimron, *The Hebrew of the Dead Sea Scrolls* (Atlanta: Scholars, 1986), 42 (§200.27.d).

[15] Baumgarten, 59, reconstructed the second line exactly as I do, and in his discussion suggests that "the first line probably alludes to the purification of the people by sprinkling after the making of the golden calf." Although he does not furnish

16 [He sprinkled o]n the people and on their garments [

17 [And the calf which the children of I]srael [had made] Mose[s] burnt[

Admittedly, my overall reconstruction of these lines is predicated, in part, on their proximity to language based on Exod 30:12–13, the command to take a census, which appears earlier in frg. 1 (lines 6–7), and the story of the golden calf in Exodus 32, as well as on the basis of our text in frg. 5. It could be argued, therefore, that there is an apparent circularity in my argumentation. But this reconstruction works not only in terms of the factors which I have just indicated, but on internal grounds as well. Furthermore, regardless of how we reconstruct and interpret them, these lines appear to break the strictly legal flow of the contents of 4Q159, and therefore already furnish at least a limited parallel to the presence of frg. 5 in the document.

In our reconstruction of line 16, something was sprinkled on the people and their garments, with the idiom following along the lines (although probably not the context) of the descriptions in Exod 29:21 והזית על אהרן ועל בגדיו ועל בניו ועל בגדי בניו אתו and Lev 8:30, ויז על אהרן על בגדיו ועל בניו ועל בגדי בניו אתו.[16] The reconstruction of line 17 is based on Exod 32:20 ויקח את העגל אשר עשו וישרף באש.[17] The only occurrences of the verb שרף in conjunction with Moses in the Pentateuch are this one and its parallel in Deut 9:21 ואת חטאתכם אשר עשיתם את העגל לקחתי ואשרף אתו באש.[18] The only other possible context for these words, if they are not based directly on biblical idiom, would appear to be the covenant ceremony in Exodus 24 where in 24:8 Moses sprinkles half of the blood on the people, but "clothing" is not mentioned in that passage. Nor is the verb שרף found there

---

a reading, it would seem that he would reconstruct the first line along the lines that I have.

[16] Baumgarten suggests, 60, that what was sprinkled could have been the purifying ashes of the red heifer, implying that the worship of idolatry (presumably the golden calf) imparts corpse impurity. The suggestion is attractive, but unprovable, and is subject to the further counterclaim that the commandment regarding the ashes of the red heifer does not appear in the Pentateuch until Numbers 19.

[17] J. Liver, "The Half-Shekel Offering in Biblical and Post-biblical Literature," *HTR* 56 (1963): 193, writes somewhat strangely, "L. 17 is apparently based on Exodus 32:20; that is to say, here also the subject matter is biblical and relates to cult practices."

[18] The verb עשה, in the context of the making of the calf and with the people as subject, is found in both of the just-cited verses, as well as in Exod 32:8, 35 and Deut 9:12, 16.

(it would have to allude, uncharacteristically for that root, to burning of sacrifices or the like which Moses is also not said to have performed and for which we should have expected the verb הקטיר). Our suggestion therefore remains the most plausible scenario based on the surviving textual material for the location of these last two lines of fragment 1.

With that reconstruction of fragment 1 in mind, if we now examine the distribution in the Pentateuch of the material found in the other fragments of 4Q159, and re-order them so that fragments 2–4 precede fragment 1, a pattern does emerge. We observe that the material deriving from passages in Deuteronomy then appears in the sequence of the biblical book, and, perhaps more significant for fragment 5, it is then followed by text which derives from Exodus 30 (census) and, according to my suggested reconstruction, from Exodus 32 (Moses and burning) as well. My hypothesis thus is that frg. 5 is to follow frg. 1 and that the link between them is their connection with the sequence of events in the narrative of the sin of the golden calf.

This narrowly focused answer to the relationship of fragment 5 with fragment 1 does not contain the answers to some of the larger questions about 4Q159, such as why it seems to move through Deuteronomy as it does, or why it then proceeds to texts from Exodus, or the largest question, what principle governs its overall selection from and readings of biblical law, but that should not vitiate its efficacy in responding to the limited question. Of course the given name of the text, "Ordinances," would then no longer be fully descriptive of the text as a whole, much in the same way as the former designation, "Joseph Apocryphon[a–c]", based only on 4Q372 frg. 1, was deemed inappropriate for the whole of 4Q371–373, now renamed "Narrative and Poetic Composition[a–c]".[19] Once again, a *prima facie* generic identification which appears reasonable for the large part of a Qumran text may be seen to be inappropriate for its entirety.[20]

---

[19] Cf. E. Schuller and M. Bernstein, "4QNarrative and Poetic Composition[a–c]: Introduction," in *Wadi Daliyeh II: The Samaria Papyri from Wadi Daliyeh and Qumran Cave 4.XXVIII: Miscellanea, Part 2* (DJD 28; Oxford: Clarendon, 2001), 151–54.

[20] Baumgarten, 60, writes similarly regarding 4Q159 and 4Q265, "The genre of these miscellaneous legal and narrative texts should now be added to the heterogeneous classifications of Qumran compositions, although their functional purpose has yet to be clarified."

Fragment 5 Reconstructed

We now proceed to our fuller reconstruction of frg. 5, suggesting
that it be read as follows:

בהקציפ[ם א-ל וימותו פשר] הדבר
vacat [בני לו]י·
[במשפט ואשר אמ]ר
[בקחת מושה את] האוהל ויט אותו מחוץ למחנה והיה כול
5 מבקשי יהוה] יצאו שמה פשר הדב]ר
לד]רוש התורה בצוקה ו?[
אש]ר דבר מושה]
[כול]

When] they [angered] God and they died. The *pesher*[of the matter
  ] *Vacat*   Sons of Lev[i
      ]in judgment. And as for that which say[s
    ] When Moses took the [tent and pitched it outside the camp,
     then all who
5 [sought the Lord] would go out thither. The *pesher* of the matte[r
  [to se]ek the Law in distress, *v*[
      whi[ch Moses spoke[
        ]all[

Notes on Reconstruction

L. 1 The assumption of my interpretation is that the passage deals
with the aftermath of the incident of the golden calf, and I have
reconstructed the first line accordingly. The verb הקציף with God as
direct object is employed of this incident in Deut 9:8 ובחרב הקצפתם
את ה'.[21]

Ll. 2–3 If the reconstruction is correct, these lines refer to the actions
of the sons of Levi in punishing the Israelite sinners after Moses'
descent from the mountain (Exod 32:26–28), or perhaps to their
reward for doing so (Exod 32:29).

L. 4 In Exodus 33, Moses, in the aftermath of the golden calf incident, establishes a tent as a "meeting tent" outside the camp where
all who sought the Lord could approach for guidance. There is lit-

---

[21] Alternatively, a form like בהכעיס[ם might be suggested, with similar meaning.
Baumgarten, "4Q265," 59, suggests reading בנגפ[ם אל, "when God plagued them,"
but I believe that my suggestion is more likely, both because of the parallel usage
in Deuteronomy and the fact that the genitive is more likely to be subjective with
אל as object, than objective, with אל as subject.

tle doubt that lines 4–5 reflect that passage and we have restored accordingly.[22]

L. 6 יד[רוש is also possible, "who seeks;" the choice would depend on the syntax of the missing material.

INTERPRETATION AND IMPLICATIONS

In a recent discussion of the role of Moses in the Dead Sea Scrolls, J. M. Bowley notes that "Quantitative evidence from the sectarian scrolls would suggest that the role of Moses merits attention if only because Moses is the biblical figure most often referred to in all of the sectarian texts found at Qumran."[23] His section on "Moses in Sacred History," divided into "Moses and the Past" and "Moses and the Future," seeks to determine which episodes in the life of Moses were prominent in the Qumran literature, and the role that they play therein. He finds that the Moses material is employed to provide historical examples of such significant issues as "the struggle between cosmic forces of life and darkness" in CD 5:17–19, to provide "a historical example with the object of encouragement," and to remember "the intercessory role of Moses" and its meaning for contemporary worship.[24] It is unfortunate that Bowley did not consider this text in his discussion of Moses in the scrolls, because it may present another way in which Moses provided a model for the later sectarians. Furthermore, the fact that the passage appears to be treated in a pesher context may be of special significance for the ideology of the Qumran group. Although based on our understanding of other Qumran texts it is reasonable to assert that pesher on historical narrative material is out of character at Qumran, this text may nonetheless be an exception to that assertion and the "pesher" in it may make perfectly good sense.[25]

---

[22] Baumgarten, *ibid.*, suggests מבקשי אל rather than מבקשי יהוה. In light of the replacement, at times, of the Tetragrammaton by אל at Qumran, this reading should be considered as well. But cf. מבקשי ה' in 4Q521 2–4 ii 3 התאמצו מבקשי אדני.

[23] J. E. Bowley, "Moses in the Dead Sea Scrolls: Living in the Shadow of God's Anointed," in *The Bible at Qumran: Text, Shape and Interpretation* (ed. P. W. Flint; Grand Rapids: Eerdmans, 2001), 159–81 (159).

[24] *Ibid.* 171–172.

[25] This line of reasoning develops a brief suggestion made by Elisha Qimron (personal communication, October, 2001) after I discussed with him my reconstruction and interpretation of fragment 5.

We noted above the oddity that the words before הדבר [פשר] in line 1 do not coincide with any biblical text which we know, so the missing preceding text cannot offer us any aid in reconstructing the main portion of frg. 5. I am inclined, therefore, to focus upon the text which follows and is more easily identifiable as the primary guideline in reconstructing even the opening line of the fragment. Since lines 4–5 clearly derive from Exod 33:7, I believe that the most reasonable reconstruction of the whole passage would place the text being commented upon within the story of the golden calf which the Israelites worshiped after the revelation at Mt. Sinai. References to the Israelites having angered God and then dying, the Levites, and "judgment" all fit plausibly into such a context before the allusion to Exodus 33.

It is those lines whose context seems clear, furthermore, that may give us the greatest insight into the goal of this "pesher." According to a straightforward reading of the narrative in Exodus 33, these biblical verses describe Moses' actions in the wake of the sin with the golden calf and involve his isolating himself from the sinful people and establishing a location outside the Israelite camp where "seekers of the Lord" could achieve their goal. This is an enigmatic passage to the modern scholar, although it may not have seemed so to the ancient reader. What might have made it particularly of interest to the Qumran interpreter is its similarity to his own situation. It is known that the Qumran group saw its habitation in the Judaean desert as analogous to the Israelite camp in the wilderness.[26] VanderKam begins his treatment of "The Judean Desert and the Community of the Dead Sea Scrolls" with the remark, "They opted to construct their communal buildings in the forbidding Judean wilderness at the northwest corner of the Dead Sea. As we might expect for a group so keenly attuned to the details and predictions of the scriptures, they found biblical warrant for their location."[27] We sug-

---

[26] Cf. Shemaryahu Talmon, "The 'Desert Motif' in the Bible and in Qumran Literature," in *Biblical Motifs, Origins and Transformations* (Texts of the Philip L. Lown Institute of Advanced Judaic Studies 3; ed. A. Altmann; Cambridge: Harvard University Press, 1966), 57–63 (31–66), G. J. Brooke, "Isaiah 40:3 and the Wilderness Community," in *New Qumran Texts and Studies: Proceedings of the First Meeting of the International Organization for Qumran Studies, Paris 1992* (ed. G. J. Brooke with F. García Martínez; Leiden: Brill, 1994), 117–32, especially 128–29, and James C. VanderKam's paper referred to in the next note.

[27] James C. VanderKam, "The Judean Desert and the Community of the Dead Sea Scrolls," *Antike Judentum und Frühes Christentum: Festschrift für Hartmut Stegemann zum*

gest that Exodus 33 was understood by 4Q159 fragment 5 in such a fashion so as to give further scriptural support for departure to the wilderness, or at least from Jerusalem to a place like the wilderness.

What might פשר mean in a text such as this one? Talmon writes,

> the *pesher* preponderantly is employed as a means by which to prove that the events which befell the 'last generation'—that is to say, the Sectaries—were actually foreshadowed in Biblical prophetic literature. . . . The *pesher* technique is rarely, if ever, applied to traditions of a definable one-time historical nature.[28]

This text may serve as a very significant exception to Talmon's rule, employing a narrative text in a *pesher* context, and indicating the need to actualize a biblical narrative text by adopting a particular course of behavior. That is to say, the pesher is not the interpretation of a text, but of an historical event, treating the event as prefiguring or typologizing an event in the future.[29] I suggest that the Qumranites (or whatever we are to call the initial group who separated themselves at that site) may have seen in this pentateuchal passage a model or precedent in Moses' separation of himself from the Israelite camp, after the biblical Israelites had sinned with the golden calf, for their own departure to the desert to isolate themselves from the sinful remainder of contemporary Israel.[30]

The biblical "camp," furthermore, in certain Qumran texts is identified with Jerusalem in halakhic contexts; e.g., 4QMMT B59–62

כי ירושלים היאה מחנה הקדש והיא המקום שבחר בו מכל שבטי ישראל כי ירושלים

---

65. *Geburtstag* (ed. B. Kollmann et al.; BZNW 97; Berlin/New York: De Gruyter, 1999), 159 (159–71). Professor VanderKam was kind enough put at my disposal also a longer, as yet unpublished, version of this essay.

[28] Talmon, 59.

[29] Might this explain the absence of a verbatim quotation from the text, since it is the event which is being "peshered" and not the text?

[30] Talmon, 60–61, suggests that initially the desert was for the Qumran group "a place of refuge from persecution," and "the flight into the desert effected their secession from their sinful contemporaries." Even if this was the historical sequence of events, subsequent reflections upon the departure to the desert need not have followed the actual order, and the scriptural "justification" may be a *post hoc* invention. Cf. also D. Schwartz, "Desert and Temple: Religion and State in Judea in the Days of the Second Temple," in *Priesthood and Monarchy: Studies in the Historical Relationships of Religion and State* [Hebrew] (ed. I. Gafni and G. Motzkin; Jerusalem: Zalman Shazar Center for Jewish History, 1987) 61–78. Beginning with Josephus' depiction of a number of Jewish leaders who led their followers to the desert in the turbulent years before the destruction, Schwartz proposes that certain groups felt that the Temple had to be abandoned and that God was to be sought in the desert (68).

היא ראש מחנות ישראל ("for Jerusalem is the holy camp and it is the place which He has chosen from all the tribes of Israel, for Jerusalem is the foremost of the camps of Israel").[31] In our passage, the author of 4Q159 might have seen Moses' pitching his tent "outside the camp" as offering a recommendation for the same type of behavior in analogous circumstances on the part of the Qumran community, signifying that they ought to move their own location to outside the camp (= Jerusalem).

It is possible, furthermore, that the words בני לו[י], if that plausible reconstruction is correct, may then be particularly significant since they would refer to the Levites' having stepped forward to exercise judgment on the sinners (perhaps the allusion in משפט?) and having been selected as a result. The Qumran group, many of whom were apparently of priestly or levitical descent, would be following the model of their ancestors in the tribe of Levi by separating themselves from rest of sinful Israel.

The potential significance of this passage for the ideology of Qumran would be heightened further if the very logical reconstruction of Exod 33:7 is accepted. The presence of the biblical phrase כול מבקש(י) ה (or מבקשי אל), even without its pesher, would point toward a theme which is found often at Qumran, that of seeking after God, at times expressed via the verb בקש and at others via דרש, both of which idioms are fairly common in biblical Hebrew.[32] Significant instances of these terms occur in the openings of both 1QS and CD.[33]

---

[31] Similarly, 4QMMT B29–32. See the discussion in Elisha Qimron and John Strugnell (eds. in consultation with Y. Sussman, with contributions by Y. Sussman and A. Yardeni), *Qumran Cave 4.V: Miqṣat Maʿaśe Ha-Torah* (DJD 10; Oxford: Clarendon, 1994), 143–45 and D. Henshke, "The Sanctity of Jerusalem: Between the Sages and Sectarian Halakhah," *Tarbiz* 67 (1998): 5–28, esp. 22–27.

[32] The Exodus passage contains the only biblical occurrence of מבקש ה; the plural מבקשי ה, which I believe is likely to have appeared in the paraphrase of the biblical text in 4Q159, is found at Isa 51:1; Ps 105:3 (= 1 Chr 16:10); and Prov 28:5.

[33] 1QS 1:1–2 לדרוש אל [בכול לב ובכול נפש]; CD 1:10 דרשוהו כי בלב שלם. Cf. also 1QS 5:10–11 להבדל מכול אנשי העול ההולכים בדרך הרשעה כיא לוא החשבו בבריתו כיא לוא בקשו ולוא דרשהו בחוקידו (modeled on Zeph 1:6 ואשר לא הנסוגים מאחרי ה' בקשו את ה' ולא דרשהו). Note that in the latter passage, "seeking God" is accomplished through his statutes. Most similar to the reconstructed text of 4Q159, however, is 4Q521 2–4 ii 3 התאמצו מבקשי אדני. I am not concerned here specifically with the use of דרש\מדרש as indicating a particular form of scriptural interpretation at Qumran; for that issue, cf. the detailed discussion by S. D. Fraade, "Looking for Legal Midrash at Qumran," in *Biblical Perspectives: Early Use and Interpretation of the Bible in Light of the Dead Sea Scrolls: Proceedings of the First International Symposium of the Orion Center for the Study of the Dead Sea Scrolls and Associated Literature, 12–14 May,*

Even more significant, however, may be the pesher on the reconstructed כול מבקש ה' of the biblical text, an interpretation which identifies "seeking for the Lord" as "seeking after the Torah."[34] It is well-known that the דורש התורה was clearly envisioned as a titled figure in the past and future history of the Qumran sect.[35] But the term דרש בתורה clearly has broader usage as well; e.g., 1QS 6:6 ואל ימש במקום אשר יהיו שם העשרה <u>איש דורש בתורה</u> יומם ולילה תמיד עליפות איש לרעהו, referring to members of the group who would take turns in being דורש the Torah.[36] Thus the pesher's employment of the language לדרוש\ידרוש התורה בצוקה to interpret the biblical מבקש ה' is certainly uniquely appropriate for a group one of whose leaders was called the דורש התורה and which saw לדרוש בתורה as one of the responsibilities of their members at all times.[37] The goal of going away

---

1996 (ed. M. E. Stone and E. G. Chazon; Leiden/Boston/Cologne: Brill, 1998), 59–79, esp. the references in nn. 1, 16, 19, 22, 24, 27, and 29.

[34] Frequently the idioms דרש ה' and בקש ה' are rendered in the Aramaic versions of the Bible as "seeking teaching from before the Lord" (cf. my "Torah and Its Study in the Targum of Psalms" *Hazon Nahum: Studies in Honor of Dr. Norman Lamm on the Occasion of His Seventieth Birthday* [ed. J. Gurock and Y. Elman; Hoboken: Yeshiva University Press, 1997], 64–65 on the employment of this term in the targum of Psalms). This, indeed, is the translation of Targum Onqelos here; מבקש ה' is rendered by דתבע אולפן מן קדם ה', "who sought teaching from before the Lord." The consonance between the Qumran document and the later targumim is striking but should not be considered unusual.

[35] The title דורש התורה, according to M. A. Knibb, "Interpreter of the Law," *Encyclopedia of the Dead Sea Scrolls* (ed. L. H. Schiffman and J. C. VanderKam; Oxford: Oxford University Press, 2000), 1.383, "occurs four times in the Dead Sea Scrolls but it is used in different ways." At times it refers to an individual who is a figure of the past and decider of the Law (CD 6:7), while at others it alludes to an eschatological priestly figure who would accompany the royal messiah (4Q174 [Florilegium] 1–2 i 11). Talmon, 58–9, actually suggests that the "very image of the 'Teacher of Righteousness,' and certainly that of the 'Law Interpreter,' undoubtedly was patterned upon the image of Moses. . . . Moses further had been entrusted with bringing 'the Law' to the Children of Israel in the desert, and again the 'Teacher' follows the same pattern." In this he was following N. Wieder, "The 'Law-Interpreter' of the Sect of the Dead Sea Scrolls: The Second Moses," *JJS* 3 (1952): 158–75.

[36] Accepting the interpretation of עליפות as the equivalent of חליפות, "in turn." Cf. also 1QS 5:9 לבני צדוק הכוהנים שומרי הברית ודורשי רצונו, "the Zadokite priests, keepers of the covenant, and *seekers of his favor.*" The term מדרש התורה also occurs in 1QS 8:15 (and parallels, in a desert context, no less) and CD 20:6.

[37] The equivalent phrase בקש תורה occurs several times at Qumran: 4Q398 11–13 7 (MMT) והם מבקשי תורה referring to the righteous kings of Israel; 4Q216 ii 13 (= *Jub.* 1:12) ובקשו את התורה וא[ת] ו[א]ת מבקשי [ה]תורה ירדופן and 4Q306 2 3 המ[צוה]. The Jubilees passage is particularly interesting as it refers to the future persecution of the "seekers of the Torah," a term and a circumstance which the Qumranites could easily have applied to themselves.

from the camp (= Jerusalem) was to find a proper way of seeking the Lord and studying the Torah away from the sinful remainder of Israel.[38] The use of בצוקה, "in distress," furthermore, may indicate a perception of a specific historical time of crisis when the act of "seeking the Torah" was being, or had been, performed.[39] But further hypothesizing regarding a possible context for these comments would be too fanciful.

We have admitted *ab initio* that this final suggestion is quite speculative, and its possible attractiveness should not allow us to forget that very important fact. The restoration of fragment 5 itself, I believe, is fairly close to certain, as far as we have attempted it. The challenge to our interpretation has to do with its relationship to the other fragments of 4Q159. If fragment 5 indeed belongs to 4Q159, and if we arrange the fragments in the order 2–4, 1, and then 5, and if we accept the restoration at fragment 1, lines 16–17, then our reading of the texts together is more than defensible, despite the problems which it might then raise regarding the mixed genre of 4Q159 as a whole. That issue must be left to a subsequent discussion.

---

[38] We might even see in 1QS 8:12–16, which, as VanderKam (168–169) notes, explains "the purpose and location of the separated group," and which contains references to separating "from the habitation of men of iniquity to go to the desert" (based on a reading of Isa 40:3) and to the "midrash of the Torah [which] he commanded through the hand of Moses," something which looks like the result of a pesher on the text in Exodus. On the Isaiah passage in 1QS, see Brooke, "Isaiah 40:3," 117–28. Our reading would also serve as a counter to the claim of N. Golb, *Who Wrote the Dead Sea Scrolls?* (New York: Scribner, 1995), 75, that nowhere "in the Qumran texts is it proposed that sectarians literally leave their habitations in order to go to the desert, either to study or for any other purpose."

[39] Could the use of צוקה be predicated on Prov 1:27 ... אשחק באידכם אני גם בבא אליכם צוקה או יקראני אז אענה ולא ישחרני ולא ימצאנני, understood as a reference to seeking God?

DEUTERONOMY 5–6 IN THE PHYLACTERIES FROM QUMRAN CAVE 4

GEORGE J. BROOKE

I. INTRODUCTION

Emanuel Tov has divided the phylacteries found in Cave 4 at Qumran into two groups according to their scribal practices.[1] He has concluded that the largest group were written according to what he has designated "the Qumran practice."[2] According to Tov there is sound evidence that the Qumran practice exists with regard to 4QPhyl A, B, G–I, J–K, L–N, O, P, and Q.[3] The second group consists of 4QPhyl C, D, E, F, H, R, and S which do not exhibit the same elements of scribal practice.[4]

---

[1] It is a pleasure to offer this short study to honour Emanuel Tov for his many contributions towards the better understanding of the transmission of the texts of Scripture in the late Second Temple period, especially as those have been influenced by his study of the so-called biblical manuscripts among the Dead Sea Scrolls.

[2] E. Tov, *Textual Criticism of the Hebrew Bible* (2nd ed.; Assen: Royal Van Gorcum; Minneapolis: Fortress, 2001), 108–10. The appearance of Qumran scribal practice does not necessarily imply that the manuscript was penned at Qumran, though such remains a strong possibility, since the majority of the clearly sectarian compositions are written according to this scribal practice; one might suppose at least that manuscripts written in this practice and showing affinities to the Qumran sectarian compositions were penned in communities affiliated with that resident at Qumran.

[3] E. Tov, *Textual Criticism of the Hebrew Bible*, 109. In an earlier study Tov laid out the evidence for the scribal practice of these phylacteries; at that time he considered that there was positive but insufficient evidence for the inclusion of 4QPhyl G–I under the umbrella of the Qumran practice: E. Tov, "The Orthography and Language of the Hebrew Scrolls Found at Qumran and the Origin of These Scrolls," *Text* 13 (1986): 54–55.

[4] For the phylacteries see: J. T. Milik, "Tefillin, Mezuzot et Targums (4Q128–157)," *Qumrân Grotte 4.II* (*DJD* 6; Oxford: Clarendon, 1977), 33–91. All references to Milik in this study are to this principal edition, ad loc. One fragment of Phyl A (Deut 11:10–17) was published in a preliminary edition by K. G. Kuhn, *Phylakterien aus Höhle 4 von Qumran* (Abhandlungen der Heidelberger Akademie der Wissenschaften Philosophisch-Historische Klasse 1957, Abh. 1; Heidelberg: Carl Winter, 1957), 15–16, as 4QPhyl[c]; Kuhn published Phyl B as 4QPhyl[b] (*Phylakterien aus Höhle 4*, 11–15), Phyl H as 4QPhyl[d] (*Phylakterien aus Höhle 4*, 16–20) and Phyl J as 4QPhyl[a] (*Phylakterien aus Höhle 4*, 5–11); Phyl I was partially published by Milik in "Fragment

It is not possible in a short paper like this to consider all the variants in all the phylacteries, so examples will be restricted to the use
of Deuteronomy 5–6 in these phylacteries from Qumran's Cave 4.[5]
The variants will be categorised and analysed to see whether there
is anything which might support the association of those phylacteries written in the Qumran scribal practice with the views presented
in the so-called sectarian compositions from Qumran, the vast majority of which are also written in the Qumran practice.

There is some ambiguity concerning the status of the texts of scripture represented in the phylacteries: should they be considered as
scripture in a narrow sense, or should they fall into some other category? If they are deemed to be scripture, then because it seems
clear that there are no sectarian manuscript copies of scriptural
books,[6] it would be straightforward to conclude that the textual variants in the phylacteries could not be closely associated with any
particular sectarian point of view. However, since phylacteries are
essentially excerpted texts, it may be more appropriate to consider
them as one of the many rewritten or reworked forms of scripture
present in the Qumran library. Since several of such rewritten scriptural compositions have clear exegetical tendencies of a particular-
ist, even sectarian kind, then it might be that the texts in the
phylacteries, especially those written in the Qumran practice, might
show signs of affinity with the explicitly sectarian compositions in
the Qumran library.

For the purposes of this paper the phylacteries are being grouped
with the rewritten Bible compositions. This can be justified not only
because they are clearly not straightforward copies of scriptural books,
being excerpted texts, but also because they have a particular function. Their function may be broadly described as liturgical. Their
use probably falls within the realm of private prayer,[7] since it is indi-

---

d'une source du Psautier (4QPs89) et fragments des Jubilés, du Document de Damas,
d'un Phylactère dans la grotte 4 de Qumran," *RB* 73 (1966): 105–106 (Pl. IIb).
    [5] Also there is not space to consider all the manuscripts of Deuteronomy itself
which have been found at Qumran.
    [6] See, e.g., G. J. Brooke, "E pluribus unum: Textual Variety and Definitive
Interpretation in the Qumran Scrolls," *The Dead Sea Scrolls in their Historical Context*
(ed. T. H. Lim with L. W. Hurtado, A. G. Auld and A. Jack; Edinburgh: T & T
Clark, 2000), 107–19.
    [7] As described, e.g., by L. H. Schiffman, "The Dead Sea Scrolls and the Early
History of Jewish Liturgy," *The Synagogue in Late Antiquity* (ed. L. I. Levine; Philadelphia:
American Schools of Oriental Research, 1987), 33–48.

viduals who wear them. Some scholars have also considered that within the context of private prayer the use of phylacteries is apo-tropaic.[8]

II. The Variants

1. *Scribal Lapses*

It needs to be said at the outset that not all scribal variants are conscious and deliberate. There are plentiful instances of scribal lapses. For example, in Phyl B 11–12 there is a clear instance of dittography with the repetition of a large section of Deut 5:23 and the first word of Deut 5:24. Not surprisingly, scribal lapses are not restricted to manuscripts written in the Qumran practice, such as B, but can also be found in the others. For example in Phyl H 7 for Deut 5:30 there are two corrections: לשוב is corrected to שובו and לאהלים is corrected to לאהליכם.[9] In terms of scribal lapses there seems to be nothing which distinguishes phylacteries written in the Qumran scribal practice from those which are not.

2. *Harmonisations*

Several variants within the phylacteries can be classed as harmonisations.[10] It is often difficult to know whether these harmonisations are deliberate and conscious, making the point that the scribe considered there to be a need to make texts consistent with one another, or whether the scribe was so well versed in scriptural materials that one text unconsciously influenced him as he wrote out another; this may have been especially the case if he was working from memory.[11]

---

[8] E.g., I. Fröhlich, "Demons, Scribes, and Exorcists in Qumran," in *Essays In Honour of Alexander Fodor On His Sixtieth Birthday* (ed. K. Dévényi and T. Iványi; Budapest Studies in Arabic 23; Budapest: Csoma de Kőrös Society, 2001), 74–75.

[9] This is wrongly presented as לאהליהם at the foot of p. 60 in *DJD* 6.

[10] On this see E. Tov, "The Nature and Background of Harmonizations in Biblical Manuscripts," JSOT 31 (1985): 3–29. Note his intriguing comment on p. 18: "The juxtaposition of these (phylactery) passages in its turn may have influenced biblical MSS, especially because of the great importance of the phylacteries in daily life."

[11] Tov (*Textual Criticism of the Hebrew Bible*, 119) comments: "The biblical texts reflected in these *tefillin* and *mezuzot* often differ from M, possibly because they were written from memory, as stated by *b. Meg.* 18b: תפלין ומזוזות נכתבות שלא מן הכתב, '*Tefillin* and *mezuzot* may be written out without a written source <that is, from memory>'."

(a) Harmonisations with Exodus.[12] For Deut 5:6–21 Phyl G, written
    in the Qumran scribal practice, represents the most consistent
    presentation of a text that seemingly harmonises the decalogues
    of Exodus and Deuteronomy. In Phyl G 13 we read וכול תמונה
    as in Phyl J 15, XQPhyl 3:15, the Samaritan Pentateuch and
    the LXX, but also in agreement with Exod 20:4. Phyl G 18 pre-
    sents nothing after לקדשו for Deut 5:12; this omission of כאשר
    צוך יהוה אלהיך effectively brings the text of Deuteronomy 5 closer
    to that of Exod 20:8. Unfortunately not enough survives of Phyl
    G to see whether the sabbath commandment opened with זכור
    (Exod 20:8) or שמור (Deut 5:12). Most significantly, like 4QDeut^n,
    Phyl G 12–13 uses the justification for the sabbath concerning
    the creation (Exod 20:11) rather than the justification from the
    servitude in Egypt (Deut 5:14b–15). In the commandment con-
    cerning the honouring of father and mother Phyl G 23–25 has
    a strange mixture of Exodus and Deuteronomy. It is important
    to note that in all these harmonisations the text of Exodus is
    being fitted into that of Deuteronomy. The decalogue of Deuteron-
    omy is the base and controlling text which is being standardised,
    to which other texts are being attached and fitted.
       An interesting variant occurs in 4QPhyl O 21. The text of
    Deut 6:8 is represented with ידיכה in the plural as it is in Exod
    13:9 and 16 in the form of the Exodus texts in Phyl B, C, E,
    H, I, M, R, and the Samaritan Pentateuch. For Deut 6:8 both
    the MT and the LXX give the word in the singular. Though
    the plural can be understood to refer to the sum of each indi-
    vidual Israelite's hand, perhaps the singular form was introduced
    into or preserved in the MT tradition to prevent a misunder-
    standing that might lead to the wearing of phylacteries on both
    forearms not just one! Whatever the case, this example shows
    that the process of harmonisation is present in both phylacteries
    written in the Qumran scribal practice and those which are not.
(b) Harmonisations within Deuteronomy. The opening of Deut 5:1
    in Phyl B appears to be different since there is probably insufficient
    space for the whole of the verse. Both Kuhn and Milik have ob-
    served that there was apparently some kind of sublinear correction
    akin to the slightly later sublinear insertion of דובר באוזניכמה היום הזה.

---

[12] There is not space to present all the harmonisations in the Cave 4 phylacteries, but key samples are noted.

This addition in Phyl B for Deut 5:1 corresponds with a similar phenomenon in Phyl G which Milik aptly compares with Deut 6:6. This harmonisation of the two parts of Deuteronomy heightens the consistency between the Decalogue and the Shema, possibly implying that both texts together form a single unit within the phylactery.

In 4QPhyl G 6–7 there is a long addition which Milik justifiably considers to make little sense. Some similar phrases occur elsewhere in Deuteronomy. To begin with Milik draws attention to Deut 4:12:

Deut 4:12a   וידבר יהוה אליכם מתוך האש קול דברים אתם שמעים

Phyl G 6   כי אל יהוה אלהים שמעים אתם מתוך האש

After a phrase that contains a repetition of מתוך האש, line 7 seems to allude to Deut 4:13:

Deut 4:13   *ויגד לכם את בריתו אשר צוה אתכם לעשות עשרת הדברים*

Phyl G 7   ואנכי אגיד דברי בריתי היום הזה

However one tries to make sense of this addition, it is clear that there is reference to the corresponding narrative of Deut 4:12–13, so that overall the addition may be considered as a harmonisation for literary consistency within Deuteronomy, even though the earlier text is not of course represented in the phylactery itself.

The same section of narrative in Deuteronomy 4 is involved in 4QPhyl B 10 where the natural phenomena accompanying the divine audition recounted in Deut 5:22 are probably three in number: וענן וערפל חושך. Though these terms are variously associated with theophanies in other biblical passages, they occur together as a threesome only in Deut 4:11 in Moses' narrative description of what happened: "And you came near and stood at the foot of the mountain, while the mountain burned with fire to the heart of heaven, wrapped in darkness, cloud, and gloom (חושך וענן וערפל); then the Lord spoke to you ... and he declared to you his covenant, which he commanded you to perform, that is the ten words" (Deut 4:11–13). Significantly this harmonisation within the text of Deuteronomy is not only also present in Phyl J 25, the Samaritan Pentateuch and the LXX, but also there is a further harmonisation involving these verses in some LXX manuscripts in which φωνη μεγαλη is present in Deut 4:11, reflecting the same phrase that occurs in Deut 5:22. This reflects how scribal traditors attempted to create narrative consistency, a well-known feature especially of the Samaritan Pentateuch. It should also be noted, however, that Phyl L 12 seems to preserve a text like that of the MT הר מתוך האש ה]. The *he* would suggest הענן like the MT over against חשך of Phyl B 10, J 25 and Deut 4:11. There is thus no overall consistency with regard to harmonisation within the phylactery texts that belong to the Qumran scribal practice.

Alongside these various examples from the phylacteries written in the Qumran practice can be set an example from Phyl H which is not. In the description of the overpowering experience of the audition of the divine voice in Phyl H 4, instead of the MT's עוד as the penultimate word of Deut 5:25, we read מדבר מתוך האש. This is an anticipation of the very same phrase in Deut 5:26 which Phyl H preserves in its entirety. Even if this variant is regarded as a scribal slip based in the scribe's eye jumping ahead in his exemplar, it is intriguing that it nevertheless provides a text which can make good sense.

A further example shows that similar harmonisations can be found in various scribal practices. In Phyl J 37 the phraseology of Deut 5:27a (כול אשר יומר יהוה אלהינו) is followed by the preposition with suffix (אליכה), a reading the phylactery shares with the versions and Phyl H 5. The reading may well be original, but in any case it is another small case of internal consistency, for with this one word the phrasing of Deut 5:27b is neatly anticipated.

A final example in this category shows how copies from two scribal practices illuminate one another. In Phyl B (Qumran practice) the phrase of Deut 5:31 (המצוה החוקים והמשפטים) is written with only one conjunction whereas in MT there is a conjunction before החוקים as well. The text of Phyl B 17 corresponds directly with the opening phrase of Deut 6:1, providing another small instance of internal narrative consistency. In part this may have been done deliberately to facilitate the exclusion of the redundant material in Deut 5:31–33 between these two phrases. A further variant is attested in 8Q3 which, in agreement with the LXX, does not have ומשפטים in Deut 6:1. A very different kind of harmonisation has happened for the same reason, internal narrative consistency, in Phyl H 8 (non-Qumran practice). There in Deut 5:31 there is a long anticipatory addition of the

similar subject in matter of Deut 6:1–2. Phyl H 9 very probably shows further harmonisation with other parts of Deuteronomy.
There after תסרו of Deut 5:32 there is an illegible addition. Milik
proposes that some wording from Deut 17:11 or 28:14 would be
suitable to fill the lacuna.

Overall instances of harmonisation can be found both in phylacteries belonging to the group assigned to Qumran practice and also in
those which are not.

3. *Abbreviation*

Abbreviation is a phenomenon well known in excerpted and rewritten texts. As with scribal lapses and harmonisations, examples can
be found in phylacteries of both groups. For example, in relation to
the group written in Qumran practice, after the expansion of Deut
5:1 with allusions to Deut 4:12–13 and 11:19, Phyl G presents a
much abbreviated form of Deut 5:2, just the two words עמנו בחורב.
Naturally it is not necessary to envisage versification as in modern
versions, so it is notable that the abbreviation produces a compre-
hensible text without any repetition of Deut 5:2–3. In addition because
of the expansion of Deut 5:1 in Phyl G 6–7 the corresponding phraseology of Deut 5:5 is omitted from line 11.

The end of line 23 in Phyl J (Qumran practice) is fragmentary,
but it seems as if there is not enough room for the whole of Deut
5:6. It appears that the final phrase of the verse is missing. This
could have been omitted through homoioteleuton. However it could
be that this phrase was omitted deliberately so that the commandment in Deut 5:16 matched the text given later, from which Deut
5:32–6:1, which also mentions the gift of the land, has effectively
been removed. If that were the case, then it might be that the similar endings were not the cause of a scribal slip, but the means
whereby a deliberate omission was made.[13]

In Phyl G 26 the prohibition against covetousness is reduced by
one phrase. It is clear from the versions and from the text of the

---

[13] On the possibility of homoioteleuton becoming the means whereby phrases
could be deliberately excluded see G. J. Brooke, *Exegesis at Qumran: 4QFlorilegium in
its Jewish Context* (JSOTSup 29; Sheffield: JSOT, 1985), 11–12. On these verses as
a whole see also the study by A. Rofé, "Deuteronomy 5:28–6:1. Composition and
Text in the Light of Deuteronomic Style and Three Tefillin from Qumran," *Henoch*
7 (1985): 3–14.

parallel version in Exod 20:17 that this is not simply a case of abbreviation, but rather that there is a history of discussion concerning whether the neighbour's wife should be included in this prohibition, and, if so, where in the order of coveted items she should be. Part of this problem may be present in Phyl J 24 where it seems that the verb חמד was used twice, thus equating all the kinds of desire that are prohibited.[14]

Phyl H provides possible examples of abbreviation in a manuscript not written according to Qumran practice. In Phyl H 2, after the strange misspelling of הקול as הקומל, the brief phrase מתוך החשך is omitted from Deut 5:23. It is impossible to determine whether or not this omission was made deliberately. Later in Phyl H 6 after הזה the rest of Deut 5:28 is not present. This may have been a deliberate omission; perhaps in some tradition a scribe disagreed with this divine approval of a people which was about to betray its commitment.

There seem to be examples of abbreviation in both types of phylactery in relation to the text of Deut 5:32–33 which is largely repeated in Deut 6:1–2. Phyl A (Qumran practice) contains a text which seems to omit much of this repetition. The text is very fragmentary at the point of the omission, though A 18 can be justifiably restored with the text of Deut 6:2. The preference for the phrasing of Deut 6:1–2 may lie in its specificity: it is not simply that one should walk in the way of all that God has commanded, but that there are particular "commandments, statutes and ordinances" which must be put into practice. These are terms common in the sectarian scrolls for rules that are deemed to be suitable interpretations and extensions of matters in the Mosaic law.[15] However, these technical legal terms were probably not used in this extended fashion solely by members of the Qumran community. This redundancy is also visible in Phyl B (Qumran practice) which, in providing a more complete text, allows us to see how the link was made between Deut 5:31 and 6:1.

Phyl J (Qumran practice) represents an omission which is also reflected in Mezuza C. Phyl J goes with Deut 5:32 until half way

---

[14] For a detailed discussion of the problems associated with this prohibition see B. S. Childs, *The Book of Exodus: A Critical, Theological Commentary* (Philadelphia: Westminster Press, 1974), 425–28.

[15] As pointed out convincingly by L. H. Schiffman, *The Halakhah at Qumran* (SJLA 16; Leiden: Brill, 1975), 42–49.

through the verse and then seems to follow with a short phrase beginning with *lamed* for which Milik plausibly proposes לשמ]ר מצאותו. Phyl J 59 then begins with a phrase from Deut 6:2. It should be noted, however, that Phyl M 20–24 preserves Deut 5:23–6:1, though with some minor variants from the MT involving orthography, the presence or absence of the conjunction, and the adjustment of the *qal* (תירשון) to the *hipʿil* (תורישון).

Phyl H 11 (not Qumran practice) omits a phrase from Deut 6:2, perhaps acidentally. Since Phyl H keeps Deut 5:32–33, which contains some similiar phraseology, it could be that whereas Phyl A and B shorten the material by effectively omitting several phrases from Deut 5:32–33, Phyl H slightly reduces the amount of repetition in these verses by omitting a phrase from Deut 6:2. 8Q3 has a similar short text.

In matters of abbreviation there seems little to choose between the phylacteries written in the Qumran practice and those which are not.

4. *Vocabulary Differences*

In matters involving particular items of vocabulary choice, some slight difference begins to emerge between those phylacteries written in the Qumran practice and those which are not.

(a) In Phyl B 18 and M 24 the end of Deut 6:1 reads: בארץ אשר אתמה באים שמה לרשתה. 8Q3 12 6 also contains באים for Deut 6:1. The use of באים apparently agrees with the *Vorlage* of the LXX (εἰσπορεύεσθε). MT reads בארץ אשר אתמה עברים שמה לרשתה. How might the difference be explained? It could be that there is the straightforward substitution of a synonym in one text or the other. Certainly both terms are common in Deuteronomy. The whole semantic range of עבר is present in the scrolls and the synonymity of עבר and בוא is demonstrated neatly from 1QS II,11–12 which reads לעבור הבא בברית. However, it is remarkable that in 1QS I–II the term עבר is used six times consistently of entering the covenant (עבר בברית).[16] In light of this one may wonder whether בוא was used in Phyl B and M and the *Vorlage* of the LXX because it was considered more appropriate for entering the

---

16 1QS I,16, 18, 20, 24; II,10, 11.

land, given that the terms of the covenant had just been stated. The difference is not necessarily narrowly sectarian, but the variant fits with what a scribe writing within the sectarian tradition of Qumran might have preferred.

(b) Another matter of vocabulary difference concerns the divine name. For Deut 5:5 Phyl G 10 reads אלהים for יהוה. Since elsewhere in Phyl G both terms are used, there may be no significance in this variation. In Phyl H 3 and Phyl J 28 אלהים of MT Deut 5:24 is represented as יהוה. Phyl H 4 reads קול יהוה אלהים over against קול אלהים חיים of the MT Deut 5:26. The scribe of Phyl H may be assimilating his text to the similar phrase in Deut 5:25 or even thinking of Gen 3:8 as he wrote. In all these variants it may be significant that only in one of the phylacteries written in the Qumran scribal practice is there a change in representing the Tetragrammaton by writing אלהים. The avoidance of the Tetragrammaton is a well-known feature of all the sectarian compositions from the Qumran library.

5. *Matters of Content*

As with the previous two items of vocabulary in the previous category, so three matters of content may illuminate something of the character of the phylacteries written in the Qumran scribal practice.

(a) Deuteronomic emphases. In his introductory remarks Milik notes that in the phylacteries the sections of Exodus usually follow those from Deuteronomy. Deuteronomy takes precedence as it does in many sectarian and other compositions found in the caves.[17] In Phyl A 2 the word order of Deut 5:3 is the same as that of Phyl J 9–10 and similar to that in Phyl G, all three being written in the Qumran scribal practice: אלה פוא כולנו חיים היום. This reflects the natural stress in the summons of Moses. It is not so much that the summons goes out to all who are alive; rather, in contrast with Israel's fathers the covenant is made with the people today, now. The present immediacy of the covenant making is stressed: it is reality here and now.

---

[17] See, e.g., G. J. Brooke, "The Deuteronomic Character of 4Q252," in *Pursuing the Text: Studies in Honor of Ben Zion Wacholder on the Occasion of His Seventieth Birthday* (ed. J. Kampen and J. C. Reeves; JSOTSup 184; Sheffield: JSOT, 1994), 121–35.

Another aspect of this Deuteronomic stress can be observed in the addition of the demonstrative adjective זה in Phyl G 5. The phylactery reads באוזניכם היום הזה; Deut 5:1 in the MT has solely באוזניכם היום. That this is not a stress restricted solely to the version written according to the Qumran scribal practice is made plain by the LXX where the demonstrative adjective is also represented. This demonstrative is also present in the sublinear correction in Phyl B 1 and in Phyl J 6. All three, B, G and J belong to the group of phylacteries penned according to the Qumran scribal practice.[18] In addition Phyl J 59 and M 26, together with 8Q3 15 4, some MT manuscripts, the Samaritan Pentateuch and the LXX, read the opening of Deut 6:2 as אשר אנוכי מצוכה היום. The phylacteries written in the Qumran scribal practice seem to have a preference for the Deuteronomic phrasing and stress on "today."

(b) The Sabbath Commandment. In Phyl B 6, Deut 5:14 opens with וביום over against the MT's ויום. In this reading Phyl B agrees with Phyl G 19, with Phyl J 20, with XPhyl 3:21, with 4QDeutⁿ III,11, as well as with both LXX Deut 5:14 and LXX Exod 20:10. 1Q13 10 has כי ביום. The significance of all this may only be syntactical in that without the preposition there is an independent free-standing statement at the start of the verse. However, it may be significant to recall that it is the form of the text with the preposition which seems to be reflected in the use of the Sabbath commandment in CD X,13b.[19] In particular, after the form of the opening of the commandment from Deut 5:12, שמור את יום השבת לקדשו, CD X,15 continues with וביום השבת. Something akin to this phrasing is also present in the elaborate development of the Sabbath commandment in the *Book of Jubilees* (50:8–13) which has several parallels with the Sabbath material in CD.

In Phyl J 20 Deut 5:14 contains a further explicatory בוא so as to read: לוא תעשה בוה כול מלאכה. This explication is present also in the Samaritan Pentateuch and the LXX and other versions. There is nothing sectarian about this reading, but it is reflected also in 11QTᵃ XXVII,6, legislation for the Day of

---

[18] Perhaps this point should not be overemphasised since a similar stress can be read in Phyl H 3 where in Deut 5:24 the phylactery has ביום הזה where the MT and Sam. have היום הזה, though in that instance there is really no difference in meaning.

[19] Cf. CD X,17, 22; XI,2, 13.

Atonement couched in the phraseology of Sabbath rest. Phyl J
20 may also show a form of an element of the sabbath commandment that is reflected in Exod 20:10. The two texts share
the reading of עבדכה without the conjunction; this also occurs in
some manuscripts of the MT, in the Samaritan Pentateuch and
in the LXX. In this way those whose rest is guaranteed by the
commandment are linked in pairs. Phyl G 20 also shares this
reading.

At the end of Deut 5:15 Phyl B reads לקדשו as does Phyl O
9–10, 4QDeut^n, and the *Vorlage* of the LXX. This may represent some kind of attempt to bring the text of Deuteronomy
closer to that of Exod 20:11 at this point, possibly even an attempt
to improve the literary construction of the commandment.

Like 4QDeut^n, Phyl G 21–23 uses the justification for the sabbath concerning the creation (Exod 20:11) rather than the justification from the servitude in Egypt (Deut 5:14b–15). Thereby,
not only is the scribal interest in harmonisation demonstrated,
but also incorporated within the text of Deuteronomy is the justification for the keeping of the Sabbath that reflects an interest
in the order of creation.

All these adjustments to the Sabbath commandment are observable in the phylacteries written according to the Qumran scribal
practice. There is nothing overtly sectarian in these readings, but
they all fit with the kind of stress on the observance of the Sabbath
which is found in the explicitly sectarian compositions.

(c) The Teaching Role. In Phyl G lines 6 and 7 (Qumran practice)
there is a complicated and lengthy addition whose purpose is to
enhance the consistency of the presentation of the Decalogue
with the narrative from which it has been extracted. As this
process is taking place, in Phyl G there appears to be a deliberate displacement of the phrase ולמדתם אותם from the start of
Deut 5:1b. In Phyl G 7–8 we read ולמדתם אותם את בניכם/[לעשו]תם<>.
As Milik has noted, this is probably a reference to Deut 11:19
(ולמדתם אותם את בניכם), the very words of instruction concerning
the commandments as phylacteries. Although this might be construed as just another example of how the text in some of these
phylacteries is being presented with attention to the internal consistency of Deuteronomy, the adjustment in this case leads to a
stress on the teaching role and the very purpose of phylacteries
themselves. Again, there is nothing exclusively sectarian in this,

but the perspective of the addition fits both with the presence of considerable numbers of phylacteries at Qumran and the emphasis in the sectarian compositions on teaching and study.

III. Conclusion

Apart from the existence of a few slips, much of the scribal activity in the phylacteries found at Qumran is the result of a desire for tidiness. The tendency in all the scribal traditions represented in the Cave 4 phylacteries was not towards preserving differences but towards enhancing consistency. Tidying up the text involved harmonisation and abbreviation as well as some stylistic improvements. These same non-sectarian scribal tendencies are evident in compositions which are deliberately organised as systematisations of the Torah, such as the Temple Scroll and so help justify the classification of the phylacteries as a kind of reworked or rewritten Bible.

Beyond this, however, there are a few features of the presentation of Deuteronomy 5 and 6 in the phylacteries found at Qumran which are exclusive to those written in the Qumran scribal practice; these features seem to reflect the ethos of a particular school of thought. Not necessarily peculiar to this school, but nevertheless characteristic of it, seems to be the priority that is given to the text of Deuteronomy itself, as indeed it is in the so-called Priestly editing of the Torah. This priority is reflected not only in the way in which it is Deuteronomy 5 and 6 that form the base texts in the phylacteries (that would be expected from Deut 6:8), but also in the way that the Deuteronomic Decalogue is variously made consistent with the narrative of the giving of the law in Deuteronomy and in the way some items of Deuteronomic vocabulary, such as "this day" or "today", recur in prominent positions in the phrasing of the text. Giving priority to Deuteronomy and its vocabulary is evident in the so-called sectarian compositions found at Qumran.

In addition there are some features which when taken together with the characteristics already mentioned, may serve as a more precise identification tag. Chief amongst these features is the particular concern with the presentation of the Sabbath commandment. Elsewhere in the compositions preserved at Qumran this concern is evident in those works which are the self-expression of those who consider themselves to be the heirs of the Holiness Code and its festal priority for the Sabbath (Lev 23:3); those works are chiefly the *Book of Jubilees*, and the *Damascus Document*.

Together with this concern for the Sabbath goes an interest in the teaching of the Law. Though common enough in biblical texts, especially Psalm 119, it is intriguing to note that in 2 Chr 17:7–9 this is predominantly the role of the Levites and according to 1Q22 1 3–4 it is the Levites who are given special charge of the Law and, more importantly, its correct interpretation (cf. CD III,21; XIII,3–4). In light of this it need be no surprise that in at least one place the phylacteries may reflect the vocabulary of 1QS I–II, a section which expounds the place of the Levite in the community. In these respects the phylacteries written in the Qumran scribal practice hint that a particular group has the right to transmit and interpret the Law.

Overall, because many of the variants in the phylacteries are held in common with other texts and versions, the phylacteries are an important group of witnesses to the transmission of the scriptural texts in the second temple period. As rewritten Bible all the phylacteries from Qumran attest to scribal activity in harmonisation, abbreviation, and other stylistic improvements to the text. In addition, however, several minor features of vocabulary choice and other matters in the rewritten aspects of the phylacteries which are penned in the Qumran scribal practice seem to witness to a group whose interests are found amongst the Qumran community, but probably cannot be restricted to it. The scribes who followed the Qumran practice seem to identify themselves from time to time as those who would indeed have been at home in the Qumran community.

THE *TEMPLE SCROLL*[a] [11Q19, 11QT[a]], COLUMNS 16 AND 17: MORE CONSONANTS REVEALED[1]

James H. Charlesworth

Introduction

The purpose of this publication is to announce the discovery of new readings—indeed more than 35 Hebrew letters—in columns 16 and 17 in the *Temple Scroll* (11Q19 or 11QT[a]), to discern their original setting, restore them to the critical text, and to perceive them in their original context.[2] These new readings are possible due to the codicological nature of 11QT[a] and to computer-enhanced digital imaging technologies.[3]

The leather of 11QT is exceedingly refined. In contrast to some leather Qumran Scrolls that are coarse or thick, 11QT[a] is thin and in places translucent.[4] The attempt to prepare a work of art in

---

[1] It is "good" to honor Professor Emanuel Tov. He has proved to be a distinguished specialist not only of the Septuagint but also of Qumranology, a remarkable editor, and a cherished friend.

[2] The spirit of the original team of editors of the Qumran Scrolls was (and continues) to encourage subsequent scholars and editors to "improve on" an *editio princeps*. See, e.g., J. Strugnell, "we editors" encouraged "other scholars . . . to improve on" our own creative work as editors. Strugnell in *On Scrolls, Artefacts and Intellectual Property* (ed. T. H. Lim, et al.; JSPS 38; Sheffield: Sheffield Academic Press, 2001), 184. What must be stressed over and over again is that although we, in lectures, refer to piecing the Qumran Scrolls together like a jigsaw puzzle, the analogy is a very poor one. We almost never have matching borders and the links are conceivable only because of a mastery of codicology, Semitic philology, orthography, and morphology. And then much more is required: the knowledge of Biblical Hebrew syntax and Qumran Hebrew syntax. To make connections among fragments and to discern consonants in ancient hand writing is nothing less than "creative work." Interpretation does not begin with the addition of vowels; it begins with perceiving consonants and meaningful forms.

[3] See K. T. Knox, R. L. Easton, and R. H. Johnston, "Digital Miracles: Revealing Invisible Scripts," in *The Hebrew Bible and Qumran* (ed. J. H. Charlesworth; The Bible and the Dead Sea Scrolls 1; N. Richland Hills, Texas: BIBAL, 2000), 43–61. For a discussion of the technical aspects of these new images, see Knox, Johnston, and Easton, "Imaging the Dead Sea Scrolls," *Optics & Photonics News* 8 (1997): 30–34.

[4] I am grateful to the Israel Antiquities Authority for permission to examine closely, over four decades, the Qumran Scrolls in the Rockefeller Museum and in the Shrine of the Book's strong room.

scraping and rubbing the animal skin, cutting the leather for horizontal and vertical lines,[5] and introducing the black ink—produced
a relatively fragile, and almost transparent, leather scroll.[6]

There is also more to observe. While Qumran Scrolls are composed of bovine, gazelle, ibex, or something else, this scroll, 11QT[a],
is the only Qumran Scroll that showed an identical DNA sequence
to goat skin (*capra hircus*) among those tested by Professor Scott R.
Woodward.[7] In contrast to domestic sheep and bovine skins, goat
skin provides the finest leather. Thus, the nineteen separate sheets
of leather that constitute 11QT[a] are exceptional in quality and refine-
ment.[8] While Y. Yadin, E. Qimron, and I had observed writings
transferred from the front of one column to the back of another,
none of us thought that Hebrew consonants could be "pulled, by
computer," through the leather. The translucent nature of 11QT[a]
reveals that this procedure is possible—as I shall now demonstrate.

The upper portions of 11QT[a]—especially in columns 16 and 17—
are now deteriorated. Often many lines of text are now missing, and
the lines with which a column begins, in editions, denotes not the
original first line of text but the extant first line of text. Since more
lines are lost in some columns than in others, this imprecise count-

---

[5] To see the clear traces of vertical and horizontal lines, see the photograph of
col. 24 in Y. Yadin, *The Temple Scroll* (Jerusalem: The Israel Exploration Society,
The Institute of Archaeology of the Hebrew University of Jerusalem, and the Shrine
of the Book, 1977), vol. 3, Plate 39.

[6] I am grateful to the Israel Antiquities Authorities, the Shrine of the Book, and
Magen Broshi for permission to examine closely 11QT[a] and to direct the re-pho-
tographing of it by B. and K. Zuckerman. I am also grateful to the Zuckerman
brothers for the work we did together in the Shrine of the Book and the photographs taken of 11QT[a].

[7] I am grateful to Professor Woodward for numerous lengthy conversations on
DNA testing of the Qumran Scrolls. See esp. S. R. Woodward, G. Kahila, P. Smith,
C. Greenblatt, J. Zias, and M. Broshi, "Analysis of Parchment Fragments from the
Judean Desert Using DNA Techniques," in *Current Research and Technological Developments
on the Dead Sea Scrolls* (ed. D. W. Parry and S. D. Ricks; STDJ 20; Leiden, New
York: Brill, 1996), 215–38, esp. Figure 2 on p. 230.

[8] See Woodward, et al., in *Current Research & Technological Developments on the Dead
Sea Scrolls*, 224. Note esp. p. 228: "We have also examined six fragments from five
different sheets of the *Temple Scroll*. These have all been shown to be derived from
goat (see fig. 2)." Woodward and I presently speculate that the goats' hides may
have been split into two portions, by pulling the leather down the middle; thus,
the result is virtually vellum. Obviously, numerous goat skins would have been
required to assemble this long scroll. Most likely the hides were taken from young
goats when the leather would be relatively soft.

ing of lines, based only on what is extant, confuses the relationship between the lines of one column and the lines of another. That is to report, although XVI,7 now appears parallel to XVII,7, it was originally parallel to XVII,5.

The *Temple Scroll*, Col. 17, first 7 lines, before digital and computer enhancement, line 5 vacat (no consonants visible).

Published by permission of Xerox Corporation, the Rochester Institute of Technology, and Princeton Theological Seminary, and thanks to Drs. Keith Knox, Robert Johnston, and Roger Easton, Jr.

Column 16: Readings in Qimron's Critical Edition

E. Qimron in his magisterial *The Temple Scroll: A Critical Edition with Extensive Reconstructions*[9] presents the following text of the *Temple Scroll*, col. 16, lines 3–7 (letters within parentheses are restored from readings in manuscripts of 11QT other than 11QT[a]):[10]

3   [תנוך האוזן] הימנית ויון] מן הדם ו(מן השמן) על בנדיו
4   [קדוש יהיה] ליהוה כול ימיו
5   לוא [י]טמא כי קדו]ש הוא vacat?
6   ויקרב על המזן]בח והקטיר א]ת חלב הפר הראישון את
7   כור ה]חלב אשר על הקרב וא]ת יותרת הכבד ואת שתי

It is clear that significant portions of these lines have been restored. Line three is restored on the basis of Exod 29:20–21. Now, thanks to digital analysis and computer enhancement of column 17, we are able to improve the text of column 16. How does column 17 help in improving column 16? It shall become obvious that Qimron surmised the key when he opined that some readings of column 16 can be seen on the back of column 17.[11]

Column 17: Clarifying Background Readings

Studying the photographs the Zuckermans and I took of column 17 eventually convinced me that some formerly unseen consonants might be seen, in light gray, behind the opaque black letters on column 17. I flew to Rochester, New York, to work on the images of 11QT[a] with some scientists, namely Dr. Keith T. Knox of Xerox Corporation, and with Dr. Robert H. Johnston and Dr. Roger L. Easton, Jr., both of the Rochester Institute of Technology. Computer enhanced photography proved that numerous consonants were clearly visible on column 17 of 11QT[a]. I soon became convinced that these consonants were not original with this column for two main reasons. They were a light gray in contrast to the dark black of letters on

---

[9] Jerusalem: Israel Exploration Society/Beer Sheva: Ben-Gurion University of the Negev Press, 1996.

[10] Since it is not possible to reproduce Qimron's use of hollow letters to denote the restored text, I shall use square brackets, as in most publications.

[11] Qimron reported that his reading of ליהוה, against Yadin's היה[י] is possible because the "*yod* and the flag of a *lamed* are extant on the back of column xvii." Qimron, *The Temple Scroll*, p. [26] note to 4a.

The *Temple Scroll*, Col. 17, first 7 lines, after digital and computer enhancement, many consonants appear for the first time.
   Published by permission of Xerox Corporation, the Rochester Institute of Technology, and Princeton Theological Seminary, and thanks to Drs. Keith Knox, Robert Johnston, and Roger Easton, Jr.

column 17. They are also on a parallel that slants downward and are below the darker consonants that hang from the visible horizontal lines.

   The consonants are also not a mirrored image; they clearly are readable as if a scribe had inscribed them on the leather of column 17. The consonants had not been put on column 17 and then washed off by water or something else that might have entered through the slit that slices upward from line six almost to line four of column 17. The consonants also were not transferred from a facing column, since if that were the explanation, they would appear in mirror image.

What then was the original source of these consonants? Several attempts to locate the original setting proved fruitless. Then I observed the periodization of the worn away margins and upper portions of columns in 11QT^a. What was the relationship between lines in columns 17 and 16? I had assumed that XVI,5 parallels XVII,5. I eventually observed that this assumption was invalid. Columns 16 and 17 are on the same continuous piece of leather, the last line of each is preserved with the lower margin, and 16.18 coincides [is roughly parallel to] XVII,16. Hence, XVI,7 was originally parallel to XVII,5.

The fact that the consonants transferred from column 16 to 17 are slightly below those on column 17 means that the transfer of consonants occurred when the scroll was rolled up in an uneven manner. I do not see now how we can discern if this transfer of consonants occurred in antiquity or during the centuries when the 11Q19 was lying in a Qumran Cave [although I would imagine the latter possibility is more likely, since the scroll was in Cave XI (if the Bedouin found it in that cave) for 19 centuries, was rolled up unevenly, and humidity was a factor since the scroll shows water damage in this section].

There should be no doubt that the faint consonants now revealed on column 17 once belonged on column 16. They had been transferred to the back of column 17 from column 16.

Column 16: The New Readings and the Restored Text
[All Alignments are as Accurate as the Computer can Supply]

There are no clear overlaps between 11QT^a and other copies or ancient versions of the Temple Scroll, specifically 11QT^b (11Q20), 11QT^c (11Q21), 4QT (4Q521), and perhaps 4QT? (4Q365a).[12]

---

[12] Of all the copies of the *Temple Scroll*, the closest overlap is between 11QT^a and 11QT^b which in Col. 2 (frags. 3 and 4) is parallel to 11QT^a XVI,1–3, 8–11 but no consonants are shared between 11QT^a and 11QT^b. See esp. S. White Crawford, *The Temple Scroll and Related Texts* (Companion to the Qumran Scrolls 2; Sheffield: Sheffield Academic Press, 2000), 12–16. Also see F. García Martínez, E. J. C. Tigchelaar, and A. S. Van der Woude, eds., *Qumran Cave 11: II 11Q2–18, 11Q20–31* (*DJD* 23; Oxford: Clarendon, 1998), 370 and Frg. 4 in Plate 42 [PAM 43.976].

Column 16, according to the text of 11QT[a] and normal photographs contains the following in lines 3 to 7:

[הימנית ויזו] 3
[הוה כול ימיו 4
[°טמא כי קדו° 5
[בֿח והקטיר א] 6
[שׁר על הקרב וא] 7

The previously unseen consonants from column 16 now discernible on column 17 provide the following transcription:[13]

[תנ[ו]ך האוזן] 3
[הוא קדוש לי] 4
[°°°כי אם י 5
[...]ה על המן] 6
[את החלב אש] 7

These readings provide the right hand portions of lines 3–7 of column 16. Lines 9 and following on column 16 disclose the right hand margin; thus, the letters preserved on column 17 actually provide the beginnings of XVI,3–7.

Here are the new readings and their original settings in column 16 (numbers for footnotes disturb the alignment):

[תנ[ו]ך[14] האוזן הימנית ויזו] 3
הוא קדוש ליהוה[15] כול ימיו 4
°°°כי[16] אם יטמא כי קדו[ש 5
]...[ה על המ[ז]בח והקטיר א] 6
את החלב אשר על הקרב וא]ת 7

In my judgment, there should be no doubt about the *waw* in 11QT[b] [that is, in my judgment it should not receive a dot above it]. I am grateful to García Martínez for suggesting improvements to an earlier draft of this publication.

[13] Professor H. Rietz worked with me in the RIT laboratory. I appreciate his skills and insights.

[14] This reading is possible only when one studies the infra red and ultraviolet computer enhanced images.

[15] With digital photography, one can see on the front of col. 17 traces of ל, ש, and ה.

[16] The כ is clear; it is not the digraph כיא that appears also in 11QT[a]; cf. esp. 45.11 and 66.6. I know of no instance of the digraph with אם; that is אם כיא does not seem to appear in the Qumran Scrolls; see Charlesworth, et al., eds., *The Graphic Concordance to the Dead Sea Scrolls*, 313–15. Of course, כי אם appears frequently in the Qumran Scrolls; see esp. 1QH; IV,31, XIV,20; 1QS V,14; CD IV,II, V,15 [*bis*]; 4QpIs[c] 6+2,13; and 11QT[a] III,6, XLVIII,12, LVII,16.

Qimron's restoration of line three ([תנוך האוזן]) is confirmed by the
enhanced photographs. His restoration of line four ([קדוש יהיה]) is
improbable; the *lamed* follows the *shin* and there is no room for יהיה
between them. The reading הוא קדוש seems likely, although not certain. Qimron's restoration at the beginning of line five ([לוא]), while
grammatically and syntactically correct, can now be improved, due
to the appearance of consonants seen on column 17, line 3.

Of all the lines, the one that is most difficult to discern is XVI,5.
Yadin had speculated the following:

[לאביו ולאמו לוא]יטמא כי קדו[ש הוא ליהוה אלוהיו [

[nor] defile himself, [even for his father or for his mother;]
for [he is] hol[y to the Lord his God].[17]

Yadin's extensive restorations are based on Leviticus 21, especially
the Septuagint reading of Lev 21:7.[18] Qimron had not only restored
the beginning of line five with [לוא] but also left the impression that
there was room for eight more consonants before it on the leather.
We can improve the reading of XVI,5 because כי אם—that was originally on it—can now be seen behind the consonants on XVII,3 (and
recall that XVI,5 = XVII,3). Using the ultraviolet photographs,[19]
altering saturation levels, and adding yellow back lighting and then
blue back lighting with the computer, it is possible to see traces of
three consonants before כי אם.[20] Thus it is possible to read ◦◦◦ כי אם.
This reading brings to mind 11QT[a] III,6: ולוא תטמאנו כי אם: "and
you shall not pollute it; No!"

The shifting and re-placing of these letters from column 17 to column 16 is aided by the observation that part of the ש of אשר is visible in XVI,7 and another part in XVII,5. That link provides the
key for aligning all the consonants as they were originally. This alignment confirms the calculation that there are approximately three
consonants or spaces to fill before כי אם in XVI,5.

While קדו[ש יטמא כי אם כי ◦◦◦ seems certain, the exact meaning of
XVI,5 is not easy to discern since the context is lost. The restrictive adverb כי אם, seems more restrictive than לוא; it indicates a pro-

---

[17] Yadin, *The Temple Scroll* (1983), 2.69.
[18] Yadin, *The Temple Scroll* (1983), 2.69.
[19] This image can be downloaded at www.ijco.org.
[20] Richard Craig Miller helped me work on the computer with images of 11QT[a].

hibition, represented by "rather" in Deut 17:3, 5 and 1 Sam 8:19. Perhaps the passage meant "he must not defile himself, because (he is) hol[y. . . ."[21] The second כי means "because," not "on the contrary" (one would expect to obtain that meaning for it to follow a negative clause).[22]

The author of the Temple Scroll seems to be reacting to or correcting a practice of the reigning High Priest. Only to a certain extent is it necessary to modify Yadin's comment about 11QT[a] columns 15 to 17: "Commands pertaining to the ordination ceremony of the High Priest start in line 15 and continue in Col. XVI and the beginning of Col. XVII."[23] Probably, the author of this section of the *Temple Scroll* was thinking about other concerns besides the High Priest's ordination ceremony.

What is the meaning of 17.5? Is the author of this section of the *Temple Scroll* warning the priests that the High Priest must not do something that defiles him? If so, what was the act or habit that gave rise to this warning or prohibition? Does the legal ruling of the author of the *Temple Scroll* differ from those of the priests in charge of sacrifices in the Jerusalem Temple? Is the author warning his readers that the High Priest must change his actions, otherwise, he would defile himself? In what ways are these thoughts of the *Temple Scroll* reminiscent of the strict interpretations of Torah found in 4QMMT?[24]

Qimron's restoration of line six (וֹיקרב על המז[בח]) also seems unlikely. There is no room for five consonants and a space before the preposition על. His restoration of the next noun however is confirmed by the appearance of the first two consonants: על המ[ז]בח.

Qimron's reading of line seven, [כול ה]חלב אשר על הקרב וא[ת], can be improved by the consonants now visible on column 17, line 5:

---

[21] For other instances where the Impf. represents the English subjunctive, see the meaning of the modal or conditional Impf. in Gesenius-Kautzsch-Cowley, §107 m-u (pp. 316–19); Waltke-O'Connor, *Biblical Hebrew Syntax*, pp. 506–09 [31.4]; Joüon-Muraoka (Subsidia biblica 14/II) §113 m-n (p. 371–72).

[22] See, e.g., Koehler-Baumgartner, 2.470.

[23] Yadin, *The Temple Scroll*, 2.61.

[24] J. Milgrom rightly points to the technique of homogenization/*binyan 'āb* in the *Temple Scroll*, and wisely claims that for "Qumran, divergent opinions are intolerable; for the rabbis, they can be declared 'the words of the living God' (*b. 'Erub.* 13b)." See Milgrom's contribution in *Temple Scroll Studies* (ed. G. J. Brooke; JSPS 7; Sheffield: JSOT Press, 1989), 178.

את החלב אשר על הקרב וא]ת[. The minor restoration of a *waw* at the beginning of line seven is conceivable, if it is influenced by the formula that appears in the next line (xvi,8):]ואת החלב אשר עליה.

Column 17: Readings in Qimron's Critical Edition

Some of Qimron's readings or restorations in column 17 are confirmed by the computer enhancement of this column. The first ה of his הכֹּוהנים[ה] in XVII.1 can now be seen; read הכֹוהנים. The first three consonants in the first visible word in XVII,2 are more certain; read וٞיٞשֹמחו not וٞיٞשٌמחו. In XVII,3 Qimron read וה]יה היום הזה להמה; now read as follows: ו]היה היום הזה להמה. Finally, בכול as the first visible letters of XVII,4 are somewhat more certain; read בֹכٞוٞל in place of בٞכٞוٞל.

Improved Translation of Column 16

The translation of 11QT^a according to the improved text is as follows:

3   the l[o]be of the right ear, and they shall sprinkle[25] [. . .]
4   He (is to be) holy to YHWH all his days [. . .]
5   . . . he must not[26] defile himself,[27] because (he is) hol[y]
6   . . . *h* upon the al[t]ar and he will cause to smoke[28] *a*[. . .]
7   the fat that (is) upon the entrails and t[he. . .]

I have first presented the text and translation without the readings found in 11QT^b (11Q20) and restorations based on Exod 29:20–21. The latter text is fundamentally important for restoring the probable text of 11QT^a, hence it is presented below:

---

[25] As Yadin suggested, "they" refer to the elders among the priests. Yadin, *The Temple Scroll*, 2.69.

[26] The restrictive adverb כי אם in this line emphasizes the prerequisite that the High Priest must be holy and ritually pure to perform sacrifices. See the discussion of restrictive adverbs in Waltke and O'Connor, *Biblical Hebrew Syntax*, 670–71.

[27] This form can be a Qal Impf. ("he shall become unclean), a Pi. Imp. ("he shall defile"), or a Niph. Impf. ("he shall defile himself"). I take this form to be a Niph. Impf. The author seems to be referring to anything that the High Priest might do or be exposed to that would defile him. The High Priest seems to be the object of these rules. Cf. Lev 21:10–15.

[28] The Hiph. Pf. literally means "make sacrificial smoke" or "make incense smoke."

ושחטת את־האיל ולקחת מדמו
ונתתה על־תנוך אזן אהרן ועל־תנוך
אזן בניו הימנית ועל־בהן ידם הימנית
ועל־בהן רגלם הימנית וזרקת את־הדם
על־המזבח סביב ולקחת מן־הדם אשר
על־המזבח ומשמן המשחה והזית על־אהרן
ועל־בגדיו ועל־בניו ועל־בגדי בניו אתו
וקדש הוא ובגדיו ובניו ובגדי בניו אתו

And slaughter the ram, and take some of its blood and place it upon the lobe of Aaron's (right) ear, and on the lobe(s) of his sons' right ear(s), and upon the thumb(s) of their right hand(s) and upon the big toe(s) of their right feet. And dash the (rest of) the blood round the altar. And take some of the blood that is upon the altar and some of the anointing oil and sprinkle (it) upon Aaron and upon his garments and upon his sons and upon his sons' garments. Thus shall he and his garments be holy, and (also) his sons and his sons' garments.

With the readings from 11QT[b] and obvious restorations we obtain the following:

תנ[ו]ך האוזן הימנית ויזו[מן הדם ו]מן השמן[29]   3
הוא קדוש[30] ליהוה כול ימיו   4
°°°כי אם יטמא כי קדו[ש   5
[..]ה על המ[ז]בח והקטיר א[6
את החלב אשר על הקרב וא]ת   7

3   the l[o]be of the right ear, and they shall sprinkle [some blood and] some oil [
4   He (is to be) holy to YHWH all his days [. . .]
5   . . . he must not defile himself, because (he is) hol[y]
6   . . . *h* upon the al[t]ar and he will cause to smoke *a*[. . .]
7   the fat that (is) upon the entrails and t[he . . .]

This translation may be compared with the rendering found in the "Study Edition" by F. García Martínez and E. J. C. Tigchelaar,[31] who follow Qimron closely:[32]

3   [. . .] right, and they shall sprinkle [some blood and some oil upon it and upon their garments.]
4   [Holy shall be] for YHWH all his days [. . .][33]

---

[29] מן השמן [ו]מ[ן] is clear in 11Q20 [see *DJD* 23].
[30] This reading is confirmed by Exod 29:21, וקדש הוא.
[31] *The Dead Sea Scrolls: Study Edition* (Leiden, Boston: Brill/Grand Rapids, Michigan: Eerdmans, 1998), 1237.
[32] The only difference from Qimron's text is their reading [והקרי־ב] for Qimron's [ויקרב]. The improved photographs disclose that neither restoration is valid.
[33] These words do not constitute an English sentence.

5 [. . .] He shall [not] defile himself, for [he is] hol[y for YHWH his
   God . . .]
6 [And he will bring upon the al]tar and he will burn the [fat of
   the first bullock,]
7 [all the fat whi]ch there is upon the entrails and th[e lobe of the
   liver and the two]

The new translation reveals the idiomatic and free translation offered
by G. Vermes in *The Complete Dead Sea Scrolls in English* (lines were
not provided [quoted without deletions]):

> [on his right ear lobe and on the thumb of his right hand and the
> big toe of his] right [foot. They shall sprinkle on him and his vest-
> ments some of the blood which was on the altar] . . . [he] shall be
> [holy] all his days. [He shall not go near any dead body]. He shall
> [not] render himself unclean [even for his father or mother,] for [he
> is] hol[y to YHWH, his God] . . . [He shall offer on the al]tar and
> burn [the fat of the first bull] . . . [all] the fat on the entrails and [the
> appendage of the liver and the two kidne]ys . . .[34]

The new readings contrast markedly with J. Maier's rendering:

3 . . . the right and . . .
4 . . . [s]hall he be all his days . . .
5 . . . he [shall not] make himself impure for ho[ly is he] . . .
6 . . . [on the alt]ar and offer up in fire t[he] . . .
7 [the fat wh]ich is on the entrails and . . .[35]

CONCLUSION

By enlisting scientists to assist in Qumranology and using digital
analysis and computer enhancement, we can now see on column 16
alone 35 Hebrew letters not obvious or visible for millennia. To be
able to read the new consonants from 11QT[a] is tantamount to discovering a once lost fragment of 11QT[a]. Qimron's unusual abilities
are confirmed in many instances; a comparison between his work
and the *editio princeps* of the text and translation reveals not only his
industriousness but also his skill.[36] In the future more consonants

---

[34] G. Vermes, *The Complete Dead Sea Scrolls in English* (New York: Penguin Press,
1997) 194.
[35] J. Maier, *The Temple Scroll: An Introduction, Translation & Commentary* (transl.
R. T. White; JSOTS 34; Sheffield: JSOT Press, 1985), 124.
[36] Contrast Qimron's text with Yadin's earlier attempt in *The Temple Scroll*, 2.69.

may be found on the front or back of 11QT^a, the longest of all the Qumran Scrolls,[37] when Knox, Johnston, and Easton travel to Jerusalem to help me re-photograph for the Israel Museum and the PTSDSS Project all of 11QT^a, front and back.

The origin of the *Temple Scroll* has been the center of much discussion and even controversy, as all Qumranologists know. The present work should help contribute to that discussion by providing a better text of columns 16 and 17. I am not claiming to have uncovered the composition written by the author of the *Temple Scroll*, or positing a better glimpse into an oral stage, if one ever existed. As Emanuel Tov states, I am only trying to clarify "that stage (those stages) of the composition(s) which is (are) attested in the textual evidence."[38] In the present context, that means a better text of the final state of composition as represented by 11QT^a.

---

[37] It is 8.148 meters long. See White Crawford, *The Temple Scroll*, 12.

[38] E. Tov, *Textual Criticism of the Hebrew* Bible (2nd rev. ed., Minneapolis: Fortress and Assen: Royal Van Gorcum, 2001), 288.

THE USE OF THE BIBLE AS A KEY TO MEANING IN PSALMS FROM QUMRAN[1]

Esther G. Chazon

In recent years we have seen an increasing sophistication in discussions of the use of the Bible in the psalms and prayers discovered at Qumran, which now number more than 200 previously unknown texts.[2] We have advanced from early characterizations of the anthological, mosaic style,[3] to systematic studies beginning in the 1980's that distinguish between and define different types of biblical use.[4] Two forthcoming articles, one by myself and the other by Adele Berlin,[5] focus on the compositional techniques used to mold the biblical text into new poetical works, and illustrate how these techniques convey the new compositions' meaning and purpose.

---

[1] I am honored to dedicate this article to my teacher, colleague and Scrolls Editor-in-Chief, Prof. Emanuel Tov, and to wish him many more fruitful years in good health, "120 עד." This article is based on the paper I delivered at the fourth meeting of the International Organization for Qumran Studies, August 2001, at which Prof. Tov participated. I thank Adele Berlin and Adele Reinhartz for their insightful comments on this paper.

[2] A catalogue of the texts appears in Esther G. Chazon, "Hymns and Prayers in the Dead Sea Scrolls," in *The Dead Sea Scrolls after Fifty Years: A Comprehensive Assessment* (eds. Peter W. Flint and James C. Vanderkam; Leiden: Brill, 1998), 244–270.

[3] For a succinct history of the early research see Eileen M. Schuller, *Non-Canonical Psalms from Qumran: A Pseudepigraphic Collection* (HSS 28; Atlanta: Scholars Press, 1986), 10–11 and the literature cited there, especially Svend Holm-Nielsen, *Hodayot: Psalms from Qumran* (ATDan 2; Aarhus, Universitatsforlaget, 1960).

[4] Bonnie Kittel, *The Hymns of Qumran: Translation and Commentary* (SBLDS 50; Chico, CA: Scholars Press, 1981), 48–55; Schuller, *Non-Canonical Psalms*, 32–38; Michael Fishbane, "Use, Authority and Interpretation of Mikra at Qumran," in *Mikra: Text, Translation, Reading and Interpretation of the Hebrew Bible in Ancient Judaism and Early Christianity* (CRINT 2,1; ed. Martin Jan Mulder; Assen/Maastricht: Van Gorcum, Philadelphia: Fortress, 1988), 339–77; Devorah Dimant, "Use and Interpretation of Mikra in the Apocrypha and Pseudepigrapha," Ibid., 379–419; Judith H. Newman, *Praying by the Book: The Scripturalization of Prayer in Second Temple Judaism* (SBLEJL 14; Atlanta: Scholars Press, 1999).

[5] Adele Berlin, "Qumran Laments and the Study of Lament Literature," in *Liturgical Perspectives: Prayer and Poetry in Light of the Dead Sea Scrolls, Proceedings of the Fifth International Symposium of the Orion Center, 19–23 January 2000* (ed. Esther G. Chazon with Ruth Clements and Avital Pinnick; STDJ series; Leiden: Brill, forthcoming). Esther G. Chazon, "Scripture and Prayer in 'The Words of the Luminaries,'" *Scripture and Prayer* (ed. James Kugel; Cambridge: Harvard Univ. Press, forthcoming).

The present study is offered as a further contribution to the theoretical and empirical treatment of this topic. The theoretical question that I wish to pursue emerges from Berlin's aforementioned article. Berlin advocates an interpretive strategy that takes seriously the biblical contexts of the allusions. She grounds this approach in her observation that, "In poetry, as in Midrash, allusive words do not lose their contexts or their connotations . . . These allusions act somewhat like a vehicle and a tenor . . . pulling meaning from one context and inserting it into another."[6] I adopt a similar interpretive strategy in this study while aiming to further assess the transference of biblical context by allusion. I will pose the specific question: How much of the biblical context does a biblical allusion pull into the new work and under what conditions? This question is crucial for evaluating the use of the Bible in the creation of new compositions, and it will be a focal point of my case studies. I will examine the use of the Bible as a key to the meaning and purpose of two psalms, and then explore what light the results shed on the nature of the two collections in which they are found. The two examples are the *Tehillah of the Man of God* in Non-Canonical Psalms B (4Q381) and the *Hymn to the Creator* in the large Psalms Scroll from Cave 11 (11QPs*ᵃ*).

Our first example is the psalm entitled *Tehillah of the Man of God* (4Q381 24 4–12). In this example, we shall see how paying close attention to the psalm's use of the Bible, and in particular to its transference of biblical context, provides valuable clues for resolving outstanding interpretive issues. I provide here the transcription and translation prepared by Eileen Schuller for *Discoveries in the Judaean Desert* XI; however, as Schuller acknowledges, the tenses of the verbs are open to interpretation:[7]

	תהלה לאיש הֹאל[הי]ֹם יהוה אלהיֹם]	4
	נאל ליהודה מכל צר ומאפרים].	5
]אֹ[	דור ויהללהו בחניו ויאמרו קום א[לוהי	6
[בֹיום א]ֹדי	שמך ישעי סלעי ומצודתי ומפלטֹ]י	7
[שנאי ויאמר]	אקרא ליהוה ויענני אלהי עזרתי]	8
שועתי ל[פֹני באזניו תבוא	כי] [הצ . . .] [לעם ואני שֹ]	9

⁶ Berlin, "Laments."

⁷ Eileen Schuller, "381. 4QNon-Canonical Psalms B," in *Qumran Cave 4.VI: Poetical and Liturgical Texts, Part 1* (*DJD* XI; ed. Esther Eshel et al.; Oxford: Clarendon, 1998), 109–12. The term "non-canonical" is used here merely as a convention for indicating that these psalms are not included in the Masoretic or Greek psalters.

‏.ת בי חרה לו עלה[וקו[ן]לי מהיכלו ישמע ות[רעש ה]ארץ [ותגעש 10
‏[ם השכיל ושכל   ] כל ...[.].[[באף]ו עשן 11
‏VACAT [12

4. A Tehillah of the Man of G[o]d. YHWH God[

5. He redeemed Judah from all distress, and from Ephraim .[

6. generation. And his tested ones praise him and say, 'Rise up [my] G[od

7. your name (is) my salvation. My rock, my fortress, and [my] deliverer [   ] On the day of [my] dis[tress]

8. I call to YHWH, and my God answers me. My help[   ]those who hate me. And he will say [

9. that[   ]ḥṣ.[   ]l'm. And I [my cry be]fore him comes to his ears.

10. And [my] voi[ce from his temple he will hear. And] the earth reeled [and rocked   ].t for he was angry. There went up

11. in [his] nostrils [smoke   ]. [ ] ... kl [   ]m he taught and instruction

12. [   ] vacat

Three of the many issues addressed by Schuller are critical for understanding the complete psalm and its pseudepigraphic attribution. Schuller asks: 1) Who is the Man of God referred to in the title, and what does his identity tell us about the nature of this collection? 2) Is the first verb we encounter in this psalm (line 5) the imperative "Redeem," or a perfect form meaning "He redeemed," or a participle perhaps referring to the "Redeemer"? 3) What are the tenses of the subsequent verbs, particularly the imperfect forms with *waw* in line 6, and do these describe future or past actions? The last two questions impact directly upon the issue of genre. I will deal with them first, before treating the separate matter of the pseudepigraphic heading.

I begin with Schuller's observation that the Tehillah of the Man of God "draws extensively upon a single biblical psalm" namely, Psalm 18 = 2 Samuel 22.[8] The extensive and apparently exclusive quotation from Psalm 18 makes the biblical reference point easily recognizable to the informed audience, ancient as well as modern. It also suggests that the later author is pulling the original biblical context into his own composition.

---

[8] Schuller, *Non-Canonical Psalms*, 121–2; a chart of the parallels is given on page 35. All references below to Psalm 18 apply equally to 2 Samuel 22.

A look at the way our new psalm appropriates Psalm 18 will reveal what biblical information it accesses and for what purpose while, at the same time, help us answer the two grammatical questions that bear on the issue of genre. Schuller already observed that lines 7–11 of the new psalm contain a sustained quotation of Ps 18:3, 7–9 and an allusion to Ps 18:19 in the reconstructed phrase, "On the day of [my] dis[tress], [ביום א]יד[י" (line 7). In addition, the new psalm's reference to "those who hate me" (שנאי in l. 8) might correspond to the biblical psalmist's enemies (אויבי) perhaps alluding to Ps 18:4 or better yet to Ps 18:18, where אויבי and שנאי occur in synonymous parallelism. What is the author's strategy here? By assimilating similar phrases in verses 3–19 and by working allusions to verses 18–19 into the citation of verses 7–9, the new psalm effectively telescopes the entire first section of Psalm 18 and sharpens the focus on the biblical psalmist's cry for deliverance and God's positive response. This message is reinforced by the freely composed lines added in between the biblical quotations, "and my God answers me, . . . And he will say [" (line 8).[9]

In a similar but more dramatic shift, the author places the extensive revised quotation of Psalm 18 into the framework of a petition opening with the imperative, "Rise up" (קום). He thereby turns the biblical royal psalm of thanksgiving into a prayer that now shares affinities with the genre of laments of the individual. Tellingly, the royal aspects of the biblical psalm are not alluded to. The new petition, which incorporates the reworked biblical psalm, is put into the mouths of the tested ones as depicted in line 6, "ויהללהו בחיניו ויאמרו, And his tested ones praise him and say."

We may draw several pertinent conclusions from this reworking of Psalm 18 into a petition to God to rise up and deliver, and as the reported speech of the tested ones, who are probably to be identified with Judah mentioned in the previous line.[10] First, the petitionary discourse opening with the imperative "Rise up" in line 6

---

[9] My working assumption is that the third person singular subject of both verbs in line 8 is the same, namely, God (ויענני אלוהי עזרתי . . . ויאמר]).

[10] On the relationship between Judah and Ephraim in line 5 see Schuller, *Non-Canonical Psalms*, 117 and "4QNon-Canonical" (*DJD* XI), 112. As Schuller notes, the *lacuna* precludes determining if Judah and Ephraim stand in synonymous parallelism or if they are contrasted and, therefore, convey either the idea that, unlike Judah, Ephraim is not to be redeemed or the idea that Judah is to be redeemed from Ephraim as from "כל צר."

strongly suggests that the verb in line 5 is also an imperative, "Redeem, גאל." The similarity, indeed continuity, in the redemption theme between the two parts of the psalm, the introduction in lines 4–6 and the reported speech in lines 6–11, is consistent with this first conclusion. Second, the entire composition may now be understood as a communal lament, which petitions for Judah's deliverance from all trouble and commits God's tested ones to recite—evidently in the future—a prayer that is a reworked version of Psalm 18.[11] Appealing to the biblical psalmist's experience of and thanksgiving for God's answer to his cry in distress thus not only lends authority and depth to the new psalm but also serves to motivate the petition for national redemption carefully crafted by the later psalmist.

This brings us to the question of the title's attribution of the new psalm to the Man of God. Whoever attached the title, whether the psalmist himself or the editor of the collection, evidently recognized the references to Psalm 18 = 2 Samuel 22, knew of that biblical psalm's ascription to David on the occasion of his deliverance from all his enemies, and exploited these connections to attribute the new psalm to the Davidic Man of God (cf. Neh 12:24, 2 Chr 8:14). The choice of this epithet highlights David's role as an inspired poet of prophetic stature, whose work is quoted in and serves as a model for the new psalm. If the Man of God in this title indeed refers to David, then, as Schuller has pointed out, the entire collection of pseudepigraphic psalms in 4Q381, which also features psalms of other kings, might be a royal collection.[12]

---

[11] Based on this understanding, I take the imperfect forms of the verb with *waw* in line 6 to be unconverted forms referring to the tested ones' liturgical recitation in the, perhaps immediate, future. The use of the root *hallel*, 'praise,' both in line 6 and in the psalm's title to designate a petition for deliverance is in character with the word's broad application as a general term for prayer during the Second Temple period. In this period *tehillah* is virtually interchangeable with *tefillah*, a term regularly associated with laments. The juxtaposition of lament elements in the thanksgiving song of Psalm 18 might have influenced the choice of *hallel*/*Tehillah* in our new psalm. See Schuller, *Non-Canonical Psalms*, 26–27 and Eileen M. Schuller, "The Use of Biblical Terms as Designations for Non-Biblical Hymnic and Prayer Compositions," *Biblical Perspectives: Early Use and Interpretation of the Bible in Light of the Dead Sea Scrolls: Proceedings of the First International Symposium of the Orion Center for the Study of the Dead Sea Scrolls and Associated Literature, 12–14 May 1996* (STDJ 28; eds. Michael E. Stone and Esther G. Chazon; Leiden: Brill, 1998), 207–22.

[12] The pseudepigraphic attributions of at least two other psalms survive: a psalm of a King of Judah, whose personal name was not preserved (4Q381 31 4) and

Our second example is the *Hymn to the Creator* (11QPs[a] XXVI, 9–15). In this case, scholarly debate has focused not on the Hymn's meaning but rather on the issue of its liturgical function and the implications for the function of the whole scroll, on the one hand, and for the history of Jewish liturgy, on the other. Specifically, Moshe Weinfeld has made a famous claim that the Hymn alludes to Isaiah's threefold proclamation of divine holiness (Isa 6:3) and also reflects an ancient form of the *Qedushah* liturgy, the centerpiece of which is that Isaianic verse.[13] I will return to this issue at the end of the discussion, and consider first the Hymn's single, sustained biblical quotation taken from the poem found in Jer 10:12–13 (51:15–16). The Hymn's adaptation of these biblical verses serves as a valuable indicator of the work's message and function. The transcription and versified translation provided below are from the *DJD* edition by James Sanders:[14]

$$ 9 \quad \text{נדול וקדוש יהוה קדוש קדושים לדור ודור }^{2}\text{לפניו הדר} $$
$$ 10 \quad \text{ילך ואחריו המון מים רבים }^{3}\text{הסד ואמת סביב פניו אמת} $$
$$ 11 \quad \text{ומשפט וצדק מכון כסאו }^{4}\text{מבדיל אור מאפלה שחר הכין בדעת} $$
$$ 12 \quad \text{לבו }^{5}\text{אזראו כול מלאכיו וירננו כי הראם את אשר לוא ידעו} $$
$$ 13 \quad ^{6}\text{מעטר הרים תנובות} \qquad \text{אוכל טוב לכול חי }^{7}\text{ברוך עושה} $$
$$ 14 \quad \text{ארץ בכוחו מכן תבל בחוכמתו }^{8}\text{בתבונתו נטה שמים ויוצא} $$
$$ 15 \quad \text{[רוח] מאו[צרותיו }^{9}\text{ברקים למט[ר עשה ויעל נשיא[ים מ]קצה} $$
$$ 16 \quad \text{[ארץ]} $$

1.   [9] Great and holy is the Lord,
       the holiest unto every generation.
2.   [9–10] Majesty precedes him,
       and following him is the rush of many waters.
3.   [10–11] Grace and truth surround his presence;
       truth and justice and righteousness are
       the foundation of his throne.

the Prayer (*Tefillah*) of Manasseh, King of Judah (4Q381 33a,b+35 8). For alternative identifications of the Man of God in our psalm (e.g., with Moses or another prophetic figure such as Elijah) see Schuller, *Non-Canonical Psalms*, 27–32.

[13] Moshe Weinfeld, "Traces of *Kedushat Yozer* and *Pesukey De-Zimra* in the Qumran Literature and in Ben-Sira," *Tarbiz* 45 (1975–1976), 15–26 (Hebrew); "The Angelic Song Over the Luminaries in the Qumran Texts," *Time to Prepare the Way in the Wilderness: Papers on the Qumran Scrolls by Fellows of the Institute for Advanced Studies of the Hebrew University, Jerusalem, 1989–1990* (STDJ 16; ed. Devorah Dimant and Lawrence H. Schiffman; Leiden: Brill, 1995), 131–57.

[14] James A. Sanders, *The Psalms Scroll of Qumran Cave 11 (11QPs[a])* (DJDJ IV; Oxford: Clarendon, 1965), 47, 89–91. Sanders notes most of the biblical parallels and variant readings there. The raised numbers in the transcription represent the verses; in the versified translation, they represent the lines of the manuscript.

4. [11-12] Separating light from deep darkness
    by the knowledge of his mind he established the dawn.
5. [12] When all his angels witnessed it they sang aloud,
    for he showed them what they had not known:
6. [13] Crowning the hills with fruit,
    good food for every living being.
7. [13-14] Blessed be he who makes the earth by his power,
    establishing the world in his wisdom.
8. [14-15] By his understanding he stretched out the heavens,
    and brought forth [wind] from his st[orehouses].
9. [15] He made [lightning for the rai]n,
    and caused mist[s] to rise [from] the end of [16][the earth].

In a subtle yet significant shift, the Hymn turns the Jeremiah verses into a doxological blessing simply by prefacing them with the word *barukh*. Moreover, the Hymn appears to end with this blessing, which now stands in the position of a closing benediction.[15] This striking, benedictory adaptation is no mere stylistic imitation of the blessings that close the books of the canonical psalter[16] but rather is a sign of liturgical reworking to be viewed against the background of the increased use of formal opening and closing benedictions during the Second Temple period. Tobit's hymn (13:19), the Psalms of Solomon (2:37, 5:19, 6:6) as well as the daily, weekly, and festival liturgies from Qumran offer some examples.[17] This liturgical development ultimately resulted in talmudic laws governing the use of the formal, liturgical benediction in the statutory Jewish liturgy.[18]

The Hymn's doxological application of the cited biblical verses in effect severs them from and breaks the continuity with their original biblical context in Jeremiah's prophecies of doom against Israel

---

[15] The last word of the quotation from Jer 10:13 (51:16) would have extended onto line 16 of col. XXVI (line 15 is the last extant line of the column). It seems that the Hymn ended on line 16 and that the rest of this column contained the psalm in 2 Sam 23:1–7, whose final six words appear at the top of col. XXVII. See James A. Sanders, *The Dead Sea Psalms Scroll* (Ithaca, NY: Cornell University Press, 1967), 10–11, 134 and Peter W. Flint, *The Dead Sea Psalms Scrolls and The Book of Psalms* (STDJ XVII; Leiden: Brill, 1997), 190, 191, n. 101.

[16] Pss 41:14, 72:18–20, 89:53, 106:48. Cf. Pss 68:20, 36 and 135:21.

[17] See Eileen M. Schuller, "Some Observations on Blessings of God in Texts from Qumran," *Of Scribes and Scrolls: Studies on the Hebrew Bible, Intertestamental Judaism, and Christian Origins Presented to John Strugnell on the Occasion of His Sixtieth Birthday* (College Theology Resources in Religion 5; eds. Harold W. Attridge, John. J. Collins and Thomas H. Tobin; Lanham: MD: University Press of America, 1990), 133–43; Bilhah Nitzan, *Qumran Prayer & Religious Poetry* (STDJ XII; Leiden: Brill, 1994), 69–80.

[18] Joseph Heinemann, *Prayer in the Talmud: Forms and Patterns* (trans. Richard S. Sarason; Studia Judaica 9; Berlin: de Gruyter, 1977), 77–103.

(chapter 10) and against Babylon (chapter 51). This last observation rests upon the plausible assumption that our text quotes the verses directly from the Book of Jeremiah rather than from an unknown "floating" piece of religious poetry.[19] Indeed, with the exception of the newly added blessing formula, the Hymn's penultimate line is identical with Jer 10:12 = 51:15 while its final line has the last three cola in Jer 10:13 = 51:16 but in a chiastic order that now depicts the bringing down of rain from heaven to earth. The story of what our author did with the first colon, Jer 10:13a = 51:16a, is bound up with the meaning, message and purpose of this beautiful psalm.

Both in the context of Jeremiah's prophecies of doom and the Hymn's concluding doxology, Jer 10:12–13 form a statement about God as creator of the world and provider of rain. The only major exegetical crux lies in the words לקול תתו (literally, "at the sound of His giving")[20] in Jer 10:13a = 51:16a. This entire colon is missing from the verse's otherwise full quotation both in Ps 135:7 and in the *Hymn to the Creator*'s concluding doxology. Both psalms seem to be skirting the exegetical problem by eliminating the difficult words![21]

In the case of our Hymn, however, the author appears to deploy the rest of this colon elsewhere—that is, in the opening stanza's depiction of the heavenly waters. Such a double reference to the same source in the Hymn's opening and closing stanzas would form a nice *inclusio*. I surmise that our author began his use of Jer 10:12–13 in the first stanza by severing off the difficult colon in v. 13 and identifying its reference to "the rush of heavenly waters" with the similar sound accompanying God's appearance on His celestial throne (compare Ezek 1:24–25, 3:12–13, 43:2). The Hymn's second verse may even entail a conflation of Jer 10:13a's המון מים בשמים with Ezek 1:24's קול מים רבים to produce ואחדיו המון מים רבים. Whether or not

---

[19] Sanders (*Dead Sea Psalms*, 129; *Psalms Scroll* [DJDJ IV], 89) suggested that the Hymn, the Book of Jeremiah and Psalm 135 made use of such a "floating" piece of liturgical poetry that was "easily quotable and frequently used." For a similar approach to the poems in Jeremiah see John Bright, *Jeremiah* (AB 21; 2d ed.; Garden City, NY: Doubleday, 1984), 79–80, 359–60. Jer 10:12–13 are partially preserved in several manuscripts from Qumran including the oldest copy, 4QJer[a]. Consult Eugene Ulrich et al., *Qumran Cave 4.X The Prophets* (DJD XV; Oxford: Clarendon, 1997).

[20] Bright (*Jeremiah*, 77–78) offers the plausible interpretation that the phrase in Jeremiah "describes God's voice as the thunder that accompanies the storm."

[21] The Septuagint and perhaps also 4QJer[c] omit this phrase in Jer 10:13. See Ulrich, *Prophets* [DJD XV], 158, 187. The phrase does occur in LXX Jer 28 = MT 51:16.

this particular Ezekiel verse is quoted directly, the prophet's *merk-abah* vision seems to lie behind the Hymn's opening portrayal of God on His heavenly throne surrounded by splendor, the tumult of many waters, and the angels.[22] It is in this context that I entertain below the possibility of the opening line's allusion to Isa 6:3. But first, I would like to suggest a comprehensive interpretation of the Hymn that accords with its biblical re-use as well as with its literary form and content.

The Hymn's opening description of the transcendent God in heaven stands in contrast to the closing praise of God as creator of the earth and provider of its sustenance. This contrast serves to heighten the worshippers' appreciation of and praise for that sustenance. The use of Jer 10:13 as an *inclusio* would tie the two ends together and reinforce this message stylistically and exegetically. In the middle stanza, the setting moves from heaven to earth and the gap between them is bridged when the angels burst into song at light's creation and at seeing earth's produce. Here, motifs of the divine throne and angelic song are subsumed into and made to serve the Hymn's praise of the Creator and Sustainer of the universe.

We now consider the proposal that the Hymn alludes to Isa 6:3 and, in addition, also attests the *Qedushah* liturgy which is built upon that verse. The angels' threefold proclamation of God's holiness in Isa 6:3 does seem to resonate in the Hymn's threefold repetition of the word "holy" in its opening line., "Great and *holy* is the Lord, the *holiest* of *holy* ones for every generation."[23] Significantly, as in Isa 6:3, the Hymn also depicts the angelic entourage (in the "holiest of holy ones" epithet), the divine throne (in v. 3), and the angelic song (in v. 5). I propose, therefore, that not only does the Hymn allude to Isa 6:3 but it also accesses and carries over the immediate context of Isaiah's throne vision. Furthermore, as suggested above, the very next verse evokes Ezekiel's *merkabah* vision, perhaps through an allusion to Ezek 1:24. The Hymn thus seems to be juxtaposing and essentially harmonizing the two prophetic throne visions in a manner typical of *merkabah* exegesis and the *Qedushah* liturgy.[24]

---

[22] Verse 3 might also allude to Pss 89:15, 97:2.

[23] I quote here from Sander's later translation in *Dead Sea Psalms*, 131, which reflects the original Hebrew's threefold repetition of "holy."

[24] For this type of *merkabah* exegesis beginning with its earliest manifestations see David Halperin, "Merkabah Midrash in the Septuagint," *JBL* 101 (1982): 351–63. The *Qedushah* is discussed below.

Is the Hymn to the Creator, then, an ancient form or attestation
of the traditional *Qedushah* liturgy, in which the earthly congregation
joins the angels in reciting Isa 6:3's *trishagion* as well as the blessing
of God's glory recorded in Ezek 3:12? The parallels with the later
Qedushah texts simply do not prove that specific claim about the
Hymn.[25] Rather, the evidence before us seems to point to some
shared exegetical and liturgical traditions as well as to a common
religious phenomenon that I call "praying with the angels."[26] The
Hymn's appropriation of Isa 6:3's angelic *trishagion* and its description of the angelic song imply that by reciting this Hymn, the human
worshippers were joining the angels in praising God. It may well be
the case that the Hymn, like the angelic song, was recited at dawn
(vv. 4–5, cf. Job 38:7). In fact, the phenomenon of joint human-
angelic praise at sunrise (and sunset) is now amply documented in
Second Temple sources.[27]

For the purposes of the present study, it suffices to note that our
appreciation of the Hymn's potential as joint praise fits in nicely
with our earlier conclusion for its liturgical function. Active liturgical use could also account for the Hymn's popularity[28] apparently
attested by its citation in *Jubilees* 2:2–3 and the *Admonition on the
Flood.*[29] The Hymn's liturgical function would be another piece of
evidence in favor of taking the entire Cave 11 Psalms Scroll as a
liturgical collection.[30]

---

[25] For that claim see Weinfeld, "Traces" and "Angelic Song." Note, however,
that the Hymn only paraphrases Isa 6:3, does not even allude to Ezek 3:12, and
lacks distinctive, precise parallels with the *Qedushah* texts cited by Weinfeld, which
are hundreds of years later than the Hymn.

[26] On this phenomenon see Esther G. Chazon, "Human and Angelic Prayer in
Light of the Dead Sea Scrolls," in *Liturgical Perspectives.* Examples of shared traditions are the harmonization of the prophets' throne visions discussed above and the
early morning human-angelic praise discussed below.

[27] See, for example, the sources cited in Weinfeld, "Angelic Song" and Esther
G. Chazon, "The Function of the Qumran Prayer Texts: An Analysis of the Daily
Prayers (4Q503)" in *The Dead Sea Scrolls: Fifty Years After Their Discovery. Proceedings of
the Jerusalem Congress, July 20–25, 1997* (ed. Lawrence H. Schiffman, Emanuel Tov,
and James C. VanderKam; Jerusalem: Israel Exploration Society, 2000), 217–25.

[28] Alternatively, authoritative, scriptural status (see n. 30 below) could explain this
popularity.

[29] See Carol A. Newsom, "370. 4QAdmonition on the Flood," in *Qumran Cave
4.XIV: Parabiblical Texts, Part 2 (DJD* XIX; ed. Magen Broshi et al.; Oxford: Clarendon,
1995), 85–94; Patrick W. Skehan, "*Jubilees* and the Qumran Psalter," *CBQ* 37 (1975):
343–7 and Flint, *Psalms Scrolls,* 222–4. The Hebrew of *Jub* 2:2–3 is partially preserved in 4Q216 II, 10–11.

[30] This conclusion does not preclude the possibility that the entire collection or

In conclusion, I shall draw out the implications from our two case studies for the theoretical question posed at the beginning of this paper: How much of the biblical context do biblical allusions carry along with them into the new literary work, and under what conditions? Admittedly, answers to this type of question will invariably entail a certain degree of subjectivity and will also be somewhat dependent upon assumptions about the author's and the audience's knowledge of Scripture. Nevertheless, we are now in a position to establish criteria that can guide us in tackling this issue. Based on my case studies, I recognize four criteria that can help us gauge when the biblical context is being accessed and to what extent.[31]

First, on the most basic level, there must be a clearly identifiable quotation from or allusion to a specific biblical passage that establishes the link between the two texts. Second, there should be an additional marker that flags that particular passage and makes it virtually impossible for the biblically acquainted reader/listener to ignore. The markers may be quantitative, for example, long quotations and sustained allusions extending over several biblical verses—such as Ps 18:7–9 in the *Tehillah of the Man of God* and Jer 10:12–13 in the *Hymn to the Creator*. Or, they may be qualitative, for example, rare words or unique expressions like Isa 6:3's thrice-holy or *'m hdrk(ym)* taken from Ezek 21:26 to make a critical point in the prelude to Joseph's prayer in Narrative and Poetic Compositions[a] (4Q372 1 9).[32] Occasionally, the author will even name a biblical figure, location, or episode such as the explicit references to the covenant at Horeb and to Moses' atonement for Israel's sin found in "The Words of the Luminaries" (4Q504 3 ii 13, 1–2 ii 9–10). A third factor is the totality of the intertextual allusions. When a work draws exclusively upon one biblical passage, as in the case of the *Tehillah of the Man of God*, then that single source tends to stand out prominently. By

---

individual psalms acquired authoritative status. By analogy, psalms in what became the canonical Masoretic psalter had a liturgical function from the earliest times on. For a summary of the debate over the liturgical versus canonical character of 11QPs[a] see Flint, *Psalms Scrolls*, 202–27.

[31] My first, second, and fourth criteria bear similarities with the four stages in "actualizing a literary allusion" delineated by Ziva Ben-Porat ("The Poetics of Literary Allusion," *PTL: A Journal for Descriptive Poetics and Theory of Literature*," 1 [1976], 105–28) and analyzed by Benjamin D. Sommer in his fine study, *A Prophet Reads Scripture: Allusion in Isaiah 40–56* (Stanford, CA: Standford University Press, 1998), 6–31.

[32] Eileen Schuller, "4Q372 1: A Text About Joseph," *RevQ* 14 (1990): 349–76.

contrast, a mosaic of diverse allusions might obscure its different sources.

The fourth and perhaps decisive criterion is the degree of similarity, indeed continuity, between the new work and its biblical source in matters of content, genre and context. Continuity—whether of identity or, as Adele Berlin has shown, of dissonance[33]—engages the biblical context and imports it into the new composition. Discontinuity, that is, severing the quotation or allusion from its biblical context and completely recontextualizing it, tends to deflect or inhibit transference of biblical images, connotations, and context. Continuity and discontinuity represent opposite ends of a spectrum. From our case studies we can see the use of Psalm 18 by the *Tehillah of the Man of God* as a case of continuity. Here, the later author continues Psalm 18's motifs of crying out in distress for divine deliverance throughout the new psalm, even in the freely composed lines that precede the biblical citation. An example of discontinuity would be the Hymn to the Creator's severance of Jer 10:12–13 from the context of prophecies of doom and its double recontextualization of those verses: one colon (10:13a) in the opening celestial throne description and the remaining cola in the concluding benediction. Other allusions in the Hymn (e.g., to Gen 1:14 in v. 4, and to Job 38:7 in v. 5) might fall in the middle range of our spectrum, carrying over their original contexts in different ways and to varying degrees.

The theoretical question examined in this study and the methodological path that I have charted here are applicable not only to ancient religious poetry but to all works of all genres and all ages that look to Scripture as a source of inspiration. It is my hope that this study will both advance our understanding of the ways the Bible is used to create new works and enhance our ability to apply those new insights as a key to unlocking the new meanings, messages, and functions of our literary treasures.

---

[33] Berlin, "Laments."

FORMS OF COMMUNITY IN THE DEAD SEA SCROLLS

John J. Collins

The idea that the Dead Sea Scrolls derive from a quasi-monastic community at the site of Qumran is widespread and deeply rooted.[1] It arose, in the first case, from the impression made by the Community Rule (*Serek ha-Yaḥad*), which was one of the first scrolls discovered, and was described in a press release in April 1948 as "a manual of discipline of some comparatively little-known sect or monastic order, possibly the Essenes."[2] The *Serek* described a tightly organized, hierarchical community, that emphasized its separation from the rest of Judaism. We are told that this community, or some of its members, were to "go into the wilderness to prepare there the way of Him" (1QS VIII,13) in accordance with the oracle of the prophet: "Prepare in the wilderness the way of the Lord" (Isa 40:3), an injunction that fitted very nicely with the site of Qumran. From a very early point, this community was identified as an Essene settlement.[3] There were numerous parallels, in manner of organization and in beliefs and ideology, between the Community Rule and the descriptions of the Essenes by Josephus and Philo.[4] Pliny the Elder had written of an Essene settlement on the western shore of the Dead Sea.[5] The view

---

[1] For recent discussions see M. Broshi, "Was Qumran, Indeed, a Monastery?" in *Caves of Enlightenment. Proceedings of the American Schools of Oriental Research Dead Sea Scrolls Jubilee Symposium (1947–97)* (ed. J. H. Charlesworth; North Richland Hills, Tex.: Bibal, 1998), 19–37; J. L. Magness, "Communal Meals and Sacred Space at Qumran," in *Shaping Community: The Art and Archaeology of Monasticism* (ed. S. McNally; British Archaeological Reports International Series 942; Oxford: Archaeopress, 2001), 15–27, especially 15–16.

[2] The release was written by Millar Burrows of Yale, and appeared in the Times of London on April 12, 1948. See J. C. VanderKam, *The Dead Sea Scrolls Today* (Grand Rapids: Eerdmans, 1994), 6.

[3] E. L. Sukenik had already proposed the Essene identification even before Burrows' press release. See N. A. Silberman, "Sukenik, Eleazar L.," in *The Encyclopedia of the Dead Sea Scrolls* (eds. L. H. Schiffman and J. C. VanderKam; New York: Oxford, 2000), 903; H. Stegemann, "The Qumran Essenes—Local Members of the Main Jewish Union in Late Second Temple Times," in *The Madrid Qumran Congress* (eds. J. Treballe Barrera and L. Vegas Montaner; Leiden: Brill, 1992), 1.84.

[4] For the sources, see G. Vermes and M. Goodman, eds. *The Essenes According to the Classical Sources* (Sheffield: JSOT, 1989).

[5] Pliny, *Natural History* 5.17.4 (73).

that Qumran was an Essene settlement was consolidated by Roland
de Vaux's interpretation of the ruins at the site.[6] It should be noted,
however, that neither the monastic analogy nor the identification
with the Essenes was originally proposed by de Vaux, or by Catholic
priests, and that both positions have commanded the allegiance of
Jewish scholars as well as Christian. The resulting consensus has
dominated the field for more than fifty years.

It has not, of course, gone unchallenged. Over the last decade
there have been animated debates over the Essene identification and
over the interpretation of the site.[7] It is not my purpose to rehearse
these debates here, but rather to re-examine what can be inferred
from the Scrolls themselves, and more especially from the Community
Rule, about the nature of the communities that they presuppose.[8]
Three issues in particular will concern us.

The first is the degree of similarity between the communities
described in the Scrolls and Hellenistic voluntary associations. Moshe
Weinfeld, in an influential study, has shown that there are indeed
significant similarities.[9] Weinfeld argued that the similarities were limited to form and structure. He still affirmed that the Qumran community was different in character from the associations because of
its sectarian nature. Matthias Klinghardt, however, has tried to go
further.[10] For Klinghardt, the Qumran *yaḥad* is a religious associa-

---

[6] R. de Vaux, *Archaeology and the Dead Sea Scrolls* (Oxford: Oxford University Press,
1973). See further Stegemann, "The Qumran Essenes," 86–88.

[7] For a recent discussion of the Essene identification, see T. S. Beall, "Essenes,"
in, *The Encyclopedia of the Dead Sea Scrolls*, 262–69; on the interpretation of the site,
see J. L. Magness, "Qumran Archaeology: Past Perspectives and Future Prospects,"
in *The Dead Sea Scrolls after Fifty Years. A Comprehensive Assessment* (eds. P. W. Flint and
J. C. VanderKam; Leiden: Brill, 1998), 1.47–77.

[8] For an overview of the issues see C. Hempel, "Community Structures in the
Dead Sea Scrolls: Admission, Organization, Disciplinary Procedures," in *The Dead
Sea Scrolls after Fifty Years*, 2.67–92.

[9] M. Weinfeld, *The Organizational Pattern and the Penal Code of the Qumran Sect. A
comparison with Guilds and Religious Associations of the Hellenistic-Roman Period* (NTOA 2;
Göttingen: Vandenhoeck & Ruprecht; Fribourg: Presses Universitaires, 1986). Analogies
with Hellenistic voluntary associations had been proposed earlier by others in a less
systematic way, e.g. H. Bardtke, "Die Rechtstellung der Qumrangemeinde," *TLZ*
86 (1961) 93–104. A good summary of the discussion can be found in C. M. Murphy,
Wealth in the Dead Sea Scrolls and in the Qumran Community (Leiden: Brill, 2002), 13–18.

[10] M. Klinghardt, "The Manual of Discipline in the Light of Statutes of Hellenistic
Associations," in *Methods of Investigation of the Dead Sea Scrolls and the Khirbet Qumran
Site. Present Realities and Future Prospects* (eds. M. O. Wise, et al.; Annals of the New
York Academy of Sciences 722; New York: The New York Academy of Sciences,
1994), 251–70; *Gemeinschaftsmahl und Mahlgemeinschaft* (Tübingen: Francke, 1996),
217–49.

tion of quite the same type as the Hellenistic associations. In the Jewish context, he refers to it as a synagogue community. The crucial issue here is the degree to which the community was cenobitic, i.e. the degree to which the members shared a common life.

The second issue is the variety of community forms attested in the Scrolls, and specifically within the Community Rule. There is provision in 1QS VI, as also in the Damascus Document and in 1QSa, for multiple small assemblies (of at least ten people) within a larger umbrella organization. The *yaḥad* in Serek ha-Yaḥad must be identified with the umbrella organization, not with an individual community such as the Qumran settlement. A distinction is made, however, in 1QS VIII, of an elite group that is set apart in the midst of the yaḥad (1QS VIII,11). This group is supposed to go out into the desert to prepare the way of the Lord. Whether or not this passage relates to the founding of the Qumran settlement, as many scholars have supposed,[11] it shows that the lifestyle of all members of the yaḥad was not necessarily identical.

Finally, we will consider the relevance of 1QSa to the development of sectarian community structures. This scroll is presented as the rule for all the congregation of Israel at the end of days, and accordingly has usually been understood as a rule that would be applicable to all Israel at a future time. Hartmut Stegemann, however, has argued that the sectarians believed that the end of days had already come, and that 1QSa was the earliest form of a community rule.[12] Charlotte Hempel has adapted this proposal, to argue that 1QSa contains an "early nucleus" that was intended as a rule for the present.[13] This rule evidently bears some relation to the Community Rule and Damascus Document, but we will argue that it is still most satisfactorily understood as a rule for a future, messianic age.

---

[11] As suggested by E. F. Sutcliffe, S. J. "The First Fifteen Members of the Qumran Community," *JSS* 4 (1959): 134–8.

[12] H. Stegemann, "Some Remarks to 1QSa, to 1QSb, and to Qumran Messianism," *RevQ* 17 (1996) 479–505; *The Library of Qumran* (Grand Rapids: Eerdmans, 1998), 113–15.

[13] C. Hempel, "The Early Essene Nucleus of 1QSa," *DSD* 3 (1996) 253–67. (The printed title of this article, which reads Earthly instead of Early, is clearly a mistake).

The analogy with voluntary associations

Hellenistic voluntary associations were of many kinds and served many purposes—religious, philosophical, or simply social. What they had in common was the custom of meeting regularly to share a meal and hold discussions. The frequency of their meetings could vary. Some of those whose statutes are preserved met once a month.[14] Even though they had procedures for admission and rules and regulations, the members of these associations did not live together, and their common life was limited.[15]

In the Dead Sea Scrolls, it is generally recognized that the Damascus Document envisions members of the new covenant who do not share a cenobitic lifestyle, although they are to "keep apart from all the sons of the pit" (CD VI,15; cf. 4Q266 3 ii, 20–21). They "live in camps according to the order of the land and marry and beget children" (CD VII,6–7). The new covenant is conceived on the model of Israel in the wilderness, organized in "thousands, hundreds, fifties and tens" (Exod 18:25). The "camps" are the smallest units, constituted by assemblies of at least ten people (CD XIII,1), including a priest. Each camp has its own Inspector (m^{c}baqqēr), who examines the members on a range of matters including their property. No one is allowed to sell or buy without consulting the Inspector. Likewise, no one is allowed to marry or divorce without consultation, and the Inspector has responsibility for instructing the children (4Q266 9 iii, 1–7; cf. CD XIII,15–18). Nonetheless, it is clear that members retain private property, since they are required to contribute two days' salary per month (CD XIV,13; 4Q266 10 i, 6). There is also an assembly of all the camps, with its own Inspector (CD XIV,3,

---

[14] E. g. the guild of Zeus Hypsistos and the Iobacchi. See A. Baumgarten "Graeco-Roman Voluntary Associations and Ancient Jewish Sects," in *Jews in a Graeco-Roman World* (ed. M. Goodman; Oxford: Clarendon, 1998), 96. See further S. Wilson and J. S. Kloppenborg, *Voluntary Associations in the Greco-Roman World* (London: Routledge, 1996).

[15] The Pythagoreans are a possible exception, although the existence of Pythagorean communities in antiquity remains elusive. See J. Dillon and J. Herschbell, *Iamblichus. On the Pythagorean Way of Life* (Atlanta: Society of Biblical Literature, 1991), 14–16. In any case, such communities would have been exceptional in the ancient world, and fall outside the range of voluntary associations invoked by Klinghardt as analogues for the *yaḥad* of the Scrolls. The analogies between the Pythagoreans and the Scrolls in the matter of common property is noted by H. J. Klauck, "Gütergemeinschaft in der Klassischen Antike, in Qumran und im Neuen Testament," *RevQ* 41 (1982): 47–79 (see especially p. 68). See also Murphy, *Wealth in the Dead Sea Scrolls*, 18–20 for a summary of older discussion on "the Pythagorean connection."

9; 4Q 266 10 i, 2; 4Q267 9 v, 6, 13). It is apparent that the authority of the Inspector over the lives of the members is more intrusive
than was usual in voluntary associations, but that the common life
of the camps stopped well short of later monastic standards.

We know from Josephus that there were two orders of Essenes,
one of which married while the other lived a communal, celibate
life.[16] It is often assumed that the Damascus Rule relates to the marrying Essenes, while the Community Rule reflects the celibate order.[17]
In fact, there is some evidence that the Damascus Rule envisions
two distinct orders. CD VII,4–8 has been interpreted as contrasting
those who live in camps with "those who walk in perfect holiness."[18]
The latter, by implication, do not marry or have children, and so
they are assured that "God's covenant is guaranteed for them that
they shall live a thousand generations." The Damascus Rule, however,
is primarily concerned with the former. Both the quasi-monastic characterization of the community and the Essene identification have
been based primarily on 1QS V–IX Since cols. I–IV are not found
in several of the 4QS manuscripts, it seems likely that cols. V–IX
constituted an early, though not necessarily the earliest, form of the
Rule book.[19] In the Community Rule, the community in question is
called the yaḥad, a term that does not occur in the fragments of
the Damascus Rule from Qumran. (In CD manuscript B, XX,32,
the reference to "the men of the yaḥîd" should presumably be read as
"men of the yaḥad" while the reference to yōreh ha-yaḥîd [the unique
teacher] in XX,14 may be a wordplay on "teacher of the yaḥad.")

The first point to be noted in the introduction to 1QS V–IX is
the degree of separation that is required. The *raison d'être* of the

---

[16] *J.W.* 2.160.

[17] E.g. G. Vermes, *The Dead Sea Scrolls. Qumran in Perspective* (Philadelphia: Fortress,
1977), 129; VanderKam, *The Dead Sea Scrolls Today*, 91.

[18] See especially J. M. Baumgarten, "Qumran-Essene Restraints on Marriage,"
in *Archaeology and History in the Dead Sea Scrolls* (ed. L. H. Schiffman; Sheffield: JSOT,
1990), 3–24; idem, "Celibacy," in *The Encyclopedia of the Dead Sea Scrolls*, 1.122–4.

[19] There is some evidence that these columns preserve material from different
stages of development. Hempel, "Community Structures," 71, has noted that "the
simple procedure of admission by swearing an oath described in 1QS 9:7c–9a contrasts with the elaborate prescriptions on the admission of new members in 1QS
6:13b–23. The simpler procedure is comparable to what is found in CD 15:5b–10a,
which seems, however, to address the case of children of members rather than pos-
tulants from the outside. The Damascus Rule also provides for a period of instruction for those who need it (CD 15:14–15; 4Q266 8 i 5–6) and for examination of
aspiring members by the Inspector (CD 13:11; 4Q267 9 iv 8–9).

community is to separate from "the congregation of the men of deceit" (1QS V,2). The primary concern here is to separate from other Jews, who know the revealed Torah, but act presumptuously with regard to it (V,12) and do not seek out the hidden things that are disclosed in the interpretation of the community. The members are warned not to eat or drink anything from the property of these people, and not to accept anything from them without payment. Outsiders cannot be rendered fit for association by purificatory baths "for they cannot be cleansed unless they turn away from their wickedness" (V,13–14). All of this bespeaks a degree of separatism that is more extreme than what we find in the statutes of Hellenistic voluntary associations.[20] The great concern for purity, however, also underlies the regulations for the Pharisaic/rabbinic *ḥaburôt*.[21] It does not in itself require a cenobitic life-style, although it does require strict rules of association.

The second point to be noted is that the members of the community are united not only in their observance of the Torah, but also in their possessions. The "merging" of possessions is described carefully in the regulations for admission to the community in VI,17–22. When the postulant first approaches the community he is not allowed "to touch the purity of the many" or to have any share in the community property.[22] At the next stage, he hands over his possessions to the mᵉbaqqēr, who registers it to his account, but it is not yet available to the community. Only when the postulant has completed a full year in the midst of the community is his property fully merged. There is nothing in the Community Rule to indicate that members retain any private property. In this regard there is a striking contrast with CD, where members hand over only two days' wages a month.

---

[20] This point is emphasized by S. Walker-Ramisch, "Graeco-Roman Voluntary Associations and the Damascus Document," in *Voluntary Associations*, 128–45. See also E. W. Larson, "Greco-Roman Guilds," in *The Encyclopedia of the Dead Sea Scrolls*, 1.321–3.

[21] As pointed out by S. Lieberman, "The Discipline in the So-Called Dead Sea Manual of Discipline," *JBL* 71 (1952): 199–206. See now A. Oppenheimer, "Haverim," in *The Encyclopedia of the Dead Sea Scrolls*, 1.333–6.

[22] The "purity of the many" is usually taken to mean "the pure food" of the community. Cf. the distinction between the purity of food and drink in rabbinic sources, noted by Lieberman, "The Discipline," 203. See however F. Avemarie, "'Tohorat ha-Rabbim' and 'Mashqeh Ha-Rabbim'. Jacob Licht Reconsidered," in *Legal Texts and Legal Issues* (eds. M. Bernstein, F. García Martínez, and J. Kampen; Leiden: Brill, 1997) 215–29, who suggests that it may have a broader sense, and imply that outsiders should not even touch members of the community.

Klinghardt has claimed that this merging of property in 1QS "is most likely what is called in Greek associations the '*eisēlysion*,' the entrance fee.[23] He argues that "it is very unlikely that the initiant had to submit all his possessions to the yachad, because otherwise the regulation about financial liablitiy for damages (1QS VII,6–8) would make no sense at all."[24] But in fact the only case where the Rule stipulates payment is when a member is neglectful of the property of the community. In that case, he is supposed to restore it, if he can. This does not require that he be able to draw on private property. He may be able to restore the damaged goods by work, or by obtaining something from other sources. Apart from this case, punishment in the Community Rule takes two forms: reduction of the food allowance or exclusion, whether temporary or permanent, from the community.[25] These penalties take the place of monetary fines in the Hellenistic associations, but they lend no support to the claim that members retained any private property.

Communal property does not necessarily require cenobitic life. Members might have the use of common property for their daily affairs, but maintain separate dwelling places. The passage most often cited as evidence of the common life is 1QS VI,2–3: "They shall eat in common and bless in common and deliberate in common." Klinghardt has argued plausibly that this sentence refers not to three separate meetings but to three stages of the evening assembly: the meal proper is followed by a blessing and then by deliberation.[26] We are not told explicitly how often common meals were to take place, but we are told that the members were to study the Torah and bless together "for a third of every night of the year." It would seem then that members of the community were expected to spend their evenings together, and this would surely require that they live in close proximity to each other. But in fact Klinghardt's idea of cenobitic life, which seems to imply living under a single roof as in a medieval monastery, is misleading in the context of the ancient world. People who lived in separate dwellings with a central meeting place could nonetheless maintain a high degree of common life.

---

[23] Klinghardt, "The Manual of Discipline," 255.
[24] Ibid.
[25] This is also true of the penal code in 4Q266 10 ii which corresponds in large part to 1QS VII.
[26] Klinghardt, *Gemeinschaftsmahl*, 229–30. He argues by analogy with the order of Hellenistic communal meals, which typically included a libation with praise of the gods, and a discussion in the form of a symposium.

The Community Rule does not require that all members of the yaḥad meet in one place. 1QS VI envisions smaller groups. We are told that wherever there were ten members, there should not lack a priest, and that someone should always be engaged in the study of the Torah, day or night. The number ten seems to constitute a quorum, as in the Damascus Rule. It should be noted that the term yaḥad, as used in 1QS V,1, refers to the umbrella organization of these smaller groups, not to a single settlement such as the Qumran community.[27] The common assumption that yaḥad is the technical name for the quasi-monastic settlement at Qumran cannnot be maintained.

There is obvious similarity between the kind of community organization found in 1QS VI and the "camps" of the Damascus Rule. The small "cell" communities of the Community Rule differ from these "camps" in two important respects. First, the Damascus Rule explicitly says that those who live in camps marry and have children. The Community Rule makes no provision for women or children at all, and is compatible with a celibate life-style, even if it does not explicitly require it. Whether members of the yaḥad were supposed to be celibate remains highly controversial.[28] In view of the contrast with the Damascus Rule, I am inclined to the view that the Community Rule did not envisage women and children in the community,[29] but then the silence of the Rule on the subject of celibacy is also surprising. Second, the Damascus Rule does not require common property, but only a contribution of two days' salary per month. It may be that the yaḥad corresponds to "those who walk in perfect holiness" in CD VII, or that the contrast between the two orders of Essenes is reflected here, but again it should be noted that the yaḥad is not restricted to a single settlement such as that of Qumran.[30]

---

[27] Stegemann, "The Qumran Essenes," 155, goes further, arguing that "Ha-yaḥad meant a confederation of all existing Jewish groups, their union in a new religious body, which had never existed before." There is no evidence that the yaḥad was ever meant to embrace all existing Jewish groups, but Stegemann was right that it was not restricted to a single settlement such as that of Qumran. Note also the conclusion of Murphy, *Wealth in the Dead Sea Scrolls*, 161–2, that the variation between different manuscripts of the rule books suggests that they were used in more than one community.

[28] For recent summaries of the issues see J. M. Baumgarten, "Celibacy," in *The Encyclopedia of the Dead Sea Scrolls*, 1.122–4; E. Schuller, "Women in the Dead Sea Scrolls," in *The Dead Sea Scrolls after Fifty Years*, 1.117–44.

[29] So also Broshi, "Was Qumran, Indeed, a Monastery?"

[30] The archeological evidence from the Dead Sea region suggests that few if any

An elite group within the yaḥad

There is, however, a further distinction made within the Community Rule. In column VIII we read that "in the council of the community there shall be twelve men and three priests," who are distinguished by their knowledge and practice of the law. The identity of this sub-group is one of the intriguing mysteries of the Scrolls. Elsewhere, they are mentioned only in 4Q265 7 line 7, which refers to fifteen men, clearly taking the three priests as additional to the twelve.[31] The council of the community cannot be distinguished from the community itself. (Compare, e.g. 1QS V,7; VI,10, 12, 14, 16). The 12+3 are members of the yaḥad, they do not constitute it. Their actions and characters bear a strong similarity to those of the whole community, but their performance is on a higher level. They undergo two further years of training, and they are trusted by the Interpreter more fully than are the other members of the community (1QS VIII,12).

In VIII,11–12, we are told that when these form a yaḥad in Israel according to all these rules, "they shall separate from the habitation of unjust men and shall go into the wilderness to prepare there the way of Him."[32] The passage goes on to cite Isa 40:3, and explicate it: "This is the study of the Law, which he commanded by the hand of Moses . . ." The explanation presumably applies to "preparing the way of the Lord," which is the focus of the biblical citation. It is not apparent, however, that any allegorical explanation is offered for the retreat to the wilderness.[33] On the contrary, the statement that the people in question should "separate from the habitation of unjust men" suggests rather strongly that the retreat to the wilderness be taken literally. This datum is highly compatible with the foundation of a settlement at Qumran, although it is impossible to prove that the reference was to this specific location.

Our concern here, however, is not primarily with the location of this group, but with its relation to the broader sect. E. F. Sutcliffe,

---

people lived in the main buildings at Qumran. Some apparently lived in caves nearby, but there were also several related sites in the vicinity. See Murphy, *Wealth in the Dead Sea Scrolls*, 344–9.

[31] The reading is reconstructed by analogy with 1QS, but the word "five" is clear. See J. Baumgarten, '265. 4QMiscellaneous Rules," in *Qumran Cave 4.XXV* (eds. J. Baumgarten et al.; *DJD* XXXV; Oxford: Clarendon, 1999), 72.

[32] Trans. Vermes.

[33] See the discussion of this passage by G. J. Brooke, "Isaiah 40:3 and the Wilderness Community," in *New Qumran Texts and Studies* (eds. G. J. Brooke and F. García Martínez; Leiden: Brill, 1994), 117–32.

in a famous article, suggested that these were the first fifteen members of the Qumran community, but, to his credit, he recognized that they were also members of a larger movement.[34] His insight was taken up by Murphy-O'Connor, who proceeded to argue that 1QS VIII was a "manifesto," and that it was the oldest stratum of the Community Rule.[35] But while the elite fifteen may be said to constitute *a* yaḥad, they cannot be the original members of *the* yaḥad: 1QS VIII,11 states clearly that they are to be "set apart as holy within the council of the men of the community." They are trained by the Instructor of the larger yaḥad, and they have his complete confidence. They complement the larger movement, and bring it to perfection. They do not "break away" from the parent group, and there is no question of a split between them. If the elite fifteen were indeed the first members of the Qumran community, as seems plausible though not certain, then it should be clear that the Qumran community did not originate because of a split, but was a harmonious offshoot of the larger yaḥad.[36]

The relation of that yaḥad to the community of the new covenant in the land of Damascus is still unclear. There evidently was some relationship, as can be seen from the references to the yaḥad in the B manuscript of CD and the presence of the 4QD manuscripts at Qumran, as well as the overlaps between the various 4QD and 4QS

---

[34] Sutcliffe, "The First Fifteen Members," 137: "Thus the text presents fifteen men as members of a larger group."

[35] J. Murphy-O'Connor, "La genèse littéraire de la Règle de la Communauté," *RB* 76 (1969) 528–49.

[36] The view that the Qumran settlement resulted from a schism within the Essene movement has been advanced by J. Murphy-O'Connor, "The Essenes and their History," *RB* 81 (1974): 235, who holds that the followers of the Man of the Lie in CD XX,14–15 were "non-Qumran Essenes" who refused to follow the Teacher to the wilderness. Murphy-O'Connor was followed by P. R. Davies, "Qumran Beginnings," in his *Behind the Essenes. History and Ideology in the Dead Sea Scrolls* (BJS 94; Atlanta: Scholars Press, 1987), 15–31, who takes the laws of the Damascus Document to reflect the parent Essene movement from which the Qumran community allegedly seceded. This alleged split is still reflected in G. Boccaccini, *Beyond the Essene Hypothesis. The Parting of the Ways between Qumran and Enochic Judaism* (Grand Rapids: Eerdmans, 1998), 119–62, who attributes the authorship of the Damascus Document to "the Enochic party" and goes on to speak of a schism between Qumran and Enochic Judaism." Boccaccini, however, holds that the parent movement was never completely condemned (p. 127). In fact there is no reason to regard the followers of the Man of the Lie as Essenes at all, or to speak of a schism between the communities reflected in the Damascus Document and in the Community Rule. See further my comments in "The Origin of the Qumran Community," in *Seers, Sibyls and Sages* (Leiden: Brill, 1997), 253–8.

manuscripts.[37] But if all these manuscripts relate to a single movement, it must have been a movement that allowed for a range of different forms of community: the camps of married people attested in CD, the "cell groups" of ten or more that we find in the Community Rule without reference to women and children, and the elite "council of holiness" who withdrew to the desert to walk in perfection of the way.

THE RULE OF THE CONGREGATION (1QSa)

A further issue in the study of forms of community in the Scrolls concerns the Rule of the Congregation, 1QSa, and its relation to the Community Rule and Damascus Rule. This short rule book is introduced as "the rule for all the congregation of Israel at the end of days." Accordingly, it is usually taken as a rule for a future, messianic age. Hartmut Stegemann, however, has argued that the authors of the sectarian scrolls believed they were living in "the end of days" and that this was not a rule for a future time but rather "an early rule-book for the Essenes."[38] The recent publication of other manuscripts of the Rule of the Congregation, in cryptic script, by Stephen Pfann, supports an early date for this document.[39] Its place in the development of the Qumran rule books, however, remains controversial.

Stegemann's suggestion that it was a rule for the present rather than for the future, appeals to the thorough study of the phrase aḥarît hayyamîm by Annette Steudel.[40] Steudel shows that the phrase can refer to events that are already past and to time continuing in the present, but she adds: "In addition to all previous implications,

---

[37] Note especially the overlaps in the penal code in 1QS VII and 4Q266 10 ii (= 4QD^a), and the complex relation of 4Q265 to both rules. C. Hempel, *The Laws of the Damascus Document: Sources, Tradition and Redaction* (Leiden: Brill, 1998) argues that the legal material in the Damascus Rule was revised so that it would be more closely aligned with the Rule of the Community.

[38] Stegemann, "Some Remarks to 1QSa," 488. In *The Library of Qumran*, 113, he calls it "The Essenes' Oldest Congregational Rule." His main argument for the antiquity of this Rule is that, on his interpretation, it does not envision a priestly messiah.

[39] S. J. Pfann, "Cryptic Texts," in *Qumran Cave 4.XXVI* (*DJD* XXXVI; Oxford: Clarendon, 2000), 515–74 (= 4Q249 a–i). Pfann dates these manuscripts to the second century B.C.E. (ibid., 522–3) and argues that the lack of any copies of the Community Rule and the Damascus Covenant in cryptic script argues for the priority of the Rule of the Congregation.

[40] A. Steudel, "'The End of Days' in the Qumran Texts," *RevQ* 62 (1993): 225–45.

there are also events which are expected *within the aḥarît hayyāmîm as lying in the future.* First of all, this concerns the coming of the messiahs, who are still awaited . . ."[41] Stegemann's contention that the Rule refers to the present time of the author is disproven by the explicit references to the messiah in 1QSa II,11–22. In no other text from Qumran is the messiah said to be actually present. This is a rule for a future age, that has not yet come to pass. In part, Stegemann is misled by his presuppositions of what a messianic age must entail. 1QSa addresses problems presented by the presence of people with various blemishes and impurities. But the messianic age is not the new creation. It is an intermediate era, which is utopian in some respects, but in which the conditions of the old order still obtain.[42]

There are also problems with Stegemann's claim that 1QSa is "the Essenes' oldest congregational rule." According to this rule, the congregation is to be governed by the regulation of the sons of Zadok, whose authority is also asserted in 1QS V. In some of the manuscripts of the Community Rule from Cave 4, however, the references to the sons of Zadok are missing. Geza Vermes and Sarianna Metso have argued convincingly that the shorter texts preserve the older form of the Community Rule, despite the fact that 1QS seems to be older palaeographically.[43] In the words of Metso: "A comparison between the manuscripts 1QS and 4QS[b,d] reveals a process of redaction in 1QS, the purpose of which was to provide a Scriptural legitimation for the regulations of the community and to reinforce the community's self-understanding."[44] The references to the sons of Zadok must be seen in the context of other scriptural allusions in 1QS that are lacking in the shorter form of the text. It is easier to understand why these allusions would have been added than to suppose that they were systematically eliminated in some manuscripts.[45]

---

[41] Ibid., 230.

[42] See my essay, "He Shall Not Judge by what His Eyes See": Messianic Authority in the Dead Sea Scrolls," *DSD* 2 (1995): 145–64. The priestly messiah is simply the High Priest of the messianic age. Stegemann's claim that 1QSa does not envision a priestly messiah would require the odd situation of a messianic age without a High Priest.

[43] G. Vermes, "Qumran Corner. Preliminary Remarks on Unpublished Fragments of the Commuity Rule from Qumran Cave 4," *JJS* 42 (1991): 250–55; S. Metso, *The Textual Development of the Qumran Community Rule* (Leiden: Brill, 1997), 105; cf. Metso, "In Search of the Sitz im Leben of the Community Rule," In *The Provo International Conference on the Dead Sea Scrolls* (eds. D. W. Parry and E. C. Ulrich; Leiden: Brill, 1999), 306–15.

[44] Metso, *The Textual Development*, 105.

[45] As proposed by P. S. Alexander, "The Redaction History of Serekh Ha-Yaḥad: A Proposal," *RevQ* 17 (1996): 437–56.

But the references to the Sons of Zadok in 1QSa are plausibly assigned to the same redactional stage as those in 1QS.[46] If this is correct, the shorter form of the Community Rule found in 4QS[b,d] is likely to be older than 1QSa. Moreover, the statement that the sons of Zadok atone for the land, in 1QSa I,3 echoes 1QS VIII,10. The allusions to the yaḥad in 1QSa are scarcely intelligible without prior acquaintance with some form of the Community Rule.

Charlotte Hempel has offered a more sophisticated variant of Stegemann's proposal. The Rule of the Congregation is messianic in its present form, but it includes an early nucleus that was intended as the rule for a community in the present, which should be associated with the community behind the Laws of the Damascus Document, which she takes to go back to "the Essene parent movement of the Qumran community."[47] The most obvious point of affinity is that both 1QSa and the Damascus Rule presuppose family life and provide for women and children. Other points of affinity adduced by Hempel include the use of "all Israel" terminology, the term "congregation" (ʿēdāh), which occurs seen times in CD, reference to the book of Hagu (1QSa I,7; CD X,6; XIII,2), and the exclusion of those who suffer from disabilities from the congregation.

That there is some relationship between 1QSa and the Damascus texts cannot be doubted, but there is also an important link between 1QSa and the Community Rule, which Hempel only acknowledges in a footnote.[48] This is the mention of "the council of the community" (ʿaṣat hayyaḥad) three times in 1QSa I,6–II,11), as well as a variant, "the council of holiness," which is found once. This terminology is familiar from the Community Rule, and is not found at all in the fragments of the Damascus Rule at Qumran, and is only reflected in Ms. B of CD. The "council of the community" is not co-terminous with the congregation. Those summoned to it are "the wi[se men] of the congregation, the learned and the intelligent, men whose way is perfect and men of ability," together with the chiefs and officials (1QSa I,28–29; trans. Vermes). These, we are told, are "the men of renown, the members of the assembly summoned to the council of the community in Israel before the sons of Zadok the priests" (1QSa II,2). It is from their assembly (1QSa II,4: qehal ʾēleh: the assembly of these)[49] that those smitten with any human uncleanness

---

[46] Hempel, "The Early Essene Nucleus," 257–9.
[47] Ibid., 253–69.
[48] Hempel, "The Early Essene Nucleus," 267, n. 31.
[49] So correctly García Martínez. Vermes translates "the assembly of God."

are excluded: "none of these shall come to hold office among the congregation of the men of renown, for the angels of holiness are [with] their [congregation]" (1QSa II,8–9). It is with this group that the messiah shall sit and eat (II,11). The rule for the assembly in the presence of the messiah in the latter part of column 2 applies whenever there is a quorum of ten, and the messiah is present. The reference is not to a single "messianic banquet," but neither is it to any gathering of ten Israelites.

In short, 1QSa, like the Damscus Rule and the Community Rule, sets some people aside as more holy than others. This elite group is called "the council of the community," which is the name of the sect in the Community Rule. The usual assumption that this rule is intended for all Israel at a future time[50] is quite correct, but fully half of the document relates to the special role that "the council of the community" retains in "the end of days." The concern of the text for "all Israel" must be seen in context. The author hoped for a time when all Israel would live "according to the law of the sons of Zadok the Priests and of the men of their covenant who have turned aside [from the] way of the people, the men of his council who keep his covenant in the midst of iniquity, offering expiation [for the land]" (1QSa I,2–3). We should expect, then, that the rules for all Israel in the future would to a great degree correspond with the rules of the new covenant in the present, at least for those members who married and had children, as envisioned in the Damascus Rule.[51] The affinities between the Rule of the Congregation and the Damascus Rule, however, must be balanced by an appreciation of the role in 1QSa of "the council of the community." The relation of this text to both the Damascus and the Community rules shows again the difficulty, if not the impossibility, of assigning these rules to different movements.

---

[50] As expounded by, e.g., L. H. Schiffman, *The Eschatological Community of the Dead Sea Scrolls* (Atlanta: Society of Biblical Literature, 1989).

[51] See further my essay "The Construction of Israel in the Sectarian Rule Books," in *Judaism in Late Antiquity. Part 5. Volume 1. The Judaism of Qumran: A Systemic Reading of the Dead Sea Scrolls* (eds. A. J. Avery-Peck, J. Neusner and B. Chilton; Leiden: Brill, 2001), 25–42.

Conclusion

It is now widely recognized that the long-regnant view of "the Qumran community" as a quasi-monastic community, corresponding to the celibate Essenes of Philo and Josephus, does not do justice to the full range of forms of community that we find in the Scrolls. The Damascus Rule provides for "camps" whose members marry and have children, but also for "men of perfect holiness," with whom these are contrasted. The Community Rule describes a yaḥad, which is not a single settlement but an umbrella "union" whose members could meet in groups of ten or more, without reference to women or children. While these groups share many organizational features of Hellenistic voluntary associations, they are distinguished by the degree of their separation from outsiders, by their common possessions, and by the extent of their common life, which required, at least, that they spend all their evenings in community. But the Community Rule also describes an elite group, set apart within the yaḥad, which goes into the wilderness to prepare the way of the Lord. In virtue of its physical separation, this group must be assumed to have had a more intensely communal life and to approximate to the "quasi-monastic" model. Finally, the Rule of the Congregation looks to a time when all Israel will follow the regulations of the sect, but still assigns special authority and status to "the council of the community" in the future age.

The identity of all or any of these groups with the Essenes lies beyond the scope of this essay. Suffice it to say that when due account is taken of the diversity within the celibate and marrying Essenes as described by Josephus, the Essene hypothesis remains by far the most plausible explanation of the data, even though it also remains an hypothesis, that must continue to be tested against the data of the Scrolls.

4Q460/4Q350 AND TAMPERING WITH QUMRAN TEXTS IN ANTIQUITY?*

HANNAH COTTON AND ERIK LARSON

INTRODUCTION

The great euphoria caused by the sensational discoveries in the mid-20th century of ancient manuscripts in the caves of Qumran has not faded to this day. Moreover, it has often eclipsed, or altogether banished from mind, the information we have that centuries earlier caves in the area had already been the source of similar finds. The earliest reference comes from Origen who mentions a discovery of manuscripts in the first quarter or so of the third century. Although transmitted by Eusebius in his account of the antecedents of Origen's *Hexapla*, it is likely to be a quotation from Origen himself informing his readers that the sixth ms. tradition for his redaction was found in an earthen jar together with other books in Hebrew and Greek near Jericho at the time of Antoninus, the son of Severus, i.e. Caracalla, 212–217.[1] About 600 years later, another cache of manuscripts was found also near Jericho. The Nestorian Patriarch Timothy I (780–823) recounts in a letter to Sergius, the Metropolitan of Elam, the discovery of 'the Books of the Old (Testament) and others in Hebrew script' in the neighbourhood of Jericho in terms which recall the finding of the Dead Sea Scrolls in 1946/47. According to Timothy, the dog of a Bedouin shepherd entered a cave while in pursuit of an animal. Following his dog, the Bedouin found scrolls

---

* It is in the nature of scholarship that previous work prepares the ground for further study by enabling one to see more clearly a given field of inquiry. In recognition of this, the present article attempts to investigate further some texts upon which both the authors and the honorand of this Festschrift have recently written. It is a pleasure to dedicate it to one who has done so much to advance the study of the ancient Jewish texts from the Judean Desert.

[1] *Hex* 6.16: ϛ' ἔκδοσις εὑρεθεῖσα μετὰ καὶ ἄλλων βιβλίων ἑβραικῶν καὶ ἑλληνικῶν ἔν τινι πίθῳ περὶ τὴν Ἰεριχώ ἐν χρόνοις τῆς βασιλείας Ἀντωνίνου τοῦ υἱοῦ Σευήρης. For the origin of this information see P. Nautin, *Origène. Sa vie et son ouvre* (Paris, 1977), 309–11, 343–4, with reference to earlier literature.

written in Hebrew, some biblical and some non-biblical, including 'more than two hundred psalms of David.'[2] It has been suggested that the scrolls mentioned by Timothy became known to a Karaite group known as the 'Cave Sect' (al-Maghariyya), whose name, we are told, derived from the fact that its doctrines were based on scrolls found in a cave (magâr).[3] And indeed there are striking similarities between Karaite doctrines and some doctrines now known from Qumran writings.[4]

In this article, we suggest that the opisthograph 4Q460/4Q350 provides further evidence for the Qumran Caves being accessed after the scrolls were originally deposited. This, however, happened in the late first or early second century—long before the discoveries of 212–217 c.e. and ca. 800 c.e. just mentioned.

DESCRIPTION OF 4Q460 AND 4Q350

The vast majority of the texts from Qumran contain writing on one side of the skin or papyrus only. The exceptions to this are sixteen in number.[5] These manuscripts are not written in codex form, in which case the *verso* would contain the same work as the *recto*, but are properly termed opisthographs in that the writings on *recto* and *verso* are completely independent. Within this small group, 4Q460/4Q350

---

[2] O. Braun, "Ein Brief des Katholikos Timotheos I über biblische Studien des 9 Jahrhunderts," *OrChr* 1 (1901) 299–313. For an English translation, see S. P. Brock, *A Brief Outline of Syriac Literature* (1997), 245–50.

[3] R. de Vaux, "A propos des manuscrits de la Mer Morte," *RB* 57 (1950): 417–29.

[4] Cf. the discussion in H. H. Rowley, *The Zadokite Fragments and the Dead Sea Scrolls* (Oxford, 1952), 22–30; P. Kahle, *The Cairo Geniza*[2] (New York, 1959), 16–28, and A. Paul, *Ecrits de Qumran et Sectes Juives aux Premières Siècles de l'Islam* (Paris, 1969), 94–95, 137–138. For a more recent discussion favoring the same conclusion, see F. Astren, "Karaites," in *Encyclopedia of the Dead Sea Scrolls* (ed. L. H. Schiffman and J. C. VanderKam; Oxford, 2000), 464. Although most of the discussion centers on the Damascus Document, Kahle suggested that Ben Sira and Aramaic Levi, both found in the Genizah, likewise came into the possession of the Karaites through this same find.

[5] For a convenient table of these, cf. M. Wise, "Accidents and Accidence: A Scribal View of Linguistic Dating of the Aramaic Scrolls from Qumran," in *Thunder in Gemini and Other Essays on the History, Language and Literature of Second Temple Palestine* (JSPSS 15; Sheffield, 1994), 133. In addition to these, there are five scrolls that have short titles on the *verso* describing the contents of the *recto*, 1QS, 4QGen[h] (4Q8c), 4QS[c] (4Q249), 4Q257, and 4Q504, but these do not fall into the category of opisthographs discussed here.

is unique in that one side contains a literary work written in Hebrew and the other a documentary text written in Greek.[6]

4Q460 consists of ten fragments.[7] The fragments offer a mixture of narrative material written in the third person combined with prayers and admonitions written in the first and second persons. In its present state of preservation it is difficult to tell whether this is some kind of historical work, perhaps rewritten Bible, with the narrative element providing the framework to situate and introduce the prayers, or whether the whole composition is a collection of prayers with some historical elements embedded within them. On balance, the former seems a little more likely because of the similarities with other Dead Sea Scrolls texts described below.

The largest portions of the text are preserved on frags. 7–9. Fragment 7 consists of twelve lines, the first five of which contain a narrative written in the third person and referring to someone being named (line 4: 'and he called his name . . .') and then apparently stating that 'Judah [was not] to be His priest' (line 5). This narrative then gives way to an exhortation in lines 6–12 that encourages some individual, probably mentioned in the previous narrative but now missing, not to fear in a time of great affliction and distress. Fragment 8 contains further admonition, the first four lines being clearly based on Jer 9:23–24 (cf. also LXX 1 Sam 2:10): 'Let not the strong man boast in his strength,' but in an expanded form and written in the plural rather than the singular. The next lines then contrast the powerlessness and helplessness of mankind with the power of God who is 'mighty to help us' (line 6). Fragment 9 is the largest piece of all holding parts of two columns, the first of which preserves the greatest amount of material. This column consists of 12 lines intentionally divided into two sections as clearly indicated by a *vacat* at the end of line 6. The first section (lines 1–6) is written in the first person singular and contains an address to God in which the speaker makes the remarkable appeal to God as 'my Father and my Lord.' (line 6). The next six lines are a rebuke, addressed to Ephraim and Israel in the second person plural, the gist of which is that God will judge them for abandoning Him.

---

[6] The uniquenes of 4Q460/4Q350 has already been pointed out by E. Tov in "The Nature of the Greek Texts from the Judean Desert," *NovT* 43 (2001): 6–9.

[7] Ed. E. Larson, "4Q460: Narrative Work and Prayer," in *Miscellanea, Part 1: Qumran Cave 4.XXVI (DJD XXXVI;* Oxford, 2000), 369–86.

Besides the clear parallel with the book of Jeremiah and a few similarities with other Biblical phrases, 4Q460 shows clear affinities in phraseology with 4Q378–379, Apocryphon of Joshua, and 4Q371–373/2Q22, Apocryphon of Joseph. The most important of these are as follows: 4Q460 9 i 3 reads למהומה בישראל ולשערוריה באפרים which is similar to 4Q379 22 ii 13 רשעה נדלה בישראל ולשערוריה באפרים and 4Q460 9 i 5–6 כיא לוא עזבתה לעבדכה [ ] אבי ואדוני which resembles 3Q372 1 16 אבי ואלהי אל תעזבני ביד הגוים. In addition, both apocryphons have the same mixture of narrative and admonition. Still, the similarities are not sufficient in nature to warrant concluding that these are all copies of a single work.

4Q350[8] is written on the *verso* of frg. 9 of 4Q460. It is a ledger which ticks off quantities of cereals. It contains several abbreviations found in similar documents in Greek from Wadi Murabba'at, Naḥal Ṣe'elim, and Naḥal Mishmar—all of them dated palaeographically, and archaeologically in the case of the last two sites, to the first part of the second century C.E. However, the abbreviation for πυροῦ is not the figure 4, as in the documents from Wadi Murabba'at, Naḥal Ṣe'elim, and Naḥal Mishmar,[9] but rather that common in Egyptian papyri, namely ꝛ. Nevertheless, as in the documents mentioned, quantities of *se'ah* are underlined, and the symbol for *kab* (one sixth of a *se'ah*), ^, above the numeral, occurs in line 9. The diagonal strokes beside the quantities of *se'ah* appear to be a type of check mark (√) inserted as the scribe ticked off items he had checked.

1	*traces*		
2	]oρ	γ	\
3	]	δ	\
4	].	γ	\
5	].	ι̣	\
6	].	δ̲	\
7	]ꝛ	δ	
8	].βω ꝛ	ς̲	
9	].πεπ	κ̂λ	\
10	]*traces*	.ο̣	∸
11	]α..υ̲	ꝛ̲	ς̲	*traces*
12	]α.[		

[8] Ed. H. M. Cotton, "4Q350: Account," in *Miscellanea, Part I. Qumran Cave 4.XXVI* (*DJD* XXXVI; Oxford, 2000), 294–5.
[9] Mur 89–107, ed. P. Benoit in P. Benoit, J. T. Milik et R. de Vaux, *Les Grottes*

The presence of documentary material among the finds said to come from Qumran has interesting implications for the question of the relationship between the community or group living on the site of Qumran and the scrolls discovered in the caves.[10] This issue is only tangential to the present discussion.[11] True, our text contains a documentary text on its *verso*, but, as we shall see, there can be no doubt that the *verso* could not have been written by the person(s) who had written or stored away the text written on its *recto*. In other words, an outsider must have used the parchment on which 4Q460 was written for writing 4Q350. Thus our documents can perhaps be used to shed some light on the fate of the texts hidden in the caves of Qumran in antiquity; they even constitute proof for the suggestion made above that the texts were already accessed in antiquity. But first it needs to be proved that our texts, though allegedly coming from Cave 4, do indeed come from there, since they belong to a group of texts whose provenance from Cave 4 and from Qumran as a whole has recently been impugned.[12]

THE QUESTION OF PROVENANCE

In the introduction to her edition of 4Q342–360, Ada Yardeni has offered grounds for thinking that some of the documentary texts included in this group said to come from Cave 4 actually come from Naḥal Ḥever.[13] More specifically she claims that 4Q437 can be physically joined with P.Hever 32, and that the names in 4Q359 and P.Hever 7 suggest a common provenance for both. In addition, recent C–14 analysis of 4Q342 and 4Q344 indicates that these two texts date from the late first to the early second century C.E.—far too late for them to have been written at Qumran. This impression is further

---

de Murabba'at (*DJD* II; Oxford, 1961), 212–5; 1 Mish 2, 34Se 5, ed. H. M. Cotton in *Miscellaneous Texts from the Judaean Desert* (*DJD* XXXVIII; Oxford, 2000), 204, 227.

[10] On this controversial issue see the balanced account by Magen Broshi in "Qumran: Archaeology," *Encyclopedia of the Dead Sea Scrolls*, 737–9.

[11] See review by Ph. Callaway in *The Qumran Chronicle* 8 (1998): 113–9 of H. M. Cotton and A. Yardeni, *Aramaic, Hebrew and Greek Texts from Naḥal Ḥever and Other Sites with an Appendix Containing Alleged Qumran Texts* (*The Seiyâl Collection* II. *DJD* XXVII; Oxford, 1997). The documents published in this edition are designated P.Hever.

[12] Until then their Qumran provenance was accepted without reservations; see e.g. J. C. VanderKam, *The Dead Sea Scrolls Today* (Michigan, 1994), 69.

[13] "Introduction to the 'Qumran Cave 4' Documentary Texts," *DJD* XXVII, 283–4.

strengthened by the fact that the cursive handwriting found in
many of the texts 4Q342–348, 4Q351–354, and 4Q356–361 is unlike
anything found at Qumran. Even the documentary nature of the
lot—so much in contrast with the rest of the material found in
Qumran—suggests, albeit circularly, a different provenance. If this
line of reasoning is followed, the documentary nature of 4Q350, the
fact that it is written in Greek and its similarity to documentary texts
from Wadi Murabbaʿat, Naḥal Ṣeʾelim and Naḥal Mishmar—all of
which can be dated palaeographically to the late first and second
centuries C.E. (see above)—could easily be used to question 4Q460/
4Q350's Qumran provenance.

However, the sweeping assignation of the provenance of texts
alleged to be from Qumran to Naḥal Ḥever must be now modified,
and each document must be examined on its own. The early 4Q343
(Nabataean) and 4Q345 (Hebrew?) are not very likely to come from
Naḥal Ḥever where occupation goes back to the second Jewish revolt
but not to an earlier period.[14] 4Q348, dated by the high priest,
Joseph son of Camydus, to 46 or 47, is also too early for Naḥal
Ḥever.[15] The use of Hebrew in documentary material may well point
to priestly circles and to Qumran.[16]

As regards 4Q350/4Q460, a fairly strong case can be made for
associating the manuscript with the caves of Qumran. It is well
known that during the excavation of the settlement at Qumran, no
one paid much attention to the caves in the marl terrace overlook-
ing the wadi. No one, that is, until the archaeologists left and the
Bedouin returned. In September of 1952 they found Cave 4. When
de Vaux got wind of this he returned to the site, which he excavated from September 22–29, recovering numerous fragments that
the Bedouin had not yet removed.[17] These excavated fragments were
photographed as a group and may be found in the PAM series numbered 40.962–985. As S. Pfann notes, 'Of the approximately 600
fragmentary manuscripts which have been identified as having come
from Cave 4, fragments of about one-fourth of these were identified

---

[14] See Cotton, *ZPE* 125 (1997): 223–4 and H. Eshel, *JJS* 52 (2001): 132–5; idem,
Leshonenu, 63 (2001): 43–52 passim. The excavations of 1999 and 2000 in the Cave
of Letters have not so far changed this picture.
[15] See Eshel, loc. cit.
[16] So Eshel in *JJS*, 134 and n. 15.
[17] R. de Vaux, *Archaeology and the Dead Sea Scrolls. The Schweich Lectures of the British
Academy 1959* (Oxford, 1973), 52.

among those found in the excavation.'[18] Examination of the relevant photos reveals that two fragments belonging to 4Q460 were found in the excavation, frg. 2 appearing on PAM 40.979 and frg. 3 on PAM 40.978. Unfortunately, however, as noted in the original publication of the manuscript, the small size of frags. 2 and 3 and the paucity of the letter forms they contain make it difficult to know for sure whether they actually come from the same manuscript as the larger fragments.

However, if the physical remains just mentioned deny us absolute certainty as to the Qumran provenance of 4Q460/4Q350, there may still be something about the contents and style of writing of 4Q460 which points convincingly to Qumran.

Emanuel Tov has raised the possibility that 4Q460 may be a sectarian composition but that 'in any event, its orthography and morphology suggest that it was copied (not necessarily authored) by a sectarian scribe.'[19] As for authorship by the Dead Sea Scrolls group, one can only say that there does not seem to be any of the distinctive terminology or ideology that would necessitate this conclusion. Moreover, the use of the Tetragrammaton in frg. 9 i 10 may militate against it since the Qumranites seem to have avoided its use.[20] What about the orthography of the text? Does it in fact point incontrovertibly to Qumran, or, more precisely to what Tov designates a Qumran Scribal School?[21]

For some years now Emanuel Tov has developed the theory of a Qumran Scribal School 'whose characteristics are visible in peculiarities in orthography, morphology, and some scribal features.'[22]

---

[18] S. Pfann, "Sites in the Judean Desert Where Texts Have Been Found," *The Dead Sea Scrolls on Microfiche: Companion Volume* (ed. E. Tov with the collaboration of S. J. Pfann; Leiden, 1993), 112.

[19] E. Tov, "The Nature of the Greek Texts," *Novum Testamentum* 43 (2001): 7.

[20] Cf. E. Larson, "4Q460: Narrative Work and Prayer," 374; in addition to the literature cited there see D. W. Parry, "Notes on Divine Name Avoidance in Scriptural Units of the Legal Texts of Qumran," in *Legal Texts and Legal Issues: Proceedings of the Second Meeting of the International Organization for Qumran Studies Published in Honour of Joseph M. Baumgarten* (eds. M. Bernstein, F. García-Martínez, and J. Kampen; STDJ 23, Leiden, 1997), 437–49.

[21] E. Tov, "The Orthography and Language of the Hebrew Scrolls Found at Qumran and the Origin of These Scrolls," *Textus* 13 (1986): 31–57; idem, "Hebrew Biblical Manuscripts from the Judaean Desert: Their Contribution to Textual Criticism," *JJS* 39 (1988): 5–37; the citation is from his "Further Evidence for the Existence of a Qumran Scribal School," *The Dead Sea Scrolls Fifty Years After Their Discovery* (ed. L. H. Schiffman, E. Tov, and J. VanderKam; Jerusalem, 2000), 199–216.

[22] "Further Evidence for the Existence of a Qumran Scribal School," 199.

Such features are present in 4Q460 in the spelling כיא, the second person pronominal suffix ‑כה, and the second person perfect verb ending with ‑תה. However, we would urge caution here since it is now apparent that some of these features have turned up in manuscripts found in Masada and Wadi Murabbaʿat as well. Thus, the copy of the Songs of the Sabbath Sacrifice found at Masada uses the form כיא (MasShirShabb i 6) that Tov lists as a feature of the Qumran Scribal School.[23] In the past, the discovery of a text already known from Qumran elsewhere led one immediately to assume a Qumran provenance. In the case of MasShirShabb it was suggested that it was brought to Masada after 68 C.E. by sectarian refugees from Qumran.[24] But Carol Newsom has rightly questioned the necessity for such a hypothesis. In what is in many ways a groundbreaking study, she enumerates various criteria for determining whether a given work was authored by the Dead Sea Scrolls group.[25] Applying these to Songs of the Sabbath Sacrifice, she concludes that there is no compelling argument for sectarian authorship. She reasons that the presence of the work at both Qumran and Masada may indicate nothing more than that it was popular with various Jewish groups in the Second Temple period. We have evidence of such popularity in the case of works like Enoch, Jubilees and Ben Sira.

But we can go further and question the necessity of an association between the so-called sectarian orthography and a Qumran provenance. The presence of כיא in the Masada manuscript may imply that such spellings were not limited to manuscripts found at Qumran. Or, to put the matter differently: Tov's 'Qumran Scribal

---

[23] See now C. Newman and Y. Yadin, "1039–200 Songs of the Sabbath Sacrifice (MasShirShabb)" in *Masada* VI (Jerusalem, 1999), 120–35.

[24] Y. Yadin, "The Excavation of Masada—1963/4. Preliminary Report," *IEJ* 15 (1965): 105. It is accepted by Tov in "Hebrew Biblical Manuscripts from the Judaean Desert," 24, n. 80; endorsed by H. M. Cotton and J. J. Price in "Who Conquered Masada in 66 C.E., and Who Lived There until the Fortress Fell?," *Zion* 55 (1990): 454 (Hebrew).

Likewise the presence of the long form of the pronoun הואה, commonly understood as a Qumran form, in the small fragment Mas1n (1063–1747) led Sh. Talmon to suggest that 'the fragment stems from a Covenanters' work,' *Masada* VI, 134, although he is more cautious about this in the title which he gives to it: "Unidentified Qumran-Type Fragment," ibid. 133.

[25] C. Newsom, "Sectually Explicit Literature from Qumran," *The Hebrew Bible and its Interpreters* (ed. W. H. Propp, B. Halpern, and D. N. Freedman; Winona Lake, 1990), 167–87, and more briefly and recently "Songs of the Sabbath Sacrifice," *Encyclopedia of the Dead Sea Scrolls*, 887.

School' may not be represented only in manuscripts found in Qumran itself. In fact, in his own study of Qumran orthography, Tov has noted parallels to the spellings רוש and לוא in two documents from Wadi Murabbaʿat (Mur 42 and Mur 47 respectively).[26]

True, if we dissociate 'the scribal school' from Qumran, the orthographic features which turn up in 4Q460 do no more than suggest a Qumran provenance, but cannot prove it. Nevertheless, when they are taken in conjunction with the physical remains discussed above, we believe that the likelihood that 4Q460/4Q350 does come from Cave 4 in Qumran is considerable.

How to account for the presence of 4Q350 on the verso of 4Q460?

Assuming then, as we probably should, that 4Q460/4Q350 was copied or deposited where it was found, namely in Qumran, the presence of the documentary 4Q350 on the *verso* of frg. 9 of 4Q460 remains to be accounted for. The reuse of the *verso* of a manuscript containing a sacred text for a profane purpose is not without parallel. P.Rylands 458, one of the earliest copies of the Septuagint, is dated palaeographically to the first half of the second century B.C.E. By the end of the second century it was reused to hold an account of expenditures,[27] and not more than a century later, the manuscript was torn up and used once again, this time as cartonnage in the wrappings of a mummy! The fragments were found wadded together with an assortment of other texts and covered with plaster.[28] We

---

[26] "Hebrew Biblical Manuscripts from the Judaean Desert," p. 24, n. 80.

E. Chazon has arrived at the same conclusion by a different route. She points out that 4QPs[a], 4QQoh[m], and 4Q504 all display the full style of orthography and language mentioned by Tov and yet are dated on palaeographic grounds to the middle of the second century B.C.E., a time earlier than the founding of the settlement at Qumran. Thus, the spellings under discussion are likely to have developed in pre-Qumranic times, later to be adopted by the group's scribes. Their presence in a given manuscript 'opens the possibility of sectarian origin,' but does not prove it. Cf. "Is *Divrei Ha-meʾorot* a Sectarian Prayer?" in *The Dead Sea Scrolls: Forty Years of Research*, ed. D. Dimant and U. Rappaport; Leiden, 1992), 7.

[27] Cf. C. H. Roberts, *Two Biblical Papyri in the John Rylands Library, Manchester* (Manchester, 1936), 16–17, 21–22.

[28] The practice of using papyri for mummification is known from the third century B.C.E. until the time of Augustus, but seldom thereafter, which would establish a likely terminus *ante quem* for the final use of the fragments. Cf. E. G. Turner, *Greek Papyri: An Introduction* (Oxford, 1980), 31.

may safely exclude the possibility that 4Q350, a ledger in Greek listing quantities of cereal, was penned by those who authored, copied,
or deposited 4Q460 in Qumran. And not merely on account of the
later date of 4Q350, suggested by its resemblance to similar documents from Wadi Murabba'at, Naḥal Mishmar and Naḥal Ṣe'elim
(see above); it is simply inconceivable that a Jew would reuse for a
profane purpose a scroll that contained the Tetragrammaton (frg. 9
i 10). Thus, if a Qumran provenance is accepted, 4Q460/4Q350
becomes evidence of a later occupation of the Qumran caves in the
wake of the destruction of the settlement in 68 c.e.

This later occupant of Qumran used the *verso* of frg. 9 of 4Q460
to make a list of items stored at the place. After the list was written and the items were checked off, it was apparently of no further
use and was allowed to remain on the floor of the cave together
with the hundreds of other texts that were not reused. Indeed, the
manuscript was re-rolled and left on the cave floor (or, less likely,
curled up on its own after being thrown down). There are clear indications that frags. 7–9 (the largest surviving fragments) lay on top
of each other in the cave.[29] This can be seen in the shape of the
lower right side frg. 7 which exactly matches the shape formed by
the transition between the darker and lighter areas of frg. 8, which
indicates that frg. 7 lay on top of frg. 8. Also, the discoloration at
the bottom of frg. 9 is similar to that of the right side of frg. 8,
again indicating that frgs. 7 and 8 lay on top of frg. 9. Apparently
4Q350 was of ephemeral importance, unlike a deed of sale or a
contract of marriage or divorce that would have been kept by its
owner for a longer period of time.

The indifference, not to say insouciance, displayed in the penning
of an ephemeral list in Greek on the back of a sacred text in Hebrew
points to non-Jewish occupants of the site; perhaps an auxiliary unit[30]
of the Roman army which occupied Qumran after its destruction in
68 c.e.[31]

---

[29] Cf. Larson, *DJD* XXXVI, 371–72.
[30] This would explain the use of Greek rather than Latin, see H. M. Cotton and
J. Geiger, *Masada* II: *The Latin and Greek Documents* (Jerusalem, 1989), 11–18.
[31] On the post-revolt period in Qumran see Broshi, *Encyclopedia of the Dead Sea
Scrolls*, 737.

FURTHER EVIDENCE FOR A SUBSEQUENT ACTIVITY IN CAVE 4?

We have argued here that 4Q460/4Q350 provides important evidence for believing that the Qumran caves were accessed fairly soon after the scrolls were deposited in Cave 4. Is there any further evidence that might support this suggestion?

One piece of evidence which could be interpreted in such a way as to support this claim, and indeed has been so interpreted in the past, is the presence of many tears in the fragments found at Qumran. In fact frg. 9 of 4Q460/4Q355 is actually two fragments, having suffered an oblique tear. Some early investigators suggested that many of the scrolls were deliberately torn up in antiquity, probably by Roman soldiers. Among those who raised this possibility were H. del Medico, Roland de Vaux, and John Allegro.

Del Medico claimed that the scrolls had been deliberately burnt or torn up, and that the Qumran caves were used as a genizah and the scrolls were deposited there in the generation after the destruction of the Temple because they were viewed as being heretical.[32] De Vaux himself was inclined to the idea that 'apart from the damage caused by natural agents and animals' the fragments found in Cave 4 had suffered at human hands in antiquity:

> It may be added that . . . a number of these fragments show signs of having been torn by human hands. These mutilations, together with the fact that fragments from the same manuscripts had been scattered about, show that the cave had been pillaged in ancient times, and before the deposit of marl had invaded the cave and sealed them off. In view of the closeness of Cave 4 to the ruins of Qumran there can hardly be any doubt that the depredation here is to be ascribed to the Roman soldiers who occupied the ruins.[33]

This view was also held by J. Allegro: 'I am myself inclined to believe that the Fourth Cave documents at least were torn up in antiquity, perhaps before being placed in the chamber.'[34] However, this sort of explanation has been used not only at Qumran to explain the deterioration of ancient manuscripts. Indeed, Shemaryahu Talmon follows a similar line of thought to account for the small size and straight

---

[32] H. del Medico, "L'état des manuscrits de Qumran I," *Vetus Testamentum* 7 (1957): 127–38 and *L'énigme des manuscrits de la Mer Morte* (Paris, 1957), 47–63, 73–75.
[33] *Archaeology and the Dead Sea Scrolls*, 100 n. 3.
[34] *The Dead Sea Scrolls: A Reappraisal* (Harmondsworth, 1964), 56.

edges of the manuscript fragments found at the 'Locus of the Scrolls' on Masada, although he wavers between this explanation and one of natural deterioration.[35] Furthermore, we should note that the manuscripts of Deuteronomy and Ezekiel, found buried under the floor of the 'synagogue' on Masada, must have been put there at some point by the Jewish inhabitants of the site. Consequently, whatever tears and breaks exist in these two manuscripts—despite their similarity to those found in the 'Locus of the Scrolls'—cannot be attributed to the Romans. This whole argument seems to break down.

To return to Qumran, Allegro gives two examples of scrolls that he believes were subject to deliberate damage. These are 4QFlorilegium (4Q174) and 4QApocryphon of Moses B[b] (4Q376). With regard to 4QFlorilegium, however, the irregular edges of the individual pieces do not bear the appearance of intentional tearing, for in that case one would expect long and somewhat straight edges. But the only straight edges on these fragments are the result of breaks along the horizontal drylines. The Apocryphon of Moses too fails to convince. This time the fragment does have long straight edges at both top and bottom. However, the straight edge at the top is due to the fact that the the column begins there, whereas the bottom shows the typical repeated pattern of damage which can be attributed to natural processes of deterioration found also in other scrolls, e.g. 1QM, 1QH[a] 11QPs[a] and 11QT. That straight edges may be the result of the natural deterioration of the scrolls over time is indicated by frg. 23 of 4Q365 (RP[c]).[36] Today, this fragment actually consists of two pieces (like frg. 9 of 4Q460) divided by a tear slanting upward from right to left; this occurs near the top of a column as the column margin is visible. Plate 28 in *DJD* XIII provides two photos, one showing the fragment before the skin split apart (PAM 41 series) and the other after (PAM 43 series), indicating that the separation occurred after it had been deposited in the museum. The long straight break was not due to cutting, it simply follows the natural creases or 'fault lines' in the manuscript skin that developed as it lay in the cave.

---

[35] S. Talmon, "Preface," *Masada* VI (Jerusalem, 1999), 20; repeated more or less in "Masada: Written Material," *Encyclopedia of the Dead Sea Scrolls*, 521. Contrary to what he says, Josephus never alleges that 'Roman soldiers . . . vented their rage on the sacred writings of the Jewish defenders after the conquest of Masada.'

[36] Cf. E. Tov and S. White, "4Q365: Reworked Pentateuch[c]," *Parabiblical Texts, Part 1: Qumran Cave 4.VIII* (*DJD* XIII; Oxford, 1994), 255–318.

We must conclude that the evidence for human hands, presumably those of Roman soldiers occupying Qumran after 68 C.E., being responsible for the state of preservation of the fragments found in Cave 4 in Qumran, among them 4Q460/4Q350, is at best inconclusive. This in its turn leaves us with nothing more than the character of the Greek document 4Q350 as the only certain evidence for Roman hands tampering with the contents of the Cave, and for human access to the Cave soon after the destruction of the settlement in Qumran.

NOT ACCORDING TO RULE:
WOMEN, THE DEAD SEA SCROLLS AND QUMRAN*

Sidnie White Crawford

Until very recently, the juxtaposition of the words "women," "Dead Sea Scrolls" and "Qumran" in the same title would have seemed like an oxymoron. From the beginning of Dead Sea Scrolls research, the people who lived at Qumran and stored the manuscripts in the eleven surrounding caves were identified with the ancient Jewish sect of the Essenes.[1] This identification was based on the descriptions of the Essenes provided by the ancient writers Josephus, Philo and Pliny the Elder. Philo (*Apol.* 14) and Pliny (*Nat. Hist.* 5.17) are unequivocal in their description of the Essenes as an all-male, celibate group. Josephus also focuses his description of the Essenes on those members who shunned marriage and embraced continence (*J.W.* 2.120–21). Thus it was almost uniformly assumed that the Qumran site housed an all-male, celibate community. This assumption was aided by the fact that one of the first non-biblical scrolls to be published, the Community Rule or *Serekh ha-Yaḥad*, contains no references to women.[2] Further, the ruins of Qumran did not disclose a settlement organized around normal family life, and the graves excavated in the adjoining cemetery had a larger proportion of men than women and children.[3]

---

* It gives me great pleasure to dedicate this article to my colleague, mentor and friend Emanuel Tov. It was written during my tenure as a Research Associate in the Women's Studies in Religion Program at the Harvard Divinity School. I would like to thank the program's director, Ann Braude, and my fellow Research Associates for their collegial support and helpful comments. I would also like to thank Frank Moore Cross, John Strugnell, Eileen Schuller and Jodi Magness who took the time to read and comment on previous drafts; any mistakes remain my own. Finally, I owe thanks to Jodi Magness, Susan Sheridan, Victor Hurowitz and Gershon Brin for sharing their research with me prior to publication.

[1] The first scholar to do so was E. Sukenik in 1948; see N. Silberman, "Sukenik, Eleazar L.," in *The Encyclopedia of the Dead Sea Scrolls* (vol. 2; ed. L. Schiffman and J. VanderKam; New York: Oxford University Press, 2000), 902–03.

[2] With the exception of the formulaic phrases לבן אמתכה, "for the son of your handmaid" (1QS XI,16) and וילוד אשה, "and one born of woman" (1QS XI, 21), which are actually variant ways to describe a male human being.

[3] R. de Vaux, *Archaeology and the Dead Sea Scrolls* (London: Oxford University Press, 1973), 45–48, 57–58.

Although it was acknowledged in the scholarly literature that Josephus describes a second group of Essenes that practiced marriage for the sake of procreation (*J.W.* 2.160–61) and that many of the Qumran scrolls, e.g. the Damascus Document, in fact do contain material concerning women, the picture of Qumran as a celibate, quasi-monastic community dominated the first forty years of research.[4]

This situation began to change in the early 1990's through the work of such scholars as H. Stegemann, L. Schiffman, E. Qimron and especially E. Schuller.[5] The change came about not so much because new evidence came to light, although certainly the pool of evidence became deeper and wider as more and more manuscripts were published, but because these scholars broadened their focus to take in the references to women and to try to understand these references in the wider context of Dead Sea Scrolls scholarship.

In this paper I will attempt a somewhat systematic look at what information the Qumran Scrolls can give us about women. This attempt is fraught with several methodological difficulties. First, the corpus of the Qumran Scrolls is not in itself coherent. Rather, the scrolls are the fragmentary remains of what I understand to be the collection or library of the group of Jews that inhabited Qumran from the late second century B.C.E. until its destruction by the Romans in 68 C.E.[6] The fact that I identify it as a collection or a library indicates a certain coherence, and these scrolls are a deliberate col-

---

[4] For the former position, see e.g. G. Vermes, *The Dead Sea Scrolls: Qumran in Perspective* (Philadelphia: Fortress Press, 1981), 96–97, 128–30; for the latter, see Edmund Wilson, *The Scrolls from the Dead Sea* (London: W. H. Allen, 1955).

[5] H. Stegemann, *The Library of Qumran: On the Essenes, Qumran, John the Baptist and Jesus* (Grand Rapids, MI: Eerdmans, 1998); L. Schiffman, "Women in the Scrolls," in *Reclaiming the Dead Sea Scrolls: The History of Judaism, the Background of Christianity, the Lost Library of Qumran* (Jerusalem/Philadelphia: Jewish Publication Society, 1994), 127–43; E. Qimron, "Celibacy in the Dead Sea Scrolls and the Two Kinds of Sectarians," in *The Madrid Qumran Congress. Proceedings of the International Congress on the Dead Sea Scrolls Madrid 18–21 March, 1991* (vol. 1; ed. J. Trebolle Barrera and L. Vegas Montaner; Leiden: E. J. Brill, 1992), 287–94; E. Schuller, "Women in the Dead Sea Scrolls," in *Methods of Investigation of the Dead Sea Scrolls and the Khirbet Qumran Site: Present Realities and Future Prospects* (ed. M. Wise et al.; New York: New York Academy of Sciences, 1994), 115–31; idem, "Women in the Dead Sea Scrolls," in *The Dead Sea Scrolls after Fifty Years: A Comprehensive Assessment* (vol. 2; ed. P. Flint and J. VanderKam; Leiden: E. J. Brill, 1999), 117–44; E. Schuller and C. Wassen, "Women: Daily Life," in *Encyclopedia of the Dead Sea Scrolls* (vol. 2; ed. L. Schiffman and J. VanderKam; New York: Oxford University Press, 2000), 981–84.

[6] M. Broshi, "Qumran: Archaeology," in *Encyclopedia of the Dead Sea Scrolls* (vol. 2; eds. L. Schiffman and J. VanderKam; New York: Oxford University Press, 2000), 733–39 (737).

lection that betrays a particular group identity within the Judaisms of the period. First, it is mainly a collection of religious documents. There are very few personal business documents that have so far surfaced among the scrolls stored in the caves, as there were at Masada, Naḥal Ḥever or Wadi Murabbaʿat.[7] These were not refugee caves, but storage caves. Second, the majority of the non-biblical scrolls, and particularly the compositions that were unknown prior to the discoveries at Qumran, betray certain traits and biases that identify them as the property of a particular Jewish group, not a random sampling of the different Judaisms of the period. These include an adherence to the solar calendar, a particular style of biblical interpretation, a distinctive vocabulary, and a distinct set of legal regulations. Further, the collection is also defined by what is not there: there are no works identified as Pharisaic (e.g. Psalms of Solomon), no "pagan" compositions,[8] and no early Christian works.[9] Thus there is an intentional collection to examine. But the fact that it is fragmentary means that at best we have only a partial picture, and the picture we do have is an accident of preservation.

Another methodological peril is the fact that we are dealing with a literary corpus. The literature within this corpus is written (composed, redacted, copied) by men for a male audience; therefore what they do have to say about women is primarily prescriptive and presents what is to them the ideal situation. It may have very little to do with the reality of women's lives in the Second Temple period.[10] It is also important to bear in mind the social location of this literature. It is the collection of a Jewish group that had the time and

---

[7] For a survey of economic or business documents found at Qumran, see H. Eshel, "4Q348, 4Q343 and 4Q345: Three Economic Documents from Qumran Cave 4?" *JJS* 52 (2001): 132–35.

[8] H. Stegemann, "The Qumran Essenes- Local Members of the Main Jewish Union in Late Second Temple Times," in *The Madrid Qumran Congress. Proceedings of the International Congress on the Dead Sea Scrolls Madrid 18–21 March, 1991* (vol. 1; eds. J. Trebolle Barrera and L. Vegas Montaner; Leiden: E. J. Brill, 1992), 83–166 (99).

[9] *Pace* O'Callaghan and Thiede, who identify fragments from Cave 7 as belonging to the Gospel of Mark. J. O'Callaghan, "New Testament Papyri in Qumran Cave 7?" *Supplement to the Journal of Biblical Literature* 91 (1972): 1–14; C. P. Thiede, *The Earliest Gospel Manuscript? The Qumran Papyrus 7Q5 and its Significance for New Testament Studies* (Exeter: Paternoster Press, 1992).

[10] Bernadette Brooten warns against this methodological pitfall in her programmatic essay "Early Christian Women and Their Cultural Context: Issues of Method in Historical Reconstruction," in *Feminist Perspectives on Biblical Scholarship* (ed. A. Y. Collins; Chico, CA: Scholars Press, 1985), 65–92 (67–73).

means to write about, meditate on and practice a particular way of life without, evidently, concerns about day-to-day existence. Further, it presupposes an androcentric social order. In other words, it is the product of a social elite. So the slice of Jewish life in the Second Temple period that we are investigating through this literature is a very narrow slice. However, with these problems in mind we may at least begin to sketch in the presence of women described by the Qumran Scrolls, from which they have been so glaringly absent.

We will begin first with the legal texts dealing with marital relations and women's biology and sexuality. Following this we will examine those texts which either discuss or assume the participation of women in the ritual and/or worship life of the community, paying particular attention to the roles that women could play and the rank, if any, that they could attain.[11]

The second major section of the paper will investigate the archaeology of Qumran, especially the small finds and the gender of the skeletons in the excavated graves, for evidence of the presence of women in that particular place during the approximately two centuries in which the settlement at Qumran existed. Finally, I will attempt to put all this evidence in a wider context, and in particular attempt to resolve the question of the identification of the Qumran community with the Essenes.

There are a large number of manuscripts that deal with legal prescriptions, in one way or another. For our purposes "legal prescriptions" or "regulations" refer to legislation that usually has a strong scriptural base, is generally applicable to all Jews (whether or not all Jews followed the particular regulation), and does not refer to a specific organized community structure.[12] For example, legislation in the Qumran scrolls concerning Sabbath observance (binding on all Jews) would fall under the rubric "legal prescription," while the initiation procedure for entrance into the community would not.

---

[11] There are two sources of texts about women in the Qumran Scrolls that we will not be able to discuss owing to space constraints. The Wisdom compositions portray in more general, less prescriptive terms Jewish society and women's place within it. The "literary" compositions (e.g. the Genesis Apocryphon) present a fictionalized view of women and are therefore only marginally relevant to determining the actual place of women in the community portrayed in the Qumran corpus.

[12] This definition follows that of Charlotte Hempel, *The Laws of the Damascus Document: Sources, Traditions and Redaction* (Leiden: E. J. Brill, 1998), 25–6.

One difficulty that arises concerns the distinction that is usually made between sectarian and non-sectarian documents.[13] For example, the book of Deuteronomy was found at Qumran in multiple copies; however, it is not considered to be the exclusive property of the community there, proclaiming their own distinct ideology, but to be an authoritative book for all Jews of the period. On the other hand, most scholars agree that the Community Rule is the exclusive property of the Qumran community, proclaiming its distinct ideology over against other Jewish groups of the period. Thus, the question of "sectarian" vs. "non-sectarian" is important in determining the particular stance of the Qumran community, concerning women or anything else. Since I view the Qumran scrolls as a deliberate and particular collection, my assumption is that overall the scrolls are ideologically in agreement (although it is always possible to discover internal contradictions). Happily, the legal texts are largely compatible with each other and do betray a bias of interpretation that often contrasts with that found in other legal systems, most prominently that of the later rabbis.[14] Therefore it is methodologically appropriate to treat them systematically.

As might be expected, much of the legislation that specifically applies to women has to do with marriage, sexuality, and women's biological functions that impinge on ritual purity (e.g. menstruation and childbirth). We will begin with the regulations concerning marriage.

It is important to emphasize from the beginning that the texts containing regulations concerning marriage regard marriage as a normal state for both men and women. The Damascus Document, which contains the majority of the marriage regulations, states, "And if they live in camps, according to the rule of the land, taking wives and begetting children, they shall walk according to the Law . . ." (CD VII, 6–7). This passage, which begins with the adversative clause ואם ("and if"), seems to distinguish those who dwell in camps, marry and have children from others who do not; that is, marriage does not seem to be considered the only legitimate path to follow. This

---

[13] For a good discussion see Carol Newsom, " 'Sectually Explicit' Literature from Qumran," in *The Hebrew Bible and its Interpreters* (ed. W. Propp, B. Halpern, D. N. Freedman; Winona Lake, IN: Eisenbrauns, 1990), 167–87.

[14] See H. K. Harrington, "Purity," in *The Encyclopedia of the Dead Sea Scrolls* (vol. 2; ed. L. H. Schiffman and J. VanderKam; New York: Oxford University Press, 2000), 726.

would imply that there are those who choose not to marry.[15] For those who do marry, the Damascus Document declares that marriage should be governed according to the Torah. In another example, the Rule of the Congregation specifies that a man is eligible to marry at the age of twenty,[16] although no comparable age is given for the female partner.

The legal regulations do, however, place restrictions on marriage. There are forbidden unions outside of those enumerated in the Torah. 4QMMT B 48–49 enjoins male Israelites to shun "any forbidden unions" (נבר]ה[ערובת]ת) and be full of reverence for the sanctuary (המקדש).[17] The Damascus Document (CD V, 9–11; 4QD^e 2 ii 16), 4QHalakhah^a (frag. 12) and the Temple Scroll (11QT^a LXVI, 15–17) forbid uncle-niece marriage; the prohibition is based on Lev 18:12–14, in which sexual relations between a nephew and his aunt are forbidden. The exegetical position of the three documents cited above is that "the commandment concerning incest, written for males, is likewise for females" (CD V, 9–10). Therefore a niece is prohibited from marrying her uncle.[18] The Damascus Document (4QD^f 3, 9–10) also contains the statement that a woman's father should not give her "to anyone who is not fit for her," evidently referring to forbidden degrees of marriage, or perhaps some overt incompatibility. The regulation is based on Lev 19:19, which forbids "mixing" (כלאים) improper kinds of animals, seeds or cloth. This prohibition of "mixing" is also used to condemn marriage between the priestly and lay

---

[15] See Qimron, "Celibacy," 289–91, who argues that "those who walk in the perfection of holiness" (CD VII, 5) abstained from sexual relations because of purity concerns. See also C. Hempel, "The Earthly Essene Nucleus of 1QSa," *DSD* 3 (1996) 253–69 (266), who states "the protasis clearly presupposes that an alternative lifestyle from the one in the camps with wives and children did exist."

[16] *Contra* Talmudic law, in which twenty is the *terminus ante quem* for marriage (*b. Qidd.* 29b).

[17] J. Strugnell, "More on Wives and Marriage in the Dead Sea Scrolls: (4Q416 2 ii 21 [Cf. *1 Thess* 4:4] and 4QMMT B)," *RevQ* 17 (1996) 537–47 (541). The tie between proper marriage (= sexual purity) and reverence for the sanctuary is a theme that recurs in the Temple Scroll and the Damascus Document.

[18] This ruling is in active contrast to the rabbis, who promoted uncle-niece marriage. See Tal Ilan, *Jewish Women in Greco-Roman Palestine* (Tübingen: Mohr/Siebeck, 1995), 76. The exegetical principle explicated by the Damascus Document, that what is written concerning males likewise applies to females, opens many doors for women to obey Torah prescriptions written from a male perspective. Unfortunately we do not have any other specific example from Qumran of another legal regulation which applies this exegetical principle.

orders (4QMMT B 80–82). All of these statements about forbidden unions appear to be polemical; that is, they are inveighing against the practices of other Jewish groups of the period.

The Qumran documents also betray a strict attitude toward polygamy and divorce. Both polygamy and divorce are allowed according to the Torah (Deut 21:15–17; Deut 24:1–4). However, according to the Damascus Document, polygamy is a form of זנות (usually translated as "fornication"):

> The 'builders of the wall' . . . are caught twice in fornication: by taking two wives in their lives, even though the principle of creation is 'male and female he created them' and the ones who went into the ark 'went in two by two.' And concerning the prince it is written 'he shall not multiply wives for himself . . .' (CD IV, 19–V, 2).

The prohibition of polygamy is made by reference to the stories of creation and the flood, as portrayals of God's real intentions for humanity, and capped by the citation from the Law of the King (Deut 17:17).[19] The Temple Scroll also prohibits polygamy for the king (11QTᵃ LVII, 17–19).

The evidence on divorce is more mixed. There are various statements that indicate that divorce was tolerated (e.g. 4QDᵃ 9 iii, 5; 11QTᵃ LIV, 4). However, the "Law of the King" in the Temple Scroll prohibits divorce for the king:

> and he shall take no other wife in addition to her for she alone will be with him all the days of her life (11QTᵃ LVII, 17–18).

It does permit remarriage after the wife's death. This passage, however, only applies to the king; it is possible that it should be extrapolated to apply to all Jews, but that may be a risky assumption. The passage from the Damascus Document discussed above may also be understood to prohibit divorce, but it may simply support serial monogamy. The interpretation of the passage hinges on the understanding of the word בחייהם ("in their lifetime") which, with a 3mpl suffix, refers to men. Are men prohibited absolutely from having more than one wife (thus precluding any second marriage, including one following divorce),[20] or does it only prohibit having two wives

---

[19] G. Vermes, "Sectarian Matrimonial Halakhah in the Damascus Rule," *JJS* 25–26 (1974–75): 197–202 (200).

[20] A. Isaksson, *Marriage and Ministry in the New Temple* (Copenhagen: C. W. K. Gleerup Lund, 1965), 59–60.

at the same time?[21] The most that can be said is that divorce is nowhere forbidden for all Israelites, although (in light of the prohibition of divorce for the king) it may have been less frequent among the Qumranites than among Jews outside the community.[22] This is, however, speculation.

The impact of these marriage regulations on the actual lives of women is difficult to gauge, but the regulations, if followed, would have resulted in fewer marriage partners for women, since more types of marriage (including polygamy) were forbidden. There is not, to my knowledge, any specific discussion of the duty of levirate marriage[23] in the Qumran scrolls, but the prohibition of polygamy would have made its fulfillment more difficult.

Closely related to the regulations concerning marriage are the rules concerning sexual relations, since for all Jews in this period marriage was the only legitimate venue for sexual intercourse. Many of the statements in the Scrolls concerning sexuality reflect general Jewish morality at the time: women must be virgins at the time of their first marriage, sexual activity for women outside of marriage was forbidden, with adultery considered especially heinous, and the main purpose of sexual activity was procreation. However, the Qumran scrolls do betray a stricter attitude toward sexual activity even within marriage. The Damascus Document declares: "And whoever approaches his wife for זנות ("fornication"), which is not according to the rule, shall leave and not return again" (4QD^b vi, 4–5; 4QD^e 7 i, 12–13). The meaning of זנות in this context is enigmatic; does it mean intercourse during pregnancy or menstruation, some form of "unnatural" sexual activity such as anal or oral intercourse, or simply sex for pleasure?[24] The Damascus Document elsewhere specifically prohibits intercourse during pregnancy (4QD^e 2 ii, 15–17; the prohibition also includes homosexual intercourse). It is possible that the Damascus Document (4QD^e 2 i, 17–18) also forbids intercourse on

[21] Vermes, "Sectarian Matrimonial Halakhah," 197.
[22] Although it is beyond the scope of this paper, it should be noted that the gospels record a logion of Jesus prohibiting divorce and remarriage (Matt 5:32 [except for fornication], 19:9; Mark 10:11–12; Luke 16:18). Paul likewise prohibits divorce and remarriage (1 Cor 6–7).
[23] The duty of a deceased husband's brother to marry a childless widow in order to produce an heir for the dead husband's estate (Deut 25:5–10).
[24] J. M. Baumgarten, *Qumran Cave 4.XIII: The Damascus Document (4Q266–273)* (*DJD* XVIII; Oxford: Clarendon, 1996), 164–65.

the Sabbath (reading [ביום [השבת as restored by Baumgarten) or perhaps during the daylight hours.[25] Both the Damascus Document (CD
XII, 1–2) and the Temple Scroll (11QT[a] XLV,11–12) forbid sexual
intercourse within the city of the Temple for purity reasons.[26] Thus
the legal regulations of the Qumran scrolls places restrictions on sexual expression for both women and men that are more severe than
those of the Torah. These rules, combined with the greater restrictions on marriage, polygamy and possibly divorce, may have resulted
in a greater proportion of unmarried persons in the community at
any given time; marriage may not have been so attractive or easy
to contract for this group.[27]

Purity regulations are of great significance for anyone who wishes
to investigate legal regulations concerning women in the Qumran
Scrolls. Since many of the purity regulations concern bodily secretions, women (who experience the regular flow of menstruation as
well as the secretions of childbirth) are particularly subject to the
rules of purity.

4QPurification Rules A places stringent restrictions on a menstruating woman or one with abnormal bleeding. They are not to
"mingle" in any way because they contaminate others; anyone who
touches another who is impure through bodily flows likewise contracts impurity for the full seven days (see also 4QD[a] 6 ii, 2–4). This
extends the commandment in the Torah, in which the person who
is touched becomes impure only until sundown (Lev 15:21–23). The
practical implications of the heightened consequences of touching an
impure person are seen in the Temple Scroll, which calls for special quarantine areas for menstruants and postpartum women (as
well as those men with genital flux or anyone with skin disease) outside every city in Israel (11QT[a] XLVIII,14–17),[28] and in the War

---

[25] Understanding ביום as an absolute; so G. Brin, *The Concept of Time in the Bible
and the Dead Sea Scrolls* (Leiden: Brill, 2001), 366. *Jub.* 50:8 forbids intercourse on
the Sabbath; Jubilees was an important text in the Qumran collection and especially for the Damascus Document, which cites it by name (CD XVI, 3–4).

[26] See above 4QMMT B 48–49, which enjoins reverence for the sanctuary within
the context of forbidden marriages.

[27] E. Qimron, "Celibacy," 287–94; H. Stegemann, *The Library of Qumran*, 193–98.

[28] The עיר המקדש ("city of the sanctuary") does not have these quarantine areas
because menstruating and postpartum women were barred from the Temple City
all together. See S. Crawford, *The Temple Scroll and Related Texts* (Sheffield: Sheffield
Academic Press, 2000), 47–49.

Scroll, where women (and children) are banned from the war camp in order to prevent impurity due to ejaculation in sexual intercourse,[29] and the impurity of menstruating women (1QM VII, 3–4; based on Num 5:1–3).

Although pregnancy itself does not cause ritual impurity, the death of a fetus *in utero* did, according to the Temple Scroll.

> And if a woman is pregnant and her child dies within her womb, all the days which it is dead within her she shall be impure like a grave; every house which she enters will be unclean with all its utensils for seven days; and everyone who comes into contact with her shall be impure up to the evening . . . (11QT[a] L,10–12).

This ruling comes from an analogy: if a person finds a human bone in an open field or a grave, they become impure; a woman is like an open field or a grave, therefore the dead thing inside her conveys corpse uncleanness.[30] All of these purity regulations would have placed a heavier burden on women in the community than would adherence only to the injunctions of the Torah.

We have been dealing with legal regulations that, while found only in the Qumran Scrolls and betraying their exegetical position, were meant to apply to all Jewish women. The Scrolls also present us with statements concerning women's participation in the life of the community that presumably adhered to those legal regulations.

There are several texts that preserve prayers and blessings applicable only to women, indicating that women participated in the ritual life of the community, at least in a limited way. 4QPurification Liturgy (4Q284) contains a purification ritual for a woman following menstruation (frgs 2, col. ii and 3). The text mentions "food" and "seven days"; presumably the woman abstained from the pure food of the community during her period. Following mention of sunset on the seventh day (the time of the ritual bath), frg. 2, ii, 5 preserves the beginning of a blessing evidently spoken by the woman: "Blessed are you, God of Israe[l . . ." Frg. 3 contains a response from a male officiant (a priest?).[31]

---

[29] Men rendered impure through involuntary ejaculation are also banned from battle (1QM VII, 6).

[30] This ruling is in direct contradiction to the rabbinic ruling in *m. Ḥul.* 4.3, which states that the womb makes the fetus a "swallowed impurity"; that is, it does not convey corpse uncleanness until it leaves the womb. See Crawford, *The Temple Scroll*, 45.

[31] 4Q512, another purification liturgy, contains a series of blessings spoken by a

4Q502 is an intriguing text belonging to the Qumran community that its editor identified as a Ritual of Marriage,[32] although others have suggested that it is a "golden age ritual" or a New Year festival.[33] In it, men and women are paired together by age group, and the names assigned to these age groups at least sometimes have the function of titles, such as "daughter of truth," (frg. 2, 6), which is parallel to the epithet "sons of truth" in 1QS IV, 5–6; "adult males and adult females," (frg. 34, 3); "brothers," (frg. 9, 11); "sisters," (frg. 96, 1); "male elders," (frg. 19, 5); "female elders," (frg. 19, 2, frg. 24, 4); "virgins," (frg. 19, 3); and "young men and young wo[men]," (frg. 19, 3). The ritual is a community rite which thanks and praises God. In frg. 24, 4 a woman is described as follows: "[and] she will stand in the assembly of male elders and female elde[rs?] . . .," thus clearly identifying "female elder" as a title for certain women in the community.[34] Whatever the true purpose of this ritual, it describes women participating in the worshipping life of the community, and belonging to particular defined groups within the community.

Another defined group of women appears in the Cave 4 fragments of the Damascus Document, which indicates that at least some women in the community were given the honorific title "Mothers." The text in question reads "[and whoever murmu]rs against the Fathers (אבות) [shall be expelled] from the congregation and never return, [but if] it is against the Mothers (אמות), he will be punished te[n] days, because the Mo[th]ers do not have authority (?) (רוקמה)[35]

---

male thanking God for purification after various types of uncleanness. However, frg. 41, 2 inserts above the line איש או אשה, thus implying that women as well as men participated in these rituals.

[32] M. Baillet, *Qumrân grotte 4, III (4Q482–4Q520) (DJD* VII; Oxford: Clarendon Press, 1982), 81–105, pls. XXIX–XXXIV. 4Q502 is certainly a sectarian text, since it contains a passage from the sectarian "Treatise Concerning the Two Spirits" found in the Community Rule (1QS IV, 4–6).

[33] J. M. Baumgarten, "4Q502, Marriage or Golden Age Ritual?" *JJS* 34 (1983): 125–135; M. L. Satlow, "4Q502 A New Year Festival?" *DSD* 5 (1998): 57–68. See most recently J. Davila, *Liturgical Works* (Grand Rapids, MI: Eerdmans, 2000), who argues that the work's identification as a wedding ritual is the "least speculative" of the three (184).

[34] Davila, *Liturgical Works*, 197. "Male elders" (זקנים) is used as a title for a distinctive group elsewhere in Qumran literature. See 1QS VI, 8–9, where the זקנים are ranked behind the priests, or CD IX, 4, where the זקנים function as judges. If the זקנים are a distinctive group, it is reasonable to suppose that the זקנות were as well. See also Josephus' and Philo's use of the term πρεσβύτεροι as honored members of the Essene community (*J.W.* 2:146; *Prob.* 87).

[35] Translations of רוקמה vary; the root רקם means "variegated, multi-colored," and the noun form usually means "embroidery" or "multi-colored fabric." It occurs

in the midst [of the congregation]" (4QD^f 7 i, 13–15). Two things are clear from these lines: women could attain the status of "Mother," and that status, although acknowledged and honored, was of less consequence than the status of "Fathers."

Women also had particular roles to play within the life of the community. The Damascus Document gives women the responsibility of examining prospective brides whose virginity prior to marriage had been questioned. These "trustworthy and knowledgeable" women were to be selected by the Overseer (מבקר), the chief officer of the community (4QD^f 3, 12–15). According to the Rule of the Congregation (1QSa), after marriage a woman "shall be received to bear witness (תקבל לעיד) concerning him (about) the commandments of the Torah . . ." (1QSa I, 11). Although there is dispute about the precise nuances of the woman's responsibility,[36] it is clear that women were considered eligible after marriage to give testimony. However, she is not eligible to give testimony generally, but only concerning her hus-

---

elsewhere in the Qumran literature with that meaning (e.g. 4QShirShabb, 1QM, 4QpIsa^a). That meaning does not appear to fit the context here; hence the variety of translations in the literature. George Brooke has recently argued that the primary meaning of the root רקם should be taken seriously, so that רוקמה would denote a tangible thing, possibly "a piece of embroidered cloth associated with priestly status" (G. Brooke, "Between Qumran and Corinth," Dead Sea Scrolls conference at the University of St. Andrews, June 26–28, 2001). J. F. Elwolde, on the other hand, has focused on the Septuagint rendering of two words from the root רקם in Ezek 17:3 and Ps 139:5, where the Greek words ηγημα ("leadership") and υποστασις ("essence") are used respectively. Thus he argues for a secondary meaning of רקם as "essential being," "authority," or "status," based on "the metonymy of expensive clothing/covering and the power represented by it." (J. F. Elwolde, "rwqmh in the Damascus Document and Ps 139:15," in *Diggers at the Well. Proceedings of a Third International Symposium on the Hebrew of the Dead Sea Scrolls and Ben Sira* [ed. T. Muraoka and J. F. Elwolde; Leiden: E. J. Brill, 2000], 72). Finally, in a recent article, Victor Hurowitz proposes that the רוקמה found here has nothing to do with the רוקמה meaning "embroidery," but instead comes from the Akkadian word *rugummû*, which means "legal claim." This would involve a *qof/gimel* interdialectical interchange. V. Hurowitz, "רוקמה in Damascus Document 4Qd^e {4Q270} 7 I 14," forthcoming in *DSD*. Elwolde's argument appears most convincing to the present author, hence the translation given above.

[36] The history of the interpretation of this phrase is in itself a lesson in gender bias. The original editors took it at face value, understanding it to mean that women could give testimony (D. Barthélemy and J. T. Milik, *Qumran Cave 1* [DJD I; Oxford: Clarendon, 1955], 112). A second generation of (male) scholars, however, proposed emending the text to a masculine verb, on the grounds that women in Judaism could not give testimony (J. M. Baumgarten, "On the Testimony of Women in 1QSa," *JBL* 76 [1957]: 266–69). Most recently the text as it stands is generally accepted without emendation (E. Schuller, "Women in the Dead Sea Scrolls," in *The Dead Sea Scrolls After Fifty Years: A Comprehensive Assessment* [vol. II; ed. P. Flint and J. VanderKam; Leiden: E. J. Brill, 1999], 133).

band.[37] This would imply that the testimony concerned matters that were private between a husband and wife. Perhaps her responsibility lay in the area of sexual purity, in which a woman would by necessity need to be fully instructed.[38]

Several texts indicate that women were expected or allowed to be present during the rituals of the community, and to participate in its daily life. The Rule of the Congregation I,4–5 gives instructions for the assembly of the congregation: "When they come they will assemble all who come, including children and women, and they will recite in [their hear]ing [a]ll the statutes of the covenant and instruct them in all their commandments lest they stray in their errors." I understand the Rule of the Congregation to be describing actual assemblies during the history of the community and not merely an assembly at some projected "end of days."[39] Therefore I would argue that women and children participated in these assemblies, as they did also in the public liturgy in 4Q502.

Finally, we should be mindful of falling into the trap of silence. Just because a text does not specifically mention women, or portray women as participating in particular aspects of community life does not mean that they were not there. As Schuller states, "many regulations, though expressed in the masculine, apply also to women, and in that sense form part of the corpus of texts about women."[40] If we "shift our focus"[41] to include women in the life of the community described in the Qumran Scrolls, our picture of that community is radically changed.

To summarize the evidence of the texts: women were present in the community life regulated by the legal prescriptions in the Scrolls. This is indicated by the number of regulations pertaining to women, especially in the areas of marriage, sexual conduct, and biological causes of impurity. That these prescriptions were not simply the general laws in force in Judaism at this time and thus can tell us nothing

---

[37] P. Davies and J. Taylor, "On the Testimony of Women in 1QSa," *DSD* 3 (1996): 223–35 (227).

[38] Isaksson, *Marriage*, 57, notes a rabbinic saying that a wife can be heard on sexual matters concerning her husband, e.g. impotence.

[39] See Hempel, "Earthly Essene Nucleus," 254–56, who argues that 1QSa I, 6–II, 11a refers to actual, not eschatological, community legislation. She also suggests that that community legislation emerges from the same social situation as the Damascus Document.

[40] Schuller, *The Dead Sea Scrolls After Fifty Years*, 122.

[41] To borrow Brooten's phrase, "Early Christian Women", 65.

about this particular community is evidenced by the fact that some of them embrace positions in opposition to other groups within Judaism of the period (e.g. the bans on uncle-niece marriage and polygamy). The regulations for community life also indicate the presence of women; in fact, women had particular roles to play in the governance of community life, and could attain special honored positions (e.g. "Mothers"). Finally, although the hierarchy of the community was male-dominated and the viewpoint of the Scrolls androcentric, there is nothing in the Scrolls themselves that indicates that women were deliberately excluded or that this was a male-only community.

Let us now turn to the site of Qumran itself, in the vicinity of which the Scrolls were found. At Qumran's lowest level its excavator, Roland de Vaux, discovered a small Iron Age II settlement, but the more important settlement was dated to the late Second Temple period. De Vaux distinguished three phases of the Second Temple period settlement: Period Ia, which began c. 135 B.C.E., Period Ib, which was a seamless outgrowth of Period Ia, and Period II. Period II ended when Qumran was destroyed by a Roman legion in 68 C.E. A short period followed during which the site was used as a Roman army camp.[42] Although there have been refinements made to de Vaux's chronology, and in particular the existence of a separate Period Ia and a long break in the habitation between Periods I and II have been questioned, de Vaux's essential chronology of a settlement existing from the late second century B.C.E. to 68 C.E. still stands.[43]

De Vaux's excavations revealed an anomalous site from the Herodian period. In de Vaux's own words,

> Khirbet Qumran is not a village or a group of houses; it is the establishment of a community. We must be still more precise: this establishment was not designed as a community residence but rather for the carrying on of certain communal activities. The number of rooms which could have served as dwellings is restricted as compared with the sites designed for group activities to be pursued ... there is only a single large kitchen, a single large washing-place, and one stable. There are several workshops and several assembly rooms (10).

De Vaux found at Qumran evidence for a communal lifestyle, including a common dining hall and a "scriptorium," a room in which he

---

[42] De Vaux, *Archeology*, 1–45.

[43] See J. Magness, "The Archaeology of Qumran," *QC* 8 (1998): 49–62 (59–60) and "The Chronology of the Settlement at Qumran in the Herodian Period," *DSD* 2 (1995): 58–65.

claimed manuscripts were copied. There was also a large cemetery, separated from the buildings by a low wall, which contained approximately 1200 graves. The graves had an unusual orientation, with the corpses buried in a north-south direction, rather than the usual east-west direction.[44] Finally, de Vaux connected the Scrolls found in the eleven caves with the site of Qumran on the basis of the paleographic date of the manuscripts, the date and type of pottery found in the caves and in the ruins, and the proximity of the caves, especially Caves 4–10, to the site of Qumran.[45] Although in recent years there have been many challenges to de Vaux's interpretation of the archaeological remains,[46] none of these theories have gained more than a handful of adherents. The scholarly consensus still centers on de Vaux's interpretation of Qumran as a site inhabited by a particular group of Jews, pursuing a communal lifestyle, who collected and preserved (and copied at least some of) the Qumran Scrolls and hid them in the caves before the site was destroyed by the Romans in 68 C.E.[47]

With that context in mind we may turn to the evidence for women at the site of Qumran. On the face of it this question is a strange one. Women make up half of the human race, and most archaeological remains are gender neutral; that is, architectural remains such as buildings are used by both sexes, and the same is true for most small finds, objects like lamps, coins or cups. Therefore the evidence for the presence of women at any given archaeological site should be the same as that for men. But Qumran, as stated above, is an anomalous site. First of all, the architectural configuration of the site does not support the normal features of family, village or city life in the Second Temple period. If women were living at Qumran, they were not living in the usual family arrangements presumed as the norm by the vast majority of Second Temple literature (and supported by archaeological investigations), including the Qumran documents themselves. Further, the archaeological remains (aside from the buildings) indicate that if women were at Qumran, they were there in much smaller numbers than men. The evidence for that statement comes from a study of the small finds and the excavated graves.

---

[44] De Vaux, *Archeology*, 46–48.

[45] De Vaux, *Archeology*, 97–102.

[46] See Broshi, "Qumran: Archeology," 737–39, for a summary of these views.

[47] J. Magness, "Qumran Archaeology: Past Perspectives and Future Prospects," in *The Dead Sea Scrolls after Fifty Years: A Comprehensive Assessment* (vol. 1; ed. P. Flint and J. VanderKam; Leiden: E. J. Brill, 1998), 47–98 (53–57).

The term "small finds" refers to objects that were used or owned by individuals. Most of these are "gender neutral"; that is, we cannot determine the gender of the user from the object itself (e.g. coins or lamps). However, women used certain special objects in the Second Temple period: combs, mirrors, cosmetic containers, jewelry and objects associated with spinning, such as spindle whorls.[48] A "male-gendered" object would be something used only by men, such as a phylactery case.[49] A survey of the records of the small finds at Qumran yields a startling discovery: there is one spindle whorl (found in locus 7, the stratum of which is unrecorded) and four beads.[50] Recall that these finds cover a period of almost two hundred years! Further, the caves in which the Scrolls were found yielded three beads and two fragments of a wooden comb.[51] This compares, for example, with the Cave of Letters at Naḥal Ḥever, inhabited by refugees during the Bar Kokhba Revolt in 132–135 C.E. In this cave there were found balls of linen thread, two mirrors, five spindle whorls, comb fragments, eighteen beads, a cosmetic spoon, a cosmetic box and a hairnet.[52] The differential between these finds, coming from a period of months, and those at Qumran, coming from a period of two hundred years, is striking. However, we must be careful of how we interpret this "small find" evidence; to claim that the lack of female-gendered objects shows that women were *not present* at Qumran is to make an argument from silence. The lack of female-gendered objects does not positively prove that women were absent from Qumran, but it does make their presence more difficult to prove. One other possible avenue of positive evidence is the gen-

---

[48] J. Taylor, "The Cemeteries of Khirbet Qumran and Women's Presence at the Site," *DSD* 6 (1999): 318.

[49] The supposition that only men used phylacteries is based on later Jewish practice. We do not actually know whether or not women in the Qumran community used phylacteries. Tal Ilan notes that *Mekhilta de-Rabbi Ishmael* states that women are exempt from wearing phylacteries, but mentions a woman by the name of Mikhal b. Kushi who did don phylacteries. Ilan, "The Attraction of Aristocratic Women to Pharisaism During the Second Temple Period," *HTR* 88 (1995): 1–33 (27).

[50] J. Magness, "Women at Qumran?" Paper presented in the Qumran section of the Society of Biblical Literature Annual Meeting; Nashville, TN, November, 2000; 11, 13. Taylor (318, "The Cemeteries," n. 117) notices a spindle whorl found in locus 20, but locus 20 is only from the period III Roman encampment. Her identification of the so-called sundial as a spindle whorl is not convincing (see also Magness, 11).

[51] Magness, "Women," 13.

[52] Y. Yadin, *The Finds from the Bar-Kokhba Period in the Cave of Letters* (Jerusalem: Israel Exploration Society, 1963), as cited by Magness, "Women," 17–18.

der of the corpses exhumed in the cemetery. Let us now turn there.

Of the ca. 1200 graves in the cemetery, de Vaux excavated only forty-three. S. Steckoll excavated nine more graves in 1966–67, but the remains have apparently disappeared.[53] The parts of the skeletons preserved from de Vaux's excavations are now housed in Munich, Paris and Jerusalem.[54] O. Röhrer-Ertl identified the twenty-two skeletons in the Munich collection as nine males, eight females and five children.[55] The remains of the Paris and Jerusalem collections have been identified by S. Sheridan et al. as sixteen males, one female (Tomb A), and one male with a question mark.[56] Further, J. Zias has challenged the antiquity of some of the skeletons from the Munich collection, arguing that six of the female skeletons (T32–36, South T1) and all of the children (South T2–4) are recent Bedouin burials and not from the period of the Qumran settlement at all.[57] While I cannot comment on his anthropological arguments, his archaeological evidence seems compelling: five of the tombs (T32–36) were oriented along an east-west axis, in accordance with Muslim burial practice;[58] the graves were particularly shallow; and the grave goods found in T32–33 and South T1 are anomalous in the Qumran cemetery.[59] If Zias is correct,[60] that would reduce the number of positively identified females buried at Qumran in the Second Temple period to three (Tombs A, 22, and 24II). It is important to emphasize

---

[53] Steckoll identified five of the burials as male (G3, 4, 5, 9 and 10), three as female (G 6, 7, 8), and one as a child (G6, buried together with the female). Steckoll, "Preliminary Excavation Report in the Qumran Cemetery," *RevQ* 6 (1968): 323–52 (335).

[54] For a history of the post-mortem journeys of these skeletons, see Taylor, "The Cemeteries," 296, n. 38 and 298.

[55] O. Röhrer-Ertl, F. Rohrhirsch, and D. Hahn, "Über die Gräberfelder von Khirbet Qumran, insbesondere die Funde der Campagne 1956, I; Anthropologische Datenvorlage und Erstauswertung aufgrund der Collection Kurth," *RevQ* 19 (1999): 3–46.

[56] S. Sheridan, J. Ullinger, J. Ramp, "Anthropological Analysis of the Human Remains from Khirbet Qumran: The French Collection," forthcoming, Table 5.

[57] J. Zias, "The Cemeteries of Qumran and Celibacy: Confusion Laid to Rest?" *DSD* 7 (2000): 220–53.

[58] F. M. Cross, *The Ancient Library of Qumran and Modern Biblical Studies* (Garden City, NY: Doubleday, 1958), comments that the north-south orientation of most of the graves at Qumran caused the Bedouin who were excavating there with de Vaux in the 1950's to identify them as non-Muslim.

[59] Zias, "The Cemeteries," 225–230. Zias argues that the jewelry found in those tombs resembles that found in Bedouin burials that have been identified with certainty.

[60] For a critique of Zias's arguments, see J. Zangenberg, "Bones of Contention. 'New' Bones from Qumran Help Settle Old Questions (and Raise New Ones)— Remarks on Two Recent Conferences," *QC* 9 (2000): 52–76.

that forty-three (or even fifty-two, including Steckoll's tombs) graves out of 1200 are not a statistically compelling sample. We are left again with an argument from silence: the percentage of women from the exhumed graves from the period of the Qumran settlement is not as large as we would otherwise expect.[61]

What conclusions can be drawn from this scanty evidence? I think the argument can be made that the demographic profile of the Qumran settlement, based on the available evidence, was overwhelmingly male. If women were present there, it was only in small numbers and for short periods of time. That is, individual women may have been there long enough to die there, but women as a group were not there in large enough numbers or for a long enough period of time to leave discernible evidence in the archaeological record. Thus the evidence of archaeology seems to be at odds with the textual evidence presented above. I will propose a solution to this problem in the final section.

Sukenik's early proposal, subsequently adopted by Cross, Milik et al.,[62] that the community that collected the Qumran Scrolls should be identified with the ancient Jewish sect of the Essenes, became the consensus position in Dead Sea Scrolls scholarship for the following reasons. 1. The location of Qumran fits with the information of Pliny the Elder, who locates the Essenes "on the west side of the Dead Sea . . ." and to the north of the oasis of Engedi (*Nat. Hist.* 5.73).[63] 2. Several of the theological concepts that Josephus and Philo attribute to the Essenes appear in the Qumran Scrolls, such as determinism and a belief in the afterlife. 3. Essene practices as described by Josephus, Philo and Pliny seem to be reflected in both the Qumran Scrolls and the archaeological record, e.g. communal property, common meals, particular initiation procedures and special purity regulations.[64] Further, it is clear from the descriptions in Josephus, Philo,

---

[61] Magness, "Women," 6.

[62] See Cross, *ALQ*, and J. T. Milik, *Ten Years of Discovery in the Wilderness of Judaea* (London: SCM Press, 1959).

[63] Pliny's use of the term *infra hos* has been the cause of some controversy. Pliny could mean that the Essene settlement was located in the hills looking down over the oasis of Ein Gedi (hence "above"). However, Pliny is naming towns and settlements along the shores of the Dead Sea beginning in the north and proceeding southwards: Jerusalem/Jericho > Essenes > Ein Gedi > Masada. Thus, the Essenes would be located to the north of ("above") Ein Gedi. This is the way in which I understand Pliny's description. See T. Beall, *Josephus' Description of the Essenes Illustrated by the Dead Sea Scrolls* (Cambridge: Cambridge University Press, 1988), 5.

[64] J. VanderKam, *The Dead Sea Scrolls Today* (Grand Rapids, MI: Eerdmans, 1994), 71–87.

rabbinic literature and the New Testament that the Scrolls do not
reflect Pharisaic beliefs and practices. Finally, although some of the
legal positions embraced by the Scrolls are the same as those attributed to the Sadducees in rabbinic literature, and the "sons of Zadok"
are an important leadership group in the Scrolls,[65] the group who
collected the Scrolls is not identical to the aristocratic Sadducees who
controlled the Temple and the High Priesthood in the late Second
Temple period.[66] Thus, the identification of the Qumran group with
the Essenes (understanding the Essenes as originating in a Zadokite
or "proto-Sadducee" movement) has much merit.

There are, however, difficulties with this Essene identification. The
evidence of Josephus and Philo and the information attainable from
the Scrolls do not always line up precisely. For our purposes the
greatest difficulty with the Essene identification is that Philo and
Pliny both declare that the Essenes were celibate. Josephus' evidence
is more nuanced; however, he does say in his main discussion concerning the Essenes that "they disdain marriage for themselves" (*J.W.*
2.120) and "they take no wives" (*Ant.* 18.21). Philo says "they banned
marriage at the same time as they ordered the practice of perfect
continence" (*Apol.* 14); and Pliny states that they are "without women,
and renouncing love entirely ... and having for company only the
palm trees" (*Nat. Hist.* 5.73).[67] As we have seen above, although the
Scrolls ban polygamy, only tolerate divorce, expand the number of
forbidden marriages, and evidently restrict the expression of sexual
intimacy within marriage, *nowhere do they advocate celibacy*. This is a
seemingly irreconcilable contradiction.

However, we also noted above that according to the archaeological
evidence women lived at Qumran in very small numbers, if at all.
Pliny is the only ancient source who places the Essenes at a specific

---

[65] Schiffman, *Reclaiming the Dead Sea Scrolls*, 83–9.

[66] Schiffman, *Reclaiming the Dead Sea Scrolls*, 73–6.

[67] Both Philo and Josephus claim that the Essenes avoid marriage for misogy-
nistic reasons, considering women to be "selfish, excessively jealous, skilful in ensnar-
ing ... and seducing ..." (*Apol.* 14) and being "convinced that none of them is
faithful to one man" (*J.W.* 2.121). This misogyny betrays the bias of Philo and
Josephus and may not at all reflect the Essene attitude. Pliny makes no such claim,
only remarking that the Essenes' sexual abstinence is "admirable" (*Nat. Hist.* 5.73).
The classical sources' emphasis on Essene celibacy may stem from a desire to present them as if they were similar to Hellenistic associations such as the Pythagoreans,
who also practiced sexual self-restraint. G. Vermes and M. Goodman, *The Essenes
According to the Classical Sources* (Sheffield: JSOT Press, 1989), 13.

geographical location (a location that seems to fit the site of Qumran); Josephus and Philo locate them more generally in the towns and villages of Judaea.[68] Further, as mentioned in the introduction, Josephus also states that "there exists another order of Essenes who, although in agreement with the others on the way of life, usages, and customs, are separated from them on the subject of marriage. Indeed, they believe that people who do not marry cut off a very important part of life, namely the propagation of the species; and all the more so that if everyone adopted the same opinion the race would very quickly disappear" (*J.W.* 2.160). In other words, some of the Essenes married. Josephus goes on to say that this group of Essenes eschewed intercourse with their pregnant wives, a practice that accords with the legal regulations from the Damascus Document discussed above. Although Josephus presents the "marrying Essenes" almost as an afterthought, his notice may give us the clue we need to reconcile the seeming contradictions of the various sources.

If one removes the word "celibacy" from the discussion concerning the identification of the Qumran community with the Essenes, then it is possible to suggest that most Essenes married and lived a family life, but that some Essenes avoided marriage primarily for purity reasons.[69] Qimron has proposed that the phrase in the Damascus Document "those who walk in the perfection of holiness," (CD VII, 4–6), describes community members who avoid marriage for purity reasons.[70] These community members are contrasted with ordinary community members, who pursue marriage: "*And if* (אם) they reside in camps in accordance with the rule of the land, and take wives and beget children..." (CD VII, 6–7; emphasis mine). The adversative clause indicates a demarcation of those described in the previous lines and those described in the following lines; in other words, two groups, one of which married, the other of which did not. It is possible that the latter group included the widowed and/or

---

[68] Philo, *Prob.* 76: "fleeing the cities... they live in villages." *Apol.* 1: "They live in a number of towns in Judaea, and also in many villages and large groups." There is an internal contradiction in Philo. Josephus, *J.W.* 2.124: "They are not in one town only, but in every town several of them form a colony."

[69] This solution was first proposed by R. Marcus, who suggested that Josephus reversed the actual situation of the Essenes, in which most were married, but a few were celibate. As cited by Cross, *Ancient Library of Qumran*, 71, n. 101.

[70] E. Qimron, "Celibacy," 289–90. See also J. Baumgarten, "The Qumran-Essene Restraints on Marriage," in *Archaeology and History in the Dead Sea Scrolls* (ed. L. Schiffman; Sheffield: Sheffield Academic Press, 1990), 23, n. 23.

divorced, as well as those who either chose not to marry or could not find suitable marriage partners; therefore abstention from marriage would not necessarily have been a lifelong choice, but more limited in scope.[71] This proposal accounts for Josephus' evidence regarding the two groups of Essenes. Could women become members of the Essenes through marriage? While it is clear from Josephus and Philo that men took the leading roles in the community, Josephus notes that before marriage "they observe their women for three years. When they have purified themselves three times and thus proved themselves capable of bearing children, they then marry them" (*J.W.* 2.161). The two halves of the last sentence have both been taken to refer to proving a woman's fertility before marriage.[72] However, the time frame in that regard makes no sense. The women "purify themselves three times"; this must refer to three menstrual cycles, a matter of months, not years! To what then do the "three years" refer? It would seem to be a period of initiation, similar to that undergone by men.[73] In fact, according to Josephus elsewhere, the Essene initiation process took three years. Perhaps only married or betrothed women were eligible to join the community;[74] certainly women could not attain the same status as men in the organization. That is, they could not serve as judges or other officers, or take part in the deliberations of the community; they could only serve as witnesses in the limited way described in the Rule of the Congregation (see above). But it is plausible that women were admitted to some form of membership. In fact, Josephus goes on to say "the women bathe wrapped in linen, while the men wear a loincloth. Such are the customs of this order." This statement seems to presume that the women of the group observed the same purification rituals as the men (as witnessed by 4QPurification Liturgy discussed above), implying membership in the order.

---

[71] Baumgarten, "Qumran-Essene Restraints," 19, has suggested that the community contained those who never married or at a later stage in life renounced sexual relations in an effort to "walk in the perfection of holiness."

[72] A. Dupont-Sommer, *The Essene Writings from Qumran* (Gloucester: Peter Smith, 1973), 35, n. 3; Beall, *Josephus' Description of the Essenes* 112. M. Kister, "Notes on Some New Texts from Qumran," *JJS* 44 (1993): 280–90 (281), suggests that the three-year period of observation took place after marriage, to see if procreation would occur. If no pregnancy resulted from the marriage, presumably it would be dissolved.

[73] Schuller and Wassen, "Women: Daily Life," 983.

[74] Davies and Taylor, "On the Testimony of Women," 226–27, suggest that women could only be part of the community by virtue of attachment to a man, specifically a husband.

The proposal concerning two groups of Essenes also helps to account for the paucity of evidence regarding women's presence at Qumran. Stegemann has observed that although Pliny limits the Essenes to one geographical location, Philo and Josephus do not,[75] but instead locate them in settlements throughout Judaea. Josephus, in fact, implies a community of Essenes in Jerusalem itself (*J.W.* 5.145). How can these contradictions be reconciled? If Qumran is understood as a study center or retreat for the Essenes,[76] then the settlement of Essenes Pliny describes can continue to be identified with Qumran, while positing other groups of Essenes living among the Jewish population of Judaea. Pliny, who was a non-native and used sources when composing his work, simply had no awareness of other Essene settlements. Josephus and Philo, who were both Jewish, had better information. It can also be argued that as a study center Qumran would have housed a large collection of manuscripts and would have been populated mainly by males, although it is possible that a very small number of women lived there as well. Thus, to outsiders, the community would have indeed looked "celibate."[77] The dwellers at Qumran, whether they lived there permanently (a small number) or temporarily, would have adhered to a rigorous degree of purity, the same degree required for the Temple in Jerusalem.[78] If this is correct, it would be impossible for women in their childbearing years or for married women or men to reside permanently at Qumran, since those groups are periodically rendered impure by bodily flows. Thus, only men abstaining from marriage (and perhaps old women; the "Mothers"?) could reside permanently at Qumran. This would account for the disproportionate number of males in the excavated graves, but also leave space for a small percentage of women.

This proposal also solves another dilemma of Scrolls scholarship, the relationship of the Damascus Document and the Community

---

[75] Stegemann, "The Qumran Essenes," 84.
[76] Stegemann, "The Qumran Essenes," 161.
[77] Qimron, "Celibacy," 288.
[78] J. Magness, "Communal Meals and Sacred Space at Qumran," in *Shaping Community: The Art and Archaeology of Monasticism* (ed. S. McNally; *BAR International Series 941*, 2001), 15–28. Magness has argued that the archaeological layout of the Qumran settlement indicates that the inhabitants organized their space into ritually pure and impure zones. She sees a parallel between the layout of Qumran and the purity regulations of the Temple Scroll, which bar the ritually impure (including menstruants) from the sacred zone of the Temple City.

Rule. Both documents exist in multiple copies at Qumran, legislate for a particular community, betray evidence of editing and redactional growth, and mutually influence one another, e.g. in the parallel sections of their penal codes.[79] However, there are also clear differences in the type of community for which they legislate, the most pertinent difference being that the Damascus Document legislates for women, while the Community Rule has no overt information about women. I propose that the Damascus Document is the rule for all Essenes living throughout Judaea, while the Community Rule applies only to those permanent dwellers at Qumran, who have chosen to pursue "the perfection of holiness." Thus the two documents existed side by side, because the two groups of Essenes existed at the same time. These groups would not have been separate or isolated, but in constant dialogue and communication.[80] This would account for the mutual influence of the Damascus Document and the Community Rule on one another, as evidenced by the 4Q copies of the Damascus Document penal code, and documents like the Serekh Damascus, which combines material from the Community Rule and the Damascus Document. Baumgarten points out that an "extensive pericope" from the 4QD penal code closely parallels that of 1QS. However, the 4QD penal code includes offenses such as זנות with a wife and murmuring against the Mothers, which presume the presence of women in the community. The Community Rule does not contain these offenses (either in 1QS or in the 4QS manuscripts), which points to a community without women.[81] I am suggesting that Qumran housed this special Essene community.

To summarize, the Qumran documents are the library or collection of the Jewish Essenes in the late Second Temple period. The Essenes included women, and its members married, but a subgroup

---

[79] See Hempel, *Laws*, and S. Metso, *The Textual Development of the Qumran Community Rule* (Leiden: E. J. Brill, 1997).

[80] The idea that the ascetic desert community (יחד) and the less ascetic communities throughout Judaea were contemporaneous is also suggested by Cross in the third revised edition of *Ancient Library at Qumran* (Minneapolis: Fortress, 1995), 186.

[81] The relation between the penal codes of the Damascus Document and the Community Rule is more complex than I am able to discuss here. See J. Baumgarten, *The Damascus Document (4Q266–273)*, P. Alexander and G. Vermes, *Qumran Cave 4: XIX: Serekh Ha-Yahad and Two Related Texts* in *DJD* XXVI (Oxford: Clarendon Press, 1998), and C. Hempel, "The Penal Code Reconsidered," in *Legal Texts and Legal Issues. Proceedings of the Second Meeting of the International Organization for Qumran Studies, Cambridge, 1995* (ed. M. Bernstein, F. García Martínez, J. Kampen; Leiden: E. J. Brill, 1997), 337–48.

within the Essenes eschewed marriage for purity reasons.[82] Qumran was a study center for the Essenes, inhabited mostly by males pursuing a rigorous standard of purity and adhering to the Rule of the Community, but the majority of the Essenes lived throughout Judaea, following the regulations of the Damascus Document. This thesis allows us to place women back into the frame of Qumran studies, and resolves the question of so-called Essene "celibacy."

---

[82] Cross, *Ancient Library of Qumran*, 72, suggests that this sexual abstinence was also rooted in the rigorous rules of Holy War, to which the Essenes adhered because of their apocalyptic expectations. J. Collins notes in the same vein that the community believed that they were companions to the heavenly host, and that "sexual activity would be difficult to reconcile with the angelic life." "Powers in Heaven: God, Gods, and Angels in the Dead Sea Scrolls," in *Religion in the Dead Sea Scrolls* (ed. J. Collins and R. Kugler; Grand Rapids, MI: Eerdmans, 2000), 24.

THE STRUCTURE OF THE APOCALYPSE OF 'SON OF GOD' (4Q246)

Frank Moore Cross

The Apocalypse of the 'Son of God' (4Q246) was first published in a preliminary edition by Émile Puech, "Fragment d'une apocalypse en araméen (4Q246 = pseudo-Dan^d) et le 'royaume de Dieu,'" *RB* 99 (1992): 98–131. Puech produced an exemplary edition of the text that was originally assigned to J. T. Milik to edit. It became widely known as early as 1972 when Milik lectured in the United States on the important text and passed out handouts recording the text and his interpretation.[1] Milik proposed a reading in which the 'Son of God' was identified with a historical figure, a self-deified king. Puech supported such a reading in part, at least the view that the figure was a historical person, presumably Antiochus IV (Epiphanes), but Puech left open the possibility that the figure was the royal messiah of the apocalyptic future.[2]

---

[1] See J. T. Milik, *The Books of Enoch: Aramaic Fragments of Qumrān Cave 4* (Oxford: Clarendon, 1976), 13, 60, 213, 261.

[2] See also the reconstructions of Joseph Fitzmyer in his several studies of the text, "4Q246: "The 'Son of God' Document from Qumran," *Bib* 74 (1993): 153–174; and "The Aramaic 'Son of God' Text from Qumran Cave 4," *Methods of Investigation of the Dead Sea Scrolls and the Khirbet Qumran Site: Present Realities and Future Prospects* (ed. M. Wise, *et al.*; Annals of the New York Academy of Sciences 722; New York: New York Academy of Sciences, 1994), 163–178. Other studies include R. Eisenman and M. Wise, *The Dead Sea Scrolls Uncovered* (Shaftsbury, Dorset; Rockport, Massachusetts; and Brisbane, Queensland: Element, 1992), 68–71; Edward M. Cook, "4Q246," *BBR* 5 (1955): 43–66; A. Chester, "Jewish Messianic Expectations and Mediatorial Figures and Pauline Christology," in *Paulus und das antike Judentum* (ed. M. Hengel and U. Heckel; Tübingen: Mohr, 1991), 17–89; Sharon L. Mattila, "Two Constrasting Eschatologies at Qumran (4Q246 and 1QM)," *Bib* 75 (1994): 518–538. John Collins shares my view that the text is messianic; he also argues eloquently, if briefly, for the closeness of the text to canonical Daniel. See his studies, "A Pre-Christian 'Son of God' among the Dead Sea Scrolls," *BRev* 9 (1993): 34–38 and 57, esp. n. 4; *Daniel: A Commentary on the Book or Daniel [Hermeneia]*: 77–79; "The Son of God Text from Qumran," in *From Jesus to John: Essays in Honour of Marinus de Jonge* (ed. M. C. de Boer; Sheffield: JSOT, 1993), 65–82. J. T. Milik has described his views most recently in "Les modèles araméens du livre d'Esther dans la grotte 4 de Qumrân," *RevQ* 15 (1992) [Mémorial Jean Starcky II]: 383–384. David Flusser has also opted for an interpretation of the "Son of God" as an Antichrist figure: "The Hubris of the Antichrist in a Fragment from Qumran," *Imm* 10 (1980): 31–37. F. García

The apocalypse is written in Aramaic, and more specifically, in the language and idiom of the Aramaic portions of Daniel. There can be no doubt that this work, along with the Additions to Daniel, belongs to a wider Daniel literature of which the canonical Daniel is a single exemplar. For common linguistic usages see the notes to the text.

The manuscript dates in the interval between the late Hasmonaean scripts and the Early Herodian scripts, between 50 B.C.E and 1 B.C.E.[3] The original composition must go back to the early second century B.C.E., coeval with the four apocalypses of Daniel (Chapters 7, 8, 9, and 10–12 of the Book of Daniel).

The clue to the understanding of the fragmentary text and the resolution of the disputed identity of the 'Son of God' is to be found, I believe, in an analysis of the poetic structure of the text. This can be diagramed as follows.

Prologue
The apocalyptist [Daniel] falls before the king and
announces that he will interpret the king's
disturbing dream.   Column I, 1–3

Martínez holds yet another view, which while seeing the figure as an eschatological savior, does not identify him with the royal messiah: "The Eschatological Figure of 4Q246," *Qumran and Apocalyptic* (Leiden: Brill, 1992), 162–179; "Two Messianic Figures in the Qumran Texts," in *Current Research and Technological Developments on the Dead Sea Scrolls* (ed. Donald W. Parry and Stephen D. Ricks; Leiden: Brill, 1996), 14–40. I have held a messianic interpretation of the "Son of God" text since J. T. Milik read a paper on the text at Harvard University in 1972. Indeed I sent to him my reconstruction of the text of 4Q246 recorded here below shortly after his American visit, arguing strongly against his interpretation of the epithets as belonging to a Seleucid king (Alexander Balas). See F. M. Cross, *The Ancient Library of Qumran* (3d ed.; Sheffield and Minneapolis: Sheffield Academic Press and Fortress Press, 1995), 188–191; and "Notes on the Doctrine of the Two Messiahs at Qumrân and the Extra-Canonical Daniel Apocalypse (4Q246)," in *Current Research and Technological Developments on the Dead Sea Scrolls* (ed. Donald W. Parry and Stephen D. Ricks; Leiden: Brill, 1996), 1–13.

[3] Its script is slightly more advanced than that of 4QSam[b] and 1QIsa[b], and slightly less advanced than the Early Herodian script of 1QM. See F. M. Cross, "The Development of the Jewish Scripts," in *The Bible and the Ancient Near East: Essays in Honor of William Foxwell Albright* (ed. G. Ernest Wright; Garden City, New York: Doubleday, 1961), 138, lines 3–4. The script charts are republished in Cross, *The Ancient Library of Qumran*, Figure 17 (between pages 128 and 129), lines 3 and 4.

A. 1: War and the Perishing of Kings
War and carnage shall come upon the earth.
At the end of days the two evil kings, the last of
the kings of Assyria [i. e., of the Seleucids], and
the last of the kings of Egypt [i. e., of the
Ptolemies] shall perish.   Column I, 4–6

B. 1: The Coming of the Messianic King
Then a great king shall arise. He shall
establish universal rule, and be called the
Son of God, the Son of the Most High.   Column I, 7–II, 1a

A. 2: War and the Perishing of Kings
(The two kings) shall rule for a time,
trampling on all nations, but ruling briefly,
flashing and falling like comets.   Column II, 1b–3

B. 2: The Coming of the Messianic King
Then the people of God shall arise, and all
will rest from the sword. His (the Son of
God's) kingdom shall be eternal, and all
peoples will worship him. The great God
shall be his patron and make war for
him, giving all peoples into his hand.   Column II, 4–9

Note the alternation of stanzas on the two themes: (1) the war and
the perishing of kings, followed by (2) the coming of the messianic
king, a pattern which repeats itself twice.

The language and idiom of 4Q246, as well as its apocalyptic genre,
and the style of apocalyptist in coming before a king, and in interpreting
the dream of the king(s), has so many contacts with the Daniel literature that we must affirm Milik's initial conclusion that we are dealing here with a lost portion of the Daniel literature. Cave 4, Qumran
has also presented us with another such document, the Prayer of
Nabonidus (4Q242 = PrNab ar) first published by Milik.[4] The most
striking parallels exist between the apocalypse of the Ancient of Days

---

[4] J. T. Milik, "'Prière de Nabonide' et autres écrits d'un cycle de Daniel," *RB*
63 (1956): 407–415; for corrections of the placements of the fragments, and corrections to the readings, together with a discussion of more recent literature, see
F. M. Cross, "Fragments of the Prayer of Nabonidus," *IEJ* 34 (1984): 260–264.

and the 'one like a son of man' in Daniel 7, and the apocalypse of the 'Son of God,' suggesting strongly that Daniel 7 too must be read as messianic. The man-like one—like Ba'al flying up on his cloud chariot to the cosmic mountain, where 'El sits enthroned, to receive kingship from the Ancient One ('Ĕl,)—is the messianic figure of the apocalypse of the Son of God and indeed of I En 46:1–4; 48:1–10; and 52:4. The holy ones of the Most High who receive the eternal kingdom (Dan 7:18) are the people of God of Column II, line 4 of the Apocalypse of the Son of God. There appears to be in the interpretation of the dream of Daniel 7 a secondary democratizing of the royal figure, notably in Dan 7:18, equating the 'one like a son of man,' with the saints of the Most High. This is not the case, I believe, in 4Q246 where the Son of God is distinct from the People of God.

The parallels (or contacts) between the Aramaic Apocalypse of the Son of God, Column I, 7–Column II, 1, and the poetic sections of the Annunciation to Mary in Luke 2 are quite remarkable. We have discussed the details in notes 17 and 18 to the text below. Note the epithets of the messiah which are common to both passages: "great" (I, 7; Luke 1:32), "son of the Most High" (II, 1; Luke 1:32), "son of God" (II, 1; Luke 1:35), and (reconstructed) "holy one" (I, 9; Luke 1:35). "His kingdom shall be an eternal kingdom" (II, 5); "Of his kingdom there shall be no end" (Luke 1:33). The Lucan hymn is not directly derived from the Apocalypse of the Son of God; but the hymn testifies to the author's knowledge of the language and thought of non-canonical Daniel literature and verse.

The text of 4Q246 can be reconstructed tentatively as follows:

Column I

ע]לוהי שרת נפל קדם כרסיא]	1
[ואמר לה חי מן]לכא [ל]עלמא אתה רגז ושנוך	2
[זיוך ואפשר מלכ]א חזוך וכלא אתה עד עולם	3
[חזיתא⁵ די י שפלון ר]ברבין עקה תתא על ארעא	4
[להוה קרב בעממיא] ונחשירון רב במדינתא	5
[ולקצת יומיא יאבדון] מלך אתור [ומ]צרין	6
[ויקום בר אנש מלך] רב להוה על ארעא	7
[כלה וכל אנש לה יע]בדון וכלא ישמשון	8
[לה קדיש אלהא ר]בא יתקרא ובשמה יתכנה	9

---

⁵ On the orthography, see II, 2, and Dan 2:41.

Column II

1 ברה די אל יתאמר ובר עלין יקרונה כזיקיא

2 די חזיתא⁶ כן מלכותהן תהוה שנ[ין] ימלכון על

3 ארעא וכלא ידשון עם לעם ומדינה למד[ינ]ה

4 vacat עד יקום עם אל וכלא ינוח מן חרב vacat

5 מלכותה מלכות עלם וכל ארחתה בקשוט ידי[ן]

6 ארעא בקשוט וכלא יעבד לשלם חרב מן ארעא יסף

7 וכל מדינתא לה יסנדון אל רבא באילה

8 הוא יעבד לה קרב עממין ינתן בידה וכלהן

9 ירמה קדמוהי שלטנה שלטן עלם וכל תהומי

Column I
(Prologue)

(1) [   ]⁷ on him settled;
He fell before the throne,
(2) [and said to him, "Live O k]ing forever!⁸
You are disturbed and your (3) [appearance] ⁹changed
[And I shall interpret ¹⁰O kin]g your dream
And all that comes to pass¹¹ unto perpetuity;¹²

---

⁶ See n. 5.

⁷ Fitzmyer following Puech for the most part, reconstructs [וכדי דחלה רבה ע[לוהי], "[When great fear] settled on him." Both compare Dan 10:7. This reading is plausible, and fits the space.

⁸ Puech reconstructs line 2 to read: [ואמר דניאל ל](?)[מן]לכא {ל} <מ><עלמא אתה רנו]. I wish to read rather, avoiding the double emendation: [ואמר לה חיי מ]לכא ושניך. For the cliché לעלמא מלכא חיי לעלמין חיי מלכא see in Dan 2:4; 3:9; 5:10. Address is to the king. Fitzmyer reconstructs [אדין אמר למלכא חיי מ]לכא. His reading is an improvement on that of Puech, but is decidedly too long for the space. One need only pen the letters proposed for the lacuna in the script of this scribe to see that his reconstruction is impossible.

⁹ At the end of line two, and the beginning of line 3, Puech reads אתה רנו ושניך [בדחלה] which he translates "*tu t'irrites et tes années se déroulent* (3) *dans la crainte!*" I believe the material reading is wrong. I read אתה רנו ושנוך [זיוך] "You are disturbed and your (3) appearance changed." The reading ושנוך זיוך I regard as certain. The lower part of the *waw* may be slightly marred, but the form is identical with the *waw* in חזוך found later in line 3. ושנוך זיוך is precisely the impersonal use with suffix as subject found in Dan 5:6 with the same terms: זיוהי שנוהי. Fitzmyer recognized that *zyw* should be read here, and *šnyk* somehow derived from *šny*, but his solution produced a grammatical anomaly as he himself recognizes. Puech and Milik's reading of *šnyk* as "your years" throws line 3 off, and in my view is impossible.

¹⁰ Puech's reconstruction בדחלה הן אש[ר]א or בדחלה הן אק[ר]א is too short for the space. Moreover, neither the verb *qr'* or *šr'* is a natural way to introduce the interpretation of a dream. We expect *pšr*. Fitzmyer's reconstruction fits the space, but leaves the dream interpretation without an introduction. In my reconstruction, the speaker (Daniel) promises to interpret the king's dream using the language of Daniel 5.

¹¹ Both Émile Puech and Joseph Fitzmyer have misunderstood the expression וכלא אתה עד עלמא, "and all that comes to pass unto perpetuity." The seer is to relate all that will happen in the future. This use of אתה, here a participle, is well known both in Hebrew and Aramaic. Note its use in line 4.

¹² The seer then relates the future events seen in the dream. Both Puech and

(A. 1: War and the Perishing of Kīngs)
(4) [You saw in your vision that[13] the] might[y shall be humbled];
Affliction shall come on earth.
(5) [There shall be war with the nations,][14]
And great carnage among the countries.
(6) [And at the end of days[15]] the king of Assyria and of Egypt [shall perish].

(B. 1: The Coming of the Messianic Kīng)
(7) [And there shall arise a son of man][16]
He shall be a great [king] [17]over the [whole][18] earth (8)

Fitzmyer have failed to recognize that the bicolon ends at the end of line 3. This throws off their reconstructions of the beginning of line 4. Puech's poetry breaks down. I believe that it is easiest to have the seer explain what the king saw.

[13] For the use of די [א]חזית to introduce the content of a vision of the future, see, for example, Dan 2:45 and 4:17.

[14] My reconstruction is very close to those of Puech and Fitzmyer.

[15] The expression לקצת יומיא appears in Dan 4:31. The line should signal the end of the war and carnage, and the perishing or defeat of the Seleucids and Ptolemies (i. e., the king of Assyria and of Egypt). Puech has no reference to the demise of the great powers in his reconstruction (nor did Milik). Fitzmyer's reconstruction of the beginning of line 6 is much too short. He too proposes no reference to the defeat of the powers.

[16] In line 7, Fitzmyer reconstructs ברם אף ברך רב לחוה על ארעא, translating "[. . . . but your son] shall also be great upon the earth." Whose son? Evidently the son of the king addressed. In an apocalypse written in the name of Daniel—as Milik correctly labeled this fragment, a conclusion I believe is clear from shared linguistic and literary traits—the king in question presumably would be either Nebuchadnezzar, Darius, Belshazzar or Cyrus, the kings addressed in the Daniel literature. But to give the son of one of these kings the eschatological titles to follow in the next lines of the text, is surely far-fetched, if not impossible. Fitzmyer ultimately rejects a messianic interpretation, to be sure, and opts for an historical Jewish king.

The reconstruction of these lines is, of course, speculative. But, I believe, certain elements must have been included in the development of the apocalypse: the war among the nations (line 5), the defeat of the great powers, Assyria and Egypt—that is, the Seleucids and Ptolemies (line 6), and the rise of the eschatological king—the Davidic messiah (line 7). Certainly lines 8, 9, and II, line 1 describe the king of the end time. Note that in II, 5, the expression מלכותה מלכות עלם echoes Dan 7:27, and recalls Luke 1, 33.

[17] In line 7, I believe we must read מלך] רב לחוה על ארעא [כלה. The epithet *mélek rāb* is found in Ps 48:3 (cf. Dan 2:10):

הר ציון ירכתי צפון
קרית מלך רב

I believe that in the apocalypse it was taken to refer to the son of David, the future king, "city of the great king" understood as equivalent to "city of David." In Luke 1:32 we read οὗτος ἔσται μέγας καὶ υἱὸς ὑψίστου κληθήσεται καὶ δώσει αὐτῷ κύριος ὁ θεὸς τὸν θρόνον Δαυὶδ τοῦ πατρὸς αὐτοῦ, "He will be great, and will be called the son of the Most High, and the Lord God will give to him the throne of David his father." I am interested here in the epithet "great," (μέγας = רב), the basis of my reconstruction.

[18] *klh*, literally "all of it" is an idiomatic usage found in Imperial Aramaic. See for example, 'Aḥiqar [2:]12, [4:] 55 (*'twr klh*, "the whole of Assyria.").

[And all of mankind] shall serve [him],
And all shall minister (9)[to him.][19]
[The Holy One of the g]reat [God] he shall be called,
And by his name he shall be surnamed.

Column II
(1) Son of God he shall be called,
And Son of the Most High he shall be surnamed.[20]

---

[19] Line 8/9 I believe must be reconstructed in a bicolon with *yʿbdwn* and *yšmšwn* in parallelism. The latter verb, *yšmšwn* is used in Dan 7:10, "Thousands upon thousands served him [the Ancient of Days]; myriads upon myriads attended him."

[וכל אנש לה יע]בדון

וכלא ישמשון [לה]

[And all of mankind shall s]erve [him]
And all shall minister (9) [to him.]

We could as well reconstruct [וכל עממיא לה יע]בדון וכלא ישמשון [לה]. Both *kl ʾnš* and *kl ʿmmyʾ* are expressions found in the Book of Daniel.

[20] In I, 9–II, line 1 I reconstruct the quatrain as follows: (note the parallelism of *ytqrʾ*, *ytknh*, *ytʾmr*, and *yqrwnh*):

[קדיש אלהא ר]בא יתקרא

ובשמה יתכנה

ברה די אל יתאמר

ובר עליון יקרונה

[The holy one of the of the g]reat [God] he shall be called,
And by His name he shall be surnamed.
(II,1) Son of God he shall be called,
And Son of the Most High he shall be surnamed.

In lines I, 7–9 and II, 1 we have a sequence of messianic epithets. We have discussed [*mlk*] *rb* above, and compared the passage in Luke 1:32. In line 9, we have reconstructed [*qdyš ʾlhʾ r*]*bʾ*, "the Holy One of the Great God." The basis of this reconstruction is twofold. In Luke 1:35b we read τὸ γεννώμενον ἅγιον κληθήσεται υἱὸς θεοῦ, ". . . the child to be born will be called the holy one, Son of God." The term *qdyš* is applied to the elect of Israel in Daniel 7. Here the man-like figure, *kbr ʾnš*, who is given eternal kingship, is interpreted in Dan 7:18–28 to be corporate Israel, or at least the holy ones of Israel, *qdyšy ʿlywnym*. However, it can be argued convincingly, I believe, that the man-like figure in Daniel 7 was originally the future king, the "holy one of the great God," namely the Son of God. In other words the editor or author of Daniel democratized the messianic figure. In origin, of course, the vision of the Ancient of Days goes back to the Canaanite myth of the young god (Baʿl-Haddu) riding his cloud chariot up to the throne on the mount of the council of the gods, there receiving kingship from the head of the pantheon, ʾEl.

We have reconstructed the titles [son of man], Great [King], [Holy One of the G]reat [God], which fit nicely into the lacunae, and which go well with the titles which are fully preserved on the leather: "Son of God," and "Son of the Most High." The epithets found in Luke 1:32–35, "Great," "Holy One, "Son of the Most High," "Son of God" (where the messianic interpretation is patent), are so striking as to suggest, if not require, that the author of the hymn quoted in Luke is dependent on a Danielic text very much like the one we have in 4Q246. I should argue this even if some of my reconstructed titles prove not to be correct. For example, an alternate reconstruction of the lacuna in line 9 might be *ʿbd ʾlh rbʾ*.

It should be noted that in the Aramaic epithets, the names of god—ʾEl and ʿElyon—are given their Hebrew forms—not their Aramaic forms. This makes it most

(A. 2: War and the Perishing of Kings)
²¹Like comets (2) that you saw (in your vision), thus will be their²²
kingdom.
For some years they will reign over (3) the earth;
And they will trample on all;
One nation shall trample on another nation,
And one province (will trample on) another province.

(B. 2: The Coming of the Messianic King)
(4)*[vacat]* Until the people of God arise
And all rest from the sword. *[vacat]*
(5) His²³ kingdom shall be an eternal kingdom,
And all his ways truth.
He shall judge (6) the earth with truth,
And all will make peace (with him).
The sword shall cease from the earth,
(7) And all the countries shall worship him.
The great God shall be his patron.
(8) He will make war for him;
People he will give in his hand
And all of them (9) he shall cast before him.
His rule shall be an eternal rule . . .

---

implausible that they be applied to any but an Israelite king. If these were pagan
titles, or rather titles claimed by a foreign king, we should expect *'lh'* and *'ly'*, the
ordinary Aramaic words for "god" and "most high." There would no reason for
the evil king, or, *a fortiori*, for a pious Jew to substitute the specifically Jewish names
of god in the epithets of a hated enemy.
²¹ The section which starts at the end of line 1 begins a new section of the interpretation of the dream of the king (mentioned in Column I, line 3–4). There is a
reversion to the sequence of the dream in the pattern $A_1B_1 : A_2B_2$. First (A_1) the
evil kingdoms and their wars are described (I, 4–6); then (B_1) there is appearance
of the great king, the Son of God who shall establish universal rule. (I, 7–II, 1).
Then the sequence is repeated. (A_2) The kings will rule briefly—some years, like
flashes in the pan, like the falling of comets (II, 1b–3); then (B_2) the people of god
arise, peace is restored and their king establishes a just, peaceful, and eternal kingdom (II, 4–9).
²² Note that in II, 2, the usage is plural: "Thus shall be their kingdom . . . they
will rule over the earth." The reference is to the two kings of Column I, the king
of Assyria and the king of Egypt.
²³ The antecedent of the third singular pronouns in II, 5–9 is not explicit. It is
clear from line 7 that the pronouns do not refer to the deity. Conceivably they
could refer to the "people of God," but the structure of the poetry described above
requires that the pronouns refer to the future king, the messiah whose kingdom is
eternal and who judges justly the nations.

SAMARITAN SCRIBAL HABITS WITH REFERENCE TO THE MASORAH AND THE DEAD SEA SCROLLS

Alan D. Crown

The discovery of the Qumran scrolls and the identification among them of proto-Samaritan text types has led to a resurgence of interest in the Samaritan Pentateuch and its value as a witness to the state of the text in the late pre-Christian eras. The current tendency is to attribute the *stabilisation* of the Samaritan text-type to the period from the second century C.E. onwards[1] but the value of the text as a witness in the pre-Christian era is not yet subject to a consensus of opinion.[2]

Until recently, the discussion has focussed on the text of the Samaritan Pentateuch and its relationship to the Hebrew masoretic and the Septuagint versions. The structure of the Pentateuch, that is, in the broadest sense of the term, the Samaritan masorah, the form and layout of the Pentateuch in which the words are presented to the reader, had not been found to be a suitable object of study, nor consequently, a source of evidence in the prime discussion until Emanuel Tov's extended work on the format of the Qumran scrolls. Tov has found the need to refer to the traditions employed in copying the Samaritan Pentateuch, but apart from Tov's work few scholars have taken account of Samaritan masoretic traditions other than a small coterie of Samaritan scholars. Moses Gaster[3] drew attention to the parallels between the section structures of the Samaritan Pentateuch and the *petuhot* and *setumot* in the Jewish masoretic text and to the lectional arrangement in *parashiyot*. However his words

---

[1] See B. K. Waltke, "Prolegomena to the Samaritan Pentateuch," Harvard Ph.D. (1965) especially pp. 86 and 132.

[2] Ibid. Introduction, pp. 1–41 for a discussion of older and contemporary views until 1965. More recently Emanuel Tov has made extensive comparisons between the scrolls and the Samaritan Pentateuch and has demonstrated the antiquity of the characteristics of the latter, See, for example, E. Tov, "Sense Divisions in the Qumran Texts, the Masoretic Text and Ancient Translations of the Bible," in *The Interpretation of the Bible*, The International Symposium in Slovenia ed. Joze Krasovac JSOTSup 289; Sheffield: Sheffield Academic Press, 1998), 121–46.

[3] See M. Gaster, "The Biblical Lessons: A Chapter in Biblical Archaeology," *Studies and Texts* 1 (Ktav reprint: New York, 1973), 503–600. See also his "Massoretisches im Samaritanischen" reprinted from the Nöldeke Festschrift, in *Studies and Texts* 1, 614–37.

were by way of a preface to a study of the lections read by the Samaritans and they seem to have been ignored until recently.[4]

B. K. Waltke seems to summarise a widely-held view in his doctoral thesis in which he wrote: "It is obvious that no school of Masoretes arose among the Samaritans."[5] In clear contrast Z. Ben-Hayyim observed:[6] 'We can glimpse an independent scientific activity of early Samaritan Masoretes and grammarians which was by no means confined to the point discussed here,' with which statement he noted his change of mind on this question.

Both of these opposing views were propounded after detailed scrutinies of the evidence which, in Waltke's case, included recourse to a computer survey of the text of the Samaritan Pentateuch and a thorough appraisal of the work of his predecessors and, in Ben-Hayyim's case, an opinion resulting from a life-long accumulation and intensive study of evidence. Waltke's conclusion seems to have been strengthened by the fact that in the earliest of the Samaritan Pentateuch manuscripts available to him he could see no signs of ongoing masoretic activity, at least as far as textual correction is concerned. It is Ben-Hayyim's view that the system of representing the vowels in Samaritan sacred texts developed after a period of masoretic activity which followed its own line of development from a common ancestry with the Jewish traditions.[7] Ben-Hayyim suggests that the creative period of the masorah of the Samaritans was in the era when they used Aramaic as their vernacular, a conclusion for which support might be adduced from other sources.[8] Written evidence for establishing a history of Samaritan literature is not abundant for the

---

[4] Ibid. note 19. See also J. M. Oesch, *Petucha und Setuma* (Vandenhoeck and Ruprecht: Göttingen, 1979).

[5] "Prolegomena," 65.

[6] Z. Ben-Hayyim, "The Samaritan Vowel System and its Graphic Representation," *Archiv Orientalni* 22 (1954): 515–30 (at page 530).

[7] Ibid. p. 526. He discusses this matter further at various places in *LOT*.

[8] On the languages spoken by the Samaritans see A. D. Crown, *Samaritan Scribes and Manuscripts*, TSA 80 (Mohr Tübingen: Siebeck, 2001) chapter one, "Literature." See also Cowley, *SL* II, p. xxxiv, and Loewenstamm, "The Samaritans," *EJ*. Cowley's view is largely substantiated and reinforced by the conclusions of Abraham Tal, in his work on the edition of the Samaritan Targum restated most succinctly in his "The Hebrew Pentateuch in the Eyes of the Samaritan Translator" in *The Interpretation of the Bible*, op. cit., pp. 341–54. Other convenient summaries of Tal's views are to be found in his "Towards a Critical Edition of the Samaritan Targum of the Pentateuch," *Aleph-Beth Samaritan News* or see his *STP*. Tal's work should be read in conjunction with Haseeb Shehadeh, "The Arabic Translation of the Samaritan Pentateuch, Prolegomena to a Critical Edition" (Ph.D. diss., Jerusalem, 1977).

early period,[9] but it is clear enough that by the tenth century Aramaic had ceased to be the vernacular or even used for religious writings and, while it remained the language of the liturgy, the concerns of the commentators and translators from the eleventh century onwards were now with the Arabic edition of the Samaritan Pentateuch.[10] The creative period of the Samaritan Masoretes would seem to have ended by the time any of the extant manuscripts was written. There are but two masoretic tracts for the Samaritan Pentateuch, the works of Ibn Darta[11] and Ibrahim al Ayyah, and they are repetitive and retrospective rather than creative and innovative.[12] One factor which has not yet been considered is whether there were substantial breaks in Samaritan masoretic activity. It has been argued elsewhere that the Samaritans followed the Jewish tradition of writing mainly scrolls of the Pentateuch in the early centuries of the first millennium C.E.[13] only later adopting the Septuagint tradition of codex writing. This course might have encouraged a break in masoretic activity with plagiarism of the Jewish traditions in the earlier part of the first millennium and a resumption of some independent activity later. The evidence on this point is ambiguous. A fundamental problem is that, for the studies of the structural features of the Samaritan text—such as the arrangement of the poetic passages, the number and location of the open and closed sections, the marking of the centre point of the Torah, the location of minor and major *tashqilim*, the counting of verses and letters and the like, one is dependent upon manuscripts which were copied when there was no visible, *active* masoretic tradition. It is possible that there was an oral masoretic tradition passed down from scribe to scribe inside the scribal families, or even that different scribal centres had their own inner traditions. If these oral traditions existed there is as yet, no proof of them, and study of manuscripts from specified schools is not yet sufficiently advanced to permit a description of any governing local masoretic traditions,

---

[9] See Crown, *Samaritan Scribes and Manuscripts*, chapter one.

[10] Ibid. Waltke, "Prolegomena," 81f., introduces a discussion of the literature to 1965. This discussion is superseded by Shehadeh's fine and exhaustive work. There is a convenient English summary at the end of volume I of Shehadeh's thesis.

[11] In Ben-Hayyim's publication of the treatise of Ibn Darta on the rules of reading (*LOT* 3), reference is made (pp. 318–319) to the fixing of some of the rules in Ascalon (coastal Diaspora) in 534 H = 1139–1140 C.E. The reference would seem to be to an evaluation rather than an establishment of the rules.

[12] Ibid.

[13] Ibid. Cf. J. Finegan, *Encountering New Testament Manuscripts* (London, 1975), 27–9.

though, doubtless, that day will come. Appearances at present suggest that scribes copied the forms of the manuscripts which they
inherited without necessarily understanding that they were transmit-
ting a specialised Samaritan masoretic tradition. As observed above,
there is a school of thought which would deny even that cautious
statement. However, it is fortunate that the material with which we
work is visual and some, at least, goes back to the very beginning
of the current millennium and must be based on older copies, which
would carry us back further still.[14] In this we are far more fortunate
than those who have been investigating the Samaritan traditions of
cantillation. They too, have come to the conclusion that there was
once an active Samaritan masoretic tradition which was later lost.
They have argued in these terms: 'The inescapable conclusion would
be that a group of people, an archaic people, after having reached
a sophisticated musical notation (neumes) reverted to an earlier stage
of musical notation, directly deriving from chieronomy.'[15] Because of
the oral nature of that material, the work on cantillation must finish
with the hypothesis with which this study begins, namely that there
was an active masoretic tradition which has left traces which can be
recovered and which will allow us to reconstruct some elements of
the Samaritan masorah.

I. OPEN AND CLOSED SECTIONS

One most important element of that masorah, in the view of the
present writer, an element which may cast light on the active period
of that masorah, is the division of the text into paragraphs and their
layout in what appears to be a version of the open and closed sections of the Masoretic Text. This division may also have some light
to shed on the age of the sentence division of the Pentateuch. The
paragraphs are known as *qiṣṣim* or *qiṣṣin* but Gaster suggests that

---

[14] This point will become more obvious from the discussion below, where it is
shown that practices described are conservative rather than innovative.

[15] Cf. Joanna Spector, "The Significance of the Samaritan Neumes," *Studia
Musicologia Academaiae Scientiarum Hungaricae* 7 (1965): 141–52. Spector was told that
the musical meaning of the *sidre miqrata* died with one of the High Priests in the
nineteenth century. This would imply that the tradition had been maintained accurately after the true priestly line died out in the seventeenth century. One may suspect that this was the latest point at which the break in the musical tradition
occurred. See especially p. 152.

they may have originally been known by the term *Piska* or *parasha*, both of which names came to have different meanings in regard to the MT.[16] The *qiṣṣim* are identified both by their separation from each other by spacing and by the use of a *qiṣṣah* mark, a combination of a tricolon, a *diplé* and a horizontal line, corresponding with the Greek *paragraphos*, to end the paragraph. The *qiṣṣim* are identified by name by the Samaritans, the name usually being the first words of the *qiṣṣah*. As Gaster points out there is early evidence for the same system to have been used for the MT.[17] These names are listed for the book of Genesis in the table. The identifying names are written down as paragraph headings or lemma in the Arabic manuscript versions of the Samaritan Pentateuch where they are set out in Samaritan Hebrew script. A similar custom is found in some manuscripts of the Samaritan Targum. A comparison of the lemma in two manuscripts Bodley Or. 345 and Bodley Marsh 209 indicates that there was a standard tradition which has been maintained in most manuscripts though it may have lapsed in the copying of some manuscripts. The indication of a standard tradition is derived from the following data. In general the title of the *qiṣṣah* is the first group of words which is unique and allows the section to be identified. For the most part these are the first words of the *qiṣṣah*. However, in Genesis *qiṣṣah* 33 (Gen 6:7–12) the opening words are the frequently repeated *vayomer yahweh* which would give no unique identification hence the lemma in the manuscripts is *emḥeh et ha'adam*. In contrast *qiṣṣim* 221 and 222, in both Marsh 209 and Or. 345, begin with the identical words *vayomer yosef*. The lemma could be made unique by the addition of a third word, but since this is not done in either manuscript it seems that an old tradition is maintained. However, while the divisions are almost the same in all manuscripts it is clear from the differences between manuscripts that there is more than one tradition. The same *qiṣṣim* are found in both scrolls and codexes. In the scrolls there is very clear evidence that the text is written to allow each new column to begin with a *qiṣṣah*. A very good illustration of this is the scroll Bodley Or. 669 where the text at the bottoms of columns is extended and spaced to allow the following columns to begin with new *qiṣṣim*. The same system is true of the

---

[16] "Biblical Lessons," 523.
[17] Idem, 527.

older columns of the renowned Abisha scroll, though in this manuscript of many ages, hands and reconstructions, there is no attempt
to differentiate between open and closed sections.

The *qiṣṣim* for each book of the Samaritan Pentateuch are numbered
at the end of each book. In many cases this is the only masoretic
note, possibly indicating that this was the prime division of the text
in ancient times. It is noteworthy that the names of the books in
the masoretic notes are simply 'First book,' 'Second book,' etc., ignor-
ing the Greek or Jewish names, testifying to the age of the division.

The number of *qiṣṣim* in each book may be given but when the
qiṣṣim are counted they differ in number from the stated number.
This would seem to indicate that progress had been made by the
Samaritan masoretes to standardising the number of *qiṣṣim* but not
in unifying the actual breaks in the text. It will be seen from the
table that in Tal's diplomatic edition of the Samaritan Pentateuch[18]
there are two *qiṣṣim* more than in most other manuscripts, numbered
159a and 238a, yet the masoretic note at the end of Genesis still
reads הספר הראישון קצים ר ונ = 250.

The recorded number of *qiṣṣim* for each book is not stable and
there are several traditions varying between 962 *qiṣṣim* (the most common number) to 968. The number of *qiṣṣim* is usually Genesis 250,
Exodus 200, Leviticus 134 [or 130 (BL Or. 6461) or 135 (BL Add.
21581, BL Or. 2688)], 136 (Shechem Synagogue 10) Numbers 218
[or 220 (BL Add. 19016 and Shechem Synagogue 10)] and Deuteronomy 160 (Vatican Samaritan 1, BL Add. 19012, Petermann 1) or
161 (Cotton Claudius B viii) or 166 (BL Or. 6461). At the end of
each book Tal's edition lists the *qiṣṣim* as 250, 200, 134, 218 and
166. Despite these figures the reality is that in Tal's edition, there
are 199 *qiṣṣim* in Exodus, 136 *qiṣṣim* in Leviticus, 219 *qiṣṣim* in Numbers
and 164 *qiṣṣim* in Deuteronomy. Gaster[19] lists these numbers as 250,
200, 135, 220 and 161 respectively.[20]

The divergence between the number of *qiṣṣim* stated and the number to be counted is evident in many manuscripts, and even within
the work of a single scribe.[21] For example, one of the most prolific

---

[18] A. Tal, *The Samaritan Pentateuch edited according to MS 6' of the Shekhem Synagogue* (Tel Aviv University, 1994).

[19] "Massoretisches," 632.

[20] Gaster may have erred. He cites his coded 800—BL 10271 which states that there are 160 *qiṣṣim* in Deuteronomy.

[21] See for example BL Or. 10131 where the *qiṣṣah* numbers have been added in the margins and differ repeatedly from the masoretic notation.

scribes of Pentateuch manuscripts, a member of the well established twelfth century Coastal Samaritan scribal school, with a old masoretic tradition, such as Abi Berakhata b. Ab Zehuta b. Ab Nefusha, there are differences between the numbers of *qiṣṣim* cited at the end of the books from manuscript to manuscript. From other evidence we are aware that Abi Berakhata copied what he found before him rather than trying to unify his manuscripts to a standard. It is probable that there was one old Samaritan masoretic tradition about the number of *qiṣṣim* in the books and that tradition was preserved by scribes in the end legends to the books of the Pentateuch, but from time to time it was modified when scribes counted the *qiṣṣim* and found that they differed from the received tradition. The number of *qiṣṣim* per manuscript cannot be correlated with the manuscript source: there seems to be no unique Damascene, Cairoene, Coastal or Nablus Samaritan tradition.

That the *qiṣṣim* are related to the open and closed sections is not immediately clear for there are more *qiṣṣim* than there are open and closed sections, though the number becomes closer when one takes account of those *petuhot* and *setumot* in the manuscripts of the MT which are close to the *qiṣṣim* of the Samaritan Pentateuch but are not identical with them or which have a *qiṣṣah* finial but no spacing. For example in Rylands 1 *qiṣṣah* 238 of Genesis is spaced to conclude at verse 49:21, but has a *qiṣṣah* mark between vv. 19 and 20, so that if one counted *qiṣṣah* marks rather than lemma and spacing, one would have an extra *qiṣṣah* here, corresponding with the division of sections in the MT. Note that the sections of the manuscripts of the MT (cp the facsimile editions of Leningrad codex with Hilleli) are not consistent here. These places are marked in Table 1 with a verse number in the MT column.

The relationship between the *qiṣṣim* and the open and closed sections is shown more closely and made certain by comparison between the Samaritan texts and such a work as *4Qpalaeo Gen-Exod*[l] where the divisions substantially exceed in number the *petuhot* and *setumot* of the MT.[22] There are many places where *qiṣṣim*, breaks in *4Qpalaeo Gen-Exod*[l] and the MT coincide. There are places where *qiṣṣim* and breaks in *4Qpalaeo Gen-Exod*[l] coincide and are not represented in the MT. Even when they do not coincide with the Samaritan *qiṣṣim* the proximity of the breaks in *4Qpalaeo Gen-Exod*[l] to the *qiṣṣim* is noteworthy.

---

[22] See table 2, p. 20 in P. W. Skeehan, E. Ulrich, J. E. Sanderson, *DJD IX, Qumran Cave 4.IV, Palaeo-Hebrew and Greek Biblical Manuscripts* (Oxford: Clarendon Press, 1992).

Thus one finds Exodus qiṣṣah 5 = 2:10/11 of *4Qpalaeo Gen-Exod^l* (not in MT); *qiṣṣah* 10 = Exod 3:18 ± 3:17–18 *4Qpalaeo Gen-Exod^l* (not MT); *qiṣṣah* 44 = Exod 9:27 i.e. 9:26–27, *4Qpalaeo Gen-Exod^l* (not MT); *qiṣṣah* 76—Exod. 17:5 ± Exod. 17:6, *4Qpalaeo Gen-Exod^l* (not MT); *qiṣṣah* 102 = Exod 23:4 = *4Qpalaeo Gen-Exod^l* (not MT). In like fashion one notes other *qiṣṣim* where there is a more remote relationship with additional paragraphing in *4Qpalaeo Gen-Exod^l* beyond that found in the MT.

The way that the *qiṣṣim* are written, with either substantial space or reduced space is redolent of the words of Maimonides about the *petuḥot* and *setumot*. Maimonides' view was that an open section could have two forms. The first is that when it ends in the middle of the line, there should be left a space of at least nine letters and then the next section should begin on the first part of the next line. If there was no space left or only a little, then the next section should begin on the third line.

A closed section could have three forms. If it ends in the middle of a line, a space of a line was left, and then the scribes begin to write at the end of the line one word of the beginning of the closed parashah so that the space lies in the middle. But if there is nothing left on the line so as to leave a space in the middle, a little space should be left at the beginning of the next line and the beginning of the closed section should be written from half way along the next line. However if the line is completed, a scribe should leave a space at the beginning of the next line and start the closed section. Maimonides admitted that there was still no unanimity on this matter. Since Maimonides' descriptions can be related to the *qiṣṣah* phenomenon in Samaritan manuscripts, it would seem that the *qiṣṣim* are an attempt to develop a system of *petuḥot* and *setumot* in Samaritan manuscripts. In the Samaritan system while it is apparent that there is a relationship with the masoretic system, it is not internally consistent.

It is clear from the inconsistencies between Samaritan manuscripts, even those penned by the same scribes, that the Samaritan system developed before the Jewish system was closed and never reached the same consistency as the Jewish system.

While at first sight the manuscripts of the Samaritan Arabic versions of the Pentateuch are helpful in determining which *qiṣṣim* represent open and which represent closed sections, this is illusory. In the Samaritan Arabic versions, the sections are seen very clearly as separated from each other not only by their lemma but also by a single complete empty line giving the appearance of open sections, whereas the closed sections appear to be those *qiṣṣim* where the lemma shares a part of a line with the text. Unfortunately, while comparison between the Arabic versions shows some stability, comparison with the Hebrew Samaritan versions does not produce any resulting consistency which would allow us to define a system of open and closed sections.

The better Samaritan Hebrew Pentateuch manuscripts write the beginning and the end of the *qiṣṣim* in various ways and these clearly relate to the open and closed section structure. The older Samaritan manuscripts such as the eleventh century Tokapi Serai G I 101, Rylands Samaritan MS 1, Chester Beatty 751, Shechem Synagogue 10, Sassoon 402 and other manuscripts in the hand of Abi Berachatah b. Ab Zehutah[23] which tend to be very well written and retain elements of the masoretic tradition, distinguish between paragraph structures and these are clearly related to the *petuhot* and *setumot* of the MT. Rylands Sam. MS 1 may complete a *qiṣṣah* with a full line and a *qiṣṣah* sign in the margin. In this case the next *qiṣṣah* is separated from the preceding by a blank line and the next line starts with a word that is unbroken except for the slight detachment to the right of the initial letter into its vertical justification column, the separation being less than the width of a single character. This is the equivalent of an open section. Another version of an open section is that of Tokapi Serai G I 101 which not only does the same as Rylands 1 but also has a system like the Maimonidean description where a *qiṣṣah* may end with one or two words on a line and the next *qiṣṣah* starts on a new line with no breaks in the new line. This should also be taken as the equivalent of an open section.

Alternatively, both Rylands 1 and G I 101 may complete its *qiṣṣim* with one or two words on a line followed by a *qiṣṣah* sign. The one or two words may be justified to the right or left of the *qiṣṣah*. In the case that the word/s are justified to the right of the *qiṣṣah* no blank line is left between the *qiṣṣah* and its following *qiṣṣah*. The first line of the following *qiṣṣah* is arranged so that there is a gap between the first and second words or between the first cluster of letters of the word and the end of the word. The effect is the creation of a *setumah* space about two to three centimetres long, the

---

[23] See Crown, *Scribes and Manuscripts*, chapter ten, entry 167.

height of one line of writing. If the first word of the *qiṣṣah* is the Tetragrammaton, there is a reluctance to split it, and the space is left between it and the following word. Should the single word be justified to the left and the *qiṣṣah* sign be in the left margin, there is no blank line before the following *qiṣṣah* as in the preceding case, and the last word of the first line of the following *qiṣṣah* is spaced. However, it is not easy to determine whether this spacing is for the sake of justification only or really represents a closed section. The same system is used in the scroll Bodley Or. 665, of a much later period, indicating a continuity of tradition.

The *qiṣṣim* of Rylands Sam 1 and Chester Beatty 751 are marked B in the table[24] where there is a blank line after the *qiṣṣah* and NB where there is no blank line. NBL is used for the case where there is no break but the justification is to the left margin. In the third column the *qiṣṣim* of the Tal edition are marked. In the fourth column the *petuhot* and *setumot* of the MT are listed where they coincide with the *qiṣṣim* of the Samaritan, and a verse number is given for proximity of a *petuhah* or *setumah* to the Samaritan.

A comparison with the published Genesis texts of the Dead Sea scrolls shows only one vacant place, which coincides with the Samaritan, which is not a *petuhah* or *setumah* in the MT. That place is Genesis 45:16 in 4QGen[j]. For the rest, the vacant places agree with the *petuhot* and *setumot*.

When all of this evidence is put together it indicates the following: The system of *petuhot* and *setumot* in the MT originated in a system of paragraph divisions in the text which was the most primitive text division and preceded any versification. This system, which allowed ease of reference to the text is still to be identified in some of the Qumran Pentateuch documents. Since the Samaritan *qiṣṣah* system relates to both the MT and the LXX paragraphing,[25] it represents the oldest form of the paragraphing system and because it has obvious attempts at creating open and closed sections, it arises from the same scribal traditions as produced the MT. It must have taken its separate way before the MT was stabilised and probably can ultimately be traced to the Samaritan texts types represented at Qumran. More work will need to be done on this with reference to the Exodus and Leviticus texts of which there is more Qumran material preserved than of

---

[24] Beginning with chapter 2 since chapter one of Genesis in Rylands 1 is defective.
[25] See Gaster, "Biblical Lessons," 518.

Genesis. The fact that some lines of text in Genesis 49, in virtually every Samaritan manuscript, in particular those lines relating to the Judean tribes, have *qiṣṣah* finials but are not separate *qiṣṣim* suggests that the *qiṣṣah* structure existed before Samaritan sectarian influences affected the text in its 'Samaritan canonisation (i.e 3rd–4th century C.E.). Alternatively, but less likely, the failure to separate these lines as *qiṣṣim* is a mark of masoretic harmonisation by scribes trying to relate *qiṣṣah* numbers to markings. The Samaritan system, then, developed between the first century B.C.E. and the third century C.E. and is a testimony to the antiquity of Samaritan masoretic activity.

Table 1

בראשית	Or. 345	Ryl'sl	Tal	MT	CB 751
1. בראשית ברא 1:1	*	*	*		
2. יהי רקיע 1:6	*	*	*	P	B
3. יקוו המים 1:9	*	*	*	P	B
4. יהי מאורות 1:14	*	*	*	P	NBL
5. ישרצו המים 1:20	*	*	*	P	B
6. תוצא הארץ 1:24	*	*NBL	*	P	B
7. ויכלו השמים 2:1	*	*NB	*	P	B
8. אלה תולדת 2:4	*	*NB	*	P	B
9. ויטע יהוה 2:8	*	*NBL	*		B
10. ויקח יהוה 2:15	*	*B	*		B
11. לא טוב 2:18	*	*B	*		B
12. ויפל יהוה 2:21	*	*B	*		B
13. והנחש היה ערום 3:1	*	*B	*		B
14. ויקרא יהוה 3:9	*	*B	*		NB
15. ויאמר יהוה 3:14	*	*B	*	3:16	B
16. ולאדם אמר 3:17	*	*B	*	S	B
17. הן האדם 3:22	*	*B	*	P	NB
18. והאדם ידע 4:1	*	*B	*	S	B
19. ויאמר יהוה אל קין 4:9	*	*B	*		B
20. וידע קין 4:17	*	*B	*		B
21. וידע אדם 4:25	*	*NB	*		B
22. ויחי אדם 5:3	*	*B	*	5:1	NB
23. ויחי שת 5:6	*	*B	*	S	B
24. ויחי אנוש 5:9	*	*B	*	S	B
25. ויחי קינן 5:12	*	*NB	*	S	B
26. ויחי מהללאל 5:15	*	*B	*	S	B
27. ויחי ירד 5:18	*	*NB	*	S	B
28. ויחי חנוך 5:21	*	*B	*	S	B
29. ויחי מתושלח 5:25	*	*B	*	S	NB
30. ויחי למך 5:28	*	*B	*	S	B

Table 1 (cont.)

בראשית	Or. 345	Ryl'sl	Tal	MT	CB 751
31. ויהי נח 5:32	*	*NB	*	S	B
32. לא ידון 6:3	*	*B	*	6:5	NB
33. אמחה את האדם 6:7	*	*B	*	6.9	B
34. לנח קץ כל בשר 6:13	*	*B	*	S	NB
35. ואני הנני 6:17	*	*B	*		B
36. אל נח בא אחה 7:1	*	*NB	*		B
37. ונח בן שש מאות שנה 7:6	*	*NB	*		NB
38. ויהי לשבעת הימים 7:10	*	*B	*		B
39. ויהי המבול 7:17	*	*B	*		B
40. ויזכר אלהים 8:1	*	*NB	*		B
41. ויהי מקץ 8:6	*	*NB	*		NBL
42. וידבר אלהים אל נח 8:15	*	*B	*	S	NB
43. ויאמר יהוה אל לבו 8:21+	*	*B	*		B
44. ויאמר אלהים אל נח 9:8	*	*B	*	S	B
45. זאת אות 9:12	*	*B	*		B
46. ויהיו בני נח 9:18	*	*B	*	P	B
47. ואלה תולדת 10:1	*	*NB	*	P	NB
48. ובני חם כוש 10:6	*	*B	*		B
49. ומצרים ילד 10:13	*	*B	*	10:15	B
50. ולשם ילד 10:21	*	*B	*	S	NB
51. ויהי כל הארץ 11:1	*	*B	*	P	B
52. אלה תולדת שם שם 11:10	*	*B	*	P	B
53. וארפכשד 11:12	*	*B	*	S	B
54. ויהי שלח 11:14	*	*B	*	S	B
55. ויהי עבר 11:16	*	*B	*	S	B
56. ויהי פלג 11:18	*	*B	*	S	B
57. ויהי רעו 11:20	*	*B	*	S	B
58. ויהי שרוג 11:22	*	*B	*	S	B
59. ויהי נחור 11:24	*	*NB	*	S	NBL
60. ויהי תרה 11:26	*	*B	*	S	NB
61. אברם לך לך 12:1	*	*B	*	P	B
62. ויראה יהוה 12:7	*	*B	*		B
63. ויהי רעב בארץ	*	*NB	*	P	B
64. ויקרא פרעה 12:18	*	*B	*		B
65. וגם ללוט 13:5	*	*NB	*		NBL
66. ויהוה אמר 13:14	*	*NB	*		B
67. ויהי בימי (א)מרפל 14:1	*	*B	*	P	NB
68. ויצא מלך סדם 14:8	*	*B	*		B
69. ויבא הפליט 14:13	*	*NB	*		NB
70. ומלכי צדק 14:18	*	*B	*		B
71. אחר הדברים 15:1	*	*B	*	S	NB
72. ויהי השמש לבוא 15:12	*	*B	*		NBL
73. ויהי השמש בא(ה) 15:17	*	*B	*		NB
74. ושרי אשת אברם 16:1	*	*B	*	S	NBL

Table 1 (*cont.*)

בראשית	Or. 345	Ryl's1	Tal	MT	CB 751
75. וימצאה מלאך 16:7	*	*B	*		B
76. ויהי אברם 17:1	*	*B	*	S	B
77. אל אברהם ואתה 17:9	*	*B	*		B
78. שרי אשתך 17:15	*	*B	*	S	NBL
79. בֿ ויעל אלהים 17:21	*	*B	*		NB
80. באלוני ממרא 18:1	*	*B	*	P	NB
81. (לי) למה זה 18:13 צחקה שרה	*	*B	*		B
82. צעקת סדם ועמרה 18:20	*	*NB	*		NB
83. אם אמצא בסדם 18:26	*	*B	*		NB
84. ויבאו שני המלאכים 19:1	*	*B	*		B
85. ויאמרו המלאכים 19:12	*	*B	*		NB
86. ויאמר לוט 19:18	*	*B	*		B
87. ויהוה המטיר 19:24	*	*NB	*		B
88. ויעל לוט 19:30	*	*NB	*		NB
89. ויסע משם 20:1	*	*B	*	S	B
90. וישכם אבימלך 20:8	*	*NB	*		B
91. ויקח אבימלך 20:14	*	*B	*		B
92. ויהוה פקד 21:1	*	*B	*	S	B
93. אל אברהם אל ירע 21:12	*	*B	*		B
94. בֿ ויקרא מלאך 21:17	*	*NB	*		NB
95. ויהי בעת ההיא 21:22	*	*NB	*	P	B
96. ויקח אברהם צאן 21:27	*	*B	*		B
97. והאלהים נסה 22:1	*	*B	*	P	B
98. ויאמר יצחק 22:7	*	*NBL	*		B
99. ויקרא אליו מלאך 22:11	*	*B	*		B
100. ויקרא מלאך 22:15	*	*B	*		B
101. וינד לאברהם 22:20	*	*NBL	*	P	B
102. ויהיו חיי שרה 23:1	*	*B	*	P	B
103. אֿ ויען עפרון 23:10	*	*B	*		NB
104. ואברהם זקן 24:1	*	*NB	*	S	B
105. ויקח העבד 24:10	*	*B	*		B
106. ויהי הוא טרם 24:15	*	*NB	*		B
107. כלו הגמלים 24:22	*	*NB	*		NB
108. ותרץ הנערה 24:28	*	*B	*		B
109. עבד אברהם 24:34	*	*B	*		NB
110. ואבוא היום 24:42	*	*B	*		B
111. ויהי כאשר שמע 24:52	*	*NB	*		NB
112. ויצחק בא 24:62	*	*NBL	*		B
113. ויסף אברהם 25:1	*	*NB	*	P	NB
114. ואלה ימי שני 25:7	*	*B	*		B
115. ואלה תולדת 25:12 ישמעאל	*	*NB	*	P	B
116. ואלה תולדת יצחק 25:19	*	*NB	*	P	NB

Table 1 (cont.)

בראשית	Or. 345	Ryl's1	Tal	MT	CB 751
117. ויזיד יעקב 25:29	*	*B	*		B
118. ויהי רעב בארץ 26:1	*	*B	*	P	B
119. וישב יצחק בגרד 26:6	*	*B	*		NB
120. ויזרע יצחק 26:12	*	*B	*		NBL
121. וירא אליו יהוה 26:24	*	*B	*		B
122. ויהי כי זקן 27:1	*	*B	*	S	NBL
123. אל רבקה אמו 27:11	*	*B	*		NB
124. אל יעקב נשה 27:21	*	*B	*		B
125. כלה יצחק 27:30	*	*NB	*		B (B)
126. ויהי כשמע עשו 27:34	*	*B	*		NB (NB)
127. ויאמר עשו בלבו 27:41ב	*	*B	*		NBL (NB)
128. ויקרא יצחק 28:1	*	*B	*		B (B)
129. ויצא יעקב 28:10	*	*B	*	S	B (NBL)
130. וי*קץ יעקב 28:16	*	*B	*		B (NB)
131. וישא יעקב 29:1	*	*B	*		B
132. ראה יעקב 29:10 (NB)	*	*B	*		NBL
133. וללבן שתי 29:16	*	*B	*		B
134. וירא יהוה 29:31	*	*B	*		B
135. ותרא רחל 30:1	*	*B	*		B
136. ותרא לאה 30:9	*	*B	*		NB
137. וילך ראובן 30:14	*	*B	*		B
138. ויזכר אלהים 30:22	*	*B	*		B
139. לא תתן לי מאומה 30:31א	*	*NB	*		B (B)
140. ויאמר מלאך 30:37א	*	*NB	*		B (B)
141. ויקח לו יעקב 30:37ב	*	*B	*		NBL
142. א [ל]יעקב שוב 31:3	*	*B	*		B
143. ויאמר [אלי] מלאך 31:11	*	*B	*		NBL
144. ויקם יעקב 31:17	*	*B	*		NBL
145. ויבא אלהים אל לבן 31:24	*	*NB	*		NBL
146. ויען יעקב 31:31	*	*B	*		B
147. ויחר ליע קב 31:36	*	*NBL	*		B
148. זה עשרים 31:38	*	*B	*		NB
149. זה לי עשרים 31:41	*	*B	*		NB
150. ויען לבן 31:43	*	*B	*		NB
151. ויאמר לבן ליעקב 31:51	*	*NB	*		B
152. וישלח יעקב 32:4	*	*B	*	P	B
153. ויאמר יעקב 32:10	*	*B	*		NB
154. ויקח מן הבא 32:14ב	*	*B	*		NBL
155. ויקם בלילה ההוא 32:23	*	*B	*		B
156. וישא יעקב עיניו 33:1	*	*B	*		B
157. ויאמר נסעה 33:12	*	*B	*		B

Table 1 (*cont.*)

בראשית	Or. 345	Ryl's1	Tal	MT	CB 751
158. ויבא יעקב שלום 33:18	*	*B	*	S	B
159. ותצא דינה 34:1	*	*B	*	S	B
159a. ויצא חמור 34:6	——	——	*		
160. וידבר חמור 34:8	*	*B	*		B
161. ויענו בני יעקב 34:13	*	*NB	*		B
162. ויבא חמור 34:20	*	*NB	*		NB
163. ויהי ביום השלישי 34:25	*	*NB	*		B
164. ויאמר אלהים אל 35:1 יעקב or קום עלה בית אל (BL Or 2683)	*	*B	*	P	B
165. ויבא יעקב לוזה 35:6		*NB	*		NB
166. וירא אלהים 35:9	*	*B	*	P	B
167. ויסע ישראל 35:21	*	*B	*	35:23	B
168. עשו הוא אדום 36:1	*	*B	*	P	B
169. עשו אבי אדום 36:9	*	*B	*		B
170. ואלה בני שעיר 36:20	*	*NB	*	S	NB
171. ואלה המלכים 36:31	*	*B	*	P	NBL
172. וישב יעקב 37:1	*	*B	*	P	B
173. ויחלם יוסף 37:5	*	*B	*		NB
174. ויחלם עוד 37:9	*	*B	*		B
175. ויאמר ישראל אל 37:13 יוסף	*	*B	*		B
176. בא יוסף 37:23	*	*NB	*		B
177. וישוב ראובן 37:29	*	*NB	*		B
178. ויהי בעת ההיא 38:1	*	*B	*	P	B
179. ויאמר יהודה 38:11	*	*NB	*		NB
180. וישלח יהודה 38:20	*	*NB	*		B
181. ויהי כמשלשת 38:24	*	*B	*		NBL
182. ויוסף הורד 39:1	*	*B	*	S	B
183. ותשא אשת אדניו 39:7	*	*B	*		NB
184. ויהי כדברה אל 39:10 יוסף	*	*B	*		B
185. ויהי כשמע אדניו 39:19	*	*B	*		NBL
186. חטאו משקה 40:1	*	*B	*	P	B
187. ויספר שר המשקים 40:9	*	*NB	*		B
188. וירא שר האפים 40:16	*	*B	*		NBL
189. ויהי מקץ 41:1	*	*B	*	P	B
190. וידבר שר המשקים 41:9	*	*NB	*		B
191. וידבר פרעה 41:17	*	*B	*		NB
192. ויאמר יוסף 41:25	*	*NB	*		NBL
193. ועתה יראה 41:33	*	*B	*		B

Table 1 (*cont.*)

בראשית	Or. 345	Ryl's1	Tal	MT	CB 751
194. ויאמר פרעה אל יוסף 41:39	*	*NB	*		B
195. ויצא יוסף 41:42	*	*NB	*		B
196. וליוסף ילדו 41:50	*	*B	*		B
197. כי יש שבר במצרים 42:1	*	*B	*		B
198. ויבאו אחי יוסף 42:6ב	*	*B	*		B
199. הוא אשר דברתי 42:14	*	*B	*		NB
200. יוסף ביום השלישי 42:18	*	*NB	*		B
201. ויצו יוסף 42:25	*	*B	*		N B
202. ויבאו אל יעקב 42:29	*	*B	*		B
203. אתי שכלתם יוסף 42:36	*	*B	*		B
204. למה הרעתם לי 43:6	*	*B	*		B
205. אם כן אפוא 43:11	*	*B	*		B
206. ויקחו האנשים 43:15	*	*B	*		B
207. וינשו אל האיש 43:19	*	*B	*		NBL
208. ויבא יוסף הביתה 43:26	*	*NBL	*		NBL
209. ויצו את אשר על 44:1 ביתו	*	*B	*		B
210. ויבא יהודה 44:14	*	*NB	*		NB
211. וינש אליו יהודה 44:18	*	*NB	*	S	B
212. ויאמר עבדך 44:27	*	*B	*		B
213. ולא יכל יוסף 45:1	*	*B	*		B
214. מ[א]הרו ועלו 45:9	*	*B	*		NBL
215. ויאמר פרעה 45:17	*	*NB	*		B
216. ויעלו ממצרים 45:25	*	*NB	*		B
217. במרא[ו]ת הלילה 46:2	*	*NB	*		NB
218. ואלה שמות 46:8	*	*NB	*	S	B
219. בני רחל 46:19	*	*B	*		NB
220. ואת יהודה 46:28	*	*B	*	S	B
221. ויבא יוסף 47:1	*	*B	*		B
222. ויבא יוסף 47:1	*	*NB	*		NB
223. ותלא 47:13ב	*	*B	*		B
224. ויקן יוסף 47:20	*	*B	*		NB
225. ויאמר יוסף 47:23	*	*B	*		B
226. וישב ישראל 47:27	*	*B	*		NB
227. ויאמר [א]ל יוסף 48:1	*	*B	*	P	B
228. ויאמר יעקב אל יוסף 48:3	*	*B	*		B
229. וירא ישראל 48:8	*	*NBL	*		NB
230. וישלח ישראל 48:14	*	*NB	*		B
231. וירא יוסף 48:17	*	*B	*		B
232. ויאמר ישראל אל יוסף 48:21	*	*NB	*		B
233. ויקרא יעקב 49:1	*	*B	*	P	NB

Table 1 (*cont.*)

בראשית	Or. 345	Ryl's1	Tal	MT	CB 751
234. שמעון ולוי 49:5	*	*NB	*	P	B
235. יהוד ה אתה 49:8	*	*B	*	P	NB
236. זבולן 49:13	*	*B	*	P	B
237. דן ידין 49:16	*	*B	*	S	B
238. נד נדוד 49:19	*	*NBL	*	S	B
238a. נפתלי 49:21	——	——	*	S	
239. בן פרת יוסף 49:22	*	*NBL	*	S	B
240. בזאת אשר דבר להם 49:28	*	*B	*	49:27	B
241. ויכל יעקב 49:33	*	*B	*	S	B
242. בוידבר יוסף 50:4	*	*B	*		B
243. ויעל יוסף 50:7	*	*NB	*		B
244. וירא יושב 50:11	*	*B	*		NBL
245. ויראו אחי יוסף 50:15	*	*B	*		B
246. ויאמר אליהם יוסף 50:19	*	*B	*		B
247. וישב יוסף 50:22	*	*NBL	*		B
248. ויאמר יוסף 50:24	*	*NB	*		NB
249. וישביע יוסף 50:25	*	*B	*		NBL
250. וימת יוסף 50:26	*	*B	*		B

הספר הראישון קצים ר ונ

The asterisk shows the *qiṣṣah* structure

II. MARGINS AND TEXT PLACEMENT

Of especial interest to scholars of the scrolls is the size of margins, the proportion of a leaf, column or folio taken up by text and the halakhic permissibility of the margins. There is a self-evident value of this information in reconstructing fragments. Unfortunately, there are no dated Samaritan texts before the eleventh century C.E. but there are reasons to argue that the Samaritan scribes drew on the same tradition as the Jewish scribes and preserved an older masoretic tradition.

Samaritan texts show a remarkable stability in the proportion of a text on a folio—or sheet of parchment in the case of a scroll—to the margin size, though there are diachronic changes and changes which are related to the nature of the material. Some of the diachronic changes relate to script. When Arabic became an important Samaritan language, the scribal traditions began to adapt to what was customary in Arabic manuscripts. Moreover, many of the later Samaritan manuscripts are on paper and the mould size in paper manufacturing governed the text size. However, even in the latter type of MS, traditions died hard, and the proportion of the text block to the margins reflected older habits.

In the opinion of the writer, traditions found in Jewish manuscripts were reflected in the older Samaritan manuscripts. The Talmudic prescriptions in regard to the margins of a sheet of sacred writing to be used for lections are that the lower margin shall be one handsbreadth in width and that the upper margin shall be three finger breadths, whereas scrolls to be used for study should be two finger breadths.[26] The margin between columns is to be two finger breadths.[27] Maimonides varies the proportions slightly by indicating all measurements in fingerbreadths alone, though it is clear from his calculations that four fingerbreadths go to make one handsbreadth.[28] The interpretation of what is a fingerbreadth must vary from scribe to scribe, unless an equivalent measure is laid down, as in the Maimonidean calculation that it is to be about an inch.[29] Such an interpretation necessitates upper, lower and medial margins of 3, 4 and 2 inches respectively.

From the following table it will be seen that these proportions and percentages of text to writing material size are preserved in the Samaritan scribal tradition, and the following data may be helpful in scroll reconstruction.

The columns in the table show the size of the document, the size of the text block, the percentage of the text block occupying the folio or column, the inner margin or margin between columns, the foredge or outer margin, the percentage of the inner margin to the outer margin, the size of the upper and lower margins and their percentage relationship to each other. In some instances trimming of material before binding has to be accounted for and reconstructions of incomplete sheets are asterisked.

The chronological data help to establish a diachronic profile.

---

[26] *Sopherim* 2:4.
[27] *Hagahot Maimuniot* 15 to *HST* 7:15.
[28] *Sopherim* 2:4.
[29] Idem.

Table 2

Date	MS	Folio size	Text size	% area	I	F	%	U	L	%
1230	Bod. Sam 3	27.5 × 33.5	22 × 19	45	3	6	50	4.8	6.8	70
1300	Bod. Sam b1	26.5 × 36.5	23.5 × 18.5	44	3	6.5	46	6	8	75
1200+	Bod. Sam c3	27 × 34	20 × 23	50	3	6	50	5.6	5.5	101
1300−	Bod. Sam c2	30* × 37	28.5 × 25.5	51	2.5	1.5*	?	3.5	6.0	58*
1390	c2 ff. 11−12	29 × 36.5	22 × 44	49	3	4.5	66	5.5	6.5	84
1362	Cot.Claud.	29.8 × 21.8	22 × 17	40	2.5	2.3	108	3.5	4.3	81
1359	BL 22369	27 × 33.8	18.2 × 21	41	2.4	6.5	36	4.8	7.0	68
1342	b5 ff. 10−14	20 × 30.5	14 × 21	47	2.5	3.5	71	4	5	80
14thc.	b3 27	22.5 × 27	15 × 17	43	2.5	5.5	45	4	5.5	72
14thc.	b3 21	29 × 23.5	18.6 × 17	51	2.5	4.0	62	3.9	6.5	60
14thc.	b3 15	28.5 × 23.5	15 × 17	38	3	6	50	4.9	6.5	75
1450	Hunt. 301	27.5 × 18.5	18 × 12	42	1.5	5.0	30	4.5	5	90
1479	Bod. Or 345	21.6 × 31.3	13.5 × 21	41	2.5	5.6	44	5	5.3	94
1484	b6	29 × 35	22 × 26	56	1.5	5	30	5	7	71
16thc.	Bod. Or 699	23.5 × 30	1.5 × 21	49	2.5	4.5	50	4	6	66
1596	Hunt 350	14.5 × 21	11 × 15.5	53	1.5	2	75	2.5	3	83
1650	Hunt 24	20 × 32	11.5 × 19	34	1	7.5	13	6.5	6.5	100

THE APOCRYPHON OF JOSHUA—4Q522 9 ii:
A REAPPRAISAL*

Devorah Dimant

לעמנואל, ידיד אמת

The Apocryphon of Joshua is the title given to a work represented by three or four copies of the Qumran scrolls, and perhaps another copy from Massada. It belongs to the genre of reworking the Bible, well documented at Qumran. The history of research into this *Apocryphon* illustrates the complex process through which the identification and understanding of an unfamiliar Qumran composition has to go. The *Apocryphon* was first identified in two copies, 4Q378 and 4Q379, published by Carol Newsom under the title the *Psalms of Joshua*.[1] Another manuscript, 4Q522, was initially published by Émile Puech without any connection to Joshua.[2] However, in a subsequent re-edition of 4Q522 9 ii Elisha Qimron identified the speaker of the discourse preserved therein as the biblical Joshua and noted its links to episodes related in the biblical Book of Joshua. In the absence of overlapping of this manuscript with 4Q378 and 4Q379, Qimron was reluctant to attribute it to the *Psalms of Joshua*. Instead he suggested assigning all the manuscripts related to Joshua to one group, which he labeled 'Joshua Cycles.'[3] Reviewing materials pertaining to Joshua at Qumran Emanuel Tov analyzed the phraseology and motifs shared by all three manuscripts and convincingly showed that their similarity

---

* The article was completed during my tenure at the Institute for Advanced Studies of the Hebrew University of Jerusalem (2001–2002). I thank the members of the Qumran group for their helpful comments.

[1] Following John Strugnell. See her publication "The 'Psalms of Joshua' from Qumran Cave 4", *JJS* 39 (1988): 56–73. But already there she noted that this title "is not entirely apt as a description of the whole work" (ibid., 58).

[2] Cf. his preliminary edition of two fragments from this manuscript, "Fragments du Psaume 122 dans un manuscrit hébreu de la grotte IV," *RevQ* 9 (1978): 547–54; idem, "La Pierre de Sion et l'autel des holocaustes d'après un manuscrit hébreu de la grotte 4 (4Q522)," *RB* 99 (1992): 676–96. While not explicitly connecting 4Q522 with *the Psalms of Joshua* Puech noted the various affinities displayed by 4Q522 9 ii to this work. Cf. ibid., 690.

[3] Cf. E. Qimron, "Concerning 'Joshua Cycles' from Qumran (4Q522)," *Tarbiz* 63 (1994): 503–8 (Hebrew).

is sufficient to postulate that they are copies of one and the same
work. He named this work the *Apocryphon of Joshua*.[4] The analysis
below lends additional support to this view and shows that the passage published by Puech is fully and correctly understood only in
terms of the activities of Joshua.[5] Another fragment with a list of
toponyms, 5Q9, may have been torn from a fourth copy of the same
work, since it is very similar to the list of toponyms preserved in
4Q522 9 i.[6] Lastly, a small fragment found at Masada perhaps came
from a fifth copy of the *Apocryphon*.[7]

---

[4] Cf. E. Tov, "The Rewritten Book of Joshua as Found at Qumran and Masada,"
in *Biblical Perspectives: Early use and Interpretation of the Bible in Light of the Dead Sea Scrolls*
(ed. M. E. Stone and E. G. Chazon; *STDJ* 28; Leiden: Brill, 1998), 233–56. This
title is also adopted by Carol Newsom in a subsequent article, "4Q378 and 4Q379:
An Apocryphon of Joshua", in *Qumranstudien* (ed. H.-J. Fabry, A. Lange, and
H. Lichtenberger; Göttingen: Vandenhoeck & Ruprecht, 1996), 35–85. It is retained
in her final publication, *Qumran Cave 4. XVII; Parabiblical Texts, Part 3* (*DJD* XXII;
Oxford: Clarendon, 1996), 237–88. Tov, ibid., 239–241, 247–250 demonstrates that
4Q522 9 ii is aligned with other Joshua materials, and rejects Puech's attempt to
center the passage on David and Solomon. See Puech, "La Pierre de Sion." One
of the most compelling arguments adduced by Tov is the list of toponyms in 4Q522
9 i, preceding the present passage about the Tent of Meeting. Toponym lists also
appear in other fragments of 4Q522 (cf. esp. frg. 8). Tov points out that such lists
are irrelevant to the context of David and Solomon, but are most pertinent to the
conquests of Joshua. See comment on line 8.

[5] In his final edition of this manuscript Émile Puech remains undecided and at
times inconsistent regarding the identification of 4Q522 as a copy of the *Apocryphon
of Joshua*. Cf. idem, *Qumrân Grotte 4.XVIII; Textes Hébreux (4Q521–4Q528, 4Q576–4Q579)*
(*DJD* XXV; Oxford: Clarendon, 1998), 55–62. On the one hand he argues that
the absence of overlapping between 4Q522 and other copies of the *Apocryphon* (4Q378
and 4Q379) militates against such identification (cf. ibid., 71). On the other hand
he admits that the biblical Book of Joshua furnishes the framework for 4Q522 and
even suggests that Joshua may be the protagonist of this "pseudepigraphic work"
(ibid., 57). By arguing against the identification of 4Q522 as a copy of the *Apocryphon
of Joshua* Puech resorts to an even less likely hypothesis, namely, the presence at
Qumran of two different, but very similar, works on the same topic.

[6] Cf. Tov, "The Rewritten Book of Joshua," 241–3; 250–51. 5Q9 is published
by Milik in *Les 'Petites Grottes' de Qumran* (ed. M. Baillet, J. T. Milik and R. de Vaux;
DJD III; Oxford: Clarendon 1962), 179–80.

[7] MS. Mas 11, as suggested by S. Talmon, *Masada VI—The Yigael Yadin Excavation
1963–1965* (Jerusalem: Israel Exploration Society, 1999) 105–16. Cf. Tov, "The
Rewritten Book of Joshua" (n. 4), 251–2. One may also add to the list the small
fragments of another scroll, 4Q123, copied in Paleo-Hebrew characters. It contains
some sort of rewriting of Joshua and is published by E. Ulrich in *Qumran Cave 4/IV:
Paleo-Hebrew and Greek Biblical Manuscripts* (ed. P. W. Skehan, E. Ulrich and J. E.
Sanderson; *DJD* IX; Oxford: Clarendon 1992), 201–3. Tov, "The Rewritten Book
of Joshua," 252 suggests that 4Q123 may come from another copy of the *Apocryphon
of Joshua*, given its similarity to certain expressions in 4Q379 1. Puech, *Textes Hébreux*,
72 thinks that they are unconnected. Tov, ibid., 233 considers the pseudepigraphic

From these copies the work appears to consist of a narrative framework, interspersed with speeches, blessings and prayers, mostly pronounced by Joshua.[8] This general characterization also covers 4Q522 9 ii re-edited below.

None of the extant fragments from the *Apocryphon* contains any term characteristic of the literature associated with the Qumran community, so it cannot be considered to have belonged to the literature of the community proper. Yet several passages espouse ideas close to those expressed in works from the circle of the Qumran community.[9] Moreover, a passage from the *Apocryphon* (4Q378 22 ii 7–15) is cited by a sectarian collection of biblical quotations, *4QTestimonia* (= 4Q175) 21–30.[10] These facts point to a closer relationship between the present work and the circles of the Qumran community, but its precise nature requires further study.[11] In any case, the members of the community were certainly interested in the *Apocryphon*. They not only read it but also copied it. For instance, the full orthography and forms typical of Qumran manuscripts (e.g. ראישון, החטיוני, מאתכה, ישוע) attest to the late linguistic environment of the copyist, who may have been a member of the Qumran community. However, these orthographic features reflect only the idiosyncrasies of the scribe of this particular manuscript and, therefore, do not necessarily attest to the provenance of the original author. So they cannot be taken as an indication of the origin of this composition.[12]

As often is the case with scrolls from Qumran, the precise date of the composition is difficult to establish, especially when the subject matter relates to biblical episodes and lacks any allusion to later

---

writing *Assumption of Moses* to be a work related to the Qumran *Apocryphon of Joshua*. However, the final judgment on this issue must be withheld until a detailed study of the *Apocryphon* is undertaken.

[8] See the list of themes suggested for the entire work by Tov, "The Rewritten Book of Joshua," 253–4.

[9] Cf. e.g. 4Q379 12, which calculates in jubilees the date of entry of the Israelites into Canaan, a calculation that coincides with that of *Jub.* 50:4.

[10] Published by J. Allegro, *DJD* V, 57–60. Cf. the corrections of J. Strugnell, "Notes en marge du volume V des 'Discoveries in the Judaean Desert of Jordan,'" *RevQ* 7 (1969–70): 225–9.

[11] Newsom, "The Psalms of Joshua," 60 had noted a general affinity between some fragments and the Aramaic *Testament of Levi* and *Jubilees*. Tov, "The Rewritten Book of Joshua," 254–5 suggests a possible sectarian provenance. I deal with this issue in a forthcoming article, "Between Sectarian and Non-sectarian: the Case of the *Apocryphon of Joshua*."

[12] Contra Tov, "The Rewritten Book of Joshua," 255 who is inclined to accept this orthography as an indication of sectarian provenance.

events or figures.[13] The extant copies were penned during the first century B.C.E.,[14] a period that constitutes the *terminus ante quem* for the composition of this work. However, the presence of several exemplars, spanning over a century, suggests that the work was authored earlier, during the last part of the second century B.C.E. at the latest. This early date is corroborated by the fact that 4Q174 (*Testimonia*), copied in a hand dated to 100–75 B.C.E., quotes a passage from the *Apocryphon*.[15]

Unfortunately, most of the surviving passages of the work are quite fragmentary. Of the few large pieces, fragment 9 from 4Q522 is one of the longest and best preserved. It contains the middle section of two successive columns. The first is a list of toponyms, connected with Joshua's conquests. The second presents a discourse of Joshua concerning the Tent of Meeting and the future Solomonic Temple. It is this second column that is re-edited and discussed below.

---

[13] At an early stage of research the quotation of 4Q379 22 ii in 4Q175 was considered to be an allusion to Simon or John Hyrcanus. Cf. J. T. Milik, *Ten Years of Discovery in the Wilderness of Judaea* (London: SCM, 1961), 61–64; F. Cross, *The Ancient Library of Qumran* (New York: Anchor Books, 1961, revised ed.), 147–52. Cf. more recently T. H. Lim, "Psalms of Joshua" (4Q379 frg. 22 col. 2): "A Reconsideration of its Text", *JJS* 44 (1993): 309–12; H. Eshel, "The Historical Background of the Pesher Interpreting Joshua's Curse on the Rebuilder of Jericho," *RevQ* 15 (1992): 409–420. However, the historical interpretation should now be reexamined in the context of the *Apocryphon of Joshua* as a whole. Eshel's suggestion that the passage attributed to Joshua originally belongs to 4Q175, which the *Apocryphon of Joshua* quotes, is incompatible with the character of the two works. For 4Q175 is a collection of quotations, whereas the *Apocryphon of Joshua* is a reworked version of Joshua's exploits. A quotation of Joshua's word is therefore quite in place within the *Apocryphon*, and therefore is part of its original text, whereas in 4Q175 it is one of several citations adduced from other sources.

[14] The earliest is 4Q379, dated by Newsom to the first half of the first century B.C.E. Cf. *DJD* XXII, 262. 4Q522 is slightly later, dated by Puech to the second third of the same century. Cf. idem in *DJD* XXV, 41. 4Q378 is assigned by Newson to the turn of the Common Era. Cf. her note in *DJD* XXII, 241.

[15] For the composition of 4Q522 Puech offers a similar date for different reasons. Cf. idem, "La Pierre de Sion," 689–691. On the basis of the assumed association of 4Q379 22 ii with Simon or John Hyrcanus Tov dates the *Apocryphon of Joshua* to the late second or early first century B.C.E. Cf. idem, "The Rewritten Book of Joshua," 255–6.

4Q522

Fragment 9, column ii

[ובני ישראל]	[נִֹתַֹתַֹ]	1
לוֹא יֹ[בוא]וֹ [לצי]וֹן להשכין שם את אהל מו[עד עד אשר יעברו]		2
העתים כי הנה בן נולד לישי בן פרץ בן יה[ודה והוא אשר ילכוד]		3
את סלע ציון ויורש משם את כֹּ^להאמורי מיר[ושלים ויהיה עם לבבו]		4
לבנות א^תהבית ליהוה אלוהי ישראל זהב וכסף [נחושת וברזל יכין]		5
ארזים וברושים יביא מ[לבנון לבנותו ובנו הקטן [הוא יבננו וצדיק]		6
יכהן שם ראישוֹןֹ מ[בני פינ]חֹס [בכורכה] ואותו [יר]צֹה ו[יברכהו יהוה]		7
[מע]ל [ממ]עֹון מן השמי[ם כי] ידיד יהו[ה] ישכון לבטח [ימינו ו]יהוה מגינו כול		8
[ה]^הימים עמו ישכון לֹעד ועתה האמורי שם והכנענ[י] בקרבנו הוא		9
יושב אשר החטיונֹי אשר לוא דרשתי אֹ[ת מ]שפטֹ הֹ[אורים והתומים]		10
מאתכה והשלוני וה[נֹ]הֹ נתחו עבד ע[בדים ליש]אֹל° ולמזבח יהוה]		11
ועתה נ[ש]כינה את אֹ[הל מו]עד רחוק מן הֹ[אמורי והכנעני וישאו]		12
אלעזֹ[ר וישו]ע את אֹ[הל מו]עד מבית [אל לשילה	[	13
ישוֹע[	שֹ[ר]° צבא מעֹ[רכות ישראל	[	14
]°שֹ[	]לֹ[ ]לֹ[	[	15

Notes on Reading

The present edition is based on PAM 41.948 and PAM 43.606, and the respective editions of Puech and Qimron.[16] As pointed out by Puech, of some twenty fragments of 4Q522 none has preserved the full length of the line, so any reconstruction of lines here is hypothetical. Nevertheless, since fragments 22–25 produce Psalm 122 the lines may be plausibly reconstructed. The length of lines thus obtained consists of 55–57 letter-spaces.[17] This approximate length is also assumed for 4Q522 9 ii edited below. In the case of fragment 9 ii such a length requires supplements of some 13–15 letter-spaces at

---

[16] The photographs are published by Puech *Textes Hébreux*, Pl. V. Puech published his final edition ibid., 38–83. An earlier version of his edition for two fragments was published in "Fragments du Psaume 122", and in "La pierre de Sion,". Qimron re-edited 4Q522 9 ii. in "Joshua Cycles". Tov, "Rewritten Book of Joshua," 237 usually reproduces Qimron's edition. Tov's edition is quoted only where it differs from Qimron's text.

[17] Cf. Puech's comments in *Textes Hébreux*, 39–40, 68. Various stylistic considerations also favor such a length. Cf. comments to lines 3, 4, 8, 12. This size should therefore be preferred to the shorter lines reconstructed by Qimron. Qimron now agrees that the lines should be longer (oral communication). Also Tov, "The Rewritten Book of Joshua," 236–7 argues for lines longer than the length proposed by Qimron. He suggests (ibid., 249–50) that Psalm 122 should be placed immediately before the discourse of Joshua preserved in 4Q522 9 ii, at the bottom of the preceding column (4Q522 9 i).

the end of each line, slightly longer than the reconstruction suggested by Qimron.[18]

L. 1].ֺהֺֺתֺ[. Only the lower strokes survived. Similarly Puech.

L. 2 יֺ[בוא]וֺ [לצי]וֺן. The edge of a vertical stroke survived in the middle of the line before the lacuna. It suits a *yod* (rather than *nun*, read by Puech, or *kaf*, read by Tov), in accordance with the short form of this letter in this manuscript. A very faint tip of a stroke further on may stand for a *waw*. The size of the entire stretch is 11–12 letter-spaces and the supplement is proposed to match it. The restorations proposed by Puech and Qimron are too long, some 14–15 letter-spaces each.

מו[עד. Qimron's מוֺעֺֺד] has no manuscript evidence.

L. 4 מיר[ושלים. Thus Puech. The reading מיר] is clear on PAM 41.948.[19]

כֺל. Apparently the word was initially omitted by the scribe and later added above its proper place. A similar insertion above the line (the word את) is observed in the following line. This is a common method of correction practiced by the scribes of the Qumran scrolls.

L. 7 וֺ[יברכהו]. A very faint trace of the first letter is seen in the photo. Qimron reads *waw*, which is preferable to *bet* (thus Puech).

L. 8 [מע]לֺ] ממ[עוֺן. A very faint tip of a stroke in the middle of the line suggests a *lamed*. Thus also Puech and Qimron. However, they supply different restorations.

L. 10 החטיוני. *Nun* and *yod* should be read at the end of the word (with Qimron), rather than a final *mem* (thus Puech).

L. 11 עבד ע[בדים ליש[רֺא]ל. The lacuna accommodates 7–8 letter-spaces. The restoration is suggested to fit it. Qimron's restoration עבד ע]ולם should be discounted because, as Puech points out, missing is the upper tip of a *lamed*, which should have survived on the remaining space had it originally been written in the scroll.[20] Puech's own restoration עבד ע[ם בני יש[רֺא]ל is awkward in this context.

---

[18] Qimron, "Joshua Cycles," 505 argues that in lines 9–10 probably only one word is missing at the end of each (accepted also by Tov, ibid., 236). But this is not necessarily so, since longer restorations are possible, which meet the requirements of both the context and the Hebrew style.

[19] Cf. Puech, *Textes Hébreux*, 58 n. 39. The photograph is reproduced ibid., plate V.

[20] Cf. Puech, *Textes Hébreux*, 62.

L. 14 מֹעֻֽרכות]. The faint upper tip of a right vertical stroke is better read as *'ayin* (with Tov), rather than *shin* (thus Puech).

L. 15]שׁׄ. Thus Puech, Tov. The traces of the upper tips of a *shin* are clearly visible on the photographs. Also an upper tip of the left stroke of another letter survived before the *shin*.

TRANSLATION

1 [   ]. . .[the Children of Israel]
2 w[ill] not [come t]o[Zi]on to install there the Tent of Mee[ting until]
3 the times [will pass], for behold, a son will be born to Jesse son of Perez son of Ju[dah and it will be he who will seize]
4 the rock of Zion and will dispossess from there <all> the Amorites from Jer[usalem, and it will be his intention]
5 to build <the> house to the Lord, God of Israel. Gold and silver, [brass and iron he will prepare],
6 cedar-trees and junipers he will bring [from] Lebanon to build it, and his youngest son [he will build it, and Zadok]
7 will minister there, first of [the sons of Phin]eas [your first-born], and him He [will fav]or [and the Lord will bless him]
8 [from ab]ove[, from the heaven[ly ab]ode[, for] "the friend of the Lo[rd] will dwell in safety and[the Lord will be his protector all]
9 [the] days. With him He will dwell forever". But now the Amorites are there and the Canaanit[es amidst us are]
10 dwelling, for they led me to sin because I did not seek th[e dec]ision of the [Urim and Thummim]
11 from you and they deceived me, and beh[o]ld I made them slaves of s[laves to Is]rae[l and to the altar of the Lord].
12 And now let us in[st]all the T[ent of Mee]ting far from the [Amorites and the Canaanites. And]
13 Eleazar [and Joshu]a [carried] the T[ent of Mee]ting from Beth[el to Shilo   ]
14 Joshua[the comman]der of the army of the batt[le arrays of Israel   ]
15 [ ] .[   ].[ ].[   ]

Comments

L. 2] יᵒ[בוא]ᵒי לֹוᵒא. The negation of the verb indicates that the entire phrase of line 1 describes an impossibility. The surviving words in lines 2–4 show that this impossibility concerns the installing of the Tent of Meeting in Jerusalem.

] יᵒ[בוא]ᵒי. The lacuna accommodates 3–4 letter-spaces, and the restoration is suggested accordingly. If this restoration is correct, the 3rd pers. plural verb may refer to the Israelites, and the supplement at the end of the previous line is restored accordingly. The entire discourse is pronounced by Joshua, as is indicated by the 1st pers. sing. verbs in lines 10–11. The 2nd pers. sing. in line 11 (מאתכה) suggests that Joshua is addressing someone, probably Eleazar, mentioned in line 13. In fact, by using the 1st pers. plural in line 12 (נ]ו[ש]כינה) Joshua includes both himself and Eleazar. Thus the 1st pers. singular verbs convey actions of Joshua alone (lines 10–11), while the 1st pers. plural refers to activity performed jointly with the priest Eleazar, who shared leadership with Joshua during the conquest of the land of Canaan (cf. Num 27:15–22; 34:17; Josh 14:1; 17:4; 19:51; 21:1).

להשכין. The author employs the *hifʿil* form of the verb שכן ("to dwell"), a form used by Josh 18:1 precisely for installing the Tent of Meeting at Shilo. The same verb is used again in line 12. The verb is thus a key word in the passage. The verb occurs also in the *qal* form, playing both on the dwelling of the divine presence in line 9 (for biblical background cf. e.g. Exod 24:16; Num 9:17–18; Deut 12:11) and on human dwelling in line 8.[21] See comment below. The reference to Josh 18:1 here and in lines 12–13 shows that this biblical episode underlies the entire passage. Cf. Discussion.

Ll. 2–3 העתים [עד אשר יעברו]. The supplement follows the locution of 1 Chr 29:30. The word עתים ("times") is often used in a general way, without apocalyptic overtones (cf. e.g. Neh 13:31; 2 Chr 15:5; 1QS(*erekh Ha-Yaḥad*) IX, 14). Such a sense has been produced here to accord with the general context. Puech and Qimron suggest עד קᵒץ [העתים, following Dan 11:13, but the distinctive apocalyptic

---

[21] The importance of this word in the passage was also noted by Tov, "The Rewritten Book of Joshua," 247.

locution קֵץ הָעִתִּים "the end of times," does not suit the context here; for the Temple of Solomon, which is the subject of the phrase, was not built "at the end of times" but at a well-defined point in the history of Israel. Inserting such a locution disagrees with the absence from the passage of any apocalyptic overtones. Significantly, none of the predictions attributed to Joshua here and in 4Q379 22 ii are eschatological.

L. 3 כִּי הִנֵּה בֵן נוֹלַד לְיִשַׁי. An allusion to the birth of David. For the formula cf. 1 Kgs 13:2; 1 Chr 22:9. The introduction כִּי הִנֵּה points to the future, a common construction in biblical usage (cf. e.g. 1 Kgs 13:3; Isa 7:14). The adverb הִנֵּה is used here together with the participle (הִנֵּה . . . . נוֹלַד) to designate the future. The same usage of this adverb is found in another passage of the *Apocryphon*, preserved in 4Q379 22 ii 9 and quoted by 4Q175 (*Testimonia*) 23 (וְהִנֵּה . . . עוֹמֵד לִהְיוֹת). In both cases the word introduces a prediction.[22] Based on biblical statements (Num 27:19–23; Deut 34:9; Josh 3:7; 4:14) the gift of prophecy is attributed to Joshua already by Sir 46:1, a notion also espoused by later sources (LXX variants, *Tg. Onk.* and *Tg.Ps.Jon*) to Num 27:18; the *L.A.B.* 21:6; 24:3; Joshephus, *Ant.*, iv, 165; v, 20; *Mek. beshalaḥ* to Ex 14:13; *Num.Rabb.* 12, 9). This view underlies the depiction of Joshua in the *Apocryphon* and provides additional evidence for the antiquity of the idea.

(לְ)יִשַׁי בֶן פֶּרֶץ בֶן יְה]וּדָה. An abbreviated version of David's genealogy. Cf. Ruth 4:18–22; 1 Chr 9:4. The full genealogy is detailed in 1 Chr 2:9–17.

[וְהוּא אֲשֶׁר יִלְכּוֹד]. Puech and Qimron provide similar supplements, following the formulation of 2 Sam 5:7; 1 Chr 11:5. But Qimron's restoration is too short for the required length of the line. It also lacks the syntactical stress laid upon David, who will carry out what Joshua did not. Compare a similar syntactical stress in line 7 (וְאוֹתוֹ), which shows that such a construction is a stylistic feature of this passage.

L. 4 סֶלַע צִיּוֹן. A non-biblical locution. As noted by Qimron, the context of the future conquest of Jerusalem favors the understanding of this expression as an allusion to the stronghold of Zion (מְצֻדַת צִיּוֹן),

---

[22] Thus Puech, "La Pierre de Sion," 680; Qimron, "Joshua Cycles," 506 n. 13; Tov, "The Rewritten Book of Joshua," 237–8.

conquered by David (cf. 2 Sam 5:7). The substitution of סלע ("rock") מצודה ("stronghold") may have been influenced by the biblical collocation, which pairs both words (cf. e.g. 2 Sam 22:2; Ps 18:3; Job 39:28). Less suitable for the immediate context is Tov's proposal to connect it with the area bought from Aravna for the future temple (2 Sam 24:18–24; compare 1 Chr 21:18–26).[23]

ויורש משם את כל⁻האמורי. The reference is to David's conquest of Jerusalem, related by 2 Sam 5:6–9. By the addition of word כל ("all") the author contrasts Joshua with David, who disposed of all the Amorites and not only some of them, as was the case with Joshua. Although according to the biblical tradition Joshua defeated the king of Jerusalem together with other Amorite kings (cf. Joshua 10), the Jebusites remained settled in Jerusalem throughout the times of Joshua and the Judges (cf. Josh 15:63; Judg 1:21; 19:10–12). The *Apocryphon* implies that only with the complete expulsion of the Amorites from Jerusalem could the Solomonic Temple have been built, a proper abode for the Tent of Meeting. According to 1 Kgs 8:4 and 2 Chr 5:5, both the Ark of Covenant and the Tent of Meeting were brought into the temple after its completion.

ויורש. As noted by Qimron, the verb stands in the short form of the conjunctive imperfect (וַיּוֹרֶשׁ). For the formulation cf. Num 21:32; 32:39. The reference is to the conquest of Jerusalem by David (2 Sam 5:6–9).

משם. "from there"; from Zion as in lines 2 and 9. מ⁻יר[ושלים stands as apposition to משם.

האמורי. The context clearly shows that the Amorites stand here for the Jebusites.[24] In the biblical tradition this name is often used as a general designation of the ancient peoples settled in Canaan (cf. Gen 15:16; Amos 2:9–10). The Amorites are also listed as a separate people side by side with the Cannanites and the Jebusites (cf. e.g. Gen 15:21; Exod 23:23; Deut 7:1; 20:17). Here, however, the Amorites are identified with the Jebusites, apparently on the basis of Joshua 10. This chapter designates the king of Jerusalem, a well-known Jebusite center (cf. Josh 15:63; Judg 1:21; 19:10–12; 2 Sam 5:6), as

---

[23] Tov, "The Rewritten Book of Joshua," 238.
[24] Noted by Puech, *Textes Hébreux* 58; Tov, "The Rewritten Book of Joshua," 238.

one of the five Amorite kings who fought Joshua (Josh 10:1–5). According to the biblical traditions the Amorite peoples settled the Land of Canaan (compare Gen 10:16; 1 Chr 1:14, where Canaan is presented as one of the offspring of Ham son of Noah), and Israel was commanded to annihilate them upon entering to the land of Israel (cf. Ex 23:23; Deut 7:2; 20:16–17). Already in Gen 15:16–21 Abraham is promised the land of Canaan, and his offspring are to and dispossess the Canaanite peoples because of their iniquity. Both the Canaanites and the Jebusites are included among these peoples. The second century B.C.E. *Book of Jubilees* (8:22–24; 10:29–34) justifies the dispossession of the indigenous Canaanites by stating that from the outset Canaan had settled unlawfully in the land of Canaan, for the provinces originally assigned to him lay elsewhere.

Ll. 4–5 לבנות [לבבו עם ויהיה]. The restoration follows the Chronicler's phraseology (1 Chr 22:7; 28:2; 2 Chr 6:8. Cf. also 1 Kgs 8:17). Other details about David and Solomon here are also taken from the Chronicler's account.

L. 5 הבית ליהוה אלוהי ישראל°. The locution echoes 1 Kgs 8:17; 1 Chr 22:6; 2 Chr 6:7.

זהב וכסף [נחושת וברזל יכין. The list of materials is reconstructed here on basis of 1 Chr 22:16; 29:2. Cf. also 1 Chr 22:14; 2 Chr 2:6. That David is the subject of these preparatory activities is clear from the separate mention of Solomon in line 6 (הקטן ובנו). David preparing materials for the building of the temple is a theme distinctive of the Chronicles' account of David's career. Cf. 1 Chr 22:3, 5, 14; 29:2–3.

L. 6 ארזים וברושים. The description follows the account of 1 Chr 22:3–4; 29:2 about the materials prepared by David for the construction of the temple. However, in this account the Chronicler mentions only cedar-trees (22:3–4) or the general word "timber" (עצים 29:2). The pairing of cedar-trees with junipers (ארזים וברושים) is borrowed from the description of Solomon's building of the temple (cf. 2 Chr 2:7. Compare 1 Kgs 5:22, 24). This is a fine illustration of the *Apocalypse*'s method of combining biblical details from similar episodes, a method widely used in contemporary Jewish literature.

יביא [מ]לבנון. Following 1 Chr 22:4. The Chronicler picks up this detail from the activities of Solomon (cf. 1 Kgs 5:22, 24; 2 Chr 2:7), and applies it to David.

ובנו הקטן. This detail refers to Solomon. The expression is reminiscent of the locution נער קטן, used by Solomon to describe himself when asking God for a gift of wisdom (1 Kgs 3:7). It also echoes David's description of Solomon נער ורך in 1 Chr 22:5; 29:1. Solomon was indeed the youngest son of David. Note the laudatory terms with which David and Solomon are depicted here. Compare 4Q385a 1 ii.

[הוא יבנו. The supplement follows 2 Chr 6:9 (cf. 1 Chr 22:6). The restoration of the pronoun for emphasis is suggested in line with the size of the lacuna and with the stylistic idiosyncrasies of the passage (cf. comment on line 3). Similarly Puech, *Textes Hébreux*, 55.

Ll. 6–7 וצרוק] יכהן שם ראישׁוֹן. The supplement is imposed by the remaining words in line 7. For Zadok as the first priest in the Solomonic temple cf. 1 Chr 29:22. The surviving phrases do not imply in any way that David or Solomon were regularly to officiate in the future temple, as suggested by Puech.[25]

L. 7 מ]בני פינ[חס. With Puech. The supplement proposed by Qimron מ]יהוה is too small for the lacuna and ill suited to the Hebrew phrase. Also unacceptable is Qimron's restoration הסד[. The partly surviving space after the letter *samech* indicates that this was the last letter of the word.

[בכורכה. The supplement is proposed to fit a lacuna of 7–8 letter-spaces. The form is restored with a long suffix, as מאתכה in line 11, forms well known from the Qumran scrolls. The word applies to Phineas, who was the firstborn of Eleazar; cf. Exod 6:25; 1 Chr 5:30; 6:35.

ואותו. Following the description of the priest as it does, this pronoun is better understood as an allusion to Zadok rather than to Solomon.

ו[יברכהו יהוה]. The supplement matches the length of line. The verb form with the suffixed pronoun (יברכהו), restored by Qimron, is to be preferred to the non-suffixed form (יברך) offered by Puech, for it yields a smoother Hebrew phrase. If this restoration is correct, the suffixed pronoun is syntactically ambivalent, for it may refer to Zadok or to Solomon, both mentioned previously. The choice between the two depends on how one understands the following quotation from

---

[25] Idem, "La Pierre de Sion," 683–5; *Textes Hébreux*, 59.

Deut 33:12. Since it is suggested below that the author reads into the quotation a reference to the priestly temple service the pronoun here may refer to Zadok.

L. 8 מע[ל] [ממ]עׄון מן השמי[ם]. The upper tip of the *lamed*, as read by Puech, is seen on a magnified photograph. It excludes Qimron's restoration מן המ[עון]. However, Puech's restoration [בכו]ל [מ]עון creates an awkward expression. The restoration proposed here matches the size of the lacunae and harmonizes with the echoes of Deut 26:15; 2 Chr 30:27, in reference to the divine abode in heaven. Accordingly the locution השמי[ם ממ]עון מן ("from the heavenly abode") stands in apposition to מע[ל] ("from above"). The formulation of the passage suggests a divine blessing descending from the heavenly abode.

כי] ידיד יהו[ה] ישכון לבטח. A quotation of Benjamin's blessing in Deut 33:12. Note that the quoted verse contains twice the verb שכן, a keyword in the passage (cf. comment on להשכין in line 2). The function of the quotation in the passage depends on the understanding of the title ידיד ה׳ from the quoted verse. While the biblical blessing is addressed to Benjamin, and thus confers the title on him, the *Apocryphon* does not mention Benjamin but adduces the verse in connection with the priestly service in the future Solomonic temple. It therefore appears to attribute the title to Levi, as seems to be the case in another passages of the *Apocryphon* (4Q379 1 2 ידיד ללוי).[26] If so, the *Apocryphon* interprets Deut 33:12 as a phrase Moses indeed addressed to Benjamin, but which speaks not of Benjamin but of Levi and his future service in the temple. Apparently Benjamin was deemed worthy of such a blessing because Jerusalem, the site of the future temple, lay within his territory (Josh 18:28; Judg 1:21).[27] Accordingly, in the understanding of the *Apocryphon* the entire blessing addressed to Benjamin in Deut 33:12 deals, in fact, with the first temple. This seems to be the sense read by the author into Deut 33:12 ידיד ה׳ ישכון לבטח.

---

[26] This collocation appears in a list of the twelve tribes, albeit in a different order from the one in Deuteronomy 33. Significantly, in 4Q379 1 Levi is placed at the head of the list. Puech, "La Pierre de Sion," 686 and *Textes Hébreux*, 60 notes this and also mentions the title ידיד אל, applied to Levi in the *Aramaic Testament of Levi* (Cambridge ms.) 43:9.

[27] Emphasizing the same link between Benjamin and the temple the rabbis applied the title "a friend of God" to Benjamin himself (e.g. *Sifre, Deut* §352; *AdRN* B, ch. 43. Compare *b. Menaḥ.* 53b).

Through such an interpretation a link is created between the blessing
to Benjamin (Deut 33:12) and the preceding blessing to Levi (Deut
33:8–11). Significantly, the blessing of Levi mentions the priestly use
of the Urim and Thummim, precisely the subject of the Qumranic
passage in lines 10–11 below. The understanding of the title ידיד נֹי
as a reference to Levi fits very well with the general concern of
4Q522 19 ii. It is therefore less likely that the title ידיד ה׳ is applied
here to Solomon through association with Solomon's name ידידיה
(2 Sam 12:25), as proposed by Puech.[28] In support of such an interpretation Puech cites Sir 47:12, which describes Solomon by alluding to Deut 33:12 ישכן לבטה. However, the fact that Ben-Sira connects
Solomon to Deut 33:12 does not prove the claim that the same association is present in our Qumranic passage. For identifying Solomon
as the subject of the passage here would imply that he was to officiate
regularly and permanently in the future temple. Puech's efforts to
demonstrate that this is indeed the case go against the character and
purpose of the present passage and against the biblical data.

Ll. 8–9 ו]יהוה מגינו כול ה]יֹמים. Since what precedes quotes the first
part of Deut 33:12 while what follows comes from the end of the
verse, the missing words at the end of the line must represent
the middle part of the quotation, namely the words חפף עליו כל היום.
The biblical verse contains the unique verb חפף, usually understood
as "to protect, to cover." The restoration suggested here replaces it
by the more common root מגן. Note the Aramaic *Tg. Onq.* Deut
33:12c יהי מגין עלוהי כל יומא.

כול ה]יֹמים. כול is restored in the full form (as Qimron and Puech) in
line with the orthography of the other occurrence of the word in
the manuscript (4Q522 9 i 4). In the correction of line 4, however,
the word is written defectively כל. The phrase takes up Deut 33:12c
כל היום. Also *Tg. Ps.-Jonathan, Neophyti* and *Fragmentary Targum* translate the locution in the plural.

L. 9 עמו ישכון לֹעד. The formulation follows and interprets the end
of Deut 33:12d, ובין כתפיו שכן adding לעד ("forever") in parallelism
with the preceding strophe. The biblical phrase was traditionally

---

[28] Cf. idem, "La Pierre de Sion," 686 and *Textes Hébreux*, 60. The suggestion is
followed by Tov, "The Rewritten Book of Joshua," 238.

understood to refer to the temple located in the high part of Benjamin's territory (cf. targums to Deut 33:12; *Sifre, Deut* §352).[29] The 3rd pers. singular theme here would establish a proper logical sequence for lines 7–9. In contrast, it would be out of character for our passage to switch abruptly to another subject, namely Solomon. Therefore the suffix of עמו ("with him") must apply to the person previously referred to by the title ידיד ה׳ ("the friend of the Lord"). Since lines 7–8 concern the priestly service, the same subject seems to be assumed here without mentioning him in the immediate context. Thus, the phrase appears to continue its treatment of the priestly function, and so seems to allude to Zadok and the blessing of eternal priesthood (Num 25:13; cf. 1 Sam 2:35). For the formulation Qimron cites 11QTᵃ XLVI, 4.

L. 9 ועתה. As observed by Qimron, the word introduces a new section which contrasts the future described in the preceding lines with the reality of Joshua's days. The same word with a similar emphasis occurs in line 12.

והכנען[י] בקרבנו. This supplement suits the context better than the ones offered by Puech (והכנען[י] את האר[ץ]) or Qimron (והכנען[י] בהר]), for it accords with the situation of the Gibeonites after they made the covenant with the Israelites (cf. Josh 9:27; 10:1; note Judg 1:29; compare Exod 34:12). This line also makes clear that the Amorites are carefully distinguished from the Canaanites. That the Amorites are equated with the Jebusites is clear from line 4. In lines 9–11 the Canaanites are explicitly equated with the people of Gibeon.[30] The two peoples are thus set apart by their different roles in relation to the Israelites. See comment on the supplement to line 12 and Discussion.

Ll. 9–10 והכנען[י] . . . אשר החטיוני. The Canaanites are clearly the Gibeonites, who by a stratagem made a covenant with Joshua and the leaders of Israel, thus escaping war and extermination during the conquests in Canaan (cf. Josh 9–10).

L. 10 החטיוני. The transitive verb "they made me sin" takes the Gibeonites as subject, but the 1st pers. singular suffixed pronoun

---

[29] An often-quoted rabbinic midrash understands the biblical phrase in the same way (e.g. *b. Yoma* 12a; *b. Sota* 37a; *y. Meg.* 1.12). Another midrash understands in the same way Deut 33:12c הפף עליו כל היום (*b. Zabaḥ* 118b).

[30] Josephus, *Ant.* v, 59 states that the Gibeonites belonged to the Canaanite people.

relates it to Joshua.[31] So this phrase shows that it was Joshua who sinned through the ploy of the men of Gibeon. By such an emphasis the text explicates the outcome of concluding the covenant with the Gibeonites. According to the biblical account (Josh 9:14, 19) the chieftains of the tribes (thus мт; the Septuagint has "the elders of the community") were those who took the oath of the covenant.[32] On the grounds of this statement one may argue that legally Joshua did not take part in the actual ratification of the covenant. Here, however, the *Apocryphon* strongly emphasizes that the transgression lies with Joshua himself.

Ll. 10–11 מאתכה [והתומים והתומים] ה[אורים ה]שפֿֿטֿ מ[ת א[ת דרשתי לוא אשר. The formulation is based on Num 27:21. The supplement completes this allusion and so is certain. Similarly Qimron and Puech. The phrase explains why the Canaanites were able to lead Joshua to sin. The reason was that Joshua had not consulted God through enquiring of the Urim and Thummim, a service that the priest Eleazar had to perform for him. In this Joshua infringed the explicit divine commandment given during Moses' lifetime (Num 27:21). The commandment decreed that Joshua must consult God through Eleazar and the Urim and Thummim in every matter. The *Apocryphon* may have drawn the idea that Joshua disobeyed this directive from the statement of Josh 9:14: "and they did not inquire of the Lord" (ואת שאלו לא ה' פי). Moreover, Joshua's faulty action led to the transgression of another injunction laid down by the Torah, namely the prohibition to make a covenant with the Canaanite peoples (cf. Exod 23:32–33; 34:12; Deut 7:2). Exod 34:12,15 and Deut 12:30; 20:17–18 warn the Israelites explicitly not to make a covenant with the Canaanite people lest they lead them to idolatry.[33] By connecting Joshua's offense with the emplacement of the Tent of Meeting the *Apocryphon* makes clear that the dispossession the Amorites was a precondition for the building of the temple and installing the Tent of Meeting in it. By not consulting God about the Gibeonites Joshua contributed to the presence of indigenous people in Canaan and Jerusalem, preventing

---

[31] The orthography ההטיוני with the dropping of the *alef* has similar parallels in the Qumran scrolls, as noted by Qimron, "Joshua Cycles," 506.

[32] According to Josephus, *Ant.* v, 55 the council of the elders and Eleazar were those who actually did it.

[33] A rabbinic midrash gives these Torah interdictions as motives for the Gibeonites' deceitful action (cf. *y. Qidd.* 4, 1; *Num. Rab.* 8, 4).

the installation of the Tent of Meeting in Jerusalem. According to some rabbinic opinions Joshua was exempted from inquiring the Urim and Thummim because he possessed prophetic powers (cf. *b Eruvin* 63a.).

L. 10 דרשתי א[ת מ]שפט ה[ל]אורים. Note the replacement of the MT biblical term of Num 27:21 ושאל by דרשתי. Compare 11QTᵃ LVIII, 18, 20 which quotes this verse in the version of the MT.

מ]שפט ה[ל]אורים והתומים]. Puech's restoration (following e.g. Exod 28:30; Neh 7:65. Cf. 4Q164 (pIsᵈ) 1 5; 4Q174 i 13)[34] meets the requirement of the line's length, and therefore should be preferred to the shorter form מ]שפט ה[ל]אורים], supplied by Qimron (following Num 27:21; 1 Sam 28:6). Note that the *L.A.B.* 22:8 states that Joshua installed in Shilo the Urim and Thummim together with the Tent of Meeting and the Ark of Covenant. Cf. Discussion.

L. 11 והשלוני. ("and they deceived me"). As noted by Qimron, שלה is rare in Hebrew (cf. 2 Kgs 4:28) but common in Aramaic. The use of this word here may indicate a relatively late linguistic environment, strongly influenced by Aramaic. The biblical Joshua story employs the common word רמיתם (Josh 9:22). If the statement here is taken together with Deut 20:10–18, the Gibeonites' ruse appears to have consisted of feigning to come from a faraway city in order to win the clemency prescribed by Deut 20:15, and to escape the extinction mandated by Deut 20:16 for neighboring cities.

וה[נ]ה נתתיו. Here the adverb הנה is used with the perfect to introduce action in the past. In line 3 it is used with a participle to refer to the future.

ל[א]יש ליש לי[בדים ע]בד. The locution takes up the curse of Canaan in Gen 9:25, but the subject is treated by Josh 9:27. Perhaps the special emphasis on the servitude of the Gibeonites implies that following Deut 23:16–17 Joshua had the obligation to protect them as slaves of Israel.

[ולמזבח יהוה]. The supplement is suggested to fit the length of the line and to follow Josh 9:27.

[34] As read and reconstructed by A. Steudel, *Der Midrasch zur Eschatologie aus der Qumran-gemeinde (4QMidrEschat^{a,b})* (*STDJ* 13; Leiden: E. J. Brill, 1994), 23.

L. 12 ‫נ[ש]כינה‬. Here Joshua includes also Eleazar, as is indicated by the following line.

‫רחוק‬. ("distant"). The choice of this word highlights the issue of the entire passage. The Tent of Meeting could not be pitched in Jerusalem because of the proximity of the Amorites, nor near the Israelites' emplacement due to the presence of the Gibeonites.

‫מן ה[אמורי והכנעני‬. Qimron has supplied ‫ה[כנעני‬ as in line 9. However, comparison of line 4 and line 9 shows that the author is concerned with two national entities, the Amorites-Jebusites and the Canaanites-Gibeonites. The statement that the Tent of Meeting was to be carried far away must imply distancing it from both, undoubtedly in order to exclude any contact with them. This is the precise reason why the Tent could not be installed in Jerusalem at the time. The supplement also adds a reference to the Canaanites-Gibeonites, in line with line 9. For being already established among the Israelites the Gibeonites' presence hindered the installation of the Tent of Meeting there.

Ll. 12–13 ‫וישא[ו‬ ‫אלעזר [וישו]ע‬. Restored on the basis of Josh 18:1. Note, however, that the biblical verse does not specify who carried the Tent. According to *L.A.B.* 22:8 it was Joshua who performed this task.

L. 13 ‫אלעזר [וישו]ע‬. Restoring the name of Joshua is most plausible here, given the surviving ʿayin, the size of the lacuna and the context. The name of Joshua is fully preserved in the next line. The mention of both Eleazar together with Joshua firmly ties the present passage to their dual role in establishing the Tent of Meeting at Shilo and in distributing the tribal territories (Josh 18:1; 19:51; 21:1–2). Eleazar with his brother Ithamar (cf. Ex 6:23; 28:1; 1 Chr 24:1) are mentioned in another fragment of the *Apocryphon*, 4Q379 17 5.

‫מבית [אל לשילה‬. Thus Qimron. The name of Shilo is restored on the basis of Josh 18:1, but the surviving letters necessitate an additional toponym, plausibly Bethel. If the restoration is correct, the author may be striving to resolve a difficulty embedded in the biblical account. Unlike the Books of Judges and of Samuel, wherein Shilo plays a prominent role, the Book of Joshua mentions it only in the last chapters, and only in connection with the distribution of territories to the tribes (18:1, 8, 10; 19:51; 21:2). Moreover, Shilo is absent from the list of conquests or tribal territories. By contrast, Bethel is mentioned in the Book of Joshua several times. Situated in the territory of Benjamin near Gibeon, Bethel was one of the cities that fought the Israelites and was conquered by them (Josh 12:16). Significantly, both Gibeon and Bethel are located in the territory of Benjamin, as is Jerusalem. Being populated by the Amorites (= Jebusites) and Canaanites (= Gibeonites) at the time, this territory was considered by the author unsuitable for the abode of the Tent of Meeting. By specifying that the Tent of Meeting was transported from Bethel to Shilo in the territory of Ephraim, the author achieves two aims: first, he bridges a gap in the biblical story by explaining how the Tent of Meeting, presumably located in Gilgal near Jericho (Josh 4:19) after crossing the Jordan, came to be established at Shilo (Josh 18:1).[35] Second, he accounts for this transportation by the need to distance the Tent of Meeting from the environs of Jericho and Jerusalem, due to the Amorites' and Canaanites' presence there. A similar need to account for gaps in the biblical account are observable in other contemporary works. Thus, according to *L.A.B.* 22:8 Joshua brought the Ark of the Covenant to Shilo from Gilgal. Josephus states that it was the Tent of Meeting, which was transported in this way (*Ant.* v, 68).[36] Also the rabbis state that the cultic center was moved from Gilgal to Shilo (*m. Zebaḥ* 14, 4–6; *Seder Olam Rabbah* 11).

מבית [אל. The restoration is plausibly suggested by Qimron and accepted by Puech in his final edition. Bethel also suits the geographical

---

[35] M. Kister apud Qimron, "Joshua Cycles," 507–8 suggests that Bethel was mentioned because it lies on the way from Gilgal to Shilo. Puech takes up this suggestion, *Textes Hébreux*, 62. Tov, "The Rewritten Book of Joshua," 247 argues that the author attempts to account for the contradictory biblical traditions about the location of the ark (according to Judg 20:26–28 it was placed in Bethel). However, two separate problems are involved here, that of the Tent of Meeting and that of the ark. Shilo is designated by Josh 18:1 as the place of the Tent of Meeting and not of the ark, while Judg 20:27 speaks of Bethel as the location of the ark without mentioning the Tent of Meeting. It is possible that the author of 4Q522, like other post-biblical sources, may have considered the ark to be included in the Tent of Meeting and its vessels. Cf. Discussion.

[36] Josephus also speaks of moving the Tabernacle and explains the choice of Shilo by its beauty.

context of the passage (cf. above). Bethel is mentioned in another copy of the *Apocryphon*, 4Q379 26 2.[37]

L. 14]יֵשׁוּעֹ. Typical of Second Temple period, the name Joshua is written in the short form, dropping the *he*. Besides the mention in the previous line the name occurs in other copies of the *Apocryphon* (4Q378 22 i 2–3; 4Q379 22 ii 7; 5Q9 1 1).

שֻׂ[ר צֹבֹא מעֹ]רכות ישׂראל The restoration follows Josh 5:14, which tells about the exchange Joshua had with a supernatural being. Note that the MT text of Joshua has שר צבא ה.

DISCUSSION

The passage that survived in this column comprises two sections, each with its distinct style. Lines 2–12 produce the final part of a discourse by a speaker who refers to himself in the first person, in the singular (lines 10–12) and in the plural (line 12). The content of lines 10–11 indicates that the speaker is Joshua, since it refers to the episode of the Gibeonites' ruse (Joshua 9), in which Joshua himself was involved. This identification is validated by the mention of the name Joshua, fully preserved in line 14, and partly preserved in line 13.

The other section, from line 13 onwards, contains a narrative about the activities of Joshua and the priest Eleazar. The transition from 1st pers. direct speech to 3rd pers. narrative must have occurred in the missing end of line 12, as has been reconstructed. Since narrative passages are preserved in other copies of the *Apocryphon of Joshua*,[38] the present fragment supplies additional evidence for the view that the *Apocryphon* as a whole is a narrative work, adapting different episodes from the Book of Joshua, interlaced with various discourses. The speech and narrative preserved in the present fragment concern the Tent of Meeting in relation to the future temple to be built by Solomon. The choice of words (cf. line 2 and comment) and the explicit reference to Josh 18:1 (lines 12–13 and com-

---

[37] Tov, "The Rewritten Book of Joshua," 249 reads this line סבו בבית אל and connects it with the ark (citing 1 Sam 5:8). However, as noted by the editor, the reading is doubtful and may alternatively be read סכי בבית אל.

[38] Other fragments that preserve narrative passages are the following: 4Q378 14; 4Q522 1; 4Q522 8.

ments) shows that the present section is built on and interprets this biblical episode. Perhaps the theme of Jerusalem in relation to the temple was introduced in context of a list of localities not conquered by the Joshua (compare the list in 4Q522 9 i).[39]

The discourse, which occupies lines 2–12, is set in the reality of Joshua's days. This is clear from elements in the discourse itself (see the expression "but now," ועתה, in lines 9, 12), and from the circumstances described in the narrative section (lines 12–13). In the speech Joshua states that the prevailing conditions in his time do not allow the establishment of the Tent of Meeting at its proper site, namely Mount Zion (lines 2, 9). The reason given for this hindrance is the presence of the Amorites in Jerusalem, undoubtedly the Jebusites, as implied by line 4. Joshua proceeds to reveal that only in the distant future will David complete the conquest of Jerusalem (line 3). It will be David who will prepare the materials for building the permanent abode for the Tent of Meeting, namely the temple, and his son, Solomon, who will actually build it. Joshua concludes his prediction about the future temple with a citation of Deut 33:12 (lines 7–8), understood here as the prophetic promise for the temple's permanence and divine blessing. The word ועתה ("and now"—line 9) contrasts the prediction about the temple with the conditions prevailing in Joshua's days. These include the incident with the Gibeonites, related in lines 9–11. Thus, the Tent of Meeting could not be installed in Jerusalem because of the Israelites' failure to dispossess the Amorites-Jebusites, nor could it remain where the Israelites were camped due to the proximity of the Canaanites-Gibeonites. The action necessitated by these circumstances is again introduced by ועתה ("and now"). It proposes to distance the Tent of Meeting, probably from both the Amorites and the Canaanites. The last phrase, which may be plausibly reconstructed (line 13), describes the accomplishment of this suggestion.

As it stands, the passage is clearly connected with various episodes in the Book of Joshua. But the relationship to the biblical text is complex. In some cases the *Apocryphon* is engaged in solving exegetical problems involved in the biblical narrative. For instance, the account of the Book of Joshua is inconsistent with regards to the whereabouts of the Tent of Meeting. The Tent is mentioned only

---

[39] Similarly Tov, "The rewritten Book of Joshua," 244.

twice, in both cases already as established at Shilo (Josh 18:1; 19:51), and never in association with the Ark of the Covenant or the Urim and Thummim. The *Apocryphon* fills this gap by stating that Joshua and Eleazar transported the Tent of Meeting to Shilo, probably from Gilgal, where the Israelites camped after crossing the Jordan (Josh 4:19). By referring to the Urim and Thummim the *Apocryphon* also makes reference to their presence and asserts that they were in the possession of Eleazar at that time. Thus, the author has amended another omission from the biblical account, which does not mention these objects in the Book of Joshua. The scriptural basis for such affirmation emerges from other ancient Jewish commentators. Since the tribal territories were allocated at Shilo in the Tent of Meeting through some procedure of casting lots (Josh 19:51), they concluded that it was carried out through the Urim and Thummim (cf. *b. B. Bat.* 122a; *y. Yoma* 4, 1; 10, 1). Therefore it was surmised that Joshua moved the Tent of Meeting from the Gilgal to Shilo. According to the *L.A.B.* 22:8–9 Joshua carried from Gilgal to Shilo both the Tent of Meeting and the Ark of Covenant, including the Urim and Thummim. The tannaim affirm that the cultic center was moved from the Gilgal to Shilo, where the Tent of Meeting was established (*m. Zebaḥ* 14, 4–6; Seder Olam Rabbah 11). According to a rabbinic baraita the Tent of Meeting remained in Gilgal fourteen years and then was installed in Shilo (*b. Zebaḥ* 118b; *Tosefta Zebahim* 13, 6, 14; cf. *Seder Olam Rabbah* 11). The occurrence in the Qumran *Apocryphon* of similar traditions attests to their great age and to the antiquity of the exegetical concerns, which shaped them.

Filling gaps in the biblical account is, however, just a corollary of the *Apocryphon*'s chief interest. First and foremost the author is engaged in reworking the Book of Joshua according to his own agenda: the centrality of Jerusalem, the status of the Land of Israel, and the interpretation of Joshua's exploits in the light of the Torah laws. All these facets are clearly reflected in the manner the episode about the Tent of Meeting is worked out. The main emphasis is laid on the fact that Jerusalem remained settled by the Jebusites until the time of David. This reality is noted by several biblical accounts (Josh 15:63; Judg 1:21; 2 Sam 5:6). However, nowhere in the Bible is it connected with the site of the Tent of Meeting or the future temple. The connection is made only by the author of the *Apocryphon of Joshua* in order to explain why the Tent of Meeting was not established at its proper site immediately following the conquest of Canaan.

Already here the *Apocryphon* implies the notion that Jerusalem is the sole location proper for the Tent. But as long as the Amorites inhabited Jerusalem the Tent could not be placed there (col. ii 1, 9) for fear of idolatrous impurity. The presence of the Gibeonites within Israel involved a similar danger. In fact, by treating the Jebusites as "Amorites" and the Gibeonites as "Canaanites", the *Apocryphon* emphasizes their character as two of the peoples Israel was commanded to dispossess and avoid contact with, for fear of idolatry and impurity (Exod 23:32–33; 34:12–16; Deut 7:1–6; 20:16–18). Thus, besides the obstacle they created by their presence the fact that these peoples remained settled within Canaan represented a grave infringement of the Torah commandment.

In the case of the covenant made with the Canaanites-Gibeonites the offense is even more serious, since Israel was explicitly forbidden to make any agreement with the indigenous population (Exod 23:32; 34:12; Deut 7:2). In addition such a covenant involved infringement of another Torah directive, namely the Torah interdiction against concluding a covenant with inhabitants of a Canaanite neighboring city (Deut 20:15–17). Indeed, these offenses are already hinted at in the biblical account of the story (Josh 9:17; cf. David Kimhi's comment ad. loc.). But the biblical account alleviates Joshua's offense by stressing that only the chieftains took the oath to ratify the covenant. The biblical story states that Joshua and the chieftains adopted this procedure without consulting God (Josh 9:14: "and they did not consult God" ואת פי ה' לא שאלו). In other biblical descriptions this formula refers to consulting God through some oracular procedure (cf. 1 Sam 22:10; 23:4), so the author of the *Apocryphon of Joshua* could have concluded from this statement that Joshua indeed transgressed in not seeking divine guidance by consulting the Urim and Thummim beforehand.[40] Yet the author wishes to emphasize an explicit Torah injunction that rendered Joshua's omission graver still, as admitted by Joshua himself (line 10). For Joshua's breach also

---

[40] For Urim and Thummim as means of ascertaining the divine will cf. Exod 28:30; Lev 8:8; Deut 33:8; Ezra 2:63; Neh 7:65. These objects are mentioned in several Qumran texts (11QT[a] LVIII 19,21; 4QpIs[d] 1 5; 4Q174 i 13). 4Q376 1 i–ii (partly overlapped by 1Q29), as well as Josephus (*Ant.* iii, 214–215), describe a similar, but probably not identical, oracular consultation. Cf. the comments by J. Strugnell, "376. 4QApocryphon of Moses[b?]," in *Qumran Cave 4. XIV; Parabiblical Texts, Part 2* (ed. M. Broshi et al.; *DJD* XIX; Oxford: Clarendon, 1995), 124–5.

constitutes an infringement of the divine commandment, given to him in Moses' lifetime, that he should consult the Urim and Thummim through Eleazar in every matter (Num 27:21). In fact, the *Apocryphon* describes Joshua's offense by the very words of Num 27:21 (cf. line 10 and comment), thereby indicating the nature of his misdeed. In this way the formulation of lines 10–11 conveys the idea that because God was not consulted in advance the Gibeonites-Canaanites were able to deceive Joshua and the Israelites. Therefore Joshua and the Israelites infringed both the commandment to expel the Canaanite peoples and the directive to consult God before any action. It seems that Joshua also bypassed a more general provision to consult God on uncertain or obscure matters.[41] So the *Apocryphon* attributes the inability to establish the Tent of Meeting in Zion to sins going back to the times of Joshua. The building of the permanent abode for the Tent, namely the temple, was to be accomplished generations later by David and his son Solomon. The detailed and laudatory reference to the two kings and their activities in relation to the temple shows the importance of this theme for the present author.

One of the characteristics of the passage under discussion is the interpretation of episodes set forth in the biblical Book of Joshua in light of the Torah commandments. This is expressed by the judgment passed on Joshua's actions considering the Torah injunctions to dispossess the Canaanite peoples and to consult God through the Urim and Thummim before taking any political or military step. Our passage implies criticism of Joshua for infringement of the Torah, and praise for David and Solomon as the ideal rulers who carried out the divine purpose to the full.

Looking at the biblical account about Joshua from the perspective of leadership, Joshua represents the first successor of Moses who

---

[41] According to Ezra 2:63 and Neh 7:65 such a practice was recommended to establish the proper genealogy of certain priestly families. However, the performance of this ceremony was left to the future for in the time of Ezra and Nehemiah the Urim and Thummim were no longer available (cf. Josephus, *Ant.* iii, 218; *m. Soṭa* 9, 12). Indeed, rabbinic midrash understood it as a reference to the messianic age (*b. Soṭa* 48b; *y. Qidd.* 4,1). Interestingly, 4Q376 mentions a similar procedure, apparently applied to decide whether a prophet is false or true (cf. Deut 13:2–6 and 4Q376 1 i–ii; 1Q29). However, due to its fragmentary state it is difficult to ascertain whether 4Q376 depicts an abstract ceremony or one that was performed by the Qumranites. In any case, the prominence of this theme in 4Q376 attests to its importance in Qumran circles. Such prominence is also reflected in the *Apocryphon of Joshua*.

is not graced with his mentor's direct access to divine guidance. The directive to consult God through the Urim and Thummim aims at providing a different more institutionalized means of contact with the divine. The Urim and Thummim, and their priestly mediator, thus acquire special importance during Joshua's lifetime. Indeed, the central role of the priest Eleazar in the distribution of territories to the tribes of Israel is repeatedly stressed in the biblical account (cf. e.g. Josh 14:1; 17:4; 19:51). It is therefore surprising that the Urim and Thummim are not mentioned at all in the Book of Joshua. Our passage amends this by implying that they were indeed in the possession of Eleazar, just as they should have been according to Num 27:21.

Rewriting the biblical narrative in light of the Torah injunctions has clear theological implications. The bearing on ideological issues, and even specific historical circumstances, emerges from comparison with a passage from the *Temple Scroll* (11QT^a). This passage too verbally incorporates the Torah directive of Num 27:21 to consult the Urim and Thummim (11QT^a LVIII, 18–21). But while the biblical instruction refers to Joshua's obligation to consult these sacred objects via the priest Eleazar, the *Temple Scroll* applies it to the king, who is to seek the decision of the Urim and Thummim through the high priest. The *Temple Scroll* prescribes the use of the Urim and Thummim only in case of war, probably an "optional war," that is, a war not prescribed by divine command.[42] Nevertheless, the application to the king of the general directive from Num 27:21 suggests that it had relevance to the king as political ruler. The *Temple Scroll* then extracts from the commandment to Joshua a general principle of government in Israel, namely, the king's obligation to act by divine guidance. It implies the view that Joshua acted as the political ruler of Israel similar to a king, an idea shared also by Philo and the Tannaim.[43] In precisely the same way the tannaitic halacha applies the directive to Joshua of Num 27:21 to the obligation of the king to consult the Urim and Thummim through the high priest in the case of

---

[42] Optional war is distinct from an "obligatory war," namely a war decreed by God, for instance, the conquest of Canaan. According to the rabbis also an "optional war" required prior consultation with the Urim and Thummim (cf. *b. Sanh.* 16a). Josephus (*Ant.* iii, 217) implies a similar procedure.

[43] Cf. Philo *Virt.* §70; *b. Yoma* 73b; *b. Sanh.* 49a. Compare Josephus, *Ant.*, iv, 165.

initiating an optional war.[44] The passage from the *Temple Scroll* shows that this is an old piece of exegesis, shared by various circles in Second Commonwealth Judaism. The author of the *Apocryphon* was undoubtedly aware of this view. Indeed, the stress laid on Joshua's offense may suggest that Joshua infringed the commandment of Num 27:21 not only in the personal sense, but also as the political ruler of Israel at the time. If this understanding is correct, the *Apocryphon of Joshua* may be expressing a notion well-known from the Qumran sectarian literature, namely, that of the ascendancy of the priestly function over the political.[45]

---

[44] Cf. e.g. *b. Yoma* 73b; *b. Sanh.* 16a.
[45] See my forthcoming article, cited in n. 11.

4Q413—A HYMN *AND* A WISDOM INSTRUCTION[1]

TORLEIF ELGVIN

This paper demonstrates that the two fragments of 4Q413 represent two separate compositions. The larger fragment may be renamed '4QExhortation,'[2] while the smaller one (hereafter 4Q413a) calls for a designation such as '4QApocryphal Psalm B.'[3]

4Q413Composition concerning Divine Providence was published by Elisha Qimron in 1995 and 1997.[4] He follows Strugnell's placement of two separate fragments as representing the right and left part of the top margin of a column, and renders the text as follows:

top margin

מזמ֗ת ד[עת מצאו] וחוכמה אלמדכמה והתבוננו בדרכי אנוש ובפועלות 1
בני אד[ם כי באהבת] ⟵ את איש הרדבה לו נחלה בדעת אמתו וכפי נועלו 2
כל רע] ההולך אחר מ[שמע אוזניו ומראה עיניו בל יחיה vacat ועתה 3
חסד [ ] ר֗ישונים ובינו בשני ד[וד ו]דור כאשר נלה ⟵ 4
vacat [ ] ל [ ][ ] ל [5

1. a plan of kn[owledge find] and wisdom let me teach you, and (thus) contemplate the conduct of man and the actions of
2. human beings. [For whenever] God [favoured] a person He increased his share in the knowledge of His truth; and as He despised
3. every wicked individual [who would follow what] his ears hear and what his eyes see (that wicked individual) would not survive (*vacat*). And now

---

[1] This paper is dedicated in gratitude to Emanuel Tov who in 1992 showed me the confidence of inviting me to join the *DJD* team. He was co-editor of my first text edition (4Q422ParaGenExod), and was the dear and patient tutor of my doctoral thesis.

[2] 'Exhortation' would distinguish 4Q413 from 4QInstruction and 4QInstruction-like Composition A, B (4Q419, 4Q424). While 4Q413 could be part of a larger wisdom instruction, the designation 'exhortation' better fits the small amount of preserved text.

[3] The inventory lists 4Q448Apocryphal Psalm and Prayer and 11Q11Apocryphal Psalm.

[4] "A Work concerning Divine Providence: 4Q413," *Solving Riddles and Untying Knots. Biblical, Epigraphic, and Semitic Studies in Honor of Jonas C. Greenfield* (ed. Z. Zevit, S. Gitin, M. Sokoloff; Winona Lake: Eisenbrauns, 1995), 191–202; *DJD* XX (Oxford: Clarendon, 1997), 169–71.

4. (sons of) grace [(the events of)]the former years and contemplate the events of past [gene]rations as God has revealed.

4Q413 and 4Q413a

In 1992 Strugnell asked me to check the structure of these two fragments and suggested that they did not belong together. After an examination of the originals I noted in the published version of my paper on the sapiential texts from the 1992 New York conference: "The proposed connection seems questionable. Close investigation of the fragments reveals that they can hardly belong together, and the texts in the two fragments cannot easily be fit together."[5] As Qimron prepared his *DJD* publication he was probably not aware of this comment of mine.

In a forthcoming article Strugnell comments:

> 4Q413 . . . may be even shorter than it appears to be from the *DJD* edition by Qimron. It was only by a *hesitant* suggestion of mine, made in 1959, that these two fragments were joined together—their text indeed seemed able to be fitted harmoniously together, but the script of each seemed very different, even if one were to assume that one of the pieces was badly shrunken. Clearly the larger fragment comes from the beginning of an exhortation, addressed *to a group* (cf. the second person plural), inviting them, in standard sapiential language, to the study of Wisdom.[6]

---

[5] "Admonition Texts from Qumran Cave 4," *Methods of Investigation of the Dead Sea Scrolls and the Khirbet Qumran Site. Present Realities and Future Prospects* (ed. M. O. Wise, N. Golb, J. J. Collins, D. G. Pardee; New York: New York Academy of Sciences, 1994), 179–94, p. 183.

[6] J. Strugnell, "The Smaller Hebrew Wisdom Texts Found at Qumran: Variations, Resemblances, and Lines of Development," in *The Wisdom Texts from Qumran and the Development of Sapiential Thought.* (BETL 159; ed. C. Hempel, A. Lange, H. Lichtenberger; Leuven: Peeters, 2002, forthcoming).

Here Strugnell is less clear in his view of the physical evidence than he was in 1992.

Daniel Harrington, who co-edited the sapiential text 4QInstruction with Strugnell, follows the photograph as does Qimron, but reads the first word or two 'a psalm, a song,' and suggests that material close to the wisdom instruction here is designated as a hymn.[7]

An examination of their physical structure by microscope shows that these two fragments cannot be placed together. The surface of frg. 4Q413a is more scraped than that of 4Q413, so that the hair structure is not visible, while it is clearly seen on 4Q413. 4Q413a has a darker brown color than 4Q413. The horizontal ruling lines are visible on 4Q413, not on 4Q413a. The curved structure of the skin of 4Q413a shows that this part of the sheet represents a curved part of the hide, close to the shank (see below), while 4Q413 has a plain surface.[8]

There are paleographical differences between the fragments. *Mem*, *lamed* and *ḥet* are clearly drawn by different hands. Further, 4Q413 represents a full orthography, while כל of 4Q413a indicates a more defective spelling. Both hands are Herodian (with 4Q413a probably earlier than 4Q413). 4Q413 measures 8.8 × 3.7 cm, 4Q413a 2.8 × 3.8 cm. The distance between the lines is 7 mm in both fragments. The skin in both fragments is relatively thick, and somewhat thicker in 4Q413 than 4Q413a.

Concluding: the text of the fragments must be read and reconstructed differently from Qimron's edition.

---

[7] D. Harrington, *Wisdom Texts from Qumran* (The Literature of the Dead Sea Scrolls; London: Routledge, 1996), 64. Similarly A. Lange, "In Diskussion mit dem Tempel. Zur Auseinandersetzung zwischen Kohelet und Weisheitlichen Kreisen am Jerusalemer Tempel," *Qohelet in the Context of Wisdom* (BETL 136; ed. A. Schoors; Leuven: Peeters, 1998), 113–59, p. 153. Strugnell originally designated 4Q413 'A Sapiential Hymn': E. M. Schuller, "The Use of Biblical Terms as Designations for Non-Biblical Hymnic and Prayer Compositions," *Biblical Perspectives: Early Use and Interpretation of the Bible in Light of the Dead Sea Scrolls* (STDJ 28; ed. M. E. Stone, E. G. Chazon; Leiden: Brill, 1998), 207–22, p. 214. In the inventory of 1992 4Q413 has the provisional title 'sapiential work': E. Tov, "The Unpublished Qumran Texts from Caves 4 and 11," *JJS* 43 (1992): 101–36.

[8] Conservator Lena Liebman of the Rockefeller Museum fully agreed on this point. She noted that it is not impossible that the fragments derive from the same sheet. But, if so, there must have been some distance between these two parts of the skin, so they cannot derive from the same column.

4Q413a (4QApocryphal Psalm B)

top] margin

A hymn, a s[ong	מזמר שׁ]ׅיר 1
the sons of *fo[l]ly*[9]	בני אוׄלׅ]ה(?) 2
all *evil*[	כל רעׄ]ׄο 3
mercy u[pon	חסד עׄ]ל 4
	]ο ∞ 5

READINGS

L. 1. Qimron reads the opening words מזׄמׄת ד]עׄת. The first three letters were fully visible under the microscope a few years ago, the quality of the original has since then deteriorated. The fourth letter is not *taw* (there is no left vertical stroke) but *reš* (cf. the shape of the *reš* in line 3). The first letter of the next word (at the edge of the fragment) is not a *daleth*, but the remnants of *šin* or *ʿayin*. Thus there is no alternative to Strugnell's reading in the *Preliminary Concordance* מזמר שׁ]ׅיר.[10] This would have been the obvious reading if Qimron had not read this fragment together with the larger one, as he was forced by the sapiential vocabulary of the neighbor to suggest related terminology at the beginning of what he perceived as the same line.

L. 2. בני אוׄלׅ]ה. The second letter of the second word is more probably *waw* than *dalet*. Two spots of ink below a crack in the skin preserve the bottom of the left leg of the ʾalep and the first stroke of the next letter. The top of a *lamed* (less probably a speck of ink) is visible on the photograph, and could earlier be seen on the original, below the *šin* of line 1. The location of the suggested *lamed* would exactly fit the reading אוׄלׅ]ה (there is space for a *waw*, not a *dalet*). If one opts for the 'speck of ink' option, בני או]ׄר would be another attractive suggestion. בני אסׄ]ף would not fit the physical evidence.

L. 3. כל רעׄ]ׄο. Of the last letter before the lacuna one can see a spot of the lower right edge (lower than the left downstroke of the *ʿayin*). 'Evil/wickedness' is not the only possible interpretation of this word, cf. words such as רעה 'shepherd' (the trace of the third letter could represent the right leg of *he*), רֵעַ 'friend/neighbor.' כל רעׄ]ן

---

[9] Italic font in the translation indicates tentative interpretation or restoration.

[10] As rendered by B. Z. Wacholder and M. G. Abegg, *A Preliminary Edition of the Unpublished Dead Sea Scrolls. The Hebrew and Aramaic Texts from Cave Four*. Fascicle Two (Washington D.C.: Biblical Archaeology Society, 1992), 43.

'every thunder' would fit the physical evidence well, but is not an easy reading in a hymnic context.

L. 4. The letter opening the word after חסד could be *śin*, or more likely *ʿayin*.

L. 5. *Pace* Qimron, there is no *vacat* in the beginning of line 5. Under the microscope one could see remnants of the top of what is most likely a two-letter word, and then of the first letter of the next one.

COMMENTARY

The opening words preserve the title of this composition, מזמר or מזמר שיר. The double expression מזמר שיר is frequent as title of biblical psalms (30:1; 67:1; 68:1; 87:1; 92:1; שיר מזמר is used in Ps 48:1; 83:1; 88:1; 108:1, cf. Ps 98:1 מזמר שירו ליהוה).

E. Schuller notes that the designation מזמר is surprisingly rare in the scrolls, compared to the 57 occurrences in the titles of biblical psalms.[11] מזמר שיר recurs in col A of 4Q448 Apocryphal Psalm and Prayer (the fragment on king Jonatan with a hymn partly parallel to Psalm 154): שיר מזמר.[12] הללויה מזמֹוֹֿ שֹֿ֗ occurs once in the Hodayot: 1QHª VII,21 (Sukenik frg. 10, 10, *Study Edition* VII,11): שׁיֿר מזמר למשׁ[כיל (מזמור] is supralinearly added).[13] Further, Schuller suggests that another hodayah opened with למשכיל מזמר שיר: the combination of the last line of 4Q427 (4QHodª) 3 with 1QHª XXV,34 (Sukenik frg. 8, 10, italic, *Study Edition* XXV bottom 10) results in the text [למשכיל] שׁיֿר [מזמר שׁ]יֿ֗רֿ לֿ].[14]

In our text one could restore a text such as מזמר שׁ]ירו לאל (cf. Ps 98:1), or see מזמר שׁ]יר as the title and let the continuation introduce the singer such as למשכיל.

---

[11] According to Schuller, מזמר occurs three times in the Hodayot: "but all in damaged or problematic contexts, and none of these readings are given in standard editions or concordances": "Use of Biblical Terms," 215.

[12] Strugnell's reading in the *Preliminary Concordance*. מזמר שיר is the original beginning of this scroll, הללויה is later added in the margin.

[13] Schuller's reading: "Use of Biblical Terms," 215.

[14] *DJD* XXIX (Oxford: Clarendon), 91, 93. In 4Q427 3a there are cancellation dots above (the first) שיר, 1QHª XXV,34 reads למשכיל מזמ]ר. The combination of these two fragments is tentative, based on the overlap of the next column of 4Q427 (frg. 7) with 1QHª XXVI,6–17 (Suk frgs 56 ii, 46 ii, 55 ii). The order of hymns in 4Q427 is different from that of 1QHª.

If בני אול[ת] is correctly restored in line 2, this hymn includes sapiential terminology, and may deal with God's different attitudes towards the sons of folly and the sons of grace, a welcome subject in the Qumran library. The alternative בני או[ר] would place this scroll clearly in the sectarian corner of the library.

Line 4 should most probably be restored with ע[ל], resulting in a text such as חסד ע[ל]ינו, חסד ע[ל כול ישראל, or חסד ע[ל בני אמתכה. The preposition עם is also possible: חסד ע[מנו, or (about God) חסד ע[מכה.

The fragment has a top margin of 6–7 mm and a wide right margin of 15 mm, cut straight at the edge. There are no traces of sowing at the edge, which means that 4Q413a preserves the beginning of a scroll and the opening of a hymnic composition.

4Q413a may belong together with fragments registered under another PAM number, e.g. 4Q451 Prayer C, which is similar to 4Q413a in script and physical appearance. 4Q451 has a similar division between the elect and another group (alternatively: Israel and the nations) as may be perceived in 4Q413a:

>]your great [na]me and let [them] not defi[le
>] and give them into the hand of your beloved ones for annihila[tion
>]and in your wonders and the might of your right hand[

The tiny amount of preserved text in 4Q451 has no sapiential terminology such as the suggested בני אול[ת] in 4Q413a 2. 4Q451 is now sown between nets, which makes a close examination difficult (the hair structure cannot be seen). Its color is a similar brown to that of 4Q413a, and both fragments are written on relatively thick skin. 4Q451 does not have the curved structure of 4Q413a, but this would be the case only on the upper right corner of the same sheet. As yet another option, 4Q413a could represent the beginning of another 4Q copy of the Hodayot, in addition to the six already known.

The structure with curved creases which spread out (visible on the photograph, even clearer under the microscope) shows the location of this fragment on the hide.[15] Provided the writing is on the hair side, the curved skin of this fragment can be located at the left part of the belly close to the shank of the front leg (see drawing).

---

[15] On this point I am indebted to S. E. Pfann.

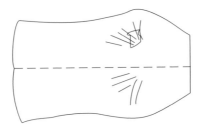

Location of fragment (4Q413a) on the hide.

4Q413 (4QExhortation)

top margin [

1] האזינו לי בני והפיקו דעת[וחוכמה אלמדכמה והתבוננו בדרכי אנוש ובפועלות

2 [אדם ונורלו תביטו כפי אהבת [⟆ את איש הרבה לו נחלה בדעת אמתו וכפי נועלו

3 [הקטין לו נחלה אשר הלך אחר מ[שמע אוזניו ומראה עינו בל יחיה *vacat* ועתה

4 [המבינים בחירי אמת הביטו ב[רי͏̈שונים ובינו בשני ד[ור ו]דור כאשר נלה ⟆

5 [רזי פלאו לבני אמתו]°[ ]°[]°°[ ]°°[ ]°[

1. [*Listen to me, my sons, and acquire knowledge!*] Then I will teach you wisdom, so you may understand the conduct of human beings and [contemplate] the actions of

2. [man and his lot. As]God [loved] a man He increased his share in the knowledge of His truth; and as He despised another

3. [*He diminished the share of one who follows* what] his ears hear and what his eyes see, so that he will not live. And now,

4. [*understanding ones and truly elect ones*, contemplate]the former things and understand the events of the past [gene]rations, as God revealed

5. [*His wondrous secrets to His true sons*]for all[

PHYSICAL DESCRIPTION

The top and left margins are preserved. The left margin is cut straight at the time of preparation, which indicates that the fragment is the end of the scroll.

COMMENTARY

For this larger fragment, Qimron's commentary in *DJD* XX is still useful. The text can be structured as follows:

Ll. 1–2. Call for attention, introductory admonition.
Ll. 2–3. Reflection on creation and election.

Ll. 3–5. Call to attention and exhortation: learn from the right understanding of history, as revealed to the elect.

The text of the first line would fit well as the opening of a wisdom
instruction, but a composition of only one column is not likely. The
physical evidence seen together with the contents point to these lines
as the beginning of a section, the closing parenetic part of a sapiential or parabiblical composition. Parabiblical compositions could
include parenetic sections, cf. the speech of Levi in Aramaic Levi
82–106;[16] and 4Q542 (4QTQahat ar).

The language of this sapiential exhortation shows affinities with the
Hodayot, 4QD, 4Q180AgesCreat A, 4Q181AgesCreat B, 4Q298Words
of the Maskil, 4Q525Beat and 4QInstruction. The divine designation El is written in paleo-Hebrew in lines 2 and 4. This fact points
to the copying of the scroll within the Qumran scribal school.[17] All
the suggested restorations are tentative. In line 1 the restoration com-
prizes 16.5 corrected letter spaces, in line 2 19 letter spaces, in line
3 21 letter spaces, and in line 4 19.5 letter spaces.

L. 1 probably opened with a call to attention such as 'Listen to
me, my sons!' The teaching style of 4Q413 with instruction in the
1st person sing. (often introduced by a call to attention) is found in
4Q298Words of the Maskil 1–2 i,1–3; 3–4 ii,3–10; CD I,1; II,2, 14;
4Q266 (4QDᵃ) 1,5–6; 4Q270 (4QDᶜ) 2 ii,19–21; 4Q185 I,13; II,3;
1Q27 (1QMyst) 9–10,3; 4Q299 (4QMystᵃ) 3a ii,9; 4Q303
(4QMeditation on Creation Aᵃ) 1,1;[18] 4Q426 (4QSapiential-Hymnic
Work A); 4Q525Beat 2 ii+3,12; 10,3; 13,6, 14 ii,18; 4Q539
(4QapocrJoseph B ar) 2–3,2; 4Q546 (4QVisions of Amramᵈ ar) 14,
4, and 4QAramaic Levi 82–106. For the tentative restoration והפיקו
דעת, cf. 4Q525 14 ii,19 הפק דעת לבטנכה. For the opening admonition, cf. 4Q426 (4QSapiential-Hymnic Work A) 1 ii,4 ואתבוננו
בפועלת אנ̇[ש. Qimron explains the somewhat unusual form פועלות as
a partly defective spelling of the assumed early form *quṭula*.[19]

---

[16] 4Q213 6 i–ii, 4Q214 6 ii, with Cambridge Geniza ms. See R. A. Kugler, *From
Patriarch to Priest. The Levi-Priestly Tradition from Aramaic Levi to Testament of Levi* (SBLEJL
9; Atlanta: Scholars Press, 1996), 118–21.

[17] E. Tov, "Further Evidence for the Existence of a Qumran Scribal School,"
*The Dead Sea Scrolls Fifty Years After their Discovery. Major Issues and New Approaches.
Proceedings of the Jerusalem Congress, July 20–25, 1997* (ed. L. Schiffman, E. Tov,
J. C. VanderKam, G. Marquis; Jerusalem, 2000), 199–216, esp. pp. 104–5.

[18] כול ה[מבינים שמעו ו]י "All you who]understand, listen and [" (interpreted different
from *DJD* XX).

[19] "Work concerning Divine Providence," Appendix 2.

Ll. 2–3 share the theology of double predestination of the sectarian scrolls: God has ordained different portions for the elect and the ungodly. Qimron points to terminological parallels in the Two-Spirit Treatise in 1QS IV,16, 24 and especially 1QHᵃ XVIII,28–29 (Suk X,28–29) הרביתה נחלתו בדעת אמתכה ולפי דעתו ו|. Cf. also 4Q181 AgesCreat B 1 ii,5 איש לפי נורלו אשר הפ[י]ל ל[ו "each man according to his lot which he as[sig]ned to [him." These lines seem to locate the fragment in the sectarian corner of the Qumran library, but also presectarian works such as 4QInstruction and 4QVisions of Amram[20] preserve similar thoughts. While line 1 and the missing beginning of line 2 contains a call to attention and an introductory admonition, line 2 is a reflection on the lot of men. The suggested restoration with נורל bridges these themes.

Ll. 3–4. The ungodly is described as one who follows 'what his ears hear and what his eyes see.' These terms from Isa 11:3 are used as a description of an ungodly person.[21] The ungodly are despised by God, and "will not live." The result clause could refer to physical life or to the hereafter. The *vacat* before ועתה signals a new paragraph. ועתה functions as call to attention, as in 4Q418 (4QInstructionᵈ) 69 ii,4.

L. 4. An exhortation to understand the meaning and mysteries of past history. Similar admonitions are found in 4QD, 4Q180AgesCreat A, and 4QInstruction (in particular the wisdom instruction in 4Q417 1 i). For parallels, see 4Q270 (4QDᵉ) 2 ii,21 ובהבינכם במעשי דור ודור["by considering the deeds of each generation"; 4QMMT C, 10–11 "so that you may study the book of Moses and the books of the Prophets and David [and the events of] ages past"—מעש[י] דור ודור. The parallel with בשני ד[ור ו]דור[indicates that ריאשנים here refer to early events of history (as ראשנות or קדמוניות in other texts), not forefathers such as CD I,4, 16; VI,2.[22] Cf. further 4Q298Words of the Maskil 3–4 ii,9–10 [תבינו בקץ עולמים ובקד[מ]וניות חביטו לדעת "that you may give heed to the end of the ages and contemplate on the for[m]er things, to know ["

---

[20] Cf. É. Puech, *DJD* XXXI (Oxford: Clarendon), 283.

[21] Qimron, "Work concerning Divine Providence," Appendix 1. 4Q161 (4QpIsaᵃ) 8–10, 21–23 represents another exegesis of this biblical verse, restricting it to the messianic king.

[22] Joseph's psalm in 4Q372 (4QNarrative and Poetic Compositionb) line 27 uses הראשנות on God's earlier acts: [הראשנות וללמד לפשעים חקך ["I will . . .] the former things, to teach sinners Your statutes." The same meaning recurs in 4Q372 9, where הראשנות is used in line 1, and the next line mentions the jubilees of history.

Ll. 4–5. *Pace* Qimron, כאשר נלה אל introduces a new sentence, either qualifying the thought of the preceding one, or an independent one (in the latter case, translate with a full period before "As God revealed"). One could restore with sectarian terminology as suggested here: כאשר נלה אל [רזי פלאו לבני אמתו, "as God revealed [His wondrous secrets to the sons of His truth (i.e. His true sons)." Alternatively, one could reconstruct based on parallels in 4QInstruction וכאשר נלה אוזנכה [אוזן מבינים ברז נהיה, כאשר נלה אל, cf. 4Q416 2 iii,17–18 אשר נלה אל אוזן מבינים ברז נהיה; 4Q418 184,2 ברז נהיה; 4Q418 123,4 א.[שר נלה אוזנכה ברז נהיה ביום].

L. 5. After לכֿוֿל[one could restore a text such as קצי עולם 'all the periods of history,' cf. the pesher on the periods in 4Q180 1.

Strugnell notes that key words in the preserved text also are characteristic of 4QInstruction; נחלה (35 in 4QI), פעולה (9× in 4QI), אמת (41× in 4QI).[23] But these terms are not infrequent in sectarian scrolls either. Our text demonstrates parallels primarily with text from the Yaḥad, but also with extra-sectarian texts such as 4QInstruction and 4Q525Beatitudes.

In principle 4Q413 could represent the end of another sapiential instruction represented in the Qumran library. However, the 1st person form of this text is rare among the sapiential writings; one finds this form in 4Q298 (written in cryptic script), 1Q/4QMysteries, 4Q185 and 4Q426Sapiential-Hymnic Work A. So more probably this fragment remains a separate composition. Theology and terminology point to a sectarian origin of the work, at the least it reflects a theology close to the world view of the Yaḥad.

---

[23] "The Smaller Hebrew Wisdom Texts."

DATING THE SAMARITAN PENTATEUCH'S COMPILATION IN LIGHT OF THE QUMRAN BIBLICAL SCROLLS

Esther Eshel and Hanan Eshel

The Samaritan Pentateuch (henceforth SP) features approximately six thousand textual variants of the Masoretic Text (MT). Rabbinic sources,[1] as well as the writings of the Church Fathers, mainly Origen,[2] and Jerome,[3] mention several of these differences. The first manuscripts from the Samaritan community in Damascus reached Europe in the seventeenth century and scholarly research on the SP subsequently developed.[4] Today we know of over 150 manuscripts of the SP; the earliest ones date to the ninth century C.E. and the latest to present times. A significant number of these manuscripts were copied between 1474–1485.[5]

The Samaritans highly esteem the Abisha Scroll. Although according to the colophon of the scroll itself, the text was written in the thirteenth year of the entrance of the tribes to Canaan, it is undoubtedly composed of fragments from several scrolls written between the twelfth and fourteenth century C.E.[6] When the SP was rediscovered in the seventeenth century, biblical scholars realized that the SP was identical to the Septuagint (LXX) as regards approximately one-third of the differences between the SP and MT. They consequently concluded that both the SP and LXX originated in a common Hebrew source, which is preferable to the MT.

---

[1] See, for example, *Sifre Deuteronomy* 11:30; *y. Soṭah* 7,3 (21c) *b. Soṭah* 33b.

[2] In the notes on the *Hexapla* to Num 13:1; See F. Field, *Origenis Hexaplorum* (Oxford, 1871–1875), I/I:239, Num, 21:13, p. 250; Prolegomena, I/II:LXXXII–LXXXIII.

[3] Prol. gal on Gal 3:10. The latest Greek reference to it is found in George Syncellus (around 800 C.E.) in his *Chronographia*, 83.

[4] J. Macdonald, *The Theology of the Samaritans* (London, 1969), 12.

[5] See R. T. Anderson, "Samaritan Pentateuch: General Account," *The Samaritans* (ed. A. D. Crown; Tübingen, 1989), 390–96.

[6] A. D. Crown, "The Abisha Scroll of the Samaritans," *BJRL* 58 (1975): 36–65.

216 E. AND H. ESHEL

I. The Nature of the Samaritan Version of the Pentateuch

In 1815 W. Gesenius published a study of the origin of the SP. In this work, Gesenius categorized the differences between the SP and the MT and demonstrated that the majority were generated by a Samaritan edition of the MT, engendered either by linguistic-stylistic objectives or religious principles in order to adapt it to the needs of the Samaritan community.[7] In the light of Gesenius' study, Bible scholars negated the importance of the textual differences documented in the SP.[8] However, P. Kahle's study, published one hundred years after Gesenius' book, questioned the existence of an ancient text of the Bible (*Urtext*). Kahle claimed that several Hebrew versions of the Bible were prevalent among Jews during the Second Temple period.[9] Kahle's investigation engendered a reexamination of the SP, with the assumption that this text-type preserves the style of a text common during the Second Temple period. The biblical scrolls found at Qumran confirmed Kahle's theory, and following the publication of the scrolls resembling the SP version,[10] scholarly research of the SP increased.

The variants between the SP and MT can be divided into intentional and unintentional variants,[11] in other words, differences with some significant value and those without. The latter category includes variants in spelling, form, and grammar, and they should be viewed as synonymous versions of the MT. Such an interchange of words or idioms is evidently not unique to the SP. Exchanging a word with a synonym as well as spelling differences were a common custom when transcribing a text, a phenomenon that is documented in the manuscripts of the MT itself.[12]

Differences encompassing the intentional variants can be divided into sectarian and non-sectarian variants.[13] The latter are mostly

---

[7] W. Gesenius, *De Pentateuchi Samaritani origine, Indole et auctorite* (Halle, 1815).

[8] See, for example, S. Kohn, "Samareitikon und Septuaginta," *MGW* 38 (1894): 61; Z. Frankel, *Über den Einfluss der Palästinischen Exeges auf die alexandrinische Hermenneutik* (Leipzyg, 1851), 231ff.

[9] P. Kahle, "Untersuchungen zur Geschichte des Pentateuchtextes," *TSK* 88 (1915):390–439 [= *Opera Minora* (Leiden, 1956), 3–37].

[10] M. Cross, "The History of the Biblical Text in the Light of Discoveries in the Judaean Desert," *HTR* 57 (1964): 288.

[11] Z. Ben-Hayyim, *The Literary and Oral Tradition of Hebrew and Aramaic Amongst the Samaritans.* Vol. V: Grammar of the Pentateuch (Jerusalem, 1977), 2–3 (Hebrew).

[12] Cf. R. Weiss, *Studies in the Text and Language of the Bible* (Jerusalem, 1981), 75–114 (Hebrew).

[13] E. Tov, *Textual Criticism of the Hebrew Bible* (Minneapolis, 1984), 84–85.

exegetical variants, which can be divided into several categories, the most important of which is harmonistic editing. Other variants include interchanging idioms, rare forms of ordinary idioms,[14] grammatical correspondence—in particular adapting the predicate to the object in terms of gender and number,[15] as well as exegetical emendations designed to resolve specific textual problems. The following passages illustrate some of these changes:[16]

Gen 2:2
MT: ויכל אלהים ביום השביעי
SP: ויכל אלהים ביום הששי

Exod 13:6
MT: שבעת ימים תאכל מצת
SP, LXX: ששת ימים תאכל מצות

Exod 24:7
MT: נעשה ונשמע
SP: נשמע ונעשה

These changes were designed to eliminate difficulties and assist the reader in understanding the Bible. In Gen 2:2 the emendation clarified that God completed the work of creation on Friday, and not on the Sabbath; in Exodus 13 the purpose was to eliminate any overlap between the expression "the day of Passover" and "the Festival of Unleavened Bread."[17] In Exodus 24 it was in order to make the text conform to a logical sequence.[18]

As previously mentioned, most of the non-sectarian exegetical changes in the SP are harmonizations. This textual phenomenon includes changes, additions, or deletions, as well as a change in the word sequence in order to resolve contradictions, discrepancies, and

---

[14] Weiss, *Studies in the Text*, 115–131; Tov, *Textual Criticism*, 70–71.

[15] Tov, *Textual Criticism*, 90–91.

[16] MT is based on Biblica Hebraica Stuttgartensia; and SP is based on A. Tal, *The Samaritan Pentateuch, Edited According to MS 6 (C) of the Shekhem Synagogue* (Tel-Aviv, 1994).

[17] The confusion between "the day of Passover" and "the festival of Unleavened Bread" can be found in Exod 12:15, where MT and SP read: שבעת ימים מצות תאכלו, while in Deut 16:8 we find ששת ימים תאכל מצה; See Hillel's saying in *y. Pesaḥ* 6,1 (33a): "One verse says: "Six days you shall eat unleavened bread" (Deut 16:8). And another verse says "Seven days you shall eat unleavened bread" (Exod 12:15). How is this possible? Six [days you shall eat] from the new grain [which is permitted after bringing the first sheaf of new grain on the second day] and seven you shall eat from the old grain [which may be consumed also on the first day of the festival, when the new grain is still prohibited]" (= Mekilta *Bo* 8,17; Sifra *Emor* 12,5; Sifre Deut 134.

[18] J. E. H. Thomson, *The Samaritans* (London, 1919), 306–12.

unevenness in the biblical text. Likewise, in certain cases a text was enriched with details from a parallel biblical description even though there appeared to be no discrepancies. Such a change was made when some connection existed between two texts—for example, collections of laws or parallel descriptions. The harmonization was usually intentional although slight changes may have been unintentional.[19] The harmonizations can be classified into several categories:

1. Changing the text in order to avoid any differences among parallel biblical texts (for example, the Decalogue).

2. The addition of a source to a biblical passage. For example, elements from Deuteronomy were sometimes added to Exodus or Numbers since Deuteronomy repeats descriptions from previous books of the Pentateuch. Such a phenomenon can be termed the completion of details in a "poor" text based upon a "rich" description.

3. A further addition is a depiction of the implementation of a certain commandment in order to emphasize its performance.[20]

The following sectarian changes in the SP reflect Samaritan beliefs: the SP states that the commandment in Deut 27:4 to establish twelve stones and an altar occurred on Mt. Gerizim while according to the MT it transpired on Mt. Eybal; the SP adds an additional commandment to the Decalogue cited in Exodus and Deuteronomy— the building of an altar on Mt. Gerizim;[21] and the future form of the verb יבחר that occurs twenty-one times in Deuteronomy is altered to the past tense—בחר. Deuteronomy does not explicitly mention Jerusalem since the city was only sanctified in Davidic times. Consequently, the expression יבחר (will choose) in the MT came to signify Jerusalem in Jewish tradition. According to Samaritan belief, however, Mt. Gerizim had been the chosen place since the time of the Patriarchs and therefore the SP systematically changed the expression from the future tense to the past. The same factor brought about the emendation in Exod 20: (21) 24:[22]

---

[19] Weiss, *Studies in the Text*, 132–33; Tov, *Textual Criticism*, 85–89.

[20] See: E. Tov, "The Nature and Background of Harmonizations in Biblical Manuscripts," *JSOT* 31 (1985): 3–29; E. Eshel, "4QDeut^n—A Text that Has Undergone Harmonistic Editing," *HUCA* 62 (1991): 120–21.

[21] The Samaritans takes the first commandment אנכי יהוה as part of the introduction to the Decalogue. Thus, adding their commandment does not increase the accepted of ten commandments.

[22] Tov, *Textual Criticism*, 94–95.

MT: בכל המקום אשר אזכיר את שמי   אבוא אליך וברכתיך

SP: במקום אשר אזכרתי (!) את שמי שמה אבוא אליך וברכתיך

II. The Connection between the Qumran Biblical Scrolls and the Samaritan Pentateuch

Up until the discovery of the Dead Sea Scrolls it was impossible to determine the date of the sp's compilation. The collection of biblical scrolls unearthed at Qumran includes some Scrolls that resemble the text of the sp. The Book of Exodus (4QPaleoExod^m) was the first scroll identified; it is written in paleo-Hebrew script and contains a text close to that of the sp.[23] Cross noted that the scroll of the Book of Numbers (4QNum^b) resembles the Hebrew background to the sp, although it also has additions that also exist in the lxx.[24] Cross later identified a scroll with parts of the Book of Deuteronomy (4QDeut^n), which is close to the sp. This scroll was finally published in 1995 by S. White Crawford.[25]

In 1968, J. A. Allegro published the first volume of texts from Cave 4,[26] including two texts with biblical passages. Allegro labeled the first text, 4Q158, a Biblical Paraphrase and the second, 4Q175, was designated 4QTestimonia. In 1970 J. Strugnell and R. Weiss proved that the biblical fragments cited in 4Q158 and 4QTest were taken from a biblical text similar to the sp.[27] In 1977 M. Cohen pointed out that the wording of a *mezuzah* uncovered in Cave 8 in Qumran and published in 1962 also resembles the sp.[28] Likewise, harmonistic additions resembling the sp also appear in 4Q364, which

---

[23] See P. W. Skehan, "Exodus in the Samaritan Recension from Qumran," *JBL* 74 (1955): 182–87; J. E. Sanderson, *An Exodus Scroll from Qumran: 4QPaleoEx^m and the Samaritan Tradition* (HSS 30; Atlanta, 1986); P. W. Shehan, E. Ulrich and J. E. Sanderson, "4QPaleoExodus^m," *Qumran Cave 4.IV* (DJD 9; Oxford, 1992), 53–130.

[24] F. M. Cross, *The Ancient Library of Qumran and Modern Biblical Studies* (Garden City, 1958), 138–39.

[25] S. White Crawford, "4QDeut^n," *Qumran Cave 4.IX* (DJD 14; eds. E. Ulrich et al.; Oxford, 1995), 117–28; See E. Eshel, 4QDeut^n.

[26] J. A. Allegro, *Qumrân Cave 4, I (4Q158–4Q186)* (DJD 5; Oxford, 1968).

[27] R. Weiss, in his review on *Discoveries in the Judaean Desert of Jordan V Qumran Cave 4,I <4Q158–4Q186>, Qiryat Sefer* 45 (1970): 61 (Hebrew); J. Strugnell, "Notes en marge du volume V des 'Discoveries in the Judaean Desert of Jordan," *RevQ* 7 (1970): 168–75, 225–29.

[28] M. Cohen, "The Orthography of the Samaritan Pentateuch, its Place in the History of Orthography and its relation with the mt," *Beth Mikra* 21 (1976): 361–39 (Hebrew).

is known as the Reworked Pentateuch.[29] The common additions to
4Q364 and the sp constitute the completion of details in a "poor"
text based upon a "rich" text, thus Gen 30:36 augments the description
of Jacob's dream with the account of that dream in Gen 36:11–13.[30]
These are named Pre-Samaritan Texts or Proto-Samaritan Texts.[31]
All the common variants documented in the Dead Sea Scrolls and the
sp contain non-sectarian differences. Sectarian changes are not documented in the scrolls under discussion. For example, the tenth commandment that appears in the sp and the commandment to build
an altar on top of Mt. Gerizim are missing in 4QPaleoExod^m, 4Q158,
and 4QDeut^n. Scholarly research has consequently deduced that these
scrolls did not belong to the Samaritans; rather, they adopted a biblical version similar to these scrolls when the sp was compiled.[32]

Inasmuch as harmonistic editing constitutes the principle feature
of these texts, the prevalent name for these texts, "Pre-Samaritan
Texts" or "Proto-Samaritan Texts," is inappropriate.[33]

Conscious of this problem, Cross refered to the sp and the above
scrolls, as "Palestinian" in type.[34] He proposed a threefold division
for the Second Temple Period biblical text-types wherein the mt represents the family of biblical texts characteristic of Babylon; the lxx
represents the family of biblical texts characteristic of Egypt; and the
sp represents the family of biblical texts characteristic of Palestine.[35]
Nonetheless, this division is schematic and imprecise since: 1. The
Nash papyrus unearthed in Egypt evidently documents a harmonis-

---

[29] E. Tov and S. White, "4QReworked Pentateuch^b," *Qumran Cave 4.VIII* (DJD
13; ed. J. VanderKam, E. Tov et al.; Oxford, 1994), 197–254.

[30] Tov and S. White, "4QReworked Pentateuch," 210–11.

[31] E. Tov, "Proto-Samaritan Texts and the Samaritan Pentateuch," in *The Samaritans*
(ed. A. D. Crown; Tübingen, 1989), 397–407.

[32] We cannot accept Baillet's opinion that these scrolls found at Qumran are
Samaritan in origin; see M. Baillet, "Le texte Samaritain de l'*Exode* dans les manuscrits de Qumrân," in *Hommages à André Dupont-Sommer* (ed. A. Caquot and
M. Philonenko; Paris, 1971), 363–81, due to the fact that none of these scrolls contains any of the Samaritan additions and changes. Having the longest and best preserved scroll among this group, 4QPaleoExod^m, written in the Paleo-Hebrew script
is, to our mind, a mere coincident; see E. Eshel, "Harmonistic Editing in the
Pentateuch in the Second Temple Period," (MA thesis, the Hebrew University,
1999), 136 (Hebrew). The Samaritans started, using the Paleo-Hebrew script only
in the third century c.e. see discussion below.

[33] E. Tov, "Proto-Samaritan Texts," 405; idem, *Textual Criticism*, 80–82.

[34] M. Cross, "The Evolution of a Theory of Local Texts," in *Qumran and the
History of the Biblical Text* (ed. F. M. Cross and S. Talmon; Cambridge and London,
1975), 308–10.

[35] Cross, "The History of the Biblical Text," 281–99.

tic text-type dating to the Hasmonean period;[36] 2. The SP endeavored to resolve the textual difficulties extant in the MT. Thus, the scribes who edited the harmonistic text presumably had a biblical text very similar to the MT in front of them. We can consequently conclude that the SP and MT were prevalent in the same region—evidently Palestine. Textual findings from Qumran also testify to the fact that all three families of texts were common in Palestine. It is therefore preferable to label the texts that underwent harmonistic revision "harmonistic texts."[37]

Cross pointed out that "Thanks to the discovery and study of the Qumran scrolls, we are able to place the Samaritan Pentateuch in the history of the Hebrew biblical texts. It proves to be a late form of an old Palestinian tradition... The Samaritan Pentateuch text broke off very late in the development of the Palestinian (Proto-Samaritan) text... The Samaritan text-type thus is a late and full exemplar of a common Palestinian tradition in use both in Jerusalem and Samaria in Hasmonaean times."[38] This hypothesis formed the basis for J. D. Purvis' doctoral thesis, written under Cross' supervision. In his thesis, Purvis dated both the Samaritan Pentateuch and the origin of the Samaritan sect as a separate community to the Hasmonean period. His rationale was as follows: 1. The Samaritan script developed from the paleo-Hebrew script of the Hasmonean period. It did not develop from the Hebrew script of the Persian or Hellenistic period preceding the Hasmoneans, nor from the Hebrew script of the Roman period, but from the paleo-Hebrew script of the Hasmonean period;[39] 2. The orthography of the SP is in *plene* Hebrew spelling, which is characteristic of the Hasmonean period and not of the preceding periods or the later Rabbinic period.[40] 3. The SP belongs to one of three textual witnesses prevalent during the Hasmonean period, which are documented in the Dead Sea Scrolls.[41]

---

[36] Eshel, "4QDeut^n," 123.

[37] Eshel, "4QDeut^n," 120.

[38] F. M. Cross, "Samaria and Jerusalem in the Era of the Restoration," *From Epic to Canon* (Baltimore and London, 1998), 173–202.

[39] J. D. Purvis, *The Samaritan Pentateuch and the Origin of the Samaritan Sect* (Cambridge MA, 1968), 18–52.

[40] Purvis, *The Samaritan Pentateuch*, 52–69.

[41] Purvis, *The Samaritan Pentateuch*, 69–87.

III. The Dating of the Samaritan Script

Purvis claims that the Samaritan script developed from the Hasmonean paleo-Hebrew script. When his investigation was published (1968), the earliest Samaritan inscription known was from Emmaus, which Purvis attributed to the first century c.e. due to the paleographical similarity with coins from the Great Revolt. However the publication of Jewish and Samaritan inscriptions written in paleo-Hebrew script following the publication of Purvis' work shed new light upon the issue of the stage of Hebrew writing from which Samaritan Script developed. Three Hebrew inscriptions discovered on Mt. Gerizim, which antedate the Emmaus inscription by over one hundred years, were recently published.[42] In view of this information, we must reexamine the origins of the so-called "Samaritan script."

We shall launch our discussion with the four Samaritan inscriptions uncovered at Emmaus,[43] with which Purvis was acquainted. The first inscription was discovered in 1881; it was engraved upon an Ionic column and consists of a bilingual inscription in Greek and Hebrew. The Greek reads: ΕΙΣ ΘΕΟΣ and the Hebrew ברוך שמו לעולם. The three other inscriptions unearthed at the site are longer and consist of passages from the Book of Exodus.[44] The first inscription was usually attributed to the first century c.e. due to paleographic considerations.[45] Nonetheless, as Pummer has recently noted, the dating of a Samaritan inscription based solely upon paleographic considerations is difficult and usually impossible since the stone's hardness, the stonecutter's artistic ability, and local epigraphic traditions engendered significant epigraphic variants. Pummer therefore concluded that one must rely principally upon historical rather than paleographic information in order to date Samaritan inscriptions.[46]

Inasmuch as the first inscription from Emmaus engraved upon an Ionic column was discovered near a church, some scholars have claimed that it belonged to a Samaritan synagogue. These scholars

---

[42] J. Naveh and Y. Magen, "Aramaic and Hebrew Inscriptions of the Second-Century BCE at Mount Gerizim," 'Atiqot 32 (1997): 9*–17*.

[43] See: J. A. Montgomery, The Samaritans: The Earliest Jewish Sect (Philadelphia, 1907), Pl. 4–6.

[44] R. Pummer, "Inscriptions," in The Samaritans (ed. A. D. Crown; Tübingen, 1989), 192–3.

[45] Purvis, The Samaritan Pentateuch, 23.

[46] Pummer, "Inscriptions," 191.

hypothesized that the three other inscriptions uncovered at Emmaus also originated in the same Samaritan synagogue.[47] Current historical and archaeological data confirm that Emmaus was a Jewish settlement up until the time of the Bar Kokhba Revolt.[48] A comparison of the letters appearing in the first inscription from Emmaus with the letters in the other inscriptions reveals significant paleographical differences. It should be noted that only a relatively small number of first century C.E. synagogues have been discovered in Palestine up until the present,[49] and no bilingual inscriptions have been uncovered within them. Accordingly, although the Ionic column upon which the inscription was engraved indubitably predates the other inscriptions, we cannot accept the hypothesis that this inscription was engraved in the first century C.E. It was more probably engraved following the Bar Kokhba Revolt, when the Samaritans settled in Emmaus.[50] If the four inscriptions from Emmaus originated in one Samaritan synagogue built at the site then we must assume that the first inscription was written in the second century C.E.—prior to the development of the Samaritan Script characteristic of the third century and prior to the other inscriptions. However, since the Samaritan inscriptions were apparently used as *mezuzot*,[51] we can therefore assume that the inscriptions belonged to various individual houses. There are no grounds to assume that the four inscriptions belonged to the same synagogue, with the first one preceding the three others. An analysis of the script of the first inscription confirms that the similarity to the coins of the Great Revolt is comparable to that of the coins of the Bar Kokhba Revolt.[52]

---

[47] On the inscriptions found in Emmaus and their possible link with the Samaritan synagogue found there, see Montgomery, *The Samaritans*, 275–76; Z. Safrai, "Samaritan Synagogues in the Roman-Byzantine Period," *Cathedra* 4 (1997): 100–101 (Hebrew); Pummer, "Inscriptions," 192. But see: J. Naveh, "Did Ancient Samaritan Inscriptions Belong to Synagogues?," in *Ancient Synagogues in Israel* (ed. R. Hachlili; BAR International Series 499; Oxford, 1989), 61–63.

[48] L. H. Vincent and F. M. Abel, *Emmaüs, sa Basilique et son histoire* (Paris, 1932); M. Gichon, "EQED, ḤORVAT," in *The New Encyclopedia of Archaeological Excavations in the Holy Land* (ed. E. Stern; Jerusalem, 1993), 416–17.

[49] L. I. Levine, "The Second Temple Synagogue: The Formative Years," in *The Synagogue in Late Antiquity* (ed. L. I. Levine; Philadelphia, 1987), 7–31.

[50] G. Alon, *The Jews in Their Land in the Talmudic Age (70–640 C.E.)* (Jerusalem, 1984), II: 742–746.

[51] Naveh, "Ancient Samaritan Inscriptions."

[52] As opposed to Purvis, *The Samaritan Pentateuch*, 22–28. The *bet* and the *resh* in the first Emmaus inscriptions is similar to the Bar-Kokhba coins; the *waw* and the *kaph* to the Great Revolt coins, but the *shin* is similar to the Bar-Kokhba ones.

Epigraphic finds published in the last two decades establish that the paleo-Hebrew script documented in inscriptions originating from the region of Samaria or attributed to the Samaritans, such as the *bulla* of "...]YHW son of [San]ballat, governor of Samaria," discovered at Wadi ed-Daliyeh,[53] inscriptions from Mt. Gerizim, and the first inscription from Emmaus, does not differ from the Paleo-Hebrew script documented in Jewish inscriptions from the same period. The writing on the *bulla* from Wadi ed-Daliyeh is identical to the writing on Jewish *bullae* published by Avigad.[54] The inscription from Emmaus resembles those on Jewish coins from the First Revolt and the Bar Kokhba Revolt.[55] On the other hand, the Samaritan Script documented in Samaritan inscriptions starting from the third century C.E., as well as in the manuscripts of the Samaritan Pentateuch, is a development of the paleo-Hebrew script used among Jews during the first century C.E. The origins of the Samaritan script can be discerned in two scrolls found at Qumran. Inasmuch as the first scroll, 1QPaleoLev,[56] is written in paleo-Hebrew script it is difficult to determine its precise date. Scholars have proposed dating it to the Hasmonean period.[57] It is easier to establish an exact date for the second scroll, 4QIsaᶜ, whose writing bears a greater resemblance to the Samaritan script. This scroll is written in the Jewish script, which developed from the Aramaic script, although the Divine names are written in paleo-Hebrew script.[58] Following the publication of Purvis' book, a transcription of the Hebrew letters interwoven within 4QIsaᶜ was published.[59] Paleographic considera-

---

Having no clear distinction in the form of the *mem*, *lamed* and *'ayin* between the script of the Great Revolt coins and those of the bar-Kokhba, one can not determine clearly whether the script of the first Emmaus inscription reflects a development of the script used at the end of the Second Temple period rather than the script used during the Bar-Kokhba Revolt. As it is well known, dating these inscriptions should be based on the later forms of the letters.

[53] F. M. Cross, "The Papyri and Their Historical Implications," in P. W. Lapp and N. L. Lapp, *Discoveries in the Wâdī ed-Dâliyeh* (AASOR 41; Cambridge MA, 1974), 18.

[54] N. Avigad, *Bullae and Seals from a Post-Exilic Judean Archive* (Qedem 4; Jerusalem, 1976).

[55] D. Purvis, *The Samaritan Pentateuch*, 23.

[56] D. Barthélemy and J. T. Milik, *Qumran Cave I* (DJD 1; Oxford, 1955), 51–54, Pl. 8.

[57] R. S. Hanson, "Paleo-Hebrew Scripts in the Hasmonean Age," *BASOR* 175 (1964): 41.

[58] P. W. Skehan, "The Text of Isaias at Qumrân," *CBQ* 17 (1955): 162. D. Green, "4QIsᶜ: A Rabbinic Production of Isaiah found at Qumran," *JJS* 53 (2002): 120–145.

[59] M. D. McLean, "The Use and Development of Paleo-Hebrew in the Hellenistic and Roman Periods," (Ph.D. Diss., Harvard University, 1982), Pl. 5.

tions, based upon the Jewish script,[60] enable us to readily date the scroll to the end of the Second Temple period.

The Abba inscription uncovered in the Givʿat ha-Mivtar neighborhood of Jerusalem provides the Jewish inscription in paleo-Hebrew script most similar to the Samaritan script. This inscription was discovered in 1970 on the wall of a side room, wherein one sole niche had been hewn. An ossuary was found in the main room of this cave. In light of the cave's archaeological findings, the tomb can be unequivocally dated to the first century C.E.[61] The inscription itself is comprised of seven lines, with red colored chiseled letters. The letters in the second and fifth lines were not colored, except for their background. The inscription's language is Aramaic and up until the present time it furnishes the only example of the use of paleo-Hebrew script in an Aramaic inscription from the Second Temple period. Saul Lieberman has identified the Abba inscription as Samaritan due to its similarity with the Samaritan script and since the Samaritans used Samaritan script for Aramaic and Arabic texts in later periods.[62] A. S. Rosenthal, who published the inscription, deliberated as to whether this is a Jewish or Samaritan inscription. He concluded that Abba was a Jew since the inscription does not contain any definitive signs of Samaritan writing, moreover, the Abba inscription significantly predates other known Samaritan inscriptions. Abba was born in Jerusalem and called his birthplace Jerusalem whereas the Samaritans scrupulously avoided using this name. He brought the remains of Mattathias son of Judah from Babylon and buried them in Jerusalem. Abba consequently appears to be Jewish.[63] Epigraphic

---

[60] Skehan, "The Text of Isaiah," 162.

[61] V. Tzaferis, "The 'ABBA' Burial Cave in Jerusalem," ʿAtiqot 7 (1974): 61–64 (Hebrew).

[62] S. Lieberman, "Notes on the Givʿat ha-Mivtar Inscription," Pʾraqim 2 (1974): 375–80 (Hebrew).

[63] E. S. Rosenthal, "The Givʿat ha-Mivtar Inscription," Pʾraqim 2 (1974): 335–6; 372–3 (Hebrew); idem, "The Givʿat ha-Mivtar Inscription," IEJ 23 (1973): 80. Based on his discussion of the script, Naveh came to the conclusion that it is a Jewish inscription; see: J. Naveh, "An Aramaic Tomb Inscription Written in Paleo-Hebrew Script," IEJ 23 (1973): 91; idem, Early History of the Alphabet (Jerusalem, 1987), 120–21. Although the Abba inscription seems to be of Jewish origin, based on the research of P. Smith, "The Human Skeletal Remains from the Abba Cave," IEJ 27 (1977): 121–24; and of T. Ilan, "The Greek Names of the Hasmoneans," JQR 78 (1987): 12–13, it is difficult to accept Grintz's opinion, identifying Mattathias son of Judah with Antigonus Mattathias, son of Aristobulus II; See Y. M. Grintz, "The Givʿat Hamivtar Inscription: A Historical Interpretation," Sinai 75 (1974): 20–23 (Hebrew).

findings from the Second Temple period attributed to Samaritans and written in Aramaic substantiate the Jewishness of the Abba inscription even more than the Samaritan inscriptions from this period written in paleo-Hebrew. The legends imprinted on the coins of the city of Samaria in the fourth century B.C.E. were written in Aramaic script, all the documents discovered in Wadi ed-Daliyeh are written in Aramaic script, and only one *bulla* on ". . .]YHW son of [San]ballat, governor of Samaria," was stamped with a seal written in Hebrew script. Over sixty fragments of Samaritan inscriptions written in Aramaic script were uncovered on Mt. Gerizim as opposed to only six inscriptions written in paleo-Hebrew script.[64] The first century C.E. tomb inscriptions unearthed at Kefar 'Illar (ten kilometers east of Tul Karem) and at Jatt are perhaps Samaritan inscriptions. This confirms Samaritan use of a Jewish script, developed from Aramaic, during the Second Temple period.[65]

Likewise, there is more evidence indicating that Jews employed the paleo-Hebrew script during the Hellenistic period than there is regarding its use by the Samaritans. Jews used Hebrew script for stamping coins, administrative stamps (such as the "Jerusalem" stamp), writing scrolls (found at Qumran and Masada), inscriptions (a column's fragment of a marble slab found near the Temple Mount in Jerusalem and the Abba inscription), on ossuaries (found on Mt. Scopus), on sarcophagi (discovered at Masada), as well as column fragments and tags (at Masada) during the Second Temple period. These finds confirm that Jews utilized the paleo-Hebrew script during the Second Temple period for official purposes (on seals, coins, and perhaps even in an inscription from the Temple Mount), religious needs (the scrolls), and even in daily life.[66] Therefore the use of the Hebrew script during the Second Temple period does not prove that an inscription was Samaritan.

The inscriptions mentioned above substantiate the widespread use of the Paleo-Hebrew script among Jews during the Second Temple

---

[64] Naveh and Magen, "Aramaic and Hebrew Inscriptions."

[65] On the inscription found at the entrance to a tomb-cave at 'Illar, see: B. Mazar, "A Hebrew Inscription from 'Illar," *BIES* 18 (1954): 154–7 (Hebrew). On the Jatt inscription see: Y. Porath, Y. Neeman and A. Boshnino, "Jatt," *Excavations and Surveys in Israel 1988/89* 7–8 (1988–89), 83–84. For the possibility of such inscription being Samaritan in origin, see: J. Naveh, "Scripts and Inscriptions in Ancient Samaria," *IEJ* 48 (1998): 94–95.

[66] Naveh, *Early History of the Alphabet*, 119–23.

period. Based upon the writing in 4QIS^c and the Abba inscription, which were unknown to Purvis, we can ascertain that the Samaritans adopted the Paleo-Hebrew script used by the Jews at the end of the Second Temple period, as suggested by Cross and Naveh' following the discovery of the Abba inscription.[67] The Hebrew script evolved into a script characteristic of the Samaritans following the Bar Kokhba Revolt. Starting from the third century C.E., there is documentation of a "Samaritan script," which developed from the Hebrew script of the end of the Second Temple period. Accordingly, the Samaritan script does not provide any confirmation for the evolution of the Samaritan Pentateuch and the Samaritan sect during the Hasmonean period.

IV. THE DATING OF THE SAMARITAN PENTATEUCH IN LIGHT OF THE DEAD SEA SCROLLS

We shall now address Purvis' other hypotheses relating to the date of the SP's formation. As regards Purvis' second premise, that the orthography of the SP is in *plene* Hebrew spelling, although most of the orthography of the SP is more full than in the MT, certain grammatical categories in the MT are more complete than in the SP.[68] Hence, the SP's orthography does not verify its development during the Hasmonean period.

When Purvis composed his book, only a sparse number of harmonistic scrolls had been published, and he therefore utilized Cross' data on the SP's textual character (Purvis' third rationale).[69] In view of the publication of four additional harmonistic scrolls from Qumran during the past decade: 4QDeut^n,[70] 4Num^b,[71] 4QPaleoExod^{m}[72] and 4Q364,[73] the hypotheses that prompted Cross' conclusion concerning the SP's formation during the Hasmonean period can now be more precisely examined.

---

[67] Cross, "Samaria and Jerusalem," 201; Naveh, "Scripts and Inscriptions in Ancient Samaria," 91–100.

[68] M. Cohen, "The Orthography of the Samaritan Pentateuch," *Beth Mikra* 21 (1976): 54–70 (Hebrew).

[69] Cross had the rights of publication to most of the harmonistic scrolls, still unpublished in 1968.

[70] White-Crawford, 4QDeut^n; Eshel, 4QDeut^n.

[71] N. Jastram, '4QNum^b,' in *Qumran Cave 4.VI* (*DJD* 12; ed. E. Ulrich et al.; Oxford, 1994), 205–67.

[72] Skehan, Ulrich and Sanderson, "4QPaleoExod^m."

[73] Tov and S. White, "4QReworked Pentateuch^b."

In 1991 E. Eshel identified additional Second Temple period texts which had undergone harmonistic editing: 4QDeut[j], 4QDeut[kl],[74] the Nash papyrus uncovered in Egypt,[75] and a collection of five sheets of *tefillin* and *mezuzot* discovered at Qumran (4QPhyl J, 4QPhyl G, 4QMezA, 8QPhyl, XQPhyl 3).[76] Therefore, we now have fifteen Second Temple period texts with harmonistic editing, similar in character to the harmonistic editing in the SP.[77] Most of the texts are fragments from the Book of Deuteronomy as well as one long scroll, several fragmentary sections containing the harmonistic editing of the Book of Exodus, and one scroll of the Book of Numbers also with harmonistic editing. In 4Q364 there is a passage from the harmonistic version of the Book of Genesis. No evidence of Second Temple period text types of the Book of Leviticus with harmonistic editing have yet been found.

The following table was formulated in order to examine when the Samaritan version of the Pentateuch developed. It contains paleographic data establishing the dating for the copying of the harmonistic texts from the Second Temple period.

SECOND TEMPLE PERIOD TEXT TYPES WITH HARMONISTIC EDITING

Version	Date of Transcription	Reference
1. 4QPaleoExod[m]	End of the second century or first half of the first century B.C.E.	McLean (above, n. 59), 66–78
2. 4Num[b]	Early Herodian, 30 B.C.E. to 20 C.E.	Jastram (above, n. 71), 211; Cross (above, n. 74), 138, *l.* 5

---

[74] J. A. Duncan, "4QDeut[j], 4QDeut[kl]," in *Qumran Cave 4.IX* (DJD 14; eds. E. Ulrich et al.; Oxford, 1995), 75–98; F. M. Cross, "The Development of the Jewish Scripts," *The Bible and the Ancient Near East: Essays in Honor of William Foxwell Albright* (ed. G. E. Wright; Garden City, New York, 1961), 174–81.

[75] W. F. Albright, "A Biblical Fragment from the Maccabaean Age: The Nash Papyrus," *JBL* 56 (1937): 145–76.

[76] For the publication of the *Tefillin* and *Mezuzot* found in Cave 4, See: J. T. Milik, *Qumrân Grotte 4.II: Tefillin, Mezuzot et Targums (4Q128–4Q157)* (DJD 6; Oxford, 1977); and of Cave 8, see: M. Baillet, J. T. Milik and R. de-Vaux, *Les 'Petites Grottes' de Qumrân* (DJD 3; Oxford, 1962). Another *Tefillin* found at Qumran was published by Y. Yadin, "Tefillin from Qumran (XQPhyl 1–4)" (Jerusalem, 1969).

[77] Eshel, "4QDeut[n]," 121–123.

3. 4QDeut^n	Early Herodian, circa 30–1 B.C.E.	White Crawford (above, n. 25), 117
4. 4QDeut^j	Late Herodian, circa 50 C.E.	Duncan (above, n. 74), 77
5. 4QDeut^{kl}	Early Herodian	Duncan (above, n. 74), 94
6. 4Q158	Late Hasmonean or Early Herodian	Strugnell (above, n. 27), 168
7. 4QTest	End of the second century B.C.E.	Cross (above, n. 74), 198, n. 116; Eshel below, n. 98
8. 4Q364	End of the Hasmonean period	Tov and White (above, n. 29), 201
9. Nash Papyrus	Hasmonean period	Albright (above, n. 75)
10. 4QMez A	Second or first century B.C.E.	Milik (above, n. 76), 80
11. 4QPhyl G	undated	Milik, *ibid.*, 58
12. 4QPhyl J	undated	Milik, *ibid.*, 64
13. 8QMez	Herodian	Baillet, Milik & de-Vaux (above, n. 76), 158
14. 8QPhyl	First century C.E.	Baillet, Milik & de-Vaux, *ibid.*, 149
15. XQPhyl 3	first half of the first century C.E.	Yadin (above, n. 76), 69

These harmonistic texts contain additions and emendations of the text in order to resolve internal contradictions or add details taken from a parallel biblical description. This was not only true for individual cases, it entailed a systematic process.[78] The scribes who augmented and changed the texts in question believed that inconsistencies in the Pentateuch somehow diminish the text's sanctity. The harmonistic version of the Ten Commandments expresses the desire to reject the traditional justification that "'Remember' and 'Observe' were spoken in a single utterance" (*b. Roš Haš.* 27a), which nullified human limitations for all things associated with Divine speech. On the other hand, like the sages, the editors of the harmonistic version also believed that the two versions of the Ten Commandments, in Exodus and in Deuteronomy, faithfully reported the words of God at Mt. Sinai. An analysis of the harmonistic texts in our possession illustrates the exegetical problems confronting Jewish sages during the Second Temple period. For example, 4QPaleoExod^m also documents

---

[78] Eshel, "4QDeut^n," 121.

the transformation of "we will do and we will hearken" in Exod 24:7 to "we will hearken and we will do" as in the SP. A comparison between the MT and text types with harmonistic editing shows that the difficulties the harmonistic editors attempted to resolve also existed in the MT. The harmonistic editors' text-type was consequently probably close to that of the MT.[79] Significantly, the SP is the only text-type with comprehensive harmonistic editing in all five books of the Pentateuch.

Second Temple period harmonistic text-types reflect an awareness of the variants among the descriptions of events in the Bible and not differences among collections of laws.[80] The exegetical changes in law compilations in the SP are not documented in Second Temple period text types, for example:

> *Exod 21:29*
> MT, 4QPaleoExod[m]: השור יסקל
> SP: הבהמה תסקל
>
> *Exod 21:31*
> MT, 4QPaleoExod[m]: או בן ינח
> SP: או בן יכה

In these two cases the law was expanded in the SP in order to clarify that not only an ox but also any animal causing injury must be stoned. Consequently, the topic is not only damages caused by an ox but by other animals as well. Some scholars have claimed that these legal expansions were due to the inadequacy of the Samaritan oral law.[81] The correspondence between the changes in the SP and in Jewish law has already been examined.[82] For example, in certain cases the word "ox" in the MT was changed to "animal" in the SP (Exod 21:28, 29, 32). In other cases, when the "ox" or "ass" were mentioned, the SP added the words "or any animal" (Exod 21:28, 32, 35; 22:3; 23:4 and Deut 22:1, 4). The generalization "or any animal" is only mentioned once in the MT (Exod 22:9). These changes in the SP were interpreted as a comprehensive judicial expansion similar to the rabbinic ruling that when the Bible mentions damages from an ox it signifies any animal (*mek. derabi Yishmael, Mishpatim*, Horowitz-Rabin edition, p. 280). However, in regards to paying four

---

[79] Eshel, "Harmonistic Editing," 6.
[80] Tov, "Proto-Samaritan Texts."
[81] Weiss, *Studies in the Text*, 160, 190–205.
[82] D. Daube, "Zur frühtalmudischen Rechtspraxis" *ZAW* 50 (1932): 148–59.

and five times the cost, which according to Jewish law is only valid for an ox and sheep (*b. B.Qam.* 7a), the SP left the original phrase "ox or sheep" (Exod 21:37) and did not add "or any animal."[83]

One such change is documented in the harmonistic texts—4Q158 and apparently 4QPaleoExod[m] as well.[84] Exod 22:4 according to 4Q158 reads:

כי יבעה [איש שדה או כרם ושלח את בעירו ובער בשדה אחר שלם ישלם
משדהו כת]בואתו אם כול השדה יבעה מיטב שדהו ומיטב כרמו י[שלם

The SP resembles 4Q158 except for the following change in the second word of the verse: it is written כי יבעה at the beginning of 4Q158 while the SP has כי יבעיר. The MT reads: כי יבער איש שדה או כרם ושלח את בעירה ובער בשדה אחר מיטב שדהו ומיטב כרמו ישלם. This verse presents two exegetical problems: 1. What does the word יבער signify? 2. What is the law—is one obligated to make restitution for any impairment to the field or only if the entire field is damaged? The objective of the emendation documented in 4Q158 and the SP was to establish that the owner of the animal must make restitution only if the entire field is destroyed. If only part of the field is destroyed then the owner must give compensation from his field for the amount of grain damaged.[85] The root בע"ר can be interpreted to refer to either a kindling a fire or the consumption of grain by an animal (see Isa 5:5). The sages viewed this verse as the judicial basis for compensation on account of animal grazing and thus the expression was interpreted to mean grazing. The LXX, the Peshiṭta, and all the Aramaic translations also translated it in this manner. However Targum Neofiti, as well as a Targum fragment found at the Geniza,[86] translated it as follows: ארום יקד נבר "If a man sets a fire", in other words, it signifies kindling a fire. The emendation from יבעיר to יבעה documented in the SP and 4Q158 is based upon the Aramaic root

---

[83] Weiss, *Studies in the Text*, 160–63.

[84] In 4QPaleoExod[m] the verse of Exod 22:4 did not survive, but there is enough space for reconstructing the Samaritan variant, found also in 4Q158, while the MT has a shorter version.

[85] A. Toeg, "Exodus XII, 4: The Text and the Law in the Light of the Ancient Sources," *Tarbiz* 39 (1970): 223–31 (Hebrew).

[86] Based on the publication of an Aramaic Targum fragment found in the Geniza, reading:

ארום יבקר נבר נבר בחקל או כרם וישלח ית יקידתה ויוקד בחקלא דאחרן בית
שפר חקלא ובית שפר כרמא ישלם

this issue was intensively dealth with, see: J. J. Weinberg, *Meḥkarim batalmud* (Berlin, 1937–8), 68–82 (Hebrew). For additional bibliography, see Toeg, Exodus XII, 4.

בע"ה which can signify either grazing or grain. The emendation of
this verse appears once in the SP and twice in 4Q158. Its objective
was to establish that the subject is damages due to animal grazing
and not from kindling a fire as the translator of the fragment from
the Geniza as well as the author of Targum Neofiti had interpreted
it.[87] In this case, 4Q158 documents a more comprehensive exegetical editing than the SP.

In light of 4Q158's version of Exod 22:4, it is doubtful whether
the absence of a Samaritan oral law engendered the few halakhic
additions in the SP. Such a change is more fully documented in the
Second Temple period text types than in the SP, which indicates that
Jews may have appended the additions and halakhic changes to the
SP during the end of the Second Temple period. The fact that other
halakhic additions were not preserved in the harmonistic scrolls uncovered at Qumran is probably purely coincidental. Therefore, it cannot be assumed that these additions postdate the adoption of the
harmonistic texts or that the Samaritans added them. The above
hypothesis explains the various cases Daube and Weiss compiled
wherein halakhic additions in the SP reflect a halakhah similar to
one documented in rabbinic sources.

The comparison between the SP and harmonistic texts from the
Second Temple period reveals that certain Second Temple period
texts underwent a more comprehensive harmonistic editing than the
SP. This point can be proved by investigating the harmonistic version
of Deuteronomy 5, documented in eight texts with harmonistic editing (the SP, 4QDeut^n, the Nash Papyrus, 4QPhyl G, 4QPhyl J,
4QMez A, 8QPhyl, and XQPhyl 3); the version of Deuteronomy 11
documented in four text-types with harmonistic editing (the SP, 4QDeut^j,
4QDeut^{kl}, and 8QMez); as well as by the harmonistic version of
Exodus 20 documented in four text types (the SP, 4QPaleoExod^m,
4QTest, and 4Q158).

Text types preserving the harmonistic version of Deuteronomy 5
are divided into three groups. The first group contains texts with
limited harmonistic editing in order to bring the version of the Ten
Commandments in Deuteronomy closer to that in Exodus. In this
editing, the commandment concerning the Sabbath resembles the MT
in Deuteronomy. This group includes the SP, XQPhyl 3, 4QPhyl J.
The changes documented in these text types are as follows:

---

[87] Eshel, "Harmonistic Editing," 106–8.

Deut 5:8
MT: כל תמונה
sp, XQPhyl 3, 4QPhyl J: וכ(ו)ל תמונה

Deut 5:9
MT: ועל שלשים
sp, XQPhyl 3: על של(י)שים
Harmonization to Exod 20:5.

Deut 5:14
MT: לא תעשה כל מלאכה
sp, 4QPhyl J: לא תעשה בו כל מלאכה
The same reading is found in sp to Exod 20:10, based on harmonization to Exod 35:2.

Deut 5:18–21
MT: ולא תנאף\תגנב\תענה\תחמד\תתאוה
sp, XQPhyl 3: לא תנאף\תגנב\תענה\תחמד\תחמד
Harmonization to Exod 20:14–17.

Deut 5:20
MT, sp: עד שוא
XQPhyl 3: עד שקר
Harmonization to Exod 20:16.

Deut 5:21
MT: ולא תתאוה בית רעך
sp, XQPhyl 3, 4QPhyl J: לא תחמ(ו)ד בית רעך
Harmonization to Exod 20:17. The MT reads: בית ... אשת, while in sp the sequence is: אשת ... בית, as harmonization to the verse.
XQPhyl 3 end with Deut 5:21, but sp and 4QPhyl J have further harmonizations:

Deut 5:22
MT: הענן והערפל
sp, 4QPhyl J: ה(ו)שך ענן וערפל
Harmonization to Deut 4:11, and to 5:23.

Deut 5:27
4QDeutʲ: [כול אשר יאמר יהוה אלוהינו אליכ]ה
MT: כל אשר יאמר יהוה אלהינו
This harmonization, found also in 4QPhyl J and 4QPhyl H, is harmonization to the next verse, 5:28.

The first ten emendations detailed above change the version in Deuteronomy 5, based upon Exodus 20. These changes are also documented in the subsequent text types, surveyed below.[88] It therefore

---

[88] Most of the variants documented in the Second Temple sources which we identified in this group, are also found in sp—but the harmonization found in Deut 5:20.

appears that this does not reflect unintentional change but rather
systematic harmonistic editing.

The second group preserves a harmonistic version of the Ten
Commandments in Deuteronomy. It includes text types with all of
the changes in the first group, as well as an almost complete harmonization of the commandment concerning the Sabbath. This group
includes the Nash Papyrus, 8QPhyl, 4QMez A, and 4QPhyl G. This
group of text types omits the rationale for keeping the Sabbath of
the bondage in Egypt, which appears in Deut 5:14. Rather, it gives
the rationale of the Creation, which appears in Exod 20:11

Deut 5:14–15
MT and SP: ... למען ינוח עבדך ... וזכרת כי עבד היית
Nash Papyrus, 8QPhyl, 4QMez A, and 4QPhyl G:
כי ששת ימים עשה יהוה את השמים ואת הארץ את הים וכל אשר בם וינח ביום
השביעי על כן ברך יהוה את יום השבת ויקדשו

The third harmonistic version of the Ten Commandments in Deuteronomy is documented in 4QDeut[n]. All the emendations documented
in the above text types appear in this scroll, however, two explanations
are given for the commandment concerning the Sabbath. The first
reason—the enslavement in Egypt—is also found in the MT version
of Deuteronomy; the second reason given also appears in the MT of
Exodus—the Sabbath as a remembrance of the Creation. This harmonistic version is also documented in Codex Vaticanus of the LXX.[89]

The SP version of the Ten Commandments consequently reflects
limited harmonistic editing, as opposed to the scrolls discovered in
Qumran and the Nash Papyrus discovered in Egypt, which reflect
more comprehensive harmonistic editing than the SP. We can summarize the differences among the three different stages of editing in
the following table:

Exod 20:8–11		Deut 5:12–15	
MT, SP	MT, SP	LXX	4QDeut[n]
זכור (שמור) את יום השבת לקרש(ה)ו	שמור את יום השבת לקרש(ה)ו כאשר צוך יהוה אלהיך	שמור את יום השבת לקדשו כאשר צוך יהוה אלהיך	שמור את יום השבת לקדשו כאשר צוך יהוה אלהיך
ששת ימים תעבד ועשית כל מלאכתך ויום השביעי שבת ליהוה	ששת ימים תעבד ועשית כל מלאכתך ויום השביעי שבת ליהוה	ששת ימים תעבוד ועשית את כל מלאכתך וביום	ששת ימים תעבור ועשית את כול מלאכתך וביום

---

[89] Eshel, "4QDeut[n]," 146.

אלהיך לא תעשה (בו) | אלהיך אל תעשה (בו) | השביעי שבת ליהוה | השביעי שבת ליהוה
כל מלאכה אתה ובנך | כל מלאכה אתה ובנך | אלוהיך לא תעשה כו | אלוהיך לוא תעשה בו
ובתך עבדך ואמתך | ובתך (ו)עבדך ואמתך | כל מלאכה אתה ובנך | כל מלאכה אתה בנך
(שורך וחמרך) | (ו)שורך וחמרך וכל | ובתך עבדך ואמתך | בתך עבדך ואמתך
(ו)בהמתך וגרך אשר | בהמתך וגרך אשר | שורך וחמורך וכל | שורך וחמורך ובהמתך
בשעריך | בשעריך | בהמתך וגרך אשר | גריך אשר בשעריך
 | | בשעריך |

Codex Vaticanus

כי ששת ימים עשה יהוה | | כי ששת ימים עשה יהוה |
את השמים ואת | | את השמים ואת |
הארץ את הים ואת כל | | הארץ את הים ואת כל |
אשר בם | | אשר בם |

למען ינוח עבדך | למען ינוח עבדך | למען ינוח עבדך | למען ינוח עבדך
ואמתך כמוך | ואמתך כמוך | ואמתך כמוך | ואמתך כמוך

וזכרת כי עבד היית | וזכרת כי עבד היית | וזכרת כי עבד היית | וזכרתה כי עבד היית
בארץ מצרים ויציאך | בארץ מצרים ויצ(י)אך | בארץ מצרים ויציאך | בארץ מצרים ויציאך
וי(צ)(י)אך יהוה אלוהיך | יהוה אלוהיך משם ביד | יהוה אלוהיך משם ביד | יהוה אלוהיך משם ביד
משם ביד חזקה | חזקה ובזרוע נטויה | חזקה ובזרוע נטויה | חזקה ובזרוע נטויה
ובזר(ו)(ע) נטויה על כן | על כן צוך יהוה אלוהיך | על כן צוך יהוה אלוהיך | על כן צוך יהוה אלוהיך
צוך יהוה אלוהיך לעשות | לשמור את יום השבת | לשמור את יום השבת | לשמור את יום השבת
את יום השבת | לקורשו | לקרשו | לקרשו

The harmonistic version of Deuteronomy 11, documented in four text types, furnishes a similar account. All three scrolls unearthed at Qumran reflect a more comprehensive harmonistic editing of this chapter than that documented in the SP. We will illustrate this with the version of Deut 11:8. The MT and SP read as follows for this verse:

ושמרתם את כל המצוה אשר אנכי מצוך (SP—מצוה אתכם) היום למען
תחזקו ובאתם וירשתם את הארץ אשר אתם עברים (SP—באים) שמה
לרשתה.

One the other hand, 4QDeut^j, 4QDeut^kl, and 8QMez contain three harmonistic additions for this verse, which supplement details based upon parallels of this passage. The three additions are documented in 4QDeut^kl. The first was preserved in 4QDeut^j, the two others were reconstructed therein, however only the first two additions are documented in 8QMez. The additions are as follows:

1. The commandment החוקים והמשפטים (the laws and the rules)— based upon Deut 7:11.

2. So that you may thrive ורביתם (and increase)—based upon Deut 8:1.

3. That you are crossing הירדן (the Jordan) to possess—based upon Deut 30:18; 31:13.

Since these harmonistic additions are not documented in the sp, the harmonistic version documented in 4QDeut^j, 4QDeut^kl, and 8QMez is apparently more comprehensive than the sp.[90]

A segment was added to the sp version of Exodus 20, following verse 21. The beginning was extracted from Deut 5:22–26 and the end from Deut 18:18–19. It is also documented in 4QPaleoExod^m, 4QTest, and 4Q158. The segment is composed of four harmonistic additions that supplement details in a "poor" text on the basis of a "rich" text. The first addition documents the rationale for the Israelites' request that Moses act as an intermediary between them and God. The mt of Exodus also hints at this rationale but does not explicitly mention it. It appears in the mt of Deut 5:25: כי נמות למה האכלנו האש הגדלה הזאת. The second addition consists of God's reaction to the request not to hear His words directly. This addition is extracted from Deut 5:28–29. The mt of Exodus does not mention God's reaction to the Israelite request although it is cited in the sp and other harmonistic versions, based upon Deuteronomy. The third part of this addition deals with the issue of a true and false prophet. The mt of Deut 18:15–16 reads: . . . נביא מקרבך מאחיך כמני יקים לך יהוה אלהיך כל אשר שאלת מעם יהוה אלהיך בחרב ביום הקהל, therefore this addition was added on to Exodus 20 since בחרב ביום הקהל was mentioned. Thus a section based upon the sp Deut 18:18–19 was added to 4QPaleoExod^m and 4QTest, after Exod 20:21. Following the text discussing a true and false prophet, God's command to Moses appears in the sp—to tell the Israelites to return to their tents—while Moses is commanded to remain and hear the laws dealing with sanctified sites and altars. This addition is taken from the mt of Deut 5:27–28.

In 4Q158 the editor preceded the Ten Commandments with the people's request to hear God's words through Moses. This request was added to the sp of Exod 20:21, in other words, following the Ten Commandments. Consequently, the request that Moses mediate between God and the Israelites appears in the sp after the revelation at Mt. Sinai while in 4Q158 it precedes the Ten Commandments. In this manner, the harmonistic editor of the version documented in 4Q158 attempted to reconcile the texts of Exodus and Deuteronomy regarding who uttered the Ten Commandments (Exod 20:1 declares that God spoke all these words while Deut 5:1–5 states that Moses uttered the Ten Commandments).

---

[90] Eshel, "Harmonistic Editing," 117–18.

In the addition to Deuteronomy, documented in 4QPaleoExod[m] and 4QTest and in the SP as well, the following sentence was added to 4Q158, based upon Deut 5:28; 5:30: ועתה כשומעכה] את קול ל [ר]אמו דברי. לחמה נביא[]. This sentence is not documented in other text types with harmonistic editing.

The preamble ויאמר יהוה אל משה is another harmonistic version that exists only in 4Q158. It was added between the section discussing true and false prophets and the command for the Israelites to return to their tents. This formula appears at the end of the large harmonistic addition to Exod 20:21 and does not appear in the SP.

The harmonizations added to 4Q158 in order to make the command correspond to the action—relating that the Israelites did indeed return to their tents while Moses did indeed remain with God—are not documented in the SP.

Another change in 4Q158 is documented in a version of Exod 20:17:

לא תחמד בית רעך (ו)לא תחמר אשת רעך ,MT, SP
לא תחמור אשת רעכה [לא תחמר בית רעך] 4Q158

This is a harmonization of Deut 5:12. In the SP and 4QPhyl G Deuteronomy was adapted to the version in Exodus while in 4Q158 the version in Exodus was adapted to Deuteronomy.

The harmonistic version documented in 4Q158 is therefore clearly different and more comprehensive than the SP. It can solve significant difficulties in the biblical version, which are encountered in the SP.[91] The aforementioned halakhic changes common to both the 4Q158 and the SP reveal that 4Q158 documents a more comprehensive editing than the SP.

In light of the above analysis, we can conclude that the harmonistic editing reflected in 4QPaleoExod[m], 8QPhyl, XQPhyl 3, 4QNum[b], 4QTest, 4Q364, and 4QPhyl J—has the same scope as that of the SP and most of the harmonistic changes documented in these scrolls also exist in the SP. However 4QDeut[n], 4QDeut[j], 4QDeut[kl], 4Q158, the Nash Papyrus, 8QPhyl, 4QMez A, 4QPhyl G, and 8QMez have a more comprehensive editing than what is documented in the SP.

In our opinion, this distinction had a crucial impact upon the issue of the SP's chronological development. The scrolls pertaining to the second group reflect a more comprehensive harmonistic editing

---

[91] Eshel, "Harmonistic Editing," 84–91.

than the SP, and were written in either late Hasmonean or Herodian script. On the other hand, scrolls featuring harmonistic editing, with the same additions and scope as the SP, were dated to the end of the second century B.C.E. or the beginning of the first century B.C.E.

No scrolls incorporating the entire Pentateuch were uncovered at Qumran.[92] It consequently seems to have been uncommon to possess large scrolls with the entire Pentateuch during the Second Temple period and rather individual books written on scrolls were the norm.[93] The Samaritans appear to have deliberately chosen five scrolls with harmonistic editing for their authoritative version of the Bible. It is improbable that other Jewish groups in Palestine possessed only harmonistic texts and the Samaritans decided to adopt their scrolls in particular.[94] The findings at Qumran reflected a very broad textual pluralism in regards to the various versions of the Bible. Yadin's publication of a phylactery compartment with three of the original parchment sheets illustrates this pluralism. One parchment sheet (XQPhyl 3) contains a harmonistic version while the other two (XQPhyl 2, XQPhyl 1) embody a pre-Masoretic version.[95] This finding reinforces the hypothesis that the Samaritans' acquisition of harmonistic texts was not accidental—their election of scrolls with harmonistic editing was intentional. The harmonistic version corresponded to the Samaritan outlook and in their opinion it could resolve the inconsistencies in the Bible. The harmonistic version was therefore chosen as the basis for the normative version of the Samaritan sect.[96]

We must now ask why the Samaritans did not choose a harmonistic version with more comprehensive editing than the one documented in the SP, why did they not select a version that solves additional difficulties extant in the biblical text? The answer to this question is essentially chronological. The Samaritan adopted scrolls with harmonistic editing, which were prevalent when the authoritative version of their Pentateuch was established. This transpired during a period when Jewish scribes continued to refine the harmonistic version. Those scrolls with more comprehensive editing than the SP

---

[92] E. Tov, "Hebrew Biblical Manuscripts from the Judaean Desert: Their Contribution to Textual Criticism," *JJS* 39 (1988): 5–37.

[93] M. Haran, "Archives, Libraries, and the Order of the Biblical Books," *JANES* 22 (1993): 51–52.

[94] Eshel, "Harmonistic Editing," 6.

[95] Eshel, "Harmonistic Editing," 116.

[96] As opposed to Tov, "Proto-Samaritan Texts," 405–7.

appear to reflect a version the editing of which was concluded after the Samaritan adoption of the scrolls which formed the basis for the SP. Once the SP was formulated, it was transcribed with great precision and no additional changes were made,[97] including harmonistic additions proposed by Jewish scribes.

4QTest, which includes sections from Exodus (the harmonistic version), Leviticus, and Deuteronomy, as well as Pesher Joshua 6, 26 plays an important role in establishing the date for the SP's formation. This scroll, which was copied at the end of the second century B.C.E. or the beginning of the first century B.C.E.; appears in the harmonistic version of Exodus,[98] which has the same amount of editing as the SP. This fact authenticates the editing, acceptance, and prevalence of this version in the second century B.C.E. Consequently, the discovery of texts with more comprehensive editing than the SP, which are written in Hasmonean and Herodian script, as well as the harmonistic section in 4QTest, prove that the primary version of the SP was created during the second century B.C.E.

This discussion of the SP cannot be concluded without exploring the issue of when sectarian changes were added to the SP (which are not documented in the Qumran scrolls). It can be presumed that these sectarian additions were carried out prior to the destruction of the Samaritan temple on Mt. Gerizim in 111 B.C.E. A recently published fragmentary Hebrew inscription uncovered in the sacred Samaritan site on Mt. Gerizim may possibly support this hypothesis.[99] The third line of this inscription reads: ‏[בה ר[‏ and we may speculate that it can be completed as: ‏אש[ר בח]ר‏. This perhaps represents one of the sectarian changes cited in Deuteronomy.[100] Even if one does not accept this reconstruction, it can be assumed that the Samaritans chose the harmonistic Jewish version of the Pentateuch prevalent prior to the Hasmonean period. The Samaritans acquired this version during the period preceding the deterioration of Jewish-Samaritan relations due to the establishment of the Hasmonean state. Samaritan

---

[97] Tov, "Proto-Samaritan Texts," 401.

[98] H. Eshel, "The Historical Background of the Pesher Interpreting Joshua's Curse On the Rebuilder of Jericho," *RevQ* 15 (1992): 409–20.

[99] Naveh and Magen, "Aramaic and Hebrew Inscriptions," *15, Inscription A.

[100] For a discussion concerning this possibility, see: H. Eshel, "The Samaritans in the Persian and Hellenistic Periods: The Origins of Samaritanism" (Ph.D. diss., Hebrew University, 1994), 86 (Hebrew).

scribes who lived near the temple on Mt. Gerizim during the second
century B.C.E. probably added sectarian additions to this version.

The Jewish version of the Pentateuch adopted by the Samaritans
in the second century B.C.E. consequently formed the nucleus of the
SP. Similar to Jewish scribes of the same period, the Samaritans also
believed in the need to resolve the internal contradictions in the
Bible. They therefore chose the harmonistic text-type of five scrolls
as the basis for their version. Once these scrolls were selected, the
Samaritans did not revise their version although some Jewish scribes
added more harmonizations and solved other difficulties extant in
the Bible. Sectarian changes establishing Mt. Gerizim as the primary
sacred site were added to the Jewish version used by the Samaritan
scribes. The SP consequently confirms a connection between Jews
and Samaritans during the second century B.C.E. As a result of these
relations, the Jewish harmonistic version, which forms the basis of
the SP, reached the Samaritans. The sectarian additions to this version demonstrate an explicit religious ideology sanctifying Mt. Gerizim
and challenging Jerusalem's holiness. During the second century
B.C.E., Jewish harmonistic scrolls probably reached the Samaritans
and the sectarian additions were made to the SP.

THE RECEPTION OF NAHUM AND HABAKKUK
IN THE SEPTUAGINT AND QUMRAN

Heinz-Josef Fabry

In antiquity, up the period of the Church Fathers, the books of Nahum and Habakkuk were read in a more pronounced manner than seems imaginable to us, especially considering their marginalization today. There can be no doubt that the message of these two minor prophets was heard to a much greater degree in earlier times. The following contribution demonstrates the reception of these two books in the Septuagint[1] and the Qumran Scrolls (and, concluding, in the archives of Naḥal Ḥever and Wadi Murabbaʿat) in order to better understand the high estimation which they were held by in contemporary communities and groups. The method of reception history, which is yet awaiting a more detailed definition, might one day enable us to elucidate and evaluate similarities as well as differences from ancient and contemporary perspectives.

Such a methodology derives its main tools from the historical-critical method. Just as *Überlieferungskritik*, literary criticism and redaction criticism search for the origins of a text, a method focusing on reception history would trace the afterlife of the final text and uncover the understanding of those who received the text. However, textual and canonical history have ceased to be of primary importance, and the original intentions cannot be uncovered in a text any more. Now, the new contextuality of the texts has become central, as are added and attached texts, additional commentaries, or even compositions of a non-biblical nature. The early reception of biblical texts enables us to examine our own exegetical methods and can serve as self-critique on the one hand, and as a positive widening of our perspective on the other. Reception history offers fuel for many a text and literary-critical question, in as far as unclear passages are often met with the argument that already the Septuagint, Qumran literature or the church fathers had run into difficulties at this point. Since

---

[1] More detailed remarks will follow in my commentary to Nahum and Habakkuk in *HThK*.

such an argument is based only on superficial impressions there is great need for a theory leading to verifiable results.

Apart from this reception history—and this is where we enter sensitive territory—intertestamental texts can also be decisive indicators regarding text- and canon-historical developments.

Nahum and Habakkuk have clearly been received at Qumran. To the Qumran Essenes or whoever has to be seen as their historical antecedents or successors, both books were obviously important enough to warrant individual commentaries. On the other hand, they were not as important as the Pentateuch or the Psalms, as the number of their preserved copies indicates.

A. The reception of the minor prophets in the Septuagint

The most essential facts concerning the differing order of the books of the twelve minor prophets in the Septuagint and Tanakh have already been discussed.[2] In contrast to this, the date of the translation of the minor prophets is still disputed at the present time. There are arguments for an early dating to the Ptolemaic period (mid-3rd c. B.C.E.),[3] for instance a softening of the concentration on Jerusalem and Judea in favor of a stronger consideration of the needs of the Diaspora. But there are also arguments supporting a late dating to the end of the 2nd and the beginning of the 1st century. Taking Micah-LXX as an example, terms, ideas and problems would point to a Maccabean context, and perhaps even presuppose the literary existence of 1 or 2 Maccabees.[4]

Exegetical scholars still argue if the minor prophets of the Septuagint were translated by one or more persons. In their *Beiträge zur Wissenschaft vom Alten Testament*, J. Herrmann and F. Baumgärtel already observed and described the uneven character of the translation and concluded cautiously that several Alexandrines stood behind the minor prophets.[5]

---

[2] E. Zenger et al., *Einleitung in das Alte Testament* (Stuttgart, 2001⁴), 33; E. Tov, *Der Text der Hebräischen Bibel. Handbuch der Textkritik* (Stuttgart, 1997), 113f.; N. van Meeteren, *Zwölfprophetenbuch*, *NBL* III (2001): 1232–35.
[3] H. Utzschneider, *Michas Reise in die Zeit. Studium zum Drama als Genre der prophetischen Literatur des Alten Testaments*, *SBS* 180 (Stuttgart, 1990), 162, note 451.
[4] H. Utzschneider, "Das griechische Michabuch—zur Probe übersetzt und erläutert," in *Im Brennpunkt: Die Septuaginta. Studien zur Entstehung und Bedeutung der Griechischen Bibel* (ed. H. J. Fabry and U. Offerhaus; *BWANT* 153, Stuttgart, 2001), 213–50, esp. 4.
[5] *BWAT N.F.* 5 (1923): 32–8.

Ziegler countered this with the observation that this unevenness which can be found throughout the minor prophets would speak against a second translator.[6]

1. *The reception of Nahum in the Septuagint*

The commentaries are generally silent when it comes to the reception of Nahum in the Septuagint. In the 1940s, it was especially J. Ziegler who discussed the reception of Nahum in several articles.[7] In 1948, F. Dingermann, too, compiled the variants in his Würzburg doctoral dissertation "Masora-Septuaginta der kleinen Propheten". The last article on this subject was penned by M. Carrez.[8]

In each case, the Septuagint differs in many places from MT. This might be traced back to a faulty understanding or to a free reproduction of the text. There are conflicting opinions between Muraoka[9] and Jones[10] on the one side and Harrison[11] on the other. Disputed is the question of whether Nahum's translator is identical with the translator of the remaining books of the minor prophets or not. A historically oriented analysis of the translation is still lacking. If one assumes one translator, the time frame would be the period of the Maccabees and Hasmoneans around 100 B.C.E.

2. *The reception of Habakkuk in the Septuagint*

The Septuagint is decisive for the question of an original connection between Habakkuk 1–2 and 3, a question asked particularly from a Qumran perspective. LXX as well as 8Ḥev XII (Greek 1st century C.E.)[12]

---

[6] J. Ziegler, "Die Einheit der Septuaginta zum Zwölfprophetenbuch," in J. Ziegler, *Sylloge. Gesammelte Aufsätze zur Septuaginta* (*MSU* 10; Göttingen, 1971), 29–42 (first as *Beilage zum Vorlesungsverzeichnis der Staatl. Akademie zu Braunsberg* 1934/35, 1–16); id., *Zur Dodekapropheton-LXX*, in *Sylloge*, 587ff.

[7] J. Ziegler, "Der griechische Dodekaprophetentext der Complutenser Polyglott," *Bibl* 26 (1945): 37–51; idem, "Studien zur Verwertung der Septuaginta im Zwölfprophetenbuch," *ZAW* 60 (1944): 107–131; idem, "Der Text der Aldina im Dodekapropheton," *Bibl* 26 (1945): 37–51.

[8] M. Carrez, "Naoum Septante", *RHPR* 70 (1990): 35–48.

[9] T. Muraoka, "In Defense of the Unity of the Septuagint Minor Prophets," *Annual of the Japanese Biblical Institute* 15 (1989): 25–36.

[10] B. A. Jones, *The Formation of the Book of the Twelve* (Atlanta, 1995).

[11] C. R. Harrison, "The Unity of the Minor Prophets in the Septuagint: A Reexamination of the Question," *BIOSCS* 21 (1988): 55–72.

[12] E. Tov, *The Greek Minor Prophets Scroll from Naḥal Ḥever (8ḤevXIIgr)*, *DJD* VIII (Oxford, 1990).

and Mur 88 (Hebrew, c. 135 c.e.)[13] contain the combination Hab 1–3 (!), while Qumran apparently knows Habakkuk 1–2 only. There are internal theological and linguistic reasons for an original unity of Habakkuk 1–3. Conversely, this does not exclude the possibility that Habakkuk 3 might later have become independent, at least in individual text traditions in order to fulfill a specific function, perhaps in the liturgy (as apparently is the case with versio Barberini, dating to the 1st century c.e.).[14]

This *versio Barberini* (only Hab 3!) is attested in six medieval manuscripts (8th–13th centuries) but can be traced back to 2nd century c.e. Alexandria.[15] It is not related to any other Greek textual traditions in any recognizable manner. At the most, there are similarities to the Coptic tradition, especially in its *Akhmimic* form, and to the Peshitta. This is a free and paraphrasing translation that was obviously produced for liturgical purposes.

lxx understands the book as a harbinger of the Last Judgment the arrival of which is unknown (2:3–4). The problem of the eschatological delay later occupies apocalyptic (here especially Qumran) and Rabbinic literatures.[16] Paul makes Hab 2:4b the basis of his doctrine of justification and uses it for his definition of faith (Rom 1:1ff.; Gal. 3:11). For the author of the Epistle to the Hebrews it becomes a call for eschatological perseverance (10:37ff.; similarly *Tg. Jonatan*).

---

[13] P. Benoit et al., *Les Grottes de Murabba'at, DJD* II (Oxford, 1961).

[14] Cf. E. M. Good, *The Barberini Greek Version of Habakkuk III, VT* 9 (1959): 11–30; Strobel; V 62–147 86 407 has an extreme version of Hab 3 that is rather different from the Septuagint cf. Ziegler, "Zur Dodekapropheton-LXX", in: *Sylloge*, 588.

[15] The text shows a textual tradition that is independent of the Septuagint and can perhaps be traced back to the 1st c. c.e. It probably originates in Egypt since this text is closely related to *versio Coptica*. The more than 20 variants are doubtless due to textual corruption of mt; others refer perhaps to a different Hebrew textual tradition (cf. Good). The suggestion to explain these tremendous variants as peculiarities of the translator (R. D. Haak, "Habakuk," *SVT* XLIV [Leiden, 1992]: 7) is of little help.

[16] A. Strobel, "Untersuchungen zum eschatologischen Verzögerungsproblem aufgrund der spätjüdisch-urchristlichen Geschichte von Habakuk 2,2ff.," *NTS* 2 (Leiden, 1961): 211ff.

B. The reception of the Twelve Minor Prophets in Qumran

At Qumran, we must principally distinguish between the reception of the twelve minor prophets in Bible manuscripts, in the *pesharim* and the quotations in the remaining writings of the community.

1. *The eight XII manuscripts of Qumran*

4Q76 (XII^a)[17] dates to the early Hasmonean period (mid 2nd century B.C.E.), and is thus the oldest preserved manuscript of the minor prophets. Textually, it cannot be attributed to any of the great biblical text traditions. The peculiar order of its individual prophetic books has elicited the greatest attention. Although only containing fragmentary texts of Zechariah (frg. 1), Malachi (frg. 2–9) and Jonah (frg. 8–21), the textual sequence Mal-Jonah is secured and poses questions. O. H. Steck, too, decided in favor of this textual reconstruction, although it is entirely unfounded in my opinion.[18] This reasoning assumes that fragment 9 (Plate XLI) contains the text of Mal 3:19–21 in the right hand column. Fragments 10 (Mal 3:22, 23) and 7 (contains 2 words from Mal 3:24) belong to this column. This last fragment obviously separates Mal 3:24 from the preceding text by an empty half-line or a space (*vacat*). It sees the text either as a final colophon of the book, in which case a combination with v. 23 would have made more sense, or as the beginning of a longer passage. As the above mentioned fragment 9 still contains traces of a left hand column and thus of a text following Mal 3:24, such a passage is indeed to be expected. The two still legible letters at the beginning of the line are ל and, underneath it, ה and should be read as לבוא (Jon 1:3) and הטיל (Jon 1:4). But this is now entirely unlikely. The editor reconstructs the suggested column with the help of fragments 11–18 (Jonah 1:1–5:7–8). He can combine הטיל which is running from fragment 9 II to fragment 15[19] while the expected לבוא is neither to be found in the text itself nor in Jonah 1:3b, the central text passage underlying this theory. לברח of v. 3a is too far away.

---

[17] R. E. Fuller, *DJD* XV (Oxford, 1997), 221–32 and Plate XL-XLII.
[18] Cf. O. H. Steck, "Zur Abfolge Maleachi-Jona in 4Q76 (4QXII^a)," *ZAW* 108 (1996): 249–53.
[19] The text of Jonah 1:3 "appears to have been shorter than MT," Fuller, 230.

According to this, the proposed reconstruction must be rejected as unfounded. The remaining traces of the two letters in the left column of fragment 9 cannot serve as evidence for the hypothesis of the order Zachariah—Malachi—Jonah!

It has to be assumed that this scroll did not conclude with Malachi if indeed it is a scroll of the minor prophets. It did not end with Mal 3:24 and so becomes crucial for the question of the origin of the second part of the canon, the *nebi'im*. However, the text following Malachi cannot be reconstructed. I very much doubt that a material reconstruction of the scroll, applying Stegemann's method, can be successful in this case.

Until the contrary has been proven, we have to assume the usual textual sequence for 4Q76 as in the remaining manuscripts of the twelve minor prophets containing this critical passage, however, are all at least 50 years younger.[20] Therefore, one should not assume that 4Q76 predates a formation of the Masoretic text and signifies a stage in which the twelve minor prophets were not yet textually finalized.[21] This manuscript possibly represents a different tradition, similar to Qumran's text tradition that was not identical with the later MT.[22]

4Q77(XII[b])[23] contains only parts of Zephaniah 1–3 and Haggai 1–2. Paleographically, it is to be dated only insignificantly later than 4Q76. The text is essentially identical with MT.

4Q78(XII[c])[24] contains Hos 2–4; 13, Joel 1–2;4; Amos 2–4; 6–7; Zeph 2–3; Mal 3:3–6. Paleographically, this manuscript should be dated to the first half of the 1st century B.C.E. Although close to the Masoretic Text, there are minor variants and a consistent plene-script.

4Q79(XII[d])[25] contains only Hos 1:6–2:5. This manuscript is difficult to date in terms of paleography. It was probably written at the end

---

[20] 4Q82 (4QXII[g]), Mur 88 and 8ḤevXIIgr.

[21] Cf. R. E. Fuller, *The Minor Prophets Manuscripts from Qumrân, Cave IX* (Ph.D. diss., Harvard, 1988; Ann Arbor, 1995), 151.

[22] Cf. J.-H. Fabry, "Der Text und seine Geschichte" in *Einleitung in das Alte Testament* (ed. E. Zenger et al.; Stuttgart, ⁴2001), 36–65, esp. 49–56; idem, "Die Qumrantexte und das biblische Kanonproblem," in *Recht und Ethos im Alten Testament. Gestalt und Wirkung. Festschrift H. Seebass* (ed. Beyerle, G. Mayer, H. Strauß; Neukirchen, 1999), 251–71.

[23] Fuller, *DJD* XV, 233–6 and Plate XLIII.

[24] Fuller, *DJD* XV, 237–51 and Plates XLIV–XLVI.

[25] Fuller, *DJD* XV, 253–6 and Plate XLVI.

of the first half of the 1st century B.C.E.[26] The preserved text is of a "mixed hand"[27] and could point towards two scribes. It is close to MT.

4Q80(XII^c)[28] contains Hag 2:18–21 and Zech 1–8; 12 on 25 fragments. The manuscript stems from the late Hasmonean period, c. 75–70 B.C.E. The text, mostly written plene is close to MT. Hag 2:20 seems to assume a different textual division than MT (Hag 2:19).

4Q81(XII^f)[29] contains Jonah 1:6–8,10–16 (4 fragments) and Mic 5:1–2 as a separate fragment, only discussed by Fuller thanks to its paleographic similarities to 4Q81. The manuscripts originate in the early Herodian period and are to be dated to c. 50 B.C.E. The text is largely identical with MT.

4Q82(XII^g)[30] consists of roughly 105 fragments with passages from Hos 2–4; 6–14; Joel 1–2, Amos 1–9; Obad; Jon 1–4; Mic 1–6; 7; Nah 1–3, Hab 2:4; Zeph 3:3–5 and Zech 10–12. The text is mostly written plene in an early Herodian script and can be dated to the last third of the first century B.C.E. The transitions from Joel (frg. 34–40) to Amos (frg. 40–75), from Amos to Obadiah (frg. 70–75), from Jonah (frg. 76–91 I) to Micah (frg. 91 II–97 verso) and to Nahum (frg. 97 recto–101) are clear. The transitions from Hosea to Joel, from Obadiah to Jonah, from Nahum to Habakkuk as well as those between Habakkuk to Zechariah are uncertain because of the fragmentary character of the text.

5Q4[31] contains Amos 1:3–5 and perhaps also Amos 1:2–3 in 14 fragments. The handwriting points to the 1st century B.C.E. The text is closer to LXX than to MT.

2. *Pesharim and quotations*

8 Pesharim on parts of the twelve minor prophets are attested in Qumran: 4Q166 (pHos^a); 4Q167 (pHos^b); 1Q14 (pMic); 4Q168 (pMic?); 1QpHab; 4Q169 (pNah) and 1Q15 (pZeph). The number

---

[26] H. W. Nebe suggests a date between 50 and 1 B.C.E.; cf. idem, "Eine neue Hosea-Handschrift aus Höhle 4 von Qumran," *ZAW* 91 (1979): 292–4.

[27] Cf. L. A. Sinclair, "A Qumran Biblical Fragment Hos 4QXII^d (Hosea 1:7–2:5)," *BASOR* 239 (1980): 61–65.

[28] Fuller, *DJD* XV, 257–65 and Plate XLVII.

[29] Fuller, *DJD* XV, 267–270 and Plate XLVIII.

[30] Fuller, *DJD* XV, 271–318 and Plates XLIX–LXIV.

[31] J. T. Milik, *DJD* III, 173–4 and Plate XXXVI.

of quotations of the XII-books in the remaining literature of Qumran is considerable. CD in particular frequently derives its arguments from the minor prophets.[32]

I. *The Reception of Nahum*

1. The XII-manuscripts
In the Qumran XII-manuscripts, Nahum is only partially attested in 4Q82(XII^g),[33] dated to the last third of the 1st century B.C.E.

Frg. 98 contains Nah 1:7–9 and agrees with MT in the preserved passages. The fragmentary evidence does not allow a decision regarding the corrections suggested in BHS.

Frg. 97 recto, 99 contains Nah 2:9–11. In v. 9, the text reads מימיה and therefore belongs to the textual tradition of LXX: τὰ ὕδατα αὐτῆς and Vg *aquarum aquae eius* both continue the metaphor of the first quarter of the verse "Ninive (is) like a water fountain" in the second quarter "are its waters". MT מימי היא is actually incomprehensible with Mur XII, and makes only sense after a complicated emendation of מימי היותה "in the days of her existence" in which case the following half verse causes new difficulties.[34] LXX and Qumran surely offer an easier text with the advantage of being clear without any serious textual correction.

Frg. 100 contains Nah 3:1–3. The few preserved letters are identical with MT.

Frg. 101 contains Nah 3:17 and agrees with MT. As they are part of the reconstruction, this manuscript cannot solve the text critical problems presented in BHS.

2. Pesher Nahum
4Q169[35] (Pesher Nahum) dates paleographically to the late Hasmonean-early Herodian period but was probably written 50 years earlier. It quotes repeatedly the late 6th century prophet Nahum who had witnessed and sung about the destruction of Nineveh. Covering Nah 1:3–3:14 in remarkable clarity, the Pesher points out historical contexts by mentioning actual names and thus allowing for exact dat-

---

[32] Cf. the list in J. Maier, *Die Qumran-Essener. Die Texte vom Toten Meer III* (*UTB* 1916; München, 1996), 173–6.

[33] Cf. Fuller, *DJD* XV, 1997, 271–318 and Plates XLIX–LXIV.

[34] For a further discussion cf. K. Spronk, *Nahum, Historical Commentary on the Old Testament* (Kampen, 1997), 100.

[35] J. M. Allegro and A. A. Anderson, *DJD* V (Reissue, Oxford, 1997).

ing. As a whole, it is a polemic directed against the Pharisees that also considers the brutal policies of Alexander Jannaeus.[36] Demetrius (frg. 4+3 I, 1–3) is mentioned at the beginning, probably Demetrius III Eucerus. He "strove to come to Jerusalem", i.e. he even attacked Jerusalem, but without success, since only the Romans succeeded in occupying the city. The Antiochus mentioned in the same context is probably Antiochus IV Epiphanes and stands at the beginning of a time period leading to the arrival of the Kittim. This is obviously a fixed date for the beginnings of the Qumran-Essene group. 4 QpNah can now probably be dated precisely because the "lion of wrath" mentioned in the following text is said to have crucified alive those who "had given smooth instructions" (frg. 4+3 I, 4–8), a form of punishment familiar from the Temple Scroll. This converges with Flavius Josephus' description (*B.J.* I 88–98 and *Ant.* XIII 372–383) and points to Alexander Jannaeus who executed 800 Pharisees in this manner.[37] But later events, too, are taken into consideration: The Pharisean loss of power hinted at in III, 6–8 calls to mind the chaos of the fraternal struggle between Hyrcanus II and Aristobulus II. The so-called Kittim have ceased to stand for the Seleucids or the Ptolemaeans but now mean the Romans who ended the civil war when they entered Jerusalem in 63 B.C.E. It is disputed if the humiliation of the kingdom of Manasseh mentioned in IV,3 alludes to the arrest of Aristobulus II. This inaccuracy of allusions might mean that the writing of Pesher Nahum should pre-date this time period but Tantlevskij's suggestion of 88 B.C.E. is too early in my opinion. In any case, the exegetical scholar finds himself in the interesting situation of being able to interpret the Pesher as an application of the Nahum text to a specific time period. This is a kind of

---

[36] In the 1st c. B.C.E., the community of Qumran turned the book into a script of war. "Sie sah in 'Ninive' eine Chiffre für ihre Gegner und erkannte darin die Partei der Pharisäer, 'No-Ammon' hingegen war für sie Symbol für die Partei der Sadduzäer. Aus der Ankündigung bzw. Schilderung ihrer Vernichtung schöpfte sie Mut für die Zukunft. Man wird fragen müssen, ob das Vor-Bild solche Identifikation zuläßt. Aber man wird sagen können, daß sie den 'Trost' des Büchleins, wie er im 1. Kap. im Blick auf Gottes Souveränität notifiziert ist, gefunden hat" (K. Seybold, *Nahum, Habakuk, Zephanja, ZBK* 24/2 (1991): 16; E. Zenger et al., *Einleitung in das Alte Testament* (Stuttgart, 2001⁴), 512.

[37] For the historical background cf. especially I. R. Tantlevskij, "The Reflection of the Political Situation in Judaea in 88 B.C.E. in the Qumran Commentary on Nahum (4QpNAH, Columns 1–4)," *St. Petersburg Journal of Oriental Studies* 6 (1994): 221–31.

exegesis in situ. The following texts will be examined according to
the Pesher procedure:

Nah 1:3–6: "He rebuked the sea and made it dry." Taking the
sea as a metaphor for the Kittim, i.e. the Romans, the Pesher understands God's power of creation as a historical power (4Q169, 2+1, 3f.).

Nah 2:12–14 contrasts the lion's powerful striding antithetically
with the Seleucid Demetrius III's failed attempt to conquer Jerusalem
(4Q169, 4+3, 1–3). Here, the Pesher does not refer to a contemporary situation but reflects the beginnings of the Essene community. The same can be seen in Pesher Habakkuk (see below). The
Pesher further associates the ironical attribute of Nineveh as "lion's
den" (Nah 2:13) with the "lion of wrath", Alexander Jannaeus (4Q169,
4+3, 6–8; cf. TR 64,6–13) who had crucified 800 Pharisees alive
according to Josephus, *Ant.* XIII 380ff. (see above).[38] The Pesher here
is based on an obvious and clear law in Deut 21:22–23. In the
Pesher, the threat against Nineveh now refers to the exploiting priests
of Jerusalem (4Q169, 4+3, 10ff.).

Nah 3:1–5, the lamentation over bloodthirsty Nineveh is clearly
transformed into a lamentation against the Pharisees (4Q169 3+4,
II, 4–10) who are obviously in the midst of a fierce dispute. The
civil war between the Pharisees and Sadducees in the 70's B.C.E. that
ceased with the Roman invasion might have served as a backdrop.

Nah 3:6–9, the threat against Nineveh is likewise directed against
the Pharisees but it considers the possibility of mass conversions in
the wake of which many would turn to the community (4Q169, 3+4
III, 3–5). This is different from the older Pesharim, as is evident in
the Isaiah-Pesharim which are dated to different periods: While the
older Isaiah Pesharim (c. 100 B.C.E.; 4QpIsa[c.e]) were still praising the
Essene community as the true people of God, the younger commentaries (c. 50–70 B.C.E., 4QIsa[a.b.d.]) have to come to terms with
the fact that large parts of Israel have still not joined the Essenes.[39]

Nah 3:10–12 compares Nineveh's fate with No-Amon, Thebes in
Upper-Egypt that had been conquered by Assurbanipal in 667 B.C.E.
The Ninevites are now identified with Manasseh (4Q169, 3+4, IV,3f.),
possibly standing for the Sadducees (?) or perhaps Aristobulus II to
whom a quick end is predicted (as *vaticinium ex eventu*).

---

[38] Cf. E. Puech, "Die Kreuzigung und die altjüdische Tradition," *Welt und Umwelt der Bibel* 9/3 (1998): 73–5.

[39] Cf. H. J. Fabry, "Qumran," *NBL* III (1998ff.): 237.

3. Quotations

CD IX,5 quotes Nah 1:2 in a context characterized by the prohibition of revenge in Lev 19:18 on the one side and the commandment of the correctio fraterna in Lev 19:17 on the other. Each
member of the community is to avoid any type of anger or revenge
towards a fellow member. Rather, he is called to rebuke him in a
brotherly manner.[40] The insertion of Nah 1:2 demonstrates that
revenge and anger are only appropriate vis-à-vis the opponent and
the enemy. If this statement of MT refers explicitly to YHWH, the
substitution of the divine name in CD with the personal pronoun
הוא only seemingly detaches it from God. In the end, revenge and
wrath are up to him (הוא), i.e. to God alone.

4Q177(4QMidrEschat[b]) X,3 quotes Nah 2:11 in its entirety according to MT. The quotation is embedded in an anthology of quotations from Deut 7:15; Ps 16:3; Joel 2:2; Ps 17:1a and Zeph 3:4. Due
to the fragmentary character of the midrash, their connection can
only be vaguely assumed. This midrash is rather late (first half of
the 1st century B.C.E.)[41] and belongs to those Pesharim that make
recourse to prophetic words in order to reflect the situation of the
Last Days. This community sees itself in opposition to the community of the Pharisees (IX,12–13) who search "smooth things". They
see themselves as those who circumcise the foreskin of their hearts,
the noble and saintly ones whose knees do not shake and whose
loins do not tremble (X,2–3). Due to the fragmentary state of the
text, it cannot be asserted if the original text indeed continued the
description of the imprisoned inhabitants of a conquered Nineveh
and transformed them into the contrary in order to contrast this to
the inner strength of the Qumran community in the Last Days.

II. *The reception of Habakkuk*

1. The XII manuscripts

In the biblical manuscripts of Qumran, only one part of Habakkuk
is to be found in 4Q82 and this reference, too, is disputed.

4Q82(XII[g])[42] dates to the last third of the 1st century B.C.E. and
contains passages of Hos 2–4; 6–14; Joel 1–2; 4; Am 1–5; 7–9; Obad;

---

[40] Cf. also 1QS VI,1.

[41] Cf. A. Steudel, "Der Midrasch zur Eschatologie aus der Qumrangemeinde
(4QMidrEschat[a.b])," *STDJ* XIII (1994): 78, 102, 199.

[42] Fuller, *DJD* XV, 271–318 and Plates XLIX–LXIV.

Jon 1–4; Micah 1–6; 7; Nah 1–3; Hab 2:4 (?); Zeph 3 and Zech 10–12 (see above). According to Fuller, frg. 102 contains two barely legible words from Hab 2:4 ישרה נפשו]. This might add to the clarification of a text critical question put forth in BHS: MT לא ישרה נפשו בו "his soul was not quite in him" is confirmed by frg. 102 but in addition to this also by יושרה in 1QpHab VII,14. 8ḤevXIIgr. with the reading ουκ ευθεια ψυχη αυτου "his soul was not upright" like-wise confirms MT. For that reason, LXX οὐκ εὐδοκεῖ ἡ ψυχή μου which is equivalent to לא רצתה נפשי "my soul finds no pleasure in him" is not supported by Qumran.[43]

4Q238 is registered as a manuscript containing "Habakkuk 3 and other poetry" in the usual inventory lists.[44] Since this manuscript does not know Habakkuk 1–2, this is taken as proof for two sepa-rate Habakkuk traditions that converged at some point. This opin-ion is no longer supported by 4Q238 (= 4QUnid.F.; Plate 1393; PAM 43.399). By now, this inventory number refers to the text "4QWords of Judgment" that has just been published.[45]

2. Pesher Habakkuk

Pesher Habakkuk originates in the middle of the 1st century B.C.E.[46] but was probably written under Alexander Jannaeus.[47] As there seem to have been older Pesharim at Qumran,[48] the community initially did not turn to this book, although the redactional use of the prophetic Words of Lamentation for the Babylonian violence surrounding the events in 587/6 B.C.E. made this book suitable for the Pesher tech-nique practiced at Qumran.[49] 1QpHab contains c. 125 variants to MT, which are mainly limited to orthography. Only 15 variants appear

---

[43] Cf. D. Cleaver-Bartholomew, *An Analysis of the Old Greek Version of Habakuk*, (Ph.D. diss., Clearmont University, 1998), 169.

[44] Maier, *Die Qumran-Essener*, 185; cf. F. García Martínez and E. J. C. Tigchelaar, *The Dead Sea Scrolls, Study Edition* I (Leiden, 1997), 485: "4QHabakkuk 3 and songs", but "details unknown."

[45] P. W. Flint and E. Ulrich, in *Wadi Daliyeh II and Qumran Miscellanea, Part 2—The Samaria Papyri from Wadi Daliyeh, DJD* XXVIII (ed. D. M. Gropp et al.; *DJD* XXVII; Oxford, 2001).

[46] For the discussion cf. A. Lange and H. Lichtenberger, "Qumran," *TRE* XXVIII (1997), 50, 61.

[47] Cf. M. A. Knibb, *The Qumran Community. Cambridge Commentaries on Writings of the Jewish and Christian World* (Cambridge, 1987), 221–46.

[48] Cf. A. Steudel, 188f.

[49] Cf. H.-J. Fabry, "Methoden der Schriftauslegung in den Qumranschriften," in *Stimuli* (Festschrift E. Dassmann; Münster, 1996), 18–33.

significant enough to warrant closer examination here. The great textual fidelity of 1QpHab might originate in the text divisions: 1QpHab usually divides the text sequence in agreement with MT, but there are occasional differences.

1QpHab continually comments upon Hab 1–2 while the message of Hab, written "for an appointed time" (2:3) was read as referring to the contemporary plundering of the Temple in 54 B.C.E. by the Romans (Josephus, *Ant.* 14,105–109) as an eschatologically interpreted situation (1QpHab II,11f.; IX,2–7), in contrast to its literal meaning (Kasdim [Chaldeans]—Kittim [Romans]). This is a binding and final interpretation of the prophetic message that not even the prophet could have been aware of (1 QpHab VII,2). This exegesis was not accidental. Rather, the prophetic text in Hab 2:3 itself indicates that its message was destined for "the end." Likewise, the "in our days" (Hab 1:5) seems to calls for a Qumranic application of Habakkuk's message to the Qumran sect's own time. 1QpHab, like the Letter to the Hebrews understands Habakkuk as referring to perseverance in the eschatological waiting period (II, 9–15: emphasis on the prophetical element instead of the Torah) and the necessity for the community to establish itself. For 1QpHab the foundation period of the community coincides with the eschatological situation, teaching us much about the Teacher of Righteousness. The enemy profile concentrates in its entirety on the "Wicked Priest" and his adherents whose downfall is now prophesied (1QpHab VIII,3–13; IX,12–X,5).

Hab 1:5, God's announcement to perform an unbelievable act "in your days", is now understood as referring to a schism within the community (1QpHab II,1–10) and describes an influential opposition figure to the Teacher of Righteousness, the "Man of the Lie." Those threatened by the verdict are not easily identified. Stegemann suggests that the Pharisees were the traitors with the Man of the Lie and that those "who had desecrated his holy name" were the Sadducees.[50] His hypothesis is not cogent, especially considering the lack of classical metaphors. The "new covenant" in particular remains unclear. Although Pesher Habakkuk can refer back to the beginnings of the history of the community (cf. below), a less recent schism

---

[50] H. Stegemann, "Die Essener, Qumran, Johannes der Täufer und Jesus," *Herder-Spektrum* 4128 (Freiburg, ⁵1996): 185.

should here be taken into consideration. The reading of the Pesher is facilitated when one recalls the problem of a large group of apostates in the Essene exclaves in Transjordan alluded to in CD XIX, 33–XX,1. The author will have thought of the dissidents who, after the death of the Teacher, had lied, betrayed and desecrated the "community of the new covenant in the land of Damascus" and were permanently excluded from reconciliation.

Hab 1:11: "Then they sweep by like the wind; they transgress and become guilty; their own might is their god!" The Pesher interprets the Chaldeans mentioned in Habakkuk consistently as the Romans. The exegesis of Hab 1:1 understands the change of the direction of the wind as a metaphor for the constantly changing consuls in Rome, following the decision of the Senate ("house of guilty [people]"), (1QpHab IV,9–13).

Hab 1:13b condemns the inactivity of the wicked who watch the attacks on the righteous. Here, the Pesher once more alludes to this little known schism and scolds the "house of Absalom" for not assisting the Teacher in his conflict with the Man of the Lie (1QpHab V,8–12). It becomes obvious that Pesher Habakkuk presents itself as a defense of the primacy of the Teacher.

Hab 1:16 talks about the sacrifice vis-à-vis the catching net. In this, the Pesher finds an allusion to the Roman sacrifices to their military standards (1QpHab VI,2–5).

Hab 2:3 "For there is still a vision for the appointed time; it speaks of the end and does not lie." The Pesher reads this as follows: "Its interpretation: the final age will be extended and go beyond all that the prophets say, because the mysteries of God are wonderful": (1QpHab VII,7f.).[51] Since, according to the Qumran sect's reckoning, the last century had begun with the violent death of Onias III in around 170 B.C.E., Pesher Habakkuk can at most be dated to 70 B.C.E. since this clearly refers to a delay of Judgement Day.

Hab 2:4 is interpreted as referring to the Qumran community, as far as it is this community, the keeper of the Torah, that will be saved by God for its fidelity to the Teacher of Righteousness. An actualizing Pesher-technique is almost palpable here.

Hab 2:15: "Woe to anyone making his companion drunk, spilling out his anger, or even making him drunk to look at their festivals!"

---

[51] García Martínez and Tigchelaar, I,17.

The Pesher does not present an updated interpretation but takes recourse to history by recalling the persecution of the Teacher by the Wicked Priest that took place on the Day of Atonement according to the Essene calendar (1QpHab XI,2–8).

3. Habakkuk quotations

It should not be overlooked that the references that were so far identified as Habakkuk quotations all originate in Hab 1–2 only: Hab 1:12 in 1QH^a XIII,8f; Hab 2:1 in CD IV,12 and Hab 2:11 in 1QH^a XIV,26 as well as Hab 2:4 in 4Q82 frg. 102 which is so difficult to identify. The occurrence of Hab 3 in Qumran is so far unproven.

1QH^a XIII,8f. "And there you established me for the judgement and strengthened in my heart the foundation of truth" alludes to Hab 1:12, even if only in a loose association of key words. Whereas the prophet still laments that the Chaldeans as God's instruments carry out the judgement, the association is now located in the Hymn of Thanksgiving of an individual ("Song of the Teacher"). Here, the Teacher emphasizes that the Judgment in particular will demonstrate the strength of his own faith and will turn him into a source of strength for the community.

CD IV,12 "But when the period corresponding to the number of these years is complete, there will no longer be any joining with the house of Judah but rather each one standing up on his watchtower" is terminologically related to Hab 2:1 where the prophet climbs the tower to keep watch for God's word. Clearly, CD puts the prophet's watch into an eschatological, apocalyptic context. At the same time, the author democratizes this task; the eschatological decision is up to all.

1QH^a XIV,26 "I have become like someone who enters a fortified city, and finds shelter on the high wall until salvation. My God, I lean on your truth, for you place the foundation upon rock, and beams to the correct size, and a true plumb line to stretch out, tested stones to build (a fortress which will not shake)." This passage adopts several motifs from the prophetic tradition of the Hebrew Bible but I would reject Maier's assertion that he took up Hab 2:11 here.

In summarizing these observations, the Qumran texts can still be seen as extremely significant for the discussion of the arguments on behalf of an original connection between Hab 3 and the remaining book of Hab (since B. Stade [1884]). Even when 4Q238 falls away, the results are nevertheless clear:

1. 1QpHab quotes only Hab 1–2 and does not seem to know Hab 3.
2. It cannot be ignored that all references that have so far been identified as Habakkuk quotations demonstrate that Qumran did not seem to know Hab 3: Hab 1:12 in 1QH XIII,8f.; Hab 2:1 in CD IV,12 and Hab 2:11 (?) in 1QH XIV,26 as well as Hab 2:4 in 4Q82 frg. 102, so difficult to identify.
3. It thus does not seem unlikely that there were two separate traditions for Hab 1–2 and Hab 3, the latter of which might not have reached Qumran. The confluence of both traditions must in any case have taken place in the text tradition that formed the basis for LXX and that was known at Qumran. According to this, Qumran could have known Hab 3, too, but apparently did not do so. There are no reasons for a Qumranic rejection of this Psalm. Clearly, this had ceased to be a problem for the rabbis and the text tradents from the Bar Kokhba circle.

The presence of Hab 3 in the Greek minor prophets from Naḥal Ḥever (8Ḥev XIIgr) cannot be overlooked.[52] This scroll dates from the time of the Bar Kokhba revolt and preserves Jonah 1–4; Mic 1–5; Nah 1:13f.; 2:5–10,13f.; 3:3,6–17; Hab 1:11.14–17; 2:1–8a.13–20; 3:9–15; Zeph 1–3; Zech 1–3; 8–9. This text is of high text critical value as it might go back to Theodotion and could thus be closer to MT than LXX, if Barthélemy was correct.

The scroll of the Twelve from Wadi Murabbaʿat (Mur 88) dates to the 2nd century B.C. and contains texts from Joel 2:3; Amos 1–2; 6–9; Obad 1–2; Jonah 1–4; Mic 1–7; Nah 1,1–14; 2,1–14; 3:1–19; Hab 1:3–13,15; 2:2f,5–11,18–20; 3:1–19; Zeph 1–3; Hag 1–2; Zech 1:1–4. Apart from slight orthographical variants, the text has few textual particularities, Hab 3:10 *zerem mayyim ʿabar* is replaced by a quotation from Ps 77:18. This scroll, too, assumes the existence of the entire book of Habakkuk. It would be wonderful to know what actually happened to the book of Habakkuk between 50 B.C.E. and 130 C.E.

---

[52] E. Tov, "The Greek Minor Prophets Scroll from Naḥal Ḥever," *DJD* VIII (Oxford, 1990).

THE INTERPRETATION OF GENESIS 15:6:
ABRAHAM'S FAITH AND RIGHTEOUSNESS
IN A QUMRAN TEXT

Joseph A. Fitzmyer

Chapter 15 in Genesis tells of the Lord's appearing to Abraham in a vision and promising him support and a great reward. The Lord assures Abraham that Eliezer of Damascus, a slave born in his house, would not become his heir but rather one of his own descendants would inherit him. "Look at the heavens and count the stars, if you can count them; so shall your descendants be" (Gen 15:5). The text then continues:

> והאמן ביהוה ויחשבה לו צדקה, And he believed in the Lord, and he reckoned it to him as righteousness/a righteous act (15:6).

This verse speaks of a new act of faith on Abraham's part. He had not only left his native land at God's behest (Gen 12:1), but now he has believed (an anomalous perfect with *waw*, והאמן) in God's promise of numberless progeny (15:5).[1] Against all appearances Abraham put his trust in God, to whom he submitted himself. This belief of Abraham was judged (חשב) by God, who is depicted as an assessor in the manner of priests in Israel assessing the offerings made in the Temple (Num 18:27; Lev 7:18; 17:4).[2] God reckoned Abraham's belief to his credit as uprightness, considering it a righteous act (צדקה). צדקה denotes the characteristic of a human being who stands in correct relationship with others and especially with God, as one who

---

[1] Following upon the *waw*-conversive imperfects in v. 5 (ויוצא, ויאמר, ויאמר), the perfect with *waw* is anomalous. It is listed as such in P. Joüon, *Grammaire de l'hébreu biblique* (2d ed.; Rome: Institut Biblique, 1947), §119z; cf. Gesenius-Kautzsch-Cowley, *Hebrew Grammar* (Oxford: Clarendon, 1946), §112ss. It is sometimes said that the perfect is used because the clause does not carry the narrative forward. See also B. K. Waltke and M. O'Connor, *An Introduction to Biblical Hebrew Syntax* (Winona Lake, IN: Eisenbrauns, 1990), §32.3d; but also §16.4f. (p. 305): "Now he trusted [the Lord] and he counted *it* to him as righteousness."

[2] See further G. von Rad, "Die Anrechnung des Glaubens zur Gerechtigkeit," *TLZ* 76 (1951) 129–32; *The Problem of the Hexateuch and Other Essays* (New York: McGraw-Hill, 1966), 125–30.

conducts himself properly and affirms the consequences of that relationship (cf. Ezek 18:5–9; Ps 24:5).[3]

So this verse has often been interpreted, but some medieval and
modern commentators have pointed out the ambiguity of the Hebrew
verbal form ויחשבה, "and he reckoned it to him." Who is meant by
"he"? The parallelism of Hebrew poetry would call for the subject
of the two verbs to be the same, viz. Abraham. Then, because "righteousness" is a relational concept and implies that one is acting in
accord with one's social obligations, the alternate meaning of the
verse would be that Abraham is acknowledging the Lord's righteousness, believing that the Lord will be true to the commitments
expressed in 15:1.[4] This alternate meaning is not adopted by the

---

[3] See E. König, *Die Genesis eingeleitet, übersetzt und erklärt* (Gütersloh: Bertelsmann,
1925) 495; J. Skinner, *Genesis* (ICC; 2d ed.; Edinburgh: Clark, 1930), 280; J. Chaine,
Le livre de la Genèse (LD 3; Paris: Cerf, 1949), 211; G. von Rad, *Genesis: A Commentary*
(rev. ed.; Philadelphia: Westminster, 1972), 184–5; C. Westermann, *Genesis 12–36:
A Commentary* (Minneapolis, MN: Augsburg, 1985), 222–23; N. M. Sarna, *Genesis*
(JPS Torah Commentary; Philadelphia, PA: Jewish Publication Society, 1989), 113;
R. D. Sacks, *A Commentary on the Book of Genesis* (Ancient Near Eastern Texts and
Studies 6; Lewiston, NY: Edwin Mellen, 1990), 92–3; H. Gunkel, *Genesis Translated
and Interpreted* (Macon, GA: Mercer University, 1997), 179.

[4] The alternate understanding of Gen 15:6, according to which Abraham credited God with righteousness, was proposed by Ramban (Nachmanides, 1194–1270),
who disagreed with Rashi; see his *Commentary on the Torah: Genesis* (trans. C. B.
Chavel; New York: Shilo Publ. House, 1971), 197–98; פרוש התורה (2 vols.; Jerusalem:
Mossad ha-Rab Kook, 1959–60), 1. 90–91. In modern times it has been proposed
by L. Gaston, "Abraham and the Righteousness of God," *Horizons in Biblical Theology*
2 (1980): 39–68; H. Mölle, *Genesis 15: Eine Erzählung von den Anfängen Israels* (FzB
62; Würzburg: Echter Verlag, 1988), 78–82; R. W. L. Moberly, "Abraham's
Righteousness (Genesis xv 6)," in *Studies in the Pentateuch* (VTSup 41; ed. J. A.
Emerton; Leiden: Brill, 1990), 103–30, esp. 106–8; R. Mosis, "'Glauben' und
'Gerechtigkeit'—zu Gen 15,6," in *Gesammelte Aufsätze zum Alten Testament* (FzB 93;
Würzburg: Echter Verlag, 1999), 55–93.
It is also found in an article by M. Oehming, "Ist Genesis 15,6 ein Beleg für
die Anrechnung des Glaubens zur Gerechtigkeit?" *ZAW* 95 (1983): 182–97, who
has judged that Paul's use of the verse is "simply wrong" (*schlicht falsch*). Oehming
criticized von Rad's treatment of חשב, maintaining that the occurrences in Num
18:27; Lev 7:18; 17:4 are niphal, not qal (as in Gen 15:6). He fails to note, however, that the qal of חשב is used in 2 Sam 19:20 and Ps 32:2 with the same meaning, "reckon, credit." This has been pointed out rightly by A. Behrens ("Gen 15,6
und das Vorverständnis des Paulus," *ZAW* 109 [1997]: 327–41, esp. 329). Behrens
translates Gen 15:6 thus: "Er [Abraham] glaubte Jahwe, und der rechnete es ihm
als Gerechtigkeitserweis an." Behrens also calls attention to the subject of ויאמר in
15:7, which can only be God; so the context supports the traditional understanding of the second verb in Gen 15:6 (p. 331).
A questionable analysis of Gen 15:6, which attempts to build on Oehming's interpretation has been proposed by D. U. Rottzoll, "Gen 15,6—Ein Beleg für den
Glauben als Werkgerechtigkeit," *ZAW* 106 (1994): 21–27. He argues from the use

majority of commentators on Genesis 15, but the ambiguity of the Hebrew verbal form has to be recalled at least, because it has affected the interpretation of this crucial verse.

This characteristic of Abraham is given a different accent when it is recalled in Neh 9:7–8, where God is addressed: "You are the Lord, the God who chose Abram and brought him out of Ur of the Chaldeans and put on him the name Abraham; you found his heart faithful before you and made a covenant with him to give his descendants the land of. . . . You have fulfilled your promise, for you are righteous." Here God is reckoned as the one who is righteous, which would give support to the alternate interpretation of Gen 15:6.

Another accent, however, is introduced in Sir 44:20:

בבשרו כרת לו חק ובניסוי נמצא נאמן,

ἐν σαρκὶ αὐτοῦ ἔστησεν διαθήκην καὶ ἐν πειρασμῷ εὑρέθη πιστός.

He established the covenant in his flesh, and when he was tested he was found faithful. (RSV)

Similarly in 1 Macc 2:52:

Ἀβραὰμ οὐχὶ ἐν πειρασμῷ εὑρέθη πιστός, καὶ ἐλογίσθη αὐτῷ εἰς δικαιοσύνην;

Was not Abraham found faithful in (his) testing, and it was reckoned to him as righteousness?

Here it is no longer a question of Abraham's faith, but rather of his faithfulness to God who tested him. Even though the authors of Sirach and First Maccabees do not specify the testing, they take it for granted that the reader would recognize the allusion to the sacrifice of Isaac, his only son at that time (Gen 22:9–18). Hence in the pre-Christian Jewish tradition reflected here, the basis of Abraham's uprightness is no longer his "faith," but his stalwart fidelity.

Gen 15:6, however, has become the classic statement about Abraham's faith and the basis of his righteous status before God, especially because of the way Paul of Tarsus used it in Gal 3:6 and Rom 4:3, 9. Before we look at those Pauline passages, however, it

---

of חשב in Job 19:11; 33:10 [cf. also Job 13:24], where the qal form is used with לו in a reflexive sense. So he prefers to translate Gen 15:6: "And he believed the Lord, and he [Abraham] counted it [his belief] as a righteous act for himself" (Und Abraham glaubte Gott und rechnete *sich* das [sc. sein Glauben] zur/als Gerechtigkeit an). See further I. Willi-Plein, "Zu A. Behrens, Gen 15,6 und das Vorverständnis des Paulus, ZAW 109 (1997), 327–341," *ZAW* 112 (2000) 396–97.

will be helpful to recall how some of the translations of Gen 15:6
have rendered it, because such translations have contributed to the
history of the interpretation of this classic statement. Moreover, some
new light has been shed on that interpretation from a recently published Qumran fragment, that should be added to the history of such
interpretation.

RENDERINGS OF GEN 15:6

We may begin with modern translations of Genesis itself, which will
point up the problem with which we are dealing:

NRSV: "And he believed the Lord; and the Lord reckoned it to him
       as righteousness."
RSV: "And he believed the Lord; and he reckoned it to him as
       righteousness."
NAB: "Abram put his faith in the Lord, who credited it to him as
       an act of righteousness."
NIV: "Abram believed the Lord, and he credited it to him as right-
       eousness."
NJPSV: "And because he put his trust in the Lord, He reckoned it
       to his merit."
BJ: "Abram crut en Yahvé, qui le lui compta comme justice."
Einheitsübersetzung: "Abram glaubte dem Herrn, und der Herr rech-
nete es ihm als Gerechtigkeit an."

The foregoing modern translations eliminate the ambiguity of the
second Hebrew verbal form either by supplying a noun as its subject, "the Lord" (NRSV, Einheitsübersetzung), or by using an equivalent rendering, "who" (NAB, BJ), or by capitalizing "He" (NJPSV).
The ambiguity is preserved, however, in the RSV and the NIV.

Although the ambiguity has been resolved in one way or another
by such modern translations of Gen 15:6, a different solution is found
in ancient versions, to which we now turn.

The Septuagint rendered the verse thus:

καὶ ἐπίστευσεν Ἀβρὰμ τῷ Θεῷ, καὶ ἐλογίσθη αὐτῷ εἰς δικαιοσύνην.

And Abram believed God, and it was reckoned to him as righteousness.[5]

---

[5] See J. W. Wevers, *Genesis* (Septuaginta . . . Gottingensis 1; Göttingen: Vandenhoeck
& Ruprecht, 1974), 168.

One should note the differences in the Septuagint version from the Masoretic Text. Here a proper noun ('Αβράμ) is supplied as subject of the verb "believed"; the anomalous perfect of that verb in the Masoretic Text (וְהֶאֱמִן) has been rendered by an aorist; the tetragrammaton is translated as τῷ Θεῷ, as it is also in 15:7;[6] and the ambiguous second Hebrew verbal form is rendered as a passive ἐλογίσθη, which is often understood as a so-called theological passive, "was reckoned" (by God).[7] The sense of the verse may not be radically changed in this Greek translation, but the use of the passive at least has eliminated the ambiguity of the original.[8]

This change to the passive is found also in *Jubilees* 14:6, where the rewriting of the Genesis story is otherwise rather faithful to the Hebrew text. The paragraph corresponding to Gen 15:1–6 ends with the sentence: "And he believed in the Lord; and it was counted to him as righteousness."[9]

The change is reflected also in the praise of Abraham recorded in 1 Macc 2:52, mentioned above, where the passive verb ἐλογίσθη

---

[6] This is somewhat unusual, because in most instances the tetragrammaton is translated as Κύριος, especially in the great Christian manuscripts of the Septuagint. Unfortunately, Gen 15:6 does not appear among the fragments of Genesis preserved in Papyrus Fuad 266, which often has the tetragrammaton written in Hebrew characters in its Greek text. See Z. Aly, *Three Rolls of the Early Septuagint: Genesis and Deuteronomy* (Papyrologische Texte und Abhandlungen 27; Bonn: R. Habelt Verlag, 1980), e.g. plates 44–45; F. Dunand, *Papyrus grecs bibliques (Papyrus F. Inv. 266): Volumina de la Genèse et du Deutéronome* (2 vols.; Cairo: Institut Français d'Archéologie Orientale, 1966), 2. plates 9–10. Cf. J. A. Fitzmyer, "The Semitic Background of the New Testament *Kyrios*-Title," in *A Wandering Aramean: Collected Aramaic Essays* (SBLMS 25; Missoula, MT: Scholars Press, 1979), 115–42, esp. 119–23; repr. in *The Semitic Background of the New Testament* (Grand Rapids, MI: Eerdmans, 1997), 115–42, esp. 119–23.

[7] See Blass-Debrunner-Funk, *A Greek Grammar of the New Testament and Other Early Christian Literature* (Chicago: University of Chicago, 1961), §130.1, 313. Such a passive is said to have been used "to avoid the divine name" (§130.1).

The use of the passive in the Septuagint may be influenced in part by the similar ascription of righteousness to Phinehas in Ps 106:30–31, which uses a niphal imperfect with *waw*-conversive and reads: וַיַּעֲמֹד פִּינְחָס וַיְפַלֵּל וַתֵּעָצַר הַמַּגֵּפָה וַתֵּחָשֶׁב לוֹ לִצְדָקָה לְדֹר וָדֹר עַד עוֹלָם, "Then Phinehas stood up and intervened, and the plague was checked. And that was reckoned to him as righteousness from generation to generation for ever." These verses refer to the apostasy of Baal-Peor in Num 25:1–13, where Phinehas intervened.

[8] See further R. Mosis, "Gen 15,6 in Qumran und in der Septuaginta," in *Gesammelte Aufsätze* (n. 4 above), 95–118, a treatment of the Septuagint that I came upon only after most of this paper was completed.

[9] Translation of R. H. Charles and C. Rabin in *The Apocryphal Old Testament* (ed. H. F. D. Sparks; Oxford: Clarendon, 1984), 52.

is employed and where it has been customary to attribute such usage to the influence of the Septuagint.

The same influence is probably to be found in Philo's reference to this Abraham passage of Genesis. In *Legum allegoria* 3.81 §228, Philo recommended that it was best to believe in God and not in unwise speculation or insecure conjecture, because Ἀβραὰμ γέ τοι ἐπίστευσε τῷ Θεῷ, καὶ δίκαιος ἐνομίσθη, "Abraham believed God and was considered righteous." Here again the passive is used, even though it is a different verb. In *De mutatione nominum* 33 §177, however, the form of the Septuagint is used verbatim, and it is the subject of Philo's comments in *Quis rerum divinarum heres* 19 §94–95.[10]

The shift in emphasis from "faith" to "fidelity," noted in Sir 44:20 and 1 Macc 2:52, may also be the reason why Josephus, in giving his résumé of Genesis 15, completely omits 15:6 (*Ant.* 1.10.3 §183). He begins his summary rather by noting that God commended Abraham's virtue (αὐτοῦ τὴν ἀρετήν): "You shall not lose the rewards that are fitting for you to receive for such good deeds" (ἐπὶ τοιαύταις εὐπραγίαις, i.e. the defeat of the four kings in Genesis 14). Thus, once again, Abraham's faith has disappeared from consideration, and his deeds are extolled.

Paul, however, breaks with this later Jewish tradition of speaking of Abraham's fidelity and returns to the sense of Genesis itself. He quotes Gen 15:6 in Gal 3:6 and in Rom 4:3, but he follows the Septuagintal rendering and makes it part of his comment on Abraham in Rom 4:9, when he says:

ἐλογίσθη τῷ Ἀβραὰμ ἡ πίστις εἰς δικαιοσύνην,

Faith was reckoned to Abraham as righteousness.

Similarly in Rom 4:22. Here Abraham's "faith" is clearly emphasized and interpreted as the basis of his righteous status before God. By faith Paul understands that Abraham has taken the Lord at his word and has been willing to abide by it even when there was no perceptible evidence of the numberless progeny promised. It thus involved his personal confidence in God's word, and so he was justified, i.e. put in a right relationship with God, not by doing deeds

---

[10] See further H. Moxnes, *Theology in Conflict: Studies in Paul's Understanding of God in Romans* (NovTSup 53; Leiden: Brill, 1980), 155–64.

prescribed by the Mosaic Law (as in Deut 6:25; 24:13c; or Ps 32:2), but by faith.[11]

Targum Onqelos preserves the earliest of the Aramaic renderings of Gen 15:6:

והימין במימרא דיוי וחשבה ליה לזכו,

> and he believed in the Word of the Lord, and he reckoned it to him as a meritorious deed.[12]

Here מימרא דיוי is used as a reverential surrogate for the tetragrammaton of the Hebrew original, and although the ambiguous Hebrew verbal form is rendered exactly in the Aramaic וחשבה, the use of לזכו, lit. "for a good deed, merit,"[13] tips the scale in the direction of Abraham; in this way this targum removes the ambiguity.

Targum Pseudo-Jonathan goes even further:

והוות ליה הימנותא במימרא דייי וחשבה ליה לזכו דלא אטה לקמיה במילין,

> And he had faith in the Word of the Lord, and he reckoned it to him as a meritorious deed in that he did not argue before him with words.[14]

The addition in this targumic rendering clearly reveals who the subject of the verb חשבה is, viz. God.[15]

Whereas the two foregoing targums preserved a form of the ambiguous Hebrew verb in וחשבה, Targum Neofiti 1 uses the passive:

---

[11] See further F. Hahn, "Genesis 15,6 im Neuen Testament," in *Probleme biblischer Theologie: Gerhard von Rad zum 70. Geburtstag* (ed. H. W. Wolff; Munich: Kaiser, 1971), 90–107.

[12] See A. Sperber, *The Bible in Aramaic* (4 vols.; Leiden: Brill, 1959–73), 1. 20; cf. B. Grossfeld, *The Targum Onqelos to Genesis: Translated, with a Critical Introduction, Apparatus, and Notes* (The Aramaic Bible 6; Wilmington, DE: M. Glazier, 1988), 70: "And he trusted *the Memra of the Lord* and He considered it for him as a meritorious deed."

[13] See J. Bowker, *The Targums and Rabbinic Literature: An Introduction to Jewish Interpretations of Scripture* (Cambridge: Cambridge University, 1969), 202: Bowker shows that זכו normally meant "plea for defense" or "verdict of acquittal," but that it came to mean "merit," or "that by which acquittal might be ensured." Cf. Sarna, *Genesis*, 113.

[14] See E. G. Clarke, *Targum Pseudo-Jonathan of the Pentateuch: Text and Concordance* (Hoboken, NJ: Ktav, 1984), 16.

[15] See M. Maher, *Targum Pseudo-Jonathan, Genesis: Translated, with Introduction and Notes* (The Aramaic Bible 1B; Collegeville, MN: Liturgical Press, 1992), 60.

וְהֵימִן אַבְרָם בְּשֵׁם מֵמְרָא דַייָ וְאִתְחַשְׁבַת לֵיהּ לְזָכוּ,

And Abram believed in the name of the Word of the Lord, and its
was reckoned to him as merit.[16]

This late targum thus reveals that its tradition was somehow tribu-
tary to the version first attested in the Septuagint as far as this verse
was concerned, even if it did retain the translation of Hebrew צְדָקָה
as לְזָכוּ, also found in the other targums.

When Genesis 15 was translated into Latin in the *Vetus Latina*,
verse 6 was rendered in a way similar to the Septuagint:

> *et credidit Abram Deo et aestimatum est ei ad iustitiam,*

> And Abram believed God, and it was credited to him for justice.

Here *Deo* corresponds to Greek τῷ Θεῷ, and the passive *aestimatum
est ei* to Greek ἐλογίσθη.[17]

The Latin Vulgate followed suit in similarly translating Gen 15:6:

> *credidit Domino et reputatum est ei ad iustitiam*, he believed the Lord, and
> it was credited to him for justice.[18]

Dominus reflects the tetragrammaton of the Hebrew original, as elsewhere in the Vulgate, but it too has rendered the ambiguous Hebrew
verbal form as a passive, *reputatum est ei*.

Likewise the Peshitta rendered Gen 15:6 in a similar way:

> *whymn 'brm b'lh' w'tḥšbt lh lzdyqw,*

> And Abram believed in God, and it was reckoned to him for right-
> eousness.

This rendering is closer to the Septuagint in using *'lh'* instead of the
tetragrammaton, but it inserts before that noun the preposition *b*,
following the Hebrew of the Masoretic text, and translates the ambiguous Hebrew verbal form as a passive, *w'tḥšbt lh*.[19]

---

[16] See A. Díez Macho, *Neophyti 1: Targum palestinense MS de la Bibliotheca Vaticana:
Tomo I Génesis* (Madrid/Barcelona: Consejo Superior de Investigaciones Científicas,
1968), 79.

[17] With variants *deputatum est ei* and *reputatum est ei* in some MSS. See B. Fischer,
Genesis (Vetus Latina 2; Freiburg im B.: Herder, 1951–54), 173.

[18] See H. Quentin, *Librum Genesis ex interpretatione sancti Hieronymi*...(Biblia Sacra
iuxta Latinam Vulgatam versionem 1; Rome: Vatican Polyglot Press, 1926), 198.

[19] See *The Old Testament in Syriac According to the Peshiṭta Version* I/1 (Leiden: Brill,
1977), 26.

The Qumran Version

Although Genesis 15 does not appear in any of the fragments of the Book of Genesis preserved among the biblical texts discovered in the Qumran caves,[20] verse 6 does figure in one of the parabiblical texts from Qumran Cave 4. The text is called 4QPseudo-Jubilees[a] (4Q225), which was part of the batch of Cave 4 fragments originally entrusted to J. T. Milik for publication, but which was finally published by J. C. VanderKam.[21] According to the latter, the text employs language familiar to and characteristic of the *Book of Jubilees*, but it is not actually a copy of that intertestamental writing. Hence the title given to this text by Milik, "Pseudo-Jubilees." *Jubilees* itself was often called in the patristic period Λεπτογένεσις, "Little Genesis," because it is a retelling of events in the Book of Genesis within a framework of jubilee years. Column 1 of fragment 2 of 4Q225 rewrites part of Genesis 15, embellishing it with details not known in the biblical form of the story.[22] Lines 3–9 of this column are pertinent to this discussion, and they run:

3   [ויאמר א]ברהם אל אלוהים אדני הנני בא ערירי ואלי[עזר]
4   [בן ביתי] הואה וירשני   (*vacat*)
5   [אמר אד]ני אל א[ב]רהם שא צפא את הכוכבים וראה
6   [וספור את]החול אשר על שפת הים ואת עפר הארץ כי אם
7   [יהיו נמ]נים אלה וא[ף] אם לוא ככה יהיה זרעכה וא[מין]
8   [אברהם ב]אלו[הי]ם ותחשב לו צדקה ויולד בן אח[רי]כן
9   [לאברה]ם ויקרא את שמו יסחק

3. [And A]braham [said] to God, "My Lord, look at me, going childless; and Eli[ezer]

4. is [the son of my household], and he will inherit me."

5. [The Lo]rd [said] to A[b]raham, "Lift up (your eyes), observe the stars; see

---

[20] See M. Abegg, Jr., P. Flint, and E. Ulrich, *The Dead Sea Scrolls Bible: The Oldest Known Bible Translated for the First Time into English* (San Francisco, CA: HarperSanFrancisco, 1999).

[21] See "**225.** 4QPseudo-Jubilees[a]," in *Qumran Cave 4: VIII. Parabiblical Texts, Part 1* (*DJD* 13; ed. H. Attridge et al.; Oxford: Clarendon, 1994), 141–55, esp. 145–49 (+ pl. X).

[22] See J. C. VanderKam, "The *Aqedah*, Jubilees, and Pseudo-Jubilees," in *The Quest for Context and Meaning: Studies in Biblical Intertextuality in Honor of James A. Sanders* (Biblical Interpretation Series 28; ed. C. A. Evans and S. Talmon; Leiden: Brill, 1997), 241–61.

6. [and count] the sands that (are) on the shore of the sea and the dust of the earth, for if

7. these [will be num]bered, and ev[en] if not, so will your descendants be.

8. [Abraham] belie[ved in] G[o]d, and righteousness was reckoned to him. A son was born af[ter] this

9. [to Abraha]m, and he named him Isaac.

What is noteworthy is the form of Gen 15:6 that appears here:

ויא[מין אברהם ב]אלו[הי]ם ותחשב לו צדקה,

And [Abraham] belie[ved in] G[o]d, and righteousness was reckoned to him.

It agrees with the Greek translation found in the Septuagint in using a passive form of the verb חשב, the 3d sg. niphal imperfect with *waw*-conversive.[23] It supplies "Abraham" as the subject of "believed," as in the Septuagint,[24] and strikingly it not only reads instead of the tetragrammaton ב]אלו[הי]ם, but uses a *waw*-conversive imperfect for the anomalous perfect of the Masoretic Text, "he believed." The one difference is the preposition εἰς before δικαιοσύνην, whereas 4Q225 has simply צדקה, as in the Masoretic text of Gen 15:6, but that has now become the subject of the passive verb. Thus it shows that the Greek translation preserved in the Septuagint is a translation of a Hebrew form of Gen 15:6, which differed from the Hebrew wording of the Masoretic tradition.

4Q225 has been dated by VanderKam to the Herodian period, roughly 30 B.C.–A.D. 20. That is the date of the Cave 4 copy, and one can only speculate about the date of the composition of the text

---

[23] The form ותחשב is not perfectly preserved, because only traces of the first three letters are extant. What I have given above is the reading in the *editio princeps*, where VanderKam notes that the "second letter is *taw*, as the sizable tick at the bottom of the left leg shows. This fact helps in interpreting the first vertical stroke as *waw*. The *ḥet* is somewhat distorted in the damaged section" (p. 147).

However, B. Z. Wacholder and M. Abegg (*A Preliminary Edition of the Unpublished Dead Sea Scrolls: The Hebrew and Aramaic Texts from Cave Four, Fascicle Two* [Washington, DC: Biblical Archaeology Society, 1992], 205) read the word as יתח<ו>שב, obviously understanding the form as a hithpael imperfect with *waw*-conversive. This reading was given also by J. T. Milik in his commentary on the Copper Scroll (3Q15) in *DJD* 3. 225 (2a [V]).—See now the elaborate explanation of the niphal reading of the *editio princeps* given by Mosis, "Gen 15,6 in Qumran", 104–9.

[24] Although the name is restored in the *editio princeps*, it is so restored with certainty because of the preceding and following contexts.

itself. Since the composition of Jubilees has been dated to about 150 B.C.,[25] this writing (4Q225) may come from a similar date. The Greek translation of the Septuagint would, then, be possibly older and probably dependent on a Hebrew *Vorlage*, which this Qumran text also uses. It reveals at least that the passive form of the verb in Gen 15:6 was known in pre-Christian Palestinian Judaism along with the active form that is preserved in the Masoretic tradition. Such evidence also shows why the passive continued to be used in the various ancient translations of Gen 15:6 cited above and provides a Palestinian Jewish background for the Pauline use of the passive verb in Gal 3:6 and Rom 4:3,9, and for the tradition that grew out of the Pauline usage.

The Jewish tradition reflected in Sir 44:20 and 1 Macc 2:52, quoted above, finds an echo in the Epistle of James 2:21, which alludes to Gen 15:6 in showing Abraham's righteous status before God: "Was not our father Abraham justified by deeds, when he offered his son Isaac on the altar?" It then quotes the text in v. 23:

> καὶ ἐπληρώθη ἡ γραφὴ ἡ λέγουσα· ἐπίστευσεν δὲ ᾽Αβραὰμ τῷ Θεῷ, καὶ ἐλογίσθη αὐτῷ εἰς δικαιοσύνην.

> And the Scripture was fulfilled that says, 'Abraham believed, and it was reckoned to him as righteousness.'

In this epistle, the author has made explicit reference to Abraham's willingness to sacrifice his son Isaac, when he was tested by God, and accordingly interprets it as a "deed" of Abraham. The emphasis has shifted from Abraham's "faith" to his "deeds," just as in 1 Maccabees and in the rabbinic tradition reflected in the targums cited above, where צדקה has become זכו, "merit."

Another Qumran text has preserved an interesting Hebrew formulation of a phrase used in Sir 44:20 and 1 Macc 2:52. There it was recorded that Abraham "was found faithful in (his) testing" (ἐν πειρασμῷ εὑρέθη πιστός). In another fragmentary copy of 4QPseudo-Jubilees[b] (4Q226) 7:1, we read:

---

[25] See J. C. VanderKam, *Textual and Historical Studies in the Book of Jubilees* (HSM 14; Missoula, MT: Scholars Press, 1977), 283–85. J. H. Charlesworth ("The Date of Jubilees and of the Temple Scroll," *SBL 1985 Seminar Papers 24* [ed. K. H. Richards; Atlanta, GA: Scholars Press, 1985], 193–204, esp. 197) dates *Jubilees* between 168/67 and 152 B.C.

‫נמצא אברהם נאמן ל[א]ל[הים]‬,

Abraham was found faithful to [G]o[d].[26]

Even though this clause is not the same as the Hebrew of Gen 15:6, it is not unrelated, when one sees the passive verb ‫נמצא‬ (niphal perfect) used and understands the way in which the Jewish tradition that grew out of Gen 15:6 actually developed. Its wording is close to that of the statement in Sir 44:20.

I am happy to contribute this study to the volume honoring Professor Emanuel Tov, because it deals with the type of problem that would interest him in his textual work on Greek and Hebrew forms of the book of Genesis.

---

[26] See "**226**. 4QPseudo-Jubilees^b," in *Qumran Cave 4: VIII. Parabilical Texts, Part 1* (*DJD* 13), 165.

SCRIPTURES IN THE DEAD SEA SCROLLS:
THE EVIDENCE FROM QUMRAN

Peter Flint

The theme of this essay, the canon of Scripture and the scrolls, has enjoyed considerable attention from scholars. Since the term *canon* is not appropriate in this context, the first section provides a definition of *canon* and offers more appropriate terms for the sacred writings under discussion. The second part of the essay compares the Jewish, Protestant, Roman Catholic, and Orthodox Canons of the Hebrew Bible/Old Testament, and the third surveys the ancient evidence apart from the Dead Sea Scrolls. The final section considers the evidence from the scrolls that were found at Qumran.

1. *Canon* and More Appropriate Terminology

1.1 *History and Definition of the Term* Canon

The term *canon* transliterates the Greek κανών, which in turn derives from a Semitic word for *reed*. Compare the Greek κάννα, Hebrew קָנֶה, and Arabic *qanāh*, as well as the English term *cane*. In classical usage, the basic sense of *reed* yields to that of *straight rod* or *bar*, with the literal meaning of a measuring tool (as used, for example, in building). Metaphorically, the term then becomes a *norm, ideal*, or *standard* of excellence (for instance, to denote the perfect human figure in sculpture, or the basis for knowing what is true or false in philosophy). Finally, the term can signify a *table* or *list* (for example, a chronological timetable or a mathematical series).[1]

In the early fourth century (in his letter to Carpian) the Church Father Eusebius uses the plural form term κανόνες for chronological timetables and for lists of Gospel references. In his *Ecclesiastical History* (3.25; 6.25), however, Eusebius refers to his own listing of New Testament books as a κατάλογος. Our earliest surviving list of

---

[1] See R. E. Brown and R. F. Collins, "Canonicity," the *NJBC*, §§66.1–101, esp. §66.5; and H. W. Beyer, "κανών," *TDNT*, 3.596–602.

books is in the *Muratorian Fragment* (late second century), but it is only with lists from the later fourth century—by Athanasius and Augustine, and from the councils of Hippo (393) and Carthage III (397)—that general agreement with respect to their contents becomes clear for most of the Church. Athanasius, for instance, distinguishes between the κανονιζόμενα (canonical books) and the Apocrypha.

The basic meaning of *canon* is a *reed*, but its two extended meanings in Classical Greek, *norm* and *list*, are pertinent for biblical studies.[2] Occurring thrice in the Septuagint[3] and four times in the New Testament,[4] its only significant usage in the present context is Gal 6:16, which says that Christians live by one κανῶν or normative rule of life. In the early Church, the notion of κανῶν as a norm soon became prominent due to early disputes,[5] and was also used for binding decisions.[6] In addition to a norm, the term sometimes denoted widely accepted lists of Scriptures. Such closed lists of κανονιζόμενα became invested with ecclesiastical status, giving rise to the twofold meaning of κανῶν that prevailed in later theology: *norm* for the Church, and *list* of sacred writings of the Old and New Testaments. Implicit is the notion of reflexive judgement on the part of the church authorities and compilers, who declared certain lists to be normative and sacred. *Canon* is thus to be regarded as a technical term with several distinct components: norm, list, and reflexive judgment.[7] I propose the following definition:

> A canon is the closed list of books that was officially accepted retrospectively by a community as supremely authoritative and binding for religious practice and doctrine.[8]

---

[2] See Brown and Collins, "Canonicity," *NJBC*, 1035 (§66.5); and Beyer, "κανῶν."

[3] Mic 7:4; Jdt 13:6; 4 Macc 7:21 (The last is a figurative reference to philosophical rule.)

[4] 2 Cor 10:13, 15, 16; and Gal 6:16.

[5] For instance, Clement (96 C.E.) employs the term in an ethical and homiletical context (1 Clement 7:2), and Irenaeus (*ca.* 180) uses the *canon of truth* to describe the binding truth of the Gospel, attested by the Scriptures and tradition (*Against Heresies* 1.9.4–5; 3.2.1; 3.11.1.).

[6] For example, the decisions reached at Nicaea (325) were termed *canons*, which functioned as normative rules of life for Christians.

[7] E. Ulrich, "The Canonical Process, Textual Criticism, and Latter Stages in the Composition of the Bible" in *"Shaʿarei Talmon." Studies in the Bible, Qumran, and the Ancient Near East Presented to Shemaryahu Talmon* (ed. M. Fishbane and E. Tov; Winona Lake, IN: Eisenbrauns, 1992), 267–912, esp. 69–70; and J. Barr, *Holy Scripture: Canon, Authority, Criticism* (Philadelphia: Westminster, 1983), 50.

[8] See P. W. Flint, *The Dead Sea Psalms Scrolls and the Book of Psalms* (STDJ 17:

This definition allows for the fact that different groups have different canons, whether in the ordering of materials (Jews versus Christians), or in the inclusion or exclusion of specific books (Roman Catholics and Orthodox versus Jews and Protestants).[9]

1.2 Appropriate Terminology

Since the term *canon* belongs to the post-biblical period, it should not be used for collections of sacred books, whether Jewish or Christian, before the second or third centuries C.E. Finding more fitting terms for sacred or authoritative writings in the Second Temple period, however, is no simple matter. The word *Bible*[10] usually denotes a book consisting of writings that are generally accepted by Jews or Christians as inspired by God and thus of divine authority, although more general,[11] narrow,[12] or technical[13] meanings are also found. The difficulty with using this term for writings prior to the second century C.E. is that it implies the completion of the Jewish Scriptures, and their existence in one book or collection at that time. This assumption, however, pertains only to a later date, since no completed Bible is known to have existed during the Qumran period or that of the New Testament writers.

While the terms *canon, canonical, Bible,* and *biblical* should not be used with reference to the Dead Sea Scrolls and other Second Temple

---

Leiden: Brill, 1997), 21; Compare the similar definition by Sid Leiman: "A canonical book is a book accepted by Jews as authoritative for religious practice and/or doctrine, and whose authority is binding upon the Jewish people for all generations" (ed., *The Canon and Masorah of the Hebrew Bible. An Introductory Reader* [New York: KTAV, 1974], 14).

[9] See the table in Part 2 below.

[10] From the Greek βιβλία, pl. of βιβλίον, the diminutive of βίβλος, *papyrus* or *book*. βίβλος is a loanword from the Egyptian, first denoting the papyrus reed, later the inscribed paper or scroll, and finally the writing as a book, letter, record, or statute. It is also used for individual books (e.g. Psalms in Acts 1:20) or groups of books (e.g. the whole Law in Mark 12:26). The diminutive form βιβλίον is used especially for a scroll or writing, for nonbiblical writings, libraries, archives, chornicles, epistles and for documents. With reference to the OT, τὸ βιβλίον can denote the Law (e.g. Gal 3:10) or a single book (cf. Luke 4:17), but the plural τὰ βιβλία seems to indicate several OT books in 2 Tim 4:13. Later, τὰ βιβλία is used for the entire canon, which for Christians includes the NT. Special senses of βιβλίον are also evident in the Book of Revelation. See G. Schrenk, "βίβλος, βιβλίον," *TDNT*, 1.615–20.

[11] "A book containing the sacred writings of [any] religion" (*Webster's Dictionary*, 211c).

[12] For example, the Torah.

[13] "A library or collection of books" (*Webster's Dictionary*, 211c).

literature, the ancient sources suggest several others that are more appropriate:[14]

(1) הַמִּקְרָא (*What is read*, cf. Neh 8:8). The form מִקְרָא is also found in the Qumran scrolls, but usually in the sense of *gathering*.[15]

(2) אֲשֶׁר כָּתוּב or כַּאֲשֶׁר כָּתוּב (*As it is written*): 1QS 5:17; 8:14; 4QFlor frg. 1.2, 12, 15, 16; *4QCatena A* frgs. 5–6.11; 7.3; 10–11.1.

(3) הַכָּתוּב (*What is written*), 11QMelch 2:19.

(4) כִּתְבֵי הַקֹּדֶשׁ (*The Holy Writings*), m. *Yad.* 4:6; cf. αἱ ἱεραὶ γραφαί (1 Clem 53:1); τὰ ἱερὰ γράμματα (2 Tim 3:15); γραφαὶ ἅγιαι (Rom 1:2).

(5) הַסְּפָרִים (*The Books*, Dan 9:2) or הַסֵּפֶר (1QS 7:2). Cf. τὰ βιβλία τὰ ἅγια (*the Holy Books*), 1 Macc 12:9; αἱ ἱεραὶ βίβλοι, Alexander Polyhistor (according to Eusebius, *Praep. ev.* 9.24).

These terms suggest that sacred material was contained in three loci or activities: reading, writing, and books. At Qumran, *writing* features most often with respect to sacred truth or teaching, with passages from holy and authoritative works regularly introduced by *as it is written* or a similar phrase. Accordingly, the term *Scripture* (with its adjective *scriptural*) seems most fitting for uniquely sacred or authoritative writings in the Second Temple period.

1.3   Can All Authoritative Writings at Qumran be Termed Scripture?

The word *Scripture* denotes a writing that was considered divinely revealed, uniquely authoritative, and believed to be ancient origin (even if it was actually quite recent). This suggests that although the Scriptures have much in common with other authoritative writings, they are more unique, especially with respect to putative older origins. This distinction is well illustrated by the *Commentary (Pesher) on Habakkuk* (1QpHab) from Qumran, in which the scriptural text is quoted and is followed by an interpretation. Both the scriptural base text (for example, Hab 2:1–2) and the interpretation were considered to be revealed and authoritative:

> So I will stand on watch [13]and station myself on my watchtower and wait for what He will say [14]to me, and [what I will reply to] His rebuke. Then the Lord

---

[14] For a survey of terms used for Scripture, see R. T. Beckwith, "Formation of the Hebrew Bible," in *Mikra. Text, Translation, Reading and Interpretation of the Hebrew Bible in Ancient Judaism and Early Christianity* (CRINT 2.1; Assen and Maastricht: Van Gorcum; Philadelphia: Fortress, 1988), 39–86, esp. 39–40.

[15] The combination מִקְרָא קֹדֶשׁ (*holy gathering*) appears twice in the *Temple Scroll* (11QT[a] 17:10; 25).

answered me [15][*and said, "Write down the vision plainly*] *on tablets, so that with ease* [16][*someone can read it*]." (Hab 2:1–2, quoted in 1QpHab 6:12–16)

[16][This refers to . . . [17]. . .] [1]then God told Habakkuk to write down what is going to happen to [2]the generation to come; but when that period would be complete He did not make known to him. [3]When it says, "so that with ease someone can read it," [4]this refers to the Teacher of Righteousness to whom God made known [5]all the mysterious revelations of his servants the prophets. (1QpHab 6:16–7:5)[16]

This passage indicates that for the Qumran community both the scriptural text and the interpretation were of divine origin and authoritative—but there is a clear distinction between the older, revealed prophecy and the later, revealed interpretation. In other words, the term *Scripture* can be used only for the excerpt from Habakkuk 2, not for the *pesher* that follows.

2. The Jewish, Protestant, Roman Catholic, and Orthodox Canons of the Hebrew Bible/Old Testament

The canon of the Hebrew Bible/Old Testament and its development are complex issues because of the different faith communities that are involved. It is evident from the accompanying table that there are in fact several canons of the First Testament.

The Jewish, Protestant, Roman Catholic, and Greek Orthodox Canons

HEB. BIBLE (TANAKH)	PROTESTANT OT	ROMAN CATHOLIC OT	GREEK ORTHODOX OT
[Total: 24 Books]	*[Total: 39 Books]*	*[Total: 46 Bks 3 Additions]*	*[Total: 49 Bks 4 Additions]*
Torah (5)	**Pentateuch** (5)	**Pentateuch** (5)	**Pentateuch** (5)
Genesis	Genesis	Genesis	Genesis
Exodus	Exodus	Exodus	Exodus
Leviticus	Leviticus	Leviticus	Leviticus
Numbers	Numbers	Numbers	Numbers
Deuteronomy	Deuteronomy	Deuteronomy	Deuteronomy

---

[16] Translation: M. O. Wise, M. G. Abegg, and E. C. Cook, *The Dead Sea Scrolls: A New Translation* (San Francisco: Harper San Francisco, 1996), 119.

(Table cont.)

HEB. BIBLE (TANAKH)	PROTESTANT OT	ROMAN CATHOLIC OT	GREEK ORTHODOX OT
[Total: 24 Books]	*[Total: 39 Books]*	*[Total: 46 Bks 3 Additions]*	*[Total: 49 Bks 4 Additions]*
Nebi'im [Prophets] (8)	**Historical Books** (12)	**Historical Books** (16)	**Historical Books** (17)
Joshua	Joshua	Joshua	Joshua
Judges	Judges	Judges	Judges
Samuel	Ruth	Ruth	Ruth
Kings	1 & 2 Samuel	1 & 2 Samuel	1 & 2 Kingdoms (1 & 2 Sam)
Isaiah	1 & 2 Kings	1 & 2 Kings	3 & 4 Kingdoms (1 & 2 Kings)
Jeremiah	1 & 2 Chronicles	1 & 2 Chronicles	1 & 2 Paralipomenon
Ezekiel	Ezra	Ezra	1 Esdras
Book of the 12 Prophets	Nehemiah	Nehemiah	2 Esdras (Ezra-Nehemiah)
Hosea		Tobit	Tobit
Joel		Judith	Judith
Amos	Esther	Esther + Additions	Esther + Additions
Obadiah		1 & 2 Maccabees	1–3 Maccabees
Jonah			
Micah	**Poetry/ Wisdom** (5)	**Poetry/ Wisdom** (7)	**Poetry/ Wisdom** (8)
Nahum	Job	Job	Job
Habakkuk	Psalms	Psalms	Psalms + Psalm 151
Zephaniah			Prayer of Manasseh
Haggai	Proverbs	Proverbs	Proverbs
Zechariah	Ecclesiastes	Ecclesiastes	Ecclesiastes
Malachi	Song of Songs	Song of Songs	Song of Songs
		Wisdom of Solomon	Wisdom of Solomon
		Ecclesiasticus	Ecclesiasticus
Kethubim [Writings] (11)	**Prophets** (17)	**Prophets** (18)	**Prophets** (18)
Psalms	Isaiah	Isaiah	Isaiah
Proverbs	Jeremiah	Jeremiah	Jeremiah
Job	Lamentations	Lamentations	Lamentations
Song of Songs		Baruch + Letter of Jeremiah	Baruch + Letter of Jeremiah
Ruth	Ezekiel	Ezekiel	Ezekiel
Lamentations	Daniel	Daniel + Additions	Daniel + Additions
Ecclesiastes	Hosea	Hosea	Hosea
Esther	Joel	Joel	Joel
Daniel	Amos	Amos	Amos

(Table cont.)

HEB. BIBLE (TANAKH)	PROTESTANT OT	ROMAN CATHOLIC OT	GREEK ORTHODOX OT
[Total: 24 Books]	*[Total: 39 Books]*	*[Total: 46 Bks 3 Additions]*	*[Total: 49 Bks 4 Additions]*
Ezra-Nehemiah	Obadiah	Obadiah	Obadiah
Chronicles	Jonah	Jonah	Jonah
	Micah	Micah	Micah
	Nahum	Nahum	Nahum
	Habakkuk	Habakkuk	Habakkuk
	Zephaniah	Zephaniah	Zephaniah
	Haggai	Haggai	Haggai
	Zechariah	Zechariah	Zechariah
	Malachi	Malachi	Malachi

This layout has been adapted from the Newsletter of the Ancient Bible Manuscript Center, The Folio *11/1 (1991) pg. 3*

2.1 *Structure of these Canons*

While the Old Testaments of the various Christian confessions follow the pattern given above, more variety is evident in Jewish tradition. According to Jack Lightstone,[17] the twenty-four books of the tripartite rabbinic Bible were arranged somewhat differently in the medieval period, with Samuel, Kings, and Chronicles each counted as two books; Ezra and Nehemiah each counted as one book; and the Song of Songs, Ruth, Lamentations, Ecclesiastes, and Esther counted as a single collection (the *Five Scrolls*). Under this arrangement, the twenty-four books are as follows:

(a) The Pentateuch or *Torah*
   (1) Genesis, (2) Exodus, (3) Leviticus, (4) Numbers, (5) Deuteronomy
(b) The Prophets or *Nebi'im*
   *The Former Prophets:
   (6) Joshua, (7) Judges, (8) 1 Samuel, (9) 2 Samuel, (10) 1 Kings, (11) 2 Kings

[17] J. N. Lightstone, "The Rabbis' Bible: The Canon of the Hebrew Bible and the Early Rabbinic Guild," in *The Canon Debate: The Origins and Formation of the Bible* (ed. L. M. McDonald and J. A. Sanders; Peabody, MA: Hendrickson, 2002), 163–84, esp. 171.

        *The Latter Prophets:
        (12) Isaiah, (13) Jeremiah, (14) Ezekiel, and (15) The Twelve Minor
            Prophets
   (c) The Writings or *Kethubim*
        (16) Psalms, (17) Proverbs, (18) Job, (19) The *Five Scrolls* (Song of
            Songs, Ruth, Lamentations, Ecclesiastes, Esther), (20) Daniel,
            (21) Ezra, (22) Nehemiah, (23) 1 Chronicles, (24) 2 Chronicles

When we compare the Jewish canon (in both listed arrangements) with the three Christian canons, a basic difference becomes evident: the arrangement of the books involved. All these canons begin with the five books of the Pentateuch (Torah), but then the Jewish Bible places Joshua through the Book of the Twelve Prophets in a second category (the *Nebi'im* or Prophets), and Psalms through Chronicles in a third division (the *Kethubim* or Writings).[18] In contrast, Christian Bibles place the books after the Pentateuch in three further groups: the Historical Books, Poetry or Wisdom, and the Prophets.

Because it ends with Ezra-Nehemiah and Chronicles, the *Hebrew Bible* culminates with a clear theological message: the return to the land of Israel after the Exile, in fulfillment of God's covenant promises to Abraham and later Israelite leaders. With the religion, city walls, and Temple being rebuilt by Ezra, Nehemiah, and Zerubbabel, and with Israel's history being recounted to the returned exiles by the Chronicler, the culminating message of the *Hebrew Bible* is very evident.

In contrast, the *Old Testament* of Christian Bibles ends not with a return, but with prophecies of judgment and the promise of the messianic age. The theological message is also clear: Jews and the nations must forsake wickedness, be aware of coming judgment, and prepare for the coming of the Messiah. For Christian readers, the coming of Jesus and the New Testament's reference to John the Baptist as preparing the way of the Lord flow from the expectations and future orientation of the final books of the Old Testament.

With respect to structure, then, the Jewish *Hebrew Bible* and the Christian *Old Testament* are quite different. These two terms are not interchangeable, which is why the rather awkward term *Hebrew Bible/ Old Testament* is sometimes used in this essay. A useful, indeed more

---

[18] There is some fluidity in Hebrew tradition as regards the order of some books in the *Kethubim*. For example, in the oldest complete manuscript of the Hebrew Bible, the Leningrad (or St. Petersburg) Codex, the order is: Chronicles, Psalms, Job, Proverbs, Ruth, Song of Songs, Ecclesiastes, Lamentations, Esther, Daniel, and Ezra-Nehemiah.

suitable, alternative has been proposed by James Sanders: the *First Testament*.[19] It remains to be seen, however, whether this will supercede the traditional terms, since *Hebrew Bible* and *Old Testament* are so familiar to scholars.

2.2 *Contents of these Canons*

First, some of the differences between the four canons presented above are accounted for in terms of simple arithmetic. Most notably, the Jewish canon of twenty-four books contains precisely the same writings as the Protestant canon of thirty-nine books. The total in the Jewish canon is far lower because Jews count each of the following groups as forming a single book: 1 & 2 Samuel, 1 & 2 Kings, the Twelve Minor Prophets, Ezra & Nehemiah, and 1 & 2 Chronicles. In contrast, Christian canons reckon each of these writings as separate books, thus yielding the higher total.

Second, while the Protestant Old Testament contains thirty-nine books, Roman Catholic Bibles contain an additional seven books, for a total of forty-six: Tobit, Judith, 1 and 2 Maccabees, the Wisdom of Solomon, Ecclesiasticus (also known as Sirach or the Wisdom of Jesus ben Sira), and Baruch (of which chapter 6 is often known as the Letter of Jeremiah). Catholic Bibles also contain "additions" or longer endings to Esther (in eight sections) and to Daniel (in three sections: the Prayer of Azariah and Song of the Three Young Men; Susanna; and Bel and the Dragon).

Books Included in all Orthodox and Catholic Bibles

Tobit
Judith
Additions to Esther
Wisdom of Solomon
Ecclesiastcus (Sirach)
Letter of Jeremiah
Additions to Daniel
1 Maccabee
2 Maccabees

---

[19] For example, in "Canon as Dialogue," in P. W. Flint (ed.), *The Bible at Qumran: Text, Shape and Interpretation* (SDSRL series; Grand Rapids: Eerdmans, 2000) 7–26, esp. 7–9.

Greek Orthodox Bible	Slavonic Orthodox Bibles
Prayer of Manasseh	Prayer of Manasseh
Psalms 151	Psalms 151
1 Edras	2 Edras
3 Maccabees	3 Esdras
4 Maccabees (in appendix)	3 Maccabees

Third, Greek Orthodox Bibles include all the writings found in the Catholic canon, plus a further three books for a total of forty-nine (*1 Esdras*, *3 Maccabees*, and the *Prayer of Manasseh*), as well as a longer ending to the Psalter (*Psalm 151*). Furthermore, in this tradition the books usually designated 1 and 2 Samuel are known as 1 and 2 Kingdoms, 1 and 2 Kings as 3 and 4 Kingdoms, 1 and 2 Chronicles as 1 and 2 Paralipomenon, and Ezra-Nehemiah together as 2 Esdras.

It should furthermore be noted that the Old Testament canons of other Orthodox Churches contain yet more differences. For example, the Slavonic Orthodox Church also includes *3 Esdras* (called *4 Ezra* in the Latin Vulgate), while the Ethiopian Church apparently recognizes *1 Enoch* and *Jubilees* as part of the Old Testament.[20]

3. Ancient Evidence outside Qumran

Passages and references found in ancient Jewish writings from about 200 b.c.e. to about 100 c.e. show that most or all Jewish people considered certain books as divinely revealed and uniquely authoritative—in other words, as Scripture. Not surprisingly, none of these writings use the word *canon* in the sense of a closed list of books that was officially accepted by a group as supremely authoritative (see section 1 above). The passages discussed below, from ancient writings other than the Dead Sea Scrolls, show that there was widespread agreement among Jewish groups on the scriptural or authoritative status of many books, and perhaps less agreement on others.

[20] Table above adapted from the *Harper Collins Study Bible (NRSV), With the Apocryphal/ Deuterocanonical Books* (New York: Harper Collins, 1993), 1435.

3.1   *From the Septuagint Apocrypha*

a. *The Prologue to Sirach (the Wisdom of Jesus ben Sira)*

Among the Apocrypha is the wisdom book Sirach (also known as Ecclesiasticus or the Wisdom of Jesus ben Sira), which was written in Hebrew about 190 or 180 B.C.E. Several passages furnish evidence about which books were considered by Ben Sira as authoritative in his day. One of these describes the activity of the scribe:

> [34]How different the one who devotes himself to the study of *the law* of the Most High! [39:1]He seeks out *the wisdom of all the ancients*, and is concerned with *prophecies*; [2]he preserves the *sayings* of the famous and penetrates the subtleties of *parables*; [3]he seeks out the hidden meanings of *proverbs* and is at home with the obscurities of *parables* (Sir 38:34–39:1).

It has been proposed that this passage points to "a tripartite structure of the canon,"[21] or even to the sequence of the divisions of Law, Wisdom Writings, and Prophets as found in Greek and Latin Bibles.[22] These suggestions seem speculative by going beyond the evidence, but the passage shows that for our author *the law of the Most High, the wisdom of all the ancients, prophecies*, and *sayings, parables and proverbs* were very authoritative.

More significant is the famous poem in praise of famous men from biblical times in chapters 44 to 50.[23] The order in which Ben Sira praises Israel's ancestors reveals the sources he drew upon and the sequence in which he found them. Our author refers to events in the five books of Moses, Joshua, Judges, 1–2 Samuel, 1–2 Kings (with some parallel material from Chronicles and Isaiah), Jeremiah, Ezekiel, possibly Job,[24] the Twelve Prophets, Ezra, and Nehemiah. If Chronicles and Job are removed from this list, it corresponds with the order of books in the first two divisions of the Hebrew Bible (the Torah and Prophets). Virtually all the books in the third division (the Writings) are absent: Psalms, possibly Job, Proverbs, Ruth, the Song of Songs, Ecclesiastes, Lamentations, Esther, Daniel, Ezra, and Nehemiah.

---

[21] Julio Trebolle, "Origins of a Tripartite Old Testament Canon," in *The Canon Debate*, 129–45, esp. 129.

[22] P. Skehan and A. Di Lella, *The Wisdom of Ben Sira* (The Anchor Bible 39; New York: Doubleday, 1987), 452.

[23] See J. VanderKam, *The Dead Sea Scrolls Today* (Grand Rapids: Eerdmans; London: SPCK, 1994), 142–43.

[24] Sir 49:9, but the text is problematic.

Half a century later, in about 132 B.C., the author's grandson translated Ben Sira's book into Greek, adding a prologue of his own. This prologue mentions three series or divisions of books that were apparently considered as Scripture by himself and his audience:

> Many great teachings have been given to us through *the Law* and *the Prophets* and *the others that followed them*, and for these we should praise Israel for instruction and wisdom. Now, those who read *the scriptures* must not only themselves understand them, but must also as lovers of learning be able through the spoken and written word to help the outsiders. So my grandfather Jesus, who had devoted himself especially to the reading of *the Law* and *the Prophets* and *the other books of our ancestors*, and had acquired considerable proficiency in them, was himself also led to write something pertaining to instruction and wisdom, so that by becoming familiar also with his book those who love learning might make even greater progress in living according to the law.
>
> You are invited therefore to read it with goodwill and attention, and to be indulgent in cases where, despite our diligent labor in translating, we may seem to have rendered some phrases imperfectly. For what was originally expressed in Hebrew does not have exactly the same sense when translated into another language. Not only this book, but even *the Law* itself, *the Prophecies*, and *the rest of the books* differ not a little when read in the original. (*NRSV*)

The passage points to *the Law* and *the Prophets* (or *the Prophecies*) as Scripture, together with an apparent third series (*the others that followed them*, *the other books of our ancestors*, or *the rest of the books*). It has been suggested that for the author's grandson—and even for Ben Sira himself—the Writings already "formed a closed collection."[25] The evidence, however, does not support such a proposal: the third series of old books is very vaguely defined, and was possibly not as authoritative for the translator as the other two.

b. *1 Maccabees 56–57*

Another apocryphal book is 1 Maccabees, which was written in the late second or early first century B.C. There we read that during the persecutions of the Jews by Antiochus IV "the books of the law that they found they tore to pieces and burned with fire. [57]Anyone found possessing the book of the covenant, or anyone who adhered to the law, was condemned to death by decree of the king" (1:56–57). The

---

[25] Beckwith, "Formation of the Hebrew Bible," 52.

following chapter refers to *the law* and *the deeds of the ancestors*, and mentions Abraham, Joseph, Phinehas, Joshua, Caleb, David, Elijah, the three Israelites in the fiery furnace, and Daniel (2:50–60). Although not very specific, this passage may point to the books of the law (Moses), some of the historical books, and the book of Daniel. Furthermore, 1 Macc 7:17 quotes Ps 79:2b–3 after introducing it with "in accordance with the word that was written," which indicates that for this author the book of Psalms was acknowledged as Scripture.

c. *2 Maccabees 2:2–3, 13–14; and 15:9*

This apocryphal book, which deals with the events leading up to and following the Jewish revolt under Judas the Maccabee, was completed in 124 B.C. After *the law* is mentioned in vv. 2–3 of chapter 2, a significant passage follows in vv. 13–14:

> [13]The same things are reported in the records and in the memoirs of Nehemiah, and also that he founded a library and collected *the books about the kings and prophets*, and *the writings of David and letters of kings about votive offerings*. [14]In the same way Judas [the Maccabee] also collected all the books that had been lost on account of the war that had come upon us, and they are in our possession.

Here *the books about the kings and the prophets* may mean the historical books (1–2 Samuel, 1–2 Kings, perhaps even Chronicles)[26] together with the prophetic books, *the writings of David* denotes the Psalms, and *letters of kings about votive offerings* may denote Ezra (which contains royal letters concerning offerings in the Temple). This proposal, however, is not certain, since our author does not clearly state which books he is describing.

Later on, 2 Maccabees mentions only two series of books: "Encouraging them from the law and the prophets, and reminding them also of the struggles they had won, [Judas] made them the more eager" (15:9). Again, the contents of these books, especially *the prophets*, is not specified; so these statements cannot be used to support a division of the biblical books into laws and prophecies.

---

[26] Compare J. A. Goldstein, *II Maccabees* (The Anchor Bible 41A; New York: Doubleday, 1983), 187.

3.2 *From the Pseudepigrapha*

a. *4 Ezra 14:23–48*

This book, which is often included as chapters 3–14 of *2 Esdras*, was
written after 70 C.E., the year that the Romans destroyed the Temple,
and finalized in about 100. Some historic churches (for example, the
Russian Orthodox) include *4 Ezra* in their Old Testament canon.
The author offers a profound meditation on the issues raised by the
destruction of the Temple, and adds that the Scriptures were lost in
this terrible event. Ezra, the putative hero of the book, prays that
God's Holy Spirit will inspire him to write down all that had been
recorded in God's *Law* (here meaning all the Scriptures). By divine
inspiration Ezra dictated ninety-four books, without a break, to five
scribes over a forty-day period:

> [45]And when the forty days were ended, the Most High spoke to me,
> saying, "Make public *the twenty-four books* that you wrote first, and let
> the worthy and the unworthy read them; [46]but keep *the seventy* that
> were written last, in order to give them to the wise among your peo-
> ple. [47]For in them is the spring of understanding, the fountain of wis-
> dom, and the river of knowledge." [48]And I did so.

In this passage the number twenty-four is one way—based on the
Greek alphabet—of counting the books of the Hebrew Bible (compare the twenty-two books in section 3 above). The fact that they
were transcribed first gives these books priority, and they are meant
for a general audience ("the worthy and the unworthy"). This is a
significant passage, since it shows that by about 100 C.E. (perhaps
earlier) the books that make up the Jewish canon were already assembled, and accepted by many Jews as a distinct collection of scriptural writings. It also suggests that this collection was near to being
closed, since it could not be expanded to include the other seventy
inspired writings, which seem to form a separate group. Yet the collection falls shy of a being Bible or a canon, since the passage does
not confirm that the twenty-four books were accepted by all Jews as
supremely authoritative.

But what is meant by the other *seventy books* that were written last
and are reserved for an exclusive audience ("the wise among your
people")? These seem to be esoteric books, possibly apocalyptic ones,[27]

---

[27] See the notes in the *Harper Collins Study Bible*, 1807.

which needed special insight to be interpreted properly. In the quoted example, which is later than all the others mentioned in this section on evidence outside Qumran, the writer does not limit the inspired writings to the twenty-four found in the Hebrew Bible. It is difficult to decide, however, if he believes that many books besides the twenty-four should also be regarded as Scripture. It is equally plausible that he is advocating a brand of Judaism not followed by all Jews (such as Enochic Judaism, with its emphasis on apocalyptic themes), or that he may be distinguishing between older, revealed Scripture and later, revealed prophecy (see the comments on the *Habakkuk Pesher* in section 2 above).

b. *4 Maccabees 18:10*

Composed sometime in the 1st century B.C.E. or the 1st century C.E., this book includes the following passage: "While he was still with you, he taught you the law and the prophets" (18:10). This is followed by references to the narratives in the Pentateuch and the books of Daniel, Isaiah, "the psalmist David," Proverbs and Ezekiel. It is possible, but by no means certain, that here *the prophets* includes David's Psalter, the book of Daniel, and (surprisingly), the book of Proverbs.

3.3   *From Hellenistic Jewish Writings*

a. *Philo, On the Contemplative Life 25*

The Jewish philosopher Philo lived in Alexandria, Egypt, from about 20 B.C.E. until around 50 C.E. In his treatise *On the Contemplative Life*, Philo describes a Jewish group called the Therapeutae, who shared several traits with the Essenes that lived at Qumran:

> In each house there is a consecrated room which is called a sanctuary or closet and closeted in this they are initiated into the mysteries of the sacred life. They take nothing into it, either drink or food or any other of the things necessary for the needs of the body, but *laws* and *oracles delivered through the mouth of prophets*, and *psalms and anything else which fosters and perfects knowledge and piety* (*Contempl. Life* 25).[28]

Philo seems familiar with the series or categories of books that were mentioned earlier by Ben Sira's grandson. The philosopher's *laws and oracles . . . of prophets* sound similar to the grandson's *Law and*

---

[28] Philo, *Contemplative Life* (Colson, LCL), 127.

Prophets, while his *psalms and anything else which fosters and perfects knowledge and piety* may correspond to the grandson's even less specific *the others, the other books of our ancestors*, or *the rest of the books*. As Philo phrases it, the third category is rather vague, but the *psalms* (presumably the book of Psalms) is considered the most prominent of the nonlegal, nonprophetic works. If his third series does denote an early form of the Writings, Philo's quotations of Scripture show that it must have contained books besides those found in the Jewish canon. Whereas the Jewish philosopher quotes almost exclusively from the Pentateuch, he sometimes cites the books of Ben Sira and Wisdom of Solomon, thereby going beyond the limits of the traditional *Kethubim*.[29]

b. *Josephus, Against Apion 1 §§37–42 (and The Jewish War 10 §35)*
Written by the Jewish historian Josephus in the 90s c.e., *Against Apion* includes a defense of the veracity of the ancient records in which the history of the Jewish people is presented. In contrast, Josephus points out, the records of Greek history are less reliable and contradict tone another:

> We do not possess myriads of inconsistent books, conflicting with each other. Our books, those which are justly accredited, are but two and twenty, and contain the record of all time.
>
> Of these, *five are the books of Moses*, comprising the laws and the traditional history from the birth of man down to the death of the lawgiver. This period falls only a little short of three thousand years. From the death of Moses until Artaxerxes, who succeeded Xerxes as king of Persia, *the prophets* subsequent to Moses wrote the history of the events of their own times *in thirteen books. The remaining four books contain hymns to God and precepts* for the conduct of human life.
>
> From Artaxerxes to our own time the complete history has been written, but has not been deemed worthy of equal credit with the earlier records, because of the failure of the exact succession of the prophets.
>
> We have given practical proof of our reverence for our own Scriptures. For, although such long ages have now passed, no one has ventured either to add, or to remove, or to alter a syllable; and it is an instinct with every Jew, from the day of his birth, to regard them as the decrees of God, to abide by them, and, if need be, cheerfully to die for them. (*Ag.Ap.*, 1 §§38–42)[30]

---

[29] See Siegert Folker, "Early Jewish Interpretation in a Hellenistic Style," in *Hebrew Bible/Old Testament: The History of Its Interpretation* (ed. Magne Saebo; vol. I/1; Göttingen: Vandenchoeck & Ruprecht, 1996), 130–98.

[30] *Against Apion or On the Antiquity of the Jews* (Thackeray, LCL), 179, 181.

At first glance, this evidence seems the most complete and explicit of all our examples, but its interpretation is by no means transparent. One clear feature is that Josephus' listing of twenty-two books is another way of counting the books in the complete Hebrew Bible, most likely based on the Hebrew alphabet which has twenty-two letters. There can also be little doubt that his first section comprises the five books of Moses (Genesis to Deuteronomy, ending with the "death of the lawgiver" in Deuteronomy 34).

The next two categories, however, are not straightforward. The second section contains the "thirteen" books written by the prophets, which contrasts markedly with the eight prophetic books of the Jewish canon outlined in section 3 above. The mention of Artaxerxes as the endpoint of prophetic succession offers a strong indication that Ezra, Nehemiah, and Esther were included in this prophetic group, since he is the latest Persian king mentioned in these books. Nevertheless, more than one grouping has been proposed for Josephus' thirteen prophets, as in the Table below:[31]

Josephus' Thirteen Prophets

St. John Thackeray (1926)	Roger Beckwith (1985)	James VanderKam (1994)
Joshua	Joshua	Joshua
Judges + Ruth	Judges (+ Ruth?)	Judges
Samuel	Samuel	1 Samuel
		2 Samuel
Kings	Kings	1 Kings
		2 Kings
Chronicles	Chronicles	
Ezra-Nehemiah	Ezra-Nehemiah	Ezra-Nehemiah
Esther	Esther	Esther
Job	Job	
Isaiah	Isaiah	Isaiah
Jeremiah + Lam	Jeremiah	Jeremiah
	(+ Lamentations?)	
Ezekiel	Ezekiel	Ezekiel
Daniel	Daniel	Daniel
Twelve Minor Prophets	Twelve Minor Prophets	Twelve Minor Prophets

---

[31] *Against Apion*, translated by H. St John Thackeray, 179 note b; R. Beckwith, *The Old Testament Canon of the New Testament Church and Its Background in Early Judaism* (London: Clowes, 1985), 119; VanderKam, *Dead Sea Scrolls Today*, 148.

In *The Jewish War*, however, Josephus mentions Isaiah and "also others, twelve in number," which do not correspond with the thirteen books of the prophets referred to in *Against Apion*. This passage most likely refers to the books of Isaiah and Twelve Prophets:

> As for the prophet [Isaiah], he was acknowledged to be a man of God and marvellously possessed of truth, and, as he was confident of never having spoken what was false, he wrote down in books all that he had prophesied and left them to be recognized as true from the event by men of future ages. And not alone *this prophet, but also others, twelve in number*, did the same. (*J.W.*, 10 §35)[32]

The compositions in Josephus' third section, the *remaining four books* that *contain hymns to God and precepts* have also found different identifications, all of them from what are now termed the Writings:[33]

The Remaining Four Books

St. John Thackeray (1926)	Roger Beckwith (1985)	James VanderKam (1994)
Psalms	Psalms (+ Ruth?)	Job
Proverbs	Proverbs	Psalms
Ecclesiastes	Ecclesiastes	Proverbs
Song of Songs	Song of Songs	Ecclesiastes

While the passage from *Against Apion* hints at an emerging third series or section of Scriptures, another possibility is that Josephus has in mind literary forms which do not correspond to canonical divisions:[34] the books of Moses "comprising the laws and the traditional history," the prophets presenting "the history of the events of their own times," and the remaining four books containing "hymns to God and precepts for the conduct of human life." If this is so, Josephus' text may indicate that the Scriptures derive from either of two sources, Moses or the prophets, which provides evidence for an essentially twofold division of Scripture.[35]

---

[32] Josephus, *Ant.* x (Marcus, LCL), 177.
[33] Beckwith (*Old Testament Canon*, 119) is somewhat vague in adding that Lamentations could replace either Ecclesiastes or Song of Songs in this list.
[34] S. Mason, "Josephus on Canon and Scriptures," in *Hebrew Bible/Old Testament*, 215–35, esp. 234.
[35] See J. Barton, *Oracles of God: Perceptions of Ancient Prophecy in Israel after the Exile* (London: Longman and Todd, 1986), 49; and Trebolle, "Origins of a Tripartite Old Testament Canon," 132.

3.4   *From the New Testament*

a. *Matt 23:34–35*

Matt 23:34–35 (= Luke 11:49–51) might be interpreted as showing that by Jesus' day the Scriptures ended with the book of Chronicles, since Jesus begins with an example of murder found in Genesis (Abel, Gen 4:8) and ends with one from Chronicles (Zechariah who was slain by Joash, 2 Chron 24:20–22):

> [34]Therefore I send you prophets, sages, and scribes, some of whom you will kill and crucify, and some you will flog in your synagogues and pursue from town to town, [35]so that upon you may come all the righteous blood shed on earth, from the blood of righteous Abel to the blood of Zechariah son of Barachiah, whom you murdered between the sanctuary and the altar.

According to this view, Jesus' words have canonical significance since he chose examples from the first and last books of the Bible to show that such murderous conduct permeated the Scriptures. The reference, however, may simply be to the last murder mentioned in the historical books of the Bible, without necessarily implying that Chronicles was the last book of the Bible.[36]

Another difficulty is that in the Chronicles passage Zechariah is called the son of Jehoiada. It is thus possible that Luke is referring to the prophet Zechariah son of Berechiah (Zech 1:1), or to Zechariah the son of Baris in Jerusalem during the first Jewish revolt as related by Josephus (*J.W.* 4 §§334–44).[37]

b. *Luke 24:44*

The New Testament often features the expression *the law (of Moses) and the prophets*, for example: Matt 5:17; 7:12; 22:40; Luke 16:16, 29, 31 (*Moses and the prophets*); John 1:45; Acts 13:15; 28:23; and Rom 3:21. Luke also mentions *Moses and all the prophets* (24:27), but a few verses later this Gospel contains a longer and intriguing expression, in a scene where the resurrected Jesus appears to his followers:

---

[36] See A. van der Kooij, ("The Canonization of Ancient Books Kept in the Temple of Jerusalem," in *Canonization and Decanonization*, edited by A. van der Kooij and K. van der Toorn (Leiden: Brill, 1998), 17–40, esp. 22.

[37] *The Jewish War*, translated by H. St John Thackeray, in *Josephus vol. III* (Loeb Classical Library 210; London: Heinemann; Cambridge MA: Harvard University Press, 1961), 99, 101; see also O. Eissfeldt, *The Old Testament, An Introduction* (Oxford: Blackwell, 1966), 568; Trebolle, "Origins of a Tripartite Old Testament Canon," 131.

> Then [Jesus] said to them, "These are my words that I spoke to you while I was still with you—that everything written about me in *the law of Moses, the prophets, and the psalms* must be fulfilled." (Luke 24:44)

In this passage *the psalms* most likely refers to the book of Psalms. It has been proposed that the term also encompasses additional books found in the Writings, but this identification extends beyond the evidence. A similar expression (*David*) is most likely found in the work known as 4QMMT; for comment on the passages from Luke 24 and 4QMMT and a third series of sacred writings, see section 5 below.

3.5   *Assessment of the Evidence Outside Qumran*

a. *Several Series of Scriptures*
The texts featured in this section offer valuable insights into Jewish perceptions of Scripture outside of Qumran from about 200 B.C.E. to about 100 C.E. The evidence indicates that already in the second century 200 B.C.E. many Jews were familiar with two series or sections of Scriptures, and with others besides.

(1) The first series was variously known as the law, the laws, Moses, the law of Moses, or the books of Moses.

(2) The second series was variously termed the Prophets, (the) prophecies, or oracles delivered through the mouth of prophets.

(3) Additional books were also regarded as Scripture, but it is not clear if an actual third series was familiar to most authors. In one case (*4 Macc* 18:15; compare verse 10), the psalmist David seems to be among the prophets. Two other sources, however, refer to the writings of David (2 Macc 2:13) or the psalms (Luke 24:44) separately from the prophets.

(4) Other terms suggest that many Jews viewed certain books beyond the Psalms as Scripture. Sometimes these writings are generally or vaguely designated: the others that followed them, the other books of our ancestors, and the rest of the books. Others seem to be poetic or wisdom books: psalms and anything else which fosters and perfects knowledge and piety; the remaining four books [which] contain hymns to God and precepts; and sayings, parables, and proverbs. Two references in 2 Macc 2:13 probably refer to writings of a narrative nature: the books about the kings and prophets, and the letters of kings about votive offerings.

b. *The Books Included*

Most scholars understand the *law of Moses* or the *books of Moses* to be the five books of the Pentateuch (Genesis to Deuteronomy). While this could mean that the first part of what was to become the Jewish Bible had been fixed by the second century B.C.E., evidence from Qumran suggests that at least some Jews believed that the *book(s) of Moses* contained more than the five books of the Pentateuch (see below).

The ancient sources are not clear as to just how many and which books made up the second series of Scriptures, the *Prophets*. There is no firm evidence that this section contained the same list of prophets found in the Jewish canon (Joshua to the Twelve Minor Prophets), although Isaiah, Jeremiah, Ezekiel, Daniel, and the Minor Prophets are obvious candidates.

The Psalms could be included among the Prophets, yet were separate from them in the eyes of some Jewish communities. There is insufficient evidence to tell whether a distinct third series containing the Psalms and other books was emerging. If this were the case, the infant series did not contain all the books now preserved in the Writings (Psalms to Chronicles).

Several more books that contained poetic and narrative material were also recognized as Scripture, but these do not belong to the second series or the possible third series.

By the close of the first century C.E., then, there was as yet no canon, in the sense of a closed list of books that was accepted retrospectively by all Jewish people as supremely authoritative. But the ancient sources do bear witness to the canonical process, or a canon in the making.

4. The Evidence from Qumran

Almost all the ancient sources that featured in the evidence outside Qumran were written in Greek, although a few (for example, Ben Sira) were originally composed in Hebrew. The Dead Sea Scrolls, however, were mainly written in Hebrew and Aramaic, the languages of the Hebrew Bible. What light do the Scrolls, especially those published during the last decade of the Twentieth Century, shed on the growth of the canon of Scripture? What do they tell us about the arrangement and contents of the Hebrew Bible/Old Testament, and were any of the apocryphal books accepted as Scripture by the Qumran community?

4.1   *The Scrolls and the Structure of the Hebrew Bible/Old Testament*

Is there any evidence in the Scrolls for the threefold division of Scripture as found in the Jewish Bible, or the fourfold arrangement found in Christian Old Testaments? Three relevant readings are found in the third section (C) of the halakhic work 4QMMT, which was composed in the mid-second century B.C. by leaders of the Qumran community, perhaps before they migrated to Qumran.

> And so we see that some of the blessings and curses have already come *²¹*that are written in the b[ook of Mo]ses. (section C, lines 20–21, from 4Q398 frgs. 11–13)

> [It is also written in *the book of*] Moses and in *the* [*books of the prophet*]s that *¹⁸*[the blessings and curses] shall come [upon you . . .]. (C, lines 17–18, from 4Q398 frgs. 11–17 i)[38]

> [And] we have [also *¹⁰*written] to you so that you may have understanding in *the book of Moses* [*and*] in *the book*[*s of the Pr*]*ophets* and in *Davi*[*d* and *¹¹in the events*] *of ages past*. . . . (C, lines 9–11, from 4Q397 frgs. 14–21)[39]

These readings from section C suggest that up to four groupings of Scripture were accepted by the authors and their audience. First, all three excerpts (two partly reconstructed) refer to the *book of Moses*. This expression is equivalent to the *law of Moses*, which also occurs in a *Juridical Text* (2Q25) and even earlier as a doublet in 2 Kgs 14:6: *the book of the law of Moses*. Second, two of the excerpts (one largely reconstructed) mention the *books of the Prophets*, which suggests two categories of Scripture. Similar terminology appears in the *Community Rule* (1QS) and in the *Damascus Document* (CD):

> [The Instructor] is to teach them to seek ²God with all their heart and with all their soul, to do that which is good and upright before Him, just as ³He commanded through *Moses* and *all His servants the prophets*. (1QS 1:1–3)[40]

---

[38] The first two translations are from Wise, Abegg, and Cook, *The Dead Sea Scrolls*, 364.

[39] My translation of the Hebrew ‫ו]בספר[י‬ ‫מושה‬ ‫בספר‬ ‫שתבין‬ ‫אליכה‬ ‫כתב]נו‬ ‫]ואף‬ ‫הנ]ביאים‬ ‫ובדוי]ד[‬. The preposition *bet* (*in*) before ‫דוי]ד[‬ is significant since it separates David from the Prophets.

[40] Translation: Wise, Abegg, Cook, *The Dead Sea Scrolls*, 126–27.

The books of the Law are the [16]tents of the king, as it says, "*I will re-erect the fallen tent of David*" (Amos 9:11). The king is [17]<Leader of> the nation and the "foundation of your images" is the *books of the prophets* [18]whose words Israel despised. (CD 7:15–18)[41]

Third, the final excerpt from 4QMMT seems to denote [the *book of*] *Moses*, the *book*[*s of the Pr*]*ophets, Davi*[*d*, and *the events*] *of ages past*. Assuming that the placement of fragments is correct,[42] this reading may well have parallels in the passages from 2 Maccabees and Luke that were discussed in section 3:

> The same things are reported in the records and in the memoirs of Nehemiah, and also that he founded a library and collected *the books about the kings and prophets*, and *the writings of David* and *letters of kings about votive offerings*. (2 Macc 2:13)

> Then [Jesus] said to them, "These are my words that I spoke to you while I was still with you—that everything written about me in *the law of Moses, the prophets*, and *the psalms* must be fulfilled." (Luke 24:44)

It seems reasonable here to equate 4QMMT's *David* with Luke's *the psalms*. (In both cases we take this to signify not the Writings or the Wisdom books as a whole, but only the Psalter.) An interesting picture then emerges: David (that is, the psalms) was considered as prophecy, yet was emerging as a book distinct from the Prophets and as the forerunner of a third section of the Scriptures as early as the mid-second century B.C.E. While the editors of 4QMMT are perhaps too bold in claiming that this passage is "a significant piece of evidence for the history of the tripartite division of the Canon,"[43] the excerpt at least suggests three series of the Scriptures for some Jews (in this case the Qumran community and their audience) in the second century B.C. For Julio Trebolle, "the book of Psalms becomes the key element in this discussion, seeing that it is a book at the borderline between Prophets and Writings."[44]

The words following *Davi*[*d* in the MMT passage are intriguing, though incomplete due to the broken text. At this point it will be helpful to compare the suggested readings by the official editors as well as other scholars.

---

[41] Translation: Wise, Abegg, Cook, *The Dead Sea Scrolls*, 57–58.

[42] בכספר[י] (*in the book*[*s of*]) is preserved on the isolated frg. 17, while [ה]נ[ב]יאים ובדו[י]ד ([*the Pr*]*ophets and in Davi*[*d*]) is on frg. 15 which does not join directly with frg. 17 (see *DJD* 10.58 and plate vi).

[43] Qimron and Strugnell, *DJD* 10.59.

[44] "Origins of a Tripartite Old Testament Canon," 133.

[*and in the events*] *of ages past*	Qimron and Strugnell[45]
[*. . . all*] *the generations*	Wise, Abegg, Cook[46]
[*and the annals of eac*]*h generation*	F. García Martínez[47]
[*and all the events*] *of every age*	G. Vermes[48]

In view of the key term *of each generation* (דור ודור) in line 11 of 4Q397 frg. 18, the missing and preserved text apparently refers to ages past, and thus probably denotes writings of a narrative nature such as annals.[49]

Such language may refer to the historical books Joshua to Kings— perhaps even to these plus the books of Chronicles, Ezra and Nehemiah. If this proposal is valid, 4QMMT suggests that, for some Jews at least, what are now the Former Prophets in modern Hebrew Bibles were grouped together as historical books (as in the Septuagint). Whether or not this is so, the absence of the non-historical wisdom books that were later included in the Writings (for example, Proverbs) should be noted. The suggestions made at this point are admittedly speculative, so caution is advised. We can state, however, that in the mid-second century B.C.E. 4QMMT seems to indicate an emerging third series of scriptural books that contained at least the Psalms, and possibly an emerging fourth series that contained historical writings.

To summarize: As was the case for with several other Jewish writings, the evidence from the Scrolls point to at least two series or sections of Scriptures for the Qumran community in the second century B.C.: (1) *Moses* or *the book of Moses*, and (2) *the Prophets* or *the books of the Prophets*. Less conclusive, but of great interest, is the evidence in 4QMMT for an emerging third series: (3) *David* (that is, the Psalms); and (4) possibly an emerging fourth series which contained historical writings.

With respect to *structure*, then, the evidence from Qumran is mixed. On the one hand, the sequence of Moses–Prophets supports the

---

[45] *DJD* 10.59.

[46] Wise, Abegg, Cook, *The Dead Sea Scrolls*, 363.

[47] F. García Martínez, *The Dead Sea Scrolls Translated. The Qumran Texts in English* (Leiden: Brill; Grand Rapids: Eerdmans, 1994), 79.

[48] G. Vermes, *The Complete Dead Sea Scrolls in English* (London: Penguin, 1997), 227.

[49] Thus E. Ulrich, "Canon," *Encyclopedia of the Dead Sea Scrolls* (ed. L. Schiffman and J. VanderKam; New York and Oxford: Oxford University Press, 2000), 117–20, esp. 119.

arrangement of Scripture as found in modern Jewish Bibles; on the other hand, the apparent grouping of historical writings lends support to the arrangement in the Septuagint and Christian Old Testaments. It could be argued that certain scrolls (notably those written in Greek) may support a different arrangement, but since these manuscripts are mostly fragmentary, this proposal is speculative. (It is worth noting that in the most extensive Greek manuscript from the Judean Desert, the Minor Prophets Scroll from Naḥal Ḥever, the sequence of books follows that of the Masoretic Text, not of the Septuagint.)[50]

These series of Scriptures do *not* necessarily mean that for the Qumran community *Moses* or *the book of Moses* contained only the five books of the Torah (Genesis to Deuteronomy) as in modern Hebrew Bibles. Neither does it follow that *the Prophets* or *the books of the Prophets* contained the books of the Prophets (Joshua to the Twelve Minor Prophets), nor *that Davi[d* contained the books of the Writings (Psalms to Chronicles), nor that *the events]* *of ages past* contained the historical books (Joshua to Esther). The issue of *contents*—that is, which books were viewed as Scripture by the Qumran community—will be explored below.

5.2 *The Scrolls and the Contents of the Hebrew Bible/Old Testament*

It is incorrect to assume that the Qumran community regarded as Scripture all the books found in traditional Hebrew Bibles or in a particular Christian Old Testament; such a decision must be based upon hard evidence found in the Scrolls. Which criteria, then, are to be used for deciding whether or not specific books were viewed as Scripture by the Qumran community? No single approach is sufficient for deciding the scriptural status of individual books or groups of books; instead, I propose the following eight criteria, with one or two examples for each. (Several of these examples are from books whose authority at Qumran may not be obvious—i.e. books represented by only few scrolls, or works found among the Apocrypha or Pseudepigrapha.)

<hr/>

[50] See E. Tov, *The Minor Prophets Scroll from Naḥal Ḥever (8ḤevXIIgr)* (*DJD* 8; Oxford: Clarendon Press, 1990), 8.

a. *Statements that Indicate Scriptural Status*

Certain terms or statements in the Qumran community's own writings show that they regarded particular writings as authoritative or sacred Scripture. Among the Prophets, for instance, Ezek 44:15 is specified in the *Damascus Document*: "as God promised them by Ezekiel the prophet, saying . . ." (CD 3:20–4:2). The authoritative and prophetic status of Daniel is indicated in the *Florilegium*, which quotes Dan 12:3 and states: "As it is written in the Book of Daniel the Prophet" (4Q174 2:3).

Two other relevant passages are in *4QText with a Citation of Jubilees* (4Q228). Although this document is poorly preserved, fragment 1 i,1 almost certainly denotes the *Book of Jubilees* by its Hebrew title במחל[ק]ו[ה העתים ([In the *Divisi*]ons *of the Times*), and fragment 1 i,9 introduces the first word of the title by a citation formula: כי כן כתוב במחלקות ("For thus it is written in the *Divisions* [*of the Times*]).[51] Finally, *Jubilees* is also specified as the source of information (the precise passage is not clear) in the *Damascus Document*, concerning the times when Israel would be blind to the law of Moses:

> [2]. . . But the specification of the times during which all Israel is blind to [3]all these rules is laid out in detail in the *Book of Time Divisions by* [4]*Jubilees and Weeks*. (CD 16:2–4)[52]

b. *The Appeal to Prophecy*

Associating a book or writing with prophecy points to authoritative or scriptural status. An important New Testament example occurs in Jude 14–15, which tells us that Enoch *prophesied* (Προεφήτευσεν), and then quotes from *1 Enoch* 1:9. A comparable case occurs in *David's Compositions*, the extended prose "epilogue" found in col. 27:2–11 of the Great Psalms Scroll (11QPs^a):

> [2]And David, the son of Jesse, was wise, and a light like the light of the sun, and literate, [3]and discerning and perfect in all his ways before God and men. And the Lord gave [4]him a discerning and enlightened spirit. And he wrote [5]3,600 psalms; and songs to sing before the altar over the whole-burnt [6]perpetual offering every day, for all the days of

---

[51] For both readings, see J. C. VanderKam and J. T. Milik, "4Q228. Text with a Citation of *Jubilees*," *DJD* 13.177–85 + plate XII.

[52] Translation: Wise, Abegg, Cook, *The Dead Sea Scrolls*, 66.

the year, 364; . . . [11]*All these he composed through prophecy* (בנבואה) which was given him from before the Most High.[53]

This passage clearly implies that all the compositions found in 11QPs[a] are products of Davidic prophecy. In addition to many Psalms found in the traditional Hebrew Bible, these include other works that form part of 11QPs[a], notably the canticle in Sirach 51:13–30, Psalms 151A, 151B, 154 and 155, and nine previously unknown compositions. The passage quoted from 11QPs[a] provides striking evidence that its compiler and, most likely, its readers viewed the entire Psalter represented by 11QPs[a] as authoritative Scripture.

c. *Claims of Divine Authority*

Besides obvious candidates such as Exodus or Isaiah, some writings found at Qumran are attributed to the forefathers and/or claim their message to be from God or from an angel. Two prominent examples are *1 Enoch* (1:2; 10:1–11:2) and *Jubilees* (1:5–18, 22–28, 26–29; 2:1), both of which also contain material that was written on heavenly tablets (see *1 Enoch* 81:1–2; 93:1; *Jub.* 3:8–14, 31). *Jubilees*, in fact, "advertises itself as divine revelation."[54] Two other very influential books that claim to be divine revelation should be mentioned. First, *Reworked Pentateuch* is nearly a verbatim quotation of material from Genesis through Deuteronomy; and *The Temple Scroll* presents itself as a new Deuteronomy directly from God, spoken in the first person.

d. *Davidic Superscriptions*

One function of Davidic superscriptions in the book of Psalms is to associate particular compositions with David, the Psalmist *par excellence*. There are very few examples among the Scrolls of Davidic titles given to Psalms not found in our traditional Psalter, which shows that adding such titles for purposes of lending authority was not practiced among the compilers of the different Psalters found at Qumran. Two rare examples of titles given to Psalms not found in

---

[53] Translation: J. Sanders, *The Dead Sea Psalms Scroll* (Ithaca, NY: Cornell University Press, 1967), 87.

[54] J. VanderKam, "The Jubilees Fragments from Qumran Cave 4," in *The Madrid Qumran Congress. Proceedings of the International Congress on the Dead Sea Scrolls, Madrid. 18–21 March 1991* (ed. J. Trebolle Barrera and L. Vegas Montaner; 2 vols., STDJ 11; Leiden: Brill; Madrid: Universidad Complutense, 1992), 2.635–48, esp. 648.

the traditional Psalter are the autobiographical Psalms 151A and
151B, whose titles are clearly Davidic and thus denote the scriptural
status of the two Psalms:

הללויה לדויו בן ישי

A Hallelujah of David the Son of Jesse (Ps 151A:0)

תהלת נב[ו]וֹרה ל[דו]יד משמשחו נביא אלוהים

At the beginning of [Da]vid's po[w]er after the prophet of God had
anointed him (Ps 151B:1)

e. *Quantity of Manuscripts Preserved*

Works that are represented by a large number of manuscripts were
extensively used at Qumran, which indicates their popularity and
most likely their authoritative status. Of all the scrolls discovered at
Qumran the books represented by the greatest number are—in descending order—the Psalms (thirty-six manuscripts), Deuteronomy
(thirty), Isaiah (twenty-one), Genesis (twenty), Exodus (seventeen),
Jubilees (about fifteen), Leviticus (fourteen), and *1 Enoch* (twelve). While
these statistics alone do not prove that the books involved were
viewed as Scripture by the Qumran community, they form an important component in making this assessment.

f. *Translation into Greek or Aramaic*

Comparatively few Qumran scrolls were written in Greek, but the
translation of a Hebrew work into Greek may indicate its importance and authoritative status for its scribe or users. Several Greek
scrolls were found in Caves 4 and 7 at Qumran, including the following: Exodus (pap7QLXXExod), Leviticus (4QLXXLev[a] and pap-
4QLXXLev[b]), Numbers (4QLXXNum), Deuteronomy (4QLXXDeut),
the Letter of Jeremiah (pap7QEpJer gr), and *1 Enoch* (pap7QEn gr).
In addition, the large Greek scroll containing the Book of the Twelve
Minor Prophets was discovered at Naḥal Ḥever.

Furthermore, only books that were regarded as Scripture—specifically as books of Moses—seem to have been translated into Aramaic. Three *targums* were found at Qumran: 4QtgLev, 4QtgJob, and
11QtgJob. (For the tradition that Moses wrote Job, see *b. B. Bat.*
14b, 15a.)

g. *Pesharim and Other Commentaries*

Books on which commentaries were written were most likely viewed
as Scripture by the commentators and their audiences. This cate-

gory includes the *pesharim*, in the form of textual citation followed by interpretation (*pesher*). At least seventeen *pesharim* are found among the Scrolls: six on Isaiah (3QpIsa and 4QpIsa^{a-e}), two each on Hosea, Micah, and Zephaniah (4QpHos^a, 4QpHos^b, 1QpMic, 4QpMic?, 1QpZeph, 4QpZeph^a), one each on Nahum, Habakkuk (4QpNah, 1QpHab), and three on the Psalms (1QpPs, 4QpPs^a, 4QpPs^b). Two more works are *Apocryphal Malachi* from Cave 5 (5Q10), which was earlier classified as a *pesher*, and another unidentified *pesher* from Cave 4 called *4QpUnidentified* (4Q172).

Other types of commentary were found at Qumran, including: *A Commentary on Genesis and Exodus* (4Q422), which may be classified as "rewritten Bible"; and *A Commentary on the Law of Moses* (4Q251), which features passages concerning the law of damages (Exod 21:19, 28–29), first-fruits (Exod 22:29), and proper sacrifice. It has also been suggested[55] that the fragmentary text *Pesher on the Apocalypse of Weeks* (4Q247) is a commentary on a section of *1 Enoch*.

h. *Books Quoted or Alluded to as Authorities*

Ways in which a book is used in later writings often point to its special authority or scriptural status. This category is very large, and its components are sometimes difficult to determine because the difference between definite allusion and general scriptural imagery is not always clear. With reference to the *Hodayot*, for example, Bonnie Kittel proposes four degrees of the use of scriptural language, ranging from definite quotations to the "free use of biblical idiom and vocabulary."[56] A few examples are discussed below. An extensive list of quotations of, or clear allusions to, scriptural passages in the nonbiblical scrolls will be provided in a work currently in press.[57]

(1) Midrashic Texts

Two examples are the *Florilegium* (4QFlor), which includes Ps 1:1 and Ps 2:1 as base texts, and *Catena A* (4Q177) which contains quotations from several Psalms (11:1–2; 12:1, 7; 5:10?; 13:2–3, 5; 6:2–5, 6; 16:3; 17:1, apparently in that order).

---

[55] J. T. Milik, *The Books of Enoch: Aramaic Fragments of Qumrân Cave 4* (Oxford: Clarendon Press, 1976), 256.

[56] *The Hymns of Qumran: Translation and Commentary* (SBLDS 50; Chico, CA: Scholars Press, 1981), 48–55.

[57] J. C. VanderKam and P. W. Flint, *The Meaning of the Dead Sea Scrolls* (San Francisco: Harper San Francisco, 2002).

(2) Quotations with Introductory Formulae

In many cases the quoted passage is preceded by a special phrase, notably *as he said* or *as it is written*, which suggests that the writer viewed the passage as especially authoritative or scriptural. Some examples are as follows:[58]

> *As God said.* The *Damascus Document* uses this phrase and refers to Mal 1:10 (CD 6:13–14).
> *As David said.* In *4QCatena A* (4Q177), this formula introduces Ps 6:2–5 (frgs. 12–13 i,2).
> *As he said.* In the *Florilegium* (4Q174), this phrase introduces 2 Sam 7:11, with God as the subject (col. 3:7).
> *It is written.* In the *Damascus Document*, this formula introduces Prov 15:8 (CD 11:19–21).
> *As it is written.* The *Isaiah Pesher* (4Q163) introduces a passage, apparently from Jeremiah, with this phrase (frg. 1,4). Another important usage is found in the *Community Rule*, where Isa 40:3 is quoted in relation to the self-identity and mission of the Qumran desert community:
> . . . they shall separate from the session of perverse men to go to the wilderness, there to prepare the way of truth, *as it is written* (Isa 40:3): "In the wilderness prepare the way of the Lord, make straight in the desert a highway for our God" (1QS 8:13–14).[59]

(3) Quotations or Allusions without Introductory Formulae

Some examples of texts that are quoted or alluded to are from the following books:

*Genesis. In criticizing the polygamy of the Pharisees, the *Damascus Document* argues on the basis of Gen 1:27 ("male and female he created them") and Gen 7:9 ("went into the ark two by two") that one wife was the biblical norm (CD 4:19–5:1).

*Leviticus. The key to understanding the Qumran community's emphasis on purity is found in Lev 15:31: "You must keep the people of Israel separate from their uncleanness, so that they might not die in their uncleanness by defiling my tabernacle which is in their midst." See the *Ritual of Purification B* (4Q512) frg. 69,2, and the *Temple Scroll* (11QT^a) 51:4b–10.

---

[58] See M. Fishbane, "Use, Authority and Interpretation of Mikra at Qumran," in *Mikra. Text, Translation, Reading and Interpretation of the Hebrew Bible in Ancient Judaism and Early Christianity* (ed. M. J. Mulder; CRINT 2.1; Assen and Maastricht: Van Gorcum; Philadelphia: Fortress, 1988), 339–77, esp. 347–48.

[59] Translation: Wise, Abegg, Cook, *The Dead Sea Scrolls*, 138.

*Jubilees. *Jub* 23:11 is quoted in the *Damascus Document* (CD 10:9–10); and *Jub.* 3:8–14—which grounds the legislation of Leviticus 12 (concerning a woman's impurity) in the story of Adam and Eve—may be the source for the same material in the *Miscellaneous Rules* (4Q265 frg. 7 ii,11–17). Furthermore, another passage in the *Damascus Document* seems to be based on *Jub.* 23:11, which refers to people's loss of knowledge in their old age:

> [7] ...No one above the age [8]of sixty shall hold the office of judge of the nation, because when Adam broke faith, [9]his life was shortened, and in the heat of anger against the earth's inhabitants, God commanded [10]their minds to regress before their life was over. (CD 10:7–10)[60]

*Isaiah: The *Community Rule* refers to the *precious corner-stone* of Isa 28:16 (1QS 8:7).

*Jeremiah. The first column (1:1–11) of the *Apocryphon of Jeremiah C* (4Q385b) draws on Jeremiah 40 to 44, although lines 4–6 recall the fall of Jerusalem as found in Jer 52:12–13.

*Psalms. The *Hodayot* cite Ps 26:12, but with some modification (1QH[a] 2:30).

*Proverbs. Prov 1:1–6 is echoed in *4QBeatitudes* (4Q525): "[to kno]w wisdom and disc[ipline], to understand [. . .]" (frg. 1,2). Two texts that treat the biblical figures of Lady Wisdom and Dame Folly at Qumran are the *Wiles of the Wicked Woman* (4Q184) and *Sapiential Work* (4Q185). For example, Prov 7:12 seems to be quoted in 4Q184 where Lady Folly "lies secretly in wait [. . .] in the city streets" (frg. 1,11–12).[61]

*Lamentations. A *Lament for Zion* (4Q179), which appears to be patterned after Lamentations, quotes Lam 1:1 (frg. 2,4). A *Prayer for Deliverance* (4Q501) capitalized on the genre of lament, although in this case the enemy was not a foreign people, but rather unbelieving Jews.

i. *Dependence on Earlier Books*
Several Qumranic texts show a more general dependence on particular earlier works, which suggests that those works were authoritative to the later writers:

---

[60] Translation: Wise, Abegg, Cook, *The Dead Sea Scrolls*, 68.

[61] See John I. Kampen, "The Diverse Aspects of Wisdom in the Qumran Texts," in *The Dead Sea Scrolls After Fifty Years: A Comprehensive Assessment* (ed. P. W. Flint and J. C. VanderKam; 2 vols., Leiden: Brill, 1998–99), 1.211–43, esp. 223–25.

*Genesis. Retelling portions of Genesis occupied more than one Qumran scribe. For example, the *Genesis Apocryphon* is an Aramaic work that rehearses the lives of Enoch, Lamech, Noah and his sons, and Abraham.

*Exodus and Leviticus. Exodus 22–35 and Leviticus, as well as Numbers and Deuteronomy, form the foundation of the largest non-biblical manuscript, the *Temple Scroll*. This work presents itself as a new Torah for the Last Days in which God speaks to Israel—evidently through Moses—in the first person.

*Leviticus. Of the approximately two dozen rulings found in 4QMMT, more than half are based on legal issues concerning ritual purity from the text of Leviticus. Furthermore, most of the Laws in the *Damascus Document* are retellings of various Levitical commands, and the assorted legal discussions in *A Commentary on the Law of Moses* (4Q251) are largely Levitical in origin.

*Jubilees. This work may well be the source for dating covenants to the third month, especially the fifteenth day, as well as the Qumranic idea that the covenant was to be renewed on the Festival of Weeks.

*Ezekiel. At least five scrolls, probably representing three separate compositions, contain rewritten versions of the book of Ezekiel: *4QPseudo-Ezekiel^{a–e}* (4Q385–88, 5Q391).

*1 Enoch. This book details a lunisolar calendar that combines a 364-day solar year with a schematic 354-day one, and which served as the model for the Qumran calendars.

*Psalms. The *Hodayot* and some other collections of hymns found among the Dead Sea Scrolls are largely modeled on the Psalms.

*Kings. At least one of the Dead Sea Scrolls contains a narrative retelling of some Elijah stories and other events that are described in 1 Kings: *4Qpap paraKings et al.* (4Q382), which was copied in the first half of the first century B.C.E. Another relevant scroll is the *Apocryphon of Elisha* (4Q481a), which presents a version of 2 Kgs 2:14–16 and other material.

*Ezra. This book provided one of the terms that the Qumran community appropriated for itself, the *yahad* ("community"); see Ezra 4:3. The designation also forms the title of one of its foundation documents, the *Serek HaYahad* or *Community Rule*.

j. *Summary*

The evidence offered above indicates that many books were viewed as Scripture by the Qumran community. In the accompanying table, for convenience we shall place these books in three general group-ings: (1) *Books Associated with Moses*, (2) *Books of the Prophets*, (3) *David and the Other Writings*.

Since not all of the non-biblical scrolls were authored by the Qumran covenanters, a quotation in a particular work does not nec-essarily mean that the book quoted was viewed as Scripture by the community. However, a survey of several of the best preserved or distinctive writings of the community itself provides a general but fairly accurate picture of just which books they regarded as scrip-tural. These distinctive works are:[62]

1QS: the *Manual of Discipline* (1QS)
DD: the *Damascus Document* (CD, 4Q266–73, 5Q12, 6Q15)
WS: the *War Scroll* (1QM, 1Q33, 4Q491–96)
1QH^a: the *Hodayot* (1QH^a)
4QFlor: the *Florilegium* (4Q174)
4QTest: the *Testimonia* (4Q175)
11QMelch: the *Melchizedek scroll* (11Q13).

To these may be added the *pesharim*: *Pesher Isaiah* (3Q4, 4Q161–65), *Pesher Hosea* (4Q166–67), *Pesher Micah* (1Q14, 4Q168), *Pesher Nahum* (4Q169), *Pesher Habakkuk* (1QpHab), *Pesher Zephaniah* (1Q15, 4Q170), and *Pesher Psalms* (1Q16, 4Q171, 4Q173). Also worth noting are *Apocryphal Malachi* (5Q10) and the *Pesher on the Apocalypse of Weeks* (4Q247).

In the three tables that follow, the second column lists the number of times that a particular book is quoted or referred in one of these distinctive works; for example, Genesis is cited three times in the *Damascus Document* (Gen 1:27 in CD 4:21, Gen 7:9 in CD 5:1, and Gen 41:40 in Gen CD:3). The exact references will be published elsewhere.[63] When a book is not cited in one of the works listed above but rather in another document found at Qumran, the num-ber of these references is presented in parentheses. For example, the book of Lamentations is cited once (Lam 1:1 in 4Q179 frg. 2.4).

On the basis of the eight criteria listed above, including the num-ber of citations (second column) and the number of manuscripts (third column), the scriptural status of each book at Qumran is given in one of three categories: *Certain*, *Uncertain*, or *Not*.

---

[62] For the methodology used here, see James VanderKam, *Dead Sea Scrolls Today*, 150–51.
[63] VanderKam and Flint, *The Meaning of the Dead Sea Scrolls* (in press).

Quantities of Scrolls and Citations at Qumran: Books Associated with Moses

Name of Book	Used in Distinctive Works	Manuscripts	Certain	Uncertain	Not
Genesis	DD (3)	20	Genesis		
Exodus	1QS, DD, 4QFlor, 4QTestim	17	Exodus		
Leviticus	1QS, DD (20), 11QMelch (2)	14	Leviticus		
Numbers	1QS, DD (12), WS (2), 4QTestim	8	Numbers		
Deuteronomy	1QS, DD (18), WS, 4QFlor (3), 4QTestim (3), 11QMelch	30	Deuteronomy		
Reworked Pentateuch		5	*R. Pentateuch*		
Jubilees	DD (2) (see also 4Q228, 4Q265)	about 15	*Jubilees*		
Temple Scroll		about 5			*Temple Scroll*

Comment: Almost all the listed books fall in the *certain* column, These were viewed as Scripture by the Qumran community, since in these cases at least two of the eight criteria apply. *Reworked Pentateuch* is included here on the grounds that it comprised the entire Pentateuch in a form that is close to the early Samaritan Pentateuch. The status of *Temple Scroll* is more difficult to decide. While this was certainly an important work for the Qumran covenanters, it falls in the *uncertain* column because only one of the eight criteria seem to apply (Claims of Divine Authority). In contrast, the book of *Jubilees* is presented as revelation, is preserved in many copies, and is quoted or referred to in other writings, which classifies it as *certain*.

Quantities of Scrolls and Citations at Qumran: Books of the Prophets

Name of Book	Used in Distinctive Works	Manuscripts	Certain	Uncertain	Not
Isaiah	1QS (4x), DD (16), WS, 4QFlor (2x), PesherIsa (51), 11QMelch (6x)	21	Isaiah		
Jeremiah	(yes, e.g. 4Q177, 4Q396, 4Q397)	6	Jeremiah		
Lamentations	(yes, 4Q179)	4	Lamentations		
Letter of Jeremiah	(no)	1			Letter of Jer

(Table cont.)

Name of Book	Used in Distinctive Works	Manuscripts	Certain	Uncertain	Not
Ezekiel	DD (4x), 4QFlor	6	Ezekiel		
12 Minor Prophets		8	12 Prophets		
Hosea	DD (6x), PesherHos (18)		Hosea		
Joel	DD (4x)		Joel		
Amos	DD (2x), 4QFlor		Amos		
Obadiah	(no)		Obadiah		
Jonah	(no)		Jonah		
Micah	DD (7x), PesherMic (8)		Micah		
Nahum	DD (2x), PesherNah (24)		Nahum		
Habakkuk	PesherHab (44)		Habakkuk		
Zephaniah	1QS, PesherZeph (3x)		Zephaniah		
Haggai	(no)		Haggai		
Zechariah	DD (2x), PesherIsa		Zechariah		
Malachi	DD (4x), ApocrMal (2x)		Malachi		
1 Enoch	PesherApocWeeks(?)	12	*1 Enoch*		
Daniel	4QFlor, 11QMelch	8	Daniel		

Comment: As we would expect, Isaiah, Jeremiah, Ezekiel, and Daniel were definitely viewed as Scripture at Qumran (*certain*). The same is true of the Minor Prophets; although not all of them are referred to in other writings, this collection was treated as a single book at Qumran. The book of *1 Enoch* is classified as *certain*, since it is presented as revelation, is preserved in many copies, served as the model for the Qumran calendars, and may be quoted in the *Pesher on the Apocalypse of Weeks* (4Q247). The book of Lamentations is likewise classified, since it is represented by four copies and is quoted once (4Q179 frg. 2:4). The Letter of Jeremiah is found only in one manuscript (pap7QEpJer gr) and is apparently not alluded to elsewhere, hence its *uncertain* scriptural status at Qumran

Quantities of Scrolls and Citations of Books at Qumran: David and Other Books

David and Other Books	Used in Distinctive Works	Manuscripts	Certain	Possible	Not
Psalms	DD (2x), 1QHª, 4QFlor (3x), PesherPs (42x), 11QMelch (3x)	36	Psalms		
Proverbs	DD (2x)	2	Proverbs		

(Table cont.)

David and Other Books	Used in Distinctive Works	Manuscripts	Certain	Possible	Not
Job	DD (cf.)	4	Job		
Song of Songs	(no)	4		Songs	
Ecclesiastes	(no)	2		Ecclesiastes	
Ben Sira	(no)	2		Ben Sira	
Joshua	4QTestim	2	Joshua		
Judges	(cf. 4Q522)	3	Judges		
Ruth	(no)	4		Ruth	
1 Samuel	DD?, WS (cf.)	4	1 Samuel		
2 Samuel	4QFlor (3)	3	2 Samuel		
1 Kings	(cf. 4Q504)	3	1 Kings		
2 Kings	(no)	1	2 Kings		
1 Chronicles	(cf. 4Q522)	0		1 Chronicles	
2 Chronicles	(cf. 4Q522)	1		2 Chronicles	
Ezra	(the *yaḥad*, Ezra 4:3)	1	Ezra		
Nehemiah	CD (cf.)	0	Nehemiah		
Esther	(no, but cf. 4Q550)	0			Esther
Tobit	(no)	4		Tobit	

Comment: Several books in the *uncertain* category are represented by comparatively few manuscripts at Qumran, and are apparently not referred to in the community's other writings: the Song of Songs, Ecclesiastes, Ben Sira, Ruth, 1 and 2 Chronicles, and Tobit. Some or all of these *may* have been viewed as Scripture by the community, but the mere existence of manuscripts of these works at Qumran is insufficient to ensure their authoritative status. As many scholars have noted, the book that was not viewed as authoritative Scripture by the Qumran community is Esther, most likely because it features a festival (Purim) that was not included in the Qumran calendar.[64]

---

[64] For discussion, see M. G. Abegg, P. W. Flint, and E. Ulrich, *The Dead Sea Scrolls Bible* (San Francisco: Harper San Francisco, 1999), 630–31.

THE PARABIBLICAL LITERATURE OF THE QUMRAN LIBRARY AND THE CANONICAL HISTORY OF THE HEBREW BIBLE*

Armin Lange

As the term "parabiblical" was introduced by Emanuel Tov,[1] it is only appropriate to contribute a study concerned with parabiblical literature to a Festschrift honoring him. He has described parabiblical literature as being "closely related to texts or themes of the Hebrew Bible."[2] In this type of literature, on the basis of biblical texts or themes, the authors employ exegetical techniques to provide answers to questions of their own time. The results of their exegetical effort are communicated in the form of new texts. Therefore, parabiblical literature should not be understood as a pseudepigraphic phenomenon (i.e. the ascription of a literary work to a biblical author),[3] but as a form of scriptural revelation, comparable to the phenomenon of literary prophecy.[4] For this purpose, the authors of parabiblical liter-

---

* I was privileged to present earlier versions of this article at Cambridge, Manchester, Durham, and Claremont as well as at conferences held in Schwerte and Tübingen. The intensive discussions following these lectures contributed significantly to what is published here. It is a pleasure for me to express my gratitude for the hospitality of my hosts (Graham I. Davies, George J. Brooke, Loren Stuckenbruck, and Christine M. Helmer), for the hospitality of the conferences' organizers (Heinz-Josef Fabry, Hartmut Stegemann, Hermann Lichtenberger, and Gebern Oegema), and for the intensive scholarly interactions following my talks. I am obliged to Prof. Dr. Randall G. Styers for improving the English of this article.

[1] *DJD* 13 (1994), ix.
[2] Op. cit.
[3] The earliest attestation of the term 'pseudepigrapha' is found with Serapion in the second century CE (see Eusebius, *Ecclesiastical History*, 6, 12). W. Speyer defines pseudepigraphy as follows: "Als Pseudepigraphen sind diejenigen Schriften des Altertums zu betrachten, die nicht von den Verfassern stammen, denen sie durch Titel, Inhalt oder Überlieferung zugewiesen sind" ("Religiöse Pseudepigraphie und literarische Fälschung im Altertum," in *Pseudepigraphie in der heidnischen und jüdisch-christlichen Antike* [ed. N. Brox; Wege der Forschung 484; Darmstadt: Wissenschaftliche Buchgesellschaft, 1977] 195–263, esp. 195; cf. also idem, *Die literarische Fälschung im heidnischen und christlichen Altertum: Ein Versuch ihrer Deutung* [Handbuch der Altertumswissenschaft I.2; Munich: C. H. Beck, 1971]; J. A. Sint, *Pseudonymität im Altertum: Ihre Formen und ihre Gründe* [Commentationes Aenipontanae 15; Innsbruck: Universitätsverlag Wagner, 1960]).
[4] For the phenomenon of literary prophecy see O. H. Steck, *The Prophetic Books and their Theological Witness* (St. Louis, Miss.: Chalice Press, 2000).

ature used different genres: rewritten Bible,[5] new stories or novellas
created on the basis of biblical items or topics, different types of
apocalypses, and testaments. In addition, there are parabiblical texts
combining different genres.[6]

In the following, I will discuss the importance of parabiblical literature for the canonical history of the Hebrew Bible in the 4th and
3rd centuries B.C.E. For this purpose, I will explore which books and
persons are the focus of parabiblical literature. Based on this analysis, I will then try to draw some conclusions regarding what was recognized as authoritative literature in late Persian and early Hellenistic
Judaism. But to begin, I need to describe briefly the parabiblical
texts known before the Qumran library was discovered.

1. What was Known before Qumran?

It is possible to enumerate 18 compositions known before the discovery of the Dead Sea Scrolls which today are dated to the 4th or
3rd centuries B.C.E. Three of these compositions cannot be dated
with certainty. With a few exceptions, this count ignores questions
of redaction criticism because of the obvious difficulties in isolating
and dating the different redactional layers of the books of the Hebrew
Bible and the necessarily speculative nature of such dates.

For reasons of space, only a few remarks concerning the more
unknown compositions are possible.

Demetrius the Chronographer tries to date the events of Israel's
history as reported in the biblical books. Preserved are five fragments
(Eusebius, *Praeparatio Evangelica* IX,19.4, 21.1–19, 29.1–3, 15, 16)
which are concerned with events reported in Genesis 22–Exodus 14.
A sixth fragment (Clemens Alexandrinus, *Stromata* 1.141.1–2) dates

---

[5] The term was introduced by G. Vermes, *Scripture and Tradition in Judaism: Haggadic Studies* (StPB 4; Leiden: E. J. Brill, 1961), 95. He defines *Sefer ha-Yashar* as follows: "In order to anticipate questions, and to solve problems in advance, the midrashist inserts haggadic development into the biblical narrative—an exegetical process which is probably as ancient as scriptural interpretation itself." As further examples for rewritten Bible, Vermes (ibid.) adds "the Palestinian Targum and Jewish Antiquities, Ps.-Philo and Jubilees, and the recently discovered 'Genesis Apocryphon.'"

[6] For this definition see A. Lange and U. Mittmann-Richert, "Annotated List of the Texts from the Judaean Desert Classified by Content and Genre," *DJD* 39 (2002) 117–8; for a list of all manuscripts from the Qumran library attesting to parabiblical literature see op. cit.

Table 1: *Texts Known Before the Dead Sea Scrolls Were Found*[7]

	History	Stories and Novellas	Prophecy	Apocalypses	Sapiential Texts	Poetic and Liturgical Texts
Hebrew Bible	Ezra/ Nehemiah 1–2Chron	Jonah Esther Daniel *2–6	Joel		Qohelet	Psalm-Collections Canticles
Early Jewish Literature	Demetrius *Artapanus* Sirach *44–49	Tobit	Epistle of Jeremiah	Astronomical Enoch Book of Watchers		*Ezekiel the Tragedian Theodotus*

the conquest of the northern realm by Senachherib and the conquest of Judah by Nebuchadnezzar according to the reign of Ptolemy IV, who was in power from 221 to 204 B.C.E.: "But from the time when the ten tribes of Samaria were taken captive to that of Ptolemy the 4th, there were 573 years and 9 months. But from the time of the captivity of Jerusalem [to Ptolemy the 4th], there were 338 years [and] 3 months."[8] Therefore Demetrius the chronographer is to be dated to the 3rd century B.C.E.[9]

Of Artapanus's work, only three fragments have been preserved in Eusebius's *Praeparatio Evangelica* (IX, 18, 23, 27) and Clemens Alexandrinus's *Stromata* (1.23.154,2f.). These fragments are concerned with events in the lives of Abraham, Joseph, and Moses. Because there is no clear evidence left in these portions of Artpanus's work, its dating is complicated. The *terminus ad quem* is set by Alexander Polyhistor who summarized Artapanus in the middle of the first century B.C.E. The *terminus post quem* can be derived from the fact that Artapanus knew the Septuagint. Thus Artapanus wrote in the years 250–100 B.C.E. J. J. Collins proposed that the policy of Ptolemy IV to permit the Egyptian peasantry to bear arms in his service is reflected in the statement that Moses included Egyptian farmers in

---

[7] In this table, compositions which cannot be dated with certainty are marked by italics.

[8] Translation according to J. Hanson, "Demetrius the Chronographer," *OTP* 2 (1985): 2, 843–54, 854.

[9] See Hanson, 844; C. R. Holladay, *Fragments from Hellenistic Jewish Authors*, vols. 1–4 (Chico, Calif./Atlanta, Ga.: Scholars Press, 1983–96), vol. 1, 51–2.

his army (*PrEv.* 9.27.7).[10] If this is correct, the work of Artapanus must be dated at the end of the 3rd century B.C.E.

Another composition which should be mentioned here is the *Praise of the Fathers* in Sirach 44–50. I admit that Ben Sira himself wrote his book in 190–180 B.C.E., as is evident by his grandson's introduction and by the mention of the high priest Simon II in Sirach 50.[11] But in my opinion, in Sirach 44–50 Ben Sira has utilized an older composition. In chapter 50, this composition was enlarged with the praise of the high priest Simon II. The redactional enlargement of the *Praise of the Fathers* is evidenced by the disproportionate accentuation of Simon II, who afterall was only of minor importance in the history of Israel. In addition, Enoch is praised in 49:14 a second time (cf. Sir 44:16), and a praise of Joseph, Shem, Seth, and Enosh is appended in Sir 49:15–6 because they were not mentioned in the *Praise of Fathers* proper. In my opinion, the best explanation for these facts is that Ben Sira incorporated in Sirach chapters 44–49 an older composition and enlarged it for his purposes. The version of the *Praise of the Fathers* reworked by Ben Sira must necessarily be dated earlier than Ben Sira's book itself, i.e. to the 3rd century B.C.E. Because a collection of the twelve minor prophets was not known before the 3rd century B.C.E., an even older date is excluded by the reference to them in Sir 49:10.

The Epistle of Jeremiah (Bar 6) claims to be a letter of Jeremiah to the Babylonian exiles, which is mainly an admonition on the topic of idols. In v. 3, the seventy years of Jer 25:11 and 29:10 are transformed to seven generations, suggesting a date in early Hellenistic times.[12]

The *Exagoge* composed by Ezekiel the Tragedian is written in the style of tragic drama using iambic trimeter. Guided by the book of

---

[10] See J. J. Collins, *Between Athens and Jerusalem: Jewish Identity in the Hellenistic Diaspora* (New York, N.Y.: Crossroad, 1983), 32–3; idem, "Artapanus," *OTP* 2 (1985), 889–903, 891.

[11] See e.g. P. W. Skehan and A. A. DiLella, *The Wisdom of Ben Sira: A New Translation with Notes, Introduction and Commentary* (AB 39; New York, N.Y.: Doubleday, 1987), 8–10; R. J. Coggins, *Sirach* (Guides to Apocrypha and Pseudepigrapha; Sheffield: Sheffield Academic Press, 1998), 18–20; O. Kaiser, *Die alttestamentlichen Apokryphen: Eine Einleitung in Grundzügen* (Gütersloh: Chr. Kaiser/Gütersloher Verlagshaus, 2000), 83–4.

[12] See C. A. Moore, *Daniel, Esther, and Jeremiah, the Additions: A New Translation with Introduction and Commentary* (AB 44; Garden City, N.Y.: Doubleday, 1977), 328; Kaiser, 60–1.

Exodus, the author creates a Greek drama written on the models of Aeschylus, Sophocles, and Euripides around Moses and the story of the Exodus. For this purpose, the author utilizes the LXX text of Exodus,[13] which excludes a date much earlier than the middle of the 3rd century B.C.E. On the other hand, the excerpts of the *Exagoge* by Alexander Polyhistor argue against a dating after the middle of the 1st century B.C.E.[14]

Of Theodotus's poem entitled "On the Jews" eight fragments have survived in Eusebius's *Praeparatio Evangelica* (IX,22,1, 2, 3, 4–6, 7, 8–9a, 9b, 10–1). The preserved text pertains to the rape of Dinah and the events following it as described in Genesis 34, but the title "On the Jews" certainly suggests a much broader topic. Theodotus's description of Shechem's wall as "smooth" (*PrEv* IX,22,1) gives us an idea of when he wrote his poem. Excavations indicate "that from the time of Alexander the Great (c. 331 B.C.) until c. 190 B.C. there was a large city wall around Shechem. However, in the following period (190–150 B.C.) the city wall was no longer maintained and stones were taken from the wall to build towers in front." Therefore, a date at the end of the 3rd or the beginning of the 2nd century B.C.E. stands to reason.[15]

At the end of this brief survey it should be noted that the now commonly accepted dates of the *Astronomical Enoch* in late 4th or early 3rd century B.C.E. and of the *Book of Watchers* in the 3rd century B.C.E. are derived from the palaeographic dates of Enoch-manuscripts found at Qumran.[16]

2. COMPOSITIONS OF THE 4TH AND 3RD CENTURIES B.C.E. FOUND IN THE QUMRAN LIBRARY

In addition to biblical books, apocrypha and pseudepigrapha already known before the finds of Qumran, I now count 23 further literary

---

[13] See e.g. Holladay, vol. 2, 313; Jacobsen, 40–1.

[14] See G. Vermes, F. Millar and M. Goodman, *The History of the Jewish People in the Age of Jesus Christ (175 B.C.–A.D. 135) by Emil Schürer: A New English Version Revised and Edited*, vol. 3.1 (Edinburgh: T. & T. Clark, 1986), 565; R. G. Robertson, "Ezekiel the Tragedian," *OTP* 2 (1985), 803–19, 803–4; H. Jacobson, *The Exagoge of Ezekiel* (Cambridge et al.: Cambridge University Press, 1983), 6; Holladay, vol. 2, 308–12 (for a comprehensive history of research see Jacobson, 6–8).

[15] F. Fallon, "Theodotus," *OTP* 2 (1985), 785–93, 787–8. For a brief history of research see Holladay, Fragments, vol. 2, 69–70.

[16] See J. T. Milik, *The Books of Enoch* (Oxford: Clarendon, 1976), 7, 22–3, 140–1, 273.

compositions of the 4th and 3rd centuries B.C.E. which were found
in the caves of Qumran (although six of these composition cannot
be dated with certainty to this period). Many of these 23 compositions are attested by several manuscripts. The total number of texts
from 4th and 3rd centuries B.C.E. is thus increased by the library of
Qumran to 32–41 compositions. One should remember by contrast
that the canon of the Hebrew Bible itself includes only 39 books.

Table 2: *Compositions from the 4th and 3rd cent. B.C.E. attested in the Qumran Library*[17]

Parabiblical Literature	Literature not Related to Authoritative Texts
Book of Giants (1Q23–4; 2Q26; 4Q203; 4Q530–3; 6Q8)	Prayer of Nabonidus (4Q242)
Admonition of the Flood (4Q370)	ProtoEster (4Q550a–e)
The Book of the Words of Noah (1QapGen ar v 29–xviii ?)	Parts of 11QPs^a
Abraham in Egypt (1QapGen ar xix 10–xx 32)	11QapocrPs
Narrative and Poetic Composition (= NPC; 2Q22; 4Q371–3)	Non-Canonical Psalms A–B (4Q380–1)
Testament of Joseph (4Q539)	Songs of the Sabbath Sacrifice (4Q400–7, 11Q17, Mas1k)
Aramaic Levi Document (4Q213.213a.213b.214.214a. 215 +1Q21?; CLev^Bodl.Cam; Koutloumousiou 39)	*Wiles of a Wicked Woman* (4Q184)
Temple Scroll (4Q524; 11Q19–21)	Sapiential Work (4Q185)
Apocryphon of Moses (1Q22; 1Q29; 4Q375–6; 4Q408)	Admonitory Parable (4Q302)
Apocryphon of Joshua (4Q378–9, 4Q522; 5Q9; Mas11 [Mas 1039–211])	Instruction (1Q26, 4Q415–8.418a.418c; 4Q423)
Vision of Samuel (4Q160)	Instruction-like Compostion B (4Q424)
New Jerusalem (1Q32; 2Q24; 4Q554–5; 5Q15; 11Q18)	

---

[17] In this table, compositions which cannot be dated with certainty are marked
by italics. 4Q374 (*Exod/Conquest Trad.*), 4Q460 (*Narrative Work and Prayer*), 4Q461
(*Narrative B*), and 4Q474 (*Text concerning Rachel and Joseph*) are not included. Although
their free use of the Tetragrammaton (4Q374 9 3; 4Q460 9 i 10; 4Q461 1 9, 10;
4Q474 4, 5) could argue for 4th or 3rd cent. B.C.E. setting, the extremely fragmentary state of preservation of these manuscripts does not allow for a more precise dating than pre-Maccabean times. In addition, in all manuscripts, no evidence
is preserved which would hint to a 4th or 3rd cent. B.C.E. setting.

In the following section, I would like to give a short description of the parabiblical literature of the 4th and 3rd centuries B.C.E. found in the Qumran caves and to discuss their dating. For reasons of space, a similar discussion of the literature not related to authoritative texts must be done elsewhere.

3. The Parabiblical Literature from Qumran from the 4th and 3rd Centuries b.c.e.

The *Book of Giants* from Qumran is preserved in nine fragmentary manuscripts (1Q23–4; 2Q26; 4Q203; 4Q530–3; 6Q8); the Manichaean *Book of Giants* used this Aramaic composition as a *Vorlage*. In the Aramaic *Book of Giants* from Qumran the descendants of the fallen watchers, the giants, experience symbolic dreams, which they are unable to understand. Therefore, they ask Enoch to interpret them. The *Book of Giants* from Qumran depends thus on the *Book of Watchers* which is to be dated to the 3rd century B.C.E. On the other hand, the *Book of Giants* from Qumran reports a dream of the giant Oyah/Uyah (4Q530 II 16–20), in which he sees how the ruler of heavens descends to earth. There, the heavenly monarch sits on his throne, books are opened in front of him and judgment is spoken. As Loren Stuckenbruck has suggested, in terms of tradition history, this might be an earlier version of Dan 7:9–10. If this is correct, the *Book of Giants* should be dated between the years 250 and 164 B.C.E.[18]

The preserved text of the *Admonition of the Flood* (4Q370) tries to impart religious values by means of the example of the deluge and the Noachide covenant. The main interest of this text is to admonish that one should not rebel against the words of YHWH. The free use of the Tetragrammaton in this text (4Q370 1 i 1–3; 1 ii 2, 7)

---

[18] L. Stuckenbruck, *The Book of Giants from Qumran: Text, Translation, and Commentary* (TSAJ 63; Tübingen: Mohr Siebeck, 1997), 121–3, and "The Book of Daniel and the Dead Sea Scrolls: The Making and Remaking of the Biblical Tradition," in *The Hebrew Bible and Qumran* (ed. J. H. Charlesworth; N. Richland Hills, Tex.: Bibal Press, 2000), 135–71, 143–9 (against Milik, 57–8); cf. J. C. Reeves, "Giants, Book of," *Encyclopedia of the Dead Sea Scrolls* 1 (2000), 309–11, 311, and E. Puech, "Livre des Géants," *DJD* 31 (2001), 9–115, 12–4, who regards a common tradition which was shared by both the *Book of Giants* and Daniel 7 as more plausible and dates the *Book of Giants* between 200 and 160 B.C.E. For the Manichean *Book of Giants* and its relation to the Qumran fragments see J. C. Reeves, *Jewish Law in Manichaean Cosmogony. Studies in the Book of Giants Traditions* (Cincinnati, Ohio: Hebrew Union College Press, 1992).

requires a date for the *Admonition of the Flood* before 150 B.C.E. In addition, in this composition Noah is named neither in connection with the deluge nor in connection with the resulting covenant. This attests to a very free use of the biblical *Vorlage* which is unlikely after the 3rd century B.C.E. On the other hand, the midrashic compilation of several different authoritative texts in 4Q370 I 1–3 (11Ps[a] XXVI 13 [Hymn to the Creator]; Ezek 36:19b, 20aß, 30a, 31a, 33aß; Deut 8:7–10)[19] as well as the incorporation of 4Q185 I 13–II 3 in 4Q370 II 5–7[20] advise against a dating of the *Admonition of the Flood* earlier than the 3rd century B.C.E.

Before I can deal with the *Book of the Words of Noah* some explanations concerning the scroll 1QapGen are necessary. When all columns of 1QapGen were published in at least preliminary editions,[21] it became evident that the scroll is not a copy of any single text but a collection of different literary compositions:

(1) It starts in columns I–V with a narrative on the birth of Noah.
(2) Afterwards a text entitled *ktb mly nḥ* "*The Book of the Words of Noah*"[22] follows in columns V–XVIII.
(3) From column XVIII onwards 1QapGen proceeds with a rewritten Bible version of the Abraham cycle.

The *Book of the Words of Noah* is a renarration of Genesis 6–9, which enlarges the Biblical story with two apocalpytic dreams of Noah and a detailed description of the apportionment of the earth to Noah's sons. The heading *ktb mly nḥ* is reminiscent of *1 En.* 14:1 (4QEn[c] 1 vi 9) where the vision of Enoch is described as *spr mly qwšṭ/ḥ* "the book of the words of truth." Similarly, in 4Q543 1 1 (par 4Q545 1 i 1), the *Vision of Amram* is entitled *ktb mly ḥzwt ʿmrm* "the book of the words of the vision of Amram." Because of the corresponding headings of the *Book of the Words of Noah*, the *Vision of Amram* and

---

[19] See C. A. Newsom, "*4Q370*": An Admonition Based on the Flood, *RevQ* 13 (1988): 23–43, 30–5; "**370**. 4QAdmonition Based on the Flood," *DJD* 19 (1995), 85–97, 88–93.

[20] See C. A. Newsom's discussion of the relation between 4Q370 and 4Q185 in *RevQ* 13 (1988): 39–42, and *DJD* 19, 89–90.

[21] J. C. Greenfield and E. Qimron, "The Genesis Apocryphon Col. XII," in: *Studies in Qumran Aramaic* (ed. T. Muraoka; AbrNSup 3; Leuven: Peeters Press, 1992), 70–7; M. Morgenstern, E. Qimron, and D. Sivan, "The Hitherto Unpublished Columns of the Genesis Apocryphon," *AbrN* 33 (1995): 30–54.

[22] Cf. R. C. Steiner, "The Heading of the *Book of the Words of Noah* on a Fragment of the Genesis Apocryphon: New Light on a 'Lost' Work," *DSD* 2 (1995): 66–71.

1 En. 14:1 as well as the relatively high amount of text dedicated to the apocalyptic dream visions of Noah in the *Book of the Words of Noah*, this composition should be understood as an apocalypse with a narrative frame. To date the *Book of the Words of Noah* to the 3rd century B.C.E. is recommended by its reception in *Jubilees* 8–9, in the 3rd book of the *Sibylline Oracles* (110–61), and in 1QM I–II.[23] According to Morgenstern, Qimron, and Sivan, this date is confirmed by the Aramaic pecularities of the *Book of the Words of Noah*.[24]

The rewritten Bible version of the Abraham cycle in 1QapGen XVIIIff. is commonly dated to the end of the 2nd century or the beginning of the 1st century B.C.E.[25] It merges an itinerary of the journey of Abraham with a sapiential didactive narrative developed out of Gen 12:10–20. The sapiential didactive narrative reports how in a symbolic dream Abraham is warned of the dangers which Sarah and he will experience in Egypt. Afterwards, three nobles from the court of the Pharaoh visit to ask the sage Abraham for his advice. Later on, the nobles describe Sarah's beauty to the Pharaoh, and he reacts by kidnapping her. By means of an incantation of a pestilential spirit, Abraham is able to inflict the Pharaoh with illness and gains back his wife. Because of the complicated redactional history of the Genesis Apocryphon's Abraham cycle, it seems appropriate to date the sapiential didactive narrative on the sojourn in Egypt to the 3rd century B.C.E.[26]

The text formerly named *Apocryphon of Joseph*[27] and now entitled *Narrative and Poetic Composition* (2Q22; 4Q371–3) is unusual not only

---

[23] For the reception of the *Book of the Words of Noah* in the literature of Second Temple Judaism see James M. Scott, "The Division of the Earth in *Jubilees* 8:11–9:15 and Early Christian Chronography," in *Studies in the Book of Jubilees* (ed. M. Albani, J. Frey, and A. Lange; TSAJ 65; Tübingen: Mohr Siebeck, 1997), 295–323, 300–3.

[24] Op. cit., 33–6.

[25] E. Y. Kutscher, "Dating the Language of the Genesis Apocryphon," *JBL* 76 (1957): 288–92, 289; idem, "The Language of the 'Genesis Apocryphon': Aspects of the Dead Sea Scrolls," *ScrHier* 4 (^{2}1965): 1–35, 22; F. Altheim and R. Stiehl, 'Die Datierung des Genesis-Apokryphons vom Toten Meer,' in: idem, *Die aramäische Sprache unter den Achämeniden*, vol. 1: Geschichtliche Untersuchungen (Frankfurt a.M.: V. Klostermann, 1963), 214–22, 215–8.

[26] For the sapiential didactic story incorporated into the Genesis Apocryphon's retelling of the Abraham cycle see my article "1QGenAp XIX$_{10}$–XX$_{32}$ as Paradigm of the Wisdom Didactive Narrative," in *Qumranstudien* (ed. H.-J. Fabry, A. Lange, and H. Lichtenberger; Schriften des Institutum Judaicum Delitzschianum 4; Göttingen: Vandenhoek & Ruprecht, 1996), 191–204.

[27] See E. Tov, "The Unpublished Qumran Texts from Caves 4 and 11," *BA* 55 (1992): 94–104, 100; idem, "The Unpublished Qumran Texts from Caves 4 and 11," *JJS* 43 (1992): 101–136, 120.

for the Qumran collection but for the literature of Second Temple Judaism more generally. The fragmentary state of preservation of its manuscripts is a serious obstacle for its analysis. It seems to be composed mostly in prose, but its narratives are interspersed with poetic sections. In 4Q372 1 11ff. the fate of Joseph is understood as a *typos* of the fate of the ten northern tribes.[28] Like Joseph, who never returned from Egypt alive, the northern tribes are still in exile.[29] This demonstrates that despite their claims, the Samaritans are not descendants of Joseph. Later in the composition (2Q22 par 4Q372 19 par 4Q373 1), a fragmentary passage is preserved whose remnants attest to the battle of David and Goliath. The date of the *Narrative and Poetic Composition* from Qumran can be deducted from the word *bmh* attested in 4Q372 1 12. Because *bmh* never refers to a roofed temple, the polemic against a Samaritan *bamah* on mount Gerizim in 4Q372 1 12 advises dating the *Narrative and Poetic Composition* before the Samaritan temple was built on Mount Gerizim, i.e. at latest in the late 4th or the 3rd century B.C.E.[30]

Of 4Q539 only five heavily damaged fragments are preserved. Their contents would suggest describing the composition as a *Testament of Joseph*. If K. Beyer[31] is correct that the *Aramaic Levi Document* incorporates this text, it should be dated to the 3rd century B.C.E. But because the evidence for this incorporation is at best meagre, much uncertainty remains concerning this dating.

The *Aramaic Levi Document* (4Q213.213a.213b.214.214a.215 + 1Q21?; CLev[Bodl.Cam]; Koutloumousiou 39) is a description of the life of Levi, based mostly on Genesis 34; Exod 32:25–9; Num 25:6–13; Deut 33:8–11; and Mal 2:4–8. It opens with the assault of Shechem (Genesis 34) and proceeds to describe in detail how Levi was appointed to the priesthood. Then follows a description of Levi's life by the

---

[28] In comparison, in Zech 10:6, the northern kingdom is designated as "the house of Joseph."

[29] Note that Zech 9:11 uses Joseph's exile in Egypt as a *typos*, too. But in Zech 9:11, it is understood as a promise for a positive end to the exile of Zion. Zion will come back just as Joseph was liberated from the pit.

[30] Only during the reign of Antiochus III at the beginning of the 2nd cent. B.C.E., a roofed temple was erected on Mt. Gerizim. For the archeological evidence see Y. Magen, "Mount Gerizim and the Samaritans," in *Early Christianity in Context: Monuments and Documents* (Studium Biblicum Franciscanum collectio maior 38; ed. F. Manns and E. Alliata; Jerusalem: Franciscan Printing Press, 1993), 91–148, 97–109, esp. 104, 139.

[31] *Die aramäischen Textfunde vom Toten Meer* (Göttingen: Vandenhoek & Ruprecht, 1984), 204 note 1.

patriarch himself and a sapiential instruction to his children. The appointment of Levi to the priesthood is justified by his zeal to exterminate the pagan elements of Israel (demonstrated by what happened in Shechem). The date of origin of the *Aramaic Levi Document* is difficult to determine. The *Book of Jubilees* depends on it (cf. *Jub.* 30:1–32:9), and in the ideas of dualism and purity of the *Aramaic Levi Document*, no response to the so-called Hellenistic religious reforms of the years 174–64 B.C.E. can be found. These factors suggest dating the *Aramaic Levi Document* to the 3rd century B.C.E. at the latest. On the other hand, the combination of Pentateuchal and prophetic scriptures in the *Aramaic Levi Document* advises against a time much earlier than the late 4th century B.C.E.[32]

The *Temple Scroll* (4Q524; 11Q19–21) combines parts of the Pentateuch and formerly unknown passages, and claims to have been revealed to Moses on Mount Sinai. Throughout the book, the speeches of God are formulated in the first person. This is the case even when in the *Vorlage* of the *Temple Scroll* the third person is used. The *Temple Scroll* is heavily influenced by an omphalological world view, according to which the world's most holy place is the Holy of Holies in the Jerusalem Temple. The remainder of the cosmos is grouped around this centre of the world in concentric circles of decreasing holiness. This world view is evident even in the structure of the *Temple Scroll*:

11QT^a I–II: Introduction: The Sinai covenant
11QT^a III–XXX: Temple buildings, altar and rituals connected with them.
11QT^a XXX ?–XLV 7: The courtyards of the Temple.
11QT^a XLV 7–XLVII: Prescriptions concerning Jerusalem as an enlarged precinct of the sanctuary.
11QT^a XLVIII–LXVII: Discussions concerning the cities of Israel and further prescriptions (mostly from Deut)

---

[32] For the date of the *Aramaic Levi Document* see P. Grelot, "Le Livre des Jubilés et le Testament de Lévi," in: *Mélanges Dominique Barthélemy* (ed. P. Cassetti, O. Keel, and A. Schenker; OBO 38; Fribourg and Göttingen: Edition Universitaires and Vandenhoek & Ruprecht, 1981), 109–133, 110; M. E. Stone, "Enoch, Aramaic Levi and Sectarian Origins," in: idem, *Selected Studies in Pseudepigrapha and Apocrypha* (SVTP 9; Leiden, New York, and Köln, 1991), 247–58, 247–8 note 2; M. de Jonge, "The Testament of Levi and 'Aramaic Levi'," *RevQ* 13 (1988) 367–85, 373–4; R. A. Kugler, *From Patriarch to Priest: The Levi-Priestly Tradition from Aramaic Levi to Testament of Levi* (SBLEJL 9; Atlanta, Ga.: Scholars Press) 131–5.

For the *Temple Scroll*, the *terminus ad quem* is set by its oldest preserved manuscript, 4QT^b (4Q524), which is dated paleographically around 150 B.C.E.[33] As M. Broshi has shown, in Palestine the spiral staircaise described in the *Temple Scroll* for the northwestern tower of the Temple (11QT^a XXX 3–XXXI 9) and the peristyles situated in the middle and the outer courtyard are attested only from Hellenistic times onwards.[34] Their occurrence in the Temple as described by the *Temple Scroll* thus determines a *terminus post quem* in the 3rd century B.C.E. In my opinion, the extremely free approach to the *Temple Scroll*'s biblical *Vorlage* and its own claim to be an authoritative legal text recommends dating the *Temple Scroll* to the 3rd century B.C.E.

The *Apocryphon of Moses* (1Q22; 1Q29; 4Q375–6; 4Q408)[35] is a deuteronomizing legal text. In its introduction, the announcement of the Torah after Israel's 40 years in the wilderness is described according to the model of the Book of Deuteronomy. Ideologically, the *Apocryphon of Moses* is also heavily influenced by deuteronomistic theology: the law has been given to the Israelites, but they despised it, turned to other Gods, and violated the Sabbath of the covenant. The deterioration of the manuscripts of the *Apocryphon of Moses* make a reliable dating of this composition impossible. The formula "in the year forty of the departure of the children of Israel from the land of Egypt, in the eleventh month, in the first day of the month" (1Q22 I 1–2) corresponds to the dating formulas of the *Songs for the Sabbath Sacrifice* and the calendrical texts from Qumran. The *Apocryphon of Moses* thus adheres to a 364–day solar calendar, which is attested after the middle of the 2nd century B.C.E. in Essene texts only. Since the free use of the Tetragrammaton in the Apocryphon of Moses advises against an Essene setting for this composition, its adherence to the 364-day solar calendar as well as the free use of the Tetragrammaton itself suggests a date before the middle of the 2nd century B.C.E.

The *Apocryphon of Joshua* (4Q378–9, 4Q522; 5Q9; Mas1l)[36] is a free

---

[33] See E. Puech, *Qumrân grotte 4 XVIII: Textes hébreux (4Q521–4Q528, 4Q576–4Q579)* (*DJD* 25; Oxford: Clarendon, 1998), 87–8.

[34] M. Broshi, "Visionary Architecture and Town Planning in the Dead Sea Scrolls," in *Time to Prepare the Way in the Wilderness* (ed. D. Dimant and L. H. Schiffman; STDJ 16; Leiden, New York, and Köln: Brill, 1995), 9–22, 19.

[35] For the identification of the different manuscripts of the apocrMoses see J. Strugnell, *DJD* 19 (1995), 129–30 and A. Steudel, *DJD* 36 (2000), 298.

[36] For the different witnesses of the *Apocryphon of Joshua* see E. Tov, "The Rewritten Book of Joshua as Found at Qumran and Masada," in *Biblical Perspectives: Early Use*

retelling of the conquest narrative with a curse upon the person who rebuilds Jericho. The dating of the composition depends on 4Q379 22 ii: If the enlarged quotation of Josh 6:26b found there alludes to the palace building in Jericho by Simon or John Hyrcanus, the *Apocryphon of Joshua* would have to be dated at the end of the 2nd or the beginning of the 1st century B.C.E.[37] But this is doubtful because 4QTestimonia has to be dated palaeographically around 100 B.C.E. If it already quotes the *Apocryphon of Joshua* in 4QTest 21–30, the latter has to be older than 4QTestimonia. When it is recognized that 4QTestimonia quotes the *Apocryphon of Joshua* parallel to biblical texts like Deut 18:18–9; Num 24:15–7; and Deut 33:8–11, this observation is of even more importance. For the Qumran covenanters, to become a text of equal authority to biblical books, the *Apocryphon of Joshua* must at least have been some decades old when 4QTestimonia was written around 100 B.C.E. Furthermore, the terms *ḥwmh* and *mgdlym* used in 4Q379 22 ii 12 designate a wall which circumvents a city and towers connected to such an instrument of defense. In my opinion, this does not agree with the building activities of Hyrcanus I at Jericho, which according to recent excavations were restricted to the erection of a palace near Jericho.[38] Thus, while 4Q379 22 ii is interpreted in 4QTest with concern for the Hasmonean palace building in Jericho, the quoted lemma from the *Apocryphon of Joshua* should be understood as a literary prophecy written before the Hasmonean building activities. A date of the *Apocryphon of Joshua* earlier than Hasmonean times is also recommended by its quotation in a text called *Narrative Work and Prayer* (4Q460 9 i 3 par 4Q379 22 ii 13–13a).[39] Because of its free use of the Tetragrammaton (4Q460

---

and Interpretation of the Bible in Light of the Dead Sea Scrolls (ed. M. E. Stone and E. G. Chazon; STDJ 28; Leiden, Boston, and Köln: Brill, 1998), 234–52. In addition to 4Q378–9, 4Q522; 5Q9; Mas 11, Tov (252–3) interprets 4Q123 (4Qpaleo paraJosh) as a further manuscript of the the *Apocryphon of Joshua*. But in my opinion, the paleo-Hebrew script in which it is written suggests that this manuscript attests to a variant form of the text of the Book of Joshua.

[37] Thus e.g. C. A. Newsom, "4Q378 and 4Q379: An Apocryphon of Joshua," in *Qumranstudien* (ed. H.-J. Fabry, A. Lange, and H. Lichtenberger; Schriften des Institutum Judaicum Delitzschianum 4; Göttingen: Vandenhoek & Ruprecht, 1996), 36, and Tov, "Rewritten Book of Joshua," 255–6; for a comprehensive discussion of the history of research, see Newsom, 76–8.

[38] See E. Netzer, *Die Paläste der Hasmonäer und Herodes' des Großen* (Mainz: Verlag Philipp von Zabern, 1999), 5–12.

[39] For further parallels between the *Apocryphon of Joshua* and *Narrative Work and Prayer* see E. Larson, "**460**. 4QNarrative Work and Prayer," *DJD* 36 (2000), 369–86, 373.

9 i 10), even *Narrative Work and Prayer* itself has to be dated before 150 B.C.E. Finally, such a dating of the *Apocryphon of Joshua* before the middle of the 2nd century B.C.E. is corroborated by its free use of the Tetragrammaton in 4Q378 3 i 8; 11 1; 12 3; 14 4; 4Q379 3 2, 4; 14 1; 22 ii 5; 4Q522 5 4; 9 ii 5, 8.

The *Vision of Samuel* (4Q160) represents an alternative version of 1 Samuel 3 which paraphrases neither the textual version of 1 Samuel attested by the MT nor the one attested by the LXX. The very free use of the biblical text in the *Vision of Samuel* may advise dating this composition in the 3rd century B.C.E.

The text called *New Jerusalem* (1Q32; 2Q24; 4Q554–5; 5Q15; 11Q18) is a description of the heavenly Jerusalem which bases itself on Ezekiel 40–48. The often used phrase "and he showed to me" (2Q24 1 3; 8 7; 5Q15 1 ii 2, 6; 11Q18 I 6–7; VI 1; X 5) suggests that we understand the *New Jerusalem* text as an other-worldly journey in which an *angellus interpres* guides a visionary through the heavenly city. Because of the reliance of the New Jerusalem text on Ezekiel 40–48, there is a strong possibility that this visionary was the prophet Ezekiel himself. The date of this Pseudo-Ezekiel text can be determined by the tower with spiral staircases mentioned in 5Q15 II 2–5. According to M. Broshi, this type of staircase is attested in Palestine from Hellenistic times onwards only.[40] The hippodamic plan of the city described in the *New Jerusalem* text points in the same direction. On the other hand, M. O. Wise has demonstrated, that the *Temple Scroll* depends in its description of the Temple on the *New Jerusalem* text.[41] Thus, the 3rd century B.C.E. seems to be the most probable date of origin for the *New Jerusalem* text.

4. Conclusion

In conjunction with the compositions already known before the discoveries of the Dead Sea Scrolls, a surprising image of Jewish literary history of the 4th and 3rd centuries B.C.E. emerges:

---

[40] See note 34.
[41] M. O. Wise, *A Critical Study of the Temple Scroll from Qumran Cave 11* (SAOC 49; Chicago, Ill.: The Oriental Institute of the University of Chicago, 1990), 71–86; cf. M. Broshi, 10–1, 22).

Table 3: *Parabiblical Literature*

	History	Stories + Novellas	Rewritten Bible	Prophecy	Apocalypses	Testaments	Didactic Speeches	Drama and Epic Poetry
	Gen-Neh	Sir *44–49						
	Gen-2Kgs	Demetrius						
	Gen-1Sam	NPC						
	Gen-Exod	*Artapanus*						
	Enoch		*Book of Giants*		Enochastr			
					Book of Watchers			
	Noah + Deluge				Words of Noah		Admon Flood	
	Gen 12:10–20		Abraham in Egypt					
	Levi		Aramaic Levi Doc.					
	Joseph					*TestJoseph*		
	Exod-Deut		Temple Scroll apocrMoses					
	Exod 1–15							*Ezek. the Tragedian*
	Josh		apocrJosh					
	1Sam-2Kgs	1–2 Chron						
	Samuel		*VisSam*					
	2Kgs 14:25			Jonah				
	Jeremiah			EpJer				
	Ezekiel			New Jerusalem				
	Ezek 14:14; 28:3	Dan *2–6						
	Unknown							*Theodotus*

Twenty-three compositions from this era must be categorized as para-biblical. Of these, only eight compositions (i.e. *Artapanus, Ezekiel the Tragedian, Theodotus,* the *Book of Giants,* the *Testament of Joseph,* the *Apocryphon of Moses,* the *Apocryphon of Joshua,* and the *Vision of Samuel*) cannot be dated with certainty. Eighteen compositions from the 4th and 3rd centuries B.C.E. have been written independently from books of the later Hebrew Bible. Of these compositions, only the so-called *Wiles of a Wicked Woman* cannot be dated with certainty. Therefore, more than 50% of the Jewish literature of the 4th and 3rd centuries B.C.E. still known today are of parabiblical nature.

Table 4: *Literature not Related to Authoritative Texts*

History	Stories and Novellas	Prophetic Literature	Poetic and Liturgical Literature	Sapietial Literature
Ezra/ Nehemiah	Esther Tobit	Joel	Pss-Collections Canticles	Qohelet *Wiles of a Wicked Woman*
	Prayer of Nabonidus		Parts of 11QPs[a]	Sapiential Work
	ProtoEsther		11QapocrPs	Admonitory Parable
			Songs of the Sabbath Sacrifice	Instruction
			Non-Canonical Psalms A–B	Instruction-like Compostion B

The evidence becomes even more remarkable if one examines which genres were written in a parabiblical manner and which genres were formulated independently from authoritative literature. In the fields of stories, historical, and revelatory literature, only six of the total twenty-seven compositions (Esra/Nehemiah, Esther, Joel, Tobit, the *Prayer of Nabonidus*, and the so-called *ProtoEsther*) are independent from authoritative texts. All other stories, historical, halakhic, and revelatory compositions must be categorized as parabiblical. The other way round, the evidence is even more emphatic: of the total eighteen compositions which were written independently from authoritative literature, twelve belong to sapiential, poetic, and liturgic genres.

The statistical result reached above calls for interpretation. In attempting this, one must keep in mind the arbitrariness of the transmission of Jewish literature from the 4th and 3rd centuries B.C.E. This arbitrariness introduces an element of chance that blurs any statistical result significantly. Nevertheless, the fact that 75% of the Jewish prose and revelatory literature preserved from 4th and 3rd centuries B.C.E. are written in a parabiblical manner cannot be attributed to chance only. It means that in the area of narrative and revelatory literature, a majority of Jewish authors felt obliged to write in relation to texts or themes of authoritative compositions. This preponderance of the parabiblical in prose and revelatory literature should be understood in the context of the process which led to the formation of the canons of the Hebrew Bible and the Greek Old Testament. Apparently, in the 4th and 3rd centuries B.C.E., at least a part of the Jewish literary tradition had gained such authority that Jewish authors felt obliged to pursue their literary creativity in the shadow of this tradition. In other words, in the 4th and 3rd centuries B.C.E. the Pentateuch, the deuteronomistic history, and prophetic literature had gained such a level of religious authority that they were well on their way in the canonical process of the Hebrews Bible.

Does this mean that compositions of which no parabiblical literature is preserved—e.g. the Book of Isaiah—did not enjoy a corresponding religious authority? And does this mean that the books written in the different poetic genres had not yet gained a high degree of religious authority? Does the evidence from the 4th and 3rd centuries B.C.E. thus indicate a dual canon? In answering these questions, the arbitrariness of what is preserved as well as matters of genre criticism urge caution. It might well be that once, for example, parabiblical compositions for the Book of Isaiah existed but are no longer known today. Or it might well be that the very nature of poetic compositions interfered with the parabiblical mode of writing. This suspicion might be corroborated by the small volume of parabiblical literature preserved for the prophetic books of the later Hebrew Bible and the Greek Old Testament. I hope to gain answers to these questions by way of an analysis of the quotations of and allusions to authoritative literature in late Persian and early Hellenistic Judaism. But for reasons of space, such an analysis will have to be pursued elsewhere.[42]

---

[42] See "From Literature to Scripture: The Unity and Plurality of the Hebrew Scriptures in Light of the Qumran Library" in *One Scripture or Many? Canon in Biblical, Theological, and Philosophical Perspectives* (ed. Christine Helmer and Christof Landmesser; Oxford: Oxford University Press, forthcoming).

QUMRAN-MESSIANISM*

Hermann Lichtenberger

A. Introduction

For the second time[1] the messianic texts from the Dead Sea Scrolls have become the focus of interest:

1) One of the first known texts, 1QSerekh ha-Yahad,[2] speaks of the "messiahs of Aaron and Israel" and thus represents a double messianic expectation, a priestly and a kingly.

2) In the course of the full availability of all the Qumran texts since 1991 many have been published which make the evidence even more colourful and manifold. Some of these "new" texts are as vividly debated as the "old" ones from the fifties.[3]

3) In anticipation we can say: The scrolls found in Qumran represent the three "classical" types of messianic expectations, the munus triplex, i.e. king, priest, prophet.[4]

Before we come to analyze the relevant texts, we have to answer the most debated question: When are we entitled to speak of a messianic figure?

---

* This paper was read at Tel Aviv University (March 11, 2001) on invitation by Prof. Dr. A. Oppenheimer. I am most grateful to the Institute of Advanced Studies of the Hebrew University of Jerusalem for inviting me to be a fellow in the Academic Year 2000/2001.

[1] Fundamental for the first phase Adam S. van der Woude, *Die messianischen Vorstellungen der Gemeinde von Qumran* (SSN 3; Assen, 1957).

[2] Millar Burrows, *The Dead Sea Scrolls of St. Mark's Monastery, Vol. II* (New Haven, 1951).

[3] See now Loren T. Stuckenbruck, "'Messias': Texte in den Schriften von Qumran," in *Papers on the Dead Sea Scrolls* (ed. Zdzislaw J. Kapera, Mogilany 1993; Kraków: Enigma Press, 1996), 129–39; Johannes Zimmermann, *Messianische Texte aus Qumran: Königliche, priesterliche und prophetische Messiasvorstellungen in den Schriften von Qumran* (WUNT II 104; Tübingen, 1998). For the state of research James H. Charlesworth, Hermann Lichtenberger and Gerbern S. Oegema, eds., *Qumran-Messianism: Studies on the Messianic Expectations in the Dead Sea Scrolls* (Tübingen, 1998). Stephan Schreiber, *Gesalbter und König: Titel und Konzeptionen der königlichen Gesalbtenerwartung in frühjüdischen und urchristlichen Schriften* (BZNW 105; Berlin/New York, 2000).

[4] See the structure of the book by Zimmermann, *Messianische Texte.*

Two basic types are advocated:

1) Of a "messiah" we only may speak if the word *mashiaḥ* or *meshiḥaʾ* or an equivalent in translation like χριστός or *unctus* occurs.[5]

2) A more general definition is oriented towards the eschatological character of the figure: "It is best to reserve the English term 'messiah' for figures who have important roles in the future hope of the people."[6] Such a rather general definition covers not only the instances with the term messiah (and its equivalents) but also figures connected with him or them or having similar eschatological functions.

Another consideration should be mentioned: In spite of the unexpected and unprecedented insight the Qumran texts give us on messianic hope, we cannot say with certainty how representative they are generally speaking. The fact that in the Qumran "library" texts of Essene origin and pre- and extra-Essene origin are represented proves that a broad spectrum of traditions is preserved. As to most of the texts, the Qumran-Essene community was not the author, but the librarian. In Jewish texts before 70 there is only one very explicit use of the term *mashiaḥ*;[7] in Psalms of Solomon. The Messiah King from the House of David, who will besiege the heathens and bring peace to Israel is portrayed according to Isaiah 11 as a just ruler, filled with the Spirit: "May God cleanse Israel for the day of mercy in blessing, for the appointed day when his Messiah will reign. Blessed

---

[5] This is the view held by Joseph A. Fitzmyer e.g. expressed in his interpretation of 4Q246: "Hence I continue to question the importation of messianism into the interpretation of this text [scil. 4Q246], and continue to insist that there is as yet nothing in the Old Testament or in the pre-Christian Palestinian Jewish tradition that we know of to show that 'Son of God' had a messianic nuance. Consequently, I consider this apocalyptic text to speak positively of a coming Jewish ruler, perhaps a member of the Hasmonean dynasty, who be a successor to the Davidic throne, but who is not envisaged as a Messiah"; J. A. Fitzmyer, "4Q246: The 'Son of God' Document from Qumran," *Bib* 74 (1993): 153–74, here: 173f.; see also J. H. Charlesworth, "Challenging the *Consensus Communis* Regarding Qumran Messianism (1QS, 4QS MSS)," in Charlesworth, Lichtenberger and Oegema, *Qumran-Messianism*, 120–34, here: 124, n. 19.

[6] This is the view of J. J. Collins, *The Scepter and the Star. The Messiahs of the Dead Sea Scrolls and Other Ancient Literature* (New York, 1995), 12f.; see also J. J. Collins, *'Messianic Expectation': Apocalypticism in the Dead Sea Scrolls* (London/New York, 1997), 71–90; J. J. Collins, "'He shall not Judge by What His Eyes See': Messianic Authority in the Dead Sea Scrolls," *DSD* 2 (1995): 145–64, 146: "By 'messiah' I mean an agent of God in the end-time, who is said somewhere in the literature to be anointed, but who is not necessarily called 'messiah' in every passage." Cf. Zimmermann, *Messianische Texte*, 17.

[7] See also J. H. Charlesworth, "Messianology in the Biblical Pseudepigrapha," in Charlesworth, Lichtenberger and Oegema, *Qumran-Messianism*, 21–52.

are those born in those days, to see the good things of the Lord which he will do for the coming generation; (which will be) under the rod of discipline of the Lord Messiah, in the fear of his God, in wisdom of spirit, and of righteousness and of strength, to direct people in righteous acts, in the fear of God, to set them all in the fear of the Lord. A good generation (living) in the fear of God, in the days of mercy." (Pss. Sol. 18:5–9).[8]

A messianic text but without the use of the messiah-title is in Philo, de praemiis et poenis 165ff.:

> For even though they dwell in the uttermost parts of the earth, in slavery to those who led them away captive, one signal, as it were, one day will bring liberty to all . . . When they have gained this unexpected liberty, those who but now were scattered in Greece and the outside world over islands and continents will arise and post from every side with one impulse to the one appointed place, guided in their pilgrimage by a vision divine and superhuman unseen by others but manifest to them as they pass from exile to their home.
>
> When they have arrived, the cities which but now lay in ruins will be cities once more; the desolate land will be inhabited; the barren will change into fruitfulness; all the prosperity of their fathers and ancestors will seem a tiny fragment, so lavish will be the abundant riches in their possession, which flowing from the gracious bounties of God as from a perennial fountain will bring to each individually and to all in common a deep stream of wealth leaving no room for envy (Deut 30:5). Everything will suddenly be reversed, God will turn the curses against the enemies of these penitents [. . .].[9]

In this short outline of messianism before and around 70 we must include historical realizations of messianic-prophetic expectations as Josephus relates them:[10]

1) Josephus reports that after the fall of Jerusalem many of the Sicarii fled to Egypt, where they continued their resistance and battle against the Roman rule and the collaborators and mentions a

---

[8] Translation according to R. B. Wright in *Old Testament Pseudepigrapha* (ed. J. H. Charlesworth; 2 vols.; New York, 1983), II, 669.

[9] LCL VIII. 417–421.

[10] See to the following M. Hengel, "Messianische Hoffnung und politischer 'Radikalismus' in der 'jüdisch-hellenistischen Diaspora.' Zur Frage der Voraussetzungen des jüdischen Aufstandes unter Trajan 115–117 n.Chr.," in *Apocalypticism in the Mediterranean World and the Near East* (ed. D. Hellholm; Tübingen, ²1989), 655–86; D. R. Schwartz, "Temple and Desert: On Religion and State in the Second Temple Period Judaea," in *Studies in the Jewish Background of Christianity* (WUNT 60; Tübingen, 1992), 29–56.

prophetic(-messianic) figure, Jonathan, a weaver: "The madness of the Sicarii further attacked, like a disease, the cities around Cyrene. Jonathan, an errant scoundrel, by trade a weaver, having taken refuge in that town, won the ear of not a few of the indigent class, and led them forth into the desert, promising them a display of signs and apparitions" (*B.J.* VII, 437ff.). Jonathan seems to have taken upon him the role of a Moses redivivus: a new Exodus, accompanied by signs and wonders, will bring salvation.[11]

2) The messianic prophet Theudas (after 44 C.E. under Fadus; cf. Acts 5:36) led a great number of followers to the Jordan valley promising that the water of the river would divide miraculously just as with the crossing of Joshua (Joshua 3) (*Ant.* XX, 97). Perhaps he wanted to lead his followers to the desert east of the Jordan river to initiate with this exodus the messianic time (see Matt 24:23–26).

3) A further example of these apocalyptic-eschatological figures is the so-called Egyptian (cf. Acts 21:38), who called his followers to the Mount of Olives by promising them that on his order—as was the case with Jericho—the walls of Jerusalem would fall down, so that they could enter the city (*Ant.* XX, 169–172).

4) In the tradition of the Prophet like Moses (Deut 18:15, 18) stands a Samaritan who rallied the mob to come with him to Mount Garizim: "He assured them that on their arrival he would show them the sacred vessels which were buried there, where Moses had deposited them" (*Ant.* XVIII, 85; time of Pilate, around 36 C.E.).

5) Simon bar Giora shows himself on the Temple Mountain at the place where the temple had stood dressed in a white garment and a purple mantle to present himself as the King-Messiah (*B.J.* VII, 29). What Josephus claims to be an intention to deceive in reality was a messianic demonstration.

6) Finally the First Jewish War seems to have received its initiating impulse by a prophecy.[12] Tacitus and Sueton confirm Josephus, that there had been an old prophecy in the "priestly scriptures" that from Judaea a world reign would begin (profectique Iudaea rerum potiretur, Tac hist V, 13.2): "But what more than all incited them to the war was an ambiguous oracle, likewise found in their sacred scriptures, to the effect that at that time one from their country would become

---

[11] See M. Hengel, *Die Zeloten. Untersuchungen zur jüdischen Freiheitsbewegung in der Zeit von Herodes I. bis 70 n.Chr.* (AGJU 1; Leiden/Köln, ²1976), 239.

[12] Hengel, *Zeloten*, 243–6.

ruler of the world. This they understood to mean someone of their own race, and many of their wise men went astray in their inter-pretation of it. The oracle, however, in reality signified the sover-eignty of Vespasian, who was proclaimed Emperor on Jewish soil."[13]

7) To the messianic uprisings no doubt belongs the Jewish Revolt in the time of Trajan (115–117), when King Lukuas led the Jews from Cyrene to Egypt, certainly with Jerusalem as goal. For sure—already because of the royal title—an eschatological-messianic back-ground must be assumed.[14]

Back to the Apocrypha and Pseudepigrapha. According to J. H. Charlesworth in *Qumran-Messianism*[15] only in five of the 65 texts included in the Old Testament Pseudepigrapha do we find before 70 A.D. the term Messiah or the Anointed-one or Christos (or equiv-alents). From the five texts *Pss. Sol.*, 2 (syr)Baruch, 4 Ezra, the Similitudes of 1 (eth)Enoch and 3 Enoch, however, only the Psalms of Solomon are without a doubt from the time before 70. This strik-ing fact requires an explanation, especially why in other pre-70-texts the title is not used, not even in "messianic" passages.

This changes totally with the publication of 1QS (IX,11) and 1QSa (II,12, XIV,20) and the discovery that the Damascus Document also (II,12; VI,1; XII,23; XIV,19; XX, 1) belongs to Qumran-Essene lit-erature. 1QS IX,11 "until the coming of the prophet and the anointed ones of Aaron and Israel" together with the long known passages from the Damascus Document especially lead to the thesis that the doc-trine of the two Messiahs was a characteristic of the Qumran-Essene community, for instance in RGG: "As savior figures the Essene com-munity not only expects the Messiah from the House of David as does the rest of Judaism, but three savior figures: the prophet (cf. Deut 18:15), the Messiah from Aaron, the eschatological anointed high-priest, and the Messiah from Israel, the eschatological King from the tribe of Judah, the Son of David."[16]

---

[13] Transl. LCL.
[14] Hengel, *Messianische Hoffnung.*
[15] Charlesworth, "Messianology," 50–52.
[16] K. G. Kuhn, "Qumran," *RGG*³, 5:740–756, here: 747 (translation by H. L.); see esp. van der Woude, *Messianische Vorstellungen*, 75–89 (ref. to 1QS IX,9–11); relat-ing the prophet to the Teacher of Righteousness and the Messiah of Aaron to Eliah is not convincing (op. cit. 86–89).

Today, as we now know all the material from the Qumran texts, we have to draw a much more complex picture. On the one hand, we realize that "a very important fragment from Cave IV, 4QS MS E, does not contain the celebrated *locus classicus* on Qumran messianism."[17] On the other hand we now count about 30 instances of "messiah" (Hebrew or Aramaic).[18] If we add terms as "the Branch of David," "the Prince of the Congregation," "the Elect of God," "the Son of God," and "the Eschatological Anointed of Spirit,"[19] we arrive at an impressive variety which warns us of speaking further of the doctrine of the two Messiahs as *the* characteristic of Qumran-Essene messianism.

B. Eschatological "Messianic" Figures in the Expectation of the Community of Qumran

1. *The Prophet and the Messiahs of Aaron and Israel*

The Prophet certainly is the "prophet like Moses" according to Deut 18:15 (cf. 4Q[Test]175), and the two Messiahs of Aaron and Israel are taken from Zech 4:14, the two "anointed ones." The traditions and functions connected with them result from the Community itself, especially concerning the superiority of the priestly Messiah (Messiah of Aaron) to the Messiah of Israel. Without dealing more deeply with the history and structure of the Qumran-Essene community, it is evident that the Community was formed of priestly and lay members, whose interaction was regulated, but among whom the priests enjoyed priority. This corresponds with the superiority of the eschatological High Priest to the Messiah of Israel in the eschatological meal in 1QSa[1Q28a] II,18ff.: (the Priest, i.e. the eschatological High Priest) shall "[stretch out] his hand to the bread first of all. And af[ter (this has occurred)] the Messiah of Israel [shall stret]ch out his hands to the bread." The three figures meet again in 4QTestimonies [4Q175], a text in which basic "messianic" passages from the Pentateuch expressing the expectation of three eschatological figures, namely the Prophet like Moses (Deut 18:18–19), the Messiah of Israel

---

[17] Charlesworth, "Challenging," 123: "עד בוא נביא ומשיחי אהרון וישראל." See P. Alexander and G. Vermes, *Qumran Cave 4, XIX* (DJD XXVI; Oxford, 1998), 148.

[18] M. G. Abegg and C. A. Evans, "Messianic Passages in the Dead Sea Scrolls," in Charlesworth, Lichtenberger and Oegema, *Qumran-Messianism*, 191–203, here: 191.

[19] Abegg and Evans, "Messianic Passages," 194–203.

(the Star from Jacob, Numb 24:15–17) and the eschatological High Priest, the Priestly Messiah (Deut 33: 8–11), are quoted. All three have juridical functions and thus show their role in the latter-day expectations of the community.

Finally a short view in the concept of the Damascus Document:

CD XII,23–XIII,2: The precepts which are given to walk in the camps are valid for this age of wickedness until the coming of the Messiah of Aaron and Israel (cf. CD XIV,18f.).

The coming of both Messiahs of Aaron and Israel appears as latter-day events in CD XIX,33–XX,1: "Thus all the men who entered the new covenant in the land of Damascus and returned and betrayed and departed from the well of living water will not be accounted among the council of the people; and when (the latter) was written, they will not be written from the day on which the unique Teacher was gathered in until there arises the Messiah from Aaron and from Israel."

Analogous figures, as is well known, are found in the Testaments of the Twelve Patriarchs: the two Messiahs connected with the names of Levi and Judah; Judah is the king, but Levi has primacy over him (*T. Jos.* 19:4). As the eschatological High Priest Levi will bring deliverance (*T. Levi* 18): "And then the Lord will raise up a new priest, to whom all the words of the Lord will be revealed. He shall effect the judgment of truth over the earth for many days (2)... This one will shine forth like the sun in the earth; he shall take away all darkness from under heaven (4)... For he shall give the majesty of the Lord to those who are his sons in truth forever. And there shall be no successor for him from generation to generation forever. And in his priesthood the nations shall be multiplied in knowledge on the earth, and they shall be illumined by the grace of the Lord... In his priesthood sin shall cease and lawless men shall rest from their evil deeds... And he (God) shall open the gates of paradise; he shall remove the sword that has threatened since Adam, and he will grant to the saints to eat of the tree of life. The spirit of holiness shall be upon them. And Beliar shall be bound by him" (8–11).[20] In short: The abundance of the time of salvation will break through with the appearance of the Eschatological High Priest.

---

[20] Translation according to Howard C. Kee, in *OTP I*, 794f.

2. *The Expectation of the Eschatological King Messiah*

(a) *The Branch of David*

According to 4QFlorilegium [4Q174] 2 Sam 7:11–14 speaks of the "Branch of David," who at the end of days will appear in Zion together with the eschatological "Teacher of the Torah." In 4Q252 (PatrBless) the "Branch of David" is identified with the "Messiah [Anointed] of Righteousness."

(b) *The "Anointed of Righteousness"*

See (a).

(c) *The "Teacher of Torah"*

As can be deduced from 4QFlor[4Q174], the "Teacher of Torah" is an eschatological figure. This becomes even clearer when the "Teacher of Torah" is interpreted as the "Star of Jacob" (Numb 24:17) in CD VII,18f. He comes together with the "Prince of all the Congregation."

(d) *The "Prince of the Congregation"*

The "Prince of the Congregation" will execute the judgement (CD VII, 18f.). In the eschatological Blessings 1QSb[1Q28b] a whole benediction formula for the "Prince of the Congregation" is imparted carrying all the features of the Davidic King-Messiah (V,20–29). Of highest importance but much disputed is 4Q285 (4QSerek ha-Milḥamah) where according to Isa 11:4 the "Prince of the Congregation" kills the leader of the hostile army leading to a time of blessing.

(e) *The "Son of God"*

In the controversies about the text 4Q246, concerning a messianic, a non-messianic, an angelologic or a collective interpretation, scholars were inclined to forget that there is an indisputable Son-of-God text in 4Q174, where 2 Sam 7:14 ("I will be to him a father and he will be to me a son") is interpreted as the "Shoot of David."

The Aramaic text gives us the "Son-of-God" notion in three variants: "Son of the great God," "the Son of God," "Son of the Most High." There are good reasons to see in him a positive figure (cf. Luke 1:32,35).

(f) *The "Elect of God" in 4Q534*

J. A. Fitzmyer has proposed that this text refers to the birth of Noah, but in light of Isa 7:14ff. it may speak of the birth of a Savior King.

3. *The Expectation of an Eschatological Priest (Messiah)*

(a) *The Messiahs from Aaron and Israel*
See above (B. 1.).

(b) *The Moses-Apocryphon 4Q375/376*
This text is without eschatological expectation. It gives ordinances for the "anointed priest" in case of false prophecy.

(c) *4Q541 (4QahA)*
J. Starcky had found in this text a "messie souffrant, dans la perspective ouverte par les poèmes du Serviteur." In fact the figure has traits of the Suffering Servant ("and he will atone for all the sons of his generation");[21] the text probably deals with the eschatological High Priest.

4. *The Expectation of the Eschatological Prophet*

(a) *The "Prophet like Moses"*
See above (B. 1.).

(b) *The "Anointed of the Holy Spirit" 4Q270*[22]
The "Anointed Ones of the Holy Spirit" are inspired teachers of the community;[23] there is no eschatological dimension.

(c) *"His Anointed One/Ones" 4Q521*[24]
This text is not only of special importance because it gives the first

---

[21] Collins, *Scepter*, 125: "The figure described in 4Q541 is said to atone for the children of his generation. The obvious implication is that he is a priest and makes atonement by means of the sacrificial cult. He does not atone by his suffering and death, as is the case with Isaiah's servant." "Finally the figure in this passage undergoes suffering, but it is mental anguish, brought on by lies and calumnies, and so it is quite a different sort from the suffering described in Isaiah 53."

[22] Edition J. M. Baumgarten, "4Q270. 4QDamascus Document^e," in *Qumran Cave 4, XIII (DJD* XVIII; Oxford, 1996), 137–68.

[23] See Baumgarten, DJD XVIII, 146.

[24] Edition E. Puech, "4Q521. 4QApocalypse messianique," in *Qumrân Grotte 4, XVIII (DJD* XXV; Oxford, 1998), 1–38. For his earlier editions and interpretations see p. 1. A detailed interpretation in J. Zimmermann, *Messianische Texte*, 343–89. Cf. esp.: F. García Martínez, "Messianische Erwartungen in den Qumranschriften," *JBTh* 8 (1993): 182–5; J. J. Collins, "The Works of the Messiah," *DSD* 1 (1994): 98–112; H. Kvalbein, "Die Wunder der Endzeit. Beobachtungen zu 4Q521 und Matth 11,5p," *ZNW* 88 (1997): 111–25; recently: E. Puech, "Some Remarks on 4Q246 and 4Q251 and Qumran Messianism," in *The Provo International Conference on*

clear notion of the resurrection of the dead[25] in the Dead Sea Scrolls, but speaks also three times of "His Anointed One/Ones." The decisive passage is in 1,II, 1: "hea]ven and earth will obey His Anointed One" (here I prefer singular). As this "Anointed One" is connected with the eschatological time of salvation, he is best understood as the messianic prophet.[26]

(d) *Melchisedeq as Heavenly Figure and the "Anointed of the Spirit"* (11QMelch[11Q13])[27]
Melchisedeq is depicted with priestly (atonement) and juridical functions. Another figure is the "Anointed of the Spirit": "And the herald (*ham-mevasser*) is the one anointed of the Spirit" (2:18), a prophetic figure of the end-time.

5. *Summary and Conclusions*

This whole inventory of eschatological figures makes evident that even for such a limited group as the Qumran Community to speak of *the* messianic expectation does not do justice to the sources. The cause of this abundance may be that the community covers a history of about 200 years, and a development or change in the messianic expectations and figures connected with them may be assumed. Even more important is the fact that only a part of the (messianic) texts found in the caves of Qumran derive from the community itself, but are of pre- or extra- (Qumran)- Essene origin. This enables us to see what was thought and taught beyond the walls of Qumran, and this seems to me to be even more important than the Qumran-Essene belief itself. It teaches us that we should not isolate Essenism from other contemporary movements.

---

the Dead Sea Scrolls. *Technological Innovation, New Texts, and Reformulated Issues* (eds. D. W. Parry and E. Ulrich; StTDJ 30; Leiden/Boston/Köln, 1999). For an overview see E. Puech, "Messianic Apocalypse," *EDSS* I: 543f.

[25] See in detail E. Puech, *La Croyance des Esséniens en la vie future: Immortalité, résurrection, vie éternelle? Histoire d'une croyance dans le judaisme ancien, Vol. 2: Les données qumraniennes et classiques* (Paris, 1993), 627–92.

[26] Pace Puech, *DJD* XXV, 12, n. 16, and "Remarks," 557, we are dealing neither with two figures nor with a priestly one. Puech assumes for Isa 61:1 a dialogue of the Highpriest with a fellow-priest and refers that to 4Q521. Luke 4:18–21 is a testimony for a prophetic interpretation of Isa 61:1f.

[27] Edition F. García Martínez, E. J. C. Tigchelaar and A. S. van der Woude, *Qumran Cave 11, II* (*DJD* XXIII; Oxford, 1998), 221–41; see there the preceding editions and interpretations. In greater detail Zimmermann, *Messianische Texte*, 389–412; see also A. Steudel, "Melchizedek," *EDSS* 1:535–7.

Another important circumstance is to be noted: The latter-day expectation in Qumran writings may not feature any messianic figure, e.g. the War Scroll according to the manuscript from cave 1:[28] The war between the Sons of Light and the Sons of Darkness, and respectively between the army of Michael and the army of Belial, ends after heavy battles in joy and rejoicing, but is fought without a messianic figure. For the coming of the age of salvation a saviour figure is not necessarily needed. Moreover, despite the abundance of eschatological saviour figures, the Qumran Community has not taken over all available traditions in the Hebrew Bible and Judaism. What is lacking, for instance, is the image of the Son of Man which, originating from the Book of Daniel, extends through the Books of Enoch to the New Testament Gospels. Add also the Temple Scroll 11Q19, Col. 29: The eschatological sanctuary, which will be created by God himself, will come without any interaction or appearance of a salvation mediator. Of utmost importance for the development of messianic concepts and the role of messianic figures are Scriptures. These are the so-called "messianic" texts as Num 24:17, Deut 15:18, 2 Sam 7:14, Isa 11:1ff. Most of them are also of greatest importance for New Testament christology, in which Psalm 110 plays—as well as in Qumran—a crucial role.[29] Isa 61:1 enables both, New Testament and Qumran, to connect a figure anointed by the spirit of God to the eschatological salvation (see for the Dead Sea Scrolls 4Q521 and 11QMelch, for the New Testament Luke 4:18–21 and Luke 7:18–23/ Matt 11:2–5). The Qumran-Essene Community, the Dead Sea Scrolls as a whole, and the New Testament draw from a common source, the Biblical and post-Biblical tradition. Neither the Dead Sea Scrolls nor the New Testament are a monolithic entity, but a living organism with basic ideas—and contradictions.

---

[28] 1QM XI,7–8 refers to Biblical prophets.
[29] M. Hengel, "Psalm 110 und die Erhöhung des Auferstandenen zur Rechten Gottes," in *Anfänge der Christologie* (eds. C. Breytenbach and H. Paulsen, Chr. Gerber; Göttingen, 1991), 43–73.

THE COMMUNITY RULE (1QS): COLUMN 4*

Takamitsu Muraoka

1QS IV,1 עולמים ‏ועדי‎[א]] The restoration at the beginning of the line as in the editions by Charlesworth and García Martínez is preferable to Licht's עדי ועלמים: there are traces of a letter and space enough for two letters.

בכול עלילותיה ירצה] The poetic noun, a synonym of מעשה (|| מעללים Ps 106:39), פעל (|| עלילות Ps 77:13), פעלה, occurring as many as 24 times in BH, is mostly used in pl. (sg. twice only). It is one of the favourite words of Ezekiel (8x), who always uses it with negative connotation: "evil deeds, practices," which manifestly does not apply here. Here the noun forms a parallelism with דרך pl. later, just as in Ps 103:7, though with God as their author and with salvation-historical connotation. Semantically closer to our text would be combinations in the prophetic language with unmistakable moral, ethical connotation: Ezek 14:22, 23 את דרכם ואת עלילותם, 24:14 כדרכיך וכעלילותיך, שפטוך‎ 20:44 כדרכיכם הרעים וכעלילותיכם הנשחתות. See further Ezek 20:43; 36:17, 19. Let us note that Jeremiah's equivalent is מַעֲלָלים: thus Jer 4:18 את דרכיכם ואת מעלליכם 7:5, דרכך ומעלליך. Also 7:5; 18:11; 17:10; 23:22; 25:5; 26:13; 32:19; 35:15.

The collocation of the verb with ב, whether c. pers. or c. rei, is common enough in BH, but one with עלילות is a hapax. One may note that in Prov 3:2 אהב and רצה occur in parallelism.

אהת תעב סודה לעד] The antithetical parallelism of שנא—אהב is a commonplace, whereas that with תעב as its negative pole as here is not. A rare example is Job 19:19 תעבוני כל־מתי סודי וזה אהבתי נהפכו־בי where the noun, though perhaps meaning something different—"people in my close circle"—, happens to occur as in our text. By contrast, the synonymic parallelism with שנא as here is attested at Ps 5:7; 119:163.

---

* I am sure that Emmanuel Tov understands better than any other the value of a thorough, philological-linguistic study of an ancient document, though such a branch of "fundamental science" is not everybody's cup of tea. Its practitioners can only get on in their work with a reliable edition of texts, for which Emmanuel, with his uncommon dedication, determination, insight, organisational skills and scholarship has put all of us in incalculable debt.

Charlesworth[1] wonders whether סודה is a scribal error for מודה = מאד, an unwarranted suggestion.

The four verbs—אהב, ירצה, תעב, שנא—are in two different tenses. The three other than ירצה can best be taken as suffix conjugation forms with stative force. It is not necessary, therefore, to attempt to reflect this morphological variation in an English translation as Charlesworth does: ". . . loves . . ., taking pleasure . . ."[2] We have here a series of four, coordinated verbal clauses in parallelism, between which there is no logical subordination.

1QS IV,2 להאיר בלבב איש] "to enlighten man's mind." In an earlier study I argued against the standard, non-sensical translation at 1QS II,3 יאר לבכה with "enlighten the heart."[3] The phrase here, however, is slightly different, being prefixed by the preposition Beth. A closer parallel may be found at 4QShir[b] 18.2.8 האיר אלהים דעת בינה בלבבי, cf. also 1QS XI,5 אור בלבבי מרזי פלאו. In other words, we may be dealing with an ellipsis of a direct object. So Licht: את אור הדעת.[4]

לפחד לבבו במשפטי אל] "to awaken awe in his heart by means of God's judgements." In BH the verb פחד, in whatever *binyan*, mostly has to do with terror and dread. Only very rarely it is used as a near synonym of ירא with the manifestly religious colouring of *awe*: e.g., Hos 3:5 וּפָחֲדוּ אֶל־יהוה אֱלֹהֵינוּ and Mic 7:17, וּפָחֲדוּ אֶל־יהוה. Cf. also Isa 60:5 וּפָחַד וְרָחַב לְבָבֵךְ. The noun פַּחַד, however, is more frequently used with this connotation, in combinations with יהוה, אלהים, and especially as פחד יצחק.

---

[1] J. M. Charlesworth, ed., *The Dead Sea Scrolls: Hebrew, Aramaic and Greek Texts with English Translation, Vol. I, Rule of the Community and Related Documents* (Tübingen/Louisville: J. C. B. Mohr/Westminster John Knox, 1994), 16.

The following translations/editions are also cited by the translator/editor's name only: M. Wise, M. Abegg, & E. Cook, *The Dead Sea Scrolls: A New Translation* (San Francisco: Harper, 1996).

F. García Martínez & E. J. C. Tigchelaar eds., *The Dead Sea Scrolls Study Edition* (2 vols.; Leiden: E. J. Brill, 1997).

A. R. C. Leaney, *The Rule of Qumran and its Meaning: Introduction, Translation and Commentary* (London: S.C.M., 1966).

E. Lohse, *Die Texte aus Qumran in Hebräisch und Deutsch* (4th ed.; Darmstadt; Wissenschaftliche Buchgesellschaft, 1986).

G. Vermes, *The Complete Dead Sea Scrolls in English* (Harmondsworth: Penguin Books, 1997).

[2] Charlesworth, *Dead Sea Scrolls*, 17.

[3] Muraoka, "Notae Qumranicae philologicae (2)," *AbrN* 33 (1995): 55–73, esp. 60–62.

[4] J. Licht, *The Rule Scroll: A Scroll from the Wilderness of Judaea: 1QS · 1QSa · 1QSb* (The Bialik Institute: Jerusalem, 1965) [Hebrew], 95.

The preposition Bet in במשפטי אל is best taken as instrumental. It is hardly an object marker: "fear of the precepts of God" (Leaney), "respect for the precepts of God" (García Martínez), "to make . . . fear the judgements . . ." (Charlesworth), 'the fear of the laws of God' (Vermes), "to fear the laws of God" (Wise-Abegg-Cook), "sein Herz in Furcht zu versetzen vor den Gerichten Gottes" (Lohse). The verb פחד nor its synonym ירא takes -ב to indicate the object of fear. The only instance, Jer 51:46 תיראו בשמועה is one of an occasion or ground for fear: "on account of the rumour." A direct object is understood: "to awaken awe *for God* in his heart . . ."

1QS IV,3 [רוח ענוה ואורך אפים ורוב רחמים וטוב עולמים] "a spirit of humility, long-suffering and plenty of compassion and eternal kindness." The noun רחמים, a plurale tantum in BH, when used with a quantifier רַב or רֹב, is always used as an attribute of God as at 2 Sam 24:14 רבים רחמיו and Ps 51:3 כרב רחמיך. It is as if the author is exhorting us to aim at this divine dimension just as we are commanded to be holy as He is holy.

The same applies to another virtue listed here, namely long-suffering or patience. In BH and QH both אֹרֶךְ אַפַּיִם and אֶרֶךְ אַפַּיִם is normally an attribute of God, and so also in Sir 5:4; all the exceptions are from the sapiential literature, Prov 14:29; 15:18; 16:32; 25:15.[5] See also an exhoratation to the righteous at 1QH^a IX,36–37: האריכו אפים. In the New Testament it is as commonly applied to humans as at Eph 4:2 μετὰ μακροθυμίας ἀντεχόμενοι ἀλλήλων 'bearing with one another with patience.'

The abstract noun of the last phrase, "eternal kindness," is also, in BH, essentially a divine attribute when indicating a moral virtue: e.g., Neh 9:25f. טוּבְךָ הגדול, 9:35 טוב הרב. The affinity with the anthropology of the Apostle Paul is striking: Gal 5:22–23 ὁ δὲ καρπὸς τοῦ πνεύματός ἐστιν ἀγάπη χαρὰ εἰρήνη, μακροθυμία χρηστότης ἀγαθωσύνη, πίστις πραΰτης ἐγκράτεια 'the fruits of the Spirit, on the other hand, are love, joy, peace, long-suffering, kindness, generosity, faith, humility and self-restraint.'

The plural עולמים, rather rare in BH (12 times in all), when used attributively as here in the sense of "enduring, everlasting" is best illustrated by Dan 9:24, צֶדֶק עֹלָמִים.

---

[5] Cf. 1QM VI,12 ארוכי רוח and Sir 5:11 (Ms B) ארך רוח (both of men).

I agree with Wernberg-Møller, who takes רוח as a *nomen regens* of each of the following noun phrases, not only of ענוה,[6] and as I argued elsewhere, the noun רוח here, just as in 1QS III,8 רוח יושר וענוה, should be taken in the sense of a spiritual principle, not some transcendental, divine being.[7]

הכמת נבורה] 'empowering wisdom' or 'mighty wisdom.' Wernberg-Møller's *wonderful wisdom* is unacceptable.[8] That the two words occur sometimes co-ordinated does not necessarily mean that they are synonymous. At CD XIII,8 the word נבורה does not mean "wonder": נבורות פלאו should be rendered "his wonderful deeds of might" and the phrase is parallel with מעשי אל. The same objection holds for Licht's contention.[9] What would one do with a statement such as Qoh 9:16 טובה הכמה מנבורה?[10]

מאמנת בכול מעשי אל] "trusting in all the deeds of God" *Pace* Yalon, who argues that מאמנת here is pu'al, meaning "supported" (נתמכת), and has to do with strength and assured existence,[11] one cannot fail to notice the parallel נשענת, hardly a real passive nip'al, cf. *sustained* (Wise-Abegg-Cook). Our author must be talking about wisdom the strength of which has its source in God's mighty deeds.[12] The community members are reminded that the requisite empowering, enabling wisdom does not lie within themselves, but must be sought from above. Thus Lohse's vocalisation (מַאֲמֶנֶת) and his translation (*vertraut*) are to be followed.

1QS IV,4 רוח דעת בכול מחשבת מעשה] "a spirit inculcating in the entire practical philosophy." This phrase is parallel with the following מחשבת קודש. The combination as a whole is innovative. The *nomen regens* is mostly taken as meaning something like "a plan, intention." Given the parallelism, Charlesworth's translation is not felicitous: "all work upon which he is intent . . . a holy intention." Nor am I happy

---

[6] P. Wernberg-Møller, *The Manual of Discipline Translated and Annotated with an Introduction* (Leiden: E. J. Brill, 1957), 74.

[7] Muraoka, "Notae Qumranicae philologicae (3)," *AbrN* 35 (1998): 47–64, esp. 52–53.

[8] Wernberg-Møller, *The Manual of Discipline*, 26, 74.

[9] Licht, *The Rule Scroll*, 95.

[10] A phrase in the reverse order also occurs: Sir 42:21 (Ms M) נבורת הכמה τὰ μεγάλεια τῆς σοφίας αὐτοῦ "the mighty works of his wisdom."

[11] H. Yalon, *Studies in the Dead Sea Scrolls: Philological Essays (1949–1952)* [Hebrew] (Jerusalem: Qiryat Sepher, 1967), 80.

[12] There is absolutely no good reason for taking recourse to Syriac or Arabic, as does Wernberg-Møller (*The Manual of Discipline*, 75), in order to arrive at *mysteries* as a translation of מעשים here.

with the use of the plural by García Martínez: "all the plans of action . . . holy plans." מחשבת can mean "a thought" or "an act of thinking," hence my proposed translation. The first phrase refers to an entire thought on how one ought to translate his faith into practical deeds, whereas the second phrase possibly refers to a religious philosophy, systematic theology, or alternatively one's thought about liturgy and cult.

The preposition Beth is best understood as a marker of a direct object of a verbal noun דעת. Cf. 1QS VIII,18 אל ידע בכול עצתם; 1QH^a XVII,9 ידעתי באמתכה. The use of *in* in most current English translations is misleading: 'knowledge of' is to be preferred.

מחשבת קודש] an equally innovative collocation. Though Licht (96) justly refers to מחשבת קודשכה at 1QS XI,19 it does not necessarily follow that מעשה here refers to God's deeds. On the contrary, the suffix on קודש does not seem to govern the entire construct phrase, but only the *nomen rectum*, as is indicated by the juxtaposed phrases: נפלאותיכה, עומק רזיכה: it is about God's sanctity, His mysteries and His wonders.

מחשבת קודש ביצר סמוך] "religious philosophy (practised) by means of a trustful creature." יצר סמוך appears to be a key phrase in the Qumran anthropology. It is thus important to understand precisely what it means. The second term is mostly taken to mean "steadfastness," "with a steadfast purpose" (Charlesworth), for instance. Licht (96) has correctly located the source of this phrase in Isa 26:3 יֵצֶר סָמוּךְ תִּצֹּר שָׁלוֹם שָׁלוֹם כִּי בְךָ בָּטוּחַ, which he has interpreted as an expression of trust in God on the part of the pious, an interpretation well-grounded on account of the parallel בָּטוּחַ. Though both סָמוּךְ and בָּטוּחַ are vocalised as passive participles, they are pseudo-participles and indicate in fact a result arising from an action already undertaken and as such they are an expression of an attitude of a person who has already placed his trust in his God. In other words, it does not signify a disposition or inclination. Cf. the Greek perfect participle πεποιθώς meaning precisely the same thing as our Hebrew participles here and derived from πείθειν "to persuade." So understood it forms an excellent parallelism with the preceding מאמנת and נשענת.

The collocation יצר סמוך occurs also elsewhere in the DSS: e.g., 1QS VIII,3 (|| רוח נשברה), 1QH X,9; ibid. X,36. The *nomen regens*, יצר, seems to mean "that which has been created, creature," as in a highly frequent collocation יצר חמר or יצר עפר in 1QH, e.g. IX,21; XXI,16, though a lexeme does not have to mean the same thing in its every occurrence. A rendering such as *purpose* seems to be unduly

influenced by the noun as used in Gen 6:5 יצר מחשבת לבו, its derivatives in QH itself such as 1QS V,5 מחשבת יצרו; 4Q370 I,3 וישפטם
כ[כול]דרכיהם וכמחשבות יצר לבם, and its use in post-biblical Hebrew
with יצר הטוב and יצר הרע. Such an analysis is practically precluded
in 1QH^a IX,35 והיו ליצר סמוך where a translation such as "seid fes-
ten Sinnes" (Lohse) or "be of staunch purpose" is rather unlikely.

1QS IV, 5 [רוב חסדים על כול בני אמת "plenty of kindnesses towards
all the men of truth." The closest parallel occurs in Isa 63:7 כרחמיו
וכרב חסדיו. The significant difference is, however, that there the phrase
refers to God's deeds. In the Bible (and the DSS) the plural form
is mostly so used. Rare exceptions are Isa 55:3 חסדי דוד הנאמנים;
2 Chr 6:42 אל־תֵּחֲמַח חַסְדֵי אֲשֶׁר עָשִׂיתִי; Neh 13:14 חסדי דוד עבדך; 2 Chr
32:32 ויתר דברי חזקיהו וחסדיו, similarly ibid. 35:26. It is to be noted
that the plural form as applied to human deeds is confined to late
books, which reminds us of a standing phrase in Rabbinic Hebrew,
גְּמִלוּת חֲסָדִים "performing of kind acts (by a man to a fellow-man),"
a phrase which harks back to the above-mentioned Isaianic passage:
חסדי יהוה .. אֲשֶׁר־גְּמָלָנוּ יהוה, though the actor is God. Here again, our
Qumran text, by using the basically same phrase as a line earlier
(רוב חסדו), exhorts the community members that their mutual relationship should reflect the way their God deals with them.

The preposition על here is probably by analogy of its use with
רַחֲמִים, a synonym of חסדים. See, for instance, Ps 145:9 רחמיו על כל
מעשיו, cf. ibid. 103:13 כְּרַחֵם אָב עַל בָּנִים רִחַם יהוה עַל יְרֵאָיו. The collocation עשה חסד in the Bible usually takes either עם or אֶת 'with' with
the sole exception at 1 Sam 20:8 עשית חסד על עבדך.[13]

טהרת כבוד a difficult phrase. The *nomen rectum* is generally taken as
an equivalent of an adjective as in הַר קֹדֶשׁ "a holy mountain," thus
Lohse's *glänzende Reinheit* and Charlesworth's *glorious purity*. The difficulty
is, however, that at least in the Bible, when the abstract noun is
used in such a way, it usually refers to outward, visible splendour
as in its applications to throne (1 Sam 2:8), chariots (Isa 22:18), trees
(Ezek 31:18) and the like, whereas here it is supposed to be qualifying an inner, spiritual feature. Wernberg-Møller's proposal to emend
the word to read עבודה "cult, worship" is therefore rather attractive,
though the spelling without a feminine ending and the resulting
incongruence with the following masculine מתעב cannot be as lightly
dismissed as he does.[14]

---

[13] Cf. LXX μετὰ τοῦ δούλου σου.
[14] Wernberg-Møller, *The Manual of Discipline*, 77.

[מתעב כול גלולי נדה] In contrast to its synonyms שׂנא and מאס is תעב, both as a verb and a noun (תּוֹעֵבָה), used in the Bible very often with reference to cultic, religious or ethical matters. Even where תעב as a verb takes a person as its direct object as in Ps 106:40 ויתעב יהוה את־נחלתו they are abhorred by God on account of their deeds. The only exception seems to be Ps 107:18 כל־אכל תתעב נפשם. The use of the verb in our 1QS passage is in line with this general semantic contour of it in BH.

Licht's (96) suggestion that מתעב is an Aramaising infinitive is rather unlikely. It would then be a *Qal*, [= *peʿal* in Aramaic]. In BH, however, this verb, which is rather frequent, is never attested in *Qal*, but only in piʿel, puʿal, *hipʿil* and *nipʿal*. A concordance by Habermann[15] lists 13 attestations of תעב as a verb, none of which can be taken as unequivocally *Qal*, although the fact that its *nipʿal*, both in BH and QH, is passive in force would leave the possibility of its use in *Qal* open. If מתעב here is a *piʿel* participle, as most scholars seem to think, its subject must be identified. Wernberg-Møller (77) invokes a *construction ad sensum*, "the virtual subject being the pious man." Here one ought to bear in mind that starting at line 3 ורוח the syntax and style of the passage began to turn a little loose, whereas earlier the properties of the spirit possessed by men of truth had been described by means of the infinitive: לפחד, להאיר. A better alternative has been suggested by Lohse (12) to adopt a variant reading מתעבת found in a 4Q fragment of the document, namely 4Q257 2 i, 2. With its repeated preposition *of* set off by a comma from the preceding, the English translations by García Martínez and Vermes assumes as many as six noun phrases as nomina recta of רוח at line 4, which definitely makes for rather awkward and heavy-footed syntax and style not quite in keeping with our author of generally elegant style. Although the noun phrases following the first construct phrase with רוח may be regarded as related or affiliated to what is expressed by the construct phrase, the strict syntactical analysis of the whole series would hardly tolerate a serial accumulation of so many noun phrases dependent on the initial רוח. The presence of two infinitives absolute in the series, הצנע לכת בערמת כול וחבא לאמת רזי דעת (lines 5–6), also speaks against such an analysis; for the use of such an infinitive as an equivalent of a *nomen rectum* is very suspect.[16]

---

[15] A. M. Habermann, *Megilloth Midbar Yehuda: The Scrolls from the Judaean Desert* (Machbaroth Lasifruth, 1959) [Hebrew].

[16] See P. Joüon – T. Muraoka, *A Grammar of Biblical Hebrew* (Rome: Pontifical Biblical Institute, 1993), § 123 *c*.

By contrast, in translating another equally long series introduced by
רוח at line 3 García Martínez and Vermes—at two different places—
repeat the preposition only once. On the other hand, the presence
of the two series one after the other and both headed by the key-
word רוח, describing virtues and properties, is certainly a feature of
the above-mentioned accomplished style of our author. Most translations[17] construe (ת)מתעב with a feminine noun in the construct state
טהרת, which is reasonable. It would mean that נלולי נדה is irreconcilable with, and totally alien to, טהרה, let alone טהרת כבוד.

What does the construct phrase נלולי נדה signify here? In the Bible
the nomen regens, rather frequent (45x), is a plurale tantum—so in
QH[18]—and highly frequent in the books of Kings and Ezekiel. It
mostly denotes idols as tangible objects of illicit worship. As far as
I know, there is no archaeological evidence suggesting that Qumran
secretarians worshipped such objects. Is this a prohibition against
importing or bringing such objects into the community? Or a polemic
against the contemporary, mainstream Judaism? The use of the noun
elsewhere in QH, however, points to a metaphorical or non-concrete
meaning of it, a linguistic manifestation of the intellectualisation and
spiritualisation of the Jewish religion as conceived by the Qumranites.
Elsewhere, starting from 1QS II,8 ארור בנלולי לבו, I have shown[19]
that this late semantic development had already been captured by
the Septuagint translator of the book of Ezekiel, in which one finds
an example such as 14:3 האנשים האלה העלו נלוליהם על לבם ומכשול עונם
ישים נכח פניהם, which hardly implies that people carried idols around
on their chests.[20] See further CD-B XX, 9 שמו נלולים על לבם. This
also accords with the way the *nomen rectum* here, נדה, is used, with

---

[17] An exception is "glorious purity combined with visceral hatred of impurity in
its every guise" by Wise, Abegg and Cook (130). The syntactical analysis as reflected
in Charlesworth's translation is rather unreliable: ". . . and a glorious purity, loathing
all unclean idols, and walking . . . about everything, concealing the truth . . ." The
morphosyntactical status of the three -*ing* forms is not clear: Are they participles or
gerunds and who are their agents? The punctuation is not illuminating, and note
an equally equivocal use of another -*ing* form, "*leaning*" (line 4).

[18] A highly rare singular occurs once in Sir 30:18.

[19] Muraoka, "Notae (2)," 68.

[20] LXX: οἱ ἄνδρες οὗτοι ἔθεντο τὰ διανοήματα αὐτῶν ἐπὶ τὰς καρδίας αὐτῶν . . .
Thus the widely accepted translation of our 1QS passage with *idols*, *Götzen* etc. needs
to be altered, and for that matter, our Hebrew dictionaries are also in need of revision in this respect. On the Septuagint in this regard, see further T. Muraoka, "Hosea
IV in the Septuagint version," *Annual of the Japanese Institute of Biblical Studies* 9 (1983):
40–41. Licht (96) justly mentioned Ezek 36:25 where טמאה is parallel with נלולים.

no reference to a highly specific application of the notion of impurity, namely menstruation. Would a rendering such as "impure ideas" be far-fetched? The phrase is possibly an ellipsis for נלולי נדה אשר על לב.

הצנע לכת בערמת כול] The first half is further expanded at V,3–4 יחד, וענוה צדקה ומשפט ואהבת חסד והצנע לכת בכל דרכיהם לעשות אמת, of course based on the famous verse in Micah (6:8). What is striking here is the following prepositional phrase of mode. The noun עָרְמָה as well as its related noun עֹרֶם, adjective עָרוּם and verb often carry a negative connotation of slyness or craftiness. Significantly in the book of Proverbs, however, where they are rather frequent, the connotation is consistently positive: e.g., 19:25 וּפֶתִי יַעֲרִם. There is even a collocation; הָכְמָה עָרוּם (14:8). The same applies to QH: see, e.g., 1QS X,25 בערמת דעת || בעצת תושיה ;X,9 ערמה לפתיים "prudence for the simple-minded" (cf. Prov 19:25 mentioned above); CD-A II,4 ערמה ודעת. This linguistic affinity with the language of the book of Proverbs is not a mere accidental play of words or association, but goes a little deeper. The book of Proverbs attests to the beginning of an important development in Ancient Israel which saw a vital connection between wisdom and religiosity, a way of thinking further cultivated in the book of Ben Sira.[21] No wonder that this contemporary sapiential book was on the list of essential reading for the sectarians, not just among later freedom fighters at Massada. The use of כול as a *nomen rectum* is unusual; the phrase probably means "all-pervasive prudence, prudence in every respect." Humility and prudence or wisdom are not mutually exclusive at all. On the contrary it is precisely those who submit themselves to the yoke of the kingdom of heaven who are the most prudent.

I do not see any compelling reason for departing from the traditional interpretation of the verb הצניע, "to conduct oneself humbly." It is granted that the verb in Rabbinic Hebrew and Jewish Aramaic means "to keep in reservation, conceal." But to apply such a meaning to the verb in our passage on the ground that Aramaic was the mother tongue of its author does not convince any more. Moreover, such a comparative semantics amounts to a semantic circus, for when used with the verb of walking as here "walk with reservation" can only refer to a diffident, not unduly self-confident demeanour, whereas the notion of reservation associated with the verb in Rabbinic Hebrew

---

[21] For instance, in Chapter 6 where we note תתחכם || חערם (vs. 32).

and Jewish Aramaic has to do with that of preserving things for future in cases of emergency or urgent needs or for some other use. To attempt to see some link between our passage and Isa 42:3 לֹא יְכַבֶּנָּה לֵאמת on the supposition that our author was not capable of keeping ה and כ without a dagesh lene apart[22] is a sheer affront to his linguistic competence.[23]

1QS IV,6 [וחבא לאמת רזי דעת] The first word is best understood as an infinitive absolute in *pi'el* parallel with הצנע. Though the verb often carries a negative connotation of stealth and evasion, it is also used in the sense of providing temporary protection from danger until a storm passes: e.g., Rahab's action (Josh 6:17) or that of Obadiah sheltering 100 prophets (1 Kgs 18:4). Here in our passage, too, one need not think of sectarians keeping the divine revelation to themselves, refusing to share it with others, nor of a hierarchy among them with second-class members barred from full access to the revelation, but it is rather about sheltering it or protecting it from corruption or contamination. The preposition Lamed of לאמת is probably a marker of direct object. Cf. 1QH^a XIII, 11–12 ותורתכה חבתה ב[ל]י ע[ל]ד קץ הגלות ישעכה לי.

[אלה סודי רוח לבני אמת תבל] According to Licht (96) the last noun is a *nomen rectum* qualifying the preceding אמת alone, referring to one specific kind of truth, an analysis which I find rather attractive, particularly in view of a related phrase later in this column, ואז תצא לנצח אמת תבל (line 19). There is little justification for analysing תבל in the latter case as a sort of adverbial accusative of place and translate, e.g., "Then shall come forth for ever truth upon the earth."[24] An alternative syntactic analysis would make the preceding construct phrase as a whole—בני אמת—a *nomen regens* dependent on תבל, somewhat like בית מקדש יהוה or כלי מלחמתנו, this latter translatable as "our weapon," and not "the weapon of our war." Only in the preceding line the members of the community were designated by this phrase.

---

[22] So Wernberg-Møller, *The Manual of Discipline*, 79. This is an issue separate from the generally recognised weakening of gutturals in QH: see E. Qimron, *The Hebrew of the Dead Sea Scrolls* (Atlanta: Scholars Press, 1986), 25–26.

[23] See Joüon—Muraoka, *A Grammar*, § 5 *k*.

[24] Leaney, *The Rule of Qumran*, 154, whereas Leaney's translation of the first passage reads: "these are the counsels of the spirit for the sons of truth on earth." The preposition *in* enclosed within the brackets in his English translation (in both passages) suggests that García Martínez also takes the Hebrew noun as an adverbial complement.

Note also a synonymous phrase אנשי (ה)אמת at 1QHᵃ VI,2 and 1QpHab VII,10. Our author is addressing the true members of the kingdom of heaven in their earthly existence (בעולם הזה). Note especially the contrast between the two spheres of existence at 1QHᵃ XI,35–36 מלחמת גבורי שמים תשוט בתבל. In the end, the general thought expressed here may be the same whichever syntactical analysis one might adopt, though the adverbial analysis is highly questionable.

[פקודת כול הולכי בה למרפא Another key-word, פקדה, is mostly trans- lated with *visitation* or, in German, *Heimsuchung*.²⁵ In the Bible it occurs about 15 times, where it is concerned with an action by God and so translated traditionally. What needs to be noted, however, is that with a single exception (Job 10:12) the connotation is negative, namely punitive, divine punishment. In QH this action takes place at a certain, predetermined time, mostly in future (eschatological), as shown by phrases such as: 1QS III,18 עד מועד פקודתו; IV,18–19 לכול קצי עולם ופקודת עד כי אתה הכינותמה מקדם במועד פקודה; 1QHᵃ V,15 עולם; CD-A VII,21 אלה מלטו בקץ הפקודה הראשון (already past). The very fact that a few lines later in our column of 1QS the destiny of the other group of mankind is described with basically identical word- ing shows that the noun is essentially neutral and that whether the consequences are going to turn out to be favourable or unfavourable is purely a function of the general context: 1QS IV,11–12 כול מלאכי חבל ופקודת כול הולכי בה לרוב נגעים ביד.²⁶ One wonders whether a ren- dering such as *stocktaking*, *evaluation* better expresses what is meant by the noun.²⁷

For this blessed group such an evaluation leads to, or results in מרפא. Since there is no question of their having been ill or injured, the verbal noun cannot really mean "healing" in the literal, med- ical sense as in most current translations. 1QS IV,18–19 במועד פקודה ישמידנה may be taken to suggest that מרפא is an antonym of השמדה

---

²⁵ An exception is "the reward" of García Martínez.

²⁶ The choice of "the visitation" by Marcía Martínez here, in contrast to "the reward" earlier, suggests that the noun *visitation* in Contemporary English, when understood as God's act, tends to be negative in connotation. Cf. also "a graceful visitation . . . the judgement" in the translation of Wise—Abegg—Cook. My copy of *Duden Deutsches Universal Wörterbuch A-Z* (Mannheim, 1989²) defines *Heimsuchung* as: "Schicksalsschlag, den man als Prüfung od. Strafe von Gott erfindet," so again not neutral. So if Qumran scholarship wishes to interest the wider general public as well, we had better abandon *visitation, Heimsuchung* etc.

²⁷ At Job 31:14 the LXX, which often uses ἐπισκοπή to render our Hebrew word, uses also ἔτασις 'examination, enquiry' in parallelism to ἐπισκοπή.

"destruction, annihilaiton," or a synonym of להחיות "to keep alive, to allow to live on." Note the following parallelism, again in the book of Proverbs: כי חיים הם למצאיהם ולכל בשרו מַרְפֵּא and at 13:17 מרפא is an antonym of רַע 'calamity, disaster, thus an antithesis of what follows מרפא in our 1QS passage.

1QS IV,7 ורוב שלום באורך ימים] The word שלום is universally taken to mean 'peace,' thus שָׁלוֹם. I wonder, however, whether the phrase can mean 'generous remuneration,' hence שִׁלּוּם. I have argued else-where[28] for such an analysis particularly when the noun occurs in conjunction with, or in the vicinity of, פקודה. Cf. Isa 57:18 "I have seen their ways, but I will heal them (וּרְפָאתִיו); I will lead them and repay (אֲשַׁלֵּם) them with comfort" (NRSV). Then our lemma may be rendered: "and generous remuneration in the form of longevity."

---

[28] Muraoka, "Notae (3)," 60.

APPROACHES TO BIBLICAL EXEGESIS IN QUMRAN LITERATURE*

Bilhah Nitzan

Pericopes containing biblical exegesis have been discerned in the Qumran texts since the discovery of the Dead Sea Scrolls in 1947. These have been observed in the versions of the biblical text, in the *pesharim* of biblical texts, and in most of the variegated texts and genres from Qumran, both sectarian and non-sectarian. Systematic study of the characteristic methods of biblical interpretation found in the Qumran scrolls has been accomplished in part, particularly in the *Pesharim* scrolls,[1] in pericopes of homilies using proof texts,[2] in the *Temple Scroll*,[3] and in reworked Pentateuchal texts.[4] However, this

---

* I am grateful to Dr. Meira Polliack for her valuable suggestions regarding the content and style of this article.

[1] See K. Elliger, *Studien zum Habakuk-Kommentar vom Toten Meer* (BHT 15; Tübingen: J. C. B. Mohr, 1953), 127–64; W. H. Brownlee, *The Midrash Pesher of Habakkuk*, SBLMS 24 (Missoula: Scholars Press, 1979); M. P. Horgan, *Pesharim: Qumran Interpretations of Biblical Books* (CBQMS 8; Washington DC: Catholic Biblical Association, 1979), 244–47; I. Rabinowits, "Pesher/Pittaron, Its Biblical Meaning and its Significance in the Qumran Literature," *RevQ* 8 (1973): 219–32; B. Nitzan, מגילת פשר חבקוק ממגילות מדבר יהודה (Jerusalem: Bialik Institute, 1986), 27–103; G. J. Brooke, *Exegesis at Qumran: 4QFlorilegium in Its Jewish Context* (Sheffield: JSOT, 1985); M. J. Bernstein, "Introductory Formulas for Citation and Re-Citation of Biblical Verses in the Qumran Pesharim," *DSD* 1 (1994): 30–70.

[2] J. Fitzmyer, "The Use of Explicit Old Testament Quotations in Qumran Literature and in the New Testament," *Essays on Semitic Background of the New Testament* (SBLSBS 5; Missoula: Scholars Press, 1974), 3–58; G. Vermes, "Bible Interpretation at Qumran," *ErIsr* 20 (Jerusalem, 1989): 184*–91*; idem, "Biblical Proof-Texts in Qumran Literature," *JSS* 34 (1989): 493–508.

[3] Y. Yadin, *The Temple Scroll* (Jerusalem: The Israel Exploration Society, 1983), I.71–88 (Hebrew original: מגילת המקדש [Jerusalem: The Israel Exploration Society, 1977], I.60–73).

[4] E. Tov, "Biblical Texts as Reworked in Some Qumran Manuscripts with Special Attention to 4QRP and 4Q ParaGen-Exod," *The Community of the Renewed Covenant* (eds. E. Ulrich and J. VanderKam; Notre Dame, IA: University of Notre Dame Press, 1994), 113–34; idem, "The Textual Status of 4Q364–367 (4QPP)," *The Madrid Qumran Congress* (ed. J. Trebolle Barrera and L. Vegas Montaner; STDJ 11; Leiden: Brill, 1992), I. 43–82; E. Tov and S. White, "4Q364–367. 4QReworked Pentateuch[b-e] and 365a. 4QTemple?, *Qumran Cave 4.VIII, Parabiblical Texts Part 1* (ed. H. Attridge et al.; *DJD* 13; Oxford: Clarendon, 1994), 187–96.

research has concentrated on certain specific texts. A comprehensive, systematic study of approaches and methods of biblical exegesis in Qumran remains to be done.

Due to the accelerated publication over the past decade of the
scrolls from Cave 4, thanks to Emanuel Tov's direction and man-
agement, the entire Qumran corpus is now available in authoritative scientific editions. Additional genres of Qumran literature
incorporating biblical exegesis are also known today. In addition to
the *Pesharim* of biblical texts and the exegetical use of biblical proof
texts for sectarian ideas, we are acquainted with parabiblical texts,
including scrolls of the reworked Pentateuch, with apocryphal and
pseudepigraphic compositions, with halakhic compositions, and with
other genres. Thus, study of the interpretive approaches to the Bible
in Qumran may be further elaborated and even reach a comprehensive classification.

Methods of biblical interpretation may be investigated with regard
to contents, textual criticism, and form criticism through use of conventional categories of biblical exegesis, but while maintaining openness towards new categories used in Qumran literature. Synchronically,
one may engage in a comparative investigation as against the exegetical methods used in the ancient translations of the Bible, with those
used in the apocryphal and Jewish-Hellenistic literature from the
Second Temple period, and with the ancient tannaitic homilies.
Diachronically, Qumran exegetical types may be studied in relation
to other Jewish sectarian exegetical types, such as those of the Middle
Ages and especially the ancient Karaite exegesis.

The importance and purpose of a systematic study of biblical interpretation in Second Temple texts is to promote our knowledge of
the history of biblical exegesis. A comprehensive study of the categories and methods of biblical exegesis in the entire corpus of the
Qumran scrolls would be very extensive, far too wide for one study.
However, an attempt to build the foundations for such a systematic
research project should be undertaken, at least of some of the interpretive approaches and methods used in the Qumran scrolls.

My first attempt to build a classification of biblical exegesis, in
terms of both formal and stylistic-critical aspects and those of content, was undertaken in my book *Pesher Habakkuk*, published in Hebrew
in 1986.[5] During the last decade I have continued, throughout my

---

[5] Nitzan, פשר הבקוק, 27–103.

teaching of the Qumran scrolls, to deal with the approaches and methods of biblical interpretation. Following the recent publication of the Qumran scrolls, and their editors' suggestions, my teaching has encompassed variegated genres. These include: some of the para-biblical texts published in the *DJD* series, such as the texts entitled *Reworked Pentateuch* (e.g. 4Q364–367)[6] and some of those texts which dealt in a freer manner with selected pericopes of biblical texts (e.g., the 4Q252–254 *Commentary on Genesis and Malachi*,[7] the 4Q370 *Admonition Based on the Flood*,[8] the 4Q378–379 *Apocryphon of Joshua*,[9] and others). Following Fitzmyer's and Vermes's analysis of biblical quotations as proof texts for sectarian ideas, I have dealt with the form and contents of homiletic pericopes in the *Damascus Documents*. Most recently, I dealt with the exegetical methods used in the *Temple Scroll*, following the suggestions of Yadin, Milgrom, Schiffman, Wise, Shemesh and others. The latter research was conducted with the able help of my research assistant, Jacob Nachmias, thanks to the help of the Internal Research Fund of Tel-Aviv University.

In this early stage of our study of the approaches and methods of biblical interpretation used in the Qumran scrolls, the following system of classification seems a reasonable hypothesis. In terms of analysis of contents, we may distinguish between an approach that tends to elucidate the biblical text according to its context and history, and one which attempts to explain the coherence and relevance of the Bible in terms of the situation of later generations.[10] Thus, types of exegesis based upon the Bible's own context and history is visible primarily in some of the reworked Pentateuch texts (e.g. 4Q158, and 4Q364–367). The type of exegesis concerning the relevance of the Bible to a later reality is apparent in the *Pesharim* scrolls and in the sectarian homilies using biblical verses as proof texts for sectarian ideas (e.g. the *Damascus Documents*, the *Rule Scroll*, and the *War Scroll*). Some scrolls, however, are guided by both approaches, especially such halakhic texts as the *Temple Scroll*.

---

[6] See above, n. 4.

[7] See G. J. Brooke, "Commentary on Genesis and Malachi, 4Q252–254," *Qumran Cave 4.XVII, Parabiblical Texts, Part 3* (ed. G. J. Brooke et al.; *DJD* 22; Oxford: Clarendon, 1996), 185–236, and the rich bibliography mentioned there.

[8] C. Newsom, "4Q370. Admonition on the Flood," *Qumran Cave 4.XIV Parabiblical Texts Part 2* (ed. M. Broshi et al.; *DJD* 19; Oxford: Clarendon, 1995), 85–98.

[9] C. Newsom, "4Q378–379. 4QApocryphon of Joshua," *Qumran Cave 4.XVII, Parabiblical Texts, Part 3* (*DJD* 22; Oxford: Clarendon, 1996), 237–88.

[10] P. Szondy, *Introduction to Literary Hermeneutics* (Cambridge: Cambridge University Press, 1995), 1–13.

From the viewpoint of form criticism, one may distinguish between those approaches that integrated the exegetical elements within the running biblical text, and those which separated between the biblical text and its commentary. This classification may partly correlate to the content of the biblical text, as may be seen in the aforementioned examples. Nevertheless, these scrolls, as in their form they appear to be specific versions of continuous biblical texts, require careful textual analysis so as to identify the exegetical elements within the biblical text and isolate their interpretive purpose and methods. Moreover, linguistic criticism is necessary in order to identify the historical literary levels in these texts.[11]

In this stage of our research, a distinction needs to be drawn between a macro-compositional approach, regarding the form of the biblical exegesis and its purposes, and micro-compositional methods regarding the literary techniques used in attaining the purpose of the exegetical process.[12] Thus, even though there is a certain degree of synchronization between form and content of the exegetical elements, the following survey will start with a suggestion for form classification and its significance.

The distinct forms of biblical exegesis in Qumran literature may be described as following:

1. A running biblical text reworked by integration of the exegetical elements within it and rearrangement of its order. This method imparts to the biblical text two variegated forms:

a. A specific version of the biblical text (e.g. parabiblical texts, such as 4Q364–367, *Reworked Pentateuch*).

b. An apocryphal edition of the biblical text (e.g. the *Temple Scroll*, and the *Book of Jubilees*).

---

[11] A. W. Wilson and L. Wills, "Literary Sources of the Temple Scroll," *HTR* 75 (1982): 275–88; G. Brin, "הערות לשוניות למגילת המקדש" in סוגיות במקרא ובמגילות (Tel-Aviv: Tel-Aviv University and the Hakibbutz Hameuchad, 1994), 162–71; E. Qimron, למילונה של מגילת המקדש, *Shnaton* 4 (1980): 239–62.

[12] See L. H. Schiffman, "The Temple Scroll in Literary and Philological Perspective," *Approaches to Ancient Judaism* (ed. W. S. Green; BJS 9; Chico CA: Scholars Press, 1980), II.143–158. Schiffman draws a distinction between macro-structure and micro-structure of the text of the *TS*, specifically regarding the role of associative editing method used both in the *TS* and in Rabbinic halakhic literature. However, he does not mention the differentiation of the literary forms used in Qumran and in Rabbinic literature.

2. Free exegetical compositions concerning a biblical book or books, or biblical subject/s (e.g. *Commentary of Genesis and Malachi*—4Q252–254; *Admonition Based on the Flood*—4Q370).

3. Biblical exegesis in distinct homiletic forms. Such forms are apparent, e.g. in the *Damascus Documents* and in the *Pesharim* Scrolls.

The following examples will explain this classification.

1. Reworked Running Biblical Text

A. *Parabiblical Texts as Specific Versions of the Bible*

This group is composed of running biblical texts that are expanded, rephrased, and reedited, probably for exegetical purposes.[13] The running text essentially reflects a known version of the Bible, but in some cases the known biblical text is rewritten by means of exegetical additions, omissions, paraphrases and rearrangements. These techniques have been classified, explained and exemplified by Tov, White, Segal, and others.[14] I shall deal with some known examples of this group in terms of exegetical purpose and form.

Completing the biblical text: in 4Q364–367, which reflect a running text from all the Pentateuch books,[15] and a parallel text in 4Q158, which reflects a specific paraphrase of Genesis and Exodus,[16] there are some prominent additions that resolve exegetical difficulties by completing the biblical text. Examples are the text of the Song of Miriam added to the biblical text of Exodus 15:20–21 (4Q365 6a ii, 1–7), and that of the angelic blessing to Jacob, added to the biblical text of Genesis 32:29 (4Q158 1, 7–9).[17] These additions reflect

---

[13] See S. White Crawford, "The 'Rewritten' Bible at Qumran: A Look at Three Texts," *ErIsr* 26 (1999): 1*–8*. She concludes: "4QReworked Pentateuch is certainly illustrative of the practice by scribes of the art of inner-biblical commentary in the late Second Temple period." Ibid., p. 5*. See also E. Ulrich, "Pluriformity in the Biblical Text, Text Groups, and Questions of Canon," *The Madrid Qumran Congress* (ed. J. Trebolle Barrera and L. V. Montaner; STDJ 11; Leiden: Brill, 1992), I.23–41, esp. pp. 32–37.

[14] See Tov's and White's works mentioned above, n. 4; M. Segal, "Biblical Exegesis in 4Q158: Techniques and Genre," *Text* 19 (1998): 45–62; idem, "4QReworked Pentateuch or 4QPentateuch?" *The Dead Sea Scrolls Fifty Years After their Discovery 1947–1997* (ed. L. H. Schiffman, E. Tov and J. C. VanderKam; Jerusalem: Israel Exploration Society, 2000), 391–99.

[15] Tov and White, "4Q364–367," 191.

[16] See Segal, "Biblical Exegesis," op. cit. n. 14.

[17] The first word of this addition appears in 4Q364 5b ii, 13.

early exegetical traditions for resolving issues of incomplete contents
within the biblical text.

As only one verse of Miriam's Song parallel to the Song of Moses
(Exod 15:1) is recorded in Exod 15:21, the question is raised "what
was Miriam's song?" This question is specifically raised by the Rabbinic
sages, who solve the issue by attributing the same song to Miriam
and the women as was sung by Moses with the men (*Mek. Beshalah*
§10; cf. Rashi on Exod 15:21). But in Qumran we find a new song
integrated within the running biblical text, imitating the biblical style
(see the poetic style in line 4), and referring freely to the motifs of
Moses' song.

A similar exegetical tradition is reflected in 4Q158, where the
angelic blessing to Jacob, which is only mentioned in Gen 32:29, is
completed. Michael Segal has shown that the words of this additional blessing, יפרכה ה' וירבכה, are taken from God's blessing to Jacob
in Gen 35:11, פרה ורבה, while the words יצילכה מכול חמס allude to 2
Sam 22:49 (= Ps 18:49).[18] Moreover, the latter phrase is appropriate
to Jacob's struggles with Laban and Esau. Thus, even though Jacob
had already received his blessing in Gen 32:28–29, and the information concerning an additional blessing of the angel may be considered as a redundancy, the fittingness of its words to Jacob's life
turn it into a reasonable story. The Rabbinic sages relate to this
issue by means of another blessing, יהי רצון שיהיו בניך צדיקים כמותך,
in the style of Rabbinic prayer stated in a separated Midrash (*Yal.
Shim'oni, Vayishlah*, §132).

A similar but not identical type of exegetical tradition appears in
4Q364 3 ii, 1–6 regarding Rebecca's anxiety for Jacob about the
possible consequences of his taking Esau's blessing from Jacob by
deception. In this passage Gen 28:6 is preceded by an additional
pericope, elaborating the elliptical biblical phrases expressing Rebecca's
anxiety, למה אשכל את שניכם יום אחד (Gen 28:45) and למה לי חיים (28:46)
by constructing a dialogue between Isaac and Rebecca. This additional pericope may be understood in relation to a parallel tradition
of this narrative, detailed in *Jub.* 27:1–18.[19]

---

[18] Segal, "Biblical Exegesis," 59–60.

[19] For more details of this additional pericope see White, "The 'Rewritten' Bible
at Qumran" (op. cit. n. 13): 3–4; B. Nitzan, "פרשנות קדומה למקרא במגילות קומראן," על
הפרק 15 (1998), 179–80. Both of them assume that the conflation in 4Q364 3 ii
relates to the detailed tradition told in *Jub.* 27.

Another form of exegetical tradition is apparent in 4Q365 6a i, 9. An interpretive problem appears in Exodus 14:19, in the redundancy by which the protection of the Israelite camp from the Egyptians is attributed to both the pillar of cloud and to the angel of God. This issue is solved in 4Q365 6a i, 9 by substituting another act for the redundant act of the pillar of cloud: ויסע ע[מוד ה]ענן מ[מחנה, מצרים להי[ו]ת במחנה [ישראל] ("[And the p]illar of c[loud moved f]rom the camp of Egypt to b[e] in the camp of [Israel]"). This exegetical replacement, integrated in the running biblical text from Qumran and written in biblical style, relates to a homiletic tradition known in *Jub.* 48:12–17. The *Book of Jubilees* relates in detail (and from a dualistic outlook)[20] how the angel of God delayed the Egyptians from pursuing the children of Israel for five days, and then hastened them to reach the Read Sea, where they were drowned. The phrase in 4Q365 only hints at this tradition, relating it to the pillar of cloud, the parallel of the angel of God (cf. Exod 13:21), thereby integrating this exegetical tradition in the running biblical text.

These pericopes, written to resolve difficulties in the biblical text, reflect ancient exegetical traditions. Nevertheless, their integration as the natural continuation of the biblical text imparts to the parabiblical text an image of a particular version of the Bible.[21]

The issue of discrepancy between parallel versions of the same narrative is resolved in 4Q364–367 by harmonizing the variegated texts into a complete and coherent description of an event.[22] This exegetical technique, in which the order of the specific pericopes in the ongoing biblical text is rearranged and variations of the relevant stories are conflated, may be considered as an exegetical tradition used within the running biblical text. Nevertheless, such an exegetical version became the basis for the Samaritan version of the Bible.

Another type of harmonized version of the biblical text appears in 4Q158. This exegetical type is created by associative combination of variegated texts on the basis of a common idea, as demonstrated by Michael Segal.[23] This technique, which also rearranges the biblical order, creates a specific version of the biblical text that

---

[20] See Nitzan, "פרשנות קדומה למקרא במגילות קומראן", 176–78, esp. n. 23, p. 178.
[21] See Ulrich, "Pluriformity in the Biblical Text" (op. cit. n. 13), 35–37; Segal, "4QReworked Pentateuch or 4QPentateuch?" (op. cit. n. 14).
[22] See some examples in Tov, "Biblical Texts as Reworked" (op. cit. n. 4), 127–29.
[23] Segal, "Biblical Exegesis".

may be defined as an exegetical, or even homiletic version; it is ear-lier than the Rabbinic homilies, which relate associatively to varie-gated biblical verses, but in the form of extra-biblical homilies. The Rabbinic exegesis was separated from the biblical text which, in accord with its canonical outlook, remained untouched.

Given the absence of any sectarian ideas or terms in these exeget-ical versions of the Bible, these may not be considered as sectarian. Such versions are on occasion parallel to Rabbinic homilies in their contents, albeit not in their exegetical form.[24] These Hebrew exeget-ical versions of the Bible may thus be described as pre-canonical phenomenon.[25] On the other hand, the integration of exegetical peri-copes within the biblical texts is apparent in some translations of the Bible,[26] including those accepted by the Rabbinic sages for inter-preting the Pentateuch in public, such as the Aramaic translations.[27] Thus, even in those cases in which there is no identity between Qumran variations of the biblical text and the known translations of the Bible, we cannot exclude the possibility that such Hebrew exegetical versions reflect pre-canonical versions used in public, which presumably could have been used as *vorlags* for biblical translations.

B. *Apocryphal Editions of the Biblical Text*

The *Temple Scroll* (*TS*) is a distinctive, salient apocryphal edition of the biblical text, even though its exegetical form and characteristics are similar, to some extent, to those of the aforementioned specific biblical versions. This scroll is based upon a running biblical text, although paraphrases, omissions, and exchanged or additional peri-copes which harmonize or complement the biblical text, rearrange

---

[24] See P. Alexander, "Retelling the Old Testament," *It is Written Scripture: Scripture Citing Scripture. FS Barnabas Linder* (ed. D. A. Carson and H. G. M. Williamson; Cambridge: Cambridge University Press, 1988), 99–121.

[25] M. Fishbane, relates the beginning of this scribal activity to the days of Josiah's reform at the 7th century B.C.E. See *Biblical Interpretation in Ancient Israel* (Oxford: Clarendon, 1985), 35–36.

[26] See, for example, A. Rofé, "תרגום השבעים לרות ד 11—דרמטיזציה מדרשית" *Text, Temples, and Traditions, FS Menahem Haran* (ed. M. V. Fox et al.; Winona Lake: Eisenbrauns, 1996), 119*–24*.

[27] See Neh 8:8: ויקראו בספר בתורת האלהים מפרש ושום שכל ויבינו במקרא ("They read from the book, from the law of God, with interpretation") and the practice mentioned in *b. Ber.* 8a to read twice from the Scriptures and once from its trans-lation (שנים מקרא ואחד תרגום). For the custom of reading the Bible and its com-mentary in public see C. Perrot, "The Reading of the Bible in Ancient Synagogue," *Mikra* (ed. M. J. Mulder; CRINT 2; Assen: Van Gorcum—Philadelphia: Fortress, 1988), 137–59, esp. pp. 137–38, 149–59.

its order, or conflate the biblical text, are selectively integrated within that text. Nevertheless, these exegetical and editorial techniques are not chance deviations from the complete running text of the Pentateuch, as in the reworked narrative sections of the Bible, but are used for specific halakhic purposes, which guide the rearrangement of the biblical text and its interpretive methods. Moreover, the scroll is considered as God's direct speech to the people of Israel. This message is attained by changing the person of God from the third to the first person singular, and the person of the children of Israel from the third person plural to the second person plural in particular parts of the scroll, as well as in its overall editorial reworking.[28]

In our investigation of the exegetical approaches used in the *Temple Scroll*, we have attempted to discern and classify its macro-compositional characteristics, regarding its purposes and form, prior to its micro-compositional characteristics, regarding the exegetical techniques used to convey the content of particular laws.

From the macro-compositional aspect, the macro-structure of the scroll as a whole is guided by the aim of presenting to the people of Israel a complete and homogeneous law of the holy worship of God and of the state of the holy people. In other words: to create a complete and homogeneous Law for the Temple, the land and state of a holy people. This purpose guides the selection of the specific pericopes of the Pentateuch chosen for the scroll as well as the basic structure and order of its subjects, as has been demonstrated by Yadin and Schiffman.[29] The extant text of 11QTS is arranged as follows:

The covenant between God and Israel based on Exod 34 and Deut 7 (cols. I–II)
A plan of the Temple, based mainly on Exod 35 and 25 (cols. III–XI, XXX, XLVII)
Sacrificial laws of daily, Sabbath and festivals (cols. XIII–XXIX)
Purification laws (cols. XLVIII–LI,10)
Laws regarding the political and juridical structure of the state of the holy people (cols. LI, 11–LXVI)[30]

---

[28] See Wilson and Wills, "Literary Sources of the Temple Scroll" (op. cit. n. 11): 276–79.

[29] See Yadin, *The Temple Scroll*, I.39–70, 81–88 (Hebrew original, I.34–60, 69–73); Schiffman, "The Temple Scroll in Literary and Philological Perspective" (op. cit. n. 12), 152–53.

[30] The extant text of 11QTS opens with the covenant between God and Israel in Exod 34, juxtaposed with Deut 7, which proscribes the worship of God in the pagan temples and altars, and commands the children of Israel to build a Temple

A redactor might have composed this over-all structure of the subjects of the *Temple Scroll* from separate sources.[31] Nevertheless, this
rearrangement of the sequence of the Pentateuch, and of the editorial and exegetical activities integrated within it, were intended to
present a comprehensive law for a holy Temple and holy land and
state consistent with a specific ideology of holiness,[32] and to "modernize"
the biblical text in light of new historical and political situations. A
similar purpose guided the composition of the Books of Deuteronomy
and Chronicles, which are included in the canonical Bible.

In order to achieve these aims of comprehensiveness, consistency
and "modernization," based upon a specific homogenous ideology,
it was necessary to abolish discrepancies noted in the Pentateuch
between parallel laws and books, as well as ambiguous and vague
formulations of the laws. This was done by means of harmonization
of the various laws to unequivocal commandments, written consistently throughout the *Scroll*. Thus, the *Scroll* is characterized by both
exegetical and editorial activities for creating a coherent law. The
pseudepigraphic form of the *Scroll* also served the aim of creating a
homogeneous and "modernized" law, being regarded as a direct commandment of God to the people of Israel. The formulation of the
exegetical and harmonized laws in pseudo-biblical form reflects the
idea that this version of the Law is a revelation of a hidden exegetical
version of the Law, given by God to his people for all generations.[33]

This classification of the law of the *Temple Scroll* from the macro-
compositional viewpoint is not intended to expose innovations of its
halakhic content and purpose, as has been successfully done by such
experts in halakhah as Milgrom, Schiffman, Baumgarten, Shemesh,

---

to the God of Israel (cols. I–II). This commandment guides the subject of a plan
of the Temple based on Exod 35 and 25, but integrated with Solomon's and
Ezekiel's Temple plans (cols. III–XI, XXX–XLVII). Following the description of
the burnt offering altar (col. XII,8–16), the subject of the laws of the regularly
sacrifices—daily, Sabbaths and festivals, based on Lev 23, and Num 28–29 (cols.
XIII–XXIX)—is stated. The subject of purification laws for keeping the holiness of
the Temple, the city of the Temple, the land of Israel and the people of Israel follows the plan of the Temple (cols. 48–51:10). Laws regarding the political and
juridical structure of the state of the holy people, based on the book of Deuteronomy,
are stated in the last part of the scroll (cols. LI,11–66).

[31] Wilson and Wills, "Literary Sources of the Temple Scroll," esp. pp. 284, 288;
M. O. Wise, *A Critical Study of the Temple Scroll from Qumran Cave 11* (Chicago: Oriental
Institute of the University of Chicago, 1990).
[32] See A. Shemesh, "The Holiness According to the Temple Scroll," *RevQ* 19
(2000): 369–82.
[33] See Alexander, "Retelling the Old Testament" (op. cit. n. 24), 100–102.

and others. Our own intention in classifying its editorial and exegetical purposes is simply to note its place and significance in the study
of the history of the biblical exegesis. We shall present here some
selected examples of this type of classification, as we have suggested
in our investigation of the festival offerings, in its present stage.

A. *Amendable Exegesis:*
Adjustment of specific commandments to a main principle

(1) *Grain-Offerings and Libations*

The principle of presenting a separate grain-offering and libation for
each animal offered as sacrifice is stated clearly in Num 15:4–12, but
its application to the sacrificial practice of the specific offerings as
specified in the Pentateuch is unclear. The commandments of the daily,
Sabbath and festival burnt offerings, as formulated in Numbers 28–29,
mention first all the animals offered for each of the burnt offerings,
and thereafter the additional grain-offerings and libations. This textual separation leaves ambiguous the practical procedure of the
sacrificial act: whether the grain offering and libation is added for
each separate sacrificed animal, or whether there is a separation
between the act of sacrificing the animals and these additional offerings.
Such a separation obscures the relationship between the sacrificed
animals and their additional offerings, a confusion that the *Temple Scroll*
intends to obviate.[34] Moreover, the offering of a he-goat as a purification
offering is stipulated in Numbers 28–29 as an addendum to the festival burnt offering, generally speaking without mentioning its grain
offering or libation. In col. XXXIV,12–13, in an additional halakhic
pericope written in the context of the entire practical process of
slaughtering the beasts in the inner court of the Temple, *TS* clarifies
the practical procedure for the sacrificial service as follows: ומקטירים
אותמה על האש אשר על המזבח פר פר ונתחיו אצלו ומנחת סולתו עליו ויין נסכו
אצלו ושמנו עליו.

   This practice is also mentioned in the law of the wood offering
(col. XXIV,7–8), where it is regarded as an ever-lasting law, a phrase
that may allude to a polemic against other practices customary in
the Second Temple. Yadin notes that this assumption may be suggested according to a different practice mentioned in *m. Menaḥ* 9.4.[35]

---

[34] Yadin, *The Temple Scroll*, I.149–50 (Hebrew original: I.118).
[35] Yadin, ibid.

However, in dealing with this issue from the viewpoint of the history of biblical interpretation, one needs to ask how this practice is to be reconciled with the biblical text in the *Temple Scroll*. In the context of the running biblical text of the festivals offering based upon the order of Numbers 28–29, the main principle involved in this procedure is recorded in the commandment of the new-moon offering, the first law of the festival offerings. However, in *TS* the commandment to add a grain offering and libation to each of the sacrificed animals enumerated in Numbers 28:12–14 is replaced by the general commandment of Num 15:4–10, in which these supplementary offerings are noted separately for each kind of animal sacrificed (col. XIV,2–8). This substitution harmonizes the general principle with the specific commandment of the festival offering within the context of the ongoing biblical text, thereby clarifying the procedure for all the following festival offerings.

In the Bible, the commandment to add a grain offering and a libation to the purification offering[36] is only specified for the leper's purification (Lev 14:10,19–20, 31), and was accepted thus in *m. Menaḥ* 9.6.[37] The biblical adaptation of these supplementary offerings to the he-goat of the festival purification offering is not consistent. The *Temple Scroll* consistently adjusts this principle to the he-goat purification offering of the festivals by removing the commandment of the purification offering from the closing phrase of the sacrificial festival laws to the continuous lists of sacrificed animals; it thereby receives its grain offering and libation as well (*TS* XV,2–3; XVII,13–14; XVIII,4–7; XX,03–05; XXIII,4–5; XXV,4–6, 14–15).[38] Yadin regards

---

[36] For the translation "purification offering" to the Hebrew term חטאת, instead of the more common "sin offering", see J. Milgrom, "Sin Offering or Purification Offering?" *VT* 21 (1971): 237–39.

[37] Yadin suggested that the principle of the addition of the grain offering to the purification offering is based on that of the leper's sin offering (Lev 14), which was regarded by the Rabbis as a particular case. This suggestion was rejected by G. A. Anderson, who hypothesized that the regulation in *TS* was based on Num 15:24, while replacing the he-goat before "a pleasing odor to the Lord" ("The Interpretation of the Purification Offering (חטאת) in the Temple Scroll (11QTemple) and Rabbinic literature," *JBL* 111 (1992): 17–35). However, based upon Num 28:6, 24, 27; 29:2,13, J. Milgrom rejected Anderson's suggestion ("On the Purification Offering in the Temple Scroll," *RevQ* 16 (1993): 99–101.

[38] In the laws of the Day of Atonement the commandment to add grain offering and libation to the he-goat of the purification offering is written precisely (*TS* XXV,14–15). This commandment is likewise added for the he-goat, which was chosen by lot to be sacrificed for the sake of God.

this literary editorial change as an exegetical act, of which there are also some traces in the ancient translations of the Bible.[39] The application of a specific principle to a specific commandment by relating the relevant biblical verses to each other is also accepted in the Rabbinic halakhah, albeit not within the ongoing biblical text, but in separate halakhic homilies. Thus, the exegetical model of providing the relationship between an halakhic principle and its practical realization within the running biblical text should be regarded as an ancient form of interpretation even earlier than the Rabbinic exegetical approach.

(2) *Adjusting the Status of the First-fruit Festival to the Day of Waving the Sheaf*

The day of waving the sheaf is mentioned among the festivals in Leviticus 23 (vv. 9–14), but the wording of this commandment is deficient. It is not defined as מִקְרָא קוֹדֶשׁ ("a holy convocation"), it lacks the proscription forbidding any work,[40] its burnt offering is limited to one sheep along with grain offering and libation (Lev 23:12), and the he-goat purification offering is not mentioned. This day is missing from the list of festivals in Numbers 28–29, and in Deuteronomy this day is only mentioned in terms of the beginning of the counting of the seven weeks towards the festival of Pentecost (16:9). Although the text of *TS* col. XVI is fragmented, it is clear that it includes at least one ram for a burnt offering (col. XVIII:2, 9) and a he-goat for a purification offering (line 4) which, according to Num 28:27, 30, are included among the festival offerings of the Pentecost. For this reason Yadin has suggested that the author of *TS* attempted to impart to this day the status of a first fruit festival, that of the first fruit of the barley,[41] by harmonizing its laws with those of the first fruit festival recorded in Num 28:26–31.

B. *Creative Exegesis: Creation of New Laws for "Modernization" of the Biblical Law, Based upon Biblical Allusions*

(1) *Festival of the First New Moon (11QTS XIV,9–18)*

No first-new-moon festival is commanded in the Bible, even though this date does have specific importance. According to a tradition

[39] Yadin, *The Temple Scroll*, I.143–46 (Hebrew original I.114–16).
[40] Cf. Lev 23:7–8, 21, 24–25, 27–28, 35–36.
[41] Cf. *m. Soṭa* 2:1; *b. Menaḥ* 68b; Josephus, *Ant.* 3, 250.

mentioned in the Bible, this was the date of the inauguration of the tabernacle of the tent of meeting (Exod 40:2, 17),[42] while in the *Book of Jubilees* this is mentioned as the date for the inauguration of the patriarchal altars (*Jub.* 13:8–9; 24:22; 27:19–26). It is also mentioned as the beginning of the journey out of Babylon (Ezra 7:9), as the end of the polemic concerning marriage with foreign women (Ezra 10:17), and the date of the purification of the Temple from Ahaz's idolatry (2 Chr 29:17).[43] However, only in the tradition of Noah, recorded in *Jub.* 7:2–4, is this day regarded as a festival, marked by a festival burnt offering and a he-goat as a purification offering, with their additional grain offering and libation. On the basis of the model of the new moon of the seventh month (Num 29:1–6), *TS* regards the first new moon as a specific festival, without specifying any reason. This creation of a new festival is accomplished by attributing other festive offerings to this day in addition to those of a regular new moon and those of the first day of the *milluim*, which falls on this date. It is not clear whether this date was considered as a special festival in the Second Temple period, at least among certain circles. If such was, the case, in fact, the creation of a specific law for this festival might have been regarded as a "modernization" of the biblical law, adjusting the law to contemporary reality.

(2) *Additional Festivals*

The author of *TS*, on the basis of certain biblical indications, created laws for additional first fruits festivals: those of the first fruits of wine and the first fruits of oil (cols. XIX,11–XXIII,2). These festivals are based on the commandments to offer to the Lord the first fruits of grain, wine and oil, as specified in Num 18:12–13; Deut 18:4; 2 Chr 31:5, and especially the ordinance, mentioned in Neh 10:35–40, according to which all these first fruits are to be brought to the Temple every year, as specified in the Law. According to Judg 21:19–20, and Hos 2:11, as well as on the basis of testimonies of wine festivals that were customary in Greek and Mari, Milgrom claims that festivals of wine at the appropriate season were also customary in Israel. If such is the case, the above-mentioned ordinances of *TS* were intended to fix these practices in the law. The author

---

[42] This date is suggested in Ezek 45:18 for the inauguration of the eschatological Temple.

[43] See Yadin, *The Temple Scroll*, I.89–91 (Hebrew original, I.74–75).

of *TS* appended to these ordinances the system of fixing the dates of the festivals at intervals of seven weeks from one another,[44] as well as the cultic purpose of the festivals, of assigning the use of the new harvest for cultic offerings. However, he deviated from the biblical model of the law of the festival of first fruit in three respects: (1) the celebration of the festival by the twelve tribes of Israel (cf. Judg 21:13–24); (2) elaborating the laws of the festival offering by details regarding the practice of the offerings (cf Lev 2:2–3, 9–13; 3:1–17); (3) creation of a law for giving the shoulder of the sacrifices for the Levites (cols. XXI,4–5, XXII,10–11). The latter ordinance is amended in the *TS* according to the biblical indications of giving "a portion" from the sacrifices to the Levites, as written in Neh 12:44–47; 13:10; 2 Chr 31:4–9, 19.[45] The author emphasizes the introduction of these ordinances as "a law for ever."

Similar innovative acts are entailed in the creation of a law for a wood offering, connected with the provision of new wood for the altar (*TS* XXIII,3–XXV,1) which, according to 4QMMT[a] v, 7–9, was to be celebrated on the last six days of the sixth month.[46] According to Neh 13:31, this festival was considered as having been mentioned in the Law. It is not mentioned in the Masoretic biblical text, but appears in a reworked Pentateuch text from Qumran, 4Q365 23, which might have been regarded as a specific version of the Pentateuch. An ordinance concerning this festival appears also in *Jub.* 21:12–14; in *m. Ta'an.* 4:5; *b. Ta'an.* 28a, and in Maimonides' *Hilkhot Kelei Mikdash* 6.5. Its celebration during the Second Temple period is mentioned by Josephus (*J.W.* 2, 17, 6. §425). Hence, the integration of this ordinance within the biblical text of the *TS* might have been regarded as an act of fixing an actual reality as a law,[47] or as "modernization" of the law.[48]

---

[44] See the dates of these festivals in the table of Sabbaths and Festivals of 4QMMT, *Qumran Cave 4.V, Miqsat Ma'ase Ha-Torah* (ed. E. Qimron and J. Strugnell; *DJD* 10; Oxford: Clarendon, 1994), 7.

[45] See Yadin, *The Temple Scroll*, I.157–58, and the Appendix written by Milgrom, ibid., I.169–76 (Hebrew original, I.123–24; 131–36).

[46] *Qumran Cave 4.V, DJD* 10, 7.

[47] See J. Milgrom, "Qumran's Biblical Hermeneutics: The Case of the Wood Offering," *RevQ* 16 (1994): 449–56.

[48] M. Fishbane has pointed out additional regulations mentioned in the Bible, of which the customary practice becomes a law. E.g. the practice of reading the Law in public (Deut 31:10–13; Neh 8:1–8), the regulations of the Tabernacle festival (Lev 23:40–43; Neh 8:14–18; 2 Macc 10:6–7; *Jub.* 16:29–31). See *Biblical Interpretation*, 107–13.

(3) *"Modernization" of the Milluim Law*

Another type of creativity is apparent in the law of the *milluim* as found in *TS*. The biblical ceremony of *milluim* (Exod 29; Lev 8–9) was a one-time ceremony for the consecration of the priests who were to serve in the Tent of Meeting. Although its adaptation for other occasions, such as the consecration of the priests in Solomon's Temple and in the Second Temple, was necessary, there is no law or narrative in the Bible concerning its renewal.[49] The Bible only describes the inauguration of the altar of Solomon's Temple (2 Chr 7:7–9), of Ezekiel's plan for the Temple (Ezek 43:18–27), and that of the Second Temple (Ezra 3:8–11). The formulation of this law in the *Temple Scroll* is intended to establish this ceremony as a permanent law. The main innovation used by the *TS* to accomplish this end is to adapt the biblical law to the form of an annual ceremony, by placing the law on a fixed date within the framework of the annual festivals, from the first to the eighth day of the first month. According to this exegetical amendment, the main role of this ceremony is to annually consecrate the new junior priests, who join the service of the Temple upon coming of age. The author of the *TS* thus changed the order of the biblical ceremony. Its ceremony begins with the consecration of the junior priests (*TS* XV,3–14), while the consecration of the high priest is described thereafter as a specific case (XV, 15–XVII,5), performed only when a new high priest is consecrated.

This small selection of examples from the *TS* does not reflect specifically sectarian ideas, but nevertheless does reflect sectarian perceptions regarding the text of the Bible and biblical exegesis. The fact that there are no quotations from the *TS* in other Qumran compositions may indicate that this book was not considered as part of the accepted traditional Scripture.[50] Nevertheless, among the Qumran community this book may have been considered as a new stage of God's words to his people, one of disclosure of the exegetical mysteries hidden within the biblical text. This perception is defined in

---

[49] See L. H. Schiffman, "The Milluim Ceremony in the Temple Scroll," *New Qumran Texts and Studies* (ed. G. J. Brooke; STDJ 15; Leiden: Brill, 1994), 255–72.

[50] The pseudepigraphical books mentioned in the Qumran texts are the *Book of Jubilees*, which is mentioned in CD XVI,3–4 only by its definition, and the *Testament of Levi*, some of the contents of which are mentioned in CD IV,15–19. The issue regarding the authoritativeness of books in Qumran is dealt with by J. C. VanderKam, *The Dead Sea Scrolls Today* (Grand Rapids, Mich.: Eerdmans, 1994), 150, and White, "The 'Rewritten' Bible in Qumran," 3*–6*.

the sectarian books from Qumran as נילוי נסתרות ("revelation of hidden matters"),[51] and is likewise characteristic of the perception in the non-sectarian, apocryphal and pseudepigraphic literature, as for example described in *4 Ezra* 14:18–26, 42–47. The literary expression of this perception was the continuation of the biblical literature by exegetical creativity, of which the most distinct phenomenon was the integration of biblical exegesis within the biblical text itself.

2. Free Exegetical Compositions

The tendency to continue the biblical literature through exegetical creativity is also apparent in those compositions incorporated in the second category mentioned above, "free exegetical compositions concerning a biblical book or books, or biblical subject/s," albeit in different literary genres. The compositions included in this category reflect their author's exegetical perceptions of a biblical issue or of a biblical subject, at times influenced by the author's perception of the reality of his own time. The specific type of paraphrase of a biblical subject expresses each author's exegetical perception of these compositions. For example: the author of the *Commentary of Genesis and Malachi* (4Q252–254) paraphrases selected pericopes from Genesis and Malachi, constituting a chain of blessings to their sons or to later generations by biblical personalities who revered the Lord, an antithesis of a chain of curses to the wicked during the same periods.[52] This chain of blessings, beginning with Noah, continuing through the patriarchs down to Malachi, also reached the members of the Yaḥad who, according to the perception of the author, revered the Lord. Thus, even though this composition ostensibly deals with

---

[51] See e.g. CD III,14; 1QS V,11; VIII,11; 1QH[a] frg. 55,1, etc., and see L. H. Schiffman. *The Halakhah at Qumran* (Leiden: Brill, 1975), 8,22–32; idem, הלכה הליכה ומשיחיות במגילות מדבר יהודה (Jerusalem: Merkaz Shazar, 1993), 45–67.

[52] See G. J. Brooke, 'The Thematic Content of 4Q252,' *JQR* 85 (1994): 33–59. The curse upon Sodom and Gomorrah, itself (4Q252 III,1–6) is explained and reconstructed by G. Barzilai, "נורל רשעי סדום על פי פירוש קדום מקומראן" *Beth Miqra* 43 (1998): 323–31. M. J. Bernstein prefers to place greater emphasis on the problems faced by the exegete of 4Q252, and the stimulations in the text of the book of Genesis which trigger his comments, than to an overall thematic content in this composition. Nevertheless he does not renounce that this composition is a series represents consecutive periods of human history. See "Themes, Structure and Genre of Pesher Genesis, A Response to G. J. Brooke," *JQR* 85 (1994): 61–90; "4Q252: From Re-Written Bible to Biblical Commentary," *JJS* 45 (1994): 1–27.

a biblical issue, presented in its biblical context, its exegetical aspect is directed to a sectarian perception of the author's own generation.[53]

The composition *4QAdmonition Based on the Flood* (4Q370) paraphrases the narratives of the paradise and the flood in a brief and partial manner, in order to express the perception about the responsibility of human beings for their position, for good and for bad. However, this outlook expresses the awareness of what befell of later generations.

3. BIBLICAL EXEGESIS IN DISTINCT HOMILETIC FORMS

Explicit sectarian ideas, which may be related indirectly and homiletically to biblical texts, are expressed in distinct homiletic forms similar to the Rabbinic homilies. This exegetical genre is especially apparent in the *Damascus Documents*.

Vermes has already noted the main literary structure of these homiletic pericopes.[54] These are structured on the basis of three or four elements: (i) an actual idea or situation, mostly sectarian; (ii) a technical formula such as כאשר כתוב to relate the new idea to a biblical verse; (iii) quotation of a biblical verse as proof text; (iv) when necessary, a *pesher* is used for further explanation of the relationship between the biblical verse and its specific actualized exegesis. One of the known homilies of this genre is that of the well, based on Num 21:18, which is used exegetically to define the Law and the exegetical activity of the teacher of righteousness and his followers to expose its hidden regulations (CD VI,2–11).[55] Such an explanation of reality based upon the specific sectarian outlook could not have been derived directly from a biblical context. Hence, the adaptation of the biblical text to such a later and specific context should be done metaphorically and homiletically.

---

[53] Cf. CD II,14–III,20, where a similar sectarian conception is written in an historical survey of generations of fathers and sons, as part of an admonition.

[54] See Vermes, "Bible Interpretation at Qumran" (op. cit. n. 2), 184*–91*.

[55] See M. Fishbane, "The Well of Living Water: A Biblical Motif and its Ancient Transformation," in *"Shaʾarei Talmon" FS Shmaryahu Talmon* (ed. M. Fishbane et al.; Winona lake: Eisenbruns, 1992), 3–16.

Conclusion

I have attempted to present and exemplify the basic outlines of a tentative classification of the characteristics of biblical exegesis in Qumran literature. The scheme of classification suggested here should be evaluated considering to the aims and techniques of biblical exegesis in a wide ensemble of literary genres and individual pericopes, synchronically for the Second Temple period, and diachronically for later periods. The justification for such a study is the understanding of the contribution of Qumran biblical exegesis to our knowledge of the history of biblical exegesis.

THE 'WORD' OR THE 'ENEMIES' OF THE LORD? REVISITING THE EUPHEMISM IN 2 SAM 12:14

Donald W. Parry

The Hebrew Bible features an abundance of euphemistic (and dys-phemistic) expressions that were found in various sectors of life. The expressions were used with regard to governmental affairs, the military, commerce, intimate relationships, disease, bodily functions, and death. More particularly, Biblical writers, as well as scribes and copyists, industriously employed them when dealing with things that pertained to God and religion, the clean, the pure, and the holy. Scholars have examined an assortment of euphemisms in the Bible, the Mishnah, and Midrashic texts,[1] and have granted much attention to the "emendations of the scribes" (תיקון סופרים).[2] Investigators have also compared biblical euphemisms with those belonging to Meso-

---

[1] The classic work on Biblical euphemisms is Christian D. Ginsburg, *Introduction to the Massoretico-Critical Edition of the Hebrew Bible* (New York: Ktav, 1966), 345–404; for a study of euphemisms in the Mishnaic and Midrashic texts, see E. Z. Melamed, "Euphemisms and Textual Alterations in the Mishnah," *Leš* 47 (1983): 3–17; I. L. Rabinowitz, "Euphemism and Dysphemism: In the Talmud," *Enc Jud* (Jerusalem: Keter, 1996), 6:961–62; E. Z. Melamed, "Euphemisms and Textual Alterations of Expressions in Talmudic Literature," *Benjamin De Vries Memorial Volume* (ed. E. Z. Melamed; Jerusalem, 1968), 119–48. Rabbinic Sages used a number of expressions when speaking of euphemisms and good words—מעליא ישנא (*b. Giṭ.* 76b; *Ketub.* 65b; *Tem.* 30b), לשון סני נהור/נוהריה (*b. Ber.* 58a; *Lev. Rab.* 34:13; *Y. Peʾah* 8,21), and לשון נקיה (*Y. Moʾed Qaṭ.* 1, 80d; *Soṭah* 1, 2, 16c; *Ketub.* 1, 25c); see Shalom M. Paul, "Euphemistically 'Speaking' and a Covetous Eye," *HAR* 14 (1994): 193.

[2] "The term תיקון סופרים is first found in an utterance of R. Joshua b. Levi, a Rabbi who flourished in the first half of the third century," writes Saul Lieberman, "Corrections of the Soferim," in *Texts and Studies, Volume XVIII: Hellenism in Jewish Palestine* (New York: Jewish Theological Seminary of America, 1962), 28. For a catalog and discussion of the emendations, which total eighteen in number, see Ginsburg, *Introduction to the Massoretico-Critical Edition of the Hebrew Bible*, 348–63; and William McKane, "Observations on the Tiḳḳûnê Sôpeʿrîm," in *On Language, Culture, and Religion: In Honour of Eugene A. Nida* (eds. M. Black and W. Smalley, *Approaches to Semiotics*, Vol. 56, The Hague/Paris: Mouton, 1974), 53–77. See for example the eleven scriptural passages presented in the *Mekilta of Rabbi Ishmael* at Exodus 15:7 (Zech 2:12; Mal 1:13; 1 Sam 3:13; Job 7:20; Hab 1:12; Jer 2:11; Ps 106:20; Num 11:15; 2 Sam 20:1; Ezek 8:17; Num 12:12). Compare also *Sifra*, Numbers 84, which is a midrash on Numbers and Deuteronomy, *Yal. Shimeoni*, an anthology of midrashic texts, and *Midrash Tanḥuma*, a midrash on the Pentateuch. An important study on

potamian literature,[3] including love poetry from Mesopotamia,[4] and they have looked at euphemisms in Greek and Latin texts[5] as well as others from the ancient Near East. Translators, too, have concerned themselves with euphemisms as they approach the task of rendering the Hebrew Bible into several modern languages,[6] and as they confront the question: Does the translator "have to translate the Hebrew euphemism literally, or should he replace it by a euphemism typical of the receptor language?"[7]

One area of research that has not been adequately examined pertains to variant readings of euphemisms in biblical texts from Qumran and the Judaean Desert as they compare with the Masoretic tradition and other ancient witnesses to the Bible. With the recent publication of *Discoveries in the Judaean Desert*,[8] a number of studies can now be conducted on the topic of euphemisms in Qumran biblical texts. This paper represents a brief study of variant readings of a euphemism that is located in 2 Samuel 12:14, and, as points of comparison, I will examine other euphemistic and dysphemistic expressions in the Bible.

THE "ENEMIES" OF THE LORD (2 SAM 12:14)

David's role in the narrative of Bathsheba and Uriah (2 Sam 11:1–27) prompted Nathan's accusation of the king (2 Sam 12:1–14). Nathan

---

the *Tiqqun Sopherim* was conducted more than a century ago. W. Emery Barnes, "Ancient Corrections in the Text of the Old Testament (*Tiqqun Sopherim*)," *JTS* 1(1900), repr. in Sid Z. Leiman, ed., *The Canon and Masorah of the Hebrew Bible* (New York: Ktav, 1974), 379–414, argues that "the tikkun tradition is not Masoretic (i.e. textual), but Midrashic (i.e. exegetical or, more accurately, homiletic). This conclusion was based on the nature of the documents in which the data of the subject are contained; it is supported further by the consideration of each passage in detail," 405.

³ Paul, "Euphemistically 'Speaking'," 193–203.

⁴ Shalom M. Paul, "The 'Plural of Ecstasy' in Mesopotamian and Biblical Love Poetry," in *Solving Riddles and Untying Knots: Biblical, Epigraphic and Semitic Studies: A Festschrift for Jonas C. Greenfield* (eds. Ziony Zevit, Seymour Gitin, Michael Sokoloff; Winona Lake, Indiana: Eisenbrauns, 1995), 585–97.

⁵ I. Opelt, *Reallexikon für Antike und Christentum VI* (Stuttgart, 1966), conducts a study of Hebrew, Greek, and Latin euphemisms.

⁶ Consult, for example, Jan de Waard, "Do You Use 'Clean Language'?" *The Bible Translator* 22: 3 (July 1971), 107–15; and Paul Ellingworth and Aloo Mojola, "Translating Euphemisms in the Bible," *BT* 37: 1 (January 1986): 139–43.

⁷ De Waard, "'Clean Language'?," 114.

⁸ All of the volumes of *Discoveries in the Judaean Desert* that deal chiefly with biblical texts have been published except for volumes XVII (which is at press) and XXXII; the former is comprised of the Samuel texts and the latter the Isaiah Scrolls.

first presented a parable to David, and then, following David's response, delivered a lengthy accusation. The final verse of the pericope
reads: אפס כי נאץ נאצת את איבי יהוה בדבר הזה גם הבן הילוד לך מות יומת,
"Yet because you have certainly spurned the enemies of the Lord
in this matter, the son that is born to you will surely die" (2 Sam
12:14). With regard to the phrase "enemies of the Lord," the majority of the Greek witnesses, the Vulgate, the Targum, and the Syriac
share the same reading as the Masoretic Text (MT). Two variant
readings for the word "enemies" will be discussed below.

Textual critics have held that "enemies" in this passage is a secondary insertion because its inclusion makes little sense contextually.
The story's setting presents no clue as to whom the Lord's enemies
are. Nathan's accusation against David pertains to the king's role in
the Uriah and Bathsheba story and does not relate directly to either
David's or the Lord's enemies. As Mulder reminds us, David's enemies could not have known about David's sin because it was committed in secret (בסתר, see 2 Sam 12:12).[9] In addition, a number of
textual critics also consider the verbal root נאץ, which preceeds איבי,
to be a Pi'el verb, but never a causative (see, for example, 1 Sam
2:17; 2 Sam 12:14 (2x); 14:11, 23; 16:30). "נאץ does not elsewhere
mean to cause to blaspheme," explains Driver.[10]

Elsewhere נאץ may have triggered a change in 1 Sam 2:17, where
it was evidently directly coupled with the Divine Name before the
insertion of the secondary, euphemistic האשים.[11] Ps 10:3 may be
included in this same discussion, because the expression "spurned"
(נאץ) was apparently changed to "blessed" (ברך).[12]

---

[9] M. J. Mulder, "Un euphémisme dans 2 Sam. XII 14?" VT 9 (1968): 111.

[10] S. R. Driver, Notes on the Hebrew Text and the Topography of the Books of Samuel
(Oxford: Clarendon, 1913), 292. See also Mulder, "Un euphémisme?" 110–12.
Others view נאץ in 2 Sam 12:14 as a causative Pi'el. See, for example, H. W.
Hertzberg, I and II Samuel: A Commentary (trans. J. S. Bowden from German, Old
Testament Library, 1960. Philadelphia: Westminster, 1964), 315; and C. F. Keil and
F. Delitzsch, Biblical Commentary on the Books of Samuel (trans. James Martin from
German, Grand Rapids, MI: Eerdmans, 1950), 391–2.

[11] See the discussion in Jean-Dominique Barthélemy, "La qualité du Texte
Massorétique de Samuel," in The Hebrew and Greek Texts of Samuel: Proceedings of the
Congress of the International Organization for Septuagint and Cognate Studies (Vienna 1980)
[Septuagint and Cognate Studies] (ed. Emanuel Tov, Jerusalem: Academon, 1980), 5.

[12] Correspondingly, there are instances where scribal changes reflect ברך rather
than קלל (see 1 Kgs 21:10, 13; Job 1:5, 11; 2:5, 9), although Reuven Yaron, "The
Coptos Decree and 2 Sam XII 14," VT IX (1959): 90, claims that "there is no
proof for the assumption that the euphemistic substitution of berekh—'to bless' for
expressions meaning 'to curse' or 'to blaspheme' is due to subsequent emendation."

"Enemies" is supplied as a euphemism elsewhere. MT 1 Sam 25:22 features a self-curse uttered by David: כה יעשה אלהים לאיבי דוד כה יסיף אם אשאיר מכל אשר לו עד הבקר משתין בקיר ("May God do thus and more to the enemies of David, if I spare any that are his until the morning any who pisses against the wall"). In this passage the MT (see also LXX[L]) supplies the reading איבי against one or more of the other witnesses (LXX[BA]) that lack it. McCarter calls this reading in the MT an "euphemistic expansion" that is "unquestionably late and scribal."[13] The expansion in David's self-curse was conveyed to his enemies by a scribe or copyist who wished to protect the king. As McCarter has explained: "This expansion is surely a deliberate attempt to distort the original meaning. The threat is never carried out, and a scribe has changed David's words to protect him (or his descendants!) from the consequences of the oath."[14] It is probable that 1 Sam 20:16b also contains a secondary plus that serves as a euphemism where the MT speaks of "the enemies of David" in Jonathan's self-curse.[15] None of the three Qumran Samuel witnesses attest either 1 Sam 20:16b or 25:22.

Yaron argues that the source for *enemies* in 2 Sam 12:14 stems from the Coptos Decree, an inscription that dates from the 18th century B.C.[16] The decree describes the punishment that was set for the rebellious Teti, son of Minhotep: "His name shall not be remembered in this temple, according as it is done toward one like him, who is hostile toward the enemies of his god."[17] According to Yaron, the arguments by scholars that enemies in 2 Sam 12:14 is secondary and a euphemism "seems rather artless and pedantic."[18] Yaron's argument breaks down on two counts—he does not reveal the variant reading of "word" in the Qumran Samuel scroll found in the same verse (on this, see below); and he fails to point out that *enemies* makes a regular appearance as a euphemism in rabbinic writ-

---

[13] P. Kyle McCarter, Jr., *II Samuel: A New Translation with Introduction, Notes and Commentary* [The Anchor Bible 9] (Garden City, NY: Doubleday, 1984), 296.

[14] P. Kyle McCarter, Jr., *I Samuel. A New Translation with Introduction, Notes and Commentary* [The Anchor Bible 8] (Garden City, NY: Doubleday, 1980), 394.

[15] "What is expected is not that Yahweh should require it from the hand of David's enemies, but from the hand of David himself, in case he should fail to fulfil the conditions of the covenant," writes Driver, *Notes on the Hebrew Text and the Topography of the Books of Samuel*, 165–6; see also, McCarter, *I Samuel*, 337.

[16] Yaron, "The Coptos Decree and 2 Sam XII 14," 89–91.

[17] Yaron, "The Coptos Decree and 2 Sam XII 14," 90.

[18] Yaron, "The Coptos Decree and 2 Sam XII 14," 91.

ings, including *Ta'an.* 7a, *Sukkah* 29a, *Soṭah* 11a, *Lev. Rab.* 25:1, and the *Mekilta of Rabbi Ishmael.*

Ta'an. 7a, for example, records a brief discussion of Jer 50:36: "R. Jose b. Ḥanina said: What is the meaning of the verse. *A sword is upon the lonely, and they shall become fools?* This means, destruction comes upon the enemies of such scholars who confine themselves to private study."[19] A footnote to this passage explains that "Enemies here is a euphemisim for the scholars themselves." Another text reads, "Our Rabbis taught, When the sun is in eclipse it is a bad omen for idolaters; when the moon is in eclipse, it is a bad omen for the enemies of Israel, since Israel reckons by the moon and idolaters by the sun" (*Sukkah* 29a). That *enemies* here is a euphemism for Israel is acknowledged by Talmudic scholars.[20] Further, in a discussion of a passage from Exod 1:10, the sages do not explicitly use the word *enemies*, but they allude to Pharaoh and the Egyptians, Israel's ancient enemies (see *Soṭah* 11a). Rabinowitz explains, "The rabbis detect . . . a euphemism in the use of the third person 'and it [the people of Israel] shall go up from the land' (Ex. 1:10). According to the Talmud Pharaoh actually meant to say 'and we shall [be forced to] go up from the land,' and they will possess it, 'but it is like a man who curses himself and hangs the curse on someone else' (*Soṭah* 11a)."[21] *Lev. Rab.* 25:1 also uses enemies euphemistically: "So also did the Holy One, blessed be He, say to Moses: 'Tell Israel: My children! Occupy yourselves with the Torah and you need not be afraid of any nation.' If the text had read, 'She is a tree of life to them that toil in her' Israel's enemies would have been unable to survive. What it says therefore is not that, but: 'To them that lay hold upon her.' If the text had read, 'Cursed be he that learneth not the words of the law' Israel's enemies would have been unable to survive."[22] The *Mekilta of Rabbi Ishmael*, not cited here, uses *enemies* euphemistically on a regular basis.

[19] Israel W. Slotki, *Hebrew-English Edition of the Babylonian Talmud, Ta'anith* (London: Soncino Press, 1984).
[20] See Slotki, *Hebrew-English Edition of the Babylonian Talmud, Ta'anith*, 1984; and Rabinowitz, "Euphemism and Dysphemism: In the Talmud," 962. See also Gustaf Dalman, *Grammatik des jüdisch-palästinischen Aramäisch* (Darmstadt: Wissenschaftliche Buchgesellschaft, 1960), 109.
[21] Rabinowitz, "Euphemism and Dysphemism: In the Talmud," 962.
[22] *Midrash Rabbah: Leviticus*, chapters XX–XXXVII (trans. by Judah J. Slotki. London: Soncino Press, 1983).

In view of the fact that *enemies* is featured regularly as a euphemistic expression in the rabbinic writings, perhaps a future study will consider such things in light of the euphemistic plus found in the MT 2 Sam 12:14.

THE "WORD" OF THE LORD (2 SAM 12:14)

4QSam[a], the best preserved of the three Qumran witnesses of Samuel,[23] has a variant to MT's reading of אנץ נאצת את איבי יהוה (2 Sam 12:14). The Qumran witness reads: נ[אץ נאצ[ת]ה] את דבר יהוה "you have certainly spurned the word of the Lord."[24] The Coptic version (*verbum Domini*), presented in the Brook, McLean, and Thackeray apparatus,[25] supports the reading of 4QSam[a] in this verse. The probable source for דבר in 4QSam[a] is found in the same pericope under discussion. In 2 Sam 12:9, Nathan asks David, מדוע בזית את דבר יהוה לעשות הרע בעינו; "why have you despised the word of the Lord, to do evil in his sight?" (2 Sam 12:9). Verses 9 and 14 have a number of corresponding points. In both verses, Nathan is the speaker and David is the addressee. Both sentences comprise an accusation in which the prophet accuses the king—in verse 9 Nathan pronounces, בזית את דבר יהוה and in verse 14 he declares, את דבר יהוה נאצת. One notes the similarity between these two phrases: they are syntactically identical—second masculine singular perfect verb, object marker, noun in construct, and Divine Name. Most significantly, יהוה דבר is found in both passages (of 4QSam[a]). It appears that a scribe belonging to the 4QSam[a] tradition was influenced by verse 9 when he copied verse 14. Whether or not דבר was an intentional or unintentional plus is difficult to determine.

Verse 9 also has a variant reading where דבר appears. Although the MT reads דבר together with the majority of Greek witnesses (LXX[BAMN]), the Syriac and the Targum, both the Lucian group (LXX[L]) and Theodotion (θ) lack דבר. Based on these last two mentioned wit-

---

[23] The other two Qumran witnesses—4QSam[b] and 4QSam[c]—are not attested at this point of the text.
[24] The apparatus of *BHS* errs with its reading of the Qumran text (ל[ ]בד). See *DJD* XVII (ed. F. C. Cross, D. W. Parry, and E. Ulrich, forthcoming).
[25] Alan England Brook, Norman McLean, and Henry St. John Thackeray, *The Old Testament in Greek* . . . (Volume II in *The Later Historical Books*, Part I, *I and II Samuel*; London: Cambridge University Press, 1927), 142.

nesses (LXX[L] and θ), it is probable that דבר is secondary in verse 9 as it is in verse 14. Unfortunately, only a small fragment of 4QSam[a] exists where 2 Sam 12:9 is found and it is unknown whether the Qumran witness attested or lacked דבר.[26]

Yet another variant to "enemies" and "word" in 2 Sam 12:14 is found in "c," a Greek cursive which is part of the Lucianic Manuscripts.[27] This cursive, with no support from other witnesses, has נאץ נאצת את יהוה, lacking both איבי and דבר. Most scholars hold that this Greek cursive presents the primitive reading—"you have certainly spurned the Lord."[28] Both of the terms "enemies" and "word," then, are secondary readings or scribal expansions that serve as euphemisms that changed an offensive reading to an inoffensive reading.

THE NAMES *BAAL* AND *BOSHET*

A number of dysphemisms[29] are found in Samuel that are associated with theophoric names that once contained the name of a Canaanite deity. Many theophoric names that include the name *baal* were changed, seemingly because the element *baal* was identical to the Canaanite deity with that same name.[30] This change of the names

---

[26] Only ten characters from 2 Sam 12:9 remain on the fragment: א[שׂתּו לֹ]קחת . . . [י]הוה לעשׂ[ות.

[27] The Larger Cambridge LXX uses the sigla boc₂e₂ to represent the Lucianic Manuscripts. The Göttingen edition, Holmes and Parsons, uses the numbers 19 + 108, 82, 127, and 93 for the same.

[28] A. Geiger, *Urschrift und Uebersetzungen der Bibel in ihrer Abhängigkeit von der innern Entwicklung des Judenthums* (Breslau: Hainauer, 1857. 2nd. ed., 1928), 267; see Driver, *Notes on the Hebrew Text and the Topography of the Books of Samuel*, 292. See Eugene C. Ulrich, *The Qumran Text of Samuel and Josephus* HSM 19; Missoula, MT: Scholars Press, 1978), 138.

[29] Paul defines dysphemism as "the substitution of an offensive or disparaging term for an inoffensive one," Shalom M. Paul, "Euphemism and Dysphemism," *Enc Jud* vol. 6 (Jerusalem: Keter, 1996), 959. For other examples of dysphemism in the Hebrew Bible, see Paul, "Euphemism and Dysphemism," 959–60. John Ellington, "Translating the Word 'Baal' in the Old Testament," *BT* 44 (October 1993), 427, explains, "Since the idea of other gods was such a shameful thing, some editors or copyists got the idea of writing the Hebrew word for 'shame' (*bosheth*) in place of the offending word *baal*."

[30] See Otto Thenius, *Die Bücher Samuels erklärt* (2nd ed.; Leipzig: n.p., 1864), 142, 175; Geiger, ZDMG, 729–31; Wellhausen, *Der Text der Bücher Samuelis*, 30–31; K. Budde, *Die Bücher Samuel* (1902), 203; Driver, *Notes on the Hebrew Text and the Topography of the Books of Samuel*, 253–55. For other examples of *baal* names that have been changed to *boshet*, see Ginsburg, *Introduction to the Massoretico-Critical Edition of the Hebrew Bible*, 400–04, and Ellington, "Translating the Word 'Baal' in the Old

accomplished two things—the blotting out of the name of *baal* from certain literary units of the religious record and also the denigrating (or the dysphemising) of this name.[31] For example, the name *Eshbaal*, belonging to Saul's fourth son (see 1 Chr 8:33; 9:39) was changed to *Ish-Boshet* in Samuel (see 2 Sam 2:8, 10, 12, 15; 3:7, 8, 14, 15; 4:5, 8 (2x), 12); the name *Merib-Baal* (1 Chr 8:34) or *Meri-baal*[32] (1 Chr 9:40), which belonged to Jonathan's son, Saul's grandson, was changed to Mephiboshet throughout Samuel (see 2 Sam 4:4; 9:6 (2x), 10, 11, 12 (2x), 13; 16:1, 4; 19:24, 25, 30; 21:7). Note too that the name Mephiboshet is also the name of one of Saul's sons (2 Sam 21:8) and perhaps it was once Meri-baal or Mephibaal.

Jerubbaal (ירבעל) (also named Gideon) is attested fourteen times in the Hebrew Bible, thirteen in Judges (Judg 6:32; 7:1; 8:29, 35; 9:1, 2, 5 (2 x), 16, 19, 24, 28, 57) and once in Samuel (1 Sam 12:11). The name is changed to Jerubbesheth (ירבשת) in MT 2 Sam 11:21 but remains Jerubbaal in the Septuagint, Syriac, and Vulgate. Note the peculiar pointing of *besheth* in the received text, of which Paul proposes that "perhaps the pointing of *beshet* was intended to suggest the word *sheqer* ('lie')."[33] The fact that the Septuagint, Syriac, and Vulgate have variant readings suggests that the MT made the change from Jerubbaal to Jerubbesheth subsequent to the translation of LXX; or it is also possible that the Septuagint belonged to a school which held the other reading.

Testament," 428–9. A small number of scholars oppose the theory that such names were changed, including M. Jastrow, *JBL* 13 (1894), 19–30; F. M. T. Böhl, *Die Sprache der Amarnabriefe* (Leipzig: Zentralantiquariat der Deutschen Demokratischen Republik, 1979), 4–5; J. Lewy, *HUCA* 32 (1961): 36–37. Matitiahu Tsevat, "Ishbosheth and Congeners: The Names and Their Study," *HUCA* 46 (1975), 71–88, challenges the theory that *boshet* was substituted for *baal* on the basis that *boshet* is related to the Akkadian *bāštu*, having the specific meaning of "guardian angel, patron saint," 76. Tsevat concludes that those men referred to in Samuel whose names were Ish-Boshet and Mephiboshet each had two names and Jerubbesheth had three names (see Tsevat 85).

[31] Hos 2:17 and Deut 12:3 have provided inspiration to rabbinic authorities to make dysphemistic name changes. As Rabinowitz explains, "the verse 'ye shall destroy their name' (Deut 12:3) is interpreted as meaning that a dysphemistic name is to be given for its correct one," and one of the reasons for euphemisms "is based on the injunction 'a man should not open his mouth to Satan' (Ber. 19a), i.e., one should not invite misfortune by ominous statements" ("Euphemism and Dysphemism: In the Talmud," 962).

[32] The name as recorded in Chronicles is מריב בעל (1 Chr 8:34) and alternatively, מריבעל (1 Chr 9:40). The name מרבעל, minus the *yod*, has been discovered on an ostracon in Samaria; see G. A. Reisner, *Harvard Expedition at Samaria I* (1924), 233, no. 2.

[33] Paul, "Euphemism and Dysphemism," 961.

In addition to these theophoric names, there are variants in other passages where *boshet* and *baal* are attested. Jer 11:13, for instance, has a plus of "altars of shame" in Hebrew which is lacking in Greek texts and 1 Kgs 18:19 has "Baal" in Hebrew where the Septuagint reads "shame."

A possible basis for *boshet* in these compound names may be found, at least in part, in a parallelism where *boshet* is set against *baal*: "because your gods, O Judah, have become the number of your cities; and the number of the streets of Jerusalem are the altars you have set up to shame (לבשת), altars to burn to Baal (לבעל)" (Jer 11:13). Owing to the attestation of these names in Chronicles, the custom of changing the names must have occurred fairly late, i.e. after the formation of Chronicles.[34]

4QSam[a], which exists in fragmentary form, presents only three readings where the theophoric names listed above in the previous paragraphs are attested in the Samuel texts. The three readings are found in 2 Samuel 4, verses 1, 2, and 12.[35] In the first reading (2 Sam 4:1), 4QSam[a] has מפי[ב]ת with the Septuagint (cf. the Syriac), versus MT and the Targum which lack it. Such an omission in the MT, reports Wellhausen, is not due to a simple whim or by chance.[36] Critics have recognized that מפיבשת is a mistake for אישבשת, itself a tendentious substitution for אשבעל. אשבעל, the primitive name, is present in 2 Sam 2:8 (and in 2 Sam 2:15) only in a single manuscript of the Lucianic group (e₂), but see also אשבעל in 1 Chr 8:33; 9:39.

In the second reading (2 Sam 4:2), למפיבשת בֿן שאול is attested in 4QSam[a] and the Septuagint, where the MT, Targum, and Syriac have בן שאול. Driver points out that the reading by the MT of הֿיו בן שאול 'is not translatable,' and submits that the text read הֿיו לאיש בשת בן שאול, based on the Septuagint.[37] A scribe, avoiding the error of reading למפיבשת, omitted the name and with it, the preposition

---

[34] Julius Wellhausen, *Der Text der Bücher Samuelis* (Göttingen: Vandenhoech and Ruprecht, 1871), 153.

[35] Compare also, our reconstruction and discussion of the name Ishboshet in 4QSam[a] at 2 Sam 2:8 [איש בשת] and 2 Sam 2:15 [איש לאיש בשת] (*DJD* XVII, ed. F. M. Cross, D. W. Parry, forthcoming).

[36] Wellhausen, *Der Text der Bücher Samuelis*, 160. See further Driver, *Notes on the Hebrew Text and the Topography of the Books of Samuel*, 252; Frank Moore Cross, Jr., *The Ancient Library of Qumran: The Haskell Lectures 1956–57* (3rd. ed.; Sheffield, England: Sheffield Academic Press, 1995), 140–45. [Previous title *The Ancient Library of Qumran and Modern Biblical Studies*. New York: 1958], 191; Ulrich, *The Qumran Text of Samuel and Josephus*, 42–5.

[37] Driver, *Notes on the Hebrew Text and the Topography of the Books of Samuel*, 253.

necessary to make sense of the expression. 4QSam^a incorrectly reads מפיבשת but correctly preserves the *lamed* used idiomatically with היו, even though the latter itself is omitted. The third reading (2 Sam 4:12) features מפיבשת in 4QSam^a and LXX, where MT, LXX^{MN}, Targum, and Vulgate read איש בשת.

ADDITIONAL EUPHEMISTIC/DYSPHEMIC FEATURES
IN THE SAMUEL TEXTS

In addition to the somewhat complex text critical aspects of euphemisms and dysphemisms that have been discussed above, there are additional points pertaining to this topic that will be dealt with briefly:

1. *Emendations of the Sopherim.* The "emendations of the sopherim" serve to illustrate the concern of the scribes or Rabbinic authorities[38] to create euphemisms with the view of showing honor to God or to avoid "anthropomorphisms and anthropopathisms which were thought to be theologically improper because they encroached in one way or another on the majesty of God."[39] Three of the emendations are from the books of Samuel:

1 Sam 3:13. כי מקללים להם בניו. Based on the Septuagint, the Hebrew text probably once read "because his sons cursed God" (cf. Exod 22:27). A simple change in the reading (omitting the *'alep* from אלהם, God) could have created the reading להם (them/themselves),[40] thus turning the sons of Eli's derogation of God on themselves.

2 Sam 16:12. יראה יהוה בעוני. The *ketib* of the third word in this phrase reads (בעוני) "on my iniquity"; the *qere* reads (בעיני) "on my eye"; and the LXX has (בעניי) "on my affliction." Note the graphic similarity of the words. Some Rabbinic authorities hold that the original reading was (יראה יהוה בעינו), "the Lord will behold with his eye,"[41] an anthropomorphism.

2 Sam 20:1. לאהליו. The primitive text allegedly read "to his gods" (לאלהיו), but was changed to "to his tents" (לאהליו). A simple metathesis of the *lamed* and *he* caused the alteration. "To his gods" implies that northern tribesmen, disaffected with David and being prompted by the Benjaminite Sheba, turned to idolatry. The similar readings

---

[38] For a significant review of the *Tiqqun Sopherim* see Barnes, "Ancient Corrections in the Text of the Old Testament (*Tiqqun Sopherim*)," 379–414.

[39] McKane, "Observations on the Tikkûnê Sôpe^crîm," 60.

[40] See Ginsburg, *Introduction to the Massoretico-Critical Edition of the Hebrew Bible*, 354.

[41] Lieberman, "Corrections of the Soferim," 32.

in 1 Kgs 12:16 (לְאֹהָלֶיךָ) and 2 Chr 10:16 (לְאֹהָלֶיךָ), both of which are listed in the emendations of the sopherim, have also allegedly experienced the change from "gods" to "tents."

2. *Ketib and Qere.* A number of euphemistic expressions are found in the *ketib* while the *qere* presents another reading. For example, 1 Sam 5:6, 12; 6:4, 5 have בַּעְפֹלִים "hemorrhoids" as the *ketib* which is substituted for בַּטְחֹרִים, an apparently unacceptable word for hemorrhoids, as the *qere*.

3. *Vocalization Methods.* Related to number 2 was the practice of the Masoretes to vocalize the *ketib* with the vowels of the *qere*. This practice indirectly altered the text presumably so that the *ketib* would not be read aloud. The substitution of vowels on יהוה so that the Divine Name would be read 'adonay, "my Lord(s)'" serves as an example. Similarly, the vowels for *boshet* were sometimes imposed on theophoric names containing *baal*, thus dysphemizing this and other names of pagan deities.[42] The vowels of clean words, too, were frequently imposed on obscene words with the *qere* presented in the margins.[43]

4. *Simple Changes to the Text.* Euphemisms are easy to install into a text by simply adding a word or phrase or by changing a single letter in a word. The Talmudic and "proverbial"[44] idea, "It is better that one letter be removed from the Torah than the Divine name be publicly profaned" (*Yebam.* 79a; cf. *Y. Sanh.* II, 20c) may have application here. There are several examples of words added or letters changed in the books of Samuel which resulted in euphemistic expressions. We have already considered the plus of the words "enemies" and "word" in two independent Hebrew witnesses in 2 Sam 12:14, the metathesis of *lamed* and *he* in 2 Sam 16:12; 20:1, and the omitting of the *'alep* in 1 Sam 3:13. Another example of a simple textual change to make a euphemism is located in 1 Sam 24:4, where the removal of a *yod* in the word לְהָסִיךְ ("to defecate") changes the reading to לְהָסֵךְ, "to cover," i.e., "covering one's legs" (cf. Jdg 3:24). Other examples of single letter changes are found in the "emendations of the soferim."[45]

---

[42] Marvin H. Pope, "Bible, Euphemism and Dysphemism in the," *The Anchor Bible Dictionary* vol. 1 (New York: Doubleday, 1992), 720; see also Ginsburg, *Introduction to the Massoretico-Critical Edition of the Hebrew Bible*, 346.

[43] One such example is located in Isa 36:12; see Pope, "Bible, Euphemism and Dysphemism in the," 720.

[44] See Lieberman, "Corrections of the Soferim," 35–36.

[45] Lieberman, "Corrections of the Soferim," 32, observes that "Nine out of the eleven euphemisms recorded in the Mekhilta involve the change of only one letter in the pronominal suffixes."

5. *Variant Readings of Euphemisms.* The focus of this paper, of course, is the variant readings of euphemisms in ancient witnesses to the biblical text. This is especially manifest where the two Hebrew witnesses (4QSam[a] and MT) employ distinct euphemistic expressions, of which "enemies" and "word" (2 Sam 12:14) are prime examples. These variant readings confirm that there was a strong tradition to create euphemisms among those who transmitted the Samuel texts, both the Qumran and the Masoretic versions.

Although it is likely that most of the euphemisms of the Bible belong to the primitive text, e.g., the earlier strands of the biblical stories, it is evident that later scribes and authorities were instrumental in producing a number of euphemisms. Euphemisms know of no geographical borders, nor are they bound to a particular historical era. They are found in all segments of life—commerce, politics, military establishments, religious systems, and in various social settings. According to Robert Burchfield, who served for a period of time as the editor of *The Oxford English Dictionary*,[46] euphemisms are universally known and belong to all languages. Most especially, as demonstrated in this paper, two scribes or scribal schools independently desired to honor God and his holiness by using variant euphemisms in 2 Sam 12:14.

---

[46] Burchfield has written that "a language without euphemisms would be a defective instrument of communication." Cited in Cullen Murphy, "The E Word," *The Atlantic Monthly* (September 1996): 16.

THE NAMES OF THE GATES OF THE
NEW JERUSALEM (4Q554)

E. Puech
Centre National de la Recherche Scientifique

In the caves of Qumran the remains of seven aramaic manuscripts were discovered which have been identified as belonging to a scroll dealing with the theme of the *New Jerusalem*: 1Q32, 2Q24, 4Q554, 4Q554a, 4Q555, 5Q15 and 11Q18.[1] According to the palaeography these copies date from between the end of the Hasmonaean period through the Herodian period, but the dating of the composition itself is still a matter of discussion. Some assume that this work stems from the *Temple Scroll*,[2]

---

[1] J. T. Milik, *The Books of Enoch. Aramaic Fragments of Qumran Cave 4* (Oxford: Oxford University Press, 1976), 59, thought that a little fragment "seems to provide us with a specimen of the Hebrew version of the Aramaic work edited under the title 'Description of the New Jerusalem,'" but it seems that this fragment eventually was not accepted as for a copy of 4QJN Hebrew. J. Starcky, the first editor, did not accept this identification proposal, and therefore turned these fragments over to J. Strugnell. Y. Yadin thought that this fragment was another copy of the *Temple Scroll* (Y. Yadin, *The Temple Scroll* [Jerusalem: The Israel Exploration Society, 1983], vol. III *Supplementary Plates*, Pl. 38* et 40*) and the editor hesitantly took up this identification, "4Q365a—4QTemple?," see S. White in *Qumran Cave 4.VIII. Parabiblical Texts, Part I* (*DJD* XIII; Oxford: Clarendon, 1994), 319–33, p. 328: 4Q365a 2 "cannot be taken as simply a third copy of the *Temple Scroll*", and again S. White Crawford, "Three Fragments from Qumran Cave 4 and Their Relationship to the Temple Scroll," *JQR* 85 (1994): 259–73. If this were correct, we would be dealing here with a shorter recension. J. Strugnell, however, already attributed these fragments to a composition of the Pentateuch with unique additions, and considered them more likely as they were a source of the *New Jerusalem* and of the *Temple Scroll*, in a letter to F. García Martínez, "The 'New Jerusalem' and the Future Temple of the Manuscripts from Qumran," in *Qumran and Apocalyptic. Studies on the Aramaic Texts from Qumran* (STDJ IX; Leiden, 1992), 180–213, p. 180, n. 1, adaptation of the note "La 'Nueva Jerusalén' y el Templo Futuro de los MSS de Qumrán," in *Salvación en la palabra. Targum-Derash-Berith. En memoria del profesor Alejandro Díez Macho* (ed. D. Muñoz León; Madrid: Cristiandad, Huesca, 30–32, 1986), 563–90, n. 2. During the preparation of the *editio princeps* of these Cave 4 manuscrits, I had to subdivide manuscrit 4Q554 which was originally planned by J. Starcky, see the note "A propos de la Jérusalem Nouvelle d'après les manuscrits de la mer Morte," *La ville de 1200 avant J.-C. à l'Hégire, Sem* 43–44 (1995): 87–102.

[2] See for example B. Z. Wacholder, *The Dawn of Qumran. The Sectarian Torah and the Teacher of Righteousness* (HUCM 8; Cincinnati: The Oriental Institute of the University of Chicago, 1983), 96.

while others consider it to be its source,[3] and still others turned it into an Essene composition.[4]

However, this conclusion concerning an Aramaic composition in the Qumran environment is more than doubtful.[5] As far as the identification of 4Q524 as the oldest copy of the *Temple Scroll* is concerned, we have shown that that last text seems to be a composition dating from the beginnings of the Community and cannot be dated as far back as the Persian period as has been proposed.[6] While the *terminus ante quem* of the *New Jerusalem* is indicated by the dating of the copies, the *terminus a quo* is lost in the absence of any historic allusion. The only indication could be found in the hippodamic or checkered map of the Hellenistic city transmitted to the east by

---

[3] For example M. O. Wise, *A Critical Study of the Temple Scroll from Qumran Cave 11* (SAOC 49; Chicago: The Oriental Institute of the University of Chicago, 1990), 64–86.

[4] F. García Martínez, "New Jerusalem," pp. 202–13, or "Nueva Jerusalén," pp. 580–90.

[5] As was recently shown by J. Frey, "The New Jerusalem Text in Its Historical and Traditio-Historical Context," in *The Dead Sea Scrolls Fifty Years after their Discovery. Proceedings of the Jerusalem Congress, July 20–25, 1997* (ed. L. H. Schiffman, E. Tov, and J. C. VanderKam; Jerusalem: Israel Exploration Society, 2000), 800–16. Since then F. García Martínez has changed his mind and now proposes a dating at the beginning of the 2nd century B.C., F. García Martínez, "The Temple Scroll and the New Jerusalem," in *The Dead Sea Scrolls after Fifty Years. A Comprehensive Assessment* (ed. P. Flint and J. C. VanderKam; Leiden: Brill, 1999), vol. II, 431–59, see also "New Jerusalem," in *Encyclopedia of the Dead Sea Scrolls* (ed. L. H. Schiffman and J. C. VanderKam; Oxford: University Press, 2000), 2:606–10.

[6] See E. Puech, *Qumrân Grotte 4.XVIII. Textes hébreux (4Q521–4Q528, 4Q576–4Q579)* (*DJD* XXV; Oxford: Clarendon, 1998), 87–89. (I put the beginnings of the Community at 152 B.C.). For a much older dating, the end of the 5th-beginning of the 3rd c., preferably the 4th c., see H. Stegemann, "The Origins of the Temple Scroll," in *Congress Volume Jerusalem 1986* (ed. J. A. Emerton; VTSup 40; Leiden: Brill, 1988), or *idem*, "The Literary Composition of the Temple Scroll and Its Status at Qumran," in *Temple Scroll Studies. Papers Presented at the International Symposium on the temple Scroll, Manchester, December, 1987* (ed. G. J. Brooke; Sheffield: JSOTSup 7, 1989), 123–48, and J. Maier, "The Architectural History of the Temple in Jerusalem in the Light of the Temple Scroll, *ibidem*, pp. 23–62, who opts for the end of the Persian period or the beginning of the Hellenistic period. An older dating, anterior to the Essene movement, is also advocated by Frey, *New Jerusalem*, 807 and n. 39. However, Yadin, *Temple Scroll*, vol. I, *Introduction*, 386–90, already dated this composition from the times of John Hyrcanus or shortly earlier, what M. Broshi, "Visionary Architecture and Town Planning in the Dead Sea Scrolls," in *Time to Prepare the Way in the Wilderness: Papers on the Qumran Scrolls* (ed. D. Dimant and L. H. Schiffman; Leiden: Brill, 1995), 9–22, p. 17, understood as "at the time of the Hasmonean king John Hyrcanus or a little later;" for still other opinions, see pp. 17–18; a note first published in Hebrew in *Avraham Biran Volume*, ErIsr 23 (1992): 286–92.

Alexander the Great and adopted especially by the Seleucids, and in the presence of spiral staircases which are well attested from the Hellenistic period on and among the Nabateans.[7] Therefore, the composition of this document could be dated at the earliest from the 3rd century, or better towards 200 B.C. or shortly afterwards, which is much more likely for an Aramaic composition found in the Qumran caves.[8] In this case, *New Jerusalem* might have been known by the author of the *Temple Scroll*, and not the opposite. But it is more difficult to form an opinion about a dependency of 4Q365a, probably one of the direct sources of the *Temple Scroll*. Is it possible to put forward an answer? The continuation of the investigation of the names of the gates of the city seems to indicate a solution which can be proposed.

THE GATES AND THE GRID PATTERN OF THE CITY

It seems likely that manuscripts 4Q554, 4Q554a and 5Q15 have preserved the remainders of the first columns of the *New Jerusalem* scroll. Before going into the inside of the city and describing its parts,[9] the measuring angel starts by showing the general map to the visionary, the rampart with its three gates on each of its four sides, and he gives the distances between them and from the

---

[7] As has been rightly shown by Broshi, "Visionary Architecture." Consequently, this author would date the composition towards 200 B.C. See also A. Negev, "The Staircase-Tower in Nabatean Architecture," *RB* 80 (1973): 365–83, even though we cannot agree with the author that this type of staircase-tower is a Nabatean invention. On the other hand, M. Chyutin, *The New Jerusalem Scroll from Qumran. A Comprehensive Reconstruction* (JSPSup 25; Sheffield: Sheffield Academic Press, 1997), 126–7, sees the map of the city as a reminiscence of the map of the royal city of David-Salomon with an Egyptian, not a Greco-Roman, influence. The description of the small *insula* remind him of the map of the city of the slaves at Kahun.

[8] The state of the Aramaic language would well accommodate this dating, see E. Y. Kutscher, "The Language of the 'Genesis Apocryphon.' A Preliminary Study," *ScrHier* 4 (1957): 1–35, pp. 6, 15: state of language comparable to that of 1QApGen.

[9] It is obvious from the indications of manuscripts 2Q24 and 11Q18 that the author deals afterwards with the inside of the city, the temple at the center of the city and the cult that has to be practised, the altar, etc. The reconstruction of the scroll by Chyutin, *New Jerusalem*, in which the description of the gates occupies colums XV–XVI, more or less in the center of the scroll, while the beginning deals with the temple and the cult, cannot be understood. It seems that the author wants to imitate the order of Ezekiel 40–48 and wants to stretch the evidence of the manuscripts, particularly that of 11Q18, which preserved the end of the scroll.

corners, with the help of a seven cubit long reed.[10] The city is not a square as in Ezek 48:30–35 or an enormous cube as in Rev 21:16, but an immense rectangle measuring 140 stades (or *res*) in length in the direction north-south and 100 stades of width in the direction east-west, that is a perimeter of 480 stades.[11] The distance between the gates or the length of a section of wall between two towers is, therefore, 35 stades on the long sides and 25 stades on the short sides.[12] There are still 480 other, smaller gates or posterns which correspond with streets in between the *insulae*,[13] meaning clearly one street for every stade (that is to say: 51 reeds for the *insula* + 6 [3 × 2] reeds of free space [peristyle or sidewalk] around the *insula* + 3 reeds for half of the street = 60 reeds of 3.15 m., that is 189 m for the stade which is indeed the expected distance).[14]

As indicated in 4Q554, the measuring angel starts at the northeast corner of the city and enumerates three main gates with a distance of 35 stades in between on the eastern and on the western sides, which correspond to three large streets or important avenues,

[10] While in Ezek 48:30–35 the reed measures six cubits of seven palms, that is the royal cubit of 52.5 cm, as is explained in Ezek 40:5 and 43:13 or also distances which can be divided by six, here the reed measures seven cubits of six palms, or the common cubit of 45 cm, but the length of the reed is not affected; it still stays the same: 3.15 m.

[11] J. T. Milik, "5Q15," in *Les 'Petites Grottes' de Qumrân* (M. Baillet, J. T. Milik et R. de Vaux; *DJD* III; Oxford: Clarendon, 1962), locates the city in the southern strip of the *terumah*. J. Licht, "An Ideal Town Plan from Qumran—The Description of the New Jerusalem," *IEJ* 29 (1979): 45–59, locates the temple in the fourth strip at the south side and therefore comes to a more or less square map of the city, in order to at best recover the ideal map of the model of Ezekiel, but this representation which does not take textual evidence into consideration, must be abandoned.

[12] P. Söllner, *Jerusalem, die hochgebaute Stadt. Eschatologisches und Himmlisches Jerusalem im Frühjudentum und im frühen Christentum* (Texte und Arbeiten zum neutestamentlichen Zeitalter 25; Tübingen: A. Francke, 1998), 121, 131, follows the translation by J. Maier, *Die Qumran-Essener: Die Texte vom Toten Meer*, Band I–II (München: Reinhart, 1995), who reads 24 cubits instead of 25 as in the manuscript, and obtains, therefore, a rectangle of 140 by 96 stades!

[13] It is in fact clear from the number of towers that are on the side of the rampart (1432), two at each postern and one half-way from the posterns, that is 480 × 3 = 1440, that the twelve large gates and their two towers are not taken into consideration and that the author substracted the eight corner towers instead of adding four. In fact, in this outline there can only be 468 posterns, plus the twelve large gates, and therefore 1440 towers or 1444 if the corner towers are double.

[14] See J. Starcky, "Jérusalem et les manuscrits de la mer Morte," *Le Monde de la Bible* 1 (1977): 38–40, E. Puech, "A propos de la Jérusalem Nouvelle," 96–98, with bibliography.

two of them measuring 10 reeds or 31.5 m. in width, and a immense boulevard (the big *decumanus* of the Roman city) extending at the north side of the temple, measuring 18 reeds, that is 126 cubits or 56.7 m. in width. He enumerates three other gates at a distance of 25 stades on the southern and northern sides, corresponding to three other large streets or avenues, two of them measuring 9 reeds and 4 cubits, that is 67 cubits or 30.15 m. in width, and a large central boulevard (the large *cardo*) measuring 13 reeds and 1 cubit, that is 92 cubits or 41.4 m. Even though the author does not specifically say so, it is very likely, as will appear from the following, that this very wide boulevard or *decumanus* extending along the northern side of the temple corresponds with the central gates of the eastern and western sides of the rampart of the city and not with the southern gates of those sides, as has been suggested.[15]

THE NAMES OF THE GATES

Only the names of five out of the twelve gates of the city, named after the twelve sons of Jacob, are preserved in 4Q554 (Gen 29:31 – 30:24 + 35:16–20; 35:22–26). The measuring angel starts out at the northeast corner and continues clockwise. The name of the first gate on the long side of the rectangle near the north-east corner has by chance been preserved. It is of SIMEON who is not the oldest but the second son of Jacob and Leah, the oldest one, Ruben, having been relegated to lesser status (4Q554 1 i 5[13]). The next preserved name is that of the first gate of the small south side of the rectangle, near the south-east corner, JOSEPH, the oldest son of Rachel (4Q554 1 i 10[18]). The following preserved name is that of the gate of the same small side, the one that is close to the south-west corner, RUBEN, the oldest son of Jacob and Lea who comes here only at the sixth place (4Q554 1 i 13[21]). Finally, the two other

---

[15] Licht, "Ideal Town Plan," 48–49: ". . . lying to the south side of the street network." Furthermore, Licht attributes a theoretical value of 0.5 m. to a cubit, without any known attestation. He is followed by Broshi, "Visionary Architecture," 12–15, and by Chyutin, "Ideal Town Plan," 81–86. In the edition of 5Q15, with the benefit of 4Q554, Milik (5Q15, *DJD* III, p. 185) rather arbitrarily situates the city and the temple in the southern strip of the *terumah*, even though he perfectly related the twelve gates of the rampart with the six described avenues. But the presentation of these boulevards takes place after the entrance to the city and the boulevards cut across from side to side, from gate to gate (4Q554 1 ii 12–23).

preserved names are those of the last two gates of the small north side, the gate of NAPHTALI in the center and the gate of ASHER at the north-east, the names of the two youngest sons of the servants Bilhah and Zilpah (4Q554 1 ii 3[8] and 5[10]). However, it is impossible to read the name of the gate of Dan in 4Q554 1 ii.[16]

The restoration or distribution of the names of the other gates, according to the twelve sons of Jacob, and not according to the names of the twelve tribes of Israel as in Rev 21:12, causes problems depending on which of the known lists is adopted. Y. Yadin restored the deficient sequence of the names of the gates of the south side of the exterior forecourt of the temple in the *Temple Scroll* (XL 14–XLI 11) with the help of the sequence of the gates of the intermediate forecourt (XXXIX 11–XL[1ff.]), a parallel listing that can be found in 4Q365a 2 ii where only the names of the west and north sides are preserved (the last five out of the six names). There the descriptions start also with the northeast corner: Simeon, Levi, Judah, Reuben, Joseph, Benjamin, Issachar, Zebulun, Gad, Dan, Naphtali and Asher.[17] In fact, this sequence differs both from that of the list of the encampment of the tribes around the tent of meeting in the desert (Num 2:3–31) and even from that of the gates of Jerusalem in Ezekiel, where the list starts at the north side and the western corner of the city wall (Ezek 48:30–35). It also differs from the list of the tribes for the wood offering festival in the *Temple Scroll* XXIII–XXIV, tribes grouped by two during the six days of the week: Levi—Judah, Benjamin—'Joseph' (represented by his sons Ephraim and Manasseh), Reuben—Simeon, Issachar—Zebulun, Gad—Asher, Dan—Naphtali, see also the preserved remains of 4Q365 23 10–12.[18]

In his search for parallels, Yadin might perhaps not have known about the list of the *New Jerusalem* according to 4Q554, since he was interested in the other alleged copy of the *Temple Scroll* (4Q365a 2). But in their research with original texts, other critics who knew about this list, have without failure noted an exact correspondence between the beginning and the end of the list of 4Q554 and the *Temple Scroll*

---

[16] Contrary to the unauthorized edition of K. Beyer, *Die aramäischen Texte vom Toten Meer, Ergänzungsband* (Göttingen: VandenHoeck & Ruprecht, 1994), 96: 129.

[17] Yadin, *Temple Scroll*, vol. I, 255–6.

[18] See White Crawford, "Three Fragments from Qumran Cave 4," and E. Tov and S. White, "4Q365," *DJD* XIII, 291–2, but read at the end of line 6 [*lt*]*ht h'wl*[*wt*]°[instead of the proposal of Yadin [*w*]*'t h'gl*[*y*]*m*[followed by the editors or *w't h'wl*[*h* by Wise and Wacholder.

(11Q19), but have too quickly drawn the conclusion that the entire list corresponds.[19] It is impossible to insist too much on an exact parallel in 4Q365a 2 because only the names of the last five gates have been preserved, a final sequence which more lists have in common: *Temple Scroll*, 4Q365a and *New Jerusalem*. However, taking into consideration the distances of three hundred and sixty cubits between the gates in 4Q365a and in the *Temple Scroll* XL–XLI, it is obvious that these two texts deal with the same subject, in both cases the gates of the exterior forecourt of the temple, which is confirmed by the continuation of the text, as opposed to *New Jerusalem* that describes the gates of the city. But it is certainly impossible to maintain that the sequence of the *Temple Scroll*, of *New Jerusalem* and of 4Q365a, which puts the gate of Levi in the middle of the east side and which omits Ephraim and Manasseh, "seems to follow a peculiar order corresponding to the sequence of tribes as it is mentioned in the context of the wood-offering (11Q19 XXIII)."[20] On the one hand, the lists are very incomplete in two out of three documents and, on the other hand, the sequence of the tribes in the wood-offering in the *Temple Scroll* differs too much from the list of the gates: Levi—Judah, Benjamin—Joseph (Ephraim et Manasseh), Reuben—Simeon,

---

[19] See Wise, *Critical Study*, 78–81, (p. 79): "It is very significant that the 4Q MS of the NJ contains twelve named gates in exactly the same order (see figure 1)"! The author provides, however, the correct list in note 58, according to the brief note by Starcky, but he does not retain it in figure 1 (p. 79) where, incorrectly, he simply identifies the two lists, and therefore concludes: "The fact that the texts agree on the order and names of the twelve gates is virtually decisive proof of their interrelatedness all by itself" (p. 81). Also García Martínez, trying to refute the conclusions of dependency proposed by Wise, notes the same agreement: "The only real instance of agreement between the two texts is the well-known correspondence of the names of the gates of the temple in *11QTemple* with those of the city in *NJ*" ("New Jerusalem," 185). This correspondence is also accepted by Broshi ("Visionary Architecture," 11) and Frey ("New Jerusalem," 806–807), both quoting García Martínez, but Frey also adds the list of 4Q365a here, and again (p. 815) where he writes that 4Q554 "shows the order of the gates corresponding to that in the Temple Scroll. (11QT^a 40:13ff.) and in the Reworked Pentateuch (4Q365a 2 ii), but differing significantly from the order of gates in Ezek 48:30–35. . . ." However, the author is supposed to have knowledge of the note by Starcky and of our study, see p. 800, n. 1! García Martínez, "New Jerusalem" (*Encyclopedia*), p. 608, now notes: "in a similar order . . . although the order is not identical."

[20] As it is described by Frey, "New Jerusalem," 815: "Moreover, it seems to follow a peculiar order corresponding to the sequence of tribes as it is mentioned in the context of the wood-offering (11QT^a 23). Therefore, the arrangement of tribes documented in these texts might correspond with certain cultic practices rather than being merely theoretical."

Issachar—Zebulun, Gad—Asher, Dan—Naphtali. It is therefore impossible to find a sequence corresponding with specific cultic practices of the tribes in these documents dealing with the names of the
gates. The sequence of the names of the gates in these particular
documents seems to be dictated by another logic.

The list of the gates of the square city in Ezekiel (48:30–35) starts,
as we have seen, at the north side, from the western corner on. We
see, in order, on the north side: 1) Reuben, 2) Judah, 3) Levi, east
side: 4) Joseph, 5) Benjamin, 6) Dan, south side: 7) Simeon, 8)
Issachar, 9) Zebulun, west side: 10) Gad, 11) Asher, 12) Naphtali.
In this list the first place is occupied by Reuben, the oldest son of
Jacob and Leah, followed by the fourth and third brother respectively (sons of Leah), while Judah takes the central position, certainly
because the Prince (nasî') of the House of David is called upon to
play a more important role than that of the priesthood (Ezek 37:25).
But Levi nevertheless remains associated with Judah as expected,
and he occupies the northeastern gate, since in the semitic world
the temple is generally orientated towards the rising sun. Thus the
order of the gates on the side of the city facing the most important
part of the territory seems to be explained. Then, on the eastern
side are placed the sons of Jacob and Rachel, in their birth order,
Joseph and Benjamin followed by Dan, the oldest son of Bilhah,
Rachel's servant. Thus the sons of Jacob, three sons of Leah and
three sons of Rachel (and of her servant), are equally divided. On
the south side are divided in order the second son of Jacob and
Leah, Simeon, and his two other brothers (sons of Leah), Issachar
and Zebulun. Finally, on the eastern side, Gad and Asher, the two
sons of Zilpah, Leah's servant, and Naphtali, the second son of
Bilhah, Rachel's servant. The order is therefore not articificial but
calculated: on the north and south sides the sons of Leah, facing
each other, and west and east, opposite each other the sons of Rachel
and of their servants, the sons of Bilhah, Rachel's servant, surrounding
the sons of Zilpah.[21]

---

[21] Yadin, *Temple Scroll*, vol. I, 255 (diagram) gives, without explanation, a reverse
order on the north and east sides, and, on p. 256, he reverses the position of the
gates on the south and east sides in Ezekiel! A comparable inversion affects the
sequence of Numbers 2 at the west and south sides, p. 255.

The list of the tribes for the wood-offering festival in the *Temple Scroll* XXIII–XXIV also answers to an order which has its own internal logic. As expected with pairs, the sons of Jacob and Leah come first, Levi with the priesthood serving in the temple and Judah, then as counterbalance the two sons of Rachel, Benjamin first this time because 'Joseph' is represented here by his two sons, Ephraim and Manasseh, then the oldest and the second sons of Jacob and Leah, Reuben and Simeon, the two last sons of Leah, Issachar and Zebulun, then the sons of the servants, Gad and Asher, sons of Zilpah, Leah's servant, and finally Dan and Naphtali, sons of Bilhah, Rachel's servant.

The order of the encampment of the tribes around the tent of meeting in the desert in Num 3:3–31 is not without significance, and since the tribe of Levi is set aside to perform the service in the tabernacle, Joseph is represented by his two sons, in order to reach the number of twelve tribes. In the first place, at the east side, come the sons of Jacob and Leah, Judah and his two younger brothers Issachar and Zebulun, at the south side, his two older brothers Reuben and Simeon, and Gad, the oldest son of Zilpah, Leah's servant. Opposite, at the west side, the sons of Jacob and Rachel, Ephraim and Manasseh, Joseph's sons, and Benjamin, finally at the north side, the other sons of the servants, Dan the oldest son of Bilhah, Rachel's servant, then Asher the youngest son of Zilpah and finally Naphtali, the youngest son of Bilhah.

Among the lists of the names of the twelve gates of the courts of the temple in the *Temple Scroll* and its likely source (4Q365a), only the list of the gates of the intermediate court is entirely preserved (11Q19 XXXIX 11–13). The context shows that the author always starts his description at the east side: 11Q19 XXXVIII 13–14, XXXIX 14–XL[1ff.], 8–9, 11, 14–XLI 11. The order is the following: at the east side 1) Simeon, 2) Levi, 3) Judah, at the south side 4) Reuben, 5) Joseph, 6) Benjamin, at the west side 7) Issachar, 8) Zebulun, 9) Gad, and at the north side 10) Dan, 11) Naphtali, 12) Asher. This order also has its own logic: Reuben is relegated to the fourth position at the south side, to make room for his younger brothers at the preferred place with Levi in the center and Judah following, maybe also because of the proximity of the territory of the tribe at the south side. Following the oldest son Reuben are the two sons of Rachel, Joseph and Benjamin. At the west side are the

two last sons of Leah, Issachar and Zebulun and Gad, the oldest
son of Zilpah, Leah's servant, and at the north side, Dan and Naphtali,
the two sons of Bilhah, Rachel's servant, and finally Asher the
youngest son of Zilpah, surrounding the two sons of Bilhah.

The Names of the Gates of the City in *New Jerusalem* (See Table 1)

Is it now possible, taking these divergent lists into consideration, to
restore the complete list of the names of the gates of the city in *New
Jerusalem*? Although only five out of them are known from the manuscript, this certainly seems to be possible. On the south side, the
names of JOSEPH at the east side and of REUBEN at the west
side are preserved. The name of the central gate must be the gate
of *BENJAMIN* because in all those lists the two brothers, sons of
Jacob and Rachel, are always together and on the same side, in the
fifth and sixth positions of the south side in the *Temple Scroll*, on the
west side of the tent of meeting in *Numbers* 2, but in the fourth and
fifth positions of the east side in *Ezekiel* 48 and also in *New Jerusalem*,
but this time on the south side, thus relegating Reuben to the sixth
position, contrary to the *Temple Scroll*. This latter correspondance
between Ezekiel 48 and *New Jerusalem* of the fourth and fifth positions of the gates in the rampart of the city of Jerusalem should not
surprise anyone. Then it is more than likely that *LEVI* and *JUDAH*
occupy the second and third positions on the east side, after the first
position of SIMEON, their elder brother. The restoration of the line
in 4Q554 which does only leave a little space for this name would
confirm the reading "Levi." Thus Levi occupies the central position
on the east side in the same order as in the *Temple Scroll*, while Judah
who is always following Levi occupies at the same time a position
of territorial proximity. After the mention of the four oldest sons of
Jacob and Leah and the two sons of Jacob and Rachel, the mention of the two other sons of Leah, *ISSACHAR* and *ZEBULUN*,
should logically follow, just as in the *Temple Scroll* and *Ezekiel* 48,
which is confirmed by what follows. The last two names on the small
north side being documented, 11) NAPHTALI the youngest son of
Bilhah and 12) ASHER the youngest son of Zilpah, the oldest one
of Zilpah, *GAD*, should be inserted first, then the oldest one of Bilha,

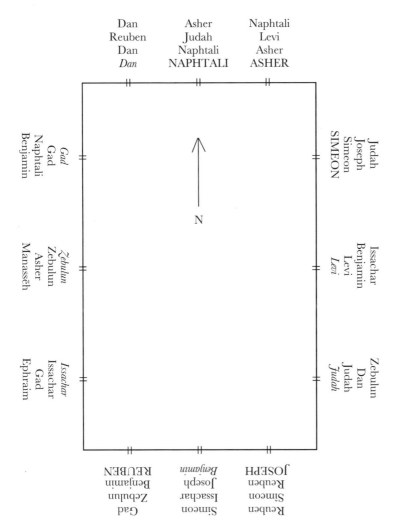

Table 1. Legend (from the inside to the outside):
New Jerusalem—4Q554 (the known names in capitals, the restored names in italics);
Temple Scroll **XXXIX** 11–XL[1ss], XL 14–XLI 11 and 4Q365a
(the last five names); Ezek 48:31–34; and Num 2:3–31.

DAN, so that the sons of the servant of Leah surround the two sons of the servant of Rachel. Thus we see again the final sequence of the names of the gates of the forecourts of the *Temple Scroll*.

The only difference with the lists of the *Temple Scroll* is located at the south side, with the priority of the two sons of Rachel over Reuben, the oldest son of Jacob and Leah. It is possible, even likely, that the order we know from 4Q365a, the source of the *Temple Scroll*, is anterior to that of *New Jerusalem*, since the oldest son Reuben has moved down to the sixth position after the two sons of Rachel, still in the birth order, Joseph—Benjamin, while he was at the first position in *Ezekiel* 48 or in the fourth position in the source of the *Temple Scroll* and already in *Numbers* 2.[22] This demotion, unique in these lists, is the source of the different designations of the three gates of the southern wall, the only differences between the lists of the *Temple Scroll* and *New Jerusalem*. Is there an allusion in this demotion to the list of the tribes apportioned to Mount Gerizim for the blessing, Simeon and Levi, Judah and Issachar, Joseph and Benjamin, and to the Mount Ebal for the curse, Reuben, Gad and Asher, Zebulun, Dan and Naphtali, the oldest and youngest sons of Leah and the sons of the servants (Deut 27:12–13)? In fact, Reuben is guilty of incest (Gen 35:22; 49:4, see *Jubilees* 33:1–20), and is the object of cursing in Deut 27:20 on the one hand and, on the other hand, Simeon, Levi and Judah are together at the east side, the side of the rising sun, as they are at Mount Gerizim, together with Joseph and Benjamin.

This restoration and identification of the gates of the city takes on its greatest importance in *New Jerusalem*, naming the openings of the big streets to the ramparts, as we suggested above. The gates of Benjamin—Naphtali (the youngest sons of Rachel and Bilhah) delimit the large south-north boulevard or large *cardo*, and the gates of Levi—Zebulun, sons of Leah, the very large east-west avenue or the large *decumanus* which runs along the north side of the temple, as it is stated expressly. This detail cannot be trivial or without effect in the naming of the gates and the arrangement of the streets leading to the temple, at the heart of the future city. It can be deduced that

---

[22] I have already provided the restoration of this list in my note, "A propos de la Jérusalem Nouvelle," 93–95, without giving a developed presentation, which was not suitable for that context.

the temple cannot occupy the southern part of the city, but must occupy a central point, with big avenues running alongside. The order of the names has therefore nothing to do with specific cultic practices,[23] or directly with the geographical proximity of the territory of the tribes, even if this can indirectly be taken into account for Judah.[24]

This restoration of the names of the gates according to the twelve sons of Jacob is important because it provides one more argument to prove that the *Temple Scroll* does not stem from *New Jerusalem* as has been claimed,[25] but from a Hebrew source similar to 4Q365a.[26] The *Temple Scroll* cannot be the source of *New Jerusalem* either.[27] And *New Jerusalem* can at most stem from the source of the *Temple Scroll*, but the dating of this source is then in question and, if the author knew it, he did not follow it in his list of gates, putting Reuben out of order, and he also did not follow it in the general description of the city, already with the mention of the measuring angel instead of the divine author. In fact, the description of the gates of the city, on the one hand, and that of the gates of the forecourts of the temple, on the other hand, cannot be the cause of this difference. The author was obviously preoccupied by another issue, the relegation of Reuben, guilty of incest, and the 'outclassing' of Simeon and Levi who revenged Dinah, their sister who was raped by the Shechemites. Contrary to Gen 49:5–7, Deut 33:8–11 praises Levi, just like the *Testament of Levi* in Aramaic which insists on purity, warning his descendants against all fornication, impurity, etc.[28] Thus *New Jerusalem* certainly is not an Essene-Qumranian composition, but it more likely comes from priestly circles which were so active in

---

[23] See Frey, "New Jerusalem," 815.

[24] See Chyutin, *New Jerusalem Scroll*, 80–81.

[25] Wise, *Critical Study*, see *supra*.

[26] J. Strugnell (see n. 1) regarded 4Q365a as a source of *New Jerusalem* and of the *Temple Scroll*, likewise F. García Martínez, "New Perspectives on the Study of the Dead Sea Scrolls," in *Perspectives in the Study of the Old Testament and Early Judaism. A Symposium in Honour of Adam S. van der Woude on the Occasion of His 70th Birthday* (ed. F. García Martínez and E. Noort; VTSup 73; Leiden: Brill, 1998), 230–48, p. 239.

[27] Wacholder, *Dawn of Qumran*, see *supra*. The composition of this text is later than that of *New Jerusalem*, as we have indicated above.

[28] The Aramaic text of the *Testament of Levi* from the Cairo Genizah preserve traces of this episode in MS Cambridge, column a; see E. Puech, "Le *Testament de Lévi* en araméen de la Geniza du Caire", *RQ* (forthcoming); see also *Testament of the XII Patriarchs, Levi* 5:1–4.

many other Aramaic compositions, such as the *Testament of Levi* and the *Testament of Qahat*, the *Visions of ʿAmram*, etc.[29] The interest of the author in the placement of the gate of Levi at the center of the east side in the New Jerusalem, as well as a similar interest regarding the temple and its cult, points in this direction. Therefore, the composition of *New Jerusalem* predates the oldest discovered copy by at least one century.[30]

---

[29] See E. Puech, *Qumrân Grotte 4.XXII. Textes araméens, Première Partie 4Q529–549* (*DJD* XXXI; Oxford: Clarendon, 2001).

[30] K. Beyer, *Die aramäischen Texte vom Toten Meer* (Götttingen: VandenHoeck & Ruprecht, 1984), 215, dates this composition at best in the first half of the 1st century B.C.E. And H. Stegemann, *Die Essener, Qumran, Johannes der Täufer und Jesus. Ein Sachbuch* (Freiburg-Basel-Wien: Herder, 1993), 141, dates it from the 4th or 3rd century B.C.E.

THE MODERN HISTORY OF THE QUMRAN PSALMS SCROLL AND CANONICAL CRITICISM

James A. Sanders

At its 2001 annual meeting the international Society of Biblical Literature celebrated the completion of the publication of the Dead Sea Scrolls. It was a gala occasion with a sense of the miraculous hovering over the some three hundred who attended. In the previous five decades eight volumes of the *Discoveries in the Judaean Desert* series had been published, but during the last decade twenty-eight more have appeared. Emanuel Tov, Magnes Professor of Hebrew Bible at the Hebrew University, made the difference. In 1990 Tov became the fourth chief editor of the international team charged with the publications, following Roland de Vaux, Pierre Benoit, and John Strugnell. Tov increased the team from twenty scholars to over sixty. Five further volumes are in the pipeline at the present, which will complete publication of thirty-nine volumes of the scrolls in the *DJD* series, over nine-hundred ancient texts all told. Reference volumes will follow.

Tov's address on the occasion was stunning. It was a tell-all, detailed history of publication of the Dead Sea Scrolls from his standpoint, and as only he with his intimate knowledge of the last phases of the enterprise could tell it.[1] It was a kind of oral history of the sort Sterling Van Wagner and Weston Fields, an editor of the present volume, and others have recently been collecting from the earlier generation of Dead Sea Scrolls scholars. One weeps over the lost, unpublished records that have languished in widows' and heirs' attics, when the source of the most intimate kind of knowledge has been totally lost in the deaths of those who failed to complete their work, or who were too modest to publish their memories of what really happened. This is all the more poignant in the case of the Scrolls about which much unconscionable nonsense has been published and said simply because there was lack of access to most of them for so long, not only to the Scrolls but also to the real histories swept

---

[1] See Hershel Shanks' interview of TOV in BAR 28/3 (May 2002) 32–35, 62.

394SANDERS

away by death and personal modesty. That situation has changed dramatically in the past ten years since open access has been the policy rather than the exception to much of the world's information, through the internet and through the fall of walls of separation and discrimination around the world. It seems appropriate to honor Tov's own openness, as well as labors of the past ten years, by offering a tell-all, modern history of the Dead Sea Psalms Scroll (11QPs^a = 11Q5).

TOV'S ADDRESS

In his address Tov mentioned that the tendency early on to give names to the Scrolls documents as they appeared meant that some might not finally be the most appropriate. He then gave examples, one of which was the Psalms Scroll from Qumran Cave Eleven. He explained that assigning numbers instead of titles obviated the problem, and that has been the practice recently. Tov was, of course, right both that early titles usually endure, and that they can be problematic. One thinks of "Manual of Discipline," "Job Targum," "Wiles of a Wicked Woman," and "Temple Scroll." The situation is true in archaeology generally. When a find on a dig comes to light, it needs to be discussed by the team and is therefore given a name or tag of some sort to be referred to, sometimes that very evening when the day's work is assessed. Often a name hastily bequeathed becomes the name that appears in eventual publication.

In the case of the Psalms Scroll, a change was made from the siglum I gave it in the first two publications. The preliminary report referred to the scroll as 11QPss.[2] The editor of *BASOR* at the time, William F. Albright, made no comment in correspondence about the designation but, on the contrary, ran the article as received in the next available issue, which appeared the following spring while we were still in Jerusalem. The second article issuing from work on the scroll during the 1961–62 winter of recovery in Jersualem was titled, "Psalm 151 in 11QPss."[3] It was not until the third article appeared that I used the more specific siglum, 11QPs^a.[4] This came partly out

---

[2] "The Scroll of Psalms (11QPss) from Cave 11: A Preliminary Report," *BASOR* 165 (February 1962): 11–15.
[3] In the *ZAW* 75 (1963): 73–86.
[4] "Two Non-Canonical Psalms in 11Ps^a," *ZAW* 75 (1964): 57–75.

of a conversation with William Brownlee, but the subtle change in sigla indicated my growing sense that the Scroll had been viewed at Qumran as "canonical" despite its differences from the much later Masoretic Psalter. And thereon hangs a tale.

THE PSALMS SCROLL

During the summer of 1959 I was a member of a New York University seminar in Israel. After the six-week course I crossed through the Mandelbaum Gate from Israeli Jerusalem to the Arab Old City where I was expected at the American School of Oriental Research (ASOR, later to be renamed The Albright Institute) on Salah ed-Dhin Street, north of Herod's Gate. I had not known that Frank Cross would be there. He was in Jerusalem along with others of the Cave Four team of scholars working on the lots of fragments assigned to each. I was very pleased to see him at the ASOR that night at dinner. We had met a couple of years earlier, before he left McCormick Seminary in Chicago in 1958 to succeed Robert Pfeiffer at Harvard. We had a good conversation at the table, then later he asked if I would like to accompany him to the Palestine Archaeological Museum nearby the next morning. I, of course, accepted with delight.

I shall never forget the visit to the museum that morning. After Cross had introduced me to other members of the team he took me to his table in "the scrollery." While there he picked up a fragment with tweezers and asked if I would identify it. I read it off. It was a portion of Jeremiah 8. I think now that he was impressed. I was not. I had earned the PhD from the Hebrew Union College in Cincinnati four years earlier, and my feeling was that if I could not read that beautiful script I should return the degree! The major emphasis at HUC was and is reading text, whether Akkadian, Ugaritic, Hebrew, Aramaic, or Greek. Many texts, daily. Reading about the sources was also required, but nothing substituted for reading original texts.

Still it was a stunning surprise a year later when Cross called my home in Rochester, N.Y. to ask if I would be interested in going to Jerusalem to unroll one of the scrolls recovered from Cave 11. I shall never in my life forget that moment. I, of course, said I would. Other factors made a good fit. I was planning a year's sabbatical leave from my post at the Colgate Rochester Divinity School for 1961–62, and Cross said that would work fine. I was applying for

a Guggenheim Fellowship for the year and Cross said he would write
a recommendation. I had applied to be Annual Professor at the
ASOR anyway, and Cross agreed to put in a word there as well.

I pause here to offer my understanding of the politics of selection. Considerable amounts of money had been taken from the
Palestine Archaeological Museum's endowment to secure the manuscripts of Caves Four and Eleven from the Ta'amri bedouin of the
area where they were found. Donations were sought from European
governments and from American philanthropists to refurbish the
endowment of the Museum, which at that point was privately owned
and endowed largely by Rockefeller family money.[5] The Cave 11
Job Targum, for instance, was financed by monies from the Netherlands
which then had the right to appoint the scholars to work on it. The
Psalms Scroll was financed by Kenneth and Elizabeth Bechtel of
San Francisco, who stipulated that the scholar appointed to unroll
and prepare the scroll for publication should be American. Père
Roland de Vaux, the head of the Ecole Biblique Française in Jerusalem,
president at the time of the Museum, the Qumran archaeologist,
and the "chef de travail" of the international team working on the
massive Cave Four fragments, asked Cross to appoint the American.
He added the stipulation that the one appointed should not be
Roman Catholic. De Vaux was sensitive already at that time to the
criticism that there were too many Catholics working on the scrolls
in Jordanian Jerusalem. The two stipulations narrowed the field of
choice for Cross.

UNROLLING THE SCROLL

I departed by ship from New York in September 1961. I had not
known it, but the USS Constitution to Naples that trip was to be a
cruise as well as passenger ship. That gave me plenty of time to re-
read and practically memorize the Masoretic Psalter (in BHK) during the nearly two weeks on board ship. Before I sailed I visited
with Cross about the assignment, and read everything I could find

---

[5] The museum was nationalized by the Jordanian government early May, 1967
just before the Six-Day War, so that when Israel assumed responsibility for it the
next month it came under the authority of the Department of Antiquities of the
State of Israel, now the Israel Antiquities Authority.

about how to unroll an ancient scroll. Then when I arrived in Beirut (on the USS Excalibur from Naples) I consulted with Abbé Milik and with Abbé Starcky at the Ecole Française there about the task ahead. I had to schlep my gear for the year by "service" taxi down from Beirut through Damascus and Amman, then across to Jordanian Jerusalem. There I took up residence as Annual Professor of the American School for 1961–62. Paul Lapp, who had been Acting Director the previous year, was now the Director. I was alone at that point; Dora and our six-year-old son, Robin David, would not arrive until spring.

Since the Jordanian Department of Antiquities had not yet issued the official release of the scroll for unrolling and study, I spent most of the first seven weeks at the ASOR functioning as Annual Professor (AP). I led archaeological visits to various important sites in the area for the appointed fellows that year, and served as AP on a three-week tour led by Lapp, up through Jordan, Syria and Lebanon to Turkey and back. Those were the Kennedy years in Near Eastern relations, the halcyon days of recent history for Americans. We were welcomed everywhere we went. Finally, not long after our return to Jerusalem official permission was received in early November from the Jordanian Department of Antiquities in Amman to begin work on the scroll.

On November 10th I was escorted by de Vaux, Lapp and Yusef Sa'ad, the secretary of the Museum, into the individual lab room that I was assigned in the museum. It was ample enough in size and looked out three large windows to the east facing the Mount of Olives and Mount Scopus. There was a built-in table-shelf that ran the length of the room under the windows. It was covered in clean, brown wrapping paper. There was an oil-burning stove with a kettle in one corner of the room, a humidifier, and a camel-hair brush on a small desk with chair in another. Sa'ad brought the scroll, which was in a Jordanian shoe box, from the Museum vault into the room. De Vaux formally handed it to me, whereupon the three gentlemen rather somberly backed out of the room and left me to my task. By their body language they made it clear that either I successfully unrolled the scroll, or it would unroll me! I was thirty-three years old, but looked considerably younger. I am sure some were wondering why Frank Cross had sent a kid over to do a man's job. In fact, I apparently put them in mind of the young John Allegro of the Cave Four team, who only a few years earlier had distinguished himself rather negatively in their minds, to the point that Sa'ad did not permit Najib Albina, the museum photographer, to take a photo of myself with the scroll. There is none.[6]

Left alone in the room I turned to the table under the windows, where the box lay, and fell to my knees with the prayer that I do as well as I possibly could and not disappoint or embarrass Frank Cross. When I extracted the scroll from the box it was daunting, to say the least. Covered in ancient bat dung and caked mud it gave an odor that my nose was to live with rather intimately the next ten days. De Vaux had estimated from the way it looked that it might take three to six months to unroll. The camel-hair brush helped somewhat in dusting it off, but I had to borrow a pen-knife from Prof. William Reed, who was also at the ASOR at the time. One third of the scroll had decomposed during its two-millenia residence in the floor of Cave 11, and one end was black and hard as ebony. Some winters during those two thousand years would have had a bit more rainfall than others, even at 1200 feet below sea level in the stark desert on the northwest shorewastes of the Dead Sea. It had been found in February, 1956, in the floor of the cave with one end partly buried. The decomposed skin had turned into mucous substance which when dried hardened into a very imporous substance, like black ivory. The skin itself was thick enough that de Vaux thought it possibly was bovine in origin, rather than ovine or capric like most of the scrolls. DNA analysis has recently indicated that some of the animal skins were from the ibex, which might account for the scroll's thickness.

Day after day I chipped away at the ebony one skin thickness at a time until I had all five sheets, plus the separable leaves and fragments that had been on the outer layers of the scroll, under square glass panes on the long table. All told there were almost fourteen feet of scroll under glass, with an average width (the length of a column) of over six inches of the extant scroll.[7] Albina and I are the only humans in modern times who have seen the linen threads that linked the five sheets of skin. By the time I arrived each morning

---

[6] This is the reason that when recently George Brooke of Manchester, who was preparing a photographic history of the Scrolls, asked me for a photo of myself with the scroll, I could not supply him with one.

[7] The exact data can be found in J. A. Sanders, "The Psalms Scroll," in *Encyclopedia of the Dead Sea Scrolls* (ed. L. Schiffman and J. VanderKam; New York: Oxford University Press, 2000), Vol. 2, 15–17.

they had disintegrated into dust. The scroll had been rolled so tightly by its last reader that the threads were amazingly well preserved—until exposure. This accounts as well, I am sure, for how well the scroll itself was preserved. The *DJD* and Cornell edition photos show that quite well. The writing surface has discolored deeply since I first saw it forty years ago. The outside leaves had probably been part of a sixth sheet at the beginning of the extant scroll. The top margin of each column in the scroll was well preserved while about a third of each column was lost in the decomposed part at the bottom. As I worked I catalogued, and carefully put all the tiny chips of ebony in the clean cigarette boxes provided by the museum, but I am morally certain that I lost nothing legible on the scroll that had been handed me. Even so, loss of a few letters would have been worth recovering the whole scroll for study after two thousand years. On the morning of the tenth day, November 20th, I had arrived at the last sheet deep inside the tightly rolled scroll. It was so tight that I was having difficulty with it.

I had had to use the humidifier only a few times up to then. The point of the humidifier was to mollify the skin in order to render it supple and pliable enough to open, but not so much as to cause it to discolor. The glass instrument had two chambers with a narrow neck between the upper and lower. There was a sponge to moisten and put in the lower chamber, a screen to put at the neck, and a lid to cover the top. The scroll would lie on the screen in the top chamber. De Vaux warned me not to leave it in the humidifier for more than twenty minutes at the time. The tenth and last morning, however, I could see that leaving it in the humidifier for longer periods would not be enough. It would not yield and lunch time was approaching. So I decided that I would put the kettle on the stove and leave it for the length of time it would take me to run over to the American School, eat lunch, and run back. I had not told anyone about the progress I was making during those ten days, nor did I at the table that noon. I certainly did not tell anyone what I had just done! I knew that de Vaux would be very upset; he had warned me against doing anything of the sort. When I returned the lab room was comfortably warm and humid, but nothing was amiss. I carefully chipped away at the bottom edge of the last rolled sheet which gradually yielded its treasures. I finally had it all under glass. It formed an arc due to the drawn, black bottom edge of the sheets, and the table-shelf was the right length and width for all of it.

On the eleventh morning at about 11:00 AM Albina, as was his custom, brought his photographic equipment into the room. Albina, a Palestinian Christian, was an artist. Everyone who has worked with his photographs says he was expert. He knew when the morning sun through those windows would be at its best angle for exposing infra-red film, the medium he used. Infra-red increases the contrast between the carbon-based ink on the scroll and the color of the skin on which it was written. I could read the bottoms of the columns through the blackened skin better in the prints than on the leather. I worked all winter with his photographs, mainly in the library at the Ecole Biblique. They were easier to read than the actual scroll. I would return to the museum only to check to see if a black dot was scribal or verminous, or for some similar concern.

PUBLICATION

Thereafter I worked rather steadily at the job of studying the scroll to prepare it for publication. It was so beautifully preserved on the inside that I had been able to read it as I unrolled it, column by column. I then worked on the photos mostly at the Ecole Biblique, a few blocks away, because it had one of the best libraries for biblical and archaeological study, if not the best, in the world. Without the family at that point I immersed myself in making sense of the scroll. The Ecole library had a special card-catalogue index to every critical study ever published for every verse of the Bible. It is now digitized, of course, but it was paper-published in the 1980s even before it became accessible by computer, and hence available to all scholars. But back then it was available only at the Ecole in Jerusalem. It was because of those index cards that I was able to identify Psalms 154 and 155 in the scroll, almost as soon as I started work on them.[8]

---

[8] I identified Psalm 151 because I had read it in the Septuagint as a student, and it was when looking up literature on it that I saw Martin Noth's work in the *ZAW* of 1930 on the Five Syriac Psalms preserved in the fly leaves of a Syrian bishop's Book of Discipline. Noth's work in retroverting the Syriac to Hebrew was so close to the original now available in the scroll, that I sent the MSS of the two articles noted above in notes 2 and 3 to the *ZAW*. The numbering of the five as Psalms 151 to 155 comes from a twelfth-century Syriac biblical MS from Mossul (Mossul 1113), of which P. A. H. deBoer graciously provided me photos before their publication by the Peshitta Institute in Leiden.

During that winter I twice read papers critically assessing the contents of the Scroll for small gatherings in the American School library of western scholars from the French and British Schools, which were also situated at that time east of the wall separating the two Jerusalems. The first paper was on Psalm 151 and the second on Psalms 154 and 155, both later published in the *ZAW*.[9] By the time of the second *ZAW* article in 1964 I had settled on the siglum, 11QPs^a, as more apt that 11QPss. A number of other apparently deviant biblical texts had already been published which used the alphabetic sequential sigla. But more than that there was and is no firm evidence of a truly proto-MT Psalter before second century C.E. On the contrary, there is literary evidence of later ancient Psalters with up to 200 psalms.

The Associated Press ran a very short public notice from Amman in early February 1962 stating that the scroll had been unrolled and was being studied in Jerusalem. *The New York Times* picked up on it and sent their correspondent, Dana Adams Schmidt, resident in Beirut at the time, down to Jerusalem for an interview. He cut a rather avuncular figure and put me completely at ease. One question he asked was what it took to unroll an ancient scroll. I told him the story above. When I had finished he asked if that was all. I realized that my answer did not sound like high science, so I responded by saying, "That, and guts." I had in mind the Yiddish word, *chutzpah*, and should have said "gall" perhaps. In his article, published on the front page of *The Times* of 8 March 1962, he wrote, "Professor Sanders says all it takes to unroll an ancient scroll is a camel-hair brush, a humidifier, a pen knife, and guts." I was often teased about it. It apparently became a "College Bowl" quiz question on the radio the following year, and was included still later in a book of quotations.

After our return to the States in the summer of 1962 I continued to work preparing the *editio princeps* of the whole scroll. The administration and faculty in Rochester were very supportive, as was my family, assisting in many ways. When I had completed the first draft I took it to the homes of the three scholars I knew would be most helpful: Frank Cross (at Harvard), John Strugnell (then at Duke), and Patrick William Skehan (at Catholic University). I showed each

---

[9] See above notes 3 and 4.

all the sections to that point, but they were especially helpful in particular areas: Cross the palaeographic section; Strugnell the apparatus to each psalm; and Skehan the non-Masoretic psalms. I have
thanked them in print several times, but feel I can never express
gratitude enough to them, and fortunately two of them are still alive.
They were very generous and helpful. The point is that none of
them disagreed with the new siglum.

I mailed the draft manuscript for *DJD* 4 to Oxford in January
1963, and the volume was published in 1965.[10] Even so, I had not
yet directly addressed the issue of the canonical status of the scroll
at Qumran, or of the Psalter itself at that point in Early Judaism;
nor did any of them raise the issue directly. I had, however, been
attempting to gather the data necessary to do so. Not only was
Skehan helpful with the manuscript of *DJD* 4, he was also very generous with transcriptions of his lot of Cave 4 fragments of Psalms.
So was van der Ploeg of Nijmegen in the Netherlands, one of the
scholars appointed by the Dutch government to work on Cave 11
materials. Van der Ploeg sent me all the information he had about
other materials from Cave 11, as did Yigael Yadin about Psalms
fragments he had from Masada. As a result, "Pre-Masoretic Psalter
Texts" was published in the same year as *DJD* 4.[11] I continued to
work on and improve that list, which was a catalogue and index of
all known texts of biblical psalms, and included it in the Cornell
edition of the Psalms Scroll two years later. In the light of such evidence I simply could not bring myself to call the Qumran Psalms
Scroll a liturgical collection of psalms derived from an already canonical, single Jewish Psalter. That was Skehan's position.[12] We stayed
in close touch through all the debates and he would send me MSS
of his work in advance, plus two copies of them when published
("one to throw darts at" he would graciously say).

Elizabeth Hay Bechtel expressed continuing interest in the Scroll.
She invited us to San Francisco, where she lived, to address the City
Club there in 1963, and often came to visit us, first in Rochester
and then in New York City where we moved in 1965. She was sup-

---

[10] *Discoveries in the Judaean Desert of Jordan IV: The Psalms Scroll of Qumrân Cave 11
(11QPsᵃ)* (Oxford: Clarendon, 1965).
[11] "Pre-Masoretic Psalter Texts," *CBQ* 27 (1965): 114–23.
[12] See, e.g., his argument in "A Liturgical Complex in 11QPsᵃ," *CBQ* 35 (1973):
195–205.

portive of the scholarly work on the scroll, but was very interested in a second edition which would be more accessible to lay folk. Before we arrived in July 1965 at Union Theological Seminary in New York, where I was invited to join the faculty, I had set to work on what I thought and hoped would satisfy her wish but also afford me the opportunity to address issues that had arisen from discussions of the early articles published, and from reviews of *DJD* 4. Henry Detweiler, president of the American Schools of Oriental Research at the time, and a dean of the school of architecture at Cornell University, also in upstate New York, suggested that I submit the second manuscript to Cornell University Press, which I did. It was published in 1967.[13] That edition included Fragment E, a fifth separable leaf from the front of the Scroll, which Yadin had published in *Textus* 5 in 1966, as well as the improved version of the catalogue and index to all pre-Masoretic Psalter texts, which had appeared in 1966 in *CBQ*.[14] The Cornell edition also has improvements in the apparatus and notes to the non-Masoretic psalms in the Scroll, in which I attempted to respond to the various critiques of the early articles and of the Oxford edition.[15] It also provided translations from the Syriac of Pss 152 and 153, lacking in the Hebrew Scroll.

In *Textus* 5 (1966) there were three responses to work on the Scroll to that point: Yadin's publication of Fragment E, a response by Shemaryahu Talmon to my reading of Ps 151, and a challenge by Moshe Goshen-Gottstein. The challenge was that I had not in the

---

[13] *The Dead Sea Psalms Scroll* (Ithaca: Cornell University Press, 1967).

[14] Yadin wired me on New Year's Eve in 1965 to inform me of his forthcoming publication of Fragment E in *Textus* 5. I was stunned. Here is another case of possibly valuable information lost because so far as I know Yadin never revealed from whom he had obtained the fragment, other than to say that it was an anonymous American who wished to remain so. Those were the days of cloak-and-dagger secrecy surrounding the scrolls, and I assumed at the time that Yadin would tell me what he could when he could. He never did. Given where it seems to fit in the scroll, just before col. 1 beneath the first four separable leaves, I am still puzzled because the fragment would have had to be within the folds of leather under the first four fragments which I had had to pry loose from the dung-encased crust on the outside. See the discussion with references and dates in the Cornell edition (note 13 above), 155–9.

[15] This has not been noted by most scholars, who apparently took the Cornell edition to be merely a popularization of the Oxford. Actually, I tried to answer, on pp. 93–117, the objections scholars had had to my readings of Ps 151 and of the Sirach canticle in Col 21, but I have seen very few references at all to the Cornell volume in the scholarly literature since.

DJD volume addressed the issue of canonicity. He was right, but in the Cornell edition, written before I had seen *Textus* 5, I did so.[16] I had thought long and hard about the issue and could not bring myself to assume, as the older generation apparently did, that the Psalter as we know it in the much later MT had already been "canonized" for all Judaism. By that time Jack Lewis had published his study of all references to Yavneh/Jamnia and uncertainty about the stabilization of the Ketuvim was in the air.[17] What we had in hand was a magnificent exemplar of a Psalter from the mid-first century C.E., and a number of fragments of Psalms from Cave 4 which also cast doubt on such an assumption. There simply was no evidence that I could see to view the Psalms Scroll as somehow derivative of an already set Psalter; there were only old assumptions that, in my view, were being called into question in various ways. Further, Yadin informed me that he thought the Temple Scroll, also from Cave 11, was probably viewed as canonical at Qumran.[18] It seemed to me that the Scrolls generally were calling many old assumptions into question, and this one in particular. To substantiate the observation, in the same year that the Cornell edition appeared, *JBL* published my first attempt at cataloguing all publications of Scroll materials to that point.[19]

In the meantime Ted Campbell at McCormick Seminary in Chicago asked me to contribute an article to a 1968 McCormick Seminary publication he was editing. I decided it was time to try again. Abbé Starcky had just published some Cave 4 Psalter fragments which also included non-Masoretic psalms and a different order of the Masoretic ones, two characteristics of 11QPs^a that raised the questions about its canonical status.[20] I had become convinced that the

---

[16] Cornell edition, pp. 10–15.

[17] J. Lewis, "What Do We Mean by Jabneh?" *JBR* 32 (1964): 125–32, and a review of discussions it has engendered in *HUCA* 70–71 (2001): 233–59.

[18] See Y. Yadin, *The Temple Scroll* (Jerusalem: The Israel Exploration Society, 1983), 390–92.

[19] "Palestinian Manuscripts 147–67," *JBL* 86 (1967): 431–40. This was supplemented in *JJS* 24 (1973): 74–83, and in *Qumran and the History of the Biblical Text* (ed. Frank Cross and Shemaryahu Talmon; Cambridge: Harvard University Press, 1975), 401–13. Since those efforts Joseph Fitzmyer published two editions of *The Dead Sea Scrolls: Major Publications and Tool for Study* (Atlanta: Scholars Press, 1975–1977, 1990), so that I could with confidence turn my attention elsewhere. I understand that he intends to update his lists even though it is a considerably more daunting task at this point.

[20] J. Starcky, *RB* 73 (1966): 356–7 (Pl. XIII).

new path had to be explored.[21] That new path, I clearly saw, could not be limited to the parameters of earlier discussions. I became interested in the whole issue of authoritative community traditions and scriptures, how they arose, and how they functioned in ancient communities. I was trying to gather and share all the data I could assemble to make informed decisions.[22]

FURTHER PROBES

In 1968 I received two invitations which I accepted because I knew they would help explore the issue further. The one was from W. D. Davies and Louis Finkelstein, who had been asked to edit a multi-volume Time-Life illustrated edition of the Bible, to write the introduction to the Old Testament or Hebrew Bible (HB). The other was from Eugene Nida who was forming a research group sponsored by the United Bible Societies (of New York, London, and Stuttgart) to be called the Hebrew Old Testament Text Project (HOTTP), and to be a companion to the one he had formed for The Greek New Testament Project in 1955. The six members of the HOTTP, plus assistants, met for a month annually from 1969 to 1980 in Germany.[23] We dealt with almost 6,000 textual problems throughout the Hebrew Bible, produced five volumes of a preliminary report on our work, and have so far published three volumes of the final report authored by Dominique Barthélemy.[24] Having to

---

[21] See "Cave 11 Surprises and the Question of Canon," *McCQ* 21 (1968): 284–98, which was reprinted in three later collections of essays on the Scrolls and on the issue of canon, by different scholars interested in the same question.

[22] See "The Dead Sea Scrolls—A Quarter Century of Study," *BA* 36 (1973): 109–48, in which I tried to give an overview of all the Scrolls recovered from all provenances, and to address the issue of canon.

[23] The six were Dominique Barthélemy, Hans Peter Rüger, Norbert Lohfink, W. D. McHardy, A. R. Hulst, and myself. All but two years we met in the Erholungsheim in Freudenstadt. We agreed to participate if we were permitted also to work out and publish a hermeneutic and method in textual criticism that we deemed indicated by the new situation caused by recent manuscript discoveries, especially the Scrolls. The UBS, including the Württembergische Bibelanstalt in Stuttgart, agreed and the final result will be BHQ. See J. Sanders, "The Hebrew University Bible and Biblia Hebraica Quinta," in *JBL* 113/3 (1999): 518–26.

[24] *Preliminary and Interim Report on the Hebrew Old Testament Text Project*, Vols. 1–5 (ed. D. Barthélemy et al.; London and New York: United Bible Societies, 1973–1980). Three volumes of the final report have appeared with the fourth, on the Psalter, in the press: Dominique Barthélemy, *Critique textuelle de l'Ancien Testament* (Göttingen:

deal in depth with the textual peculiarities of all the books of the HB gave us a comprehensive perspective on the effect of the Scrolls on the varying textual situations of all the books of the HB. The hermeneutic being pursued by Biblia Hebraica Quinta, the fifth volume in the Biblia Hebraica series of critical texts of the Hebrew Bible that started in 1902, is based on the work of the HOTTP.[25]

I wrote the introduction for the Time-Life project, which was, however, abandonned in 1971. I then sent the MS I had generated for it to Fortress Press, which published it in 1972 as *Torah and Canon*. In it I tried to deal with how and why canons arose, and how early oral traditions that later became part of the Jewish canon had already functioned authoritatively, like later Scripture in early Jewish communities, which gave shape to the Torah and the Prophets.[26] This was followed soon thereafter by a study probing canon as function in order to respond to ensuing discussions. The presidential address to the Society of Biblical Literature in November 1978 then probed the relation between text and canon, and how study in each discipline had changed since the discovery of the Scrolls.[27] This was followed by other studies pressing the relationship.[28] It was important

Vandenhoeck & Ruprecht, 1982, 1986, 1992). The introductions to *CTAT* are rich in discussions of the whole history of the transmission of the text from antiquity to the latest critical studies, but is seldom referred to in scholarly literature; see J. Sanders, "Hermeneutics of Text Criticism," *Text* 18 (1995): 1–26, and "The Hebrew University Bible and Biblia Hebraica Quinta". In the few that have made reference to it one comment has been made that we dealt with only scattered problems. And yet they represent the most problematic texts in the HB and gave the committee a comprehensive perspective on the textual situation of all the books of the HB. Our mandate was to provide assistance to modern translation committees throughout the world who often do exactly what ancient translators did, follow already extant translations for difficult textual problems. We have provided critical in-depth studies to each problem treated in order to break that cycle, which is evident in modern scholarship as well. In addition the lengthy introductions provide extensive studies of the whole discipline of textual criticism unavailable elsewhere. Not only so, but every textual problem will indeed be treated in the forthcoming BHQ apparatuses and in the accompanying critical commentaries to each biblical book.

[25] BHQ should be published by 2006. The first Biblia Hebraica was published in 1902 and the fourth, BHS, in 1972. See J. Sanders, "Keep Each Tradition Separate," *BRev* 16/4 (2000): 40–49, 58.

[26] *Torah and Canon* (Philadelphia: Fortress Press, 1972), which went into eleven printings before it was remaindered. It has since been republished by Wipf and Stock.

[27] "Text and Canon: Concepts and Method," *JBL* 98 (1979): 5–29.

[28] *Canon and Community* (Philadelphia: Fortress Press, 1984) and *From Sacred Story*

to find the interface between the move in Early Judaism from oral and textual fluidity to textual stability, and the move from authoritative oral traditions to later fixed canons. Work in this area continues.[29]

COMPARATIVE MIDRASH AND THE CANONICAL PROCESS

Seeking that interface as well as the relation between text and canon, created the subdiscipline called comparative midrash. It is important to trace the Nachleben of early oral traditions and of nascent Scripture through the literature of Early Judaism, including early Christian and even Tannaitic literature, in order to discern the forms and function of citations and allusions, just as we had tried to do in the pre-exilic and exilic biblical literature.[30] It became clear that the two were in fact the same exercise or function. Even the citations showed the same kinds of fluidity, or lack of verbal "accuracy." References in the earlier literature to Exodus or Davidic or patriarchal stories exhibited "poetic license," so to speak, but clear enough that the point of the reference was not lost in doing so. The adaptability of the text to ever-changing situations required a measure of stability of reference to be effective. Early Jewish literature exhibits the same adaptability/stability quotient.

Parallel work in textual criticism showed that the early history of transmission of the text, the pre-Masoretic period, was one of textual fluidity as well: tradents could modify or adapt a passage cited to fit the later use not only in citations but also in translation and in copying; textual stability in this regard was not clear until the proto-Masoretic period beginning in the second century of the common era. The focus of early tradents clearly was in getting their communities to understand the text, copied, translated or cited, in their later contexts. The focus of the later tradents in the proto-

---

to Sacred Text: Canon as Paradigm (Philadelphia: Fortress Press, 1987). These are also available through Wipf and Stock.

[29] Note the bibliographies attached to *A Gift of God in Due Season: Essays on Scripture and Community in Honor of James A. Sanders* (ed. Richard Weis and David Carr; Sheffield: The Academic Press, 1996), 274–85, and *The Quest for Context & Meaning: Studies in Biblical Intertextuality in Honor Of James A. Sanders* (ed. Craig Evans and Shemaryahu Talmon; Leiden: Brill, 1997), xxv–xxxix.

[30] See above notes 26–28.

Masoretic period shifted to textual accuracy. The Scrolls have made this point abundantly clear, and it resonated well with the move in Greek translations from the fluidity of early Greek translations (the so-called Septuagint) to the stability and even rigidity of the second-century c.e. Greek translations.[31] It was clear that there were many pseudo-variants in the pre-Masoretic MSS and translations, unrelated to distinct Vorlage, due to the earlier tradents' freedom to focus on Community understanding instead of on verbal accuracy.

The Greek Minor Prophets Scroll from Naḥal Ḥever provided, according to Barthélemy, the missing link between the fluidity and the stability.[32] Something must have happened in the basic Jewish hermeneutic, or understanding of the nature of the text, evidenced in both textual transmission and in textual citations. The basic understanding or hermeneutic of the text of Scripture shifted from an early shamanistic or dynamic understanding of the inspiration or provenance of the text generally, to a view of the text as verbally inspired, and hence no longer textually adaptable to new situations.[33] The view of literal inspiration of Scripture followed very soon. The rise of the Tannaitic and Rabbinic *middot* about the same time give testimony as well to the shift.[34] Tradents could no longer slightly modify or adapt a passage of Scripture to make its message clear, but they could and did engage in all sorts of midrashic techniques to render the stable text adaptable and relevant in commentaries to the on-going believing communities. All this was happening precisely in the crisis period of Roman occupation and then destruction of Palestinian Jewish institutions.

---

[31] See Martin Hengel's very helpful survey of Greek textual fluidity in *The Septuagint as Christian Scripture: Its Prehistory and the Problem of its Canon* (New York: T & T Clark, 2002) pp. 43, 86, 89, et passim.

[32] D. Barthélemy, "Redécouverte d'un chainon manquant de l'histoire de la Septante," *RB* 60 (1953): 18–29. This was more fully developed in *Les Devanciers d'Aquila: Première publication intégrale du texte des fragments du Dodécaprophéton* (Leiden: E. J. Brill, 1963). See the critical praise of Barthélemy's work in Emanuel Tov's full edition of the Dodecapropheton in *The Greek Minor Prophets Scroll From Naḥal Ḥever (8ḤevXIIgr)* (*DJD* VIII; Oxford: Clarendon Press, 1990), ix, and throughout the volume.

[33] The thesis of the *JBL* 98 (1979) article, pursued in J. Sanders, "Stability and Fluidity in Text and Canon," in *Tradition of the Text: Studies offered to Dominique Barthélemy in Celebration of his 70th Birthday* (Göttingen: Vandenhoeck & Ruprecht, 1991), 203–17.

[34] See J. Sanders, "The Issue of Closure," in *The Canon Debate*, ed. Lee McDonald and James Sanders (Peabody: Hendrickson, 2002) 252–66.

Comparative midrash developed out of the basic meaning of the term "midrash" probed by Renée Bloch, followed by Roger Le Déaut.[35] The focus was on midrash as function in early believing communities rather than on the literary form of the later rabbinic midrashim. The question was how a passage cited or alluded to functioned in the literature where the reference occurred. The question generated the hermeneutic triangle, that is, appreciation of the importance of three basic factors necessary to seek out in each case studied: a. the passage called upon or cited; b. the socio-political situation of the community for whom the new writing was intended; and c. the hermeneutic of the tradent writing it for that community.[36] It applies to early fluid copies of Scripture, to translations of Scripture, and to new literature based on it. All Early Jewish literature was written Scripturally, that is, was based on or arose out of one or more Scriptural books or passages. The later writers knew to base what they had to say for and to their communities on "Torah" or received Scripture, oral or written. If what they had to say was important enough in their minds to share it they told it in Scriptural terms and cadences. The critical triangle proved to be a sharp tool for understanding this kind of canonical process through the Early Jewish period. It is also an antidote to the hermeneutic circle that entraps most readers of the Bible, whereby they find in Scripture what their community already teaches them is there.

Comparative midrash also developed a perspective on biblical intertextuality. Scripture, even the earliest, is full of echoes, citations, and allusions to earlier tradition and Scripture. Tradition in this sense would include Ancient Near Eastern literature resignified into biblical literature, creation myths, flood stories, and the like. No two rereadings and reapplications are ever quite the same. Each addressed different community needs when retold or rephrased. While it is often very difficult to reconstruct what those needs were the result when valid is well worth the effort. When that is discerned then the

---

[35] See R. Bloch's article on "Midrash" in *Supplément au Dictionnaire de la Bible* (SDB), vol. 5 (1957) cols 1263–81; and R. LeDéaut, "Apropos a Definition of Midrash," *Int* 25 (1971): 259–82, translated by Mary Howard Calloway. The latter was in part a response to Addison Wright's *The Literary Genre Midrash* (Staten Island: Alba House, 1967) which opposed Bloch's broader definitions of "midrash."

[36] Despite the dramatic rise in interest in recent years in the Nachleben of Scripture in Early Judaism and Early Christianity, rarely are the reprises of Scripture studied in the light of these three basic factors. See, e.g., James L. Kugel, *Traditions*

hermeneutics, or understanding of the tradition, by which the re-signification came about is also discernable. There are three kinds of intertextuality: the interrelation of blocs of text; the function of citations and allusions within a text; and the interrelation of reader and text. When different texts are bound together by redactional activity or canonical compression they tend to interact in the readings of the communities for which the binding was effected. A kind of chemistry emerges between them. When earlier texts are cited or echoed in later writings they obviously were intended by the tradent to function in some authoritative mode, and they cast light on each other. And when a text is read its own texture interacts with the texture of the reader, and a kind of chemistry emerges between them as well. Again, no two readings are ever exactly the same. Because this kind of activity surrounded texts that made them into a canon, it is important to probe as much of it as possible. Comparative midrash illumines the canonical process in Early Judaism and Christianity.[37]

When the debate about the status of the Psalms Scroll seemed to have abated, an article and a dissertation were published in 1985 which reopened it.[38] In them Gerald Wilson considerably supported the editor's view of the status of the Scroll. Not long thereafter another dissertation appeared that provided an in-depth analysis of all the Psalter manuscripts from Qumran, seeing the Psalms Scroll as a Davidic Psalter designed to authenticate the solar calendar in use at Quman and elsewhere in Early Judaism, and a marker on the path toward the eventual MT-150 Psalter.[39] The Psalms Scroll,

---

of the Bible: A Guide to the Bible as It Was at the Start of the Common Era (Cambridge: Harvard University Press, 1998), whose focus is on "interpretation" instead of on the crucial factors of socio-political situations and the hermeneutics used in them.

[37] The second type of intertextuality, that of reference to earlier tradition and literature, has seven modes: 1) citation with formula; 2) citation without formula; 3) weaving familiar phrases into the new composition; 4) paraphrasing; 5) allusion to persons and events of the past; 6) echoes; 7) mimesis of literary structure. See J. Sanders, "The Dead Sea Scrolls and Biblical Studies," in Sha'arei Talmon: Studies in the Bible, Qumran, and the Ancient Near East Presented to Shemaryahu Talmon (ed. Michael Fishbane, Emanuel Tov, and Weston Fields; Winona Lake: Eisenbrauns, 1992), 37–42. The canonical process is also described by Magne Saebo in On the Way to Canon: Creative Tradition History in the Old Testament (Sheffield Academic Press, 1998); and see his contribution to The Canon Debate.

[38] Gerald H. Wilson, "The Qumran Psalms Scroll Reconsidered: Analysis of the Debate," CBQ 47 (1985): 624–42, and The Editing of the Hebrew Psalter (SBLDS 76; Chico CA: Scholars Press, 1985).

[39] Peter W. Flint, The Dead Sea Psalms Scrolls and the Book of Psalms (Leiden: Brill,

dating from the second quarter of the first century of the common era, highlights both the textual and the canonical fluidity of pre-Masoretic biblical manuscripts. Due to the nature of the Psalter its canonical fluidity is more in evidence perhaps than in the case of other books of the Bible.[40] It provides a road mark on the multi-track move toward the eventual MT-150 collection.[41]

1997). The dissertation had been defended at Notre Dame in 1993. See the editor's review in *DSD* 6/1 (1999): 84–89, and that of Shemaryahu Talmon in the *JBL* 118/3 (1999): 545–7.

[40] There are only a few fragments of Proverbs that were part of only two exemplars (4QPrv[a] and 4QPrv[b]). By contrast there are thirty-nine manuscripts of Psalters among hundreds of fragments plus the Cave 11 Psalms Scroll.

[41] See the incisive study of the multi-track canonical process in David Carr's "Canonization in the Context of Community: An Outline of the Formation of the Tanakh and the Christian Bible," in *A Gift of God in Due Season*, 22–64.

UTOPIA AND REALITY: POLITICAL LEADERSHIP AND ORGANIZATION IN THE DEAD SEA SCROLLS COMMUNITY

Larry Schiffman

The corpus of some 800 scrolls or, in most cases, fragments of scrolls which emerged from the Qumran caves, can generally be classified into three groups: (1) Hebrew Bible, (2) apocryphal compositions, including many previously unknown texts, and (3) the literature of the Qumran sect, considered by many scholars to be identical with the Essenes described by Philo, Josephus and a number of Greek authors. This study will concentrate primarily on the last group of texts, those which tell us of the teachings, beliefs, and way of life of the Qumran sect.[1]

In a variety of ways, these texts exhibit a sense of the separation of powers which the sectarians believed was required by biblical law. During the period in which the Qumran sect flourished, we can also discern a shift in political power and leadership from an elite group of Zadokite priests to a broader-based constituency. We will examine the manner in which the separation of powers affected a number of areas of sectarian thought: the division of king and priest, the division of executive and legislative functions, and the interrelationship of religious and temporal power (what we term "church and state") in the ideal Jewish polity.

Kings and Priests

We will begin with a text which lies somewhere on the borderline between the sectarian corpus and the literature which preexisted it. Among the most enigmatic of the Qumran documents is the well-

---

[1] See the detailed study of the Qumran library in D. Dimant, "The Qumran Manuscripts: Contents and Significance," *Time to Prepare the Way in the Wilderness: Papers on the Qumran Scrolls by Fellows of the Institute for Advanced Studies of the Hebrew University, Jerusalem, 1989–90* (ed. D. Dimant and L. H. Schiffman; Leiden: E. J. Brill, 1995), 23–58.

preserved Temple Scroll, a kind of rewritten and reedited Torah. Its author/redactor rewrote the sacrificial and legal sections of the Pentateuch in order to express his own particular views on the nature of the Temple and its sacrifices, the political system of Hasmonean times, and Jewish law on a variety of topics. The text was compiled some time in the latter half of the reign of the Hasmonean King John Hyrcanus (134–104 B.C.E.), or early in the reign of Alexander Janneus (103–76 B.C.E.).[2]

This document was initially thought to reflect the teachings of the Qumran sect. Nevertheless, numerous differences between the approach of this document and those of the Qumran sectarian texts were immediately clear after it was published.[3] When the existence of 4QMMT, also known as the "Halakhic Letter," a foundation document of the Qumran sect, became known in 1984,[4] the true nature of the Temple Scroll became clear. It turned out that, despite the date of its completion some time in the Hasmonean period, this scroll was actually composed of a variety of sources which were earlier than the complete scroll.[5] These sources were most probably Sadducean in nature and provenance.[6] Among the latest of the sources of the Temple Scroll, reflecting Hasmonean times in a variety of its polemics, is that known as the Law of the King.[7]

This section of the scroll, actually a rewriting and expansion of the Law of the King of Deuteronomy (Deut 17:14–20), puts forward a demand for a thoroughgoing reform of the existing political

---

[2] See L. H. Schiffman, "The Temple Scroll and the Nature of its Law: The Status of the Question," *The Community of the Renewed Covenant, the Notre Dame Symposium on the Dead Sea Scrolls* (ed. E. Ulrich and J. VanderKam; Notre Dame: University of Notre Dame Press, 1994), 37–55.

[3] First noted by B. A. Levine, "The Temple Scroll: Aspects of its Historical Provenance and Literary Character," *BASOR* 232 (1978): 5–23; cf. H. Stegemann, "The Origins of the Temple Scroll," VTSup 40 (1988), 235–56.

[4] Cf. L. H. Schiffman, *Reclaiming the Dead Sea Scrolls: The History of Judaism, the Background of Christianity, the Lost Library of Qumran* (Philadelphia: Jewish Publication Society, 1994), xvii–xviii.

[5] A. M. Wilson and L. Wills, "Literary Sources of the Temple Scroll," *HTR* 75 (1982): 275–88; M. O. Wise, *A Critical Study of the Temple Scroll from Qumran Cave 11* (SAOC 49; Chicago: Oriental Institute of the University of Chicago, 1990), 35–194.

[6] See Schiffman, "The Temple Scroll," 46–8.

[7] A full discussion of this text is found in L. H. Schiffman, "The King, His Guard and the Royal Council in the Temple Scroll," *PAAJR* 54 (1987): 237–59. Cf. M. Weinfeld, "'Megillat Miqdash' 'o 'Torah la-Melekh,'" *Shnaton* 7 (1987/9): 214–37.

order in the Hasmonean period. Following Deuteronomy, the text requires that, upon assuming office, the monarch must have a Torah scroll written for him which he is to have with him at all times. Here the text is calling for restoration of a constitution based on the Torah which the author sees as violated by the Hasmoneans. We must remember that by this time, the descendants of the Maccabees who had fought so valiantly against Hellenism and foreign influence were already conducting themselves in a Hellenistic manner.

Among the clearest demands of this scroll is that the position of king be separated from that of high priest. Indeed, this text demands that there be a royal council, the supreme legislative and judicial body, to consist of 12 priests, 12 Levites and 12 Israelites. All decisions of the king are to be subject to ratification by this body. In this way, the power of the king is severely limited by the proposed "constitutional monarchy." Further, the document makes clear that the king is forbidden to conduct an offensive war without the approval of the high priest and consultation of the Urim ye-Tummim, the oracle which the high priest wore on his breastplate.

All of this is clearly a reflection of the severe objection of the circles that produced this document to the system of Hasmonean kingship in which those actually of priestly lineage were for all intents and purposes functioning as kings. In fact, in later Hasmonean times, the priestly rulers even styled themselves kings on their coins. The authors of the Law of the King of the Temple Scroll, no doubt followed by the members of the Qumran sect, saw this usurpation as a violation of biblical constitutional law. What was at stake here was the separation of temporal and religious powers, and the authors objected to their confluence in the hands of the Maccabean priest-kings. At the same time, according to this scroll, the king, who would not have been a priest, had to answer to a mostly Levitical council, and the high priest was in some matters the king's superior. So even this separation of powers bordered to some extent on a kind of constitutional theocracy, if we may coin such a phrase.

Those who produced this text, and the Qumran sectarians who read and preserved it, were not the only ones to object to the Hasmonean arrogation of both priestly and royal powers. The MMT document itself, in our view, testifies to unhappiness on the part of Sadducean priests with the Hasmoneans' having taken control of the high priesthood when they had originally been rural members of the lower clergy, not descended from the Zadokite high-priestly family.[8] But for the most part, this document indicates specific objections to the legal rulings which guided the Hasmonean Temple.[9]

Yet the strongest opposition to the Hasmoneans came from the Pharisees, the forerunners of the talmudic sages, as described in a *baraita* preserved in the Babylonian Talmud.[10] This source informs us that the Pharisees were willing to tolerate Hasmonean kingship, even though this Aaronide priestly family was not of the house of David, as required for a true Jewish king. However, they disputed the rights of this family to serve as high priests, asserting that the mother (or grandmother) of Alexander Janneus (John Hyrcanus in the account preserved in Josephus[11]) had been a captive and, hence, that her descendants were disqualified from the high priesthood. The Pharisaic objection to the Hasmoneans as priests eventually led to civil strife and later to war and devastation in Judea, but that is a story beyond the scope of this study.[12]

The opposition of the Temple Scroll and other such documents to the Hasmonean house resulted from the fact that the Hasmoneans served as kings. They were regarded as having violated the age-old separation of royal and priestly powers which the Bible had required. A similar separation was carried over into the complex organizational structure of the Dead Sea sectarians as well.

PRIESTS AND LAYMEN

The Qumran sect came into being as a discrete group in the aftermath of the Maccabean revolt when the Hasmonean high priests decided to ally themselves with the Pharisees against the Hellenizing priests, many of whom had been Sadducees.[13] A group of pious

---

[8] See L. H. Schiffman, "The New Halakhic Letter (4QMMT) and the Origins of the Dead Sea Sect," *BA* 53 (1990): 64–73.

[9] A full discussion of the laws in this document is found in E. Qimron and J. Strugnell, *Qumran Cave 4.V: Miqṣat Ma'aśe Ha-Torah (DJD* 10; Oxford: Clarendon Press, 1994), 123–77.

[10] B. *Qidd.* 66a.

[11] *Ant.* 18, 288–96.

[12] See Schiffman, *Reclaiming*, 236–38. See also, D. R. Schwartz, *Studies in the Jewish Background of Christianity* (Tübingen: J. C. B. Mohr [Paul Siebeck], 1992), 44–56.

[13] Cf. F. M. Cross, "The Early History of the Qumran Community," *New Directions in Biblical Archaeology* (ed. D. N. Freedman and J. C. Greenfield; Garden City, NY: Doubleday, 1971), 70–89.

Sadducees left the Temple and protested to no avail the abandonment of Sadducean priestly practice for the halakhic rulings of the
Pharisees. This group, after failing to sway their colleagues and the
Hasmonean leaders by means of the Halakhic Letter (4QMMT),
eventually relocated to Qumran where they lived lives of piety and
holiness, preparing for the end of days.

The sectarian group that eventually came into being, certainly by
the sect's heyday after ca. 134 B.C.E., saw itself as a corporate group.
This is clear from the various names of the sect. It is often called
yaḥad, "community," a nominal use of an adverb usually meaning
"together," and this term may occur in a construct together with
other terms.[14] This is the case with *'aṣat ha-yaḥad*, "council of the
community," probably identical with the assembly to be discussed
below, and *berit ha-yaḥad*, "covenant of the community," a term indicating that the sectarians saw themselves as banding together to
observe the "renewed covenant" of God with His chosen ones, the
members of the sect.[15] Further, we should note that the term *'edah*,
"congregation," designates the community of the end of days to
which we will return below.

The corporate nature of the group is further indicated by the
archaeological remains of Qumran, which apparently functioned as
a sectarian center for those who left their scrolls in the nearby caves.
Here we can observe facilities for the meals that the sectarians sometimes ate communally as well as for the various occupations such as
pottery making, husbandry, and small farming, pursued by members. While the actual sleeping quarters cannot be identified, it seems
that the members of the group lived either in the nearby caves or
tent shelters.[16]

The initial leadership of the sect was made up of Sadducean
priests, termed the Sons of Zadok over and over in the scrolls.[17] This
family descended from Zadok, high priest at the time of Solomon,

[14] S. Talmon, "The Sectarian *yḥd*—a Biblical Noun," *VT* 3 (1953): 133–40.
[15] This phrase is taken from S. Talmon, "The Community of the Renewed
Covenant: Between Judaism and Christianity," *The Community of the Renewed Covenant*,
3–24. Talmon's essay provided the title for the volume.
[16] R. de Vaux, *Archaeology and the Dead Sea Scrolls* (London: Oxford University
Press, 1973), 1–48; Schiffman, *Reclaiming*, 37–57.
[17] J. Liver; "Bene Ṣadoq shebe-Khat Midbar Yehudah," *ErIsr* 8 (1966/7): 71–81;
L. H. Schiffman, *Halakhah at Qumran* (Leiden: E. J. Brill, 1975), 72–5.

whose descendants had virtually uninterruptedly held the high priest-hood in first and second temple times. For this reason they felt that they were entitled to continue in office, even after the Maccabean victory and the appointment of Jonathan, the brother of Judah the Maccabee, as ruler in 152 B.C.E.

The Zadokite priests who started the sect were apparently soon sharing power with laymen as part of the general tendency toward lay power and democratization in Judaism during the second tem-ple period. This general trend abetted the transfer of leadership from the priesthood to lay sages also in Pharisaic-rabbinic Judaism, lay-ing the groundwork for the institution of the rabbinate. Evidence for this transition in the scrolls is found in the requirement of the Rule of the Community that decisions be made according to the rulings of the Sons of Zadok[18] and the majority of the men of their covenant.[19] Apparently, at a later stage in the history of this group, this formula and the political reality behind it were replaced by the *rabbim*, the "many," an assembly of members of the sect.[20] All those who had completed the stages of the initiation process into the sect, attaining ascending levels of ritual purity and knowledge of the sect's teach-ings, could participate in the assembly.[21] Besides its legislative func-tions, which were linked to its ability to properly interpret scripture under divine inspiration, the *rabbim* also served as the supreme judi-cial body, and it appears to have been predominantly lay.

We cannot see this assembly as truly a democratic institution because it did not grant rights beyond a small circle. Only full-fledged members of the sect were permitted to join, and, of course, women could take no role in this body. This form of "democracy for the minority" was typical of the so-called democracies of ancient Greece and the Hellenistic cites, in which voting rights were extended only to a minority that attained the required status.

We have some indication of how this assembly functioned. Each person who wanted to speak had to get the permission of the pre-siding *mevaqqer* ("examiner"), and it was forbidden to speak out of

---

[18] Rule of the Community 5:2–3, 9–10.
[19] Rule of the Community 6:19.
[20] Schiffman, *Halakhah at Qumran*, 68–70.
[21] For the initiation rites, see Schiffman, *Reclaiming the Dead Sea Scrolls*, 97–103; C. Rabin, *Qumran Studies* (Oxford: Oxford University Press, 1957); S. Lieberman, "The Discipline in the So-Called Dead Sea Manual of Discipline," *JBL* 71 (1951): 199–206.

turn. Generally, members spoke in order from highest to lowest status. Anyone who fell asleep during sessions was penalized with a reduction of his food ration. According to most interpretations, decisions were made by voting, following majority rule, a principle thought by the rabbis to have been enshrined in the Bible (Exod 23:2).[22]

While it is not possible to trace the exact historical development of the increase in lay power, it seems that the Zadokite priestly leadership was increasingly eclipsed as the sect developed, even if to some extent they retained formalistic symbols of their earlier oligarchic—or better hieroarchic—prerogatives. By some time in the Roman period (after 63 B.C.E.), what we might term legislative power had shifted almost entirely from priestly hands to those of the lay members of the sect. Even so, it seems that a priest continued to preside over the meetings of the assembly.

When it came to the everyday functioning of the group, however, members were not all equal. There was a roster which listed members from those of highest to lowest status, and those lower on the list had to follow the directives of those above in regard to matters of sectarian law or the conduct of the sect's affairs.[23]

The courts of the sect are described in the Zadokite Fragments, also known as the Damascus Document. This text was first discovered in two manuscripts in the Cairo genizah, and later ten manuscripts emerged from the caves of Qumran.[24] The composition of the sectarian courts as prescribed here provides for a balanced grouping.[25] The basic sectarian courts were of ten judges, probably patterned on the court of ten which appears in the book of Ruth (4:2). The ten were to consist of four of the tribe of Aaron and six from Israel. It has been rightly concluded that the four Levitical members represented the Aaronide priests and the three families of Levites—Gershon, Kohath and Merari. Accordingly, the basic court consisted of one priest, three Levites and six Israelites, not an unfair distribution of clerical and lay power for an ancient Jewish court. Indeed, the Talmud required the presence of all three classes—priests,

---

[22] Cf. Rabin, *Qumran Studies*, 102–7.

[23] Schiffman, *Halakhah at Qumran*, 66–7.

[24] J. M. Baumgarten, *Qumran Cave 4.XIII: The Damascus Document (4Q266–273)* (*DJD* 18; Oxford: Clarendon Press, 1996).

[25] See L. H. Schiffman, *Sectarian Law in the Dead Sea Scrolls: Courts, Testimony and the Penal Code* (Chico, CA: Scholars Press, 1983), 23–30.

Levites and Israelites—in the Great Sanhedrin, the high court.[26]

These various elements indicate that the Qumran sect sought to create a balance between the power of the priesthood with its God-given prerogatives and aristocratic connections, and the common Israelites who, after all, were the vast majority of Jews. Even in this biblicizing, conservative group, the forces of democratization were at work long before the destruction of the Temple.

COURTS AND THE RIGHTS OF THE ACCUSED

Although we have concentrated so far on the issue of separation of powers in Qumran sectarian literature, some remarks about the rights of members of the sect before the courts will also be of interest. Just as in the Pharisaic-rabbinic system enshrined in talmudic literature, in the legal system of the Dead Sea Scrolls there were specific requirements for witnesses to ensure that only reliable individuals could testify.[27] While some have suggested that women were permitted to testify, this view is based on a corrupt passage,[28] and it must be admitted that the Qumran sect disqualified the testimony of women. To be sure, women could not serve as judges or sectarian leaders either, although the texts flatly contradict the suggestion of many scholars that the sect was celibate.[29] Witnesses had to be at least twenty year old males and full members of the group, thus guaranteeing that they were truly observant Jews who would testify honestly. Age requirements also existed to guarantee that judges would be experienced enough for the job yet at the same time to exclude those who had become senile.[30]

Ancient Jewish law was concerned to guarantee that the accused had been fully cognizant that his actions violated the law and that he knew of the punishment for his crime before committing the forbidden action. Otherwise, he could not be considered a purposeful violator and could not be punished. To deal with this problem, the sectarians required that the offender be reproved for a previous commission of the same offense before he or she could be punished for

---

[26] *Sifre Deut.* 153.
[27] Schiffman, *Sectarian Law*, 55–63.
[28] J. M. Baumgarten, *Studies in Qumran Law* (Leiden: E. J. Brill, 1977), 183–86.
[29] Schiffman, *Reclaiming*, 127–43.
[30] Schiffman, *Sectarian Law*, 63–5.

the infraction. For the same reason, the rabbis instituted the requirement of *hatra'ah*, "warning," by which the witnesses had to warn the
offender and appraise him of the punishment for his act before the
commission of the crime.[31]

As in all Jewish legal systems, circumstantial evidence, hearsay,
and evidence not based on testimony (forensic evidence) was excluded.
All these regulations tipped the scales way in favor of the accused
and guaranteed a fair trial to the greatest extent possible. The Temple
Scroll (11QT 51:11–18) prohibits judicial corruption and commands
the death penalty for corrupt judges who take bribes.[32] Further, it
prohibits the king from taking the property of his subjects by the
use of trumped up legal procedures (11QT 57:19–21).

While human rights as we know them were not a subject of discussion in ancient Israel, it is clear that in continuing the system of
biblical jurisprudence and expanding on it, the sectarians continued
to guarantee a fair trial and an equitable system of justice. Accordingly,
some form of due process was provided by sectarian law.

SECTARIAN LEADERSHIP

In discussing the issue of separation and balance of powers, it is
important to note the nature of the sectarian leadership. The Teacher
of Righteousness was the leader who led the group from its initial
opposition to the manner in which Temple worship was being
conducted in the early Hasmonean period to its full-fledged incorporation as a sectarian body with distinct ideology and organization.[33] The Teacher must have functioned in the early years of the
Hasmonean dynasty, in the days of Jonathan (152–143 B.C.E.) or
Simon (142–134 B.C.E.), one of whom was regarded by the sect as
the Wicked Priest, the sworn opponent of the Teacher. The Teacher

---

[31] Schiffman, *Sectarian Law*, 97–98.

[32] L. H. Schiffman, "The Prohibition of Judicial Corruption in the Dead Sea
Scrolls, Philo, Josephus and Talmudic Law," *Hesed ve-Emet: Studies in Honor of Ernest
S. Frerichs* (ed. J. Magness and S. Gitin; Brown Judaic Studies 320; Atlanta, GA:
Scholars Press, 1998), 155–78.

[33] Schiffman, *Reclaiming*, 117–21; G. Jeremias, *Der Lehrer der Gerechtigkeit* (Göttingen:
Vandenhoeck & Ruprecht, 1963); G. Lambert, *Le Maître de justice et la communauté
de l'alliance* (ALBO II.28; Louvain: Publications universitaires, 1952); F. F. Bruce,
Second Thoughts on the Dead Sea Scrolls (Grand Rapids, MI: Eerdmans, 1977), 92–97;
G. W. Buchanan, "The Office of Teacher of Righteousness," *RevQ* 9 (1977): 237–40.

of Righteousness was clearly a priest as we know from direct evidence in the Habakkuk Pesher.[34] Part of his duties included that of legislator. He showed his followers how to put the Torah into effect by revealing to them the *nistar*, the hidden or secret interpretation, which was known only to the sect. It was this body of law with which the Teacher had endowed the sect. Therefore, his teachings had as much validity as the Torah itself. The sect always believed that it would be rewarded for its steadfast adherence to the Teacher's authority.

Though it is difficult to be specific on this matter, it seems that the sect suffered a crisis with the death of its first leader. It had expected that the messianic era was soon to dawn and that no successor to the Teacher of Righteousness would be needed. Nonetheless, the sect weathered this crisis and was able to replace its leader with various officers who later managed its affairs.

The duties of the Teacher of Righteousness were apparently carried out after his passing by two officials of the sect, the *mevaqqer* and the *paqid*.[35] The *mevaqqer*, "examiner," may very well have been a priest, although there is no direct evidence of his status. The *mevaqqer* was a teacher and guide to his followers, responsible for their spiritual and physical welfare. He tested new members and had to approve their entrance into the community. He supervised all members' business transactions, was responsible for approving marriages and divorces, and he was required to treat his people with love and kindness. The examiner had to be between thirty and fifty years of age. He organized the members in the order of their ranks, from the senior to the most junior, which determined the order in which they spoke at the sectarian assembly and their mustering for the annual covenant renewal ceremony.

The *paqid*, literally, "appointed one," was a priest as well. He is known from the Rule of the Community as the official who administered the initial test of those wishing to join the sect. The Zadokite Fragments calls him "the priest who musters at the head of the community" and says that he must be between thirty and sixty years old. This detail confirms that he must be a different person from the *mevaqqer* although scant information is available about him.

---

[34] Pesher Habakkuk 2:8.
[35] Cf. J. Priest, "*Mebaqqer, Paqqid* and the Messiah," *JBL* 81 (1962): 55–61; R. Marcus, "*Mebaqqer* and *Rabbim* in the *Manual of Discipline* VI, 11–13," *JBL* 75 (1956): 398–402.

The sect also had various lay leaders known as *maskilim* who are described in the Rule of the Community.[36] This name derives from the verb meaning "to enlighten or instruct." The *maskil* was to enlighten the sectarians about the nature of the Sons of Light, those who follow the sectarian ways, and the Sons of Darkness, the rest of the peoples of the world, both Jewish and non-Jewish. Presumably, the *maskil* was responsible for conveying the ideology and theology of the Qumran community to other members of the group. The *maskil* was also expected to be a master of the sectarian legal tradition. He also led the recitation of blessings found in the Rule of Benedictions which apply to those who fear the Lord,[37] the Zadokite priests,[38] and the Prince of the Congregation.[39] The *maskilim* were a class of scholars but not priests, and although they shared their knowledge with their fellow sectarians and were perhaps role models for them, they do not seem to have been assigned any specific administrative functions: the *mevaqqer* and *paqid* filled this role.[40]

All in all, in regard to the conduct of the affairs of the group and its decisions concerning Jewish law, a process of laicization and, hence, democratization was going on throughout the sect's history—from Hasmonean times through the destruction of the Temple in 70 c.e.—similar to that in evidence in the Pharisaic-rabbinic context as well. Further, it is interesting that the sect seemed to tend toward a division of executive, judicial and legislative powers. Yet this division was limited in that the assembly, which was primarily legislative in function, served also as the highest court. Indeed, the same was the situation in the rabbinic legal system described in the Mishnah and Talmud.

ROYAL AND PRIESTLY MESSIAHS

An entirely different arena in which to look at these questions is that of the sect's dreams for the messianic future.[41] This is especially the case since we know that the sect modeled its life in the present

---

[36] Cf. L. Kosmala, "Maskil," *JANES* 5 (1973): 235–41.
[37] Rule of Benedictions 1:1.
[38] Rule of Benedictions 3:22–28.
[39] Rule of Benedictions 5:20–29.
[40] Schiffman, *Reclaiming*, 121–25.
[41] For messianic ideas in the Qumran scrolls see, S. Talmon, *The World of Qumran*

pre-messianic age on its eschatological aspirations. It sought to create in the present the experience of purity and holiness which it
expected would finally commence with the dawn of the end of days.[42]

Equally important to the sectarians was the immediacy of the end
of days. They anticipated that the old order would soon die and the
messianic era would be established in their lifetimes. The sect lived
on the verge of the end of days, with one foot, as it were, in the
present age, and one foot in the future.

Two separate messianic ideologies coexisted in the sectarian documents. One, like that of rabbinic Judaism, speaks of an individual
messiah who is to be a "branch of David," that is, a Davidic scion.
A totally different approach speaks of an Aaronide priestly messiah,
who is effectively an eschatological high priest, and a temporal messiah of Israel who is to rule over political matters.[43] Both messiahs
would preside over the eschatological banquet. Described in the Rule
of the Congregation, it would usher in the new age that would
include worship at the eschatological Temple. Sacrificial worship
would be conducted according to sectarian law.

This messianic paradigm of two leaders, based on the Moses/Aaron
and Joshua/Zerubbabel model, would later be applied to Bar Kokhba
and the High Priest Eleazar in the Bar Kokhba Revolt (132–135
C.E.). To the sect, the coming of the messiahs of Israel and Aaron
and the eschatological prophet augured the restoration of the old
order.

These restorative tendencies are based on biblical prophetic visions,
but the Qumran sect went much further. Reflecting the apocalyptic

---

from Within (Jerusalem: Magnes Press, 1989), 273–300; F. García Martínez, "Messia-
nische Erwartungen in den Qumranschriften," *JBTh* 8 (1993): 171–208; J. J. Collins,
The Scepter and the Star: The Messiahs of the Dead Sea Scrolls and Other Ancient Literature
(New York: Doubleday, 1995).

[42] L. H. Schiffman, *The Eschatological Community of the Dead Sea Scrolls* (Atlanta:
Scholars Press, 1989), 68–71.

[43] L. H. Schiffman, "Messianic Figures and Ideas in the Qumran Scrolls," *The
Messiah: Developments in Earliest Judaism and Christianity* (ed. J. H. Charlesworth;
Minneapolis: Fortress Press, 1992), 116–29; W. S. LaSor, "The Messiah of Aaron
and Israel," *VT* 6 (1956): 425–9; J. Liver, "The Doctrine of the Two Messiahs in
Sectarian Literature in the Time of the Second Commonwealth," *HTR* 52 (1959):
149–85; K. G. Kuhn, "The Two Messiahs of Aaron and Israel," *The Scrolls and the
New Testament* (ed. K. Stendahl; New York: Crossroad, 1992), 54–64; L. Silberman,
"Two Messiahs of the Manual of Discipline," *VT* 5 (1955): 77–82; R. B. Laurin,
"The Problem of the Two Messiahs in the Qumran Scrolls," *RevQ* 4 (1963): 39–52;
G. J. Brooke, "Messiah of Aaron in the Damascus Document," *RevQ* 15 (1991):
215–31.

trend,[44] it anticipated that the advent of the messianic age would be heralded by the great cataclysmic battle described in the War Scroll and radical changes in the world order resulting in the victory of the forces of good over those of evil, in heaven above and on earth below. After forty years the period of wickedness would come to an end; then the elect would attain glory. In essence, Jews in the messianic age would surpass their current level of purity and perfection in observing Jewish law. Here in the sphere of Jewish law we again find the utopian trend. Only in the future age will it be possible properly to observe the Torah as interpreted by the sect.

In addition to the dual messiahs of Aaron and Israel and the single messiah of the House of David, the Qumran texts also mention other eschatological figures who will appear in the end of days.[45] The Teacher of Righteousness is expected to arise to interpret the law, and the Prince of the Congregation (*nesi' ha-'edah*) will serve as the sect's military leader in the eschatological battle described in the War Scroll. It is also possible that "prince" simply is an alternate name for the king who will rule in the messianic era. Some texts also speak about an eschatological prophet who will announce the coming of the messiah, a figure similar to Elijah in the rabbinic tradition.

The concept of the dual-messiahs certainly envisages a division of powers between the religious and temporal, but, as we noticed before in our discussion of the Temple Scroll, the priest holds the superior status of the pair. This is reflected when he is commanded to enter first in the description of the messianic communal meal in the Rule

---

[44] On apocalypticism at Qumran, see C. A. Newsom, "Apocalyptic and the Discourse of the Qumran Community," *JNES* 49 (1990): 135–44; H. Stegemann, "Die Bedeutung der Qumranfunde für die Erforschung der Apokalyptik," *Apocalypticism in the Mediterranean World and the Near East: Proceedings of the International Colloquium on Apocalypticism* (ed. D. Hellholm; Tübingen: J. C. B. Mohr, 1983), 495–530; J. J. Collins, *The Apocalyptic Imagination* (New York: Crossroad, 1984), 115–41; J. J. Collins, "Was the Dead Sea Sect an Apocalyptic Movement?" *Archaeology and History in the Dead Sea Scrolls: The New York University Conference in Memory of Yigael Yadin* (ed. L. H. Schiffman; JSOTSup 8; Sheffield: JSOT Press, 1990), 25–51; J. J. Collins, *Apocalypticism in the Dead Sea Scrolls* (London and New York: Routledge, 1997); P. R. Davies, "Qumran and Apocalyptic or Obscurum Per Obscurius," *JNES* 49 (1990): 127–34; J. Starcky, "Les quatre étapes du messianisme à Qumran," *RB* 70 (1963): 481–505.

[45] L. H. Schiffman, "Messianic Figures and Ideas in the Qumran Scrolls," *The Messiah: Developments in Earliest Judaism and Christianity* (ed. J. H. Charlesworth; First Princeton Symposium on Judaism and Christian Origins; Minneapolis: Fortress Press, 1992), 116–29.

of the Congregation,[46] an eschatological appendix to the Rule of the Community.[47] So again we have the expectation of constitutional theocracy.

Even when a Davidic messiah is indicated in Qumran texts, it is expected that there will also be a messianic high priest. But in these texts there is no sense of the superiority of the priest as there is in those Qumran sectarian texts which expect two messiahs. Just as the sectarians demanded a balance of power in the present between priestly and temporal power, they looked forward to the same in the end of days.

THE MESSIANIC ASSEMBLY

According to the Rule of the Congregation, in the end of days there will also be an assembly, which will have specifically defined powers: This group will serve as the highest court; it will also be the legislative assembly, but in addition, it will have the power to declare war.[48]

In this regulation, we again see that the king is limited in his powers, so that he may not commit the nation to war without the approval of the assembly. This may very well be a further polemic against, or better, reaction to, the Hasmonean rulers who attacked neighboring territory simply to expand their empire. A similar regulation in the Zadokite Fragments, for the present age, requires that offensive war only be undertaken with the approval of a council or gerousia, the *ḥever yiśra'el*.[49]

The community of the end of days would reflect all of the sect's aspirations and dreams. The assembly, therefore, would govern the sect under the leadership of the messianic leaders, expanding the functions and procedures of the assembly of the present, and allowing all sectarians to participate in the shaping of the society of the end of days.

---

[46] Rule of the Congregation 2:11–22.
[47] Schiffman, *Eschatological Community*, 53–67.
[48] Ibid., 29–32.
[49] L. H. Schiffman, "Legislation Concerning Relations with Non-Jews in the Zadokite Fragments and in Tannaitic Literature," *RevQ* 11 (1983): 382–85.

CONCLUSIONS

The authors of the Qumran sectarian documents and related texts dealt with a variety of issues pertaining to the organization of the Jewish people as a whole as well as of their own sectarian community in the present age and the future. They saw their community as the ideal Israel, structured and organized politically and religiously in a way that mirrored their utopian views of the ideal world of the end of days.

The sectarians knew all too well from their own understanding of the Hasmonean dynasty that the concentration of temporal and religious power in the hands of the same people was unjust. Accordingly, they hoped for the day when the two powers would be separated as they understood the Torah to require. They further distinguished the powers of the executive from the legislative, expecting different individuals to be involved in each.

Over time, greater democratization of the sect can be observed, such that lay members attained greater power while that of the priests was reduced. The sectarians balanced priestly and lay members in the courts and in the king's council, protected the rights of the accused to a trial before honest and competent judges, and called for the death penalty for judicial corruption. Only the most reliable witnesses could be employed to convict an offender. In the end of days they expected similar regulations to be in force and, therefore, expected a division of power between priestly and lay messiahs.

In enacting all these various regulations, the Dead Sea sectarians were following their interpretation of the Hebrew biblical tradition, which to them constituted a guide for life in the present age and in the utopian era of the end of days. They earnestly sought a society following the biblical ideal in which powers would be balanced and separated, as a means to the attainment of the perfect holiness of the end of days.

ARAMAIC LEVI DOCUMENT AND GREEK TESTAMENT OF LEVI

Michael E. Stone

The question of the relationship between the *Aramaic Levi Document (ALD)* known chiefly from the Cairo Geniza, the Greek Athos fragments and seven fragmentary Qumran manuscripts on the one hand, and the Greek *Testament of Levi (TPL)* from the *Testaments of the Twelve Patriarchs* on the other, is complex and much debated. The question has been particularly important for two reasons: the antiquity of *ALD* and the disputed nature of *TPL*.[1] It is our view that *ALD* is of the third century B.C.E. and, in any case, one of the oldest of the extra-biblical pseudepigrapha from Qumran or elsewhere.[2] None would deny that it is one of the sources used by the author/redactor of *TPL* (and, by the way, of *Jubilees, pace* Kugel),[3] and presumably, therefore, of the *Testaments of the Twelve Patriarchs*. What is debated, is whether *Testaments of the Twelve Patriarchs* is a Christian document using Jewish sources or a Jewish document with Christian interpolations. The present writer finds himself, basically, on Marinus de Jonge's side of that discussion, i.e., that the present form of the *Testaments of the Twelve Patriarchs*, including the *TPL*, is the work of a Christian author/redactor. This means that a complete Jewish *Testaments of the Twelve Patriarchs* never existed, or at least cannot be argued to have existed from the existing document called *Testaments*

---

[1] A bibliography of older editions and translations of *ALD* is to be found in J. C. Greenfield and M. E. Stone, "Remarks on the Aramaic Testament of Levi," *RB* 86 (1979): 214–230, especially 214–215. See also J. C. Greenfield and M. E. Stone, "The Aramaic Levi Document," in *The Testaments of the Twelve Patriarchs: A Commentary* (ed. H. W. Hollander and M. de Jonge; SVTP 8; Leiden: Brill, 1985), 457–469, especially p. 457. The Dead Sea Scrolls manuscripts are edited by J. T. Milik in *DJD* 1, 87–91 and by Greenfield and Stone in *DJD* 22.17,1–82.

[2] M. E. Stone, "The Dead Sea Scrolls and the Pseudepigrapha," *DSD* 3 (1996) 279 and M. E. Stone, *Studies in the Pseudepigrapha, with Special Reference to the Armenian* (SVTP; Leiden: Brill, 1991), 247–48 where arguments for this dating are set forth.

[3] J. Kugel, "Levi's Elevation to the Priesthood in Second Temple Writings," *HTR* 86 (1993): 1–64; on pp. 52–58 he argues for *Jubilees*, precedence to *Aramaic Levi Document*.

of the Twelve Patriarchs. The Christian author/redactor of that work used varied Jewish sources in Semitic languages or Greek.

Through a careful, synoptic study of *ALD* and *TPL* it is possible to show how the author (I shall use this term for convenience's sake) of *TPL* adapted and used *ALD*. This is worth understanding for the following reasons. It is common for students of ancient Jewish literature to say that one or another work used pre-existent sources. Indeed, this is an essential factor in many analyses of works in the apocryphal and pseudepigraphical literature and, of course, in biblical studies. An example of a source and its use in the Hebrew Bible is Kings and Chronicles. Like Kings and Chronicles, in the case of *ALD* and *TPL*, both the source and the document using it survive. Surely understanding that process from an extant instance might show how a similar process might have happened in other works. More specifically, whether *Testaments of the Twelve Patriarchs* is a Jewish document with Christian interpolations, or a Christian document using Jewish sources, it is indubitably using sources, and not only *ALD*. Moreover, studying the one testament of which we do actually have the source may cast light onto authorial procedure adopted by the author of *Testaments of the Twelve Patriarchs* throughout.

The research presented here is part of a project originally undertaken by the writer with the late Jonas C. Greenfield and now being continued with the collaboration of Esther Eshel. The aspect of the research presented here, however, is the writer's. The project itself is complex but, nonetheless, some advances can be made from the study of one example. So, we have chosen to examine the sequence of events surrounding the prayer of Levi in *ALD* and how these events were reworked in *TPL*. The texts discussed are to be found in the Geniza fragments (Cambridge and Oxford), in Qumran manuscripts, and in Greek. We use de Jonge's edition of the Athos fragment and of *TPL*, and our own edition of the Aramaic text. The main points of the argument are the following:

1. The surviving fragments of *ALD* open with the story of Shechem. A codicological analysis of the Geniza manuscript shows that a substantial amount of text must have preceded the extant fragment. A section of a conversation between the sons of Jacob and the Shechemites survives and we may infer that the complete narrative of the event must have been considerably longer originally, because the surviving fragment of the conversation is very detailed. In contrast, *TPL* opens with the usual testamentary scene; it then gives brief bio-

graphic details of Levi and recounts the Shechem story in a summary fashion. (Even its longer recapitulation of the Shechem incident in chapter 6 is far less detailed than *ALD*'s text.)

2. In *ALD* a substantial lacuna, two columns and 14 lines to be exact, ensues and then a fragment of text (designated Cambridge col. b) that refers to an unknown incident. Nothing corresponds to it in *TPL*. In our view, the fragment of 4QLevi[a] aram known as the "Prayer of Levi" as well as one or two further small Qumran fragments followed this unknown incident and preceded the surviving first column of the Bodleian leaves (Bodleian col. a).[4]

3. In the prayer in *ALD* Levi launders his garments and washes his body, a purification ritual such as commonly follows a ritual act or corpse uncleanness. As Greenfield and I wrote some years ago: "[T]he laundering of garments and washing of the body, actions [that] are typical of Levitical purity (see Num 8:21), do not occur anywhere else preceding a prayer or an apocalyptic vision experience, but instead usually follow a cultic, priestly act" or, I may add, on uncleanliness, such as corpse uncleanliness.[5] E. Eshel and I propose that the purification is consequent on the Shechem incident, though that is quite a long way before it in the text. Alternatively, it follows on some other event, such as the wars of the sons of Jacob referred to in *Jubilees*, *Testament of Judah* 3–7 and in *Midrash Wayyisaʿu*, which might have been the context of the Cambridge, col. b fragment.[6] These lines (§§*1–*2), then, are not the opening of the prayer but the conclusion of another, prior incident.[7]

4. According to *ALD* *3ff., after the above purification, Levi assumes the spiritual and bodily stance of a person praying and he commences the prayer. Functionally parallel but differing, in *TPL* 2:3–4 Levi describes an incident of inspiration, grief and consequent prayer. The geographical setting is given there, Abel Meholah which is near

---

[4] See J. C. Greenfield and M. E. Stone, "The Prayer of Levi," *JBL* 112 (1993): 247–66.

[5] J. C. Greenfield and M. E. Stone, "Two Notes on the Aramaic Levi Document," in *Of Scribes and Scrolls: Studies on the Hebrew Bible, Intertestamental Judaism and Christian Origins* (ed. H. W. Attridge, J. J. Collins, and T. H. Tobin; College Theology Society Resources in Religion 5; Lanham: University Press of America, 1990), 153–62: see p. 156.

[6] Jub. 34:1–9, cf. *T. Jud.* 3–7 and *Midrash wayyisaʿu* (A. Jellinek, *Bet Ha-Midrasch* [repr. Jerusalem: Bamberger and Wahrmann, 1938], 3:1–5).

[7] See Greenfield and Stone, "Two Notes," 156.

Shechem (see *TPL* 2:1). *ALD* does not identify the site. The actual text of the prayer is omitted by *TPL* but occurs in *ALD* both in Aramaic and in Greek.

5. In *ALD* three fragmentary lines follow the prayer. They read "Then I continued on[" (l. 11); "to my father Jacob" (l. 12); and "from Abel Mayin" (l. 13). Levi apparently went to Jacob (ll. 11–12) though we do not know to what end. Line 13 relates that Levi was in Abel Mayin and traveled from there to somewhere else. Great edifices have been constructed on "Abel Mayin,"[8] but it is not clear whether Abel Mayin was the site of the prayer, or the place where Levi found Jacob, or some third location. If Levi pronounced the prayer there, it corresponds functionally to Abel Meholah in *TPL* 2:1. He almost certainly departs from there ("from Abel Mayin. Then" [l. 13]) before receiving the vision which is related in lines 14–18. The word "Then" in line 13 commences the narration of the events leading up to the vision; that does not take place at Abel Mayin.

6. In both texts Levi, probably prone according to *ALD* and explicitly asleep in *TPL*, receives the vision. In the vision in *ALD*, Levi sees something (lost in a lacuna) below him, high until it reached to the heavens. If what was below him was the mountain, which is likely if we compare the text with *TPL* 3:5, he is above it and situated before the gates of heaven. In *Apocalypse of Abraham* the seer describes an experience of rapture. Before seeing the Deity, he says "I desired to fall down upon the earth, and the high place, on which we stood [at one moment rose upright,] but at another rolled downwards" (*Apocalypse of Abraham* 17).[9] In his vision, from this position, Levi sees the gates of heavens (*ALD* 4QLevi[a] aram 2, 16–18) "and an angel . . ." (here the manuscript breaks off).

7. In *TPL* 2:5–6, but not in *ALD*, the mountain is given the name "Aspis in Abelmaoul, i.e., Abel-Mehola." In our view, the introduction of the mountain's name by *TPL* is secondary. In the original text, the mountain was part of the vision. In *TPL* though in the context of the vision, the mountain is identified as "Mount Aspis in

---

[8] See J. T. Milik, "Le Testament de Lévi en araméen," *RB* 62 (1955): 403–5. This will be discussed in detail in Greenfield, Stone and Eshel (forthcoming).

[9] This mystical state of standing on high and having bottomless space below is discussed by G. Scholem, *Major Trends in Jewish Mysticism* (New York: Schocken, 1941), 52 and footnote 43.

Abelmaoul" (*TPL* 2:5), a specific mountain drawn from real geography. This is secondary, whether the vision took place at Abel Mayin or not. In *TPL* the mountain has been moved from the vision into geographic reality.

8. The identification of Abel Mayin (*ALD*) with Abel-Meholah (*TPL*) also creates a considerable problem. The facts are the following. First, the name Abel-Meholah occurs nowhere at all in *ALD* while it is found in the biographical preliminary to the vision in *TPL* 2:3 and 2:5.[10] Second, the known site Abel-Meholah is nowhere near a high mountain; it is in the center of the country. Third, the name Abel Mayin found in *ALD* is otherwise known only (in a Hebrew form) as a hapaxlegomenon in 2 Chr 16:4 where it corresponds to Abel-Beth-Maacah of 1 K 15:20. This identification would indeed put Abel Mayin in the North of the country and, doubtless, for this reason the secondary identification of the high mountain as Aspis is made in *TPL* 2:5. This happens for the following reason: the name Aspis results from a name midrash on the mountain name Sirion (also known as Si'on) read as Shirion "armor," and, in turn, Sirion / Si'on was identified with Mt. Hermon. Thus we have the following development: Aspis < Shirion <Sirion < Hermon.

9. The text of *TPL* may, then, have arisen as follows.

- First, in *ALD*, since the events discussed are in the environs of Shechem, Bethel and, apparently, Hebron, we would expect that Abel Mayin should also be in the center of the country.
- Second, Abel Meholah as the place of the prayer in *TPL* 2:5 corresponds to Abel Mayin which is somehow related to the prayer in *ALD* (4QLevi[a] aram 2, 13). The location of mount Aspis in Abel Meholah (*TPL* 2:5) implies that *TPL*'s author / redactor has taken two sequential steps. The first was to apply Chronicles' identification of Abel Mayim with the northern site Abel-Beth Maacah to the place name Abel Mayin in his source. Thus, since he thought that Abel Mayin was in the north, he identified the mountain, which he said was nearby, as the Hermon/Sirion/Aspis.[11] Second, perhaps as a result of the geographical inconsistency thus created,

---

[10] In this and the following geographical remarks, we follow in a several respects proposals of E. Eshel, to whom we are much indebted.

[11] Note the "high mountain" in Mark 9:2 which many scholars today identify as Mt. Hermon.

northern Abel Mayim, a rare name, was identified as Abel-Meholah a good distance to the south. This produced the anomalous geography we have in *TPL* 2:5. The Shechem story was introduced into the text of *TPL* a second time (chaps. 6–7) and there the mountain tradition was introduced again, adding in *TPL* 6:1, Abila's connection with Gebal and Mount Aspis.

- Esther Eshel will address the issue of the location of Abel Mayin separately. Here I will just say that the geographical problem only arises if Chronicles' isolated and unparalleled identification of Abel-Beth-Maachah of Kings as Abel Mayim is accepted, for that puts Abel Mayin in the north. There are good reasons, however, to doubt that *ALD* accepted this identification and to seek *ALD's* Abel Mayin much further south.

10. Observe that in *TPL* the vision in chapter three, though complicated, seems to be composed of a beginning, a visionary section, and a concluding prophecy.[12] Levi is led from one heaven to another until he reaches the highest heaven of all, where he sees the "Great Glory" (3:4). The heavenly vision experience is followed by an eschatological prophecy, and by a blessing at the end of chapter 4. Then, in chapter 5:1 we read what sounds like the beginning of another vision experience, "And then the angel opened to me the gates of

---

[12] The structural anomaly, the doubling of the heavenly ascent within chapter 2, is a separate issue, and will not be analyzed here. The full series of heavens occurs in 3:1–8; a preliminary and somewhat different treatment of the seven heavens occurs in 2:7–9. The structure of the two descriptions is quite similar:

2:7–9 three + four heavens	3:1–8 three + four heavens; God is in the seventh.
2:10, 12 prophecy to Levi	3:9 God's awesome presence; 3:10 hidden from sinful men.
2:9 prophecy to Levi and Judah about Christ's appearance and salvation, cf. 4:3–4.	4:1 Prophecy of judgement.
	4:2 God has answered your prayer; 4:3–4a Prophecy to Levi. 4:4b Sons of Levi will lay hands upon Christ. 4:5–6 Levi's teaching function is so he can instruct his sons about Christ. Conclusion.

Clearly there is a sort of doublet here, with chapter 4 repeating more expansively the vision of chapter 3.

heaven, and I saw the holy temple, and the Most High sitting on a throne of Glory."[13] This follows very strangely on chap. 2:5–4:6, for at the start of the vision in 2:6 the heavens had already been opened to Levi and he was invited in by an angel. Moreover, no descent, awakening or vision conclusion is to be found at the end of chapter 4, and he is not said to leave the heavens. So 5:1, which says the heavens were opened and Levi saw the Most High seated on the Throne of Glory, is odd. That is compounded by the fact that there is no further vision of the heavens following *TPL* 5:1, but instead Levi receives a blessing of priesthood and a promise of the incarnation of Christ.

11. Then, in 5:3 the vision concludes. Levi is brought to earth, the angel gives him a shield and sword and commissions him to destroy Shechem. In response to Levi's request for his name (5:5) the angel only says that he is protector of Israel. The word used for shield in this passage is not ἀσπίς but ὅπλον. In the narrative of chapter 6, Levi finds the shield (there called ἀσπίς), which is said to be the reason for the name of the mountain, and in the rest of chapter 6 and 7 the Shechem incident is described.[14]

Clearly the same hand that introduced the name midrash in *TPL* chapter 2 and moved the mountain from the visionary to earthly geography, was responsible at least for the second half of the vision (chap. 5) and for the detailed Shechem narrative in chapters 6 and 7. What we cannot know is how much of this repetitive narrative was drawn from the missing parts of *ALD* preceding 4QLevi[a] aram. Possibly quite a lot of it, for we saw that that part of *ALD* was rather detailed. We do know that the phrase, "to me the gates of heaven," which occurs at the beginning of the vision in *ALD*, has been used to open the second part of the vision in *TPL* 5:1. Yet the content of the angelic command to take vengeance that follows this in *TPL* certainly did not come in this position in *ALD* in which the Shechem incident had preceded the prayer.

M. de Jonge makes a number of observations about the relationship of the two writings, which have contributed substantially to our developed view set forth above.[15]

---

[13] This brief vision description, of course, recalls Isaiah 6.

[14] Is it possible that this is an indication of a further complexity in the composition of this section?

[15] M. de Jonge, "Notes on Testament of Levi II–VII," *Travels in the World of the*

a. The narrative in 4QLevi^a aram differs from the order of events in *TPL* which also omits most of the text of the prayer. All it preserves is ηὐξάμην Κυρίῳ ὅπως σωθῶ "I was praying to the Lord that I might be saved" (2:4) which at most is a passing allusion to the extensive prayer found in *ALD*.[16] To this observation, we may add that the angelic words in 4:2 also refer to the prayer and this is shown in detail by Stone and Greenfield.[17]

b. M. de Jonge considers, correctly, that there are definite points of contact between *ALD* col. 2, lines 14–18 (the narrative following the prayer) and *TPL*. He points to 2:5 τότε ἐπέσεν ἐπ᾽ ἐμὲ ὕπνος "then sleep fell upon me" and *TPL* 5:1 τὰς πύλας τοῦ οὐρανοῦ "the gates of heaven". De Jonge points out that the words τὰς πύλας τοῦ οὐρανοῦ are "in any case awkward after the descriptions of several heavens in the previous chapters" of *TPL*, thus strengthening the argument for the dependence of *TPL* 5:1 on *ALD*.[18] De Jonge's observation supports the view that *TPL* uses *ALD*.[19] Notable is de Jonge's conclusion that *ALD* "belongs to an earlier stage in the transmission of the document."[20]

The following further observations may be made about the fragment of 4QTLevi^a and its position within *ALD*.

1. As it stands it is impossible to identify the broad context in which the prayer is offered. However, §6 implies that Levi is surrounded by his children. This is reminiscent of an *Abschiedsrede* context but, if such a context existed, it is lost.[21]

2. A copyist interpolated the Greek translation of the Prayer of Levi into manuscript *e* of *TPL* preceding 2:4. This, scholars have

---

Old Testament (ed. M. S. H. G. Heerma van Voss, Ph. H. J. Houwink ten Cate, and N. A. van Uchelen; Assen: 1974), 132–45, especially 138.

[16] Greenfield and Stone, "Two Notes," 155. It was this phrase, of course, that provided the occasion for the scribe to introduce the prayer into the Koutoumlous manuscript (manuscript *e*) of *Testaments of the Twelve Patriarchs*.

[17] *Ibid.*

[18] "Notes," 138. He argues, persuasively, that all these verses must be integral to *TPL* and that the dependence on *Aramaic Levi* is at the compositional level (p. 139).

[19] The words "Neither, it may be noted by way of corollary, does the shared phrase 'gates of heaven' show that the vision which follows the prayer directly in *ALD*, was in fact the event alluded to in *TPL* 5:1" were written before we had fully understood the relationship between the two documents. See "Prayer of Levi," 249.

[20] "Notes," 142.

[21] After an analysis of content and codicology, I have concluded that the Prayer followed the Shechem incident and/or the incident related in Cambridge b, and preceded Bodleian a.

assumed, is a reflection of its original position in the full Greek translation of the *ALD*. In view of our research, we are inclined to support this assertion, but more because of our analysis of *ALD* than because of where a medieval scribe may have decided to interpolate a fragment of the Greek translation of *ALD*.

The editorial process, which introduced redundancy, confusion, and geographic duplication into the story line of *ALD* is, therefore, quite evident. It involves re-arrangement, omission, and the introduction of learned glosses at least. Indeed, very much of the language and phraseology of *ALD* has been incorporated into *TPL*, perhaps more than was previously hypothesized. The reason for the re-arrangement of the material by the author/redactor of *TPL* remains unclear. That is a question of very considerable interest, to which the answer must still be sought. That it was purposeful and designed to achieve a goal or goals cannot be doubted.

IN SEARCH OF THE SCRIBE OF 1QS*

Eibert Tigchelaar

Documents Copied or Corrected by the Scribe of 1QS

In his studies Emanuel Tov has called attention not only to scribal schools, but also to the identity of scribes. Repeatedly he refers to the scribe of 1QS, who also copied several other manuscripts.[1] Scholars soon claimed that this scribe also copied the other texts from that scroll, 1QSa and 1QSb,[2] as well as 4Q175 (4QTest)[3] and 4Q53 (4QSam^c). Cross assigned the script to ca. 100–75 B.C.E., and characterises this scribe as "one of the most energetic at Qumrân,"[4] responsible for copying "4QSam^c; 4QTestimonia, et al."[5] and for some of the corrections in 1QIsa^a.[6] He did not specify which other documents ("et al.") stem from the hand of this scribe, but the Reed Catalogue, based upon the notes of Strugnell, qualifies 4Q441 and 4Q443 as "in hand of 1QS."[7] Chazon records that Strugnell noted that the hand of 4Q443 resembles that of 1QS,[8] and that Strugnell

---

* My thanks are due to Wout van Bekkum who commented on a first draft of this paper.

[1] E. Tov, "The Orthography and Language of the Hebrew Scrolls Found at Qumran and the Origin of These Scrolls," *Text* 13 (1986): 31–57, at 48; "Hebrew Biblical Manuscripts from the Judaean Desert: Their Contribution to Textual Criticism," *JJS* 39 (1988): 5–37, at 23.

[2] J. T. Milik, *DJD I*, 107.

[3] "Le travail d'édition des fragments manuscrits de Qumrân: Communication de J. M. Allegro," *RB* 63 (1956): 62–64, at 63.

[4] F. M. Cross, "Introduction" in *Scrolls from Qumrân Cave I. The Great Isaiah Scroll, The Order of the Community, The Pesher to Habakkuk from photographs by John C. Trever*, (Albright Institute of Archaeological Research and The Shrine of the Book, Jerusalem, 1972), 1–5, at 4 n. 8.

[5] F. M. Cross, 'The Development of the Jewish Scripts', in *The Bible and the Ancient Near East: Essays in Honor of W. F. Albright* (ed. G. E. Wright; Garden City, NY: Doubleday, 1961), 133–202, at 198 n. 116. Scholars generally adopt Cross's datings; thus, for example, *DJD XXVI*, 20, but G. J. Brooke, *DJD XXVI*, 229: '125–75 B.C.E.'.

[6] Cross, "Introduction," 4 n. 8, mentions 'XXVIII.25 (?), XXXIII.7 (and left margin), XLIV.15, 16 (one letter, *taw*).'

[7] S. A. Reed, M. J. Lundberg, eds., *The Dead Sea Scrolls Catalogue. Documents, Photographs and Museum Inventory Numbers* (Atlanta, GA: Scholars Press, 1994), 114.

[8] *DJD XXIX*, 349.

identified 4Q457b "as one of the numerous groups written in the hand of 1QS, 1QSa, 4QTest, 4QSam^c etc."[9] Here it is not clear whether "in the hand of 1QS" means copied by the scribe of 1QS, or merely a specific type of semiformal Hasmonaean script like that of 1QS. The latter is the case for other manuscripts that have been likened palaeographically to 1QS, such as 4Q382,[10] 4Q502 and 4Q257.[11]

I will not compare the hands of these documents, but shall proceed from the commonly held view that 1QS, 1QSa, 1QSb, 4Q53, some of the corrections in 1QIsa^a, as well as the less carefully written 4Q175, were written by the same scribe.[12] I think it is plausible that 4Q443 and 4Q457b were written by the scribe of 1QS, whereas not enough of 4Q441 remains for a judgment.[13]

Early contestants of the identification of the scribe of these texts are Martin, who discerned two different hands in 1QS (hand A), 1QSa (hand B), and 1QSb (hands A and B),[14] and Siegel who claims that "the bizarre orthography of 4Q175 leads one to suspect two different scribes for 1QS and 4Q175."[15] No scholars have questioned the palaeographic judgments of Cross and Strugnell, even though the hand of 4Q175 varies at points (most notably in the *samek*) from that of 1QS.

The language, orthography, and scribal practices of 1QS, 1QSa, 1QSb, 4QSam^c, and 4QTest, have been analysed by many scholars, but rarely in relation to the other documents of the scribe. The one exception is Ulrich who identifies the following "idiosyncratic

---

[9] *DJD XXIX*, 410.

[10] S. Olyan, *DJD XIII*, 363.

[11] F. M. Cross, 'Palaeographical Dates of the Manuscripts,' in *Rule of the Community and Related Documents* (ed. J. H. Charlesworth; PTSDSSP 1; Tübingen: Mohr, 1994), 57.

[12] 2QJer is not to be included in this list. Baillet, *DJD III*, 62, compares the hand of 2QJer to that of the corrections in 1QIsa^a XXVIII, 18–20, not to the hand of the scribe of 1QS who was responsible for other corrections in 1QIsa^a.

[13] With regard to the closed *samek* in 4Q443 1, 7 (*DJD XXIX*, 350), see the completely similar *samek* in 4Q175 14 הסידך.

[14] M. Martin, *The Scribal Character of the Dead Sea Scrolls* (Bibliothèque du Muséon 44–45; Louvain: Publications Universitaires, Institut Orientaliste, 1958, 2 vols.), 55.

[15] J. Siegel, 'The Scribes of Qumran. Studies in the Early History of Jewish Scribal Customs, with Special Reference to the Qumran Biblical Scrolls and to the Tannaitic Traditions of Massekheth Soferim' (Ph.D. diss., Brandeis University, 1972), 129.

features: the bold, relatively undisciplined calligraphy, proliferation of *matres lectionis*, run-on words, frequent errors and supralinear insertions, and the rare device of four dots used to represent the divine name."[16] In his discussion of 4QSam[c] he often refers to similar features in documents copied by the same scribe.

IDIOSYNCRASIES OF THE SCRIBE OF 1QS

1. *The Use of Four Dots to Represent the Divine Name*

The scribe of 1QS uses four dots as a surrogate of the Tetragrammaton in 1QS VIII, 14; 4Q53 1, 3 (1 Sam 25:31); III, 7 (*bis*) (2 Sam 15:8); 4Q175 1, 19. Cross attributes the supralinear correction with the four dots in 1QIsa[a] XXXIII, 7 (40:7) to the same scribe. One may assume that the four (not five) supralinear dots in 1QIsa[a] XXXV, 15 (42:6) for the divine name were also added by our scribe. It is virtually certain that the two dots in 4Q443 1, 5 before קֹ אלוהי[are not remains of two letters (as suggested by the editor), but the last two dots of a series of four representing the divine name. Since almost all examples concern biblical quotations, one may consider there a quote from Hab 1:12.

Other manuscripts which use the four dots are 4Q176, 4Q196, 4Q382, 4Q391, 4Q462, and 4Q524.[17] The oldest ones, 4Q391 and 4Q524, are from the second part of the second century B.C.E., the youngest one, 4Q462, is from the late Hasmonaean to early Herodian period.[18] Apart from the Aramaic 4Q196, all these manuscripts display orthographic features common to the Qumran scribal practice. The early Herodian 4Q248 (4QGreek King) forms a different

---

[16] E. C. Ulrich, '4QSam[c]: A Fragmentary Manuscript of 2 Samuel 14–15 from the Scribe of the *Serek Hay-yahad* (1QS),' *BASOR* 235 (1979): 1–25, at 1.

[17] Cf. É. Puech, *DJD XXV*, 89 and E. Tov, 'Further Evidence for the Existence of a Qumran Scribal School,' in, *The Dead Sea Scrolls: Fifty Years after Their Discovery. Proceedings of the Jerusalem Congress, July 20–25, 1997* (ed. L. H. Schiffman, E. Tov, and J. C. VanderKam; Jerusalem: Israel Exploration Society in cooperation with The Shrine of the Book, Israel Museum, 2000), 199–216, at 208. Older discussions could not take all the data into account. Cf. H. Stegemann, 'Religionsgeschichtliche Erwägungen zu den Gottesbezeichnungen in den Qumrantexten,' in *Qumrân: Sa piété, sa théologie et son milieu* (ed. M. Delcor; Paris-Gembloux: Duculot, 1978), 195–217, and P. W. Skehan, 'The Divine Name at Qumran, in the Masada Scroll, and in the Septuagint,' *BIOSCS* 13 (1980): 14–44.

[18] M. Smith, *DJD XIX*, 196.

case: there are not four dots, but five strokes, representing the Tetragrammaton.

In short, the four dots are found in eleven manuscripts, all from the Hasmonaean period, and probably all copied at Qumran. At least four (1QS, 4Q53, 4Q175, 1QIsaᵃ corrections), and plausibly a fifth (4Q443) were copied by one scribe, who was the only scribe to use the four dots in biblical manuscripts.

2. *The Marginal* Paragraphos *Sign*

A *paragraphos* sign, probably a cryptic *'ayin*, is found in 1QS, 1QSa, 1QSb,[19] and 4Q175, but the rounded form of 4Q175 is somewhat different from the angular one in the 1QS scroll. Tov cautions that "it cannot usually be determined whether these *paragraphos* signs were written by the original scribes, later scribes, or readers of the text."[20] The partial erasure of the *paragraphos* sign in 1QS X, 5–6, where the initial scribe erased the letters at the beginning of line 6, indicates that in this manuscript the signs were written by the original scribe.

3. *Correction Procedures*

Discussions of corrections in 1QS, 4Q175 and 4Q53 are provided by Martin,[21] Allegro (*DJD V*), Strugnell,[22] and Ulrich. Tov has supplied overviews of different categories of scribal corrections in the Dead Sea Scrolls.[23] Several categories of corrections are found in the documents copied by the scribe of 1QS.

---

[19] 1QSb I, 21, cf. the remainder of the sign in the right margin of 1QSb I on the photograph of 1QSa II.

[20] E. Tov, 'Scribal Markings in the Texts of the Judaean Desert,' in *Current Research and Technological Developments. Conference on the Texts from the Judean Desert, Jerusalem, 30 April 1995* (ed. D. W. Parry, S. D. Ricks; STDJ 20; Leiden: E. J. Brill, 1996), 41–77, at 46.

[21] Martin, *Scribal Character*, 432–47, though not all cases presented there are certain.

[22] J. Strugnell, "Notes en Marge du Volume V des 'Discoveries in the Judaean Desert of Jordan,'" *RevQ* 7/26 (1970): 163–276, at 226. Not all of these notes are correct, though.

[23] E. Tov, 'Correction Procedures in the Texts from the Judaean Desert,' in *The Provo International Conference on the Dead Sea Scrolls. Technological Innovations, New Texts, and Reformulated Issues* (ed. D. W. Parry, E. Ulrich; STDJ 30; Leiden, Boston, Köln: Brill, 1999), 232–63; 'Further Evidence,' 202–4.

Some examples show how the scribe started a word, then realized a mistake, and fixed this mistake by reshaping or overwriting the letters, occasionally in combination with supralinear writing. See, for example, 4Q53 I, 23 הנער; II, 12 ויאמר; 4Q175 2 אליכה; 1QS V, 16 מאומה. One may assume that many other reshapings or overwritings happened during the process of copying. In 1QS some erasures seem to have been done by the scribe during the process of writing (see, for example, 1QS X, 9). A special phenomenon is the interruption of writing a wrong word, followed by a *vacat*, as in 1QS X, 4 and 1QSa I, 27.

In view of the large number of unmarked erasures and overwritings, the dots, above and below letters, presumably were added in a second proof-reading stage. Correction dots are found in 1QS, 1QSa, 4Q53 and 4Q443, but not in 4Q175. The phenomenon of dots only below, and not above, the letters, cancelling the word, is only found in documents copied by the scribe of 1QS (1QS VII, 20; X, 24; 1QIsaᵃ XXXIII, 7 where the scribe of 1QS corrected the text), and may therefore be an idiosyncrasy of that scribe. The phenomenon of subsequent erasure of letters marked by dots is found in 1QS, but not in the other documents copied by the scribe.[24]

Some of the unusual correction procedures in 1QS, such as parentheses signs (VII, 8), dots to the right and left (VII, 1, 6; XI, 9) were probably done by later correctors (see the different hand of VII, 7).

Ulrich and Tov call attention to the large number of corrections in 1QS and 4Q175.[25] Even in the fragmentary text of 4Q53, there are at least thirteen cases of scribal intervention, most of which "are presumably attributable to the scribe himself."[26] This suggests that the scribe of 1QS was "more prone to error than others."[27]

---

[24] In 1QSa I, 18 the two 'dots' after עבודה are the top and bottom of an erased *waw*.

[25] Ulrich, '4QSamᶜ,' 1; Tov, 'Correction Procedures,' 260–61, mentions an average of one correction for every four lines in 4QTest, but there are some 24 corrections in 30 lines. Tov seems to refer to supralinear corrections only.

[26] Ulrich, '4QSamᶜ,' 20.

[27] Tov, 'Correction Procedures,' 261. Cf. also Ph. Alexander and G. Vermes, *DJD XXVI*, 16: "1QS is not a particularly careful exemplar of S. It contains numerous changes and corrections, as well as obvious, uncorrected scribal errors."

4. *Weakening and Confusion of Gutturals*

Qimron refers to spelling irregularities involving gutturals in non-formal, and very occasionally in formal manuscripts, but also allows for differences between scribes.[28] One should distinguish between corrections and non-corrected spelling "irregularities."

In many cases corrections, mostly by the initial scribe, involve gutturals, indicating that the original spelling was regarded as incorrect. Confusions between ʿ*ayin* and ʾ*alep* are found in 1QS I, 16 יעבורו corrected from יאבורו; V, 2 יעל corrected from אל; 26 ואל corrected from ועל; VI, 1 ביללה second hand correction, possibly from בעלה; 20 על corrected from, or to, אל; 27 תג{א}נעש (for ותענש); VII, 3 על corrected from אל; 14 ונראתה corrected from ונרעתה; 4Q175 7 אל corrected from על; 4Q53 II, 24 (2 Sam 15:3) עליו corrected to אליו. The frequent confusion between על and אל may, however, partly be due to uncertainty with regard to the proper use of the prepositions.

Corrections involving ʾ*alep* and *ḥet* are 1QS IV, 6 וחבא possibly corrected from ואבא; VII, 11 וחנם corrected from ואנם (or ועגם?). Corrections involving *he* and *ḥet* are 1QS IV, 4 מחשבת corrected from מהשבת; VII, 14 ישחק corrected from ישהק. In the supralinear and intramarginal correction to 1QIsaᵃ XXXIII, 7 (40:7–8) the scribe of 1QS twice wrote הציר which afterwards was corrected to הציר. Corrections involving *he* and ʾ*alep* are 4Q175 9 וישא corrected from וישה and נאום corrected from נהום; 1QS IV, 24 ישנא corrected from ישנה; V, 16 מאומה corrected from מאומא. Corrections concerning addition or omission of ʾ*alep* are: 4QSamᶜ II, 2 (2 Sam 14:22) בˣלא; III, 6 (15:8) בˣרם; 1QS III, 2 וניˣלים; X, 10 אבˣאה corrected from אבˣה; 19 ואפיא corrected to ואפי. Secondary addition or deletion of *he* is found in 1QS I, 25 לכתנו{ה}ב; VI, 22 ולטˣורה.

It is difficult to assess the nature of non-corrected spelling irregularities. One may proceed from the assumption that if a similar type of error has been corrected elsewhere, we may be dealing with uncorrected errors; on the other hand, if specific types of non-standard spelling occur frequently, without being corrected, they were probably not regarded as incorrect. Some of these forms, however, may be hypercorrections.

---

[28] E. Qimron, *The Hebrew of the Dead Sea Scrolls* (HSS 29; Atlanta, GA: Scholars Press, 1986), §200.11 and note 1.

The first category (uncorrected errors) probably includes 1QS VII, 2 and 4Q53 II, 12 *bis* (2 Sam 14:30) על for אל; 1QS VIII, 2 אם for עם;[29] 1QS III, 15 מהשבתם for מחשבתם; VI, 11 להפץ for לחפץ. Possibly also 1QSa I, 11 התורא; II, 22 עשרא.[30]

On the other hand, one encounters several types of "irregular" spellings which were apparently not regarded as incorrect. First, elision of *he* of infinitives *nip'al*, *hip'il* and *hitpa'el* after *le* (לעלות for להעלות, ולסתר, להיסד, לקריב). Second, spellings where radical quiescent *'alep* has been dropped (*passim* רוש, רשונה, רשית, שרית, חטתו, שרית, מודה; 1QS I, 7 להבי; 4Q175 5 נבי; 7 הנבי).[31] Third, elision of *'alep*, especially after ה: 1QSa I, 1 בהספם; 27 הנשים for האנשים;[32] 4Q175 22 היש for האיש; 28 ונצה = ונאצה (see 4Q379 22 ii, 14). Fourth, interchange of *'alep* and *he* in word-initial position, perhaps sometimes as hypercorrection (1QS VI, 26 באמרות, VIII, 13 הנשי, X, 2 באופיע, 6 הברכנו, 12 הבחרה; 4Q175 23 ואנה). Fifth, interchanging of לוא and לו (לוא for לו in 1QS VI, 27, 4Q53 1, 3; II, 20; III, 7; and לו for לוא, perhaps arising from hypercorrection, in 1QS IX, 24; בלו in 1QS VII, 4; XI, 17). The first two types are quite common in the Dead Sea Scrolls, whereas the other three types are rather rare.

A special case are the three forms 4Q175 11 עתהא; 1QS VII, 4 בדעהא; VIII, 13 הואהא. הא- endings are found in 1QIsaᵃ (thrice היהא),[33] and in the 3 f.s. suffixes in 4Q176 1-2 i, 6 חטותיהא; 10 ומאציהא; 4Q222 1, 4 דיהא[י']. The three forms belong to different categories. 1QS VIII, 13 הואהא seems to be a substitute for the Tetragrammaton,[34] and 4Q175 11 עתהא is a reading error: עתה אשורנו was read as עתהא שורנו. In a second hand, the missing *'alep* was placed before שורנו in the right margin of line 12.

Well-known are the exceptional spellings with plene *'alep* for /a/ in 4Q175 4 למעאן; 5 לאהמה.[35]

---

[29] Cf. 4Q377 2 ii, 7 איש עם רעהו.

[30] For examples from other texts, see Qimron, *Hebrew*, §100.7 and 4Q286 1 ii, 6 חוכמא, and E. Y. Kutscher, *The Language and Linguistic Background of the Isaiah Scroll (1QIsaᵃ)* (STDJ 6; Leiden: E. J. Brill, 1974), 163–4.

[31] Kutscher, *Language*, 204.

[32] Kutscher, *Language*, 509 for an explanation. Similar cases are הרץ for הארץ in 1QpHab XIII, 1 and 4Q79 (4QXIIᵈ) 1–2, 9 (Hos 2:2).

[33] Kutscher, *Language*, 185.

[34] See 4Q259 (4QSᵉ) III, 4, and *DJD XXVI*, 148.

[35] Kutscher, *Language*, 160–2.

Statistical data on spellings in the Scrolls are hardly available. Yet, spelling irregularities involving gutturals seem to be disproportionately frequent in the documents of the scribe of 1QS, perhaps even more than in 1QIsaᵃ. This suggests that the gutturals in the scribe's pronunciation were weakened, and that the scribe was less careful or less trained than other scribes. The interchange of ʾalep and he in word-initial position, as well as the use of ʾalep for final /a/ may suggest influence of Aramaic orthography on the scribe's spelling.

Aramaic Influence on the Scribe of 1QS

Kutscher attributed many of the peculiarities of the orthography of 1QIsaᵃ to Aramaic influence in the dialect of its scribe. Apart from the weakening of gutturals, it is difficult to judge which non-standard features reflect the scribe's own orthography or linguistic background, and which were found in the text the scribe copied. Thus, the sixfold use of אנוש (or איש׳) in 1QSa contrasts with the use of אנש׳ in 1QS, and it is possible that the scribe was here copying the spelling of the *Vorlage*. On the other hand, non-standard features which are found in several documents of the scribe are probably idiosyncrasies of the scribe. Irregularities which may reflect Aramaic influence on the scribe's dialect or orthography are the following.

a. The plural of יום is written יומים in 1QS II, 19 and III, 5 (יומי), V, 26 ביומיו corrected to ביום, 1QSa I, 7 יומיו and 4Q175 4 היומים. The same plural is found in 1QIsaᵃ I, 1 (1:1) where בימי is (mis)corrected to בי׳מי (and perhaps in XXXII, 2). The *waw*s were added by the original scribe, or perhaps by the scribe of 1QS.[36] To my knowledge, this plural יומים occurs only in 1QIsaᵃ and in documents copied by the scribe of 1QS.

Other examples of irregular spellings of plurals are 1QSa I, 14 בראשי,[37] and six times אנוש or איש׳ (1QSa I, 2, 3, 28; II, 2, 8, 13).

b. Most of the confusions between על and אל (see above) occur

---

[36] S. Talmon, 'Aspects of the Textual Transmission of the Bible in the Light of Qumran Manuscripts,' reprinted in *Qumran and the History of the Biblical Text* (ed. F.M. Cross, S. Talmon; Cambridge, MA: Harvard University Press, 1975), 226–63, at 232, refers to "the Aramaic determined morphology of the sectarian copyist" of the Isaiah scroll, and claims that the (mis)correction in I, 1 "may be ascribed [. . .] with absolute certainty" to the initial scribe.

[37] See also Isa 15:2 רֹאשָׁיו (1QIsaᵃ ראושו).

where Aramaic uses על and Standard Hebrew אל. This confusion is widespread in late-biblical and post-biblical texts.

c. הם- for the pronominal suffix 3 m.pl. may reflect the Aramaic vowel of the suffix (cf. הם- in Ezra and twice in 4QDanᵃ, and הון- in Daniel). See 1QS I, 21 נבורתום; III, 25 עליהון (3 f.pl.); V, 20 הונם corrected to הונם; IX, 14 רוחום; 1QSa I, 4 בבואום. See also 4Q382 1, 2 ויהביאום (1 Kgs 18:4 וַיַּחְבִּיאֵם) where the editor reads ויהביאים. These forms have been explained differently. Qimron suggests for נבורתום and רוחום the addition of an enclitic *mem*, but also discusses the possibility of *waw* (for *o, u*) instead of *a, e*.[38] Other explanations deal with isolated cases, for example the explanation of נבורתום as a miswriting, by a kind of dittography, for נבורתו.[39]

d. The Aramaic suffix 3 m.sg. והי- is found mainly in documents written by the scribe of 1QS and in 1QIsaᵃ.[40]

e. The Aramaic dissimilation of gemination in ינתן (corresponding to MT יתן) in 4Q175 3.

f. The occasional use of *'alep* as mater lectionis for -*a*, as well as interchange of initial *he* and *'alep*, reflect spelling practices which are common in Aramaic, but rare in standard Hebrew and other Qumran scrolls.

g. Isolated cases have been, or may be, explained on the basis of Aramaic. Thus, אלה in 1QSa II, 4 בקהל אלה may be an Aramaism.[41] שמעת in 4Q175 1 for MT שמעתי may be due to an accidental omission of the *yod*, or reflect the Aramaic ending of the 1 c.sg. form. The strange 2 f.sg. pronominal suffix כה- in 4Q175 16 may be a scribal error, or perhaps influenced by the Aramaic ending כי-.

QUMRAN SCRIBAL PRACTICES AND THE CASE OF 4Q175

1. *The Scribe of 1QS and Qumran Scribal Practices*

The scribe of 1QS wrote according to the Qumran practice of orthography and morphology. In a discussion of the 'Qumran system' *vis-à-vis* scribal individuality, Tov refers to 1QS which "lacks forms of the type מלכמה," as well as to "[s]upralinear corrections which

[38] Qimron, *Hebrew*, §200.143 and §200.26.
[39] *DJD XXVI*, 49.
[40] Qimron, *Hebrew*, §322.144.
[41] See L. H. Schiffman, *The Eschatological Community of the Dead Sea Scrolls* (SBLMS 38; Atlanta, GA, 1989), 37 for other explanations.

render the Qumran orthography even more 'Qumranic' than it was."[42] Examples of the latter are the supralinear addition of *'alep* in 4Q53 II, 2 כֹּ̊אֿ, and of *waw* in 1QS II, 13; IV, 3; XI, 6; 1QSb I, 1; 4QSamᶜ I, 5. Statistical data on 1QS, 4Q175 and 4Q53 are included in Tov's tables.[43] Comparison of those data shows differences between 1QS and 4Q53 on the one hand, and 4Q175 on the other hand, both with regard to orthography and morphology.

The spelling of words as כול and לוא is generally plene.[44] The Qumran orthography כיא is found in the 1QS-1QSa-1QSb scroll (except for כי אם in 1QS V, 14 and 1QSa I, 10) and 4QSamᶜ II, 2 (2 Sam 14:22) כֹּ̊אֿ. 4Q175 17 and 4Q443 1, 10 have כי. The scribe writes the "Qumran" long form כה- of the 2 m.sg. pronominal suffix. Exceptions are עוונך in 1QS II, 8 and פיך in 4Q443 2, 5. Only in 4Q175 there are seven cases of ך- (all in lines 14-18; see below), against four cases of כה-.

The linguistic criteria of lengthened 2 and 3 m.pl. pronominal suffixes shows diverging statistics. 1QS has הם- more than thirty times against one (VIII, 21) המה-. In 1QSa two (or three if one reads במ]שנותיהמ[ה) lengthened suffixes are found in I, 5-8; the remainder of 1QSa has six forms with הם-. In 1QSb the only lengthened form might be found in I, 3 if יברככה has been corrected from יברכֹמֿה. 4Q175 has four 'short' forms in lines 3-4, three lengthened forms written המה- in 5-6; and שניהמה in 25. 4Q443 has one plural suffix, 12 i, 3 ללהמה[; 4Q457b I, 7 בצעם but II, 6 עליהמה.

2. *The Case of 4Q175*

4Q175 (4QTestimonia) is generally listed as a non-biblical, sectarian, composition, but it consists of quotations of four partially expanded biblical texts. On the whole, the text and orthography of 4Q175 seem to be based on the texts copied by the scribe.

Instructive is the quotation of Deut 33:8–11 in 4Q175 14–20. The remains of Deut 33:8–11 in 4Q35 (4QDeutʰ) help us to reassess the

---

[42] Tov, 'Hebrew Biblical Manuscripts,' 25.

[43] Tov, 'Orthography,' 51–52 (Tables 1a–b).

[44] A special case of defective spelling are plural verbal forms with omission of the *waw* before the suffix: 1QS V, 11 הדרשהו (cf. Zeph 1:6); VI, 17 ידרושהו; 21 פקודהו; 22 כתובהו; 25 ויבדילהו; VII, 1 והבדילהו; 16 והבדילהו; 17 ישלחהו; 21 יקרבהו; VIII, 18 יקרבהו; 22 ישלחהו; 1QSa I, 7 יל[מֿדהו]. The only *plene* writing of this form is 1QSa I, 7 ישכילוהו. See M. G. Abegg, 'The Hebrew of the Dead Sea Scrolls,' in *The Dead Sea Scrolls after Fifty Years. A Comprehensive Assessment. Vol. I* (ed. P. W. Flint & J. C. VanderKam; Leiden, Boston, Köln: Brill, 1998), 325–58, at 331.

scribal practice of our scribe, as well as the subsequent corrections of the text. These few lines have 9 scribal corrections, most of which stem from a second hand. Whereas the scribe elsewhere spells the 2 m.sg. pronominal suffix as כה-, in 4Q175 14–20 the text has ך- seven times, and כה- only twice. Also, in this section the scribe writes כי, and not כיא.

In a comparison of 4QDeut^h, 4Q175, MT and the versions, Duncan identifies six agreements between the initial text of 4Q175 and the preserved text of 4QDeut^h against MT, but only one disagreement between the original text of 4Q175 and 4QDeut^h.[45] In two other cases the scribe simply forgot an entire word. Duncan demonstrates that the initial text of 4Q175 18–19 was corrected towards the text known from MT.

There are some aspects not mentioned explicitly by Duncan. First, the *waw* of ובריתך in 4Q175 17 is an addition by a second hand, which gives yet another example of 4Q175 first corresponding to the text of 4QDeut^h, but then corrected towards an MT-like text. Second, 4Q175 14-20 has the full Qumran spelling in לוא and יעקוב as opposed to MT and 4QDeut^h, but a defective spelling against MT in 14 ואורך, 15 ותרבהו, 19 ידו, קמו, and ומשנאו. This can be compared to 4QDeut^h, which in Deuteronomy 33 has a spelling which is more defective than MT. In other words, the text presents a confusing picture. On a few occasions, the scribe uses the Qumran orthography (twice כה-, and several times a plene spelling of -*o*-), but the same scribe also spells ך- and כי, and follows the archaic spelling practice of the manuscript from which the quote was copied. We see a scribe who takes care to copy the defective spelling of the *Vorlage*, but at the same times omits two words.

Perhaps one may explain the differences in the first quote in a similar manner. Lines 3–4 have 'short' pronominal suffixes: לבבם, להם,[46] and ולבניהם, whereas lines 5–6 have three lengthened suffixes, with final *mem* before *he*: לאהמה, אהיהמה, and אליהמה. Siegel's description and explanation of this ending המה- in 4Q175 must be dismissed:[47] the *he*s have definitely *not* been squeezed in, and it seems

---

[45] J. A. Duncan, 'New Readings for the "Blessing of Moses" from Qumran', *JBL* 114 (1995): 273–90, esp. 289–90. Her lists do not include *plene* versus defective spelling, or variants involving the conjunction.

[46] Not {ה}להם as suggested by Strugnell, "Notes en Marge," 226.

[47] *Contra* Siegel, "Scribes of Qumran," 149.

unlikely that three times, within a range of eight words, the final *he* was added "as afterthought."

The transition from 'short' to lengthened 3 m.pl. suffixes concurs with the transition from Deut 5:29 to 18:18 as in the sequence of Exod 20:21b in the Samaritan Pentateuch. We know there existed different expanded versions: 4Q158 also expands Exodus 20 with passages from Deuteronomy 5 and 18, but in a different manner and sequence. The example of 1QIsaᵃ (1QIsaᵃ–I has mainly short forms; 1QIsaᵃ–II many lengthened forms) shows that within one manuscript the orthography may change. One may hypothesise that either the scribe of 4Q175, or an earlier scribe of the expanded text used by the scribe of 4Q175, copied from two sections of Deuteronomy written in a different orthography. Apparently this scribe carefully or mechanically copied the medial and final *mem*s of the *Vorlage*, which itself may have been a text where *he* was added secondarily.

These examples show that it is difficult to judge which special features were introduced into the documents by the scribe of 1QS, and which were copied from a *Vorlage*. One should attribute the spelling of היומים to the scribe, because it also is found in other documents written by the scribe. Likewise, one may explain יתן against the Aramaic influence on the scribe. But what about the strange spellings למעאן and ללאהסה? Such spellings are rare in the Scrolls, and are mainly found in 1QIsaᵃ-II. Since the scribe of 1QS does not use such spellings elsewhere, one may hypothesise that these spellings derive from a *Vorlage* with a spelling not unlike that of 1QIsaᵃ.

THE SCRIBE OF 1QS

What kind of a scribe was the scribe of 1QS? Scholars use qualifications as "careless," "less competent," and "prone to error." Tov once characterised the documents written by the Qumran scribes (especially 1QIsaᵃ and the documents of our scribe) as follows: "[t]he writing is frequently careless and the text full of errors, and in many cases these were corrected in sundry ways,"[48] a view which he phrased with more sophistication in later studies. This judgment is true to some extent. In the documents copied by the scribe of 1QS there are disproportionately many scribal corrections. The erasures and

---

[48] Tov, 'Orthography,' 43.

interlinear corrections in 1QS VII and VIII are conspicuous, but more telling are the many remodellings, erasures or additions of one or two letters throughout the documents. The number of corrections and errors varies in 1QS, and is relatively small in cols. I–III and in VIII, 15–IX, 11, and extremely high in cols. V–VIII. To a certain extent the scribe may have been less competent, but the accumulation of errors and corrections in specific sections may reflect a complicated textual tradition.

Many errors are related to gutturals, whereas other non-standard forms are Aramaicizing. This reminds one of 1QIsaᵃ. Goshen-Gottstein argued that 1QIsaᵃ "stands in a category of its own as the most deviating manuscript among [the] Q[umran] S[crolls]."[49] Yet, of all the Cave 1 scrolls which he studied, he considered 1QS to stand linguistically nearest to 1QIsaᵃ "in spite of the considerable distance," especially with regard to the weakening of gutturals and the tendency towards Aramaisms.[50] This view still holds after the publication of all the other Dead Sea Scrolls. We may assume that both scribes had the same linguistic background, a dialect which Kutscher called "a Hebrew-Aramaic patois."[51]

The scribe, presumably a man, was a member of the (Qumran) Community at the beginning of the first century B.C.E. His documents are written in accordance to the practices of the Qumran scribal school. The main exception is 4Q175. The lack of care for a consistent orthography and the undisciplined script in 4Q175 suggest that this single sheet was written for private use. The scribe copied "biblical" passages from different manuscripts; on the whole he simply adopted the orthography of his *Vorlage*, but a few times he (automatically?) used the Qumran orthography. 4Q175 stands in contrast to the 1QS scroll which is more consistent and written more carefully. The series of subsequent corrections, and the almost perfect preservation of the scroll, suggests that this scroll was kept in honour, perhaps even as the model scroll of the Rule of the Community.

The ideological correspondence between 4Q175 (the compilation refers to a prophet, a royal and a priestly messiah, and an anti-messianic figure) and 1QS IX, 11 (with its reference to the prophet and

---

[49] M. H. Goshen-Gottstein, 'Linguistic Structure and Tradition in the Qumran Documents,' *ScrHier* 4 (1958): 101–36, at 105.

[50] Goshen-Gottstein, 'Linguistic Structure,' 131.

[51] Kutscher, *Language*, 61.

the Messiahs of Aaron and Israel) is well-known. Metso argues convincingly that 1QS VIII, 15b–IX, 11, which is missing in 4Q259, consists of three interpolations, namely two already existing penal code sections, and, in IX, 3–11, a duplicate of VIII, 1–15.[52] The spelling מהמה in VIII, 21 is found in the inserted already existing material, and may reflect the orthography of the *Vorlage*. The reference to the first directives of the Community in IX, 10 shows that this duplicate was composed in later times.

Why did the scribe of 1QS compile the quotations of 4Q175?[53] Perhaps because he gathered scriptural evidence for the motif of the eschatological prophet and messiahs in the text he copied. Or may one assume the opposite? The quotations in 4Q175 were used by the composer of 1QS IX, 3–11. Perhaps the scribe of 1QS composed this duplicate and inserted it together with the penal code material in his scroll. If that is the case, the scribe may have been one of the leaders of the Community, entitled to insert his scriptural interpretation in the Community's Rulebook. This might explain why someone who was "careless" and "less competent" as a scribe was nonetheless entrusted to copy the 1QS scroll, and why this scroll was preserved so well.

[52] S. Metso, *The Textual Development of the Qumran Community Rule* (STDJ 21; Leiden, New York, Köln: E. J. Brill, 1997), 71–73, 124–8.
[53] Thanks are due to Geza Xeravits who stimulated my thinking by suggesting that the scribe of 1QS was the compiler of the *Testimonia*.

TWO PERSPECTIVES ON TWO PENTATEUCHAL MANUSCRIPTS FROM MASADA

Eugene Ulrich

I am grateful for this opportunity to honor and celebrate Emanuel Tov—an admired scholar, an enriching colleague, and a trusted friend. For over thirty years we have been walking the same road together, and I thank him for teaching me much. In this article I would like simply to offer another episode in our ongoing conversation concerning the history of the biblical text. As with most good conversations, I hope that this study offers some new light and that our future conversations will push and refine our knowledge yet further.

Specifically, I would like to inquire more closely into the textual nature of two of the Pentateuchal MSS found at Masada and recently published.[1] Just as the prevailing view of the scriptural scrolls from Qumran is that they portray a pluriform text with variant literary editions of many books, so too the prevailing view of the scriptural scrolls from Masada is that, in contrast, they uniformly display a close relationship to the proto-Masoretic Text.[2] Tov himself has already led the way in formulating some of the nuanced context that should be kept in mind:

> The fact that all the texts left by the Zealots at Masada (dating until 73 C.E.) reflect 𝔐 is also important.
>
> But there is a snag in this description. While on the one hand it was claimed . . . that those involved in the transmission of 𝔐 did not insert any change in 𝔐 and as a result its inconsistency in spelling as well as its mistakes have been preserved for posterity, on the other

---

[1] Shemaryahu Talmon and Yigael Yadin, *Masada VI: Yigael Yadin Excavations 1963–1965: Final Reports* (Jerusalem: Israel Exploration Society/Hebrew University of Jerusalem, 1999).

[2] See, as representative examples, Shemaryahu Talmon, "Masada: Written Material," *Encyclopedia of the Dead Sea Scrolls* (ed. L. H. Schiffman and J. C. VanderKam; New York: Oxford University Press, 2000), 1.521–25, esp. 523; Talmon and Yadin, *Masada VI*, 25, 38, 46, 55, 68, 89, 93; Lawrence H. Schiffman, *Reclaiming the Dead Sea Scrolls* (Philadelphia: Jewish Publication Society, 1994), 172.

hand, there never existed any one single text that could be named *the* Masoretic Text. In fact at a certain stage there was a *group* of Masoretic texts and naturally this situation requires a more precise formulation. Although at one time an attempt was made not to insert any changes in 𝔐, at that time the texts within the group of Masoretic texts already differed internally one from another. . . . The wish to preserve a unified textual tradition thus remained an abstract ideal which could not be accomplished in reality.[3]

In an attempt to gain even sharper focus for categorizing the Masada scrolls, we can study two of the MSS from the Pentateuch that survived there: MasGen and MasLev[a].

I. Genesis (MasGen)

Only one tiny fragment of Genesis, 5.6 × 4.5 cm, was found at Masada.[4] It contains merely eight complete words and six other letters from three broken words, but it can be identified as containing parts of Gen 46:7–11.[5] Talmon offers the following transcription, altered here only by the insertion of the brackets at the end of the first line (since the MS is broken off) and by the shift to the left side plus the insertion of brackets at the right to indicate, as Talmon notes, that the words constitute the ends of the lines:

[ ] מצרים[	]	1
מצרי[ם את יעקוב	]	2
[ו[בנ]י ראובן חנוך	]	3
ימ[ן]ואל וימין	]	4
[ובני לוי	]	5

Talmon gives the following reconstruction, again altered only by the insertion of the brackets at the end of the first line, the brackets at the beginning of the lines, and the verse numbers:

[ובנות בניו וכול זרעו הביא אתו [מצרים [vac]	]	1
[8]ואלה שמות בני ישראל הבאים מצרי[ם את יעקוב		2

---

[3] Emanuel Tov, *Textual Criticism of the Hebrew Bible* (2d ed.; Minneapolis: Fortress; Assen: Royal Van Gorcum, 2001), 28–29; emphasis in the original.

[4] For the edition of MasGen, see Talmon and Yadin, *Masada VI*, 31–35.

[5] Unfortunately, no other biblical MS from the Judean Desert is preserved for Genesis 46.

3 [אביהם בכור יעקוב ראובן] ⁹ו[בנ] ראובן חנוך

4 [ופלוא וחצרון וכרבי ¹⁰ובני שמעון ימ[ו]נל וימין

5 [ואהד ויכין וצוחר ושאול בן הכנענית] ¹¹ובני לוי

There is one orthographic difference from the MT (and on the basis
of this longer reading Talmon reconstructs longer readings for other
words where appropriate):

46:8 (line 2) יעקוב MasGen] יעקב MT SP

There are three variants preserved:

46:7 (1) מצרים MasGen] מצרימה MT SP
46:8 (2) מצרי[ם MasGen] מצרימה MT SP
46:8 (2) את יעקוב MasGen] יעקב MT SP LXX

The first two variants are morphological and do not involve a shift
in meaning, but the third variant ("with Jacob") involves a different
syntactic pattern and requires Talmon to restore אביהם as the next
word, in agreement with *Jub.* 44:11 את יעקב אביהם, as opposed to
the more awkward יעקב ובניו in MT SP LXX.

This means that, of the eight complete and three broken words
in MasGen, there are three variants (plus a fourth reconstructed)
and an orthographic difference which suggests a pattern of differing
orthography.

Finally, Talmon suggests that "MasGen exhibits an important
agreement with MT . . . a break . . . [which] dovetails with the masoretic
section-divider (*parašah*) after Gen 46:7."[6] One should observe, however, that blank space is extant for only the width of one letter (or
inter-word space) after מצרים and then breaks off. It is very likely,
of course, that the scribe did leave an intentional interval here, but
it would have been a short interval of only 1 cm, enough for only
three or four letters. Moreover, most scribes or translators would
independently start a new section here (see below).

Consideration of how to describe the textual profile of MasGen
leads in two directions. The detailed and nuanced observations made
by editors of texts are sometimes lost on the wider array of scholars, who will often not work from the original MS or photographs
but rely on the transcription and description given by the specialist.
Thus, on the one hand, since the MT is the center for much of the

---

[6] Talmon and Yadin, *Masada VI*, 33.

academic and religious use of the Hebrew Bible, it can be argued
that description from the point of view of the traditional MT is a
good way to proceed. Since the MT provides the only complete collection of texts in the original language, it indeed functions in practice as the standard text of the Hebrew Bible. It has also long been
the reference-point for text-critical mapping.

On the other hand, one could make the case that for the Second
Temple period the reference-point of textual discussions should be
the situation as it existed at the time. How would the people who
were producing or hearing or reading the texts have described them?
What were the operative categories, classifications, and worldview
with which they were working? Though the MT has been amazingly
faithfully copied from texts well attested in the late Second Temple
period, it represents only one form of the text of many books as
Judaism knew them; and it is difficult to find convincing evidence
that the collection of individual texts that the rabbis received and
handed on were carefully selected in contradistinction to other forms
of the texts used by other Jews.

From the first perspective, one can classify a text under observation primarily by its relationship to the MT, aided by contrast with
the SP and the presumed Hebrew behind the LXX or other versions.
From the second perspective, one questions whether the people who
penned the texts or lived by them would have known about the
"proto-MT," thought of it as textually or religiously preferable to the
"SP" or "LXX(-*Vorlage*)," or thought they should compare their texts
to it as a "standard text."[7]

Returning specifically to MasGen, is it appropriate to classify this
fragment as generally Masoretic? From the first perspective, yes: it
agrees with the MT except for five letters in four words, and, noting
Tov's careful remarks in the quotation at the beginning, such small
variants are to be expected even within the Masoretic group.

From the second perspective, no. First, "(proto-)MT" was probably
not a concept or category at the time, nor would "LXX(-*Vorlage*)" have
been. Jews would probably have known about the Samaritans' Torah,

---

[7] Were this the case, one would expect that 𝔐 would consistently be a superior
form of the text; but, as Tov (*Textual Criticism*, 24) says, "... the preference of 𝔐
by a central stream in Judaism does not necessarily imply that it contains the best
text of the Bible. Both the Hebrew parent text of 𝔊 ... and certain of the Qumran
texts ... reflect excellent texts, often better than that of 𝔐."

but the only aspects they would probably have been aware of would be the paleo-Hebrew script and the specifically Samaritan-faith variants regarding Mount Gerizim.[8] They would probably not have had a problem with the script, but they would have rejected the entire corpus due to the sensitive Mount Gerizim variants.

Secondly, the SP and the LXX are identical with the MT for all the preserved text of MasGen, so that "agreements with the MT" would equally be agreements with the SP or agreements with the LXX. Would it be acceptable to classify MasGen as "basically Samaritan" or as "aligned with the LXX"?

Similarly, the short interval of 3–4 letters at the end of line 1 is not well characterized as "an important agreement with MT,"[9] since the SP also has a qiṣṣah and Rahlfs' and Wevers' editions of the LXX as well as most translations display a break before the new section. Gen 46:8–27 breaks into the Genesis narrative with a different genre. It is a genealogical list which was inserted into the story, interrupting the narrative that breaks after 46:7 and resumes in 46:28. Most ancient scribes or modern editors would independently place a section break at this point.

Finally, of the eleven words (eight complete plus three partial) in MasGen, there are three variants from the MT (plus a fourth reconstructed); should a variant rate of 27% (or 36% if orthography is included) be considered closely aligned?

In sum, if one's stand-point is the present outcome of history, or the medieval world, or the MT as a cherished religious text, or *BHS* as a practical tool for ease of comparison, one could legitimately conclude that MasGen is quite close to the MT. On the other hand, if one's standpoint is the world represented by Masada and the wider Jewish world of the time, one would conclude that MasGen appears

---

[8] There is no evidence to suppose that they would have been aware of the main distinguishing features of the Samaritan (as opposed to the MT-LXX) form of Exodus and Numbers, since those features would have been identical with Jewish MSS presumably in use, such as 4QpaleoExod^m and 4QNum^b.

[9] Talmon and Yadin, *Masada VI*, 33. Talmon also mentions a break in a *Jubilees* MS, but none appears to be extant for *Jub.* 44:11–12; see James C. VanderKam, "The Jubilees Fragments from Qumran Cave 4," *The Madrid Qumran Congress: Proceedings of the International Congress on the Dead Sea Scrolls—Madrid, 18–21 March 1991* (ed. J. Trebolle Barrera and L. Vegas Montaner; STDJ 11/2; Leiden: Brill; Madrid: Editorial Complutense, 1992), 635–48, esp. 642. I thank Professor VanderKam for a recent private communication updating the list in his article.

to be a good representative of the single then-current (and hence-forward enduring) edition of Genesis, which nonetheless showed a relatively high number of the minor variants typical of mss of authoritative Scriptures in that period. Four of its eleven preserved words show minor variations in comparison with other current texts which also differed from each other. One is purely orthographic, two are morphological with no change in meaning, and one shows a sentence structure different from that in the received MT, SP, and LXX but aligned with the one on which *Jubilees* was also based.

II. The First Leviticus Scroll (MasLev^a)

For MasLev^a only a pair of contiguous fragments is extant, preserving the left half of eight lines containing Lev 4:3–9.[10] When compared with the MT and SP, the only two orthographic differences that emerge are:

4:7 (6) יִשְׁפֹּךְ MasLev^a] יִשְׁפֹּךְ MT SP
4:9 (8) הַיֹּתֶרֶת MasLev^a MT] הַיּוֹתֶרֶת SP

When compared with the MT, SP, and LXX, there are three preserved variants:

4:7 (5) מִן הַדָּם MasLev^a MT SP] *מִדַּם הַפָּר (ἀπὸ τοῦ αἵματος τοῦ μόσχου) LXX
4:7 (6) דַּם הַפָּר MasLev^a MT LXX] הַדָּם SP
4:8 (7) עַל MasLev^a MT^L] אֵת MT^{mss} SP LXX (τὰ [ἐνδόσθια])

But the extant left half of the lines permits a reasonably confident restoration of the right half which argues for these probable, reconstructed variants:

4:4 (3) [רֹאשׁ הַפָּר] MasLev^a MT SP] + *לִפְנֵי יהוה (ἔναντι κυρίου) LXX[11]
4:5 (3–4) [ ]\ הַמָּשִׁיחַ MasLev^a MT] + אֲשֶׁר מִלֵּא אֶת יָדוֹ SP LXX[12]
4:6 (5) [פְּעָמִים] MasLev^a MT LXX$^{B,A\ Rahlfs}$] + בְּאֶצְבָּעוֹ SP 4QLXXLev^b OG

---

[10] For the text and edition of MasLev^a, see Talmon and Yadin, *Masada VI*, 36–39. See also the edition of 4QLev^c by Emanuel Tov in *DJD* 12.189–92 and pl. XXXV; it has one fragment that overlaps with MasLev^a but no clear variants preserved.

[11] It may be questioned whether the OG translation included ἔναντι κυρίου here as well as ἐνώπιον κυρίου a few words later (where the Hebrew texts do have לִפְנֵי יהוה). Since ἔναντι(ον) κυρίου is used repeatedly in this section and ἐνώπιον κυρίου occurs only here (but note in the later sections 4:18 and 24), one suspects that ἔναντι κυρίου may have originally translated לִפְנֵי יהוה but was transposed, and ἐνώπιον κυρίου was a later addition to reflect the emergent MT.

[12] Note the anomalous interlinear writing of אֵת יָדוֹ °°°° above הֹכֹּ[הֵ]ן in וֹלָקַח⁵ in

Again, is it appropriate to classify MasLev^a as generally Masoretic? From the first perspective, certainly yes, since MasLev^a agrees with the MT in all preserved and reconstructable variants, differing only in a single orthographic detail. From the second perspective, it is also easy to agree that, when MasLev^a is compared specifically with the MT, SP, and LXX, only the MT consistently agrees with it in every textual variant (though it disagrees with many MT^{mss} at 4:8; see *BHS* note). On the other hand, one can ask whether the MT, SP, and LXX are the proper and sufficient measuring sticks in the first century C.E. by which to measure MasLev^a. All the orthography and variants listed are minor and routine, involving no change in meaning, and exhibiting erratically changing patterns of affiliation. The SP has only two tiny and insignificant variants from MasLev^a in the 63 (56 completely and 7 partly) preserved words; this is a variant rate of only 3.17%.[13]

My suggestion for a description of affiliation would begin by noting that the remaining evidence from the late Second Temple period indicates that only one literary edition of the Hebrew Leviticus was in circulation, with minor variants exhibited randomly by the various copies, including those at Qumran, the one that served as the *Vorlage* for the LXX, the one that the rabbis inherited, the one that the Samaritans adopted, and assorted other copies.[14] When considered in contrast to Exodus and Numbers, which exhibit variant literary editions,[15] it is plausible to suggest that the Jerusalem priesthood guarded a more or less uniform tradition for the Book of Leviticus— not as a "standard text of Scripture" (otherwise, how explain Exodus and Numbers?), but for the correct and consistent praxis in the

---

4QLev^c; see *DJD* 12, pl. XXXV (lower part of frg. 2) and pp. 190–91. For the addition of אשר מלא את ידו in the SP and LXX *Vorlage*, see Lev 8:33; 21:10; and esp. 16:32.

[13] The SP also probably disagrees in two reconstructed variants, but compared with the fully reconstructed text of MasLev^a, the variant rate would not rise significantly.

[14] Perhaps the largest Leviticus variants from Qumran are the two complete verses missing from 4QLev-Num^a at Lev 14:24 and 45, but both are probably meaningless simple omissions by parablepsis (and a later hand secondarily inserted the latter verse); see *DJD* 12.156–57 and pl. XXIII.

[15] Three variant editions are preserved for Exodus and two for Numbers: for Exodus, the OG of Exodus 35–40 (vs. secondary MT-SP), the MT-OG for the rest of the book, and the later expanded 4QpaleoExod^m-SP edition; for Numbers, the MT-OG and the expanded 4QNum^b-SP edition.

sacrificial rituals of the Temple. The part of MasLev^a that survives displays a copy that was virtually identical with the one that the rabbis inherited and that formed the consonantal text for what eventually became the MT. Thus, it serves, like 1QIsa^b for the most part, to demonstrate the startling fidelity with which the MT preserves an ancient form of the text. But, as MasGen and other indicators show, that does not mean that the proto-MT had become the standard text.[16]

III. Observations on the Text in the Second Temple Period

The Qumran biblical MSS show that at least six books (or possibly ten) of the twenty-four in the Masoretic canon circulated in variant literary editions in the closing centuries of the Second Temple period: Exodus, Numbers, Joshua, Judges(?), Samuel(?), Jeremiah, the Twelve Prophets(?), Psalms, Song, and Lamentations(?). When the study is widened to include the witness of the LXX and SP, seven (or eight) more can be added or become clear: Genesis (chapters 5 and 11), Samuel (at least 1 Samuel 16–17), Kings, Ezekiel, the Twelve Prophets, Job(?), Proverbs, and Daniel. Thus, we have MS evidence that Judaism during the last two and a half centuries while the Second Temple stood knew variant literary editions for half or more of the books that would become Tanakh: thirteen (or up to sixteen) of the traditional twenty-four books.

But this synchronic perspective can be viewed diachronically as well. The double or multiple literary editions are products of the latter stages of the compositional process of the Scriptures. The composition of the various books took place in numerous stages that were different for each book (consider the growth, e.g., of Isaiah, Jeremiah, the Twelve, Psalms, Proverbs) or set of books (e.g., the Tetrateuch, the Deuteronomistic History). Each new edition resulted from the creative efforts of some author/scribe/priest/teacher who

---

[16] See Eugene Ulrich, "The Qumran Biblical Scrolls—The Scriptures of Late Second Temple Judaism," *The Dead Sea Scrolls in Their Historical Context* (ed. Timothy H. Lim et al.; Edinburgh: T&T Clark, 2000), 67–87. See also the insightful discussion of Julio Trebolle Barrera, "Qumran Evidence for a Biblical Standard Text and for Non-Standard and Parabiblical Texts," ibid., 89–106.

took the current edition and intentionally revised it in light of the new opportunity or need, whether religious or national, of the time. The literary and redactional analysis that has accumulated since the Enlightenment richly charts this history for each of the books, from their hazy beginnings to their final form. But those analyses, while persuasive in varying degrees, did not have benefit of MS evidence. The Qumran scrolls have now provided MS evidence for the latter stages of this dynamic process of the growth of the biblical books, and allowed us to recognize the collateral evidence that the SP and the LXX furnish. If we had evidence from earlier centuries, it is not overly sanguine to expect that we would see variant editions of the other books as well.

Usually, the newer edition eventually replaced the older one(s), but sometimes not, presumably because the newer one was not yet sufficiently established, or was known to be recent, or conflicted with current beliefs (e.g., 4QpaleoExod^m and 4QNum^b with their affinities to the SP, or 11QPs^a and *Jubilees* advocating a 364-day solar calendar).

When attempting to sort out the various witnesses, one can diachronically label the variant editions "text traditions," and synchronically label them "text types." Within the same text tradition or text type, one can speak of "text families," insofar as the witnesses somewhat regularly agree on minor variants; insofar as they display more disagreement, they would belong to different text families. Thus, on an ideal stemma (which is different for each book), the main lines would be drawn according to variant editions (i.e., different text traditions), while the secondary lines would be drawn according to the pattern of individual variants between or within text families. The variant editions (i.e., large-scale *patterns* of variants) arose as the products of intentional creative work in the on-going composition of the books; the individual variants arose more as a function of the perceptiveness and clarifying moves, or the inadequacies and mistakes, of scribal copyists.

IV. The Scriptural Manuscripts from Masada

When viewed from the first (i.e., MT-oriented) perspective described above, it is possible to describe the Pentateuchal MSS from Masada, and indeed the remaining scriptural MSS from there, as generally witnessing to the proto-Masoretic tradition. We have seen that this is a legitimate conclusion, especially for MasLev[a], if less so for MasGen. That conclusion gains in persuasiveness the more one emphasizes the nuance articulated by Tov at the beginning of this paper, that "there never existed any one single text that could be named *the* Masoretic Text,"[17] and the more one insists that the (proto-)MT is "an abstract ideal" that includes the modest array of variants exhibited in the collection of Masoretic MSS.

But the observations in part III above invite focus on the second perspective as well. It may have been noticed that the short list of scriptural books found at Masada—Genesis, Leviticus, Deuteronomy, Ezekiel, and Psalms—has little or no practical overlap with the list of books found in variant editions at Qumran and in the SP and LXX. That is, for Genesis,[18] Leviticus, and Deuteronomy,[19] the evidence that survives attests only a single edition. For Ezekiel, even though the OG shows signs of a variant edition,[20] the small remains of the few Hebrew MSS from Qumran offer almost no possibility of comparison where the variation between editions occurs.[21] And for the Psalter, though there are variant editions, the variation is mainly on the macro level (the order and the inclusion or not of full compositions), not the micro level (individual variant readings); i.e., the wording of individual Psalms of one edition is for the most part identical to that of the other edition.[22]

Thus, from the first perspective, the Masada remains may be described as close to the (proto-)MT. But from the second perspective, they would be described as preserving only a very limited amount of useful evidence for the history of the biblical text. Fragments from only five books are extant, and three of those books do not show

---

[17] Tov, *Textual Criticism*, 28.

[18] That is, except for the triple edition or recension in chapters 5 and 11, which do not appear in MasGen. See Ralph W. Klein "Archaic Chronologies and the Textual History of the Old Testament," *HTR* 67 (1974): 255–63; and Ronald S. Hendel, *The Text of Genesis 1–11: Textual Studies and Critical Edition* (New York: Oxford University Press, 1998), 61–80.

[19] The agreement of 4QDeut[q] with the LXX is limited to Deuteronomy 32.

[20] See Emanuel Tov, "Recensional Differences Between the MT and LXX of Ezekiel," *ETL* 62 (1986): 89–101; idem, *Textual Criticism*, 333–34, 349–50.

[21] 4QEzek[b] at 1:22 does attest the interpolation הנורא = MT, > LXX (see *DJD* 15.218, and Tov, *Textual Criticism*, 333); however, the small MS did not contain the full book, but apparently only chapter 1 and perhaps a few other small passages (see *DJD* 15.215–16).

[22] See Peter W. Flint, *The Dead Sea Psalms Scrolls and the Book of Psalms* (STDJ 17; Leiden: Brill, 1997).

the pluriform nature typical of the text of Scripture in that period; that is, the possibility for significant differentiating information is quite limited. For Ezekiel, though the evidence is slim, it is not impossible that the earlier, shorter edition that formed the *Vorlage* of the OG in the third or early second century B.C.E. was becoming less popular in the first century than the later, longer edition inherited by the rabbis and the MT.[23] More importantly, there is very little text of Ezekiel preserved at either Qumran or Masada that is capable of clearly indicating one edition as opposed to another.

For the Psalter, though it is argued that "MasPs[a] corresponds to all intents and purposes to MT," the case is less strong than the edition suggests.[24] Nonetheless, for MasPs[b], it should be stated clearly that it unambiguously shows agreement with the edition preserved in the MT against 11QPs[a] and LXX, since a blank column follows traditional Psalm 150. On the other hand, the individual wording—as opposed to the edition—is not identical to the MT. Of the 21 complete and 6 partial words preserved, MasPs[b] has six or seven differences from the MT. It reads הללהו vs. הללוהו MT five times, שפר vs. שופר, and וענוב (= 11QPs[a] MT[L]) vs. וענב in the Aleppo Codex of the MT. It is possible, but unlikely, that the first represents a textual variant (singular verb; note the collective singular in v. 6); it is more likely, as Talmon suggests, simply orthographic, as are the remaining two instances. But it was argued with respect to MasLev[b] that the "textual identity of MasLev[b] with MT is evinced by the meticulous preservation of the defective and plene spellings," and even "the same inconsistency as MT in the employment of defective and plene spellings."[25] By that same criterion, MasPs[b] would be categorized, with regard to text, as not especially closely related to the proto-MT within the text family, but, with regard to edition, as sharing the same general text tradition as the proto-MT (in contrast to that of 11QPs[a] and the LXX).

---

[23] This may have been the case also for Jeremiah and Joshua.

[24] Some of the examples listed on page 89 in Talmon and Yadin, *Masada VI* should be scrutinized. The variant, e.g., at Psalm 81:13 (singular suffix vs. plural) is not a true variant but simply translation technique on the part of the LXX, as the context shows. The antecedent is עמי/ישראל; therefore the LXX naturally uses the plural, as does the MT two words later: לבם. Even the JPS translation of the MT (as well as the NRSV) uses the plural: "My people . . ., I let *them* go after their willful heart."

[25] Talmon and Yadin, *Masada VI*, 46.

In conclusion, from one perspective the scriptural MSS from Masada can be characterized as in agreement with the MT (or proto-MT) to varying degrees. From an alternate perspective, it seems that that description can be enhanced with a more detailed characterization that is first-century oriented and more attuned to the variant-edition status of the Scriptures in the closing centuries of the Second Temple period.

THOSE WHO LOOK FOR SMOOTH THINGS, PHARISEES, AND ORAL LAW

James C. VanderKam

The scholar of the Qumran scrolls has a number of means available for situating the texts and their authors in their proper historical setting. Archeological data from the Qumran site and caves have revealed the general period in which the texts belong, while paleographical analyses and carbon-14 tests have confirmed and added their own kinds of precision to the dating of the manuscripts. Another type of evidence for indicating the time of the scrolls is the internal references, whether to historical individuals or to groups and events.

While some texts mention known individuals, the writers of the scrolls more often referred to people, friend and foe alike, not by names that we recognize, but by nicknames or epithets. Naturally, these have proved somewhat frustrating to decipher. Not only are the names unfamiliar, but the traits ascribed to the individuals and groups can be too general to permit firm identifications. The long history of trying to name the Teacher of Righteousness and the Wicked Priest is testimony to the difficulties involved. No one has succeeded in identifying the Teacher (though there have been proposals), and the clues about the Wicked Priest in the *pesharim* have led to sundry theories involving nearly all of the Hasmonean high priests and a few others. In fact, the Groningen Hypothesis holds that there was a series of Wicked Priests on the grounds that the descriptions fit no single individual. As for groups, the House of Absalom may serve as an example. They are charged with not coming to the Teacher's assistance at the time of his rebuke (1QpHab 5, 8–12); other than that we know nothing about them. Hence we do not know whether the term designates a group that was associated with one of the Absaloms attested in the late second temple period or whether it is a symbolic term, meant to recall the son who rebelled against David.[1]

---

[1] For a summary of the evidence and positions on it, see B. Nitzan, "Absalom,

One exception to the great uncertainty engendered by the epithets for groups has been the designation דורשי החלקות. Although the term is clearly one of opprobrium, the relatively large number of charges leveled against these seekers and the other names associated with them have led many scholars to identify them as Pharisees and to see the name as punning on their scholarly quest for הלכות. The identification and the explanation of the play on words go back to the early days of scrolls scholarship.[2]

Decoding the דורשי החלקות as Pharisees rests most securely on the use of the phrase in Pesher Nahum, the first Qumran text with personal names to be published. In 4QpNah 3–4 i, 1–8 where Nah 2:12–13 are under consideration, the commentator mentions two events that have clinched the identification to the satisfaction of many. First, the Greek king Demetrius, taken to be Demetrius III Eukerus (96/95–88), tried to enter Jerusalem "on the counsel of those who seek smooth things" (3–4 i, 2).[3] He did not succeed in entering the city, just as no king did from the time of Antiochus (IV) until the rulers of the Kittim. Second, the Furious Young Lion (understood to be Alexander Jannaeus) is depicted as one who takes revenge "on those who seek smooth things and hangs men alive, . . . formerly in Israel." (3–4, i 7–8). The two events are then explained by turning to Josephus who, both in the *Antiquities* (13.376–418) and in *War* (1.92–114), narrates the circumstances in which enemies of Jannaeus invited Demetrius to come to their assistance, his invasion of Judea, his victory over Jannaeus, his eventual withdrawal, and the revenge Jannaeus took on his enemies by crucifying 800 of them.[4]

House of," in *Encyclopedia of the Dead Sea Scrolls* (ed. L. Schiffman and J. VanderKam; 2 vols.; New York and Oxford: Oxford University Press, 2000), 4–5.

[2] See, for example, W. Brownlee, "Biblical Interpretation among the Sectaries of the Dead Sea Scrolls," *BA* 14 (1951): 59; J. Allegro, "Further Light on the History of the Qumran Sect," *JBL* 75 (1956): 92.

[3] Quotations of the scrolls are from G. Vermes, *The Complete Dead Sea Scrolls in English* (New York: Penguin, 1997).

[4] After Allegro suggested this interpretation ("Further Light," 92), it was widely accepted. Cf. J. Milik, *Ten Years of Discovery in the Wilderness of Judaea* (SBT 26; London: SCM, 1959), 72–73. For additional bibliography, see the surveys in M. Horgan, *Pesharim: Qumran Interpretations of Biblical Books* (CBQMS 8; Washington, DC: Catholic Biblical Association of America, 1979), 175–78; A. Baumgarten, "Seekers After Smooth Things," *Encyclopedia of the Dead Sea Scrolls*, 857–59; and H. Bengtsson, *What's in a Name? A Study of the Sobriquets in the Pesharim* (Uppsala: Uppsala University, 2000), 110–35.

While the evidence from this passage in the Nahum Pesher has been crucial in discerning Pharisees behind the title "those who seek smooth things," other uses of the epithet have contributed additional support. Here the argument is somewhat more indirect because in the Qumran texts specific legal positions are not attributed to the ones who look for smooth things. In the Damascus Document, the exact phrase דורשי החלקות does not occur but a variant of it does— דרשו בחלקות (I,18). The term is lodged in a passage directed against early opponents of the group behind the Damascus Document— called "the congregation of traitors" in I,12. After a "plant root" sprang up and a Teacher of Righteousness came to lead them, "the Scoffer [איש הלצון] arose who shed [הטיף] over Israel waters of lies [מימי כזב]. He caused them to wander in a pathless wilderness, laying low the everlasting heights, abolishing the ways of righteousness and removing the boundary with which the forefathers had marked out their inheritance. . . . For they sought smooth things [דרשו בחלקות] and preferred illusions. . . ." (I,14–18) The Scoffer appears to be connected here with the ones looking for smooth things, and he is accused of lying and misusing speech in various ways, including "tearing down firmly established teachings."[5] These enemies are said to constitute a "congregation" (בעדתם [II,1]).

Later in the Damascus Document, in the section regarding the nets of Belial (see IV,13–V,11), the writer refers to a group he dubs "the builders of the wall . . . who have followed after 'Precept'— 'Precept' was a spouter [מטיף] of whom it is written, *They shall surely spout* (Mic ii, 6). . . ." (IV,19–20) Their leader is designated with the term (מטיף) employed for the Scoffer in col. I. Among the charges made against them is that they marry their nieces (V,7–8), in direct violation of the group's understanding of Lev 18:13. Since in Rabbinic literature niece marriages are permitted and even commended, and since the Rabbis are often seen as the successors of the Pharisees, some experts have inferred that the Pharisees too permitted niece marriages and are thus the seekers after smooth things and the builders of the wall in the Damascus Document.[6]

---

[5] This is L. Ginzberg's explanation of ולסיע נבול (*An Unknown Jewish Sect* [Moreshet Series 1; New York: Ktav, 1970; translation of *Eine unbekannte jüdische Sekte* (1922)], 6).

[6] See, for example, A. S. van der Woude, *Die messianischen Vorstellungen der Gemeinde von Qumrân* (SSN 3; Assen: van Gorcum, 1957), 240. Ginzberg (*An Unknown Jewish*

The argument from the Nahum pesher, while it has convinced most, has not won universal consent, or at least some questions have been raised regarding it. A. Saldarini, for one, wrote: "The identification of the 'seekers after smooth things' and 'Ephraim' with the Pharisees is common in the literature, but hardly certain. The eight hundred opponents crucified by Jannaeus are not called Pharisees by Josephus . . . and the opponents of Jannaeus in Josephus and the pesharim need not be identified with one of the three schools of thought listed by Josephus."[7] He is willing to allow only that the "Qumran polemics against their opponents testify to the diversity and conflicts in Jewish society but not that their opponents were Pharisees."[8] Actually, a study of the passages in *Antiquities* makes it overwhelmingly likely that the people crucified by Jannaeus were Pharisees, even though Josephus does not say that explicitly in the passage.

This indirect argument from legal positions attributed to a group—wall builders—that may be identified with the seekers of smooth things (see below) has also aroused some misgivings. Not only is it unclear, for example, that only Pharisees would have accepted niece marriages,[9] but also, as a number of scholars have pointed out, great care must be taken in extrapolating from Rabbinic to Pharisaic views and practices.[10]

In this paper I take a different approach that supports those who identify the ones who seek smooth things (and associated terms) as Pharisees but does so by relating some of the words used for them

---

Sect), who denied that the wall builders were Phariseees (see p. 36, where he also rejects the idea that "wall builders" is a reference to the "hedge around the law" of *m. Avot* 1.1), nevertheless interpreted the position of the Damascus Document regarding niece marriages as directed against the Pharisaic one set forth in Rabbinic texts (23–24).

[7] A. Saldarini, *Pharisees, Scribes and Sadducees in Palestinian Society* (Wilmington, DE: Michael Glazier, 1988), 279 (reissued as a paperback reprint in The Biblical Resource Series; Grand Rapids: Eerdmans/Livonia, MI: Dove, 2001). The pagination is the same in the reprint. For the same position, see G. Jeremias, *Der Lehrer der Gerechtigkeit* (SUNT 2; Göttingen: Vandenhoeck & Ruprecht, 1963), 129–31.

[8] *Pharisees, Scribes and Sadducees*, 280. F. Cross (*The Ancient Library of Qumran & Modern Biblical Studies* [rev. ed.; Grand Rapids: Baker, 1980], 123 n. 25, 124–26) suggested the seekers of smooth things might be Jews with Hellenistic leanings. He speaks more definitely about this in *The Ancient Library of Qumran* (3rd ed.; Minneapolis: Fortress, 1995), 97 n. 2.

[9] So Jeremias, *Der Lehrer der Gerechtigkeit*, 103–5.

[10] For a recent discussion of this much debated issue, see G. Stemberger, "Qumran, die Pharisäer und das Rabbinat," in *Antikes Judentum und Frühes Christentum: Festschrift für Hartmut Stegemann zum 65. Geburtstag* (ed. B. Kollmann, W. Reinbold, and A. Steudel;

to a problem connected with the Pharisees as described in second-temple sources. It seems likely that the person reproached as the Scoffer/the Man of the Lie/the Spouter of the Lie and his followers are included among or are the same as the ones who look for smooth things. From the profile for each a consistent picture emerges that may contribute to the existing evidence about the historical Pharisees.

Did the Pharisees, like the later sages of Rabbinic literature, have an oral law? That is, did they develop elaborations and other explanations of the Mosaic Torah that they transmitted from generation to generation in oral, not written form? For this some have found evidence in Josephus who took the time to explain the Pharisaic position on certain laws, a position opposed by the Sadducees. As he tells the story about the rift that sundered the alliance between John Hyrcanus (134–104 B.C.E.) and the Pharisees, he relates that a certain Eleazar urged him to give up the high priesthood. When the priest-king became convinced that Eleazar had criticized him with Pharisaic approval, he abrogated "the regulations [νόμιμα] which they had established for the people." (*Ant.* 13.296)[11] The historian then clarifies the point: "For the present I wish merely to explain that the Pharisees had passed on [παρέδοσαν] to the people certain regulations [νόμιμα] handed down [διαδοχῆς] by former generations and not recorded in the laws of Moses, for which reason they are rejected by the Sadducaean group, who hold that only those regulations should be considered valid which were written down [νόμιμα τὰ γεγραμμένα] (in Scripture), and that those which had been handed down by former generations [ἐκ παραδοσέως τῶν πατέρων] need not be observed." (13.297) This much-studied passage has been taken by some to contrast written and unwritten regulations and thus to attest a Pharisaic doctrine of oral law.[12]

BZAW 97; Berlin/New York: de Gruyter, 1999), 210–24. J. Meier has written a commendably careful overview of the issue in connection with a study of the Pharisees in the New Testament in his *A Marginal Jew: Rethinking the Historical Jesus*, vol. III: *Companions and Competitors* (ABRL; New York: Doubleday, 2001), 289–388.

[11] *Antiquities* is cited from R. Marcus, *Josephus VII Jewish Antiquities Books XII–XIV* (LCL; Cambridge: Harvard University Press, London: Heinemann, 1966).

[12] See, for example, J. Baumgarten, "The Unwritten Law in the Pre-Rabbinic Period," in his *Studies in Qumran Law* (SJLA 24; Leiden: Brill, 1977), 18–20 (the essay originally appeared in *JSJ* 3 [1972]: 7–29).

The passage ushers us into a large, complex problem which scholars have attempted to solve in different ways. Does Josephus suggest
that the Pharisees had an oral tradition of regulations, an oral tradition like the one that emerges from some Rabbinic texts? What
the historian says may be consistent with such an interpretation, but
his words do not make the point explicit. He speaks of a Pharisaic
tradition, not of an oral tradition.[13] Of course, the Pharisees as teachers of the people would have carried out their work orally in a
largely illiterate society; but from Josephus's words we cannot tell
whether they transmitted their teachings from generation to generation by word of mouth or in written form.

If, with many scholars, we accept the identification of the ones
who look for smooth things with Pharisees, do the descriptions of
them in the scrolls make any contribution to the issue of whether
the Pharisees had an oral tradition? I suggest that that they do make
a very modest contribution in that the charges leveled against the
Pharisees through various code names and other insults focus on
abuses of speech, not on writing. This is not the same as saying the
descriptions document an oral tradition for the Pharisees; it does,
however, show that they were known to their enemies for their oral
labors which may not have been confined simply to daily teaching.

The derogatory title דורשי החלקות already points in this direction.
The participle expresses the general actions of "seeking, consulting,
inquiring, investigating, studying, interpreting",[14] all of which can be
done for negative or positive reasons. So, for example, one may seek
gods (Deut 12:30) or one may seek/study the Torah (Ezra 7:10).
The second term in our phrase (החלקות) makes the epithet negative
and does so by accusing the opponents of misusing speech and relax-
ing legal requirements, as shown by other uses of the word.[15] The
scriptural basis for the title seems to be Isa 30:10–11, part of a

---

[13] Among many treatments, see J. Neusner, "Josephus' Pharisees: A Complete
Repertoire," in *Josephus, Judaism, and Christianity* (ed. L. Feldman and G. Hata,
Detroit: Wayne State University Press, 1987), 291–92; E. Sanders, "Did the Pharisees
Have Oral Law?" in his *Jewish Law from Jesus to the Mishnah: Five Studies* (London:
SCM, Philadelphia: Trinity, 1990), 99–100; and S. Mason, *Flavius Josephus on the
Pharisees: A Composition-Critical Study* (SPB 39; Leiden: Brill, 1991), 240–45.

[14] These are some of the definitions suggested in *DCH* 2.473–74.

[15] H. Stegemann has defended translating the expression as "Missdeuter (der
Thora)" and thinks it does not connote an easing of the requirements in scriptural
legislation as is often suggested (*Die Entstehung der Qumrangemeinde* [Ph.D. diss., Bonn,
1971], A56–59 n. 176). A. Baumgarten seems correct when he rejects this understanding and favors the idea that through this nickname they were accused of "light-

reproof directed at the rebellious people. In it the prophet quotes them:

> For it is a rebellious people,
> Faithless children,
> Children who refused to heed
> The instruction [תורת] of the Lord;
> Who said to seers,
> "Do not see,"
> To the prophets, "Do not prophesy truth to us;
> Speak to us falsehoods [חלקות],
> Prophesy delusions.
> Leave the way!
> Get off the path!
> Let us hear no more
> About the Holy one of Israel."[16]

The term חלקות is often used in in the Bible for dubious kinds of speech. So, in Ps 12:3–4 we read:

> Men speak lies to one another;
> their speech is smooth [שפת חלקות];
> they talk with duplicity.
> May the Lord cut off all flattering lips [כל שפתי חלקות],
> every tongue that speaks arrogance.

Such uses of the term can be documented in a number of biblical and non-biblical passages.[17] The smooth words of the דורשי החלקות were appealing because they advocated looser constructions of the Torah (see CD I,18–19).

In the Qumran texts the דורשי החלקות appear in contexts that associate them with other insulting titles and terms of reproach. We may begin with the Damascus Document where people charged with looking for smooth things share a context with an individual who is described as איש הלצון אשר הטיף לישראל מימי כזב ויתעם בתוהו לא דרך (I,14–15). The man characterized by the quality לצון ("scorning, babbling")[18] is joined in the Damascus Document and elsewhere in the scrolls by a group qualified as the אנשי הלצון. According to CD XX,11–12 they are to be judged, and perhaps they—perhaps

---

ening the yoke of the Torah" ("The Name of the Pharisees," *JBL* 102 [1983]: 421 n. 42).

[16] Scriptural citations are from the New JPS Translation, second edition.

[17] See *DCH* 3.242–43 for a rather full listing, and Bengtsson, *What's in a Name?*, 118–20.

[18] *DCH* 4.564.

others who will be judged with them—are accused of speaking falsely
[דברו תועה][19] against righteous precepts[20] and rejecting the covenant
made in Damascus (ומאסו). The verb "reject" recurs in 4QpIsa[b]
(4Q162) 2,6–8 where the wasteful people of Isa 5:11–14 who give
no thought to what God is doing are said to be the אנשי הלצון אשר
בירושלים הם אשר מאסו את תורת יהוה. Here their mockery, their abuse
of speech, is coupled with rejection of the Torah.[21] The title and
chararacterization point one to Isa 28:14–15 where we meet the
men of mockery (see also v. 22) who govern the people in Jerusalem.
Among the accusations the prophet makes against them are their
boasts

> For we have made falsehood [כזב] our refuge,
> Taken shelter in treachery [שקר].[22]

The fact that the איש הלצון is said to have הטיף לישראל מימי כזב brings
him into contact with another series of epithets. He shares an attachment to lying with the person called the Liar (איש הכזב) who figures
in Pesher Habakkuk, the Damascus Document, and 4QpPs[a] (4Q171).
He, as was the Scoffer, is associated with traitors who appear not
to have accepted the words of the Teacher of Righteousness that
came from God's mouth (1QpHab II,1–3). He and the Teacher were
involved in the situation lamented in 1QpHab V,9–12 where the
traitors of Hab 1:13b are said to be "the House of Absalom and
the members of its council who were silent at the time of the chas-
tisement of the Teacher of Righteousness and gave him no help
against the Liar who flouted [מאס] the Law in the midst of their
whole [congregation]." So, like the Scoffer, he was a contemporary
of the Teacher; in fact, the two titles probably point to the same

---

[19] The phrase is found in Isa 32:6.

[20] In CD V,11–12 the writer says of the wall builders: "they defile their holy
spirit and open their mouth with a blaspheming tongue against the laws of the
Covenant of God saying, 'They are not sure.'"

[21] The same accusation is made against the איש הכזב in 1QpHab V,11–12. The
אנשי הלצון are also mentioned in 4Q162 II,10; most of the context is lost but they
are said to consititute a community (עדה).

[22] In 4Q177 VIII,7 הלצון is preserved after a break in the leather. One cannot
therefore determine whether איש or אנשי appeared before it, though one or the
other is likely. It is significant that the phrase there is used to clarify Isa 32:7, perhaps especially the words אמרי שקר. See A. Steudel, *Der Midrasch zur Eschatologie aus
der Qumrangemeinde (4QMidrEschat[a.b])* (STDJ 13; Leiden: Brill, 1994), 71, 83.

individual[23] and both appear in the same context in CD XX,11, 15.[24]

The person dubbed the מטיף הכזב shares the same family trait as the Liar and the Scoffer. We have seen that the Scoffer in CD I,14–15 הטיף לישראל מימי כזב. The hip'il form of נטף, while it can mean "drip" and is thus appropriate with "waters", has the sense of "preach, teach, prophesy." The usage is attested in several passages, but Mic 2:11 seems especially to have been the scriptural inspiration behind the insult. There the prophet details the traits that would make a prophet popular in his day:

> If a man were to go about uttering
> Windy, baseless falsehoods [ושקר כזב]:
> "I'll preach [אטף] to you in favor of wine and liquor"—
> He would be a preacher [מטיף] [acceptable] to that people.

While הטיף . . . מימי כזב forms a natural contrast to the title מורה הצדק,[25] the word "waters" had wider associations. As Ginzberg commented on the passage: "Similar expressions for false doctrines are מים הרעים 'bad water' in the saying of Abtalion, Avoth 1,12 and מים עכורים 'troubled water,' Sifre Deut. 48 = Midrash Tannaim p. 42. As in the Rabbinic sources, so in our text 'deceitful water' is to be understood as the false doctrines of Jewish teachers and not something like pagan doctrines."[26]

The dripper of false waters should be associated with the מטיף הכזב who is castigated in several passages. In 1QpHab X,5–13, commenting on Hab 2:12–13 (a woe-oracle against one who builds a city on blood and wickedness), we learn: "Interpreted, this concerns the Spouter of Lies [מטיף הכזב] who led many astray [התעה][27] that he might build his city of vanity with blood and raise a congregation on deceit [בשקר]." The last two clauses appear to parallel each other.

---

[23] B. Nitzan, *Pesher Habakkuk: A Scroll from the Wilderness of Judaea* (1QpHab) (Jerusalem: Bialik, 1986), 136–38 (Hebrew). She includes the איש הכזב in the equation. Stegemann (*Die Entstehung der Qumrangemeinde*, 41–87) also identifies these and other titles as denoting one enemy group and its leader.

[24] The איש הכזב is mentioned in 4QpPs[a] (4Q171) I,26–27 where the successful man who carries out schemes in Ps 37:7 is explained as meaning the Liar.

[25] It is usually thought that the title derives from Joel 2:23 where המורה לצדקה means "the early rain". But it may come from ירה צדק in Hos 10:12 (Jeremias, *Der Lehrer der Gerechtigkeit*, 313).

[26] *An Unknown Jewish Sect*, 6. He directed the point against those who understood the Scoffer to be a non-Jew like Antiochus IV.

[27] The verb is common in the descriptions of the enemies: CD I,15; 1QH[a] XII,7; 4QpNah 3–4 ii, 8. See Stegemann, *Die Entstehung der Qumrangemeinde*, 69–72.

That is, the city in question is understood to be the community that the lying preacher founded.[28] The Man of Mockery who drips lies in the Damascus Document also has a community (II,1) and leads people astray (I,15). Again, the terms characterize the same person.[29]

This מטיף הכזב plays a role in the Damascus Document in suggestive contexts. As the Admonition deals with the nets of Belial (with reference to Isa 24:17), it mentions the builders of the wall and says they "have followed after 'Precept'—'Precept' was a spouter [מטיף] of whom it was written, *They shall surely spout* (Mic ii, 6)" (IV,19–20). While the double forms of hip'il נטף are quoted from the Micah passage, the צו is from Hos 5:11:

> Ephraim is defrauded,
> Robbed of redress,
> Because he has witlessly
> Gone after futility [צו].

The author takes צו as referring to a person, the מטיף and in so doing links the wall builders with the group treated above. He was not alone in personifying צו. "Das Wort 'Zaw' ist schon sehr früh auf eine Person gedeutet werden, sowohl bei Aq., Sym., Targ., Pesch. als auch bei den Rabbinen. Entsprechen wird an unserer Stelle der צו auf den Leiter der Gegner, den uns hinlänglich bekannten מטיף gedeutet, . . ."[30] The connection with the wall builders continues in CD VIII,12–13 (with a parallel in XIX,25–26), following a series of harsh condemnations against such people. After predicting that the chief of the Greek kings would take vengeance on them, he says: "But all these things the builders of the wall and those who daub it with plaster (Ezek xiii, 10) have not understood because a follower of the wind, one who raised storms and rained down lies [ומטיף כזב],[31] had preached [הטיף] to them (Mic ii, 11), against all of whose assembly [עדתו] the anger of God was kindled." This passage brings together

---

[28] So Stegemann, *Die Entstehung der Qumrangemeinde*, 73–74; Nitzan, *Pesher Habakkuk*, 187–88. Brownlee ("The Wicked Priest, the Man of Lies, and the Righteous Teacher—The Problem of Identity," *JQR* 73 [1982]: 14) thought the last section of 4QTestimonia (4Q175) clinched the literal interpretation.

[29] Jeremias, *Der Lehrer der Gerechtigkeit*, 118–21.

[30] Jeremias, *Der Lehrer der Gerechtigkeit*, 97. Ginzberg understood him to be the איש הלצון of CD I,14 (*An Unknown Jewish Sect*, 18). Perhaps the overlap in letters between צו and לצון is not accidental.

[31] The parallel in XIX,25–26 has ומטיף אדם לכזב. Vermes's translation of the

a range of terms associating the builders, the preacher, and his community with the same leader and group met in the contexts already examined.[32] By appealing to expressions from Ezek 13:10, the writer calls to mind a chapter directed against prophets whose messages are characterized as lies and falsehood.

That we are dealing with the same group follows from the way in which אפרים is employed in Pesher Nahum. In 4QpNah 3–4 ii, 1–2 we find an interesting equation: "*Woe to the city of blood; it is full of lies and rapine* (iii, 1a–b). Interpreted, this is the city of Ephraim, those who seek smooth things [דורשי החלקות] during the last days, who walk in lies and falsehood [אשר בכחש ושקר]ים י[תהלכו]." The titles are used in apposition, indicating that "those who seek smooth things" and "Ephraim" refer to the same people. They are again associated with abuse of speech, and their way is depicted by using a form of הלך, perhaps hinting at the Pharisaic הלכה.[33]

The next passage in Pesher Nahum in which Ephraim as a code name appears has engendered some debate. As he explicates Nah 3:4 (the many harlotries and sorceries of the city of blood), the commentator writes: "Interpreted, this concerns those who lead Ephraim astray [מתעי אפרים], who lead many astray [יתעו רבים] through their false teaching [בתלמוד שקרם], their lying tongue [ולשון כוזיהם], and deceitful lips [ושפת מרמה]. . . ." (3–4 ii, 8) Amid the many negative speech terms, the word תלמוד has of course attracted attention. What does it mean in the context? It may be the earliest occurrence of the noun[34] and presumably does not mean the later corpora that we called the talmuds.[35] Perhaps it points to the activity that lies behind the written texts that were to appear centuries later. B.-Z. Wacholder has given a helpful clarification of the meaning. He points out that

---

context is something of a composite from the two versions in manuscripts A and B.

[32] 1Q14 (1QpMic) 8–10, 4–5 also mentions the מטיף הכזב[, perhaps charging him with misleading the simple.

[33] See, for one, L. Schiffman, "Pharisees and Sadducees in *Pesher Nahum*," in *Minhah le-Nahum: Biblical and Other Studies Presented to Nahum M. Sarna in Honour of his 70th Birthday* (ed. M. Brettler and M. Fishbane; JSOTSup 154; Sheffield: Sheffield Academic Press, 1993), 276.

[34] See also 4Q525 14 ii, 15 where it figures in a positive context: ובתלמודכה יתהלכו יחד כול יודעיכה (É. Puech, *Qumrân Grotte 4 XVIII Textes Hébreux [4Q521–4Q528, 4Q576–4Q579]* [DJD 25; Oxford: Clarendon, 1998], 146, with pl. XI). It may also occur in 1QH[a] X.19, again in a favorable setting.

[35] The word was one of the pieces of evidence used by S. Zeitlin to argue the scrolls were later texts (e.g., in "The Expression BeTalmud in the Scrolls militates against the View of the Protagonists of their Antiquity," *JQR* 54 [1963]: 89–98).

the three terms בתלמוד שקרם ,ולשון כזביהם, and ושפת מרמה are parallel
and are encased between expressions about misleading (מתעי אפרים
and יתעו רבים). Hence, for the sense of תלמוד we should look to the
two terms with which it is related—לשון and שפה.[36] "Since neither
the biblical nor Qumran texts supply any examples, we may *provi-sionally* interpret the phrase as if it were part of rabbinic terminol-ogy. It was shown that 'betalmud' is to 'tongue' and 'lip' what 'false'
is to 'lie' and 'deceit.' It follows that the *Pesher of Nahum* was denounc-ing something oral when using the term 'betalmud.' Hence, 'ŠR
BTLMWD ŠQRM appears to mean roughly: 'those who by their
false oral teaching (or oral interpretation).'"[37] This is an interpreta-tion that is true to the context, and it is at least intriguing that it
is connected with a sobriquet for the Pharisees.[38]

It is likely that these abusers of speech also lurk behind the epi-thet מליצי כזב. It figures in the Hodayot, again in suggestive contexts.
In 1QH[a] X,31–32 the poet declares: "I thank Thee, O Lord, for
Thou hast [fastened] Thine eye upon me. Thou hast saved me from
the zeal of lying interpreters [מליצי כזב], and from the congregation
of those who seek smooth things [ומעדת דורשי חלקות]." The two titles
appear to be poetic parallels. 1QH[a] X,14–15 includes among the
psalmist's enemies מליצי תעות and דורשי חל[קות]. Something similar
emerges from 1QH[a] XII,6–11. There the two epithets are not a
poetic pair, but lines 6–7 speak of opponents: "[Teachers of li]es
have smoothed them [with words] [החליקו], and false prophets have
led them astray [ומליצי רמיה ה[תעום]."[39] The verb related to חלקות
here expresses the same idea regarding the deceitful words the mis-leading teachers use and reflects biblical usage.[40]

---

[36] B.-Z. Wacholder, "A Qumran Attack on the oral Exegesis? The phrase *'šr btlmwd šqrm* in 4 Q Pesher Nahum," *RevQ* 5 (1966): 576–77.

[37] "A Qumran Attack on the oral Exegesis?" 578. Schiffman ("Pharisees and Sadducees," 283) says it means "the method of logical analysis which must have already been part of the intellectual equipment of Pharisaic endeavor."

[38] *Ephraim* occurs again in 4QpNah 3–4 iii, 4–5 where the commentator predicts that when the glory of Judah (= the writer's group) is revealed the simple of Ephraim will leave the ones who have misled them and join themselves to the majority of Israel. See also 3–4, iv 5 where it may be used in the phrase "the wicked of E[phraim."

[39] I have moved the brackets in Vermes's translation where they mistakenly sur-round what is preserved and are absent for what is restored. I have also replaced his "Thy people" with "them" as in the text.

[40] See *DCH* 3.242 for the examples. It appears a number of times in Psalms and Proverbs and is used in 4QWiles of the Wicked Woman (4Q184) I,2.

All of these insulting titles for a group and its founder or leader seem to refer to the same entities, and the titles themselves and their descriptive contexts leave the reader with an overwhelming impression: through their smooth, lying, deceptive, deceitful talk, these people mislead many. Here are the words used to describe their oral activity:

חלקות
כזב
כחש
לצון
מרמה
רמיה
שקר
תלמוד
תעות

The verbs used with these nouns and adjectives also highlight the oral way in which they communicated their lies so that they rejected the Torah and righteous statutes: נטף (*hip̄ʿil*), ליץ (*hip̄ʿil*).

Perhaps all of this is relevant for the question whether the Pharisees already were associated with an oral law. At the least we may say that their Essene opponents from Qumran and those who produced the Damascus Document consistently insulted them by using epithets that highlight abuse of speech—something that is not the case for their treatment of other enemies. The Qumran references do not prove that they had an oral law in a stronger sense, that is, that it came from Moses on Mt. Sinai and was of equal importance to the written Torah. They do, though, indicate that the Pharisees were especially associated with oral teaching in late second temple times.[41]

---

[41] I wish to thank my colleague, John Meier, for reading and commenting on a draft of this paper.

ESCHATOLOGICAL WORLD VIEW IN THE DEAD SEA SCROLLS AND IN THE NEW TESTAMENT

Geza Vermes

To Emanuel Tov
in friendship and gratitude

Eschatology does not flourish in a politically and socially secure world. People living in circumstances of peace and prosperity look forward optimistically to a predictable and safe future. Uncertainty, danger and continuous political and social unrest generate the eschatological atmosphere and the consequent eschatological outlook. It goes without saying that the problem is complex, and all that I can offer here is a sketch of its salient features.

Biblical eschatology in the form of the expectation of the Kingdom of God modelled itself on the image of divine sovereignty over Israel by extending it over the whole of mankind. It was to be achieved either (a) by the Jewish king through his conquest of all the nations, or through their religious subjection to the God of Israel; or (b) directly by God himself without human mediatorship, messianic or otherwise. In this paper, however, I do not intend to deal specifically with Messianism as such.[1]

I. The Eschatological World View of Biblical and Post-biblical Judaism

The *onset* of the eschatological era is imagined in late Second Temple Judaism in three ways.

---

[1] For general works of reference see Paul Volz, *Die Eschatologie der jüdischen Gemeinde im neutestamentlichen Zeitalter* (J. C. B. Mohr: Tübingen, 1934); E. Schürer, G. Vermes, F. Millar, M. Goodman, *The history of the Jewish People in the Age of Jesus Christ* II (T. & T. Clark: Edinburgh, 1979), 494–96, 531–47; "Eschatology" in *Anchor Bible Dictionary* (ed. D. N. Freedman; New York, 1992), 579–609; John J. Collins, "Eschatology" in *Encyclopedia of the Dead Sea Scrolls* (ed. by L. H. Schiffman & J. C. VanderKam; OUP: New York, 2000), 256–261.

a) It was envisaged as *cataclysmic*. The classic biblical example is
Noah's flood. But the same concept was revived again in the intertestamental age. One of the Qumran Hodayot speaks of fiery torrents
of Belial:[2]

> [They] shall reach to all sides of the world. In all their channels a
> consuming fire shall destroy every tree, green and barren, on their
> banks; unto the end of their courses it shall scourge with flames of
> fire, and shall consume the foundations of the earth and their expanse
> of the dry land. The bases of the mountains shall blaze and the roots
> of the rocks shall turn to torrents of pitch; it shall devour as far as
> the great Abyss (1QH 11[3], 29–31).

Josephus in turn refers to two types of annihilation of the world:
"Adam predicted a destruction of the universe, at one time by a
violent fire and at another by a mighty deluge of water" (*Ant.* i. 70).[3]

b) The onset of the eschatological era was also depicted as *semi-
cataclysmic* in the form of world wars. The picture is familiar ever
since the biblical prophets. The principal example in the late Second
Temple period is Daniel chapters 11 and 12, on which the Qumran
War Scroll is modelled as will be shown later.

c) The third form of the arrival of the eschatological era is a *transformation* without an antecedent annihilation. The old universe is
replaced by another world descending from the celestial heights. At
Qumran the Aramaic Heavenly Jerusalem texts describing the new
Holy City according to the measurements of an angelic surveyor
definitely represent this genre (1Q32, 2Q24, 4Q232, 4Q554–555,
5Q15 and 11Q18), and so possibly does the Temple Scroll (11Q19–20
and 4Q365a).

The ancient Jewish attitude to eschatology was twofold: *speculative*
or *inspirational*.

1. *The Speculative Approach*

The first and more common approach derives from religious speculation. Its principal topics relate to the time of the advent of the
Kingdom of God and to the premonitory signs which signal its

---

[2] All the Qumran excerpts are borrowed from Geza Vermes, *The Complete Dead
Sea Scrolls in English* (Penguin: London, 1998).
[3] The same tradition is attested also in *The Life of Adam and Eve* 49:3 among the
Pseudepigrapha. For the biblical and New Testament idea of a fiery destruction of
the world see Deut 32:22; Isa 34:9; Am 7:4; Zeph 1:18; Pss 18:8; 2 Pet 3:10, 12.

arrival. Formulated in plain language: When will the Kingdom come and what are the portents marking its nearness?

Once more the main pattern is provided by the Book of Daniel which represents the final age of the present era as consisting of seventy year weeks, i.e. *490 years*. Its theory is based on Jeremiah's prophecy announcing that after the conquest of Jerusalem by Nebuchadnezzar, Babylon will rule for 70 years, followed by a divine visitation for redemption (Jer 29:10). By means of a pesher-type interpretation, the angel Gabriel explains to Daniel that the 70 years must be understood as 70 weeks of years (Dan 9:24). The seventy year weeks are then broken down to three periods: seven weeks [49 years] plus 62 weeks [434 years] plus the final week [7 years]. Daniel is informed that he is in the middle of this last week. By then he will have witnessed the murder of an anointed one [a high priest] as well as the conquest of Jerusalem and the installation of the "abomination of desolation." But after another half of a week, three and a half years, final salvation will dawn on Israel (Dan 9:25–27). This figure roughly corresponds to 1335 days of Dan 12:12, marking the end. By using these fairly clear landmarks it is possible to determine exactly where the reader stands in regard to the eschatological D-day. It would seem that a very short period of waiting was forecast.

Despite one missing element, it is reasonable to assume that the eschatological chronology of the Qumran *Damascus Document* also follows the same seventy weeks of years pattern if we put together two separate passages.

The first of these figures at the opening of the work:

> For when they were unfaithful and forsook Him, He hid His face from Israel and His Sanctuary and delivered them up to the sword. But remembering the Covenant of the forefathers, He left a remnant to Israel and did not deliver it up to be destroyed. And in the age of wrath, *three hundred and ninety years* after He had given them into the hand of King Nebuchadnezzar of Babylon, He visited them, and He caused a plant root to spring from Israel and Aaron to inherit His Land and to prosper on the good things of His earth. And they perceived their iniquity and recognized that they were guilty men, yet for *twenty years* they were like blind men groping for the way. And God observed their deeds, that they sought Him with a whole heart, and He raised for them a Teacher of Righteousness to guide them in the way of His heart (CD 1:3–11).

The second identifies the length of the final period:

> From the day of the gathering in of the Teacher of the Community
> until the end of all the men of war who deserted to the Liar there
> shall pass about *forty years* (CD 20:13–15).

Taking these figures at face value, the author of the manuscript dates
the beginnings of the Community, the "remnant of Israel," 390 years
after the fall of Jerusalem to Nebuchadnezzar. The birth of the group
was followed by a period of leaderless wandering lasting twenty
years when the Teacher of Righteousness appeared 410 years after
Nebuchadnezzar. At some later point this Teacher was "gathered
in" and the end period, in the course of which the wicked opponents of the Community would perish, was forecast as lasting 40
years. The only figure lacking in this reckoning is the length of the
ministry of the Teacher of Righteousness. Without it the sum total
is 450 years, but assuming that his public activity was symbolized
by the forty years of wandering of the Jews in the wilderness, we
arrive at the mystical number of 490. But note again that the author
responsible for the calculation places himself close to the end of the
final 40 years. So the writer of the Damascus Document like Daniel
imagined that the onset of eschatology was at hand.[4]

As a final illustration of the 490 year pattern, let me take the
work of rabbinic chronology dating to the second century C.E. and
known as *Seder 'Olam Rabba* §30. Its author breaks down the period
separating the fall of the first Temple under Nebuchadnezzar (586
B.C.E.) from the fall of the Second Temple under Titus (70 C.E.) –
i.e 656 years under our reckoning—as follows: Babylonian rule =
70 years; Persian rule = 34 years; Greek rule = 180 years; Hasmonaean
rule = 103 years; Herodian rule = 103 years. Surprise, surprise,
these sums also add up to 490. In other words, the fall of the Second
Temple was seen as the fulfilment of Daniel's prediction. In sum,
the chief aim of writers engaged in eschatological speculation was
to determine with the help of data borrowed from the Bible the
approximate distance of the respective author from the start of the
eschaton.

---

[4] Although the date obtained from the 390 years after Nebuchadnezzar, i.e. the
opening years of the second century B.C.E., for the start of the Qumran movement
is perfectly plausible, it would be most unwise to take this computation *à la lettre*.
All the extant evidence proves that Jews of the early post-biblical age possessed no
correct knowledge of the length of the duration of the Persian rule. The author of
Daniel got it wrong by about 70 years. Demetrius, the Jewish Hellenist also made
a mistake of 73 years in his calculation of the length of the period separating the

It is worth recalling that without following the strict seventy weeks of years model, the First Book of Enoch in chapters 89 and 90 assigns the government of Israel to *seventy shepherds* during the final age starting with the Babylonian empire via Cyrus and Alexander the Great to the Messiah. Likewise the Testament of Levi divides the history of the Jewish priesthood into *seven weeks* from Levi, Moses and Aaron to the priestly Messiah.

490 (70 × 7) is not the only mystical figure in Jewish eschatological speculation. The Damascus Document mentions, as has been noted, that the final unit of the breakdown is *forty years* (CD 20:15). The same number is encountered again in the Qumran War Scroll, which pictures the eschatological war as lasting 40 years. Yet again the real purpose of the standard figure appears in its detailed division into time units which indicate precisely how far the present moment is from the final apogee. According to 1QM cols 1–2 the first phase of the war (years 1 to 6) ends with the liberation of the land of Israel and Jerusalem by the Sons of Light. Their next activity consists in reorganizing the worship in the Temple during the first sabbatical year (year 7). During the remaining thirty-three years the Sons of Light will overcome: Aram-Naharaim (year 8), Lud (year 9), Uz, Hul et al. (year 10), Arphachshad (years 11–12) and Assyria (year 13). Next comes the second sabbatical year with suspension of fighting (year 14). The third period will see the defeat of Persia (year 15), Elam (year 16), Ishmael (year 17). The nine-year-long war against the sons of Ham (years 18–20 and 22–27) will be interrupted by the third sabbatical year (year 21) and followed by the fourth (year 28). The final ten-year period will be occupied by hostilities against the Japhetites (years 29–34 and 36–40) plus the last sabbatical year (year 35). The ultimate stage of the warfare culminates in the defeat of the final foe, the Kittim, by the Jewish and angelic forces under the

---

accession of Ptolemy IV (221 B.C.E.) from the fall of Samaria (722/21 B.C.E.) [Clement of Alexandria, *Stromateis* I, 141,2]. Josephus did not fare better either. He counted 481 or 471 years between the return from the Babylonian exile (538 B.C.E.) and the death of the Hasmonaean priest-king Aristobulus I (103 B.C.E.) [Ant 13:301; War 1:70]. The correct figure is 435 years. He also wrote that the Jewish schismatic Temple of Leontopolis in Egypt had lasted 343 years whereas the difference between 160 B.C.E. and 73 C.E. is 233 years. Hence it is much safer to consider the 390 years of the Damascus Document as part of a theological rather than a historical chronology.

joint leadership of the archangel Michael and of the Nasi or Prince of the Congregation.[5]

To recapitulate briefly, the speculative approach to eschatology aims to reassure Jews in the midst of their trials and sufferings by providing them with a time table of the events of the final age. Indeed, there is a tendency to place the day of the Lord within the life time of the author. In Daniel only three and a half years remain of the present era and in the Damascus Document the forty years after the death of the Teacher of Righteousness are nearly elapsed. Such an adventurous and incautious forecast carries with it an element of serious risk; what is the author to say if by the end of say three and a half years nothing has happened. We shall come to this presently.

2. *The Inspirational Approach*

By inspirational approach I mean to define the specific religious action prompted by the conviction that the writer and his contemporaries were living in the final phase of the present age. More simply, what is one to do in the eschatological situation? The answer to this question, easily obtainable from the study of the Scrolls, amounts to a sketch of the eschatological piety prevalent at Qumran. This eschatological piety is strictly biblically based and arises from the special interpretation of the appropriate passages of Scripture, especially of the prophets. Let us begin with the classic text of Isaiah 40:3.

> When these shall become members of the Community in Israel according to all these rules, they shall separate from the habitation of unjust men and shall go into the wilderness to prepare the way of Him as it is written, *Prepare in the wilderness the way of ****, make straight in the desert a path for our God* (Isa 40:3). This (path) is the study of the Law which He commanded by the hand of Moses, that they may do according to all that has been revealed from age to age, and as the Prophets have revealed by His holy Spirit (1QS 8: 12–16).

The Isaiah quotation, in which the four asterisks stand for the Tetragram,[6] is understood as conveying a double instruction relative to the end of time. Literally, the sectaries saw in it a divine com-

---

[5] The Nasi is mentioned only once in the surviving section of the War Scroll (1QM 5:1) but appears in 4Q285.
[6] Instead of the Tetragram, 4Q259 has the substitute divine name, *ha'emet*, the Truth.

mand to withdraw from the society of the wicked and settle in the solitude conducive to inward spirituality. The same teaching is repeated a little further:

> This is the time for the preparation of the way into the wilderness, and he (the Master or Maskil) shall teach them to do all that is required at that time and to separate from all those who have not turned aside from all injustice (1QS 9:20–21).

The implied message is that there are peculiar doctrines and rules that apply in the eschatological age. In fact, the "way" which is to be prepared in the silence and remoteness of the desert consists in an intense study of the Torah and the Prophets according the particular exegesis of the Zadokite priestly leaders of the Community (see 1QS 5:2, 9).[7]

Eschatological spirituality as a rule entails revelations appropriate for the end of time and presupposes a revealer to guide the disturbed and confused people living through the hard times of the approaching *eschaton*. According to the Habakkuk Commentary, the priestly master of the Dead Sea Community was commissioned by God to instruct his followers in the divine message concealed in biblical prophecy:

> The men of violence and the breakers of the Covenant will not believe when they hear all that [is to happen to] the final generation from the priest [in whose heart] God set [understanding] that he might interpret all the words of His servants the prophets through whom He foretold all that would happen to His people ... (1QpHab 2:6–10).

The eschatological instruction entailed the communication in an intelligible form of all the secrets and coded messages in the Bible with the help of which the pupils of the Teacher of Righteousness were enabled to conduct themselves in the correct manner among the unforeseen circumstances of the end time. The clue to the prophetic mysteries entrusted by God to the Teacher was believed to be indispensable for salvation. It related also to the proper understanding of the length of the final age.

---

[7] 4Q256 and 258 do not contain the mention of the Sons of Zadok and refer to *ha-rabbim*, the Congregation, instead. I discuss the significance of these variants in "The Leadership of the Qumran Community: Sons of Zadok—Priests—Congregation" in *Geschichte—Tradition—Reflexion. Festschrift für Martin Hengel* (ed. H. Cancik, H. Lichtenberger, P. Schäfer; Mohr Siebeck: Tübingen, 1996), 375–84.

> As for that which He said, '*That he who reads may read it speedily* (Hab 2:2),' interpreted this concerns the Teacher of Righteousness to whom God made known all the mysteries of his servants, the prophets (1QpHab 7:3–5)

Thus the members of the Qumran community believed that the privileged knowledge conveyed by the Teacher permitted them to adopt the right religious behaviour while all the outsiders were bound to go astray even when they imagined themselves following literally the scriptural teaching.

The inspirational approach to eschatology provided also a necessary corrective to the speculative approach. The latter, as I have shown, tended to foreshorten the period leading to the end, so that within a certain number of years some kind of explanation or rectification was needed. In any case sooner or later, and generally sooner rather than later, unfulfilled eschatological frenzy unavoidably led to frustration and disappointment necessitating further inspirational reassurance and encouragement.

Such a situation of confusion occurred in the Qumran sect by the time of the composition of the Habakkuk Commentary (c. mid-first century B.C.E.). The prophetic prediction of the extent of the final age was thought to be liable to misunderstanding and the Teacher of Righteousness was credited with the revelation of the true significance of the mystery of the *eschaton*, namely that the waiting period would be longer than expected.

> *For there shall be another vision concerning the appointed time. It shall tell of the end and shall not lie* (Hab 2:3a). Interpreted this means that the final age shall be prolonged and shall exceed all that the prophets have said; for the mysteries of God are astounding. *If it tarries, wait for it for it shall surely come and shall not be late* (Hab 2:3b). Interpreted this concerns the men of truth who keep the Law, whose hands shall not slacken in the service of truth when the final age is prolonged. For all the ages of God reach their appointed end as He determines for them in the mysteries of His wisdom (1QpHab 7:5–14).

The central message is that of total confidence in God and exhortation to patience. So ultimately Qumran eschatological piety can be summed up as faith and perseverance: in due course "all the ages of God reach their appointed end."

A rather different picture emerges from the study of *early rabbinic literature*. It is generally thought to lack eschatological fervour. Yet despite two calamitous uprisings against Rome, traces of a quasi-political concept of the *eschaton* survived, contrasting the Kingdom of Heaven to the wicked Roman empire. Likewise political messianism theoretically at least lingered on. R. Akiva apparently recognized Bar Kokhba (Simeon bar Kosiba) as the King Messiah (*y. Ta'an.* 68d). However, other sages, such as Yohanan ben Torta, preferred to pour cold water on, indeed ridicule such enthusiasm: "Akiva, grass will grow out of your cheek bones before the son of David comes" (ibid.). The politically more sophisticated R. Simeon bar Yohai advanced a more down-to-earth opinion: "When you see a Persian horse tethered in the Land of Israel, then you may look for the Messiah" (*Lam. Rab.* 1:13 [41]). Indeed, from the second century Tannaim onwards, the rabbis were inclined to spiritualize eschatology and imagined entry into its reality in a non-violent form, through taking on the "yoke of the Kingdom of Heaven" by means of whole-hearted obedience to the Torah. Thus R. Joshua b. Qorha explained that the order of the paragraphs of the *Shema*—first "Hear o Israel" and then "If you obey my commandments"—indicates that obedience to the *mitzvot* must follow at once any self-subjection to the "yoke of the Kingdom" (*m. Ber.* 2:2)

II. The Eschatological World View of the New Testament

Eschatology is the domain in which, in spite of their substantially different religious aspirations, the Qumran writings and the New Testament come very close to one another. In both, the Kingdom of God is seen as imminent. In both, prophecies regarding the end are believed to be fulfilled in their respective leaders and institutions. In both, the leader is held to be the conveyer of the ultimate revelation. But while in the eschatological outlook of the Old Testament and intertestamental Judaism, speculation about signs and times was in general the dominating tendency, the religious vision of Jesus and of John the Baptist focussed rather on the right conduct under the pressure of eschatological urgency. The eyes of Jesus were fixed on the Kingdom of God which he proclaimed as being "at hand." However, as the Kingdom was not realized during his lifetime, primitive Christianity substituted for it the Parousia: the return of Christ was expected to mark the inauguration of God's universal dominion. The longing for the Parousia was accompanied by a search for signs which could be built up into a schedule of the final events.

Also, like the expectation of the Qumran people, that of the New Testament was also to exhibit symptoms of declining eschatological fervour.

The survey will proceed in four stages: 1. John the Baptist; 2. Jesus; 3. Saint Paul; 4. Early Christianity. An appendix will consider the eschatological outlook of the Book of Revelation.

1. *The Eschatological Outlook of John the Baptist*

a) According to the Synoptic Gospels, the prophecy of Isa 40:3, "The voice of one crying in the wilderness: Prepare the way of the Lord" (Mk 1:3; Mt 3:3), was realized in John the Baptist. The interpretation entails an exegetical twist: The herald is not proclaiming that the way of the Lord is to be prepared in the wilderness; it is he who is is in the wilderness where he enjoins people to prepare themselves for the coming of the Kingdom. Both here and in 1QS, Isa 40:3 is the biblical basis of an eschatological manifesto. John's appearance in the wilderness, like the Qumran community's move to the Judaean desert, was understood as a prophecy come true. The passage represents a New Testament version of the Qumran *pesher.*

b) John's eschatological appeal was addressed to all Jews, not just the few chosen ones at Qumran It called for *immediacy and urgency.* The preparation of the way of the Lord demands instant repentance together with subjection to Johannine baptism leading to forgiveness of sins (Mk 1:4; Mt 3:2; Lk 3:3). John's emphatic call was followed by prompt action: at once all Judaea and Jerusalem (Mk 1:5; Mt 3:5–6; Lk 3:7), and even Jesus from Galilee (Mk 1:9; Mt 3:13; Lk 3:21), flocked to him and sought to be baptized. The timetable in the Gospels is compressed; there is no need or room for premonitory signs. John's programme consists of pure eschatological action.

2. *The Eschatological Outlook of Jesus*

a) Like the Baptist, Jesus began with a powerful eschatological manifesto: "The time is fulfilled and the Kingdom of God is *at hand"* (Mk 1:15; Mt 4:17). The verb and adverb *engizein* and *engus* (to be near, near) as well as *phthanein* (to arrive) hint at eschatological presence. For the latter, see Mt 12:28; Lk 11:20: "If it is by the spirit (or finger) of God that I cast out demons, the Kingdom of God has come (*ephthasen*) upon you." Once more the event is seen as imminent or even incipient. Premonitory signs would be superfluous.

As a result, Jesus' proclamation is "inspirational" and demands prompt and whole-hearted action: "Repent and believe"—at once (Mk 1:15; Mt 4:17). The same urgency surrounds the order given to the disciples to proclaim the closeness or near-presence of the Kingdom of heaven (Mt 10:7; Lk 10:11). If their appeal provokes no instantaneous positive answer, they must not waste their time on trying to persuade unresponsive Jews: "And if . . . they refuse to hear you, . . . shake off the dust that is on your feet for a testimony against them" (Mk 6:11; Mt 10:14; Lk 9:5; 10:11).

b) The battle cry of Jesus is a demand for eschatological presence. He was convinced that the Kingdom would be established in his own generation: "Behold the kingdom of God is in the midst of you" (Lk 17:20–21). "The kingdom of God has come upon you" (Mt 12:28; Lk 11:20) and "There are some standing here who will not taste death before they see that the kingdom of God has come with power (Mk 9:1; Lk 9:27). Holding such views, he felt it inappropriate to give clues regarding the future. He shunned signs: "The Kingdom of God is not coming with signs to be observed" (Lk 17:20). Or more succinctly, "No sign shall be given to this generation" (Mk 8:11–13). Positively—and in flat contradiction to all the forewarnings ascribed to him in the rest of the eschatological discourse— Jesus firmly denied any precise knowledge of the date of the advent of the Kingdom.: "But of that day and that hour no one knows, not even the angels of heaven, nor the son, but only the Father" (Mk 13:32; Mt 24:36).

This assertion is fully in harmony with Jesus' stress on concern with the immediate: "Do not be anxious about tomorrow . . . Let the day's own trouble be sufficient for the day" (Mt 6:34; Lk 12:22–31). Those who recite the Lord's Prayer are enjoined to ask for the bread of today (Mt 6:11; Lk 11:3). If his words are taken in their most obvious sense, it follows that Jesus refused to contemplate eventualities lying far ahead. For him, the Kingdom of God was already there, revealed in his charismatic healings and exorcisms, and its full manifestation was due any moment. In such a perspective it would have been nonsensical to be concerned with matters of the present age. This is shown in the parable about a wealthy farmer who, expecting a particularly rich harvest, decided to demolish his old barns and construct larger ones only to discover that he, like the time of this world, had no tomorrow. "Fool!" he was told, "This night your soul is required of you" (Lk 12:16–20).

Hence Jesus did not tolerate any procrastination in the march towards the Kingdom, hyperbolically speaking not even on the pretext of burying one's father (Lk 9:60; Mt 8:22). Once recruited, a labourer for the cause of heaven was to press ahead: "No one who puts his hand to the plough and looks back is fit for the Kingdom of God" (Lk 9:62). In short, the religious outlook and piety of Jesus can be summed up as pure eschatological enthusiasm cut short by the tragedy of the cross.

3. *The Eschatological Outlook of Saint Paul*

A quarter of a century after the historical reality of Jesus, Saint Paul was still fully motivated by eschatological enthusiasm, but it was framed in revised terms. In continuity with the outlook of Jesus and of the primitive church reflected in the Acts of the Apostles, the idea of an impending Kingdom of God was still central in Paul's thinking as can be seen in 1 and 2 Thessalonians, Galatians, 1 Corinthians and Romans, all written between 50 and 56 C.E. In regard to the imminent arrival of the eschatological age, or "the day of our Lord Jesus Christ" (1 Cor 1:8; 2:16), Paul's hope only slightly differed from the expectation of Jesus, who saw the Kingdom of God as hidden beyond the nearest corner, but also often as already disclosing its presence.

Similarly, envisaging the Parousia of Christ as the gateway to the Kingdom, Paul and his Thessalonian and Corinthian Christians were convinced that the return of the Lord would occur during their life. "The appointed time (has) grown very short" Paul writes to the Corinthians (1 Cor 7:29). Christ will burst in suddenly "like a thief in the night" (1 Thess 5:2), and "We declare to you by the word of the Lord, that we who are alive, . . . are left until the coming of the Lord . . ." (1 Thess 4:15). The precision of the language precludes any explaining away: the arrival of the Parousia was believed to be due at any moment.

Paul's theology and his eschatological ethics are to be envisaged in this almost-no-future perspective. They resulted in eschatological action, including some ephemeral oddities. First there were some members of the Corinthian Church who, anxious about the ultimate fate of their deceased friends and relations, introduced the custom of baptism on behalf of the dead (1 Cor 15:29). Through this legal fiction, of which Paul did not disapprove, unbaptized pagans were presumed to gain Christian status and entitlement to resurrection as "those who belong to Christ" (1 Cor 15:23).

Even more curiously, in the early fifties C.E. rumours began to circulate in Thessalonica that Christ had already returned and that Paul had announced it in a letter. As a result, some Christians laid down tools in the certainty of an immediate manifestation of the Lord. Paul had to intervene in this religiously and socially dangerous situation, and denied the actual reappearance of Christ.

Yet on one notable point Paul departed from the total trust in God advocated by Jesus. He, like intertestamental Jews in general, believed that the Parousia would be heralded by a series of premonitory warning signs. Confronting the idle Thessalonians, he gave a precise scenario of the second coming of Jesus and thus produced one of the most detailed programmes of speculative eschatology:

> For that day will not come, unless the rebellion comes first, and the man of lawlessness is revealed, the son of perdition, who opposes and exalts himself against every so-called god or object of worship, so that he takes his seat in the temple of God, proclaiming himself to be God. . . . For the mystery of lawlessness is already at work; only he who now restrains it will do so until he is out of the way. And then the lawless one will be revealed, and the Lord Jesus will slay him with the breath of his mouth and destroy him by the manifestation of his Parousia. The coming of the lawless one by the activity of Satan will be with all power and with pretended signs and wonders (2 Th 2:3–9).

4. *The Eschatological Outlook of Early Christianity*

With the delay of the Parousia, the early church was compelled to devise fresh means to deal with the anxiety and impatience of the faithful, especially after the destruction of Jerusalem and the Temple which might have provided the most apt preliminaries for the inauguration of the Kingdom of God in the wake of the return of Christ. First the events of the catastrophe of 70 C.E. were utilized in combination with the traditional eschatological imagery of Daniel to support the flagging Parousia hope in the midrashically re-interpreted Son of Man figure descending on the clouds in the company of the angels. To endow this image with greater authority, Jesus himself is credited with the prediction of the events heralding the arrival of the Son of Man. This is in total contrast to his stated unwillingness to give premonitory signs.

The signs of the approach of the Parousia are listed in the Eschatological Discourse in the Synoptic Gospels. They include:

i) The destruction of the Temple of Jerusalem (Mk 13:2–4; Mt 24:2–3; Lk 21:6–7).

ii) Wars, earthquakes, famines, i.e. the general prophetic signs of doom (Mk 13:5–8; Mt 24:4–8; Lk 21:8–11).

iii) Internal conflicts in the community (Mk 13:9–13; Mt 24:9–14; Lk 21:12–19).

iv) The setting up of the Abomination of Desolation, a pagan object of cult, in the Temple in fulfilment of Daniel 9:27; 11:31; 12:12, followed by great upheavals (Mk 13:14–20; Mt 24:15–22; Lk 21:20–24).

v) The appearance of false Messiahs (Mk 13:21–23; Mt 24:23–28; Lk 17:23–24) cf. Josephus' sign-prophets, Theudas (Ant. 20:97–99), the Egyptian (War 2:261–263; Ant. 20:169–172), etc.

vi) Darkness, another prophetic sign of doom (Mk 13:24–25; Mt 24:29; Lk 21:25–26)

vii) The Parousia, viz. the Son of Man's descent from heaven on the clouds (Dan 7:13–14; Mk 13:26–27; Mt 24:30–31; Lk 21:27–28), heralding the advent of the Kingdom which is "at the very gates . . . This generation will not pass away before all these things take place" (Mk 13:29–30; Mt 24:33–34; Lk 21:31–32).

Thus from the pure eschatological enthusiasm of Jesus, we are once more back in the decades following the fall of Jerusalem to speculative calculation.

With the prolonged delay of the Parousia, eschatological enthusiasm was progressively defused in late New Testament writings. The Fourth Gospel ignores the eschatologically crucial notion of the Kingdom of God. Even in Jesus' conversation with Nicodemus, the Kingdom concept is de-eschatologized and, as it were, sacramentilized. The Jesus of John tells Nicodemus: "Unless one is born of water and spirit [symbol of baptism], he cannot enter the kingdom of God" (Jn 3:3, 5).

The best example of the death of eschatological fervour is furnished by 2 Peter, usually dated to about 125 C.E. or later. The writer himself expected to die before the Parousia: "I know that the putting of my body [literally, my tent] will be soon, as our Lord Jesus Christ showed me. And I will see to it that after my departure you may be able at any time to recall these things" (2 Pet 1:14–15).

2 Peter practically extinguishes the last cinders of the eschatological exuberance so characteristic of the religion of Jesus. Its author was compelled to enter the dangerous arena of the delay of the Parousia because by that time, after the passing of several Christian generations, sceptics in the church were making sarcastic remarks on the subject: "Where is the promise of his (Christ's) coming? For ever since the fathers fell asleep, all things have continued as they were from the beginning of the creation" (2 Pet 3:4).

Pseudo-Peter offers a twofold evasive answer. First, God's view of time is not the same as man's. Secondly, people should be grateful for the postponement of the return of Christ as it grants them more opportunity to turn away from sin. "But do not ignore this one fact, beloved, that with the Lord one day is as a thousand years, and a thousand years as one day. The Lord is not slow about his promise as some count slowness, but is forbearing toward you, not wishing that any should perish, but that all should reach repentance" (2 Pet 3:8–10). Here we hear the echo of the Habakkuk Commentary written probably a century after the death of the Teacher of Righteousness.

To sum up, intense eschatological fervour is unsustainable for an extended period in a closed religious community, be it the Essene sect or the Christian church. In the normal course of events, apocalyptic fever is progressively transformed into institutional certainty. To quote freely Alfred Loisy's famous dictum, "The disciples of Jesus expected the Kingdom of God, but it was the church that arrived instead."

APPENDIX

Let me end with a brief comment on the totally different vision, in line with mainstream Jewish eschatology, disclosed in the Book of Revelation.

1. Contrary to the Jesus of the Synoptic Gospels, Revelation contains a celestial *bellicose* Christ, riding on a white horse, with his robe dipped in blood, and as "King of kings and Lord of Lords" annihilating all the nations (Rev 19:11–16).

> And I saw the beast and the kings of the earth with their armies gathered to make war against him who sits upon the horse and against his army. And the beast was captured and ... thrown alive into the

lake of fire that burns with brimstone. And the rest were slain by the
sword of him who sits upon the horse, the sword that issues from his
mouth; and all the birds were gorged with their flesh (Rev 19:19–21).

2. It introduces the idea of millenarism. Millenarism implies that the
return of Christ and the first resurrection which is granted only to
Christians would be followed by a thousand-year reign of the saints
during which Satan would be imprisoned. At the end of the millennium, Satan would be let loose once more against the nations
of the earth only to be defeated for a second time by God's army.
The fall of the rule of evil would then be accompanied by another
judgement, and those found guilty would suffer a second death in
the lake of fire. This notion of second death, meaning a situation
out of which no further resurrection would provide an escape, appears
also in the Aramaic paraphrases of Deuteronomy, Isaiah and Jeremiah
of a later vintage though in the light of the testimony of Revelation,
it must have had a clandestine existence since at least the first century C.E.

3. Revelation, like the Qumran New Jerusalem texts, envisages
the end in the form of a new heaven and a new earth and a new
Jerusalem descending from heaven (cf. Rev 21).

The eschatology of Revelation made little inroads on church dogma,
but became a lasting source of inspiration for Christian mysticism
and for the representation of heaven and hell in Western literature
and art over the centuries.

PART TWO

SEPTUAGINT

THE SIGNIFICANCE OF SEPTUAGINT STUDIES

Raija Sollamo

When writing about the beginnings of Septuagint studies in Finland, I once expressed the following opinion: "In this specialist area the future belongs to those optimists who believe in the significance of LXX studies."[1] Septuagint studies comprise the main field in which I have worked all my academic life. From the human angle, this paper is a justification of my career, or a critical evaluation of whether it has been worthwhile dedicating the best decades of one's life to the study of the Septuagint.

THE SEPTUAGINT AND THE HEBREW CANON OF THE OLD TESTAMENT

I shall begin by defining the term "Septuagint." The designation Septuagint originally referred to the Greek translation of the Torah (LXX proper), produced in Alexandria in Egypt in the middle of the third century B.C.E. But since the first centuries C.E. the term "Septuagint" has taken on an extended sense to indicate the Christian Greek "Old Testament" in its entirety,[2] including not only the LXX proper, but various "Old Greek" (OG) translations and editions of other Jewish writing, including many books ("apocrypha") not found in what came to be standardized as the Hebrew Bible.

What was it that made this enlargement possible? The books of this extended "Septuagint" (LXX/OG) were translated into Greek, or in some cases originally written in Greek during the last centuries B.C.E.[3] At that time no generally accepted canon of the Old Testament

---

[1] Raija Sollamo, "The Origins of Septuagint Studies in Finland," *SJOT* 10 (1996): 159–168, the quotation on p. 168.

[2] Sidney Jellicoe, *The Septuagint and Modern Study* (Oxford, 1968), 41–42.

[3] Emanuel Tov, "The Septuagint," in *Mikra, Text, Translation, Reading and Interpretation of the Hebrew Bible in Ancient Judaism and Early Christianity* (ed. M. J. Mulder. Assen-Maastricht/Philadelphia, 1988), 161–88.

yet existed. Canon is a Greek word meaning "norm" or "rule."[4] The limits of the Jewish scriptural canon were established, for what became mainstream Judaism, not earlier than the discussions at the Jamnia academy around 90 c.e. Only the Pharisees of the Jewish religious groups and movements had survived the disaster of the Jewish War against the Romans. After the war the Pharisees represented "normative Judaism" and dominated the discussion on the limits of the canon. Apparently even Jamnia decisions were merely a preliminary attempt towards defining a Hebrew canon, and a final list of books appeared at the time of the second Revolt against Rome in 132–135 c.e., when Rabbi Aqiba strenuously argued that the Song of Songs, too, was scripture.[5]

In order to see how the Greek canon of the Old Testament developed we must return to Alexandria. In the hellenistic communities in Alexandria and elsewhere in the Diaspora the Jews possessed an extensive collection of religious literature. The first two parts of the Hebrew scriptures, the Law (Torah) and the Prophets were held as authoritative by both the Hellenistic and Palestinian Jews, but the latest part of the canon, the collection of so called hagiographa or "holy writings," remained open for a very long time, finally comprising a larger number of books among Hellenistic Jews than among Hebrew- or Aramaic-speaking Jews. The Dead Sea Scrolls show that the Bible of the Qumran community was still in the making from the second century b.c.e. through the first century c.e.[6] When the members of the community quoted biblical texts, they used the technical terms "as it is written" or referred to "the law and the prophets" rather than the Bible or scripture.[7] At times they also employed the designation "the law and the prophets and David" (4QMMT C 17). The number of authoritative books grew step by step over the course of time. Actually, we cannot adequately study the existence

---

[4] The word became a technical term for a collection of scriptural writings in christianity by the time of the synod of Laodicea in 360 c.e. It also appears in the Easter letter by Athanasius of Alexandria in 367 c.e.

[5] Eugene Ulrich, "The Bible in the Making: The Scriptures at Qumran", in *The Community of the Renewed Covenant* (ed. Eugene Ulrich and James VanderKam. Notre Dame, Indiana, 1994), 77–93; Bertil Albrektson, "Reflections on the Emergence of a Standard Text of the Hebrew Bible," *VT* (1978): 49–65.

[6] Ulrich, "The Bible in the Making," 77–93.

[7] The book of Daniel was included among the prophets at Qumran, 4Q174, II, 3.

or development of authoritative texts without considering the religious community, religious group or subgroup that was acquainted with the texts and appealed to their authority.[8] The core collection of authoritative texts is always established by a religious community, and therefore the selection varies from community to community, such as the hellenistic Jewish community in Alexandria, the Qumran community and other Palestinian Judaism(s).

As for the material form of the scriptural texts, it is probable that in the early period the law, for instance, consisted of a collection of at least five scrolls. With regard to the Greek collection(s), apparently no formal decision was ever made as to its limits or as to how many scrolls it contained. From the third or fourth century C.E. onwards, however, the manuscripts which had been copied from one scroll to another for centuries began to be written in codex form, primitive books, and when in the fourth century these were gathered together under one cover, as it were, the apocryphal books were included in the same codex with the other books of Jewish scriptures. The number of books varied but the Greek collection was always much more extensive than the Hebrew canon. *Codex Vaticanus*, often considered the best single manuscript of the Greek scriptures, dating from the fourth century, contains, in addition to the books of the Hebrew canon, all the apocrypha, except for 1–4 Maccabees. 1–4 Maccabees are included in the fifth century *Codex Alexandrinus*. As long as the biblical texts were written on scrolls, and a scroll normally contained a single book or a small collection of works (e.g. the minor prophets), the order of the scrolls was not a relevant issue. The order of the books of the canon varied considerably in both traditions, and the final order of the Greek Bible differed from that of the Hebrew Bible. Only those books whose place is determined by the chronological sequence of the story have always had a fixed order, e.g. the books of the Pentateuch and the books of Samuel and Kings. With the production of the first comprehensive Christian Greek biblical codices in the 4th century, which included the New Testament along with the Hebrew Bible in Greek and the Jewish "apocrypha," the "canon" became a physical object, a single book, possibly bound in two or more volumes.[9]

---

[8] Julio Trebolle Barrera, "Authoritative Functions of Scriptural Works," in *The Community of the Renewed Covenant* (see note 5), 95–110.

[9] *Codex Alexandrinus* was probably originally bound in two volumes. Jellicoe, 183.

During the two first centuries of our era the authors of the New Testament often referred to the Jewish scriptural books in the same way as the members of the Qumran community did. Their Bible consisted mainly of the law (= Moses) and the prophets,[10] while at times the Psalms were also mentioned as a special category (Luke 24:44). The following formulas are commonly used in the New Testament: ἡ γραφὴ λέγει or λέγει γὰρ ἡ γραφή,[11] καθὼς γέγραπται[12] or γέγραπται γάρ,[13] which demonstrate that ἡ γραφή "the scripture" was developing into a designation for the collection of writings which later, after the formation of the New Testament, was called "the Old Testament" by the Christian church. More interesting, in my opinion, is the fact that the writers of the New Testament cited the apocryphal or even pseudepigraphical books using the same formulas as when quoting the Law and prophets. For instance, Jude 14 "And Enoch also ... *prophesied* of these, *saying* ..." προεφήτευσεν ... Ἐνώχ λέγων (ἐπροφήτευσεν P[72] B*). The writer attributes the same authority to a book of Enoch as to a scripture. He also employs almost the same formula as Mark, for instance, when he quotes the prophet Isaiah in 7:6 καλῶς ἐπροφήτευσεν Ἡσαΐας (par Matt 15:7). The authors of the New Testament referred to a selection of biblical books that was more extensive than what became the Hebrew canon.

The Greek collection of Jewish scriptures became very influential, because the Greek translation of the Scriptures was more suitable for the needs of the early Christian missionary and maintenance enterprise. During the hellenistic era Greek was the *lingua franca* of the whole civilized world and in particular around the eastern Mediterranean, while Hebrew had almost been forgotten, even by the Jews, most of whom spoke Aramaic. Thus only a few members of the Christian church were able to read the Scriptures in Hebrew. The first scriptures of the Greek speaking early Christians were therefore what became the "Septuagint" (LXX/OG), which also later received the New Testament as its companion, while the Hebrew scriptures remained as the basis of the Jewish canonical collections. The Hebrew scriptures, however, were viewed by some Christians

---

[10] The law and the prophets, for instance, in Matt 11:13, Rom 3:21, Moses and the prophets Luke 16:29, Acts 26:22, John 1:45.
[11] E.g. Rom 9:17, 10:11, 1 Tim 5:18.
[12] E.g. Rom 1:17, 2:24, 3:4, 3:10, 4:17, 8:36, 9:33, 10:15 etc.
[13] E.g. Rom 12:19, 14:11, 1 Cor 1:19, 3:19, etc.

as of abiding importance as representing the supposed "original text" of most of the Greek translations, against which "norm" the translations could be amended and revised. The work of revision began already in Greek Jewish circles as early as the first centuries B.C.E.,[14] and the original stimulus was by no means polemical interaction between Jews and Christians, although later on each group did indeed attempt to take advantage of the differences between the Greek and Hebrew texts.

THE TRANSMISSION HISTORY OF THE BIBLE

As an integral part of the Christian Bible from the fourth century onward, this hybrid Septuagint (LXX/OG) greatly influenced the transmission history of the Bible. First of all, the high prestige of the Greek Bible as an inspired translation, enjoying the same authority as the Hebrew source text, contributed to establishing the conviction that a Greek translation of the law and prophets and Psalms was not only of value for those who did not know Hebrew, but also very acceptable as the sacred text of a Greek-speaking religious community instead of the source text. The favorable reception of the original Septuagint (Pentateuch), promoted by the Letter of Aristeas in the second century B.C.E., was of crucial importance as an encouraging model for all future Bible translations in whatever language. A translation, too, could be inspired and so replace the original. In the first century C.E., the Alexandrian Jewish philosopher commentator Philo was the first to attribute the translation process of the Septuagint to divine guidance. While the Letter of Aristeas emphasized the agreement of the members of the first Bible translation

---

[14] According to Robert Hanhart it is obvious that the papyrus manuscript 848 contains corrections towards the Hebrew parent text. See his review of Francoise Dunad's edition of P. Fouad 266 in OLZ 73 (1978), 39–45. John Wevers cautiously arrived at the same conclusion in his *Text History of the Greek Deuteronomy* (MSU 13; Goettingen, 1978), p. 141. Ludwig Koenen in his introduction to Koenen and Zaki Aly, *Three Rolls of the Early Septuagint: Genesis and Deuteronomy* (Bonn: Habelt, 1980), p. 9, takes it for granted that both 847 and 848 harmonize the text of the Septuagint with the Hebrew parent text. See also my review in OLZ 82 (1986), 355–357. The father of the idea that in some Jewish circles previous to the Christian era the MSS of the Septuagint were being assimilated to the Hebrew text(s) was Dominique Barthelemy in his *Les Devanciers d'Aquila* (VT Suppl., 1963).

commission as sufficient proof that the translation was accurate,[15] Philo did not hesitate to speak of the original Septuagint (LXX) as a work produced by divine inspiration, so that it was believed to be completely identical with the original Hebrew and so truly God's word.[16] Thus the Septuagint opened the door for further Bible translations. The acceptance of a translation was a very important decision of principle and quite contrary to later decisions made, for instance, by Muslims concerning their holy book, the Qur'an. The history of the Christian church came to be a history of Bible translations, and it contributed to the recognition and literary standardization of vernaculars, even though—as is well known—the Roman Catholic church with its Latin Vulgate opposed this principle during the middle ages. The protestant reformation returned to the old principle of making the Bible available to people in their own native language.

During the first centuries C.E. most Bible translations were made from the Septuagint, and for this reason they are designated as daughter versions, such as the *Vetus Latina* or Old Latin, the Sahidic and Bohairic Coptic, Ethiopic and Armenian translations. The Vulgate, the work of Jerome (346–420), which gradually achieved the status of the official translation of the Roman Catholic Church, was originally a revision of the Old Latin translations by comparison with the Septuagint, but Jerome later became more interested in the Hebrew Bible, because he realized the unsatisfactory state of the Septuagint and became acquainted with its major variations from the Hebrew. When Jerome decided to use the Hebrew Bible as the basis of his translation, he did not work in a systematic manner, but only desired to satisfy the immediate requests of friends and inquirers.[17] In his introduction to the books of Samuel and Kings he wrote that only the books of the Hebrew canon were now of real concern. "Whatever is beyond these must be placed among the apocrypha."[18] Thus Jerome was very much aware which books belonged to the Hebrew Bible and which did not, and the same applies to many of the Greek fathers (e.g. Origen and Athanasius), but this knowledge

---

[15] Arist. 312–317.
[16] Philo, *Mos.* 2. 25–44.
[17] Jellicoe, *The Septuagint*, 251–6.
[18] ". . . quidquid extra hos est inter ἀπόκρυφα esse ponendum." *Prologus Galeatus in lib. Sam et Malachim.*

did not affect their conviction that it was the Greek Bible that was holy scripture.

After Jerome, the question of the extent of the Old Testament canon was not revived until the reformation. The general attitude of the humanist scholars was characterised by the slogan "ad fontes," "to the sources." Within biblical studies this led to the restitution of the *Hebraica veritas*, because this was thought to be the more original of the two Old Testament canons. Consequently, the position of the Septuagint was weakened and the apocrypha or deuterocanonical books were excluded from canonical authority in protestant churches, whereas the eastern Orthodox churches and the Roman Catholic church preserved them in their canon.

Let me summarize the first part of this paper in the form of a thesis: The significance of Septuagint studies today grows from the fruitful soil of the history of ancient Bible translations. The original Septuagint (Greek Pentateuch) was the first translation of Jewish scriptures of which we know. As such it for the first time conveyed the terms and ideas of Semitic Jahwistic religion in an Indo-European language. As a result the Septuagint (LXX/OG) came to be the vehicle that contributed to the integration of vital elements of Hebraic Judaism into European culture. These Greek scriptures also made available to the writers of the New Testament much of the religious terminology and fundamental beliefs of the Hebrew scriptures in Greek form, in the international language of the hellenistic world. The impact of this material on the New Testament and thereby on European languages and cultures has been great. It has often been said that European culture has grown from two roots: one in Greek and Roman antiquity and the other in Judaeo-Christian soil. The Septuagint anthology (LXX/OG) is one of the corner-stones upon which our European culture is built. In European languages the first human beings are not called Adam and Hawah as in the Hebrew Bible, but Adam and Eve (Ewa) as in the original Septuagint.

THE SEPTUAGINT AS A BRIDGE BETWEEN THE TWO TESTAMENTS

My second thesis is closely connected with the first one. The larger Septuagint corpus became the first part of the Christian Bible and formed a bridge from the Hebrew Scriptures ("Old Testament") to the New Testaments. It represented the form of Jewish Scriptures

known to the writers of the New Testament. The septuagintal translations, although usually very literal, resulted in some degree of hellenization of the Hebrew scriptures. The words and expressions were
typical of koiné Greek. Without intending to, the translators gave
their work a hellenistic flavour as regards its language and conceptual framework. Since these Greek scriptures were a source for the
New Testament writers as regards their language and theology, the
study of the Septuagint (LXX/OG) is necessary for anyone who desires
to specialize in the Greek New Testament and its language. These
two anthologies, the Septuagint and the New Testament, are closely
related and are our main representatives of semitic translation Greek.
For the studies of the language, textual history and theology of the
New Testament the study of the Septuagint is 'a must' or *conditio
sine qua non*. Several examples could be provided. Here we must
confine ourselves to only one. For the author of Luke-Acts, the Greek
Jewish Scriptures provided a model that he attempted to imitate in
various ways.[19] He not only employed "Septuagintisms," but created
at least one "hyperseptuagintism" in Acts 13:24 by extending the
use of the Hebraism πρὸ προσώπου beyond its LXX/OG parallels.[20]

The semitic flavour of New Testament Greek is not totally due
to the "foreign" influence of the Septuagint translations. Semitisms
may also have had their origin in Aramaic, the mother tongue of
many of the earliest followers of Jesus, whose influence may be
detected in some of the New Testament writings. Quite often, the
result or the actual equivalent for a Semitic expression is the same
in LXX/OG and in the New Testament, but we cannot be sure whether
the New Testament writers depend on the septuagintal language or
whether a similar, but independent translation process produced the
same equivalent. The Hebrew and Aramaic preposition ב, for instance,
is mostly rendered both in LXX/OG and in the New Testament by
the Greek equivalent ἐν, even when it has an instrumental function,
which is unidiomatic Greek. The New Testament practice possibly
arose independently of the Septuagint translations. The same concerns pleonastic use of *participium conjunctum* with verbs expressing

---

[19] Albert Wifstrand, "Lukas och Septuaginta," *STK* 16 (1940): 243–262.
[20] Raija Sollamo, "Semitic Interference in Words meaning 'before' in the New
Testament," in: *Glaube und Gerechtigkeit, in memoriam Rafael Gyllenberg, SESJ* 38 (1983),
181–200.

movement or speaking. The two Testaments frequently use unidiomatic expressions such as ἀπεκρίθη λέγων, ἀπεκριθεὶς εἶπεν, and
ἀναστὰς ἀπῆλθεν "answered saying," "said answering," and "he arose
and went" or "arising he went." These phrases indicate the semitic
practice of dissolving the actual event into smaller segments than is
idiomatic in Greek or any Indo-European language. German grammars call it "enumerative Redeweise (resumptive narration)".[21] To
produce idiomatic Greek, and theology, translations would have
required a very good knowledge of Greek on the part of the translators, and they would also have had to abandon their literal method
of translation. However, literalism remains the prevailing norm
throughout the Septuagint corpus and in the New Testament with
few exceptions, and the Greek translations of specific words or constructions are often very similar in both. And influence of septuagintal language on the language of the New Testament gradually
increased, as can be seen with reference to words meaning "before"
in Luke—Acts, the Pastoral Epistles and Revelation.[22]

THE THEOLOGY OF THE SEPTUAGINT?

Many scholars have expressed an opinion concerning the theologies
of the Septuagint translators and their relationship to the theologies
of the Hebrew scriptures.[23] They are usually ready to admit that
there is a difference between them, but opinions are divided as to
the depth and extent of the differences. Bertram found evidence to
support his conviction that there was a special septuagintal theology,[24] whereas Robert Hanhart, the dean of modern Septuagint

---

[21] Carl Brockelmann, *Hebräische Syntax* (Neukirchen, 1956), 133.

[22] Sollamo, "Semitic Interference," 199–200.

[23] Some Septuagint scholars speak about the theology of the Septuagint, whereas
some others prefer the term ideology to theology. The decision depends on whether
one considers it adequate to speak about the theology of the Old Testament and
how one defines the terms theology and ideology. See the variation of terminology
in articles by Johann Cook, "Ideology and Translation Technique: Two Sides of
the Same Coin?," and Frank Austermann, "ἀνομία im Septuaginta-Psalter: Ein
Beitrag zum Verhältnis von Übersetzungsweise und Theologie," both in *Helsinki
Perspectives on the Translation Technique of the Septuagint*, Proceedings of the IOSCS
Congress in Helsinki 1999 (ed. Raija Sollamo and Seppo Sipilä; SESJ 82; The
Finnish Exegetical Society in Helsinki; Göttingen, 2001).

[24] Georg Bertram, "*Praeparatio evangelica* in der Septuaginta," *VT* 7 (1957): 225–49.

studies in Germany, definitely argued that there exists no septuagintal
theology as a separate entity, but whenever Old Testament theology is investigated, the theology of the Septuagint should be given
a special section or a place of honour.[25] The discrepancy between
Bertram and Hanhart is not as wide as it might seem at first sight,
although there is a difference of emphasis. Hanhart points out that
the theology of the Septuagint has no independent existence beyond
the Hebrew Bible, and its theology is only a new hellenistic and
Alexandrian interpretation of the old theology of the Hebrew Bible.
Bertram insists that the Septuagint has a theology of its own. My
view is more in agreement with Hanhart than with Bertram. The
Septuagint translators had enough work to do in translating—theology was not a primary concern for them—but in interpreting the
Hebrew source texts they also needed to understand and adequately
express the conceptual and theological information of their Vorlagen.
As a rule they attempted to be very literal. But when, for instance,
they were embarrassed by the archaic anthropomorphic image of
God in their source text, they translated more freely. The correct
explanation of this freer practice seems to be quite simple. Due to
their theological understanding, the translators interpreted the expressions referring to God in Hebrew in a metaphorical rather than concrete way. To take just one example, the Hebrew idiom בעיני יהוה
"in the eyes of Yahweh" or "before the very eyes of Yahweh" is
seldom rendered literally ἐν ὀφθαλμοῖς κυρίου, but usually more freely
by such phrases as ἐνώπιον, ἔναντίον, ἔναντι τοῦ κυρίου "before the
Lord" (e.g. 1 Kgs 15:26 and 16:7). This time the ideology and linguistics coincided, for the phrase ἐν ὀφθαλμοῖς seldom occurred in
genuine koiné Greek.[26] Small changes of similar kinds do not justify
one in speaking of a special septuagintal theology or ideology, but
in the study of the Hebrew scriptures the evidence from the septu-

---

[25] Robert Hanhart, "Die Septuaginta als Problem der Textgeschichte, der
Forschungsgeschichte und der Theologie," 32 (1972; Congress Volume Uppsala,
1971), 185–200.

[26] Cf. Raija Sollamo, *Renderings of Hebrew Semiprepositions in the Septuagint* (AASF;
Diss. Hum.Litt. 19; Helsinki, 1979). The idiom בעיני יהוה is not rendered by ἐν
ὀφθαλμοῖς κυρίου anywhere else in the LXX/OG, except in the KAIGE sections (pp.
141–145 and 272). The translator of the KAIGE recension was not afraid of anthropomorphisms. See also James Donald Shenkel, *Chronology and Recensional Development
in the Greek Text of Kings* (Cambridge MA, 1968), 11–18.

agintal materials is important for anticipating later theological or ideological development.

The Septuagint translations as a whole represented a small step in the direction of Greek culture. Minor details of the Greek Bible also came to be influential. One of the most influential renderings was the regular use of the term κύριος "the Lord" for the Hebrew proper name Yahweh, the "tetragrammaton" (four lettered name). This was on a par with the Jewish practice of replacing the holy name of God by reading אדני, the Lord. This decision originally followed Jewish traditions, but nevertheless shows how septuagintal language gradually became detached from its national Jewish background. The new *terminus technicus*, κύριος, was very suitable as a designation of a deity in the hellenistic world. There were many other κύριοι or lords.

In some of the earliest Greek scriptural fragments and in some of the Qumran texts, the tetragram is written in ancient Hebrew letters, also in the middle of the Greek text. The best example is the Greek scroll of the Twelve Prophets, found at Wadi Murabba'at and published by Emanuel Tov in volume 8 of *DJD*. As an example of the Qumran texts we may refer to a biblical quotation in the pesher on Habakkuk (1QpHab 6,14) with Yahweh written in ancient Hebrew letters.[27] There are also Greek scriptural texts in which the tetragram is written in "square" Hebrew script. And at least in pap4QLxx-Lev[b] the Greek triagram ιαω appears. The first conclusion to be drawn from these data was that the tetragram written in ancient Hebrew letters must have been the original practice of the Septuagint translators as well. This was maintained as early as Origen. Following on the steps of Wolf Wilhelm Graf Baudissin's massive work *Kyrios als Gottesname im Judentum und seine Stelle in der Religionsgeschichte* (1929), Albert Pietersma, John Wevers' pupil from Toronto, demonstrated in his fine 1984 article "Kyrios or Tetragram: A renewed Quest for the Original LXX," that κύριος was the original rendering of the Septuagint translators, whereas the Hebrew tetragram is typical of later recensional activity attempting to adhere to the wording of the

---

[27] A complete list of instances was compiled by Emanuel Tov, "Scribal Features of Early Witnesses of Greek Scripture", in *The Old Greek Psalter. Studies in Honour of Albert Pietersma* (ed. Robert J. V. Hiebert, Claude E. Cox and Peter J. Gentry; *JSOTSup* 332; Sheffield, 2001), 146–8.

presumed Hebrew original as strictly as possible.[28] Pietersma refuted the arguments put forward in 1977 by George Howard in his article "Tetragram and the New Testament."[29] The practice of employing κύριος "the Lord" instead of Yahweh, first launched by the Septuagint translators, was then adopted by most Bible translators, and it is still observed in modern translations of the Bible.

The title κύριος as a surrogate for Yahweh proved very suitable for use by Christians. They ascribed the same title to the risen Christ present in the worship of the congregation. Jesus Christ probably did not receive this title through the influence of the Greek scriptures, but once it had been conferred on him, many things that those scriptures said about "the Lord" could be attributed to the new Lord, Jesus the Christ. When Paul or the authors of Acts refer to Joel 3:5 in identifying the followers of the Christ, they can substitute the name of Jesus Christ for Yahweh, the "Lord" of that old Greek translation—see Acts 2:21 and 1 Cor. 1:2.

Joel 3:5 καὶ ἔσται πᾶς, ὃς ἂν ἐπικαλέσηται τὸ ὄνομα κυρίου, σωθήσεται.
1 Cor 1:2 σὺν πᾶσιν τοῖς ἐπικαλουμένοις τὸ ὄνομα τοῦ κυρίου ἡμῶν Ἰησοῦ Χριστοῦ ἐν παντὶ τόπῳ.

Another small step in this process of hellenization of Hebrew Scriptures was the frequent use of the equivalent ψυχή for נפש. This implied that the Greek conception of "soul" (ψυχή) was introduced into the Bible, and the dualistic distinction between the soul and the body (ψυχή and σῶμα) spread to many other translations through the influence of the Septuagint. When we recently translated the Bible into Finnish a decade or so ago, we realized, when we had almost finished our task, that we had seldom used the Finnish equivalent for soul/ψυχή either in the Old or New Testament. Other equivalents were much more idiomatic in Finnish, such as "life," "mind," and different personal pronouns, because "my soul" is "I," "your soul" is "you," etc.[30]

---

[28] Albert Pietersma, "Kyrios or Tetragram: A renewed Quest for the Original LXX." In *De Septuaginta. Studies in Honour of John William Wevers on his sixty-fifth birthday* (Mississauga, Ont., 1984), pp. 85–101.
[29] George Howard, "The Tetragram and the New Testament," *JBL* 96 (1977): 63–68.
[30] Pyhä Raamattu. Suomen Evankelis-Luterilaisen Kirkon Kirkolliskokouksen vuonna 1992 käyttöön ottama suomennos.

Textual Criticism

My third thesis maintains that the Septuagint corpus is an indispensable tool in the textual criticism of the Hebrew scriptures (Old Testament)[31] and has an eminent bearing upon the text of the New Testament as well. As for the present, we are very fortunate in having at our disposal a vast collection of biblical manuscripts from Qumran. The publication of these manuscripts has taken 50 years, and the work still continues, but it will soon be brought to completion. New editions come out at a hectic pace. With each edition of the Qumran manuscripts, the *Biblia Hebraica Stuttgartensia*, our standard text for the Hebrew Bible becomes more and more outdated. The information in its apparatus no longer suffices for scholarly purposes. As for the textual criticism of the Pentateuch, we also benefit from the Samaritan Pentateuch, which, in addition to the Qumran manuscripts, is a witness to a pre-Masoretic text. These Hebrew sources cover only a small portion of the Hebrew Bible; other parts must be studied primarily with the aid of the septuagintal evidence. The Septuagint corpus, although translated material, is of great significance for those who want to recover the earlier stages of the Hebrew scriptures, in quest of the "original text." Just as the apparatus of the *Biblia Hebraica Stuttgartensia* is inadequate with reference to the Qumran manuscripts, it is equally inadequate for the septuagintal evidence. The apparatus cannot possibly include the most recent material of the latest editions, and the notes referring to the Septuagint translations lack consistency and care. Besides such elementary faults, the apparatus offers misleading or wrong interpretations of the translation techniques employed by the translators.[32]

Now finally, we come to the issue of translation technique, which is the field with which I am best acquainted. The term "translation technique" must be understood as meaning the different methods and ways that the translators used when translating their Hebrew *Vorlagen*. Every translator had methods and practices, typical of him

---

[31] Emanuel Tov has made one of his chief contributions to scholarship in the field of the textual criticism of the Hebrew Bible. I only need to mention his *The Text-critical Use of the Septuagint in Biblical Research* (rev. and enl. 2nd ed.; Jerusalem, 1997).

[32] John Wm. Wevers, "Text History and Text Criticism of the Septuagint," (VTSup. 29; *Congress Volume Göttingen 1977*; Leiden, 1978), 392–402.

and diverging from those of others. These methods and practices constituted his translation technique. A translator by himself may not have been fully aware of the translation technique he followed. He and his colleagues probably had no fixed rules or principles, which they attempted to observe. No instructions were given before-hand or no guidelines ever existed, as far as we know. The meth-ods, how they worked when translating, must be determined by scrutinizing their completed piece of work. When their translation is compared with their presumed Hebrew *Vorlage* in great detail, their methods or their usual ways of translating become evident. Such knowledge of translation technique is necessary in textual criticism, because one has to be able to make a retroversion from a Greek reading back to the Hebrew. The usefulness of the Septuagint evi-dence in textual criticism is due to the literalness of the translation, so that it is not totally impossible to deduce from it the wording of the Hebrew original. Only through such retroversion is a scholar able to recreate to produce the Hebrew reading represented by the Greek expression, and only the retroverted Hebrew reading can be compared with other Hebrew variants. The readings of the Septuagint translations are very significant, because the oldest of them go as far back in time as the third century B.C.E. and all of them antedate the Masoretic text.

In these years after the second beginning of Qumran studies, when the texts were opened up to all scholars in 1991, it has become evi-dent that the Masoretic text was only one of several Hebrew texts that existed and circulated before the consolidation of the Masoretic text. Thus, the value of the Masoretic text has been overestimated. Actually, we should use the plural instead of the singular when refer-ring to the Masoretic text. The plural, the Masoretic texts, is far more appropriate to indicate the fact that the so-called Masoretic text has no inner coherence, but its quality varies greatly from book to book. The Masoretic collection arose as a result of combining the texts of many different scrolls in one manuscript. The same uneven nature is also typical of the large Greek codices such as the *codex Vaticanus, codex Alexandrinus*, etc. The textual quality of the Masoretic texts must be examined separately for every single book, as we also have to ponder book by book the textual value of the various Greek translations included in the septuagint tradition, whether in the large early codices such as *Vaticanus* or elsewhere. It has also emerged that many of the biblical books circulated in multiple editions; for example the book of Jeremiah is attested in an earlier and shorter Old Greek form (in LXX/OG) and in a longer and later form (in MT). The shorter Greek form of Jeremiah is not due to a laconic or manipulative translator, but to a shorter Hebrew vorlage which the translator had at his disposal. The fragments from Qumran (4Q Jer[b,d]) also provide evidence of a shorter LXX/OG-like edition.[33]

SEPTUAGINT STUDIES IN THEIR OWN RIGHT

So far, we have discussed the significance of Septuagint studies for other disciplines, such as the study of ancient Bible translations and their aftermath in European civilization, the textual criticism of the Hebrew Bible, Old and New Testament studies in general, and the philology of the New Testament in particular. Last but not least, it is high time to say a few words about Septuagint studies in their own right. It might sound odd, but the greater the significance we would hope to assign to Septuagint studies, the more we have to concentrate on all areas of Septuagint research. It is essential to publish new critical text editions, it is important to write grammars and compile lexica and describe the translation technique of the different translators. Thorough-going basic research, and only that, can provide solid ground for applied studies. There is no short cut.

When many years ago my teacher Professor Ilmari Soisalon-Soininen began to urge me to pursue Septuagint studies, my first question was whether there was any value in doing so. He became embarrassed and referred to its importance for the textual criticism of the Old Testament and for the linguistic study of the New Testament, but I realised that for him my honest question was a sacrilege. All research is valuable in its own right; doubly valuable is research in such a crucial field as the bridge between the Old and New Testament. I decided in favour of Septuagint studies in the belief that I was dedicating myself to invisible and laborious basic research in order to lay the foundation for other scholars' more

---

[33] E. Tov, "Jeremiah Scrolls from Qumran," *RevQ* 14 (1989): 189–206; Idem, "Three Fragments of Jeremiah from Qumran Cave 4," *RevQ* 15 (1992): 531–41; Idem, "The Literary History of the Book of Jeremiah in Light of its Textual History" In *The Greek and Hebrew Bible. Collected Essays on the Septuagint* (ed. E. Tov; *VTSup.* 72; 1999), 363–7.

significant work. I could not predict the great actual advantage that
I was to gain from my Septuagint studies in the huge task of translating the Bible into Finnish in which I participated as a member
of one of the Old Testament translation units (see above n. 30). It
was again obvious, as it had been so often before, that one never
knows when and how basic research turns out to be of unforeseen
importance. The future always belongs to those optimists who trust
in the significance of exhaustive basic research, whatever the subject might be—without excluding "the Septuagint," the mother of
all Bible translations and one of Egypt's greatest gifts to Western
civilization.

A LEXICAL STUDY THIRTY YEARS ON, WITH OBSERVATIONS ON "ORDER" WORDS IN THE LXX PENTATEUCH[1]

John A. L. Lee

My doctoral dissertation entitled *A Lexical Study of the Septuagint Version of the Pentateuch* was published in 1983.[2] This was an unrevised version of a work that had been completed and submitted in 1970, from research begun in 1966. Its main objective was to demonstrate the links between the vocabulary of the LXX Pentateuch and that of contemporary Koine Greek, especially as evidenced in the Egyptian papyri. This contributed to the debate about the nature of LXX Greek, in support of the view that the Greek of the LXX is essentially the Greek of its time. It was not a new idea to use the documentary evidence for this purpose: the initial discovery had been made by Deissmann. But it had not been followed up for the LXX (unlike the New Testament) after the first enthusiasm. On the contrary, a reaction had set in and the phantom of "Jewish-Greek" had made a comeback. Moreover, the evidence had not been thoroughly exploited by Deissmann and had continued to grow in the meantime. There was clearly a need to pursue the question further and make the case stronger.

The work was well received by most reviewers and is regularly referred to in the literature. There seems to be general acceptance that the case has been proved.[3] This is gratifying, but it is not the end of the story. There is much still to be done to make full use of this evidence, not only in order to strengthen the case further but, perhaps more importantly, to throw light in all sorts of ways on the meaning and usage of LXX words. In this paper I want to look back

---

[1] An earlier form of this paper was presented at a Language Colloquium at Macquarie University, 14 September, 2001. I thank Trevor Evans for the invitation to participate and for running an observant eye over this final version.

[2] See bibliography for details.

[3] See, e.g., LEH, VIII; Muraoka, IX; Dorival, Harl and Munnich, 234; Jobes and Silva, 263.

and set that study in the context of its time, consider developments since, and present a specimen of the kind of work that is still waiting to be done.

My training at Sydney, where I did my first degree, was primarily in Classical Greek, and as part of it I was introduced to Koine Greek in a course conducted by G. P. Shipp. I had also spent some years learning Hebrew, and did some work on the LXX in my honours year. Even before I left Australia to go to Cambridge, it struck me that there was a topic of interest in some combination of the LXX and the language of the papyri, though I did not have a clear idea of how it could be focused.[4]

Early in the century Cambridge had been a centre of LXX studies, but by 1966 the great names of the past, Swete, Thackeray, Brooke and McLean, were a distant memory.[5] Sebastian Brock, who had known Peter Walters, and had recently arrived in Cambridge, was, I think, the only LXX specialist there at the time. My supervisor, Barnabas Lindars, SSF, a fine scholar who was subsequently elected to the Rylands Chair of Biblical Criticism and Exegesis at Manchester, was primarily a New Testament expert and a little mystified by my approach. Important help came to me from John Chadwick, who taught me the basics of lexicography.

Although there was contemporary debate about the nature of LXX Greek, the issue was not a priority in current LXX research, and the idea of harvesting the rich documentary evidence did not seem to be much on anyone's mind.[6] This despite the fact that Deissmann's discovery dated from 1895, and the subsequent work of Moulton and Milligan was focused on the New Testament (and covered that only partially) and was itself well out of date. I felt isolated in choosing this topic; it even seemed that I was venturing into strange and

---

[4] Shipp (1900–1980), Professor of Greek 1954–1965, best known for his work on Homer, but a philologist whose range covered all of Greek and Latin. The Sydney BA provided (as it still does) the opportunity to mix subjects from different areas. I had done enough Latin as a schoolboy to satisfy me.

[5] For a helpful summary of the life and work of these scholars, see Jobes and Silva, 247–52. On one occasion, in 1970, I dined as a guest in Christ's College; when I mentioned my work on the LXX to one of the older Fellows, he recalled McLean, who had been a Fellow of the College (he died in 1947).

[6] The papyrologist Orsolina Montevecchi was a notable exception. She had already drawn attention to the links and continued to do so. See Dorival, Harl and Munnich, 233, 243, 248; Lee, *Lexical Study*, 6.

dubious territory. As to the lexicography of the lxx, though every-one said that a new lexicon was needed, there was no project in place to make it a reality.

lxx studies at that time were quiet compared with the remark-able burgeoning that has occurred since. Much of the work was on the text—as it had been in the previous generation also—and the important Göttingen edition was a focus of effort. Sidney Jellicoe's 1968 book, which marks a sort of turning-point, being the first gen-eral book since Swete's 1902 classic, appeared during the time I was working. The IOSCS only began at the same time, holding its inau-gural meeting in December, 1968.[7] Contact between scholars in those days was not what it is today. Email did not exist, and flying to and fro between countries was yet to become common (my trip from Australia to England in 1966 was actually a sea voyage of four weeks). My first visit to the USA did not take place until 1985.

My work in Cambridge of course predated the computer. Those who have not lived through that revolution may not fully appreci-ate how far-reaching are the changes it has wrought. Electronic tools and resources did not exist. Not just hours or weeks, but months were spent searching for words in the indexes of documentary vol-umes and confirming occurrences. Every text had to be laboriously copied by hand in the library, then recopied into the manuscript when written, before finally being handed over for typing (typing of Greek could just be achieved by the latest advance in technology, the IBM "golf ball;" even so, accents and other diacritics had to be inserted by hand). Photocopying was only just beginning to be pos-sible. As to other tools, even such a basic thing as a list of editions of documentary papyri was not to hand when I began.[8]

These remarks indicate the practical constraints under which work of this kind proceeded. Today searches for words in both inscrip-tions and papyri can be done in seconds via the CD ROM PHI 7, texts can be inspected on screen and portions copied, and the whole lxx is available electronically. There are also two commentaries on

---

[7] For an account of the IOSCS, see Jobes and Silva, 311–3. I still possess a copy of the original first Bulletin, of June 1968, consisting of four sides of mimeographed foolscap. This was reprinted in *BIOSCS* 2.

[8] I remember the kindness of E. G. Turner, Professor of Papyrology at University College, London, in showing me an advance copy of the list in his *Greek Papyri: An Introduction* (Oxford: Clarendon, 1968) and marking for me the volumes that con-tained Ptolemaic papyri.

the Pentateuch, a lexicon (or two) of the LXX, an English translation project in progress, and for good measure a CD ROM containing most of Greek literature to 1453.

Obviously the book has limitations. In general it lacks the comprehensiveness that could be achieved today (even within the length limit imposed). Moreover, it was restricted to a certain kind of parallel, namely *new* developments in the language, so as to establish the point as persuasively as possible; and I was at all times very cautious to include only the most convincing examples. A less restrained collection of evidence (even if limited to the Pentateuch) could be twice as long, and even then would not exhaust the potential of this line of enquiry.[9]

What has happened since? What sort of follow-up work has there been? It is safe to say not very much. There have been minor studies in articles, but there has been no book or major work that pursues the subject thoroughly.[10] There is no "Moulton and Milligan" for the LXX. The two lexicons that have appeared since I completed my study (Lust, Eynikel and Hauspie for the whole LXX and Muraoka for the Twelve Prophets) have performed important service in providing tools after such a long time when the only lexicon was Schleusner (1820–21), but, as their authors admit, they have not attempted fresh searching of documentary sources: they have relied on existing collections. For myself, one discovery in *A Lexical Study* (on ὕω and βρέχω) was the inspiration for a line of investigation on "formality" in the New Testament; but my interests generally since 1970 have gone in other directions.[11]

---

[9] I think the decision to publish the work as it stood was right, though the delay was regrettable. Even so, nothing occurred up to 1983 to change the picture significantly; it is not as if the book has been replaced even now. Various minor weaknesses were pointed out by reviewers, mostly rightly. But Ina Willi-Plein's wholly negative review (*TLZ* 110 [1985]: 94–5) occasions as much perplexity ("Ratlosigkeit") as she says she felt in trying to review the book.

[10] A noteworthy article is that of Hélène Cadell, "Vocabulaire de la législation ptolemaïque: problème du sens de *dikaiôma* dans le Pentateuque," in *Κατὰ τοὺς ο´: Selon les Septante*, 207–21. For further bibliography, see Dorival, Harl and Munnich, 243. Documentary evidence is used sporadically in the papers of Tov, Swinn and Lee in *Melbourne Symposium*. That memorable occasion was one of many valued contacts with the honorand of the present volume.

[11] The NT study was published as: "Some Features of the Speech of Jesus in Mark's Gospel," *NovT* 27 (1985): 1–26. This could still be followed further in the LXX. Chapter 8 on linguistic evidence for dating the LXX Pentateuch was very experimental and limited (as I knew full well). Gathering the data for this purpose could

I turn now to a specimen of what might still be done to illuminate the LXX vocabulary using contemporary documentary evidence.
I have selected the group of words for "to order." One naturally
expects to begin with the ordinary word for "to order" in ancient
Greek, κελεύω. It is a surprising fact that there is not a single example in the LXX Pentateuch. Opportunities to express the idea were
certainly not lacking: the usual Hebrew word (צוה) occurs many times.
The translators must have been using something other than κελεύω.
What they were using is soon discovered. The following three verbs
account for almost all expressions of the idea in the Pentateuch:
ἐντέλλομαι (156 times), συντάσσω (82), and προστάσσω (12).[12] Not so
obvious is why this should be so. Why not κελεύω? What has happened to it? I think the documentary evidence helps considerably in
finding an answer.

Let us begin with a summary of the usage of the two common-
est words in the LXX Pentateuch and a selection of examples. A look
through the occurrences soon shows that ἐντέλλομαι and συντάσσω
are semantically close; it is difficult to find any grounds for giving
them separate lexical meanings. Both are used for orders given by
an authority figure (God, Moses, Pharaoh, a parent, a priest). The
manner of ordering is oral, rather than written, in both. Both are
used for instructions to be immediately acted on as well as longer-
term directions, and both are used to order any kind of action.
ἐντέλλομαι with the law (or provisions of the law) as object is notice-
ably frequent. Finally, it is easy to find places in which the translators use the two interchangeably in near proximity, referring to the
same event and rendering the same Hebrew word.[13]

A selection of typical examples first of ἐντέλλομαι (with one of
προστάσσω), and then of συντάσσω:

---

be done much more thoroughly and with less effort now; finding valid tests is the
tricky part.

[12] Figures from LEH, drawn in turn from the CATSS files. Other words used in
Pent.: ἐπιτάσσω (x 1); ἐξηγοῦμαι (x 1); also λέγω/εἶπον, of which possible examples
are: Exod 35:1 (cf. Boulluec and Sandevoir, L'Exode, ad loc.), Lev 9:6, Num 32:27
(cf. LEH). Not in Pent.: διατάσσω, παραγγέλλω. Not in this sense in Pent.: διαστέλλω.
Outside the Pent., κελεύω occurs 29 times, but only in books not in the Hebrew
Bible; ἐντέλλομαι is by far the favourite word.

[13] E.g., Exod 31:6 (συντ.), 11 (ἐντ.); Lev 8:4 (συντ.), 5 (ἐντ.), 9 (συντ.); Num 2:33
(ἐντ.), 34 (συντ.); Deut 5:12 (ἐντ.), 15 (συντ.), 16 (ἐντ.). All ~ צוה pi. Cf. Dorival
et al., Les Nombres, 54, 56. Wevers (Numbers, 31, 494) says he can find no distinction between ἐντέλλομαι and συντάσσω. A full translation-technical study is not

Gen 3:11 καὶ εἶπεν αὐτῷ Τίς ἀνήγγειλέν σοι ὅτι γυμνὸς εἶ, εἰ μὴ ἀπὸ τοῦ ξύλου, οὗ **ἐνετειλάμην** σοι τούτου μόνου μὴ φαγεῖν ἀπ᾽ αὐτοῦ, ἔφαγες;
And he said to him: Who declared to you that you are naked, unless you have eaten of the tree of which alone I **commanded** you not to eat?

Gen 12:20 καὶ **ἐνετείλατο** Φαραὼ ἀνδράσιν περὶ ᾿Αβρὰμ συμπροπέμψαι αὐτὸν καὶ τὴν γυναῖκα αὐτοῦ καὶ πάντα, ὅσα ἦν αὐτῷ, καὶ Λὼτ μετ᾽ αὐτοῦ.
And Pharao **gave orders** to some men regarding Abram to conduct him on his way and his wife and all his property, and Lot with him.

Gen 28:1 προσκαλεσάμενος δὲ ᾿Ισαὰκ τὸν ᾿Ιακὼβ εὐλόγησεν αὐτόν, καὶ **ἐνετείλατο** αὐτῷ λέγων Οὐ λήμψῃ γυναῖκα ἐκ τῶν θυγατέρων Χανάαν·
Isaak summoned Iakob and blessed him and **ordered** him saying, You shall not take a wife from the daughters of Khanaan.

Exod 7:6 ἐποίησεν δὲ Μωυσῆς καὶ ᾿Ααρών, καθάπερ **ἐνετείλατο** αὐτοῖς κύριος, οὕτως ἐποίησαν.
Moyses and Aaron did as the Lord **instructed** them, thus they did.

Deut 27:1 καὶ **προσέταξεν** Μωυσῆς καὶ ἡ γερουσία ᾿Ισραὴλ λέγων Φυλάσσεσθε πάσας τὰς ἐντολὰς ταύτας, ὅσας ἐγὼ **ἐντέλλομαι** ὑμῖν σήμερον.
Moyses and the council of elders of Israel **ordered** [them] saying, Keep all these commandments which I **command** you today.

Exod 1:17 ἐφοβήθησαν δὲ αἱ μαῖαι τὸν θεόν, καὶ οὐκ ἐποίησαν καθότι **συνέταξεν** αὐταῖς ὁ βασιλεὺς Αἰγύπτου, καὶ ἐζωογόνουν τὰ ἄρσενα.
The midwives feared God and did not do as the king of Egypt **directed** them, and they kept the male children alive.

Exod 12:35 οἱ δὲ υἱοὶ ᾿Ισραὴλ ἐποίησαν καθὰ **συνέταξεν** αὐτοῖς Μωυσῆς, καὶ ᾔτησαν παρὰ τῶν Αἰγυπτίων σκεύη ἀργυρᾶ καὶ χρυσᾶ καὶ ἱματισμόν·
The sons of Israel did as Moyses **ordered** them and asked for silver and gold objects and clothing from the Egyptians.

Lev 13:54 καὶ **συντάξει** ὁ ἱερεύς, καὶ πλυνεῖ ἐφ᾽ οὗ ἂν ᾖ ἐπ᾽ αὐτοῦ ἡ ἁφή, καὶ ἀφοριεῖ ὁ ἱερεὺς τὴν ἁφὴν ἑπτὰ ἡμέρας τὸ δεύτερον·
The priest **shall give directions** and shall wash [i.e., get someone to wash] the article on which the mark of infection was, and the priest shall set apart the mark of infection for seven days a second time.

Num 2:34 καὶ ἐποίησαν οἱ υἱοὶ ᾿Ισραὴλ πάντα, ὅσα **συνέταξεν** κύριος τῷ Μωυσῇ, οὕτως παρενέβαλον κατὰ τάγμα αὐτῶν καὶ οὕτως ἐξῆρον....[14]

---

undertaken here, but would complete the picture. In two of my examples below (Exod 1:17, 12:35) συντάσσω ~ דבר pi./subst.

[14] ἐξῆρον sic Rahlfs; Wevers, Göttingen ed.; but a 2nd aor. of αἴρω and compounds is unusual if not unknown. Read ἐξῆραν?

The sons of Israel did everything that the Lord **instructed** Moyses, thus they encamped according to their units and thus they set out on the march. . . .

Now for the documentary evidence. A search (via PHI 7) in nineteen volumes of papyri produced these numbers of occurrences in 3rd B.C.E. texts: ἐντέλλομαι 22; κελεύω 25; προστάσσω 32; συντάσσω 285.[15] Let me summarise what a perusal of this evidence indicates, and then give some representative examples.

It is obvious at once that συντάσσω was a favourite word in Ptolemaic officialese in the time of the LXX Pentateuch. In meaning it is definitely in the "order" field with the other verbs. This is a somewhat unexpected flourishing: the word is old, but in Classical usage it mostly means "arrange," "organise" and the like, though the beginnings of the development to "order" can just be seen in some occurrences.[16]

ἐντέλλομαι goes back to earlier Greek, though it was not very common, it seems, outside Herodotus. It is still running along in Ptolemaic Greek with its meaning as before ("command," etc.) but less favoured than συντάσσω in the kind of language found in papyrus documents.

προστάσσω was well established in Classical usage as one of the "order" words and maintains its ground.

κελεύω is the oldest member of the group, being the standard word from Homer onwards. It is well known, however, that it may show a weaker sense translatable as "request," "urge," "tell." It loses some of its vigour as a result of long and frequent use. In the Ptolemaic documents it has clearly suffered something of an eclipse, when compared with the overwhelming popularity of its new rival συντάσσω. But this does not mean it had dropped out: it was always still available in both its weaker and its full sense. Later, from I C.E. onwards, it makes a comeback alongside other words, and συντάσσω in its turn fades away.[17]

---

[15] PHib 1, 2; PLille 1, 2; PSI 4, 5, 6; PPetr 1–3; PMich 1; PCol 3, 4; PCorn; PCairZen 1–5. The counts cannot be absolutely precise. I have dropped grossly restored examples, but opinions would differ. Only 3rd B.C.E. texts are counted. I have not made any attempt on the inscriptions for the usual reasons: 3rd B.C.E. texts are scattered through numerous volumes; they come from a variety of ancient localities, not just Egypt; and their genres vary markedly.

[16] See LSJ II.4.a and b. (but Aeschin. 2.22 is quite different). More examples and comment in Anz, *Subsidia*, 324–5.

[17] A full study of the history of these words, from Classical to Modern, is a desideratum. It would include the curious later development of κελεύω to "please."

All of these verbs are close semantically. The difference between them is not one of lexical meaning so much as of connotation, of "flavour" or "tone." To determine this exactly is a difficult exercise; only a speaker of the time could appreciate it fully. We can choose, then, to give up the attempt altogether, or do what we can, relying on the hints gleaned from context and situation.

I suggest the key is this: ἐντέλλομαι, προστάσσω and συντάσσω are more formal and official-sounding than κελεύω. They are in, or have come into, use to meet the need for words with just that flavour as compared to the plain, slightly worn-out feel of κελεύω. συντάσσω is the newcomer and still fresh; it is businesslike, with some hint of its origin in the meaning "arrange." προστάσσω is not markedly different in flavour from συντάσσω. How ἐντέλλομαι differs from these two is not obvious; perhaps it is a little elevated. At the same time as all this, we have to allow for the use of κελεύω in its original sense with full force, especially in literary writing. This is why most of the lxx examples are in the more literary books (2–4 Macc account for two-thirds), and a writer like Polybius uses it 124 times.[18]

A turn-over in "order" words is in fact a general phenomenon: they tend to lose their punch and become weak, or to lack the authoritative sound felt desirable in certain contexts. In English we have a kaleidoscope of words and expressions of different ages and flavours at our disposal: *bid, enjoin, charge, command, prescribe, direct, order, instruct, issue instructions, issue orders, issue a directive, tell.*[19]

Next a selection of examples from 3rd b.c.e. papyri:

1) PCairZen 2.59155.1–3 (Philadelpheia, 256 b.c.e., letter)
Ἀπολλώνιος Ζήνωνι χαίρειν. ὁ βασιλεὺς **συνέτασσεν** ἡμῖν | διαπορῆσαι τὴν γῆν. ὡς ἂν οὖν ἐχθερίσῃς τὸν πρώιον σῖτον, | εὐθέως πότισον τὴν γῆν ἀπὸ χερός, . . .

---

[18] Mauersberger, *Polybios-Lexikon*. Figures for the other words in Polybius: ἐντέλλομαι 17, προστάσσω 60, συντάσσω 84 (the last two from my own search via TLG). Other attempts to distinguish "order" words have generally looked for differences in the manner or substance of the order. For Pelletier, κελεύω "tend à se réserver pour les cas où l'ordre est donné de vive voix," and ἐντέλλομαι "a été choisi pour exprimer le ton d'autorité bienveillante" (*VT* 32 [1982]: 239, 240). Pelletier proceeds entirely without reference to the papyrus evidence, and uses *one* inscription from Teos. The idea that κελεύω refers to oral orders is an old one, found already in Schmidt's treatment (*Synonymik*, 1:199–214). Harl (*La Genèse*, 54, 103) follows Pelletier on ἐντέλλομαι. Cf. another treatment in Louw and Nida, 33.323, 325, 329.

[19] Cf. Buck 19.45. Note esp. developments from Latin to Romance.

Apollonios to Zenon greetings. The king **has issued instructions** to us to do the second sowing of the land. When therefore you have finished harvesting the early grain, at once irrigate the land by hand, . . .

A nice parallel to Exod 1:17 above.

2) PCairZen 5.59816.1–4 (Philadelpheia, 257 B.C.E., letter)
Ἀρτεμίδωρος Πανακέστορι χαίρειν. παραγινομένου μου ἐγ Βουβάστου εἰς Μέμ[φιν] | **ἐνετέλλετο** Ἀπολλώνιος μάλιστα μὲν αὐτὸν διελθεῖν πρὸς σέ, εἰ δὲ μή, ἀποστεῖλα[ί] | τινα παρ᾽ ἐμοῦ ὃς ἀναγγελεῖ σοι τὰ παρ᾽ αὐτοῦ. ἠκηκόει γὰρ ὅτι οὐ πᾶσα κατασπείρετα[ι] | ἡ γῆ αἱ μύριαι ἄρουραι. **συνέτασσεν** οὖν ἀναγγέλλειν σοι ἵνα ξυλοκοπηθῆι πᾶσα καὶ ποτισθῆι . . .

Artemidoros to Panakestor greetings. When I arrived at Memphis from Boubastos, Apollonios **instructed** that preferably I myself should come to you, but failing that to send someone from me to convey to you his wishes. For he heard that not all the land, the ten thousand arourai, are sown. He **gave instructions** therefore to convey to you that all of it is to be cleared and irrigated. . . .

This passage illustrates the interchangeability of the two verbs as well as their general character. Apollonios, also met in 1), was a high official in the administration.

3) PCairZen 1.59057.1–4 (Philadelpheia, 257 B.C.E., letter)
Ζωίλος Ἀλεξάνδρωι χαίρειν. καλῶς ἂν ἔχοι εἰ ἔρρωσαι· ὑγιαίνομεν δὲ καὶ αὐτοί. | ἐκομισάμην τὰς ἐπιστολὰς καὶ οὐκ ἀμελῶ περὶ ὧν ἂν ἡμῖν γράφηις. σὺ δὲ καλῶς | ποιήσεις ἐκπονήσας ἵνα ἡμῖν γίνηται ἃ σοι **ἐνετειλάμεθα** κατὰ τὸ ὑπόμνημα, | τούτου δὲ γενομένου ἐπί[στ]ασο ὅτι ὀφειλήσω σοι χάριν ἱκανήν.

Zoilos to Alexandros greetings. It would be good if you are well; we too are in good health. I have received your letters and I am not neglecting the matters about which you wrote to us. You will do well to ensure that what we **instructed** you according to the memorandum is done for us, and if this happens, know that I will owe you considerable gratitude.

An ordinary example of ἐντέλλομαι in a friendly though businesslike letter.

4) PCairZen 5.59852.7–10 (Philadelpheia, 3rd B.C.E., polite letter to Zenon asking for placement)
εἰ δ᾽ ἐπὶ τοῦ παρόντος ἡσυχίαν ἄγειν **κελεύεις**, τὸμ μὲν καιρὸν αὐτὸς | εἰδήσεις, ἐμοὶ δὲ καλῶς ἂν ποιήσαις **συντάξας** ὅπως ἂν παρα|δειχθῆι μεθ᾽ ὧν οἰκίαν τε ἔξω καὶ τὰ λοιπὰ δέοντα, ἵνα μὴ πρεσ|βύτερος ὢν ῥέμβωμαι.

But if for the present you **direct** me to do nothing, you will know when it is the right time, but as for me please be kind enough to **give directions** that it be indicated with whom I am to live and the other necessary matters, so that, being an old man, I may not be left unattached.

κελεύω seems to function the same way as συντάσσω here. The writer is an older man, and the style shows touches of "better" Greek (μὲν ... δέ, τε, ὅπως ἄν).

5) PSI 4.420.1–19 (Philadelpheia, 3rd B.C.E., letter)
Ζήνωνι χαίρειν | Σεμθεύς. **συνέτα** | **ξάς** μοι κεραμεῦ | σαι ἅπαν⟨τα⟩ τὸν κέ | ραμον ἕως τοῦ | ἰσιόντος ⟨μηνὸς⟩ ε΄ τὴν | ἡμέραν ν΄. ποιῶ | οὖν κατὰ ταῦτα. | **ἐκελεύοσαν** δέ με | καταβαίνοντα | συγχωνεύειν. ἐγὼ | οὖν οὐκ ᾠχόμην, | ἕως ἄν μοι σὺ **συντά** | **ξηις**. νῦν οὖν ἄλλοι | πάρισιν κεραμεῖς· καὶ | γὰρ ὁ χωνεύων με | μαλάκισται, ὁ ξένος. | τί οὖν μοι **συντάσσεις**; | ὅπως ἂν οὕτω ποιῶ.

Semtheus to Zenon greetings. You **ordered** me to make pots and nothing else until the 5th of the ensuing month, 50 per day. So I am doing that. But they **told** me to go down and join in glazing. I did not go [and will not], until you **order** me. Now other potters have come; and the glazer has fallen ill, the foreigner. What do you **order** me, then? so that I may do that.

συντάσσω is what Zenon does, κελεύω describes the others' action. I detect a difference: συντάσσω is formal and polite in reference to the authority figure, κελεύω is informal.

6) PCol 4.66.1–9 (Philadelpheia, 256/5 B.C.E., letter)
... Ζήνωνι χαίρειν. καλῶς ποιεῖς εἰ ἔρρωσαι. ἔρρω | μαι δὲ καὶ αὐτός. ἐπίστασαι ὡς κατέλιπές με ἐν Συρίαι μετὰ | Κρότου καὶ ἐποίουν πάντα τὰ **προστασσόμενα** τὰ κα | τὰ ⟨τὰ⟩ς καμήλους καὶ ἤμην σο[ι] ἀνέγκλητ[ο]ς. σοῦ δὲ **προστά** | **ξαντός** μοι ὀψώνιον διδόναι ἃ σὺ **συνέταξας** οὐκ ἐδίδου | μοι οὐθέν. ἐπεὶ δὴ πολλάκ[ι]ς μου δεομένου διδόναι μοι | ἃ σὺ **συνέταξας** οὐκ ἐδίδου μοι οὐθὲν Κρότος, ἀλλ᾽ **ἐκέλευ** | **έμ** με ἀπαλλάσσεσθαι, χρόνον μὲν οὖν πολὺν ἐκαρτέ | ρουν σε προσδεχόμενος, ...

... to Zenon greetings. You do well if you are in good health. I also am well. You know that you left me in Syria with Krotos and I did everything that was **ordered** in regard to the camels and you found no fault with me. But though you **gave orders** to give me wages/provisions, what you **ordered** he did not give me any [of it]. When then, though I asked him often to give me what you **ordered**, Krotos did not give me anything but **told** me to leave off, I held on for a long time waiting for you, ...

Examples of προστάσσω as well as συντάσσω, all for Zenon's action without much distinction between them. κελεύω, as in 5), is for the person cast as the bad guy.

Let us draw our conclusions for the LXX. If nothing else, we have a clear explanation why the somewhat unexpected word συντάσσω makes such a strong showing in the Pentateuch: it was a standard word in Ptolemaic Egypt in the time of the translators.

προστάσσω needs little comment: it is one of the staple formal words, but less frequently used than συντάσσω in the Pentateuch just as in contemporary sources.

As to ἐντέλλομαι, while the contemporary evidence confirms that it is alive and well, the high frequency in the Pentateuch (156, as against 22 in papyri) calls for explanation. One reason can certainly be discerned. This verb is often (26 times) joined with ἐντολή, giving a neat etymological combination that matches the Hebrew (צוה ... מצוה). Most of these occur in one book (Deuteronomy), which also has a very large proportion of all the examples (85). Personal taste may well come into it: this translator, like the translator of Genesis, strongly prefers ἐντέλλομαι to συντάσσω.[20]

Finally, κελεύω. The total absence remains a little surprising, but my conclusion is that it was just not suitable in tone. Formal-sounding words were felt more appropriate in the dignified contexts the translators were dealing with throughout the Pentateuch. They availed themselves of those in use, notably συντάσσω, the characteristic word of Ptolemaic officialdom and business.

This is merely a specimen of what the documentary evidence still has to offer for illuminating the LXX. Further follow-up could certainly be done even on these words. There is a need for such work to continue in order to place LXX lexicography on as sound a footing as possible, especially as translation and commentary work on the LXX gathers pace and calls for more refined understanding of the vocabulary. Finding the best way to collect (and store) the material systematically is the challenge for the coming generation of LXX scholars.

---

[20] Distribution in Pent.: ἐντέλλομαι: Gen 20, Exod 19, Lev 16, Num 19, Deut 85: total 156. συντάσσω: Gen 2, Exod 39, Lev 12, Num 26, Deut 2: total 82.

Bibliography

Anz, H. *Subsidia ad cognoscendum graecorum sermonem vulgarem e Pentateuchi versione alexandrina repetita.* Diss. Phil. Halenses, 12.2. Halle: 1894.

Buck, Carl Darling. *A Dictionary of Selected Synonyms in the Principal Indo-European Languages.* Chicago: University of Chicago Press, 1949.

Dorival, Gilles, Marguerite Harl and Olivier Munnich. *La Bible grecque des Septante: du judaïsme hellénistique au christianisme ancien.* Paris: Éditions du Cerf, 1988.

Dorival, Gilles, *et al. La Bible d'Alexandrie: Les Nombres.* Paris: Éditions du Cerf, 1994.

Dorival, Gilles, and Olivier Munnich, eds. Κατὰ τοὺς ο΄: *Selon les Septante. Trente études sur la Bible grecque des Septante en hommage à Marguerite Harl.* Paris: Les Éditions du Cerf, 1995.

Harl, Marguerite. *La Bible d'Alexandrie: La Genèse.* Paris: Éditions du Cerf, 1986.

Jobes, Karen H., and Moisés Silva. *Invitation to the Septuagint.* Grand Rapids: Baker Academic, 2000.

Le Boulluec, Alain, and Pierre Sandevoir. *La Bible d'Alexandrie: L'Exode.* Paris: Éditions du Cerf, 1989.

Lee, J. A. L. *A Lexical Study of the Septuagint Version of the Pentateuch.* Septuagint and Cognate Studies, 14. Chico, CA: Scholars Press, 1983.

Lust, J., E. Eynikel, and K. Hauspie. *A Greek-English Lexicon of the Septuagint.* 2 vols. Stuttgart: Deutsche Bibelgesellschaft, 1992–96.

Louw, Johannes P., and Eugene A. Nida, *et al. Greek-English Lexicon of the New Testament Based on Semantic Domains.* 2 vols. New York: United Bible Societies, 1988.

Muraoka, T. *A Greek-English Lexicon of the Septuagint (Twelve Prophets).* Louvain: Peeters, 1993.

———. ed. *Melbourne Symposium on Septuagint Lexicography.* Septuagint and Cognate Studies, 28. Atlanta: Scholars Press, 1990.

Pelletier, A. "Le vocabulaire du commandement dans le Pentateuque des LXX et dans le Nouveau Testament." *RSR* 41 (1953): 519–24.

———. "L'autorité divine d'après le Pentateuque grec." *VT* 32 (1982): 236–42.

Schmidt, J. H. H. *Synonymik der griechischen Sprache.* 4 vols. Leipzig: Teubner, 1876–86.

Wevers, John W. *Notes on the Greek Text of Numbers.* Atlanta: Scholars Press, 1998.

CONTEXT SENSITIVE TRANSLATION AND
PARATAXIS IN BIBLICAL NARRATIVE

FRANK H. POLAK

לאוהב אמונה אין מחיר ואין משקל לטובתו
φίλου πιστοῦ οὐκ ἔστιν ἀντάλλαγμα
καὶ οὐκ ἔστιν σταθμὸς τῆς καλλονῆς αὐτοῦ

Sirach 6:15

One of the characteristic problems in the rendering of biblical Hebrew into Greek is the treatment of the clause connection. In biblical Hebrew this connection is often expressed, syndetically, by the copula, in a variety of functions, e.g., as *wāw* consecutive or *wāw* conjunctive, but coordination can also be indicated by an asyndetic junction, implicitly suggesting the sequence in context.

The various ways in which these connections are treated in the Septuagint have been analyzed by Aejmelaeus, who points to the standard rendering of the copula by the common connective καί, the less mechanical rendering by the postpositive particle δέ or other particles (e.g., οὖν), and various participle constructions that make use of morpho-syntactic features of the Greek which are far less developed in biblical Hebrew.[1] Syndetic junctures are also used at places where the MT presents an asyndetic connection. Wevers often notes the contextual use of δέ to suggest contrast with the previous pericope or to underline the change of subject, whereas Harl points out that it is frequently employed to indicate the paragraph opening.[2]

---

[1] A. Aejmelaeus, *Parataxis in the Septuagint: A Study of the Renderings of the Hebrew Coordinate Clauses in the Greek Pentateuch* (AASF, DHL 11; Helsinki: Suomalainen Tiedeakatemia, 1982).

[2] J. W. Wevers, *Notes on the Greek Text of Genesis* (SBLSCS 35; Scholars Press: Atlanta GA, 1993), 1, 53, 57, 60, 61, 65 (on Gen 1:2; 4:1, 2, 5, 9b, 16, 25 respectively); M. Harl, *La Genèse* (La Bible d'Alexandrie 1; Paris: Éditions du Cerf, 1986), 71.

The point of departure for the present discussion is the insight that the connection between clauses and sentences pertains to a broad context beyond the single clause or sentence.[3] Since the clauses or sentences thus connected constitute a contextual system, the preferable framework for a discussion of parataxis is that of discourse, viewed as the utterance in its entirety, beyond the sentence boundary.[4]

To this purpose parataxis is defined as the multifaceted connection between clauses by a simple copula (in Hebrew *wāw*; in Septuagintal Greek mainly καί or δέ) or by asyndetic junction.[5] In both cases the logical relationship between the clauses must be inferred from the context (and, in spoken discourse, also from intonation and body language).[6]

---

[3] Aejmelaeus (*Parataxis in the Septuagint*, 30) is aware of the importance of the "wide segmentation" but limits it to the connection between two clauses or sentences. However, in a later discussion, she points to "the translator's ability to handle larger units of text:" A. Aejmelaeus, "The Significance of Clause Connectors in the Syntactical and Translation-Technical Study of the Septuagint," *On the Trail of the Septuagint* (Kampen; Kok Pharos, 1993), 49–64, esp. p. 57.

[4] Numerous definitions of discourse are discussed by D. Schiffrin, *Approaches to Discourse* (Oxford: Blackwell, 1994), 20–43; see also A. Jaworski and N. Coupland, "Introduction: Perspectives on Discourse Analysis," in *The Discourse Reader* (ed. A. Jaworski and N. Coupland; London; Routledge, 1999), 1–3, 12–14; D. A. Dawson, *Text-Linguistics and Biblical Hebrew* (JSOTSup 177; Sheffield: Sheffield Academic Press, 1994), 13–15; K. E. Lowery, "The Theoretical Foundations of Hebrew Discourse Grammar," *Discourse Analysis of Biblical Literature. What it is and what it offers* (ed. W. R. Bodine; SBLSS; Atlanta GA: Scholars Press, 1995), 103–30. Ultimately Schiffrin (*Approaches to Discourse*, 39–42) adopts the general definition of discourse as "utterance," which already was preferred by J. E. Grimes, *The Thread of Discourse* (Ianua Linguarum, Series Minor 207; The Hague: Mouton, 1975), 21–25, 30–32. Thus, a single cry, e.g., "Wow," also is defined as discourse. Grimes (*Thread of Discourse*, 21) regards discourse as primitive term, to be circumscribed as a verbal unit of behavior (a verbal "behavioreme"). The basic point is that a person expresses his intentions in a complete utterance rather than in isolated sentences. Hence, the connective is related to discourse structure rather than to the connection between single clauses.

[5] The problems surrounding the definition of parataxis have been discussed by Aejmelaeus, *Parataxis in the Septuagint*, 2–7, 10–11; and in particular by A. Rynell, *Parataxis and Hypotaxis as a Criterion of Syntax and Style, especially in Old English Poetry* (Lunds Universitets Årsskrift. N F. Avd. 1. Bd. 48,3; Lund: Gleerup, 1952), 3–18. This definition implies, that "non-introduced subordinate clauses" represent parataxis ("it seems, he won't come").

[6] See H. Isenberg, "Überlegungen zur Texttheorie," *Lektürekolleg zur Textlinguistik* (ed. W. Kallmeyer et al.; 2 vols.; Frankfurt: Athenäum Fischer, 1974), 2.191–212; M. Shiro, "Inferences in Discourse Comprehension," *Advances in Written Discourse Analysis* (ed. M. Coulthard; London: Routledge, 1994), 167–78. Such connectors as אך, ועתה and οὖν do indicate the logic of the connection.

However, a series of clauses or sentences in parataxis is far more differentiated than this description would suggest. The backbone of biblical Hebrew narrative is the story line that is dominated by the sequence of event clauses.[7] Thus we may define the "narrative framework" as a text describing a series of actions and events, opened by and intermingled with expository notes (or other statements to introduce the main participants in the action, as well as salient details concerning the situation in general) and narrator's comments.[8] The series of events is for the most part represented by a sequence of clauses with the preterite (imperfect consecutive) as predicate ("*wayyiqtol* clause"), and is thus characterized as "action chain" (or "story line"). The action chain may include dialogue, that is to say, an exchange (or a series of exchanges) between two parties of which the one is the initiator, and the other the addressee/respondent. Within the action chain we encounter embedded details concerning the situation, that is to say, circumstantial clauses (e.g., והוא עמד עליהם תחת העץ, Gen 18:8b), references to the past ("*qātal*" as plusquamperfectum), or clauses that are contrasted with a *wayyiqtol* clause (ולחשך קרא לילה).[9]

Thus the narrative text includes various different sections, part of them representing distinctive types of discourse, and part of them related to different action stages. These subunits are set off one from another by various morpho-syntactic features, such as the use of the tenses, or the different connectors. In discourse, such features serve

---

[7] A. Niccacci, *The Syntax of the Verb in Classical Hebrew Prose* (JSOTSup 86; Sheffield: Sheffield Academic Press, 1990); R. E. Longacre, *Joseph: A Story of Divine Providence. A Text Theoretical and Textlinguistic Analysis of Genesis 37 and 39–48* (Winona Lake, Ind.: Eisenbrauns, 1989), 64–118.

[8] For this description of the narrative framework see W. Labov, *Language in the Inner City: Studies in the Black English Vernacular* (Philadelphia: University of Pennsylvania Press, 1972), 359–71, 375–78; R. E. Longacre, *The Grammar of Discourse.* (2nd ed.; New York: Plenum Press, 1996), 16–23, 29–31; Longacre, *Joseph*, 59–82.

[9] The present discussion follows the system of Niccacci and Longacre in focusing on the action chain. But unlike those systems the present proposal does not speak of a secondary story-line for static information or as background. The difference between ויקרא אלהים לאור יום and ולחשך קרא לילה is the thematization of חשך in opposition to יום. In the exposition and circumstantial clauses the order w-(pro)noun phrase—verb (mostly *qātal*) is also dependent on topicalization of the (pro)noun phrase by fronting. In this respect the present discussion is largely in agreement with the approach of M. Eskhult, *Studies in Verbal Aspect and Narrative Technique in Biblical Hebrew Prose* (Acta Universitatis Upsaliensis: Studia Semitica Upsaliensia 12; Uppsala and Stockholm: Almqvist & Amsell, 1990), 45–57, 102.

the articulation of the text, underlining the linkage between the paragraphs of which the text consists and their internal structure. Sicking describes the usage of δέ and καί in Lysias' speeches as: "articulating the discourse in question and marking the relation between the successive sections within the narrower or wider context of which they form part."[10]

The structuring of subunits may be illustrated by means of the Moses tale (Exod 2:11–25). The *setting* is introduced by the opening verse: "Some time after that, when Moses had grown up, he went out to his kinsfolk" (Exod 2:11, NJPS).[11] After the episode of the killing of the Egyptian (vv. 11b-14: action chain with dialogue), the narrator opens the next section with a *back reference* "Now when Pharaoh heard this thing, he sought to slay Moses" (v. 15a; linkage), and continues to tell the story of Moses' flight (v. 15b: "but Moses fled from Pharaoh. He arrived in the land of Midian, and sat down beside a well"). The opening of the next section takes this note up by the introduction of "the priest of Midian" as having "seven daughters" who "came to draw water" at the well. The narrator may also *focus* on a known person, when he wishes to single him out. The story of the revelation to Moses opens with a note on the hero who is thus drawn into focus: "Now Moses was keeping the flock of Jethro his father-in-law, the priest of Midian" (3:1). The mention of the "flock of Jethro his father-in-law, the priest of Midian" refers back to previous information (linkage). *The articulation of the information flow by back reference, by pointing to new information, and by focusing on a particular character or situation is called "staging."*[12] The paratactic constructions so typical for biblical Hebrew narrative, then, pertain to staging as a discourse phenomenon rather than to syntactic structure. In consequence, the various ways in which these constructions are treated by the LXX also relate to staging.[13]

---

[10] C. M. J. Sicking, "Devices for Text Articulation in Lysias I and XII," in *Two Studies in Attic Particle Usage* (ed. Sicking and J. M. van Ophuizen; Mnemosyne Supplementum 129; Leiden; E. J. Brill, 1993), 3–50, esp. p. 45.

[11] R. E. Longacre, "Discourse Perspective on the Hebrew Verb: Affirmation and Restatement," *Linguistics and Biblical Hebrew* (ed. W. R. Bodine; Winona Lake, Ind.: Eisenbrauns, 1992), 177–87, esp. 178–80; idem, *Joseph*, 83–96.

[12] G. Brown and G. Yule, *Discourse Analysis* (Cambridge: Cambridge University Press, 1983), 133–44; Grimes, *The Thread of Discourse*, 337–48; M. Kroeken, "Thematic Linkage in Nambiquara Narrative," apud Grimes, ibidem, 361–68.

[13] On staging in Greek see Sicking, "Devices for Text Articulation," 3–50;

Is the staging of the Hebrew text taken into account in the Greek version? Some of the data suggest that in a few books that is indeed the case. In the LXX on Genesis and Exodus one can find a number of indications that the Greek translator positively endeavors to utilize the rich possibilities which the Greek language offers him in order to do justice to the particularities of the Hebrew text. For instance, the circumstantial clause that was quoted above (Gen 18:8b והוא עמד עליהם תחת העץ), is rendered as αὐτὸς δὲ παρειστήκει αὐτοῖς ὑπὸ τὸ δένδρον,[14] a construction in which the particle δέ sets the pronominal subject off from the preceding sequence,[15] and thus highlights its position (topicalization).[16] In the opening verse the clause והוא ישב פתח האהל כחם היום is rendered as a genitive absolute,[17] καθημένου αὐτοῦ ἐπὶ τῆς θύρας τῆς σκηνῆς αὐτοῦ μεσημβρίας. These details give

---

A. Rijksbaron, "Introduction," *New Approaches to Greek Particles* (ed. A. Rijksbaron; Amsterdam: Gieben, 1997), 3.

[14] The use of the tenses in Gen 18:8b is matched by *v.* 2: τρεῖς ἄνδρες εἱστήκεισαν ἐπάνω αὐτοῦ/עליו אנשים נצבים שלשה; see also 28:13; 40:3; 45:1. The use of δέ in the opening of a circumstantial clause is matched by, e.g., Gen 12:4, 6; 13:7; 14:13, 18.

[15] A. Rijksbaron analyzes δέ as "setting off," and rendering "distinct," thus indicating topicalization, and in particular the introduction of new topics or themes: "Adverb or Connector? The case of καί ... δέ," in *New Approaches to Greek Particles*, 187–208, especially p. 191, n. 11–12, 193–4. On the articulation of marriage agreements see note 39 below. The discourse orientation gives new sense to the view of δέ as a "weak intensifier" and as "underlining" as proposed by J. Humbert, *Syntaxe Grecque* (3e Edition, Paris; Klincksieck; 1960), 398–99; J. D. Denniston speaks of the continuum between "pure connection" and "opposition,"' and in particular "weak contrast" (*The Greek Particles* 2nd ed.; Oxford: Clarendon Press, 1954], 163). The approach adopted by Aejmelaeus (*Parataxis in the Septuagint*, 34–36) is basically similar to Denniston's, while Harl's view (see note 2 above) is closer to that of discourse analysis.

[16] Topicalization is defined as the highlighting ("marking") of the theme, that is, the subject or the psychological subject. The theme can be highlighted by the *casus pendens* (החכם) in: בראשו עיניו החכם), or the main word of the fronted object/modifier, e.g., נתנך and עפר in Gen 3:14: חייך ימי כל האכל ועפר תלך נתנך על. For this definition see M. A. K. Halliday, "Theme and Information in the English Clause," *Halliday: System and Function in Language* (ed. G. Kress; London: Oxford University Press, 1976), 174–88, esp. pp. 179–84; Halliday's approach has been carried further by P. H. Fries, "On Theme, Rheme and Discourse Goals," *Written Discourse Analysis*, 229–49. For biblical Hebrew see B. L. Bandstra, "Word Order and Emphasis in Biblical Hebrew Narrative: Syntactic Observations on Genesis 22 from a Discourse Perspective," *Linguistics and Biblical Hebrew*, 109–123. Unlike in English and other modern European languages, in biblical Hebrew the fronting of the pronominal subject is a way of highlighting, since it is redundant in the verbal clause.

[17] The use of the genitive absolute where a *participium coniunctum* would be expected is not uncommon in Classical Greek; see Humbert, *Syntaxe Grecque*, 130–31; on Exod 2:10 see p. 533 below.

us some impression of the differentiation made possible by the syntactic repertoire of the Greek.

The intriguing staging of the birth tale of Moses is demonstrated by the introduction of Moses' parents (Exod 2:1):[18]

ἦν δέ τις ἐκ τῆς φυλῆς λευί ὃς ἔλαβεν τῶν θυγατέρων λευὶ καὶ ἔσχεν αὐτήν

The opening clause introduces the initiator of the action, the anonymous Levite ("someone"). The formulation ἦν δέ is typical for introductory exposition and for highlighted description, e.g.,[19]

Job 42:12 ὁ δὲ κύριος εὐλόγησεν τὰ ἔσχατα ἰὼβ ἢ τὰ ἔμπροσθεν
ἦν δὲ τὰ κτήνη αὐτοῦ πρόβατα μύρια τετρακισχίλια.

וה' ברך את אחרית איוב מראשתו ויהי לו ארבעה עשר אלף צאן.

2 Macc 1:24 ἦν δὲ ἡ προσευχὴ τὸν τρόπον ἔχουσα τοῦτον.
2 Macc 3:14 ταξάμενος δὲ ἡμέραν εἰσῄει τὴν περὶ τούτων ἐπίσκεψιν οἰκονομήσων
ἦν δὲ οὐ μικρὰ καθ᾽ ὅλην τὴν πόλιν ἀγωνία.

Thus the narrative opens with a typical exposition that is set off from the previous pericopes by δέ,[20] a use which is considered characteristic for Greek narrative and legal prose.[21] This opening could reflect a Hebrew variant such as ויהי איש מבית לוי ויקח את בת לוי. However, the use of the relative particle (ὃς ἔλαβεν) with a partitive genitive (τῶν θυγατέρων Λευί) strongly suggests free initiative on the part of the translator.

The opening of the tale in the MT also introduces man and wife as the two participants in the action (וילך איש מבית לוי ויקח את בת לוי). In the style of ancient Hebrew narrative the introduction of the par-

---

[18] On this verse see J. W. Wevers, *Notes on the Greek Text of Exodus* (SBLSCS 30; Scholars Press: Atlanta GA, 1990), 12.

[19] Or, with fronted subject; ἀβράμ δὲ ἦν πλούσιος σφόδρα κτήνεσιν (Gen 13:2: ואברם כבד מאד במקנה); Wevers (*Notes Genesis*, 175) remarks that in this verse δέ is used in spite of the fact that there is no subject change.

[20] Duly recognized by M. Harl, *La Genèse* (La Bible d'Alexandrie 1; Paris: Éditions du Cerf, 1986), 71; A. le Boulluec et P. Sandevoir, *L'Exode* (La Bible d'Alexandrie 2; Paris: Éditions du Cerf, 1989), 80. So also, e.g., Exod 2:11, 16, and cf, e.g., Hdt. I 23, 25, 26; Plato, Prot. 310 A, B, 315 B, C; Xenophon Ephesiacus, *Ephesiaca* A, I 3,4; II 2.

[21] The use of δέ to articulate a new section opening is discussed by Sicking, "Devices for Text Articulation," 11–13. On the indication of topic shifts by δέ see Rijksbaron, "Adverb or Connector," 196–99; see also Denniston, *Greek Particles*, 170–71; M. E. Thrall, *Greek Particles in the New Testament* (Leiden; E. J. Brill, 1962), 63–64, whose conclusions should be reviewed in the light of discourse analysis.

ticipants is a way to indicate the formal opening of the action sequence.[22] The Greek translator has used his own formulation in order to present the expository information more clearly.

In the LXX, the next stages of the narrative continue with the birth of a baby:

Exod 2:2a καὶ ἐν γαστρὶ ἔλαβεν καὶ ἔτεκεν ἄρσεν.

According to the findings of Greek stylistics καί indicates direct connection with the previous sequence.[23] Thus, in the translator's perspective the present event forms the straight continuation of the previous actions, and in particular of the marital act καὶ ἔσχεν αὐτήν. In the Hebrew text the formal indication of the subject (הָאִשָּׁה) highlights the particular position of the mother, and accentuates thereby a new stage, whereas the Greek text indicates continuity.

In the LXX, the new stage is once again opened with δέ:

2:2b ἰδόντες δὲ αὐτὸ ἀστεῖον ἐσκέπασαν αὐτὸ μῆνας τρεῖς.

This action introduces a new stage in the sequence, since both parents are now acting together. The differentiation is accentuated by the participle construction that centers on the new circumstances, highlighted by δέ. In the MT, on the other hand, this action is represented as the continuation of the previous one (וַתֵּרֶא אֹתוֹ כִּי טוֹב הוּא), all the more so as the mother is represented as the initiator.

In the Greek, a third stage is marked by the note ἐπεὶ δὲ οὐκ ἠδύναντο αὐτὸ ἔτι κρύπτειν, ἔλαβεν ἡ μήτηρ αὐτοῦ θῖβιν (v. 3a). Now the baby's mother has to prepare a basket to hold him before placing him among the reeds, while his sister watches over him: καὶ κατέχρισεν αὐτὴν ἀσφαλτοπίσσῃ καὶ ἐνέβαλεν τὸ παιδίον εἰς αὐτὴν καὶ ἔθηκεν αὐτὴν εἰς τὸ ἕλος παρὰ τὸν ποταμόν. καὶ κατεσκόπευεν ἡ ἀδελφὴ αὐτοῦ μακρόθεν μαθεῖν τί τὸ ἀποβησόμενον αὐτῷ (v. 3b–4). The use of καί characterizes the entire episode as a concatenated string of actions, which continues the topicalized opening ἐπεὶ δὲ οὐκ ἠδύναντο. From

---

[22] Longacre, *Joseph*, 143–74, 162–63; L. J. de Regt, *Participants in Old Testament Texts and the Translator* (Assen: Van Gorcum, 1999), 2–5, 13–20.

[23] Sicking ("Devices for Text Articulation," 14) mentions the use of καί to "include several predicates within a context sharing the same subject, or at least topic"; see also Rijksbaron, "Adverb or Connector," 191, n. 11; A. Carnoy, *Manuel de Linguistique Grecque* (Louvain: Éditions Universitas; Paris: Champion, 1924), 334–35; Humbert, *Syntaxe Grecque*, 412–13.

a syntactic point of view this construction differs from that of the
MT, where this stage opens with a stative clause ולא יכלה עוד הצפינו.
But with regard to narrative organization both constructions serve
to indicate a new stage. Thus the translator uses different morpho-
syntactic means to suggest the same staging as found in the MT.

A new stage is opened by the arrival of Pharaoh's daughter:

2:5 κατέβη δὲ ἡ θυγάτηρ φαραὼ λούσασθαι ἐπὶ τὸν ποταμόν καὶ αἱ
ἅβραι αὐτῆς παρεπορεύοντο παρὰ τὸν ποταμόν καὶ ἰδοῦσα τὴν θῖβιν
ἐν τῷ ἕλει ἀποστείλασα τὴν ἅβραν ἀνείλατο αὐτήν.

Once again the stage is opened by a δέ clause,[24] whereas the ensuing sequence, including the circumstantial description,[25] is connected
by καί. In the MT the staging is indicated by the mention of Pharaoh's
daughter, which refers to a new participant, all the more so as a
circumstantial clause describes part of the scene. The Hebrew narrator, then, indicates the setting in a way which, from a discourse
point of view, marks a new stage in the action sequence.

In the LXX the sight of the crying baby brings a decisive change
as marked by a participle construction that is highlighted by δέ:

2:6 ἀνοίξασα δὲ ὁρᾷ παιδίον κλαῖον ἐν τῇ θίβει.

In this case the staging of the LXX differs from that suggested by
the MT for in the latter this action is no more than a continuation
of the preceding one. The LXX continues to represent the ensuing
dialogue with the baby's sister as the direct continuation of this
development:[26]

2:7 καὶ εἶπεν ἡ ἀδελφὴ αὐτοῦ τῇ θυγατρὶ φαραὼ θέλεις καλέσω σοι
γυναῖκα τροφεύουσαν ἐκ τῶν ἐβραίων καὶ θηλάσει σοι τὸ παιδίον.

Such construction fits the internal logic of the narrative since both
the representation of the viewpoint of the princess and the exchange
with the sister deal with the boy's fate. Though formally similar to

---

[24] Wevers (*Notes Exodus*, 14) points to the change in subject.

[25] It is a notable detail that the circumstantial clause is rendered by an imper-
fect. The sensitivity to tense usage in Biblical Greek has been described by A.
Niccacci, "Dall'aoristo all'imperfetto o dal primo piano allo sfondo," *Liber Annuus.
Studium Biblicum Fransiscanum* 42 (1992), 85–105.

[26] For the use of καί to introduce a logical consequence, see Humbert, *Syntaxe
Grecque* 412–13, 416; cf., e.g., Thuc. I:108, 2; 126, 2. In Exod 3:1 the use of καί
as section opener characterizes the entire pericope as issuing from the preceding
section (2:23–25).

the LXX, the Hebrew phrase ותאמר אחתו אל בת פרעה constitutes itself as opening clause by the very mention of the two participants, and thus indicates a new stage in the action chain.[27]

In the LXX the distinction between the action sequence and the dialogue is indicated by the δέ clause which, as usual in the Greek dialogue mode, introduces the response of Pharaoh's daughter:

2:8a ἡ δὲ εἶπεν αὐτῇ ἡ θυγάτηρ φαραώ πορεύου.

When the sister acts upon this permission, the narrator marks her action by a participle clause that is highlighted once again by δέ:

2:8b ἐλθοῦσα δὲ ἡ νεᾶνις ἐκάλεσεν τὴν μητέρα τοῦ παιδίου.

This use functions to mark the transition from the dialogue exchange to the following action chain.

The same order is followed in the exchange between the princess and the child's mother:

2:9a εἶπεν δὲ πρὸς αὐτὴν ἡ θυγάτηρ φαραώ διατήρησόν μοι τὸ παιδίον τοῦτο καὶ θήλασόν μοι αὐτό ἐγὼ δὲ δώσω σοι τὸν μισθόν.

Upon this invitation the mother takes the child into her care:

2:9b ἔλαβεν δὲ ἡ γυνὴ τὸ παιδίον καὶ ἐθήλαζεν αὐτό.

When the mother returns the child to Pharaoh's daughter, this stage is once again indicated by a participle construction that is accentuated by δέ:

2:10a ἁδρυνθέντος δὲ τοῦ παιδίου[28] εἰσήγαγεν αὐτὸ πρὸς τὴν θυγατέρα φαραώ καὶ ἐγενήθη αὐτῇ εἰς υἱόν.

This construction fits the Hebrew, in which the new development is accentuated by the mention of the child as subject (ויגדל הילד). The introduction of the adoption by καί indicates a continuity which in the Hebrew is suggested by the preterite with the implicit subject (ויהי לה לבן).

The name giving ceremony is the simple continuation of the action sequence in the Hebrew (but with implicit change of subject: ותקרא שמו משה). However, the Greek highlights this ceremony with the introductory δέ, which sets this action off from the preceding sequence:[29]

---

[27] On the approach of Longacre and De Regt see note 22 above.

[28] On the genitive absolute see note 17 above.

[29] In Wevers' view (*Notes Exodus*, 16) δέ indicates the change of subject.

2:10b ἐπωνόμασεν δὲ τὸ ὄνομα αὐτοῦ μωυσῆν λέγουσα ἐκ τοῦ ὕδατος
αὐτὸν ἀνειλόμην.

Thus the ceremony is accorded a place of its own in the narrative.

In this tale, then, judicious use of δέ and the *participium coniunctum*
enables the translator to create a differentiated structure in which
various stages of the action sequence, dialogue, exposition, and setting are clearly set off each from another.

To which extent is this differentiation comparable with the staging of the Hebrew text (according to the MT),[30] and in how far is it
an independent construction on the part of the translator? The present text suggests a number of possibilities:

a) In a number of cases the LXX seems to reflect the same sense
of discourse order as the MT, though in a different way (vv. 1, 3, 5,
9, 10a). Within the dialogue the LXX uses its own means in order
to reflect the speakers' roles.[31]

b) In some cases the LXX indicates a new stage where the MT suggests continuation (v. 2b, 6, 10b).

c) New stages in the MT which the LXX indicates as continuation
of the previous stage, are found in v. 2, 7.

Additional attempts of the LXX to indicate differentiated staging
may be observed, for example, in the narrative of Moses' flight to
Sinai (vv. 11–15), or his marriage (vv. 16–22), although the Greek does
not always employ the same morpho-syntactic means as the MT.[32]

In the book of Genesis, where we have already referred to the
scene at Mamre, we can point to the opening of the tale of Sarai
and Hagar according to the LXX (Gen 16:1):

σάρα δὲ ἡ γυνὴ ἀβρὰμ οὐκ ἔτικτεν αὐτῷ.
ἦν δὲ αὐτῇ παιδίσκη αἰγυπτία ᾗ ὄνομα ἀγάρ.

Here the particle δέ sets the subject, Sarai, off from the preceding
context, and thus marks her present role.[33] In the MT the topical-

---

[30] The restriction of the comparison to the MT is problematic, since the text of
4QExod[b] clearly indicates the existence of a Hebrew text that is closer to the LXX
than the MT. However, this scroll does not contain any details that are pertinent
to the kind of staging represented by the LXX.

[31] So also, e.g., Exod 4:1–3.

[32] But the dialogue episode of Exod 5:1–5 does not indicate the distinct stages
(including change of subject in v. 2, 3, 4), although the new stages in vv. 6 and
10 are underlined by δέ.

[33] A similar structure is noted in 16:7.

ization of Sarai is indicated by the *qāṭal* clause with fronted subject (וְשָׂרַי אֵשֶׁת אַבְרָם לֹא יָלְדָה לוֹ), and the information concerning Hagar is dependent on this clause (וְלָהּ שִׁפְחָה מִצְרִית). The LXX, however, uses δέ to introduce the information concerning Hagar, thus dividing the information into a number of distinct stages.

The particle δέ is used again in the opening of the action chain following the exposition: εἶπεν δὲ σάρα πρὸς ἀβράμ, as well as in the description of Abram's reaction: ὑπήκουσεν δὲ ἀβρὰμ τῆς φωνῆς σάρας. Thus the diverse stages of the action are set off each from another. In the Hebrew a similar staging is suggested by explicit mentioning the participants even though their identity is already well-known (וַיִּשְׁמַע אַבְרָם לְקוֹל שָׂרָי; וַתֹּאמֶר שָׂרַי אֶל אַבְרָם).[34] However, these references could also indicate the authority of the participants.[35]

In the LXX the next stages are introduced by καί:

> 16:3–4 καὶ λαβοῦσα σάρα ἡ γυνὴ ἀβρὰμ ἀγὰρ τὴν αἰγυπτίαν . . . καὶ[36] ἔδωκεν αὐτὴν ἀβρὰμ τῷ ἀνδρὶ αὐτῆς αὐτῷ γυναῖκα (v. 4) καὶ εἰσῆλθεν πρὸς ἀγάρ.

These actions, then, are represented as the logical consequence of the preceding confrontation. Some internal differentiation is achieved by the use of the participle (καὶ λαβοῦσα σάρα), whereas in the Hebrew the distinction between the action chain and the exchange is suggested by the specific indication of the participants. However, in the MT the clause וַיָּבֹא אֶל הָגָר (v. 4) does not specify the subject, but depends on the previous clause for this information, thus suggesting continuity of action. In the LXX this effect is underlined by the use of καί. With regard to discourse structure, then, the MT and the LXX reflect the same perspective.

In the LXX δέ indicates a new stage in Sarai's complaint to Abram:

> 16:5 εἶπεν δὲ σάρα πρὸς ἀβρὰμ ἀδικοῦμαι ἐκ σοῦ . . .

The use of δέ is hardly surprising considering that this complaint opens an exchange between two parties. In the MT staging is indicated

---

[34] On the approach of Longacre and De Regt see note 22 above.

[35] The status of initiator and respondent is one of the main parameters in the indication of the parties in dialogue, according to F. Polak, "On Dialogue and Speaker Status in the Scroll of Ruth," *Beit Mikra* 46 (2001), 193–208 (Hebrew, with English Summary, p. 288).

[36] On the apodotic use of καί see Wevers, *Notes Genesis*, 218; Aejmelaeus, *Parataxis in the Septuagint*, 126–33.

by the mention of Sarai as initiator: ותאמר שרי אל אברם, balanced by the mention of the respondent, Abram: ויאמר אברם אל שרי (v. 6). Accordingly the Greek translator introduces Abram's response in the same way:

16:6 εἶπεν δὲ ἀβρὰμ πρὸς σάραν ἰδοὺ ἡ παιδίσκη σου ἐν ταῖς χερσίν σου χρῶ αὐτῇ ὡς ἄν σοι ἀρεστὸν ᾖ.

The ensuing clauses are introduced by καί, thus marking them as belonging to the same stage of the narrative: καὶ ἐκάκωσεν αὐτὴν σάρα, with the logical consequence καὶ ἀπέδρα ἀπὸ προσώπου αὐτῆς. The same structure is suggested by the мт, since Sarai is mentioned by name, while Hagar is not: ותענה שרי ותברח מפניה. In this case, specific mention of the one but not the other party reflects their relative authority, since Sarai is able to carry out her intentions, whereas Hagar remains powerless.

The method of "differentiated staging" is not followed in all books. In such narratives as the Balaam tale (for instance, Numbers 22), καί is the predominant clause connector. In the action sequence δέ is only used to indicate surprising developments (22:31: ἀπεκάλυψεν δὲ ὁ θεὸς τοὺς ὀφθαλμοὺς βαλαάμ) or response (v. 30: ὁ δὲ εἶπεν οὐχί). Within the dialogue it is used, with μέν, to indicate contrast (v. 33; σὲ μὲν ἀπέκτεινα ἐκείνην δὲ περιεποιησάμην; so also 23:13, 15). On the other hand, the *participium coniunctum* is frequently used to render inceptive verbs (Num 22:1, 2, 13, 14; 23:7, 18; 24:1, 25 and passim).

Were the translators of books like Genesis aware from the outset of the staging of the Hebrew text and the possibilities to reflect it by the differentiation between δέ and καί? It seems that in some of the opening tales in Genesis the translator limits the use of δέ to specific constructions, such as expository clauses with fronted subject, contrastive clauses, the alternation of speaker and respondent,[37] and surprising developments.[38] The dominant connector is καί, which

---

[37] For the fronted subject cf. Gen 1:2 ἡ δὲ γῆ ἦν ἀόρατος καὶ ἀκατασκεύαστος, rendering והארץ היתה תהו ובהו; Gen 2:6 πηγὴ δὲ ἀνέβαινεν ἐκ τῆς γῆς (cf. 2:12, 14; 3:1; 4:1, 2). In 2:20; 3:17, 4:5 one notes the topicalization of the fronted indirect object. For the indication of contrast see 2:17, 3:3, 4:7 (in dialogue); 2:20, 3:17, 4:5 (in the action chain); for the alternation of speaker and respondent see 4:9.

[38] For the highlighting of surprising developments see Gen 4:16; 9:24. Wevers (*Notes Genesis*, 218) explains the example in 4:16 as a change of subject, which in the preceding verses, however, is not indicated by δέ (vv. 9a, 10, 13, 15).

is used even for contrastive clauses and indications of new developments, e.g.,

> Gen 2:7 καὶ ἔπλασεν ὁ θεὸς τὸν ἄνθρωπον χοῦν ἀπὸ τῆς γῆς καὶ ἐνεφύσησεν εἰς τὸ πρόσωπον αὐτοῦ πνοὴν ζωῆς καὶ ἐγένετο ὁ ἄνθρωπος εἰς ψυχὴν ζῶσαν.
> 4:3–4 καὶ ἐγένετο μεθ' ἡμέρας ἤνεγκεν κάιν ἀπὸ τῶν καρπῶν τῆς γῆς θυσίαν τῳ κυρίῳ. καὶ ἄβελ ἤνεγκεν καὶ αὐτὸς ἀπὸ τῶν πρωτοτόκων τῶν προβάτων αὐτοῦ.

In cases of this type it is hardly likely that the translator intended to represent these actions as the logical consequence of the preceding events. The assumption that the use of δέ was restricted in the same way as evidenced by such narratives as the Balaam tale, seems far more plausible. It is only in the lists that the use of this particle becomes frequent, probably to indicate the distinct status of the various actors:[39]

> 4:18 ἐγενήθη δὲ τῷ ἐνὼχ γαιδάδ.
> 4:22 σελλὰ δὲ ἔτεκεν καὶ αὐτὴ τὸν θοβέλ.
> 4:23 εἶπεν δὲ λάμεχ ταῖς ἑαυτοῦ γυναιξίν.

On the other hand in the tale of the birth of Seth δέ is used in order to introduce differentiated staging: ἔγνω δὲ ἀδὰμ εὔαν τὴν γυναῖκα αὐτοῦ (4:25, corresponding with the Hebrew וידע אדם עוד את אשתו).[40] It is a notable fact that in this case the new stage in the action sequence is only marked by the indication of both participants, but not by fronting (unlike 4:1). This passage, then, represents the first instance of "differentiated staging" on the part of the translator.

One may infer that in the initial stages of his work the translator probably had only limited notions about the differences between discourse structure in Hebrew and Greek, such as marking the fronted subject of the Hebrew by the use of δέ. Working through different genres and narratives sharpened his sensitivity, so that in the sequel

---

[39] This use of δέ is frequent in agreements from the Ptolemaean and Roman period, e.g., the marriage contract P. Eleph. 1, ll. 4–13; P. Tebt. 104, ll. 13, 16, 23, 27, 30, 32; B. G. U. 11052, ll. 7, 22; quoted according to A. S. Hunt and C. C. Edgar, *Select Papyri* (3 vols.; Loeb; Cambridge MA: Harvard University Press and London: Heinemann, 1932), 1.2–3, 6–8, 10.

[40] Wevers (*Notes Genesis*, 65) speaks of the contrast between this note and the preceding Kain genealogy. Even though the wording of the Greek at 4:25 closely resembles that of 4:1, the fronted subject of the latter passage has not been adopted in our verse. Hence this similarity could hardly explain the use of δέ.

he was able gradually to increase his use of differentiated staging. Thus we encounter such verses as:[41]

Gen 6:2 ἰδόντες δὲ οἱ υἱοὶ τοῦ θεοῦ τὰς θυγατέρας τῶν ἀνθρώπων ὅτι καλαί εἰσιν ἔλαβον ἑαυτοῖς γυναῖκας ἀπὸ πασῶν ὧν ἐξελέξαντο.
6:5–6 ἰδὼν δὲ κύριος ὁ θεὸς ὅτι ἐπληθύνθησαν αἱ κακίαι τῶν ἀνθρώπων ἐπὶ τῆς γῆς ... καὶ ἐνεθυμήθη ὁ θεὸς ὅτι ἐποίησεν τὸν ἄνθρωπον ἐπὶ τῆς γῆς καὶ διενοήθη.
6:10 ἐγέννησεν δὲ νῶε τρεῖς υἱούς τὸν σήμ τὸν χάμ τὸν ἰάφεθ.[42]
6:11 ἐφθάρη δὲ ἡ γῆ ἐναντίον τοῦ θεοῦ καὶ ἐπλήσθη ἡ γῆ ἀδικίας.
7:7 εἰσῆλθεν δὲ νῶε καὶ οἱ υἱοὶ αὐτοῦ καὶ ... εἰς τὴν κιβωτόν ...

Even so the translator still employs the phrase καὶ ἐγένετο in order to match the Hebrew ויהי, e.g.,

7:10 καὶ ἐγένετο μετὰ τὰς ἑπτὰ ἡμέρας καὶ τὸ ὕδωρ τοῦ κατακλυσμοῦ ἐγένετο ἐπὶ τῆς γῆς (ויהי לשבעת הימים ומי המבול היו על הארץ).[43]
12:10 καὶ ἐγένετο λιμὸς ἐπὶ τῆς γῆς καὶ κατέβη ἀβρὰμ εἰς Αἴγυπτον παροικῆσαι ἐκεῖ.

Only in the tale of the sojourn at Pharaoh's court does the translator start to use the phrase ἐγένετο δέ:[44]

12:11 ἐγένετο δὲ ἡνίκα ἤγγισεν ἀβρὰμ εἰσελθεῖν εἰς Αἴγυπτον εἶπεν ἀβρὰμ σάρᾳ τῇ γυναικὶ αὐτοῦ ...
12:14–15 ἐγένετο δὲ ἡνίκα εἰσῆλθεν ἀβρὰμ εἰς αἴγυπτον ἰδόντες οἱ αἰγύπτιοι τὴν γυναῖκα ὅτι καλὴ ἦν σφόδρα καὶ εἶδον αὐτὴν οἱ ἄρχοντες ...

It seems, then, that the translator of Genesis had to acquire considerable experience in translating biblical Hebrew into Hellenistic Greek, before he felt confident enough to try to reflect the staging by the means put at his disposal by Greek syntax. In Exodus, by contrast, differentiated staging is used immediately in the opening verses:[45]

---

[41] In Gen 6:4, 8, 9 the LXX uses this construction for a fronted subject of the MT.
[42] Wevers (*Notes Genesis*, 81) does not detect any special meaning in the use of the particle in 6:10.
[43] So also 8:6, 13; 11:2; 19:17, 29; 22:1; 24:15, 30; and in passages in which היה serves as a copula or predicate: 7:12, 17; 10:19, 30, 11:1 (καὶ ἦν πᾶσα ἡ γῆ χεῖλος ἕν); 12:10, 16; 13:7.
[44] So also 14:1, 19:34, 20:13, 22:20, etc.; and with γίγνομαι as copula or predicate: 17:1; 21:20; 23:1, etc.
[45] Staging is paramount in in Exodus (in particular in chapters 21–23), apart from chs. 35–40, where we note only 35:2; 36:30 (39:23 MT); 39:11 (LXX plus); 40:36–37.

Exod 1:5 ἰωσὴφ δὲ ἦν ἐν αἰγύπτῳ. ἦσαν δὲ πᾶσαι ψυχαὶ ἐξ ιακὼβ πέντε καὶ ἑβδομήκοντα.
1:6 ἐτελεύτησεν δὲ ἰωσὴφ καὶ πάντες οἱ ἀδελφοὶ αὐτοῦ καὶ πᾶσα ἡ γενεὰ ἐκείνη.

We conclude, then, that discourse structure conditions the way in which the LXX uses καί, δέ and the various participle constructions in order to render clauses which in the MT are opened by *wāw*, or which are asyndetically connected to the previous clause. In such books as Genesis and Exodus the translator uses these resources in order to make the organization of the narrative more transparent. This approach develops gradually in the first twelve chapters of Genesis and is in full use in Exodus.

THE TEXTUAL CHARACTER OF MS 106 IN (NUMBERS AND) DEUTERONOMY

John W. Wevers

That *d* and *t* are very closely related, in fact at times hardly distinguishable, is clear throughout the Pentateuch.[1] No separate study of their relations was made for Deuteronomy, but a glance at Apparatus I of the Göttingen Septuaginta of Deuteronomy[2] quickly shows how closely they are related. "Deut" throughout this essay refers to the critical text of this volume. The two groups only rarely attest to different readings, often, though by no means always, joined by *n*, and sometimes by *b* as well.

The two groups are remarkably homogeneous in membership throughout the Pentateuch. The five manuscripts, 44–106–107–125–610, are always classified as *d*, with 370 joining it for Gen 25:5—fin libri. The *t* group is not as consistent. Ms 46 has a *t* text only up to Exod 13:9; mss 74–84–134 always belong to *t*, and 370 does so as well except for Gen 25:5—fin libri where it is *d*. 602 only has the Deut text complete and there it is also *t*, and 799 was clearly *t* up to Gen 36:8; in Deut it was also assigned to *t*, but it could equally validly have been called a codex mixtus.

Though *d t* are difficult to distinguish at times, they do represent distinct texts.

LIST 1: UNIQUE READINGS IN *d*

3:18 om τὴν γῆν; 4:19 αὐτά αυται; 4:41 om πέραν; 9:21 καταλέσας] καὶ κατηναλωσα; 10:4 αὐτάς] ad fin tr; 10:7 comma] (c var) κακειθεν απηραν και παρενεβαλον εις εβρωνα ειτα (εκειθεν απηραν και παρενεβαλον

[1] Cf. J. W. Wevers, *Text History of the Greek Genesis*, chh. 1 and 8; idem, *Exodus*, ch. 2; idem, *Leviticus*, ch. 2; idem, *Numbers*, ch. 2, and idem, *Deuteronomy*, pp. 21–25.

[2] SEPTUAGINTA Vetus Testamentum Graecum Auctoritate Academiae Scientiarum Gottingensis editum. III.3. *Deuteronomum* (ed. John William Wevers; Göttingen, 1977). For Numbers, see idem, III.1 *Numeri* (ed. J. W. Wevers; Göttingen, 1982).

106) εν γασιων γαβερ κακειθεν (εκειθεν απηραν και 106) παρενεβαλον εν τη ερημω σιν αυτη καδης ειτα (κακειθεν απηραν και παρενεβαλον 106) εν τω ορει ωρ (σιωρ 610) και (> 106); 11:3,6,7 ἐποίησεν] εποιει; 11:17 om κύριος 2°; 11:21 om τοῦ d⁽⁻¹²⁵⁾; 12:6 om τάς 1°; 12:17 om τά— εὐχάς; 12:26 ἐπικληθῆναι] αποκληθηναι d⁻⁴⁴; 13:16 αὐτῆς 3°] αυτου; 18:7 λειτουργήσει] -ργει σοι; 23:13 om σου 2°; 27:8 τῶν λίθων] τον λιθον τουτον; 28:48 τοῖς ἐχθροῖς] τους εχθρους; 30:3 om εἰς; 31:25 κυρίου]∩ (26) d⁽⁻¹²⁵⁾; 31:28 λαλήσω] λυσω (λαλυσω 44–106ᶜ); 32:5 οὐκ] επ; 33:2 om ἄγγελοι; 34:4 om καί 4°. In all but 9:21 the t text supported Deut.

The variant text of d also contrasts with t in the following list in which t (unless otherwise indicated) supports Deut but the variant is supported by more witnesses than d.[3]

List 2: Non-unique Readings of d

1:36 τούτῳ] τουτο; 2:29 om ἡμῶν; 2:37 γῆν] pr την; 3:16 τοῦ 2°] της; 4:10 ἤν] η; 4:25 ποιήσητε 2°] ποιησετε; 4:32 om τὸ μέγα; 5:32 οὐδέ] η; 6:2 φυλάσσεσθαι] φυλασεσθε; 6:18 κληρονομήσῃς] -σεις; 6:20 om ἡμῶν; 8:14 ὑψωθῇς] -θεις; 10:11 om κύριος

11:17 ἔδωκεν] διδωσιν; 11:18 ἀφάψετε] -ψατε; 11:23 κληρονομήσετε] -σητε; 11:24 om ποταμοῦ 2°; 11:29 ὄρος 1°] ορους; 12:12 om ὑμων 4°; 12:29 κατακληρονομήσῃς] -σεις; 14:20 ἀποδώσῃ] -σει; 15:4 ἔσται] εστιν; 15:6 σοῦ] συ; 15:9 τό 1°]∩ 2°; 17:5 αὐτούς] αυτοις; 17:14 κατοικήσῃς] -σεις; 18:7 om ἐκεῖ; 20:10 ἐκκαλέσῃ] -σει; 20:17 om καί 1° 3° 4° 6°.

21:17 om υἱόν; 22:3 om οὕτως ποιήσεις 2°; 23:13 ἐπαγαγών] απαγαγων; 24:19 om δέ; 25:3 οὐ] pr και; 25:13 στάθμιον 1°]∩ 2°; 25:16 κυρίῳ] + τω θεω σου εστιν; 26:10 σου 1°]∩ 2°; 27:6 om ἐπ᾽ αὐτό; 28:6 om εὐλογημένος σύ 2°; 28:8 ἐπί 1°] προς; 28:16 om ἐπικατάρατος σύ 2°; 28:20 om ἕως ἄν 2° d⁽⁻¹²⁵⁾; 28:41 om γάρ d⁽⁻¹²⁵⁾; 28:48 om ἐν 3°; 28:61 τοῦ νόμου τούτου] τουτου; 29:21 κατά] και; 30:3 om σε 3°; 30:9 om ἐν τοῖς ἐκγόνοις 2°; 30:10 εἰσακούσῃς] -ση; 30:15 πρὸ προσώπου σου/σήμερον] tr; 30:18 γένησθε] γινεσθε d⁻¹²⁵

---

[3] The evidence for variants is not given throughout this paper except where the indicated support is incomplete. For the evidence the reader is referred to the G"ttingen volume listed in the preceding note. For the purpose of this paper it is irrelevant.

31:6 ἐγκαταλίπῃ] -λειπη d⁻¹²⁵; 31:8 ἐγκαταλίπῃ] -λειπη d⁻⁽¹²⁵⁾; 31:21 στόματος] et σπέρματος tr d⁻¹²⁵; 32:11 αὐτοῦ 1°] εαυτου; 32:25 ταμιείων] + αυτων d⁻⁴⁴; 32:29 ταῦτα] + παντα; 32:43 μισοῦσιν] + αυτον; 33:13 ὠρῶν] ορων; 33:17 γῆς] pr της; 33:27 σκέπασις] -σης; 34:7 om καί.

Over against this the *t* group also shows itself to be a distinct entity.

LIST 3: UNIQUE READINGS OF *t*

4:25 γεννήσῃς] -ση t⁻⁷⁹⁹; 7:20 ἕως] ως t⁻⁷⁹⁹; 10:7 ἐκεῖθεν] κακειθεν; 11:17 ἔδωκεν κύριος] κυριος διδωσιν; 23:13 καί 3°]∩ 4°; 26:4 κυρίου] pr εναντι. In all cases but 11:17, for which see List 2, Deut is supported by the *d* mss.

In List 4 the *t* variant is not unique but has further support in the tradition. The lemmata, however, are fully supported by *d* except for those references which are starred.

LIST 4: NON-UNIQUE READINGS OF *t*

9:3 σου 3°] + και εξολεθρευσει αυτους t⁻⁷⁹⁹; 9:11* τεσσαράκοντα 2°] pr δια; 9:21* καταλέσας] και κατηλασα; 10:4* πυρός] + εν τη ημερα της εκκλησιας; 10:4 αὐτάς] post κύριος 2° tr; 12:6 ὑμῶν 5°] + και τας ομολογιας υμων; 12:17 εὐχας] + σου; 15:3 τοῦ] + δε; 17:10 τό 1°] παν; 17:10 ἄν 1°] εαν

22:1 fin] + και αποδωσεις αυτα τω αδελφω σου; 23:13 διακαθιζάνῃς] καθιζ.; 24:2 init] pr και εξελθη εκ της οικιας αυτου; 27:8* τῶν λίθων] + τουτων t⁻⁷⁹⁹; 28:1* σου 1°] υμων; 28:7 ἀπό] προ; 28:35 πατάξαι] -σει t⁻⁷⁶* ³⁷⁰; 31:9* ἔδωκεν] + αυτο; 31:21 στόματος] pr του; 33:27* σκέπασις] -σεις t⁻⁷⁹⁹.

From the above lists it is clear that *d* and *t* are distinct groups. These lists are all short, however, because of the aberrancy of ms. 106. In fact, sometimes this ms. has a unique reading. These are given in List 5.

LIST 5: UNIQUE READINGS OF Ms 106

1:17 om τόν 2°; 1:20 ἡμῶν] ημιν; 1:27 διεγογγύσατε] -σετε; 1:28 ἑωράκαμεν] ευρομεν; 2:6 μέτρῳ] εκ μετρου; 2:9 Ἀροήρ] γαρ 106ᶜ: 106* has σιειρ with 4 mss; 2:13 Ζάρεδ 1°]∩ (14) 106ᵗˣᵗ; 2:13,14 παρήλθομεν]

δηεπερασαμεν 106⁽ᵐᵍ⁾; 2:14 ἅς] ης 106⁽ᵐᵍ⁾; 2:14 ἀπό] ε<κ> 106⁽ᵐᵍ⁾; 6:24 ποιεῖν πάντα] tr; 7:22 σου 2°] + ου τρωθηση απ αυτων; 7:24 ἀντιστήσεται] αναστ.; 9:11 om τεσσαράκοντα 2°; 9:12 κατάβηθι] καταβα

11:30 δυσμῶν 1°] δεσμων; 12:6 om τάς 2°; 12:6 om καὶ τά 2°; 12:10 κατακληρονομεῖ] -μησαι; 13:16 σου] ημων; 13:17 πληθυνεῖ] -ναι; 13:18 om σοι; 14:8 ὑν] υιον; 14:14 αὐτῷ 1°]∩ (17); 19:8 ἥν] η; 20:14 fin] + κληρονομειν την γην αυτων

22:6 νοσσῶν] ωων, et ᾠῶν] νεοσσων; 23:13 ὅταν] ως αν; 23:15 προστέθειταί] προτεθησεται; 24:4 ὅτι] pr και; 24:19 ἵνα—(20)fin] post (21)fin tr; 26:13 χήρᾳ] + και φαγονται (εφαγον 106ᶜ) εν ταις πολεσι σου (μου 106ᶜ) και εμπλησθησαν; 27:5 om κυρίῳ—(6) σου 1°; 28:68 αὐτήν] αυτον; 29:23 ἀνατελεῖ] ανασtελει; 29:25 αὐτῶν 1°] αυτου; 30:16 om αὐτοῦ 3°; 30:16 om τάς 3°.

This list could easily be doubled if one were to include all variants supported by 106 over against d⁻¹⁰⁶ and t but little purpose would be served by it.

Of much more interest would be an examination of readings of d⁻¹⁰⁶, i.e. readings which contrast with 106 t. A large number of these involve omissions by d⁻¹⁰⁶. In List 6 all omissions uniquely attested by d⁻¹⁰⁶ are given.

LIST 6: UNIQUE OMISSIONS BY d⁻¹⁰⁶

1:21 om ὑμῶν 1°; 2:11 om ὥσπερ οἱ Ἐνακίμ; 2:14 παρεμβολῆς]∩ (15); 2:16 om ἀποθνῄσκοντες—(17) καί; 2:27 om πορεύσομαι; 3:6 om ὥσπερ—ἐξωλεθρεύσαμεν 2°; 3:18 om ὑμῖν 2°; 4:29 σου 1°]∩ 2°; 4:47 om κατά—fin; 5:21 οὔτε 3°]∩ 4°; 5:27 om ὅσα 2°—σέ d⁻¹⁰⁶; 6:2 om πάσας—fin; 6:7 om καί 2°—αὐτοῖς; 6:8 καί 1°]∩ 2°; 6:12 om ἐξ—fin; 6:15 om μή—fin; 6:21 om ἐν 2°—fin; 6:22 om ἐν 2°—fin; 6:24 om ἐνετείλατο—ταῦτα; 7:10 om τοῖς 2°—fin; 7:12 om ἄν—καί 2°; 7:12 om καὶ ποιήσητε; 7:19 om init—σου 1°; 7:21 om init—(22) σου 2°: homoiot; 8:12 καί 2°]∩ (13) 1°; 9:3 om αὐτούς 1°; 9:3 om καί 3°—fin; 9:16 om ὑμῖν ἑαυτοῖς; 9:25 om ἔναντι κυρίου

11:3 om πάσῃ—(4) ἐποίησεν; 11:10 om ὅθεν ἐπορεύεσθε ἐκεῖθεν; 12:3 om αὐτῶν 2°; 12:6 ὑμῶν 4°]∩ 5°; 13:2 om τό 1°—τέρας; 13:5 om καί 2°—fin; 13:6 om ὁ 4°—σου 7°; 13:6 om ἡ ἐν κόλπῳ σου; 13:10 om ὅτι—fin; 13:14 καί 1°]∩ 3°; 13:16 om πάντα 1°; 13:18 om ὅσας—σήμερον; 14:28 om οὐδὲ κλῆρος; 15:5 om φυλάσσειν καί; 16:14 om init—(15) αὐτόν; 16:18 om αἷς—σοι; 16:20 om καί—fin; 17:9

σοι]∩ (10) 1°; 17:14 καί 1°]∩ 2°; 17:15 om καθιστῶν; 17:19 καί 1°]∩ 2°; 17:20 om ἀπό 2°; 19:17 om οἵ—fin; 19:18 om ἀκριβῶς; 19:18 om ἀντέστη—fin; 19:20 om ἀκούσαντες; 19:20 om κατά—fin; 20:3 μηδέ 1°]∩ 2°; 20:14 om πάντα τά et πάντα 3°; 20:18 om ὅσα—fin

21:5 om ὅτι—fin; 21:6 om οἱ—τραυματίᾳ; 21:16 om τὸν υἱόν; 21:20 om ἐρεθίζει; 21:23 om αὐτόν; 22:3 om αὐτοῦ 2°—ποιήσεις 3°; 22:4 om comma; 22:6 om ἐπὶ παντί; 22:6 om τῆς; 22:18 om ἡ—ἐκείνης; 22:27 om comma; 23:5 om ὅτι—fin; 23:20 om ἵνα—σου 3°; 24:3 καί 3°]∩ 4°; 24:3 om ἐκ—αὐτοῦ; 24:3 om ἑαυτῷ γυναῖκα; 24:4 om μετά—αὐτήν 3°; 24:8 om φυλάξῃ σφόδρα; 24:12 om ὁ ἄνθρωπος; 24:13 om καί 3°—fin; 24:15 om καί ult—fin; 24:18 om διά—fin; 24:19 ἐν 2°—σου 2°] εν αυτω; 25:9 om καί 1°; 25:11 om ἐκ—αὐτόν; 26:6 om καί 3°—fin: homoiot; 27:4 om οὕς—σήμερον; 27:4 om καί 2° fin; 27:10 om ὅσα—fin; 27:22 om ἤ—(23)fin; 28:4 om καί 1°, 2°; 28:11 σου 2°]∩ 3°; 28:13 om ἐάν—(14)fin; 28:18 om καί 2°; 28:22 om καί 1°, 5°; 28:28 καί 2°]∩ (29)1°; 28:32 om καί 2°—fin; 28:39 om οὐδέ—fin; 28:40 om ὅτι—fin; 28:43 om ὅς ἐστιν ἐν; 28:44 om οὗτος 2°—fin; 28:48 om καί 4°—πάντων; 28:48 om ἕως—fin; 28:53 ἐν 1°]∩ 2°; 28:53 om ἤ—fin; 28:56—57 om commata: homoiot; 28:58 τό 2°]∩ 3°; 28:65 om ἐν; 29:13 om Ἀβραάμ—fin; 29:19 om τῇ 1°; 29:20 om καί 1°—αὐτοῦ 1°; 29:21 om init—Ἰσραήλ; 29:23 om Ἀδαμά—fin; 29:26 καί 2°]∩ (27); 30:6 σου 1°]∩ 2°; 31:17 καί 4°]∩ 5°.

That the *d* text should frequently abbreviate the Deut text is not surprising. Already in 1914 Rahlfs[4] characterized one of the mss, 125, in comparing it to 107, as "auf das willkürlichste verkürst" (abridged in a most arbitrary manner), a judgement which might well apply to the *d* text of the Pentateuch as a whole.

If one were to add to the above list the omissions which *d*[-106] attests in company with other witnesses, i.e., non-unique omissions of text by *d*[-106], the list would be at least doubled, but no real purpose would be served by making such, since its point has already been made.

It is, however, not only in omissions that 106 departs from *d*. List 7 details other cases in which *d*[-106] uniquely supports the variant

[4] A. Rahlfs, *Verzeichnis der griechischen Handschriften des Alten Testaments. Nachr. von d. Königl. Ges. d. Wiss. zu Göttingen.* Philol.-hist. Kl. 1914. Beiheft. (Berlin, 1914), 144. Today the statement is known to be equally true of the other members of the group, especially of 107 and 610.

text. Instances in which 106 *t* do not support the lemma will be starred.

<h2 style="text-align:center">LIST 7: OTHER UNIQUE READINGS OF d⁻¹⁰⁶</h2>

1:31 ἥν 2°] η; 1:35 ὄψεται] οψεσθε; 1:41 κατά] και; 1:41 ἀναλαβόντες] αναλαμβανοντες; 2:1 εἰς] προς; 2:26 Κεδμωθ] κηδεθμων; 3:2 ὥσπερ] ως; 3:6 πᾶσαν] pr και; 3:13 Μανασσῆ] βενιαμιν; 3:15 τήν] τω; 5:21* οὔτε 2°] η; 5:28 σέ] + ο λαος ουτος; 6:9 γράψετε] -ψον; 6:20 ἔσται] + σοι; 7:19 καὶ τὰ τέρατα] post ἐκεῖνα tr; 9:12 χώνευμα] χωρευμα

11:11 ἡ δέ] αλλ η; 11:11* εἰσπορεύῃ] πορευησθε (-εσθε 44); 12:3 τοὺς βωμοὺς αὐτῶν/ καὶ συντρίψετε] tr; 12:5* εἰσελεύσεσθε] εξελ.; 13:12 κατοικεῖν] κατωκει; 13:16 σκῦλα 2°] σκελη; 14:21 ἀγροῦ] αγιου; 15:3 ἄφεσιν] pr οτι επικεκληται; 16:3 ἑπτὰ ἡμέρας φάγῃ/ ἐπ᾽ αὐτοῦ] tr; 16:6 πρός] επι; 16:18 κατὰ φυλάς] post λαόν tr; 17:7 ἐξ ὑμῶν] tr; 17:19 φυλάσσεσθαι] και; 17:19 ποιεῖν] + και φυλαττειν; 17:20 ἵνα μή 2°] και; 17:20 παραβῇ] post ἐντολῶν tr; 18:18 λαλήσει] -σω 44-107′-125*; 19:20 ἔτι] + τουτο; 20:12 ποιήσωσιν] ποιησω; 20:14 ὑπάρχῃ] post πόλει tr; 20:17 ἀναθεματιεῖτε αὐτούς] tr

21:2 κριταί] + σου οι πρωτιστοι; 21:17 διπλᾶ] διπλω; 22:9 τόν] παν; 22:20 γένηται/ ὁ λόγος] tr; 22:25 τὴν παῖδα τήν] παιδα; 23:4 ὅτι] οτε; 23:10 τὴν παρεμβολήν] αυτην; 24:4 γυναῖκα] pr εις; 24:15 ὅτι— ἐλπίδα] ad fin tr; 24:15 κατὰ σοῦ] post κύριον tr; 24:20 ἐπαναστρέψεις] αναστρ.; 25:6* τοῦ τετελευτηκότος] + αδελφου αυτου; 25:11 αὐτοῦ 2°] του τυπτοντος τον ανδρα αυτης; 26:6 οἱ Αἰγύπτιοι] ad fin tr; 26:12 ἔτει] ορει; 27:22* ἐκ πατρός] η πατρος αδελφης; 28:4 εὐλογημένα] και; 28:60 ὀδύνην] οδον; 28:65 σοι κύριος ἐκεῖ] κυριος ο θεος σου επι σου; 29:13 ὤμοσεν] post σου 2° tr.

This group represents readings unique to *d*⁻¹⁰⁶. To give a fuller picture of *d*⁻¹⁰⁶ as contrasting with 106 *t* the next list gives readings which *d*⁻¹⁰⁶ shares with other witnesses. If the text of 106 *t* does not support the lemma the citation is starred.

<h2 style="text-align:center">LIST 8: OTHER NON-UNIQUE READINGS OF d⁻¹⁰⁶</h2>

1:8 ἐνώπιον ὑμῶν] υμιν ενωπιον; 1:21 δειλιάσητε] -σετε; 1:26 τῷ ῥήματι] το ρημα; 1:31 ἐτροφοφόρησέν] ετροποφορησεν; 1:44 ἐτίτρωσκον]-σκεν; 2:30 σου] ημων; 3:21 ὑμῶν 1°] ημων; 4:30 αὐτοῦ] σου; 5:28 τὴν φωνήν 1°] της φωνης; 6:12 ἐξαγάγοντος] -γαγων; 8:19 λατρεύσῃς] -σεις; 9:15

δυσίν] δυο; 11:22 πορεύεσθαι] πορευεσθε; 11:26 δίδωμι] + υμιν; 11:32 ταύτας] αυτου; 12:3 τάς] pr και; 13:15 ἀναθέματι] και; 15:2 ὅ] η; 15:11 σοι ἐντέλλομαι] tr; 15:15 σοι ἐντελλομαι] tr; 15:20 φάγῃ] σφαγη; 17:5* ἐκείνην] οι εποιησαν το ρημα το πονηρον τουτο προς πυλαις σου

18:3 ἐάν τε 2°] η; 18:13 ἔναντι] εναντιον; 19:11 αὐτοῦ ψυχήν] την ψυχην αυτου; 19:12 χεῖρας] pr τας; 19:15 καὶ ἐπὶ στόματος] η; 20:1 ἐξέλοῃς] -λθη; 20:3 πόλεμον] pr τον; 20:3 φοβεῖσθε] -σθω; 20:4 συνεκπολεμῆσαι] -μηδει; 20:7 ἀποστραφήτω] επιοτρ.; 20:9 προηγουμένους] προσηγ.; 21:3 οὐχ εἵλυσεν/ ζυγόν] tr; 21:18 καὶ φωνήν] η; 22:5 οὐδέ] ουδ ου; 22:21 τὴν νεᾶνιν] αυτην; 23:12 ἐκεῖ ἔξω] tr; 25:15 καί 1°] + μετρον; 27:12 Ἰσσαχάρ] ισαχαρ; 28:15* εἰτακούῃς] ακουσητε d⁽⁻¹⁰⁶ᵗˣᵗ⁾; 28:52 καί 1°] εως αν; 30:16 σοι] υμιν; 31:19 τοὺς υἱούς] τοις υιοις; 32:7 ἔτη] ετι; 32:19 ἐζήλωσεν] παρεζ.; 34:3 Σηγώρ] σιγωρ; 34:7 οὐκ] pr και.

It is by now clear that 106 cannot really be considered a proper witness to the *d* text. It is, however, true that for the majority of Byzantine readings, in fact in hundreds of cases the pair *d t* without exception, i.e., including 106, witnesses to variant readings. The conclusion that 106 is thus actually a witness to the *t* text in Dt seems inescapable.

This conclusion is substantiated by variant readings supported by 106 and *t* but opposed by *d*. Only a few of these are unique. Unless the citation is starred *d⁻¹⁰⁶* supports the lemma.

LIST 9: UNIQUE READINGS OF MS 106 AND *t*

1:43* καὶ παρέβητε] ουδε εποιησατε; 2:26* Κεδμώθ] κηδεμωθ; 8:12 αὐταῖς] αυτοις 106 74′–799; 11:19 om καὶ διανισταμένους; 17:11 ἀριστερά] ευωνυμα; 18:5 λειτουργεῖν] + αυτω; 22:27 ἀγρῷ] πεδιω; 28:65 κύριος] + ο θεος σου; 29:23 οὐδέ 2°] ου.

There are, however, many more cases in which 106 and *t* support a variant also supported by other witnesses, but against *d⁻¹⁰⁶*. As in the earlier lists unless the citation is starred *d⁻¹⁰⁶* supports the text of the lemma.

LIST 10: NON-UNIQUE READINGS OF MS 106 AND *t*

1:42 πολεμήσητε] -σετε; 2:11* οἱ Ἐνακίμ] pr και 106 t⁻⁷⁹⁹; 2:15 τῆς] pr μεσου; 2:27* πορεύσομαι] παρελευσομαι; 4:1 ὑμῶν] ημων 106 *t*⁻⁷⁹⁹; 5:24 αὐτοῦ 1°] + καὶ τὴν μεγαλωσυνην αυτου; 5:29 τάς 1°] pr πασας 106 *t*⁻⁷⁹⁹; 6:4 κύριος 1°] μωυσης; 6:7 om ἐν 1°; 6:15 μή] + ποτε 106 *t*⁽⁻⁷⁹⁹⁾; 6:17 δικαιώματα] + αυτου; 6:18 ἔναντι] εναντιον; 6:22 τῷ] pr ολω 106 *t*⁻³⁷⁰; 7:10 μισοῦσιν 2°] + αυτον; 7:12 om πάντα; 7:21 μέγας] pr ο; 7:21 κραταιός] pr ο; 8:2 ἐκπειράσῃ] πειρ.; 9:8 ὑμῖν] υμων 106 74'–76(vid)–602–799; 9:16 ὑμῶν] ημων 106 *t*⁻⁷⁹⁹; 9:26 κληρονομίαν] μεριδα.

13:5 ἐκ τῆς 1°] εξ οικου; 15:10 ἄν 2°] εαν; 15:11* σοι ἐντέλλομαι] + σημερον; 15:12 καὶ τῷ] + ετει; 16:15 αὐτόν] εν αυτω; 17:5* ἐκείνην] + οι εποιησαν το ρημα το πονηρον τουτο προς πυλαις σου τον ανδρα η την γυναικα; 19:18 οἱ κριταί/ἀκριβῶς] tr; 19:19 ποιῆσαι] pr του 106 74'–602–799; 19:21 ὀφθαλμόν] pr και; 20:7 μή] + ποτε; 20:16 δέ] δη 106 *t*⁻¹³⁴⁽ᶜ⁾

21:13 πατέρα] + αυτης; 22:2 ἀποδώσεις αὐτῷ] απ. αυτα αυτω (αυτα αυτω tr 799); 22:14 ἐπιθῇ] -θηται (-θητε 74; -θησει 799); 22:25 βιασάμενος] + αυτην; 24:4 αὐτήν 2°] + του ειναι; 24:4* ἑαυτῷ] αυτω; 24:8 φυλάξῃ] pr και; 24:15 αὐτοῦ] αυτω 106 *t*⁻⁷⁹⁹; 24:15 ἔχει] pr αυτος; 25:6* τοῦ τετελευτηκότος] pr του αδελφου αυτου; 25:7 γυνή] + του αδελφου αυτου; 25:16 ἄδικον] αδικα; 26:3 ἔσται] εαν η; 26:8 om ἐν ult; 26:15 om τόν 2°; 27:22* ἐκ πατρός] + αυτου; 28:34 βλέψῃ] οψη; 28:43 ὅς] οστις; 28:8 ἐπαποστελεῖ] + αυτους; 28:52 σου 4°] + εν παση τη γη σου; 28:52 αἷς] η; 28:53 fin] + εν (aut επι) πασαις ταις πολεσι σου; 29:1 οὕς] οσα; 29:3* σου] υμων; 29:13 σε] + σημερον; 29:16 οὕς] ως; 29:18 ἐξέκλινεν] + σημερον; 29:21* τῆς διαθήκης] + ταυτης; 29:28 παροξυσμῷ] pr εν; 30:10 τά] pr παντα; 31:15 fin] + του μαρτυριου 106 *t*⁽⁻⁷⁹⁹⁾; 31:20* κορήσουσιν] και κορεσουσιν (κορησ. 799); 32:17 καινοί] κενοι; 32:24 εἰς] επ; 32:27 ὑψηλή] pr η 106 *t*⁻⁷⁹⁹; 32:38 ὑμῖν 2°] υμων; 32:43 ἄγγελοι] υιοι.

Only one conclusion is possible in view of the above evidence: 106 is a witness to the *t* text, not to *d*.

One question still remains. Does the 106 support of *t* rather than of *d* begin at Deut 1:1 or did the change in allegiance begin earlier in Numbers, and if so where?

That in the latter part of Numbers, 106 belongs to *t* is clear. Note the following evidence from a randomly selected short passage: Num 30:16 αὐτῆς] pr ο ανηρ 106 *t*; 31:5 om χιλίους ἐκ φυλῆς *d*⁻¹⁰⁶; 31:5 om χιλιάδες ἐνωπλισμένοι 106 *t*; 31:8 om σύν—fin *d*⁻¹⁰⁶; 31:9 ἐπρονόμευσαν 1°] προενομ. 106 *t*; 31:13 αὐτοῖς] αυτων *d*⁻¹⁰⁶; 31:13 om ἔξω—fin *d*⁻¹⁰⁶. None of these instances is a unique reading, but the conclusion is certain.

Already as early as Num 22 and 23 the conclusion reached for Deuteronomy seems to be correct here as well. Note e.g. the following unique rewrites by d^{-106}: 22:15 init—ἄρχοντας] και ανασταν-τες οι αρχοντες μωαβ εστειλαν and 23:2 init—Βαλαάμ] και ετοιμασεν αυτους.

Actually the change from d to t support in 106 apparently does not occur abruptly at an obvious juncture, but if one must state group membership categorically one might note that at Num 14:28, 106 is clearly a member of d. For εἶπον, d has ειπε, but t has ειπον δη. And in the same verse note: λέγει] λεγω d^{-125} 370; > 125. Obviously in v. 28 d and t contrast with 106 firmly supporting d. The two groups do not contrast otherwise until v. 37 where καί is supported by 106 t but is omitted by d^{-106}. The two groups also part company in the same way at v. 43 where for οὗ εἵνεκεν d^{-106} uniquely reads διοτι; in the same verse the omission of καί 3°—fin is also uniquely attested by d^{-106}. One might therefore provisionally suggest that 106 becomes a supporter of t between Num 14:28 and 14:37. Somewhere in the ancestry of 106 a copyist changed his parent text at this point.

It now appears that it would have been more accurate if 106 had been assigned to t after Num 14:36 through the end of Deuteronomy, rather than to d.

SOME NEWLY IDENTIFIED LXX/OG FRAGMENTS AMONG THE AMHERST PAPYRI AT THE PIERPONT MORGAN LIBRARY IN NEW YORK CITY

ROBERT A. KRAFT

THE SETTING

When Grenfell and Hunt published the papyri from Lord Amherst's collection a century ago, they described a number of LXX/OG fragments and suspected that there may be other scraps from the same sources among the unidentified pieces.[1] They did not attempt to provide complete transcriptions of most of these unidentified fragments, but did include some selected lines, and some paleographic comments. The pieces that they were able to identify as from Jewish Greek scriptures (including Aquila) are as follows:

> PAmherst 003(c1) LXX Genesis 1:1–5 (first half of 4th C.E.; Göttingen #912)
> PAmherst 003(c2) Aquila Genesis 1:1–5 (first half of 4th C.E.)
> PAmherst 191(a) LXX Exodus 19 (6th C.E.; Göttingen #914)
> PAmherst 192 LXX Deuteronomy 32 (6th C.E.; Göttingen #916)
> PAmherst 004 OG Job 1–2 (stichometric, 7th C.E.; Göttingen #913)
> PAmherst 005 OG Psalm 5 (stichoi marked in line, 5/6th C.E.; Göttingen #2008)
> PAmherst 007 OG Psalm 58–59 (stichometric, 5th C.E.; Göttingen #2010)

---

[1] *The Amherst Papyri, being an account of The Greek Papyri in the collection of the Right Hon. Lord Amherst of Hackney, F.S.A., at Didlington Hall, Norfolk*, by Bernard P. Greenfell and Arthur S. Hunt. *Part I: The Ascension of Isaiah, and other Theological Fragments, with nine plates* (London, 1900) and *Part II: Classical Fragments and Documents of the Ptolemaic, Roman and Byzantine Periods, with an Appendix containing additional Theological Fragments; twenty-five plates* (London, 1901). I would like to express my appreciation to Dr. William Voelkle and the staff at the Pierpont Morgan Library in New York City for helping me to obtain photos and electronic images of pertinent items in the collection. For a more general survey of some of those materials, see my forthcoming article "The Amherst Papyri Revisited: Fragments of LXX/OG MSS" in a 2003 volume of O.L.A. (also on my Amherst Papyri web page, which also includes some images: http://ccat.sas.upenn.edu/rs/rak/amherstpap/).

PAmherst 006 oɢ Psalms 108, 118, 135, 138–140 (stichometric, 7–9th
  c.e.; Göttingen #2009)
PAmherst 193 (vellum) oɢ Proverbs 10 (stichometric, 6th c.e.; Göttingen
  #917)

To this list may now be added, as discussed below:

PAmherst 200—further fragments from PAmherst 006 of Psalms (see
  above)
PAmherst 191(b) and 194(a)—oɢ Isaiah 58:11–14 (Göttingen #915)
PAmherst 198—oɢ "A Text" Judges (Göttingen #876)

1. PAmherst 006 + 200: Pages from the Psalms
(Göttingen # 2009)

Grenfell and Hunt describe the plate labelled PAmh 200 as "fourteen small fragments . . . belonging to the papyrus of the Psalms (Amh.
Pap. I. 6)." The editors were not able to place any of these fragments. The larger, identified materials in PAmh 6 represent parts of
four double-sided pages "from one manuscript which . . . was a papyrus
book. The [original] pages were of considerable size and each contained a single broad column. The handwriting is a large uncial,
heavy and upright and carefully formed—a typical example of the
later Byzantine style. . . . We are unwilling, in the present state of
the evidence, to be definite concerning the dates of Byzantine uncials,
especially of this variety which extends over a very long period. . . .
Provisionally, we do not think that this specimen was written before
the seventh century, and it may be one or two centuries later. The
ink is of the brown colour common at this period. A middle or high
point is irregularly used to mark a pause. Single or double dots
denote diaeresis."

They continue with a paragraph describing the format of this
codex: "The stichometric arrangement of the Psalms . . . is followed
in these fragments. A fresh line is always begun for each στιχος, and
the initial letter is considerably enlarged. When a στιχος is too long
to be contained in a single line, the succeeding lines are commenced
further to the right, by the space of a couple of letters, until the
next στιχος is reached. By this method the divisions of the verse are
sharply distinguished. Above each Psalm is written its title, enclosed
within small wedge-shaped signs; and to the left of this is the number of the Psalm, above which is a horizontal stroke surmounted by
a wavy flourish."

Much of this information is useful in attempting to identify the further small fragments in PAmh 200.[2] Some of those pieces clearly preserve letters on the margin, and need to be viewed with the above formatting features in mind. It thus became apparent quite quickly that *PAmh 200.1* could be fitted nicely onto the upper part of the final page, "d," of PAmh 6 at Psalm 138:21–24 and 139:10–12, although a textual variant at the start of Psalm 139:11 doubtless obstructed the original editors from making this identification. Fragment 3, and possibly also 4, 8, 10, and 13 of PAmh 200 come from the same page. The resulting reconstruction of *PAmh 6(d)* is thus as follows (transcription of newly identified fragments appears in upper case):

Psalm 138(139):20–139(140).9a (written against the fibers, "verso"; 37 lines, up to about 30 letters in the longest lines)

(top and left margins preserved at the top, and parts at the right)

01	λημψονται εΝ[ματαιοτητι]ΠΟΛΙΣ ΣΟΥ	{138:20b}
02	ουχι τους μισουν[τας σε κ̅ε̅ εμισησα]	{21}
03	και επι τοις εχθρ[οις σου εξετηκο]ΜΗΝ	
04	τ[ελι]ον μισος εμ[ισουν αυτους](blank)	{22}
05	εις εκχθρους εγ[ενοντο μοι](blank)	
06	δοκιμασον με κ̅[ε̅ και γνοθι]ΤΗΝ	{23}
07	καρδιαν μου [(blank)](blank)	
08	ετασον με και γ[νωθι τας τριβου]Σ ΜΟΥ	
09	και ϊδε ϊ ειδες α[νομιας εν ε]ΜΟΙ	{24}
10	και οδηγησον μ[ε εν οδω αιωνια]	
11	ρ̅λ̅θ̅ >>>> ψαλμ[ος τω δα(υει)δ >>>>]>>>	{139:01/title}
12	εξελου [μ]ε [κ̅ε̅ εξ α̅ν̅ο̅υ̅ πον]ηρου	{02}
13	απ[ο α]νδ[ρος αδικου ρυσαι με](blank)	
14	[οιτινες ελογισαντο αδικ]ΙΑΝ[ε]ν καρδΙΑ	{03}
15	[ολην την ημεραν π]αρετασσοντο	
16	[πολεμους](blank)	

[2] For the Psalm materials, textcritical information is dependent on Alfred Rahlfs, *Psalmi cum Odis* (Göttingen *Septuaginta* 10; Vandenhoeck & Ruprecht, 1967²). I am indebted to the careful work of Bryan Harmelink, a doctoral student at the Westminster Theological Seminary, in attempting to place more of these small fragments. He is almost certainly correct in locating fragment 6 on the original plate as also from the page represented by PAmherst 6(d), just above the larger fragment from PAmherst 200 noted below. These are items 1 and 4 on the rearranged images of PAmherst 200 found at http://ccat.sas.upenn.edu/rs/rak/amherstpap/images/PAmh200.JPG— top and bottom of the left hand vertical row. Once that page of the original papyrus could be reconstructed visually, some other small pieces also seemed to fall into place, as can be seen at http://ccat.sas.upenn.edu/rs/rak/amherstpap/images/PAmh6(d)s.JPG.

17 [ηκονησαν γλ]ωσσ[αν] αυτω[ν   {04}
18 [ωσει οφεως](blank)
19 [ιος ασπιδων υπο]τα χιλη αυτων
20 [φυλαξον με κ̄ε̄ εκ]χιρος αμαρτωλου   {05}
21 [απο αν̄ω̄ν̄ αδικω]ν εξελου με
22 [οιτινες ελογισαντο υ]ποσκελισε τα δι
23 [αβηματα μου](blank)
24 [εκρυψαν υπερηφανοι πα]γιδα μοι   {06}
25 [και σχοινια διετιναν παγιδας]τοις
26 [ποσιν μου](blank)
27 [εχομενα τριβου σκανδα]λον εθεν
28 [το μοι](blank)
29 [ειπα τω κ̄ω̄ θ̄ς̄ μου ει συ](blank)   {07}
30 [ενωτισαι κ̄ε̄ την φωνη]ν της δεη
31 [σεως μου](blank)
32 [κ̄ε̄ κ̄ε̄ δυναμις της σωτηριας]ΜΟΥ   {08}
33 [επεσκιασας επι την κεφαλην]ΜΟΥ
34 [εν ημερα πολεμου](blank)
35 [μη παραδως με κ̄ε̄ απο της επι]Θ[υ   {09]
36 [μιας μου αμαρτωλω]
37 [διελογισαντο κατ εμου μη εγκαταλι]

line 1: The tops of the letters at the end of the line on this side of PAmh 200.4 are difficult to decipher, and cannot with confidence be equated with the expected text of the Psalm. Without reference to the expected text, I would have read the letters as ΠΕΡΛΙ or similarly, but ΠΟΛΙ is not impossible and traces of SOU can be imagined. The itacism ΠΟΛΙΣ for ΠΟΛΕΙΣ would not be surprising. In the Rahlfs edition (also for the original editors of PAmh 6) the words εις ματαιοτητα τας precede πολεις σου, but this is too long for the reconstructed gap, which covers only the space of 9 letters on the other side of the fragment. The variant εν ματαιοτητι (attested by "R" and probably by several Latin witnesses) fits better, and possibly our text did not include the definite article τας (a variant not noted by Rahlfs)? There also seems to be an isolated letter or two (vertical strokes, resembling the sides of an "N") above the conjectured "PO" on the fragment, perhaps part of a page number?

line 2: Nothing of the end of this line is preserved. In keeping with the attested practice elsewhere in this manuscript, the expected *nomen sacrum* abbreviation probably occurred here.

line 3: Rahlfs notes the variant τους εχθρους in R and a few other witnesses. Our fragment seems to have τοις although the word appears to be carelessly written, and the "I" is especially unusual at the top, although it does not resemble the normal form for "Y." The end of the line is represented in PAmh 200.1, where the letter eta is quite clear, and the mu and nu are probable.

line 4: The original editors reconstruct τελιον rather than τελειον, but either is possible. The end of this line is blank on PAmh 200.1.

line 5: Our fragment has εκχθρους where εχθρους is expected (see line 3). The end of this line is blank on PAmh 200.1.

line 6: After the με the original editors conjectured abbreviated $\overline{\text{KE}}$ (κυριε) with witnesses ART and a few others. B and several other witnesses have Ο ΘΕΟΣ (in abbreviated form $\overline{\text{ΘΣ}}$) in agreement with the MT. While the initial letter is only faintly preserved in our text, it seems to be a vertical stroke consistent with K. There would be enough room in the lacuna for a fully written KYPIE. The final word of this line is reasonably clear in PAmh 200.1.

line 7: This line is slightly indented on PAmh 6, and the end of the line is blank on PAmh 200.1.

line 8: The final letters are clear in PAmh 200.1.

line 9: The letters ΚΑΙΙΔΕΙΕΙΔΕΣ are clear, with a normal dieresis over the second iota and a single dot over the third. Rahlfs prints και ιδε ει οδος, citing variants to ει οδος, which is in agreement with MT and several Greek witnesses including the R group. Most of the Greek texts for which this detail is recorded have ει (MS A and a few L MSS have a single eta), and many follow it with ειδες as here; A shows conflation (ει ειδες οδον). Itacistic confusion and its results are obvious (ει/ι/η and ειδες/οδος). The end of this line on PAmh 200.1 is virtually illegible, but is not inconsistent with the expected reading.

line 10: The line begins with the marginal marker denoting the end of one Psalm and start of another. The papyrus is misaligned as mounted in this area.

line 11: There is a short horizontal stroke in the left margin between lines 10 and 11, then the number "139" (ΡΛΘ) in the margin at line 11, followed by four fillers (>>>>) and the title, which is also followed by such fillers. The beginning of the title itself is barely legible. The original editors reconstruct as above (perhaps with the name abbreviated to $\overline{\text{ΔΑΔ}}$), in agreement with a few "Lucianic" witnesses; all other witnesses represented by Rahlfs apparently begin the title line with εις το τελος which would be too long for this lacuna.

line 12: Probably both "nomina sacra" terms ($\overline{\text{KE}}$ = κυριε and

$\overline{\text{ANOY}}$ = ανθρωπου) were abbreviated here (judging by the expected size of the lacuna).

line 13: There is no clear evidence of writing at the preserved end of this line, despite the length of the expected line (but perhaps some traces are visible at the top of the small scrap PAmh 200.10)..

line 14: PAmh 200.3 fits nicely at the end of this line, with the letters ΔΙΑ extending far into the right margin. To the left of this section, PAmh 200.10 can be placed with some degree of probability, thus attesting the variant αδικιαν (with families R, L, and A') rather than αδικιας as preferred by Rahlfs (with the B family, Sa, and most Old Latin witnesses).

line 17: The lacuna from the left margin should be able to accommodate about 13 letters, but the known texts have only 10. Rahlfs records no variants here. Thus the original editors place ellipses dots at the left margin and suggest in a note that perhaps the MS had a compound verb such as εξηκονησαν (see Ps 51:4, Ezek 21:11). The expected text contains several letters that are normally broad in width (eta, kappa, nu, gamma, lamda), so perhaps nothing more need be supplied.

line 19: Read χειλη (itacism). Rahlfs reads διαψαλμα at the end of this line, and does not note any variants. Our text has no room for it (see also line 28 below and line 1 of the other side).

line 20: Read χειρος (itacism). Rahlfs records some variations in this line, but none seem significant for our purposes. The *nomen sacrum* was doubtless abbreviated again here (MS S omits it).

line 21: Our MS almost certainly abbreviated ανθρωπων (see also above, line 12), and had ανθρωπων αδικων not the variant ανθρωπου αδικου (Bo, some of L'He, A'). The original editors place a full stop after the N, before εξελου (MS A has ρυσαι here, as in verse 2 above), but it is not obvious in the MS.

line 22: Read υποσκελισαι (itacism). Some witnesses have του before this word (R L' 1219'), but that is unlikely here.

line 25: Nothing is preserved to adjudicate the variant of παγιδας (B' La A) or παγιδα (Bo R GaHi L'-Su 1219' = ΜΤ). The original editors help us restore the original position of parts of these fragments by noting that the "τ of τοις is immediately under δ of πα]γιδα in 24 and over the first ε of εθεν in 26 [sic! 27]." Thus as now mounted, the lower section has slipped to the left the width of about two letters, and the final N is no longer visible.

line 28: There is room at the end of the lacuna for διαψαλμα (so Rahlfs, who notes no variant), but the original editors think it probable that our MS omitted it here (with T), as also above in line 19 and in the first line of the other side of this page.

line 29: Possibly PAmh 200.8 fits here, with the letters ΑΤΩ. If so, our text would not reflect the variant ειπον reported for T.

lines 30–37 are poorly preserved, and no pertinent variants are noted by Rahlfs for this section.

Psalm 139(140):9b–140(141):5a (with the fibers, "recto")

(upper and right margins preserved at the top, and portions of the left margin)

01	ΠΗΣ[με μη ποτε υ]ψωθωσιν·	{139:9b}
02	Η ΚΕΦ[αλη του κυκ]λωματος μου	{10}
03	[κοπος των χειλε]ων αυτων κα[λ]υ	
04	ΨΕΙ[αυτους] (blank)	
05	ΚΑ[ι πεσουνται επ αυτο]υς ανθρακες πυρος	{11}
06	ΕΠΙ[της γης και κα]ταβαλεις αυτους	
07	ΕΝ Τ[αλαιπωριαις ο]υ μη ὑποστωσῑ	
08	ΑΝΗ[ρ γλωσσωδης ο]υ κατευθυνθησ	{12}
09	ΕΤ[αι επι της γης] (blank)	
10	[α]νδρα α[δικον κακ]α θηρευσει	
11	[ε]ις διαφ[θοραν] (blank)	
12	εγνων ο[τι ποιησει κ̅ς̅ την]κρισιν	{13}
13	του πτΩ[χου και την δικ]ην[των	
14	πενητων	
15	πλην δικαι[οι εξομολογησονται τω	{14}
16	ονοματι σου[	
17	και κατοι[κ]ησου[σιν ευθεις συν τω π]ΡΟ	
18	σ]ωπου σ[ο]υ (blank)	
——]		
19	ρ̅]μ̅ ψαλμος τω δ[α(υει)δ	{140:title}
20	κ̅ε̅ προς σε εκκεκ[ραξα εισακουσον μου	{01}
21	προσχες τη φω[νη της δεησεως	
22	μου εν τω κ[εκραγεναι με προς σε	
23	κατευθυν[θητω η προσευχη μου	{02}
24	ως θυμι[αμα ενωπιον σου	
25	επ[αρσις των χειρον μου θυσια	
26	ε[σπερινη	
27	θο[υ κ̅ε̅]φ[υλακην το στοματι μου	{03}
28	και θυρ[αν περιοχης περι τα χειλη μου	
29	μη εκκλ[ινης την καρδιαν μου	{04}
30	εις λογου[ς πονηριας	
31	Τ[ου προφασιζεσθαι προφασεις	

32   Ε[ν αμαρτιαις
33   ΣΥ[ν ανοις εργαζομενοις ανομιαν
34   Κ[αι ου μη συνδυασω μετα των εκ
35   [λεκτων αυτων
36   [παιδευσει με δικαιος εν ελεει και   {05}
37   [ελεγξει με

line 1: The line begins with the ending of the word εγκαταλιπης, and does not include, at the end, διαψαλμα which is found there in most witnesses (see also the other side, lines 19 and 28). A medial dot is visible at the end of the line.

line 2: The tops of the first four letters of this line are visible in PAmh 200.4 and the expected reconstruction is highly probable. The final word, μου, is unique according to Rahlfs (see мт, those who surround me!); other witnesses have αυτων (their head?).

line 3: The end of the line is badly damaged, but the reconstruction is supported by the evidence of the new fragment, PAmh 200.1, for the next line.

line 4: The end is blank.

lines 5–7: This section clearly begins with ΚΑ, followed by the lower part of a vertical stroke. The textual situation for this section is confused, including how the stichoi are divided. Our text presents two στιχοι, and its wording is identical to MS B, although according to Rahlfs, B has και καταβαλεις αυτους as a separate στιχος. Where Rahlfs' B group has πυρος, as in our text, many other witnesses have εν πυρι (as in мт) or have both. After this, some texts such as ours include επι της γης (notably B) or εν τη γη (notably R)—the pi is clear on PAmh 200.1—and some (again, notably B) continue with και which is almost certainly the situation here as well. So in its general contours, our text is closely allied to MS B and some of its allies here. But the problem of how the section began is not solved by referring to the variants recorded in Rahlfs. It is an obvious solution to read και at the start of line 5, but that leaves us with a very long "filler" if the expected text is simply added— 15 letters where the other extant lines average about 12. Still, no other solution is as obvious at this point.

line 7: The final nu is indicated by a supralinear line over the iota. The upsilon has a rough breathing over it.

lines 8–9: The first hand of MS B omits this material, which is then added in the margin.

line 10: The original editors read confidently θηρευσει, with most other known texts (T has -σαι), but I am unable to correlate those letters with the visible ink marks, which look more like ΗΣΩΡΙΣΕΙ.

line 11: MS B uniquely reads καταφθοραν.

line 12: The initial large letter epsilon is supplied convincingly by PAmh 200.3.

lines 12–14: A single stichos, with R' T A(cf), but divided into two stichoi by B´ Sa La^G Ga SyHe 1219 (Rahlfs).

line 13: Variant των πτωχων (L'Sy^{mg} 55).

line 14: Variant του πενητος (S Sa).

line 17: The original editors printed ευθεις . . . προ/σωπου here, and noted the variants εν τω προσωπω (B´) and συν τω προσωπω (the majority), with S having προσωπου instead of προσωπω. The -ου ending is quite clear in our MS, and thus they conjecture that it must have agreed with S here in what appears to be an orthographic peculiarity. Rahlfs notes only the συν/εν variation.

line 19: The lower right foot of the expected number PM (140) is visible at the left side. Probably the name ΔAY(E)IΔ was abbreviated to ΔAΔ, as frequently happens. The "filler" marks noted in the previous heading do not appear here.

line 20: Read εκεκραξα. Most witnesses transpose this word before the προς σε (so also Rahlfs), while the order in our text is attested by B´ La^G.

lines 21–22: Our text agrees with Rahlfs and the majority of witnesses by presenting a single stichos here (line 22 is indented), where B T divide into two stichoi (μου/εν).

line 25: Variant η επαρσις (R).

line 27: Variant εθου (S Sa).

lines 32–33: In Sa, these are presented as a single stichos.

2. The Exodus, Deuteronomy, and Isaiah Fragments: An Anthology?

One set of fragments that the editors thought may have come from a single 6th century codex or set of codices written in the same scribal hand, is found in their items 191, 192, and 194. The editors were a bit perplexed by the range of texts that they were able to identify in this set, since PAmh 191(a) was from Exodus 19 while

PAmh 192 was from Deuteronomy 32, and they were unable to identify PAmh 191(b), which they did transcribe, although they were convinced that it also must have come from the same codex. Thus they imagined a relatively large work that may have contained the entire Pentateuch and perhaps even more.[3]

They did comment briefly on the unusual top line of the fragment designated PAmh 191(a): "at the top of the *recto* where the chapter [Exod 19] begins is a title of some kind." Regarding the unidentified PAmh 191(b) they noted that "it is from the lower part of a leaf, and the *recto* formed the conclusion of a chapter or section."

Not long after publication of the PAmherst 2 volume, A. Deissmann was able to identify the fragment designated PAmh 191(b) as from Isaiah 58.[4] It is already included as such in Rahlfs' *Verzeichnis* (1914) where it received the Göttingen number 915 and it was used by Joseph Ziegler in his 1939 critical edition of Isaiah, although he seems unaware that the Amherst Papyri had already been relocated to New York City at the Pierpont Morgan Library many years before.

At least one of the three fragments designated PAmh 194 also comes from this same page of Isaiah, and that material will be tran-

---

[3] Regarding PAmh 191(a) [Ex 19]: "The fragment is from a very handsome MS., written in large round uncials of calligraphic type, of about the sixth century. The following fragment of Deuteronomy (192) is in a similar handwriting, and probably it as well as the unplaced piece printed below [191(b)] and three smaller fragments (194) belonged to the same manuscript, which may have extended to several volumes including the whole of the Pentateuch. The ink is of the brown colour common at this period." To PAmh 191(b): "The following fragment is certainly from the same MS., and should be readily identified, but we have not succeeded in doing so." On PAmh 192 [Deut 32, two fragments]: "The large upright hand in which these fragments are written is apparently identical with that of the preceding fragment of Exodus, and they probably belonged to the same manuscript." Finally, for PAmh 194: "Three small fragments from a papyrus book . . . in a large uncial hand resembling that of 191 and 192, perhaps forming part of the same manuscript."

[4] I am indebted to Detlef Fraenkel of the Göttingen Septuagint Project for this information. See A. Deissmann, Beilage 251 of the *Allgemeinen Zeitung Muenchen* from 31 October 1901. Deissmann reconstructed the Isaiah fragment, and this information was included in C. Schmidt's "Referat Christliche Texte" in APF 2 (1903) 382. On this basis, Alfred Rahlfs listed the fragment in his *Verzeichnis der griechischen Handschriften des Alten Testaments* (Berlin 1914); Rahlfs quotes the original editors about the relationship of the two fragments included under the 191 label and comments "that a papyrus book had contained both Exodus and Isaiah is not very probable." He does not note Schmidt's observation that in a Christian liturgical context, Isaiah 58 may have connections with the Exodus passage (ibid.). For Isaiah, textcritical information is based on Joseph Ziegler, *Isaias* (Göttingen *Septuaginta* 14; Vandenhoeck & Ruprecht, 1939).

scribed below. Thus far, the other two fragments on the PAmh 194 plate remain unidentified.

The available clues suggest that these three passages—Exodus 19, Deuteronomy 32, and Isaiah 58—were indeed from the same codex, but it was a codex of extensive excerpts rather than of complete biblical books. The heading at the top of the Exodus page ended with the words α]πο μερους (in part), set off visually from what follows by the use of underlining and overlining. The bottom of the Isaiah page has the same distinctive features (filler marks plus under and overlining). How many other passages would have been included, and how extensive these three passages were, remain mysteries. A detailed investigation of the use of these passages in (Jewish and) Christian literature from that period might prove rewarding in this connection. The passages all relate to God's covenant with Israel, and Israel's response. This may well have been a theme deserving such special treatment among some (Jews and) Christians.

What remains of the page of Isaiah is as follows. PAmh 191(b) is the larger fragment (from the middle of the column), PAmh 194.1 the smaller (from the margin, represented in upper case letters). There are no unambiguous variants from the text of Ziegler's Göttingen edition:

Isaiah 58:11–14 (end)

side 1 (against the fibers = verso)

01 ...   παντος κ]αι εμ[πλησθη   {58:11}
02 ση   καθαπ]ερ επ[ιθυμει η ψυ
03 ΧΗ[σου και]τα οσ[τα σου πιαν
04 ΘΗ[σεται κ]αι εστ[αι ως κηπος
05 Μ[εθυων   ]και ω[ς πηγη ην
06 ΜΗ[εξελι]πεν[υδωρ
 ──────
07 ΚΑ[ι οικοδο]μηθ[ησονται σου   {58:12}
08 αι ερημοι α]ιων[ιοι ...
(lower margin)

line 2: the ending of καθαπερ is visible, precluding the well attested early variant καθα (S*, Just., Tht., etc.)

line 4: the letters εστ are probable, rather than the variant εση (Ziegler's oI, L, etc. = MT)

line 5: there does not seem to be room for πηγη υδατος found in many witnesses

lines 6–7: between 58:11 and 58:12 is a marginal horizontal stroke, and there is no room at the end of verse 11 for the long plus variant recorded in Ziegler's apparatus.

side 2 (with the fibers = recto)

[about 11 lines missing]

```
00 και καλεσις τα σαββατα τρυφ          {58:13b}
01 ερα αγια τ]ω      [θω σου ουκ
02 αρεις      το]ν ποδ[α σου επ εργω
03 ουδε λαλη]σεις λ[ογον εν ]ΟΡ
04 γη εκ του ]στομ[ατος σ]ΟΥ ΚΑΙ      {58:14}
05 εση     πεπο]ιθως[ επι    κ]Ν ΚΑΙ
06 αναβιβα]σε επι[ τα αγαθ]Α ΤΗΣ
07 γης και ψ]ωμιει[    σε την_]ΚΛΗ
08 ρονομια]ν ιακω[β      του ]ΠΡΣ
09 σου το γαρ ]στομ[α κυ ελαση
10 σεν    ταυτ]α >>>>>>[. . .
11 . . . . . .] . . . . [
(lower margin)
```

line 1: after the final loop of omega, there is a blank space of about three letters width before the break (perhaps following θω rather than the definite article); none of the variants recorded by Ziegler suggest an explanation—one could conjecture that the tetragrammaton was expected, although κυριω is not among the variants.

line 4: the final word of 58:13 is not clear, and possibly there was a mark of some sort before the start of verse 14 (και).

line 5: there is not enough room for the full form of κυριον here (see also line 9), so I have assumed that the normal *nomina sacra* of this period were used; see also lines 8–9 below.

line 8: the word πατρος seems to have been abbreviated and over-lined, although the fragment is not very clear at this point; there does not seem to be sufficient room for the unabbreviated word.

line 9: again, the normal *nomen sacrum* for κυριου is expected.

line 11: the tops of some letters appear below the filler marks in line 10, but defy decipherment. We might expect them to indicate the end of the excerpt.

3. Fragments from the "A Text" of Judges

The original editors transcribed enough of one fragment from PAmherst 198 to permit identification by searching the TLG LXX/OG texts, which include both of the main Greek recensions of Judges ("A" and "B"). Apparently the original editors' tools were not sufficiently sophisticated to allow them to identify the "A Text" of that book.[5] In any event, what we have in *PAmherst 198* are several fragments of that recension, in a codex that the original editors dated to the 5th century c.e. The format of the text is interesting, in that new sections (often corresponding to modern verses) often begin on a new line, leaving the preceding line shorter than the others. Whether there were also marginal markers at those points cannot be determined. Probably there is such a marker at Judg 13:11, but that may be because the new section began with the last word of the previous line. At Judg 3:20, the marginal alignment on the left also seems disrupted, perhaps to mark the new section ("verse"). Fragments from at least two folia at Judges 16 are preserved, with two columns of writing missing from between them, and it is not immediately clear whether another folio (containing a column on each side) originally came between these preserved sections, or whether the original pages may have contained double columns (see further below).

The codex contained about 32 lines per column, with an average of 20 letters per line, judging from the best preserved sections in chapter 16. In chapter 13, there may have been only 30–31 lines, and in chapter 3 (if that identification is correct), as few as 29 lines. The outer and lower margins were fairly wide (3–4 cm), and each column of writing (without the margins) would have been about 10 cm wide and 18–19 cm tall. If it was a single column codex, the size would have been about 15 cm wide by perhaps 26 cm tall, similar to Turner's groups 6–8; if double columned, then perhaps almost 30 cm wide by 26 cm tall (which would be virtually unprecedented). Turner mentions some similarly formatted single column codices, such as his C 7 (P. Vogliano 5, Pauline Epistles, 5th c.), C 30 (PChester-Beatty, Manichaean Psalm Book, 4–5th c.), Lit 2 (6th c. Euchologium), P 35 (3–4th c. Matthew), P 46 (3rd c. Pauline Epistles), P 47 (3rd c. Revelation), among others.[6]

---

[5] "Six fragments, the largest measuring 4.2 × 6.2 cm, from a papyrus book.... About the fifth century A.D." The present plate numbered 198 contains seven fragments, one of which is too small to place with any confidence, and another of which does not seem to come from the A text of Judges (see below, "fragment 6"). Textcritical information for the book of Joshua is based mainly on Alan England Brooke and Norman McLean, *The Old Testament in Greek* 1.4 ("Cambridge Larger Septuagint"; Cambridge University Press, 1917); see also Alfred Rahlfs, *Septuaginta* (Privileg. Wuertt. Bibelanstalt, Stuttgart, 1952[5] [1935]).

[6] Eric G. Turner, *The Typology of the Early Codex* (University of Pennsylvania Press,

As has been noted, the textual affinities of these fragments are with the "A-group" for Judges, which is conveniently printed separately in Rahlfs' *Septuaginta*, and reproduced in the TLG electronic materials. Close analysis of the exact alignment within the witnesses to the "A-text" must await further study, and depends in part on careful conjectural restoration of some of the lacunae, especially in Judg 16. My quick impression is that the PAmherst 198 fragments stand closest to the group AGbckxz^{mg} where there are significant variations in the "A-text."[7]

Fragment 1 recto (along the fibers), Judg 3:15

This small fragment (5 cm wide x 3 cm high) contains mostly blank margin, but also some interesting features. The recto almost certainly was filled with standard *nomina sacra* abbreviations (for "son," "Israel," and "Lord"), and the overlining for YIOY is still visible at the end of the last preserved line in 3:15. The ink remnants from the lower part of the end of the first preserved line are consistent with the expected KN (κυριον), but are by no means unambiguous. If the proposed reconstruction is correct, 3:15 did not begin on a new line (see also 13:11, 16:23).

εκεκραξαν οι υ̅ι̅ Ι̅η̅λ̅ προς]Κ̅Ν̅
και ηγειρεν αυτοις κ̅ς̅]ΣΩ
τηρα τον Αωδ υ̅ν̅ Γηρ]Α Υ̅Υ̅

Fragment 1 verso (against the fibers), Judg 3:20

The left margin is 2.5 cm wide at the first preserved line, but uncharacteristically, the next line seems to be indented by the width of about two letters (almost 1 cm), perhaps suggesting that the beginning of the new verse on "line one" was actually extended into the left margin here. Traces of the bottom of a letter or two are visible above the "first line," but cannot be identified with confidence.

1977), especially "Table 1: Papyrus Codices Grouped by Dimension," and "Table 16: Consolidated List of Codices Consulted."

[7] For a brief and convenient summary of the textual situation in Judges, see Walter Ray Bodine, *The Greek Text of Judges: Recensional Developments* (HSM 23; Scholars Press, 1980), 2–3: he notes that the group A(G)abc(k)x has been identified by several scholars (e.g. Pretzl, Billen, Soisalon-Soininen) as the primary witness to the "A-text."

ΚΑΙ ΑΩ[δ εισηλθεν προς αυ
ΤΟ[ν και αυτος εκαθητο εν

Fragment 2 verso (against the fibers), Judg 13:10b–11a

This fragment measures 3.7 cm wide by 5.2 cm high, with a pre-served left margin (doubtless damaged) of only 1.5 cm and a lower margin of 4 cm on the verso. It is noteworthy that although the practice of starting new "verse" sections on new lines is not found here, there is a marginal mark to the left an slightly above line two, which may serve to indicate a sense break in the previous line, where our "verse 11" begins.

[μοι ο ανηρ ο ελθων προς]
ΜΕ ΤΗ[ημερα εκεινη {11} και
ΑΝΕΣ[τη Μανωε και επορευθη
(lower left margin)

Fragment 2 recto (along the fibers), Judg 13:16 (middle)

The final word of the last line in this column extends well into the margin and the final two letters are much smaller than usual. The margin for the preceding line is 1.5 cm, but for this line only 0.5 cm; the lower margin is about 4 cm, as on the other side. Rahlfs has anarthrous κυριω here, but if it was abbreviated to $\overline{\text{ΚΩ}}$, as expected, the reconstructed last line would be unusually short (18–21 letters is normal, plus the overrun into the right margin), which sug-gests that τω κ(υρι)ω appeared here, in agreement with the "B-text" and most witnesses to the "A-text" as well (not Aglnow Cyr2/3).

[ου φαγομαι των αρτων σου]
και εαν ποιησης ο]ΛΟΚΑΥ
τωμα τω $\overline{\text{κω}}$ ανοι]ΣΕΙΣ ΑΥΤΟ
(lower right margin)

Fragments 3 and 4 recto (along the fibers), Judg 16:6–8a

These fragments were once part of the same column, but there is a break of about 4 lines between them. The first and smaller piece is 3.2 cm wide by 2.3 cm high, and shows no margins; the second piece comes from the bottom of the column and is about 9 cm wide by 7 cm high, with a lower margin of 4.2 cm (the writing at the outer margin is not well preserved, but that margin seems to have been 3 cm or slightly more). The final line of 16:6 has space to the right, indicating a break between "verses." That may also be true at the end of 16:7, although the surface of the papyrus is too badly abraded to be sure. This material shows ample evidence of representing the main "A-text" in general.

```
00 {6}  [και ειπεν Δαλιδα προς Σαμ]
01      ψων αναγγει]ΛΟΝ[ μοι εν τινι
02      η ισχυς σ]ΟΫ Η Μ[εγαλη και
03      εν τινι δε]ΘΗΣΗ ΤΟ[υ ταπει
04      νωθηναι ]ΣΕ (blank)
05 {7}  και ειπεν π]ΡΟΣ ΑΥΤ[ην Σαμ
06      [ψων εαν δησωσιν με εν Z̄]
07      [νευραις υγραις μη ηρη]
08      [μωμεναις και ασθενησω ]
09      [και εσομαι ως εις των]
10      [α̅ν̅ω̅ν̅] (blank?)
11 {8}  και ανηνεγκα]Ν ΑΥΤ[η οι
12      σατραπαι τω]Ν ΑΛ[λοφ]Υ[λων
13      Z̄ νευρας ]ΥΓΡΑΣ[ μ]Η Η[ρη
```
(lower and right margin preserved)

line 0 {16:6}: in most Greek texts, Dalila (or Daleila) has become Dal(e)ida.

line 1: the bottoms of two or three letters are visible, but not easily decipherable; possibly ΛΟΝ.

line 4: after ΣΕ the remaining line is blank (about 4–5 letter widths).

line 5 {16:7}: the spacing is consistent with a new section starting here.

lines 6–8: nothing is preserved of lines 6–8, but assuming consistency with Rahlfs' A-text, these lines would be approximately as displayed above, although the number seven (line 6, επτα) probably was represented by overlined Z̄ (see also the final line of the column); traces of the bottom of line 9 and part of line 10 are preserved on the second fragment, but the latter is either badly abraded or was blank at that point (after the final word of the section, presumably an abbreviated form of ανθρωπων).

line 11 {16:8}: probably begins a new section.

line 12: these letters are very damaged, and cannot be read with confidence.

line 13: the letters ΫΓΡΑ are fairly clear (dieresis over the Ϋ), but the piece is badly damaged (and needs to be remounted) for the last part of the line; it is unlikely that the entire word ηρημωμενας would fit on the line; the number seven (επτα) at the start of the line probably was represented by overlined $\overline{Z}$ (see also above, line 6).

The lower margin including probably the right lower corner is preserved

Fragments 3 and 4 verso (against the fibers), Judg 16:11b–13a

```
00      [εν οις ουκ εγενηθη εργον]
01      και αστενη]ΣΩ ΚΑΙ[ εσομαι
02      ως εις τω]Ν ΑΝΩΝ[ (blank)
03 {12} και ελαβε]Ν ΑΥΤΩ[ Δαλιδα
04      καλωδια κα]ΙΝΑ˙ ΚΑ[ι εδησεν
05      [αυτον εν αυτοις και ειπεν]
06      [προς αυτον οι αλλοφυλοι]
07      [επι σε Σαμψων και το ενε]
08      [δρον εκαθητο εν τω ταμι]
09      [ειω και διεσπασεν αυτα]
10      [απο των βραχιονων αυτου]
11      [ως ραμμα (blank?)]
12 {13} κα]Ι ΕΙΠ[εν Δαλι]Δ[α προς Σαμ
(lower and left margin preserved)
```

line 1 {16:11b}: traces of the bottom of a letter or two are visible above this line, but cannot be identified

line 2: the final word of the section (16:11), ανθρωπων, is clearly abbreviated and overlined

line 4 {16:12}: there seems to be a high dot punctuation mark after κα]ΙΝΑ

lines 5–7 are missing completely (as with the recto fragments)

lines 8–12 five lines have left traces on the badly damaged and abraded lower fragment, but hardly any letters can be read with confidence; possibly the last line began with και ειπεν {16:13}, and the last visible letter on the line appears to be a Δ (probably part of Δαλιδα or Δαλειδα)

As with the other side, the lower margin and probably the lower left corner is preserved

[one leaf, recto and verso (or two inner columns), are missing here]

Fragment 5 recto (along the fibers), Judg 16:21b–23a

This piece contains the largest amount of writing among the fragments, and probably for that reason was called "the largest" by the original editors—6.5 cm wide by 4.5 high. The outer margin is about 4 cm wide on the verso (beginnings of lines), and varies from 3.5 to 4 cm on the recto (ends of lines). This fragment contains many readings characteristic of the "A-text," which deserve detailed treatment elsewhere. A short line clearly ended 16:21, but 16:22–23 are run together.

```
         [και κατηγαγον αυτον εις]
01       γαζαν και εδησαν α]ΥΤΟΝ
02       εν πεδαις χαλκαις] ΚΑΙ
03       ην αληθων εν οικ]Ω ΤΗΣ
04       φυλακης(blank)] (blank)
05 {22}  και ηρξατο η θριξ της] ΚΕΦΑ
06       λης αυτου ανατειλ]ΑΙ ΗΝΙ
07 {23}  κα εξυρηθη και οι σα]ΤΡΑΠΑΙ
08       των αλλοφυλων συνηχθ]Η
09       σαν του θυσαι θυσιαν . . .
         (about 6 lines more to bottom of column)
```

line 4 is blank in the preserved fragment, presumably as the end of the previous section (16:21)

line 5 {16:22} seems to have an overline above the letters ΕΦ (perhaps an elongation to the left of the top stroke of the Φ)

Fragment 5 verso (against the fibers), Judg 16:26

```
01 {26}  ΚΑΙ ΕΙΠΕ[ν Σαμψων προς το
02       ΠΑΙΔΑ[ριον τον χειραγωγουν
03       ΤΑ ΑΥΤ[ον επαναπαυσον με
04       ΔΗ ΚΑ[ι ποιησον ψηλαφη
05       ΣΑΙ ΜΕ[ επι τους στυλους εφ᾽
06       ΩΝ Ο Ο[ικος επεστηρικτα
07       ΕΠ ΑΥΤ[ων και επιστηρισο
         [μαι επ αυτους . . .]
         (about 6 more lines to bottom of column
```

line 1 is badly damaged, but probably was the start of 16:26 as reconstructed here; approximately 17–18 lines would have preceded it in this column

Fragments 6 and 7 (unidentified)

Two small fragments also mounted in the PAmherst 198 glass plate remain unidentified. I will call the largest fragment 6—it is 2.4 cm wide by 3.1 high, with portions of 5–6 lines from the center of a column (no margins visible). The hand is very similar to the Joshua fragments, with possible differences in the shape of upsilon and epsilon. I have not been able to identify either fragment by searching the TLG electronic texts of LXX/OG.

On the recto (along the fibers) of fragment 6:

line 1: the bottom of a vertical stroke, perhaps iota or nun or eta (among the numerous possibilities)

line 2: YO—a clear upsilon followed by a curved left part of a letter (sigma, omicron, omega; probably not epsilon or theta)

line 3: APM—alpha, rho, and a damaged letter or letters resembling upper parts of a mu

line 4: TAE—faint strokes (upsilon?) followed by tau, alpha, and a rounded letter (epsilon, theta, perhaps omicron or omega)

line 5: ΛΙΠΑ—part of an alpha or lamda, iota, pi, alpha

line 6: traces of ink from the top of the next line

verso (against the fibers), fragment 6

line 1: nothing visible in the topmost position

line 2: M—a large mu

line 3: MEM—mu, epsilon, and the start of another mu (on nu or eta) partly covered by a small scrap

line 4: ΣΕΣΤ—very clear sigma, epsilon, sigma and a trace of the top stroke of the next letter, possibly tau

line 5: NHΘ—nun, then a less clearly written nun or mem or eta, followed by epsilon or theta

Fragment 7

Fragment 7 is smaller still, 1.2 cm wide by 2.2 cm high, with no margins showing

recto (along the fibers)

line 1: IΣ—a vertical stroke (top missing) and the start of a rounded stroke (top and right side missing)

line 2:—apparently blank, perhaps the end of a section of Joshua?

line 3: T—possibly the right side of a kappa, and/or the left part of the top stroke of a tau

line 4: WM—three angled tops of letters, such as mu (or even the right side of omega) followed by nun or mu

verso (against the fibers)

line 1: AO—the lower right of possibly alpha or lamda followed by omicron (or theta)

line 2: ΕΣ—epsilon, and almost certainly sigma (or omicron)
line 3: Η—badly damaged, but there seems to be a horizontal mid stroke as in epsilon or eta
line 4: Μ—the top of a large mu

Afterword

For the scholar, young or old, who likes puzzles and the thrill of discovery, there are numerous fragments in the various collections that can now be identified by using the available electronic texts and tools. Many of these are listed by Joseph van Haelst in his 1976 *Catalog*.[8] Obtaining legible images, digitized at a suitable resolution and in color if possible, is becoming easier, but is still the main obstacle to making significant progress. Hopefully projects such as the Advanced Papyrological Information System (APIS) will help solve even that problem![9]

---

[8] Joseph van Haelst, *Catalogue des Papyrus Littéraires Juifs et Chrétiens* (Paris, 1976), chapter 10 ("Textes non identifiés" = ##1082–1190; see also ##1214–1215 [Latin] and 1223–1226); this provides an excellent starting point from the mid 1970s. I hope to summarize this information and supplement it on an appropriate internet folder on my own papyri page. The temporary location of this material is gopher:// ccat.sas.upenn.edu:70/00/journals/kraftpub/Papyri/Other%20Locations/.
[9] For information on the APIS project, see http://www.columbia.edu/cu/lweb/projects/digital/apis/index.html.

DID JOSHUA HAVE A CRYSTAL BALL?
THE OLD GREEK AND THE MT OF
JOSHUA 10:15, 17 AND 23

Kristin De Troyer

When I was collating the variants of MS 2648 (a.k.a. Göttingen, Rahlfs Verzeichnis 816),[1] I also looked at one of the most beautiful witnesses to the Old Greek text of Joshua: the so-called Joshua-roll of the *Bibliotheca Apostolica Vaticana* at Vatican City (Italy). Brooke and McLean, the editors of the *Cambridge Old Testament in Greek* critical edition used the roll in their 1917 publication of Part 4 of their project: the books Joshua, Judges and Ruth.[2] The roll was already known at the Vatican in the 17th century. More precisely, E. Schelstrate, director of the Vatican Library from 1683 to 1692, mentioned it already in his inventory of the Palatine Greek manuscripts "redatto," re-donated to the Vatican. After its re-donation to the library, it was sold again. But finally, in 1814, the roll again appeared in the Vatican collection. The Vatican published a book and parts of the roll in 1950.[3] In 1984 a facsimile edition of the roll and a better introduction were published.[4]

---

[1] Kristin De Troyer and Rosario Pintaudi, *The Schøyen Papyrus of Joshua*, in *Papyri from the Schøyen Collection. Part 1. Literary Texts* (ed. Rosario Pintaudi; Oslo, forthcoming).
[2] Alan England Brooke and Norman McLean, *The Old Testament in Greek according to the text of codex Vaticanus supplemented from other uncial manuscripts, with a critical apparatus containing the variants of the chief ancient authorities for the text of the septuagint. Part 4. Joshua, Judges and Ruth* (Cambridge: Cambridge University Press, 1917).
[3] Bibliotheca Vaticana, *Il Rotulo di Giosuè: Codice Vaticano Palatino greco 431* (Milano: Ulrico Hoepli, 1950).
[4] Let me clarify the "publicatons." There is first the Joshua roll, containing the pictures and the text. The roll is known as Palatinus graecus 431 (Rahlfs 661). A facsimile edition of this book was published in 1984 as: *Codices Selecti. Phototypice impressi. Facsimile volumen LXXVII. Commentarium Volumen LXXVII*. CODICES E VATICANIS SELECTI quam simillime expressi. Jussu Joannis Pauli P. II, consilio et opera curatorum bibliothecae apostolicae vaticanae. Volumen XLIII* (Graz, Austria: Akademische Druck- u. Verlagsanstalt, 1984). Together with this facsimile, an introduction and commentary to the roll was published: *Josua-Rolle: Vollständige Faksimile-Ausgabe im Originalformat des Codex Vaticanus Palatinus Graecus 431 der Bibliotheca Apostolica Vaticana. Kommentar: Otto Mazal* (Graz, Austria: Akademische Druck- u. Verlagsanstalt, 1984). In 1950,

Dated to the 9th or 10th century, the roll contains pictures and text. As I was working on Josh 9:27 to 11:3, I checked the roll and found out that it contained a couple of pictures with the appropriate texts of my pericope.[5] Table 13 pictures a battlefield, huge hailstones, and Joshua who makes the sun stand still. Under the picture one can read the text of Josh 10:9–14 (folio 453). This passage is the famous passage about the sun and the moon standing still and Joshua obtaining a victory over the Amorites.

Under the victory picture, there is another picture: Joshua is taking a rest after the battle and is explaining the victory. To the right of the picture, the five Ammorite kings flee for their lives (folio 453). The text that is placed right under this depiction starts with Joshua ordering to search for the five kings. That is part of Josh 10:17.

Two more pictures complete the story: in the first, Joshua is sitting on an even larger throne and judging the five kings, who are lying on the ground in front of Joshua (folio 453). In the second, there are the five kings, wearing a yoke. They are standing amidst a crowd of celebrating people (folio 454, respectively table 14 and 15). The editor of the book correctly connects the text from the first mentioned picture on table 13 with the following pictures. He writes: "Il lungo estratto del libro di Giosuè, comincia a tav. XIII e dice" (The long excerpt from the book of Joshua begins at Table XIII and says; p. 35) and then he quotes the text of Josh 10:16–26. In this passage the five kings are brought before Joshua.

Along with the four pictures, the roll provides a continuous text that contains the following material from Josh 10:9–14 (part of verse

---

however, a less exhaustive book was published on the roll, namely the above-mentioned Bibliotheca Vaticana, *Il Rotulo di Giosuè*. Then, there is also Palatinus graecus 431 A: The book is an explanation or commentary on the roll. After its chapter number, it describes what is on the picture. Then the biblical text follows, and in the margin the precise text reference is given. E.g. its chapter XXV lists: πόλις, Γαβαών, Ισραηλῖται, ιησοῦς ὁ του Ναυή, ισραηλῖτας, ἀλλόφυλοι. I have consulted the following chapters of this work: chapter XXIV, containing 10:6, chapter XXV: 10:9, 10, 11, 12, 13, 14, chapter XXVI: 10:16, 17, 22, 23, 24, 25, 26, and chapter XXVII: 10:26. This accompanying volume is probably from a later date than the roll. This, however, is still being discussed. Moreover, it is still debated whether or not the text on the roll, accompanying the pictures was original. Maybe the texts were added later to the pictures? As the accompanying volume sometimes offers a text different from the one on the roll, I have baptised the Palat. graecus 431 A: Rahlfs 661[A].

[5] Tables 13 to 15 on folios 453–454, which are numbered as Tav. E and F in the 1950 book, see also the 1950 publication, pp. 33–35.

12 is missing), 16–17, 22–26. Although the absence of 10:18–21 also is of special interest (especially verse 18), it was the absence of 10:15 that caught my eye. Indeed, 10:15 is lacking in many Greek witnesses (see further below), and seems not to be an original reading of the Old Greek, so its absence here was not a major surprise.

With the omission of verse 15 in mind, I turned to MS 2648.[6] There, another verse was missing. Not only was there no verse 15, but also verse 17 was missing from my text. I wondered: where did verse 17 go? And how to explain the text of verse 23, which is both in the Old Greek and MS 2648 a bit shorter than the Hebrew text? In this contribution, I will look at the text critical and literary critical issues of this part of the book of Joshua, both in Greek and in Hebrew, and formulate a challenging proposal as to why verse 15 and verse 17, and part of verse 23 are missing.

A. The Texts

1. *The MT as printed in BHS: Joshua 10:14–19a, 22–24*

ולא היה כיום ההוא לפניו ואחריו
לשמע יהוה בקול איש
כי יהוה נלחם לישראל
וישב יהושע וכל־ישראל עמו אל־המחנה הגלגלה
וינסו חמשת המלכים האלה ויחבאו במערה במקדה
וינד ליהושע לאמר נמצאו חמשת המלכים נחבאים במערה במקדה
ויאמר יהושע גלו אבנים גדלות אל־פי המערה והפקידו עליה אנשים לשמרם
ואתם אל־תעמדו רדפו אחרי איביכם
...
ויאמר יהושע פתחו את־פי המערה
והוציאו אלי את־חמשת המלכים האלה מן־המערה
ויעשו כן ויציאו אליו את־חמשת המלכים האלה מן־המערה ...
ויהי כהוציאם את־המלכים האלה אל־יהושע ויקרא יהושע אל־כל־איש ישראל
ויאמר אל־קציני אנשי המלחמה ההלכוא אתו
קרבו שימו את־רגליכם על־צוארי המלכם האלה
ויקרבו וישימו את־רגליהם על־צואריהם

NRSV:
[14]There has been no day like it before or since, when the LORD heeded a human voice; for the LORD fought for Israel. [15]Then Joshua returned and all Israel with him, to the camp at Gilgal. [16]Meanwhile, these five

---

[6] De Troyer and Pintaudi, *The Schøyen Papyrus of Joshua*.

kings fled and hid themselves in the cave at Makkedah. ¹⁷And it was told Joshua, "The five kings have been found, hidden in the cave at Makkedah." ¹⁸Joshua said, "Roll large stones against the mouth of the cave, and set men by it to guard them; ¹⁹but do not stay there yourselves; pursue your enemies and attack them from the rear. [. . .] ²²Then Joshua said, "Open the mouth of the cave, and bring those five kings out to me from the cave." ²³They did so, and brought the five kings out to him from the cave, . . . ²⁴When they brought the kings out to Joshua, Joshua summoned all the Israelites, and said to the chiefs of the warriors who had gone with him, "Come near, put your feet on the necks of these kings." Then they came near and put their feet on their necks.

2. The Old Greek as printed in Brooke-McLean: Joshua 10:14–19a, 22–24

¹⁴καὶ οὐκ ἐγένετο ἡμέρα τοιαύτη οὐδὲ τὸ πρότερον οὐδὲ τὸ ἔσχατον ὥστε ἐπακοῦσαι θεὸν ἀνθρώπου· ὅτι Κύριος συνεπολέμησεν τῷ Ἰσραήλ. ¹⁶Καὶ ἔφυγον οἱ πέντε βασιλεῖς οὗτοι, καὶ κατεκρύβησαν εἰς τὸ σπήλαιον τὸ ἐν Μακηδά. ¹⁷καὶ ἀπηγγέλη τῷ Ἰησοῦ λέγοντες Εὕρηνται οἱ πέντε βασιλεῖς κεκρυμμένοι ἐν τῷ σπηλαίῳ τῷ ἐν Μακηδα. ¹⁸καὶ εἶπεν Ἰησοῦς Κυλίσατε λίθους ἐπὶ τὸ στόμα τοῦ σπηλαίου, καὶ καταστήσατε ἄνδρας φυλάσσειν ἐπ' αὐτούς· ¹⁹ὑμεῖς δὲ μὴ ἐστήκατε καταδιώκοντες ὀπίσω τῶν ἐχθρῶν ὑμῶν [. . .]. ²²καὶ εἶπεν Ἰησοῦς Ἀνοίξατε τὸ σπήλαιον, καὶ ἐξαγάγετε τοὺς πέντε βασιλεῖς τούτους ἐκ τοῦ σπηλαίου. ²³καὶ ἐξηγάγοσαν τοὺς πέντε βασιλεῖς ἐκ τοῦ σπηλαίου . . . ²⁴καὶ ἐπεὶ ἐξήγαγον αὐτοὺς πρὸς Ἰησοῦν, καὶ συνεκάλεσεν Ἰησοῦς πάντα Ἰσραὴλ καὶ τοὺς ἐναρχομένους τοῦ πολέμου τοὺς συνπορευομένους αὐτῷ λέγων αὐτοῖς Προπορεύεσθε καὶ ἐπίθετε τοὺς πόδας ὑμῶν ἐπὶ τοὺς τραχήλους αὐτῶν. καὶ προσελθόντες ἐπέθηκαν τοὺς πόδας αὐτῶν ἐπὶ τοὺς τραχήλους αὐτῶν.

Brenton's translation runs as follows:[7]
And there was not such a day either before or after, so that God should hearken to a man, because the Lord fought on the side of Israel. And these five kings fled, and hid themselves in a cave that is in Makeda. And it was told Joshua, saying, The five kings have been found hid in the cave that is in Makeda. And Joshua said, Roll stones to the mouth of the cave, and set men to watch over them. But do not ye stand, but pursue after your enemies, and attack the rear of

---

[7] Sir Lancelot Charles Lee Brenton, *The Septuagint Version of the Old Testament and Apocrypha with an English Translation and with Various Readings and Critical Notes* (London: Bagster & sons, 1851; Grand Rapids, MI: Zondervan, 1978).

them, [. . .] And Joshua said, Open the cave, and bring out these five
kings out of the cave. And they brought out the five kings out of the
cave . . . And when they brought them out to Joshua, then Joshua called
together all Israel, and the chiefs of the army that went with him, saying to them, Come forward and set your feet on their necks; and they
came and set their feet on their necks.

B. Text Critical Remarks

1. *The Hebrew Text*[8]

Verse 15

The apparatus to Joshua 10:15 mentions that the Old Greek has
omitted this verse. There is also a problem with the *Masora Parva*.
In verse 15, there is a note attached to וכל־ישראל: the *Masora Parva*
reads: לה ר"פ דבות. The Masoretic note hence observes that the
expression appears 35 times at the beginning of a verse, like this.[9]
At the other 34 appearances of וכל־ישראל the note is similar.[10] In the
notes in the margins of the Cairo codex, however, the number mentioned is different. It is not 35, but 34.[11] The note of the editor

---

[8] R. Meyer, *Josua et Judices* (*BHS* 4; Stuttgart: Deutsche Bibelgesellschaft, 1972/77,
1983).

[9] The following passages have the note: Josh 3:17; 7:24; 8:15; 8:21; 10:15; 10:29;
10:31; 10:34; 10:36; 10:38; 10:43; 1 Sam 17:11; 2 Sam 3:37; 2 Sam 4:1; 2 Sam
18:17; 1 Kgs 8:62; 1 Reg 8:65; 1 Reg 11:16; 1 Reg 15:27; 1 Reg 16:17; 2 Reg
9:14; Esdr 2:70; 8:25; 10:5; Neh 7:72; 1 Chr 11:4; 13:6; 13:8; 2 Chr 7:6; 7:8; 10:3;
12:1; 13:4; 13:15.

[10] Weil, however, added in a couple instances his famous words "sub loco." This
note "indicates that we corrected an error in the Mp of L, or that the difficulty is
due to the absence of a related list in the Mm of L. These instances are discussed
fully in our Massorah Gedolah, vol. iii." Cf. Page H. Kelley, Daniel S. Mynatt,
and Timothy G. Crawford, *The Masorah of Biblia Hebraica Stuttgartensia: Introduction
and Annotated Glossary* (Grand Rapids, MI: Eerdmans, 1998), 54, with reference to
the BHS Introduction, p. xvii. There is, indeed, no list of the passages in the work
of Gérard E. Weil. *Massorah Gedolah iuxta Codicem Leningradensem B 19ᵃ, Vol. 1. Catalogi*
(Rome: Pontificium Institutum Biblicum, 1971; reprint 2001). Hence, the note refers
to a correction made by Weil. The sub loco note is added to Esr 2:70; 8:25; 10:5;
Neh 7:72; 1 Chr 11:4; 13:8; 2 Chr 10:3; 12:1; 13:4; 13:15, not by accident all references from the last part of the Bible. Moreover, the first *sub loco* note comes at
1 Chr 11:4 the Rabbinic Bible mentions that the discussed expression appears 34
times. I checked different editions of the Rabbinic Bible and all have 34 in the
note to 1 Chr 11:4.

[11] Cf. F. Perez Castro, *El Codice de Profetas de El Cairo* (Textos Estudios "Cardenal
Cisneros" 26; Madrid: Instituto Arias Montano, 1980), esp. p. 58.

Perez Castro, reads: "C en todos los pasajes de Ios (excepto Ios 10,29 que carece de nota) dice que el número de veces es 34. Sin embargo en todo Sam y Reg da un caso más: Deut 21,21. En efecto las veces que aparace en la Biblia וכל־ישראל en medio de vers son 35, si bien en el pasaje de Deut la versión de los LXX (ed. Wevers) presenta la variante ἐπίλοιποι respecto al texto hebraico masorético" (the Codex says, in all the passages of Joshua—except for Josh 10:29 which has no note—that the number of times it appears is 34. Outside of Samuel and Kings, there is one more case, namely Deut 21:21. Indeed, the total amount that the Hebrew phrase appears in the middle of a verse is 35, even if the Septuagint translation of Deuteronomy [edited by Wevers] presents the variant ἐπίλοιποι which reflects the Hebrew Masoretic text).[12] The editor of the Cairo codex, thus, believes that the case of Deut 21:21 was originally not counted, for it seems to have had a Hebrew text without וכל־ישראל. Although I have reason to believe that this issue is related to the Old Greek of Joshua and not to the text of Deut 21:21, I will discuss this problem in another publication.[13]

Verses 17 and 23
There are no notes attached to the verses 16–25, which might deserve our text critical attention.

2. *The Greek Text*

Verse 15
Καὶ ἐπέστρεψεν ἰησοῦς καὶ πᾶς ιηλ μετ᾽ αὐτοῦ εἰς τὴν παρεμβολὴν εἰς γάλγαλα omitted in BAF^bVOldLatSah^bSah^t; present in B^mgF^bmgGW 18 19 30 38 54 56 58 68 75 82 85^mg 108 120 121^mg 122 126 129 246 343^mg 344^mg 346^mg 370 376 426 458 488 489 628 630 646 669 707 730 ArmEth^fSyh (sub ÷; in *O* sub ※)[14]

It is clearly a hexaplaric addition to the Old Greek of Joshua. Its omission is absolutely not due to homoioteleuton.

---

[12] Ibidem, p. 58, note b. Perez Castro repeats this note at Josh 3:17; 7:24; 8:15; 8:21; 10:15; 10:31; 10:34; 10:36; 10:38; 10:43, hence everywhere in Joshua except for 10:29.

[13] This issue is also difficult from a text critical and text historical perspective. Codex Vaticanus e.g. has πας ο λαος in 7:24 whereas AFMVW read πας ισραηλ. Codex B also omits πας in 8:15.

[14] For the exhaustive list of witnesses I am most grateful to Udo Quast of the Septuagint Institute in Göttingen.

Verse 17

Καὶ ἀπηγγέλη τῷ Ἰησοῦ λέγοντες Εὕρηνται οἱ πέντε βασιλεῖς κεκρυμμένοι ἐν τῷ σπηλαίῳ τῷ ἐν Μακηδά omitted in 53 125 246 392 799; present in BAFᵇGVW et rell.

The omission of this verse can be explained by homoioteleuton: the last two words of verse 16 are precisely the same as the last two words of verse 17. While reading, the copyist could have jumped from the end of v. 16 to the end of v. 17, and thus, have omitted verse 17. Homoioteleuton, however, does not explain the absence of the verse in the above-mentioned witnesses, some of which are independent of one another.[15]

Verse 23

Καὶ ἐξηγάγοσαν τοὺς πέντε βασιλεῖς ἐκ τοῦ σπηλαίου ... (followed by the list of the names of the five kings).

Καὶ (1°)—σπηλαίου is omitted by the following witnesses: B*W 15 18 29 30 64 126 128 246 381 407 488 616 618 628 630 646 669 730. Rahlfs adds in his note to verse 22: σπηλαιου ⌒ 23 σπηλαιου B*, and thus explains the omission as due to homoioteleuton.[16] The text, without the text, is hence a mistake made by the scribe of B. The text of the Old Greek as printed by Brooke-McLean is based on a correction of the original text of the Vaticanus. Indeed, a note under the text states και (1°)—σπηλαιου Bᵃ ᵐᵍ ⁱⁿᶠ] om B*. In Codex Vaticanus the correction is clearly legible. The text in the bottom margin is precisely the text missing, except that the initial και is abbreviated.

For the sake of completeness, we have to mention that a series of witnesses has at the end of verse 22: καὶ ἐποίησαν οὕτως, namely: G 19 55 58 68 74 76 82 84 106 108 120 122 134 370 376 426 707 799 ArmSahSyh (sub ※ in G and Syh).

3. *Additional Witnesses*

Sabatier does not offer the text of the Vetus Latina, verses 15 and 16. The notes state that vv. 17–25 conform to the Greek text. There

---

[15] For instance: 125 belongs to the Byzantine group d, 799 to the Byzantine group t, and 392 is a good, but mixed, witness to the Old Greek.

[16] Alfred Rahlfs, *Septuaginta, id est vetus testamentum graece iuxta lxx interpretes* (Stuttgart: Deutsche Bibelgesellschaft, 1979).

is no note about vv. 15 and 16.[17] The Lyon manuscript of the Vetus Latina[18] does not include v. 15. Verse 17 reads: "Et renuntiauerunt Iesu, dicentes: Inuenti sunt toti quinque reges absconditi in spelunca quae est in Mageda." Verse 23 has: "Et produxerunt quinque reges istos de spelunca" (followed by the list of names).

The Peshitta edition includes vv. 15, 17 and v. 23 like the MT. In verse 23, the Peshitta adds after "and they did so" the words: "as Joshua had told them" ܐܝܟܪܐ ܠܗܘܢ ܝܫܘܥ.[19]

The Vulgate renders vv. 15 and 17 faithfully. Verse 23 starts, however, with: "fecerunt ministri ut sibi fuerat imperatum."[20]

In verses 15, 17, and 23, Targum Jonathan offers an Aramaic text close to the Hebrew text.[21]

C. Forms, Structures, and Literary and Redactional Skills of the Authors and/or Interpreters

1. MT

The Hebrew text has the following structure and forms:

> v. 14: conclusion of the former story 1: statement about what happened.
> v. 15: conclusion of the former story 2: the people gather at Gilgal.
> v. 16: new action: the five kings flee to Makedah and they hide in the cave.
> v. 17: reaction: a report is made to Joshua that the five kings have fled to Makedah and that they are hiding in the cave.
> v. 18: immediate reaction of Joshua regarding the kings: Joshua gives

---

[17] Petrus Sabatier, *Bibliorum sacrorum latinae versiones antiquae seu Vetus Italica et caeterae quaecumque in codicibus Mss et antiquorum libris reperiri potuerunt: quae cum Vulgata Latina et cum textu graeco comparantur, Vol. 1* (Reims, 1743).

[18] Ulysse Robert, *Heptateuchi partis posterioris versio latina antiquissima e codice Lugdunensi* (Lyon: Librairie de A. Rey et Cⁱᵉ, 1900).

[19] Johann E. Erbes, *Joshua*, In *Leviticus—Numbers—Deuteronomy—Joshua*. The Old Testament in Syriac according to the Peshitta Version, Part I, fascicle 2; Part II, fascicle 1b) (ed. D. J. Lane, A. P. Hayman, W. M. van Vliet, J. H. Hospers, H. J. W. Drijvers and J. E. Erbes; Leiden: Brill, 1991), 26.

[20] Robert Weber, ed., *Biblia Sacra iuxta Vulgatam Versionem* (Stuttgart: Würtembergische Bibelanstalt, 1969).

[21] B. Walton, *Biblia Polyglotta, Tomus 2* (London, 1657; photomech. reprint: Graz: Akademische Druck- und Verlagsanstalt, 1964). See also: Daniel J. Harrington, and Anthony J. Saldarini, *Targum Jonathan of the Former Prophets* (ArBib 10; Edinburgh: T. & T. Clark; Wilmington, Delaware: Michael Glazier, 1987), 33–34.

a double command: block the exit of the cave and appoint some men to guard the cave.

    vv. 19–21: additional instruction of Joshua: he directs his people to yet another action—additional story.

v. 22: later reaction of Joshua regarding the kings: Joshua gives a double command: open the cave and bring out the kings.

v. 23: response: the command is heeded and the kings are brought out.

v. 24a: action of Joshua: Joshua gives a double command: come here and put your feet on their necks.

v. 24b: response: double response: they come and they put their feet on their necks.

Verse 15 contains a reference to the camp at Gilgal. The ה-localis is added to Gilgal. Gilgal with ה-localis only appears 6 times in the Bible, three times in Joshua: 10:6, 10:15 and 10:43. In 10:6 men are sent to Joshua at the camp at Gilgal; in 10:15: Joshua returned, and all the Israelites with him, to the camp at Gilgal; in 10:43: again it is said that Joshua returned, and all the Israelites with him, to the camp at Gilgal. In between, Joshua is in Makedah dealing with the kings (Joshua 10:16–28) and in the entire country conquering the land (10:29–42). This is a survey of Joshua's whereabouts:

Gilgal	Makedah	rest of land
10:6		
10:15		
	10:21–28	
		10:29–42
10:43		

In verse 21, Joshua "returns" to Makedah. Hence, Joshua moved earlier from Gilgal to Makedah. But when did he do so?

    Verses 16 & 17 contain another problem. First the narrator reports that the five kings flee to Makedah. The reader knows that they are gone. But Joshua needs to know too. Hence, verse 17 states that it was reported to Joshua. Now, both the reader and the leading character in the story seem to know the same fact. Verse 17, however, is not constructed in an obvious manner: it opens with a Hophal "it was told to Joshua," then, the verse continues with "saying" followed by a direct quote in the third plural "they have found." Hence, verse 17 not only reports on the fleeing of the five kings, it also states that they were found hiding in the cave. Verse 17 offers the necessary facts for the continuation of the story. If it were not for verse 17, how would Joshua have found out? Verse 17 is truly a perfect verse!

It is very characteristic of this text to have commands and executions. Verse 22 and verse 23 both have a double command and a double execution of the command. Verse 24 can be split up into a double command in v. 24a and a double execution in v. 24b. Some commands, however, do not seem to be executed: the command regarding blocking the exit and appointing people does not have a counterpart in the text. Moreover, what does "and they did so" in verse 23 refer to? Does it refer to both the commands given by Joshua? The text, however, continues and states: and they brought the five kings. Does "and they did so" only refer to opening the cave? I will return to this problem.

2. *Old Greek*

The structure of the Greek text is very similar.

> v. 14: conclusion of the former story.
> v. 15: not in Greek
> v. 16: new action: the kings have fled and they hide in a cave in Makedah.
> v. 17: report to Joshua: that the kings have fled and that they hide.
> v. 18: immediate reaction of Joshua regarding the kings: double command: block the exit and appoint some guards.
>> vv. 19–21: additional instruction of Joshua to do something else— side story
> v. 22: later reaction of Joshua regarding the kings: command to open the cave and to bring the kings.
> v. 23: response: the kings are brought out.
> v. 24a: action of Joshua: Joshua gives a double command: come and put your feet on their necks.
> v. 24b: response: double response: they come and they put their feet on their necks.

I note the following obvious differences with the Hebrew text. Regarding the whereabouts of Joshua.

Galgala	Makedah	rest of land
10:6		
–		
	10:21–28	
		10:29–42
–		

Verse 15, the report of the people gathering together at Gilgal is missing in the Greek. Joshua simply calls it a day in verse 14. That he and the people with him take off for Gilgal is not mentioned. On the other hand, verse 21 does mention that the people return to the camp, to Joshua at Makedah. At first sight, verse 21, both the MT and the LXX, give the appropriate information:

וישבו כל־העם אל־המחנה אל־יהושע מקדה בשלום
Καὶ ἀπεστράφη πᾶς ὁ λαὸς πρὸς Ἰησοῦν εἰς Μακηδα ὑγιεῖς.

Only in the Greek text, however, is this information appropriate: after all that happened, Joshua and his compatriots seem to be in Makedah. The same information, though, makes the Hebrew text very complicated, for in verse 15 Joshua and his people are in Gilgal, whereas in verse 21 Joshua and his people are in Makedah. Hence, the Greek text has avoided the difficulty and omitted verse 15. The Greek text, however, has also omitted the reference to Gilgal at the end of the chapter. There is no verse 43 in the Greek text.[22] Hence, the translator interpreted the text and made Joshua move to Makedah somewhere before verse 21, so that Joshua was able "to return" to Makedah in verse 21. After Makedah, Joshua takes on the rest of the land. There is no return to Gilgal.

Second, the Greek text rather literally translates verses 16–17.

Third, verse 23 has only one part of the Hebrew execution line. The Hebrew text seems to have the report of the double execution—they did so and they brought out the kings—whereas the Greek text simply states: and they brought out the kings. There are three explanations for this phenomenon—or maybe even a fourth one, which I will propose later. Possibility one: the Greek text omitted the first part of the sentence—and they did so. Possibility two: the Greek did not find this short sentence in the Vorlage. Still another solution comes to mind. The Greek translator might have read "and they did so" in the Vorlage but thought it would be clearer to repeat Joshua's command "and they brought out the five kings." Given the understandable omission of verse 15, one is inclined to opt for the

---

[22] The Cambridge text critical apparatus reads as follows: καὶ ἀνέστρεψεν ῑς καὶ πᾶς ιηλ μετ᾽ αὐτοῦ εἰς τὴν παρεμβολὴν εἰς γάλγαλα Gbcxz(mg)ArmEthᶜSyh. The editor adds that the sentence is indicated with an ※ in both G and the SyroHexapla. It is clear that this Greek line has been supplied secondarily from the Hebrew. In "das Kollationsheft" from Udo Quast in Göttingen the following witnesses are listed as having verse 43: G 19 85ᵐᵍ 108 376 426 (G sub ※).

first possibility: the translator found the double phrase in the Vorlage, but decided to omit the least fitting, and rather uncolorful first part "and they did so."

The analysis of the differences between the MT and the Old Greek of Joshua 10:14–24 seems to have strengthened the conviction that the translator of Joshua was a wise and gifted translator. The omission of a misleading verse, namely the concluding statement in verse 15 and the omission of part of a possibly misleading execution line in verse 23 on the one hand, and the faithful translation of verses 16–17 on the other hand, call for a translator who cares for the Hebrew text but avoids contradictions and unclear elements. In short, the translator seems quite alert to the context. Or, was (s)he not?

3. A Closer Look at "The Line of Command"

In Josh 4:5 Joshua gives a command: "Joshua said to them, 'Pass on before the ark of the LORD your God into the middle of the Jordan, and each of you take up a stone on his shoulder, one for each of the tribes of the Israelites.'" The command is heeded, the children of Israel do so. This is reported in 4:8. The verse starts precisely with the same words as 10:23: "and they did so." In between, verses 6–7, it is told how one should interpret the stones. The focus, hence, is on the stones. Verse 8: "And the children of Israel did so, as the Lord commanded Joshua; and they took up twelve stones out of the midst of Jordan (as the Lord commanded Joshua, when the children of Israel had completely passed over), and carried these stones with them into the camp, and laid them down there." The twelve stones are set up at Gilgal precisely as the Lord commanded Joshua. These verses strongly resemble 10:24—a command is given and the command is literally executed. The narrator repeats the words of the command in the execution line. In 10:24, however, the words "and they did so" are not in the text. The execution of the command precisely follows the command. The command of verse 24a "Come and put your feet on their necks" is followed in verse 24b by "And while they were coming they put their feet on their necks." In verse 22, though, the text first states the command and the execution line in verse 23 starts with "and they did so."

There is still another passage where the words "and they did so" are used: Joshua 5:15. In this vision, "the 'commander of the army of the Lord' said to Joshua, 'Remove the sandals from your feet, for the place where you stand is holy.' And Joshua did so." This passage reminds the reader of the famous passage in Exod 3:5, where Moses is ordered to remove his sandals. Joshua, like Moses, receives the same command: remove your sandals. In the execution-line of the command, the narrator of the book of Joshua, however, does not repeat the words of the command, but simply writes: "and he did so." The funny thing with Exodus is that there is no execution-line at all. God commands, but the reader does not really know whether or not Moses took off his sandals. Joshua, however, did so! This passage is one of the few passages in the book of Joshua where the line of command is not literally repeated in the line of execution.

Looking at the Greek text, I notice OG that 4:5 and 8 preserve both the line of command and the line of execution. OG 10:24 also has the command and its execution. As in MT 5:15 the command given to Joshua to take off his sandals is not repeated in an execution line. Moreover, OG 5:15 does not have the words typical for MT 5:15: "and he did so." The words "and he did so" are not in the Greek text. Similarly in Joshua 10:22–23: Joshua gives a command to open the cave and to bring out the kings, but in v. 23 only the kings are brought. The words: "and they did so" are not in the text. I conclude that the repetition of the line of command in the execution seems more typical of the MT than of the Greek.

Schematically:

		MT	Old Greek
4:5	command	pass on before . . .	=
		pick up stones	=
4:8	execution	and they did so	=
		& they picked up stones	=
5:15	command	remove your sandals	=
	execution	and Joshua did so	no par
10:22	command	open the cave	=
		bring out the kings	=
10:23	execution	and they did so	no par
		and they brought out	=
10:24a	command	come	=
		and put your feet	=
10:24b	execution	while coming	(change in form)[23]
		they put their feet	=

---

[23] I also note that the following witnesses have omitted this element: 16 52

There is yet another line of command in the Hebrew text. Not only
does the writer repeat more or less literally the command in its execution, but also the line of command becomes clear: God-Moses-
Joshua-people. A good example of a line of command is Josh 11:15:
As the Lord had commanded his servant Moses, so Moses commanded Joshua, and so Joshua did; he left nothing undone of all
that the Lord had commanded Moses. Similarly in 1:17; 8:34; and
14:5 the line of command is indicated. The Old Greek of Joshua
represents this line of command.

4. *Summarizing the Results and Taking a Leap Forward*

The Hebrew text has an elaborate itinerary for Joshua. Moreover,
it makes sure that Joshua knows what is going on. Finally, its lines
of execution resemble the lines of commands. The Old Greek avoids
the Gilgal problem, keeps the report-to-Joshua-line, and removes
some of the (misleading) elements in the execution lines. All this suggests a Greek translator who carefully interpreted the Hebrew Vorlage.
This Hebrew Vorlage is more or less the Massoretic text.

This sort of Greek interpreter, however, does not seem to fit my
impression of LXX/OG translators. This interpreter seems to look at
entire stories. And a couple of studies of the Old Greek of Joshua
precisely point to the contrary. The translators of Joshua seem to
work with clauses, not with large pieces of text.[24] When dealing with
Gilgal in the beginning of the chapter, the interpreter seems to be
aware of the problem called "Makedah." When deciding on omitting verse 15, the translator knew of the problem in verse 21. And
when dealing with Gilgal in verse 43, the translator remembers the
omission in verse 15. That is, in my opinion, more than a LXX/OG
translator normally does.

Maybe we should look from a different perspective on these problems. Maybe the Hebrew Vorlage that was in front of the translator
did not have verse 15? Maybe it had no reference to a report made
to Joshua in verse 17? Maybe it only had a short sentence in verse
23: "and they did so"?

---

68 77 120 122 128 131* 236 328 392 500 509 527 529 530 616 739 761 799
Eth[f].

[24] Michael N. van der Meer, *Formation and Reformulation: The Redaction of the Book
of Joshua in the Light of the Oldest Textual Witnesses* (Ph.D. Dissertation, Leiden University,
2001), 79–91.

If verse 15 was absent in the Hebrew Vorlage underlying the Old Greek—and also verse 43—this might explain the "counting-problem" of the Cairo Codex or at least raise questions regarding the Hebrew text of Joshua on which the Codex is based.[25]

If the underlying Hebrew text had only the second part of verse 23, namely: ויציאו אליו את־המשת המלכים האלה מן־המערה, that would explain why the Old Greek of Joshua only has this sentence, and not the "and they did so." Moreover, if we accept that the "and they did so" is more typical of the MT, then we could suggest that it reflects a later redactional layer to the MT. If the words "and they did so" are the result of a later revisor, who made all passages similar: 4:8; 5:15, and 10:23, then the omissions in the Old Greek (5:15 and 10:23) are evidence of plusses in the MT. But 10:23 is very complex. As we noted in the textcritical part, precisely the sentence καὶ ἐξηγάγοσαν τοὺς πέντε βασιλεῖς ἐκ τοῦ σπηλαίου is missing in the original text of Vaticanus and in the Washington Codex, as well as in a couple of cursives. If the text of Vaticanus was due to homoioteleuton and the copyist, indeed, corrected the mistake immediately, then we ought to accept the sentence as belonging to the Old Greek. The Washington codex and a series of cursives, however, also do not include this sentence. Homoioteleuton—though entirely possible— might not be adequate to explain this case of omission. The textcritical apparatus also mentioned that a series of witnesses, which are different from the ones mentioned above, has at the end of verse 22: καὶ ἐποίησαν οὕτως, precisely as in the Hebrew text.

As the latter series of witnesses might reflect corrections towards the (later) Hebrew text, I tend to conclude that the Hebrew text underlying the Old Greek did not have the words "and they did so," but the longer sentence "And they brought the five kings out of the cave." The Old Greek, thus, did not choose this sentence for stylistic reasons, but simply translated the Hebrew text.

Finally, the "perfect" verse 17: according to the Masoretic note, the expression "and it was told" appears 24 times in the Hebrew Bible.[26]

---

[25] As this solution, however, does not fully explain the difference in total numbers, we need to do some further study here. With thanks to Christoph Levin for pointing to this problem.

[26] Gen 22:20, 27:42, 31:22, 38:13; Ex 4:5; Josh 10:17; Judg 9:25, 9:47; 1 Sam 15:12, 19:19, 23:7, 27:4; 2 Sam 6:12, 10:17, 19:1, 21:11; 1 Kgs 1:51, 2:29, 2:41; 2 Kgs 6:13, 8:7; 1 Chr 19:17, and Isa 7:2.

Of all these passages, two repeat elements of the aforementioned material: 1 Kgs 2:29 and Josh 10:17. 1 Kgs 2:29 repeats a part of the aforementioned line. 1 Kgs 2:28 states: ". . . Joab fled to the tent of the Lord and grasped the horns of the altar." Verse 29 reads: "When it was told King Solomon, 'Joab has fled to the tent of the Lord and now is beside the altar' . . ." Joshua 10:17, however, is the only verse that almost completely repeats the aforementioned verse.[27]

וינסו   חמשת המלכים האלה ויחבאו במערה במקדה v. 16
וינד ליהושע לאמר נמצאו חמשת המלכים   נחבאים במערה במקדה v. 17

This comparison not only sheds light on verses 16–17, it also confirms that the second part of verse 23 must have been in the text underlying both MT and OG. Verse 23 continues verse 16.

וינסו   חמשת המלכים האלה ויחבאו במערה במקדה v. 16
מן־המערה   ויציאו אלי את־חמשת המלכים האלה v. 23b

The author who created verse 17 has combined elements from verse 16 and 23:

וינסו   חמשת המלכים האלה ויחבאו במערה במקדה v. 16
וינד ליהושע לאמר נמצאו חמשת המלכים נחבאים במערה במקדה v. 17
ויציאו אלי   את־חמשת המלכים האלה   מן־המערה v. 23b[28]

In a sense, verse 17 fills out a gap left by the report on the five fleeing kings (verse 16) and the reaction it provoked (v. 18). From a text critical perspective, the following Greek witnesses support the omission of this verse: 53 125 246 392 799.

E. The Contribution of MS 2648

In this final section, I would like to compare the Old Greek of Joshua 10:14ff. with the text of MS 2648. Manuscript 2648 does not have

---

[27] Note that the participium of verse 17, made of the verb used in verse 16, is a hapax in the Hebrew Bible.

[28] Tov also characterizes האלה as secondary. Cf. Emanuel Tov, "The Growth of the Book of Joshua in the Light of the Evidence of the LXX Translation," *ScrHier* 31 (1986): 321–39 (= Id. *The Greek and the Hebrew Bible: Collected Essays* [VTSup 72; Leiden: Brill, 1999], 385–396). This occurs in verses 16 and 23, and not in verse 17.

verse 15. It also does not have verse 17. Regarding the text of vv. 22–23. The text reads as follows:

..]αηλτηγλωσσηαυτουκ[
.]πενι̅η̅ϲανοιξατετοσπηλ[
.]αιεξαγαγετετουϲε̅βαϲ[
τουτουϲεκτουϲπηλαιου[
εξηγαγοντουϲε̅[.]αϲιλει[
τουϲεκτουϲπη[

My reconstruction:

Ισρ]αηλ τῇ γλώσσῃ αὐτοῦ. κ̣[αὶ
εἶ]πεν Ἰησοῦς· ἀνοίξατε τὸ σπήλ[αιον
κ]α̣ὶ ἐξαγάγετε τοὺς πέντε βασ[ιλεῖς
τού̣τους ἐκ τοῦ σ̣πηλαίου. [καὶ
ἐξήγαγον τοὺς πέντε [β]α̣σιλεῖ[ς τού-
τ̣ους ἐκ τοῦ σπη[λαίου, τὸν βα-

I note that the *vacat* at the end of line 4 does not allow for a text "and they did so." To the contrary, there is only space for a text like the Old Greek, without "and they did so." Joshua gives a double command, but the execution-line only mentions the kings being brought forth.

Manuscript 2648 thus proves to be a valuable witness to an Old Greek text without verse 15, verse 17, and the words "and they did so" of verse 23.

CONCLUSION

1. *Text Critical and Literary Critical Conclusions*

1. In the Old Greek of the book of Joshua, there is no verse 15. I believe that this verse was absent in the Hebrew Vorlage underlying the Old Greek.

2. In the Old Greek of the book of Joshua, there was no verse 17. I believe that this verse was absent in the Hebrew Vorlage underlying the Old Greek.

3. In the Old Greek of the book of Joshua, the execution line of verse 23 certainly did not contain the words "and they did so." I believe these words were also absent in the Hebrew Vorlage of the Old Greek.

4. The Old Greek of the book of Joshua is characterized by a "lesser" developed command-execution form.

5. The MT reflects a text different from the Old Greek of Joshua. At a pretty late stage in the literary development of the book of Joshua, a reviser focused on the executions of commands given by leading figures. The execution of commands needed to repeat the words of the commands. Hence, a later revisor added to verse 23 the words "and they did so." Moreover, the reviser filled out the gap between verses 16 and 18, namely composed verse 17: Joshua was given a precise report on what had happened. Finally, the revisor turned Gilgal into Joshua's headquarters, and thus created verse 15.

2. *Hermeneutical Conclusions*

1. The different texts are different interpretations of the past history. They offer different perspectives. They both, however, underline the importance of the "line of command." Whether or not the "line of command"—God, Moses, Joshua—is similar or different in both texts, and whether or not it reflects an additional revisioning process, prior to the revisioning of the command-execution form, is beyond the scope of the current contribution.

2. It did become clear that the preciseness of the executions of commands became an issue. The author of the "MT" and probably also the community for which this text was meant were interested in the preciseness of the execution of commands. The word (of God or whomever was in charge) needed not only to be heard, it needed to be executed in a very precise manner.

3. The different texts also point to differences in ideologies regarding the conquering of the land. Did it happen from a central point, was Gilgal the pivot, the dispatching headquarters?[29] Even if the mentioning of Gilgal at places turned the text incredible, the MT author stressed its role. One can wonder why? For whom was Gilgal

---

[29] Cf. van der Meer, *Formation and Reformulation*, 65: "Most of these redactional additions were introduced in the MT of Josh. 1–12 for the purpose of presenting the various conquest narratives as a unified Israelite campaign with Gilgal as base for the military operations; hence the contextually intrusive additions in MT-Josh 10:15,43, which are contradicted in verse 21 by the reference to a camp at Makkedah." With reference to Leah Mazor, *The Septuagint Translation of the Book of Joshua: Its Contribution to the Understanding of the Textual Transmission of the Book and Its Literary and Ideological Development* (Heb) (Ph.D. diss., Jerusalem, 1994), 167–8.

important? Which community was fortified by stressing Gilgal? For whom was MT intended?

4. Which community needed the clearness of executions? For whom was the Vorlage of the Old Greek not precise enough? I do not know the answers to these questions. One thing comes to my mind: in the MT, there is no space left for guesses, whereas in the Old Greek Joshua sometimes needs a crystal ball.

ON DOUBLE READINGS, PSEUDO-VARIANTS AND GHOST-NAMES IN THE HISTORICAL BOOKS

Natalio Fernández Marcos

One of the fields explored by E. Tov has been the relationship between the Greek texts of what has come to be known as "the Septuagint" (henceforth LXX/OG or mainstream Greek) and the underlying Hebrew, especially in the book of Jeremiah. As a tribute to this eminent scholar I wish to consider some peculiar phenomena of the textual history for the historical books. These examples are relevant not only to textual criticism but also to translation technique and text transmission. In addition, they may help to clarify some disputed passages and the complex process of formation and transmission of the biblical text.

Since the investigations of Wellhausen, Thenius, Driver, and Rahlfs the double readings have been emphasized as one of the main characteristics of the Lucianic or Antiochene recension.[1] This device has been confirmed by subsequent studies and especially throughout our new edition of the text for the historical books.[2] These variant readings originated affect not only the transmission of the standard Greek text; the Antiochene text, which is rooted in the Hebrew, was also exposed between the 2nd century B.C.E. and the 1st C.E. to the further influence of and interaction with the Hebrew. Consequently, some of these doublets may go back to synonymous readings or alternative variants already in the Hebrew itself.[3] In other words, it can be said that this recension is in some ways doubly rooted in the Hebrew textual developments. This can scarcely be doubted since some of

---

[1] *Der Text der Bücher Samuelis* (Göttingen, 1871); O. Thenius, *Die Bücher Samuels erklärt* (2d. ed., Leipzig, 1864); S. R. Driver, *Notes on the Hebrew Text and the Topography of the Books of Samuel* (Oxford, 1890) and A. Rahlfs, *Septuaginta-Studien. 3 Heft. Lucians Rezension der Königsbücher* (Göttingen: Vandenhoeck & Ruprecht, 1911).

[2] N. Fernández Marcos and J. R. Busto Saiz, *El texto antioqueno de la Biblia griega* I–III (TECC 50, 53, 60; Madrid: CSIC, 1989–1996).

[3] Cf. S. Talmon, "Double Readings in the Massoretic Text," *Text* 1 (1960): 144–184 and idem, "Synonymous readings in the textual traditions of the Old Testament", *ScrHier* 8 (1961): 335–83.

the Antiochene variants have been confirmed by and are extant in the fragments of 4QSam[a-c].[4] Nevertheless most of the double readings in the mainstream Greek tradition have been produced at the level of the translation, as a result of a different approach to the parent language. They are due to diverse translation techniques. They usually represent conflate readings that transmit the transliteration plus the translation of the same Hebrew word or expression and, occasionally, they offer different meanings or alternate renderings of the same consonantal text. Z. Talshir has largely reflected on this phenomenon as a feature of the translation technique and part of the exegetical process. The translator does not want to give up one of the possible meanings and finally retains both. Moreover, its double reading may be at the beginning of a process that transforms, through a chain reaction, the whole sentence restores the sense and develops new meanings.[5] The translation technique cannot be separated from the process of subsequent revisions in the transmission of the text. In the Antiochene text, notorious for its double readings, it is clear that these function as a means of interpretation and exegesis of the text. The diverse equivalents are employed by the scribe or copyist in a creative way as a means to express the different shades of meaning of a difficult word in the *Vorlage*, whether by means of a synonymous word or the substitution of more stylistic Greek for a literal translation. I would, however, emphasize that the double readings form a continuum in the history of the biblical text from the source language to their reception in the target language and in the daughter translations (especially the Old Latin and the Armenian versions).

There are some major doublets or pluses that correspond to alternative renderings of the Greek manuscript tradition and have been treated extensively by S. Pisano.[6] My purpose is to deal with some

---

[4] Cf. E. Ulrich, *The Qumran Text of Samuel and Josephus* (HSM 19; Missoula MO: Scholars Press, 1978), 95–117 and *The Dead Sea Scrolls Bible* (Translated and with Commentary by M. Abegg, Jr., P. Flint and E. Ulrich; New York: HarperSanFrancisco 1999) 246–259.

[5] Z. Talshir, "Double Translations in the LXX," in *VI Congress of the International Organization for Septuagint and Cognate Studies, Jerusalem 1986* (ed. Claude E. Cox; SBLSCS 23; Atlanta GA: Scholars Press, 1987), 21–63, pp. 27–32.

[6] S. Pisano, *Additions or Omissions in the Books of Samuel. The Significant Pluses and Minuses in the Massoretic, LXX and Qumran Texts* (OBO 57; Fribourg/Göttingen: Universitäts Verlag/Vandenhoeck & Ruprecht, 1984), 119–56.

examples of minor doublets that can be detected as double translations or the result of including translation plus transliteration of the
same Hebrew word into the sentence. One should not forget that
"whenever the translator just transliterates, he inevitably offers an
interpretation."[7]

–1 Sam 10:5 ἀνάστεμα / Νασίβ

MT reads אֲשֶׁר־שָׁם נְצִבֵי פְלִשְׁתִּים for which the entire Greek tradition
translates: οὗ ἐστὶν ἐκεῖ τὸ ἀνάστεμα τῶν ἀλλοφύλων· ἐκεῖ Νασὶβ ὁ
ἀλλόφυλλος.[8] MT can be translated "at the place where the Philistine
garrison is," reading נְצִיב as singular (cf. 13:3 and versions). The
greek has a doublet. Probably the first part is secondary, because in
13:3.4 Antiochene translates נְצִיב by ὑπόστεμα a word taken probably from Aquila.[9] The result is a text in Greek that not only duplicates the sentence but also transforms the semantic aspects of the
phrase. The Hebrew *hapax* נְצִיב has not only been transliterated in
Greek but it has been converted into a proper name as well. The
Greek reader is informed that there is the Philistine garrison plus
one personified name easily transformed by the context into the chief
of the garrison or one of its famous heroes.

–2 Kgs 11:4, οἱ παρατρέχοντες / Ῥασείμ

In this verse, the last two words of the sentence לְכָרִי וְלָרָצִים in MT
('Jehodaia summoned the captains of the Carites and of the guards')
have been transliterated by the mainstream Greek: ἀπέστειλεν Ἰωδᾶε
καὶ ἔλαβεν τοὺς ἑκατοντάρχους τῶν Χορρεὶ καὶ τῶν Ῥασείμ.[10] But
there was also a current of the Greek tradition that understood the
second word as derived from the root רוּץ, 'to hasten, to run.' Symmachus, the most recent of the translators, is one of those witnesses.
The Antiochene recension incorporates this doublet and with other
small changes produces a sentence far removed from that of the parent text: ἀπέστειλε Ἰωδᾶε ὁ ἱερεύς καὶ ἔλαβε τοὺς ἑκατοντάρχους τῶν

---

[7] B. Kedar-Kopfstein, "The Interpretative Element in Transliteration," *Text* 8
(1973): 55–77, p. 55.

[8] The Hebrew text according to *Biblia Hebraica Stuttgartensia*, 1977 (BHS); the
Greek text according to our edition of the Antiochene text quoted in note 2.

[9] Cf. S. Brock, *The Recensions of the Septuaginta Version of 1 Samuel* (Torino: Silvio
Zamorani, 1996), p. 162.

[10] In codex Vaticanus probably understood as proper names, τὸν Χορρεὶ καὶ τὸν
Ῥασείν.

παρατρεχόντων καὶ τὸν Χορρεὶ καὶ τὸν Ῥασείμ. There can be little doubt that παρατρεχόντων is a translation of רצים. It is the stereotyped equivalent in the Septuagint for the verb רוץ according to the Hatch-Redpath's Concordance. Fortunately, for this passage, we have Theodoret's question explaining how a Greek reader of Antioch understood the text, once it was circulating without reference to the Hebrew. Accordingly the three terms are understood as collective denominations referring to the chiefs of the king, the shield-bearers and the spear-bearers.[11]

–2 Chr 34:22 ἱματιοφύλαξ/φυλάσσουσα τὰς ἐντολάς (corrupted from στολάς) in Antiochene.

According to MT, Hilkiah and his messengers "went to the prophet Huldah, the wife of Shallum son of Tokhath son of Hasrah, keeper of the wardrobe." The last part of the sentence in MT runs as follows:

MT: וילך ... אל־חלדה הנביאה אשת שלם בן־תוקהת בן־חסרה שומר הבגדים
Greek: καὶ ἐπορεύθη ... πρὸς Ὀλδὰν τὴν προφῆτιν γυναῖκα Σελλὴμ υἱοῦ Καθουὰλ υἱοῦ Χελλῆς φυλάσσουσαν τὰς ἐντολάς.
Ant: καὶ ἐπορεύθη ... πρὸς Ὀλδὰν τὴν προφῆτιν γυναῖκα Σελλὴμ υἱοῦ Θεκῶε υἱοῦ Ἀσὲρ τοῦ ἱματιοφύλακος τὴν φυλάσσουσαν τὰς ἐντολάς.

ἱματιοφύλαξ is the correct translation for the Hebrew expression שומר הבגדים and as such is found in the entire mainstream Greek tradition in the parallel passage of 2 Kgs 22:14. It has been preserved in the Antiochene text. The words φυλάσσουσαν τὰς ἐντολάς of the mainstream Greek tradition represent a second and secondary translation based on a paleographic corruption of the original στολάς into ἐντολάς, since στολή is the second most frequent equivalent (after ἱμάτιον) for בגד in the LXX/OG materials.[12] In this passage Antiochene is the only witness that preserves the correct translation going back

---

[11] It is the question 36 to 2 Kings: "Παρατρέχοντας" τίνας καλεῖ; Τοὺς ἡγουμένους τοῦ βασιλέως· "Χορρὶ" δὲ καὶ "Ῥασίμ", ἀσπιδηφόρους καὶ δορυφόρους. Τούτους τριχῆ διελών, τοὺς μὲν ἐκέλευσε φυλάττειν τοῦ βασιλέως τὸν οἶκον, τοὺς δὲ τὴν εἴσοδον τοῦ θείου νεώ, τοὺς δὲ τὴν πύλην τὴν ἑτέραν (whom does he call "paratrechontas"? The King's officers: "Chorri" and "Rasim"—shield-bearers and spear-bearers—dividing them into three groups; he ordered some to guard the king's house, others the entrance to the divine Temple and others the other gate.) Cf. N. Fernández Marcos and J. R. Busto Saiz, *Theodoreti Cyrensis Quaestiones in Reges et Paralipomena. Editio Critica* (TECC 32; Madrid: CSIC, 1984), 219.
[12] Cf. E. Hatch and H. A. Redpath, *A Concordance to the Septuagint* (Oxford:

probably to the Old Greek. At an earlier stage, attested by the Old Latin (*Asara custodis vestium*), there was no trace of the doublet. Moreover, the reading of the mainstream Greek tradition has φυλάσσουσαν, a feminine participle in the accusative, making Huldah the subject of the action not Hasrah. When Antiochene incorporates the doublet with small changes (addition of the article) to its current text, it results in an obvious expansion of the meaning which is absent from the original. Consequently, the sentence in Antiochene can be translated as follows: "And went . . . to the prophet Olda, the wife of Sellem son of Tecoe son of Aser, keeper of the wardrobe, who was keeping the commandments and. . . ."

In Kgs 15:44 Elijah's servant says according to MT: "Look, a little cloud no bigger than a person's hand is rising out of the sea" (עֹלָה מִיָּם). The Antiochene text with most of the mainstream Greek tradition, going back probably to the Old Greek, translates: καὶ ἰδοὺ νεφέλη μικρὰ ὡς ἴχνος ἀνδρὸς ἀνάγουσα ὕδωρ ἀπὸ θαλάσσης. The double translation of מִיָּם by ὕδωρ and ἀπὸ θαλάσσης has resulted in the modification and widening of the sense of the parent text.

These examples remind us of the semantic value of the double readings which, whether through transliteration or double translation, contribute to enlarge the meaning of the Greek biblical text. In this aspect the Antiochene recension is paradigmatic: the doublets have been incorporated into the context in such a way that the readers no longer understand them as doublets but as current parts of the biblical text.

−1 Chr 26:14 Ἰωάδ/βουλευτής
The text of Chronicles informs of the different service cycles of the gatekeepers of the Temple. This verse in MT means literally: "And the lot for the east fell to Shelemiah. And for Zechariah,[13] his son, a prudent counselor, they cast lots, and his lot came out for the north". It is worth analysing in detail the second part of the verse in Hebrew and Greek. There are different variants in the majority text of the Greek, but the double reading is transmitted by the Antiochene text and the Armenian version only.

Clarendon, 1897) and T. Muraoka, *Hebrew/Aramaic Index to the Septuagint Keyed to the Hatch-Redpath Concordance* (Grand Rapids, Michigan: Baker Books, 1998).
[13] Reading וְלִזְכַרְיָהוּ with the Antiochene recension and Vulgate.

וזכריהו בנו יועץ בשכל הפילו נורלות ויצא נורלו צפנה :MT

Main Greek: καὶ Ζαχαριά, υἱοὶ Ἰωάς· τῷ Μελχειὰ ἔβαλον κλήρους, καὶ ἐξῆλθεν ὁ κλῆρος βορρᾶ.

Ant: καὶ Ζαχαριὰ υἱῷ αὐτοῦ. Ἰωὰδ βουλευτὴς ἐν συνέσει. ἔβαλον κλήρους καὶ ἐξῆλθεν αὐτοῦ ὁ κλῆρος κατὰ βορρᾶν.

Leaving aside the variant readings of the mainstream Greek tradition that can be explained as diverse corruptions from a text similar to MT (confusion of similar letters as י/ו in the case of υἱοί, transliteration in the case of Ἰωάς corresponding to the participle יועץ understood as proper name, probably transliteration with metathesis and paleographic confusion of בשכל plus inner Greek corruption that led to the new name Μελχειὰ), I want to focus on the Antiochene doublet that transforms the sense of the phrase. Ant translates correctly the participle of יעץ 'to advise' by βουλευτής, a derivative of βουλεύειν, almost the stereotyped equivalent in the LXX/OG materials for this Hebrew verb.[14] Then, the transliteration of the same word as a proper name, present in some witnesses to the mainstream Greek tradition, was incorporated into the sentence. The result of the process is a new ghost-name into (see further, below), absent from the parent text, and a new meaning as a consequence of the reworked sentence. In the Antiochene text the lot for the east fell to Zechariah, but Yoad is the prudent counselor, not Zechariah as in the original. And the lot for the north belongs, according to the Antiochene recension, also to Yoad not to Zechariah. This interpretation, as occurs in other examples, is attested and confirmed by the Armenian version: *Yovab consiliarius in mente sua*.

−1 Sam 15:33 υἱοῦ Σασέρ/καὶ ἔσφαξε

Samuel says to Agag, king of the Amalekites, who had been captured alive by Saul: "'As your sword has made women childless, so your mother shall be childless among women.' And Samuel hewed Agag in pieces before the Lord in Gilgal."

כאשר שכלה נשים חרבך כן־תשכל מנשים אמך וישסף שמואל את־אגג לפני :MT
יהוה בגלגל

Main Greek: Καθότι ἠτέκνωσεν γυναῖκας ἡ ρομφαία σου, οὕτως ἀτεκνωθήσεται ἐκ γυναικῶν ἡ μήτηρ σου· καὶ ἔσφαξεν Σαμουὴλ τὸν Ἀγὰγ ἐνώπιον Κυρίου ἐν Γαλγάλοις.

---

[14] Cf. Hatch-Redpath, *Concordance to the Septuagint*.

Ant: Καθὼς ἠτέκνωσε γυναῖκας ἡ ῥομφαία σου, οὕτως ἀτεκνωθήσεται ἐκ γυναικῶν ἡ μήτηρ σου υἱοῦ Σασέρ· καὶ ἔσφαξε Σαμουὴλ τὸν Ἀγὰγ ἐνώπιον Κυρίου ἐν Γαλγάλοις.

Antiochene introduces a new name, Saser, somehow associated with Agag and his mother. Given the literal translation of the rest of the verse it would not be too much to speculate that the origin of this variant reading could be found in a double translation of the verb וישסף by καὶ ἔσφαξε as attested in the entire mainstream Greek tradition, and the remnants of a transliteration in Σασερ. The presence of the name Saser with two sigmas in the place of וישסף, is sufficient evidence, in my opinion, of the transliteration of this *hapax*, in the Hebrew Bible, a *pi'el* of שסף, of uncertain meaning.[15] There is no need to recur to the hypothesis of a different underlying Hebrew; even the verb σφάζειν is probably a guess-translation. The Old Latin of the marginal glosses records the variant *mater tua filius doloris* but it does not help to explain its genesis and it might also be a translation from perplexity.[16]

This device of the Antiochene recension is confirmed by many other double readings constructed as a conflation of transliteration and translation of the same Hebrew word, plus the indispensable small modification to restore the sense of the whole sentence, a sense that has resulted to be quite different from that of the parent language. In another contribution I pointed to some of these doublets especially significant as ἐν Γεθθάιμ/Ἡμάρτετε (1 Sam 14:33); Αἰούν/οἱ ἀδελφοὶ αὐτοῦ (1 Chr 9:37); Δωδεί/πατραδέλφου αὐτοῦ (1 Chr 11:26).[17]

The term "pseudo-variant" has been coined and developed by Tov[18] for those variants reflected in the LXX/OG materials as a result of a translation process that may have existed only in the mind of the translator and were not actually derived from a specific Hebrew *Vorlage*. They were created by the translators themselves by means of an interchange of similar letters that could make sense in a difficult

---

[15] υἱοῦ can be an inner Greek corruption and doublet of σου.

[16] The Greek biblical equivalents for dolor are ὠδίν, ὀδύνη and πόνος, cf. T. A. Bergren, *A Latin-Greek Index of the Vulgate New Testament* (SBLRBS 26; Atlanta: GA, Scholars Press, 1991).

[17] Cf. N. Fernández Marcos, "On the Borderline of Translation Greek Lexicography: the Proper Names," *JNSL* (2001), 1–22.

[18] E. Tov, "On 'Pseudo-Variants' Reflected in the Septuagint," *JSS* 20 (1975): 165–77 and idem, *The Text-Critical Use of the Septuagint in Biblical Research* (rev. and enl. 2nd ed.; Jerusalem: Simor Ltd., 1997), 228–40.

text. The translators were guided for their purposes by contextual
exegesis as well as by the form of the letters. The concept could
also be applied to some apparent deviations from the Masoretic Text
in the ancient translations based on misreadings, misunderstandings
of the text, inner Greek corruptions, etc. But the borderline cannot
be traced between this terminology of Tov and what I would prefer
to call, following the patterns of Greek lexicography, "ghost-words"
or "ghost-names."

"Ghost-names/words" have been known to Greek lexicography
since the 19th century. The term was invented to indicate the erroneous interpretation or conjectured readings proposed by modern
editors of texts (especially in the case of the papyri and inscriptions).
Those readings, in the light of subsequent studies and the publication of new documents (that is, submitted to the rules of textual criticism), finally proved to be false readings. They are usually recorded
in the lexica between brackets.[19] By analogy, but only thus, one could
apply the term to some lexicographical phenomena in translation
Greek. Such "pseudo-variants" also probably never existed in the
Vorlage of the translators and call into question the value of any retroverted text based on them for the restoration of the Hebrew. The
ghost-word may have diverse spurious origins—inaccurate reading of
the parent text (e.g. interchange of similar letters, conjectural vocalization, different division of words, metathesis), misunderstanding of
the parent text (problems of language as well as context), erroneous
interpretation (missing the point, applying to different situations),
inner Greek corruption, etc.—but in any event reflects the standpoint of the receptor. These words were integrated into the target
language and were never recognized as ghost-words by the readers
or the audience. They may be ghost-words for the text critic but
not for the readers. Moreover, they were transmitted and read
throughout centuries as part of the biblical text and, as such, were
even translated into other secondary versions.

We have already seen a couple of examples of such ghost-words
in the double readings discussed above. But much more can be said

---

[19] Cf. P. Bonet Colera and J. Rodríguez Somolinos, *Repertorio Bibliográfico de la
Lexicografía Griega* (Madrid: CSIC, 1998), XVI–XVII, and H. Rodríguez Somolinos,
"El DGE y la epigrafía griega: el problema de las 'palabras fantasma' (ejemplificación
y tipología)," in Τῆς φιλίης τάδε δῶρα. *Miscelánea léxica en memoria de Conchita Serrano*
(Manuales y Anejos de Emerita 41; Madrid: CSIC, 1999), 187–98.

about these pseudo-variants, which emerge at the first level of contact with the parent text and are not always motivated by the text itself, but also by the way it is interpreted. In other words, it was the complex process of translation that provoked such readings or representations of the text in the mind of the translator when confronted with various types of translational difficulties. Several times the context was able to absorb the semantic shifts produced by a pseudo-variant but occasionally the first deviation in the translation caused further deviations in order to readjust the sentence. Since this is a field extensively dealt with by Tov,[20] I will content myself with some comments on a few examples drawn from the Antiochene recension. Chapter 22 of 2 Samuel is appropriate to illustrate this hermeneutical device. It has the advantage of being attested by different Hebrew and Greek texts: MT and the parallel Psalm 18; the mainstream Greek tradition and Antiochene recension of Samuel; and the parallel Greek texts of Psalm 18 (17). Another source of interest lies in the fact that this section is part of the *kaige* revision of 2 Samuel. Moreover, it is widely represented in 4QSam[a].

It can be said that the Antiochene recension of 2 Samuel 22 follows a Hebrew text closer to that of Psalm 18 than to the MT of Samuel.[21] But in spite of its frequent agreement with the Hebrew text of Psalm 18 there are some Antiochene readings that can be explained at the level of the Hebrew *Vorlage* with a slight change of similar letters. In 22:2 the reading ἐκ θλίψεώς μου of Antiochene instead of καὶ ὀχύρωμά μου of the rest of the Septuagint implies a different reading of MT מצרתי with *res* and not with *daleth* (ומצדתי MT).

---

[20] Cf. Tov, *The Text-Critical Use of the Septuagint*, 162–71 and idem, "Did the Septuagint Translators always understand their Hebrew Text?," in *De Septuaginta. Studies in honour of John William Wevers on his sixty-fifth birthday* (eds. A. Pietersma and C. Cox; Mississauga, Ontario: Benben Publications, 1984), 53–70, reprinted in E. Tov, *The Greek and Hebrew Bible. Collected Essays on the Septuagint* (Leiden: E. J. Brill, 1999), 203–18.

[21] Cf. J. R. Busto Saiz, "The Antiochene Text in 2 Samuel 22," in *VIII Congress of the International Organization for Septuagint and Cognate Studies. Paris 1992* (eds. L. Greenspoon and O. Munnich; SBLSCS 41; Atlanta, GA: Scholars Press, 1995), 131–43. The most salient case is the first hemistich of verse 43, in Hebrew "I beat them fine *like the dust of the earth*" (כעפר־ארץ), translated literally by the majority text of the Greek tradition by ἐλέανα αὐτοὺς ὡς χνοῦν γῆς. Instead the Antiochene recension translates διασκορπιῶ αὐτοὺς ὡς χνοῦν ἐπὶ πρόσωπον ἀνέμου, just following the reading of Ps 18:43: על־פני־רוח ('before the wind?'). There is yet another variant reading attested by 4QSam[a]: על[פני ארח ('on the surface of the path').

The same confusion of similar letters has produced a different reading in Antiochene in verse 21: δόξαν (it implies a reading כבד instead of כבר of מт) and in v. 30: πεφραγμένος (it supposes a reading נדור instead of נדד of мт).

The reading ὑδάτων of Antiochene in verse 5 is difficult to explain as an inner Greek corruption from the θανάτου of the mainstream Greek. However, at the level of the Hebrew text the confusion (or intended change) י/ו is understandable. The supposed text for the translator was מים instead of the мт מות. The same can be said of other pseudo-variants of this chapter such as the reading of Antiochene μνησθήσομαι instead of the ψαλῶ of the mainstream Greek. To explain this change one has to go back to the Hebrew and detect the implied reading אזכר instead of the Masoretic one אזמר.

Chapter 22 of 2 Samuel is a mine of pseudo-variants. Some of them may have some echo in the Qumran documents (cf v. 48 καὶ ἐταπείνωσε of Ant. and ומרדד of 4QSamª). But most of them can be explained as a result of the process of translation, while it is not necessary to postulate a different underlying Hebrew text.

We have already encountered that special type of pseudo-variant that I have called ghost-names. These occur especially in the genealogical material at the start of 1 Chronicles, where the absence of a meaningful context cause major confusion of similar letters in Hebrew and throughout the Greek tradition.

–1 Chr 3:7: мт mentions among David's sons ונגה ונפג ויפיע ('Nogah, Nepheg and Japhia'). The majority greek text transliterates those names as καὶ Νάγαι καὶ Νάφαθ καὶ Ἰανοῦε/Ἰαφίε. But the Antiochene recension has converted the original names into the following: καὶ Νέεμ καὶ Νέεγ καὶ Ἀχικάμ without variants. They can scarcely be recognized in the original language. But in view of the frequent deformations which occur in the transmission of proper names in those chapters of Chronicles, the possibility of a different *Vorlage* should be excluded, unless it is confirmed by other sources. The result is a list of quite different names not only transmitted by Antiochene but passing also from this text to the Armenian version: *Neem... Neeg... Akʿikam*.

–1 Chr 3:22: мт mentions five sons of Shemaiah but gives the figure of six at the end of the verse: "Hattush, Igal, Bariah, Neariah, and Shaphat, six." In the majority Greek text the five names of мт can

be recognised in spite of some deformations in the Greek transliteration: Χαττούς καὶ Ἰωὴλ καὶ Μαρεὶ καὶ Νωαδειὰ καὶ Σαφάθ, ἕξ.
Antiochene removes this inconsistency by introducing a ghost-name,
probably a doublet of שׁפם, that completes the number six and plays
with the sound in the target language using an alliteration especially
appropriate to be recited aloud: Ἀττοὺς καὶ Ἰεγαὰλ καὶ Βεριὰ καὶ
Νεαρία καὶ Σωφὴτ καὶ Σαφάτ, ἕξ υἱοί.

–1 Chr 4:3: In this case Antiochene introduces a fourth name beyond
MT and the rest of the Greek tradition as a result of its tendency to
incorporate variants of diverse origin into its text. MT offers a probably corrupt text at the beginning of the verse אבי עיטם interpreted
by the Old Greek as υἱοὶ Ἀιτάν and as *stirps Hetam* by the Vulgate.
Whether it is the sons of Etam or the fathers of Etam (with the
sense of ancestors) as Antiochene translates, it is worth exploring the
genesis of the fourth ghost-name in the Antiochene recension:

MT: ואלה אבי עיטם יזרעאל וישׁמא וידבשׁ
Main Greek: καὶ οὗτοι υἱοὶ Ἐτάμ· Ἰεζραὴλ καὶ Ιεσμὰ καὶ Ἰγαβής[22]
Ant: καὶ οὗτοι πατέρες Ἠτάμ· Ἰεζραήλ, Σαμαά, Ῥαδαμαά, Ἰεδεβάς.

The fourth name Ῥαδαμαά might be a Greek corruption of the reading of Vaticanus Ῥαγμά for the second name of the series. But even
this name does not correspond to any of the Hebrew words of the
verse. It probably never existed in the Hebrew *Vorlage* and is a pure
result of an inner Greek corruption. Be that as it may, in Antiochene
it appears as a ghost-name that has been added to the sequence of
proper names attested by the rest of the witnesses.

The examples of ghost-names could be multiplied in chapters 1–12
of 1 Chronicles. There are cases such as 1 Chr 4:17b where the
whole sentence is duplicated in the Antiochene recension resulting
in a total of eight proper names instead of the four of MT and the
Old Greek. It is not easy to decide which form of the doublet is to
be preferred, the closest to the Hebrew or the most distant from it,
taking into account that in proper names the corruption throughout
the text transmission has been very strong. In this case Lagarde's
principle of taking as original the form more distant from the Hebrew
could conflict with other rules of text criticism.

---

[22] They are not the readings of *Vaticanus* but what I consider to be the Old
Greek in this passage.

–2 Sam 21:15–16: MT can be translated "and David grew weary. Ishbi-benob, one of the descendants of the giants. . . ." It is worth adducing for comparison the diverse forms of the Greek text as a replica to the MT.

MT: ויעף דוד וישבו בנב אשר בילידי הרפה

Main Greek: καὶ ἐξελύθη Δαυείδ, καὶ Ιεσβὶ ὃς ἦν ἐν τοῖς ἐκγόνοις τοῦ Ραφά.

Ant: καὶ ἐξελύθη Δαυίδ. καὶ Δαδοὺ ὁ υἱὸς Ιωὰς ἐκ τῶν ἀπογόνων τῶν γιγάντων.

This case is more complicated and has been discussed in detail by Pisano.[23] This sentence is a duplicate of the similar one placed in the mainstream Greek text at the end of verse 11 and in the Antiochene recension at the end of verse 10. This plus in verses 11 (10) without an equivalent in MT represents, in Pisano's opinion, the oldest Greek text here. My interest focusses on the name Δαδού of Antiochene. In the Greek text of verse 11 (10) it appears as Δὰν υἱὸς Ιωάς. Is it a corruption of Δάν or of the abbreviation of Δαυίδ, very close in the sentence to Δαδού? In any case, a new form of the name has emerged in Greek, resulting in a fuller text, more plural and diverse than the MT.

This category should also include some names that have arisen in Greek through inner Greek corruption or misunderstanding of the parent text as the reading Ἀχήμ in the Antiochene recension to 1 Chr 2:21 (probably corruption of the αὐτήν of the mainstream Greek tradition) and the reading εἰς Ἐνακείμ of the entire Greek tradition to 1 Kgs 15:22, understood as a name of place which, in the Hebrew text, was represented by אֵין נָקִי, 'no one excepted."

Double readings, pseudo-variants and ghost-names represent different aspects of a phenomenon that affects the translation and transmission of the biblical text. They pose a problem for the text critic interested in restoring a text that is as close as possible to the original Hebrew, and they belong to the kind of errors that can be accumulated in the process of text transmission. Many of them can be recognised as a product of palaeographic corruption, whether at the Hebrew stage or in the diverse stages transmitted by the versions.

---

[23] Pisano, *Additions or Omissions*, 151–54.

As secondary mistakes they can help the text critic to restore the genuine biblical text and refine the history of the text. From the standpoint of the text critic they can be detected as mistakes and be considered as ghost-names or pseudo-variants. But other double readings instead can attest real, alternative variants of a Hebrew text that has not yet reached standardization. In this case the quest for the original reading is translated to the level of the different competing Hebrew texts. The Vorlage of LXX/OG represents one of these Hebrew forms that preceded the standardization of the text. The main aim of Tov's studies on pseudo-variants was to help recover this dimension of the Greek translational activity, susceptible of being retroverted into Hebrew and used in the text criticism of the Hebrew Bible.

I would, however, like to highlight other aspects of these variants: their consolidation and continuity in the receptor's language, the development of meaning and the semantic shifts caused by them in the whole narrative. Most of these double readings, pseudo-variants and ghost-names were incorporated into the biblical text in one of the diverse forms of the Greek tradition, especially in the Antiochene recension. They achieved, with small modifications of the phrase, a new sense in the target language and were read throughout centuries in public in some communities. Indeed, the double names did not cause any specific problems because in the biblical traditions there were many cases of people known by a double name.[24] Not only were they consolidated and assimilated to the context of the narrative but they were further translated as part of the biblical text

---

[24] Yacob/Israel, Simon/Petros, etc. In 1 Chr 8:7 an original transliteration of a verb not understood as such is converted into a second name by the majority text of the Greek: Γερά· οὗτος Ἰγλαάμ (for the Hebrew הגלם = 'he carried them into the exile'). In this case the Antiochene recension restores and translates the original meaning of the Hebrew: Γηρά· αὐτὸς ἀπῴκισεν αὐτούς. The double name of several biblical characters was deeply rooted in the tradition as confirmed by the following question and answer of Theodoret: Διὰ τί τὸν κηδεστὴν ὁ θεῖος Μωυσῆς Ἰοθὼρ ὀνομάσας ἐν τῇ Ἐξόδῳ, νῦν αὐτὸν ἐκάλεσε Ῥαγουήλ; Διώνυμος ἦν, ὡς Ἰακὼβ καὶ Ἰσραήλ, ὡς Σίμων Πέτρος, ὡς Θωμᾶς ὁ λεγόμενος Δίδυμος, ὡς Θαδδαῖος ὁ καὶ Λεββαῖος. τούτου υἱὸς ἦν ὁ Ἰωβάβ (why, although the divine Moses in the [book of] Exodus named his father-in-law Iothor, has he now called him Ragouel? He had two names, like Jacob and Israel, like Simon Peter, like Thomas who was called Didymos, like Thaddaios who was also Lebbaios. Jobab was his son). Cf. N. Fernández Marcos and A. Sáenz-Badillos, *Theodoreti Cyrensis Quaestiones in Octateuchum. Editio Critica* (TECC 17; Madrid: CSIC, 1979), 202–03.

to other daughter versions. The consolidation of these names through the text history is confirmed by their survival in the Old Latin and Armenian versions. Moreover, they constitute the starting point of new exegesis as can be confirmed by the commentaries of the fathers and the development genre of *Onomastica Sacra*. In other words, they may belong to a marginal aspect of the transmission of the Hebrew with little significance for its text criticism, but they have had a strong influence otherwise on the history and exegesis of the biblical text.

THE GREEK OF PROVERBS—EVIDENCE OF A RECENSIONALLY DEVIATING HEBREW TEXT?

JOHANN COOK

1. INTRODUCTION

Few if any scholars, have contributed towards the textual criticism of the Hebrew Bible as has Prof. Emanuel Tov. The multitude of seminal and original contributions act as evidence of the consistency of this productive scholar. His research into the area of the Dead Sea Scrolls, but also of the Septuagint, will act as a firm basis for future research.

In this contribution which I am honored to offer as a homage I want to enter into discussion with him on one of his brilliant insights, namely that many[1] of the differences between the Greek of Proverbs and the Hebrew (as represented in MT) are the result of a deviating parent text. He phrases his view as follows: "When the book of Proverbs was translated into Greek, presumably in the second century B.C.E., a scroll was used that contained an editorial stage of the book differing from the one now contained in the MT."[2]

To be sure, Tov has a methodologically sound approach in this regard. He bases his interpretations on sound translation technical analyses and, as usual, is extremely cautious and reserved with his interpretations. I will follow his cue by commencing with a general analysis of the translation technique of this complicated translated unit based upon some of my previous studies. Thereafter I will deal with the most conspicuous characteristic of Greek Proverbs, the different sequence of chapters towards the end of the book. While I am convinced that the situation concerning Greek Proverbs is more

---

[1] He does not contend that ALL differences between OG and LXX are to be ascribed to a different parent text (cf. E. Tov, "Recensional Differences between the Masoretic Text and the Septuagint of Proverbs," in: H. W. Attridge *et al.*, *Of Scribes and Scrolls, Studies on the Hebrew Bible, Intertestamental Judaism, and Christian Origins Presented to John Strugnell* [Lanham, Maryland, 1990], 43–56).

[2] Tov, "Recensional Differences," 56.

complicated than most other books in the corpus of Septuagint writings, one has consistently to keep in mind the unique problems that the researcher faces in connection with this unit. The main obstacle remains that the Old Greek of this fascinating book has not yet been established. This unfortunately complicates endeavours to find acceptable explanations to a variety of remarkable textual phenomena. I have demonstrated that this book has many textual problems.[3]

2. THE TRANSLATION TECHNIQUE OF GREEK PROVERBS

It is universally accepted that this unit exhibits a free translation technique.[4] I have demonstrated that the translator(s)[5] of the Greek of Proverbs seem to have had a unique approach towards its parent text. This is observed, firstly, on a *micro-level* but also on a *macro-level*.[6] As far as the first goes, some individual lexical items are rendered consistently, whereas many are varied. I have defined this translational approach as one of *diversity* and *unity*[7] after initially using the formulation unity and diversity.[8] I am now convinced that diversity is thé characteristic of this unit. This is underscored by the rather large number of *hapax legomena* and neologisms that occur in OG Proverbs (Proceedings of IOSCS—Basel forthcoming).[9] Even though one has to be cautious in utilising these criteria uncritically as an

---

[3] J. Cook, "Textual Problems in the Septuagint of Proverbs," *JNSL* 26/1 (2000): 163–73.

[4] E. Tov & B. Wright, "Computer-Assisted study of the criteria for assessing the literalness of translation units in the LXX," *Textus* 12 (1985): 186.

[5] In this contribution I will refer to the translator in the singular even though it is possible that more than one person were involved (J. Cook, *THE SEPTUAGINT OF PROVERBS—Jewish and/or Hellenistic Proverbs? (concerning the Hellenistic colouring of Proverbs). VTSup* 69; Leiden, 1997), 322.

[6] J. Cook, "The Ideological Stance of the Greek Translator of Proverbs," in B. A. Taylor, ed., *X Congress of the International Organization for Septuagint and Cognate Studies: Oslo, 1998 (Septuagint and Cognate Studies)* (Atlanta, GA, 2001a), 463–79.

[7] J. Cook, "Ideology and Translation Technique—two sides of the same coin?," in: R. Sollamo and S. Sipilä, ed., *Proceedings of the IOSCS congress held in Helsinki, July 1999* (SESJ 82; Goettingen: Vandenhoeck & Ruprecht, 2001), 195–210.

[8] Cook, *The Septuagint of Proverbs*, 316. Cf. also J. Cook, "Lexical Issues in the Septuagint of Proverbs," *JNSL* 26/2 (2000a): 163–73.

[9] J. Cook, "Theological/ideological *Tendenz* in the Septuagint—LXX Proverbs: a case study," in: S. Sipilä, ed., *XI Congress of the International Organization for Septuagint and Cognate Studies: Basel, 2001 (Septuagint and Cognate Studies)* (Atlanta, GA, 2002, forthcoming).

indication of translation technique,[10] it is, nevertheless, striking that a high percentage of these textual phenomena indeed occur in those books that are rendered freely.[11]

It would, however, be a mistake to use this general definition as a *procrustean* bed for estimating the way a given word or passage has been rendered. Even though it is correct to use as a general point of departure the rule of thumb of diversity, it is simply not an easy task to predict in all instances what the translator would have been inclined to do. This attitude of diversity and consistency does not, for example, prevent the translator from following his own direction in individual instances, for instance where a general consistent way of translation is followed in respect of a specific Hebrew word. I recently demonstrated this issue by studying the Greek word ἀσεβής that appears in 1:7 (אֱוִיל); 1:10 (חַטָּא); 1:22 (כְּסִיל); 1:32 (כְּסִיל); 2:22 (רָשָׁע); 3:25 (רָשָׁע); 3:33 (רָשָׁע); 3:35; 4:14; 4:19; 9:7; 10:3, 6, 7, 11, 15, 16, 20, 24, 24, 25, 27, 28, 30, 32; 11:4, 7, 8, 9, 10, 10, 18, 19, 23, 31 etc.[12] It appears 92 times in Proverbs and it represents the Hebrew lexeme רָשָׁע 67 times. This is 73% of the total occurrences. At face value this seems to be stereotyping; however, when the individual equivalents are analysed, a different picture appears. Practically all the deviations from this pattern appear in Proverbs chapter 1, as listed above. Whereas the Hebrew refers to 3 categories of people—the fools, the sinners and the foolish—the Greek has only one category, namely the impious, a religious category. It would therefore be foolish, to say the least, to accept, on the basis of apparent stereotyping, that this Greek lexeme automatically acts as a rendering of רָשָׁע. It should be clear that the broader picture, in this case that of Proverbs 1 should be taken into account.

Also on the *macro-level* this translation unit exhibits unique features. I have demonstrated that the sequence of some chapters towards the end of the book that differs from, inter alia, MT, should be ascribed to its translator(s). In the final analysis I have ascribed this interpretative approach to the translator's ideology,[13] which is characterised

---

[10] C. Wagner, *Die Septuaginta-Hapaxlegomena im Buch Jesus Sirach* (BZAW 283; Berlin-New York: De Gruyter, 1999), 6 and E. Tov, *The Text-Critical Use of the Septuagint in Biblical Research* (Jerusalem: Simor, 1997), 173.

[11] Wagner, *Die Septuaginta-Hapaxlegomena*, 5.

[12] Cook, "Theological/ideological *Tendenz* in the Septuagint," (forthcoming).

[13] Cook, "The Ideological Stance of the Greek Translator of Proverbs," 472.

by a fundamentally conservative Jewish religious attitude. This infer-
ence is, inter alia, based upon the prominent role of the law of
Moses in OG Proverbs.[14] This is, as is the case with the deliberate
removal of the names of other authors than Solomon as creators of
the Proverbs, a sign of the Jewishness of the translator(s).

With this general orientation as background I will now deal with
the different sequence of chapters in Greek Proverbs *vis-à-vis* MT.

3. THE ORDER DIFFERENCES IN CHAPTERS 24–31

Tov has made us aware of the unique sequence of chapters that
appears in Greek Proverbs in comparison to all the other extant textual witnesses.[15] The latter part of this book has a different sequence
of chapters from that found in the MT. Whereas the first 23 chapters are the same as MT, the last 8 chapters differ in order.

1:1–24:1–22	
30:1–14	(The words of Agur, 1st part)
24:23–34	(Words of the wise)
30:15–33	(The words of Agur, 2nd part)
31:1–9	(The words of Lemuel, 1st part)
25–29	
31:10–31	(The words of Lemuel, 2nd part)

Parts of chapters 24, 30 and 31 appear in two different positions in
the Greek. Various possible explanations could be suggested for these
conspicuous textual differences. A differing Hebrew parent text, translational activity and inner-Greek corruptions are the most probable.
In this specific case the intricate transmission history of Greek Proverbs
is a complicating factor. This unit is riddled with textual problems[16]
and as stated already the fact that the OG text has not been established systematically unfortunately undermines endeavours at understanding these textual phenomena.

I have argued that the second possibility, the translation process
seems the most likely explanation of the major sequence differences.[17]

---

[14] J. Cook, "The Law of Moses in the Septuagint Proverbs," *VT* 49/4 (1999):
448–461.

[15] E. Tov, *Textual Criticism of the Hebrew Bible* (Minneapolis & Assen, 1992), 337.

[16] Cook, "Textual Problems in the Septuagint of Proverbs."

[17] Cook, *The Septuagint of Proverbs*, 316.

The gist of my argument is that the person(s) responsible for Greek Proverbs seems prepared to interpret extremely freely in some instances. This was already demonstrated in connection with the unique translation technique followed by the translator(s). There are also other applicable examples. Firstly, the Greek has eliminated all references to other authors of Proverbs than Solomon. There is no reference to be found in Proverbs 30 to Agur. This applies to Lemuel in chapter 31 as well. I think the particular translator is taking seriously the statement in chapter 1 that this book contains the Proverbs of *king Solomon*. He also adapted the text in chapter 10 where, to him it would seem, there occurs a redundant statement about the fact that these are the proverbs of Solomon.[18] Against the background of this remarkable freedom of interpretation I have demonstrated that some of the differences referred to above were deliberately introduced by the translator(s).

3.1 *Order differences on account of thematic considerations*

Chapter 31 in the Hebrew can be divided into two clearly distinguishable parts. The first 9 verses contain the instruction of Lemuel. The second part (verses 10–31) deals with more than one related topic. The most striking characteristic of this latter section is the acrostic form in which it has been moulded. I think it is possible that this clear dichotomy could have had an influence on the translator's rendering, for these two parts are differently placed in OG and MT.

The central theme of the first pericope is the king. Hence in verse 1 these sayings are called "an oracular answer of the king" (βασιλέως χρηματισμός). In verse 3 people are mentioned who destroy kings in the MT; an idea that apparently was unacceptable to the translator(s). Verse 4 refers to rulers who are prone to anger and who should not drink wine lest they forget wisdom and are not able to judge rightly. The most significant feature of this passage is the apparently deliberate omission of references to Lemuel to which I have already referred.

In Proverbs 25 in the Hebrew (MT) the first 8 verses are also aimed at the king. Consequently verse 2 speaks of the glory of the king; verse 3 mentions the king's heart; in verses 5–6 the presence of a king and in verse 7 that of a prince are mentioned. As I demonstrated

---

[18] Cook, "The Ideological Stance," 479.

above, Prov 31 verses 1–9 also contain references to the king. There
is clearly a relationship between these passages. To me it is therefore evident that there is a logical and especially thematic relationship between the first 9 verses of Prov 31 and the passage that follows
immediately thereafter in the Greek, Prov 25. I have, therefore,
argued that this example is indeed the result of the work of the
translator, who simply observed that these passages belong together
thematically and consequently rearranged these sections.[19]

3.2. *Order differences on account of contrastive considerations*

I also identified a contextual reason for a second major order difference,
Proverbs 31 verses 10–31 that follows directly after chapter 29. The
acrosticon in Proverbs 31 is preceded by chapter 29 in the Greek. In
the Hebrew this chapter has been constructed primarily by means
of antithetical parallelisms.[20] A whole array of relationships is dealt
with in this chapter, expressed primarily in contrastive terminology.
The immediate context of these passages, the last verse of Prov 29,
is significant in this regard.

> Verse 27
>
> תּוֹעֲבַת צַדִּיקִים אִישׁ עָוֶל וְתוֹעֲבַת רָשָׁע יְשַׁר־דָּרֶךְ׃
>
> An unjust man is an abomination to the righteous,
> but he whose way is straight is an abomination to the wicked.
>
> βδέλυγμα δικαίοις ἀνὴρ ἄδικος
> βδέλυγμα δὲ ἀνόμῳ κατευθύνουσα ὁδός
>
> An unrighteous man is an abomination to the righteous,
> and the direct way is an abomination to the wicked.

Prov 31 verse 10 follows immediately after this verse and contains
a contrast to this "unrighteous man."

> אֵשֶׁת־חַיִל מִי יִמְצָא וְרָחֹק מִפְּנִינִים מִכְרָהּ׃
>
> A good wife who can find?
> She is far more precious than jewels.
>
> Γυναῖκα ἀνδρείαν τίς εὑρήσει
> τιμιωτέρα δέ ἐστιν λίθων πολυτελῶν ἡ τοιαύτη

---

[19] Cook, *The Septuagint of Proverbs*, 316.
[20] W. McKane, *Proverbs—a new approach* (London, 1970), 632.

Who shall find a virtuous woman?
For such a one is more valuable than precious stones.

This subsection is representative of the whole pericope from verses 10–31. The virtuous woman is the exclusive focus of attention. She is described in her relationship with her husband (verses 11–12; 23 and 28); she is diligent (verses 13–18 and 24–25) and merciful (verse 20); she looks after her household (verses 15, 19, 20 and 27); she is also an ideal mother for her children (verses 26 and 28).

So the author of Prov 29 in the Hebrew expresses himself in contrasts—the righteous and the wicked, the just and the unjust, the foolish and the wise, etc. The last verse in this chapter indeed contrasts the unjust and the upright. When this last verse in Prov 29 and the following verse 10 in Prov 31 are compared, a definite relationship becomes apparent. ἀνὴρ ἄδικος and γυναῖκα ἀνδρείαν are clearly related or rather contrasted. Whereas the end of Prov 29 refers to the unrighteous man, the tenth verse of Prov 31 commences with the virtuous wife. Here is an evident contrast between these two persons. This is another example of the remarkably free approach of this translator who seemingly decided to fit two passages together that appear to be related. To me it is clear that he thus rearranged the order of the text in order to contrast the ἀνὴρ ἄδικος and the γυναῖκα ἀνδρείαν. In the *Festschrift* for James Sanders I demonstrated that contrasting takes place in this unit to the extent that one could see it as a translation technique.[21] My conclusion as to the difference of the sequence of Prov 31 in the OG compared to the MT therefore is that the translator deliberately adapted his parent text.

In my view these two examples are of critical significance for the issue at stake, whether the mentioned order differences are the result of the approach of the translator or of a different Hebrew *Vorlage*. However, I must concede that I have so far been able to find explanations for only two of these differences. The burden of proof certainly lies with me as far as the rest of the examples are concerned. I will now deal with all the deviating passages systematically in order to determine whether there is additional evidence in this regard. For methodological reasons I will concentrate on smaller contexts.

---

[21] J. Cook, "Contrasting as a Translation Technique," in: Evans C. A. & Talmon S., eds., *From Tradition to Interpretation: Studies in Intertextuality in Honor of James A. Sanders* (Leiden, 1997), 403–14.

4. Themes in the order differences

4.1. *Proverbs 24 A (verses 1–22)*

In this chapter the translator interprets to some extent. One example is in verses 7 and 8 where the explicating tendency of this translator is clearly observed:

> Verse 7
>
> רָאמוֹת לֶאֱוִיל חָכְמוֹת בַּשַּׁעַר לֹא יִפְתַּח־פִּיהוּ:
>
> Wisdom is too high for fools;
> in the gate they do not open their mouths.
>
> σοφία καὶ ἔννοια ἀγαθὴ ἐν πύλαις σοφῶν
> σοφοὶ οὐκ ἐκκλίνουσιν ἐκ στόματος κυρίου
>
> Wisdom *and good understanding*[22] are to be found in the gates *of the wise;*
> *and the wise do not turn away from the mouth of the Lord.*
>
> Verse 8
>
> מְחַשֵּׁב לְהָרֵעַ לוֹ בַּעַל־מְזִמּוֹת יִקְרָאוּ:
>
> Whoever plans to do evil
> will be called a mischief-maker.
>
> ἀλλὰ λογίζονται ἐν συνεδρίοις
> ἀπαιδεύτοις συναντᾷ θάνατος
>
> *But they caucus in the assemblies;*
> *death meets the uninstructed;*

The most striking difference between MT and OG appears in verse 22 where 11 strophes are added in OG compared to MT:

> Verse 22
>
> כִּי־פִּתְאֹם יָקוּם אֵידָם וּפִיד שְׁנֵיהֶם מִי יוֹדֵעַ: ס
>
> for disaster comes from them suddenly,
> and who knows the ruin that both can bring?
>
> ἐξαίφνης γὰρ τείσονται τοὺς ἀσεβεῖς
> τὰς δὲ τιμωρίας ἀμφοτέρων τίς γνώσεται
> 22a λόγον φυλασσόμενος υἱὸς ἀπωλείας ἐκτὸς ἔσται
> δεχόμενος δὲ ἐδέξατο αὐτόν
> 22b μηδὲν ψεῦδος ἀπὸ γλώσσης βασιλεῖ λεγέσθω
> καὶ οὐδὲν ψεῦδος ἀπὸ γλώσσης αὐτοῦ οὐ μὴ ἐξέλθῃ

---

[22] Italics indicates interpretation by the translator.

22c μάχαιρα γλῶσσα βασιλέως καὶ οὐ σαρκίνη
ὅς δ᾽ ἂν παραδοθῇ συντριβήσεται
22d ἐὰν γὰρ ὀξυνθῇ ὁ θυμὸς αὐτοῦ
σὺν νεύροις ἀνθρώπους ἀναλίσκει
22e καὶ ὀστᾶ ἀνθρώπων κατατρώγει
καὶ συγκαίει ὥσπερ φλὸξ
ὥστε ἄβρωτα εἶναι νεοσσοῖς ἀετῶν

For they can unexpectedly punish *the impious*
and who can know both their punishments?
22a A son who keeps the word will be far away from destruction,
for he received it willingly.
22b Let no falsehood be spoken from the tongue of the king;
and let no falsehood come forth from his tongue.
22c The tongue of the king is a sword and not flesh;
whoever is handed over to him will be destroyed.
22d For if his anger is sharpened
it kills people with thongs;
22e and the bones of people are devoured
and burned like a flame;
so that it cannot be eaten by young eagles!

For the sake of contextuality I deal with the final verses in this passage only. The following themes predominate:

Verse 21. *God and the king.*
Verse 22a. *An obedient son.*
Verse 22b–e. *The king.*

4.2. *Proverbs 30 A (verses 1–14)*

The following themes are addressed in this pericope.

Verse 1. Any reference to Agur that occurs in MT is removed by the translator.
Verse 2. Foolishness.
Verse 3. Wisdom (*God has taught me wisdom, and I know the knowledge of the holy*).
Verse 4. God in creation.
Verse 5. God as a shield.
Verse 6. The word of God.
Verse 7. Two things requested.
Verse 8. Remove far from me falsehood and lying,
Verse 9. falsehood and theft,
Verse 10. servant and master,

Verse 11. cursing of the father and mother,
Verse 12. unclean persons,
Verse 13. the high and mighty.
Verse 14. Wicked generation with swords for teeth.

Even though there is no reference to the king in the opening verses of chapter 30, there is a thematical relationship of sorts in that God is addressed at the end of chapter 24 and again is the focus of attention in the first couple of verses in chapter 30. God is moreover referred to more explicitly in these passages. That extensive interpretation is going on here is clear from the fact that the name of Agur has been removed deliberately, as I stated already. However, this example is not as clear cut as the others that I have discussed earlier.

The situation is different as far as the second part of Proverbs 24 goes that follows upon chapter 30 verse 14. There is a clear contrast between the wicked things mentioned in chapter 30 and the good things (wise words) of chapter 24 B (verses 23–34).

4.3. *Proverbs 24 B (verses 23–34)*

Verse 23. The sayings of the wise.
Verse 24. The wicked: "You are innocent"
Verse 25. but those who rebuke the wicked will have delight.
Verse 26. Good works.
Verse 27. Work outside, prepare the field and build the house.
Verses 28–29. False witnessing and injustice.
Verses 30–34. The sluggard.

In this case one could argue that the contrast between wicked and wise is already found in the Hebrew and that it is therefore possible that it could reflect a deviating parent text. However, that the translator could actually be at work here is evident to me in that he, as is his custom, emphasizes specific "ideological/theological" issues in the text. Chapter 30, the previous passage, contains a classical example of exegetical interpretations by this translator. The Hebrew in verses 11–14 contains references to wicked people, those who curse their parents, who are impure, haughty, etc. The Greek translator consistently calls these persons a wicked progeny (ἔκγονον κακόν), a collective singular treated as plural below. This forms a direct and marked contrast to what follows in chapter 24 B.

Verse 11

דּוֹר אָבִיו יְקַלֵּל וְאֶת־אִמּוֹ לֹא יְבָרֵךְ׃

There are those who curse their fathers
and do not bless their mothers.

ἔκγονον κακὸν πατέρα καταρᾶται
τὴν δὲ μητέρα οὐκ εὐλογεῖ

A *wicked* progeny curse their father
and do not bless their mother.

Verse 12

דּוֹר טָהוֹר בְּעֵינָיו וּמִצֹּאָתוֹ לֹא רֻחָץ׃

There are those who are pure in their own eyes
but are not cleansed of their filth.

ἔκγονον κακὸν δίκαιον ἑαυτὸν κρίνει
τὴν δὲ ἔξοδον αὐτοῦ οὐκ ἀπένιψεν

A *wicked* progeny judge themselves righteous;
but have not cleansed their ways.

Verse 13

דּוֹר מָה־רָמוּ עֵינָיו וְעַפְעַפָּיו יִנָּשֵׂאוּ׃

There are those — how lofty are their eyes,
how high their eyelids lift!

ἔκγονον κακὸν ὑψηλοὺς ὀφθαλμοὺς ἔχει
τοῖς δὲ βλεφάροις αὐτοῦ ἐπαίρεται

A *wicked* progeny have lofty eyes
and they lift their eyebrows.

Verse 14

דּוֹר חֲרָבוֹת שִׁנָּיו וּמַאֲכָלוֹת מְתַלְּעֹתָיו
לֶאֱכֹל עֲנִיִּים מֵאֶרֶץ וְאֶבְיוֹנִים מֵאָדָם׃ פ

There are those whose teeth are swords,
whose teeth are knives,
to devour the poor from off the earth,
the needy from among men.

ἔκγονον κακὸν μαχαίρας τοὺς ὀδόντας ἔχει
καὶ τὰς μύλας τομίδας ὥστε ἀναλίσκειν
καὶ κατεσθίειν τοὺς ταπεινοὺς ἀπὸ τῆς γῆς
καὶ τοὺς πένητας αὐτῶν ἐξ ἀνθρώπων

A *wicked progeny* have teeth *like* swords;
and grinders *like* knives *in order to destroy*

and to devour the poor from the earth;
and the needy from among men.

On the face of it there seems to be no obvious thematic or contrastive considerations for the next deviating passages compared to MT; the end of chapter 24B and the beginning of chapter 30B. Whereas the latter contains a number of loose aphorisms, initially, as said already, concerning the wicked, but later regarding the erection of buildings and the preparation of a field and a vineyard, as well as laziness, Proverbs 30B sets out with a number of numerical sayings.

4.4. *Proverbs 30 B (verses 15–33)*

Verse 15. The leech has two/three (OG) daughters.
Verse 16. Sheol/Hades.
Verse 17. Mocking of father and mother.
Verse 18. Three things and four.
Verse 19. Eagle, serpent, ship, man and a maiden.
Verse 20. Adulteress.
Verse 21. Three things and four.
Verse 22. Slave and king.
Verse 23. Woman and husband.
Verse 24. Four wise things on earth.
Verse 25. Ants.
Verse 26. Badgers.
Verse 27. Locusts.
Verse 28. The lizard.
Verse 29. Three and four things.
Verse 30. The lion.
Verse 31. The strutting cock, the he-goat, and a king.
Verse 32. Foolish/merriment.
Verse 33. Milk, nostrils.

The numerical sayings that occur towards the end of this chapter (verses 21f.) do contain a theme that links up with the next passage, chapter 31 verses 1–9, namely the king. This applies to the next passage as well, Proverbs chapter 25 of which the first 6 verses center around the king, as I demonstrated above.

4.5. *Proverbs 31 (verses 1–9)*

Verse 1. (MT) Lemuel.
Verse 1. (OG) Words of God.
Verses 2–3. Words to the son.
Verses 4–5. Lemuel and king.
Verses 4–5. (OG) princes.
Verses 6–7. Strong drink and wine.
Verses 8–9. Judge fairly.

4.6. *Proverbs 25 (verses 1–8)*

God and the King
Verse 1. Solomon and men of Hezekiah (MT);
Verse 1. just Solomon (OG).
Verse 2. God and the king.
Verse 3. King.
Verse 4. Silver and the smith.
Verses 5–8. King.

4.7. *Proverbs 29 (verses 25–27)*

Ruler and King
Verse 25. Snare and trust in God.
Verse 26. Ruler and God.
Verse 27. Unrighteous man.

4.8. *Proverbs 31 (verses 10–31)*

Verses 10–12. Virtuous woman.
I have already dealt with these passages above.

5. CONCLUSION

From the discussion thus far it would seem clear to me that the person(s) responsible for the Greek version of Proverbs indeed rendered the subject matter freely. My conclusion as to the difference of the sequence of Prov 31 *vis-à-vis* chapters 29 and 30 in the OG compared to the MT therefore is that the translator deliberately adapted his parent text. It is therefore not the result of either a deviating, recensionally different parent Hebrew text, nor of inner Greek corruptions,

but is based upon a different understanding of whole passages. I
have to concede that the example at the beginning of Proverbs 30A
is not too convincing. However, I think there could be a plausible
explanation for the fact that only one side of this chapter actually
fits the thematic argument. It is possible that the translator was only
interested in matching, so to speak, the one passage. There is ample
evidence that this translator does not adapt systematically in every
instance.[23]

I feel relatively confident that the explanation offered above for
the difference in the order of chapters in OG compared to MT is as
plausible as any other explanation. Tov's claim that the differences
reflect a different Hebrew *Vorlage* surely is possible, but there is no
primary evidence of such a recensionally different Hebrew text of
these passages, except the Greek itself. This appears to be a circu-
lar argument. The text-critical value of OG Proverbs, moreover, is
extremely problematic, and, I, at least, would not be willing to retro-
vert the parent text of this unit too readily. Thus, until primary evidence is available of the sequence differences discussed above
(unfortunately the Dead Sea Scrolls have not yet yielded any primary
evidence of Proverbs, excepting minor fragments), I would suggest
that the aforementioned explanation be accepted as the "default."
There is naturally another *provisio*, the complicated transmission history of Greek Proverbs must be sorted out first of all before a more
definitive word can be spoken on this issue.

---

[23] Cook, *The Septuagint of Proverbs*, 318.

MESSIANISM IN EZEKIEL IN HEBREW AND IN GREEK, EZEK 21:15(10) AND 20(15)

J. LUST

MESSIANISM IN SEPTUAGINTAL MATERIALS

It is often said that the Septuagint shows signs of a developing messianism, especially in as far as royal messianism is concerned.[1] J. Coppens, one of the protagonists of this view defines messianism as follows. It is the expectation of an individual human and yet transcendent saviour. He is to come in a final eschatological period and will establish God's Kingdom on earth. Royal messianism is the expectation of a royal Davidic saviour at the end time.[2] According to the Christian tradition, some of the main texts witnessing to this royal messianism are to be found in Isaiah: the "Immanuel" oracle in 7:14, the "Unto us a child is born" oracle in 9:1–5. In Coppens' view, a comparison between the Masoretic and Septuagint texts of these and similar passages[3] shows a clear evolution towards a more personal, more supernatural, and more transcendent messianism.

This view should be revised. One cannot treat the Septuagint as a unified entity, and draw general conclusions based on the study of one text or one book. Moreover, one should avoid arbitrary selections of proof texts. The numerous passages in the Greek texts where a "messianizing" translation might have been expected, but where it is not found, should not be overlooked. Each relevant text should

---

[1] J. Coppens, *Le messianisme royal* (Lectio divina 54; Paris: Cerf, 1968), 119: "Il suffit de comparer les textes hébreux et grecs d'Is 7,14; 9,1–5; du Ps 110,3 pour se rendre compte de l'évolution accomplie dans le sens d'un messianisme plus personel, plus surnaturel, plus transcendant." For other protagonists of this view see J. Lust, "Messianism and Septuagint. Ez 21,30–32," in *Congress Volume Salamanca 1983* (ed. J. Emerton; VTSup 36; Leiden: Brill, 1985), 174–91, esp. 174, note 2.

[2] Coppens, *Messianisme*, 14–15.

[3] Coppens also refers to Ps 110(109):3; others add Gen 3:15; 49:10; Num 24:7,17; 2 Sam 7:16: Is 11:4; 14:19–32; Ezek 17:23; 21:30–32; 43:3; Dan 7:13; Hos 8:10; Amos 4:13; Zech 9:10; for bibliographical references, see Lust, "Messianism. Ez 21," 174 note 2.

be studied on its own, and in its context. At the present stage of the research, one cannot conclude that the Septuagint as a whole displays a messianic exegesis.[4]

Focussing upon the Psalms, J. Schaper,[5] however, recently revived the thesis that the Septuagint reflects an increased degree of messianism, influenced by the "intellectual, religious and political climate" of its environment. He is convinced that current Septuagint scholarship needs a corrective. It's approach is too one-sided in its preoccupation with detailed analyses of the translation technique used by particular translators in the respective books or in parts of them. It needs to be replaced by a broader understanding of the Greek text as a literary document in its own right and expressive of its own cultural and historical milieu. Only with an open eye for this larger background can one detect the interpretative character of the translation and the main facts of its theological "Tendenz."

---

[4] See M. Harl a.o., *La Bible grecque des Septante* (Init. au christianisme ancien; Paris: Éditions du Cerf, 1988), 219–20; K. H. Jobes and M. Silva, *Invitation to the Septuagint* (Grand Rapids: Baker, 2000), 96–97; 297–300. See also my earlier contributions on this topic: "Daniel 7,13 and the Septuagint," *ETL* 54 (1978): 62–69; "Messianism and Septuagint." 174–91; "Le Messianisme et la Septante d'Ézéchiel," *Tsafon* 2/3 (1990): 3–14; "Messianism and the Greek Version of Jeremiah: Jer 23:5–6," in *VII Congress of the International Organisation for Septuagint and Cognate Studies, Leuven 1989* (ed. C. E. Cox; Septuagint and Cognate Studies 31; Atlanta: Scholars Press, 1991), 87–122; "The Diverse Text forms of Jeremiah and History Writing with Jer 33 as a Test Case," *JNSL* 20 (1994): 31–48; "The Greek Version of Balaam's Third and Fourth Oracles. The ἄνθρωπος in Num 24:7 and 17. Messianism and Lexicography," in *VIII Congress of the International Organization for Septuagint and Cognate Studies, Paris 1992* (ed. L. Greenspoon & O. Munnich; Septuagint and Cognate Studies 41; Atlanta: Scholars Press, 1995), 233–57; "Mic 5,1–3 in Qumran and in the New Testament, and Messianism in the Septuagint," in *The Scriptures in the Gospels* (eds. C. M. Tucket; BETL 131; Leuven, Univ. Press & Peeters, 1997), 65–88; "'And I Shall Hang Him on a Lofty Mountain'. Ezek 17:22–24 and Messianism in the Septuagint," in *Proceedings of the IX Congress of the International Organization for Septuagint and Cognate Studies, Cambridge 1995* (ed. B. Taylor; Septuagint and Cognate Studies 45; Atlanta: Scholars Press, 1997), 231–50; "Septuagint and Messianism, with a Special Emphasis on the Pentateuch," in *Theologische Probleme der Septuaginta und der hellenistischen Hermeneutik* (ed. H. G. Reventlow; Gütersloh, C. Kaiser, 1997), 26–45; "Messianism in the Septuagint: Is 8,23b–9,6 (9,1–7)," in *Interpretation of the Bible* (ed. J. Kracovec; Ljubljana: Slovenska akademija znanosti in umetnosti; Sheffield: Academic Press, 1998), 147–63.

[5] J. Schaper, *Eschatology in the Greek Psalter* (WUNT 2 Reihe 76; Tübingen: J. C. B. Mohr, 1995); see also his contribution on "Der Septuaginta-Psalter als Document jüdischer Eschatologie," in *Die Septuaginta zwischen Judentum und Christentum* (ed. M. Hengel and A. M. Schwemer; WUNT 2 Reihe 72; Tübingen: J. C. B. Mohr, 1994), 38–61.

In his review of Schaper's monograph, A. Pietersma rightly observes that "Septuaginta hermeneutics needs to be firmly rooted in, and informed by, detailed translation technical analysis." Schaper tends to overlook that "translators are not authors, unless proven to be so, and one can only prove them to be more than mediums by painstakingly delineating unmarked/default renderings from marked/non-default renderings."[6]

We will not here join Pietersma in a direct debate with Schapers. Analysing two messianic passages in Ezekiel[7] we will check the theory of the allegedly developed messianism in the Septuagint, completing our earlier studies on the subject.

Messianism and the Hebrew text of Ezek 21:15b, 18b, The שבט

15b: "Or shall we rejoice, 'the sceptre of my son, despises every stick'?"
18b: "'and what if even the sceptre who despises will not be?' says the Lord God."

Several scholars recognize in 21:15b, 18b an allusion to the Messiah. According to A. van den Born, both texts are to be understood as allusions to the messianic saying of Gen 49:8–12.[8] W. Zimmerli found this suggestion interesting, but had serious objections against it. L. C. Allen accepted van den Born's hypothesis as very relevant, and further developed it. In his view both phrases are editorial notes to 21:3 and 32. They became displaced and attached to the wrong side of the column.[9] Without reference to van den Born, Block accepts the connection with Genesis 49 and emphasizes the implications of

---

[6] *Bibliotheca Orientalis* 54 (1997): 185–90.

[7] Among the recent commentaries on Ezekiel giving attention to the passages in question, special mention should be made of W. Zimmerli, *Ezechiel* (2 vols. BKAT 13; Neukirchen-Vluyn: Neukirchener Verlag, 1969); B. Maarsingh, *Ezechiël* (3 vols. POT; Nijkerk: Callenbach, 1985, 1988 and 1991); L. C. Allen, *Ezekiel* (2 vols. WBC, Waco TX: Word, 1994 and 1990); M. Greenberg, *Ezekiel 1–20* (AB, Garden City, NY: Doubleday, 1983); *Ezekiel 21–37* (AB, Garden City, NY: Doubleday, 1997); D. I. Block, *The Book of Ezekiel* (2 vols. NICOT; Grand Rapids MI: Eerdmans, 1997 and 1998); see also D. Barthélemy, *Critique textuelle de l'Ancien Testament* (OBO 50/3; Fribourg: Éd. Univ.; Göttingen: Vandenhoeck, 1992) = CTAT.

[8] A. van den Born, *Ezechiël* (BOT; Roermond: Romen & zonen, 1954), 135–6.

[9] L. C. Allen, "The Rejected Sceptre in Ezekiel xxi 15b, 18a," *VT* 29 (1989): 67–71.

the use of the term שבט and its connections with the messianic prophecy in 2 Samuel 7.[10] Perhaps the most detailed investigation of the problematic passages has been produced by D. Barthélemy. He seems to be unaware of Allen's proposals, and ignores the theory of van den Born but comes to similar conclusions, based on sound argumentation.[11] M. Greenberg also ignores van den Born, rejects Allen's views, and joins a long series of exegetes who consider both verses as unintelligible.[12]

This is not the place for a full analysis of the Hebrew text of these verses. Nevertheless, some introductory remarks as well as some text-critical observations are in order. The verses belong to Ezek 21:13–22 which is often entitled the "Song of the Sword."[13] It consists of two strophes (14b–18 and 19–22a) embedded within the usual formulae characteristic of the framework of a prophetic oracle (13, 14a, 18b and 22b). The alleged messianic allusions in vv. 15 and 18 belong to the first strophe. In MT this strophe falls into three parts: (a) a presentation of a sword and of its preparation for its work of devastation (14b–16), interrupted by a rather cryptic rhetorical question, referring to the שבט (15b); (b) a renewed command, given to the prophet, to show dismay 17–18a, followed by a succinct, and again rather cryptic, aside referring to the שבט (18b).

Who are the actors? According to the context, the sword must be interpreted as the sword of the Lord (21:10), who intervenes through the instrumental help of the king of Babylon (21:24). The prophet's public are those who asked him "why do you sigh with breaking heart" (21:11). The oracle in 21:13–18 explains his behaviour: war is at hand. Verse 15b is a rhetorical question of the prophet addressed to his public "or should we rejoice?." They suggest that joy is called for, rather than sighing. Their reasoning is given in a quotation expressing the feelings of security among his public over against the threatening tidings of an aggression planned by the king of Babylon. They are convinced that the Lord will save them, and quote in support of their views one of the (lost) oracles of their (false) prophets:

---

[10] Block, *Ezekiel I*, 677–9.
[11] Barthélemy, *Critique textuelle*, 161–4.
[12] Greenberg *Ezekiel II*, 424; so also Pohlmann 2001, 325.
[13] See, e.g., Block, *Ezekiel I*, 674; Allen, *Ezekiel II*, 23; B. Maarsingh, "Das Schwertlied in Ez 21,13–22 und das Erra-Gedicht," in *Ezekiel and His Book* (ed. J. Lust; BETL 74; Leuven: Univ. Press & Peeters, 1986), 350–58.

"The sceptre of my son despises all sticks." The oracle is put in the mouth of the Lord. "His son" refers to the Messiah who will defeat all Israel's enemies. The end of the passage (18b) returns to the objection of the public, questioning its convictions: "what if the sceptre that despises does not show up?." This explanation of the passage corresponds to a large extent to Barthélemy's views on it.[14]

In this interpretation, שבט is taken to mean "sceptre,"[15] a symbol of leadership, as in Gen 49:10, where the Lord promises that the sceptre will never depart from Judah.[16] In Ezek 21:15 the Lord calls "my son" the one who has the שבט.[17] This reinforces the connection with Gen 49:9–10 where Judah is called "my son." The connection becomes more relevant when one notices that Ezek 21:32 makes use of the same messianic prophecy: "Until he comes to whom the משפט belongs," a verse that is undoubtedly reminiscent of the announcement of a ruler or Messiah of Judah in Gen 49:10 "Until he comes to whom it belongs and to him shall be the obedience of the peoples."

Our reading implies that שבט in Ezek 21:15 is a *status constructus* connected with בני. Also it presumes that שבט is the subject of the feminine participle מאסת: the sceptre despises. This was hardly acceptable to Zimmerli, since elsewhere שבט seems to be treated as masculine.[18] Barthélemy, however, countered the objection noting that the two cases in which שבט is said to be masculine are not convincing.[19]

It must be admitted that the interpretation of the initial phrase או נשיש remains a problem. Most translations, including ours, treat או as an interrogative particle: "Or shall we rejoice." Nowhere else in the Bible, however, is this use attested. Recently, D. Block adopted Garfinkel's explanation of the particle as a corruption of the Akkadian

---

[14] See Barthélemy, *Critique textuelle*, 163–4.
[15] D. M. Fouts, שבט, in NIDOT 4 (1997): 27–29; H.-J. Zobel, שבט in TWAT 8 (1993): 966–74.
[16] See however Zobel 1993, 968 who holds that in Gen 49:10 reference is made, not to a sceptre of a Judaean king, but to the ruler's stick of the head of a tribe.
[17] Note that the Targum offers a different interpretation in which שבט is taken to mean tribe: "Because the tribe of the House of Judah and Benjamin rejoiced over the tribes of Israel when they were exiled for having worshipped idols, they in turn went astray after images of wood," *The Targum of Ezekiel* (transl. S. H. Levey, Aramaic Bible, 13; Wilmington, Del.: Glazier, 1987), 66.
[18] Zimmerli, *Ezekiel*, 470.
[19] Barthélemy, *Critique textuelle*, 163.

prohibitive *ai* "(Let us) not (rejoice)."[20] This, however, does not only necessitate a correction of the Hebrew, it also complicates the reading of the remainder of the verse. According to L. Allen, אוֹ bears the sense "in other words," "or." The following word נִשִׂיא is then to be split up into נְשׂ and שׂי which are abbreviations for נִשִׂיא יִשְׂרָאֵל. The sentence as a whole is a note, explaining כָּל עֵץ in 21:3: "Every tree: *or* the ruler(s) of Israel."[21] M. Greenberg rejects this proposal and joins the large group of exegetes who consider the passage unintelligible. D. Barthélemy presents a list of that group.[22] He also gives a useful survey of the attempts towards emendation.[23] In his view, however, MT does not need any correction. We are inclined to follow his lead, suggesting that the use of the interrogative particle אוֹ (or אִי) is a symptom of late Hebrew or Aramaic.

Although v. 18b is equally difficult our comments can be shorter. What has been said about שֵׁבֶט "sceptre," and מֹאֶסֶת "who despises," in v. 15b applies also here. The subject of לֹא יִהְיֶה is taken to be the sceptre, or Messiah, whose coming is questioned.[24] Verses 15 and 18 prepare for v. 32 in which the coming of the Messiah is replaced by the coming of Nebuchadnessar, the one to whom belongs the מִשְׁפָּט.

Messianism and the Greek text of
Ezek 21:15b, 18b. The φυλή

In the Septuagint, the first part of the Song of the Sword (21:13–18) displays a slightly different subdivision from that in MT: (a) the sword is directly addressed and commanded to prepare itself for slaughter (14b–15); (b) a report is given of the handing over of the sword to the killer (16); (c) the prophet is commanded to show dismay 17–18a; (d) a rhetorical question concludes the composition (18b).

In this composition of the Greek, vv. 15b and 18b, are not formulated as asides alluding to the Messiah, they are incorporated in

---

[20] Block, *Ezekiel*, 672, note 79; S. P. Garfinkel, *Studies in Akkadien Influences in the Book of Ezekiel* (Ann Arbor: Univ. Microfilms, 1983), 31–33.

[21] Allen, "Rejected Sceptre," 69.

[22] *Critique Textuelle*, 162: Herrmann, Cooke, Eichrodt, Fohrer, König. The names of Zimmerli, Wevers, and Hals can be added to that list.

[23] *Ibidem*, 69.

[24] The masoretic sentence dividers confirm this. Compare Ezek 30:13 "there shall be no more prince from the land of Egypt."

the Lord's threatening address to the sword (15b), and in the final rhetorical question.

Focussing on vv. 15 and 18, the main difference with MT is perhaps the absence of any allusion to a royal sceptre or Messiah. This discrepancy is to a large extent connected with the Hebrew word שבט. In v. 18 the Greek text renders this key term by φυλή "tribe," and in v. 15 it has no equivalent for it. It must be admitted that שבט is an ambiguous word. Originally it seems to have referred to sticks or branches of a tree from which a rod of discipline or a staff could be made. A ruler was singled out by his שבט. In a derived sense, the people under his leadership became known as his שבט. Hence the most prevalent meaning of שבט in the OT is that of "tribe." On the other hand, the word retained great theological significance as term of authority, depicting the rod of discipline or the sceptre of a king or Messiah.

The Greek Bible translators used a variety of words when rendering the Hebrew term. Trying to catch the correct meaning, the interpretation was not always evident. In many instances their interpretive choices deviate from those preferred by modern translations and commentaries. Striking examples are to be found in the books of Samuel and Kings. In 1 Samuel and 1 Kings, the Hebrew term is almost always rendered by σκῆπτρον, even when the context makes it clear that reference is made to a tribe or to tribes.[25] The situation is totally different in 2 Samuel and 2 Kings where in similar contexts φυλή is used.[26] In an elaborate and ingenious attempt B. Grillet and M. Lestienne try to explain the behaviour of the translator of 1 Samuel.[27] According to them, in Jewish literature σκῆπτρον had both the meaning of "staff" and of "tribe." They do not, however, explain how it acquired that double meaning, nor do they account for the different behaviour of the translator in 2 Samuel and 2 Kings.[28]

---

[25] 1 Sam 2:28; 9:21; 10:19.20.21; 15:17; 1 Kgs 8:15; 11:13,31,32,35,36; 12:20,21. Exceptionally 1 Kgs 18:31 φυλή is preferred.

[26] 2 Sam 5:1; 7:7; 15:2,10; 18:14; 19:10; 20:14; 24:2; 2 Kgs 17:18; 21:7.

[27] B. Grillet and M. Lestienne, *Premier Livre des Règnes* (La Bible d'Alexandrie IX/1; Paris: Cerf, 1997), 48–49.

[28] It is tempting to ascribe the differences to the different translators detected by Thackeray according to whom 1 Samuel; 2 Sam 1–11:1 and 1 Kgs 2:13–21:29 belong to an early translation, whereas the rest belongs to a late translation. However, 2 Sam 5:1 and 7:7 do not seem to fit this theory.

Some of the Prophetic Books display exactly the opposite phenomenon. In several instances, they use φυλή where σκῆπτρον is expected.[29] Ezekiel, and more specifically Ezek 21:18, fits this category.[30] Ezek 21:15 is different. It does not seem to have a direct counterpart for MT שׁבט. For both verses, a close comparison with MT is called for.

Ezek 21:15b in the Septuagint[31]

> so that you may slaughter, be sharpened so that you may be flashing, ready *for destruction; slaughter, reject, push aside everything of wood.*

The Septuagint translation of this verse not only lacks a counterpart for MT שׁבט, it also displays an important difference in the style and structure of the verse.[32] Where MT reads a rhetorical question "or do we rejoice," LXX has the second part of a non-verbal clause "(ready) for destruction"—<ἑτοίμη> εἰς παράλυσιν with the sword as implicit subject. The first term, ἑτοίμη, probably renders MT מרוטה, a word belonging to the end of the foregoing sentence in MT.[33] The second

---

[29] See Amos 1:5,8; Mic 5:1. Jeremiah uses שׁבט twice, but the translator does not render it: both in 10:16 and in 51(28):19 he translates שׁבט נחלתו by κληρονομία αὐτοῦ. In the pre-messianic prophecy of Gen 49:10, the symbol of power שׁבט is rendered by the symbolized ἄρχων, and in Num 24:17 by the cryptic ἄνθρωπος; see Lust "Balaam's Third and Fourth Oracles," 233–57.

[30] See also Ezek 19:11 "into *sceptres* of rulers אל שׁבטי משׁלים" (MT); "for a *tribe* of rulers ἐπὶ φυλὴν ἡγουμένων" (OG); 19:14 "a *sceptre* for a ruler אל שׁבט משׁלים" (MT); "a *tribe* became a parable φυλὴ εἰς παραβολήν." (In this context it may be noted that in 37:19 the translator twice uses φυλή where MT has עץ referring to a stick or branch representing a tribe.) In most of the remaining 14 cases in which שׁבט is attested, the context makes it clear that "tribe" is meant; in all these cases LXX has φυλή. In 20:37 reference is made to the "rod of discipline," adequately rendered by ῥάβδος in OG.

[31] In the following translation of v. 15, the section corresponding to the Hebrew verse 15b is *italicized*. The translation and notes to vv. 15 and 18 have been discussed with K. Hauspie and A. Ternier in our *Centre for Septuagint and Textual Criticism.*

[32] The Syrohexaplaric version of Symmachus, although unclear, certainly brings the text of 15b (ἑτοίμη ... ξυλον) closer to MT: εξεσπασμενη η φευξομεν απο του ραβδου υιε μου απεδοκιμασας απο παντος ξυλου "drawn forth, or shall we flee away from the stick, my son? Keep away(?) from all wood"; Theodotion has εστιλβωμενη<ν> η κ<ε>ινουσα ραβδον υιων μου απωθουμενη ... Note that both Symmachus and Theodotion render שׁבט by ῥάβδος.

[33] The correspondence between these Hebrew and Greek terms is confirmed by v. 16, and probably also by v. 14, see P. Walters, *The Text of the Septuagint. Its Corruptions and their Emendation* (ed., D. W. Gooding; Cambridge: Cambridge Univ. Press, 1973), 326, n. 16.

term παράλυσις is a *hapax* in the Bible; the construction εἰς παράλυσιν, which we translated "for destruction," means literally "for loosening." The relation to its counterpart in MT אוֹ נָשִׂישׂ "or do we rejoice" is cryptic; the translator may have read, or thought he read, a form of the root מסס "to melt, to dissolve." Symmachus interprets the Hebrew verb as a form of נסס or נוס and reads φεύξομεν "(or) shall we flee."

The following word in the Septuagint is a verb: "slaughter"— σφάζε. This imperative probably translates טבחי[34] whereas MT has שׁבט "sceptre," a substantive loaded with theological meaning. LXX continues with two more imperatives. The first one, "set at naught/ reject"—ἐξουδένει, seems to render the imperative בזי,[35] whereas MT has the suffixed noun בני "my son." The second, "push aside"— ἀπωθοῦ, may render the Hebrew imperative מאסי, where MT reads the participle מאסת "the one who despises."

The final phrase "everything of wood"—πᾶν ξύλον, lit. "all wood," corresponds perfectly to MT כל עץ. In the context of the Septuagint, where no mention is made of the שׁבט "sceptre," the reference is probably to idols made of wood, calling to mind 20:32, whereas in MT the editor most likely refers to sceptres of rulers.

In favour of the original character of the Greek composition, and of the underlaying variant Hebrew text, it has to be noted that Ezekiel often works with series of imperatives.[36] Nowhere else does he work with asides bringing up rhetorical questions introduced by the particle א. The use of that particle in this context is untypical of biblical Hebrew, and perhaps fits better later Hebrew. Moreover, in contrast with MT, the Greek text does not imply an interruption of the song of the sword with a line whose meaning is rather uncertain.

EZEK 21:18b IN THE SEPTUAGINT[37]

for it has been justified. *'And what, even if a tribe is rejected, shall it not be?' says the Lord.*

---

[34] The verb טבח does occur in the beginning of the sentence, and is there also translated by σφάζω; see also 21:33.

[35] בזה "despise"; the same translation equivalent is used in 2 Kgs 19:21 and 2 Chr 36:16.

[36] In the present chapter, see verses 17, 19, 21.

[37] In the following translation of v. 18, the section corresponding to the Hebrew verse 18b is *italicized*.

In this verse, the Septuagint appears to offer a wooden word for word translation of a cryptic Hebrew text corresponding to that of MT.[38]

Here the translator obviously found שבט in his *Vorlage*, and interpreted it as meaning "tribe," referring to Israel mentioned in v. 17, distinguishing it from its ruler. The sentence beginning with "And what" (καὶ τί) can be subdivided and interpreted in different ways. The opening (καὶ τί) can be read as an independent verbless clause: a question in the form of an exclamation: "and what?," or as an introduction to the main clause formulated as a question: "and why (, even when . . .,) shall it not be?." The following two verbal clauses are to be understood as a subordinate concessive clause "even when a tribe is rejected,"[39] followed by a main clause, phrased as a rhetorical question "shall it not be?" In contrast with the "sceptre" in MT, the "tribe" (φυλή) does not despise, but is despised or rejected. The subject of the verb "to be" is not the tribe, but the coming of the sword announced in the foregoing verses. The Lord goes on with his threatening language, even if a tribe is to be rejected, shall it not happen? It certainly shall. In the following oracle (23–32) the threat is described more fully: war is at hand.

DEVELOPED MESSIANISM?

In MT, Ezek 21:15 and 18 evoke Gen 49:9–10. In LXX the connections between Ezek 21:15, 18 and Gen 49:9–10 are non-existent. In v. 15, no mention is made of the sceptre or staff, nor of the Lord's son. No positive expectation appears to be expressed. In v. 18 the Greek translation reflects Hebrew שבט, but renders it by φυλή "tribe," and not by σκῆπτρον "sceptre."[40] No allusion to a future saviour is

---

[38] According to Fields's retroversion of the Syrohexapla Symmachus reads: καὶ τι η δοκιμασια και τι ει και ραβδος. Going against LXX, Symmachus renders שבט again by ραβδος.

[39] In Classical Greek εἰ + imperfect usually introduces an *irrealis*, in Biblical Greek, however, the exceptions to that rule are numerous, see, e.g., Gen 18:3; 27:37; 30:27.

[40] In his commentary Jerome duly notes the differences between MT and LXX, but does not seem to be impressed. He focuses on his Latin translation of the Hebrew "et hoc cum sceptrum subverterit" in v. 18, and "succedisti omne lignum" in v. 15. In the "scepter" he sees a reference to the kingdom of Israel, and in "all wood" he finds an allusion to the whole people of Israel. The subject of both verbs is the destroying sword of the king of Babylon. Jerome does not seem to detect any messianic connotations in these passages; see *In Hiezechielem* (Corpus Christianorum, Series Latina 75; Turnhout: Brepols, 1964), 285–6.

to be detected. If we correctly interpreted "everything of wood" as referring to the idols of wood in 20:32, then the "tribe" φυλή in 21:18 may also allude to that passage where Ezekiel's opponents want to be like the "tribes" φυλαί of the world worshipping wood and stone.

How are the two traditions related to each other? How are the differences between MT and LXX to be explained? Are they mainly due to errors in the translation, perhaps due to ignorance, or errors in the transmission of the Hebrew manuscripts on which MT and OG were based, or do they reveal intentional changes? If they were intentional, who made them: the translator, the editor of the Hebrew text he worked with, or the Masoretes and their predecessors? Straightforward answers to these questions are hazardous. Nevertheless, some suggestions can be made.

It is unlikely that the deviations in the Septuagint were due to intentional changes introduced by the translator. As a rule, translators were no authors nor editors. They tried to render their *Vorlage* as faithfully as possible.[41] Moreover, the translator(s) of Ezekiel, as a rule, produced a rather wooden translation, following the word order of the Hebrew. Most likely, the translation of vv. 15 and 18 obeyed the same rule. Subconsciously, however, the cultural and religious background of the translator may have influenced his choice of words.

In v. 18, the translator obviously did have before him a Hebrew text that corresponded word for word to the un-vocalized MT. He rendered each word according to the word order of the Hebrew verse. He read the word שבט, but his rendition of that term by φυλή "tribe" strongly suggests that he did not see in it an allusion to Gen 49:10 with its messianic connotations.[42] Admittedly, the context is not very clear for today's readers. It may have been unclear for the Greek translator as well. Even then, his choice of the term φυλή may seem to be puzzling.

One might opine that the translator was not aware of the full semantic range of meanings of the Hebrew term. That is rather unlikely, however, since elsewhere, he knows how to use ῥαβδός

---

[41] See A. Pietersma, *Bibliotheca Orientalis* 54 (1997): 185–90; the rule certainly applies to the translation of Ezekiel, which most often rendered its *Vorlage* word for word.

[42] In 49:10 שבט is translated (and interpreted) as ἄρχων "leader."

"stick" as a translation of שֵׁבֶט.[43] Moreover, we already noted that translators of other biblical books did use σκῆπτρον "sceptre" when the context invited them to do so, or even when it did not.[44]

Why then did he use "tribe" instead of "sceptre"? The reason may be found in the context. We noted that MT and OG display drastic differences in v. 15b. In his Hebrew *Vorlage* of that verse, the translator did not find the term שֵׁבֶט, nor its immediate context pointing to a royal sceptre. He rather heard in it a command addressed to the sword, inviting it to slaughter people, identified in v. 17 with Israel and its leaders. He probably also found in it an allusion to 20:32 where Israel expressed the wish to be like the "tribes (φυλαί) of the world" worshipping wood and stone. Given this context he may have correctly interpreted שֵׁבֶט as meaning "tribe."

In v. 15 the style of the Septuagint, and of its underlying Hebrew, fits better the context than that of MT. In this verse, one has the impression that the *Vorlage* of the Greek preserved the earlier text form. Reworking that text, the editor of MT made allusions to a type of messianic expectation that he himself refused to accept. In his choice of words he was inspired by the vocabulary of v. 18.

In an earlier contribution, I tried to demonstrate that the Septuagint text of Ezek 21:31–32, as well as its underlaying Hebrew *Vorlage* referred to the Maccabees. They were the rejected leaders, threatened by the sword. More specifically Jonathan, who wanted to become a king, was accused of diminishing and abasing the priestly headdress, preferring the royal crown. The oracle announced that the priestly crown would remain abased until the coming of someone to whom it belonged. This can be interpreted as a messianic promise, not of the royal kind, but priestly.

The same background may be reflected in verses 15–18, in the Septuagint and in its *Vorlage*. In v. 15 allusion is made to Israel wishing to be like the pagan "tribes" or nations. In v. 17 the people and their leaders are said to live as strangers in the land: παροικήσουσιν. They behave themselves like the Greeks. Moreover, they live "on" or "with" the sword. These data may refer to the same situation as that decried in vv. 30–32. It should be admitted, however, that the evidence is not overwhelming.

---

[43] Ezek 20:37.
[44] See our note 18.

In MT 30–32 other nuances were brought to the fore. The attention was shifted from the royal aspirations of the priestly Maccabean leaders to Jerusalem's evil kings in general. They were contrasted with a coming king-Messiah.

My suggestion now is that the editor of MT is also to a large extent responsible for the differences with the Hebrew *Vorlage* of the Septuagint in v. 15. He inserted the messianic allusions. It may have been his intention to question the shortsighted messianic expectations of the false prophets. The Messiah was not to come and deliver them from immediate foreign invasions.

Much of what has been suggested in the final lines of this paper remains very hypothetical. On the other hand, a theory attributing the divergencies between LXX and MT to the editor of the *Vorlage* of the Greek may prove to be even more hazardous. It is indeed difficult to see why an editor would have eliminated the messianic allusions in vv. 15 and 18.

CONCLUSIONS

The following conclusions are listed according to a descending scale of probability.

1. The Septuagint version of Ezek 21:15 and 18 displays no traces of messianic expectation, whereas MT appears to allude to the messianic promise in Gen 49:9–10.

2. The differences between LXX and MT are most noticeable in v. 15. They are not due to a conscious intervention of the Greek translator.

3. In v. 15, LXX is probably based on a Hebrew text form that predates MT. In v. 18 the *Vorlage* of LXX was identical with that of MT.

4. LXX as well as its Hebrew *Vorlage* reflects a Maccabean background.

WHY A PROLOGUE? BEN SIRA'S GRANDSON AND HIS GREEK TRANSLATION*

Benjamin G. Wright III

Translation was an art fairly commonly practiced in antiquity. The evidence for translation in various Near Eastern social contexts from the Hellenistic period onward is widespread, especially throughout the Roman period. What is lacking are extended reflections on the nature of translation and how to do it, in other words any translation theory. One Latin author, Cicero, makes numerous comments on his own translations from Greek to Latin, and a number of studies of the development of translation theory in the West regard him as the first translation theorist. But Cicero is the prominent exception, not the rule for ancient translations. Most ancient translations, the Septuagint being the best example, provide no explicit information on who the translators were and what their approach to the enterprise was. That is left for modern scholars to debate. Thus, even a modest statement ruminating on translation, like that contained in the translator's Prologue to the Greek of the Wisdom of Ben Sira, has the potential of providing important insights into how ancient translators worked and is most welcome.

The reading that I give in this paper to the prologue to the translation of the Wisdom of Ben Sira originates in a longer study that applies some insights from the modern field of "Translation Studies" to the relationship between translation, source text and anticipated readership in Cicero, Ben Sira and the Septuagint.[1] Essentially, in that study I examined the extent to which a translator's expectation

---

* I am delighted to contribute an article on Ben Sira to a volume honoring Emanuel Tov, a teacher and friend for close to twenty-five years, who was one of the readers of my dissertation, written on Ben Sira. I met Emanuel in my first year of graduate school, and he has had a profound influence on my education and career for which I am grateful.

[1] "Access to the Source: Cicero, Ben Sira, The Septuagint and Their Audiences," given at "From Hellenistic Judaism to Christian Hellenism: International Colloquium," 26–28 March 2001, Institute for Advanced Studies, Jerusalem, Israel. It will appear in *Journal for the Study of Judaism* (forthcoming).

that his audience knew and could consult the source text affected the kind of translation he produced. In Cicero's case, for example, his presumption that his readers would be able to read the Greek originals allowed him to make creative use of his Greek source for his own rhetorical purposes in Latin. Thus, the abilities of Cicero's audience allowed him to make what might be called, at one end of the spectrum, "free" translations, and at the other, works that could even be called brand new literary creations.

Although the translation of the Wisdom of Ben Sira, produced somewhere shortly after the death of Ptolemy VII Euergetes II in 117 B.C.E. by a translator claiming to be the author's grandson (he calls the author ὁ πάππος μου Ἰησοῦς, "my grandfather Jesus"),[2] does not achieve anything like Cicero's literary heights, its prologue is so important because it sheds valuable light on three important aspects of this translation. First, the grandson makes some remarks about his reasons for making the translation and the audience for whom he intended it. Second, he reflects briefly on the process of translation, although, as we shall see, his reflections may not make matters as clear as we might like. Third, the fact that the grandson writes fairly elegant *koine* Greek in the prologue and resorts to an often wooden Greek translationese for the actual translation reveals something of his translation ability and/or his expectations of what constitutes translation.

Unfortunately, however, most commentators on Sirach do not usually look to the prologue for what it says about ancient translation activity. They, of course, take account of the evidence it provides for the date of the Hebrew of the book, and they note the implications of the grandson's reference to "the Law, the Prophets and the others that followed them" for understanding the development of the biblical canon. They also usually note the grandson's *apologia* about the relationship between the Hebrew original and his Greek translation, especially as it bears on the possibility of recovering the original Hebrew of the book in those places where it is not extant.

---

[2] See the argument in Patrick W. Skehan and Alexander A. Di Lella, *The Wisdom of Ben Sira* (Anchor Bible 39; New York: Doubleday, 1987), 8–9. The argument for Ben Sira's early second century *floruit* is founded on the date of the grandson's migration to Egypt in the "thirty-eighth year of Euergetes" (about 132 B.C.E.), Ben Sira's description of the high priest Simon in chapter 50, usually thought to be Simon II, and the complete absence of any awareness of the events in Jerusalem during the reign of Antiochus IV.

Thus, they look to the prologue primarily as a source of information for investigating the book's Hebrew original and not necessarily for its value in understanding the Greek version as an example of ancient translation activity. Even scholars who are interested in the history and theory of translation give little notice to Ben Sira's grandson. Whereas they frequently cite the legend of the Septuagint (most often Philo's version) and list it in collections of texts about translation, they almost never include the prologue to Ben Sira.[3] I am not sure why this is, but a careful reading of the grandson's statements in the prologue provides fascinating insight into his attitude towards his work.

The first question to ask is why the grandson decided to translate his grandfather's book into Greek. The answer actually helps us to understand the audience for whom he intended the translation. The grandson begins his prologue by noting that "Many and great things have been given to us through the Law, the Prophets and the others that followed them; for these it is necessary to praise the instruction and wisdom of Israel" (1–2).[4] But the grandson recognizes that those truths contained in the great books of Israel must be mediated to others. He says in the next clause, "Indeed it is necessary for those who read (ἀναγινώσκοντας) them to have understanding, but for those who are without them (τοῖς ἐκτός), lovers of learning must be able to be useful through both speaking and writing" (4–6).[5] The grandson emphasizes that those who know these books and their truths must "be useful" to those who do not have them. His grandfather, Jesus, was someone who was useful in this way, because, beyond devoting himself to the study of "the Law, the Prophets and the other ancestral books" and acquiring his own expertise in them, he

---

[3] The two collections that I have used primarily, Andre Lefevere, ed., *Translation/ History/ Culture; A Sourcebook* (London: Routledge, 1992) and Douglas Robinson, ed., *Western Translation Theory from Herodotus to Nietzsche* (Manchester: St. Jerome Publishing, 1997), do not include or even refer to the grandson's prologue.

[4] I cite the prologue using the line numbers given in Joseph Ziegler's critical edition of Ben Sira, *Sapientia Iesu Filii Sirach* (SEPTUAGINTA. Vetus Testamentum Graecum Auctoritate Academiae Litterarum Gottingensis editum vol. XII, 2; Göttingen: Vandenhoeck & Ruprecht, 1965).

[5] In each case in this clause the object "them" has to be supplied in English because none is explicit in Greek. The question might be raised concerning what the unstated object of these phrases is. The "them" could refer to the books of "the Law, the Prophets and the others" or to the "wisdom and instruction of Israel." For the purposes of the argument here the exact object intended by the grandson is not too crucial.

"also came to write something pertaining to wisdom and instruction, so that those who love learning, who also become familiar with these things, might add considerably to a life lived according to the Law" (7–14). The grandson saw his grandfather's intended audience comprised of Jews to whom he might communicate the insights that he had acquired through his study of the Jewish scriptures.

Such statements about Ben Sira's motivation for his teaching suggest that the grandson directed his translation to an audience like his grandfather's, in his case Jews that he encountered in Egypt who he thought could benefit from his grandfather's wisdom and instruction. The idea for the translation seems to have been sparked by the grandson's encounter with similar kinds of instruction that he most likely found among the Jews in Egypt. He says that after arriving in Egypt and "having spent some time there, I found a copy (ἀφόμοιον) of a good deal that was instructive" (28–29). The Greek word ἀφόμοιον probably here indicates that he found actual manuscript copies of works of instruction similar to his grandfather's.[6] Thus, the occasion for the translation seems to have been the desire to add his grandfather's instruction and wisdom to that already available to Greek-speaking Jews in Egypt who otherwise would not have access to his grandfather's Hebrew original. He makes a direct reference to his intended audience toward the end of the prologue when he says that he lost a lot of sleep making the translation for "for those living abroad (ἐν τῇ παροικίᾳ) who wish to gain learning and who are prepared to live by the dispositions of the Law" (34–36). Taken together, these various statements indicate that the grandson made his translation to benefit a Greek-speaking Egyptian Jewish readership that did not know Hebrew and could not read his grandfather's work in the original.

The Greek of the prologue demonstrates that Ben Sira's grandson had the ability to write in what Patrick Skehan and Alexander Di Lella call "carefully crafted prose, employing the grammar and syntax of literary *koine* Greek." He constructs his prologue using "three fairly elegant periodic sentences."[7] The first sentence provided evidence cited above for the grandson's motivation for taking on the

---

[6] Here I follow Ziegler's critical text. A number of manuscripts have the reading ἀφόρμην, indicating that the grandson had access to instruction without necessarily seeing copies of manuscripts. For an argument supporting the reading of ἀφόμοιον, see Skehan and Di Lella, *Wisdom of Ben Sira*, 134.

[7] Skehan and Di Lella, *Wisdom of Ben Sira*, 132.

translation. The third reveals the audience for whom it was intended. In the second sentence the grandson expresses, in the form of a short *apologia* for his work, the frustration of many translators over the centuries. Since the sentence is both important for our under- standing of the grandson's translation and difficult in some ways to interpret, I give it in full here in the form I have translated it for the New English Translation of the Septuagint.[8]

> You are invited, therefore, to give a reading with goodwill and atten- tion and to have forbearance for those things where we may seem to lack ability in certain phrases, despite having labored diligently in the translation. For those things originally in Hebrew do not have the same force when rendered into another language; and not only these things, but also the Law itself and the Prophets and the rest of the books are not a little different when expressed in the originals (15–26).

Scholars frequently understand this statement to concern fidelity to the Hebrew original. In such a reading of the passage, the grand- son fears that some people might claim that in places his transla- tion does not render the meaning of the Hebrew accurately. To this perceived criticism, he responds by saying that as a matter of method it is very difficult to render Hebrew into Greek. But if the potential critic is not willing to believe him on this score, he attempts to deflect the criticism by citing evidence beyond his own translation that the Law, the Prophets and the other books also suffer from this same deficiency—a statement that could be construed as critical of the Jewish-Greek scriptures.

Another possible reading would be to interpret the passage as a purely rhetorical disclaimer that aims to head off any criticism of the work. That the grandson is simply resorting to a rhetorical *apologia* makes little sense to me, however. Given what he says about the importance of those truths found in the Jewish scriptures for those who love learning and who wish to live a life according to the Law, I would find it surprising if, as a matter of rhetorical protection of his own translation, he would invent a criticism that the Greek trans- lation of those same scriptures itself is somehow deficient. Why would he employ a criticism aimed at precisely the version of the Jewish

---

[8] The New English Translation of the Septuagint (NETS) is a complete English translation of the Jewish-Greek Scriptures being undertaken by the International Organization for Septuagint and Cognate Studies. For the initial NETS publication, see Albert Pietersma, *A New English Translation of the Septuagint and Other Greek Translations Traditionally Included Under That Title: The Psalms* (New York: Oxford, 2000).

scriptures used by his reading audience? In fact, I do not think that
this passage constitutes a criticism of the Jewish-Greek scriptures at all.

Although these readings of the prologue are plausible, in view of
the constituency for whom the grandson claims he is translating, I
want to suggest an alternative reading of the prologue. The three key
phrases in it that require some explanation are: (1) "for those things
where we may seem to lack ability in certain phrases" (20); (2) "for
those things originally in Hebrew do not have the same force when
rendered in another language" (21–22); (3) "but also the Law and
the Prophets and the rest of the books are not a little different when
expressed in the originals" (23–26).

I do think, however, that the grandson expresses genuine nervous-
ness about the reception of his translation. He does expect criticism
of his work. But if his anticipated readership is made up of Greek-
speaking Jews, who presumably would not be reading his grandfather's
Hebrew original, how would they be in a position to know whether
he was being faithful to his original or not? Although I can imagine
that there might be Jewish scholars in the community who knew
Hebrew and who could level such criticism, why would such people
worry about the translation of a wisdom book like Ben Sira's? The
grandson is not claiming any special status for what he has translated that might conceivably warrant scrutiny of it for "faithfulness,"
whatever that might mean in such a case. He says explicitly that he
hopes his grandfather's wisdom would "add considerably to a life
lived according to the Law." Nothing in the prologue suggests that
the grandson is attempting to address any sort of dispute about what
it meant to live according to the Law. He simply thinks his grandfather's wisdom teaching will be helpful to the Egyptian Jews among
whom he now lives.

I suspect that the primary clue to the grandson's anxiety resides
not in any presumed unfaithfulness of his Greek translation to the
Hebrew original, but in the difference between the quality of the
Greek of the prologue and that of the translation. The prologue, as
noted above, is written in fairly good, literary Greek style. The translation, by contrast, is executed in a more or less stilted translationese
that is often at pains to represent certain formal aspects of the Hebrew
very closely—matters such as word order, for example.[9] One criti-

---

[9] On the translation of the Greek of Ben Sira, see my *No Small Difference: Sirach's
Relationship to its Hebrew Parent Text* (SBLSCS 26; Atlanta: Scholars Press, 1989).

cism that could be leveled at the grandson, and one of which he might indeed be wary, is that the Greek of his translation is not very good. And, in fact, it is not, especially if measured against the kind of Greek he uses in the prologue. His appeal to the Jewish scriptures as a response to this possible criticism would make eminent sense, then. The type of Greek (and translation approach) that he utilizes for his translation is not very different from the Greek of the Law, the Prophets and the other books, which his audience already uses. In the context of this reading of the prologue, the grandson's reference to the Jewish-Greek scriptures would not have to be construed as a negative evaluation of them, but rather as a comparison with them.[10]

An examination of the key Greek terms used in the three passages listed above can sustain my reading of the prologue. In the first (#1 above), the major issue is the grandson's self-confessed inability "in certain phrases" (τισὶν τῶν λέξεων). The verbs δοκῶμεν . . . ἀδυναμεῖν express what some see as the grandson's admitted weakness as a translator. Liddell-Scott-Jones give the earliest occurrence of the *verb* ἀδυναμέω, "to be incapable," as occurring in the prologue to Sirach.[11] The much more common *noun* form of the root indicates generally "inability" or "incapacity." The ambiguous "certain phrases" stands as the object of the infinitive. But are these "certain phrases" in Greek or Hebrew? The qualifying participial phrase κατὰ τὴν ἑρμηνείαν πεφιλοπονημένων, "despite having labored diligently in the translation (or, interpretation)" provides the key for my interpretation. The Greek ἑρμηνεία indicates an "interpretation" or "explanation," especially of thoughts by words; it can also refer to an expression. The emphasis on "interpretation/explanation," or perhaps even "expression," directs the focus of the clause on "certain phrases" in the grandson's Greek translation, rather than in his grandfather's Hebrew. If the intention is to talk about Greek phrases, the grandson in this passage appears to be asking the reader to forgive any perceived inability of his *in the way he expresses things in Greek.*

---

[10] Skehan and Di Lella claim that the grandson is here "criticizing freely not only his translation but also the LXX . . ." (*Wisdom of Ben Sira*, 134).

[11] They list only two other occurrences: one in Simplicius (6th century C.E.) and one in PLond. 2.361 (1st century C.E.). Henry George Liddell, Robert Scott, Henry Stuart Jones, eds., *A Greek-English Lexicon* (Ninth ed.; Oxford: Clarendon, 1940). A search of the TLG CD-ROM turns up a few additional references, all later than Sirach.

The second key term, ἰσοδυναμεῖ, is the verb of the second crucial clause (#2 above). The grandson remarks, "things expressed originally in Hebrew do not have the same force when rendered into
another language." This verb appears very infrequently in Greek,
and it means "to have equal force or power; to be equivalent to."
It creates so much difficulty in this passage because its semantic
range not only indicates equivalence of force or strength, but also
equivalence generally, and perhaps even equivalence of meaning (as
can the noun and adjective derived from it). But does the term have
to refer to equivalence of meaning in this passage as so many commentators have understood it? If we keep in mind that the grandson's audience is made up of Egyptian Jews who most likely did not
know Hebrew and that he has just addressed any perceived inability on his part in writing Greek, then I think that this phrase must
also be part of the grandson's defense of his *translation* to those who
will read it. As part of a longer *apologia*, I think the grandson is
claiming that because his product is a *translation* it does not have the
same *rhetorical power or force* in Greek as the original Hebrew, not necessarily that things in Hebrew do not have the same *meaning* when
translated into another language.[12] And, in fact, the lack of rhetorical power in the Greek of the translation is apparent throughout.
This interpretation fits well within the viable semantic range of the
verb ἰσοδυναμεῖ, and it is consistent with the social context that the
prologue presents us for the translation. So, we do not have to understand this passage as an expression of the grandson's anxiety about
not getting the meaning of the Hebrew right, but we can read it as
a statement, addressed to an audience that is about to read his work,
of his frustration with a translation process that seems inevitably to
produce inelegant Greek that is not rhetorically powerful or pleasing.

The third key term (#3 above) is embedded in the clause that
immediately follows the grandson's statement about the difference in

---

[12] The verb is often taken this way, however. See most recently, for example,
John F. A. Sawyer (*Sacred Languages and Sacred Texts* [London/New York: Routledge,
1999], 79), who translates the beginning of this second sentence, "Please read carefully and with good will; excuse me where I have got the meaning wrong despite
my efforts to translate. When translated into another language, words do not have
the same meaning as they have in Hebrew." Louis Kelly (*True Interpreter* [New York:
St. Martin's, 1979], 214) also seems to understand the passage in this manner,
although his translation does not make it so explicit.

rhetorical force between the Hebrew original and the Greek, and its meaning in this clause is dependent on the meaning of ἰσοδυναμεῖ in the preceding clause. The translator says, "And (δέ) not only these things, but also the Law itself and the Prophets and the rest of the books are not a little different (οὐ μικρὰν ἔχει τὴν διαφοράν) when expressed in the original." The use of δέ establishes a close grammatical relationship with the prior clause, and the neuter plural "these things" refers to the "things expressed originally in Hebrew" about which the grandson just spoke. So when the grandson claims that even the translations of the Jewish scriptures "are not a little different," what exactly is that difference? If we read the clause without considering (1) what the prologue indicates about the grandson's intended audience generally and (2) what immediately precedes it in particular, we might conclude that the grandson is speaking in this clause about differences of meaning between the source text and its translation. If, however, the clause is read within these two contexts, as I have articulated them, then we might conclude that the grandson is saying that the same difference in the rhetorical force or power between the Hebrew original and the Greek that characterizes his translation also characterizes the Jewish-Greek scriptures. Here again, my reading of the prologue finds the grandson concerned with the Greek of his own translation, its deficiencies as a Greek text, and his desire to justify it to his potential audience, not as a translation that is deficient with regard to its source text.

So, if we conclude that the grandson is making an *apologia* for the Greek of his translation, the obvious question arises—why did he translate that way? He clearly could write good literary Greek. Why not render his grandfather's Hebrew into the same sort of Greek that he used to introduce his translation? Louis Kelly has argued that a translator assumes one of two stances of authority vis-à-vis the source text, which he calls "personal" and "positional."

> Within personal authority structures, one takes responsible autonomy and retains power of decision, while positional structures impose formal patterns of obligation. Commitment, then, based on a personal authority structure, gives rise to translation behaviours akin to an elaborated sociolinguistic code: the translator's approach to text is multidimensional, author or reader-centered and subjective. Where, however, the translator sees the relation between him and the text as positional, the approach is that of restricted sociolinguistic code: unidimensional, text- and object-centered and objective. Thus, depending on the type

of authority his text exercises over the translator, fidelity will mean
either collaboration or servitude.[13]

Whereas both types of authority structures assume a communicative
purpose, the goals and methods of translation that result from assuming one structure or the other can vary dramatically.

If we look at Ben Sira's grandson through the lens of Kelly's two
authority structures, he certainly adopts a positional authority vis-à-
vis his source text. The translation can easily be described as largely
"unidimensional," "text-centered" and "objective." Or, to use Kelly's
language from above, the grandson does not collaborate with the
text; he serves it. But such a characterization alone cannot suffice
to understand fully the grandson's approach to his work. Given his
obvious abilities to compose good, rhetorically pleasing *koine* Greek, why
should he assume a positional authority toward his source text? Part
of my answer to this question takes into account what the grandson
tells us in the prologue; the other part is somewhat more speculative.

The grandson tells us that his motivation for translating his grandfather's book was to make it available to those "living abroad" who
wanted to live their lives according to the Law. He apparently came
to this decision after going to Egypt and encountering "a copy of a
good deal that was instructive." He then determined that he ought
to "contribute some effort and diligence to translating this book."
This much we know. If we read between the lines of his remarks
about how he decided to make the translation, we can infer that
the grandson was no experienced translator. He apparently made an
ad hoc decision to translate his grandfather's book for those Greek-
speaking Jews whom he met in Egypt who he thought could benefit
from its wisdom and instruction. But making the decision to translate was only the beginning of the process. Where would he learn
how to translate? How would he go about it?

It seems to me that he comes close to telling us outright. He refers
to "the Law and the Prophets and the other books" three separate
times (1–2, 7–10, 24–25). As we saw above, he compares his translation Greek to that of the Jewish-Greek scriptures. My guess is that
in his own work he adopted a positional authority stance (to use

---

[13] Kelly, *True Interpreter*, 206–207. Kelly's analysis of the two authority structures
here depends on the work of Basil Bernstein in "Social Class, Language and
Socialisation" in *Language and Social Context* (ed. P. P. Giglioli; New York: Penguin,
1972) 157–78 (cited in Kelly, *True Interpreter*, 252, n. 1).

Kelly's phrase) toward his Hebrew original because it was the same stance he saw taken in these translations.[14] They also utilize a kind of translationese that seems to have formal representation of the Hebrew as one of its primary objectives and that reveals a positional authority stance toward the source text. As he cast about for a way to approach his recently formulated project, Ben Sira's grandson seized upon a readily available model, one the Jewish community was already using and with which it was familiar. If the character of his Greek is like that of the Jewish-Greek scriptures, as he himself points out, that may be more intentional than accidental.

The result is, of course, that what he produced was a fairly literal translation. But can we say about this literal product what many who discuss translation say about literal translations generally—that it is intended to bring the original to the reader, to give the reader access to the source language/text?[15] It seems clear, for instance, that this was the intention of the Septuagint translators.[16] The reading that I have given the prologue suggests that the grandson was not troubled by some sense that he might not have rendered the meaning of his Hebrew original with fidelity. His frustration is with a translation process whose product is Greek that is not very elegant. What is interesting is that it does not seem to have occurred to him that he could translate any other way. My reading of the prologue also indicates that the grandson was not somehow as a matter of method trying to give his readers access to the Hebrew of his grandfather. His need to find a way to translate and his adoption of an authority stance he found in the Septuagint both point to the resulting literalness of his work as an unintended consequence of his decision to translate.

I will conclude by way of summary. The prologue to the translation of the Wisdom of Ben Sira contains evidence that suggests that Ben Sira's grandson translated his grandfather's book of wisdom

---

[14] The grandson does not, however, depend on the Jewish-Greek scriptures for the details of his own work. See Wright, *No Small Difference*, chap. 3.

[15] For studies of translation generally, see Eric Jacobsen, *Translation: A Traditional Craft* (Copenhagen: Gyldendalske Boghandel-Nordisk Forlag, 1958); Kelly, *True Interpreter*; Michel Ballard, *De Cicéron a Benjamin: Traducteurs, traductions, réflexions* (Paris: Presses Universitaires de Lille, 1995); Jean Delisle and Judith Woodsworth, *Les Traducteurs dans l'Histoire* (Ottawa: Les Presses de l'Université d'Ottawa, 1995). In addition to these general studies of translation, see Sebastian Brock, "The Phenomenon of Biblical Translation in Antiquity," Alta II 8 (1969): 99.

[16] On this issue, see my "Access to the Source."

on an *ad hoc* basis, not as part of some carefully preplanned translation project. Once he made the decision to translate, he probably
thought a fair amount about what it meant to undertake such a task.
I think, however, that in those places where he is often understood
to be defending the potentially problematic relationship between his
Hebrew original and the Greek translation, he turns out in actual-
ity to be worried about the possibility that his readers might think
his translation to be inadequate *as a Greek text*. In addition to his
admission that he knew his Greek could be considered inadequate,
he noted further that his Greek was of similar quality to that of the
translation of the Bible. His comments to his prospective reading
audience indicate that he believed such a result to be inherent to
the nature of the translation process. Indeed, he may well have developed his own approach to translating by adopting the same stance
towards the relationship between source text and target language
that he discovered in the Greek translations of the "Law, the Prophets
and the other books." One does get the feeling, however, that the
grandson never encountered translation of the caliber and style that
Cicero would later advocate. As a result, although the grandson
might appear at first glance to be reflecting on the difficulty of rendering Hebrew into Greek because the two languages are so different,
I think in the end he reveals to us something of his own insecuri-
ties about the reception of his work as a Greek text due to the inelegance of the product, an inelegance he perceives as unavoidable.

WHEN DAUID FLED ABESSALOM:
A COMMENTARY ON THE THIRD PSALM IN GREEK

ALBERT PIETERSMA

It is a distinct pleasure for me to contribute to a celebratory volume for Emanuel Tov who, inter alia, has become one of the most productive contemporary scholars in the field of Septuagint Studies. Since he himself, together with S. Talmon, many years ago put his hand to writing a commentary on a Septuagint text,[1] it is perhaps not inappropriate for me to follow in those footsteps and to seek to honor him with an attempt at a commentary on the third psalm.

The International Organization for Septuagint and Cognate Studies (IOSCS) has decided to sponsor a commentary series on all the books of the Septuagint corpus. A Prospectus, published in 1999,[2] has delineated a set of principles for the series, and it is these I would like to cite as a context for what appears below. They are the following:

(1) the principle of original text, which is understood to mean that though for any given book the best available critical edition will form the basis of interpretation, commentators shall improve upon that text where deemed necessary, and thus assist in the ongoing quest for the pristine Greek text.

(2) the principle of original meaning, which is understood to mean that although commentators may make use of reception history in an effort to ascertain what the Greek text meant at its point of inception and may from time to time digress to comment on secondary interpretations, the focus shall be on what is perceived to be the original meaning of the text.

(3) the principle of the parent text as arbiter of meaning, which is understood to mean that though as much as possible the translated text is read like an original composition in Greek, the commentator will need

---

[1] S. Talmon and E. Tov, "A Commentary on the Text of Jeremiah. I. The LXX of Jer. 1:1–7," *Text* 9 (1981): 1–15.

[2] *BIOSCS* 31 (1998): 43–48. See also the website of the IOSCS: http://ccat.sas.upenn.edu/ioscs/.

to have recourse to the parent text for linguistic information essential to the proper understanding of the Greek.

(4) the principle of "translator's intent," which is understood to mean that, since the language of the translated text is the only accessible expression of "the translator's mind," the linguistic information—whatever its source—embedded in the Greek text shall form the sole basis of interpretation. Stated differently, any linguistic information not already seen to be embedded in the Greek text, even though perhaps recognized as such, on the practical level, only by recourse to the parent text, shall be deemed inadmissible.

(5) the principle of linguistic parsimony, which is understood to mean that, as a general rule, no words or constructions of translation-Greek shall be considered normal Greek, unless attested in non-translation writings.[3]

It should further be noted that any retroversions from the Greek, thought to reflect a parent text different from the Masoretic Text, appear in enlarged print in the Hebrew text printed below. Since the Greek text is the point of reference, all numbers are those of the Greek psalms.

Psalm 3

Synopsis

The psalmist, alarmed at his present opposition (2–3) but conscious of divine help in the past (5, 8b–c), expresses his confidence in God's continued support (4, 6b–7, 9) which he urgently requests (8a) at the start of a new day (6a–6bα).

Psalm 3 as a whole

Based on *v.* 6, this psalm is commonly described as a morning prayer (e.g. Briggs, Weiser, Craigie), a characterization perhaps underlined by G's past tense in 6a–bα. For G, if not for the original poet, the superscription would have assigned the psalm to a particular episode in the life of King Dauid. Within that episode he might have thought of the fortuitously rejected advice of Achitophel to pursue Dauid by night (2 Kgdms 17:1; cf. 16).

---

[3] Ibid. 44.

Because of G's frequent pairing of the Hebrew perfect with the Greek aorist, the Greek psalm takes on a decidedly more historical slant, i.e. it underscores the psalmist's past experience. So in 2a we are told what occurred in time past (evidently with present effect), and this is even extended to the Hebrew imperfect verbs of 5a, although G regularly glosses these with a future. Whatever the precise reason, the Greek text reads more like a description of a past incident than does MT.

Sigla and Bibliography

AGD = W. F. Arndt, F. W. Gingrich, F. W. Danker, *A Greek-English Lexicon of the NT* (1979); Barr = J. Barr, "The Meaning of ἐπακούω and Cognates in the LXX," *JTS* 31 (1980): 67–72; BHS = *Biblia Hebraica Stuttgartensia* (1969); Briggs = C. A. Briggs & E. G. Briggs, *International Critical Commentary* (1906); Broyles = C. C., *New International Biblical Commentary* (1999); Cox, C. "Εἰσακούω and ἐπακούω in the Greek Psalter," *Bibl* 62 (1981): 251–8; Craigie = P. C. Craigie, *Word Biblical Commentary* (1983); Dahood = M. Dahood, *The Anchor Bible* (1966); Flashar = M. Flashar, "Exegetische Studien zum Septuaginta-psalter," *ZAW* 32 (1912): 81–116, 161–89, 241–68; Flint = P. W. Flint, *The Dead Sea Psalms Scrolls & the Book of Psalms* (1997); Gesenius-Kautzsch = E. Kautzsch, *Gesenius' Hebrew Grammar* (1910 [Cowley]); Keil-Delitzsch = C. F. Keil and F. Delitzsch, *Biblical Commentary* (1949); Kraus = H.-J. Kraus, *A Continental Commentary* (1988); LSJ = H. G. Liddell, R. Scott, H. S. Jones, *A Greek-English Lexicon* (1940); MM = J. H. Moulton and G. Milligan, *Vocabulary of the Greek Testament* (1997); Montevecchi = O. Montevecchi "Quaedam de graecitate psalmorum cum papyris comparata," *IX International Congress of Papyrology Oslo* (1958), 293–310; Mozley = F. W. Mozley, *The Psalter of the Church* (1905); Munnich = Olivier Munnich, "Etude lexicographique du Psautier des Septante" (1982); Muraoka = T. Muraoka, *A Greek-English Lexicon of the Septuagint* (1993); NETS = *A New English Translation of the Septuagint. The Psalms* (2000); Pietersma = A. Pietersma, "Exegesis and Liturgy in the Superscriptions of the Greek Psalter," *X Congress of the IOSCS Studies Oslo* (2001), 99–138; Robertson = A. T. Robertson, *A Grammar of the Greek New Testament* (1934); Smyth = H. W. Smyth, *Greek Grammar* (1959); Thackeray = H. St. J. Thackeray, *Grammar of the OT in Greek* (1909); TLG = *Thesaurus Linguae Graecae E* (1999); Weiser = A. Weiser, *Old Testament Library* (1962).

Commentary: v. 1

Hebrew Text

מזמור לדוד בברחו מפני **אבשלום** בנו

Greek Text

Ψαλμὸς τῷ Δαυίδ, ὁπότε ἀπεδίδρασκεν ἀπὸ προσώπου
Ἀβεσσαλὼμ τοῦ υἱοῦ αὐτοῦ.

NETS Translation

A Psalm. Pertaining to Dauid. When he was running away
from his son Abessalom.

Since MT features the same superscription, there is good reason to
assume that it belonged to G's parent text and that therefore any
kind of perceived linkage between King Dauid and the psalm proper
should be sought in the Hebrew.

Ψαλμός. As is clear both from its formation and its use in Classical
Greek sources, this word referred initially to the activity of making
music (or any comparable sound) rather than to a piece of music in
set form. That it continued to have primarily this sense in later literature is clear from such passages as Amos 5:23, which speaks of
the "psalming" of instruments (see below). Also of interest is that
Josephus consistently so uses it (*Ant.* 6.214; 7.80; 9.35; 12.323), and
Philo never uses it at all, preferring the common Greek ὕμνος instead.
A more concrete meaning ("psalm"), however, is also attested and
may therefore be what G intended in the Psalter (cf. e.g. Isa 66:20;
Zech 6:14 where it appears without warrant in MT; Ps 151:1). In
any case, there is little doubt that it developed this meaning based
on its appearance in the Greek Psalter. As is clear from its cognates,
ψάλλω "to pluck" and ψαλτήριον "harp" or "psalter," its primary
reference was to instrumental in distinction from vocal activity, in
others words, to playing rather than to singing. That it still had this
instrumental sense in our period is suggested by the fact that in several references it stands in parallel to musical instruments (Job 21:12,
30:31, Jdt 16:1) and it furthermore is regularly used to translate
Hebrew instrumental terms, for example in Job עוגב, a flute of some
description. The phrase ψαλμὸς ὀργάνων ("plucking of instruments")

in contrast to ἦχος ᾠδῶν ("sound of songs") in Amos 5:23 gives further confirmation (see Muraoka *sub* ψαλμός). NETS uses a transcription of the Greek with initial capital in agreement with NRSV, though not with the suggestion that its sense in the Greek Psalter fully equates with its use in modern English.

τῷ Δαυίδ. That this phrase serves to indicate Davidic authorship, whatever its Hebrew counterpart may be thought to mean, is most unlikely (cf. Pietersma, 103). In spite of the recognized intimate bond between Dauid and the Psalms, Greek exegetical tradition did not uniformly construe it as a *nota auctoris*, and neither did the translator himself. So Didymus the Blind in comment on Ps 24:1 writes:

εἰς τὸν Δαυὶδ ὁ ψαλμὸς λέγεται· ἄλλο γάρ ἐστιν τοῦ Δαυὶδ εἶναι καὶ ἄλλο τῷ Δαυίδ. τοῦ Δαυὶδ λέγεται, ὅταν ᾖ αὐτὸς αὐτὸν πεποιηκὼς ἢ ψάλλων. αὐτῷ δὲ λέγεται, ὅταν εἰς αὐτὸν φέρηται

the psalm is said to have reference to Dauid. For 'of Dauid' and 'to Dauid' mean different things; 'of Dauid' is used when he himself composed it or played it, whereas 'to him' is used when it refers to him.

A similar point is made by G himself when he labels the closing psalm (151) as εἰς Δαυίδ ("pertaining to Dauid") but also ἰδιόγραφος, i.e. "written by Dauid himself" in contrast to all the psalms that precede. Interestingly, Didymus' criterion for authorship, namely composition or performance, are uniquely combined in Psalm 151, since the first person account of Dauid's early life includes in *v.* 3 a direct reference to his performing on the harp: "My hands made an instrument;/my fingers tuned a harp" (NETS). Didymus' other conclusion, namely, that the dative indicated that the psalm in question "pertained to Dauid," left ample room for typological and messianic interpretation, as is clear from his own commentary on Psalms.

ὁπότε ἀπεδίδρασκεν. G uses this grammatical construction exclusively in superscriptions, though it appears only when MT has a counterpart. That could reflect a more overtly historical stance on the part of G. The relatively rare conjunction ὁπότε (only 10× in the LXX/OG) often has iterative force and as such tends to be followed by verbs that are durative in aspect. Xenophon, *Anabasis* 4.2.25–28 supplies an interesting series of examples. G, however, in all instances (3:1; 33:1; 55:1; 58:1; 59:2), except the present one, employs it with the aorist indicative. That may possibly indicate that after having used ὁπότε + impf indicative to express repeated action in 3:1, G simply stuck with the conjunction when later prompted by the same Hebrew construction (but contrast 56:1; 62:1; 141:1 where he makes use of ἐν + infinitive, which simply marks general [rather than specifically temporal] circumstance). The exclusive use of ὁπότε in the superscriptions may further indicate what the earliest Greek manuscripts show in any case, namely, that the superscriptions were regarded as entities quite distinct from the psalm per se. In any case, the durative aspect of the verb in 3:1 explicitly portrays Dauid's flight as a withdrawal in progress. As for the specific verb in our phrase—it is of interest that in both 3:1 and 55:1 G uses it to gloss ברח ("to flee") while in 138:7 he opts for φεύγω ("to flee"). Both Hebrew-Greek equations, however, appear circa 25× each in the lxx/og. (Note that the identical Hebrew construction, with Dauid as subject, is glossed in 3 Kgdms 2:7 as ἐν τῷ με ἀποδιδράσκειν ἀπὸ προσώπου 'Αβεσσαλωμ.)

v. 2–3

Hebrew Text

יהוה מה רבו צרי רבים קמים עלי
רבים אמרים לנפשי אין ישועתה לו באלהו̇ סלה

Greek Text

Κύριε, τί ἐπληθύνθησαν οἱ θλίβοντές με;
πολλοὶ ἐπανίστανται ἐπ' ἐμέ·
πολλοὶ λέγουσιν τῇ ψυχῇ μου
Οὐκ ἔστιν σωτηρία αὐτῷ ἐν τῷ θεῷ αὐτοῦ.
διάψαλμα.

NETS Translation

O Lord, why did those who afflict me multiply?
Many are rising against me;
many are saying to me,
"There is no salvation for him in his God."

Interlude on strings

τί ἐπληθύνθησαν. Since the verb is intransitive, τί must be adverbial. Rahlfs read 2a as a question, though mt is commonly read as an exclamation (e.g. NRSV, Kraus, Craigie, Dahood, Weiser). Since adverbial τί regularly has the sense of "why" rather than "how," there is good reason to read this opening line of the psalm not as the psalmist's bewildered cry about his present plight but as an agonized question as to why it is that he has landed in his current predicament. Had he wanted to express the former he would likely have used ὡς (see e.g. 65:3). Consequently, the placement of Ps 3:2 under 3b. by AGD is not justified. G's choice detracts somewhat from 2–3 as a complaint per se.

τῇ ψυχῇ μου. The grammatical role of the phrase is as ambiguous in the Greek as it is in MT, but given the fact that, in both, the direct speech that follows is couched in the third person, one might construe the dative as indicating general reference ("with respect to") rather than as an indirect object. NETS follows NRSV since there is insufficient reason to demur. Yet the possibility of general reference cannot be precluded.

αὐτοῦ. As Kraus notes, G's pronoun heightens the mocking tone of the psalmist's opponents, and perhaps for that very reason it was added, though the change is more likely to have occurred in the parent text than in the process of translation. It is also true that a third person reference has those that afflict the psalmist talk behind his back (so Craigie).

διάψαλμα. The meaning and function of its Hebrew counterpart (סלה), were apparently as unfamiliar to G as they are to modern commentators. The Greek term, however, is reasonably transparent, since it is derived from διαψάλλω, an intensive form of ψάλλω (see Munnich 72–75). Literalistically it would therefore have to mean something like "plucked/played through," as a result of which it is commonly glossed as "musical interlude" (e.g. LSJ, Muraoka). Muraoka sensibly describes it as occurring "between two contiguous passages of a poem." Since the musical interlude, by virtue of the Greek root ψαλ-, can be further specified as an interlude on a stringed instrument, NETS has added this further specification. Though the word is common in Psalms, it also appears in Hab 3:3, 9, 13 in both the OG and the so-called Venetus text (see Ziegler, *Duodecim prophetae*), but apparently never in extra-biblical Greek apart from dependent literature. In all likelihood, then, it is a neologism in Psalms (so Munnich). If that is indeed the case, G shows here a surprising level of creativity, since the link he forges between ψάλλω/ψαλμός and διάψαλμα finds no support in his parent text. In formal terms it was evidently thought to signal a pause in the singing while the music continued, and as such would have had a questionable role to play at the end of an entire piece. Presumably for that reason it was not placed by G at the close of 3:9; 23:10 and 45:12, even though in all three instances MT features סלה. As interlude it makes good sense after both verse 3 and verse 5, since both points mark a break in the sense of the psalm, the first being the close of the statement of complaint, and the second the midpoint of the statement of trust in the Lord, marking a transition from confession to confidence. The perceived function of διάψαλμα was evidently like that of a διαύλιον in drama, an interlude played on the flute (αὐλός) between choruses (cf. Keil-Delitzsch) (see also μεσαύλιον). Interestingly, a scholion on Aristophanes (1263bis 1) notes: "someone blows a διαύλιον, so called just like the διάψαλμα" (διαύλιον προσαυλεῖ τις. ὥσπερ τὸ διάψαλμα λέγεται, οὕτω καὶ τοῦτο) (TLG). It is thus possible that if G was the first to use διάψαλμα he patterned it after (δια)ψάλλω/ψαλμός, prompted by the flute interlude of Greek drama.

vv. 4–5

Hebrew Text

ואתה יהוה מגן בעדי כבודי ומרים ראשי
קולי אל יהוה אקרא ויענני מהר קדשו סלה

Greek Text

σὺ δέ, κύριε, ἀντιλήμπτωρ μου εἶ,
δόξα μου καὶ ὑψῶν τὴν κεφαλήν μου.
φωνῇ μου πρὸς κύριον ἐκέκραξα,
καὶ ἐπήκουσέν μου ἐξ ὄρους ἁγίου αὐτοῦ.
διάψαλμα.

NETS Translation

But you, O Lord, are my supporter,
my glory, and the one who lifts up my head.
I cried with my voice to the Lord,
and he hearkened to me from his holy mountain.
Interlude on strings

δέ. Even though G normally represents Hebrew ו ("and") by conjunctive καί, other conjunctions appear from time to time when the context strongly suggests them. So here the Psalmist's own expression of faith in God is counterposed to the doubt voiced by his opponents. MT is not explicitly so marked.

ἀντιλήμπτωρ μου εἶ. Kraus wonders whether G read סעדי in place of MT's מגן בעדי ("a shield around me"). There is little to support this. While it is true that G typically dissolves the"shield" metaphor—most often when it refers to God but also in most other instances (7:11 βοήθεια ["help"]; 17:36 ὑπερασπισμός ["protection"]; 46:10 κραταῖος ["strong"]; 83:12 ἀλήθεια ["truth"]; 88:19 ἀντίλημψις ["support"])—it is equally true that he uses several epithets in its place. The most common of these is ὑπερασπιστής ("protector"; 10×), but here as well as in 118:114 he uses ἀντιλήμπτωρ (cf. also 88:19 supra). Furthermore, if Kraus took his cue from the equation of ἀντιλαμβάνομαι—סעד in 17:36 and 19:3, it should be noted as well that this Hebrew verb is glossed by βοηθέω ("help" 40:4; 93:18; 118:117) and στηρίζω ("sustain" 103:15). Once G had decided to pair מגן with ἀντιλήμπτωρ, בעדי would have had to follow suit. Though the reason for G's option in 3:4 and 118:114 is not certain, it is of interest that the cognate verb ἀντιλαμβάνομαι reappears in 3:6 and 118:116, where Hebrew סמך is uniquely so translated. Thus in both cases G has a verbal echo which MT lacks. G has an obvious liking for the concept of giving support, since the verb (ἀντιλαμβάνομαι) translates six Hebrew roots, the verbal noun (ἀντίλημψις) five and the agent noun (ἀντιλήμπτωρ) seven. Montevecchi identified it as being at home in Graeco-Roman petitions and MM §482 gives some good examples. (For ἀντιλήμπτωρ see further BGU 4. 1139, 1182, 1200; CPR 7.1; PMich 3.174; POslo 3.27; POxy 50.3555, in most of which it appears with σωτήρ.) It is clearly appropiate in Psalm 3, and as a consequence of G's choice of ἀντιλήμπτωρ for Hebrew מגן, instead of ὑπερασπιστής ("protector", "one who shields"), his default in the rest of the book, the military image has been replaced by one of rendering help to a petitioner. Flashar (165) maintains that ἀντιλήμπτωρ, like σωτήρ ("savior") is a divine epithet, and indeed UPZ 14 (158 B.C.E.) lends support to that.

εἶ. Though the verb "to be" has no explicit warrant in MT, it is nonetheless not infrequently supplied by G when the context strongly suggests it. So here, without the equative verb the preceding phrase might inadvertently be construed as vocative, appositional to "Lord" and parallel to the two vocatives that follow in 4b.

ἐπήκουσεν. As Cox has shown, Hebrew ענה ("answer") is always translated in Psalms by either ἐπακούω or εἰσακούω when God is the grammatical subject. While Barr has argued that ἐπακούω can indeed meaning "to answer" and while it is true that ענה and -ακούω can have a certain semantic overlap, seeing that already in Classical Greek ὑπακούω regularly means "to answer/counter," it is nonetheless of interest that G employs ἀποκρίνομαι when God is not perceived to be the subject (87:1; 101:24; 118:42). As a result, Cox is justified in seeing an interpretive shift in Psalms from a God who answers to a God who heeds or listens, even though this shift may well pre-date the Psalter (cf. MM §1873). Of interest again is that the verb is in the past tense, hence descriptive of what happened on a previous occasion.

vv. 6–7

Hebrew Text

אני שכבתי ואישנה הקיצותי כי יהוה יסמכני
לא אירא מרבבות עם אשר סביב שתו עלי

Greek Text

ἐγὼ ἐκοιμήθην καὶ ὕπνωσα·
ἐξηγέρθην, ὅτι κύριος ἀντιλήμψεταί μου.
οὐ φοβηθήσομαι ἀπὸ μυριάδων λαοῦ
τῶν κύκλῳ συνεπιτιθεμένων μοι.

NETS Translation

I lay down and slept;
I woke again, for the Lord will support me.
I shall not be afraid of ten thousands of people
who are setting themselves against me all around.

ἀντιλήμψεται. As already noted, G links 6bβ to 4aβ, with the result that the psalmist's earlier confession in verse 4 is explicitly cited as his motivation in 6. Whereas the final verb of verse 6 in MT (יסמכני)

is commonly glossed by an English present (e.g. NRSV, Craigie, Kraus, Weiser) or a durative past (e.g. Briggs) and God's sustenance is thus taken to be the cause of the psalmist's making it through the night, the future verb of the Greek suggests instead that it is the psalmist's motivation for starting a new day. In other words, had it not been for his faith in God's continued support, he might have stayed in bed.

φοβηθήσομαι ἀπό. The grammatical construction here is an isomorphic representation of the Hebrew. Regularly in Psalms it mimics the Hebrew construction (but see 26:1 and 32:8); consequently, here -מ gives rise to ἀπό (Thackeray 47; MM §5399). As in the Hebrew so in the Greek, the prepositional phrase functions as an adverbial (not a direct object), a usage known from extra-biblical literature as well. Not surprisingly we also find it in OG Job 5:21, 22, a book not known for its Hebraisms.

συνεπιτιθεμένων. G opts for a durative participle and thus portrays what the psalmist's besiegers keep doing to him, underscoring also gang-style action by the συν- prefix. This doubly-prefixed verb appears only here in Psalms.

μυριάδων λαοῦ. Though Greek μυριάς can have the numerical value of ten-thousand, here no doubt, like Hebrew רבבות, it simply refers to a very large number. Thus the Greek matches the Hebrew idiom for idiom.

v. 8

Hebrew Text

קומה יהוה הושיעני אלהי
כי הכית את כל איבי לחי שני רשעים שברת

Greek Text

ἀνάστα, κύριε, σῶσόν με, ὁ θεός μου,
ὅτι σὺ ἐπάταξας πάντας τοὺς ἐχθραίνοντάς μοι ματαίως,
ὀδόντας ἁμαρτωλῶν συνέτριψας.

NETS Translation

Rise up, O Lord! Save me, O my God!
For you are the one who struck all who are hostile to me for
   nothing;
you shattered the teeth of sinners.

ἀνάστα. Though G uses predominantly the older imperative ἀνάστηθι
(< ἀνίστημι) (7×), the later form ἀνάστα (< ἀνιστάω) also appears
(43:27; 73:22; 81:8), and both are virtually uncontested. Not unexpectedly, the distinction in form has no warrant in the Hebrew.

ὁ θεὸς μου. Though this is appropriately glossed in English as direct
address, in Greek it is more strictly an arthrous nominative in apposition to a vocative (see Smyth §1287, Robertson §465). That we
have here a Semitism is unlikely for two reasons: (a) in Psalms Hebrew
אלהים is never arthrous as vocative, and (b) Hebrew suffixed nouns
are never arthrous.

σύ. Strictly speaking MT has no equivalent, though it is not without
interest that it features the so-called *nota accusativi* after the first verb.
Thus it is not unlikely that G's parent text was identical to MT, but
that G construed את as אָתָּ (for this form see e.g. Ps 6:4) 2 sg m pronoun ("you"), as does Dahood but without reference to the Greek.
In 144:16 G does the same thing, though MT has a preceding participle and 11QPs^a reads אתה followed by את + participle (Flint), and
in 39:6 both MT and LXX feature finite vb + pronoun. Of further
interest is 75:5 where G represents MT's participle + pronoun by
finite verb + pronoun. Though in biblical Hebrew the pronoun is
commonly placed before rather than after the finite verb, the latter
is common in Qoheleth and may thus be characteristic of late biblical Hebrew (see Gesenius-Kautzsch §135.1). Whether such instances
be labeled emphatic or pleonastic (ibid.) is not important for Ps 3:8.
Not improbably G was responsible for the switch in word order (note
that in 55:9 he splits up the same sequence of fin vb + pron between
9a and 9b). Since the context in any case lends itself to emphasis,
it is not difficult to see why G did what he did.

ἐπάταξας … συνέτριψας. MT has a perfect in both cases, and as a
result Kraus writes that the meaning of the Hebrew verse depends
on how one interprets the tenses. That is to say, should 8b and c

be read as an expression of unshakable certainty of being heard (so
J. Botterweck) or as a statement of what has already happened to
the psalmist (so H. Schmidt)? Kraus decides in favor of the latter,
as do Briggs and Weiser. The NRSV, on the other hand, by rendering the verbs as presents opts for the former interpretation. Different
from both of these Craigie, following Dahood, renders both verbs
as fond wishes ("Oh, that you would . . ."). In formal terms the aorists
of the Greek place it with Kraus though, since the aorist is G's
default for the Hebrew perfect, this may be more a matter of inad-
vertence than of deliberate interpretation. For the reader of the psalm
the past verbs nonetheless raise the question of the opponents's identity. While in MT they may simply be identified with the afflicters of
2–3, in the Greek the latter appear to constitute a second wave of
opposition.

τοὺς ἐχθραίνοντάς μοι. Only here and in 34:19a, a line not unlike
the present one, does G use the verbal form ἐχθραίνω ("be hostile")
to gloss אֹיֵב ("enemy"), which otherwise virtually exclusively gives rise
to ἐχθρός (71×). Similarly in 2a G opts for θλίβω to render צַר ("adversary"), even though the latter is slightly more often glossed as ἐχθρός
(14/12). Together with the disappearance of MT's military metaphor
in 4a, this has the effect of, on the one hand, softening the portrayal of God as warrior and, on the other hand, of weakening the
impression that the psalmist's opponents are *ipso facto* God's enemies.

ματαίως. That this equates with חִנָּם, as BHS suggests (cf. also Mozley),
is unlikely since the latter is routinely translated by δωρεάν (34:7,
19; 68:5; 108:3; 118:161), with the sole exception of the second
occurrence in 34:7 where μάτην is used, presumably to avoid δωρεάν
in consecutive lines. ματαίως, on the other hand, glosses רִיק (72:13)
and שָׁוְא (88:48). Given the fact that the latter is most often translated by (εἰς) μάτην (40:7; 126:1[2×], 2), רִיק would be a better conjecture for the parent text. One may note further that in 4:2 רִיק is
rendered as ματαιότης ("vanity"). There is, however, no good reason to posit a reading different from MT. Since לְחִי ("jaw") does not
occur elsewhere in Psalms, G may not have been familiar with it.
More likely, however, G's choice flows from his having construed
אֹיְבַי as a verbal. Consequently, the adverbial is read with the participle (ἐχθραίνοντας) as an adverb of manner, rather than as an
adverb of place with the preceding finite verb (ἐπάταξας). Whatever

the precise reason, any overt reference to the opponents' mouth (so Dahood; cf v. 3) is obscured in the Greek.

ὀδόντας . . . συνέτριψας. The identical metaphor reappears in 57:7, though there MT uses a different verb (הרס "to break").

ἁμαρτωλῶν. G's default for both √רשע and √חטא is ἁμαρτ- (66× and 31× respectively). That being the case, it is scarcely surprising that the "wicked" of MT have become the "sinners" in the Greek. Yet whereas in the Hebrew the focus is primarily on these people as opponents of the psalmist himself and only secondarily as being at odds with God (3b), that latter characterization is underscored by G's word choice in 8c.

v. 9

Hebrew Text

ליהוה הישועה ועל עמך ברכתך סלה

Greek Text

τοῦ κυρίου ἡ σωτηρία, καὶ ἐπὶ τὸν λαόν σου ἡ εὐλογία σου.

NETS Translation

Salvation is the Lord's, and may your blessing be on your people!

τοῦ κυρίου. Though the Hebrew construction of ליהוה here and of לדוד in the superscription is the same, G treats them differently, with interesting results. Greek grammars are well aware that the genitive and the dative cases, although they have a measure of semantic overlap, nevertheless typically mark distinct relationships. So Smyth in discussing the genitive of possession in contrast to what he terms the dative of the possessor remarks that whereas the dative "denotes that something is at the disposal of a person or has fallen to his share temporarily" (§1480) or "the person for whom a thing exists" (§1476), the genitive, on the other hand, "lays stress on the *person* who owns something" (§1480) or "denotes ownership, possession, or belonging" (§1297). Due to this difference in denotation, a ל- construction in Hebrew might demand differentiation along these lines. Thus if the text was perceived to indicate ownership or possesion a Greek-speaker would likely opt for a genitive; but if the Hebrew was thought to refer to an entity at someone's disposal, that same Greek-speaker would likely favor the genitive. Not surpisingly, therefore, when a Hebrew -ל construction was perceived to convey divine possession, G typically used an arthrous genitive: "kingdom" (3:9; 21:29); "the earth" (23:1); "the strong of the earth" (46:10); "escape from death" (67:21); "might" (61:13); "support" (88:19); "king" (88:19); "gate" (117:20).

ἡ εὐλογία σου. Whether the closing line of the psalm is to be read as a benediction (so e.g. NRSV, Kraus, Weiser, Broyles) or as a declaration (e.g. Craigie) is as uncertain from the Greek as it is from MT. While in general terms it is true that the unmarked form of "to be" (ἐστιν) is more easily left implicit (see 9a) than the marked form (including the subjunctive and optative), the latter is nevertheless often enough left out. Thus only context can decide. Craigie reads 9b with 9a as an expression of supreme confidence and the Greek does not prohibit that, though the conjunction (καί) perhaps makes 9b more distinct than it is in MT.

CONCLUSION

Textually, it is quite clear, there is virtually no evidence in Psalm 3 that its parent text was different from MT's consonantal text. On the interpretive level, it is difficult not to conclude that Psalm 3, with few possible exceptions, offers little evidence of what might be termed deliberate exegesis. Most of the interpretation that does occur is either by vitrue of the fact that all translation is perforce interpretation or due to the fact that G opted for certain Hebrew-Greek equations and then tended to stick with them. Exegesis in Psalm 3 is not unlike its Greek poetics: features of what Hugh Lloyd-Jones[4] calls "formal prose" do occur but seem more inadvertent than deliberate. When all is said and done, what did emerge, however, nevertheless created a certain potential for future understanding.

---

[4] *Greek Metre* (Oxford, Clarendon: 1962), 2. The German original of this work by Paul Maas speaks of Kunstprosa.

THE "HOLY LAND" IN PSEUDO-PHILO, 4 EZRA, AND 2 BARUCH

Daniel J. Harrington

The expression the "holy land" appears only once in the Hebrew Bible: "The Lord will inherit Judah as his portion in the holy land, and will again choose Jerusalem" (Zech 2:12). It also occurs in the Greek text of 2 Maccabees in the first "cover letter" to that work: "Jason and his company revolted from the holy land and the kingdom" (1:7).

One of the many features that link together Pseudo-Philo's *Biblical Antiquities* (*Liber Antiquitatum Biblicarum* = LAB), *4 Ezra*, and *2 Baruch* are their explicit references to the "holy land" (see LAB 19:10; 4 Ezra 13:48; 2 Bar 63:10).[1] In examining the theme in each of the three works this paper will explore how the motif of the "holy land" functions and how each work treats Jerusalem and Mount Zion in relation to the holy land. The works are treated in the order in which I think that they were composed. Finally it will consider briefly what the developments of this theme might tell us about their historical setting and relations to one another.

I have known Emanuel Tov since the late 1960's when we were graduate students at Harvard. I worked closely with Emanuel in editing Qumran wisdom texts for several years during the 1990's (DJD XXXIV). The topic of this paper touches on Emanuel's longstanding interests in the figure of Baruch and in the genre of "biblical paraphrase" or "rewritten Bible," as well as his love for the land of Israel where he has lived for most of his adult life.

PSEUDO-PHILO'S BIBLICAL ANTIQUITIES

Also known by its Latin title *Liber Antiquitatum Biblicarum* (= LAB), this book is a selective retelling of the biblical narrative from Adam to

---

[1] For a full account of the links among LAB, 4 Ezra, and 2 Baruch, see M. R. James, *The Biblical Antiquities of Philo* (London: SPCK, 1917; reprinted with a Prolegomenon by L. H. Feldman, New York: Ktav, 1971), 46–59.

David.[2] It interweaves biblical incidents and imaginative expansions, and so is often classified as "rewritten Bible." It now exists in eighteen complete and three fragmentary Latin manuscripts. But it was composed in Hebrew and then translated into Greek before reaching its Latin version. A Palestinian origin in the first century C.E. is very likely. Whether it was composed before or after 70 C.E. remains a matter of dispute among scholars.

The predominant theme of LAB has been summarized by Howard Jacobson in this way: "No matter how much the Jewish people suffer, no matter how bleak the outlook appears, God will never completely abandon His people and in the end salvation and triumph will be the lot of the Jews."[3] In this framework the disasters that Israel experiences are just punishments for the people's sins. But, Jacobson continues, "when the Jews cease sinning grievously and devote themselves faithfully to God and His Law—which is within their power and will at some point happen—salvation will come."

The only explicit reference to the "holy land" (*terra sancta*) in LAB occurs in the context of God's showing the promised land to Moses (see Deut 34:1, 4). Here God points out "the place in the firmament from which only the holy land drinks" (19:10). There are, however, many references to the "land" in the work, and these are best viewed with reference to the predominant theme as enunciated by Jacobson.

The first important references appear in LAB 7:4 as part of the Tower of Babel episode in which God promises to bring Abraham "into the land upon which my eye has looked from of old." God goes on to observe that the holy land had alone escaped the destruction wrought by the waters of the flood in the days of Noah: "For neither did the springs of my wrath burst forth in it, nor did my water of destruction descend on it."

Several mentions of the holy land in LAB are associated with Israel's entry into the promised land. At the exodus when the people find themselves trapped between the Red Sea and the Egyptian armies, they wonder whether they will ever reach the land promised

---

[2] For a critical edition of the Latin text of LAB, see D. J. Harrington et al., *Les Antiquités Bibliques* (SC 229–230; Paris: Cerf., 1976). The English translations are taken from Harrington, "Pseudo-Philo," in J. H. Charlesworth. *The Old Testament Pseudepigrapha* (ed., J. H. Charlesworth; Garden City, NY: Doubleday, 1985) 2.297–377.

[3] H. Jacobson, *A Commentary on Pseudo-Philo's* Liber Antiquitatum Biblicarum (AGAJU 31; Leiden: Brill, 1996), 1.241–42. See also F. J. Murphy, *Pseudo-Philo. Rewriting the Bible* (New York-Oxford: Oxford University Press, 1993), 244–61.

to the seed of Abraham in Genesis 12:7 (see LAB 10:2). The same biblical text (Gen 12:7) is taken up in the episode of the golden calf where God points out to Moses that "the people have not even entered the land yet and now even have the Law with them, and they have forsaken me" (12:4). And as the people stand ready to enter the promised land (see Num 1:1–3), God instructs Moses to make a census of them: "By number they will enter the land, and in a short time they will become without number" (14:2; see Gen 22:17).

The richest source for references to the holy land is the account of Moses' farewell address, prayer, and death in LAB 19. First Moses warns the people that they will forsake God's commandments and that in response "God will be angry at you and abandon you and depart from your land" (19:2). However, since God's commitment to the covenant is unconditional, he will eventually remember his covenant and rescue his people. Moreover, God's virtual tour of the holy land for Moses includes a vision of "the place where they will serve me for 740 years" (19:7). God also shows to Moses the special water supply reserved for the holy land: "the place in the firmament from which only the holy land drinks" (19:10).

At the altar across the Jordan (see Josh 22:10–12), Joshua scolds those who built a sanctuary there: "What are these deeds that are done among you, when we have not yet even settled in our land?" (22:2). When in the time of the Judges the people faced a crisis because they had transgressed "the ways that Moses and Joshua the servants of the Lord had commanded them," they describe their plight in this way: "We say that we are more blessed than other nations, and behold now we have been humiliated more than all peoples so that we cannot dwell in our own land and our enemies have power over us" (30:4). God responds to their confession ("our own wicked deeds") and fasting by raising up Deborah to lead them to victory, and restores them to their land.

There are very few references to Jerusalem and its Temple in LAB. The Latin text breaks off awkwardly with the death of Saul (65:5). In this narrative framework (from Adam to David) the Jerusalem Temple is not yet built, and one could hardly expect that much attention would be given to it. But one of the author's favorite literary devices is to link the biblical episode currently under discussion with what went before (flashbacks) and what will come afterward (anticipations). So, for example, in God's remarks to Moses about the golden calf episode there is a preview of the First Temple and its destruction: "I will turn again and make peace with them so that a house may be built for me among them, a house that will be destroyed because they will sin against me" (12:4).

The only explicit mention of Jerusalem in LAB appears in 22:9. In describing the worship that took place at Shiloh, the narrator explains that "until the house of the Lord was built in Jerusalem and sacrifice offered on the new altar, the people were not prohibited from offering sacrifice there."

Was the Second Temple standing when LAB was written? The notice in 22:8 that Joshua decreed what holocausts were to be offered "even unto this day" suggests that when the author wrote, sacrifices were still (i.e., before 70 C.E.) being offered in the Jerusalem Temple. Likewise, in the hymn of Deborah the flashback to Abraham's sacrifice of Isaac in Genesis 22 assumes that "for the wicked deeds of men animals are appointed to be killed" (32:3).

There is a clear "prophecy" of the destruction of the Jerusalem Temple in LAB 19:7. Speaking to Moses, God says: "I will show you the place where they will serve me for 740 years. And after this it will be turned over into the hands of their enemies, and they will destroy it, and foreigners will encircle it." This description could apply to either the First Temple or the Second Temple. The event is said to coincide on the calendar with God's destruction of the tablets of the covenant at Mount Horeb (see Exod 32:19) on "the seventeenth day of the fourth month." Although some rabbinic traditions say that in 70 C.E. Jerusalem was breached on the seventeenth day of Tammuz (see *m. Taʿan.* 4:6; *t. Taʿan.* 4:6; *b. Taʿan.* 28b), it is not completely certain that LAB 19:7 refers to the destruction of the Second Temple.[4]

Fourth Ezra

The work known as 4 Ezra is the central part of a larger book called 2 Esdras that consists of a second-century C.E. Christian prophecy and apocalypse (chaps. 1–2 = 5 Ezra), a late first-century Jewish apocalypse (chaps. 3–14 = 4 Ezra), and a third-century C.E. Christian prophecy and apocalypse (chaps. 15–16 = 6 Ezra). The composite

---

[4] For a defense of the pre-70 C.E. dating, see P.-M. Bogaert in *Les Antiquités Bibliques*, 2.66–74. For a post-70 dating, see Jacobson, *A Commentary*, 1.199–200.

text appears in Slavonic Bibles as 3 Esdras and in Latin Bibles as 4 Esdras.

The Jewish apocalypse presented in chapters 3–14 reflects the historical conditions and theological concerns associated with the destruction of Jerusalem and its temple in 70 c.e.[5] The narrative setting is the Babylonian exile in the sixth century b.c.e., and Ezra serves as the spokesman for the Jewish community there. However, the historical setting is the late first century c.e., as the vision of the Eagle and the Lion (chaps. 11–12) with its many references to Roman emperors makes clear.

Although the primary version is now the Latin text, there is a consensus that the work was composed in Hebrew and translated into Greek first. The content of the work and its composition in Hebrew point to its origin in the land of Israel in the late first century c.e.

This Jewish apocalypse consists of three dialogues (3:1–5:20; 5:21–6:34; 6:35–9:25), three visions (9:26–10:59; 11:1–12:51; 13:1–58), and a final narrative about Ezra's activity as a scribe (14:1–48). The angel Uriel serves as Ezra's guide and interpreter, though at some points Uriel speaks for God in first-person singular language. Ezra wants to know why God has allowed such terrible things to happen to Zion and what God plans to do in the future.

The one explicit reference to the holy land in 4 Ezra appears near the end of the third vision in which Ezra is promised that those "who are left of our people, who are found within my holy borders (*intra terminum meum sanctum*), shall be saved" (13:48). The most convenient way to treat the theme of the holy land and Jerusalem (the Old and the New) in 4 Ezra is to trace them through the various parts of the book.

The occasion for the first dialogue (3:1–5:20) is that Ezra has seen "the desolation of Zion and the wealth of those who live in Babylon" (3:2). He wants to understand how God could have "handed over your city to your enemies" (3:27), especially since the deeds of Babylon are worse than those of Zion. He seeks to know "why Israel has been given over to the Gentiles in disgrace" (4:23).

The second dialogue (5:21–6:34) begins with Ezra's meditation on God's election of Israel. He reminds his "sovereign Lord" that "from

---

[5] The translations of 4 Ezra are taken from the New Revised Standard Version. For a full commentary, see M. E. Stone, *Fourth Ezra* (Hermeneia; Minneapolis: Fortress, 1990).

all the lands of the world you have chosen for yourself one region . . . and from all the cities that have been built you have consecrated Zion for yourself" (5:24–25). This emphasis on the unique character of the holy land and the holy city is balanced off by the promise that God will visit the earth only when "the humiliation of Zion is complete" (6:19).

The third dialogue (6:35–9:25) is a very long conversation that treats in detail many of the theological issues arising from the destruction of Jerusalem. One passage that is pertinent to our theme concerns the appearance of the New Jerusalem and the new earth as a prelude to the revelation of "my son the Messiah" and his four-hundred-year reign: "the city that now is not seen shall appear, and the land that now is hidden shall be disclosed" (7:26). Furthermore, when the angel tries to encourage Ezra to look toward the bliss that awaits him personally, he speaks about the "paradise that is opened . . . a city built" (8:52). The most characteristic emphasis regarding the holy land in 4 Ezra is its role as the place of safety and refuge for those who by their deeds and faith will survive the eschatological tribulations: "and [they] will see my salvation in my land and within my borders, which I have sanctified for myself from the beginning" (9:8). The place of eschatological refuge will be the holy land (see also 12:34; 13:48).

In the Vision of the Woman in Mourning (9:26–10:59) Ezra counsels the woman against spending all her energies in lamenting over her dead son at a time when "Zion, the mother of us all, is in deep grief and great distress" (10:7). When she rebuffs Ezra, he tries to console her further by pointing to the even greater "adversities of Zion and . . . the sorrows of Jerusalem" (10:20). However, Ezra soon witnesses the transformation of the woman into a great city: "the woman was no longer visible to me, but a city was being built, and a place of huge foundations showed itself" (10:27). With Uriel's help, Ezra comes to understand that "the woman whom you saw is Zion" (10:44), and the city being built is "no work of human construction" (10:54). The transformation of the woman in mourning brings about the transformation of Ezra. Because God is impressed with Ezra's sensitivity ("you are sincerely grieved and profoundly distressed for her," 10:49–50), he decides to give Ezra a preview of the New Jerusalem and so helps him to move from relentless questioning about past and present misfortunes into hopeful visions of the future.

The Vision of the Eagle and the Lion in 11:1–12:51 reaches its climax when the Lion (the Messiah) brings the enemies of God's people (the Eagle = the Roman empire) before his judgment seat and destroys them (12:33). At the same time, the Lion sets up a messianic kingdom for "the remnant of my people, those who have been saved throughout my borders, and he will make them joyful until the end comes, the day of judgment" (12:34). The holy land becomes a protected zone or territory (*terminus sanctus*) during the trials of the end-time (see 9:8; 13:48). When the people complain that Ezra is abandoning them during their present exile in Babylon, he responds that he left them "to pray on account of the desolation of Zion, and to seek mercy on account of the humiliation of our sanctuary" (12:48).

In the third vision (13:1–58) the manifestation of the Man from the Sea ("my son, the Messiah") takes place on Mount Zion and becomes visible to all the world. The Messiah will gather to himself a great crowd, including members of the nine tribes who went into exile under the Assyrians. Again the holy land serves as a safe territory: "But those who are left of your people, who are found within my holy borders, shall be saved" (13:48). The Messiah will destroy the multitude of nations that come against him but "will defend the people who remain" (13:49), presumably within the holy land.

The concluding narrative about Ezra the scribe (14:1–48) explains the exile in terms of the holy land. The "land of Zion" was given to Israel as a gift, and it was taken away on account of the people's sins: "you and your ancestors committed iniquity and did not keep the ways that the Most High commanded you" (14:31). Acting as a righteous judge, God "took away from you what he had given" (14:32).

In summary, according to 4 Ezra, the holy land was a gift from God that God took away due to the people's sins. The land chosen by God now endures humiliation. But God remains faithful, and will bring about a new and better Jerusalem (see 9:26–10:59). And in the time of "my son, the Messiah" the holy land will serve as the place of refuge and safety for God's people (see 9:8; 12:34; 13:48).

Second Baruch

Second Baruch is also known as the Syriac Apocalypse of Baruch.[6] The full text is known from one Syriac manuscript (Bibliotheca

---

[6] The translations are taken from A. F. J. Klijn, "2 (Syriac Apocalypse of) Baruch," in *The Old Testament Pseudepigrapha*, 1.615–52. For a full commentary, see

Ambrosiana in Milan, B. 21 Inf., fols 257a–265b) that is dated to the sixth or seventh century C.E. However, it appears that the book was composed in Hebrew in the late first century C.E. and then translated into Greek (some Greek fragments were found among the Oxyrhynchus Papyri). In addition to revelations from "the word of the Lord" there are laments, prayers, dialogues, addresses to the people, and even a "letter" (in 78:1–87:1).

At the heart of the book are the three apocalypses that appear in 26–30; 35–43; and 53–76, respectively. Each of these visions features a reference to the "holy land" and those who dwell in it (29:2; 40:2; 71:1) as being protected during the tribulations that accompany the coming of the Messiah and the end-time events.

Like 4 Ezra, 2 Baruch takes as its literary setting the destruction of Jerusalem and its Temple in 587 B.C.E. However, the references to the destruction of the First and the Second Temples in 32:2–4 suggest a date of composition around 100 C.E. Indeed, the whole book is a theological reflection on how God could have allowed these events to have happened and on what God might have in store for his people Israel in the future. The situation and the spirituality of the whole book is expressed near the end: "Zion has been taken away from us, and we have nothing now apart from the Mighty One and his Law" (85:3).

The first reference to the holy land in 2 Baruch appears in the "Apocalypse of the Twelve Calamities and the Coming of the Messiah" (26–30). After hearing the list of calamities, Baruch asks: "Is it in one place or in one part of the earth that these things will come or will they be noticed by the whole earth?" (28:7). He is told that whatever happens at that time concerns the whole earth and all who are alive will notice it. However, those who live in the holy land at that time seem to be exempt from the immediate effects of the calamities: "For at that time I shall only protect those found in this land at that time" (29:2). In the context of 2 Baruch the expression "in this land" must be the land of Israel, not the earth in general. The protection afforded the inhabitants of the holy land in turn sets the stage for the manifestation of the Anointed One (or Messiah)

P.-M. Bogaert, *L'Apocalypse de Baruch* (SC 144–145; Paris: Cerf, 1969). See also F. J. Murphy, *The Structure and Meaning of Second Baruch* (SBLDS 78; Atlanta: Scholars Press, 1985).

and the appearance of the two great monsters Behemoth and Leviathan who in themselves will provide the main course for the messianic banquet (29:4).

The second reference to the holy land occurs in the "Apocalypse of the Forest, the Vine, the Fountain, and the Cedar" (35–43). In this apocalypse the mighty cedar tree remaining from the forest of wickedness is a symbol for the Roman empire. Adopting the four-empire scheme of world history, the apocalypse describes the fourth kingdom (which is clearly Rome in the context) as "harsher and more evil than those which were before it" and as exalting itself "more than the cedars of Lebanon" (39:5). The climax of this apocalypse is a judgment scene in which the last ruler (the Roman emperor) is to be brought in fetters to Mount Zion where the Messiah is to convict and kill him. In this setting the Messiah will also "protect the rest of my people who will be found in the place that I have chosen" (40:2). The apocalypse suggests that the messianic era takes place in the holy land and among the people that God has made to be his own. This peaceable kingdom will then "last forever until the world of corruption has ended and until the times which have been mentioned before have been fulfilled" (40:3).

The third and fourth references to the holy land appear as part of the "Apocalypse of the Clouds and the Twelve Bright and Dark Waters" (53–76). In the explanation of the eighth bright waters, the sudden and overwhelming defeat of Sennacharib and his huge army in the time of Hezekiah (see 2 Kings 18–19; Isaiah 36–37), the angel Ramael who is serving as Baruch's interpreter describes how he destroyed the 185,000 chiefs and their soldiers: "I burned their bodies within, but I preserved their clothes and their arms outside." The point of this peculiar strategy was to show that God and his angel (and not human defenders) had preserved the holy city. When it became clear that God had saved Zion and delivered Jerusalem from its tribulations, "all those who were in the holy land rejoiced, and the name of the Mighty One was praised so that it was spoken of" (63:10). Here the inhabitants of the holy land serve as witnesses to the mighty action of God in protecting the holy city of Jerusalem in the days of King Hezekiah.

The holy land is mentioned again in 71:1 in connection with the "last black waters" and the calamities that accompany them: war, earthquake, fire, and famine. Those who survive such catastrophes will in the end be "delivered into the hands of my Servant, the

Anointed One" (70:9). Whereas the whole earth will devour its inhabitants, "the holy land will have mercy on its own and will protect
its inhabitants at that time" (71:1).

Apart from the reference to the holy land as a witness to God's
action in defeating Sennacharib (63:10), the references to the holy
land in 2 Baruch appear in descriptions of end-time events in general and in connection with the revelation of the Messiah in particular (see 29:2; 40:2; 71:1). The dominant motif is the idea of the
holy land as a place especially favored and protected by God in the
times of eschatological tribulation and as the place where the Messiah
exercises his rule and judgment.

Although the narrative context of 2 Baruch is the destruction of
the First Temple, the historical context is the destruction of the
Second Temple. And so what the author says about events in the
early sixth century B.C.E. presumably has significance for readers in
the first or early second century C.E. Since the most holy part of the
holy land is Jerusalem and its temple, the author has to explain why
and how it could have been destroyed in 587 B.C.E. and in 70 C.E.

The first main section of 2 Baruch concerns the destruction of
Jerusalem and the First Temple. The reason for their destruction
was the sinfulness of the people: "Have you seen all that this people are doing to me, the evil things which the two tribes that remained
have done?" (1:2). Whereas the tribes of the northern kingdom were
forced by their kings to sin, the tribes of the southern kingdom "have
themselves forced and compelled their kings to sin" (1:3).

Baruch raises an objection to God: "If you destroy your city and
deliver up your country to those who hate us, how will the name of
Israel be remembered again?" (3:5). God's honor is at stake here. The
response is that God's honor does not depend on the Jerusalem Temple. In fact, what God really has in mind as his final dwelling place
is the New Jerusalem, the city that existed before the creation of the
world. God has already revealed the New Jerusalem to Adam before
he sinned, to Abraham "in the night between the portions of the
victims," and to Moses on Mount Sinai (4:3–5). For the present the
New Jerusalem "is preserved with me [God]—as also paradise" (4:6).

However, so that Israel's enemies might not have the satisfaction
of destroying the holy city and its temple, God devised a strategy
by which the enemies of Israel could not say: "We have overthrown
the wall of Zion, and we have burnt down the place of the mighty

God" (7:11). The plan was to have the angels first break down the walls and overturn the foundations, and only then to let Israel's enemies come in and do their work as instruments of God's wrath: "the enemy shall not destroy Zion and burn Jerusalem, but they shall serve the Judge for a time" (5:3).

There is also provision in God's plan for the sacred vessels used at the temple (the veil, the holy ephod, the mercy seat, the two tables, etc.) to be preserved and buried in the ground (presumably in the holy land) "so that strangers may not get possession of them" (6:8). These sacred vessels are to remain in the earth—in the holy land—until "the last times" (6:8) when Jerusalem "will be restored forever" (6:9).

These and related points about the destruction(s) of the holy city are repeated throughout the rest of 2 Baruch. In 32:2–7 Baruch prepares the people for the destructions of both the First Temple and the Second Temple, but holds out hope for the perfect temple of the future: "it will be renewed in glory and . . . will be perfected into eternity" (32:4). Although the sins of the people were responsible for the First Temple's destruction, there is the promise that in the time of the twelfth bright waters "Zion will be rebuilt again, and the offering will be restored, and the priests will again return to their ministry. And the nations will again come to honor it" (68:5). Nevertheless, with the phrase "but not as fully as before" (68:6) it is acknowledged that the Second Temple will not be as glorious as the First Temple was.

In 77:8–10 Baruch explains to the people that it was because of their sins that the catastrophes occur: "Or do you think that the place has sinned . . . or that the country has done some crime . . .?" It is not the fault of the holy city or of the holy land that such punishments have befallen Israel. It is the fault of the people who inhabit the city and the land.

In his letter to the nine and a half tribes in exile, Baruch explains why the First Temple was destroyed: "For we had sinned against him who created us, and had not observed the commandments which he ordered us" (79:2). He also summarizes God's strategy in having the angels do the preparatory work for Nebuchadnezzar's armies and in preserving the sacred vessels used in the tenple: "when the enemies surrounded the city, angels were sent from the Most High. And they demolished the fortifications of the strong wall, and he destroyed their solid iron corners which could not be loosened. Nevertheless, they hid the holy vessels lest they be polluted by the enemies" (80:1–2).

Baruch closes his letter by reminding the nine and a half tribes that "Zion has been taken away from us, and we have nothing now apart from the Mighty One and his Law" (85:3). This sentence summarizes the entire theology of 2 Baruch. However, there is hope that what was taken away will be restored in an incorruptible form: "For that which we lost was subjected to corruption, and that which we receive will not be corruptible" (85:5). There is also hope for a new and perfect holy city, one that has existed from before creation and will be made manifest in the New Jerusalem.

GENERAL OBSERVATIONS

These three first-century C.E. Jewish works contain colorful and interesting traditions about the holy land. Not only was the holy land especially chosen by God (see LAB 7:4; 4 Ezra 5:24–25), but it also escaped destruction from the flood in the days of Noah (LAB 7:4) and has a special water supply in the firmament (LAB 19:10). All three books regard the holy land as God's gift, but one that could be lost through the sins of the people. In 4 Ezra and 2 Baruch the holy land is the place of refuge and safety during the tribulations leading to the messianic age and the manifestation of the New Jerusalem as the resting place for God's people.

What these books say about the holy land fits well with the late-first-century C.E. dates assigned to them on other grounds. They agree in their special interest in the holy land. The links are strongest between 4 Ezra and 2 Baruch, two apocalypses that clearly reflect a post-70 C.E. setting. Despite its different literary genre ("biblical paraphrase" or "rewritten Bible") and perhaps earlier (pre-70 C.E.) setting, LAB deserves to be studied alongside the two apocalypses as reflecting the same "school" or "circle" (as M. R. James suggested long ago).

PART THREE

HEBREW BIBLE

BLOOD IN ISRAEL AND MESOPOTAMIA*

Tzvi Abusch

My paper will focus on the significance of blood in Israel and Mesopotamia. I begin with Israel or, rather, with the biblical text. That blood plays an important role in biblical cultic ritual is well known and hardly requires documentation. It is not an exaggeration to state that blood "is sprinkled, splashed, poured, and smeared on altars, persons, on the veil of the Holy of Holies, even, once a year, on the Ark of the Covenant itself."[1] Many passages could be cited as examples, but here, let me simply quote a well-known passage from the Holiness Code that contains important reflections on blood and expresses some of the beliefs regarding the significance of animal and human blood.

> And if anyone of the house of Israel or of the strangers who reside among them partakes of any blood,[2] I will set My face against the person who partakes of the blood, and I will cut him off from among his kin. For the life of the flesh is in the blood, and I have assigned it to you for making expiation for your lives upon the altar; it is the blood, as life, that effects expiation.[3]

* It is a great pleasure to dedicate this paper to Emanuel Tov and thereby to celebrate Emanuel's great contribution to biblical scholarship as well as a personal friendship that has been sustained and developed over thirty-five years on three continents.

This paper was first presented in April, 1998 at the conference "Text, Artifact, and Image: Revealing Ancient Israelite Religion," sponsored by the Center for Judaic Studies of the University of Pennsylvania. The explanation of the difference between Israel and Mesopotamia as regards blood was first worked out in the context of a lecture on "Sacrifice in Mesopotamia" that I delivered in Israel in February, 1998 at the conference "Sacrifice: A Comparative Inquiry" sponsored by the Jacob Taubes Minerva Center of Bar Ilan University. That lecture was published in the conference proceedings: T. Abusch, "Sacrifice in Mesopotamia," in *Sacrifice in Religious Experience*, ed. A. I. Baumgarten, SHR 93 (Leiden: E. J. Brill, 2002), 39–48. I wish to thank Kathryn Kravitz for her helpful comments on this paper.

[1] S. A. Geller, *Sacred Enigmas: Literary Religion in the Hebrew Bible* (London: Routledge, 1996), 64.
[2] For the prohibition against eating blood, see also Gen 9:4, Deut 12:16, and 1 Sam 14:32–34.
[3] Lev 17:10–11, translation: NJPS.

Many scholars have studied the significance of blood in the Israelite cult.[4] Among others, B. A. Levine has contributed significantly to our understanding of this topic. He maintains that blood is life and serves as a representation of the human person. Because it is the life force, blood can substitute for a life, *pars pro toto*. God accepts the blood of the sacrifice in lieu of human blood. Accordingly, Levine understands a verse such as Lev. 17:11 just quoted as meaning that blood is a ransom for life. He translates *kî haddām hûʾ bannepeš yəkappēr* there as "it is the blood that effects expiation in exchange for life," taking the *beth* in *bannepeš* as the *beth* of price, and not of means. Similarly, when used with the phrase *ləkappēr ʿal nepeš*, the blood serves as a ransom for human life. Thus, the offering of animal blood on the altar as part of the sacrifice serves to give a substitution, or ransom, for the human life. The sprinkling of blood thus protects the human being who has sinned or who needs protection. The blood is given to God, but it is a development of the earlier offering of blood to chthonic deities.[5] The aforementioned use of blood protects human beings from divine anger, but of course, this is not the only use of blood, and Levine also recognizes that in certain circumstances it also functions to protect the divine from contamination (e.g., Lev. 16).[6]

In any case, I find Levine's interpretation attractive and accept the idea that blood as a representation of life may serve as a substitute for the person and that this is one of its functions in the cult. But blood as a representation of life can also be used to create relationships between persons. And, thus, it is unfortunate that Levine sets up his interpretation as an alternative to W. Robertson Smith's well-known ideas propounded in his *Lectures on the Religion of the Semites* (1889),[7] as if substitution and communion could not be two complementary aspects of the use of sacrificial blood but need rather be mutually exclusive.

---

[4] E.g., D. J. McCarthy, "The Symbolism of Blood and Sacrifice," *JBL* 88 (1969): 166–76, and "Further Notes on the Symbolism of Blood and Sacrifice," *JBL* 92 (1973): 205–10; and Geller, *Sacred Enigmas*, 62–86 and 205–7.

[5] B. A. Levine, "Prolegomenon" to G. B. Gray, *Sacrifice in the Old Testament: Its Theory and Practice* (New York: Ktav, 1971 [reprint]), xxvii–xxviii; *In the Presence of the Lord*, SJLA 5 (Leiden: E. J. Brill, 1974), 67–69; *The JPS Torah Commentary: Leviticus* (Philadelphia: Jewish Publication Society, 1989), 115–16 on Lev. 17:11 and 6–7 on Lev. 1:4.

[6] See "Prolegomenon," xxviii; *Presence*, 73–78, cf. 103.

[7] Reprinted as *The Religion of the Semites: The Fundamental Institutions* (New York: Schocken, 1972).

Levine notes Robertson Smith's proposal that "the predominant factor in 'Semitic' sacrifice was the experience of communion actualized in the blood rites of the animal sacrifice,"[8] that is, communion through blood, but then contends that a weak point in Robertson Smith's argument is that "if the blood rite was an expression of kinship, the kinship of covenant brothers, then the covenant should, in itself, represent a kinship arrangement."[9] Levine states that Robertson Smith sensed this weakness in his own position[10] and seems to feel that he can dismiss Robertson Smith's position on the grounds that the latter believed "that the covenant between Yahweh and Israel was a relationship created artificially, an adoptive relationship."[11] For Levine believes that "The fatherhood of Yahweh, like his kingship, was not based on blood kinship, but on a type of contract in which the terminology of kinship was proverbially metaphorical,"[12] and thus concludes that since Israelite religion is based on a covenant with a vassal lord or king, a covenant that is thus artificial, the cult cannot be understood in terms of a commensality model or as an expression of the kinship of blood.[13]

In my opinion, this argument is somewhat misleading. First of all, kinship may be artificially constructed by legal and/or metaphorical means. In this context, we note that a relationship is no less powerful for being metaphorical. Moreover, one may mix types of metaphor—the Israelite God may be both kin and king. Second, in a clan context, he may, in fact, be a kin. For example, in the patriarchal accounts of Genesis, God is presented as a kin with whom the patriarch and his family bear a family relationship. In fact, in a tribal context, the relationship between man and god created by sacrifice may be one of kinship.[14] Let us also not forget that the

---

[8] "Prolegomenon," xxiii.

[9] "Prolegomenon," xxv.

[10] In my reading, I do not find that Robertson Smith recognized as a weakness that which Levine ascribes to him (*Religion of the Semites*, 312–20; cf. Levine, "Prolegomenon," xli, n. 48, where he cites *Lectures*, 319, n. 2 and additional note H).

[11] "Prolegomenon," xxv. Actually, this constitutes a form of kinship relationship. Cf. now, e.g., F. M. Cross's discussion of Kinship-in-Law in "Kinship and Covenant in Ancient Israel," in his *From Epic to Canon: History and Literature in Ancient Israel* (Baltimore: Johns Hopkins University Press, 1998), 3–21, esp. 7ff.

[12] "Prolegomenon," xxv.

[13] "Prolegomenon," xxv–xxvi.

[14] Cf. N. Jay, *Throughout Your Generations Forever: Sacrifice, Religion, and Paternity* (Chicago: University of Chicago Press, 1992), 33: "It is on the father-son relation that the sacrificial relation of deity to worshiper is founded, although it was later expanded to include . . . king-subject."

blood-covenant between Israel and God as found, for example, in Exodus 24 is not only retributive but also creates ties of consanguinity between man and god. In this context, I need hardly remind the reader of the rite of circumcision. In Exodus 4, for example, the blood of circumcision turns Yhwh into a *ḥātān dāmîm*, a kinsman (vs. 25).

Finally, and perhaps most important, the kinship established by sacrifice is not simply between man and god.[15] For sacrifice is also a social act that brings men into relationship with each other. Through blood covenants, human parties artificially create a tie of consanguinity between themselves by mixing their blood, blood that represents themselves. That is, sacrifice and the use of blood may also establish or reaffirm blood brother-ship; it is a form of commensality between blood kin, but it sometimes creates the relationship itself. If anything, blood sacrifice, in and of itself, actually stands in opposition to the natural relationship created by birth. It creates relations between men, and places these artificial relationships on a higher level than the natural relationship of mother and child created in the blood of birth.[16]

---

[15] In fact, social bonds in the Bible are often translated into kinship relationships (e.g., the people Israel are described as the descendants of one father); some of these relationships derive from actual kinship relationships, others are created. Cf. Cross, "Kinship and Covenant," 3–21, esp. 7–13. On the creation of kinship, I may repeat Robertson Smith's comment in his *Kinship and Marriage*, recently quoted by Cross, ibid., 8:

> The commingling of blood [in the oath and covenant ritual] by which two men became brothers or two kins allies, and the [legal] fiction of adoption by which a new tribesman was feigned to be the veritable son of a member of the tribe, are both evidences of the highest value, that the Arabs were incapable of conceiving any absolute social obligations of social unity which was not based on kinship; for a legal fiction is always adopted to reconcile an act with a principle too firmly established to be simply ignored.... We see that two groups might make themselves of one blood by a process of which the essence was that they commingled their blood, at the same time applying the blood to the god or fetish so as to make him a party to the covenant also. Quite similar is the ritual in Exodus 24 where blood is applied to the people of Israel and to the altar.

[16] Thus, Levine's contention that "Once the artificiality of the Israelite covenant is acknowledged, we can no longer maintain that the cult, as the supposed actualization of the covenant, expresses the kinship of blood" ("Prolegomenon," xxvi) seems not to be true. Actually, Levine's argument may be more complex than this summary indicates, but is perhaps also self-contradictory. Levine denies the kinship aspect of covenant and asserts its political nature (cf. "Prolegomenon," xxv–xxvi; *Presence*, 78). He then claims that covenant and sacrificial systems belong to different categories, and he argues that blood functions differently in covenant and in the

The insight that blood sacrifice is an artificial means of creating relationships has been developed recently by the late Nancy Jay in her posthumously published book *Throughout Your Generations Forever: Sacrifice, Religion, and Paternity.*[17] Jay argues that "sacrifice is at home in societies where families are integrated into extended kin groups of various kinds,"[18] and that "sacrificing identifies, legitimates, and maintains enduring structures of intergenerational continuity between males that transcend their absolute dependence on women's reproductive powers."[19] Jay notes that while sacrifice may serve to define both matrilineal and patrilineal descent systems, it is especially prevalent and significant in patrilineal societies, where "sacrificing orders relations within and between lines of human fathers and sons, between men and men, at least as effectively as it does relations between men and their divinities."[20] Sacrifice establishes blood-ties among men that supercede the natural blood-ties produced through women's childbirth.[21]

---

sacrificial system ("Prolegomenon," xxvi; *Presence*, 78–79). But initially interpreting the basis of the sacrificial system as a relationship between master and servant, he then notes that the same terminology is used for vassal relationships and implicitly acknowledges. the equation of God the master and man the servant with God the suzerain and man the vassal (cf. "Prolegomenon," xxviii–xxix), and thus brings together what he had claimed to separate, the covenantal and sacrificial systems. He also acknowledges the connections between the covenantal and sacrificial systems (cf. *Presence*, 37, 41: "The covenant (or covenants) merely served as the charter, or commission under the terms of which the cult, as well as the other establishments within Israelite society operated"; 103: "The covenant . . . represent[s] the larger framework within which the *ḥaṭṭā't* sacrifice functioned"). Note further that while dismissing the kinship dimension of covenant as merely metaphorical, he acknowledges the communal or bonding function of blood in the covenant ceremony and relationship of Sinai (*Presence*, 78).

I accept the expiatory function of the sacrificial cult but cannot understand why, especially in view of the connections between the covenantal and sacrificial systems, both the expiatory and communal functions of blood cannot be present in the sacrificial system, especially in view of the communal function of the *zebaḥ* and/or *šəlāmîm*. Hence, for example, the blood of *ḥaṭṭā't* is expiatory, and that of the *šəlāmîm* may also serve a binding function.

[17] See note 14.

[18] So K. E. Fields in the Foreword to Jay, *Generations*, xxiv.

[19] Fields, xxvii. That is, "[S]acrificing produces and reproduces forms of intergenerational continuity generated by males, transmitted through males, and transcending continuity through women" (Jay, *Generations*, 32).

[20] Jay, *Generations*, 34. Cf.: "When membership in patrilineal descent groups is identified by rights of participation in blood sacrifice, evidence of 'paternity' is created which is as certain as evidence of maternity, but far more flexible" (Jay, *Generations*, 36).

[21] In sum, according to Jay:

Thus, it is not sufficient to take a phenomenological approach to blood; rather, we must also look for its cultural or social functions. But to understand why I believe that a social explanation derived in some way from Robertson Smith provides a productive approach, we must place the question into a comparative context. We should examine blood and sacrifice in Mesopotamia, whose culture undoubtedly influenced Israel in many ways, but where there seems to be little use of blood in the cult, and we should ask: Why does blood play such an important role in the Israelite cult but hardly any role in the Mesopotamian?

First, then, some background and context about Mesopotamian sacrifice. When we think of sacrifice we tend to think of slaughtering animals or consuming an offering by means of fire. But to approach the topic of sacrifice in Mesopotamia we must look at things a bit differently, for our Mesopotamian religious sources emphasize neither the slaughter of animals nor the process of consumption. Rather, they usually focus on the presentation of the offering.

To understand the Mesopotamian view of sacrifice, we do well to understand the culture's view of the gods.[22] The purpose of human life, the purpose of the community, was to serve the gods, to provide them with whatever care a powerful ruling class, a landed aristocracy, would require. Paramount among these needs are shelter and food. This represents the developed or classical form of Mesopotamian theology and was probably not the original ideology or theology of god and temple. But certainly by the early part of the third millennium, the characteristic and defining forms of classical Mesopotamian theology had emerged. This new ideology was part of the evolution of early civilization and of the development of hierarchical structures within the cities.

Originally temples may have served as communal storehouses, but by the classical period, we have moved from storage to presenta-

---

The twofold movement of sacrifice, integration and differentiation, communion and expiation, is beautifully suited for identifying and maintaining patrilineal descent. Sacrifice can expiate, get rid of, the consequences of having been born of woman (along with countless other dangers) and at the same time integrate the pure and eternal patrilineage. Sacrificially constituted descent, incorporating women's mortal children into an 'eternal' (enduring through generations) kin group, in which membership is recognized by participation in sacrificial ritual, not merely by birth, enables a patrilineal group to transcend mortality in the same process in which it transcends birth (*Generations*, 40).

[22] My understanding of earliest Mesopotamian religious history follows in the tradition of several scholars, notably that of the late Thorkild Jacobsen.

tion. Gods formerly understood as naturalistic forces were now seen as manorial lords, as the divine equivalents to the newly emerging human chieftains and kings. Along with a human form, the gods were given families and households. Most importantly, their homes were now seen as manors or palaces, that is, the temples were now treated as the divine equivalent of the human ruler's abode. Hence, older cultic centers now became the classic Mesopotamian temples in which the god and his family were treated by his subjects as the ruling class of the city. For its part, the city and its inhabitants were required to care for these anthropomorphized deities.

The central act of the daily cult was not sacrifice in the sense of giving the food over to be consumed by fire, nor was it acts of slaughter and pouring out of blood. Food was placed before the god and consumed by him through that mysterious act that characterizes Babylonian religiosity. After being placed on the god's table and somehow magically eaten by the god, it was distributed to the temple personnel and to the king.

The act of killing the animal is almost hidden behind the construct of feeding the god, a construct which emerges out of a combination of the earlier offering and storage and the later image of feeding a divine king in his palace.

The temple is the center of an urban world. The temple and the feeding and care of its gods define the primary community of the dwellers in the land between the two rivers. To serve the god by supporting and participating in the economy of the temple constitutes the mark of membership in the urban community, a community which thus replaces or, at least, overshadows membership in one or another kinship community such as the family or clan.

We return now to the question of blood. A. Leo Oppenheim observed that a "difference that separates the sacrificial rituals in the two cultures [scil. Mesopotamia and the West, "represented best by the Old Testament"] is the 'blood consciousness' of the West, its awareness of the magic power of blood, which is not paralleled in Mesopotamia."[23] This observation seems to be correct so far as the major urban temples of Mesopotamia are concerned. And yet one can find an important place where blood does play a role in Mesopotamia, and this place may provide a clue to the significance

---

[23] A. L. Oppenheim, *Ancient Mesopotamia: Portrait of a Dead Civilization*, rev. edit. (Chicago: University of Chicago Press, 1977), 192.

of the emphasis on blood at least in the Semitic West and its apparent absence in Mesopotamia.

This clue can be found, I think, in texts that tell the story of the
creation of man for the service of the gods. For example, in the
Atrahasis epic, the god who led the rebellion was slaughtered and his
flesh and blood mixed together with clay in order to create the
human creature whose service was necessary for the welfare of the
gods. The use of flesh and blood in addition to clay in the formation of humanity represents a *novum*. In this mythic tradition, the
original model for the creation of humanity was that of a potter who
creates statues by forming them out of wet clay.[24] The killing of a
god and the use of his flesh and blood to create humanity are an
intrusion into the Mesopotamian system of thought. This intrusion
affects the two major early Mesopotamian mythological traditions,
those of Eridu and of Nippur,[25] and is probably due to western
Semitic influences. The killing of a god seems to be depicted already
on seals dating to the Akkadian period,[26] but it enters the literary
tradition in the Old Babylonian period possibly as a consequence of
the settlement of the tribal Amorites in Mesopotamia.

In the new construct, the clay still serves to form the physical person, while the flesh and blood of the slaughtered god add qualities
to the clay and to the human who was created therefrom. While

---

[24] Compare the earlier Sumerian myth *Enki and Ninmah*, which, like *Atrahasis*,
describes the discontent of the divine workers and the subsequent creation of human
beings by means of clay. But see now W. G. Lambert, "The Relationship of
Sumerian and Babylonian Myth as Seen in Accounts of Creation," in *La circulation
des biens, des personnes et des idées dans le Proche-Orient ancien*, ed. D. Charpin and F.
Joannès (Paris: Editions Recherche sur les Civilisations, 1992), 129–35. Basing himself upon a bilingual version of *Enki and Ninmah*, Lambert argues that Enki created
man by mixing clay and blood. If Lambert's understanding also applies to the original Sumerian text, the episode in *Enki and Ninmah* would then represent an earlier
example of the mixing of blood and clay.

[25] Thus gods are killed in order to create human beings not only in *Atrahasis* and
texts related to it, like *Enuma Elish*, but also in the Nippur text *KAR* 4. For these
texts and traditions, see G. Pettinato, *Das altorientalische Menschenbild und die sumerischen
und akkadischen Schöpfungsmythen* (Heidelberg: Carl Winter, 1971), esp. 29–32 and
39–46; as well as M. Dietrich, "Die Tötung einer Gottheit in der Eridu-Babylon-
Mythologie," in *Ernten, was man sät: Festschrift für Klaus Koch zu seinem 65. Geburtstag*,
ed. D. R. Daniels, et al. (Neukirchen-Vluyn: Neukirchener-Verlag, 1991), 49–73;
and W. G. Lambert, "Myth and Mythmaking in Sumer and Akkad," in *Civilizations
of the Ancient Near East*, ed. J. M. Sasson et al. (New York: Scribners, 1995), vol. 3,
1832–1834.

[26] See F. A. M. Wiggermann, "Discussion" in E. Porada, *Man and Images in the
Ancient Near East* (Wakefield, RI: Moyer Bell, 1995), 78–79.

the flesh is the source of the human ghost, the blood, as I have argued elsewhere,[27] is the origin of an ability to plan, that is, of human intelligence, and is ultimately the source and etiology of the personal god. The personal god is not simply the god of an isolated individual; rather, he is the god of the individual as a social being. He is both the divine personification of individual procreation and achievement as well as the god of the tribal or family group who is passed down from generation to generation by the male progenitor. The god is the blood or is in the blood, and his transmission from father to son creates a relationship of kinship between generations of men by the emphasis on the tie of blood.[28]

For the Semites it was the family, the tribe, and the wider tribal territory that defined identity and power. This remained true even of the Semites of northern Babylonia and northeastern Syria who absorbed the culture of urban Mesopotamia, for they did not fully give up their own identities, but instead transformed the culture that they had assimilated and introduced new images. One of these images was that of blood, but this image could not dominate the Mesopotamian cultic landscape, whose form was and remained fundamentally urban.

The classical Mesopotamian city defined itself not as a community of kinsmen, but rather as a community of service which had grown out of and around a female center, the fertility of the earth. Its admission rules were based on a willingness to serve the city god, not on family ties. In Mesopotamia the basic form was created in Sumer: That society seems to have descended directly from the Neolithic villages of the same area where the Sumerians lived in historical times, and saw itself as indigenous to the land. Hence, the central forms of the Mesopotamian temple had little use for blood. They emphasized offerings, first to natural forces and then to the divine owners of the city. And in any case, in contrast to the West, the distribution and consumption of meat were several steps removed from the process of slaughter.

---

[27] T. Abusch, "Ghost and God: Some Observations on a Babylonian Understanding of Human Nature," in *Self, Soul and Body in Religious Experience*, ed. A. I. Baumgarten, et al., SHR 78 (Leiden: E. J. Brill, 1998), 363–83.

[28] It is not a coincidence that in Gen 9:6, we read that "He who sheds the blood of man, by man shall his blood be shed; for in the image of god was he created"; that is to say, the shedding of human blood is prohibited because man is created in the image of god, or put differently, human blood is equated with the god.

By contrast, the tribal shepherds and herdsmen who spread out over the ancient Near East and entered Palestine and Mesopotamia during the Middle and Late Bronze Age were primarily organized according to family and clan. It is the Semites for whom the family god is important, a god represented by blood; it is they who created and cemented alliances by means of the bloody splitting of animals, a splitting evident, for example, in the "Covenant of Parts" of Genesis 15; and it is the Semites to whom we owe the image of divine blood in the *Atrahasis* epic. Especially in light of our earlier citations from Nancy Jay, I think that we should give serious consideration to the possibility that for these Semites the systems of sacrifice that emphasize blood served to maintain family groups, groups that were organized along common blood lines that were usually tribal and patrilineal. That is, blood sacrifice maintains a relationship of kinship between men by the emphasis on a tie of blood and would be consonant with the emphasis on blood in a clan context.

Thus, it is difficult to escape the conclusion that it is in the context of the contrasting forms of social organization of Semitic/Israelite tribal society and Mesopotamian urban society that we should view the blood-consciousness in the Israelite cult and its apparent absence in the Mesopotamian temple. The importance of blood in the West would seem to reflect the fact that an important element in Israelite society derived from a pastoral semi-nomadic element which defined itself in tribal terms. And it is significant, moreover, that the livelihood of this group was involved in the flesh and blood of animals of the herd. Moreover, at least in the case of the Israelites, this semi-nomadic element saw itself as different from the indigenous, autochthonous element of the population and tried to maintain that separateness by means of blood rituals. For, in the main, Israel did not see itself as indigenous dwellers of the land of Canaan; rather, it defined itself by means of its distinctiveness from the Canaanites and asserted that its origin lay elsewhere.

Israelite communities defined themselves as communities of kinsmen. The "Children of Israel" thought of themselves as bound together by ties of blood. Blood served many purposes in the Israelite cult. Surely one of them was that of creating or maintaining bonds of kinship which were defined in terms of covenant.

We recognize that our solution is a speculative and tentative one. It is really no more than a suggestion intended to provoke further discussion.

IS THE SHORTER READING BETTER?
HAPLOGRAPHY IN THE FIRST BOOK OF CHRONICLES

David Noel Freedman and David Miano

It has been said that the worst kind of error is an error of omission. In the handwritten duplication of manuscripts, this type of error is extremely common, and, unfortunately, the Bible has not been immune to it. The ancient scribes were human. Even the most disciplined and diligent mind is susceptible to wandering, and copying becomes automatic after a time. What the eye sees, the hand writes. It would have been very easy for a copyist, in the midst of his exacting task and under the pressure of time, unintentionally to skip a word, a phrase, an entire line, or even an entire paragraph without giving it a second thought. The phenomenon is known as parablepsis, and parablepsis is most often caused by the repetition of similar elements in a text. The result is haplography, which may be broadly defined as the act, in the process of copying, of writing only once something that occurs two or more times in the source text.[1] Parablepsis, therefore, refers to what the eye does, and haplography refers to what the hand does.[2] Haplography is encouraged by *homoeogrammaton*, when two or more letters of similar appearance are in the same context, *homoeologon*, when two or more whole words of similar appearance are in the same context, *homoeoarcton*, when two words have a similar beginning, and *homoeoteleuton*, when two words have a similar ending. The more alike two elements in close proximity are, the greater the chance of parablepsis.[3]

A handful of biblical text critics have given due consideration to this manner of error in the history of manuscript transmission, highlighting its frequency among the variants, but most of these have

---

[1] Emanuel Tov discusses this form of textual error in *Textual Criticism of the Hebrew Bible* (2nd ed.; Minneapolis: Fortress Press, 2001), 237–40.

[2] We use these terms somewhat differently than does Tov.

[3] See our discussion of these terms in "Slip of the Eye: Accidental Omission in the Masoretic Tradition," in *The Task of Bible Translation: Essays in Honor of Ronald F. Youngblood* (ed. G. Scorgie *et al.*; forthcoming).

been New Testament scholars.[4] Accidental omission in the text of
the Hebrew Bible deserves greater study. The phenomenon is more
widespread than a great number of scholars seem to appreciate. We
find it strange that, although haplography is recognized conceptu-
ally by all textual critics, when it comes to the analysis of specific
passages, it is largely dismissed. Many prefer to find other explanations for the differences between manuscripts, primarily guided by
longstanding (and relatively unchallenged) principles of text criticism.
One such principle, that is still adhered to by many, states that when
two manuscripts, or parallel passages in the same manuscript, offer
different readings, the shorter and more difficult reading is to be
preferred (*lectio brevior et difficilior praeferenda est*). The basis for this reasoning is that words or phrases were probably added by scribes to
clarify the meaning of the text, so the shorter and more difficult
reading is likely to be closer to the original. This principle, however,
relies on the assumption that scribes actively engaged in free composition while they were copying manuscripts. We acknowledge that
in the process of *translation*, the scribes may have been inclined to
add or subtract minor elements to improve the sense of a reading,
and in the case of the Targums, we have ample evidence of the
addition of expository notes and commentary directly into sacred
texts. However, we do not know how common this practice was,
and there is far less evidence of such activity in the duplication of
manuscripts in the same language.[5] Should we view scribes as com-
posers or simply as paid secretaries with little on their mind except
accurate duplication and the completion of their assignment in a
reasonable amount of time? Because of the prevalence of mistakes
in every known manuscript, we feel that due consideration should
be given to the likelihood of scribal oversight when explaining a variant *before* resorting to any theory based on intentional alteration.
Given the innumerable times the Bible has been copied and recopied,

---

[4] James R. Royce, "Scribal Habits in the Transmission of New Testament Texts,"
in *The Critical Study of Sacred Texts* (ed. O'Flaherty and Doniger; Berkeley Religious
Studies Series, 1979), 139–61; "Scribal Tendencies in the Transmission of the Text
of the New Testament," in *The Text of the New Testament in Contemporary Research* (ed.
Ehrman and Holmes; Grand Rapids: Eerdmans, 1995), 239–52; J. K. Elliott, "Can
We Recover the Original Text of the New Testament? An Examination of the Role
of Thoroughgoing Eclecticism," in *Essays and Studies in New Testament Textual Criticism*
(ed. Mateos; Cordoba: Ediciones el Almendro, 1992), 17–43.

[5] See Tov, *Textual Criticism*, 265–67.

either in whole or in part, over the last two to three millennia, the odds are that the occasional scribe did not always give the text its due attention, and that errors of omission have added up over time and taken their toll on biblical texts (in Hebrew, Greek, or any language). Where evidence of deliberate manipulation is lacking, appeal to and argument from a mechanical error is always the best approach.[6] Tov puts the matter in perspective, stating: "The validity of this [*lectio brevior*] rule cannot be maintained in all instances. In fact, in neither the NT nor the Hebrew Bible can it be decided automatically that the shorter reading is original. . . . The rule does not cover scribal omissions. Therefore, since it is often hard to distinguish between a scribal phenomenon and the addition or omission of a detail, the suggested rule is impractical."[7]

In order to make our point clear, we shall examine a biblical text and its transcriptional history.[8] We have chosen 1 Chr 1:1–2:5, which is almost exclusively a list of old and well-known names and therefore less subject to deliberate expansion. It is a suitable choice also because not only may we check MT's reading against the Greek Septuagint, but we also possess a copy of the Chronicler's source text, which is now found in the book of Genesis. We may use the following passages for comparison:

> Gen 10:2–4 (= 1 Chr 1:5–7)
> Gen 10:6–8 (= 1 Chr 1:8–10)
> Gen 10:15–18a (= 1 Chr 1:11–16)
> Gen 10:22–29 (= 1 Chr 1:17–23)
> Gen 25:13–16a (= 1 Chr 1:29–31)
> Gen 25:2–4 (= 1 Chr 1:32–33)
> Gen 36:4–5, 11–13a (= 1 Chr 1:35–37)
> Gen 36:20–28 (= 1 Chr 1:38–42)
> Gen 36:31–43 (= 1 Chr 1:43–54)
> Gen 46:12; 38:1–10 (= 1 Chr 2:3–5)

---

[6] See D. N. Freedman and S. Dolansky Overton, "Omitting the Omissions: The Case for Haplography in the Transmission of Biblical Manuscripts," in *'Imagining' Biblical Worlds: Spatial, Social, and Historical Constructs* (ed. D. Gunn and P. McNutt; forthcoming).

[7] Tov, *Textual Criticism*, 306.

[8] Previous studies of this nature can be found in the following articles: D. N. Freedman and J. Lundbom, "Haplography in Jeremiah 1–20," in *ErIsr* 24, Avraham Malamat Volume (Jerusalem: Israel Exploration Society, 1993), *28–*38; Freedman and Miano, "Slip of the Eye: Accidental Omission in the Masoretic Tradition."

An examination of the variants will reveal a considerable number of discrepancies attributable to haplography in both the Greek and Hebrew recensions, many of which have remained unacknowledged by modern scholarship. We encourage the reader to use the accompanying charts for easy reference.

A. In 1 Chr 1:4, we find an instance where the Masoretic Text is clearly defective. The LXX indicates that two words have been accidentally omitted by parablepsis (see H1 on chart). The repeated word נֹחַ caused a scribe's eye to skip ahead, and the copied text suffered a loss (נֹחַ בְּנֵי נֹחַ > נֹחַ).

B. Perhaps influenced by Gen 10:9, a translator of LXX added the word κυνηγός (= צַיִד) after γίγας (= נִבֹּר) in 1 Chr 1:10. The reading of the Chronicler's source text (Gen 10:8), which lacks the word, seems to support this conclusion. Another possibility is that the Chronicler himself was influenced by Gen 10:9, and the word is original. We favor this interpretation, because the Greek translators no doubt were working from a Chronicles scroll, but the Chronicler was working from the text now found in Genesis. He was more likely to be influenced by Gen 10:9. The word fell out due to haplography. The final letter in נִבֹּר resembles that צַיִד (*homoeoteleuton*), and this repetition may be responsible for the omission (see H2 on chart).

C. There is a large omission in the Greek text of the Codex Vaticanus, corresponding to 1 Chr 1:11–16, that consists of not fewer than 63 words (see G1 on chart). The scribe's eyes dropped down several lines in this case (*katablepsis*). There is no obvious duplication of words or letters that would explain the copyist's oversight, but there is no reason to doubt that the omission is accidental. Codex Alexandrinus preserves the missing section. This example illustrates the fact that accidental omissions may be nonhaplographic in nature (that is, not prompted by a repeated element).

D. The testimony of Gen 10:22–23 in Hebrew and the Codex Alexandrinus in Greek indicates that MT of 1 Chr 1:17 is missing two words (see H3 on chart). The error may be attributed to the duplication of three letters (וַאֲרָם וּבְנֵי אֲרָם עוּץ > וַאֲרָם עוּץ). The *waw* that now stands before עוּץ in MT was probably added by a subsequent copyist after the omission occurred in order to smooth out the reading.

E. A spectacular omission occurs in the Codex Vaticanus of LXX that spans 8 verses (1 Chr 1:17–24) and amounts to 96 words! The repetition of the word Αρφαξαδ coaxed an unwary scribe to resume copying several lines below the point where he left off (see G2 on chart).

F. Both 1 Chr 1:18 and Gen 10:24 (MT) contain shorter readings than their respective counterparts in LXX. The Hebrew version reads: "And Arpakshad became father to Shelach, and Shelach became father to Eber." The Greek version reads: "And Arpakshad became father to Kainan, and Kainan became father to Shelach, and Shelach became father to Eber." Which reading is original, the longer or the shorter? A comparison of the genealogy at Gen 11:12–13 does not prove to be helpful. It too reads longer in the Greek text than in the Hebrew, the birth of Kainan being recounted in full. Some might think that the consistent agreement of the Greek against the Hebrew is too great a coincidence for the variant to be accidental. However, the large number of repeated elements in these passages would certainly encourage parablepsis. Haplography can explain the shorter readings in all three texts. In Gen 11:12–13, the repetition of three whole words (את ויולד שנה) could easily have been responsible for a slip of the eye. In 1 Chr 1:24 and Gen 10:24, two repeated words (את ילד) may be to blame (see H4 on chart).[9]

G. A comparison of LXX (Codex Alexandrinus) with MT reveals an omission in the Greek text at 1 Chr 1:20. The phrase και τον Ιαραδ was apparently left out when the repeated words και τον induced parablepsis (see G3 on chart). It is also possible that such an omission occurred in the Hebrew *Vorlage* of LXX by a repetition of the word ואת (ואת הדרם ואת ירח ואת).

H. Two words (Αβραμ αυτος) are missing in the Greek text of 1 Chr 1:27 in Codex Vaticanus, when a *homeoeoarcton* of four letters (Αβρα-) misled a scribe (see G4 on chart). Codex Alexandrinus carries the original reading.

---

[9] The name of Kainan is missing in both MT and LXX at 1 Chr 1:24. If the name was accidentally omitted in this verse, there is no clear rationale for the mistake.

I. In the MT of 1 Chr 1:32, we find a shorter reading than in the corresponding passage at Gen 25:3. The repetition of the word וּבְנֵי no doubt caused the loss (see H5 on chart). A similar omission took place in Greek. The witness of Codex Alexandrinus preserves the original reading, while Codex Vaticanus has suffered from haplography because of the repeated element και υιοι (see G5 on chart). However, even after MT is restored, it still is shorter than the restored LXX, which contains two extra names (Ραγουηλ και Ναβδαιηλ). These two names are evidenced in the Greek text at both 1 Chr 1:32 and Gen 25:3. In neither of these places do they appear in MT. Yet a repeated *waw* (*homoeogrammaton*) could explain the shorter variant (see H5 on chart).

J. The phrase וְאֹהֶל יְבָמָה בַּת עֲנָה is missing in MT at 1 Chr 1:41, as is seen by the testimony of Gen 36:25 and of LXX (Codex Alexandrinus). The omission is likely the result of a single letter *homoeoarcton* (וּבְנֵי . . . וְאָהֳלִיבָמָה). (See H6 on chart.) In Greek, Codex Vaticanus also omits this phrase (και Ελιβαμα θυγατηρ Ανα), which may have come about by the repetition of the word και, if the reading of Codex A is superior. Otherwise, the omission is difficult to explain (see G6 on chart).

K. In LXX, Codex A carries a longer reading than Codex B in 1 Chr 1:43; the former is supported by MT at both 1 Chr 1:43 and Gen 36:31 and by LXX at Gen 36:31 (see G7 on chart). There is no clear rationale for the omission, but so many witnesses urge us to accept the longer reading.

L. Another lengthy section consisting of 23 words is absent in Codex B of LXX, but present in Codex A. There can be no doubt that it is a case of haplography, since a repetition of four complete words (και εβασιλευσεν αντ αυτου) occurs precisely where we would expect a repetition (see G8 on chart).

M. The LXX has the patronym "son of Achbor" after the name Hanan in 1 Chr 1:50, whereas MT does not. The reading at Gen 36:39 suggests that the longer reading is preferable, although we cannot find a clear rationale for the omission (see H7 on chart).

N. Another patronym in the same verse is lacking in Codex A of LXX (υιος Βαραδ). The omitted elements can be explained by a *homoeoteleuton* of two letters (Αδαδ υιος Βαραδ). (See G9 on chart.) The corresponding phrase in Hebrew is missing also in MT. It's reading too was probably the result of a double *homoeoteleuton* (הדד בן ברד). (see H8 on chart).

O. Again in 1 Chr 1:50, the phrase και ονομα τη γυναικι αυτου Μεταβεηλ θυγατηρ Ματραδ is present in Codex A of LXX, but not Codex B. No doubt the omission resulted from the repetition of the word και (see G10 on chart).

P. The full reading of LXX in verse 50 is still somewhat shorter than MT. A Greek rendering of בת מי זהב is not present. There is no repeated element that can be blamed for the omission (see H9 on chart).

Q. A phrase of 13 words in verse 51, found in Codex B of LXX, is not attested in Codex A. The haplography occurred because the copyist's eye skipped from one και to another (see G11 on chart).

R. In verse 3 of Chapter 2, the sons of Judah are listed. It is notable that Er's punishment of death is recounted, but not that of Onan. In the Targums, such a statement is included. BHS suggests that a line fell out by accidental omission. The missing phrase would likely have read as follows: וגם אונן משנהן רע בעיני והוה וימתהן. The last four words of the line are identical to the last four words of the previous line and could easily be responsible for the error (see H10 on chart).

Our study of the text of 1 Chronicles has produced the following results: In MT (Codex L), the section has 472 words, while comparison with parallel texts and the testimony of the versions shows or indicates that many words have been lost during the process of scribal transmission. We calculate that 34 words have been omitted in MT and that the presumed original had a total of 506 words. In the Greek text, we find a considerable difference between Codex A and Codex B. Normally viewed as a superior text, Codex Vaticanus has a word count of 473, which we calculate to be 223 words short of a presumed original text! Codex Alexandrinus, on the other hand, has a count of 678 words, only 18 words less than the estimated total count of 696 for the original. Whether Codex A is simply a better representation of an older source than is B or is a "correction" of a defective text similar to B is not easy to tell. Nevertheless, its readings are superior to B, in this passage at least. These data allow us to reconstruct a hypothetical Hebrew *Vorlage* of LXX (LXX[H] in the charts), which turns out to be somewhat longer than MT, but still ten words short of a presumed original.

While the sample is relatively small, it reflects our experience with passages taken randomly from the books of the Bible. The Greek texts here considered range between a loss of 2.6% (Codex A) and an amazing 32.0% (Codex B). LXX's Hebrew source appears to be short by 2.0%. As far as MT is concerned, Codex L is missing 6.7% of the total word count. Coupling these data with that of our previous study on the MT of Genesis, the percentage of loss in Codex L ranges between 6.5 and 7.5. If a 7% figure is maintained for the entire Hebrew Bible, it would mean that at least 20,000 words have been lost or the equivalent of a book the size of Genesis or Psalms.

Variant Readings in the Greek Versions of 1 Chr 1:1–2:5 Showing Possible Instances of Haplography

(G1) 1:10–17

της γης και Μεσραιμ... και Αμαθι υιοι Σημ	A
υιοι Σημ	B

no rationale
63 missing words

(G2) 1:17–24

και Ασσουρ και Αρφαξαδ και Λουδ... υιοι Ιεκταν Σημ	Αρφαξαδ Σαλα	A
και Ασσουρ και	Αρφαξαδ Σαλα	B

B = *homoeologon* (Αρφαξαδ/Αρφαξαδ)
97 missing words

(G3) 1:20–21

και τον Αραμωθ και τον Ιαραδ και τον Κεδουραν	LXX^H (cf. Gen 10:26)
και τον Αραμωθ και γον Κεδουραν	A

B = double *homoeologon* (και τον/και τον)
3 missing words

(G4) 1:27

θαρα Αβραμ αυτος	Αβρααμ	A
θαρα	Αβρααμ	B

B = quadruple *homoeoarcton* (Αβρα-/Αβρα-)
2 missing words

(G5) 1:32–33

Σαβα και Δαιδαν	και υιοι Δαιδαν Ραγουηλ και Ναβδαιηλ ... και Ασσουειν	και υιοι Μαδιαμ	A
Δαιδαν και Σαβαι		και υιοι Μαδιαμ	B

B = double *homoeologon* (και υιοι/και υιοι)
12 missing words

(G6) 1:41
Δαισον και Ελιβαμα θυγατηρ Ανα   και υιοι Δαισον   A
Δαισον   υιοι δε Δαισον (original reading και υιοι Δαισον?)   B
B = *homoeologon* (και/και)?
4 missing words

(G7) 1:43
αυτου οι βασιλευσαντες εν Εδομ προ του βασιλευσαι βασιλεα τοις υιοις Ισραηλ Βαλακ   A
αυτου   Βαλακ   B
no rationale
11 missing words

(G8) 1:47–49
και εβασιλευσεν αντ αυτου Σαμαα εκ Μασεκκας απεθανεν . . . και εβασιλευσεν αντ αυτου   Βαλαεννω   A
και εβασιλευσεν αντ αυτου   Βαλαεννωρ   B
B = quadruple *homoeologon* (και εβασιλευσεν αντ αυτου/και εβασιλευσεν αντ αυτου)
23 missing words

(G9) 1:50
Αδαδ υιος Βαραδ   και ονομα   B
Αδαδ   και ονομα   A
A = double *homoeoteleuton* (-αδ/-αδ)
2 missing words

(G10) 1:50–51
Φογορ και ονομα τη γυναικι αυτου Μεταβεηλ θυγατηρ Ματραδ   και απεθανεν   A
Φογορ   και απεθανεν   B
B = *homoeologon* (και/και)
8 missing words

(G11) 1:51

Σαμαα και εβασιλευσεν αντ αυτου Σαουλ εκ Ροβωθ της παρα ποταμον και απεθανεν Σαουλ και ησαν B

Σαμαα και ησαν A

A = *homoeologon* (και/ και)

13 missing words

Codex Alexandrinus word count = 678
Codex Vaticanus word count = 473
Reconstructed original word count = 696
18 words missing from A = (2.6%)
223 words missing from B (32.0%)

Variant Readings of 1 Chr 1:1–2:5 in Hebrew Showing Possible Instances of Haplography

(H1) 1:3–4

לֶפֶךְ הֲ בְּנִ הֲ שֵׁם   LXX^H, MT (Gen 10:1)
לֶפֶךְ הֲ   MT

MT = *homoeologon* (הֲ/הֲ)
2 missing words

(H2) 1:10

אֶת נִמְרֹד הֵחֵל לִהְיוֹת צָיִד בָּאָרֶץ   LXX^H
בָּאָרֶץ לִהְיוֹת הֵחֵל   MT

MT = *homoeoteleuton* (ד-/ד-)
1 missing word

(H3) 1:17

וְלוּד וְאֲרָם וְעוּץ וְחוּל וְגֶתֶר וּמֶשֶׁךְ   LXX^H, MT (Gen 10:22–23)
וְלוּד וְאֲרָם   MT

MT = triple *homoeoteleuton* (אֲרָם/אֲרָם-)
2 missing words

(H4) 1:18

לוֹ אֶת קֵינָן וְקֵינָן יָלַד אֶת שֶׁלַח   LXX^H
אֶת שֶׁלַח   MT, MT (Gen 10:24)

MT = double *homoeologon* (אֶת יָלַד/אֶת יָלַד)
4 missing words

(H5) 1:32

ואת ידן ואת האישבן ואת אלדעה ואת המשה ואת דים ואת הדפלים ואת האבדים ואת מדין	LXXᴴ (1 Chr 1:32; Gen 25:34)
ואת ידן ואת שבא ואת הדפלים ואת האבדים ואת מדין	MT (Gen 25:34)
ואת דין	MT

MT (Gen 25:3)=*homoeogrammaton* (ן-/-ז)
2 missing words
MT = *homoeologon* (וכני/נבי)
6 or 8 missing words

(H6) 1:41

קלה מזר ומבד יתן חם ובני אלהביבזמה מזר ומבד יתן מזבר ובני דישון	LXXᴴ, MT (Gen 36:25–26)
ובני דישן	MT

MT = *homoeoarcton* (-ו/-ז)
3 missing words

(H7) 1:50

בכרו ודהב מן בעל דדר ודהב מלך	LXXᴴ, MT (Gen 36:39)
מן ודהב מלך	MT

MT = no rationale
2 missing words

(H8) 1:50

התהו דרד בן בעל משם ושם	LXXᴴ
התהו דרד ושם	MT, MT (Gen 36:39)

MT, A = double *homoeoteleuton* (רד-/רד-)
2 missing words

(H9) 1:50–51

שם מרד שה בן מן כ מה זרח בן אלשבעים ואשמ ושם ושם מרד שה בן   MT
ושם מרד שה   LXX^H

LXX^H = no rationale
3 missing words

(H10) 2:3–4

חמל ותהרהן יהד מעבד הר ושמה פן אתם הל ותהרהן יהד הר מעבד יהד ותהרהן   reconstructed text (cf. T, Gen 38:10)
ותהרהן יהד הר מעבד יהד ותהרהן   MT, LXX^H
חמל

MT, LXX^H = quadruple *homoeologon* (ותהרהן יהד מעבד הר/ותהרהן הר מעבד הר)
7 missing words

Leningrad word count = 472
LXX^H word count = 496
Reconstructed original word count = 506
34 words missing from Leningrad codex (6.7%)
10 words missing from LXX^H (2.0%)

THE PLACE OF THE PROPHECIES AGAINST THE NATIONS IN THE BOOK OF JEREMIAH

Menahem Haran

I

There are several striking differences between the MT and LXX versions of the Book of Jeremiah, the first of which is their size: MT is longer than LXX by about one-seventh, exceeding the latter by more than three thousand words. The Qumran discoveries demonstrated that the Greek of LXX was not an abridgement of the Hebrew of MT, but that two Hebrew editions of the Book of Jeremiah existed in parallel. Fragments of the Book of Jeremiah (4QJer[b,d]) from the Hasmonean period found in Qumran are quite proximate to the text of LXX, while other fragments (4QJer[a,c]; 2QJer), either pre- or postdating the Hasmoneans, closely resemble MT. Another major difference between the two versions is that the prophecies against the nations, that is, chaps. 46–51, in LXX follow 25:13, thus resulting in a different numbering of these chapters than in MT. Furthermore, the internal order of these prophecies in each of the versions is markedly disparate. In contrast with the order of MT: Egypt (two prophecies), Philistines, Moab, Ammon, Edom, Damascus, Kedar, Elam, and Babylon, the order of LXX is: Elam, Egypt (two prophecies), Babylon, Philistines, Edom, Ammon, Kedar, Damascus, and Moab. The fourth major difference between the two versions is that LXX seems to be divided into two parts: chaps. 1–28 and 29–52 (following the chapter numbers in the order of MT), with distinct differences between the Greek of each part.

As regards the disparity between the two parts of the Greek translation of Jeremiah, H. S. J. Thackeray determined that this was the work of two translators, with the second taking up where the first ended. The honoree of this Festschrift, E. Tov, posited a single translator, assuming, however, that with the introduction of the codex, a revision was made in the second part, that also included Baruch 1:1–3:8, while the first part was not handed over in this revised edition.[1]

---

[1] See: H. S. J. Thackeray, "The Greek Translation of Jeremiah," *JTS* 4 (1902–1903):

Tov's opinion may be supported by the fact that the division of LXX into two parts apparently had a tangible basis in the partition of this book into two scrolls, not necessarily into two codices. The Greek and Latin Bible translations were originally written on papyrus scrolls, the length of which was less than that of the parchment scrolls that made their entry into Jewish life in the Second Temple period and were used for the copying of Scripture.[2] The bipartite division of each of the Books of Samuel, Kings, and Chronicles is a legacy of the Greek and Latin renditions (as is well-known, the Rabbis were not cognizant of this division). Jeremiah is the fourth largest book in the Hebrew Bible, but its bisection in LXX did not take place in the Hebrew editions.[3]

Scholars who seek to explain the differences between MT and LXX in the internal order of the prophecies against the nations, as well as the question of their proper place as a group in Jeremiah, whether their location shifted from the center of the book (as in LXX) to the end, or whether, vice versa, they moved from the end of the book (as in MT) to its center, frequently find themselves perplexed, since every proposed solution is based upon pure conjecture. At this juncture, we will excuse ourselves from the need to explain how, and to what end, a change took place in the internal order of the prophecies. We will content ourselves with asking the question: Which of the two orders, as they are, seems more reasonable and authentic, that of LXX, or that of MT? The unescapable impression is that the MT provides the primary order, while LXX offers a sequence that is essentially secondary and artificial. A reason sufficient to justify this impression is the position of the prophecies against Babylon (50:1–51:58), that in MT follow all the other prophecies in this assemblage.

245–66; E. Tov, *The Septuagint Translation of Jeremiah and Baruch: A Discussion of an Early Revision of the LXX of Jeremiah 29–52 and Baruch 1:1–3:8* (Missoula, Montana, 1976).

[2] For the transition from papyrus, as the primary material for preparing scrolls in the First Temple period, to parchment during the Second Temple period, see my article: "Book-Scrolls at the Beginning of the Second Temple Period: The Transition from Papyrus to Skins," *HUCA* 54 (1983): 111–22.

[3] Jeremiah's position as the fourth largest book of the Hebrew Bible is proven by the number of words it contains, in comparison with the three books preceding Jeremiah in their size (cf. F. I. Anderson and A. D. Forbes, *The Vocabulary of the OT* [2nd ed.; Rome, 1992], 23–29): Kings—25,421; Samuel—24,301; Chronicles—24,059; Jeremiah—21,835. The next largest book after Jeremiah is Genesis, with 20,614 words. Thus, it is not surprising that the Berlin papyrus of Genesis is divided into two (see F. Kenyon, *Books and Readers in Ancient Greece and Rome*[2] [Oxford, 1951] [1970], 55, n. 1).

Indeed, these prophecies on Babylon stand out in their distinctive character, in the political-prophetic conception characterizing them, in their linguistic contacts with prophecies outside the Book of Jeremiah, in the absence of any Deuteronomistic touch in them, and it is quite obvious that initially they made up a separate scroll.

The distinctive existence of the prophecies against Babylon as a separate scroll is proved, among other things, by the short narrative that is attached to them (51:59–64) and relates that Jeremiah wrote "in one scroll all the disaster that would come upon Babylon." After this he requested Seraiah son of Neriah that upon his arrival in Babylon to read out "all these words" and throw "this scroll" into the Euphrates. In the ardor of enmity for Babylon, the prophecies in "this scroll" contradict Jeremiah's position in other parts of his book. All the prophecies in this scroll speak of the fall of Babylon, but in poetical images that were not realized literally in the historical conquest by Cyrus in 539 B.C.E. It appears that Babylon was perceived as a symbol of pagan pride even after its fall, with no connection with historical details.[4] The Deuteronomistic redaction did not interfere with the prophecies in this scroll, just because this scroll was incorporated into the Book of Jeremiah after the latter's Deuteronomistic editing. The relative lateness of this scroll is especially evident in the passages that are included in it, even though they appear in the previous chapters of Jeremiah (50:41–43; 50:44–46; 51:15–19). While this scroll existed independently by itself, the fact that several of its sections appear elsewhere posed no difficulty. These sections, however, did not prevent the appending of the scroll in its entirety to the Book of Jeremiah, thus resulting in the duplication of passages. Since the prophecies about Babylon were initially an independent scroll, it is fitting that they come after chaps. 46–49 (which apparently also had been primarily an autonomous scroll). In LXX, however, these prophecies are located in the first part of the group of prophecies against the nations (46–51), where their position, between the prophecies about Egypt and the Philistines, is clearly out of place, and they certainly did not belong there originally.[5]

---

[4] Cf. W. McKane, *Jeremiah* (ICC) (Edinburgh, 1996), 1285, who, following R. P. Carroll, points out rightly that "Babylon as a symbol of imperial hubris inviting Yahweh's revenge probably had a life of its own disengaged from precise historical moorings."

[5] This opinion that the MT internal order of the prophecies against the nations

II

Let us now focus on the question of the place of the prophecies against the nations within the Book of Jeremiah, and which of the two arrangements is the more correct. Some scholars refrain from expressing an opinion on this question. Since, however, LXX contains many good readings, while the additional material in MT is frequently taken to be expansions, many scholars take for granted that the order in LXX is superior regarding the place of the prophecies in the book as well.[6] Rudolph made a distinction of four typological divisions within the Book of Jeremiah, but, following the prevalent convention, he preferred to base the four divisions on the LXX order, a preference that proved to be detrimental. Rudolph's partition of the Book of Jeremiah into four divisions is as follows:

1) 1:1–25:14 are, according to his definition, prophecies of doom, *Unheils Weissagungen*. Thus, the first half of chap. 25 becomes a continuation of this division.
2) Chaps. 46–51 (according to their numbering in MT) as well as 25:15–38 are prophecies of doom to the nations.
3) The chapters from 26 (sic! [see below]) to 35 are prophecies of salvation, *Heilsweissagungen* for Israel and Judah.
4) Chaps. 36–45 consist of the narrative by Baruch relating the tribulations of Jeremiah.[7]

---

is preferable to that of LXX is also shared by, e.g., A. W. Streane, *Jeremiah* (CBSC) (Cambridge, 1913) (1952), 262, and W. L. Holladay, *Jeremiah 2* (Hermeneia) (Minneapolis, 1989), 5, 313–14. See also J. G. Janzen, *Studies in the Text of Jeremiah* (Cambridge, Mass., 1973), 115.

[6] Thus, e.g., Janzen, loc. cit.; E. Tov, "The Literary History of the Book of Jeremiah in the Light of its Textual History," in *Empirical Models for Biblical Criticism* (ed. J. H. Tigay; Philadelphia, 1985), 217, although he is well aware of the difficulty in explaining how the prophecies were moved from the middle of Jeremiah to the end of the book. Similarly W. Rudolph, *Jeremia*³ (HAT) (Tübingen, 1968), XIX–XX; C. Rietzschel, *Das Problem der Urrolle* (Gütersloh, 1966), esp. pp. 16–17; R. P. Carroll, *Jeremiah* (OTL) (London, 1986), 757–59. Holladay (*Jeremia 2*, loc. cit.) also prefers MT on the internal order of the prophecies, and LXX on the question of their place in the Book of Jeremiah. His strange opinion (p. 314) is, however, that "the turmoil of the Maccabean revolt is the setting for both [changes]," that of the internal order of the prophecies and that of their place in the book—as if social and military upheaval has to be the reason for the "turmoil," or the two "turmoils," in the arrangement of a book.

[7] See Rudolph, op. cit., p. XIX.

This partition is basically acceptable to me, albeit with certain amendments. First of all, the first division contains not only prophecies of doom, but also reproaches, since the reproaches at times preface predictions of doom, so that the two cannot be detached from each other.[8] Secondly, the partition into four typological divisions is not restricted to the Book of Jeremiah and, in principle, it underlies the arrangement of all the Books of the Latter Prophets. Moreover, from the aspect of contents, prophecies cannot be sorted out into more than those four types. If a prophecy is directed to Israel, it can be of either positive or negative content (containing reproaches and doom). It is possible, however, that it is not addressed to Israel at all, and it then becomes a prophecy to the nations. If it is not a prophecy at all, but rather a narrative of what happened to the prophet, we come to the fourth category of Rudolph's classification (which is why it is preferable to apply to the fourth category the general appellation: "narratives about the prophet"). Not all four types, however, have been preserved for every prophet. Some books of the latter prophets contain only three division-types, others, only two, while yet others have only a single such division (for instance, the Book of Nahum consists solely of prophecies on the nations). Needless to say, a single literary unit may contain expressions of both doom and consolation. In such cases, the center of gravity may be determined, with an according decision in which division the unit should be included. The compilers of the Books of Latter Prophets undoubtedly acted in such a manner.[9]

Thirdly, the partition of Jeremiah into typological divisions in accordance with the LXX order misses the mark. In the Book of Jeremiah this partition is based on MT, the order of whose chapters (as distinct from the text itself) is authentic and correct. The typological divisions of Jeremiah, according to MT, are as follows: (1)

---

[8] Thus, e.g., concerning the two passages: 9:22–23, 24–25, Rudolph (op. cit., p. XX) declares that he was incapable of finding a reasonable cause for their placement here, that is, in this division of prophecies. These passages, however, possess an element of reproach ("But only in this should one glory [. . .] for in these I delight"; "but all the House of Israel are uncircumcised of heart"), and the reproaches are a preface to doom. The term that Rudolph applied to this division, *Unheils Weissagungen*, "prophecies of doom" (without reproaches) misled him.

[9] See, provisionally, my observations in *Ages and Institutions in the Bible* (Tel Aviv, 1972), pp. 269–80 (Hebrew). An elaborate discussion will be devoted to this issue in the second part of my work *The Biblical Collection* (Hebrew), to be published shortly.

chaps. 1–26, the division of reproaches and doom; (2) chaps. 27–35, prophecies of consolation; (3) chaps. 36–45, narratives; and (4) chaps. 46–51, prophecies against the nations (chapter 52 is an appendix assembled and arranged by the Deuteronomistic School in order to demonstrate that Jeremiah's predictions came true).

The twisted character of Rudolph's partition of Jeremiah into typological divisions is evident in his attempt to ascribe chap. 26 to the "prophecies of salvation." The content of this chapter, containing the speech by Jeremiah in the Temple court in which he destines the Temple and Jerusalem to the fate of Shiloh, and for which he was about to be put to death, is the diametrical opposite of the promise of salvation. In order to resolve this absurdity, Rudolph would have us believe that in chap. 26 Jeremiah is acknowledged as a true prophet, and this therefore serves as a sort of prelude to what is related in chaps. 27–28 concerning Jeremiah's struggle with the false prophets.[10] The truth of the matter is, however, that Jeremiah is not acknowledged as a true prophet in chap. 26, since the Temple has not yet been destroyed, but only his right to be a prophet of doom is admitted (he was allowed, as it were, to "talk" as much as he wished). If it had not been for the officials, especially Aḥikam son of Shaphan and the people, who saved him from the hands of the prophets and priests, he would have been executed. It is inconceivable that such a chapter be accounted as part of the division of consolations. Rudolph was forced to define chap. 26 as a prophecy of "salvation" because in LXX it is preceded by the prophecies against the nations, and following it begin the prophecies containing an element of consolation. Thus the chapter is isolated from the group to which it naturally belongs, severed as it is by the intervening prophecies against the nations, and ostensibly connected to the prophecies of consolation. The attempt by Rudolph only proves the flawed nature of the foundation on which he sought to rest the partition into four divisions. That is to say, the apportioning into four divisions, in itself, is not incorrect. It is quite correct, but it cannot be based on the LXX order of the chapters, which is mechanical and derivative.

The mechanical and secondary nature of the chapter order in LXX could be confirmed by the fact that the second half of chap. 25 (vv.

---

[10] Rudolph, op. cit., p. XX.

15–38), that according to LXX and Rudolph's opinion constitutes a conclusion to the prophecies on the nations, turns to, and addresses, Jerusalem and the cities of Judah and the Judean kings and officials (v. 18; cf. v. 29) and also the neighboring nations round about. This half of the chapter bears no resemblance to the prophecies against the nations as a genre (that, at least in the Book of Jeremiah, is directed to each of the nations separately). It goes without saying that the first half of this chapter (vv. 1–13; v. 14 is absent from LXX), according to MT and LXX, is the patent continuation of the prophecies of doom on Israel, and this is its simple meaning. A minor turning point, however, occurs in v. 9, where the text is directed not only to "this land" and its inhabitants, but *also* to "all these [*ha'ēleh*, absent from LXX] nations round about." This dual address, to Judah and to its neighbors, is carried on in the second half of the chapter, thus attesting to the unity and internal continuity of this chapter as it is in MT, with its massive Deuteronomistic overload. The Greek translators of Jeremiah apparently assumed that the text in v. 13: ". . . all that is written in this book, all that Jeremiah prophesied about [*'al*] all [*kol*, but absent from LXX] the nations" refers to what is stated at the beginning of the group of prophecies on the nations (46:1: ". . . the word of the Lord to the prophet Jeremiah about [*'al*] the nations"), and allowed themselves to take a shortcut. "In this book" (25:13), *bassēfer hazzeh*, with the assimilation of the defining *h* before *sēfer* and the demonstrative pronoun, was taken by them as referring to the group of prophecies on the nations, so that they shifted this group into chap. 25.

But the phrase "in this book" of Jer 25:13 does not refer to the group of prophecies against the nations. This is one of the instances in which the substantive *sēfer, hassēfer* appears in several places in the Book of Jeremiah, in each case implying a certain scroll to which the statements in that context refer (cf. Jer 29:1; 30:2; 51:60, 63). Chapter 45, at the beginning of which mention also is made of "writing these words in a *sēfer*" (v. 1), is a fragment from Baruch's scroll of the fourth year of Jehoiakim, a portion from the *end* of that scroll, that reached the editor after its text had already come under the hand of the Deuteronomist. In just the same way, 25:1–13 (and, in fact, chap. 25 in its entirety) is the product of Deuteronomistic patching and expansions, but its initial core is also a fragment that survived from Baruch's scroll of the fourth year of Jehoiakim. This belonged at the scroll's *beginning*, not at its end. The reference to "all that is written in this book, all that Jeremiah has prophesied" in verse 13 of this chapter is one of the remnants of the wording of Baruch's scroll, and it is to that scroll that this verse refers. "About [all] the nations" at the end of the verse is apparently from the quill of the Deuteronomist.[11] Consequently, the appearance of the prophecies against the nations in the middle of chap. 25 in LXX of Jeremiah is a secondary insertion, mechanical in nature, and restricted to the transmission of this translation. It therefore does not seem that the order of the chapters of Jeremiah in LXX could serve as a correct basis for an examination of the typological divisions in this book. The readings of LXX, however, as opposed to the chapter order, are frequently very good, and at times are superior to those of MT.

---

[11] Scholarly opinion is divided regarding the question of whether or not the scroll of Baruch from the fourth year of Jehoiakim contained prophecies on the nations, and if its contents can be determined with certainty. Nonetheless, it is noteworthy that Jer 25:1–8 is addressed solely to Judah and Jerusalem, who have been warned by the Lord for "these twenty-three years," but they have not heeded Him. Only beginning with v. 9 is the threat of destruction by "the peoples of the north" and the king of Babylon (Nebuchadrezzar) extended to "all the nations," and is expressed in phrases typical of the Deuteronomistic diction. According to Jer 36:2, as well, Jeremiah is commanded to collect all that the Lord had told him "about Israel [LXX: Jerusalem] and Judah," while the words, "and all the nations" are widely thought to be a Deuteronomistic addition. That is to say, we possess no evidence of the inclusion of prophecies about the nations in Baruch's scroll from the fourth year of Jehoiakim, and it is highly plausible that it contained no such prophecies. This does not prove, however, that the prophecies about the nations in the Book of Jeremiah are not authentic, or that they lack any authentic element. Prophecies about the nations, formulated in an impersonal language and containing no allusion to the personality of the prophet, could also belong to Jeremiah, as they do to other prophets.

"LEBANON" IN THE TRANSITION FROM DERASH TO PESHAT: SOURCES, ETYMOLOGY AND MEANING (WITH SPECIAL ATTENTION TO THE SONG OF SONGS)

Sara Japhet

The name "Lebanon," basically a name of a "wooded mountain-range on the northern border of Israel"[1] is employed already in the Bible, by itself or in compound phrases, in multiple literary tropes: as a simile,[2] metonymy,[3] metaphor,[4] and allegory.[5] It is therefore not surprising that this usage continues in the post-biblical literature, either in the same functions (like the Wisdom of Jesus Sirach)[6] or in further allegorical developments. We find such usage in the writings of the Qumran sect and the Targum literature, and later in the Midrash, in all its literary manifestations.

The dominant allegory for "Lebanon" in later sources, not explicitly found in the biblical texts, is that of "Temple" (בית מקדשא). This understanding of the name is probably already underlying the well-

---

[1] BDB, 527.

[2] As in Ps 92:13: "The righteous bloom like a date-palm, they thrive like a cedar in Lebanon"; or Song 7:5: "your neck is like a tower of ivory . . . Your nose like the Lebanon tower," and more. The English translation of the biblical texts generally follows NJPS.

[3] As in Isa 10:34: "And the Lebanon shall fall" (meaning: the trees of Lebanon); or Hos 14:6: "He shall strike roots like the Lebanon"—again, the Lebanon tree (as indeed represented by the NJPS), and more.

[4] As in Jer 22:6: "You are Gilead to me, the summit of Lebanon" (the NJPS adds twice "as"); or Jer 22:23: "You who dwell in Lebanon, nestled among the cedars," and more.

[5] As in 2 Kgs 14:9 (= 2 Chr 25:18); Ezek 17:3–24; 31:3, and more.

[6] See Sir 24:10; 50:8–9; 50:12. Vermès compares the usage here to that of the Targum of the Song of Songs: "in Ecclesiasticus, as in the Targum of the Song of Songs, the word Lebanon is used in relation to the Temple," but I fail to see this connection, either between Sirach and the (late) Targum of the Song of Songs, or of Sirach to the Temple. The use of the simile is similar to its use in the biblical phrases. (See: Géza Vermès, "Lebanon: The Historical Development of an Exegetical Tradition", in *Scripture and Tradition in Judaism* (StPB 4; (Leiden and New York: E. J. Brill, 1961), 26–39. The quotation is from p. 31. The article is a revised and elaborated version of an earlier work; see: Géza Vermès, "The Symbolic Interpretation of Lebanon in the Targums," *JTS*, N.S. 9 (1958): 1–12.

known statement of Pesher Habakkuk: "The Lebanon is the council of the community (כי הלבנון הוא עצת היחד)."[7] The route that led to this equation has been correctly illuminated by Géza Vermès as the combining of two interpretative axioms: Lebanon = Temple, and Temple = the Community.[8]

In the Aramaic Targums some of the representations of "Lebanon" simply spell out the tenor, the signified meaning, of the biblical metaphors,[9] such as "those who make war against the land of Israel" (Isa 10:34); "kings" (Ezek 31:15); or "nations" (Zech 11:1). "Cedars of Lebanon" are represented by "leaders of nations" (Isa 2:13), or "those who own much property" (Isa 14:8), and the latter represents also the "good of Lebanon" (Ezek 31:16).[10] However, the Temple as the symbolic value of "Lebanon" is the dominant feature in the Aramaic Targums.

The name Lebanon appears three times in the Pentateuch, another twenty-three times in the prose sections of Joshua, Judges, Kings, Ezra, and Chronicles; seven times in the poetic passages of Judges and Kings, and thirty-eight times in the poetry of the Prophets and the Hagiographa: in Isaiah, Jeremiah, Ezekiel, Nahum, Habakkuk, Zechariah, Psalms, and the Song of Songs.

Targum Onkelos represents the name "Lebanon" by its equivalent Aramaic form ליבן in two of its occurrences in the Pentateuch (Deut 1:7; 11:24), while in the third occurrence (Deut 3:25) it is represented by the allegorical meaning, "the Temple." The words of Moses: "Let me, I pray, cross over and see the good land on the other side of the Jordan, that good hill country, and the Lebanon"

---

[7] 1QpHab 12:3–4; See Géza Vermès, "Car le Liban c'est le Conseil de la Communauté," in Mélange Bibliques rédigés en l'honneur de André Robert (Paris: Bloud and Gay, 1957), 316–25. For a follow-up of Vermés study regarding the Ancient Christian exegesis, see: H. F. D. Sparks, "The Symbolical Interpretation of Lebanon in the Fathers," *JTS* N.S. 10 (1959): 254–79.

[8] Ibid, 324–5. Also idem, *Scripture and Tradition*, 32–33. This evidence refutes the former view that the allegory was first introduced by Rabbi Johanan ben Zakkai, after the destruction of the second Temple in 70 c.e. See Yehuda Komlosh, *The Bible in the Light of the Aramaic Translations* (Tel Aviv: Dvir Publishing House, 1973 [Hebrew]), 229, following Wilhelm Bacher, *Die Agadah der Tannaiten* (Strassburg: K. J. Trubner, 1884), 26, n. 2. According to Vermés, the homily of Johanan ben Zakkai represents a transformation of the tradition rather than its origin (*Scripture and Tradition*, 34–35).

[9] As is the standard procedure in the Targums; see, among others, Komlosh, *Aramaic Translations*, 230–238.

[10] עתידי נכסיא; רברבני עממיא; עממיא; מלכיא; ועבדי קרבא על ארעא דישראל respectively.

are translated by Onkelos as: "the good land on the other side of the Jordan, that good hill country and the Temple (וּבֵית מקדשא)." The Palestinian Targum to the Pentateuch (Pseudo-Jonathan) has this allegorical sense in all three occurrences of Lebanon in the Pentateuch, phrased differently in each case, and standing side by side with the literal equivalent: "and Lebanon, the place of the mountains of the Temple" (בית מקדשא ולבנן אתר טוורי; Deut 1:7); "the mountain of Lebanon, where the Shekina is to dwell" (עתיד למישרי שכינתא טוור לבנן דביה; 3:25); and "the mountains of the Lebanon are the mountains of the Temple" (הנון טוורי בית מקדשא וטוור לבנן; 11:24).

In the Jonathan Targum to the Prophets and in the Targum to the Hagiographa, the picture is similar to that of Onkelos, that is, mixed. In the Former Prophets (with the exception of 2 Kgs 19:23, parallel to Isa 37:24), in the Targum of Chronicles, and in all of the occurrences of the name in the Psalms, the translation is always literal.[11] In the other parts of the Prophets there is an alternation between the literal meaning, represented by the Aramaic form of the name (לבנן),[12] the various spelling-outs of the poetic tropes illustrated above,[13] and most frequently, the standard allegorical equivalent "Temple:" in Isa 37:24 = 2 Kgs 19:23; Jer 22:20, 23; Hos 14:8; Hab 2:17; Zech 10:10.[14] The same picture is found also in the late midrashic Targum of the Song of Songs:[15] the Targum has the literal meaning in 3:9; a double interpretation, both literal and allegorical, in 4:15 ("water that flows from Lebanon . . . the Temple in Jerusalem called Lebanon"); the Temple in 4:8; and other metaphorical

---

[11] See Josh 1:4; 9:1; 11:17; 12:7; 13:5, 6; Judg 3:3; 9:15; 1 Kgs 5:20, 23, 28; 9:19; 2 Kgs 14:9 (three times).; 2 Chr 2:7, 15; 8:6; 25:18 (three times); Ps 29:5, 6; 72:16; 92:13; 104:16. However, 'The Lebanon Forest' (בית יער הלבנון) in 1 Kgs 7:2; 10:17, 21 and in the parallels of the last two in 2 Chr 9:16, 20, is represented as "The house of the kings' cooling" (בית מקירת מלכיא), that is, the kings summer house, reflecting perhaps the coolness of the Lebanon forests.

[12] Such as Isa 29:17; 35:2; 40:16; 60:13; Jer 18:14; Ezek 17:3; 27:5; 31:3; Hos 14:6; Nah 1:4.

[13] P. 00.

[14] In Jer 22:6 "the Temple" is the equivalent of "Gilead," while "the summit of Lebanon" is represented by: "the summit of the mountains." It seems that in the version of the *Sipre* (section 6) both names are taken to refer to the Temple. Vermès sees this meaning of the name Lebanon already in the Targum (*Scripture and Tradition*, 29).

[15] See: Ezra Zion Melammed, "The Targum of the Song of Songs," *Tarbiz* 40 (1971): 201–15; Komlosh, *Aramaic Translations*, 77–81; Raphael J. Loewe, "Apologetic Motives in the Targum of the Song of Songs," *Studies and Texts* III (Cambridge: Harvard University Press, 1966), 159–96.

representations in 5:5 and 7:5. In 4:11 the Targum testifies to a variant reading, for which see below.[16] Although the rendering of Lebanon as "Temple" is not attested in the Bible itself, the antiquity and broad diffusion of this tradition seem self-evident.[17]

This allegorical representation of the name Lebanon is manifest throughout the Midrashic literature, in various combinations and elaborations.[18] In certain cases, the allegory is substantiated by a word-play on the name Lebanon, in line with the traditional practice of homiletic literature. The most common basis for the word-play is the combination of a literal interpretation and a metaphorical one: the etymology of the name in the root לבן = white, and Isaiah's prophecy in 1:18: "Be your sins like crimson, They can turn snow-white:" "Why is it called Lebanon? Because it turns white the sins of Israel" (שמלבין עוונותיהם של ישראל).[19] Other, less frequent, word-plays take their clue from the word לב = heart: "Why is it called Leba-

---

[16] Song 4:11; see p. 721, n. 52.

[17] Vermès suggests that the origin of this explanation is the association of Deut 3:25 with Isa 40:13 and Ps 92:13–14, which received its impulse from the canonization of the Song of Songs. His conclusion is based on the fact that "[The Song of Songs] is the only post-exilic book of the Bible in which Lebanon has special importance" and on the assertion that "since it was inserted into the canon of the Scripture . . . this must surely have been on the basis of its symbolical significance" (*Scripture and Tradition*, 37–38). Although the claim that the symbolic understanding of the Song preceded its canonization may be true, it does not necessarily apply to each individual allegorical detail in the book. The understanding of Lebanon as Temple is neither attested nor hinted in the occurrences of the name in the Song of Songs. Moreover, the verses from the Song play only a marginal role in this specific homiletic tradition. They are alluded to in the context of this tradition quite late in the Midrashic literature: in the *Song of Songs Rabbah* and *Zuta*, in the Aramaic Targum of the book, and in *Exodus Rabbah* (23:5, on Song 4:8). All these seem to be derivatives of the already established tradition rather than its origin. The origin of this allegory is explained by Rabbi Joseph Bechor Shor of the 12th century in his comment on Deut 3:26 (referring to v. 25): "Onkelos . . . translated 'and the Lebanon' the Temple, because it was built from the trees of Lebanon."

[18] See, among others: *Abot R. Nat.* Version A, 4; Version B, 7, 25; *Mek. de Rabbi Ishmael*, Amalek, Beshalach, 2. (ET: J. Z. Lauterbach, *Mekilta de-Rabbi Ishmael*, Philadelphia: Jewish Publication Society, 1933); *Mek. de-Rabbi Simon Bar Johai*, 17:14; *Siphre, Num*, 134; *Siphre Deut*, 6; 28; *Gen Rabbah*, 15:2; *Exod Rabbah*, 35:1; *Lev Rabbah*, 1:2; *Num Rabbah*, 8:1; 12:4; *Song Rabbah* 3:3; *Song Zuta*, 4:8; *b. Yoma* 21:2; 39:2; *b. Git* 56:2; *y. Yoma*, 4:4; 6:3; and more. It is attested also in the Christian exegetical tradition. For early examples, see Sparks (above note 7), 271. For later examples, see A. Saltman, "Jewish Exegetical Material in Alexander Nequam's Commentary on the Song of Songs," in *The Bible in the Light of its Interpreters: Sarah Kamin Memorial Volume* (ed. Sara Japhet; Jerusalem: Magnes Press, 1994), 436.

[19] *Abot R. Nat.*, Version B, 25; *Siphre Deut*, 6; *Lev Rabbah* 1:2 (In the name of Rabbi Shimon Bar Johai); *b. Yoma* 39:2; and more.

non? . . . Rabbi Tabyumi says: Because all hearts are happy with it, as it is said: 'Fair crested, joy of the earth,' etc. (Ps 48:3). The Rabbis say: Because it is said: 'My eyes and My heart shall ever be there' (1 Kgs 9:3)."[20]

It should be mentioned, however, that although "Temple" is certainly the dominant allegorical interpretation of "Lebanon" throughout the midrashic literature, it was not the only one; next to it are "King," "Jerusalem," and "the Torah."[21]

The allegorical representations of the name "Lebanon" dominated the field of biblical interpretation in the many centers of Jewish learning as long as the homiletic method was the vehicle of interpretation. However, with the emergence and consolidation of the "plain meaning" (Peshat)[22] school, these long-standing methods and traditions had to give way to whatever the plain meaning demanded: a straightforward geographical designation in some texts, or the representation of the tenor of the poetical tropes as determined by the context, in others. Without aiming at a complete picture of this process, I will try to illustrate the method followed by the major representatives of this school. The discussion of this single, rather limited item may uncover some of the broader characteristics of the Peshat school and its important protagonists.

Defined in the broadest lines, there were three major schools of Peshat exegesis in the classical period of Jewish exegesis: in Spain (including other communities under Arabic cultural influence, such as Mesopotamia); Northern France/Ashkenaz; and Provence.[23] Of

---

[20] *Lev Rabbah*, 1:2 and parallels; for the etymology 'brick' (לבנה), see *Exod Rabbah*, 23:5.

[21] For Lebanon meaning king, or kingdoms, see: *Siphre, Deut*, 6, *Tanaitic Midrash to Deuteronomy*, 1:7; *Exod Rabbah*, 23:5. For Jerusalem, see *Song Zuta* 1:1: "Jerusalem was called seventy names: Jerusalem, Shalom . . . Jebus, Gilead, Lebanon, Zion, etc." The Targum of the Song of Songs to 7:5: "The citadel of Zion which is called the tower of Lebanon." For Torah, see *Exod Rabbah*, 17:2; *Song Rabbah* 4:2 and more.

[22] I am using the rather ambiguous term "plain meaning" for the untranslatable Hebrew/Aramaic term Peshat. The more commonly used terms "literal meaning" or "contextual meaning" are misleading, in that they refer only to partial aspects of the Peshat. Peshat may be "literal" but also figurative, and "context" is certainly of significance in the establishment of the Peshat, but is just one of the factors which determine it. "Plain" in this term is not "simple" but rather the text as it is. For a broader definition, see Sarah Kamin, *Rashi's Exegetical Categorization in Respect to the Distinction between Peshat and Derash* (Jerusalem: Magnes Press, 1986), 268.

[23] See the general review of these schools, as well as other aspects of Jewish exegesis, in Moshe Greenberg, ed., *Jewish Bible Exegesis, An Introduction* (Jerusalem: Mosad

the works of the two most important representatives of the Spanish school, R. Saʿadia Gaon and Abraham Ibn Ezra, I found no comment on this matter in Saʿadia's commentary on the Pentateuch, while Ibn Ezra displays only limited interest in the subject. Ibn Ezra is strict in his adherence to the Peshat, and as the need may arise, explains briefly the tenor of the biblical simile or metaphor, alluding to the strength or magnitude of the cedars in Lebanon.[24]

The point of departure for the French/Ashkenazi school are the commentaries of Rashi, who refers to the meaning of Lebanon several times. By and large, Rashi's comments follow the example of the Babylonian Targums, Onkelos to the Pentateuch and Jonathan to the Prophets. Differently from the Targums, however, he is not compelled to render a full representation of the text, and comments only on selective verses. He refers to the geographical position of Lebanon once, rather vaguely, in his comment on Josh 13:5, where he adduces the geographical orientation from the context, the proximity of Lebanon to Lebo' Hamath: "And on the eastern side, what was left to conquer in the north was all the Lebanon, from Baal Gad . . . this is all the northern side, for Lebo' Hamath is in the northwestern side [as mentioned] in 'these were the marches' (that is, Num 33.)" In several more verses Rashi offers a literal meaning, mainly in the wake of the Aramaic Targums.[25] Most of Rashi's interpretations, however, are metaphorical or allegorical, and draw heavily on the Targumic and Midrashic traditions. In certain cases he

---

Bialik, ²1992). Another center of Jewish interpretation, which has only recently begun to be known, are the communities of Greek speaking Jews in the Byzantine empire. See Nicholas de Lange, *Greek Jewish Texts from the Cairo Genizah* (Tübingen: J. C. B. Mohr, 1996); Yisrael M. Ta-Shma, "Early Byzantine Hebrew Bible Exegesis, from Around 1000 C.E., from the Genizah," *Tarbiz* 69 (2000): 247–256; Richard C. Steiner, *The Byzantine Commentaries from the Genizah: A "Missing Link" in the Evolution of Biblical Exegesis* (forthcoming). The Italian school may then be related to the Byzantine rather than the other schools of exegesis.

[24] He does not comment on the occurrences of Lebanon in the Pentateuch, and has only short remarks on Isa 10:34; 29:17; 40:16; 60:13; Hab 2:17; Ps 29:5; 72:16; 92:13; 104:16. In the Song of Songs he comments only on 5:15: "'His aspect is like Lebanon': he is nice to look at," and then in the allegorical section of the commentary: "There are trees without number in the Lebanon . . . and when one sees one tree he may think that it is incomparable to any other, but if he walks further in the Lebanon he may find more wonderful and significant ones . . . these are the deeds of God."

[25] As on Isa 29:17 ("Lebanon is a forest of trees"); 60:13 ("these are the names of the trees in the forest of Lebanon"); Ezek 27:5 ("a name of a forest where cedars are found"); Hos 14:6; and Ps 29:6 ("Lebanon and Sirion are names of mountains").

may try to uncover the tenor of the poetic trope, either specific to the context or by the standard homiletic equivalent, Temple. These interpretations may include an explicit reference to the Aramaic Targum,[26] follow the Targum with no reference,[27] suggest different interpretations derived from other homiletic sources[28] or are Rashi's own.[29]

In his commentary to the Song of Songs Rashi follows the same method.[30] However, although the Temple (and the Tabernacle) plays an important role in this commentary, it is not connected with the name Lebanon. Of the seven occurrences (in six verses) of the name Lebanon in the book, Rashi ignores "the trees of Lebanon" in 3:9; in three verses (4:15; 5:15; 7:5) he provides the interpretation of the poetical trope in accord with the specific context.[31] The traditional equivalent "Temple" is presupposed only once, following a rather less-known homily. Rashi explains the lover's address in 4:8 "From Lebanon come with me, from Lebanon my bride, with me" as follows: "When you are exiled from this Lebanon you will be exiled with me, because I will go into exile with you . . . And when you come back from exile I will come with you . . . from the time of your going out from here until the time of your coming back here,

---

[26] I.e. 1 Kgs 7:2 ("Jonathan translated: the house of the kings' cooling"); Zech 11:1: "Jonathan translated: nations, open your gates."

[27] I.e. 2 Kgs 19:23 (= Isa 37:24: "Temple"); Isa 2:13 ("'The cedars of Lebanon': it is a metaphor [דונמא] for the strong ones"); Jer 22:6, 20; Hos 14:7–8 (the Aramaic text referring to the Temple is quoted); Hab 2:17; Zech 10:10 (Temple).

[28] I.e. 2 Kgs 14:9: "'The thistle of Lebanon:' Shechem the son of Hamor; 'sent to the cedar': Jacob;" Nah 1:4: "The sages of Israel interpreted it in regard to all sorts of fruits which Solomon planted in the Temple . . ."

[29] These seem to be a minority among his comments; see Isa 10:34: "'Lebanon': the bulk of his forest and vineyards are the majority of his troops"; Isa 35:2 "'Lebanon': The temple" (Jonathan: literally: יקר לבנן).

[30] For the uniqueness of Rashi's commentary among his exegetical works, see Sarah Kamin, "דונמא in Rashi's Commentary on the Song of Songs," Tarbiz 52 (1983): 41–58 (reprinted in idem: Jews and Christians Interpret the Bible (Jerusalem: Magnes Press, 1991), 13–30; Idem, "Rashi's Commentary on the Song of Songs and Jewish-Christian Polemic," in Moshe Weinfeld (ed.) Shnaton, An Annual for Bible and the Ancient Near East, 7–8 (1983–1984), 218–48 (reprinted in Jews and Christians, 31–61). Also idem, Rashi, 247–62.

[31] 4:15: "'Flowing waters from Lebanon': from a clean place, where there is no muddiness;" (5:15): "His appearance is tall, like the cedars of Lebanon." For 7:5 he offers several comments, "He speaks about the forehead . . . your forehead is strong . . .," ending with a citation from the Midrash: "I saw in the Midrash: this is the Lebanon Forest House that Solomon built; anyone standing on it may see and count the houses in Damascus."

I am with you. . . ." In this context, Lebanon as Temple is presupposed by the preceding "mountain of myrrh" (v. 6) interpreted (following *Gen Rabbah* 55:7; Rashi to Gen 22:2) as "the mountain of
Moriah, the eternal House," and by the contents of the homily.
Although the main point of the interpretation is drawn from the
Midrash, the phrasing is Rashi's own.[32] On 4:11 Rashi offers his
own allegorical interpretation, for which I have not found as yet any
midrashic source.[33] Rabbi Joseph Kara, the younger contemporary
of Rashi and one of the pillars of Peshat exegesis in northern France,
displays a similar picture to that of Rashi, at least as could be learned
from his extant commentaries.[34] In several comments he presents the
literal meaning of Lebanon: geographically in his comment on Ezek
27:5: "'They took a cedar from Lebanon:' . . . Because Lebanon is
near Tyre, as we learned from the book of Kings . . .," as "a forest
of trees" in Isa 29:17 (assumed also in 37:24; 40:16). More often,
however, he presents the tenor of the poetic tropes—similes, or
metaphors—either following Jonathan's Targum or providing his own
interpretation.[35] In three occurrences of the name Lebanon Kara
represents its meaning as "Temple." After explaining literally the
names Gilead and Lebanon in Jer 22:6, as denoting the land of

---

[32] The source may have been either *Exod Rabbah* 23:5 or *Song Zuta* 4:8.

[33] "'And the scent of your robes': worthy commandments relating to your robes:
blue fringes, priestly vestments and the prohibition of Sha'atnez" (cloth combining
wool and linen). In the matter of "Lebanon" there are no contacts between Rashi's
interpretations and the Aramaic Targum, in stark contrast to his practice in both
the Pentateuch and the Prophets.

[34] Relevant to our discussion are his commentaries on the Prophets (from which
only Jeremiah is missing). For the proposal to identify Kara as the author of one
of the anonymous commentaries on the Song of Songs, see below p. 000). On his
life and works see, Samuel Poznanski, *Kommentar zu Ezechiel und den XII Kleinen
Propheten von Eliezer aus Beaugency* (Warsaw: Druck von H. Eppelberg, 1913), XXV–
XXXIX (Hebrew); Moshe M. Ahrend, *Le Commentaire sur Job de Rabbi Yoseph Qara'*
(Hildesheim: Gerstenberg, 1978), 1–25, Avraham Grossman, *The Early Sages of France:
their Lives, leadership and Works* (Jerusalem: Magnes Press, 1995), 254–346 (Hebrew).

[35] Thus, in commenting on 1 Kgs 7:2: "'The Lebanon Forest House': Jonathan
translated: the house for the kings' cooling;" on Isa 2:13, "these are the high
kings . . .; they are compared to the cedars of Lebanon . . ." (similarly on Isa 14:8;
37:24). In Isa 10:34: "He compared the hosts of Sennacherib to Lebanon" (Similar
to T.-J.), and in Jer 22:20, 26 Lebanon is seen as a metaphor for "big houses of
cedar trees." In the allegory of Ezek 17:3 Lebanon stands for "the Land of Israel,"
and in 31:3 he views "The cedar of Lebanon" as a parable (דמיון), "to the king of
Assur," while in v. 15 another simile is added (from a different author?): "The
phrase 'Lebanon' refers to the branches," a simile repeated in the comment on Hos
14:16 (here following Targum Jonathan). Again following Jonathan, in Zech 11:1
"Lebanon" is interpreted as "the nations."

Gilead and the land of Lebanon, Kara cites the Targum: "And Jonathan translated: If you were loved by me as the Temple which is high on the top of mountains . . .," and then refers back to it in his comment on Zech 10:10. He adopts this interpretation also in his comment on Hab 2:17: "'For the violence done to Lebanon shall cover you': The violence that you did to the Temple, which is called Lebanon, as it is said: 'The good hill country and the Lebanon'" (Deut 3:25).

Kara's treatment of the name Lebanon, differing from Rashi in degree rather than in principle, seems to be an intermediate stage on the way from the conventional midrashic approach to the full dominance of the plain meaning. Kara is certainly aware of the plain meaning of the name, and is very conscious of its function in the poetic language. Nevertheless, he still adheres to the traditional midrashic view, representing "Lebanon" as "Temple" even when this is not called for by the obvious meaning of the text.

An enlightening comparison to Kara's (and Rashi's) practice are the few comments of R. Eliezer of Beaugency, whose commentaries on Isaiah, Ezekiel, and the Twelve Minor Prophets are relevant to our discussion.[36]

In the representation of the name Lebanon R. Eliezer's adherence to the plain meaning is absolute. This meaning is either explicitly stated, or implied by the general contents of the interpretation. In commenting on the poetic tropes he tries to adhere as much as possible to the literal meaning, and consciously uncovers the tenor as related to the specific context. Nowhere in his commentaries is "Lebanon" represented by the standard equivalent "Temple." In Isa 14:8 R. Eliezer does not even see a simile: "All your life you did not cease to fell cypresses and cedars," and he remains in the realm of the literal meaning also in his comments on Hos 14:6–8. In Isa 29:17 he first explains the metonymy: "'The Lebanon will turn into Carmel': a forest of fruitless trees will become fruit trees," and then

---

[36] For his life and works see Poznanski, *Kommentar zu Ezechiel*, CXXV–CLXVI; his commentaries on Isaiah and Ezekiel have been recently republished in: Menahem Cohen, ed., *Mikra'oth Gedoloth Haketer* (Ramat Gan: Bar Ilan University Publications; *Isaiah*—1996, *Ezekiel*—2000). To the same "fourth generation" of Northern French biblical exegesis belongs also R. Joseph Bechor Shor of Orleans, the student of Rabbenu Tam and in many ways a follower of Rashbam. In his extant commentary on the Pentateuch there is only one remark relating to our discussion (above, n. 17).

goes on to explain the simile: "those low and needy will become
strong and full with riches and honor." Similarly in Ezek 17:3: "The
Lebanon is the place of cedars. Likewise, the Land of Israel is the
place of great kings." In Hab 2:17 he first explains "The violence
done to Lebanon" as: "The violence . . . that you killed the animals
of Lebanon," and then proceeds to spell out the simile: "He compared the earth to Lebanon which is a forest, and the peoples on
the earth to the animals of Lebanon."[37]

By moving from Joseph Kara to R. Eliezer, our discussion skipped
one generation of the French/Ashkenazi Peshat school, that is
Rashbam, the strongest advocate of the Peshat methodology. However,
because of the uniqueness of his position on this matter I have left
it to the end of the paper[38] and will turn now to the most important representative of the Provence school, whose work is certainly
relevant to our discussion, Rabbi David Kimhi, Radak.[39] Radak
shows great interest in the definition of Lebanon and repeatedly
refers to it. Taking his lead from Deut 3:25 (see below, on Hab
2:17) he views "Lebanon" as a name of a territory or a forest inside
the Land of Israel. At the first occurrence of the name in the Former
Prophets (Josh 1:4) he explains: "'And this Lebanon': This is a well-
known place in the Land of Israel; it is said 'this' although it is on
the other side of the Jordan because they could see it from there;
and so did Moses say: 'This good hill country and the Lebanon'
(Deut 3:25)." Then again in his comment on 1 Kgs 5:20: "'From
Lebanon': Lebanon was inside the Land of Israel, and he [Solomon]
did not ask him for the timber but only that he [Hiram] sent him
carpenters, who would know how to fell the trees." Even in his comment on 1 Kgs 7:2, where he accepts Jonathan's interpretation, he
repeats this claim: "'The Lebanon Forest House': Jonathan translated: 'the house for the kings' cooling'. It seems that this was the
kings' custom at that period, to build a house in the forest to cool
themselves during the summertime. Solomon built (such a house) in

---

[37] We could not examine his comments on the two occurrences in Zechariah,
included in the two missing pages of the commentary (chs. 10:3–14:4). Poznanski,
Kommentar zu Ezechiel, 209.
[38] See below, p. 000.
[39] On the Provence school see Frank E. Talmage, "The Provence Commentators
in the 12th and the Beginning of the 13th Centuries", in Greenberg, *Introduction*,
86–91. More specifically on Radak, idem, *David Kimhi, the Man and the Commentaries*
(Cambridge: Harvard University Press, 1975).

the well-known forest in the Land of Israel, the name of which was Lebanon." Then, again, on 2 Kgs 19:23: "he compared the Land of Israel to Lebanon because Lebanon is a forest of trees in the Land of Israel . . .," and again on Isa 10:34: "Lebanon is a name of a forest in the Land of Israel," and similarly explicitly on Isa 29:17; 40:16; Ps 29:5; 92:3; and implicitly on Hos 14:6–8. In his comment on Ezek 17:3 Radak refers to the name Lebanon in explaining the parable and in uncovering the tenor: "'Came to the Lebanon': Lebanon is the place of many trees . . . This is the Land of Israel, in which there is a good forest called Lebanon, and the entire Land of Israel is called after it: Lebanon."

Radak is aware of the traditional rendering of Lebanon as Temple, but does not adopt it. He refers to it in his elaborate comment on Hab 2:17: "'The violence of Lebanon will cover you': means: The violence that you did to Lebanon, which is the Land of Israel, as it is said: 'this good hill country and the Lebanon' (Deut 3:25). After he compared the land to Lebanon he compared those who inhabit it to beasts which live in Lebanon, which is a forest of trees . . .; Jonathan translated: Lebanon: the Temple, as did Onkelos: 'this good hill country and the Lebanon': and the Temple." The same interpretation is repeated in a more concise phrasing in the comment on Zech 10:10.

Radak's interpretation was adopted by some later commentators, but a certain turn of this interpretation is of particular interest. The anonymous medieval commentary on the Song of Songs, published by Adolf Hübsch in 1866,[40] refers to the meaning of Lebanon in explicit opposition to the Midrash. In his comment on Song 3:9 he explains: "'Of the trees of Lebanon': according to its plain meaning, it was a forest in the vicinity of Jerusalem and it had beautiful trees; from these trees he built a palace." He refers to this matter again in his comment on 7:5: "'Like the tower of Lebanon that faces

---

[40] Adolf Hübsch, *Die fünf Megilloth* (Prague: Druck Sender and Brandeis, 1866). Hübsch published the commentaries of all the Five Scrolls from a manuscript in the University of Prague, known as "the Eger Pentateuch," but did not identify their authors. Later scholars identified Rabbi Joseph Kara as the author of the commentaries on Ruth, Esther, Lamentations and Qoheleth, and suggested that he was also the author of the commentary on the Song of Songs (see Ahrend, *Le Commentaire*, 182–183). This attribution is questionable (Ahrend, ibid; Poznanski, *Kommentar zu Ezechiel*, XXX–XXXI; Grossman, *The Early Sages of France*, 308), and a more thorough study of the commentary is necessary.

etc.': A certain tower, highly built, from the beautiful trees of Lebanon, that can be seen from Damascus," and in the same spirit, without the mention of Lebanon, in 1:17: "'Cedars are the beams of our house': there was a forest in the vicinity of Jerusalem, the trees of which were precious; from them Solomon built his houses." According to this commentator, then, Lebanon was "A forest in the vicinity of Jerusalem." While the view of Lebanon as a name of a forest could be supported by the constant reference to its trees, the idea that it was "in the vicinity of Jerusalem" is quite peculiar. Should this view be seen as an extension of Radak's understanding of "Lebanon" as "the Land of Israel," or did it derive from the connection of the "cedars of Lebanon" to Solomon's buildings in Jerusalem? The author seems to retain the Midrashic concept of Lebanon as attached to the Temple, but ascribes to it a geographical meaning.[41]

This unexpected interpretation is repeated by Gersonides.[42] He refers to it in his short comment on 1 Kgs 7:2: "'He built the Lebanon Forest House': I think that the forest of Lebanon was close to the Temple; this is why the Temple is called Lebanon," and similarly in the introduction to his commentary on the Song of Songs: "It is known that the temple was in the forest of Lebanon (1 Kgs 7:2, etc.) and thus the Temple is called Lebanon."[43] The relationship between the Hübsch "anonymous" commentator of the Song of Songs and Radak on the one hand and Gersonides on the other cannot be further elaborated at this point, as he remains, at least for the time being, utterly anonymous.

---

[41] The lead for this view might have been taken from texts relating to the building of the Second Temple in Ezra and Haggai. According to Ezra 3:7, the returned exiles "paid . . . the Sydonians and the Tyrians with food . . . to bring cedar wood from Lebanon," whereas according to Hag 1:8 the timber was taken from the hills around Jerusalem: "Go up to the hills and get timber and rebuild the House." The conjunction of the two texts may suggest, without entering into details, that "Lebanon" was in fact "the hill" near Jerusalem.

[42] For his life and works, see the articles in the important volume: Gad Freudenthal, ed., *Studies on Gersonides: A Fourteenth-Century Jewish Philosopher-Scientist* (Leiden: E. J. Brill, 1996). For his commentary on the Song of Songs, see Menachem Kelner, *Commentary of the Song of Songs: Levi ben Gershom* (Gersonides) (New Haven and London: Yale University Press, 1998).

[43] English translation by Kelner, ibid., 12.

As we saw so far, while the commentators belonging to the "Peshat" school display different views on the meaning of "Lebanon," they have one characteristic in common: the avoidance of any attempt to explain the name by itself. One may regard this avoidance as a (conscious or unconscious) reaction to the widespread homiletic procedure, of deriving or substantiating the homiletic interpretation by etymological word-plays, many of them rather peculiar.[44] The only commentator who deviates from this rule is Rashbam, who tries to explain the name "Lebanon" itself, following the methodology of the Peshat.[45]

Rashbam refers to this matter several times in his commentary on the Song of Songs,[46] and perhaps also in his lost commentary on Hosea.[47] He makes two comments on this matter in the interpretation of Song 4:11 ("and the scent of your robes is like the scent of Lebanon"), in the paraphrastic presentation of the contents of the passage and in the discussion of the details.[48] The first comment is: "The scent of your robes and clothes is better and more pleasant

---

[44] See above, pp. 710–11.

[45] On his life and works, see in particular David Rosin, *R. Samuel ben Meir (רשב״ם) als Schrifterklärer*, Breslau: Verlag von Wilhelm Koebner, 1880; Poznanski, *Kommentar zu Ezechiel*, XXXIX–XLIX; Melammed, *Bible Commentators* I, 449–513; Sara Japhet & Robert. B. Salters, *The Commentary of R. Samuel ben Meir (Rashbam) on Qoheleth* (Jerusalem and Leiden: Magnes Press and E. J. Brill, 1985), 11–18; Sara Japhet, *The Commentary of Rabbi Samuel ben Meir on the Book of Job* (Jerusalem: Magnes Press, 2000), 13–48.

[46] The commentary was published from Ms. Hamburg 32 and attributed to Rashbam by Jellinek. See: Adolph Jellinek, *Commentar zu Kohelet und den Hohen Liede von R. Samuel ben Meir* (Leipzig: Verlag von Leopold Schnauss, 1855). Subsequent scholars, most notably Rosin followed by Poznanski questioned this attribution. (See Rosin, *Schrifterklärer*, 18–19; Poznanski, *Kommentar zu Ezechiel*, LXXXVIII–LXXXIX). My own studies so far have convinced me that this is indeed Rashbam's commentary, and I hope to discuss the matter at length in the future. For the time being see Yaakov Thompson, "The Commentary of Samuel ben Meir on the Song of Songs" (D.H.L. Thesis, The Jewish Theological Seminary of America, 1988), 170–223. The complete commentary is now known in three manuscripts, as well as two short passages from chapter 1. See Barry D. Walfisch, "An Annotated Bibliography of Medieval Jewish Commentaries on the Song of Songs," in *Sara Kamin Memorial Volume*, 541.

[47] Ephraim E. Urbach, *Sefer Arugat Habosem Auctore R. Abraham b. R. Azriel I–IV* (Jerusalem: Mekize Nirdamim, 1939–1963); II 1947, 110, n. 13.

[48] On the specific literary structure of the commentary see for the time being Thompson, *Rashbam on the Song of Songs*, 134–38. The topic deserves a fuller discussion, which I hope to undertake in the near future.

to me than the trees of frankincense (לבונה);" and the second: "'like the scent of Lebanon': A tree which bears frankincense and its scent spreads."

Rashbam follows the same line of interpretation in his comments on the phrase "flowing water from Lebanon" in 4:15. According to his view the passage of 4:13–15 draws a comparison between "your irrigated field" (שלחיך) and a "fruit garden of others" (פרדס של אחרים), implying that "your irrigated field" is better than the best fruit-gardens, the description of which is presented in vv. 13–15. V. 13 describes the fruit trees; v. 14 refers to the variety of perfumes that grow in the garden, among which are also "trees of frankincense" (עצי לבונה); and v. 15 describes its source of water, ending with "flowing water from Lebanon." In his paraphrase of the passage Rashbam combines all these elements together, thus explaining v. 15: "In it there is a garden spring, a source of fresh water, whose water is dripping and flowing from between the trees of frankincense that are in the fruit-garden. The spring-head is between these trees, and therefore the water is scented and its fragrance spreads because of the scent of the frankincense which is absorbed in it."

The "water from Lebanon" then, is the scented water which flows from among the "trees of Lebanon," which are, according to this interpretation "trees of frankincense," as he explained already in his comment on 4:11.

Rashbam's conclusion illustrates the methodology which characterizes his entire exegetical enterprise: the consistent search for the "plain meaning" by means of grammatical, semantic, and contextual considerations.[49] The starting point is the question, the need to get to the roots of the text's meaning, in this case, the meaning of "Lebanon," and more specifically, the origin of the unusual phrase: "scent of Lebanon."[50] The road to the answer begins with etymology—the understanding of the root as לבן (white)—and the search for other cognate words that may shed light on the use of this name

---

[49] Discussed by all those who studied his work, among others those referred to above in note 45. For a specific example of this methodology, see Sara Japhet, "Rashbam's Commentary on Genesis 22: 'Peshat' or 'Derash'," in *Sarah Kamin Memorial Volume*, 349–66.

[50] The difficulty of this simile is illustrated by two matters: the repeated textual variants, and the modern suggestions for emendation of the text. See, e.g., David J. A. Clines, ed., *The Dictionary of Classical Hebrew IV* (Sheffield: Sheffield Academic Press, 1998), 516.

in this context. Of the extant cognate nouns, the choice of לבונה (frankincense) seems almost "natural." It is suggested by two factors: the aspect of "scent," which is the most characteristic feature of לבונה in all of its occurrences;[51] and the wording of the specific passage in the Song of Songs, in which perfumes and scents (among them frankincense) are placed together with "Lebanon." Given all these considerations, the conclusion that "Lebanon" belongs to the same semantic field as "Lebonah" seems indicated. The explicit description of "Lebanon" as "tree" (3:9) completes the interpretation: "Lebanon is a tree that bears frankincense" (4:11).

While this line of reasoning is characteristic of Rashbam's method and may stand by itself in explaining his exegetical conclusion, one is tempted nevertheless to ask whether there were additional sources or incentives for this idiosyncratic interpretation. What comes immediately to mind is the evidence of the Septuagint, and the Greek in general. Throughout the Septuagint the two Hebrew nouns, לבנון and לבונה are represented by the same Greek word, λίβανος: לבונה with a small λ, and לבנון with a capital Λ: λιβανος is frankincense; and Λιβανος is Lebanon. This similarity has resulted in a multitude of textual variants, as illustrated by many manuscripts and leading to the conclusion of Jay Curry Treat: "confusion of the two surely reigned in antiquity."[52] Moreover, according to the Greek dictionary, the meaning of the semitic loan-word λίβανος is "a frankincense tree," and only secondarily, frankincense itself.[53] Thus, Rashbam's comment on "Lebanon" sounds like a citation of the dictionary entry on λίβανος, representing in the Septuagint both לבנון and לבונה.

---

[51] On the meaning and origin of לבונה see: D. Kellermann, "לבנה (lebonah)," *TDOT* 7 (1995), 441–7.

[52] See: Jay Curry Treat, "Lost Keys: Text and Interpretation in Old Greek Song of Songs and its Earliest Manuscript Witnesses" (Ph.D. diss., University of Pennsylvania, 1996), 364. See also pp. 195, 267. Such a textual variant is attested also in non-Greek Versions, i.e., the Aramaic Targum and the Vulgate to Song 4:11, where both Versions read "Like the scent of frankincense" (Vulgate: *sicut odor turis*; Aramaic Targum: כריח אולבנין), rather than "like the scent of Lebanon." Their reading may point to a different Hebrew *Vorlage*. Rashbam's comment, however, is based on the MT.

[53] LSJ, 1047. Müller, by contrast (below, p. 53) regards the meaning 'frankincense' as primary, and 'frankincense-tree' as secondary. See his extensive discussion of the origin of the word in Old South Arabic and its diffusion into other semitic languages and Greek. W. W. Müller, "Zur Herkunft von λίβανος and λιβανωτός," *Glotta* 52 (1974): 53–59.

Was Rashbam aware of these linguistic data? As far as our knowledge goes, it is hard to assume that Rashbam actually knew Greek.
However, the possibility that he had access to traditions stemming
from the Byzantine Greek-speaking Jewish communities seems less
imaginative and far-fetched now than it could have been in the past.
As the exegetical tradition of the Greek speaking Jews is gradually
coming to light, contacts with this world may not seem so impossible.[54]
As I have shown elsewhere, on at least two occasions in Rashbam's
commentary on Qoheleth, his comments reflect the Greek text (in
this case, Aquila), rather than the Massoretic text.[55] Of significance
in this context is Rashbam's reference to information on the biblical textual tradition which he received from "Rabbi Jacob ben Shabtai
from the land of Greece," the only person he mentions by name in
his grammar book, Dayyaqut.[56] Although at this point no conclusive
statements may be made, further studies may shed more light on
this interesting question.[57]

Did Rashbam regard this interpretation of Lebanon as exclusive,
namely, as the only explanation of the name in all its occurrences?
In the absence of direct evidence (he did not refer to this matter in
his commentary on the Pentateuch, and his commentaries on the
other biblical books are now lost), we may perhaps learn from his
comment on Song 7:5. He explains the simile "your nose is like the
tower of Lebanon" as: "your nose is upright like the tower which is
in Lebanon, which rises and faces Damascus," which may indicate
that in this context "Lebanon" is a place-name. This would mean
that Rashbam distinguished between two different meanings of the
name Lebanon, following the general semantic rule which he coined
in his commentary on the Pentateuch: "Most words in the Bible
have two categories of meaning."[58]

---

[54] See above, note 23.
[55] Japhet & Salters, *R. Samuel ben Meir on Qoheleth*, p. 179; Sara Japhet, "'Goes
to the South and Turns to the North (Ecclesiastes 1:6)': The Sources and History
of the Exegetical Traditions," *JSQ* 1 (1993/4), 311–12.
[56] Ronela Merdler, *Dayyaqut MeRabbenu Shemuel [Ben Meir (Rashbam)]* (Jerusalem:
Institute of Jewish Studies, the Hebrew University of Jerusalem, 1999, 23:17–18; vii.
[57] See now: Yisrael Ta-Shma, "Toward a History of the Cultural Links Between
Byzantine and Ashkenazic Jewry," in *Me'ah She'arim: Studies in Medieval Jewish Spiritual
Life in Memory of Isadore Twersky* (eds. E. Fleischer et al.; Jerusalem: Magnes Press,
2001), 61–70 (Hebrew section).
[58] On Exod 34:29. Lockshin translates more emphatically: "[at least] two [sepa-
rate, distinct] categories." (Martin L. Lockshin, *Rashbam's Commentary on Exodus: An
Annotated Translation* (Atlanta: Scholars Press, 1997), 423.

Rashbam's exegetical suggestion comes up again in two later works, one of which explicitly identifies the interpretation as Rashbam's. The anonymous commentary on the Song of Songs published by Mathews in 1896 is dependent on Rashbam in several ways but, similar to his treatment of other sources, does not refer to him by name.[59] The author repeats the interpretation of "Lebanon = a tree bearing frankincense" several times, beginning already with the first occurrence of Lebanon in the book (Song 3:9): "'Lebanon': A tree from which frankincense is extracted and has a good smell." Accordingly he explains "With me from Lebanon" (4:8) as: "from the palanquin made from the trees of Lebanon," and on "the scent of Lebanon" (4:11) "like the scent of frankincense." On 4:15, "flowing water from Lebanon" he explains: "Its spring-head is under the trees of frankincense mentioned above." Even for the simile in 7:5 an interpretation on this basis is suggested: "'Your nose is like the tower of Lebanon': ... some explain: the scent of your nose is like the scent of frankincense, similar to 'the scent of your nose is like apples' (7:9)."

The same interpretation is referred to again in a different context, in Arugat Habosem, the famous commentary on the Piyyutim by Rabbi Abraham ben Azriel.[60] In one of his comments Rabbi Abraham refers to Hos 14:7; he first presents Jonathan's Targum, which is based on the traditional midrashic interpretation of Lebanon as "Temple," and then goes on to cite Rashbam's view on this matter: "Rashbam explains: 'his fragrance like that of Lebanon': like a forest of frankincense trees."[61] This same interpretation is referred to a second time, in reference to Hos 14:8. Here again, Rabbi Abraham brings first the lengthy Targum of Jonathan, based on the traditional rendering of Lebanon as "Temple," and then cites Rashbam's comment: "And Rashbam explained: 'His scent shall be like the wine of Lebanon', like the wine of vines which are planted among trees of perfume and frankincense, the scent of which is absorbed in the grapes. According to the Targum, Lebanon is the Temple."[62]

---

[59] H. J. Mathews, "Anonymous Commentary on the Song of Songs," *Festschrift zum achtzigsten Geburtstage Moritz Steinschneider* (Leipzig, 1896), 238–40, Hebrew section 164–185. Although the author derived his comments from many sources, he refers explicitly only to Ibn Ezra and Parhon. See Mathews, ibid., 239, and Poznanski, *Kommentar zu Ezechiel*, XC.

[60] See above, note 47.

[61] *Arugat Habosem*, II (1947); 108–09.

[62] Ibid., 110.

The quotation from Rashbam relates to the specific context of Hos 14:6–8, and may have been taken, as Urbach suggests, from Rashbam's now lost commentary on Hosea.[63] It highlights Rashbam's consistency in connecting the name "Lebanon" to frankincense whenever the context is that of "scent," and confirms, among other considerations, his authorship of the commentary on the Song of Songs.

Is Rashbam's interpretation the "true Peshat" of the text? Do the other interpretations provide the "plain meaning?" Our answer is determined by the meaning of the term. "Peshat" does not equal "correct" and is not to be evaluated by the contents of any interpretation. "Peshat" is an exegetical method, a way, rather than an object. The means by which this method is applied are changing and varying as we go along, and its results are forever temporary, never absolute or final. The commentator who adopts this method, whether medieval or modern, sees his task as a constant effort to achieve it, but he can go about it only from his own point in time and with the tools at his disposal. While later generations can better judge whether or not he was faithful to his commitment and whether or not his methodology was "Peshat," they already stand at a different point in time, and have their own perspective. The evaluation of the achievements of medieval biblical Peshat exegesis is indeed an intriguing question, but I will let the reader be the judge and allow him to provide his own answer.

---

[63] Ibid., n. 13, referring to Poznanski, *Kommentar zu Ezechiel*, XL n. 2.

RELIGION AND POLITICS IN PSALM 2

ISRAEL KNOHL

The most explicit reference to the messiah as a "son of God" in the Hebrew Bible, is to be found in Psalm 2:7 **"You are my son, today I have begotten you".** Psalm 2 has been a subject of long scholarly debate. Besides the traditional eschatological interpretation,[1] two other views have become predominant in modern scholarship. The first one is that Psalm 2 is a part of a cult drama connected with the enthronement of the king. According to this view the enemies, who are mentioned in this Psalm, are not real political enemies, but rather chaos powers. The Psalm was supposedly read during the New Year Festival in celebration of the enthronement of the reigning king. Gunkel,[2] Mowinckel,[3] Ringgren[4] Engnell[5] and other members of the school of "Myth and Ritual" held this view. The main problems with this interpretation are two:

1. We do not have enough evidence for the reconstruction of this New Year celebration in ancient Israel.[6]

2. There is no hint in the Psalm that the enemies are forces of nature and not real political rivals.

The second view prevailing among biblical scholars is that Psalm 2 originated in an actual historical setting. Various suggestions were given with regard to this specific historical event.[7] These diverse proposals show that the exact historical background cannot be determined. In what follows I would like rather to suggest another historical setting, pointing to the specific political situation where the claim

---

[1] For review of this interpretation and its problems, see J. T. Willis, 'A Cry of Defiance—Psalm 2', *JASOT*, 47 (1990), 35–36.

[2] H. Gunkel, *Die Psalmen* (Göttingen, 1929), 5.

[3] S. Mowinkel, *He That Cometh* (Oxford 1956), 96–98; idem, *The Psalms in Israel's Worship* (Nashville, 1967), Vol. 1, 152–3.

[4] H. Ringgren, *The Messiah in the Old Testament* (London, 1956), 8–13.

[5] I. Engnell, *Critical Essays on the Old Testament* (Nashville, 1969), 227.

[6] See Y. Kaufmann, *History of Israelite Religion*, Vol. 1 (Jerusalem-Tel Aviv, 1969), 580–84 (Heb.).

[7] See the survey of Willis, (above no. 1), 37–38.

that a king is "son of God" was made in ancient cultures. In my view, this may shed new light on our Psalm.

It is well known that the Pharaoh was perceived as having a divine origin.[8] The most literal description of the king's physical engenderment by the deity is to be found in the parallel accounts of the coronation of Hatshepsut and Amnehotep III.[9] According to these texts, the god Amon took the form of the reigning king, had intercourse with the queen, filled her with "his dew", and thus begot the new ruler. A stress on the divine origin and qualities of the young Pharaoh is also to be found in the case of Haremhab.[10] However, as was noted by J. J. M. Roberts, there is some thing common to the above-mentioned three rulers—"In all three cases the succession was contested and irregular. Thus the accounts sought to bolster shaky claims to the throne".[11]

Our next example comes from the Hellenistic period. The Seleucid monarch Alexander Balas (150–145 B.C.E.) called himself "son of God". Also in this case the succession was contested and irregular. Alexander Balas pretended to be the son of Antiochus IV, and he was in a constant struggle with the legitimate heirs of that king.[12]

The final example is the case of the Roman Emperor Octavian—Augustus. In the year 44 B.C.E., Julius Caesar was murdered. In his will, Caesar had adopted Octavian, the son of his niece, as his son. Octavian who wished to stress that he was the son of the "divine Julius", called himself "*divi filius*". The title means "son of God" or "son of the deified" and this title appeared on his coins.[13] Octavian begun to use this title around the year 40 B.C.E. It is clear that this title was used in order to help him in his struggle with Marc Anthony for the throne of Rome.

Thus, in all the cases that we have seen, the claim to be the "son of God" had a very specific aim. It was a political tool for supporting a ruler in his struggle with his enemies.

Psalm 2 opens with a description of a problematic political situation:

---

[8] See, H. Frankfort, *Kingship and the Gods* (Chicago, 1948), 44–5.

[9] *ARE* 2, pp. 75–100, 334.

[10] *ARE* 3, pp. 12–9, A. H. Gardiner, 'The Coronation of King Haremhab', *JEA* 39 (1953), 13–31.

[11] J. J. M. Roberts, "Whose Child Is This? Reflections on the Speaking Voice in Isaiah 9:5", *HTR* 90 (1997), 126.

[12] See A. Bouche-Leclerq, *Hist. Des Seleucides* (Paris, 1913), Vol. 1, pp. 332–46.

[13] See L. R. Tailor, *The Divinity of the Roman Emperor* (Middletown, 1931), 106; D. Fishwick, *The Imperial Cult in the Latin West* (Leiden, 1987), 76.

Why do the nations conspire,
and the peoples plot in vain?
The kings of the earth set themselves,
 and the rulers take counsel together,
against the Lord and his anointed,
saying,
"Let us burst their bonds asunder, and cast their cords from us" (Ps.
2:1–3).

As was pointed out by Victor Sasson,[14] these verses depict conspiracy
and rebellion against the Judean king. Probably some nations that
were subordinate to that king, or to his father, were seeking a way
to rebel and to throw off his yoke. Such a rebellion would shake
the throne of any king. It is no wonder then that at this difficult
moment a claim of divine origin of the king is made:

I will tell of the decree of the Lord:
He said to me,
"You are my son, today I have begotten you.
Ask of me, and I will make the nations your heritage,
and the ends of the earth your possession.
You shall break them with a rod of iron,
and dash them in pieces like a potter's vessel" (ibid. 7–9).

It seems that similar to the above-mentioned cases of the Egyptian,
Seleucid and Roman monarchs, so, too, in our Psalm the claim to
be the "Son of God" is mainly a political device. It was probably
intended for Israelite ears, rather than for the enemies.[15] It was meant
to strengthen the rule and legitimacy of the king among his people
in a time of an external threat.

I do not want to reduce the theological significance of this Psalm.
The very fact that the Judean king is depicted as a "son of God"
is important regardless of the immediate context of this expression.
Yet one should pay attention to the context in order to decide what
was the significance of this expression in biblical thought.

---

[14] V. Sasson, "The Language of Rebellion in Psalm 2 and in the Plaster Texts
from Deir Alla", *Andrews University Seminary Studies*, 24 (1986), 147–54.
[15] Contra to J. T. Willis who has suggested (above, no. 1, p. 44) that ". . . the
second psalm is best understood in the *Sitz im Leben* of impending military conflict, at
a time just prior to the joining together of enemy armies in battle, when it is customary for the kings or leaders of the two sides to taunt their opponents with threats
of severe defeat and boasts of certain victory." While this interpretation is possible,
it seems that the language of the psalm fits more to the Judean ears an address.

TEXTUAL CRITICISM OF THE HEBREW BIBLE:
ITS AIM AND METHOD

ARIE VAN DER KOOIJ

I

The manuscripts on which modern editions of the Hebrew Bible, the Old Testament, are based are of a relatively late date, viz. tenth and eleventh centuries C.E. The most important witnesses are the codex of Aleppo and the codex Leningradensis; the former is used as the basis of the edition of *The Hebrew University Bible*, whereas the latter forms the basis of the third edition of the *Biblia Hebraica* edited by R. Kittel, and of the *Biblica Hebraica Stuttgartensia*. Since, as is generally assumed, the biblical books in Hebrew (and Aramaic) go back to a period of a much earlier date—that of the seventh up to the second centuries B.C.E.—the question immediately arises whether their actual text, the so-called Masoretic text (MT), has been transmitted, through the ages up to its attestation in the early Middle Ages, accurately, or not. It is the task of textual criticism to examine its reliability from the perspective of the transmission history. To this end, textual witnesses of an earlier date than the MT—ancient versions (translations) and early witnesses in Hebrew (and Aramaic) as well—are of crucial importance. As a result of the findings in the Dead Sea area, and new developments in the research of witnesses such as the Septuagint (LXX) and the Targumim (Tg), in the last decades textual criticism has become more and more an advanced and specialized field of research. The work of a textual critic has become more exciting, but also more complicated. Emanuel Tov has provided us with an excellent introduction to the many aspects and questions involved: *Textual Criticism of the Hebrew Bible*.[1] In this contribution in honour to Emanuel I would like to make some comments on the issue of the aim of textual criticism, and on that of its method.

---

[1] (Minneapolis: Fortress Press; Assen/Maastricht: Van Gorcum, 1992; 2nd rev. ed., 2001).

II

Textual criticism of the Old Testament deals with matters pertaining to the transmission of the biblical text. It is its task to test the quality of the attested text (MT) within the framework of the long history of transmission before the MT did emerge. But what is the purpose of doing this? Generally speaking, textual criticism is a field of study which aims at reconstructing and establishing the original wording of a text by evaluating critically the text as attested in several and often diverging manuscripts. Scholars have applied this view, rightly so, to the study of the Old Testament text. As to the question of the original wording of a given biblical book, most exegetes have in mind the final redaction of a book, or, since this aim is difficult to realize, its earliest attainable form. The expression 'final redaction' is meant as a reference to the literary completion of the original text of a book.[2]

In discussing the relationship between textual criticism and literary criticism Tov has come to another conclusion regarding the aim of textual criticism. In his view, its task is "to aim at that literary composition which has been accepted as binding (authoritative) by Jewish tradition" (p. 317). He has in mind the edition "that was later to become M" (p. 316), that is to say, the proto-masoretic text. This point of view is based on the assumption that "sizable differences between the textual witnesses, as a rule between M... on the one hand and G... or a Qumran text on the other" (p. 314), testify, in several cases, to "different literary strata in the composition of the biblical books up to the stage of the edition (recension, composition) contained in M" (p. 316). In his view, large scale differences pertaining to a textual tradition which is earlier than proto-MT, are part of the literary history of a book, that is to say, they are not to be considered as belonging to the transmission history, and thus as falling outside the scope of textual criticism.

One wonders, however, whether one should define the proto-MT as the purpose of textual criticism. Admittedly, large differences do not derive from copyists, but rather from "authors-scribes" (p. 314), and the reworkings involved may be similar to—though not neces-

---

[2] See, e.g., R. S. Hendel, *The Text of Genesis 1–11. Textual Studies and Critical Edition* (New York and Oxford: Oxford University Press, 1998), 11.

sarily identical with—large scale redactional elaborations which are characteristic of the literary history of a book. These considerations are, however, no compelling reasons for the idea that particular 'sizable differences' should to be seen as reflecting a stage in the literary history of a book. On the contrary, the reworkings resulting in differences which may precede proto-MT, are very similar to reworkings which can be regarded as "subsequent to the edition of M" (for this phrase, see Tov, p. 316). Furthermore, it is to be asked whether 'sizable differences' attested by early witnesses should be termed as 'literary strata'. The idea of stratum, or layer, suggests some redactional type of work throughout a book as a whole, whereas 'sizable differences' in most cases seem to be more of an occasional nature. (I will turn to this issue below.) Moreover, it would be an unusual procedure to regard a *textus receptus* like MT, or proto-MT, as the purpose of textual criticism. Thus, in my view, it stands more to reason to consider all available textual data (Qumran; ancient versions) as pertaining to the transmission history.[3] The task of textual criticism then is to try to account for all these data in order to establish, as far as possible, the earliest attainable text of a book, be it proto-MT, or earlier (pre-MT), that is to say, the wording of a text which lay at the root of attested differences between the witnesses, including different 'editions' of chapters, or the book concerned.[4]

The search for the earliest attainable of a text, or, *idealiter*, its original wording, is most important for reasons of historical research. The study and interpretation of texts in the Hebrew Bible is as a rule based on the assumption that a given text, if critically assessed, may go back to the Persian, or Babylonian, or even to the Assyrian period. It is on the basis of such a claim that the texts concerned are used for the study of the history and of the religion of ancient Israel. This underlines the need of a critical study of the Old Testament texts aiming at its 'original' wording.[5]

---

[3] Cf. A. van der Kooij, "Textgeschichte/Textkritik der Bibel," in *TRE* Bd. XXXIII, Lief. 1/2 (Berlin: De Gruyter, 2001), 154. For a similar view, see H. J. Stipp, "Das Verhältnis von Textkritik und Literarkritik in neueren alttestamentlichen Veröffentlichungen," *BZ* NT 34 (1990): 33.

[4] An interesting example is the textual history of the Life of Adam and Eve that is marked by different 'editions' which are not to be seen as stages towards the final redaction, but as stages in the transmission history of an underlying primary text. See, e.g., J. Tromp, "The textual history of the Life of Adam and Eve in the light of a newly discovered Latin text-form," *JSJ* 33 (2002): 28–41.

[5] This concerns the final redaction in the sense of the literary completion of the

III

It is quite another issue whether, or to which extent, the above stated purpose can be realized. There are many obstacles, such as the fact that the number of ancient witnesses in Hebrew is very limited indeed. Surely, we now have an impressive number of biblical texts from the Dead Sea area, but for most books this material is very fragmentary. Besides, there are cases which are complicated, and cases which, in the end, are difficult to decide as to which reading or wording might have been the (more) original one. All this means that textual criticism can only be carried out by trial and error, including, as is usual in textual and historical research, an element of subjectivity. Or to put it with a Dutch saying: "we moeten roeien met de riemen die we hebben" (One must try to make the best of it).

The question of how to reach one's goal as a textual critic concerns the matter of method. As is well-known, the first step is to collect the relevant data in a case, or in a group of cases. The reasons to do so may be, first, the availability of a variant reading, and/or secondly, a difficulty in MT. After having studied the relevant data, each in its own context (LXX, or Qumran text, etc.), the crucial thing is to evaluate the evidence, in view of the question which reading may be the preferred one, in the sense of the (more) original one.

As to the weighing of the evidence several factors are involved, which may differ from case to case, such as linguistic, philological, exegetical, literary, and cultural considerations. As a rule, one factor will not be sufficient for an evaluation. This also applies to the well-known rule *lectio difficilior potior*. This rule is helpful, but in many instances one needs additional arguments or considerations, such as that the non-harmonized reading is to be preferred to the harmonized one. An important matter concerns the characteristics of the witnesses involved, including MT itself. For instance, for the weighing of variant readings it is important to know that a text like 1QIsaᵃ (henceforth 1Qa) represents a witness which from a linguistic point of view displays many readings of a secondary nature in comparison to MT. However, although an overall view of a witness may help

---

original text which, of course, may contain passages that go back to an earlier date than that of the completion of the original edition (as is the case, e.g., in the Pentateuch, or in the book of Isaiah).

us in weighing the evidence, this is not to say that it is decisive in every case. On the contrary, although a text such as 1Qa contains many readings which linguistically speaking are of a secondary nature, one can not exclude the possibility that this scroll also offers readings which are most important and which are to be preferred to MT. This leads us to the following statement by S. Brock: "Variants, . . ., like human beings, should be treated as individuals."[6] It is actually the art of textual criticism, in assessing the evidence, to keep the balance between overall considerations regarding the witnesses involved and detail observations in a particular case.

In the following I will give some (six) examples which are meant as illustrations of a multidimensional approach, and of the variety of the factors involved in the evaluation of the evidence.

1) Isaiah 1:20: MT חרב תאכלו] 1Qa בחרב תאכלו, LXX μάχαιρα ὑμᾶς κατέδεται, Targ. "by the sword (בחרב) of the enemy you will be killed," Pesh. "by the sword you will be killed," Vulg. *gladius devorabit vos*.

All textual witnesses have taken Hebrew חרב in the sense of 'sword,' either by taking it as subject (LXX, Vulg.; for the corresponding expression in Hebrew, see Deut 32:42), or in the sense of 'by the sword' (1Qa בחרב, cf. Targ., Pesh.). Grammatically speaking, MT is often regarded as the better text on the basis of the argument given by Gesenius-Kautzsch, par. 121c: "חרב is not an *accus. instrumenti*, but most probably an accusative of the object retained from the active construction."[7] The question, however, arises what might have been the construction in the active. If one takes the Hiphil of אכל (the Piel is not attested) the sentence would be "I will cause the sword to devour you," but in the passive, this would become "the sword shall be made to devour you," or if the active sentence would be "I will cause you to devour the sword," one would expect as the

---

[6] S. Brock, *The Recensions of the Septuaginta Version of I Samuel* (Quaderni di Henoch 9; Torino: Zamorani, 1996), 173. See also E. Tov, *The Text-Critical Use of the Septuagint in Biblical Research. Revised and Enlarged Edition* (Jerusalem Biblical Studies 8; Jerusalem: Simor, 1997), 222.

[7] *Gesenius' Hebrew Grammar as edited and enlarged by the late E. Kautzsch.* Second English edition revised in accordance with the twenty-eighth German Edition (1909) by A. E. Cowley (Oxford: Clarendon Press, 1910), 388. See also D. Barthélemy, *Critique textuelle de l'Ancien Testament. Vol. 2: Isaïe, Jérémie, Lamentations* (OB 50/2; Fribourg: Editions Universitaires; Göttingen: Vandenhoeck & Ruprecht, 1986), 8.

alternative construction "you will eat the sword."⁸ The problem is that in both cases one is left with a reading different from MT. Quite another proposal that has been made is to interpret Hebrew חרב with the help of Akkadian *ḫarūbu*, 'carob,' and to translate MT-Ketib as follows: "you will eat carobs." The carob is the food of poverty and misery. This is a most elegant solution to the problem, which in addition creates a phrase parallel to verse 19:

> If you are obedient, you will eat the good of the land,
> but if you disobey, you will eat carobs.⁹

2) Isaiah 45:2: MT הדורים] 1Qa הררים, 1Qb הרורים, LXX ὄρη, Targ. "the walls," Pesh. "rocky place" (cf. 40:4 for MT העקב), Vulg. *gloriosos* ("notables").

Hebrew הדורים presents a difficulty since its meaning is uncertain and disputed ('spiral roads,' 'uneven places'?).¹⁰ Scholars, therefore, have argued that the variant reading attested by 1Qa and LXX (1Qb?), "mountains," is to be preferred, as this one makes good sense in the context. However, the difficulty with this solution is that the reduplicated plural (הררים) does not occur in biblical Hebrew in the absolute state.¹¹ As has been argued by other scholars, MT-Ketib may well represent the original reading if taken in the sense of 'the walls,' in line with Akkadian *dūru* (cf. Targ).¹² Contextually, this would fit even better because of the 'doors of bronze' and 'bars of iron' in the rest of the verse.

As may be clear from these two cases the rule that MT might represent the *lectio difficilior* would not do, unless one takes "the more

---

⁸ For these difficulties, see Gesenius-Kautzsch-Cowley, 388. See also P. Joüon – T. Muraoka, *A Grammar of Biblical Hebrew. Part Three: Syntax* (Subsidia biblica 14/II; Rome: Editrice Pontificio Istituto Biblico, 1991), 128c (Isa 1:20 with question mark).

⁹ See M. Held, "Studies in Comparative Semitic Lexicography," in: *Studies in Honor of Benno Landsberger on His Seventy-Fifth Birthday, April 21*, 1965, eds. H. G. Güterbock and T. Joeshen (Chicago, 1965), 398, and now R. Borger, "Johannisbrot in der Bibel und im Midrasch: Über Fortschritt, Rückschritt und Stillstand in der biblischen Philologie," *ZAH* 14 (2001): 1–19.

¹⁰ For a detailed discussion, see J. L. Koole, *Isaiah. Part 3, Volume 1: Isaiah 40–48* (Historical Commentary on the Old Testament; Kampen: Kok Pharos, 1997), 434–35.

¹¹ Koole, *Isaiah*, 435.

¹² See C. H. Southwood, "The problematic *hᵃdūrîm* of Isaiah xlv 2," *VT* 25 (1975): 801–02.

difficult reading" in the sense of the Ketib. In both cases, a broader perspective, that of Semitic philology, turns out to be helpful to explain the transmitted Hebrew text, while the textual witnesses are testifying to the history of transmission and of interpretation as well. For another interesting case which belongs to this category, see D. M. Levinson, "Textual Criticism, Assyriology, and the History of Interpretation: Deuteronomy 13:7a as a Test Case in Method," *JBL* 120 (2001): 211–43.

The following cases do not concern a single reading (word, *lectio*), but are examples of 'sizable differences.'

3) Isaiah 38:21–22 MT, cf. LXX, Targ., Pesh. (in reversed order), Vulg.] in 1Qa these two verses have been added by a later hand.

The final verses of Isaiah 38 read thus (in translation):

21. Isaiah said/had said, "Let them take a cake of figs, and apply it to the boil, that he may recover." 22. Hezekiah said/had said, "What is the sign that I shall go up to the house of the Lord?"

These verses raise questions about their placement (after the psalm of Hezekiah, vv. 9–20) and their meaning. One wonders whether the question by Hezekiah about the sign makes any sense at the end of the chapter, whereas the answer is given in v. 7. The two verses concerned also occur in the parallel version, 2 Kings 20, albeit contextually at a different place (vv. 7–8). On the basis of 1Qa where both verses have been added by a later hand, scholars have argued that, originally, the text of Isaiah 38 did not contain vv. 21–22.[13] However, it could well be that vv. 21–22 were left out due to homoioteleuton (ending of v. 20 = ending of v. 22), either by the first scribe of 1Qa, or at an earlier stage in the transmission history.[14] This actually seems the more plausible option since, as has been argued by scholars,[15] the placement of vv. 21–22 is related to

---

[13] See S. Talmon, "The Textual Study of the Bible—A New Outlook" in *Qumran and the History of the Biblical Text* (ed. F. M. Cross and S. Talmon; Cambridge, Mass. and London: Harvard University Press, 1975), 330–31; Barthélemy, *Critique textuelle de l'Ancien Testament*, Vol. 2, 261; Tov, Textual Criticism, 340 ("1QIsa-a *may* reflect different stages"); R. F. Person, *The Kings—Isaiah and Kings-Jeremiah Recensions* (BZAW 252; Berlin: De Gruyter, 1997), 72; E. Ulrich, "The Developmental Composition of the Book of Isaiah: Light from 1QIsa-a on Additions in the MT," in *Qumran Studies Presented to Emanuel Tov on His Sixtieth Birthday, DSD* 8 (2001): 298–99.

[14] See e.g. Tov, *Textual Criticism*, 341.

[15] See e.g. V. Hoffer, "An Exegesis of Isaiah 38.21", *JSOT* 56 (1992): 69–84;

the insertion of the psalm (vv. 9–20): v. 21 ("that he may live") is connected with *v.* 16b ("Lord, make me live"), and the motif of going up to the house of the Lord in v. 22 goes together with the ending of v. 20. More importantly, these verses could not be placed before the psalm, partly for a theological reason (v. 21) and partly for a logical one (v. 22): the healing of Hezekiah should first of all be attributed to God, as is done in the psalm, and only secondary to the prophet (v. 21), and the question of v. 22, about the going up to the temple, could only be made after v. 20. (There is, of course, the exegetical question how to understand v. 22. It seems clear that the sign of this verse has no relation at all with the sign of vv. 7–8.[16] Why ends the chapter without an answer to the question put by Hezekiah? The most early interpretation we know of, is found in LXX, where v. 22 reads, "This is the sign . . ." [Τοῦτο τὸ σημεῖον]. Apparently, the author-translator has interpreted the sign of v. 22 as referring to the fig therapy in the preceding verse.[17] This idea is also reflected in Pesh., where v. 22 is put before v. 21.)

The following two examples belong to another category, viz. that of cases which ask for a multidimensional approach, such as a combination of text critical and literary critical methods.

4) Joshua 20

The Old Greek of Joshua 20, the chapter about the cities of refuge, is much shorter than MT (= Targ., Pesh., Vulg.): vv. 4–5, most of v. 6, and one expression in v. 3 ("unintentionally") are not attested in LXX. The latter witness reflects a text of Josh 20 which is fully in line with the related passage in Num 35:11–12. This might evoke the idea of a harmonization, but since both texts belong to the same stratum, viz. the priestly one (P), this is not plausible. As has been pointed out by scholars, from a literary-critical point of view, the pluses in MT are of a secondary nature.[18] Thus, most importantly

---

H. G. M. Williamson, "Hezekiah and the temple," in *Texts, Temples, and Traditions. A Tribute to Menahem Haran* (ed. M. V. Fox and others; Winona Lake: Eisenbrauns, 1996), 47–52.

[16] Cf. W. A. M. Beuken, *Isaiah II, Vol. 2: Isaiah 28–39* (HCOT; Leuven: Peeters, 2000), 387–89.

[17] For a similar interpretation, see e.g. Beuken, *Isaiah*, 387. 404.

[18] See, e.g., E. Cortese, *Josua 13–21. Ein priesterschriftlicher Abschnitt im Deuteronomistischen Geschichtswerk* (OBO 94; Freiburg: Editions Universitaires; Göttingen: Vandenhoeck &

from a methodological perspective, the text atttested by LXX corresponds with the results of a literary-critical analysis of MT.[19]

As to the pluses in MT-Josh 20, the question arises whether they are part of a stratum, or layer, in the book. A. Rofé and E. Tov regard these pluses as 'deuteronomistic.'[20] According to the latter, "[t]he layer of additions . . . in Joshua contains words and sections from Deuteronomy 19 which are meant to adapt the earlier layer to Deuteronomy—an assumption which is not surprising regarding the book of Joshua, whose present shape displays a deuteronomistic revision elsewhere in the book" (p. 330). However, the pluses actually contain elements from D (Deut 19) and P (in v. 6, compare Num 35:25, 28) as well. Consequently, the reworking of the text is of a late date when P and D elements were easily combined (as, e.g., is the case in the book of Chronicles, or in the Temple Scroll). It is therefore not plausible to assign the pluses in Josh 20 to a stratum such as a 'deuteronomistic' redaction of the book. Moreover, if this were the case, one would expect that LXX would attest at other 'dtr' places in Joshua a pre- or proto-dtr text, which actually is not the case, at least not in terms of sizable differences. The pluses of Josh 20 seem to be more of an occasional character than part of a redaction of the book as a whole.

5) 1 Samuel 17

The text critical issue concerning 1 Sam 17, the story of David and Goliath, represents another most interesting example in terms of the relationship between textual criticism and literary criticism. It is a well known theory that the short form of the story, as attested by LXX, reflects the earlier version of the text, whereas the longer version of MT is the result of a later expansion. The crucial question is whether a literary-cricital analysis of the longer version would confirm, just as in the case of Josh 20, the idea that the shorter version may well be considered as the (more) original form of the text. In my

---

Ruprecht, 1990), 79–80. For a different view, see V. Fritz, *Das Buch Josua* (HAT I/7; Tübingen: Mohr, 1994), 203–06.

[19] See also A. van der Kooij, "Zum Verhältnis von Textkritik und Literarkritik: Überlegungen anhand einiger Beispiele," in *Congress Volume Cambridge 1995* (ed. J. A. Emerton; SVT 66; Leiden: Brill, 1997), 189–90.

[20] A. Rofé, "Joshua 20: Historico-Literary Criticism Illustrated," in *Empirical Models for Biblical Criticism* (ed. J. H. Tigay; Philadelphia: University of Pennsylvania Press, 1985), 145; Tov, *Textual Criticism*, 330 (see the quotation given in the text).

view, such an analysis does not support the idea that the version reflected by LXX would converge with a source-component of the MT version.[21] This would imply that LXX attests a version of the story which belongs to the history of reception and not to that of the redaction-history of the book.

Finally, an example from the book of Jeremiah may be in order. The text of this book is attested in two versions, a longer one (MT, 4QJer[a], Theod, Aq, Sym, Targ, Pesh, Vulg), and a shorter one (LXX, 4QJer[b]). Many scholars are of the opinion that the shorter version represents the older one, but the whole issue is not yet settled. Whatever theory one adheres to, in line with the statement made above, each case should be treated, first of all, in its own right.[22] The following case is meant to serve as an example.

6) Jeremiah 31:38–40

> MT: Behold, the days are coming, says the Lord,
> when the city shall be rebuilt for the Lord
> from the tower of Hananel to the Corner Gate.
> And the measuring line shall go out farther,
> straight to the hill Gareb,
> and shall then turn to Goah.
> *The whole valley of the dead bodies and the ashes,*
> and all the fields as far as the brook Kidron,
> to the corner of the Horse Gate toward the east,
> shall be sacred to the Lord.
> It shall not be uprooted or overthrown any more for ever (RSV).

> LXX: Behold, the days come, says the Lord,
> when (the) city shall be built to the Lord
> from the tower of Ananeel to the gate of the corner.
> And the measurement of it shall proceed in front of them
> as far as the hills of Gareb,
> and it shall be compassed with a circle out of precious stones
> (καὶ περικυκλωθήσεται κύκλῳ ἐξ ἐκλεκτῶν λίθων).
> And all the Asaremoth even to Nachal Kedron
> as far as the corner of the horse-gate eastward,
> shall be (the) sanctuary (ἁγίασμα) to the Lord;
> and it shall not fail any more, and shall not be destroyed for ever.

---

[21] See A. van der Kooij, "The Story of David and Goliath: The Early History of Its Text", *ETL* 68 (1992): 118–31.

[22] This does not distract, of course, from the important question whether a particular case might be related to other cases in a book.

A remarkable difference between the two texts concerns the beginning of v. 40 (MT): 'the whole valley of the dead bodies and the ashes,' which is not found in LXX. It may well be that this phrase was not present in the parent text of LXX, but even then the question remains whether it represents a secondary addition, or whether it was left out for one reason or another. In the text attested by MT (cf. Targ, Pesh, Vulg) the phrase about the dead bodies and the ashes is part of a context in which the city (Jerusalem) is described as a territory 'sacred to the Lord.' Since a place with dead bodies and ashes (graves?) in Jerusalem as holy city creates serious difficulties for reasons of purity, it is more easily to imagine that this phrase was left out than that it was added at a later date. As we know from Jewish sources of the Hellenistic era (4QMMT, Temple Scroll), the issue of the purity of Jerusalem as holy city was a matter of serious concern,[23] particularly after the dramatic events in the seventies and sixties of the second century B.C. (profanation of the temple).

It is to be noted that LXX-Jeremia, which dates to the second century B.C., presents a version according to which the sacred area has been interpreted as the 'sanctuary' (ἀγίασμα). Hebrew קדש has been taken here in the sense of 'sanctuary', and not as 'sacred (to the Lord)' as in LXX-Zech 14:20, 21 (ἅγιον). The ending of v. 39 in Greek which, unlike MT, refers to an encircling wall of precious stones, is in line with this interpretation. It seems that a particular wall is meant here, viz. the περίβολος, the enclosing wall of the temple, as in LXX-Isa 54:12: καὶ τὸν περίβολόν σου λίθους ἐκλεκτούς. Whether one would consider the translator the one who left out the phrase under discussion, or not, it is clear that this phrase does not fit the interpretation of the text as attested by LXX.

---

[23] See J. Murphy-O'Connor, "Jerusalem" in *Encyclopedia of the Dead Sea Scrolls*, Vol. I (ed. L. H. Schiffman and J. C. VanderKam; New York and Oxford: Oxford University Press, 2000), 403.

FROM THE WORKSHOP OF THE REDACTOR H_R: AN EGALITARIAN THRUST

Jacob Milgrom

I. Identification

I shall not examine all the possible H$_R$ passages but only those that, in my opinion, most likely stem from his hand. They are subdivided into three groups: within Leviticus (H), within Leviticus (P), and outside Leviticus.

A. *H$_R$ Within H (Lev 17–27)*[1]

1. *Lev 18:1–5, 24–30.* This is H$_R$'s frame for the sexual prohibitions, 18:6–23. That the latter probably represents an older list is shown by the term תועבה. Only one prohibition in the list is called תועבה (v. 22), whereas all the prohibitions are labeled תועבה in the closing exhortation of the frame (vv. 26, 27, 29). Their combination in chapter 18 is the achievement of H$_R$.

2. *19:5–8.* H$_R$ placed this pericope on the שלמים sacrifice near the top of chapter 19 so as to have its rationale כי-את קדש יהרה חלל correspond with the equivalent expression וחללו את שם קדשי (22:32), thereby encompassing all the commands enjoining Israel to be holy (קדש; see no. 6, below).

3. *19:33–36.* The units on the גר (vv. 33–34) and honest trading (vv. 35–36) may be supplements.[2] Once removed, the chapter's original close forms an inclusion with its opening (vv. 3–4). The insertion of this supplement can be attributed to H$_R$.

4. *Chapters 20 and 18* contain similar prohibitions (20:9–21; 18:6–23) and initial and final exhortations (20:7–8, 22–26; 18:2b–5, 24–30),

---

[1] The following verses are discussed in J. Milgrom, *Leviticus 17–22* (AB 3a. New York: Doubleday), (2000), and *Leviticus 23–27* (AB 3b. New York: Doubleday), (2001). They are mostly assigned to h. Here the H$_R$ designation is more precise.

[2] Cf. B. J. Schwartz, *The Holiness Legislation* (vv. 30–32) (Jerusalem: Magnes), (1999), 277 (Hebrew).

thereby projecting chapter 19 as the pinnacle of Leviticus (P + H)—the work of the redactor H_R.

5. *21:24*. This compliance report is clearly H_R's addition, since nowhere in chapter 21 is Moses commanded to speak to the Israelites. It signifies that the priests' bodily defects (chapter 21) just as the high priests' rites on the Day of Purgation (לכם, 16:29, 31, 34 [H]) fall under the supervision of all Israel.

6. *22:29–30*. H_R split the two main sacrifices of the זבח, the שלמים and the תודה (cf. 7:11), placing the former at the head of chapter 19 (cf. no. 2) and the latter at the end of chapter 22, thereby creating an envelope for encompassing all H occurrences of spatial קדש.

7. *23:2ab–3, 42–43*. H_R, who probably resides in the Babylonian exile, composed the pericopes on the שבת and סכות in order to salvage some observance of the defunct cultic calendar (vv. 4–38) so that Israel might retain its religious and ethnic identity.

8. *24:4*. This verse, H_R's redactional supplement to vv. 2–3, clarifies that the lampstand comprises more than a single lamp.

9. *25:1*. This verse forms an envelope with 26:46. Since all the preceding chapters (Lev 1–24) were revealed to Moses from the Tent of Meeting, these two chapters (25 and 26), revealed at Mt. Sinai, are anomalous. They form a distinct מגילה. They show none of the verbal hallmarks of H (e.g. holiness [קדש], impurity [טמא] of the person or the land).

10. *25:5–6*. These two verses ostensibly contradict each other. The contradiction vanishes once it is realized that vv. 1–5 are a reworking by H_R of Exod 21:10–11. H_R excises the sabbatical beneficiaries in the latter. Instead, H_R provides its own beneficiary list, vv. 6–7.

11. *26:1–2*. H_R—alluding to the Decalogue (cf. also 19:3–4, 12a [H])—sums up the divine laws determinative of Israel's continuous presence in the land.

12. *26:33b–35*. Compensation must be made for the sabbaticals neglected in the past. That is, the land must remain barren before Israel can be restored.

13. *Chapter 27 (and 17)*. H_R concludes the book of Leviticus as it opens (chapter 1) with a chapter (27) on voluntary contributions to the sanctuary. It also serves as a close to the bloc of H passages beginning with chapter 17.

B. *H_R Within P*³

14. *Lev 3:16b–17.* כל חלב in v. 16⁴ and all of v. 17 are additions. They insist that all meat for the table must initially be a sacrifice (שלמים) so that its blood and suet will not be eaten but be offered on the altar. This is the viewpoint of H (see 17:3–7) to ransom Israel for slaying an animal for its meat (17:11), and its placement here at the end of the שלמים pericope (chapter 3) is probably the contribution of H_R.

15. *6:12–18aα.* This pericope is not a תודה. It was probably inserted here by H_R because it follows a passage on the מנחה (6:7–12) to which a lengthy introduction was added (vv. 12–13aαβ) to set it off from its context.

16. *7:22–27.* Like the preceding 6:12–18aα (no. 15), this pericope is an even more obvious intrusion. It severs the original continuous passage on the thanksgiving and well-being offerings (vv. 11–21) and their priestly prebends (vv. 28–36).⁵ It bears the hallmark of H: It differs from the rest of the chapter (P) by employing the second person plural. Its ban on the suet of sacrificial animals (vv. 23–25) represents the unmistakable imprint of H (cf. 17:6). Its placement here is the work of H_R.

17. *10:10–11.* These verses were most likely set in their place in chapter 10 as a proleptic introduction to chapters 11–15. That they are a late interpolation—and, hence, the work of H_R—is demonstrated by the masculine plural החקים, which occurs in the priestly texts only in two more instances, Lev 26:46 and Num 30:17, which are postpositional in their contexts. The fact that Lev 10:10–11 was imparted by YHWH to the Israelites, but not to the priests, is another hallmark of H, whose interpolation here is due to H_R.

18. *11:43–45.* This passage is replete with H expressions. Like H, it uses P idioms imprecisely. For example, שקץ and טמא are used synonymously (v. 43; contrast 11:10–38). That this passage is postpostional in chapter 11 indicates that H_R is responsible for its placement. Its purpose is to stress that obedience of the dietary laws leads

---

³ The following verses are discussed in J. Milgrom, *Leviticus 1–16* (AB 3. New York: Doubleday, (1991), where they are assigned to H. Here they are assigned more precisely to H_R.

⁴ Cf. I. Knohl, *The Sanctuary of Silence* (Jerusalem: Magnes, 1995).

⁵ Cf. Milgrom, *Leviticus 1–16*, 296–34.

to holiness. This is repeated in 20:25–26 (H), which adds the further point that holiness is contingent upon separation from the nations.

19. *16:29–34a.* This pericope bears many signs of H:

1. The second-person direct address to Israel.
2. Its terminology at times differs from the rest of chapter 16 (P): מקדש instead of הקדש; עם הקהל instead of עם or קהל; the description of the high priest is that of H (21:10) and not of P (4:3); the purgation rites (כפר) purify (טהר) the people, whereas in P they only purify the sanctuary.
3. The mention of גר is an unmistakable sign of H. The Day of Purgation is the only festival whose date is specified postpositionally, at the end of its prescription (vv. 29, 34a), whereas the date of all other festival prescriptions begin pre-positionally.

Thus, we are dealing with an appendix inserted by H$_R$. Its purpose is to abolish the privilege heretofore vested in the high priest to purge the sanctuary "whenever he chooses" (v. 2). Instead, it establishes the sanctuary purgation only "once a year" (v. 34) on the tenth of Tishri (v. 29), it imposes a national day of self-denial and abstinence from work (v. 29), and it vests control of the ritual with the people (v. 34a; cf. no. 5).

C. *H$_R$ Outside Leviticus*

20. *Exod 27:20–21 and Num 8:1–4.* These two passages on the menorah were inserted by H$_R$ between the P prescriptions on the Tabernacle (Exod 25:1–27:19) and the consecration of the priests (Exodus 28), and between the gifts of the chieftains (Numbers 7) and the ordinations of the Levites (Numbers 8). In my opinion, it was the presence of Lev 24:1–4 (H) that compelled H$_R$ to infix a duplicate of these verses in Exod 27:20–21, at a point immediately after the prescription to build the sanctuary and its sanctums (Exod 25:1–27:19: see Ibn Ezra [long explanation]).[6]

21. *Exod 29:38–46.* H$_R$ appends a prescription on the תמיד (vv. 38–42) and a rationale for the Tabernacle (vv. 43–46) to a passage on the altar (vv. 36–37). The תמיד is copied and condensed mainly from Num 28:3–8 (P). In the condensation H$_R$ eliminated the golden

---

[6] Concerning the placement of Num 8:1–4, see J. Milgrom *Numbers* (Philadelphia: Jewish Publication Society, 1990), 60 and Y. Ts. Moshqovitz, *The Book of Numbers* (Jerusalem: Mosad Harav Kook, 1988), 87 (Hebrew).

libation vessels (v. 7) and explicitly prohibited their use because of their implication that YHWH imbibed drink in His chambers.[7]

22. *Exod 31:12–17; 35:1–3.* The attachment of the Sabbath injunctions at the end of the prescriptions for the Tabernacle construction and priestly consecration (Exod 25:1–31:11), and at the beginning of the prescriptions for the manufacture of the Tabernacle furniture and priestly clothing (Exod 35:4–39:43), with their quintessential H characteristics—מקדש ישראל, אני ה׳ (Lev 20:8; 21:8,15, 23; 22:16, 32), plural construct שבתות (Lev 19:3,30;23:38), superlative שבת שבתרן (Lev 16:31; 23:3, 32; 25:4) and direct address to Israel (Exod 31; 15; 35:2, 3 LXX)—all testify to the work of H_R.[8] These Sabbath passages share, with the passage inserted at the end of the festival calendar (Lev 23:1–3; no. 7), the aim of highlighting the central importance of the Sabbath.

23. *Exod 6:2–8.* A host of scholars[9] have identified this passage as H. Its dependency on Lev 26:13[10] in addition to its incorporation of the JE term סבלת מצדים[11] make it more likely that this is the handiwork of H_R.

24. *Exod 12:18–20.* Knohl[12] has argued that Exod 12:1–20 comprise two H strata, the older stratum, vv. 1–17, and an editorial stratum, vv. 18–20. According to Bar-On[13] this text is more complex. Vv. 2, 4–6a, 9–11bα are a midrashic elaboration of the original פסח law (vv. 1, 3, 6b*, 7–8, 11ba [?]), and vv. 12–13 are the latest component to the text. Both scholars, nonetheless, agree that vv. 18–20 are a late editorial component, and I harbor no hesitations to assign them to H_R[14] since they reflect a post-deuteronomic and, possibly, exilic period.

25. *Num 3:11–13.* This is an H interpretation, as shown by YHWH's first person address with the subject אני (3:12, 13) and the object לי

---

[7] See J. Milgrom, *Leviticus 17–22*, 1338, 2093.

[8] Ibid., 1338–39.

[9] Cited by Knohl, *The Sanctuary*, 17 n. 24

[10] Demonstrated by N. F. Lohfink, "Abänderung der Theologie der priesterlichen Geschictswerks im Segen des heiligkeitsgesetzes: Zu Lev. 26, 9.11–13," in *Wort und Geschichte* (Fst. K. Elliger, eds. H. Gese and H. P. Rüger; Neukirchen: Neukirchener Verlag, 1993), 129–36. Amended by J. Milgrom, *Leviticus 23–27*, 2298.

[11] Knohl, *Sanctuary*, 17 n. 24.

[12] Ibid., 19–21.

[13] S. Bar-On (Gesundheit), *Festival Legislation in the Torah* (Ph.D. diss., Hebrew University of Jerusalem, 1999, Hebrew).

[14] See Milgrom, *Leviticus 23–27* (n. 1), 1974.

(3:12, 13), the characteristic H formula אני ה' (3:13), and the use of rationales (3:12, 13). The passage 3:11–13 is an insertion explaining 3:5–10, namely, the right of the Levites to assume a cultic office.[15] Thus, H informs us that the Levites replaced the firstborn, who hitherto had officiated at the family hearth to worship the departed ancestors.[16] Since this passage is an insertion, it most likely stems from H$_R$.

26. *Num 3:40–51*. The idea of the replacement of the firstborn by the Levites is again picked up in this pericope (see vv. 11–13, above), bearing typical H expressions: אני ה', לי (v. 41aα); והיו-לי הלוים אני ה' (v. 45b).[17] The rest of chapter 3 deals with the subordination of Levites under the priests (vv. 5–10), the Levitic census, and their assignment to guard duty of the Tabernacle (vv. 14–40). Vv. 40–51 are a postpositional insert. If removed they allow the chapter to flow smoothly. Their insertion is probably due to H$_R$.

27. *Num 5:1–4*. This is an H passage.[18] The צדוע, זב, and טמא לנפש (H) are banished from the camp, whereas Leviticus 15 and Numbers 19 (P) allow the latter two to remain at home within the settlement.[19] Can H, a later source, represent such an early tradition? Indeed it can. In this case, the discrepancy is chimerical. Numbers prescribes for the wilderness war camp in which the divine presence rests (v. 3) and more stringent impurity rules exist (1 Sam 21:5–7; 2 Sam 11:11). Thus, H and P are legislating for two different times and locales in which variant rules prevail. Note that Num 5:1–4 (H) banishes bearers of abnormal impurities. D's war camp excludes not only bearers of usual impurities, such as the menstruant and the parturient, but even those possessing a seminal emission (Deut 23:10–15). I assign this insertion to H$_R$.

28. *Num 8:14, 15b–19*. That the Levites replaced the firstborn (Num 3:11–13, 40–51, nos. 25, 26, H$_R$) is repeated here (vv. 16–17). Furthermore, v. 19 provides a rationale—a bona fide H characteristic—explaining the purpose of the Levites' service, to ransom the

---

[15] S. E. Loewenstam, "Law, Biblical," (*WHJP*, ed. B. Mazer; Tel Aviv: Massada), 3:231–67.

[16] Cf. Milgrom, *Numbers* (Philadelphia: Jewish Publication Society), 17–18.

[17] Cf. Knohl, *Sanctuary*, 54.

[18] Ibid., 86 and n. 78.

[19] Cf. Milgrom, *Leviticus 1–16*, 909–10, 995.

Israelites.[20] Remove vv. 14, 15b–19 and the text reads smoothly: vv. 20–22 reports Israel's compliance with the prescriptions of vv. 5–15a. Thus vv. 14, 15a–19 have been inserted by H_R.[21]

29. *Num 9:9–14*. It is difficult to accept Knohl's verdict on Num 9:1–14[22] that the narrative (vv. 1–8) was composed at a later stage than the legal unit (vv. 9–14). The law cites two criteria for postponing the פסח offering: distance and impurity. The narrative, however, speaks only of impurity. Thus the formulation of the latter must be subsequent to the text of the narrative. Since the narrative (vv. 1–8) is clearly a product of H,[23] the law (vv. 9–14) can be attributed to H_R. Again, a post-deuteronomic date must be postulated when distance from the one legitimate (Jerusalem) sanctuary became a major deterrent.

30. *Num 13:1–17a; 14:26–38*. As shown by Knohl,[24] the deity's direct address to Israel introduced by the subject אני, a telltale H word (13:2; 14:35), as well as interspersed P and JE expressions, which were editorially fused in these passages, point to the work of the editor H_R.[25]

31. *Numbers 15*. That this entire chapter stems from H was first observed by Kuenen.[26] This can be substantiated by examining each of this chapter's pericopes,[27] in particular, the last one, vv. 27–31. This pericope concludes not only chapter 15 but also the larger unit chapters 13–15, the failure of the scouts chosen by YHWH to report objectively their reconnaissance of Canaan. It also points forward to the adjoining Korahite rebellions (chapter 16). H_R anticipates Korah's challenge by unfurling its quintessential kerygma: All Israel can become holy if it fulfills the divine commandments. Thus, Num 15:37–41 serves as a transition between two large blocs, Numbers 13–15 and Numbers 16–18.[28]

---

[20] Cf. Milgrom, *Numbers*, 369–71.

[21] See further Milgrom, *Leviticus 17–22*, 1340–41.

[22] *Sanctuary*, 121.

[23] See the evidence compiled by Knohl, ibid., 21–22, 90.

[24] Ibid., 91–92.

[25] It is illogical, however, to assume (Knohl, ibid.). Ezekiel's use of other passages from this pericope is proof of their h origin.

[26] W. Kuenen, *An Historico-Critical Inquiry into the Origin and Composition of the Hexateuch* (Trans. P. H. Wicksteed; London: Macmillan, 1886), 96.

[27] See Milgrom, *Leviticus 17–22*, 1341–45.

[28] See Knohl, *Sanctuary*, 90.

32. *Num 19:10b.* The insertion of the גר is a telltale sign of H. Its insertion into Num 19, a P passage, is probably due to H_R.[29]

33. *Num 28:2b.* That this pre-positional verse is an H_R insertion is neatly caught by Knohl.[30]

34. *Num 29:39.* This postpositional summary of the cultic calendar would ordinarily be expected (see Lev 23:37–38). However, neither the Sabbath (28:9–10) nor the new moon (28:11–15) would be called a מועד. This verse, then, is the handiwork of H_R.[31]

35. *Num 33:50–56.* The mention of משכית and במות, both H terms,[32] as well as the first person to address Israel, testify that the insertion of this passage stems from H_R.

36. *Num 35:11–36; 36.* The plethora of H expressions in these two chapters[33] create a likelihood that their placement as an appendix to the book of Numbers should be attributed to H_R. If correct, this would mean that their legal provisions: the growth of the Levitic cities (cf. 35:1–8),[34] unintended homicide and the asylum city (35:9–29), and the requirement that daughters (and widows) who inherit ancestral land may not marry outside their tribe,[35] are H_R additions.

II. Loci

Pinpointing the location of the 36 above passages will lead to some of H_R's redactional methods.

A. *Postpositional and/or Supplementary*	B. *Pre-positional*	C. *Bi-positional (envelope)*
Within H (Leviticus)	Exod 6:2–8 (no. 23)	*Within H (Leviticus)*
19:30–36 (no. 3)	Num 5:1–4 (no. 27)	18:1–5, 24–30 (no. 1)
21:24 (no. 5)		19:5–8; 22:29–30 (nos. 3,5)
24:4 (no. 8)		18 and 20 (no. 4)
Within P (Leviticus)	D. *Interpositional*	23:2–3,42–43 (no. 7)
3:16b–17 (no. 14)	*Within P (Leviticus)*	25:1; 26:46 (no. 9)
	7:22–27 (no. 16)	*Outside Leviticus*

---

[29] I cannot follow Knohl's claim (ibid., 93) that H_R's insertion comprises 19:10b–13. Without vv. 11–12 we would not know how a corpse-contaminated person would purify himself.

[30] Ibid., 30.

[31] See J. Milgrom, *Leviticus 23–27*, 56.

[32] Cf. Milgrom, *Leviticus 17–22*, 1506.

[33] Cf. Knohl, *Sanctuary*, 99–100.

[34] Cf. M. Greenberg, "Idealism and Practicality in Numbers 4–5 and Ezekiel 48," *JAOS* 88 (1968): 59–63; J. Milgrom, "The Levitic Town: An Exercise in Realistic Planning," *JSS* 33 (1982): 185–8.

[35] Cf. Milgrom, *Numbers*, 511–12.

6:12–18aa (no. 15)	10:10–11 (no. 17)	Num 13:1–17a; 14: 26–28
11:43–48 (no. 18)	*Outside Leviticus*	(no. 30)
16:29–34 (no. 19)	Exod 27:20–21 (no. 20)	Num 28:2b ;29:39
Outside Leviticus	Exod 31:12–17; 35:1–3	(nos. 33, 34)
Exod 29:38–46 (no. 21)	(no. 22)	Num 35:1; 36:46 (no. 36)
Exod 12:18–20 (no. 24)	Num 3:11–13 (no. 25)	
Num 3:40–51 (no. 26)	Num 8:14–19 (no. 20)	
Num 9:9–14 (no. 29)	Num 15 (no. 31)	
Num 33:50–56 (no. 35)	Num 19:10b (no. 32)	

It can immediately be deduced that H$_R$ has made a studious attempt not to disturb the congealed texts of H, P, and JE. There ostensibly exists one slight exception: Num 8:14–19 (no. 28), where H$_R$ has wrapped itself around v. 15a (P). However this is one of H$_R$'s editorial techniques, as exemplified by Lev 3:16b (no. 14), where H$_R$ inserts בל חלב before ליהוה (P). Thus it is no exception. In all other instances, H$_R$ imposes his own text pre- post- bi- and inter-positionally, fourteen times in Leviticus (P and H), and sixteen times outside Leviticus (P and H; once P plus JE, no. 30). Thus, H$_R$ is clearly the redactor of Leviticus and likely the editor of Exodus and Numbers. Moreover, H$_R$ does more than edit (rearrange) the text. Whenever H$_R$ is of few words it is probably their author (e.g. nos. 5, 7, 8, 32, 36).

III. EGALITARIANISM

H$_R$ is characterized by an egalitarian thrust.

1^a. The purpose of the prohibitions against incest and other sexual violations (Lev 18:6–23; 20:10–21) is to protect the single woman against predatory males in her kin group. The result of such nationwide violations is the pollution of the land (18:24–30; 20:22), forcing the inhabitants into exile (no. 1).[36]

2^a. The universally accepted opinion that ואהבת לרעך כמוך "you shall love your fellow (Israelite!) as yourself," (Lev 19:18) is the summit of biblical ethics[37] is challenged and corrected by H$_R$ in the supplement to the same chapter, ואהבת לו כמוך "you shall love him (the נר) as yourself," (Lev 19:34) (no. 3).

---

[36] See Milgrom, *Leviticus 17–22*, 1572–84.
[37] For Judaism, see R. Akiva 4:12 קדושים ספרא and for Christianity, see Jesus, Matt 7:12.

3ᵃ. Lev 19 is structurally and ideologically the center of Leviticus and possibly the entire Torah (no. 4). Its major theme is holiness, available to all Israel—and not only the priests (see nos. 4ᵃ, 7ᵃ, 13ᵃ below).

4ᵃ. A priestly supplement (Lev 21:24) inserted by H_R ordains that the eligibility of priests to officiate in the sanctuary (Lev 21) is determined by the laity (no. 5; cf. nos. 8ᵃ and 15ᵃ, below).

5ᵃ. H_R added the pericopes on שבה and סבה (Lev 23:2aα–3, 42–43) to the festival calendar (23:4–38) to enable Israel to survive in exile (no. 7).

6ᵃ. H_R added the prohibition against eating blood and suet (Lev 3:16b–17) to the pericope on the שלמים offering (Lev 3) in order to anticipate the warning that שלמים blood not brought to the altar constitutes murder (Lev 17:3–4 [H]; cf. no. 12ᵃ, below).

7ᵃ. Holiness (Lev 11:43–45) is achieved by following the dietary laws (Lev 11), because they only permit a few herbivorous animals as food (no. 18), and they deter having a common table with non-Israelites (Lev 20:25–26). These additions are attributable to H_R.

8ᵃ. H_R (Lev 16:29–34a) transfers the supervision of the rites of the Day of Purgation from the high priest—heretofore his monopoly (cf. Lev 26:3–28)—to the laity (cf. לכם, vv. 29, 30, 31, 34a; details in no. 19).

9ᵃ. God addresses Moses (no. 21) while Israel is present *in the sanctuary* (Exod 29:42b–43, H_R's addition to the תמיד prescription vv. 39–42a), in opposition to P, which insists that lay persons are barred from the sanctuary except when they engage in the preparatory rites of their sacrifices (cf. Lev 1:3–5a, 6, 9).

10ᵃ. H_R claims that Levites replaced the first born (Num 3:11–13, 40–51). No reason is given. I surmise that the first born possessed the right and requirement to officiate at the family hearth to worship the ancestors (no. 25).[38]

11ᵃ. The Levites assumed the responsibility for lay encroachment upon the sanctums (Num 8:14–19; esp. v. 19—H_R addition). This role for the Levites is expressed by H's innovative root כפר (pi'el) "ransom."[39] (see no. 12ᵃ, below).

[38] Cf. Milgrom, *Leviticus 17–22*, 1379–82; 1772–85.
[39] Cf. Milgrom, *Numbers*, 342–43.

12^a. The root כפר meaning "ransom"[40] in the expression לכפר על נפשתיכם "to ransom your lives" (Lev 17:11) explain the function of the שלמים to ransom the lives of the Israelites when they slaughter animals for their food. Animal slaughter is declared murder (vv. 3–4) unless the animal's blood is brought to the authorized altar as a sacrifice.[41]

13^a. The laity is required to attach fringes, each of which contain a blue cord, to their outer garments (Num 15:37–41). The blue cord is a symbol of royalty and priesthood. Every Israelite is a royal priest who can attain holiness by observing the divine commandments.[42]

These additions by H$_R$ aspire to egalitarianism by: assigning a holy dimension—heretofore the exclusive prerogative of the priests—to all Israel (nos. 3^a, 4^a, 5^a, 7^a, 8^a); sharing Moses' right to witness the divine revelation (no. 9^a); granting the resident alien (גר) equivalent civil rights with Israelite citizens (no. 2^a); protecting the single woman against sexual violation by males from her kin group (no. 1^a); labeling the slaughter of animals for food as murder unless their blood is brought to the altar to ransom (כפר) the life of the slayer (nos. 6^a, 12^a); substituting the Levites for the firstborn who had heretofore worshiped the ancestors at the family hearth (no. 10^a); requiring every Israelite to wear a "thread of holiness" on each of the four fringes of the outer garment (no. 13^a)

At once, it should be noticed that six of the above passages—nearly half of H$_R$'s concerns (6 of 13)—endow every Israelite with the ability to attain holiness. H$_R$ himself is also a priest, and yet his chief desire is to share his birthright of holiness with his fellow Israelite! It should not be forgotten that priests retain the exclusive right to officiate at the altar. Note, however, that the holiness attainable by the laity is not that of the priests but of God himself, as expressed by H's kerygmatic formula קדשים תהיו כי קדש אני ה׳ אלהיכם "Be holy for I YHWH your God am holy" (Lev 19:2). All of Israel can attain the positive attributes of the deity (cf. Exod 34:6–7a; exemplified in Lev 19:11–18) by following God's commandments.

---

[40] Cf. Milgrom, *Leviticus 17–22*, 1474
[41] Ibid., 1472–78.
[42] Ibid., 1397–1400.

What contemporary message did H_R impart by declaring that all of Israel shared the divine revelation with Moses (9ª)? Perhaps H_R had court prophets in mind. Court prophets are evidenced in the time of David and Solomon (e.g., Gad, 2 Sam 24:11; Nathan, 2 Sam 11:1). Most likely, court prophets had to enter the royal sanctuary (cf. Moses, Exod 29:42b) in order to be spiritually receptive to gain the divine word.

The evidence for court prophets during the divided kingdom is scant but firm. Jezebel maintained 450 Baal prophets and 400 Asherah prophets אבלי שלחן איזבל "who ate at Jezebel's table" (1 Kgs 18:19). The 400 prophets who opposed the prophet Micaiah (1 Kgs 22:6) were probably wards of the king. The institution of the court prophet is reflected in the tradition preserved in the Book of Chronicles that among Levite singers, who were retainers of the court, there were prophets. Thus Heman the Levite was חזה המלך "the seer of the king" (1 Chr 25:5), and "The spirit of YHWH came upon Jahaziel," the Levite, who prophesized before King Jehoshaphat (2 Chr 20:14–17).[43] Thus, H_R is saying that God's message to Moses and to subsequent (court) prophets must be witnessed by the people.

H_R (and H) pound away at the equality of the גר (Exod 12:49; Lev 16:29; 17:15; 18:26; 19:34; 24:16, 22; Num 15:13, 29, 30). That the גר is required to obey the prohibitive commandments is due to his presence in the Promised (holy) Land.[44] However, that he is entitled to equal civil rights has nothing to do with his residence, but is due to H's egalitarian principles (2ª). It may well be that Ezekiel was influenced by this H doctrine when he envisioned that the one missing element in the equality of the גר—the right to possess and bequeath inherited land—would finally be granted (Ezek 47:22–23).

That the single woman receives divine protection against predatory males (1ª) may have an economic basis: She constitutes nearly 40 percent of the work force.[45] Yet to make sexual violations responsible for the pollution of the land and the expulsion of its inhabitants (Lev 18:24–30) goes far beyond the demands of egalitarianism.

---

[43] Cf. S. Mowinckel, *The Psalms in Israel's Worship*, vol. 2 (trans. D. R. Ap-Thomas; Oxford: Blackwell, 1967), 53–58.

[44] Cf. Milgrom, *Leviticus 17–22*, 1493–1501.

[45] See C. Meyers, "Procreation, Production and Protection: Male and Female Balance in Early Israel," *JAAR* 51:584–7.

It indicates, first, that such sexual abuses were probably rampant and, second, that H$_R$, by divine command, was intent on wiping them out.

H$_R$ agreed with earlier priestly tradition (P and H) that Israel should be limited to the few eligible sacrificial animals (and some species of game) for its food (7^a). This principle is also egalitarian: all life—animal as well as human—is inviolable.

The function H$_R$ assigns to the Levites—assuming the priestly role of the firstborn—bespeaks an attempt to expand the role of the Levites. Again, one can speak of an egalitarian thrust. H$_R$ is apparently unhappy with the wide disparity between the priests and Levites and tries to bridge these two cultic officials. H$_R$ does not spell out the new cultic duties to be assigned to the Levites. This task is assumed by D, for example: blessing the people (Deut 10:8); sharing the priestly sacrificial portions (Deut 18:1); sacrificing burnt offerings and incense (Deut 33:10).

Assuming that H$_R$ lived and worked in the Babylonian exile,[46] one of his goals would have been to refashion the structure of the society so that the disparities (and abuses) among the people would be reduced. This he was able to accomplish—at least in theory—mainly through the redaction of the book of Leviticus. In his workshop he structured extant passages of H and composed supplementary passages, seeking to bridge priests and laity, cultic prophets and laity, resident aliens and laity, priests and Levites, disadvantaged women and males. He also offers his solution to the widening gap between creditors and debtors, a subject I have already examined.[47]

---

[46] Cf. Milgrom, *Leviticus 23–27*, 1954–64.
[47] Ibid., 2191–2256.

A DOUBLE ENTENDRE IN JOB 15:32 IN
THE LIGHT OF AKKADIAN*

Shalom M. Paul

The Hebrew phrases מלא ימים and מלא שנה,[1] and their interdialectal semantic and etymological cognates in Akkadian: *ūmē/ šanāti malû/ mullû*,[2] and Ugaritic: *šnt mla*,[3] are well known expressions meaning "to reach fullness in time." It is interesting to note, moreover, that in both Hebrew as well as Akkadian the term is employed to refer to the forthcoming demise of an individual. Compare 2 Sam 7:12 (= 1 Chr 17:11): "When your days are complete (כִּ[י]מָלְאוּ יָמֶיךָ) and you lie down (וְשָׁכַבְתָּ)[4] with your forefathers,[5] I will raise up your offspring after you (אַחֲרֶיךָ),[6] one of your own issue, and I will establish his kingship"; Lam 4:18, "Our end is near (קָרֵב קִצֵּנוּ), our days are complete (מָלְאוּ יָמֵינוּ)."[7] Compare similarly in Assyrian royal inscriptions, *ūmē[ka imlû šanāt(ka)] ikšudamma ukkipu adanka*, "The days [of your life are over, the years of your (death)] has arrived; your

---

* It is my great privilege to be a member of the Editorial Committee of this volume, as well as to dedicate this brief contribution to Emanuel Tov, friend and colleague, whose scholarly mastery encompasses the Septuagint, Qumranic texts, and the textual criticism of the Hebrew Bible.

[1] מלא ימים—amongst the many examples that may be cited, see Gen 50:3; Lev 8:33; Num 6:5; Ezek 5:2; Esth 1:5; and for מלא(ו)את שנה, see Lev 25:30; Jer 25:12; 29:10.

[2] *CAD*, *M*, 1.180, 186.

[3] *KTU*² 1.12.ii:44–45, *šbʿ.šnt.mla wṯmn.nqpt*, "Seven years have been filled, eight cycles."

[4] For the verb שכב, "to lie down," which euphemistically means "to die," see Isa 14:8; 43:17; Ezek 31:18, 32:21, 27, 30; Job 3:13, 14:12. Cf. also its Akkadian interdialectal equivalents: *nâlu* (*CAD*, *N*, 1.204–206), *sakāpu* (= שכב) (*CAD*, *S*, 74), and *ṣalālu* (*CAD*, *Ṣ* 9, 68–69). For similar euphemisms, see W. W. Hallo, "Disturbing the Dead," *Minḥah le-Naḥum: Biblical and Other Studies Presented to Nahum M. Sarna in Honour of His 70th Birthday* (JSOT 154; ed. M. Brettler and M. Fishbane; Sheffield: JSOT, 1993), 183–92.

[5] This last phrase is absent from the Chronicles' passage.

[6] Heb. אחריך, similar to its Akkadian semantic and etymological cognate, *(w)arki*, has the connotation of "after one's demise." Cf. Laws of Hammurabi 150:17, 157:19; 158:25. For additional examples, see *CAD*, *A*, 2.279.

[7] Cf., somewhat similarly, Jer 25:34, "For the day of your slaughter draws near (מלאו ימיכם לטבוח)."

appointed time has drawn near" (Esarhaddon);[8] *ūmē imlû ukkipu adannu*,[9] "The days are complete, the appointed time has drawn near" (Ašurbanipal).[10] These two royal inscriptions contain the exact two equivalent phrases as found in the passage from Lamentations cited above: קָרַב קִצֵּנוּ[11] = *ukkipu adannu/adanka* and מָלְאוּ יָמֵינוּ = *ūmē(ka) imlû*, parallel expressions for indicating the imminent death of the persons involved. So, too, the following neo-Babylonian inscription of Nabonidus: "When (his) day was complete (*ištu ūm imlû*), Labašti-Marduk, his son, succeeded to the throne."[12]

In light of the above, we can now further appreciate the deft play on words found in Job 15:32 as part of the second discourse of Eliphaz, who picturesquely depicts the premature doom of the wicked man: בְּלֹא יוֹמוֹ תִּמָּלֵא וְכִפָּתוֹ לֹא רַעֲנָנָה. The second half of the verse, "His frond[13] never having flourished,"[14] begins the botanical imagery that continues in the next verse (33): "He will be like a vine that sheds its unripe grapes, like an olive tree that drops its blossoms." The first half of the verse, however, is problematic, since there is no feminine antecedent for the verb תִּמָּלֵא. Thus most commentators assume that the last word of the preceding verse (31), תְּמוּרָתוֹ, either dropped out by haplography or should be read at the beginning of v. 32[15] with a change of vocalization, תִּמֹרָתוֹ, meaning "his palm tree."[16] Others suggest that the female referent is יֹנַקְתּוֹ, "his shoots," which

---

[8] R. Borger, *Die Inschriften Asarhaddons Königs von Assyrien* (Graz: Selbstverlage, 1956) 105, col. i, line 32.

[9] For Akk. *ekēpu*, "to draw near, to approach," see *CAD*, E, 69; and for Akk. *adannu* (= Aram. עֶדָּן), "a moment in time at the end of a specific period," see *CAD*, A, 1.97–98. For its use in reference to the natural end of human life, see ibid., 98. It, too, is employed with the verb *malû*, "to be fulfilled, ended in time" (but not in reference to death; see ibid., 99).

[10] M. Streck, *Assurbanipal und die letzten assyrischen Könige bis zum Untergange Niniveh's* (VAB 7; Leipzig: J. C. Hinrichs, 1916), 178, line 15.

[11] For Heb. קֵץ, referring to the appointed time for the end of life, see Gen 6:13; Jer 51:13; Amos 8:2; Ezek 7:2 (twice), 3, 6 (twice); and elsewhere.

[12] S. H. Langdon, *Die neubabylonischen Königsinschriften* (VAB 4; Leipzig: J. C. Hinrichs, 1912), 276, col. i, line 26; 276, col. iv, line 35.

[13] For Heb. כִּפָּה, in connection with palm trees, see Lev 23:40, כַּפֹּת תְּמָרִים (which some commentators vocalize: כִּפֹּת תְּמָרִים).

[14] Heb. רַעֲנָנָה, accented on the penult, is the only example of the employment of this word as a verb. All other occurrences relate to the adjective. This translation follows the *NJPS*.

[15] Thus, M. H. Pope, *Job* (AB 15; Garden City, NJ: Doubleday, 1973), 119.

[16] N. H. Tur-Sinai *The Book of Job* (Tel-Aviv: Yavneh, 1954), 157 (Hebrew). See also S. R. Driver and G. B. Gray (*The Book of Job* [Edinburgh: T. & T. Clark, 1971], 102 of the notes) who compare the Peshitta translation, מוֹעִיתָא. For Heb. תִּמֹרָה, referring to "palm trees," see Ezek 41:18, 19 (twice) and elsewhere.

appears in v. 30.[17] And as for the verb itself, תִּמָּלֵא, most read תִּמַּל (*nifʿal* of the geminate verb, מלל; cf. Job 14:2, וַיִּמָּל; 24:24, יִמָּלוּ) or תִּמְלַל, "shall wither,"[18] thereby creating a parallel to לֹא רַעֲנָנָה in the parallel stich. It is suggested here, however, that the form תִּמָּלֵא was deliberately written in order to create a clever double entendre. On the one hand, the verb is related to the geminate מלל and thus commences the ensuing botanical description. But with the addition of the *aleph*, which derives the verb from the stem מלא, the scribe also intended to allude to the expression מלא ימים, with the meaning attested above in both Hebrew and Akkadian, "to reach the end of one's days, to die,"[19] in this case, "prematurely" (בלא יומו).[20] This, in turn, is the exact opposite of the blessings found in Exod 23:26, אֶת מִסְפַּר יָמֶיךָ אֲמַלֵּא, "I will grant you the full span of your days (i.e., of your life)"; and Isa 65:20, "No more shall there be an infant or old man who does not live out his days (אֲשֶׁר לֹא יְמַלֵּא אֶת יָמָיו)."

---

[17] See Driver and Gray, *Book of Job*, 102 of the notes.

[18] Most commentators read תִּמַּל; for תִּמְלַל, see, for example, Ibn Ganah, *Sepher Haschoraschim* (Berlin: Meqitzei Nirdamim, 1896), 261 (Hebrew).

[19] Cf. also the various suggestions offered by Rabbi Davidis Kimchi, *Radicum Liber* (= ספר השרשים) (ed. H. R. Biesenthal and F. Lebrecht; photocopy of Berlin edition 1847; Jerusalem: no publisher, 1965), 192 (Hebrew).

[20] See S. M. Paul, "Premature Death in Semitic Languages," *The Bible in the Light of Its Interpreters: Sarah Kamin Memorial Volume* (ed. S. Japhet, Jerusalem: Magnes, 1994), 575–86 (Hebrew).

THE HISTORY OF ISRAELITE RELIGION AND THE BIBLICAL TEXT: CORRECTIONS DUE TO THE UNIFICATION OF WORSHIP*

Alexander Rofé

I

The present article is premised on the understanding that there is an intimate relationship between religion and text, namely—between the beliefs held by scribes and copyists of holy scriptures and the texts that they produce. It is well known that the intellectual world of a copyist may leave its stamp on his handiwork.[1] If this rule applies to the scribe's universe of thoughts, feelings and mental associations,[2] how much more so when articles of faith are at stake and when the texts in question are not merely secular compositions, but rather holy writings, which both the copyist and his community expect to conform with their beliefs. In applying this principle to our area of research, I wish to discuss the transmission of the biblical text in light of the history of Israelite religion.[3]

---

* Translated by Ilana Goldberg, M.A. Excerpts from the Hebrew Bible and Talmud have been adapted from the NJPS and the Soncino Talmud, respectively. Retroversions from the LXX are marked with an asterisk.

[1] G. Pasquali, *Storia della tradizione e critica del testo* (2nd ed.; Firenze: Le Monnier, 1952); S. Timpanaro, *Il lapsus freudiano: psicanalisi e critica testuale* (Firenze: La Nuova Italia, 1974, repr. 1975). In Timpanaro's opinion, the Freudian lapsus is not present in the copying of texts.

[2] An interesting instance how present-day associations cause textual corruptions can be found in: R. Weiss, *Studies in the Text and Language of the Bible* (Jerusalem: Magnes, 1981) [IV], n*. חנוך ילון was corrupted into חנוך לוין, since Hanoch Lewin was a well-known Israeli playwright.

[3] A pioneer in this field was Abraham Geiger; cf. his *Urschrift und Uebersetzungen der Bibel in ihrer Abhaengigkeit von der innern Entwickelung des Judenthums* (Breslau: Hainauer, 1857). Seminal work was done in the last generation by Isac Leo Seeligmann; cf. his "Studies in the History of the Biblical Text," *Text* 20 (2000): 1–30; idem, "Indications of Editorial Alteration and Adaptation in the Massoretic text and the Septuagint," *VT* 11 (1961), 202–21. Cf. also: E. Tov, *Textual Criticism of the Hebrew Bible* (Minneapolis-Assen/Maastricht: Fortress-Van Gorcum, 1992), 264–69. From my own work in this field I quote two titles only: A. Rofé "The Methods of Late Biblical Scribes as Evidenced by the Septuagint Compared with the Other Textual Witnesses," in *Tehillah le-Moshe: Biblical and Judaic Studies in Honor of Moshe Greenberg*

The relationship between religion and text must be seen as one dimension of a larger complex of cultural relations. Any crucial development in the religious life of a faith community will inevitably have an impact on several areas—law and administration, historiography and storytelling, and also upon the area that concerns us here—textual transmission.[4] We wish to trace developments and transformations as they occurred in these different cultural realms. Moreover, one can expect that each one of these areas will illuminate the other, by supplying the context for understanding the full extent of any given transformation.[5] Religion, law, historiography, literature and text will mutually inform one another, interweaving to create a unified picture.

This sort of comprehensive contextual approach is sorely needed in biblical studies. The discipline's problems are well known: the Bible is a limited literary corpus; external sources which illuminate scripture are few; archaeological discoveries from the Land of Israel are mostly mute, i.e. epigraphic findings are scanty; entire historical epochs remain enigmas. As far as the text—our current subject of inquiry—is concerned, the textual witnesses are late (e.g. the Massoretic Text = MT), or tendentious (the Samaritan Pentateuch = SP), or fragmentary (Qumran scrolls) or secondary and indirect (the Septuagint = LXX, and other ancient translations, citations and paraphrases in later literature). Given this predicament, scholars are obliged to complete the evidence through conjecture. Conjecture, I wish to emphasize, is permissible and even necessary in every branch of historical science. This applies to conjectural text emendations as well. But which conjectures should be considered legitimate in textual criticism? In my opinion, only a conjecture which is consistent with

(ed. M. Cogan et al.; Winona Lake, Ind.: Eisenbrauns, 1997) 259–70; idem, "The Historical Significance of Secondary Readings," in *The Quest for Context and Meaning: Studies in Honor of James A. Sanders* (ed. C. A. Evans and S. Talmon; Leiden etc.: Brill, 1997) 393–402.

[4] Menachem Cohen offered a broad description about the impact of religious life and technical innovations on Jewish conceptions of the Biblical text and its transmission in the Modern and Contemporary Ages; cf. M. Cohen, "The Idea of the Sanctity of the Biblical Text and the Science of Textual Criticism," in *The Bible and Us* (ed. U. Simon; Tel Aviv: Devir, 1979), 42–69 (Hebrew). Available in English on internet: http://cs. anu.edu.au/%7Ebdm/dilugim/CohenArt.

[5] Indeed, when scholars challenge the presence of religious corrections, they provide an alternative context for the textual variance; cf. Y. M. Grintz, "Between Ugarit and Qumran," *Scholia* (*Eshkolot*) 4 (1962): 146–61 (Hebrew); M. Tsevat, "Ishbosheth and Congeners," *HUCA* 46 (1975): 71–87.

trends that have been recognized in the milieu of the Bible. Therefore, if we are able to identify the existence of a trend in a broad enough context—religion, law, literature and text in their ramified forms—this will provide a suitable background for proposing a conjectural emendation, even without supporting evidence from any textual witnesses. We will have recourse to such emendations in the course of this article.[6]

II

The crucial development, which concerns us in this study, is the unification of the cult carried out by Josiah, king of Judah. According to the Book of Kings, in the eighteenth year of his reign (622 B.C.E.) Josiah effected a series of cultic reforms (2 Kgs 23:2–24). He was moved to this action after the discovery of a book of Torah in the temple, which was read aloud before the king (22:8–11). One of the reforms carried out by Josiah was unusual: the defiling of all the shrines where the Lord had been worshiped before, the gathering of all the priests of Judah to Jerusalem, and the unification of the cult therein (23:8–9, 15–23). This induced scholars to speculate that the book of Torah that had been discovered in the Temple was Deuteronomy, since it is the only book in the Pentateuch which enjoins the unification of the cult in one site. Scholars speculated further, that an ancient edition of Deuteronomy, which evidently included the laws calling for the unification of the cult, was composed some time before the discovery of the book of Torah, i.e in the seventh century B.C.E.

Of the various Deuteronomic laws prescribing cult unification, one in particular seems most suited to have served as the platform for the reforms of 622 B.C.E. (a platform that preceded the reforms themselves). It is the passage in Deut 12:8–12, which begins, "You shall not act at all as we now act here, every man as he pleases, because

---

[6] Against the present trend of negating the legitimacy of conjectural emendations, I would refer the reader to the textual critics of classic literature; cf. H. Fränkel, *Testo critico e critica del testo* (a cura di C. F. Russo; trad. di L. Canfora; Firenze: Le Monnier, 1983), esp. 42–46; D'A. S. Avalle, *Principi di critica testuale* (Padova: Antenore, 1978), 111–19: 'emendatio ope ingenii'; P. Mass, *Textkritik* (3rd ed.; Leipzig: B. G. Teubner, 1957), 12–13; trans. B. Flower, *Textual Criticism* (Oxford: Clarendon, 1958), 15–17.

you have not yet come to the rest and inheritance that the Lord your God is giving you." Here the lawmaker admits that in the past, even in Moses' times, cult unification was not in practice! Apparently, the plurality of places of worship was a reality that the lawmaker was obliged to acknowledge, even though this plurality was meant to have disappeared once the people achieved rest and inheritance some time after the Settlement. If this reasoning is correct, then we can identify Deut 12:8–12 as the legal formulation of the radical platform for unifying the cult in Josiah's day.[7]

It is difficult to trace the aftermath of the unification reforms from 622 onwards. To what extent were they upheld after Josiah's death in 609, and to what extent did they endure after the destruction of Jerusalem in 587? On the other hand, we do possess knowledge of the resulting situation during the course of the Second Temple period: a single Jewish Temple in Jerusalem and a single Samaritan Temple on Mt. Gerizim.[8] The existence of other temples in Egypt—one in Elephantine at the beginning of the Second Temple period, and one in Leontopolis at its end—does not alter the general picture, although it does imply that the act of unification did not go unchallenged, and was certainly met with many doubts at the time of its institution.

On the other hand, the implication the reforms had for Israelite historiography are quite clear to us. The Book of Kings, which was compiled for the most part just before the Exile, and shortly thereafter, identified in Jerusalem "the site where the Lord your God will choose to establish his name" (Deut 12:11). And so the Book of Kings tells us that Rehoboam, the son of Solomon, "reigned in Jerusalem—the city the Lord had chosen out of all the tribes of Israel to establish His name there" (1 Kgs 14:21). Besides, the author of the Book of Kings accepted the claim in the aforementioned Deuteronomic law, that the unification of the cult should have been enforced at the beginning of Solomon's reign, when, as the king says, "The Lord my God has given me respite all around: there is no adversary and no mischance. And so I propose to build a house for the name of the Lord my God" (1 Kgs 5:18–19). From here

---

[7] For a fuller treatment cf.: A. Rofé, "The Strata of the Law about the Centralization of Worship in Deuteronomy etc.," *SVT* 22 (*Congress Volume, Uppsala 1971*; Leiden: Brill, 1972): 221–26.

[8] This is the starting point of Julius Wellhausen in his chapter on the place of worship; cf. J. Wellhausen, *Prolegomena zur Geschichte Israels* (6th ed.; Berlin und Leipzig: De Gruyter, 1927), 17–52.

onwards the law of the unification of the cult became positive law in Israel, and the author of the Book of Kings used it as a yardstick for evaluating all the kings of Judah, judging them as pious, middling, or wicked.

The literature that was written from this point onwards fell in line with this position. The Book of Tobit, for example, opens with a description of the piety of the protagonist's father, Tobit of the tribe of Napthali. Before he was exiled by Shalmaneser, king of Assyria, Tobit adhered strictly to the requirement of making regular pilgrimages to Jerusalem. All of his brethren in Israel rebelled against Jerusalem, but he remained loyal to the city and performed the yearly pilgrimages with gifts for the priesthood and tithes in hand (Tob 1:4–8). Loyalty to Jerusalem, the only Temple city, became an indispensable element of the characterization of a pious Israelite in the literature of the Second Commonwealth.[9]

The creative domain of law did not stagnate either. When King Josiah arrived at Bethel and slaughtered priests upon their altars, in the zeal of the unification reforms (2 Kgs 23:15–20), legal formulations too were radicalized. The altars and temples outside of "the site that the Lord your God will choose" were now considered past sites of Canaanite idolatry, or at least places where worship was carried out according to the ways of the Amorites (Deut 12:2–4). Simultaneously, the date when the laws became effective was pushed back. For, on the one hand, it was not conceivable that upon their entry to the land the Israelites would have tolerated the existence of idolatry for even one hour, but they must have eradicated it at once. And on the other hand, a law such as this one, which was reason enough to kill (and be killed for) could not possibly have been contingent upon achieving "rest and inheritance", but must have been an absolute commandment, effective immediately upon entrance to the land. And so reads Deut 11:31–12:7: "When you cross the Jordan to enter and possess the land . . . and you have taken possession of it and settled in it, take care to observe all the laws and the rules. . . . These are the laws and the rules that you must carefully observe . . .

---

[9] To the rich literature on the Book of Tobit I would like to add an item cherished by Israelis: Enzo Sereni, who was parachuted behind the German lines in 1944, captured and murdered in Dachau by the Nazis, had written his Ph.D. dissertation at the University of Rome on Tobit. Cf. E. Sereni, "Il libro di Tobit," *Ricerche Religiose* 4 (1928) 43–55, 97–117, 420–439; 5 (1929): 35–49.

You must destroy all the sites at which the nations you are to dispossess worshiped their gods . . . ." The law became effective, therefore,
immediately upon entry to the land. The Priestly Code continued
this trend, and took it back even one more step: the unification of
the cult was in existence from the time of the erection of the
Tabernacle in the desert, "in the first month of the second year, on
the first of the month" (Exod 40:17).

Here again, historiography aligned itself with the legal literature.
Most of the Book of Joshua (chapters 1–23) speaks of a single and
unique cultic center, the tabernacle the Israelites established in Shiloh
(18:1–10; 19:51; 22:29). This fact explains the book's silence: it contains no stories of epiphanies or etiological tales that might have
established the sanctity of various places in the land. The one exception is the story in Josh 5:13–15, which recounts the epiphany of
the Captain of the Lord's hosts to Joshua; however this story is
clearly fragmented, which only serves to confirm our contention. In
addition the book does not mention any alternative places of worship other than Shiloh. And again here there is one exception that
confirms the rule: the story in Josh 8:30–35, is a rather late accretion , which seeks to describe how Joshua realized the law in Deut
27:4–8.[10] But this cultic act does not continue on later. Most of the
Book of Joshua, as we received it in its current form—a Deuteronomic
work with priestly expansions—relates the history of ancient Israel
in congruity with the law of unification of the cult, as it is formulated in Deut 11:31–12:7, and with the practices of the Tent of
Meeting as they are described in Exodus 35–40. It appears, therefore, that Israelite historiography rewrote the period of the Conquest,
to describe it as an ancient period of cult unification, in conformity
to the legal sources.

The books of Judges and Samuel, however, and in particular the
ancient composition (called by scholars the "Elohist" or "Ephraimite"
document)[11] which extends from Joshua 24 to 1 Samuel 12, were

---

[10] Cf. A. Rofé, "The Editing of the Book of Joshua in the Light of 4QJoshᵃ,"
in *New Qumran Texts and Studies* (ed. G. J. Brooke; STD 15; Leiden: Brill, 1994),
73–80; M. N. van der Meer, *Formation and Reformulation: The Redaction of the Book of
Joshua in the Light of the Oldest Textual Witnesses* (Ph.D. diss., Leiden, 2001), 402–35.

[11] Cf. K. Budde, *Die Bücher Richter und Samuel, ihre Quellen und ihr Aufbau* (Giessen:
J. Ricker, 1890); C. F. Burney, *The Book of Judges with Introduction and Notes* (2nd ed.;
London, 1920, Repr. New York: Ktav, 1970) xli–l; A. Rofé, "Ephraimite versus
Deuteronomistic History", in *Storia e tradizioni di Israele—Scritti in onore di J. Alberto
Soggin* (a cura di D. Garrone e F. Israel; Brescia: Paideia, 1991), 221–35.

not guided by the principle of the unification of the cult. On the contrary, the literary assemblage reaching from Joshua 24 to 1 Kings 2 often mentions various places of worship in Israel—Shechem, Ophra of Abiezer, Mizpeh Gilad, Bethel, Mizpah (in Benjaminite territory), Gilgal, Ramah, Hebron, and others. And these places, which contravene the law of cult-unification, are mentioned with neither censure nor justification. The implication is that the author or redactor was not aware of the existence of even one of the laws of Deut 11:31–12:28. The editing of the literary assemblage Joshua 24–1 Kings 2 apparently preceded the acceptance of the laws of cult unification as positive law in Israel.

As a result, the historiography of the Former Prophets bequeathed future generations a complex outlook on the history of the Israelite cult: unification at first, a multitude of places of worship later at the time of the Judges, Saul and David, and unification again from the time of Solomon onwards, after the establishment of the Temple in Jerusalem.

Within Jewish law, this complex outlook became a systematized historical theory. Thus the Mishna recounts (*Zebaḥ* 14:4–8):

> Before the tabernacle was erected high places were permitted . . . After the tabernacle was erected the high places were forbidden . . . .They came to Gilgal, the high places were permitted . . . .They came to Shiloh, the high places were forbidden; there was no ceiling there, but a building of stone below and cloth overhead, and that was "Rest" . . . They came to Nob and Gibeon, the high places were permitted . . . They came to Jerusalem and the high places were forbidden and never again were they permitted, for that was "Inheritance".

In this manner the Rabbis were able to resolve a good part of the difficulties arising in the Former Prophets.[12] Here we hear of Samuel, an undoubtedly righteous leader, who gathered the people for a fast "at Mizpah . . . before the Lord" (an idiom which indicates a place of worship) (1 Sam 7:6), who built an altar for the Lord at Ramah (ibid. *v.* 17), who held sacrifices of the people at the shrine above the city (9:12–13, 19–24), and who wished to sacrifice at Gilgal (10:8; 13:8–14). However, since all the acts were performed after the destruction of Shiloh, when "they came to Nob and Gibeon," as it

---

[12] A modern tentative to uphold the Rabbinic interpretation was done by B. Uffenheimer, "On the Question of Centralisation of Worship in Ancient Israel," *Tarbiz* 28 (1958/9): 138–53. Cf. also the note by S. E. Loewenstamm, ibid., 393.

were, it follows that they were performed during "the time when high places were permitted," and that they are considered completely legitimate.

Unresolved difficulties arising from incidents when a righteous leader or a prophet of the Lord sacrifice outside of Shiloh or Jerusalem, during "the time when high places are forbidden," were resolved through midrashic interpretation. Gideon erected an altar in Ophra and sacrificed a young bull on it (Judg 6:25–32). This was addressed in the Talmud by Rabbi Abba bar Kahana, who said:

> Eight things were permitted that night: [The sacrifice] outside [the tabernacle], at night, [by] a non-priest, [without] ministering vessels, [with] vessels of Asherah, [with] woods of Asherah, *muqṣeh* and [an animal] used for work.[13]

The first allowance was made for חוץ—sacrifice outside the single sanctuary. And similarly, Elijah's sacrifice on Mount Carmel (1 Kgs 18:30–39) was interpreted: "Him you shall heed" (Deut 18:15), "Although he says to you, 'Transgress one of the commandments in the Torah, like Elijah on Mt Carmel', at that moment you shall heed him."[14]

For the sake of our discussion, it is necessary to clarify the inter-mediate links between the erection of the tabernacle in the desert and the construction of the Temple in Jerusalem, according to the Rabbinical interpretation. According to the Book of Joshua (18:1) the tent of meeting was installed at Shiloh; there the land was divided into tribes "before the Lord" (ibid. vv. 6, 8, 10, 19:51), and there too was the only legitimate altar, "the altar of the Lord our God which stands before his Tabernacle" (22:29). The tabernacle in Shiloh is mentioned also in Psalm 78 (v. 60) and the entrance to the tent of meeting is mentioned in 2 Sam 2:22 (a verse which we will treat below). Ostensibly, these verses are congruent with the description of the sanctuary in Shiloh in the stories of Eli and Samuel in 1 Samuel 1–3, but in fact there is a discrepancy, because the Shiloh of Eli and his sons is called "the palace of the Lord (1 Sam 1:9; 3:3) or "the house of the Lord" (1:24, 3:15), a house with doors

---

[13] B. Tem. 28b–29a. I have mainly followed L. Miller, *Temurah: Trans. into English* (*The Babylonian Talmud: Seder ḳodashim*, ed. I. Epstein; London: Soncino, 1960), 211.

[14] *Sipre Devarim* 175. Cf. also par. 70: "However, you sacrifice in all places sanctioned by a prophet, as done by Elijah on Mount Carmel."

(ibid.) and doorposts (1:9). What then stood there—a house or a tent? The Rabbis resolved the problem as we saw above: "They came to Shiloh . . . there was no ceiling but a building of stone below and cloth overhead . . . ." Historical criticism obliges us to acknowledge, however, that the ancient sources described the temple at Shiloh as a house or a palace, while later sources, influenced by the principle of cult unification and by the Priestly story that pushed back the unification of the cult to the Mosaic tabernacle in the desert, described Shiloh as a tent or a tabernacle.

The next intermediary links in the Rabbinical scheme are Nob and Gibeon. As for Nob, tradition relied upon the fact that Nob was inhabited by a family of legitimate priests from Eli's dynasty, who kept proper cult practices, such as "the bread of display, which had been removed from the presence of the Lord"[15] (1 Sam 21:2–10; 22:9–3). As for Gibeon, the tradition relied on Solomon's act described as follows:

> And Solomon, though he loved the Lord and followed the practices of his father David, also sacrificed and offered at the high places. The King went to Gibeon to sacrifice there, for that was the largest high place; on that altar Solomon presented a thousand burnt offerings. (1 Kgs 3:3–4).

However the author of Chronicles was not content with having Solomon worship at any of the high places, even before the Lord's Temple was built in Jerusalem, and therefore the verse was reworked:

> Then Solomon, and all the assemblage with him, went to the high place at Gibeon, for the Lord's Tent of Meeting, which Moses the servant of the Lord had made in the wilderness was there . . . The bronze altar, which Bezalel son of Uri son of Hur had made, was also there before the Tabernacle of the Lord, and Solomon and the assemblage resorted to it. There Solomon ascended the bronze altar before the Lord, which was at the Tent of Meeting, and on it sacrificed a thousand burnt offerings (2 Chr 1:3, 5–6).

Thus, by stating that the tent of meeting stood in Gibeon, the book of Chronicles bestowed a temporary sanctity to Gibeon and turned it into an intermediate link in the history of Israelite worship. It may

---

[15] The right reading has been preserved in 4QSam[b]; cf. F. M. Cross "The Oldest Manuscripts from Qumran", *JBL* 74 (1955): 147–72; repr. in: *Qumran and the History of the Biblical Text* (ed. F. M. Cross and S. Talmon; Cambridge, Mass. and London: Harvard University Press, 1975), 147–76.

be said that what the redactor of Joshua 18–22 does for Shiloh, by turning the House of the Lord into the Tent of Meeting, the author of Chronicles does for Gibeon by turning the high place into "the Lord's Tent of Meeting."

Moreover, it appears that the author of Chronicles presents Gibeon as the sole legitimate place of worship, in the very same way Shiloh is presented in the book of Joshua. At the margins of the story of Ornan the Jebusite he writes:

> At that time, when David saw that the Lord had answered him at the threshing floor of Ornan the Jebusite, then he sacrificed there. For the Tabernacle of the Lord, which Moses had made in the wilderness and the altar of burnt offerings were at that time in the high place at Gibeon, and David was unable to go to it to worship the Lord because he was terrified by the sword of the angel of the Lord. David said, "Here will be the House of the Lord God and here the altar of burnt offerings for Israel" (1 Chr 21:29–22:1).

In other words, David really ought to have gone to Gibeon, where the legitimate cult was in practice, but because of the exigencies of the moment, he was compelled to sacrifice at the threshing floor of Ornan. Only in retrospect did he realize that Ornan's threshing floor was the place that the Lord desired and he decided that it should become "the house of the Lord God." From the perspective of the book of Chronicles, Gibeon was not only a link within the chain of Israelite worship, but actually a link within the chain of the unified cult! Here there is an apparent attempt to describe the unification of the cult as a positive law that was upheld in an unbroken continuum throughout Israelite history.[16] The systemized history put forth by the Rabbis in Mishnah Zebaḥim 14—"They came to Nob and Gibeon and the high places were permitted"—seems, then, to be an indulgence on the part of the Rabbis, in order to reconcile with the tradition preserved in the Former Prophets between 1 Samuel 5 and 1 Kings 6.

Another notice in the book of Chronicles which relates to this matter is 1 Chr 16:39–40: "Also Zadok the priest and his fellow

---

[16] Aliter: S. Zalewski, *Solomon's Ascension to the Throne* (Hebrew; Jerusalem: Marcus, 1981), 338–50; M. Garsiel, "The Portrayal of David's Census in 1 Chr. 21 in Light of the Parallel Account in 2 Sam 24" (Hebrew), in *Studies in Bible and Exegesis*, vol. 5, *Presented to Uriel Simon* (ed. M. Garsiel et al.; Ramat Gan: Bar-Ilan University Press, 2000), 137–60, esp. 156–60.

priests before the Tabernacle of the Lord at the high place which was in Gibeon; to sacrifice burnt offerings to the Lord on the altar of the burnt offering regularly, morning and evening, in accordance with what was prescribed in the Torah of the Lord with which he charged Israel." This information is embedded in a passage (16:37–42) which tells how, after bringing the ark up to Jerusalem, David installed the Levitical worship "before the Ark of the Covenant"—servants, gatekeepers, and musicians. This sequence is interrupted by the mention of the Lord's Tabernacle in Gibeon, and therefore verses 39–40 must be viewed as an interpolation. This addition serves to emphasize that the legitimate cult headed by the legitimate priest was in effect at the tabernacle in Gibeon and not before the Ark in Jerusalem.[17] This is another example of how Second Temple scribes were engaged in interpreting the history of cult unification at its various stages, well before the formulation of the Mishnah by the Rabbis.

The history of unification of the cult continued to engage scribes during the Second Commonwealth even after the canonization of the book of Chronicles. This is evidenced in a recently published fragment of a manuscript from Qumran, 4Q522, which, however, was not authored there. A translation of the fragment is cited below:[18]

1. [   ] . . . [   ]
2. We [cannot come to Zi]on to establish there the Tent of Mee[ting until the end of]
3. time. For behold a son is born to Jesse son of Perez son of Ju[dah and he will seize]
4. the rock of Zion and disinherit the Amorites lest [they mislead him;[19] and he will decide]
5. to build a house to the Lord God of Israel. Gold silver and [copper he will prepare]

---

[17] Cf. J. W. Rothstein-J. Hänel, *Kommentar zum ersten Buch der Chronik* (KAT: Leipzig: Deichertsche, 1927), 393; S. Japhet, *I & II Chronicles: A Commentary* (OTL; Louisville, Kentucky: Westminster/John Knox, 1993) ad loc. Japhet, however, did not notice that 1 Chr 16:39–40 were interpolated. Besides, in her history of the Tabernacle according to the Priestly sources she did not take into account Josh 18–19, 21–22.

[18] Cf. E. Qimron, "Concerning 'Joshua Cycles' from Qumran", *Tarbiz* 63 (1994) 503–508 (Hebrew). His reconstructions are generally preferable to those of Puech, quoted therein. Puech's subsequent edition took account of Qimron's corrections; cf. E. Puech, *Qumran Grotte 4 xviii* (DJD XXV; Oxford: Clarendon, 1998), 55–62.

[19] At this point Qimron reconstructs [יניחוהו לוא] פן. However, the compound of *pen lo'* + imperfect does not sound Hebrew. It is better to restore as suggested in my translation: [יחטיאוהו] פן.

6. bringing cedars and cypresses [from the] Lebanon to build it; and his youngest son [will build it and Zadok]

7. will minister there first. [The Lord will show] him good[will and favor and bless him]

8. [from His dwel]ling in the heavens, for [the beloved of the Lord] will dwell safely and for [all]

9. days He will dwell with him forever. But now the Amorite is there and [in the hills] the Canaanit[e

10. dwell who misled me when I did not ask for the judgment of the [Urim]

11. from you and they deceived me and h[er]e I have made them [eternal] slaves to Israel

12. And now let us establish the Tent of Meeting far from the Canaanite and

13. Elazar and Joshua [carried] the Tent of Meeting from Beth [El to Shiloh]

14. Joshua [Capt]ain of the hosts of the ar[mies of Israel]

15. x[ ]x[ ]x[ ]

This passage answers the question, why the Tent of Meeting was installed in Shiloh at the time of the conquest of the land (Josh 18:1), for the site was neither sanctified by an epiphany, nor was it designated as holy by a prophetic utterance. The answer lies in Joshua's desire to distance the people from the Amorites and the Canaanites, namely the Gibeonites, who deceived him, misleading him into transgression. If the reconstruction of lines 12–13 is correct, then Elazar and Joshua carried the tent of meeting from Beth-El to Shiloh. This ties into the admonishment of the angel of the Lord at Bochim (Judg 2:1–5), which according to the LXX was near Beth-El (see below), and whose remonstrance was for the sin of making a covenant with the inhabitants of the land. Unlike its present context, it seems that that admonishment was directed against one particular instance of covenant making, the case of the Gibeonites.[20] In any event, the removal of the Tent of Meeting from Beth-El and its installation in Shiloh (according to the reconstruction) rejects Beth-El as the chosen cultic site. It should not be assumed that these words were directed toward the high place of Gibeon, since the passage at stake is tied closely with the story stemming from Chronicles concerning preparations for building the Temple,[21] and Chronicles,

---

[20] Cf. A. Rofé, *Belief in Angels in Ancient Israel* (Hebrew; Jerusalem: Makor, 1979), 256–71.

[21] Cf. I. Kalimi, "History of Interpretation. The Book of Chronicles in Jewish Tradition from Daniel to Spinoza," *RB* 105 (1998): 5–41, esp. 21–22.

as we saw, emphasizes that the Tent of Meeting stood at Gibeon, until its final removal to the Temple in Jerusalem.

III

The fundamental concepts about the history of the Israelite cult and the "chosen place," that we have encountered thus far, made their mark on the transmission of the text, as indicated by the textual variants among the major textual witnesses. And, as mentioned above, we contend that the accumulative evidence of these textual variants—when considered together with the history of law, including later legal interpretations, historiography and literature—all these together allow us to conjecture textual emendations to those verses, for which no witnesses testify against the Massoretic text.[22]

Let us begin with the subject of the ancient chosen site, Shiloh.

1. Josh 24:1 מת: ‏ויאסף יהושע את־כל־שבטי ישראל שכמה . . . ויתיצבו לפני האלהים

LXX:[23] *. ‏ויאסף יהושע את כל שבטי ישראל שילה . . . ויציבם לפני האלהים

Ibid. 25–26 מת: ‏ויכרת יהושע ברית לעם ביום ההוא, וישם לו חק ומשפט בשכם

‏. . . ויקח אבן גדולה ויקימה שם תחת האלה אשר במקדש ה'.

LXX:[24] ‏ויכרת יהושע ברית לעם ביום ההוא, וישם לו חק ומשפט בשילה, לפני משכן

*. ‏אלהי ישראל . . . ויקח אבן גדולה ויקימה יהושע תחת האלה לפני ה'.

Shechem is replaced twice by Shiloh, and instead of "the Sanctuary of the Lord" (MT v. 26)" we encounter "the Tabernacle of the God of Israel" (LXX v. 25). The phraseology smacks of translated Greek. And indeed, since at that time, as far as we know, the issue of cult unification at Shiloh was the concern of Palestinian Hebrew scribes, but not of the Hellenistic Jewish translators in Egypt, or of the copyists who came in their wake, it appears that the Septuagint translated here a reading that was in their Hebrew *Vorlage*. This is a

---

[22] Cf. *supra*, n. 6.

[23] Καὶ συνήγαγεν Ἰησοῦς πάσας φυλὰς Ισραηλ εἰς Σηλω . . . καὶ ἔστησεν αὐτοὺς ἀπέναντι τοῦ θεοῦ.

[24] Καὶ διέθετο Ἰησοῦς διαθήκην πρὸς τὸν λαὸν ἐν τῇ ἡμέρα ἐκείνη καὶ ἔδωκεν αὐτῷ νόμον καὶ κρίσιν ἐν Σηλω ἐνώπιον τῆς σκηνῆς τοῦ θεοῦ Ισραηλ.

(. . .) καὶ ἔλαβεν λίθον μέγαν καὶ ἔστησεν αὐτὸν Ἰησοῦς ὑπὸ τὴν τερέμινθον ἀπέναντι κυρίου.

secondary version that arose out of a nomistic correction, intended to harmonize the act of the righteous leader, Joshua, with the Priestly formulation of the law of cult unification, which described the erection of the Tabernacle in the wilderness.[25] For the nomistic scribe, the sanctuary of the Lord in Shiloh is the only legitimate place of worship.

2. These textual variants, and their underlying ideology, explain the problem of the verse in 1 Sam 2:22b:

MT: ‎ועלי זקן מאד ושמע את כל אשר יעשון בניו לכל ישראל ואת אשר ישכבן את
הנשים הצבאות פתח אהל מועד ויאמר להם למה תעשון

4QSam[a]:[26] ‎ועלי זקן בן תשעים שנה [ושמנה שנים] וישמע [את] אשר
[יע]שום בניו לבני ישראל [ויאמר למה] תעשו[ן].

LXX B:[27] ‎ועלי זקן מאד ושמע את אשר יעשו בניו לבני ישראל ויאמר להם למה
‎תעשו . . . *

The Septuagint and the Qumran scroll transmit a version that does not include ‎ואת אשר ישכבן את הנשים וגו' "how they lay with the women, etc.." And indeed the latter phrase is suspect as an interpolation. It describes the sin of Eli's sons, although this was mentioned neither earlier, when their deeds were described (2:12–17), nor later, in the reproach of the man of God (2:27–36), nor finally in the vision of Samuel (3:11–14). The sentence's appearance at the margins of what Eli heard, seems to be a secondary accretion. And why was it added here? It seems that a later scribe did not consider the sin of Eli's sons involving the sacrifices to be so grave, and he enhanced their sin by adding prostitution or adultery to it.

An interesting question in its own right is the hypothetical identity of the interpolator. Ostensibly this is a scribe from the priestly circles. After all, he writes using terms taken from the Priestly code, in Exod 38:8: "He made the laver of copper and its stand of copper, from the mirrors of the women who performed tasks at the

---

[25] Concerning this trend cf. *supra*, n. 10. And in addition: L. Mazor, "A Nomistic Reworking of the Jericho Conquest Narrative Reflected in LXX to Joshua 6:1–20," *Text* 18 (1995): 47–62.

[26] Cf. E. C. Ulrich, *The Qumran Text of Samuel and Josephus* (HSM 19; Missoula, Mont: Scholars, 1978), 57.

[27] Καὶ Ηλι πρεσβύτης σφόδρα· καὶ ἤκουσεν ἃ ἐποίουν οἱ υἱοὶ αὐτοῦ τοῖς υἱοῖς Ισραηλ, καὶ εἶπεν αὐτοῖς Ἵνα τί ποιεῖτε . . .

entrance of the Tent of Meeting." Actually, however, the interpolator is not a vehicle of priestly ideology in this instance. For, in his opinion, the disregard Eli's sons had for the Lord's portion of the sacrifice did not warrant punishment by death for Hofni and Phinehas, and therefore he felt the need to attribute an additional sin to them. This is an interesting example of how Priestly concepts left the exclusive domain of their original authors and became common currency for ordinary scribes.

However, in the context of this article, we are focusing on the definition of the Lord's Temple in Shiloh as "the Tent of Meeting." The identification is not deliberate, it seems, but was made only half-consciously, because this particular interpolator was really interested in another issue. However, he incidentally reveals his conceptual world, that of Jewish scribes in the Persian and Hellenistic period; for them the Temple in Shiloh was the Tent of Meeting, an expression of the continuity of the unification of the cult since ancient times: "They came to Shiloh ... the high places were forbidden."

3. The non-apparent can be deduced from the apparent. 1 Kgs 8:1–11 relates the story of the transferral of the Ark of God from the City of David to the inner sanctum of the Temple built by Solomon. In this act lies the focus of the whole story, and the ark is mentioned in vss. 1, 3, 4, 5, 6, 7, 9. Suddenly with no warning, in vs. 4, after "the priests ... carried up the ark of the Lord," we are told, "Then the priests and the Levites brought the Tent of Meeting and all the holy vessels that were in the Tent." The Tent of Meeting was not mentioned until here since 1 Sam 2:22 (MT). And if all its holy appurtenances were brought, what is the use of the vessels made for Solomon by Hiram (1 K 7:13–51)? It seems, therefore, that this too is an interpolation made in the spirit of the emendations and additions examined above. It is couched in these very words in 2 Chr 5:5. There are no textual variants to confirm our conclusion, but the logic requires it no less, in this instance.[28]

4. By analogy we suggest the conjectural emendation of the following verse in Judg 18:30–31: ויקימו להם בני דן את הפסל ויהונתן בן נרשם
בן משה הוא ובניו היו כהנים לשבט הדני עד יום נלות הארץ. וישימו להם את פסל
מיכה אשר עשה כל ימי היות בית האלהים בשלה.

---

[28] Cf. Wellhausen (*supra*, n. 8), 43–44.

The Danites set up the sculptured image for themselves; and Jonathan
son of Gershom son of Manasseh, and his descendants, served as priests
to the Danite tribe until the land went into exile. They maintained
the sculptured image that Micah had made throughout the time that
the House of God stood at Shiloh.

'Until the land (הָאָרֶץ) went into exile' probably refers to the first
exile from the times of Tiglat Pileser III, King of Assyria, in 733
B.C.E. But herein arises another difficulty concerning the end of verse
31. Shiloh was destroyed, as far as we know, after the battle at
Aphek (1 Samuel 4) in the 11th century, 300 years before the first
Assyrian exile. This also emerges from Psalm 78, which mentions
the Lord's abandonment of Shiloh (v. 60) before His election of
Mount Zion and David (vv. 68–70). How then was the existence of
a temple in Shiloh conjoined with the date "the land went into
exile"? The attempts to amend this verse to the "until the ark (הָאָרוֹן)
went into exile" (cf. 1 Sam 4:21–22),[29] are of no use, because the
words "throughout the time that the House of God stood at Shiloh"
present a difficulty in themselves. What does this have to do with
the existence of Micha's statue in the far north? How does the fate
of Shiloh affect Dan in the era before the establishment of the
monarchy?[30]

For these reasons, Smend suggested, around 100 years ago, to
emend בשלה into בלישה (in Laish, i.e. Dan).[31] In this manner both
difficulties are obviated: Michah's idol stood "throughout the time
that the House of God stood in Laish*", and they both existed until
"the land went into exile." The emendation displays great acumen,
yet it is unclear how the corruption would have occurred: while
metathesis is a common phenomeon,[32] a difficult secondary variant
like בשלה will not readily replace an original and perfectly clear reading, such as לישה. And note that the city Laish was already mentioned in this chapter in v. 7, 27, 29; it was not unfamiliar to the
copyists.

---

[29] This was Houbigant's suggestion, reported by Burney (*supra*, n. 11), at 415.

[30] In my opinion, Hauret's suggestion, to find here the theological intention of
juxtaposing legitimate Shilo to idolatrous Dan, is farfetched; cf. Ch. Hauret, "Aux
origines du sacerdoce danite: à propos de Jud. 18.30–31," *Melanges Bibliques Rédigés
en l'Honneur de André Robert* (Tournai: Bloud & Gay, n.d. [1957]), 105–13, ad 112.

[31] Cf. R. Smend, "Miscellen: 2. Jdc. 18,31," *ZAW* 22 (1902): 161; J. A. Soggin,
Judges: A Commentary (OTL; Philadelphia: Westminster, 1981), ad loc.

[32] Cf. N. H. Tur-Sinai, "Scribal Metathesis in the Biblical Text," (Hebrew) in
his: *Ha-lashon Weha-sefer* (3 vols.; Jerusalem: Bialik, 1949–1955), 2.106–149.

However, if we have identified the tendency to replace names of allegedly illegitimate sites of worship with the names of the "chosen places," as we saw in Joshua 24, then Smend's suggestion attains a great degree of probability. This is not a mere technical error, but a theological correction, even though the conjectural emendation *בלישה rests on the graphic similarity of the two words; we shall see a similar example of this sort of correction below בית ישראל – בית אל. In any event, whoever corrected the text did not pay attention to the internal logic of the passage, but was rather concerned with the legitimacy of cultic sites. Below we shall see more evidence of this kind of editing in biblical manuscripts.

5. At this juncture we ought to mention the question of the short passage in Gen 33:18–20: ויבא יעקב שלם עיר שכם אשר בארץ כנען בבאו מפדן ארם, ויחן את פני העיר. ויקן את חלקת השדה, אשר נטה שם אהלו, מיד בני חמור אבי שכם במאה קשיטה. ויצב שם מזבח ויקרא לו אל אלהי ישראל.

> Jacob arrived at Shalem the city of Shechem which is in the land of Canaan—having come thus from Paddan-aram—and he encamped before the city. The parcel of land where he pitched his tent he purchased from the children of Hamor, Shechem's father, for a hundred kesitahs. He set up an altar there and called it El-Elohe-Yisrael.

The story in Josh 24:32 about the burial of Joseph's bones in the same plot indicates that the plot was in Shechem itself, or at least in its outskirts. Therefore, even if there is a village in the area of Shechem (Nablus) named Salim, one may doubt whether the verse intended to indicate such a place. Moreover, a collocation such as שלם עיר שכם does not exist anywhere else in the Bible. Even the attempt to understand שלם as an adverb (the SP reads שלום here) would create a deviation from standard Biblical Hebrew. I believe, therefore, that Abraham Geiger was correct in suggesting, nearly 150 years ago, that שלם עיר is a corrective addition to the text, by the hand of a scribe who wished to emphasize that the first place Jacob arrived at, upon returning from Padan-Aram was not Shechem, but rather Shalem, i.e. Jerusalem.[33] Here too, according to this hypothesis, the copyist created an awkward locution, not only from the linguistic standpoint, but also from the standpoint of content and logic,

---

[33] Geiger (*supra*, n. 3), 74–76.

because the narrative sequence of the story in 33:18 through 35:8 situates Jacob in the region of Shechem.

Two methodological remarks are in order here. The first relates to the degree of consistency in textual emendations. The reader might wonder what use the scribe had for adding עיר שלם, according to this conjecture, when later on he kept the mention of בני חמור אבי שכם intact? And we shall see below that at times the mention of Beth-El is completely elided, while later in the same book, and even in the same narrative sequence it is kept in place. The reason is, that these corrections are partial, sometimes even sporadic.[34] Anyone familiar with contemporary publishing knows that even professional copyeditors can rarely produce an utterly consistent manuscript.

The second remark relates to the effect of theological corrections on the narrative sequence. The kind of emendations that we have suggested, and others we are yet to examine, create a contextual problem. "The house of God in Shiloh" and שלם עיר שכם are examples of this. These are difficult readings, although secondary ones. This implies that for the discipline of textual criticism, the identification of theological emendations contradicts the rule of *lectio difficilior prae-ferenda*, for theological emendations created variants which disturb the sequence. These are not difficult and therefore preferable variants, says one scholar, these variants are impossible.[35]

6. Back to the scriptures, we turn to the conjectural reconstruction of the original passage in Deut 27:1–8. This passage presents a borderline problem for textual criticism, verging as it does, on historico-literary criticism. The passage includes two commandments: the

---

[34] Cf. Seeligmann (*supra*, n. 3), 9 n. 20: "Continued inquiry into the matter has taught me that there have indeed been reworking processes in the MT, yet they never evince any degree of consistency (the same applies to the many text reworkings in the LXX)." Having submitted a few instances, Seeligmann concludes: "These inconsistencies are of consequence regarding a common apologetical challenge: Is one justified in assuming that a certain text underwent reworking when we do not find it in a similar text where it could be expected? And indeed, we must take into account that lack of consistency is a feature characterizing all literary activity in the Orient." These statements are, in my view, fundamental in our discipline. At the same time, I wonder if inconsistency is limited to the transmission of Oriental literatures. Moreover, one reworking process has been made thoroughly in the MT: it is the deletion of *ṣeba'ot* in the first seven books of the Bible. The LXX has it in Josh 6:17 only.

[35] Cf. B. Albrektson, "Difficilior Lectio Probabilior—A Rule of Textual Criticism and Its Use in Old Testament Studies," *OTS* 21 (1981): 3–18.

erection of large stones, and the construction of an altar. The construction of the altar is mentioned once, in vv. 5–7, while the establishment of the large stones is prescribed twice, in vv. 2–3 and in
verses 4, 8, as follows:

4. והיה בעברכם את הירדן	2. והיה ביום אשר תעברו את הירדן
	אל הארץ אשר ה׳ אלהיך נתן לך
תקימו את האבנים האלה	והקמת לך אבנים גדלות
אשר אנכי מצוה אתכם היום בהר עיבל	
ושדת אותם בשיד	ושדת אתם בשיד
8. וכתבת על האבנים	3. וכתבת עליהן
את כל דברי התורה הזאת באר היטב	את כל דברי התורה הזאת בעברך
	למען אשר תבא אל הארץ
	אשר ה׳ אלהיך נתן לך
	ארץ זבת חלב ודבש
	כאשר דבר ה׳ אלהי אבתיך לך.

4. Upon crossing the Jordan	2. As soon as you have crossed the Jordan
	into the land that the Lord your God is giving you,
you shall set up these stones	you shall set up large stones.
about which I charge you this day on Mount Ebal	
and coat them with plaster	Coat them with plaster
8. and on those stones you shall inscribe	3. and inscribe upon them
all the words of this Torah most distinctly.	all the words of this Torah,
	when you cross over
	to enter the land that the Lord your God is giving you, a land flowing with milk and honey, as the Lord, the God of your fathers, promised you.

A holisitic interpretation would see this as a prescription for two
series of stones, one on the day of the crossing of the Jordan, at a
place near the river (Gilgal?), and one on Mt. Ebal, at a later point.
But in a critical-historical view these are but two formulations of the
same commandment. The ancient formulation in vv. 4, 8, enjoined

the erection of the stones on Mt. Ebal (and next—an altar on the
same spot), while the later formulation, vv. 2.3, which is indeed more
detailed, suppressed the name of Mt. Ebal, thus blurring the place
for the erection of the stones (and the altar).[36] Both formulations, at
first probably transmitted on different scrolls, were combined together,
through the method of double readings; the ancient formulation,
however, was probably noted between the lines and in the margins,
and this is how v. 8 was copied outside of its proper place.[37] The
suppression of the name of a cult site which eventually came to be
considered illegitimate, hampers the comprehension of the sequence
of the passage. In this case, again, it must be admitted, we have no
textual witnesses to substantiate the process of transmission conjectured here.

IV

7. What about the Samaritan Pentateuch (SP)? In the passage under
discussion it goes along with the MT, apart from one difference—
v. 4, where it reads Mount Gerizim, instead of Mount Ebal. Another
significant textual witness—the Vetus Latina—supports it. There are
scholars, contemporary ones too, who prefer the reading "Mount
Gerizim" over the Massoretic one,[38] which is supported by all the
other textual witnesses, including the scribe who composed Josh
8:30–35.

Two considerations, in my view, militate in favor of the variant
"Mt. Ebal." Ancient Shechem, Tel Balaṭa, was built on the endmost
southern slopes of Mt. Ebal,—a fact more pronounced in Biblical

---

[36] B. W. Bacon, *The Triple Tradition of the Exodus* (Hartford, Conn.: The Student
Publishing Company, 1894), 255–65; M. Anbar, "The Story about the Building of
an Altar on Mount Ebal," in *Das Deuteronomium: Entstehung, Gestalt und Botschaft* (ed.
N. Lohfink, BETL 68; Louvain: Peeters, 1985), 304–309.

[37] Cf. S. Talmon, "Double Readings in the Masoretic Text," *Text* 1 (1960):
144–84; idem, "Aspects of the Textual Transmission of the Bible in the Light of
Qumran Manuscripts," *Text* 4 (1964): 95–132; R. Gordis, "The Origin of the
Masoretic Text in the Light of Rabbinic Literature and the Dead Sea Scrolls,"
Tarbiz 27 (1957/8): 444–69, esp. 453, 467–69; (Hebrew) A. Roifer, "The End of
Psalm 80," *Tarbiz* 29 (1959/60): 113–24 (Hebrew); A. Rofé, "The End of the Song
of Moses (Deuteronomy 32:43)," in *Liebe und Gebot—Studien zum Deuteronomium Festschrift . . . Lothar Perlitt* (ed. R. G. Kratz et al.; Göttingen: Vandenhoeck & Ruprecht,
2000), 164–72, ad 168–69.

[38] So *BH* and *BHS*; also E. Tov (*supra*, n. 3), 95, n. 67.

times, before three thousand years of soil erosion filled the bottom of the valley. And we have ample accounts in the Bible of an ancient cult site in Shechem, or nearby—Gen 12:6–7, 33:18–20; Josh 24:1–28. The injunction to erect a cult site on Mt. Ebal suits this reality well.

The second consideration is the well-known tendentiousness of the SP. Its tendency to continuously proclaim the holiness of Mount Gerizim may be recognized in the commandment to erect the stones and the altar on Mount Gerizim appended to the Ten Commandments, both in Exodus 20 and in Deuteronomy 5, thus creating what is essentially an incongruous context. And what's more: the ancient cultic injunction, "In every place where I cause my name to be mentioned I will come to you and bless you" (Exod 20:24), which took into account the worship of God in many sites, was emended by the SP to, "The place where I mentioned my name, there I will come to you and bless you;"[39] thus they disavowed the plurality of places of worhip, referring back to the mention of Mount Gerizim. In addition, they included an explicit identification with the place of the Blessing and Curse in Deut 11:30: "(by the terebinths of Moreh) in front of Shechem." In light of the above, the SP mention of Mount Gerizim in Deut 27:4 is part of a broad trend, which accentuates the sanctity of the new place of worship, which began to be constructed, it appears, around the middle of the Persian era, in the fifth century B.C.E.[40] But not even a random mention of a holy site on Mt. Gerizim is extant in any pre-exilic texts.

These variants from the SP ought to be viewed within the comprehensive framework of the cult unification reforms. The SP and the MT both share the tendency to harmonize scripture with what was percieved as the legitimate history of the Israelite cult. However, within the MT this is accomplished with a light finishing touch—minor additions or elisions. This is most obvious when one considers the fact that there is not one verse in the Torah which equates the "chosen place" with Jerusalem! In the SP, by contrast, the transmitters' interventions were much more drastic. This might be due to the fact that the Samaritans did not develop an oral tradition of the same scope that Judaism did, and therefore they felt the need

---

[39] Cf. A. von Gall, *Der Hebraeische Pentateuch der Samaritaner* (Giessen: Töpelmann, 1918).

[40] Cf. Y. Magen, "Mt. Gerizim—A Temple City," *Qad* 33 (2000): 74–118 esp. 113–14. (Hebrew)

to spell out things in their Scripture. The difference is aptly expressed in the words of the Rabbis:

> ... as the Terebinth of Moreh, mentioned in the latter verse [Gen 12:6] is Shechem, so in the former verse [Deut 11:30] it means Shechem. It has been taught: R. Elazar ben R. Yose said: In this matter, I proved the Samaritan scribes to be forgers. I said to them: You have falsified your Torah, but you gained nothing thereby. You declared that the Terebinths of Moreh means Shechem; we too admit that the Terebinths of Moreh means Shechem. We learned this be an inference from analogy, but you, how have you learned it?[41]

"Analogy" (גזירה שווה) and other rules for interpreting scripture are what makes the difference between Jews and Samaritans.[42]

8. The problem of the Samaritan emendations leads us to another textual correction, which also deals with a competing cultic center to Jerusalem, established later in the Second Temple period, the Onias Temple in Egypt. Isa 19:18 reads. "In that day, there shall be several towns in Egypt speaking the language of Canaan, and swearing loyalty to the Lord of Hosts; one shall be called the Town of Heres."

But the name of city has several significant variants

MT: עיר ההרס
MT, mss: עיר החרס
1QIsᵃ: עיר החרס
LXX (S) *עיר הצד חרס—πόλις ασεδ ηλιου
LXX: *עיר הצדק   πόλις/ασεδεκ
Targum: קרתא בית שמש דעתידא למחרב[43]

---

[41] *B. Soṭa* 33b; I have mainly followed A. Cohen, *Soṭah, transl. into English* (*The Babylonian Talmud: Seder Nashim in Four Volumes*, vol. 3, ed. I. Epstein; London: Soncino, 1936), 165. Parallel passages are *Sipre Deb.* 56 and *y. Soṭa* 7.3 where the saying has been attributed to R. Elazar ben R. Shimʿon.

[42] Cf. R. Weiss, "Concerning One Type of Revision in the Samaritan Pentateuch," in his: *Studies* (*supra* n. 2), 199–205 (Hebrew). The English version was published first in: *Armenian and Biblical Studies* (ed. M. E. Stone; Jerusalem: St. James 1976), 154–64. On p. 164 Weiss wrote: "The lack of binding legal exegesis among the Samaritans, i.e. Oral Law, such as is known in Judaism, which developed as an accompaniment to Written Law, resulted in the Samaritan practice of inserting interpretations into the Pentateuch text itself."

[43] According to *Mikraʾot Gedolot ʾHaketerʾ: Isaiah* (ed. M. Cohen; Ramat-Gan: Bar-Ilan University Press, 1996) a.l.

In my opinion, the original version was: עִיר הַחֶרֶס and it referred to the Egyptian city Heliopolis, where a large Jewish community existed. Originally, this verse made no mention of a cultic site in connection with the city. Later, when the son of the high priest Onias III fled to Egypt and established a Temple to the Lord modeled after the Jerusalem Temple, an attempt was made to find an allusion to it in Scripture, and Hebrew manuscripts were emended to עִיר הַצֶּדֶק, after the Zadokite dynasty. Jerusalem loyalists among the scribes came back with a rejoinder: not עִיר הַחֶרֶס, the city of the sun, but rather עִיר הַהֶרֶס, the city of destruction! If our interpretation of these textual variants is correct, this is a unique case where an originally "neutral" text was emended in two different ways, positively and negatively, as it were, reflecting the course of a religious dispute.

V

The largest group of emendations relating to the unification of worship appears in connection with the site of Beth-El. The reason for this lies in Beth-El's importance as a cultic center both in the days of the Israelite Monarchy—"a king's sanctuary and a royal palace" (Amos 7:13)—and after the destruction of the monarchy as well, when Beth-El was the seat of an Israelite priest who taught "the practices of the god of the land" (2 Kgs 17:27–28). Therefore, the cult unifiers in Josiah's day spent all their zeal and rage on Beth-El's altars and priests (2 Kgs 23:15–20; see vs. 16 in LXX). From here on we do not hear about Beth-El in the historical books, but archaeologists claim, that it was settled until approximately 500 B.C.E., that is until the reign of Darius, after the Restoration.[44]

On the other hand, the Book of Jubilees, a document from the second century B.C.E., includes one intriguing episode relating to Beth-El. According to Jub. 32:16, 22, Jacob planned to build the site of Beth-El, surround it with a garden and sanctify it in perpetuity for him and his sons after him. Then an angel descended from heaven and said to him: "Do not build this place and do not turn it into an eternal sanctuary and do not settle it, for this is not the

---

[44] Cf. H. Eshel, "The Historical Background of Building Temples for the God of Israel in Bethel and Samaria following the Destruction of the First Temple" (Hebrew University M.A. dissertation, 1989) (Hebrew).

place. Go to the house of Abraham your father and reside with your father Isaac until the day of your father's death."[45] It is not clear whether this rejection of Beth-El is a reflection of a contemporary historical reality,[46] or whether it is only a reaction to the over-emphasis of its sanctity in the Jacob narratives in the book of Genesis (28:10–22; 35:1–15). In either case, this brief episode shows us that the problem of whether Beth-El should be considered holy or should be rejected as a place of worship, was still a burning issue in the Hellenistic period, when the Biblical text was still being transmitted in a rather free manner.

Four methods can be identified in the work of copyists in dealing with the problem of Beth El. I list them here in their supposed order of appearance: (a) Beth-El is turned into a blasphemy (b) The name Beth-El is elided or (c) it is emended so as to obscure its presence (d) justification of the cult in Beth-El as a practice that was appropriate for its time.

(a) *Beth-El is turned into a blasphemy*

Amos 5:5: לא תבאו ובאר שבע לא תעברו, כי הגלגל גלה יגלה ובית אל יהיה לאון ואל תדרשו בית אל והגלגל. "Do not seek Beth-El, nor go to Gilgal, nor cross over to Beer-sheba, For Gilgal shall go into exile, and Beth-El shall become a delusion." The first part of the verse "For Gilgal shall go into exile" suggests that the meaning of און at the end of the verse is " null, chaos, nothingness."[47] In any event, this verse is proof that the name of the sanctuary in Beth-El was punned on in a derogatory sense to mean: nothingness. The name בית און does not occur in the book of Amos, but it does appear in the book of Hosea three times; and once more in the collocation במות און, as follows:

Hos 4:15:   ... ואל תבאו הגלגל ואל תעלו בית און ...
Hos 5:8:   תקעו שופר בנבעה הצצרה ברמה

---

[45] Following Littmann and Charles; cf. E. Littmann, "Das Buch der Jubilaeen," in *Die Apokryphen und Pseudepigraphen des AT* (ed. E. Kautzsch, 2 vols.; Leipzig: J. C. B. Mohr, 1900), 2.31–119; R. H. Charles, "The Book of Jubilees," *The Apocrypha and Pseudepigrapha of the OT*, 2 vols. (ed. R. H. Charles; Oxford: Clarendon, 1913; repr. 1968), 2.1–82.

[46] Cf. J. Schwartz, "Jubilees, Bethel and the Temple of Jacob," *HUCA* 56 (1985): 63–85.

[47] Cf. Isa 41:29 where *'awen* parallels *'epes* and *rûaḥ watohu*. And see: M. Weiss, *The Book of Amos* (Hebrew, 2 vols.; Jerusalem: Magnes, 1992), 1.140; 2.247.

הריעו בית און   אחריך בנימין

Hos 10:5:   לעגלות בית און   ינורו שכן שמרון
כי אבל עליו עמו וכמריו עליו יגילו על כבודו כי גלה ממנו

Hos 10:8: ונשמדו במות און חטאת ישראל
קוץ ודרדר יעלה על מזבחותם

Did scribes copying the prophecies of Hosea change the name Beth-El to Beth-Aven? This question must be answered while taking two contradictory pieces of data into account. The first is that the name Beth-El is mentioned in Hosea in the MT only once in 12:5 "At Beth-El [he] would meet him, there to commune with him," since the Beth-El mentioned in 10:5 apparently refers to a deity.[48] In LXX Beth-El is not mentioned at all. Consequently the suspicion arises that the book was reworked to have בית אל replaced by בית און. The other fact that needs to be taken into consideration is that there really was a town named בית און, although its precise location is unknown. According to the book of Joshua it was situated east of Beth-El, while the Book of Samuel locates it to the west of Michmas.[49] In any case, the existence of such a town is supported by the story of the naming of Benjamin at his birth, בן-אוני (Gen 35:18). And so, the possibility arises that בית און was actually original in some verses. Above all, one must take into account the possibility, that the prophet Hosea himself or the compiler of his book used the blasphemous name בית און for polemical reasons, and therefore it can not be seen as an emendation by a copyist.

9. The key to solving the problem lies, in my opinion, in the LXX version of Hos 12:5, which against Beth-El of the MT reads ἐν τῷ οἴκῳ Ὤν, a reading that obviously reflects the Hebrew Vorlage of LXX: *בבית און.[50] This then constitutes proof that the Hebrew copyists of this book changed בית אל to בית און. And beginning with this

---

[48] Cf. Rofé (supra, n. 20), 219–38.

[49] Cf. Josh 7:2; 18:12; 1 Sam 13:5; 14:23. Kallai tried to solve the problem by identifying Beth-awen with Tel-el-'askar, 1 km NNE of Michmas. Cf. Z. Kallai, "Beth-El-Luz and Beth-Aven," in *Prophetie und geschichtliche Wirklichkeit im Alten Israel: Fs. S. Herrmann* (ed. R. Liwak and S. Wagner; Stuttgart etc.: Kohlhammer, 1991) 171–88. An additional study was done by Na'aman; cf. N. Na'aman "Bethel and Beth-aven: An Investigation into the Location of the Early Israelite Cult Places," *Zion* 50 (1984/5): 15–25 (Hebrew). But his hypothesis that the name of the temple in Bethel was *Beit-'Eben* is farfetched, in my opinion.

[50] J. Ziegler, *Duodecim prophetae*[2] (Septuaginta, vol. XIII, Göttingen: Vandenhoeck & Ruprecht, 1967), 130.

datum, one may revisit all the verses mentioning בית און in Hosea and classify them as either original or emended verses.

10. Hos 4:15, seems to have originally read בית אל. The exhortation requires a particular object: "Do not come to Gilgal, do not make pilgrimages to Beth El," for the addressees need to know exactly what they are being warned about. Moreover, according to our hypothesis, an original בית אל makes for an effective pun: ואל תעלו בית אל. In addition, Beth-El's topographic situation at an altitude of 880 meters well suits the verb "to go up" (compare Judg 20:18, 26; 1 Sam 10:3). The copyist, who was rightly aware of the cultic reference, altered בית אל to בית און.

On the other hand, in Hos 5:8, the author seems to have originally used the name בית און, outside of any cultic reference and in relation to Benjamin,[51] whose name was בן-אוני at first. This brings to mind the possibility that the original place name was Beth-On, and indeed, it seems unlikely that a place would be called Beth-Aven by its own inhabitants.

11. Hos 10:5 is an obscure verse. It refers, apparently, to a calf which stood in Beth-El and was taken as spoil by the enemy. ("The glory that is departed from it" compare 1 Sam 4:21–22: "The glory has departed from Israel"—referring to capture of the Ark of God). "The people and the priestlings" are mournful over the exile of this "glory."[52] It is difficult to decide whether the author used the words "the calves of Beth-El" which was altered by the copyists or whether the prophet already has used this pejorative terms, as in the next example.

As for Hos 10:8, the parallelism במות און//חטאת ישראל preserves the text. "That sin of Israel" in Hosea was apparently interpreted by his disciples, the redactors of the book of Kings as "the sins that Jeroboam committed and led Israel to commit" (1 Kgs 14:16, and elsewhere); this is the sin of the calves of which it is said ויהי הדבר הזה לחטאת (1 Kgs 12:30; compare 13:34). Now, the calves were

---

[51] In spite of the similarity to Judg 5:14, I believe we should follow Wellhausen and read here *yeḥerad binyamin* or the like, instead of the MT. The LXX has ἐξέστη And cf. A. A. Macintosh, *Commentary on Hosea* (ICC; Edinburgh: Clark, 1997) 199. Note also the usage of *h.r.d* in 1 Sam 13:7; 14:15.

[52] Instead of the awkward *yagilu*, I read *yiggalu* = 'they uncover themselves' (in mourning). A fuller discussion will be presented elsewhere.

installed in Beth-El and Dan. However, the continuation of the verse in Hosea ("their altars") contains no suggestion that Beth El was referred to. And in Hos 12:12 Gilead is also connected to אָוֶן.[53]

The situation can be summed up as follows: The appellation בֵּית אָוֶן was popular in prophetic circles as early as the 8th century B.C.E., as evidenced in Amos 5:5. The prophet Hosea used the word אָוֶן in reference to Israelite cultic sites (10:8), and therefore it is likely that he too used בֵּית אָוֶן as an appellation for Beth El (10:5). On the other hand, Hosea mentions בֵּית אָוֶן (Beth-On), a town that carried the name of Ben-Oni (5:8) in a military context,[54] not a cultic one. And there is no doubt that a copyist of the Book of Hosea altered, once at least, the name בֵּית אֵל (Beth-El) to בֵּית אָוֶן (Beth-Aven) (12:5 LXX), which supports the hypothesis that such a reworking of the text was also performed on Hos 4:15 (MT and LXX).[55]

In my opinion, the emendations of Beth-El to Beth Aven were made at a relatively early date, in late pre-exilic times. This can be deduced from the way in which the copyists of the book of Hosea related to the prophets' own polemic (Amos 5:5; Hos 10:8). The textual emendation reflected the ideology shared by the first generations of the prophets' disciples, an outlook that in time became congenial to the cult unification movement that was gaining ground in Jerusalem. Such a connection exists between Jeremiah's original words, "The Shameful Thing [Boshet] has consumed the possession of our fathers ... Let us lie down in our shame, let our disgrace cover us ... " (Jer 3:24–25), on one hand, and the Baal/ Boshet emendations in the books of Jeremiah and Samuel, on the other.[56]

---

[53] Apparently, one should follow Ginsberg and read: נֹם נִלְעַד אָוֶן . . . בַּגִּלְגָּל לַשְּׁוָדִים וְזִבְּחוּ; cf. H. L. Ginsberg, "Hosea's Ephraim, More Fool than Knave: A New Interpretation of Hosea 12:1–14," *JBL* 80 (1961): 339–47, ad 342–43.

[54] On the meaning of the passage within its historical framework see: H. Tadmor, "The Historical Background of Hosea's Prophecies" in *Y. Kaufmann Jubilee Volume* (ed. M. Haran; Jerusalem: Magnes, 1960) פה-פד (Hebrew).

[55] Cf. Kallai (*supra*, n. 49). He too regarded בֵּית אָוֶן as original in Hos 5:8. Generally, however, he does not distinguish between original and secondary (scribal) blasphemies.

[56] Cf. Seeligmann (*supra*, n. 3), 6–7 and n. 16.

(b) *The elision or* (c) *emendation of the name Beth-El*

12. Clear-cut evidence for the elision of the name Beth-El can be seen in Judg 2:1

MT: ויעל מלאך ה׳ מן הגלגל אל הבכים

LXX:[57] *ויעל מלאך ה׳ מן הגלגל אל הבכים ואל בית אל ואל בית ישראל.

It is difficult to imagine that either the translators or the Greek copyists added the additional words of their own accord, and it is also difficult to attribute them to a loose copying of a Hebrew scribe. One must consider, therefore, that there was an original Hebrew version underlying this translation. A likely reconstruction would be: ויעל מלאך ה׳ מן הגלגל אל הבכים לבית אל, meaning "Bochim (a place name, see verse 5) which belongs to Beth-El. In the MT Beth-El's name was obliterated; an alternative attempt was made to emend "Beth El" to "Beth Israel." The LXX presents a concatenation of these two versions. At the root of these textual operations—the elision of Beth El or its emendation to "Beth Israel"—lies the opposition to mentioning it as a legitimate place of worship.[58]

13. In keeping with our method, we shall use the textual witness of Judg 2:1 to conjecture the original version of two other difficult verses.

Judg 20:23: ויעלו בני ישראל ויבכו לפני ה׳ עד הערב וישאלו בה׳ לאמר

But it does not say where they went up to. According to the analogy from verse 18 and 26, it appears that they went up to Beth El.[59] The name was elided, either by an accident such as homoioteleuton, or—which seems more likely in this context—on purpose, due to opposition to Beth-El as a legitimate place of worship for all of Israel.

---

[57] Καὶ ἀνέβη ἄγγελος κυρίου ἀπὸ Γαλγαλ ἐπὶ τὸν Κλαυθμῶνα καὶ ἐπὶ Βαιθηλ καὶ ἐπὶ τὸν οἶκον Ισραηλ.

[58] My arguments are stated in detail in my *Belief in Angels* (*supra*, n. 20). Commentators usually read בית-אל instead of הבכים. Cf. e.g. M.-J. Lagrange, *Le livre des Juges* (*EBib*, Paris: Lecoffre, 1903), 22.

[59] *BH* attributes this reading to the versions. This is an error. *BHS* reports it as a conjecture.

14. In Hos 6:6, the prophet declares: "For I desire goodness, not sacrifice, obedience to God, rather than burnt offerings." Later on he enumerates a deprecatory list of Israelite temples: "In Adam[60] they have transgressed the covenant" (v. 7), "Gilead is a city of evil-doers' (v. 8) "murder on the road to Shechem" (v. 9). The list ends with "In the House of Israel I saw a horrible thing, Ephraim for-nicated there, Israel has defiled himself" (v. 10). "In the House of Israel" is an exception in the line, and it duplicates "Israel" that appears at the end of the verse; furthermore, what does "there" refer to in the beginning of v. 10b? The Targum transmits the verse as follows:

בבית ישראל חזיתי שנו אשניאו קימא דנזיר עמהון דלא למפלח לטעוותא. חבו
אנון למטעי בתר עגליא בבית אל; חמן טעו בית אפרם אסתאבו בית ישראל.

Here it is possible that two translations of the same verse were con-catenated together. The first translation reflects the MT and the sec-ond reflects "In Beth-El I saw a horrible thing." Ibn Ezra's comments: "Ephraim fornicated there: this is an allusion to the calves of Beth El, which belong to Ephraim." This supposed reading of the Targum ties into the other arguments for positing an original reading of v. 10: בבית אל ראיתי שערוריה שם זנות לאפרים נטמא ישראל.

The emendation of Beth-El—Beth Israel, attested by the LXX in Judg 2:1, is evidenced also in LXX for Hosea and Amos.[61]

15. Hos 10:15

MT: ככה עשה לכם בית-אל מפני רעת רעתכם
LXX: *בית ישראל

---

[60] This is an accepted textual correction instead of כאדם read by all ancient wit-nesses. No tradition reports about Adam entering and breaking a covenant. What is meant here is the city Adam (Josh 3:16) in which stood a sanctuary. This is referred to in Ps 78:60 where one should vocalize באדם as be'adam; cf. S. D. Goitein, "The City of Adam in the Book of Psalms?," *BJPES* 13 (1946/7): 86–88 (Hebrew); also Y. Kutscher, "They Were Destroyed at En-Dor, They Became Dung at Adma," ibid. 2 (1934/5): 40–42 (Hebrew). Both essays were reprinted in: *Bulletin of the Israel Exploration Society Reader* (2 vols.; Jerusalem: Israel Exploration Society, 1965), 2.274–279

[61] The two following passages were discussed by Y. Zakowitch, "The Synonymous Word and Synonymous Name in Name-Midrashim", *Shnaton* 2 (1977): 100–115, at 113 and n. 55 (Hebrew). Zakowitch, however, preferred the reading of LXX in Amos 5:6.

16. Amos 5:6

פֶּן יצלח כאש בית יוסף ואכלה ואין מכבה לבית-אל :MT
LXX: *לבית ישראל

Another verse that belongs to this section is Gen 35:9, which will
be discussed below at the end of the article.

As for the date of the elision and emendation of Beth El, I submit that these editorial operations are characteristic of a later era
than those mentioned in the earlier section. The existence of a cultic place in Beth-El is still disturbing to a Jerusalem loyalist, but it
is not the same bitter polemic of the prophets and their disciples.
And most importantly, this sort of elision and emendation is common to several books of the Bible—Genesis (35:9), Deuteronomy
(32:8, 43) Joshua (24:1, 25) Judges (2:1). If so, this is a relatively late
phase in transmission, when several different books of the Bible were
collected together.

(d) *Justifying the cult in Beth-El as appropriate for its time*

17. Judg 20:26–28:

(26) ויעלו כל בני ישראל וכל העם ויבאו בית-אל ויבכו וישבו שם לפני ה' ויצומו
ביום ההוא עד הערב ויעלו עלות ושלמים לפני ה'. (27) וישאלו בני ישראל בה'
ושם ארון ברית האלהים בימים ההם. (28) *ופינחס בן אלעזר בן אהרן עמד*
לפניו בימים ההם לאמר האוסף עוד לצאת למלחמה עם בני בנימין אחי אם
אחדל . . .

> Then all the Israelites, all the army, went up and came to Beth-El and they
> sat there, weeping before the Lord. They fasted that day until evening, and
> presented burnt offerings and offering of well being to the Lord. The Israelites
> inquired of the Lord (*for the Ark of God's Covenant was there in those days, and
> Phinehas son of Elazar son of Aaron the priest ministered before Him in those days*), say-
> ing 'Shall we again take the field against our kinsmen the Benjaminites, or
> shall we not?'

Now here it is clear that the entire italicisized passage is an interpolation, which interrupts the continuous phrase וישאלו בני ישראל בה' לאמר.
Indeed, in LXX it actually appears before that phrase (beginning of
v. 27 in MT). Experience tells that when a verse occupies a different
location in two different textual witnesses, this is evidence of an interpolation. This increases the suspicion that the double information
about the location of the Ark of the Lord and about Phinehas' priesthood is secondary in this context. And the suspicion becomes a near
certainty when we see that these pieces of information are not reflected

in the Vetus Latina. If so, why was the information about the Ark and about Phinehas added here?

In my view, we face here an attempt to justify the cult at Beth-El:[62] The cult there was legitimate because the Ark of the Lord, which had been constructed by divine imperative at Mount Sinai, resided at Beth-El. The Ark justifies the cult at Beth El, the same way that the Tent of Meeting justified the cult in Shiloh at the time of Joshua (Josh 18:1–10), and the cult in Gibeon in Davidic and early Solomonic times (1 Chr 21:29–30; 2 Chr 1:3, 5–6). In my opinion this is an attempt to describe an alternative history of the legitimate cult in Israel, as distinct from the history that was codified in Jewish tradition: there through the stations of the Tent of Meeting, here through the peregrinations of the Ark.[63]

This interpretation is supported by LXX at the end of the book of Joshua. Immediately after the news of the death of Elazar the son of Aaron (24:33) LXX supplies

ἐν ἐκείνῃ τῇ ἡμέρᾳ λαβόντες οἱ υἱοὶ Ισραηλ τὴν κιβωτὸν τοῦ θεοῦ περιεφέροσαν ἐν ἑαυτοῖς, καὶ Φινεες ἱεράτευσεν ἀντὶ Ελεαζαρ τοῦ πατρὸς αὐτοῦ, ἕως ἀπέθανεν καὶ κατωρύγη ἐν Γαβααθ τῇ ἑαυτοῦ.

(in retroversion): ביום ההוא לקחו בני ישראל את ארון האלוהים (ס"א: ארון האלוהים) ויסבו אותו בתוכם ופנחס כהן תחת אלעזר אביו עד אשר מת ויקבר בגבעה אשר לו. Whether or not I have been correct in trying to reconstruct a somewhat different Hebrew reading out of this passage,[64] in any event there are traces here of further records of the history of the Ark's peregrinations, inasmuch as it confers legitimacy to the cult. And it should be noted that here too the Ark is mentioned in conjunction with Phinehas' priesthood.

I would estimate that the interpolation of Josh 24:33 and Judg 20:27–28 should be dated near the time of the writing of Chronicles, in the middle of the fourth century BCE or slightly later. Here the same trend is at work, reconstructing the history of the legitimate

---

[62] Cf. K. Budde, *Das Buch der Richter erklaert* (KHAT; Freiburg i.B.: J. C. B. Mohr, 1897), 136.

[63] Cf. A. B. Ehrlich, *Mikrâ ki-Pheschutô* (Hebrew; Berlin: Poppelauer, 1900; repr. Jerusalem: no publisher, 1969), 94. Ehrlich did not repeat his argument in his *Randglossen zur hebräischen Bibel* (7 vols.; repr. Hildesheim: G. Olms, 1968), 3.155.

[64] Cf. A. Rofé, "The End of the Book of Joshua according to the Septuagint," *Hen* 4 (1982): 17–36.

cult in relation to the location of the holy properties, either the Tent of Meeting or the Ark of the Covenant. An illustrative example of this approach is evident in the fragment 4Q522, quoted above.

18. We will conclude our study by looking at Gen 35:9.

MT: וירא אלהים אל יעקב עוד בבאו מפדן ארם ויברך אתו

LXX[65] Ὤφθη δὲ ὁ θεὸς Ιακωβ ἔτι ἐν Λουζα ὅτε παρεγένετο ἐκ Μεσοποταμίας τῆς Συρίας καὶ ηὐλόγησεν αὐτὸν ὁ θεός.

*וירא האלהים אל יעקב עוד בלוזה בבאו מפדן ארם ויברך אותו האלהים

For the sake of the discussion, let us ignore the question of whether the Vorlage of LXX read אלהים or האלהים. And we shall not consider the end of the verse, where *האלהים of LXX is supported by אלהים of the SP. Instead we will direct our attention to the graph בלוזה reconstructed from the Greek ἐν Λουζα. What is the nature of this plus? In our discussion we must take into account the verses in Gen 48:3–4 which relate directly to our passage:

ויאמר יעקב אל יוסף: אל שדי נראה אלי בלוז בארץ כנען ויברך אתי ויאמר אלי: הנני מפרך והרביתך ונתתיך לקהל עמים ונתתי את הארץ הזאת לזרעך אחריך אחזת עולם.

> And Jacob said to Joseph, "El Shaddai appeared to me at Luz in the land of Canaan, and He blessed me, and said to me, 'I will make you fertile and numerous, making of you a community of peoples; and I will assign this land to your offspring to come for an everlasting possession.'"

There is no doubt that these two passages are related to each other in terms of both content and style. Neither of them contain the Lord as name of god, but rather use Elohim and El-Shaddai (35:9, 10, 11, 48:3). The revelation is described in the *nipʿal* conjugation of the root *rʾh* (וירא, נראה), the promise of many offspring is given with the terms, פר"ה, רב"ה, a community of peoples, and later the land is promised to the offspring of Jacob (35:12; 48:3). The conjunction of

---

[65] On the value of the LXX to Genesis cf. the recent contribution: M. A. Zipor, "The Septuagint as a Textual Witness: Some Considerations on its Use," *Shnaton* 12 (2000): 203–220 (Hebrew). The misgivings of Rösel were put to rest by Hendel; cf.: M. Rösel, "The Text-Critical Value of Septuagint-Genesis," *BIOSCS* 31 (1988) 62–70; R. S. Hendel, "On the Text-Critical Value of Septuagint Genesis: A Reply to Rösel," *BIOSCS* 32 (1999): 31–34.

these characteristics—foremost among them the use of the name El-Shaddai—defines these two passages as belonging to the Priestly Document (P), a fact whose importance will become apparent to us later.

Then, how should the reading בלוזה be considered? Ostensibly one could argue that a copyist of Genesis 35 was influenced by the passage in chap. 48 and supplied the name לוז in Gen 35:9. But it is highly unlikely that a copyist was sophisticated enough to complete the verse in view of a passage at the end of the book. It must be remembered that copyists were not aware of the Documentary Hypothesis, and would not readily make a connection between different episodes from the same document. Therefore it is better to conclude that LXX reflects the original version and that the word בלוזה was elided from the archetype of the Massoretic text. The elision could have been a result of a copyist's mistake, but since we have already identified other deliberate elisions of the name Beth-El, and their theological motivation, it is reasonable to conclude that here too the word בלוזה was deliberately dropped, in order to undermine Beth-El's authority. This too, then, is an emendation motivated by the principle of Cult Unification.

Our conclusion about the originality of the text בלוזה has significant implications. The passage from Gen 35:9ff. derives, as mentioned above, from the Priestly Document. Biblical scholars have generally put forth the view that this source did not describe the revelations to the patriarchs as tied to any specific locations in the land of Canaan, because it did not want to attribute sanctity to these places. This view is certainly correct in regard to the Priestly account of the revelation to Abraham in Genesis 17. But here, in Gen 35:9ff. the case is different. The story ends in vv. 14–15:

ויצב יעקב מצבה במקום אשר דבר אתו, מצבת אבן, ויסך עליה נסך, ויצק עליה
שמן. ויקרא יעקב את שם המקום אשר דבר אתו שם אלהים בית-אל.

And Jacob set up a pillar at the site where He had spoken to him, a pillar of stone, and he offered a libation on it and poured oil upon it. Jacob gave the site, where God had spoken to him, the name of Beth-El.

Here, then, is an epiphany that is directly tied to a place and to the dedication of a pillar in commemoration of the event, as well as a place naming of Beth-El. How does this fit in to the religious tenets of the Priestly Document?

Critics have generally isolated vv. 14–15 from their context, and
thus minimized the significance of the passage as sanctifying a site
and its sacred objects (the pillar). They did indeed admit, that this
was done to conform with the method, since it would be impossible for the Priestly code to speak of the erection of pillars.[66] But
now, when the mention of Luz in Gen 35:9 is added to verse 15
and to the repeated mention in 48:3, it appears that the Priestly
code in fact gives great emphasis to the epiphany at Luz-Beth-El![67]
P sanctions the holiness of one site in the Land, and that is Beth-
El.[68] Consequently, there is no reason to exclude from this source
the story of the erection of the pillar in *v.* 14.

In summary, if we ask about the original provenance of the authors
of the Priestly Document, we find the answer in the one place in
Genesis where P describes an epiphany (and the dedication of a pillar): that is Beth-El. The Priestly document originated in Beth-El,
until the milieu where it was forged relocated to Jerusalem, and there
it was completed.[69]

At this point, we should complete the evidence pointing to Beth-
El as the origin of the Priestly Document. This will be aided by
noticing who are the protagonists of this document. For the Priestly
Code granted an eternal priesthood to Aaron and his sons, and its
chief protagonist is Phinehas, son of Elazar, son of Aaron the Priest:
"It shall be for him and his descendants after him a pact of priesthood for all time, because he took impassioned action for his God,
thus making expiation for the Israelites." (Num 25:13). The con-

---

[66] Cf. A. Kuenen, *The Origin and Composition of the Hexateuch* (trans. from Dutch
by P. H. Wicksteed; London: Macmillan, 1886), 228; A. Dillmann, *Die Genesis*
(KEHAT[6]; Leipzig: S. Hirzel, 1892), 378; J. Wellhausen, *Die Composition des Hexateuchs*[3]
(Berlin: De Gruyter, 1899, repr. 1963), 322.

[67] Therefore Holzinger rejected the retroverted reading בלוז, arguing: "Doch
Wird sich fragen, ob P selbst die Theophanie so ausdrücklich lokalisiert hat"; cf.
H. Holzinger, *Genesis erklaert* (KHAT; Freiburg i.B.: J. C. B. Mohr, 1898), 184. The
only one, to my knowledge, who accepted the witness of the LXX was C. J. Ball,
The Book of Genesis (SBOT; Leipzig: Hinrichs, 1896), 30.

[68] A most accurate discussion of Gen 35:9–15 is E. Blum, *Die Komposition der
Vaetergeschichte* (WMANT 57; Neukirchen-Vluyn: Neukirchener Verlag, 1984), 265–70.
In his view, P detracted from the significance of Bethel's consecration (Gen 28:
10–22). All the same, the fact remains that one single site is mentioned by P as a
place of divine revelation, and that is Luz-Bethel!

[69] Cf. A. Rofé, *Introduction to the Composition of the Pentateuch* (trans. H. N. Bock;
Sheffield: Sheffield Academic Press, 1999), 75–76, and the literature listed at n. 11,
ibidem.

nections between these three personages are clear: the addition in Judg 20:27–28 says that Phinehas served before the Ark of the Covenant in Beth El, Josh 24:33 reports that Elazar was buried on "the hill of his son Phinehas, which had been assigned to him in the hill country of Ephraim"; and Aaron is described as the one who created the calf, built an altar and convoked a festival for the Lord (Exod 32:2–5), exactly like Jeroboam, son of Nebat, when he initiated the cult in Beth El. These traditions all confirm the hypothesis that arises from Gen 35:9–15: Beth-El was the original home of the Priestly Document in the Pentateuch.

History and text go hand in hand. Historical processes that left their mark on the law, historiography and literature explicate difficulties in the Biblical text; and textual criticism, in turn, contributes to the unraveling of problems relating to the history of Biblical literature. Textual criticism is an historical discipline: relying on history, its results return to history, bringing with them their own particular contributions.

THE SIGNIFICATION OF אחרית AND אחרית הימים IN THE HEBREW BIBLE

Shemaryahu Talmon

A

The meaning of the expression (ב)אחרית ימים, which occurs thirteen times in the Hebrew Bible,[1] in the past was determined by the standard translations in the vss—LXX: (ἐπ') ἐσχάτου τῶν ἡμερῶν; VL: *extremo tempore*; *diebus novissimis* (*novissimis diebus*); Targum: בסוף יומיא; Peshitta: בחרתא דיומתא (ביומתא אחריא)—and by the later use of ἔσχατος in apocalypticism.[2] Thus, the term was invested with a 'meta-historical' dimension and was rendered 'last days', 'end of time', 'Endzeit', 'la fin des jours',[3] *et sim.* However, a detailed analysis of the thirteen occurrences of אחרית הימים, and the Aramaic *hap. leg.* באחרית יומיא (Dan 2:28), the employment of the term in the Covenanters' literature, and its analogy to Accadian *ina/ana aḥrât ûmī*, since the 1960s led scholars to conclude that the collocation pertains to 'history' proper, and connotes 'in the course of time' or 'in the future,' even in the immediate future, in distinction from 'the present (days).'[4]

The real-historical interpretation of the term אחרית הימים still predominates in contemporary research, but in some recent discussions,

---

[1] There are actually eleven basic instances, since two occur in identical texts: Gen 49:1; Num 24:14; Deut 4:30; 31:29; Isa 2:2 = Mic 4:1; Jer 23:20 = 30:24; 48:47; 49:39; Ezek 38:8,16; Hos 3:5; Dan 10:14.

[2] E. Jenni, "אחר *'ḥr* danach," *THAT* I (1978), 110–18 = *TLOT* I (1997), 83–88, with a concise survey of the discussion in pertinent literature.

[3] E.g. J. Carmignac, "Le retour du Docteur de Justice à la fin des jours," *RevQ* 2 (1958): 233–48.

[4] Int. al. G. W. Buchanan, "Eschatology and the End of Days," *JNES* 20/21 (1960): 188–92; J. Carmignac, "La notion d'eschatologie dans la Bible et à Qumran," *RevQ* 7 (1969): 17–39; H. Kosmala, "At the End of the Days," *ASTI* 2 (Leiden: Brill, 1965), 27–37; S. Talmon, "Eschatology and History in Biblical Thought" in idem, *Literary Studies in the Hebrew Bible* (Jerusalem: Magnes Press/Leiden: Brill, 1993), 160–91, esp. 170–77. This understanding of אחרית הימים was already suggested by W. F. Albright, "The Oracles of Balaam," *JBL* 63 (1944): 207–33, and B. D. Eerdmans, *The Religion of Israel*, transl. from the Dutch (Leiden: Universitaire Press, 1947), 222–23, and before them by W. Staerk, "Der Gebrauch der Wendung באחרית הימים im at. Kanon," *ZAW* 11 (1891): 247–93.

796 TALMON

for example of Qumran documents, the expression is again being 're-eschatologized',[5] and likewise its Aramaic equivalent באחרית יומיא.[6] Thus, in his edition of the 4QCommentary on Genesis A (4Q252 i v 5 2), George Brooke carefully translates באחרית הימים, which there is paraphrastically prefixed to a quotation of the biblical verse תמחה את זכר עמלק מתחת השמים (Deut 25:19, cf. Exod 17:14), '*in the latter days*.'[7] In contrast, García Martínez and E. J. C. Tigchelaar in their study edition of the scrolls,[8] and Moshe Bernstein in his discussion of the document,[9] translate באחרית הימים '*in the last days*.' The tendency to invest the term with an eschatological dimension comes into light in the *Encyclopedia of the Dead Sea Scrolls*. Here, John Collin's discussion of אחרית הימים is translated 'the End of Days,' and is subsumed under 'Eschatology.'[10]

In view of this trend, a new examination of the signification of אחרית הימים in the Hebrew Scriptures aimed at reinforcing the 'real-historical' connotation of the term and of related phrases, such as אחרית השנים, אחרית העת, and אחרית הקץ,[11] appears to be warranted.[12]

---

[5] A. Steudel, "אחרית הימים in the Texts From Qumran,' *RevQ* 16 (1993–94): 225–46, esp. 225–26.

[6] See, e.g. L. E. Hartman and A. A. Di Lella, *The Book of Daniel*. AB 23 (Garden City, NY: Doubleday, 1978), 140: "The Aramaic expression *bᵉʾaharît yômayyâ*, corresponding to the common Hebrew expression *bᵉʾaharît hayyâmîm* (Hos 3:5; Isa 2:2; Dan 10:14, etc.) literally 'in the end of days', is a typically eschatological term." Cf. J. A. Montgomery, *The Book of Daniel*, ICC (Edinburgh: Clark, 1927), 162: "For the end of days, so correctly JV, *vs.* AV RVV the latter days." But see below.

[7] G. Brooke, "4QCommentary on Genesis A," *Qumran Cave 4 XVII. Parabiblical Texts, Part 3. DJD XXII* (Oxford: Clarendon, 1996), 204 (and see below).

[8] F. García Martínez & E. J. C. Tigchelaar, *The Dead Sea Scrolls Study Edition*, Vol. I (Leiden/New York/Köln, 1997), 505.

[9] M. J. Bernstein, "4Q252: From Re-Written Bible to Biblical Commentary," *JJS* XLV (1994): 1–28.

[10] J. J. Collins, "Eschatology," *EDSS*, vol. I (2000), 256–61. The reverse is the case in the Hebrew *Encyclopaedia Biblica*, in which אסכטולוניה is subsumed under אחרית הימים (H. Z. Hirschberg, *Ency. Miq.* vol. I (1950), 230–34. A more adequate discussion of the term may be found in *The Theological Dictionary of the Old Testament* (translated from the German *Theologisches Wörterbuch zum Alten Testament*), vol. I (1970–73), which offers separate entries for אחרי by F. J. Helfmeyer, vol. I (1977) 204–7, and for אחרית, including a paragraph (III,1) by H. Seebass (207–12) in which the non-eschatological connotation of אחרית הימים is adequately presented.

[11] In the Covenanters' vocabulary, קץ signifies "period" or "appointed time" rather than "end" in turns of speech like באחרית הקץ (ה)(קץ), קץ (ה)אחרון, נמר הקץ, שלום הקץ (4Q169 2 iii 3) or לאחרית הקץ] (4Q173 1, 5), and in the restored expression קץ אחרית [הימים] (5Q16 Frag. 3, 5). This signification of the term derives from its employment in the Book of Ezekiel (7:2,3,6; 21:30,34; 35:5), and its frequent use in various components of the Book of Daniel, mostly in combination with one of the qualifying vocables עת and מועד. See S. Talmon, "קץ *qes*", *TWAT* VII (1993)

I propose to concentrate my necessarily compressed discussion on an analysis of several biblical occurrences of the term אחרית הימים, reserving for another occasion a fuller investigation of its employment in the Hebrew Scriptures and in the Covenanters' writings. In the present context, a few biblical occurrences of the component אחרית will be reviewed. Above all instances in which it connotes 'posterity' like Nabatean אחר and Imperial Aramaic אחרה,[13] throw light on the intrinsic meaning of the construct אחרית הימים.

B

My ensuing deliberations are based on the following exegetical premise: The signification of a word or a phrase which signifies a concept in the biblical literature is unavoidably coloured by the context in which it is employed. Therefore, the range of meanings of the opaque term אחרית הימים must first be ascertained contextually and intertextually through comparisons with synonyms and expressions of a similar content[14] which occur next to it in pertinent scriptural texts, foremost in *parallelismus membrorum*, and help in elucidating its essential connotation,[15] before having recourse to analogies in other Semitic languages. In this procedure the concordance takes precedence over the dictionary.

In the attempt to define the intrinsic meaning of the component אחרית in the construct אחרית הימים help can be derived from the

---

col. 84–92. By translating קץ "appointed time" or "period" rather then "The End" much speculation about varying concepts of "eschatology" in the various components of the Book of Daniel becomes redundant. J. J. Collins, "The Meaning of 'The End' in the Book of Daniel," *Of Scribes and Scrolls. Studies in the Hebrew Bible, Intertestamental Judaism, and Christian Origins, presented to J. Strugnell at his Sixtieth Birthday* (ed. H. W. Attridge, J. J. Collins, Th. T. Tobin, SJ; *College Theology Society Resources in Religion* 5 (Lanham/New York/London: University Press of America, 1990), 91–98.

[12] The required investigation of the wider semantic field of the root אח״ר and the derivatives אחר/אחרון cannot be attempted in the present framework.

[13] See: C. F. Jean and J. Hoftijzer, *Dictionnaires des Inscription Sémitiques de l'Ouest* (Leiden: Brill, 1965).

[14] I have illustrated this investigative technique in an analysis of the *hap. leg.* תרמת שדי (2 Sam 1:21) in: "Emendation of Biblical Texts on the Basis of Ugaritic Parallels," *Studies in Bible* (ed. S. Japhet; ScrHier XXXI; Jerusalem: Magnes Press, 1986), 279–300.

[15] It appears that only insufficient attention was given to this facet of research in scholarly publications.

vocables אחר, אחרון/אחרונים. These terms often connote 'second,' 'tomorrow,' or 'later/after/next,' relative to the time of the speaker or writer, as in יום אחר or יום אחרון, which indicate temporal proximity and do not point to an absolute final end.[16]

The occasional equivalence of יום אחר/אחרון with מחר = 'tomorrow' in biblical and also in post-biblical Hebrew was rightly compared with Aramaic מחר או יום אחרן in documents from Elephantine,[17] למחר וליומא אחרנא in early rabbinic sources, and Syriac יומא אחרנא.[18] However, when it comes to gauging the connotation of the term יום אחרון in Scripture, biblical texts outweigh parallels in other Semitic languages:

1. The signification 'tomorrow' of יום אחר comes into full light in the tale of the woman who in a time of severe food shortage implores King Jehoram of Samaria to come to her assistance in her dispute with a neighbor whom she accuses of having cheated her (2 Kgs 6:24–31): 'That woman said to me, give up your son for us to eat today, and we will eat mine מחר, *tomorrow*. So we cooked my son and ate him; but when I said to her *the next day*, ביום האחר, give up your son for us to eat, she hid him' (6:28–30).

2. The same meaning attaches to יום אחרון in the acrostic of the proverbial 'capable wife,' אשת חיל. She takes care of her husband's needs (Prov 31:11,12,16,23), and keeps her eyes on the doings of her household. She toils from before daybreak, ותקם בעוד לילה (31:15a), to make sure that everyone in her home is properly fed and clad (31:13,14,15b,19,21). Therefore, 'she can afford to laugh at the day ahead,' (ו)תשחק ליום אחרון (31:25). By translating יום אחרון 'last day' instead of 'next day' or 'tomorrow,' the term is invested with a notion of finality, which is totally out of place in the context.

3. Similarly, biblical law decrees that a divorced woman who married another man, after the death of that man or after being divorced by him, may not be remarried to her first husband:
Deut 24:1–3: כי יקח איש אשה ובעלה . . . וכתב לה ספר כריתת . . . והיתה לאיש אחר . . . ושנאה האיש האחרון . . . ושלחה מביתו או כי ימות האיש האחרון לא יוכל בעלה הראשון לשוב לקחתה, 'When a man married a wife and had

---

[16] Likewise, ראשון/ראשונים often do not refer to an absolute 'first,' but rather to a relative 'before.'

[17] E. Cowley, ed., *Aramaic Papyri of the Fifth Century B.C.* (Oxford: Clarendon, 1923), 5:6,8; 8:18,26 et al.; E. G. Kraeling, *The Brooklyn Museum Aramaic Papyri* (New Haven: Princeton University Press, 1955), 2:7,9, 10, 12, 13, et al.

[18] See Jenni, *THAT* (above, n. 2), 84.

intercourse with her . . . and (later) writes her a note of divorce . . . and she becomes the wife of **another man** . . . and the **other** (second) **man** . . . hates her . . . and dismisses her . . . or the **other** (second) **man** dies, then her **first** husband may not again take her to be his wife.' In this instance, like in similar cases, the coupling of האחרון with הראשון shows that the term must be translated 'second,' not 'last,' since the law does not restrain the woman from becoming the wife of a third husband.

4. In some specially persuasive cases, the connotation 'next,' 'sequent' or 'in the near future' of אחרון/אחרונים is inner-textually ascertained through an added explanatory reference to 'posterity':

a. Deut 29:21: ואמר הדור האחרון בניכם אשר יקומו אחריכם, '**The next generation—your sons** who will arise after you—will ask.' The LXX avoids the use of ἐσχάτου and correctly renders הדור האחרון by ἡ γενεὰ ἡ ἑτέρα. VL likewise has *sequens generatio* and not a form of *novissimus*, which it regularly uses in the translation of אחרון (cf. Ps 48:14: למען תספרו לדור אחרון, LXX [47:14]: εἰς γενεὰν ἑτέραν, but VL: *in generatione novissima*; Targum: לדר אוחרן).

b. The same applies to Ps 78:3–6: אשר שמענו ונדעם ואבתינו ספרו לנו, לא נכחד מבניהם לדור אחרון מספרים תהלות יהוה . . . אשר צוה את אבותינו להודיעם לבניהם,[19] למען ידעו דור אחרון בנים יולדו יקמו ויספרו לבניהם 'Things we have heard and known, that our fathers have told us. We will not withhold them from their **children**, telling the **future generation** the praises of the Lord . . . charging our fathers to make known to their **children**, so that a **future generation** (LXX: εἰς γενεὰν ἑτέραν . . . ἡ γενεὰ ἡ ἑτέρα; VL (twice): *generatio subsequens*; and Targum: דר בתרי) will know—**children** to be born (to you)—who will arise and tell it to **their children**' (cf. vv. 3–5).

c. In the hyperbolical promise that the glory of the post-exilic sanctuary, built by the returning exiles, eventually will surpass the grandeur of Solomon's temple, גדול יהיה כבוד הבית האחרון מן הראשון (Hag 2:9), the term הבית האחרון does not refer to the 'last,' but rather to the 'later,' that is to say to the Second Temple. On its part, הבית האחרון could yet be followed by another sanctuary, like the one which the Covenanters aspired to erect in the 'New Jerusalem.'[20] However,

---

[19] Cf. Joel 1:3: עליה לבניכם ספרו ובניכם לבניהם ובניהם לדור אחר.
[20] Cf. also Jer 50:17: הראשון אכלו מלך אשור וזה האחרון עצמו נבוכדראצר מלך בבל. Here the term ראשון refers to the Assyrians' capture of the Northern Kingdom, and האחרון to the Babylonians' later conquest of Judah.

in this case, the LXX translation ἡ δόξα τοῦ οἴκου τούτου ἡ ἐσχάτη and VL's *domus istius novissimae* reveal an eschatological emphasis, possibly caused by a theological bias.

d. Haggai's contemporary Zechariah similarly refers twice to the pre-exilic prophets by the title נביאים ראשונים (Zech 1:4; 7:12), thereby implicitly identifying himself and his post-exilic contemporaries Haggai and Malachi as נביאים אחרונים.[21] The ראשונים are not 'the first' but 'the former,' since they were preceded by pre-classical prophets like Samuel, Nathan, and Gad. The אחרונים are not 'the last' but 'the latter,'[22] who were expected to be succeeded by Elijah *redivivus* (Mal 3:23–24). In these instances, the end of the First Temple period constitutes the demarcation line between ראשון/ראשונים and אחרון/אחרונים.

C

We can now bring under review the employment of אחרית in reference to a future, even imminent period in history, similar to the above illustrated signification of אחרון.

In the biblical generation-pattern terminology, the noun אחרית connotes 'progeny': (A) in threats of punishment and woe, in which the loss of offspring signals the termination of a societal unit, and (B) in pronouncements of well-being and success, in which the blessing of (numerous) children is extolled as guaranteeing the continuance of a family, a clan or a people.

Both these aspects are commemorated in Ps 37:37–38: שמר תם וראה ישר כי אחרית לאיש שלום ופשעים נשמדו יחדו אחרית רשעים נכרתה, 'watch the good man look at him who is honest, for **the man of peace leaves (has) descendants**, and transgressors are wiped out altogether, **the offspring of the wicked is cut** off' (LXX translate אחרית

---

[21] This division is reflected in CD XIX (ms B). There a quotation from Zech 13:7 (XIX,7–9) is connected with "the Messiah of Aaron and Israel" (XIX, 10–11), who arose 390 years after Nebuchadnezzar's conquest of Jerusalem (CD I, 7), and is followed by a quotation from Ezek 9:4 pertaining to events which occurred בקץ הפקדה הראשון, "at the first time of visitation" (XIX,11–12), viz. at the end of the monarchic period. Cf. further *b. Soṭah* 48b: 'who are the נביאים הראשונים? (all), with the exception of Haggai, Zechariah and Malachi who are אחרונים.' For more examples see M. Jastrow, *Dictionary of Talmud Babli, Yerushalmi* etc., vol. I (New York: Title Publishing Company, 1943), 40–41.

[22] There is a reference to 'the prophetess Noadiah and all the other prophets' who joined forces with Nehemiah's enemies (Neh 6:14).

twice by ἐγκατάλειμμα; the VL has once *ad extremum*, and once *novissimum*). Like in similar texts, the verb כרת serves here as a *terminus technicus*, which equals שמד and מחה, 'to destroy' or 'wipe out.'

A.1) Ps 109:13: יהי אחריתו להכרית בדור אחר ימח שמם, 'may **his** (family) **line be cut off**, may their name be wiped out within **the next generation**' (cf. Ps 34:17: פני יהוה בעשי רע להכרית מארץ זכרם). The reference to the present generation of evildoers, collectively designated רשע (109:2,6,7), by שמם, and the possesive pronoun of אחריתו (LXX: τὰ τέκνα αὐτοῦ; but VL: *novissimum eius*), is complemented in the next verse by a mention of their forebears, אבתיו and אמו, so that the text speaks in fact of three generations.

A.2) Prov 24:20: כי לא תהיה אחרית לרע נר רשעים ידעך, 'the wicked will not have **offspring** (LXX: ἔκγονα; VL: *futurorum spem*), the **light** of the evildoers will be put out'. The term נר, like אור, serves as a metaphor for 'progeny', as in Job 18:5–6: ... גם אור רשעים ידעך אור חשך באהלו ונרו עליו ידעך, 'the wicked's **light** is extinguished ... the **light** fades in his tent and **his candle**(light) goes dark' (cf. Prov 13:9: אור צדיקים ישמח ונר רשעים ידעך, 'the **light** of the righteous gives pleasure [by burning brightly], the **candle** of the wicked will be put out'). The metaphor is explained in Job 18:17–19: זכרו אבד מני ארץ ולא שם לו על פני חוץ ... לא נין לו ולא נכד בעמו ואין שריד במגוריו, 'the **memory** (of the wicked) vanishes from the face of the earth, he leaves no **name** in public ... he leaves no **descendant** or **grandchild** among his people, no **survivor** in his dwellings.'

A.3) Am 4:2: כי הנה ימים באים עליכם ונשא אתכם בצנות ואחריתכן בסירות דונה (LXX translate ואחריתכן καὶ τοὺς μεθ' ὑμῶν; Theodion: τὰ ἔκγονα ὑμῶν; VL: *reliquias vestras*). The picture is self-explanatory. The prophet warns the women of Samaria that in the near future they will be carried into exile in baskets or on shields, and their **offspring** (daughters; Targum: ובנותכון) will be dragged away with fish-hooks.[23] אחריתכן was thus correctly understood by the medieval commentators Rashi (in the name of Dunash ibn Labrat), Ibn Ezra (who compares לאחריתו

---

[23] For the various interpretation of צנות and סירות דונה see the detailed and exceedingly well documented discussion by S. M. Paul, *Amos. Hermeneia* (Minneapolis: Fortress, 1991), 130–35, and M. Weiss, *The Book of Amos* (Jerusalem: Magnes Press, 1992), vol. I, 103–4; vol II, 168–74, nn. 74–128 (Hebrew).

in Dan 11:4 and explains the term by שהוא בנו), Kimchi,[24] and most modern exegetes.[25] The rendition of ואחריתכן by 'your Hintern' or 'your posterior,' suggested by some scholars,[26] misses altogether the thrust of the prophet's woe oracle. The threat that two generations of Samarian women or possibly more will be exiled is especially severe, since their deportation spells in fact the total annihilation of the population of the Northern Kingdom.

The same warning of imminent doom resounds in another of the prophet's oracles:

A.4) Am 9:1–2: ראיתי את אדני נצב על המזבח ויאמר הך הכפתור וירעשו הספים ובצעם בראש כלם ואחריתם בחרב אהרג. Notwithstanding the somewhat veiled wording, the basic sense of the message is evident: God is said to stand on the altar, presumably in Bethel, announcing the destruction of the local sanctuary and the killing of all habitants of the city or the country, כלם, together with their offspring, אחריתם. The LXX rendition καὶ τοὺς καταλοίπους αὐτῶν correctly reflects the realistic-tangible meaning of the term, but in the VL's *novissimum eorum* an eschatological thrust comes to the fore (cf. 4:30; Ps 109:13).

A.5) In Ezek 23:25: ועשו אותך בחמה אפך ואזניך יסירו ואחריתך בחרב תפול המה בניך ובנותיך יקחו ואחריתך תאכל באש, the meaning 'offspring' of the twice reiterated term אחרית is ascertained through the explanatory phrase המה בניך ובנותיך. The prophet threatens the city or kingdom of Samaria, here named Oholibah, with destruction by the enemy, the inhabitants of the realm with mutilation, and their descendants with death by the sword: 'they will deal **with you** in anger, they will cut off **your nose and your ears**, **your offspring** will fall by the sword, **your sons and your daughters** they will take (away), **your offspring** will be devoured by fire.' This understanding of אחרית again is mirrored twice in the Greek rendition καὶ τοὺς καταλοίπους σου. The VL translates the term in the first half of the verse by *et quae remanserint*, but in the second half invests the term

---

[24] See J. Ratzahbi, 'Reflections on Biblical Expressions,' *Beit Miqra* 160 (1999): 71 (Hebrew).

[25] Paul's translation 'the very last one of yours' (*Amos*, 135), suggests a similar understanding of the phrase, but lacks the concreteness of 'offspring/posterity.'

[26] Th. R. Robinson and F Horst, *Die Zwölf Kleinen Propheten*. HAT I, 14 (1954), 53–54; E. Hammershaimb, *The Book of Amos. A Commentary* (transl. from the Danish by J. Sturdy; Oxford: Blackwell, 1970) ad loc.

with an unwarranted eschatological dimension by rendering it *novissimum tuum*.

A.6) A woe oracle of the imminent downfall of Taḥpanḥes in Egypt in Ezek 30:18, in which the city and her satellites are designated by the 'mother-daughter' metaphor, is almost identically worded, albeit without a mention of the term: ובתחפנחס חשך היום . . . ונשבת בה נאון עזה **היא** ענן יכסנה **ובנותיה** בשבי תלכנה, 'in Taḥpanḥes daylight shall fail . . . her mighty power shall be subdued, a cloud shall cover **her**, and **her daughters** shall go into captivity' (cf. Am 4:2).

A.7) Jer 50:26: A very similar phraseology is employed in an oracle of doom against Babylon: סלוה כמו ערמים **והחרימוה** אל תהי לה **שארית**. The third person pronouns in סלוה and החרימוה refer to the population of the city, and the term שארית to the next generation: 'Pile **her** up as in heaps, destroy **her**, that there will not be (left) to **her posterity**.'

The threat of the implied total annihilation of the citizenry of Babylon suggests that the MT of Jer 50:21: על־הארץ מרתים עלה עליה **והחרם אחריתם** ואל יושבי פקוד חרב והחרם אחריהם, should be restored to read **והחרם אחריתם** instead of **אחריהם**, on the basis of the Targum's **שארהון**, 'their offspring.'[27]

B.1) Jer 29:11: כי אנכי ידעתי את המחשבת אשר אנכי חשב עליכם . . . לתת לכם **אחרית ותקוה**, 'I know the (good) plans which I have made concerning you . . . to give you **offspring and a (long) line of descendants**.'[28] LXX[OL] correctly translate **אחרית** τὰ μετὰ ταῦτα, cf. 5:31; but the VL has *finem*.

B.2) Jer 31:16–17: מנעי קולך מבכי . . . כי יש שכר לפעלתך . . . ושבו מארץ אויב ויש **תקוה לאחריתך** . . . ושבו **בנים** לגבלם, 'Cease your sound of weeping . . . for there shall be a reward for your toil . . . they shall return from the land of the enemy, **a line (generations) of your descendants,** (your) **sons** (LXX: τοῖς σοῖς τέκνοις; but VL: *ad terminos suos*) . . . shall return to their land.'[29]

B.3) Prov 23:18: כי אם יש יש **אחרית ותקותך** לא תכרת, '(if you fear God) there will be **progeny** (for you) (LXX: ἔσται σοι ἔκγονα; VL: *habebis spem in novissimo*) **and your** (family) **line** will not be cut off'.

---

[27] Cf. v. 34; Jer 29:11; 31:6; Prov 23:18; and see below.

[28] Possibly a 'double entendre' of two meanings of תקוה, 'hope' and 'line.'

[29] In Jer 33:14–16 a contextually related vision to 29:11 and 31:16–17 is introduced by a 'history-riveted' date: הנה ימים באים נאם יהוה והקמתי את הדבר הטוב אשר דברתי אל בית ישראל ועל בית יהודה בימים ההם אצמיח לדוד צמח צדיק . . . (cf. 23:5–6).

B.4) Job 42:12–13, 16: ויהוה ברך את אחרית איוב מראשיתו, 'God blessed Job's (later) **progeny** (LXX: τὰ ἔσχατα; VL: *novissimis*) more than **his former**,' as proverbially promised to the God fearing (Job 8:7): והיה ראשיתך מצער ואחריתך ישׂגה מאד '(though) your beginnings were humble, your offspring will be great' (LXX: τὰ δὲ ἔσχατά σου; VL: *novissima tua*). 'He had (again) **seven sons and three daughters**, ויהי לו שׁבעה בנים ושׁלושׁ בנות (cf. 1:2), 'And he saw his **sons and grandsons to four generations**,' וירא את בניו ואת בני בניו ארבעה דורות. Like Joseph (Gen 50:23), Job experienced the very limit of mankind's historical horizon, seen as extending to the fourth generation (cf. Exod 20:5; 34:7; Num 14:18; Deut 5:9; 2 Kgs 10:31; cf. *KAI* 226.8). That generation marks a caesura in history, the end of one major phase and the beginning of another. In the lifetime of the fourth generation of enslaved Israelites the period of slavery in Egypt would be terminated. After their Exodus they will return here, to the promised land: ודור רביעי ישׁובו הנה (Gen 15:16).[30]

Likewise, Jeremiah admonishes the Judean expatriates to adjust to life in Babylon for three generations, for 'a full seventy years' (Jer 29:10; cf. 25:11):

קחו נשׁים והולידו בנים ובנות וקחו לבניכם נשׁים ואת בנותיכם תנו לאנשׁים ותלדנה בנים ובנות, 'Marry wives and beget sons and daughters; take wives for your sons and give your daughters to husbands, so that they may bear sons and daughters' (29:6).

After that, in the fourth generation, says God 'when Babylon's seventy years are over, I will take up your cause . . . by bringing you back to this place' . . . giving you 'a long line of children after you,' לפי מלאת לבבל שׁבעים שׁנה אפקד אתכם . . . להשׁיב אתכם למקום הזה . . . לתת לכם אחרית ותקוה (29:10–11). Historical time is not seen then to end, but rather to take a critical turn. The text does not speak of a *Zeitenende* but rather of a *Zeitenwende*, opening up an entirely new phase in history.[31]

---

[30] See S. Talmon, "<400 Jahre> oder <Vier Generationen> (Gen 15,13–15): Geschichtliche Zeitangaben oder literarische Motive?," *Die Hebräische Bibel und ihre zweifache Nachgeschichte. FS für R. Rendtorff* (ed. E. Blum, Chr. Macholz and E. Stegemann; Neukirchen-Vluyn: Neukirchener Verlag, 1990), 13–25.

[31] See S. Talmon, "The 'Topped Triad': A Biblical Literary Convention and the 'Ascending Numerical Pattern'," *Let Your Colleagues Praise You: Studies in Memory of S. Gevirtz*, Part II (ed. R. J. Ratner, L. M. Barth, M. L. Gevirtz, B. Zuckerman; *Maarav* 8; 1993), 181–98.

D

At this juncture, we can bring under scrutiny the character and the status of the time or period designated אחרית הימים. The diffusion of the term in several books of the Bible strongly suggests that its employment with the pronounced history-related signification 'imminent future' is an integral component of the vocabulary of various biblical authors and is not limited to specific literary strata. Some exemplary texts highlight the pertinence of the term to events that are fervently expected to occur in the near future, in the lifetime of the next generation or of one of the next generations. The term אחרית הימים actually serves as a *Kennwort* which denotes 'in the days, הימים, of (our) progeny, אחרית.'[32] At the same time I do not wish to preclude altogether the possibility that in some instances the collocation (ב)אחרית הימים was invested with a 'meta-historical' thrust. However, the ascription of an eschatological content to the term in a specific context must be proven in every particular instance.[33]

The reference to אחרית הימים is a distinct feature of the advice or admonition in a poetically worded 'last testament,' which a father or a 'visionary' who stands for the 'present,' addresses to his children or to members of the next generation who represent the 'future.' The following texts illustrate this characteristic conjunction of 'death' and 'future generation,' or more concretely 'progeny':

1. Deut 31:27: בעודני חי עמכם היום ממרים היתם עם יהוה ואף כי אחרי מותי, '(even) during **my lifetime** you have defied YHWH, how much more (will you do so) after **my death**.'

Deut 31:29: ידעתי אחרי מותי כי השחת תשחתון וסרתם מן-הדרך אשר צויתי אתכם וקראת אתכם הרעה באחרית הימים,[34] 'I know that **after my death** you will certainly do evil and turn aside from the way which I commanded

---

[32] It is tempting to conjecture a metathesis of the components of the construct אחרית הימים = ימי (ה)אחרית, like e.g. in בפשתי העץ (Josh 2:6), LXX: ἐν τῇ λινοκαλάμῃ = בעצי פשתים; similarly Targum: כתנא במטעוני = 'in loads of flax'; cf. *m. Šabb.* 2:2: כל היוצא מן העץ אין מדליקין בו אלא פשתן, 'one may not kindle the Sabbath candle with anything growing out of העץ, except פשתן.

[33] Scholars tend to differentiate between occurrences of אחרית הימים which have a 'real-historical' thrust and others in which the idiom has an 'eschatological' signification. See int. al. S. R. Driver, *Deuteronomy.* ICC (Edinburgh: Clark, 1902), 74; Th. C. Vriezen, "Prophecy and Eschatology," *Congress Volume Copenhagen* 1953 (VTSup I; Leiden: 1973), 199–229; 202–03, 227–29.

[34] Cf. 4Q504:1–2 iii 12–14 (*DJD VII*, 141): אשר כתב מושה ועבדיכה הנביאם אש[ר ש]לחתה ל[קר]תנו הרעה באחרית הימים.

you (to follow), and in **days to come** disaster will come upon you.'

ומצאוך כל הדברים האלה **באחרית הימים** ושבת עד יהוה אלהיך :Deut 4:30,
'When all these (bad) events get hold of you[35] in **days to come**,
you will turn back to YHWH your God.'

In Moses' review of past history and his admonitions to the Israelites
on the eve of their entering Cis-Jordan, the trenchant 'real-historical,' non-eschatological signification of באחרית הימים is ascertained
through allusions to his lifetime, בעודני חי, and his imminent death,
אחרי מותי (cf. 31:1,14–16: הנך שכב עם אבתיך . . . למות ימיך קרבו הן). These
references lead up to events באחרית הימים after Moses' demise (34:5–7),
which pertain to the offspring of the present generation, תוליד כי
בנים ובני בנים (4:25), and to their close at hand settlement in the Land
of Canaan (31:3–13).

2. An essentially identical situation is portrayed in the account of
the days preceding Jacob's death in Egypt (Gen 48–49). The dying
patriarch, who represents the 'present,' foretells his offspring that in
the near future, באחרית הימים, they will 'return' to the land of their
forefathers, והשיב אתכם אל-ארץ אבתיכם (48:21), implicitly in the lifetime
of the fourth generation of his son's Joseph descendants (50:22–23,
cf. 15:16). Gen 47:29–30: ויקרבו ימי ישראל **למות** ויקרא לבנו ליוסף ויאמר לו
. . . תקברני במצרים נא אל . . ., 'When the time of **his death** drew near,
he summoned his son Joseph and said to him . . . do not bury me
in Egypt.'

Gen 48:21: ויאמר ישראל אל-יוסף הנה **אנכי מת** והיה אלהים עמכם והשיב
אתכם אל-ארץ אבתיכם, 'Then Israel said to Joseph, "**I am dying**. God
will be with you and bring you back to the land of your fathers.'

Gen 49:1: ויקרא יעקב אל-בניו ויאמר האספו ואגידה לכם את אשר-יקרא אתכם
באחרית הימים, 'Jacob summoned his sons and said, Come together,
and I will tell you what will happen to you **in the days to come**.'

After that, 'when Jacob had finished instructing his sons . . . he
died and was gathered to his kin', ויכל יעקב לצות את בניו . . . **ויגוע**
ויאסף אל עמיו (49:33).

3. The presence of the above motifs and connotative terminology,
which reveal the 'history-riveted' signification of the expression באחרית
הימים, put the visionary 'curses turned blessings' of the seer Balaam[36]

---

[35] For the meaning 'get hold of/capture,' rather than 'find/come upon,' see for the
present S. Iwry, "והנמצאא—A Striking Variant Reading in 1QIs^a," *Textus* V (1966): 34–45.
[36] In a discussion of the question who authored, כתב, the several biblical books

(Num 22:6,11; 23:11,25; 24:1,10; cf. Deut 23:5–6; Josh 24:9–10; Neh 13:2) into one category with the poetic 'last words' of Jacob and Moses. Also Balaam connects a wish that his progeny may be numerous like Israel's offspring with a mention of his own death: Num 23:10: מי מנה **עפר יעקב** ומספר[37] **את-רבע ישראל** תמת נפשי מות ישרים ותהי **אחריתי כמהו**, 'who can count **the host of Jacob** or number **the multitude of Israel**, may I die the death of *yesharim*,[38] and may **my offspring** (LXX: τὸ σπέρμα μου; VL: *novissima mea*) be like his' (viz. Israel's).

> The prevalent translations of ישרים by 'men who are righteous' (*NEB*) or 'the upright' are out of tune in the literary and conceptual context. I suggest to connect the term with the 'Book of *Yashar*, ספר הישר, which is twice quoted in the Bible (Josh 10:13; 2 Sam 1:18). In this ספר were recorded poetic compositions of war and death, which extolled the feats and told of the fates of ancient heroes. This type of poetry is exemplified by David's elegy, קינה, over Saul and Jonathan (2 Sam 1:17–27), with which Balaam's parables have some resemblance in tune and texture (cf. Num 23:24; 24:8–9,17–22).[39]

The theme of the seer's death presumably is picked up once again towards the end of the pericope in a double entendre of the phrase ועתה הנני הולך לעמי, 'Now **I am going to my kin**.' The expression indeed can simply mean 'I am going home,' like ויקם בלעם וילך וישב למקומו, 'then Balaam arose and returned home' (24:25). However, at the same time, it may echo Jacob's request of Joseph that after his demise he should be buried with his fathers: אני נאסף אל עמי קברו אתי אל אבתי (Gen 49:29). Balaam's words הנני הולך לעמי thus proleptically point to the brief mention of his death in the Israelites' battle against the Midianites, ואת בלעם בן בעור הרנו בחרב (Num 31:8,[40] cf. Josh 13:22).

---

or included them in the biblical corpus of כתבי הקדש, the authorship of the Balaam pericope (Num 22:2–24:25) is ascribed to Moses in addition to the Torah: משה כתב ספרו ופרשת בלעם (*b. B. Bat.* 14b).

[37] Read possibly ומי ספר.

[38] For explanations of ישרים see S. E. Loewenstamm, "The Death of the Upright and the World to Come," *JSS* 16 (1965): 183–86.

[39] See below.

[40] The thread of the tale of the Israelites' fornication with Moabite and Midianite women (25:6–15) in the wake of the Balak-Bileam episode is inserted after the divine command to make war on the Midianites who were struck by a plague (25:16–18). After a lengthy interpolation of quite different legal materials (26:1–30:17), the account of the plague and the ensuing war is resumed in 31:1 with the apocopated half verse ויהי אחרי המנפה, marked by a *pisqah be'emṣaʿ pasuq*, which by right should be placed before 31:1. However, at the time of the splicing in of the interpolation

This remark again is followed by the seer's expectable vaticination of the fate of the Israelites and their historical adversaries 'in the days ahead': באחרית הימים לכה איעצך אשר יעשה העם הזה לעמך (24:14ᵇ). In the ensuing cluster of Balaam's 'last words' against the nations (24:15–25), the one about Amalek is the most important for our present concern. The seer's 'prophecies' concerning Moab, Edom, the Kenites, etc. are uttered against Israel's 'present' enemies. In contrast, in the oracle about Amalek also the annihilation of that nation's off-spring, אחריתו עדי אבד, is announced. The event is foreseen to materialize באחרית הימים. In view of the signification of the term אחרית as extrapolated in part B of this essay, this means in an appreciably near future time.

Num 24:20: וירא את עמלק וישא את משלו ויאמר **ראשית גוים** עמלק **ואחריתו** עדי אבד, 'He saw Amalek and uttered his oracle, "**First of the nations** is Amalek (presently), but his **offspring** will perish"' (cf. int. al. Ps 109:12–13: כי **אחריתו** להכרית בדור **אחר** ימח שמו; further *KAI* 226:9–10: שחר ונכל ונשך יהבאשו ממתתה **ואחרתה האבד**, 'may Shahar and Nikkal and Nashku make his death miserable, and **his offspring** shall perish').

The author of the 4QCommentary on Genesis A (4Q252 i v 1–3)[41] correctly conceived of the terms **ראשית** and אחרית **אחרית** as pointers to two historical periods in the inimical relations of Israel and Amalek. He took **ראשית** to refer to the days of Moses, and אחרית **אחרית** to the days of Saul, באחרית: ותמנע היתה פילגש לאליפז בן עשו ותלד לו את עמלק הוא אשר הכ[הו] שאול כאשר דבר למושה **באחרית הימים** תמחה את זכר[42] עמלק מתחת השמים, 'Timnah was the concubine of Eliphaz, the son of Esau. And she bore him Amalek (Gen 36:12a), he whom Saul vanquished (cf.

---

the 'resumptive repetition' was erroneously appended to the report of the plague (26:19). For *p.b.p.* see *int. al.* S. Talmon, "Pisqah Be'emṣa' Pasuq and 11QPsᵃ," *Textus* V (1966): 11–21; idem, "Extra-Canonical Hebrew Psalms From Qumran—Psalm 151," in idem, *The World of Qumran From Within* (Jerusalem: Magnes Press, 1989), 244–72, esp. 264–72. For the literary technique of 'resumptive repetition' see: H. M. Wiener, *The Composition of Judges II 11 to 1 Kings II 46* (Leipzig: Hinrichs, 1929), C. Kuhl, 'Die "Wiederaufnahme"—ein literarkritisches Prinzip?," *ZAW* 64 (1962): 1–11; idem, "Die drei Männer im Feuer," *BZAW* 40 (1930): 130; S. Talmon, "The Presentation of Synchroneity and Simultaneity in Biblical Narrative," in *Literary Studies in the Hebrew Bible* (Jerusalem: Magnes Press, 1993), 112–33, et alii.

[41] See Brooke, op. cit., above, n. 7.

[42] Like in similar contexts, זכר serves here as a synonym of אחרית. See e.g. 4Q416 frg. 2 iii,7: ובמותך יפר[ח] לעו[ל]ם זכרכה **ואחריתכה** תנחל שמחה, 'when you die your offspring will blos[som for ev]er, and your progeny will inherit joy.'

1 Sam 14:48; 15:3,7)[43] *vacat* as he spoke to Moses, "In the latter days you will wipe out the memory of Amalek from under the heavens"' (Deut 25:19).[44]

4. The persuasive contextual combination or intertextual affiliation of באחרית הימים with references to future generations suggests that also in texts which are considered prime witnesses to its 'eschatological' signification, the expression actually pertains to 'real history'. In this respect, the באחרית הימים vision preserved in the books of Isaiah and Micah takes pride of place.[45]

Isa 2:2–4 = Mic 4:1–4

והיה באחרית הימים (נכון)[46] יהיה הר בית יהוה (נכון) בראש ההרים . . . ונהרו אליו כל הגוים . . . לא ישא גוי אל גוי חרב ולא ילמדו עוד מלחמה, 'In days to come the mountain of the house of YHWH shall be set over all other mountains . . . all nations shall come streaming to it . . . nation shall not lift sword against nation, nor ever again be trained for war.'

Isa 7:14: הנה העלמה הרה וילדת בן וקראת שמו עמנו אל, 'A young woman is with child, and she will bear a son, and will call him Immanuel.'[47]	Mic 5:1–4: ואתה בית לחם אפרתה . . . ממך לי יצא להיות מושל בישראל . . . לכן יתנם[48] עד עת יולדה ילדה . . . כי עתה ינדל עד אפסי ארץ . . . והיה זה שלום, 'But you, Bethlehem (in)

---

[43] Bernstein (above, n. 9) failed to recognize the real-historical connotation of אחרית הימים and had difficulties with explaining the presumably eschatological signification of the term in the context, as correctly pointed out by I. M. Ta-Shma, "Hebrew-Byzantine Bible Exegesis ca. 1000, from the Cairo Geniza," *Tarbiz* LXIX, 2 (2000): 247–56, n. 11 (Hebrew).

[44] Biblical tradition actually offers the possibility of setting in the days of Joshua the realization of the divine declaration that Amalek will be annihilated: ויאמר יהוה אל משה כתב זאת זכרון בספר ושים באזני יהושע כי מחה אמחה את זכר עמלק מתחת השמים . . . מלחמה ליהוה בעמלק מדר לדר' (Exod 17:14–16, cf. Josh 24:9–10).

[45] It is immaterial for our present concern whether the Isaiah version was 'borrowed' from Micah or *vice versa*, or whether both derive from one common *Vorlage*.

[46] The slight textual difference between the two versions of the verse does not affect our argument.

[47] Cf. Isa 8:3: ואקרב אל הנביאה ותהר ותלד בן, 'Then I lay with the prophetess, and she conceived and bore a son'; Isa 8:18: הנה אנכי והילדים שנתן לי יהוה לאתות ולמופתים בישראל, 'I and the sons whom whom YHWH has given me are to be signs and portents in Israel'.

[48] Read possibly יתנו. A ligature of נו resulted in its being misread as final mem, and doubled. The phrase לכן יתנהו is connected to the Davidic scion from Bethlehem Efratah, but it still remains a *crux interpretum*.

Isa 9:6: כי ילד ילד לנו בן נתן לנו   Efratah . . . out of you shall come
ותהי המשרה על שכמו . . . ויקרא שמו   forth for me a governor of Israel
שר שלום . . ., 'for a boy has been   . . . until the time that a woman
born for us, a son given to us,   in labour gives birth . . . for now
the symbol of dominion will be   (then) his greatness shall reach
on his shoulder . . . and he shall   to the ends of the earth . . . and
be called . . . Prince of Peace.'   he shall be (a man or sign) of
                                           peace.'

The linkage of the picture of the world at peace with motifs of birth
and posterity is meant to indicate that the vision will not materialize in the days of the present generation, but rather באהרית הימים, in
the days to come, the days of the next or a future generation.

In conclusion: The biblical expression אהרית הימים denotes an eter-
nally yearned for **historic** 'tomorrow,' which forever is held in
abeyance and never experienced in reality. The term implicitly reveals
a dissatisfaction with the present generation, and an ever recurring
shift of 'hope' to the next or a future generation, in the proverbial
time span of seventy years, (cf. Jer 48:47; 49:39 and Isa 23:15–17).
The term אהרית הימים denotes a future period in history, of peace
and well-being for the god-fearing, of doom and perdition for all
evildoers (Mal 3:13–24; LXX: 3:13–4:6).

SHARING WEAL AND WOE:
EXPRESSIONS OF SOLIDARITY*

Jeffrey H. Tigay

The Old Babylonian adoption contract from Mari, ARM 8:1, records the terms of the adoption of one Iahatti-Il by the couple Hillalum and Alitum. After declaring that Iahatti-Il is the couple's son it states that *damāqišunu idammiq lemēnišunu ilemmin*, "he shall share their good fortune and share their bad fortune" (lit. "he shall do well as they do well, he shall do poorly as they do poorly").[1] As G. Boyer, the first editor of the text observes, the clause is intended to give the adoption the same effect that natural filiation would: "to expressly associate the adoptee with the life and good or bad fortune of the adopters."[2]

In a study of this clause R. Yaron, who terms it a "solidarity clause," cites other types of solidarity clauses that resemble it.[3] Two Old Babylonian marriage contracts, both dealing with the same individuals,[4] concern a certain married man who was now marrying his

---

* It is a great pleasure for me to take part in this expression of admiration and affection for Emanuel Tov in appreciation for his friendship, for his many scholarly achievements, and for the tact, wisdom, and skill with which he has accomplished them.

[1] G. Boyer, *Textes juridiques* (ARMT 8), p. 2 no. 1, lines 4–5. For the translation see *CAD* D, 61d; *CAD* L, 116d. For the syntax see the citations of this passage in *AHw*, p. 156ab, end of (2), and 542cd beginning of (5a); and, with reference to the clauses in the marriage contracts cited below, *GAG* § 150a and R. Westbrook, *Old Babylonian Marriage Law* (AFOB 23; Horn Austria: Ferdinand Berger & Söhne, 1988), p. 79. I am grateful to my colleague, Barry L. Eichler, for clarifying issues involved in this and other Akkadian texts cited here. Obviously, any misunderstandings are my own. Pages in *CAD* and *AHw* are cited by quadrants (a,b,c,d).

[2] Boyer, *Textes juridiques*, p. 179.

[3] R. Yaron, "Varia on Adoption," *JJP* 15 (1965): 173–75.

[4] CT 2 no. 44:21–23 and Meissner, BAP 89:7–8, cited by Yaron from M. Schorr, UAZP [*Urkunden des altbabylonischen Zivil- und Prozessrechts* (Leipzig, 1913)] nos. 4 and 5; see now R. Harris, "The Case of Three Babylonian Marriage Contracts," JNES 33 (1974): 363–69; Westbrook, *Old Babylonian Marriage Law*, pp. 79, 116–17, 127. Compare, in an obscure context: *pīštī pīšatka u ṣaburti ṣaburta[ka]*, "an insult against me is an insult against you, malice against me is malice against you," G. Boyer, *Contribution à l'histoire juridique de la Iʳᵉ dynastie babylonienne* (Paris: Librairie Orientaliste Paul Geuthner, 1928), 119:17–18 (cited in *CAD* A II, 189 end; *CAD* Ṣ, 55c; AHw 869ab).

first wife's sister. According to the contracts, "whenever she (the first wife) is angry, she (the second wife) shall be angry, whenever she is friendly, she shall be friendly" (*zenîša izenni salāmiša isallim*),[5] meaning essentially "with whomever the first wife is angry, the second wife shall be angry, with whomever she is at peace, she shall be at peace."[6] Yaron finds parallels to this in two Latin passages from Plautus. In one, a slave says, "an honest servant ought to stick to this principle: be like what his betters are, model his expression on theirs, be in the dumps if they are in the dumps, and jolly if they are happy" (*tristis sit, si eri sint tristes; hilarus sit, si gaudeant*).[7] In the other a husband says to his wife, "if you weren't stupid . . . what you see displeases your husband would be displeasing to you, too" (*quód viro esse odió videas, túte tibi odio habeas*).[8] Yaron also cites Ruth's pledge of solidarity to Naomi: "Wherever you go, I will go; wherever you lodge, I will lodge; your people shall be my people, and your God my God. Where you die, I will die, and there I will be buried. Thus

---

[5] The translation essentially follows Westbrook, *Old Babylonian Marriage Law*, p. 109.

[6] S. E. Loewenstamm apud Yaron, p. 175. Yaron argues that ARM 8:1, 4–5 should be understood in the same way: "the true import of the clause is less to give the adoptee a share in the family fortunes, but to impose upon him the duty of associating himself, of adjusting himself. His joy, just as much as his sorrow, are duties rather than rights. It is the adoptive parents who determine the mood, the adoptee will have to follow suit." Following Yaron, J. J. Finkelstein translated: "he shall rejoice in their joys and commiserate in their miseries" ("Documents from the Practice of Law," ANET 3d ed., 545). The definitions of *damāqu* and *lemēnu* under which ARM 8:1 is cited in *AHw* (see n. 1, above) also see the adoptee as required to follow the adopters' moods, but they assume a meaning closer to that of the marriage contracts cited in n. 4: "freundlich sein," "böse sein gegen jmd." However, apart from the facts that "prosper" and "fall into misfortune" are more common meanings of *damāqu* and *lemēnu* than the other meanings proposed (*CAD* D, 61bc–62a; *CAD* L, 116d; *AHw*, 156b, *AHw*, 542b; *lemēnu* means "be angry" mostly in combination with *libbu*), and that the terminology of the marriage contracts is in any case entirely different, adoption and marriage to a co-wife seek to create different kinds of solidarity, and the clauses in the two genres should not be presumed to be synonymous. In adoption the adopters seek, among other things, someone to provide for them in old age and bury and mourn them, and the adoptee expects a share in the new parents' estate. The contract, accordingly, prevents the child from opting out of the relationship if the parents become poor or burdensome, and it guarantees him his share when they prosper. The contract for marriage to a co-wife, on the other hand, seeks to preserve the first wife's superiority in her relationship to a new potential rival, a danger expressed in the Semitic terms for co-wife, Heb. צָרָה; (1 Sam 1:6; Sir 37:11) and Akk. *ṣerretu* (*AHw* 1093a; *CAD* Ṣ: 137a–138b), both literally "enemy," Arab. *ḍarra*, from *ḍarra*, "harm, impair, prejudice, injure," etc.

[7] *Amphitryon*, 960f. in P. Nixon, *Plautus*. Loeb Classical Library (London: W. Heinemann, and Cambridge MA: Harvard University, 1956), 1.98–99.

[8] *The Two Menaechmuses*, 110f., in Nixon, *Plautus* 2.374–75.

and more may the LORD do to me if anything but death parts me
from you" (בַּאֲשֶׁר: אֶל־אֲשֶׁר תֵּלְכִי אֵלֵךְ וּבַאֲשֶׁר תָּלִינִי אָלִין עַמֵּךְ עַמִּי וֵאלֹהַיִךְ אֱלֹהָי:
תָּמוּתִי אָמוּת וְשָׁם אֶקָּבֵר כֹּה יַעֲשֶׂה ה' לִי וְכֹה יֹסִיף כִּי הַמָּוֶת יַפְרִיד בֵּינִי וּבֵינֵךְ: ; Ruth
1:16–17). Finally, Yaron cites the solidarity clause that appears fre-
quently in treaties, both parity treaties and vassal treaties: "to my
enemy you shall be an enemy and to my ally you shall be an ally"
(*itti nakrija lu nakrāta u itti salamija lu salmāta*).[9]

Yaron's brief study is very useful in demonstrating that such solidarity clauses and similar statements appear in various genres and
in different cultures. As similar as they are in formulation, however,
they fall into different types. Those in the Mari adoption contract
and in the book of Ruth refer to sharing of existential circumstances:
weal and woe, domicile, nation, religion, and burial.[10] The passages
dealing with co-wives and slaves refer to shared attitudes and moods:
friendship and anger, pleasure and displeasure, likes and dislikes. The
passages from treaties refer to alliance and enmity. We may refer to
these types of solidarity, respectively, as circumstantial, empathetic,
and political.

Among Biblical scholars, perhaps the best known parallel to these
clauses are the verses in the Bible that echo the political solidarity
clauses found in treaties, such as God's declarations in Exod 23:22,

---

[9] J. Nougayrol, *Le Palais royal d'Ugarit* IV (Paris: Imprimerie Nationale and Lib-
rarie C. Klincksieck, 1956), p. 36, lines 11–13. For lists of such clauses see *CAD*
N I 193a; *CAD* S, 90cd, 104c; M. Weinfeld, "The Covenant of Grant in the Old
Testament and in the Ancient Near East," JAOS 90 (1970):194; J. Tigay, "Psalm
7:5 and Ancient Near Eastern Treaties," *JBL* 89 (1970): 183, n. 26. Note *CAD*'s
dynamic translation of the clause: "I am at war with my lord's enemy, I am at
peace with my lord's friend" (*CAD* N I, 193 b,c). For reflexes of this formula in
the Bible, Greece, Rome and elsewhere, see the articles by Weinfeld and Tigay
just cited and M. Weinfeld, "The Loyalty Oath in the Ancient Near East," *Shnaton*
1 (1975): 63–64 [Hebrew] (Weinfeld cites the oath to "have the same friends and
enemies" mentioned in Plutarch, *Eumenes* 12 [B. Perrin, *Plutarch's Lives*. LCL
(Cambridge: Harvard University Press, 1969–1982)], 8.115). In contemporary par-
lance Article 5 of the North Atlantic Treaty is called the "solidarity clause": "The
Parties agree that an armed attack against one or more of them . . . shall be considered an attack against them all and consequently they agree that, if such an
armed attack occurs, each of them . . . will assist the Party or Parties so attacked . . ."
(http://www.nato.int/docu/basictxt/treaty.htm).

[10] Sasson aptly captures Ruth's point: ". . . the emphasis is on the *type of dwelling*
which will ultimately become [Naomi's] home. Ruth's statement concerns events,
situations, and relationships which will permanently bind the two women. *Whether
Naomi's future home is in a palace or in a hut*, Ruth is determined to share her mother-
in-law's dwelling" (Jack M. Sasson, *Ruth. A New Translation with a Philological Commentary
and a Formalist-Folklorist Interpretation*. 2d ed. [Sheffield, England: Sheffield Academic
Press, 1995], p. 30 [first emphasis original; second emphasis added]).

"I will be an enemy to your enemies and a foe to your foes" (וְאָיַבְתִּי אֶת־אֹיְבֶיךָ וְצַרְתִּי אֶת־צֹרְרֶיךָ),[11] and Gen 12:3, "I will bless those who bless you and curse him that curses you" (אֲבָרְכָה מְבָרְכֶיךָ וּמְקַלֶּלְךָ אָאֹר), and the psalmist's declaration in Ps 139:21–22: "O LORD, You know I hate those who hate You, and loathe Your adversaries. I feel a perfect hatred toward them; I count them my enemies" (הֲלוֹא־מְשַׂנְאֶיךָ ה׳ אֶשְׂנָא וּבִתְקוֹמְמֶיךָ אֶתְקוֹטָט: תַּכְלִית שִׂנְאָה שְׂנֵאתִים לְאוֹיְבִים הָיוּ לִי). Here I would like to call attention to several interesting parallels, mostly from later times, to the circumstantial and empathetic solidarity clauses in the Old Babylonian adoption and marriage contracts cited above. Some of these parallels are stylistically similar to the Akkadian and Latin ones, in that both parties' actions are described by the same terms (such as *damāqišunu idammiq lemēnišunu ilemmin*, "he shall do well as they do well, he shall do poorly as they do poorly"), as in many of the Hebrew examples from the Bible and Qumran. In other cases they are expressed with synonyms, as in other examples from Qumran, while in others the mutual obligations are indicated only by paraphrase, as in the Greek examples from Hellenistic and Christian literature. In all cases, the mutuality of the parties' obligations and actions is clear.

CIRCUMSTANTIAL SOLIDARITY

A close parallel to the clause in the Mari adoption contract is found in the New Testament, in Rom 8:14–17:

> All who are guided by the Spirit of God are sons of God; for what you received was not the spirit of slavery to bring you back into fear; you received the Spirit of adoption (υἱοθεσίας), enabling us to cry out, "Abba, Father!" The Spirit himself joins with our spirit to bear witness that we are children of God. And if we are children, then we are heirs, heirs of God and joint-heirs with Christ, provided that we share his suffering (συμπάσχομεν), so as to share his glory (συνδο-ξασθῶμεν).[12]

---

[11] The midrash elaborates on the theme that God considers Israel's enemies His own. See *Mekilta, Shirta,* 6 (J. Z. Lauterbach, *Mekilta de-Rabbi Ishmael* [Philadelphia: Jewish Publication Society, 1933] 2.42–47; H. S. Horovitz and I. A. Rabin, *Mechilta d'Rabbi Ismael* [Jerusalem: Bamberger & Wahrman, 1960] pp. 134–36); *Sifre Num.* 84 (H. S. Horovitz, *Siphre d'Be Rab* [Jerusalem: Wahrmann, 1966] pp. 81–2). See S. Schechter, *Aspects of Rabbinic Theology* (New York: Schocken, 1961), p. 50 top; J. Goldin, *The Song at the Sea* (New Haven: Yale University Press, 1971), p. 152 s.v. "Thy children," par. 2.

[12] Translation from *The New Jerusalem Bible*. Cf. Gal 4:4–7; Eph 1:5.

The basic idea here is that those who become Christians have been redeemed from slavery and adopted by God, whom they are inspired to call "Father," and as His children they have become His heirs, co-heirs with Jesus, entitled to share in his future glory provided that they first share his suffering. In this passage, adoption, sharing weal and woe, being an heir, and calling God "Father" stand in close connection, as at Mari. There are, of course, differences: (1) In Romans, sharing woe and weal are sequential; the one is the pre-requisite for the other, unlike the Mari contract where they are pre-sented as parallel statements. This is merely a difference in formulation due to the fact that ARM 8:1 is a contract while Rom 8:14 is an exhortation and promise. ARM 8:1 certainly implies that the one is a prerequisite for the other: an adoptee who repudiates the adopters in adversity will not be entitled to share in their estate ("If [he] should say [to them]: 'You are not my father; you are not my mother,' they shall ... sell him for money," lines 12–18). (2) In Romans, the adoptees share the woe and weal of the elder son, with whom they are co-heirs, and not that of the parent.[13] (3) In Romans, being inspired to call God "Father" is mentioned as proof of the adoption,[14] whereas in ARM 8:1, declaring that the adoptive father and mother are *not* his parents is, as noted, grounds for selling the adoptee as a slave.

The idea of sharing in Jesus's suffering and glory is also echoed in Rom 6:3–8:

> ... all of us, when we were baptised into Christ Jesus, were baptised into his death. So by our baptism into his death we were buried with him, so that as Christ was raised from the dead by our Father's glo-rious power, we too should begin living a new life. If we have been joined to him by dying a death like his, so we shall be by a resur-rection like his ... [W]e believe that, if we died with Christ, then we shall live with him too.[15]

---

[13] On adoption in the New Testament, see F. Lyall, "Roman Law in the Writings of Paul—Adoption," *JBL* 88 (1969): 458–66 and earlier studies cited by him on p. 463 n. 22. These studies debate whether Paul's use of adoption alludes to a "Semitic" or a Greco-Roman institution. The Mari adoption contract should be taken into account in future consideration of this question.

[14] *The New Oxford Annotated Bible* [with NRSV] (ed. B. M. Metzger and R. E. Murphy; New York: Oxford, 1994) ad loc. Cf. the NRSV translation of vv. 15–16: "When we cry 'Abba! Father!' it is that very Spirit bearing witness with our spirit that we are children of God." Cf. Gal 4:6.

[15] Translation from *The New Jerusalem Bible* in *The Complete Parallel Bible* (New York: Oxford University Press, 1993).

These two passages inform the wording of the Christian baptism ceremony to this day. In the Episcopal *Book of Common Prayer*, part of the ceremony involves the minister saying

> We yield thee hearty thanks, most merciful Father, that it hath pleased thee to regenerate this Child . . . with thy Holy Spirit, to receive him for thine own Child, and to incorporate him into thy holy Church. And humbly we beseech thee to grant, that he, being dead unto sin, may live unto righteousness, and being buried with Christ in his death, may also be partaker of his resurrection; so that finally, with the residue of thy holy Church, he may be an inheritor of thine everlasting kingdom . . .[16]

Note here the association of God adopting the child ("receive him for thine own child"), granting that the child, who has shared in Jesus's death, share also in his resurrection, and that he be an inheritor of God's kingdom.

The Jewish conversion ceremony also contains echoes of this idea, though less explicitly. The would-be proselyte is warned about present-day Jewish suffering. If he or she persists in becoming a Jew, he/she is instructed in selected commandments and told of the punishment for violating them and the reward for observing them, including the fact that the next world is reserved only for the righteous, and that although the Jews are suffering now, good (טובה) is in store for them in the next world.[17] In other words, if he or she persists in converting and sharing the Jews' present suffering, he/she will share in their future good fortune. (This is stated explicitly by Judah Halevi: "any Gentile who joins us . . . shares our good fortune," though he adds the qualification "without, however, being quite equal to us").[18] This has more in common with the Mari adoption contract and Christian conversion than meets the eye, since Jewish conversion is likewise an adoption: the convert becomes the child of Abraham who is the father of the Jewish people and "father of pros-

---

[16] *The Book of Common Prayer*, 1928 ed. (New York: Church Pension Fund, 1945), 280–81.

[17] *b. Yeb.* 46a–47b; Maimonides, *Hilkhot 'Issurei Biʾah* 14:1–5; *Shulḥan Arukh, Yoreh Deah* 268:2. The details in *Gerim* 1:1–5 are different.

[18] Kuzari 1.27 (H. Hirschfeld, ספר הכוזרי *Kitab al-Khazari. The Book of Kuzari by Rabbi Judah Halevi* [Brooklyn: P. Shalom, 1969], Eng. section, p. 47; Arabic: ומן אנצאף אלינא מן אל אמם כאצה יצלה מן כירנא ולם יסחו מענא, Hirschfeld, Heb. section, p. 18; Hebrew [Judah ibn Tibbon]: וכל הנלוה אלינו מן האמות בפרט יניעהו מן הטובה אשר ייטיב הבורא אלינו, אך לא יהיה שוה עמנו (A. Tsifroni, ed. Sefer ha-Kuzari [Tel-Aviv: Mahbarot le-sifrut, n.d. (repr. 1988)], p. 21).

elytes" (אב הגרים).[19] This conception was made more explicit by the later practice of the convert taking a new name with the patronym "son or daughter of Abraham our father,"[20] which is still the practice today.

A later, but more explicit, parallel to the clause "he shall share their good fortune and share their bad fortune" is found in the Christian marriage ceremony in which the husband and wife declare that they take each other "to have and to hold from this day forward, for better for worse, for richer for poorer, in sickness and in health, to love and to cherish, till death us do part."[21] This formula is attested in pre-Reformation English liturgical texts, and undoubtedly goes back to older sources.[22]

The motif of circumstantial solidarity is also reflected in the well-known midrashic theme that God shares Israel's suffering and redemption:

וכן אתה מוצא כל זמן שישראל משועבדין כביכול שכינה משועבדת עמהם
שנאמר . . . בכל צרתם לו צר (ישעיה סג:ט קרי). אין לי אלא צרת
ציבור צרת יחיד מנין ת″ל (תהלים צא:טו) . . . עמו אנכי בצרה . . . וכן הוא אומר
(ש″ב ז′כ″ג) מפני עמך אשר פדית לך ממצרים גוי ואלהיו . . . רבי עקיבא
אומר אלמלא מקרא כתוב אי איפשר לאומרו כביכול אמרו ישראל לפני המקום
עצמך פדית. וכן את מוצא שבכל מקום שגלו ישראל כביכול שכינה גלתה עמהם

---

[19] *Tanḥuma, Lekh Lekha* 6 (ed. Hanokh Zundel), p. 20a end = *Tanḥuma* Buber, *Lekh Lekha* 6, p. 32a (63) end; Maimonides, *Letter to Obadiah the Proselyte* (I. Twersky, *A Maimonides Reader* [New York: Behrman House, 1972], p. 476); see also Maimonides as cited by Bertinoro (commentary to *m. Bik* 1:4) and by S. Lieberman, *Tosefta Kifshuṭah* (New York: Jewish Theological Seminary, 1955–1988), 2. *Zeraim*, p. 824; 7. *Nashim*, pp. 421–25. That Jewish conversion is formally an adoption is also indicated by the statement that "a proselyte is like a newborn child" (שנתגייר כקטן שנולד דמי נר), *b. Yeb.* 22a, 48b, etc., which is comparable to the idea of "regeneration" in the Christian baptism ceremony (see above). Adoption as rebirth is a common notion expressed in adoption ceremonies; see J. G. Frazer, *Folkore in the Old Testament.* Abridged ed. (New York: Tudor, 1923), 216–18.

[20] *Shulhan Arukh. Even HaEzer*, 129:20.

[21] *The Book of Common Prayer*, 301–02.

[22] "I, N. take thee, N. for my wedded wife, to have and to hold, from this day forward, for better for worse, for richer for poorer, in sickness and in health, till death do us part ... and thereto I plight thee my troth" (from the Use of Sarum, cited in *The Catholic Encyclopedia*, 9, art. "Ritual of Marriage"); "Here I take thee N. to my wedded wife, to have and to hold at bed and at board, for fairer for fouler, for better for worse, in sickness and in health, till death us do part and thereto I plight thee my troth ..." (from the Use of York, cited in *The Catholic Encyclopedia*, 15, art. "Use of York") (both cited from the online edition [Copyright © 1999 by Kevin Knight]; see http://www.newadvent.org/cathen/09703b.htm and http://www.newadvent.org/cathen/15735a.htm.

נלו למצרים נלתה שכינה עמהם . . . נלו לבבל נלתה שכינה עמהם . . . נלו
לעילם נלתה שכינה עמהם . . . נלו לאדום נלתה שכינה עמהם . . . וכשעתידין
לחזור כביכול שכינה חוזרת עמהם . . .

And so you find that whenever Israel is enslaved, the Shekhinah, as
it were, is enslaved with them, as it is said . . . "In all their affliction
He was afflicted" (Isa 63:9 Qere)[23] . . . So far I know only that He
shares in the affliction of the community. How about the affliction of
the individual? Scripture says: ". . . I will be with him in trouble" (Ps
91:15) . . . And thus it says: "From before Thy people whom Thou
didst redeem to Thee out of Egypt, the nation and its God" (2 Sam.
7:23)[24] . . . Rabbi Akiba says: Were it not expressly written in Scripture,
it would be impossible to say it. Israel said to God: Thou hadst
redeemed thyself, as though one could conceive such a thing. Likewise
you find that whithersoever Israel was exiled, the Shekhinah, as it
were, went into exile with them. When they went into exile in Egypt,
the Shekhinah went into exile with them . . . When they were exiled
to Babylon, the Shekhinah went into exile with them . . . When they
were exiled to Elam, the Shekhinah went into exile with them . . .
When they were exiled to Edom, the Shekhinah went into exile with
them . . . And when they return in the future, the Shekhinah, as it
were, will return with them . . .[25]

Similarly:

ויבן משה מזבח ויקרא שמו ייי נסי . . . רבי אלעזר המודעי אומר המקום קראו
נסי שכל זמן שישראל שרויין בנס כאלו נס לפניו שרויין בצרה כאלו צרה היא
לפניו. שרויין בשמחה שמחה היא לפניו וכן הוא אומר כי שמחתי בישועתך
(ש״א ב:א)[26]

---

[23] As is well known, the midrashic interpretation of Isa 63:9 is based on the *Qere*,
בכל צרתם לו צר, "in all their troubles He was troubled," which must be construed
as an independent clause, whereas the *Ketiv* (= LXX, Vulg. and Pesh.), בכל צרתם
לא צר, requires that these words be read as part of a longer sentence beginning
with v. 8b, וַיְהִי לָהֶם לְמוֹשִׁיעַ בְּכָל־צָרָתָם/לֹא צָר וּמַלְאַךְ פָּנָיו הוֹשִׁיעָם, "So He was their
Deliverer in all their troubles, No angel or messenger, His own Presence delivered
them" (thus LXX). See I. L. Seeligmann, *The Septuagint Version of Isaiah* (Leiden:
Brill, 1948), p. 62.

[24] For the reading נוי (singular), see Lauterbach, *Mekilta*, 1.114 n. 4a.

[25] *Mekilta, Pisḥa*, ch. 14 (ed. Lauterbach 1.113–115; ed. Horowitz-Rabin, pp.
51–52). For parallels see *Sifre Num.* 84 (ed. Horovitz, pp. 81–83); *Yalqut* 2.92; *b. Meg.*
29a; etc.

[26] *Mekhilta d'Rabbi Šimʿon b. Jochai*, ed. J. N. Epstein and E. Z. Melamed (Jerusalem:
Mekize Nirdamim, 1956), p. 126 = *Midrash Hagadol*, Exodus to Exod 17:15 (ed.
M. Margulies [Jerusalem: Mosad Harav Kook, n.d.], p. 345). See also *Tg. Pseudo-
Jon.* ad loc.: "And the Memra of the Lord named it, 'This Miracle is Mine,' for
the miracle . . . was for My sake" (בניני); see M. M. Kasher, *Torah Shelemah* 14 (New
York: American Biblical Encyclopedia Society, 1944), p. 272 n. 123; R. Le Déaut,
Targum du Pentateuque. 2. Exode et Lévitique (Paris, 1979), 145 (contra J. W. Etheridge,

"And Moses built an altar and called its name Adonai-Nissi" (Exod 7:15) ... Rabbi Elazar of Modi'im said, "God[27] called it 'Nissi' [My miracle], for whenever Israel is affected by a miracle, the miracle, as it were, befalls Him. When they are afflicted it is as if the affliction befell Him. When Israel has joy, it is as if the joy befalls Him. And so it says, "For I rejoice in Your [i.e., God's] salvation" (1 Sam 2:1).[28]

In these passages, the remarkable thing is that, unlike the earlier passages where the inferior party must share the weal and woe of the superior party, or equals must share each other's weal and woe, here the superior party, God, shares the suffering and redemption of the inferior party. Rabbinic sources see this as a sign of God's great love for Israel.[29]

The idea of sharing weal and woe also appears in a metaphoric sense in 2 Macc 5:19f. God allowed Antiochus IV to defile the Temple because of Israel's sins; He did not protect the Temple ("the Place") because

it was not for the sake of the Place that the Lord chose the nation; rather, He chose the Place for the sake of the nation. Therefore, even the Place itself partook in the misfortunes (δυσπετημάτων) of the nation but then shared in the benefits (εὐεργετημάτων) which came later. The

---

The Targums of Onkelos and Jonathan Ben Uzziel on the Pentateuch [London: Longman, Green, 1865], 1.503–504, and M. Maher in M. McNamara et al., *The Aramaic Bible* 2 [Collegeville, Minnesota: Michael Glazier, 1994], p. 211 [but see n. 23]). See also *Tanḥuma Beshallaḥ* sec. 28 (ed. Zundel, p. 93); *Yalqut* 1.267; *Yalqut* 2.82 (to 1 Sam 2:1), 507 end (to Isa 63:9). The text of the parallel in *Mekilta, Amalek*, ch. 2 ad loc. (ed. Lauterbach 2.159–60; ed. Horowitz-Rabin, p. 186) and parallels (*Beshallaḥ* sec. 28 (ed. Buber p. 93); *Sekhel Tov* ed. Buber 2.324–325; *Yalqut* ad loc., sec. 267) is difficult, as noted by Kasher, *Torah Shelemah* 14.272 n. 123 and A. J. Heschel, תורה מן השמים באספקלריה של הדורות (*Theology of Ancient Judaism*) (London and New York: Soncino, 1962), 1.65 n. 1.

[27] In other words God, not Moses, is the subject of "called."

[28] Assuming that "When Israel has joy, it is as if the joy befalls Him" means the same thing as "whenever Israel is affected by a miracle, the miracle, as it were, befalls Him," the midrash takes 1 Sam 2:1 to mean that God is saved. This is how this verse and others referring to God's salvation are commonly interpreted in midrashic texts. See *Yalqut* 2.82 (to 1 Sam 2:1); 2.577 (to Zech 9:9); *Midrash Tehillim* 91 end; *Exod. R.* 30:24; other passages cited by Heschel, *Theology*, pp. 69–70, 71–72. In that case, "joy" must mean "joyous conditions," i.e., salvation. Assuming the common meaning of "joy," Lauterbach states that "Presumably the verse is interpreted as if God said this to Israel" (Lauterbach, *Mekilta*, 2.160 n. 9). In that case, God is rejoicing over Israel's salvation. Although this would make the end of the midrash inconsistent with the rest of it, this interpretation cannot be ruled out. In that case, the end of the midrash refers to God's empathetic, rather than circumstantial, solidarity with Israel. See below, n. 32.

[29] *b. Meg.* 29a; *Yalqut* 2.92.

Place, which had been abandoned at the moment of the Almighty's wrath was restored to full glory at the time of the great Lord's forgiveness.[30]

In contrast to the cases cited above, the *absence* of solidarity between Israel and the nations is expressed in a midrashic explication of (appropriately) Num. 23:9, "there is a people that dwells apart":

כשהוא משמחן אין אומה שמחה עמהן, אלא הכל לוקין, [שנאמר] ה'בדד ינחנו ... (דברים לב:יב), וכשהאומות שמחין בעולם הזה, הם אוכלים עם כל מלכות ומלכות, ואינן עולה להם מן החשבון, שנאמר ובגוים לא יתחשב (במדבר כג:ט).

When God gives them joy, no other nation shares their joy, rather, they are all punished, as it says "the Lord guides them alone" (Deut 32:12), but when the nations rejoice in this world, they (Israel) (are enabled) to eat with every single kingdom and it is not reckoned against them (that is, it is not deducted from their future reward), as it is written, "not reckoned among the nations."[31]

Empathetic Solidarity

Some midrashic passages citing Isa 63:9 and Ps 91:15 speak of God's empathetic, rather than circumstantial, solidarity with Israel, that is, He shares Israel's sorrow and joy.[32] For example:

א"ר ינאי מה התאומים הללו אם חשש אחד בראשו חבירו מרגיש כן אמר הקב"ה כביכול (תהלים צא:טו) עמו אנכי בצרה ... ואומר (ישעיה סג:ט קרי) בכל צרתם לו צר, א"ל הקב"ה למשה אי אתה מרגיש שאני שרוי בצער כשם שישראל שרוים בצער הוי יודע ממקום שאני מדבר עמך מתוך הקצים כביכול אני שותף בצערן.

R. Yannai said: Just as in the case of twins, if one has a pain in his head the other feels it, so did God say, as it were, "I am with him in trouble" (Ps 91:15) ... And it also says: "In all their affliction He is afflicted" (Isa 63:9 Qere). Said God to Moses: Don't you realize that I am in sorrow just as Israel is in sorrow? Know that from the place whence I speak to you, from among the thorns, I share, as it were, their sorrow.[33]

---

[30] Translation from J. Goldstein, *II Maccabees*. AB 41A (New York: Doubleday, 1983), 245 (slightly modified).

[31] *Tanḥuma* Buber, *Balak*, 19 (p. 143) and parallels; cf. Rashi at Num 23:9.

[32] Heschel distinguished (though without using these terms) between these two types of solidarity in rabbinic sources. See his *Theology*, 1.65–66, and his broader discussion and collection of sources, Chap. 5, pp. 65–72. It is not always clear which type a particular midrashic text has in mind.

[33] *Exod. R.* 2:5. See Maharzu, ad loc., s.v. בכל צרתם לו צר, in *Midrash Rabbah*,

According to Philo, empathetic solidarity prevailed among the animals in primordial times:

> The tale is that in old days all animals, whether on land or in water or winged, had the same language, and . . . every creature conversed with every other about all that happened to be done to them or by them, and in this way they mourned together at misfortunes (κακο-πραγίαις), and rejoiced together when anything of advantage (λυσι-τελὲς) came their way. For since community of language led them to impart to each other their pleasures and discomforts, both emotions were shared by them in common. As a result they gained a similarity of temperament and feeling . . .[34]

The Talmud expands on the theme of empathetic solidarity proclaimed by the exilic prophet in Isa 66:10–11:

שִׂמְחוּ אֶת־יְרוּשָׁלַם וְגִילוּ בָהּ כָּל־אֹהֲבֶיהָ שִׂישׂוּ אִתָּהּ מָשׂוֹשׂ כָּל־הַמִּתְאַבְּלִים עָלֶיהָ:
לְמַעַן תִּינְקוּ וּשְׂבַעְתֶּם מִשֹּׁד תַּנְחֻמֶיהָ לְמַעַן תָּמֹצּוּ וְהִתְעַנַּגְתֶּם מִזִּיו כְּבוֹדָהּ:

Rejoice with Jerusalem and be glad for her, all you who love her! Join in her jubilation, all you who mourned over her—That you may suck from her breast consolation to the full, that you may draw from her bosom glory to your delight.[35]

כל העושה מלאכה בט' באב ואינו מתאבל על ירושלים - אינו רואה בשמחתה,
שנאמר (ישעיהו סו:י) שמחו את ירושלים וגילו בה כל אהביה שישו אתה משוש
כל המתאבלים עליה. מכאן אמרו: כל המתאבל על ירושלים זוכה ורואה בשמחתה,
ושאינו מתאבל על ירושלים - אינו רואה בשמחתה.

Whoever does work on the Ninth of Ab and does not mourn for Jerusalem will not share in her joy, as it is said, "Rejoice with Jerusalem and be glad for her, all you who love her! Join in her jubilation, all you who mourned over her" (Isa 66:10). On the basis of this [the Rabbis] said: Everyone who mourns for Jerusalem merits to share in her joy, and anyone who does not mourn for her will not share in her joy.[36]

The Qumran scrolls demand another type of solidarity, a sharing of attitudes of the type required of a servant according to Plautus. One of the fundamental principles of the sect, stated at the beginning of

---

ed. Vilna (repr., Jerusalem, 1961), Exodus p. 18 (9b) (contra M. Mirkin, *Midrash Rabbah* [Tel Aviv: Yavneh, 1972] ad loc.).

[34] *On the Confusion of Tongues*, §§6–7, in F. H. Colson and G. H. Whitaker, *Philo* 4 (Cambridge, MA: Harvard University Press, 1968), 12–13.

[35] Translation from *Tanakh* (Philadelphia: Jewish Publication Society, 1999).

[36] *b. Ta'an.* 30b; see also b. B.B. 60b.

the *Rule of the Community* and repeated frequently, is that, as servants of God, members of the sect must adopt the attitudes of God: לאהוב כול אשר בחר ולשנוא את כול אשר מאס, "to love everything that He has chosen and hate everything that He has rejected."[37] The wicked, in contrast, לא רצו בכול אשר צויתה ויבחרו באשר שנאתה, "take no pleasure in all that You command, but have chosen what You hate."[38] This motif is also paraphrased in Rabbi Hiyya bar Abba's prayer in the Palestinian Talmud ותרחקינו מכל מה ששנאת ותקרבינו לכל מה שאהבת, "Keep us far from all that You hate and bring us close to all that You love."[39]

The same motif emerges several centuries later in the medieval English oath of fealty which requires that the vassal share his lord's attitudes:

> Thus shall a man swear fealty oaths. 1. By the Lord, before whom this relic [or: sanctuary] is holy, I will be to N. faithful and true, and love all that he loves, and shun all that he shuns, according to God's law and according to the world's principles, and never, by will nor by force, by word nor by work, do aught of what is loathful to him . . .[40]

MOSES'S INVITATION TO HOBAB

The theme of circumstantial solidarity may shed light on Moses's invitation to Hobab in Num 10:29–32.

כט וַיֹּאמֶר מֹשֶׁה לְחֹבָב בֶּן־רְעוּאֵל הַמִּדְיָנִי חֹתֵן מֹשֶׁה נֹסְעִים אֲנַחְנוּ אֶל־הַמָּקוֹם אֲשֶׁר אָמַר ה' אֹתוֹ אֶתֵּן לָכֶם לְכָה אִתָּנוּ וְהֵטַבְנוּ לָךְ כִּי־ה' דִּבֶּר־טוֹב עַל־יִשְׂרָאֵל: ל וַיֹּאמֶר אֵלָיו לֹא אֵלֵךְ כִּי אִם־אֶל־אַרְצִי וְאֶל־מוֹלַדְתִּי אֵלֵךְ: לא וַיֹּאמֶר אַל־נָא תַּעֲזֹב אֹתָנוּ כִּי עַל־כֵּן יָדַעְתָּ חֲנֹתֵנוּ בַּמִּדְבָּר וְהָיִיתָ לָּנוּ לְעֵינָיִם: לב וְהָיָה כִּי־תֵלֵךְ עִמָּנוּ וְהָיָה הַטּוֹב הַהוּא אֲשֶׁר יֵיטִיב ה' עִמָּנוּ וְהֵטַבְנוּ לָךְ:

²⁹Moses said to Hobab son of Reuel the Midianite, Moses's father-in-law, "We are setting out for the place of which the Lord has said, 'I

---

[37] 1QS I, 3–5. See also CD II, 15; 1QHod XIV (F. G. Martinez, *The Dead Sea Scrolls Translated*. Trans. W. G. E. Watson [Leiden: Brill, 1994], p. 321: VI), 10–11; XVII (Martinez [p. 317]: IV), 24. See J. Licht, *The Rule Scroll* (Jerusalem: Bialik Institute, 1965), 59 [Hebrew]; *The Thanksgiving Scroll* (Jerusalem: Bialik Institute, 1957), 188 [Hebrew].

[38] 1QHod XV, 18–19 (Martinez [p. 322]: VII, 22–23).

[39] *y. Ber.* 4.2, p. 7d; Licht, *The Rule Scroll*, 59.

[40] *Ancient Laws and Institutes of England* (London: G. E. Eyre and A. Spottiswoode) 1.178–79. As my colleague Donald A. Ringe informs me, the verb rendered "shun" (*onscunian*) can also mean "avoid, fear, detest, hate" (John R. Clark Hall, *A Concise Anglo-Saxon Dictionary*. 2d ed. [New York: Macmillan, 1916], p. 229).

will give it to you.' Come with us and we will do good to you; for the Lord has promised good to Israel." [30]"I will not go," he replied to him, "but will return to my land and my kindred." [31]He said, "Please do not leave us, inasmuch as you know where we should camp in the wilderness and can be our guide. So if you come with us, we will grant you the same good that the Lord grants us."[41]

At first glance Moses's offer to do good to Jethro looks very similar to Ammunenshi's offer to Sinuhe in the Egyptian *Tale of Sinuhe* (ca. 20th century B.C.E.). Sinuhe, an Egyptian courtier, flees to Syria-Palestine and is taken in by a local sheikh, Ammunenshi, who declares: "You shall stay with me. What I shall do for you is good." Ammunenshi then places Sinuhe at the head of his children, marries him to his eldest daughter, lets him choose some of his land, and makes him ruler of a tribe.[42] But the phraseology in Numbers 10 expresses another dimension beyond simply treating generously. What Moses offers is not only to "do good," but to share the good that Israel expects. Hobab will prosper as Israel prospers. This points to the beneficial aspect of solidarity: *sharing* good fortune. Judah ibn Tibbon, who translated Judah Halevi's *Kuzari* from Arabic to Hebrew, sensed the connection between Moses's offer and the concept of solidarity, though he did not use that phrase. The Arabic original of Judah Halevi's comment about conversion to Judaism, quoted above, reads literally, "any Gentile who joins us . . . shares our good fortune," but ibn Tibbon translated "our good fortune" as "the good that the LORD grants us" (הטובה אשר ייטיב הבורא אלינו), paraphrasing the wording of Num 10:32, הַטּוֹב הַהוּא אֲשֶׁר יֵיטִיב ה' עִמָּנוּ. Ibn Tibbon was doubtless aware of the Talmudic tradition that Jethro (Hobab) and his descendants converted to Judaism,[43] and hence he saw Moses's phraseology as applicable to proselytes. Although to speak of conversion in the pre-exilic period is anachronistic,[44] Moses is clearly inviting Jethro/Hobab, to whom he is already tied by marriage and who had already expressed empathetic solidarity with Israel (וַיִּחַדְּ

---

[41] Translation from *Tanakh*, slightly modified.

[42] M. Lichtheim, *Ancient Egyptian Literature*. 1 (Berkeley: University of California Press, 1973), 226.

[43] *Tg. Pseudo-Jon.* Ps. Exod 18:6, 27 and Num 10:29; *t Bik.* 1:2; *y. Bik.* 1:4 p. 64a (see Penei Moshe ad loc.); *Sanh.* 94a; *Sifre Num.* sec. 78 (ed. Horovitz, pp. 72–76); *Exod. Rab.* 1:32; *Tanḥ. Yitro*, 7; *Yalqut* 268 (to Exod 18:9); *Tanḥ.* Buber *Yitro*, 5 (see Buber's note 27 ad loc.).

[44] See J. Milgrom, "Religious Conversion and the Revolt Model for the Formation of Israel," *JBL* 101 (1982): 169–176, following and refining Yehezkel Kaufmann; idem, *Leviticus 17–22*. AB 3A (New York: Doubleday, 2000), 1495–1501.

יִתְרוֹ עַל כָּל־הַטּוֹבָה אֲשֶׁר־עָשָׂה ה׳ לְיִשְׂרָאֵל, "Jethro rejoiced over all the kind-ness that the Lord had shown Israel," Exod 18:9), to join the Israelites and live among them in a relationship that would create some form of circumstantial solidarity between them. This invitation would account for the Kenite descendants of Hobab living in Judah, the Negev and north Israel,[45] and the acts of friendship between them and Israel mentioned in Judges and 1 Samuel.[46]

The relationship proposed by Moses to Hobab has elements in common with that which Ruth proposes to Naomi in Ruth 1:8–19. Just as Moses proposed that Hobab "come with us" (לְכָה אִתָּנוּ) to the place God promised to give Israel, Ruth insisted on "going with" Naomi (לָלֶכֶת אִתָּהּ, v. 18) to Judah, declaring "wherever you go, I will go" (אֶל־אֲשֶׁר תֵּלְכִי אֵלֵךְ, v. 16). Just as Hobab declined, saying that he wished to "return to my land and my kindred" (אֶל־אַרְצִי וְאֶל־מוֹלַדְתִּי אֵלֵךְ), Naomi urged her daughters-in-law to "return to your mother's house/family" (לְבֵית אִמָּהּ, v. 8) and Orpah did return to her "people and her gods" (אֶל־עַמָּהּ וְאֶל־אֱלֹהֶיהָ, v. 15). Just as Moses implored Hobab "do not leave us" (אַל־נָא תַּעֲזֹב אֹתָנוּ), so Ruth asked Naomi not to urge her "to leave you, to turn back and not follow you" (לְעָזְבֵךְ לָשׁוּב מֵאַחֲרָיִךְ, v. 16). Ruth declared her intention to join Naomi's peo-ple (עַמֵּךְ עַמִּי, v. 17), much as the Shechemites had proposed that they and Jacob's family live together, intermarry, and become "one kindred" (עַם אֶחָד, Gen 34:16, 21–22). Moses and Hobab already had ties of intermarriage, and although Moses does not explicitly propose becoming "one kindred," Hobab's reply that he wished to "return to my land and my kindred" (אֶל־אַרְצִי וְאֶל־מוֹלַדְתִּי אֵלֵךְ), may suggest that that is what he understood Moses to mean. In any case, their relationship certainly constituted an alliance of some type.[47] Moses's

---

[45] Judg 1:16; 4:11; 1 Sam 15:6; 27:10; 30:29. On the location of the Kenites mentioned in Judg 4:11, see Y. Kaufmann, *Sefer Shoftim* (Jerusalem: Kiryat Sepher, 1962), p. 117. That Moses's invitation to Hobab includes a promise of territory in Israel—namely, Jericho—is assumed by rabbinic exegesis (*t. Bik.* 1:2; *y. Bik.* 1:4 p. 64a (see Penei Moshe ad loc.); *Sifre Num.* sec. 81 (ed. Horovitz, p. 77); Yalqut, sec. 726; followed by Rashi, Ramban, etc. (Hazzekuni at Num 10:29 end disagrees).

[46] Judg 4:21; 1 Sam 15:6.

[47] I do not believe, however, that טוֹב in vv. 29 and 32 refers to a treaty/covenant, as suggested by J. Milgrom, *The JPS Torah Commentary. Numbers* (Philadelphia: Jewish Publication Society, 1990), 79 s.v. "to be generous." Milgrom holds that "part of [v. 29] may also be rendered "for the Lord has negotiated a treaty with Israel" (דִּבֶּר־טוֹב עַל־יִשְׂרָאֵל) and implies that the following clause, "we will be good to you" means that Israel would include Hobab in the covenant. But it is clear from v. 32 that the "good" promised by God is a future good, not a past action like the covenant, and that דִּבֶּר־טוֹב עַל־יִשְׂרָאֵל means "promised good fortune" (B. A. Levine,

offer to share Israel's good fortune with Hobab would have been part of that relationship, just as an adopted son would share in the good fortune of his adoptive parents. Naturally, given Moses's optimism at that point (not to mention his desire to convince Hobab), he did not mention the complementary dimension of solidarity, sharing misfortune as well.

SAMUEL DAVID LUZZATTO

The human dimension of solidarity is nowhere expressed more movingly than in Samuel David Luzzatto's introduction to his theological work *Yesodei HaTorah* (*Foundations of the Torah*, 1880), in which he dedicates the book to his father-in-law, R. Raphael Baruch Segrè, Luzzatto's former teacher and father of his first and second wives. As is clear from the dedication, Luzzatto and Segrè shared a relationship of both circumstantial and empathetic solidarity.

אבי אבי!

אתה אשר זה שלשים שנה לשון אשכנז ולשון רומי למדתני, אתה אשר מאז והלאה
אהבתני וקרבתני; אתה אשר נדלת וחנכת שלש בנותיך לאות ולמופת בחכמה
וביראת ה' אהבת חסד והצנע לכת; אתה אשר נתת בחיקי את בלהה בת-שבע אשר
למעלת מדותיה אין ערוך זולתי באחיותיה; אתה אשר במשך ימים ושנים שבעת
עמי מרורים, וכוס התרעלה שתית עמי, במחלתה הקשה ממות; אתה אשר בכל ימי
הרעה עזרתני ונחמתני, ובך ובכל בני ביתך ברוכי ה' עזרה בצרות מצאתי מאד
אני ואשתי וכל זרעי; אתה אשר בעלות הצדקת השמימה חמלת עלי ועל
ילדי, ותתן את לאה למלא מקום אחותה, ולהיות לאם לילדים אשר זה ימים
ושנים כבנים היו לה: לך אביא היום תשורה את מבחר פרי יגיעי, הוא
מאמרי יסודי התורה. לך אתננהו, כי לך יאה, כי כוס חמת ה' אשר עברה עלי
ועליך, היא אולי היתה סבה גדולה לפקוח עיני, ולהכשירני להכיר האמת בעניינים
ההמה; ואתה אשר היית עמי בסבלותי, לך אכול בשמחה עמי הדבש הזה אשר
רדיתי מבטן תלאותי.

My father, My father!

To you, who taught me German and Latin thirty years ago; who loved and befriended me ever since; who raised and reared three daughters and taught them wisdom, piety, love of justice, and humility; who gave me Bilhah Bath-Sheva in marriage, whose remarkable qualities only her sisters can equal; who for many years shared my bitterness and during her dreadful illness drank with me the cup of poison; who

---

Numbers 1–20. AB 4A [New York: Doubleday, 1993] ad loc.). Nevertheless, though the verse does not mention it, it is entirely plausible that the relationship proposed by Moses would have been sealed by a treaty.

helped and consoled me in my adversity and, together with your God-blessed family, assisted me, my wife and children in times of need; who had compassion upon me and my children and gave me, after my saintly wife's death, her sister, Leah, to take her place and be a mother to her children, who since became like her own; to you I bring today my best work, my essay, *The Foundations of the Torah*, as a gift. I present it to you because you deserve it. For the cup of Divine wrath which we shared may have been the main factor that opened my eyes and made me realize the truth in these matters. Having endured with me in my troubles, may you, in joy, partake with me in the honey I extracted from my tribulations.[48]

*   *   *   *   *

The expressions of solidarity surveyed here[49] span nearly four millennia, from Syria and Mesopotamia of the Old Babylonian period, through Biblical, classical Latin, Hellenistic, Rabbinic, Christian, Old English, medieval Jewish and English sources, down to modern Christian and Jewish sources. While some of these expressions appear in historically connected bodies of literature and are certainly or probably related, in other cases the wording is different enough to make a relationship very difficult to prove. Luzzatto's wording—though he was certainly familiar with almost all the cultures from which the other examples came—is so different from all the others that influence seems unlikely. Circumstantial and empathetic solidarity are universal human experiences that even unrelated cultures would find ways to express, and given the similarity of the experiences the content of the expressions, if not their wording, would almost inevitably be similar.[50]

---

[48] A. Z. Eshkoli, *Yesode ha-Torah* (Jerusalem: Mosad ha-Rav Kook, 1947), 19; N. H. Rosenbloom, *Luzzatto's Ethico-Psychological Interpretation of Judaism* (New York: Yeshiva University, 1965), 147.

[49] The examples surveyed here are not the result of a systematic search but are simply cases that I began to notice and collect after studying ARM 8:1 years ago. Certainly, I have only scratched the surface.

[50] My son Chanan was kind enough to critique this article for me. The day after doing so he opened a Chinese fortune cookie and found the following advice: "Remember to share good fortune as well as bad with your friends." (I do not mean to imply that the advice is from China. Fortune cookies originated in the United States, and their messages are composed there, too. The incident merely shows that the advice is a commonplace.)

HIGH TREASON IN THE TEMPLE SCROLL AND IN THE ANCIENT NEAR EASTERN SOURCES

Moshe Weinfeld

As I have indicated elsewhere,[1] the Temple Scroll of Qumran contains—besides the prescriptions concerning the Temple—materials from the book of Deuteronomy, supplemented with additions, interpolations and clarifications. The Temple Scroll constitutes, to my opinion, the so called "treatise of the king" (= פרשת המלך) which had to be recited by the national leader every seven years (in the year of Shemiṭṭah), during the festival of Sukkoth (Deut 31:10–11, compare m. Soṭah 7:8).[2] Being designated for the king, it is appropriate that this scroll should expand the prescriptions that concern kingship. Indeed we find in this scroll a lengthy treatment of royal matters which spreads over three columns. These include the following paragraphs:

1) The organization of the military (57:1–5)
2) The body-guard of the King (57:5–11)
3) The advising council (57:11–15)
4) The prohibition of bigamy (57:15–19)
5) The forbidding of perverting justice (57:19–20)
6) The prohibition of covetousness (57:20–21)
7) The manners of mobilization of the people in case of war (58:3–21)
8) Blessings and curses (59:1–21)

---

[1] M. Weinfeld, "Temple Scroll" or "King's Law," *Shnaton, An Annual for Biblical and Ancient Near Eastern Studies*, vol. 3 (1978–79), 214–37 (Heb.)

[2] An identical tradition has been preserved in the city of Emar (on the Euphrates) in the framework of the *Zukru* festival celebrated every seventh year on the New Year festival. Like the gathering of all the people (great and small) every seventh year in the festival of Sukkoth (Deut 31:10–13), the *Zukru* festival in Emar is also celebrated every seventh year at the beginning of the year; cf. D. E. Fleming, *The Time at Emar; The Cultic Calendar and the Rituals from the Diviner's House* (Winona Lake, Indiana, 2000). A seven year cycle has been posited recently for the synagogue ritual of the reading of the Torah every Sabbath. According to S. Naeh, "The Torah Reading Cycle in Early Palestine: A Re-examination," *Tarbiz* 67 (1998): 167–88 (Heb.), the system of the Palestinian Torah reading was septennial and was based on the *Haqhel* custom (Deut 31:10) that was still in practice in Palestine during the Tannaitic period.

These paragraphs reflect a manual designated for the king (περὶ βασιλείας) in the Hellenistic period,[3] the period in which the Temple Scroll was composed. The Hellenistic influence may be learned especially from paragraph 2 that deals with the body-guard.[4] Hecataios of Abdera cited by Diodorus of Sicily,[5] tells us that the behavior of the Egyptian kings was regulated by prescriptions set forth in the Laws (70:91), and the observance of these should lead the king to fear the gods (cf. Deut 17:19). The Diodorus' passage most pertinent to our subject (= the Temple Scroll), is paragraph two that describes the conduct of kings in Ancient Egypt.

It reads:

> In the matter of their guard (θεραπεία), for instance, not one was a slave, such as had been acquired by purchase or a slave or born in the home, but all were sons of the most distinction, over twenty years old and the best educated of their fellow countrymen, in order that the king by virtue of his having the noblest men to care for his person and to attend him throughout both day and night, might not follow low practices.

Similar to the Hellenistic regulations we read in the Temple Scroll:

> The guards shall be with him (the king) always, day and night, in order to keep him away from any sinful thing (דבר חטא) and from a foreign people (גוי נכר) that he might not be caught in their hand (57:8–9).

An ideology like that of the Temple Scroll is thus found in a contemporaneous society. Furthermore, as will be demonstrated below, the law of high treason found in the Temple Scroll was common all over the ancient Near East during hundreds of years.

Let us analyze in detail the clauses of high treason.

כי יהיה איש רכיל בעמו ומשלים את עמו לגוי נכר ועושה רעה בעמו ותליתמה אותו
על העץ וימת . . . כי יהיה באיש חטא משפט מות ויברח אל תוך הגואים ויקלל את
עמו את בני ישראל ותליתמה גם אותו על העל העץ וימות.

---

[3] Cf. my article cited in note 1.

[4] On the body guard in the Hellenistic period, see P. M. Frazer, *Ptolemaic Alexandria* (Oxford, 1972), vol. II, p. 152, n. 224.

[5] Book I 70; cf. the commentary of A. Burton, *Diodorus Siculus* (1972), 209ff.

> If a man slanders his people and delivers his people to a foreign nation and does evil to his people you shall hang him on a tree and he shall die ... If a man is guilty of a capital crime and flees to the nations and curses his people, the children of Israel, you shall hang him also on the tree and he shall die ... (64:6–13).[6]

As we shall see, the phraseology of all these injunctions overlaps that of legal sources of other nations and one should not see the Hellenistic period as the beginning of the punishment of impalement for high treason. On the contrary, high treason and its punishment (impalement on trees) is frequently described in the annalistic literature as well as in the royal iconography of the second and the first millennia B.C.E.[7]

Thus we read in the treaty between Shattiwaza of Mittani and Šuppiluliuma I of Hatti:

> He destroyed the palace and exhausted the households of the Hurrians. He had the noblemen brought and extradited them to the land of Assyria and the land of Alši. They were turned over and impaled (*ana isē izakapšunūti*) in the city of Taite.[8]

Similarly we read in the Assyrian annals:

> I destroyed them, tore down (the walls) and burned (the towns) with fire. I caught the survivors and impaled them on trees[9]

The common denominator of these injunctions is the betrayal of its own nation: 1) Slander against *his own nation* (רכיל בעמו). 2) The delivering of *his people* to the enemy (משלים עמו לגוי נכר).[10] 3) Doing evil *to his people*. 4) Fleeing to *foreign peoples*. 5) Cursing one's own people and the children of Israel.

The term הלך רכיל, "to slander," is attested in Neo-Assyrian grants where the informer is warned not "to follow" (*la tallak*) the words of

---

[6] The expressions "his people" (בעמו) appear here four times to emphasize the crime which is done against the nation as such. Compare Exod 22:27: "You shall not revile God, nor curse a chief *of your own people*"; Lev 19:16: "You shall not spread slander *among your people*". Cf. G. Brin, *Issues in the Bible and the Dead Sea Scrolls* (Tel Aviv, 1994), 191ff.

[7] For the iconography, see H. Tadmor, *The Inscriptions of Tiglath–Pileser III, King of Assyria* (Jerusalem, 1994), pl. XXXIX.

[8] G. Beckman, *Hittite Diplomatic Texts* (ed. Harry A. Hoffner, Jr.; Atlanta, Georgia 1996), 45.

[9] *ANET* 2, 1955, 276 (Assurnasirpal II [859–889]).

[10] On אשלם as extradition see Yadin, *The Temple Scroll* (Jerusalem, 1983), 64, line 7.

the rebels, but to investigate and establish whether that statement is true.[11]

> *Šumma mamma ana* LUGAL EN-*šú iḫṭiṭi u lú* ŠU.2.*su ina* ŠÀ-*bi* DIN-GIR *ittubil . . . ina* UGU *pî ša ākil karṣī zāʾirāni la tallak; šâl kēn šumma abutu šalintu šî . . .*[12]

> If one of them has sinned against the king his lord or lifted his hand against god, do not go on the word of a hostile informer, but investigate, and establish whether that statement is true.

This reminds us Deuteronomy 13 where rumors are discharged about people who incited a whole city to rebel i.e., to worship foreign gods (vv. 13–16). Similar to the Assyrian grants the people of the city are commanded to investigate, inquire and interrogate thoroughly and only when the charge is established will they punish the inhabitants of the city.[13]

Verse 16 in Leviticus 19 comes to warn the Israelites not to succumb to subversive trends, which may involve the execution of innocent people. The gossip will surely result in bloodshed as is proven by verse 16b: "Do not stand idle by the blood of your fellow" (לא תעמד על דם רעך).[14] This interpretation is supported by Ezek 22:9: "Informers were amongst you in order to cause bloodshed." In the Temple Scroll we also find slander next to delivering Israelite people to a foreign nation, which is high treason.

ועושה רעה בעמו "He does evil to his people" (64:7)

"Good thing" and its opposite "bad thing" express covenantal relations. This has been correctly seen by W. L. Moran.[15] See for instance in the Mari letters: *awātim damqātim birītīya u birtišu nīš ilim u riksātim dannātim nišakkan,* "We will establish 'good things,'" a divine oath, a valid covenantal before me and him."[16] The same applies to the

---

[11] See L. Kataja and R. Whiting, *Grants, Decrees and Gifts of the Neo-Assyrian Period,* SAA vol. XII (Helsinki, 1995), 24ff. And see there the grants no. 25, 26, 30.

[12] Cf. Kataja and Whiting, *grants, Decrees and Gifts,* 25–26, compare pp. 33–34.

[13] See M. Weinfeld, *Deuteronomy and the Deuteronomic School* (Oxford, 1972), 92ff.

[14] For verse 16 as a unit see Baruch N. Schwartz, *The Holiness Legislation* (Jerusalem, 1999): 316–317.

[15] W. L. Moran, "A Note on the Treaty Terminology of the Sefire Stelas," *JNES* 22 (1963): 173–76.

[16] Cf. e.g. *anāku u ahiya itti aḥāmeš ṭābūta nidabbub.* "My brother and I made a mutual declaration of friendship."

Aramaic treaties (טבחא). Similar expressions are found in the Amarna letters and later Assyrian sources. Thus we read in the vassal treaties of Esarhaddon: "If you hear any improper, unsuitable or unseemly word against Ashurbanipal."[17] Identical phraseology is attested in the Hittite treaties: *idaluš memiyaš*, and מלין לחית in the Sefire treaties.[18] To "do evil" in the sense of betrayal is found also in 2 Kgs 8:12; 1 Sam 27:12.[19]

ויברח אל הגואים ויקלל את עמו ואת בני ישראל *"And he will flee to the nations and will curse his people and the children of Israel"*

Here we encounter a situation of high treason as defined in the Old Assyrian,[20] Middle Assyrian and Neo Assyrian periods. Thus we read in the Laws of Eshnunna (paragraph 30)[21]: "If a man hates (*izêrma*) his city (*ālšu*) and his master (*bēlšu*) and then flees...."

Similarly we find in the code of Hammurabi (paragraph 136)[22]: "If a man deserts (*iddîma*) his city and flees... because he hated (*izêruma*) his city and fled...."

The city and its master represent here the patron deity (the god of Ashur) and the prince.[23] This resembles the curse of God and king in the monarchic period of ancient Israel (1 Kgs 21:10,13; Isa 8:21) and אלהים ונשיא in the pre-monarchic time of Israel (Exod 22:27). As shown by Sh. M. Paul[24] we find in Middle Assyrian documents the crime of reviling of God and king as in ancient Israel.

---

[17] S. Parpola and K. Watanabe, *Neo-Assyrian Treaties and Loyalty Oaths* (Helsinki, 1988), 31.

[18] Cf. M. Weinfeld, "The Loyalty Oath in the Ancient Near East", *Ugarit Forschungen* 8 (1978), 412, n. 288–89.

[19] See G. Brin, *Issues in the Bible and the Dead Sea Scrolls* (Tel Aviv, 1994), 216, n. 50.

[20] For the Old-Assyrian traces of the formula: *ālum* and *bēlum*, see G. Eisser and J. Lewy, *Die altassyrischen Rechtsurkunden von Kültepe* (Leipzig, 1930–1935), no. 253, 298, 325, 326.

[21] Cf. R.Yaron, *The Laws of Eshnuna* (Jerusalem, 1988). See §30, p. 61; M. E. Roth, *Law Collections from Mesopotamia and Asia Minor* (Atlanta, Georgia, 1995), §30, p. 68.

[22] Roth, *Law Collections*, §136, p. 107.

[23] See the discussion of Yaron, *Eshnuna*, 115–17.

[24] Sh. M. Paul, "Biblical Analogues to Middle Assyrian Law", *Religion and Law: Biblical-Judaic and Islamic Perspectives*, (ed. E. B. Firmage et al., Winona Lake, IN, 1990), 333–50.

IMPLIED SYNONYMS AND ANTONYMS:
TEXTUAL CRITICISM VS. THE LITERARY APPROACH

Yair Zakovitch

It is well known that in biblical parallelism, the words in the second hemistich present either the synonym or the antonym to the first hemistich. Yet in many cases we find that instead of the anticipated synonym or antonym appears a different word—similar to the expected one either phonetically or graphically. The predominant tendency amongst philologists has been to emend the text in order to 'restore' the lost parallelism, with support for the restoration found, in many instances, in textual witnesses.

In this article, dedicated to my good friend and colleague Emanuel Tov, one of the most important textual critics of our generation, I, who represent the literary approach, wish to claim that the hands of these textual critics are too quick on the trigger. Indeed we deal here with a sophisticated and well-designed literary phenomenon in which the poet writes the unexpected word, knowing full well that his reader (who is obviously familiar with the rules of biblical parallelism and word-pairs) will notice the discrepancy and will in fact hear both words: the written and the implied, both of which contribute their parts to the complete meaning of the poet's words. The phenomenon can be likened to a palimpsest in which the erased text was left slightly visible underneath the newly written one, so that it supplies both readings. The poet actually poses a riddle to his readers, while providing two clear hints to the riddle's resolution: first, there is the broken parallelism, when the expected word does not appear; second, the word that does appear is similar—either graphically or phonetically—to the implied, expected word. These riddles of implied and written words remind us of a well-known phenomenon in rabbinic literature, the exegetical method called 'אל תקרא' (*'al tiqrê*),[1]

---

[1] For a collection of the *'al tiqrê* occurrences, see N. H. Torczyner, *'al Tiqrê'*, in *Encyclopedia Eshkol*, vol. 2 (Berlin, 1932), 376–86. For a classification of these *drashot*, see A. Rosenzweig, 'Die Al-tikre-Deutungen', in *Festschrift zu Israel Lewy's siebzigsten Gelburtstag* (ed. M. Brann and J. Elbogen; Breslau, 1911), 204–53; S. Talmon, 'Aspects

whereby the reader is told to read—instead of the written word—a similar word which in fact may bring a very different meaning to the verse.

What is the difference, in the end, between a textual critic and a reader like myself? We both sense the broken parallelism, and we both immediately think of the expected word that seems to lie right under the written one. But the textual critic then changes the text— in the belief that the text is thereby *restored*—whereas I deem the Masoretic Text reliable and see no reason for changing it. On the contrary, I find here an intentional, literary technique by which the poet has succeeded in planting two meanings in one word.

Before continuing, I must emphasize the importance of the work of textual critics. I am the last to underestimate the work of these scholars, without whom many biblical verses would have been left beyond our understanding. However, with regard to the present discussion, when we find so many examples of this phenomenon, I want to erect a sign of caution: Caution! Literary Phenomenon at Work!

Because of limitations of space I will bring here only a very few examples of this phenomenon, ten in number. I have elected not to graze from the entire corpus of biblical poetry, but to limit myself to one small pasture: the book of Proverbs. I will bring the examples according to their order as they appear in that book. Other examples, from Proverbs and other books, will remain hidden for future readers to discover.

1. If they say, Come with us,
   Let us set an ambush to shed blood (דם),
   Let us lie in wait for the innocent (לנקי) without cause. (Prov 1:11)

Many commentators have suggested replacing דם, 'blood,' with תם, 'innocent'[2]—a synonym for נקי in the second hemistich. The emendation is based on the assumption that the phonetic resemblance between *dalet* and *taw* caused a scribe to mistakenly write דם in place

---

of the Textual Transmission of the Bible in the Light of Qumran Manuscripts,' *Text* 6 (1964): 95–132.

[2] See B. Gemser, *Sprüche Salomos* (2nd ed.; HAT 16; Tübingen, 1963), 20; A. B. Ehrlich, *Randglossen zur Hebräischen Bibel*, vol. 6 (Leipzig, 1908), 10; C. H. Toy, *Proverbs* (ICC; Edinburgh, 1977), 15.

of חם—like the famous switch in Rabbi Meir's Torah of Gen 1:31 from MT טוב מאד, 'very good,' to טוב מות, 'death is good.'[3]

However the emendation is unnecessary once we realize that our verse intentionally splits the idiomatic דם נקי, 'blood of the innocent' (see e.g. Deut 19:10, 13; 21:8; 2 Kgs 21:16; Prov 6:17).[4] Moreover, in the continuation of the literary unit, the expression ארב לדם, 'ambush for blood,' reappears in reference to the measure-for-measure punishment of the sinners: 'But they lie in ambush for their own blood, in wait for their own lives' (1:18). The relationship between these two verses is clear also from their shared use of the verb צפן, 'waiting'. Further evidence of the correctness of MT is found in Prov 12:6, where one hears an echo of our verse when it refers to the words of the sinners: 'The words of the wicked are ambushing for blood' (see also Mic 7:2, 'All lie in wait for blood').

Though we disagree regarding the need to correct the text, those who suggested the correction helped to uncover the deliberately implied word play with the expression נארבה לתם, 'We lie in ambush for the innocent one.' The word for 'innocent one,' תם, (or, in the plural, תמימם) returns (though with a different meaning) in verse 12: 'Like Sheol let us swallow them alive, whole [תמימם] like those who go down into the Pit.' That is, the evil seek to swallow the innocent ones whole, leaving not even their memory remaining. תם in relation with נקי, 'innocent', appears once again, in Job 9:22.

It is therefore clear that the writer who wrote 'let us ambush for blood' fully intended for his readers to hear also the reading 'let us ambush for the innocent,' which expresses the wish to harm a righteous person. Readers are expected to uncover this second reading, but not to dismiss altogether the reading 'ambush for blood.'

2. It will be a cure for your navel (לשרך?)
   A tonic for your bones. (Prov 3:8)

This verse refers to the benefits of fearing God: God-fearing will benefit the youth who listens to this wise advice. It will be for him as a drink (see Hos 2:7; Ps 102:10), a remedy (רפאות) to strengthen his body and promise good health. שרך is derived from the noun

---

[3] E. Tov, *Textual Criticism of the Hebrew Bible* (Minneapolis, 1992), 120.

[4] On the splitting of an idiom into its two components, see E. Z. Melamed, 'שנים שהם אחד שהם במקרא,' *Tarbiz* 16 (1945): 173–89 (Hebrew). On our verse, see M. V. Fox, *Proverbs 1–9* (AB; New York, 2000), 85.

שׁר, 'navel' (see Ezek 16:4; and Rashi on our verse); an alternate form, שׁרֶר, appears in Song 7:3, 'Your navel is like a round goblet—Let mixed wine not be lacking!' The verse in Song of Songs likens the navel to a goblet, a vessel into which wine is poured. אַגָּן, 'goblet', appears in a similar context in a letter from Arad (Letter 1 lines 9–10): 'you should give from the goblet's wine.'[5] And so also in our verse the poet has chosen the navel as the organ that can contain the liquid remedy. The navel, the center of the body, serves also as a *pars pro toto* of the entire body in the same way that the bones will function in the second hemistich (see e.g. Ps 6:3; 31:11).

While the image of the navel-goblet for the body's remedy is beautiful, the expectation set up by the verse's parallelism also invites the form שְׁאֵרְךָ (the same letters only with different vocalization),[6] that is שְׁאֵרְךָ, 'your flesh,' with a dropped *'alep* (as in שְׁלָתֵךְ instead of שְׁאֵלָתֵךְ in 1 Sam 1:17).[7] The reading שׁרְךָ/שְׁאֵרְךָ finds support in the Septuagint, *Peshitta*, and modern commentators.[8] Concerning the expression 'healing of the flesh' we find another verse, also from Proverbs: '. . . healing for his whole flesh (בְּשָׂרוֹ)' (Prov 4:22). Even more, the parallelism of flesh (שְׁאֵר) and bones is found in Mic 3:3, 'You have devoured my people's flesh, you have flayed the skin off them, and their flesh off their bones' (see also verse 2 there). More frequent is the parallel of בָּשָׂר, 'flesh' and bone, e.g. Ps 38:4; Prov 14:30; Job 33:21. 'Bone and flesh' is a common expression for referring to a family relation, e.g. Gen 29:14; 2 Sam 5:1. שׁר as a shortened version of שְׁאֵר appears also in Sir 30:15–16, 'I had rather sturdy health than gold, and a blithe spirit than coral. No riches surpass a healthy body, no happiness matches that of a joyful heart'. G. R. Driver interprets שׁר both in Ben Sira and our verse as 'health.'[9] Thus also the Greek

---

[5] Y. Aharoni (in cooperation with J. Naveh), *Arad Inscriptions* (Jerusalem, 1981), 12–14.

[6] On textual emendation based on changes in vocalization, see Tov, *Textual Criticism*, 235.

[7] On textual emendations related to the assumption of the dropping of gutturals, see J. Weingreen, *Introduction to the Critical Study of the Text of the Hebrew Bible* (Oxford, 1982), 66; Tov, *Textual Criticism*, 255.

[8] See e.g. N. H. Tur-Sinai, מִשְׁלֵי שְׁלֹמֹה (Tel Aviv, 1947), 53 (Hebrew). There is no need to emend to בִּשְׂרְךָ; see Ehrlich, *Randglossen*, 19; Fox (*Proverbs 1–9*, 151) brings both options.

[9] G. R. Driver, 'Problems in the Hebrew Text of Proverbs', *Bib* 32 (1951): 175. See also W. McKane, *Proverbs* (OTL; Philadelphia, 1970), 293.

translation of Ben Sirah (ὑγίεια). With this meaning of שׁרֹד, the first hemistich of our verse means 'a cure for your health.'

Keeping the present vocalization while hearing also the implied שׁרֹד־שׁאֵרֹד extends to the verse greater meaning. שֹׁר i.e. the 'navel' and 'goblet' for the tonic; שֵׁר i.e. שְׁאֵר, man's flesh, body, and health that is protected from all harm by the tonic poured into it: the fear of God.

3. Do not envy (תְקַנֵּא) a lawless man,
   Or choose (תִבְחַר) any of his ways. (3:31)

A hasty reading leads one to ignore the relation between קנא, in the first half of the verse, and תבחר, from the second. We find the synonyms קנא, 'envy,' and אוה, 'desire,' in the verse whose beginning resembles that of our verse, 'Do not envy (תְקַנֵּא) evil men; Do not desire (תִּתְאָו) to be with them' (Prov 24:1). The root אוה is synonymous with בחר in Ps 132:13, 'For the Lord has chosen Zion, He has desired it for his seat.' From here we see that קנא and בחר present acceptable parallels. Add to this our knowledge that בחר בדרך, 'choose a way,' is a common expression (see Isa 66:3; Ps 25:12), and we see that there is no reason to change תבחר, 'choose,' to תתחר, 'compete'[10]—as we find in the Septuagint to our verse and also verses similar to ours in the Masoretic Text (e.g. 'Do not compete with evildoers, don't envy the wicked' Prov 24:19; 'Do not compete with evil men; do not envy wrongdoers' Ps 37:1).

The sensitive reader, aware of the verses we've just quoted, will detect the implied reading, 'compete,' תתחר, behind the written תבחר, 'choose.' The combination of these two readings adds, once again, to the meaning of the verse, whereby the young listener is advised not to choose the ways of the wicked, neither out of envy nor out of a desire to compete with him.

4. The memory (זכר) of the righteous is invoked in blessing (לברכה),
   But the name (שׁם) of the wicked will rot (ירקב). (10:7)

The first hemistich expresses the idea that many people will bless the memory (literally, 'the name') of the righteous person and will praise him, as we find, also, in the previous verse: 'Blessings upon

---

[10] See e.g. Ehrlich, *Randglossen*, 21.

the head of the righteous . . .'. In a similar way, God promises
Abraham, 'I will make your name great and bless you' (Gen 12:2),
and then continues, '. . . and all the families of the earth shall bless
themselves by you' (v. 3), describing how Abraham will become the
paradigm of the blessed among men. That is similar to what is said
about Jacob: 'By you shall Israel invoke blessings' (Gen 48:20). This
meaning also—that the righteous person is the paradigm of the
blessed—is found in our verse. Another meaning of our verse, and
perhaps it is the most important, is that the memory of the righteous will remain blessed for the coming generations, similar to what
is said in Esth 9:28: 'and the memory of them shall never perish
among their descendants,' i.e. future generations will continue mentioning the good deeds and character of the righteous person. The
name/memory of the wicked person, on the other hand, will rot; it
will be lost and will disappear after his death, since others will not
want to remember him (see e.g. Ps 34:17; 109:15; Job 18:17).[11]

The verse is written in antithetic parallelism: the memory of the
righteous is juxtaposed against the name of the wicked. (For the synonymous nature of name and memory, see Exod 3:15; Isa 26:8; Ps
135:13; for the order memory–name, see Job 18:17.) The parallelism
appears lacking, however, since ירקב, though indeed creating a nice
paranomasia with לברכה, is not a true antonym. For this reason, it
was suggested to read יוקב, 'will be cursed', instead of ירקב.[12] (For
the antithetic nature of the roots ברך and קבה, see Num 23:11; 24:10;
Prov 11:26.) The temptation to adopt this emendation is great also
because of the strong graphic similarity between the letters *reš* and
waw (see e.g. the tendentious interchange between יושע, 'has saved'
[LXX, representing the original reading], and ירשע, 'has been wicked'
[I Sam 14:47].[13] Another example of this interchangeability is found
between MT 'son of a perverse [נעות], rebellious [woman]' and 'son
of a young [נערת], rebellious [woman]' [4QSam^b and LXX]).[14]

Against the change stands the fact that the verb ירקב, 'will rot,'
fits the context very well. שם, 'name,' in the second hemistich, can

---

[11] Mckane, *Proverbs*, 432.
[12] See e.g. Ehrlich, *Randglossen*, 47.
[13] See I. L. Seeligmann, 'Menschliches Heldentum und Göttliche Hilfe: Die
Doppelte Kausalität im alttestamentlichen Geschichtsdenken,' *ThZ* 19 (1963): 399.
[14] Tov, *Textual Criticism*, 305.

carry a similar meaning as עצם, 'bone.' We see this from the conflate
reading in Ezek 24:2: 'O mortal, record the name of this day, this
exact day [lit.: 'the bone of this day];'[15] the words 'this exact day'
are absent from the Syriac and Vulgate. Bones do indeed rot (see
Hab 3:16; Prov 12:4; 14:30).

All this argues against emending the text. Rather, whoever reads
ירקב, 'will rot,' is expected also to think of the implied version, יוקב,
thereby extracting the intended, double meaning: the name of the
wicked will not only rot, i.e. disappear, but even worse: it will be
cursed and will be the paradigm for others who deserve to be cursed.
Both meanings found in the second hemistich represent the antithesis of meanings that are clearly stated in the first.

5. He who trusts in his wealth (בעשרו) shall fall (יפל),
   But the righteous shall flourish (יפרחו) like foliage (11:28)

Prov 11:28 differs from the previous examples in that here two words
carry alternative readings, both in the first hemistich. The first: under
the phrase בוטח בעשרו, 'trusts in his wealth,' lies בוטח בעשק, 'trusts in
fraudulence.'[16] We uncover the implied meaning first by way of the
resemblance between *reš* and *qop* in the ancient Hebrew script, but
also since both expressions are known to us from biblical literature:
בטח בעשר (Ps 52:9);[17] בטח בעשק (Isa 30:12; Ps 62:11). עשק, 'fraudulence,' is the opposite of צדק, 'righteousness': 'You shall be established by righteousness, you shall be saved from fraudulence . . .' (Isa
54:14).[18] Also עשר represents the opposite of 'righteousness,' since the
righteous person is sometimes identified with the poor: 'Because they
have sold the righteous for silver and the poor for a pair of sandals'
(Amos 2:6); 'You enemies of the righteous, you takers of bribes, you
who subvert in the gate the cause of the poor' (Amos 5:12). The
conclusion is that whoever reads בטח בעשרו will hear also בטח בעשק
and will thus conclude, as the poet intended, that the wealth was
gained through fraudulence, making its bearer deserving of the fall
that awaits him.

The second word that carries an alternate reading is the last in

---

[15] For the phenomenon of conflate readings, see S. Talmon, 'Double Readings
in the Massoretic Text,' *Text* 1 (1960): 144–85.

[16] Ehrlich, *Randglossen*, 57.

[17] See also the expression בטח באוצר, 'trusting in treasures' (Jer 48:7; 49:4).

[18] See also Jer 22:15–17.

the first hemistich: instead of יפל one can read יבל, 'will whither.'[19] The reading יפל fits the context: the evil one—the opposite of the righteous one mentioned in the second hemistich—will fall, as in 'The righteousness of the blameless men will smooth his way, but the wicked man will fall by his wickedness' (Prov 11:5). On the other hand, the reading יבל fits as the antonym of יפרח, 'will flourish,' from the second hemistich: just as the leaf flourishes, so it also withers (see Isa 34:4; 64:5; Jer 8:13; Ezek 47:12; Ps 1:3). The phonetic resemblance between נפול and נבול is strong, and the switch between *bet* and *pe* is common.[20] We see this especially well in Job 14:18: ואולם הר נופל יבול, 'Mountains collapse and whither.' While the Septuagint and Syriac read נפול יפול, 'collapse and fall,' nonetheless I believe that the Masoretic text of Job, which brings together these two roots, is the original reading (for the meaning of יבל in Job as, actually, 'crumbling, falling,' see Isa 24:4). M. Dahood has assumed that יפל in our verse is a dialectic form for יבל.[21] But both verbs together serve our verse, and enable it to reach its full meaning: whoever trusts his wealth—or the fraudulence by which he made his wealth—will fall and whither.

6. A man's steps are from the Lord,
   And man won't understand (יבין) his own way. (20:24)

The intention of the verse is that God determines man's path, while man himself does not understand (the meaning of מה is 'not')[22] the path of his own life. The first part of the verse is, itself, a well-known one-hemistich saying, 'A man's steps are from the Lord.' In Psalms the saying is completed differently, 'A man's steps are from the Lord, when He delights in his ways' (Ps 37:23). Our writer in Proverbs, on the other hand, completed the maxim with his own pessimistic comment.[23] The expression 'understand a way' is familiar—e.g. 'It is the wisdom of a clever man to understand his way'

---

[19] See e.g. Gemser, *Sprüche Salomos*, 56.
[20] See Tov, *Textual Criticism*, 251; Aharoni, *Arad*, Inscription 24 lines 14–15, 18 (pp. 46–8); J. Naveh, 'Hebrew Graffiti from the First Temple Period,' *IEJ* 51 (2001): 204.
[21] M. Dahood, *Proverbs and Northwest Semitic Philology* (Rome, 1963), 24.
[22] For this meaning of מה, see e.g. Num 23:8; Judg 11:12; 2 Sam 20:1; Job 16:6.
[23] See R. N. Whybray, *Proverbs, The New Century Bible Commentary* (Grand Rapids, 1994), 301.

(Prov 14:8)—so that there is clearly no need to accept the reading of some Hebrew manuscripts and the Syriac where instead of יבין we find, יכין, 'direct' (the switch between *bet* and *kap* is common due to the obvious graphic resemblance between the letters).[24] Commentators who preferred the reading יכין[25] bring support from such texts as 'A man may plot out his course, but it is the Lord who directs his steps' (Prov 16:9), and 'I know, O Lord, that man's road is not his [to choose], That man, as he walks, cannot direct his own steps' (Jer 10:23). The confusion amongst textual witnesses between יכין and יבין appears in yet another verse from Proverbs: 'The wicked man is brazen-faced; the upright man understands (יבין *Qere* MT[mss]LXX; יכין *Ketib*, Syr., Tg., Vulg.) his way' (Prov 21:29). Reading יכין grants to the verse a positive meaning: it is not man who lays solid foundations for his way: only God[26] (for this meaning of the root כון, see e.g. Judg 16:26, 29; 2 Sam 7:16; Ps 24:2).

A different understanding comes from reading מה not negatively, as 'not,' but interrogatively, 'what.' In this sense, the verse yields the meaning, 'God is the one who determines the way of man, What can man understand of his path?,' i.e. does man think he is even capable of making such decisions regarding his life? This sort of meaning of the verse is similar to other verses, e.g. Prov 19:21: 'Many designs are in a man's mind, But it is the Lord's plan that is accomplished.'

Once again, I find it unnecessary and even erroneous to emend the text. Instead it is clear that the biblical writer intended for his readers to hear the similarity between his verse, 'What does a man understand (יבין),' and other verses where יכין appears. By taking advantage of that similarity, he opens different options of meaning. Through his word-play, we in fact receive both meanings, יכין and יבין.

7. Do not remove ancient boundary stones (גבול עולם);
    Do not encroach upon the field of orphans (יתומים). (23:10)

The first hemistich of this verse is shared also with Prov 22:28: 'Do not remove ancient boundary stones; That your ancestors set up,'

---

[24] Tov, *Textual Criticism*, 248.
[25] See e.g. Ehrlich, *Randglossen*, 118.
[26] For the expression כון דרך, see also Deut 19:3; Prov 4:26.

where the second hemistich explains עוֹלָם, 'ancient': the ancestors are those who placed the stones in ancient times—border-stones that should not be removed. A similar idea appears in the law of Deut 19:14, 'You shall not move your countryman's landmarks, set up by previous generations.' (On the relation between 'previous generations' in Deuteronomy and the 'ancestors' in Prov 22:28, see Jer 11:10, 'They have returned to the iniquities of their fathers of old [אֲבוֹתָם הָרִאשֹׁנִים].')[27] It is not impossible that Prov 23:10 and 22:28 share a common beginning as a one-hemistich proverb, that was then developed in two different ways.[28] In our verse, the parallel element between the two hemistichs may appear to be weak: do not take from another's land. This thought is expressed in two ways: not to remove the borders left by the ancients; and not to take advantage of the weak in society i.e. orphans, by assuming their portion.

In rabbinic literature we find evidence of a different reading of the first hemistich, where the parallel between the two hemistichs is strengthened: 'If a man will not suffer the poor to glean or suffers one and not another, or aids one of them, he is a robber of the poor. Of such a one it is written, *Do not remove the landmark of the poor* (עוֹלִים)' (*m. Pe'ah* 5:6). Another example is found in the same tractate: 'If a man put a basket beneath the vine while he was gathering the grapes, such a one is a robber of the poor. Of him it is written, *Do not remove the landmark of the poor* (עוֹלִים)' (7:3). In *y. Pe'ah* 19a, an explanation is given for the term עוֹלִים = 'poor' by way of *sagi nahor* (i.e. the use of the antonym for describing, in fact, its opposite): 'R. Jeremiah and R. Joseph: one said, 'Those are the ones who ascended (עוֹלִים) from Egypt.' And the other said, 'Those are the ones who descended from (meaning: lost) their property.' The second rabbi reads the last word of the hemistich as עוֹלִים but understanding it as its antonym: descending, with the meaning of becoming impoverished.[29] However, apparently we should understand עָלִים as 'poor' not because of *sagi nahor*, but because of the root as it appears

---

[27] See M. Weinfeld, *Deuteronomy and the Deuteronomic School* (Oxford, 1972), 265.

[28] See N. H. Tur-Sinai, פְּשׁוּטוֹ שֶׁל מִקְרָא, vol. d–1 (Jerusalem, 1967), 344 (Hebrew). On the phenomenon of alternative developments of one-hemistich proverbs into two-hemistich proverbs, see Y. Zakovitch, *Introduction to Inner-Biblical Interpretation* (Even Yehuda, 1992), 115–20 (Hebrew).

[29] See H. Albeck, שִׁשָּׁה סִדְרֵי מִשְׁנָה. סֵדֶר זְרָעִים (Jerusalem Tel-Aviv, 1958), 54.

in Arabic, where the root עול means 'to be poor.'[30] The parallel between עול, 'poor,' and יתום, 'orphan,' makes sense, as we see from verses that pair עני with יתום in poetic parallelism (see Zech 7:10; Ps 82:3).

In Job we find the construct form of עול and עני representing the superlative, 'the poorest': 'They snatch the fatherless from the breast and the poorest one (עול־עני) as a pledge' (Job 24:9).[31] The word עול in Job can carry an additional meaning of עולל, 'baby,' in which case the verse in Job would mean, 'and the baby of the poor as a pledge.' In our verse, reading עולם as עולים (a difference of the vowels only),[32] carries then also the reading עוללים, 'infants' (see also Isa 49:15; 69:20). In this way we see that the author of Prov 23:10 in fact divided the term עולים יתומים—babies who are orphans, babies who have no one to protect them—between the two hemistichs of the verse.

So far we have dealt with the rabbinic reading of עולם as עולים, along with its different vocalizations that opened up several possible translations, each strengthening the parallelism in our verse. The need to strengthen the parallelism led some scholars to suggest a different emendation: אלמנה, 'widow,' instead of עולם. This is based on a number of considerations. We find the expression גבול אלמנה in Prov 15:25: 'The Lord will tear down the house of the proud, but He will establish the boundaries (= land) of the widow.'[33] Moreover, the pairing of 'widow' and 'orphan' is common, sometimes in that order (e.g. Exod 22:23; Ps 94:6). The emendation is based also on the assumption that the distinction between the gutturals 'alep and ayin was not strong, and indeed different textual witnesses attest to changes between 'alep and 'ayin.[34] Another contributing factor for the assumed corruption is the scribal custom of abbreviating words

---

[30] Albeck, משנה, 54.

[31] For the construct form of synonymous words as a superlative, see Y. Avishur, סמיכות הנרדפים במליצה המקראית (Jerusalem, 1977).

[32] For textual emendations based on changes in vocalization, see Tov, *Textual Criticism*, 41.

[33] See e.g. Gemser, *Sprüche Salomos*, 87; Toy, *Proverbs*, 341; Ehrlich, *Randglossen*, 136.

[34] On the exchange between 'alep and 'ayin, see e.g. the famous variation in the Torah of Rabbi Meir: from כתנות עור to כתנות אור (Gen 3:21); see Tov, *Textual Criticism*, 119–20; 251.

whereby אלמ is written in place of אלמנה.[35] From here it is not difficult to understand the change, then, to עולם. In the Egyptian collection of proverbs *Amen-em-Opet*—proverbs which parallel those in the section of Proverbs beginning with Prov 22:17—one finds indeed a warning against the taking of a widow's land: 'Be not greedy after a cubit of land, nor encroach upon the boundaries of a widow.'[36]

In my opinion, there is no need to emend the text, neither to עלים, עולים, nor אלמנה. The careful reader will sense the tension between נבול עולם, 'ancient boundaries,' and שדה יתומים, 'orphans' field,' and will create in his mind a sort of *'al tiqrê*: playing with the optional readings for עולם, עולים, עלים, אלמנה. The preservation of the Masoretic text on the one hand, while playing with the implied meanings on the other hand, grants to the verse intended depth and significance.

8. A deep pit (is) a harlot (זונה)
   A narrow well (is) an alien woman. (23:27)

It may seem that the synonymous parallelism encourages replacing זונה with זרה, 'foreign woman,' a synonym to נכריה, 'alien woman' (see Prov 2:16; 5:20; 7:5).[37] Support for this change can be found in Prov 22:14 where the first hemistich of 23:27 is repeated but with the change to זרות, 'A deep pit (is) a foreign woman.' This encouraged scholars to adopt that reading also in Prov 23:27,[38] a reading that is also supported by the Septuagint.[39]

Yet the meanings of the two hemistiches of 23:27 are not identical. The first speaks of the depth of the pit, while the second of the narrowness of the well. In this way the two join together to illustrate the misery of the one who will fall in. So also with regard to women. It is precisely in the variation—both deep and narrow—that the exact nature of the danger is depicted. We don't need an emendation here, but awareness of the implied meaning of זרה, 'foreign,' alongside the overt זונה, 'harlot'.

---

[34] On the possible existence of abbreviations in the biblical text, see G. R. Driver, 'Abbreviations in the Massoretic Text,' and 'Once Again Abbreviations' in *Text* 1 (1960): 112–31 and 4 (1964): 76–94.

[35] See J. B. Pritchard, *Ancient Near Eastern Texts Relating to the Old Testament* (Princeton, 1955), 422.

[36] Also the parallel coupling of זר and נכרי is common, e.g. Prov 27:2; Job 19:15.

[37] E.g. Gemser, *Sprüche Salomos*, 87; Ehrlich, *Randglossen*, 137.

[39] See R. J. Clifford, *Proverbs* (OTL; Louisville, 1999), 205.

The relation between זונה and זרה is found in a number of verses. Prov 6:24 mentions a 'foreign woman' (נכריה), while in the continuation of the literary unit, in verse 26, we find 'harlot' (זונה). In Prov 7:5, the youth is warned against the 'foreign woman' (זרה), 'the alien woman' (הנכריה), but in verse 10 it is stated that 'a woman comes toward him dressed like a harlot . . .'. Outside of Proverbs, the mother of the judge Jephtah is called 'harlot' (אשה זונה; Judg 11:1), but in the next verse she is referred to as 'foreigner' (אשה אחרת).

While זרה (LXX) sounds similar to זונה and rhymes with צרה, 'narrow,' from the second hemistich, still only the Masoretic זונה teaches us that the foreign temptress is, indeed, a harlot.

9. Open rebuke (תוכחת) is better than concealed love (אהבה). (27:5)

The connection between 'love' and 'rebuke' is illustrated in Prov 3:12, 'For whom the Lord loves, He rebukes.' Our verse can accordingly be understood as meaning that open rebuke is helpful since it can return the person to the correct path, whereas concealed love— or actually *concealing* love (a completely legitimate understanding of the word since the passive can be understood actively)—may in fact prove damaging, since whoever loves the wayward person shares responsibility for returning him to the right path.[40] The use of the passive form מְסֻתֶּרֶת was influenced by the passive form מְגֻלָּה in the first hemistich.

There are some who prefer emending אהבה to איבה, 'hatred.'[41] According to this reading, 'open rebuke' is the behavior of one who loves, as we saw already in Prov 3:12, and is better than 'concealed hatred,' which is dangerous and non-productive. The emendation seemingly finds approval in Lev 19:17, 'You shall not hate your kinfolk in your heart [this resembles 'concealed hatred]. Rebuke your kinsmen [which is a proof of your love for him]. But incur no guilt because of it.' The emendation is based on a graphic similarity between *he* and *yod* in the ancient Hebrew script (see e.g. Ps 19:5 'He placed in them (בהם) a tent for the sun,' which should be emended to 'He placed in the sea (בים) a tent for the sun').[42] The substitution of 'hatred,' איבה, for 'love,' אהבה, is found also in Ezek 25:15, where

---

[40] See Toy, *Proverbs*, 483.
[41] See e.g. Tur-Sinai, פשוטו, 367.
[42] See E. Würthwein, *The Text of the Old Testament* (Grand Rapids, 1995), 108.

MT preserves איבת עולם, 'ancient hatred', but Syr. reads אהבת עולם, 'ancient love.'

Along with the graphic resemblance between אהבה and איבה there is also the phonetic similarity. In the Bible we find several word-plays between איב and אהב, e.g. 'So may all Your enemies (אויביך) perish . . . But may His lovers (אהביו) be as the sun rising in might' Judg 5:31;[43] '. . . in His love (באהבתו) and pity He Himself redeemed them, . . . but they rebelled and grieved His holy spirit, then He became their enemy (לאויב)' Isa 63:9–10; '. . . All her lovers have betrayed her; They have become her enemies', Lam 1:2 (and see also how Saul who loved David [1 Sam 16:21] became later his enemy [18:29].

Emending the verse is needless also since the verse, as it is, con-nects elegantly with the following one in which the verb אהב reap-pears—'Wounds by a loved one are long lasting; The kisses of an enemy (שונא) are profuse.' Also the idea of verse 6 is similar to that of verse 5—'wounds by a loved one' being like 'open rebuke.'[44]

Verse 5 as it appears in MT expresses the idea that love which hides criticism is useless. Another meaning, revealed through an awareness of the intended wordplay between אהבה and איבה, is that also hidden hatred is damaging, because the hated one is unaware of his enemy, so that he can neither protect himself nor try to take action to change the other's opinion of him.

10. A generation whose teeth are swords, Whose jaws are knives,
    Ready to devour the poor from the land (מארץ), The needy from
    among men (מאדם). (30:14)

This verse ends the literary unit that speaks about the moral sins of the 'generation,' a unit in which each of its four verses starts with the anaphora 'A generation. . . .' Like its predecessors, it is written in synonymous parallelism. Matching 'swords' from the first hemistich is 'knives' in the second, because the sword 'eats' (e.g. 46:10–14) and it has a mouth (e.g. Jos 8:24; 10:28); against 'teeth' we have 'jaws' (compare Joel 1:6; Job 29:17). In the second half of the verse, the 'poor' are paired against the 'needy' (cf. e.g. Ps 12:6; 140:13).

---

[43] This verse was corrupted in Syr. and Vulg. which read ואיביך, 'your enemies.'
[44] For the juxtaposition of verses 5 and 6, see R. C. van Leeuwen, *Context and Meaning in Proverbs 25–27* (SBLDS 96; Atlanta, 1988), 128.

The completeness of the parallel seems to be interrupted, however, by the placement of 'men' as the parallel to 'land.' This provoked B. Gemser to read מאדמה, 'from the ground,' instead of מאדם, 'from among men.'[45] We find אדמה as a synonym to ארץ e.g. in the free exchange between them in the story of Korah, where we read 'the ground (האדמה) opens its mouth' (Num 16:30) and 'the earth (הארץ) opened its mouth' (verse 32); compare also the expression 'the ground yields its produce' (Deut 11:17), and 'the earth yields its produce' (Lev 26:20).[46] Indeed, one can understand a scribal error in which מאדמה became מאדם, 'from among men,' as the result of the scribal practice of abbreviation by the omission of last letter of words.[47]

However, the reader of מאדם in Prov 30:14 will think of the word אדמה, the obvious synonym to ארץ, also because the Hebrew Bible is filled with examples where there is a relationship between אדם and אדמה, e.g. 'and there was no man to till the soil' Gen 2:5; 'the Lord God formed man from the dust of the earth' (v. 7). Whether אדם represents in fact the *ad hoc* masculine form of אדמה, as has been suggested,[48] or whether אדם refers only to the human race, in which case the word אדמה is heard only in the reader's mind under the influence of the parallel with ארץ, the emendation is unnecessary. Not only does מאדם 'give sufficient parallelism to ארץ,'[49] but it even adds to the verse a new and intended dimension: the poor will be cut off not only from the face of the earth, but also from human society. Murder not only eliminates the poor, but also mortally injures the society of which they form an integral part. The moral sin is apparent precisely when we read מאדם, 'from among men', since in that way we are reminded of the humanity of the poor, while the murder of man is forbidden, 'Whoever sheds the blood of man (האדם), By man (באדם) shall his blood be shed' (Gen 90:6).

*

---

[45] Gemser, *Sprüche Salomos*, 104.

[46] The parallelism אדמה/ארץ is found in the Septuagint to Mic 5:4, where the Hebrew בארמנתינו is replaced by באדמתנו. It is interesting that the word בארמנתינו appears as באדמתנו also in the Septuagint to Jer 9:20.

[47] Driver ('Abbreviations', 123–4) brings examples of abbreviations made by the omission of the last letter.

[48] Dahood, *Proverbs*, 57–8.

[49] Whybray, *Proverbs*, 413.

The limited selection of examples that I have brought is not in any way representative. And still, a clear picture emerges from them (see table). The phenomenon of 'implied parallelism' appears both in synonymous parallelism and antithetic parallelism. The implied word can appear either in the first or the second hemistich.

At times the riddle's resolution lies in a change in the vocalization of the word, or in a phonetic similarity between the written and the implied word. Other times the similarity is graphic, evidence that these riddles were aimed at a reading public: to the literate, who knew these sayings as written literature, and not oral. At times, it is the similarity to other biblical verses which leads the reader to the implied word and to the solution of the riddle. The appearance of several solutions in different textual witnesses (each were based on different Hebrew *Vorlage*) does not signify a corrupted Masoretic Text, but rather that early copyists solved the riddles and were attracted to the expected and exact parallels.

In all ten verses examined here the emendations are not necessary for understanding the verse. Yet those who change the text—whether textual witnesses or modern scholars—showed us the solutions to the riddles, helping us to see the double or even multiple meanings imbedded in the verses, as in the rabbinic practice of *'al tiqrê*.

It is my hope that this article, which opens a window to much work on the implied parallelism in biblical poetry, also opens a gate to a dialogue and cooperation between text critics and literary critics of the Bible. And may this gift from a literary scholar happily satisfy my friend, the text critic Emanuel Tov.

Table 1: Summary

	Type of Parallelism		Location of implied word (by hemistich)		Revealing the implied word is based on:					Support found in textual witnesses
					similarity:					
	synonymous	antithetic	first	second	graphic	phonetic	to other verse(s)	vocaliztion	abbreviation	
1	•		•			•		•		•
2	•		•							•
3	•			•			•			
4		•		•	•					
5		•	•		•	•				•
6		•		•	•		•	•		•
7	•		•			•			•	•
8	•			•	•		•			
9		•		•						
10	•			•					•